토익 기본서

20일 만에 끝내는 기적의 토익 RC

목차

DAY	PAGE	PART 5 문법	PART 5 어휘
DAY 01	10	명사	명사 어휘 (1)
DAY 02	36	대명사	명사 어휘 (2)
DAY 03	62	형용사	명사 어휘 (3)
DAY 04	88	부사 (1)	명사 어휘 (4)
DAY 05	114	부사 (2)	명사 어휘 (5)
DAY 06	140	전치사 (1)	형용사 어휘 (1)
DAY 07	164	전치사 (2)	형용사 어휘 (2)
DAY 08	188	동사의 형태 변화와 종류	형용사 어휘 (3)
DAY 09	212	주어와 동사의 수 일치	형용사 어휘 (4)
DAY 10	236	능동태와 수동태	형용사 어휘 (5)
DAY 11	260	시제	동사 어휘 (1)
DAY 12	284	to부정사	동사 어휘 (2)
DAY 13	308	동명사	동사 어휘 (3)
DAY 14	332	분사	동사 어휘 (4)
DAY 15	356	등위접속사와 상관접속사	부사 어휘 (1)
DAY 16	380	명사절 접속사	부사 어휘 (2)
DAY 17	404	형용사절 접속사	부사 어휘 (3)
DAY 18	428	부사절 접속사	부사 어휘 (4)
DAY 19	452	비교 구문	빈출 숙어 (1)
DAY 20	476	가정법/도치	빈출 숙어 (2)

PART 6	PART 7
앞의 내용이 단서인 명사 어휘	주제·목적 문제/세부사항 문제
뒤의 내용이 단서인 명사 어휘	True·Not True 문제/추론 문제
앞 문장의 명사를 받는 인칭대명사	의도 파악 문제/문장 삽입 문제
지시형용사 뒤 명사 어휘	이중 지문 연계 문제
앞 문장의 내용을 요약하는 지시대명사	삼중 지문 연계 문제
알맞은 문장 고르기 – 선택지에 대명사	이메일 (1) 문제 제기 이메일
순서를 나타내는 형용사 어휘	이메일 (2) 정보 전달 이메일
앞의 내용이 단서인 동사 어휘	편지
뒤의 내용이 단서인 동사 어휘	광고 (1) 제품 및 서비스 광고
앞의 내용이 단서인 동사 시제	광고 (2) 구인 광고
뒤의 내용이 단서인 동사 시제	공지 (1) 사내 공지
일반적인 사실을 나타내는 현재 시제	공지 (2) 공공장소에서의 공지
Thank you for/apologize for + 명사	회람
시간 표현이 없는 현재완료 시제	기사 (1) 비즈니스 기사
접속부사 – 첨가	기사 (2) 문화/예술/지역사회 관련 기사
접속부사 – 인과	문자 메시지
접속부사 – 역접	온라인 채팅
알맞은 문장 고르기 – 선택지에 접속부사	양식 – 일정표/초대장/영수증 등
알맞은 문장 고르기 – 빈칸 뒤에 접속부사	후기/설문조사
알맞은 문장 고르기 – 선택지의 시제	웹페이지

[해설집] 정답·해석·해설

토익 RC, 이제 〈기적의 토익 RC〉로 학습하세요.

포인트 1

매일 PART 5, 6, 7을 학습하는 구성

PART 5 문법 학습에만 치중된 토익 공부는 이제 그만! 20일 동안 매일 PART 5, 6, 7을 골고루 학습할 수 있게 구성하여 학습 성취도를 높일 수 있도록 하였습니다.

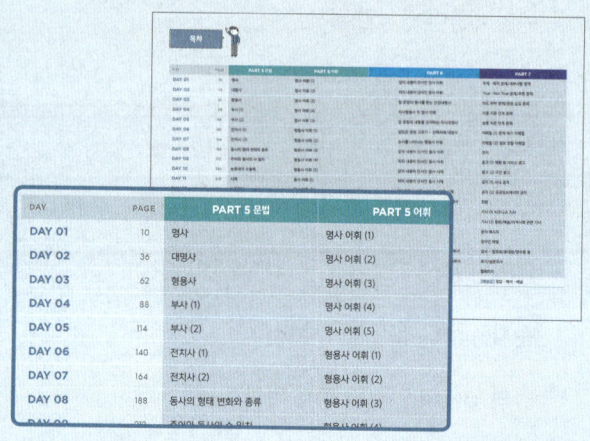

포인트 2

하루의 학습 포인트 미리보기

하루에 학습할 주요 내용을 미리 보며 큰 그림을 그릴 수 있도록 보기 쉽게 정리하였습니다. 토익 시험 직전에는 이 부분만 훑어보며 마무리 학습용으로도 활용할 수 있습니다.

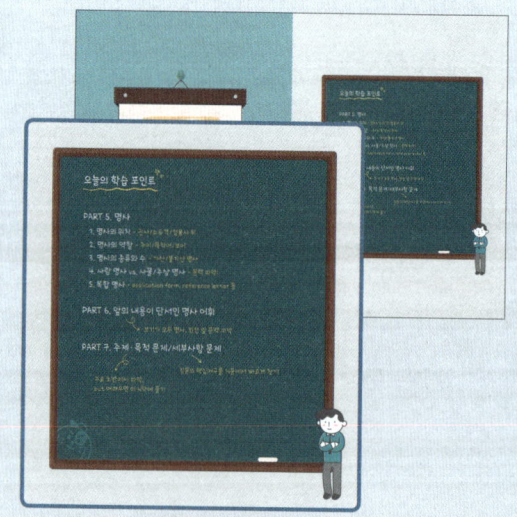

포인트 3

800⁺, 900⁺를 위한
고득점 포인트

목표 점수대에 따라 학습해야 할 출제 유형 및 개념을 구분하여, 800~900점 이상의 고득점을 위해 정복해야 하는 개념에는 '800⁺', '900⁺'를 표시하였습니다. 목표 점수에 따라 필요한 내용들만 우선 학습하여 좀 더 빠르게 효과적으로 학습할 수 있습니다.

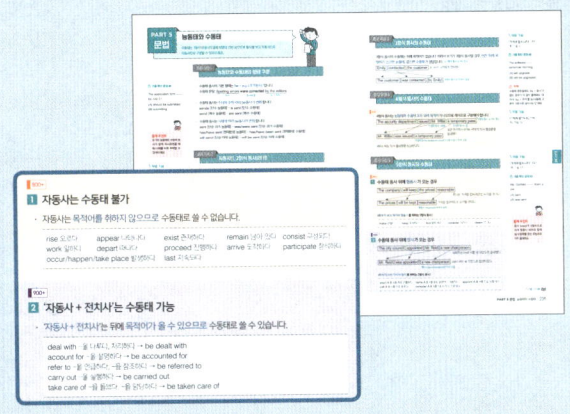

포인트 4

[PART 5] 꼭 나오는 문법 유형만,
알찬 보조 학습 코너까지!

방대한 문법 이론 학습은 이제 그만! 토익을 위해 필요한 문법 출제 유형만 선별하여 수록하였습니다. 또한 보조 학습 코너의 <확인 문제>를 풀어보며 학습한 내용을 바로바로 점검해 볼 수 있고, 토익 출제 경향을 알려주는 <출제 포인트>, 실수할 수 있는 부분을 짚어주는 <주의!> 코너를 통해 더욱 알차게 학습할 수 있습니다.

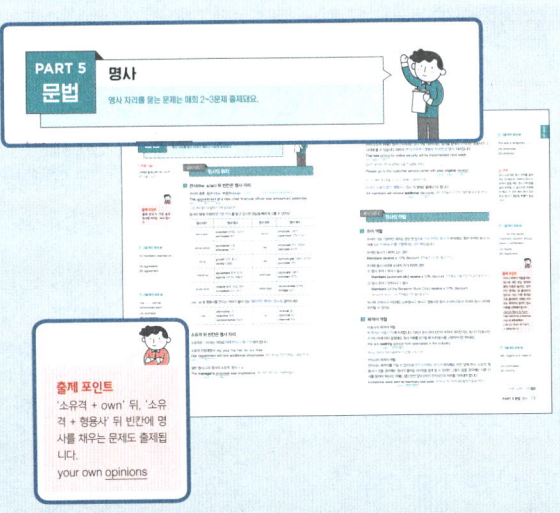

토익 RC, 이제 〈기적의 토익 RC〉로 학습하세요.

포인트 5

[PART 5] 짝꿍 표현으로 외우는 어휘 학습

PART 5 어휘 문제를 소홀히 하지 말자! 주요 기출 단어를 짝꿍 표현과 함께 학습할 수 있도록 하였습니다. 토익 선생님이 고른 빈출 PICK! 어휘도 확인해 보세요.

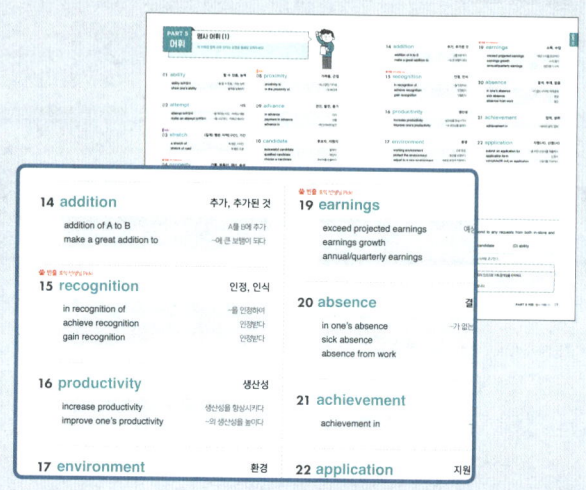

포인트 6

[PART 7] 풀기만 하면 저절로 외워지는 패러프레이징 반복 연습

PART 7은 패러프레이징만 잘하면 반은 성공입니다! PART 7에서 꼭 연습해야 하는 패러프레이징을 모든 실전 문제에서 학습할 수 있도록 별도의 코너로 구성하였습니다.

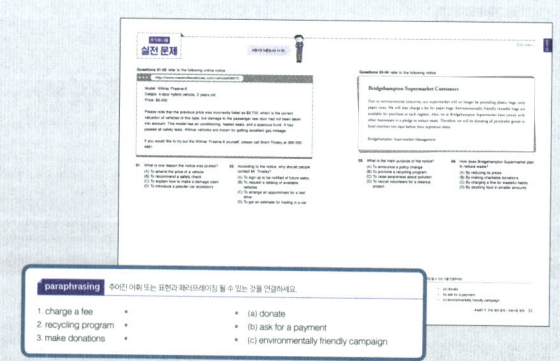

포인트 7

내 옆의 선생님 같은
친절한 풀이 방법

앞에서 학습한 출제 유형이 실제 토익 시험에서는 어떻게 문제로 출제되는지 알 수 있습니다. '이렇게 풀어요'에 제시된 풀이 방법을 따라 하다 보면 쉽게 문제가 풀리는 경험을 할 수 있을 거예요!

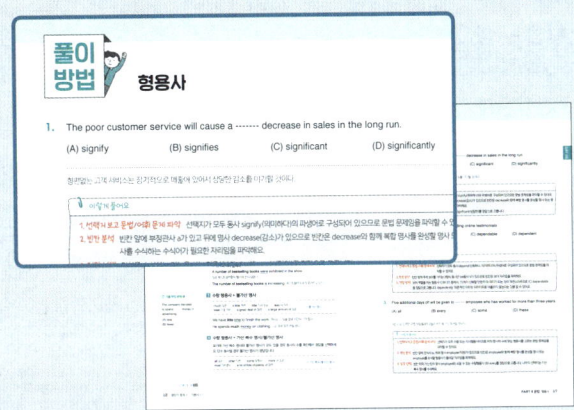

포인트 8

학습 시너지 효과를 높이는
적용 기술

개념이 실제로 적용되는 기술을 참고할 수 있도록 <영단기 700+ 기적의 필기노트>의 관련 페이지와 기술 넘버를 표시했습니다. <영단기 700+ 기적의 필기노트>와 함께 공부하면 학습 시너지 효과를 높일 수 있습니다.

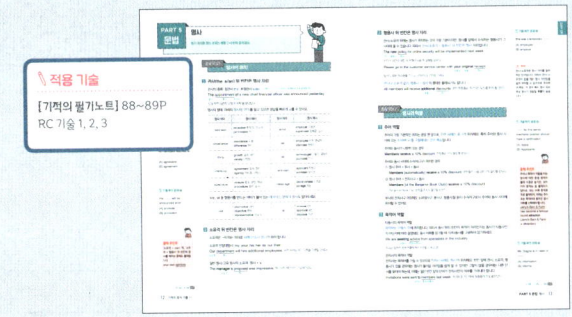

토익 시험의 모든 것

토익 시험 개요

TOEIC 시험이란?
TEST OF ENGLISH FOR INTERNATIONAL COMMUNICATION의 약자로, 모국어가 영어가 아닌 사람이 일상적인 생활 또는 업무에서 의사소통이 가능한지를 평가하는 시험입니다.

시험 구성
듣기(LC) 4개 파트 100문제와 읽기(RC) 3개 파트 100문제로 총 7개 파트에 걸쳐 200문제가 출제됩니다. 200문제 모두 선택지 중에서 정답을 찾는 객관식 문제로 출제됩니다.

구성	PART 구성	출제 내용	문항수	시간	점수
LC (Listening Comprehension)	PART 1	사진 묘사 (사진 보고 문제 풀기)	6	45분 내외	495점
	PART 2	질문-대답 (질문 듣고 답변 고르기)	25		
	PART 3	짧은 대화 (두 사람의 대화를 듣고 질문에 답하기)	39		
	PART 4	설명문 (전화 메시지, 연설문, 안내방송, 일기예보 등을 듣고 질문에 답하기)	30		
RC (Reading Comprehension)	PART 5	문장 빈칸 채우기 (하나의 문장 안에 있는 빈칸에 알맞은 말(문법 & 어휘) 고르기)	30	75분	495점
	PART 6	지문 빈칸 채우기 (짧은 지문 안에 있는 빈칸에 알맞은 말(문법&어휘&문장) 고르기)	16		
	PART 7	싱글 지문 (1개의 지문을 읽고 질문에 답하기)	29		
		더블 지문 (2개의 지문을 읽고 질문에 답하기)	10		
		트리플 지문 (3개의 지문을 읽고 질문에 답하기)	15		
총계			200	약 120분	990점

출제 범위 및 주제
일상생활 및 업무에 대한 영어 의사소통 능력을 평가하기 때문에 특정 분야의 전문 지식 또는 이와 관련된 어휘는 출제하지 않습니다. 국제 업무 환경에 맞게 다양한 국가의 지명과 성명이 등장하며, 듣기 평가에서는 미국, 영국, 호주 발음이 고르게 섞여 출제됩니다. 다음의 주제를 참고해 봅시다.

기업 일반	이사회, 편지, 공지, 전화, 팩스, 이메일, 사무실 장비 및 가구, 사무실 규정, 계약, 협상, 합병 및 인수, 판매, 보증, 사업계획, 회의
공식 연회	식사 및 연회, 장소 예약
엔터테인먼트	영화, 공연, 전시
재무	은행업무, 투자, 세금, 회계, 청구
의료	건강보험, 병원 방문 및 예약
부동산	건설 및 보수 내역, 부동산 구매 및 임대, 기타 설비
제조	제품 조립, 공장 경영, 품질 관리
채용	모집, 고용, 퇴임, 승진, 급여, 일자리 지원서, 구인광고, 연금, 시상
구매	쇼핑, 주문, 배송, 송장
기술	전자장비, 기술지원, 컴퓨터, 연구실과 관련 장비
여행	교통 관련 일정, 교통 관련 각종 공지, 렌터카, 호텔 예약, 연착 및 취소

시험 접수부터 성적 확인까지! 토익 가이드

1 토익 접수 방법
- 토익 시험의 인터넷 접수 기간을 한국 TOEIC 위원회 사이트(www.toeic.co.kr)에서 확인합니다.
- 사이트에서 인터넷 접수를 선택하고 시험일, 고사장, 수험정보 등의 정보를 입력합니다.
- 시험 접수 시 최근 6개월 이내 사진(JPG 형식)이 필요하오니 미리 준비합니다.

TIP 시험 D-30부터는 특별추가접수에 해당하여 약 5천원 정도의 추가 비용이 발생합니다. 미리 시험을 접수하는 것이 좋습니다.

2 시험 당일 꼭! 챙겨야 할 준비물
- 규정 신분증
  성인의 경우, 주민등록증, 운전면허증, 기간 만료 전 여권, 공무원증 등이 인정됩니다. 중고등학생에 한하여 학생증(국내 학생증만 허용)도 신분증으로 인정됩니다.
- 연필 (볼펜, 사인펜은 No!)
  연필 끝을 뭉뚝하게 만들어 준비하면 답안 마킹을 더 쉽게 할 수 있습니다.
- 지우개
- 아날로그 손목시계 (전자식 시계는 No!)

3 입실 전 유의사항
- 시험 시간이 오전일 경우, 오전 9:20까지, 시험 시간이 오후일 경우 오후 2:20까지 입실합니다.

TIP 오전 시험은 오전 9:50 이후, 오후 시험은 오후 2:50 이후로는 절대 입실할 수 없으니 꼭 시간을 지켜 미리 입실합니다.
TIP 시험 시간 직전에는 독해 문제를 풀기보다는 듣기 연습을 충분히 하여 귀를 훈련시키는 게 더 효과적입니다.

4 시험 진행 안내

오전 시험	오후 시험	시험 진행
9:30~9:45 (15분)	2:30~2:45 (15분)	답안지 작성 오리엔테이션
9:45~9:50 (5분)	2:45~2:50 (5분)	쉬는 시간
9:50~10:05 (15분)	2:50~3:05 (15분)	신분증 확인
10:05~10:10 (5분)	3:05~3:10 (5분)	문제지 배부, 파본 확인
10:10~10:55 (45분)	3:10~3:55 (45분)	듣기 평가 (LC)
10:55~12:10 (75분)	3:55~5:10 (75분)	독해 평가 (RC)

5 성적 확인 및 성적표 발급 방법 알아보기
- 시험일로부터 10일 후 낮 12시에 한국 TOEIC 위원회 사이트(www.toeic.co.kr)에서 성적 확인이 가능합니다.
  (토요일 시행 시험 등 일부 회차 시험은 11일 후에 발표될 수 있습니다.)
- 성적 수령은 온라인 출력이나 우편 수령을 택할 수 있습니다.
- 온라인 출력 시, 성적 유효기간 내 홈페이지를 통해 출력 가능합니다.
- 우편 수령 시, 성적발표 후 접수 시 기입한 주소로 성적표가 우편 발송됩니다. (약 7~10일 소요)
- 온라인 출력과 우편 수령은 1회 발급만 무료이며, 이후에는 유료로 발급됩니다.

'멋진 당신, 오늘도 화이팅'

DAY 01

오늘의 학습 포인트

PART 5. 명사
1. 명사의 인지 - 관사/소유격/형용사 뒤
2. 명사의 역할 - 주어/목적어/보어
3. 명사의 쓸만한 수 - 가산/불가산 명사
4. 사람 명사 vs. 사물/추상 명사 - 문맥 파악
5. 복합 명사 - application form, reference letter 등

PART 6. 앞의 내용이 단서인 명사 어휘!
↳ 단서가 되는 명사, 반복 및 관계 파악

PART 7. 공지 · 공지 공지/회사사상 공지
↳ 전문 해석이 지문에서 빠르게 찾기
↳ 주로 앞단에서 파악,
but 아래쪽은 마지막에 풀기

PART 5 문법

명사

명사 자리를 묻는 문제는 매회 2~3문제 출제돼요.

📎 적용 기술

[기적의 필기노트] 88~89P
RC 기술 1, 2, 3

출제 유형 1

명사의 위치

1 관사(the, a/an) 뒤 빈칸은 명사 자리

- 관사의 종류: 정관사 the, 부정관사 a/an → '관사 + ------ + 전치사'의 형태로 주로 출제됩니다.

  The <u>appointment</u> of a new chief financial officer was announced yesterday.
  관사　　명사　　전치사
  신임 재무 장관의 임명이 어제 발표되었다.

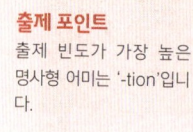

출제 포인트
출제 빈도가 가장 높은 명사형 어미는 '-tion'입니다.

- 명사의 형태: 아래의 **명사형 어미**를 알고 있으면 정답을 빠르게 고를 수 있어요.

명사 어미	명사 예시	명사 어미	명사 예시
-tion/-sion	reception 환영회, 접수처 permission 허가	-er/-or	employer 고용주 supervisor 감독관, 상사
-ance/-ence	assistance 도움 difference 차이	-ee	employee 직원, 종업원 attendee 참석자
-th/-ty	growth 성장, 증가 variety 다양함	-ist	technologist 기술자, 공학자 journalist 기자
-ment/-cy	agreement 협정, 합의 agency 대리점, 대행사	-ant/-cian	applicant 지원자 politician 정치인
-sure/-dure	closure 종료, 폐점, 폐쇄 procedure 절차, 순서	-ness/-age	decisiveness 단호함 storage 보관

🔒 확인 문제 ❶

All members reached an
-------.

(A) agreeable
(B) agreement

- -ive, -al 등 형용사를 만드는 어미가 붙어 있는 **예외적인 형태의 명사**도 알아두세요.

-ive	alternative 대안 objective 목적 representative 대표자	-al	renewal 갱신 approval 승인 disposal 처리

🔒 확인 문제 ❷

His ------- will be
announced soon.

(A) promote
(B) promotion

2 소유격 뒤 빈칸은 명사 자리

소유격은 '~의'라는 의미로 **뒤에 반드시 명사**가 와야 합니다.

- 소유격 인칭대명사: my, your, his, her, its, our, their

  Our <u>department</u> will hire additional employees. 우리 부서는 추가 직원을 고용할 것이다.
  소유격　　명사

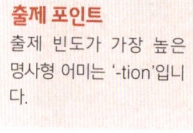

출제 포인트
'소유격 + own' 뒤, '소유격 + 형용사' 뒤 빈칸에 명사를 채우는 문제도 출제됩니다.
your own opinions

- 일반 명사/고유 명사의 소유격: 명사 + 's

  The **manager's** <u>proposal</u> was impressive. 매니저의 제안서는 인상적이었다.
  소유격　　　명사

정답 ❶ (B) ❷ (B)

12　기적의 토익 RC

3 형용사 뒤 빈칸은 명사 자리

· 관사/소유격 뒤에는 명사가 위치하는 것이 가장 기본이지만, 명사를 앞에서 수식하는 형용사가 그 사이에 올 수 있습니다. 따라서 '관사/소유격 + 형용사' 뒤 빈칸은 명사 자리입니다.

The new policy for online security will be implemented next week.
관사 형용사 명사

온라인 보안에 대한 새 정책이 다음 주 실행될 것이다.

Please go to the customer service center with **your original** receipt.
소유격 형용사 명사

당신의 원본 영수증을 가지고 고객서비스 센터로 가세요.

· 관사나 소유격 없이 '형용사 + 명사'의 형태로 출제되기도 합니다.

All members will receive **additional** discounts. 모든 회원들은 추가적인 할인을 받게 될 것이다.
형용사 명사

출제 유형 2
명사의 역할

1 주어 역할

· 주어의 가장 기본적인 위치는 문장 맨 앞으로, **주어 뒤에는 동사**가 위치해요. 특히 주어와 동사 사이에 오는 **수식어(구)를 구별해내는 것이 핵심**입니다.

· 주어와 동사가 나란히 오는 경우
Members receive a 10% discount. 회원들은 10% 할인을 받는다.

· 주어와 동사 사이에 수식어(구)가 위치한 경우
① 명사 주어 + 부사 + 동사
Members [automatically] **receive** a 10% discount. 회원들은 자동으로 10% 할인을 받는다.

② 명사 주어 + 전치사구 + 동사
Members [of the Benjamin Book Club] **receive** a 10% discount.
Benjamin Book Club 회원들은 10% 할인을 받는다.

· 부사와 전치사구 이외에도 to부정사구, 분사구, 형용사절 등이 수식어구로서 주어와 동사 사이에 위치할 수 있어요.

2 목적어 역할

· 타동사의 목적어 역할
목적어는 타동사 뒤에 위치합니다. 따라서 동사 뒤의 빈칸이 목적어 자리인지는 동사가 타동사인지 아닌지에 따라 결정돼요. 동사 어휘를 암기할 때 자/타동사를 구분하여 암기하세요.

We are **seeking** advice from specialists in the industry.
타동사 목적어(명사)

우리는 업계의 전문가들에게서 조언을 구하고 있다.

· 전치사의 목적어 역할
전치사는 목적어를 가질 수 있으므로 **전치사 뒤에도 명사**가 위치해요. 빈칸 앞에 관사, 소유격, 형용사가 있을 경우에는 명사가 들어갈 자리임을 쉽게 알 수 있지만 그렇지 않을 경우에는 다른 단서를 찾아야 하는데, 이때는 일단 빈칸 앞의 단어가 전치사인지 여부를 가려내야 합니다.

Invitations were sent **to** members last week. 초대장은 지난주에 회원들에게 발송되었다.
전치사 목적어(명사)

🔒 확인 문제 ❸

She was a temporary -------.

(A) employee
(B) employs

⚠ 주의

관사/소유격은 명사 자리를 알려주는 단서입니다. 따라서 관사/소유격이 없을 때는 명사 자리임을 쉽게 파악할 수 없으므로 주의해야 해요. 이 경우 복수 명사 또는 추상 명사가 정답일 확률이 높습니다.

🔒 확인 문제 ❹

------- for this senior mechanic position should have a certification.

(A) Apply
(B) Applicants

출제 포인트

주어나 목적어 역할을 하는 명사에 대한 문법 문제의 출제 비중은 높지만, 보어 자리 문제는 잘 출제되지 않아요. 대신 어휘 문제로 주로 출제되며, 이때는 주어 또는 목적어와 동격인 명사 어휘를 선택해야 합니다.
Jerry's Barn & Farm has become a famous tourist **attraction**.
(Jerry's Barn & Farm = attraction)

🔒 확인 문제 ❺

Ms. Gagne is in need of -------.

(A) information
(B) informs

정답 ❸ (A) ❹ (B) ❺ (A)

PART 5 문법 명사 13

적용 기술

[기적의 필기노트] 91P
RC 기술 5

🔒 확인 문제 ❻

Vincent Lab is now hiring an -------.

(A) intern
(B) interns

🔒 확인 문제 ❼

The ------- are invited to the reception.

(A) speaker
(B) speakers

🔒 확인 문제 ❽

This position requires extensive ------- in the computer science.

(A) expert
(B) expertise

⚠️ 주의

사람 명사는 가산 명사이므로 빈칸 앞에 관사/소유격이 없을 경우 반드시 복수 명사로 쓰여야 해요.

출제 유형 3

명사의 종류와 수

1 a/an 뒤에는 가산 단수 명사

- 부정관사 a/an 뒤는 명사 자리이며 가산 **단수 명사**가 위치해야 합니다.
- 이 유형의 문제는 선택지에 명사가 2개 이상 있으며, 단/복수 또는 가산 명사/불가산 명사가 혼재된 형태로 출제됩니다.
- 부정관사와 빈칸 사이에 형용사가 위치할 수 있으니 혼동하지 않도록 주의하세요.

|빈출 가산 명사|

증감	an increase 증가 a rise 증가 an advance 발전 a decrease 감소 a decline 하락
돈/금액	a refund 환불 a price 가격 a discount 할인 a benefit 수당 a profit 이익금
규정	a regulation 규제 a procedure 절차 a measure 수단 a standard 기준
기타	a relation 관계 a statement 진술 a source 출처 a request 요청

- **사람을 나타내는 명사는 모두 가산 명사입니다.**

2 the/소유격과 명사의 수

- 정관사 the 또는 소유격 뒤에 빈칸이 있고, 선택지로 단수 명사와 복수 명사가 모두 제시될 경우에는 둘 다 빈칸에 올 수 있으므로 또 다른 단서가 필요합니다.
- 빈칸이 **주어** 자리일 경우에는 **동사와 수를 일치시켜야** 합니다.
  The **items** are temporarily out of stock. 이 제품들은 일시적으로 품절입니다.
- 빈칸이 **목적어** 자리일 경우에는 **대명사와 수를 일치시켜야** 합니다.
  Please send me the **printers** tomorrow and I will install them.
  프린터를 내일 보내주시면 제가 설치할게요.

800+

3 관사/소유격 없는 명사 자리

- 빈칸 앞에 관사/소유격이 없는 경우 **명사의 종류를 구분**할 수 있는지 묻는 문제가 출제됩니다.
  빈칸 앞에 관사/소유격이 없고 선택지가 가산 명사의 단/복수 형태로 제시될 경우 반드시 복수 형태가 정답입니다.
  We offer free shipping for online (~~purchase~~ / **purchases**).
  우리는 온라인 구매에 대해 무료 배송을 제공합니다.
- 빈칸 앞에 관사/소유격이 없고 선택지가 가산 단수 명사와 불가산 명사로 제시될 경우 불가산 명사가 정답입니다.
  Evertech Software offers technical (~~assistant~~ / **assistance**) around the clock.
  Evertech 소프트웨어는 24시간 내내 기술 지원을 제공한다.

|빈출 불가산 명사|

advice 조언	access 접근	information 정보	notice 통지	clothing 의류
consent 동의	equipment 장비	luggage/baggage 수하물	news 뉴스	

- 빈칸 앞에 관사/소유격이 없고 선택지가 가산 복수 명사와 불가산 명사로 제시될 경우 문맥상 적절한 의미를 가진 명사가 정답입니다.
  Jefferson & Associates is now hiring (**professionals** / ~~professionalism~~) in tax laws.
  Jefferson & Associates는 현재 세법 전문가를 고용하고 있다.

정답 ❻ (A) ❼ (B) ❽ (B)

14   기적의 토익 RC

4 수량형용사에 따른 명사의 종류

빈칸 앞의 수량형용사가 명사의 종류를 결정합니다.

each 각각의 every 모든 another 다른 하나의	+ 가산 단수 명사

each item 각각의 제품 every employee 전 직원

(a) few 몇 개의 many 많은 several 몇몇의 various 다양한, 여러 both 둘 다 numerous 많은 a number of 많은 a couple of 두(세) 개의	+ 가산 복수 명사

a few questions 몇 가지 질문 various services 다양한 서비스들

(a) little 적은 less 더 적은 much 많은	+ 불가산 명사

a little time 적은 시간 less information 더 적은 정보 much money 많은 돈

all 모든 lots of/a lot of/plenty of 많은 some/any 약간의	+ 가산/불가산 명사 모두 가능

all employees 모든 직원들(가산 명사) all equipment 모든 장비들(불가산 명사)

출제 유형 4
사람 명사 vs. 사물/추상 명사

· 빈칸이 명사 자리이며 선택지에 사람 명사와 사물/추상 명사가 함께 제시될 경우 문맥에 알맞은 명사를 찾으면 됩니다.

You can purchase all (**products** / ~~producers~~) on our Web site at discounted prices. 당신은 우리 웹사이트에 있는 모든 제품을 할인된 가격에 구매할 수 있습니다.

A complete event schedule will be sent to all session (~~leadership~~ / **leaders**). 전체 이벤트 일정이 모든 모임 리더들에게 송부될 것입니다.

|사람 명사 – 사물/추상 명사| 중요!

an applicant/applicants 지원자 — application 지원
a founder/founders 설립자 — foundation 토대
an investor/investors 투자자 — investment 투자
an analyst/analysts 분석가 — analysis 분석
an assistant/assistants 조수 — assistance 도움
a resident/residents 거주자 — residence 주택, 거주
a user/users 사용자 — use/usage 사용
an operator/operators 운영자 — operation 운영
a contributor/contributors 공헌자 — contribution 공헌
a supervisor/supervisors 상사, 감독관 — supervision 관리, 지도, 감독
a negotiator/negotiators 협상가 — negotiation 협상, 교섭
an architect/architects 건축가 — architecture 건축
a representative/representatives 직원, 대표자 — representation 대표
a distributor/distributors 유통업체, 유통업자 — distribution 배급, 유통
a journalist/journalists 기자 — a journal/journals 잡지 — journalism 언론
an employer/employers 고용주 — an employee/employees 직원 — employment 고용
an attendant/attendants 종업원 — an attendee/attendees 참석자 — attendance 참석, 참석자 수

🔒 확인 문제 ❾

Many ------- will attend the afternoon sessions.

(A) participant
(B) participants

✎ 적용 기술

[기적의 필기노트] 90P
RC 기술 4

🔒 확인 문제 ❿

The floor plan will be checked by the -------.

(A) architect
(B) architecture

출제 포인트
사람 명사는 앞에 관사가 있거나 복수형으로 써야 합니다.

(A) ❿ (B) ❾ 답정

PART 5 문법 명사 15

출제 유형 5

복합 명사(명사1 + 명사2)

출제 포인트
명사 1 부분이 주로 빈칸으로 출제돼요.

- 명사 앞에 빈칸이 올 경우 형용사 자리인지 복합 명사를 이루는 명사 자리인지 구별할 수 있어야 합니다.

  All factory workers should follow the (~~safe~~ / **safety**) regulations.
  모든 공장 직원들은 안전 규정을 따라야 한다.

|빈출 복합 명사|

application form 신청서	reference letter 추천서
customer satisfaction 고객 만족	safety regulations 안전 규정
expansion project 확장 계획	building permit 건축 허가
travel arrangement 출장(여행) 준비	payment option 지불 옵션
performance evaluation 업무 성과 평가	expiration date 만기일
safety inspection 안전 점검	construction site 건축 부지
maintenance work 유지보수 작업	office supplies 사무용품
job opportunity 직무 기회	meal preference 식사 선호도
job vacancy 공석	clearance sale 정리 세일
attendance records 출석률	sales figures 매출액
employee performance 직원 실적	

🔒 확인 문제 ⑪

You have to fill out this ------- form.

(A) applicable
(B) application

⚠ 주의
복합 명사의 복수형은 명사2에 -(e)s를 붙여요.

`800+`

- 복합 명사에서 명사 1은 주로 단수이지만 복수 형태가 오는 아래와 같은 단어도 있어요.

  customs office 세관
  savings account/plan 예금 계좌/상품
  electronics company 전자 회사

  earnings growth 수익 증가
  awards ceremony 시상식
  sales representative 영업 사원

16 기적의 토익 RC

 명사

1. Mr. Williams submitted his ------- for a mortgage loan last week.

(A) apply   (B) application   (C) applied   (D) applies

Williams 씨는 지난주에 주택담보대출 신청서를 제출했다.

> **이렇게 풀어요**
>
> **1. 선택지 보고 문법/어휘 문제 파악** 선택지가 동사 apply(신청하다)의 다양한 형태로 구성되어 있으므로 품사를 구분하는 문법 문제임을 파악할 수 있어요.
>
> **2. 빈칸 분석** 빈칸 앞에 소유격 his가 있는데, 소유격 뒤에는 명사가 온다는 개념을 떠올려요.
>
> **3. 정답 선택** 명사인 (B) application(신청서)을 정답으로 고릅니다.

2. Judges are required to review ------- for the writing competition.

(A) enter   (B) entries   (C) entry   (D) entered

심사위원들은 글쓰기 대회의 출품작을 검토해야 한다.

> **이렇게 풀어요**
>
> **1. 선택지 보고 문법/어휘 문제 파악** 선택지가 동사 enter(출품하다)의 다양한 형태로 구성되어 있으므로 품사를 구분하는 문법 문제임을 파악할 수 있어요.
>
> **2. 빈칸 분석** 빈칸 앞에 타동사 review(검토하다)가 있으므로 목적어 역할을 할 수 있는 명사가 들어가야 함을 파악해요.
>
> **3. 정답 선택** (B)와 (C)가 명사인데, 빈칸 앞에 a/an/the나 소유격이 없으므로 복수 명사인 (B) entries(출품작)를 정답으로 고릅니다.

3. The regular ------- evaluation will be scheduled at the end of June.

(A) perform   (B) performed   (C) performing   (D) performance

정기 성과 평가는 6월 말로 일정이 잡힐 것이다.

> **이렇게 풀어요**
>
> **1. 선택지 보고 문법/어휘 문제 파악** 선택지가 동사 perform(수행하다)의 다양한 형태로 구성되어 있으므로 품사를 구분하는 문법 문제임을 파악할 수 있어요.
>
> **2. 빈칸 분석** 빈칸 뒤에 명사 evaluation(평가)이 있으므로 빈칸은 evaluation을 수식하는 형용사 또는 evaluation과 함께 복합 명사를 완성할 명사 자리임을 파악해요.
>
> **3. 정답 선택** evaluation은 performance와 함께 쓰여 '업무 성과 평가'라는 의미의 복합 명사로 쓰이므로 (D) performance를 정답으로 고릅니다.

PART 5 어휘
명사 어휘 (1)

각 어휘와 함께 자주 쓰이는 표현을 통째로 외워두세요.

01 ability — 할 수 있음, 능력

ability to부정사	~을 할 수 있음, ~하는 능력
show one's ability	실력을 발휘하다

02 attempt — 시도

attempt to부정사	~을 하려는 시도, ~하려고 애씀
make an attempt to부정사	~을 시도하다, ~하려고 애쓰다

900+
03 stretch — (길게) 뻗은 지역[구간], 기간

a stretch of	쭉 뻗은, 이어진
stretch of road	쭉 뻗은 도로

♣ 빈출 토익 선생님 Pick!
04 property — 건물, 부동산, 재산, 속성

historic property	역사적인 건물
private property	사유 재산
surrounding property	주위의 건물
property manager	건물 관리자

05 entry — 입장, 출입, 가입, 참가

limit entries to	~로의 입장을 제한하다
winning entry	결승전 참가자

♣ 빈출 토익 선생님 Pick!
06 effort — 노력, 수고

in an effort to부정사	~해 보려는 노력으로
make an effort	노력하다

07 patience — 참을성, 인내력

appreciate one's patience	양해해 주셔서 감사하다
with patience	인내심을 가지고, 참을성 있게

800+
08 proximity — 가까움, 근접

proximity to	~에 근접한, 가까운
in the proximity of	~의 부근에

09 advance — 전진, 발전, 증가

in advance	미리
payment in advance	선불
advance in	~에 있어서의 발전

10 candidate — 후보자, 지원자

successful candidate	합격자
qualified candidate	적임자
choose a candidate	후보자를 선출하다

11 permission — 허가, 승인

obtain permission	허가를 얻다
permission from	~로부터의 허가
permission for	~에 대한 허가

♣ 빈출 토익 선생님 Pick!
12 regulation — 규정, 규제

follow regulations	규정을 따르다
safety regulation	안전 수칙

800+
13 perspective — 관점, 시각

have a perspective on	~에 대한 견해를 갖다
broaden one's perspective	~의 시야를 넓히다
from a different perspective	다른 관점에서

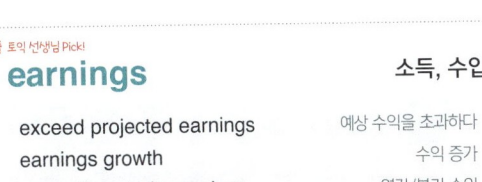

14 addition
추가, 추가된 것

addition of A to B — A를 B에 추가
make a great addition to — ~에 큰 보탬이 되다

👣 빈출 토익 선생님 Pick!
15 recognition
인정, 인식

in recognition of — ~을 인정하여
achieve recognition — 인정받다
gain recognition — 인정받다

16 productivity
생산성

increase productivity — 생산성을 향상시키다
improve one's productivity — ~의 생산성을 높이다

17 environment
환경

working environment — 근로 환경
protect the environment — 환경을 보호하다
adjust to a new environment — 새로운 환경에 적응하다

900+
18 concentration
집중

boost concentration — 집중을 돋우다
concentration on — ~에 대한 집중
require concentration — 집중을 필요로 하다

👣 빈출 토익 선생님 Pick!
19 earnings
소득, 수입

exceed projected earnings — 예상 수익을 초과하다
earnings growth — 수익 증가
annual/quarterly earnings — 연간/분기 수익

20 absence
결석, 부재, 없음

in one's absence — ~가 없는 사이에, 부재중에
sick absence — 병결
absence from work — 결근

21 achievement
업적, 성취

achievement in — ~에서의 공적, 업적

22 application
지원(서), 신청(서)

submit an application for — ~을 위한 신청서를 제출하다
application form — 신청서
complete[fill out] an application — 신청서를 작성하다

🧑 풀이 방법

This managerial position requires the ------- to respond to any requests from both in-store and online customers.

(A) concentration　　(B) regulation　　(C) candidate　　(D) ability

이 매니저 직책은 매장 고객과 온라인 고객들의 어떠한 요청에도 응대할 수 있는 능력을 요구한다.

> 🦋 이렇게 풀어요
>
> **1. 선택지 보고 문법/어휘 문제 파악** 선택지가 서로 다른 명사 어휘로 구성되어 있으므로 어휘 문제임을 파악해요.
> **2. 빈칸 분석** 빈칸 뒤에 to부정사가 있음을 파악합니다.
> **3. 정답 선택** to부정사와 함께 쓰이는 명사인 (D) ability를 정답으로 선택합니다.

PART 5 어휘 명사 어휘 (1)　19

따라 하면 문제가 풀리는

연습 문제

앞서 학습한 문제 풀이법을 적용하여 맞는 것에 ✔ 표시 하거나 괄호 안에
적절한 답을 쓰고 정답을 선택하세요.

01 The board members' ------- is built on the expansion into the European market.

(A) expects
(B) expected
(C) expecting
(D) expectation

1. 선택지 보고 문법/어휘 문제 파악하기 ☐문법 문제 ☐어휘 문제
2. 빈칸 분석하기 빈칸 앞에 있는 것 ☐관사 ☐명사 ☐소유격
          → 빈칸은 ☐명사 ☐동사 자리이다.
3. 정답 선택하기 정답 (   )

02 If you want to save more at Kent Market, please complete an ------- for our membership.

(A) addition
(B) application
(C) experience
(D) attendance

1. 선택지 보고 문법/어휘 문제 파악하기 ☐문법 문제 ☐어휘 문제
2. 빈칸 분석하기 빈칸 앞 동사 (   )
          → 동사의 의미 (   )
          → 이 동사와 어울려 쓰일 수 있는 명사가 답이다.
3. 정답 선택하기 정답 (   )

03 You must get ------- from your immediate supervisor before exchanging work shifts.

(A) permit
(B) permission
(C) permitted
(D) permitting

1. 선택지 보고 문법/어휘 문제 파악하기 ☐문법 문제 ☐어휘 문제
2. 빈칸 분석하기 빈칸 앞에 있는 것 ☐관사 ☐타동사 ☐자동사
          → 빈칸은 ☐명사 ☐동사 자리이다.
3. 정답 선택하기 정답 (   )

04 The Hancock family founded a charitable ------- over a century ago.

(A) establishing
(B) establishment
(C) established
(D) establisher

1. 선택지 보고 문법/어휘 문제 파악하기 ☐ 문법 문제 ☐ 어휘 문제
2. 빈칸 분석하기 빈칸 앞에 있는 것 ☐ 소유격 ☐ 형용사 ☐ 부사
   → 빈칸은 ☐ 명사 ☐ 동사 자리이다.
   → 정답이 될 수 있는 후보 2개 (,   )
3. 정답 선택하기 정답 (   )

05 All ------- will receive a name tag, pen, and notepad after the lecture.

(A) attend
(B) attendee
(C) attendees
(D) attended

1. 선택지 보고 문법/어휘 문제 파악하기 ☐ 문법 문제 ☐ 어휘 문제
2. 빈칸 분석하기 빈칸 앞에 있는 것 ☐ 소유격 ☐ 형용사 ☐ 부사
   → 빈칸은 ☐ 복수 명사 ☐ 단수 명사 ☐ 동사 자리이다.
3. 정답 선택하기 정답 (   )

06 This workshop is specifically intended to aid anyone who is currently seeking -------.

(A) employment
(B) employee
(C) employer
(D) employed

1. 선택지 보고 문법/어휘 문제 파악하기 ☐ 문법 문제 ☐ 어휘 문제
2. 빈칸 분석하기 빈칸 앞에 있는 것 ☐ 형용사 ☐ 타동사 ☐ 자동사
   → 빈칸은 ☐ 명사 ☐ 동사 자리이다.
   → 정답이 될 수 있는 후보 3개 (,   ,   )
   → 빈칸 앞에 an이 없으므로 ☐ 불가산 명사 ☐ 가산 명사가 들어가야 한다.
3. 정답 선택하기 정답 (   )

토익에 나올
실전 문제

제한시간 9분입니다! 시~작!

01. Please refer to your contract with Horizon Mobile for a full ------- of your service plan's details.

(A) describe
(B) descriptive
(C) to describe
(D) description

02. ------- commuting to the branch office in Daytona are entitled to receive an allowance.

(A) Supervised
(B) Supervising
(C) Supervisors
(D) Supervisor

03. Donner Cable gives lower ------- to clients with contracts of two years or more.

(A) rated
(B) rates
(C) rate
(D) rater

04. Guests at Longwood Hotel & Spa are often delighted by the wide ------- of services that are provided.

(A) variation
(B) various
(C) variety
(D) to vary

05. Thanks to a ------- in profits, the board of directors has agreed upon a company-wide bonus.

(A) rise
(B) risen
(C) rising
(D) to rise

06. Due to its popularity, you are strongly recommended to purchase tickets in -------.

(A) view
(B) environment
(C) advance
(D) perspective

07. Lenny's Farm has been the largest ------- of organic produce in the region for over a decade.

(A) to supply
(B) supplying
(C) supplier
(D) supplies

08. All tenants are asked to make a ------- before or on the due date.

(A) be paid
(B) payment
(C) pays
(D) to pay

09. Your ------- handles any problems related to defective merchandise at our store.

(A) depart
(B) departed
(C) department
(D) departing

10. The rapid growth of Tacoma Industrial over the past year has attracted much -------.

(A) interests
(B) interested
(C) to interest
(D) interest

11. Please be sure to check our service coverage map for any ------- that may apply to your area.

(A) restrictions
(B) restrict
(C) restricting
(D) restrictive

12. This two-bedroom apartment is a lot more expensive due to its ------- to the subway station.

(A) cost
(B) proximity
(C) attempt
(D) reminder

22 기적의 토익 RC

13. Many staff members consult Mr. Douglass for ------- about how to improve their professional lives.
    (A) advise
    (B) advises
    (C) advisory
    (D) advice

14. Famous Fashion is holding a massive ------- sale to make room for new merchandise.
    (A) clear
    (B) clearance
    (C) to clear
    (D) clearing

15. A report published on the ------- of Washington Furniture helped attract the attention of many investors.
    (A) profitably
    (B) profited
    (C) profitable
    (D) profitability

16. Attempts to enter foreign ------- should consider factors such as cultural differences.
    (A) marketing
    (B) to market
    (C) market
    (D) markets

17. The city of Petersburgh has experienced tremendous ------- in population since it attracted some major IT companies.
    (A) grows
    (B) to grow
    (C) growth
    (D) grown

18. The companies will merge sometime this year if the owners can come to a mutual -------.
    (A) agree
    (B) agreed
    (C) agreeable
    (D) agreement

19. In an ------- to publicize the local festival, most businesses in town have agreed to put its posters in their stores and offices.
    (A) entry
    (B) effort
    (C) advance
    (D) earning

20. Due to a ------- of required experience, Ms. Hillman didn't move to the second round of the job interview.
    (A) lacked
    (B) lacks
    (C) lack
    (D) lacking

21. In order to use a company car, you have to obtain written ------- from your supervisor.
    (A) permission
    (B) concentration
    (C) application
    (D) notice

22. VitaBlast is a popular dietary ------- for people who normally skip breakfast.
    (A) supplementary
    (B) supplementing
    (C) supplement
    (D) supplemented

23. Her assistant will take care of the vacation request in Mr. Prince's -------.
    (A) property
    (B) ability
    (C) load
    (D) absence

24. Our new automated tracking system will increase your company's -------.
    (A) productivity
    (B) achievement
    (C) patience
    (D) addition

PART 5 명사 / 명사 어휘 (1)   23

PART 6

앞의 내용이 단서인 명사 어휘 [800+]

선택지가 서로 다른 명사 어휘로 이루어져 있으면 앞뒤 문맥을 파악합니다.

적용 기술

[기적의 필기노트] 158P
RC 기술 76

VOCA

scores of 많은
mark 표시하다
founder 설립자
based on ~에 기반하여
properly 제대로, 적절히
express 나타내다, 표현하다
relocate 이전하다
branch 지점

풀이 방법   article

해석 p.5

Decatur's Deep Dish

Pirelli's Pizza & Pie, attracts scores of tourists and is marked on almost every local map. Located downtown on Main Street here in Decatur, it has been a -------
                                                                                    01.
here since 2005. Luigi Pirelli, the founder, wanted to open a restaurant with a creative menu based on Chicago's famous deep dish pizzas, and it has proved to be a huge -------.
          PART 5

To cook the items on the menu properly, a large brick oven is required. Pirelli's Pizza & Pie's kitchen actually has several of them, and they are kept hot throughout the day. They are fired up at 10 a.m. every day, one hour before the restaurant opens.

Mr. Pirelli has expressed no desire to relocate or open another branch. So, next time you're in Decatur, be sure to visit this local hotspot!

01. (A) cafeteria
    (B) preference
    (C) history
    (D) landmark

이렇게 풀어요

1. **선택지 보고 문법/어휘 문제 파악** 선택지가 같은 품사의 서로 다른 어휘로 이루어져 있으므로 어휘 문제임을 파악해요.
   (A) 구내식당   (B) 선호(도)   (C) 역사   (D) 랜드마크, 명소

2. **빈칸 분석** 어휘 문제이므로 문맥을 파악합니다. 빈칸 앞에 Pirelli's Pizza and Pie 레스토랑이 많은 관광객들을 끌어들이고 지역의 거의 모든 지도에 표시되어 있다는 내용이 있으므로 이와 관련된 어휘가 들어가야 함을 파악합니다.

3. **정답 선택** 빈칸 앞 내용을 단서로 하여 문맥상 가장 적절한 (D) landmark를 정답으로 선택합니다.

해설

빈칸 앞에 '관사 + 형용사'가 있으므로 빈칸은 명사 자리입니다. 따라서 보기 중 유일한 명사인 (B)가 정답입니다.

PART 5 문법 적용 문제

Luigi Pirelli, the founder, wanted to open a restaurant with a creative menu based on Chicago's famous deep dish pizzas, and it has proved to be a huge -------.

(A) successful   (B) success   (C) successfully   (D) succeed

24 기적의 토익 RC

따라 하면 문제가 풀리는

연습 문제

빈칸 앞 내용에서 단서가 될 부분을 찾아 표시하세요.
표시한 것을 바탕으로 정답 어휘를 선택하세요.

정답 및 해설 p.5

DAY 01

01
The Loganville Theater is open again after its 2-month renovation! Now locals have a place to enjoy ------- once again.

(A) performances   (B) interiors

02
The CEO of Blackburn Marketing, Martin Blackburn, announced at a press conference that his company will take over Arizona Ads. "The ------- will help us compete on a national level with their employees' experience," he told reporters.

(A) establishment   (B) acquisition

03
Dear Mr. Han,

I'm sorry to hear that your order was not delivered today as scheduled. The ------- was caused by the insufficient number of drivers.

(A) delay   (B) replacement

04
Hancock Kids' manager announced that the band will be coming to Lodi for the benefit performance. All of the ------- will go to the Lodi Children's Hospital where a cancer center is being constructed.

(A) proceeds   (B) sales

PART 6 앞의 내용이 단서인 명사 어휘   25

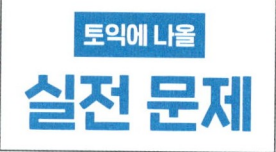

토익에 나올

실전 문제

제한시간 4분입니다! 시~작!

Questions 01-04 refer to the following article.

Monster Meats in Bristol

If you've been to Bristol, you've probably heard of Monster Meats, the famous restaurant located on Oak Drive and managed by Danielle Greene. Tables fill up quickly, so it is highly recommended to call -------. On some evenings, the entire place is ------- for private parties or special events.
     01.   **02.**

To promote her menu, Ms. Greene holds eating contests based on whatever new dish she decides to add to it. ------- are then given in the form of coupons to participants. -------.
     03.   **04.**

Be sure to make a reservation at Monster Meats if you plan to visit Bristol. Just don't forget to call first!

01. (A) as well
      (B) in addition
      (C) instead
      (D) in advance

유형 적용 문제

03. (A) Prizes
      (B) Sales
      (C) Classes
      (D) Receipts

02. (A) reserves
      (B) reservation
      (C) reserving
      (D) reserved

04. (A) Most customers prefer taking their orders to go.
      (B) All of the food must be consumed within a specified time limit.
      (C) This encourages people with big appetites to return with friends.
      (D) Discounts are given to those who eat and leave quickly to seat others.

26 기적의 토익 RC

정답 및 해설 p.5

DAY 01

Questions 05-08 refer to the following article.

Veggie Village: A New Star in West Hill

Veggie Village opened a café last year under the ownership of Jaycee Andrade, who began renting the space with the intention of providing locally sourced organic products. The source of all of the natural ------- are listed on the menus of the café. She does so partially to help promote her -------
05.
06.
suppliers.

------- members of high society, Ms. Andrade serves a variety of herbal tees and vegetarian salads.
07.
Also, she provides a very pet-friendly environment so that customers can bring their dogs and cats into the café with them. -------.
08.

Although the prices may be a bit on the high end, Veggie Village has a comfortable atmosphere that is great for a healthy brunch with friends or pets.

유형 적용 문제

05. (A) ingredients
(B) furniture
(C) energy
(D) seafoods

06. (A) partners
(B) partnership
(C) partnered
(D) partnering

07. (A) Attraction
(B) Attracts
(C) Had attracted
(D) To attract

08. (A) They even provide water bowls for pets and have treats for sale.
(B) Not all of the options on the menu are vegetarian dishes, though.
(C) Menu item availability can change depending on the season.
(D) Customers can choose to be seated either inside or on the back patio.

PART 6 앞의 내용이 단서인 명사 어휘   27

PART 7

주제·목적 문제 / 세부사항 문제

PART 7에서 가장 많이 출제되는 두 유형이므로 단서를 빠르게 캐치하는 연습을 해 두세요.

✎ 적용 기술

[기적의 필기노트] 168P
RC 기술 86

🔒 기출 표현 확인

목적 문제 정답으로 출제된 보기
· To detail adjustments~
· To offer a discount
· To provide an overview~
· To announce upcoming
  schedule~

출제 유형 1

주제·목적 문제

주제·목적 문제는 매 시험 4~9문제가 출제될 정도로 출제 빈도가 높습니다. 주로 지문 초반부에 단서가 제시되지만, 처음 두세 줄에서 명확히 파악되지 않는 경우에는 전체 내용을 파악한 후 주제를 찾아야 합니다.

1️ 질문 유형

What is the memo **mainly about**? 회람은 주로 무엇에 관한 것인가?

What is the **purpose** of the letter? 편지의 목적은 무엇인가?

Why was the e-mail **sent[written]**? 이메일은 왜 보내졌는가[쓰여졌는가]?

2️ 핵심 전략

· 지문 초반부에 inform(알리다), remind(상기시키다), announce(발표하다), change(변경하다) 등의 동사가 있을 경우 그 주변 내용을 선택지와 대조하며 답을 찾습니다.

· 지문 초반부에서 주제·목적을 파악하기 어려울 경우, 나머지 문제를 모두 풀고 다시 돌아와 풀면 정답을 파악하기 수월합니다.

✎ 적용 기술

[기적의 필기노트] 170P
RC 기술 87

출제 유형 2

세부사항 문제

PART 7에서 가장 많이 출제되는 유형으로 인물, 장소, 이유, 미래에 발생할 일 등 다양한 것을 묻습니다. 지문 전체를 정독하지 않고 일부만 읽어도 풀 수 있는 유형이므로 질문의 핵심어구를 지문에서 빠르게 찾아내는 것이 중요해요.

1️ 질문 유형

Who is Ms. White? White 씨는 누구인가?

When should the **package arrive**? 소포는 언제 도착해야 하는가?

Where did Mr. Chen study art? Chen 씨는 어디서 미술을 공부했는가?

How long has the bank been **in business**? 은행은 얼마나 오랫동안 사업을 해 왔는가?

🔒 기출 표현 확인

패러프레이징 표현
· state-of-the-art
  technology → up-to-date
  equipment
· high-volume order
  → a large order

2️ 핵심 전략

· 세부사항 문제는 문제의 핵심어구를 확인한 후 동그라미 표시를 해두고 지문에서 문제의 핵심어구와 관련된 내용을 빠르게 찾아야 합니다.

· 지문의 단서를 선택지에 그대로 사용하거나 패러프레이징하여 표현한 것을 정답으로 선택합니다.

풀이방법 주제·목적 문제

DAY 01

e-mail

해석 p.6

From: Deborah Watson <d.watson@littech.com>
To: Sales Team <sales@littech.com>
Subject: Future Travel
Date: 24 September

Attention Sales Team Members,

Please note that there will be some revisions made to our company's official policy regarding business trips as of 1 October. Receipts must still be submitted, but electronic ones will be accepted in place of printed ones. Also, some of you have mentioned that your per diem pay of $20 for daily expenses is no longer sufficient. After consideration, the management has agreed to raise it to $25. If you have any questions or concerns about this issue, feel free to contact me at your convenience.

Sincerely,

Deborah Watson
Personnel Manager, LIT Tech

Q. What is the purpose of the e-mail?

(A) To announce a travel policy change
(B) To provide upcoming trip details
(C) To request some vacation time
(D) To explain employee benefits

이렇게 풀어요

1. **문제 먼저 파악** purpose → 목적 문제임을 파악해요.

2. **핵심어를 캐치하여 지문 내용 종합적으로 파악** 지문 초반부에서 회사의 출장 관련 공식 방침에 몇 가지 수정 사항이 있을 예정이니 참고하시기 바란다고 했습니다.

   핵심어 확인! some revisions, company's official policy regarding business trips

3. **정답 선택** revisions, official policy regarding business trips 등을 a travel policy change로 표현한 (A)를 정답으로 선택합니다.

PART 7 주제·목적 문제 / 세부사항 문제   29

세부사항 문제

Advertisement   🔍 해석 p.7

Tucson Culinary School

Trujillo Education's Leadership Seminars

Trujillo Education (TE) is an internationally renowned educational company that specializes in professional development. All of our programs include:
– Talks given by industry specialists
– Active workshop sessions that allow everyone to participate
– Supplementary materials available for participants to download

HR and training staff are invited to take advantage of a new special offer. As of the first month of next year, any companies that invite TE to conduct a special session for their staff will receive a 20% discount. Visit our Web site at www.te.edu to learn more about our programs.

Q. What will happen in January?

(A) A workshop schedule will be revised.
(B) A new speaker will join Trujillo Education.
(C) Completion certificates will be issued.
(D) A corporate discount will be offered.

이렇게 풀어요

1. 문제 먼저 파악   happen in January → 1월에 일어날 일을 묻는 세부 사항 문제임을 파악해요.

2. 문제의 핵심어구를 지문에서 찾아 주변 내용 파악   문제의 핵심어구(in January)와 관련된 표현을 찾습니다. 마지막 단락에서 내년 1월부로, TE를 초청해 직원 대상 특별 세션을 실시하는 어떤 기업이든 20% 할인 혜택을 받을 것이라고 했습니다.

핵심어 확인! As of the first month of next year, any companies, discount

3. 정답 선택   any companies, receive a 20% discount 등을 A corporate discount will be offered로 바꾸어 표현한 (D)를 정답으로 선택합니다.

30   기적의 토익 RC

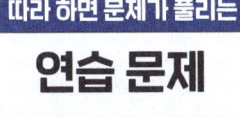

따라 하면 문제가 풀리는

연습 문제

먼저 문제의 키워드에 표시한 후,
지문에서 단서를 찾아 적절한 답을 고르세요.

정답 및 해설 p.7

DAY 01

---

01 article

> Risor Stadium Will Host a Big Event.
>
> RISOR (5 May)—The Agder Amateur Baseball League (AABL) has selected Risor Stadium as the location to hold this year's Championship Series. The stadium was chosen for its comfortable and spacious seating, along with its convenient location near both bus and metro lines. As always, the series will be played between the two AABL teams with the best records. Of course, the Risor Raiders are hoping to be one of those teams to enjoy a homefield advantage for the biggest game of the season. Updates on team records and tickets for upcoming games can be found on the AABL Web site.

Q. What is the article mainly about?

(A) A sports competition
(B) A music concert

---

02 advertisement

> RG Homecare puts the safety and convenience of our customers first. We understand that a broken boiler can be stressful. That's why we offer a 24-hour customer helpline to all members, and there is no limit to the number of technician visits you can have. We will always make the necessary repairs for no additional charge.
>
> Along with Standard Membership, we also offer Premium Membership, which entitles customers to the following:
> • No additional charge for clearing blockages from your drains or pipes
> • A routine maintenance check of your boiler and heating system once a year
> • Priority scheduling for repairs

Q. What is available exclusively to Premium Members?

(A) Unlimited repairs
(B) An annual inspection

PART 7 주제·목적 문제 / 세부사항 문제   31

토익에 나올

실전 문제

제한시간 10분입니다! 시~작!

Questions 01-02 refer to the following online notice.

http://www.2ndhandxchange.com/appliance#627464

Item: Chez Chef brand slow cooker (3.5L)
Price: $20

I received this product as a housewarming gift last year and have never used it. The original retail price is $45. This was originally listed under used items, but after explaining the situation to the Web site's service department that has been corrected. The item also comes with a booklet of slow cooker recipes from Chez Chef.

Those who are interested in purchasing an item on 2nd Hand Xchange but need to receive it urgently should contact Lori Dickson at 555-6752. She will contact the seller regarding the possibility of express shipping. Please note that extra fees may apply.

01. What is one reason the notice was posted?

(A) To clarify the condition of a product
(B) To explain how to use a product
(C) To promote the Chez Chef brand
(D) To introduce a kitchen appliance

02. According to the notice, why should people call Ms. Dickson?

(A) To apply a coupon
(B) To get some recipes
(C) To expedite shipping
(D) To negotiate the price

---

paraphrasing 주어진 어휘 또는 표현과 패러프레이징 될 수 있는 것을 연결하세요.

1. incorrectly listed •   • (a) revise
2. call •   • (b) contact
3. amend •   • (c) given the wrong information

32   기적의 토익 RC

Questions 03-04 refer to the following notice.

Bridgehampton Supermarket Customers

Due to environmental concerns, our supermarket will no longer be providing plastic bags, only paper ones. We will also charge a fee for paper bags. Environmentally friendly reusable bags are available for purchase at each register. Also, we at Bridgehampton Supermarket have joined with other businesses in a pledge to reduce waste. Therefore, we will be donating all perishable goods to food charities two days before their expiration dates.

Bridgehampton Supermarket Management

03. What is the main purpose of the notice?
(A) To announce a policy change
(B) To promote a recycling program
(C) To raise awareness about pollution
(D) To recruit volunteers for a cleanup project

04. How does Bridgehampton Supermarket plan to reduce waste?
(A) By reducing its prices
(B) By making charitable donations
(C) By charging a fine for wasteful habits
(D) By stocking food in smaller amounts

paraphrasing 주어진 어휘 또는 표현과 패러프레이징 될 수 있는 것을 연결하세요.

1. charge a fee •   • (a) donate
2. recycling program •   • (b) ask for a payment
3. make donations •   • (c) environmentally friendly campaign

PART 7 주제·목적 문제 / 세부사항 문제 **33**

 **실전 문제**

Questions 05-07 refer to the following advertisement.

Working around the clock? Give yourself a rest at Sunset Valley!

Modern Facilities: Immerse yourself in relaxation at our newly built facility, which was designed by an internationally recognized architect. We are situated on 20 acres of woodland — getting you in touch with nature and away from the hectic schedule of the city — and we have more visitors than any other facility in the area.

Naturemade Products: We exclusively use Naturemade, a line of skincare products developed from natural and organically grown ingredients. All customers receive several trial-size bottles of Naturemade products that are theirs to keep.

Inclusive Package: Let our experienced staff pamper you and help you to relieve stress. With our All-Day Package, we offer six one-hour treatments such as steam baths, massages, beauty treatments, and more. You can mix and match these treatments to make the combination that best suits you, all for one low price. There is an additional overall health assessment offered for a nominal fee. If you are traveling from out of town, we will even pick you up from the airport for free in our reliable airport shuttle.

Call us today at 555-3389.

05. What most likely is Sunset Valley?

(A) A convention center
(B) A health spa
(C) A fitness facility
(D) A job recruitment agency

06. What does the advertisement indicate about Sunset Valley?

(A) It has recently won an award.
(B) It will be featured on a television show.
(C) It was recently sold to a former architect.
(D) It is more popular than its competitors.

07. What can customers of the All-Day Package pay an extra charge for?

(A) Overnight accommodations
(B) Skincare products to take home
(C) A health evaluation
(D) Transportation from an airport

---

paraphrasing 주어진 어휘 또는 표현과 패러프레이징 될 수 있는 것을 연결하세요.

1. more visitors •   • (a) more popular
2. pick you up from the airport •   • (b) evaluation
3. assessment •   • (c) offer transportation

34 기적의 토익 RC

Questions 08-10 refer to the following information from a brochure.

Welcome to Paradise Hotel & Resort! While you enjoy your stay here, be sure to make use of some of our award-winning amenities, all of which are open on weekends:

Supreme Spa (Ages 13& up)
Get a relaxing sports massage, skin treatment, and mud bath right here in our hotel. For a nominal fee, they also bring aroma therapy to your room. You can choose the scents of candles and oils from our wide selection. (Every day)

Mini-Pool (Ages 4-10)
We have plenty of pool noodles and toys for the kids, but guests are welcome to bring their own. This area is only open when lifeguards are on duty. (Friday through Tuesday)

Ball Play Room (Ages 3-12)
A long-time favorite, let your kids loose to jump and play with others in our ball pit. Each group of children needs at least one adult supervisor. (Every day)

Dance Floor (All ages)
The dance floor welcomes singles, couples, families, and friends. Dance all night to live music by local performers. (Friday through Wednesday)

08. What is the purpose of the brochure?

(A) To inform guests about facilities
(B) To announce a special event
(C) To recruit some volunteers
(D) To give directions to tourists

09. What is true about Supreme Spa?

(A) It employs certified employees.
(B) It requires a reservation.
(C) It may incur an extra charge.
(D) It is located outside of the hotel.

10. According to the brochure, what common characteristic do Mini-Pool and Ball Play Room have in common?

(A) They are both intended for children.
(B) They are both open every day of the week.
(C) They both need an adult to supervise each child.
(D) They both encourage visitors to bring their own equipment.

---

paraphrasing 주어진 어휘 또는 표현과 패러프레이징 될 수 있는 것을 연결하세요.

1. free •
2. opened just last month •
3. have a great reputation •

• (a) be widely known
• (b) complimentary
• (c) been in operation for a short time

PART 7 주제·목적 문제 / 세부사항 문제   35

'멋진 당신, 오늘도 화이팅'

DAY

02

오늘의 학습 포인트

PART 5. 대명사

1. 인칭대명사 - 주격/소유격/목적격/소유대명사

2. 재귀대명사 - myself, himself 등/재귀 용법(주어=목적어)/강조 용법

3. 지시대명사 - that of/those of/those who

4. 부정대명사 - one/another/the other/any 등

5. 전체 중 일부를 나타내는 대명사 - 단수/복수/단·복수 둘다 가능한 것 구분하기

PART 6. 뒤의 내용이 단서인 명사 어휘

보기가 모두 명사, 빈칸 앞뒤 문맥 파악

PART 7. True·Not True 문제/추론 문제

보기 먼저 읽고 지문 읽기, 패러프레이징 연습 중요!

PART 5
문법

대명사

인칭대명사의 격을 구분하는 문제가 가장 많이 출제됩니다.
부정대명사와 재귀대명사도 확실히 학습해두세요.

🖊 적용 기술

[기적의 필기노트] 92P
RC 기술 6

출제 포인트
최근 소유대명사가 자주 출제됩니다.

⚠️ **주의**
소유격과 목적격의 형태가 같은 her, 소유격과 소유대명사의 형태가 같은 his에 주의하세요.

🔒 **확인 문제 ❶**

------- are asked to join the event.

(A) Their
(B) They

🔒 **확인 문제 ❷**

Ms. Park will send ------- package by express mail.

(A) her
(B) she

정답 ❶ (B) ❷ (A)

출제 유형 1
인칭대명사의 종류와 위치

1 인칭대명사의 종류

- 인칭대명사는 대신하는 명사와 수/성/격을 일치시켜야 합니다.

인칭	수/성		주격 (~은, 이, 가)	소유격 (~의)	목적격 (~을)	소유대명사 (~의 것)
1인칭	단수		I	my	me	mine
	복수		we	our	us	ours
2인칭	단수		you	your	you	yours
	복수					
3인칭	단수	남성	he	his	him	his
		여성	she	her	her	hers
		사물	it	its	it	–
	복수		they	their	them	theirs

2 주격 인칭대명사: 주어 자리

- 보기에 주격, 소유격, 목적격, 소유대명사, 재귀대명사가 주어지고 알맞은 것을 고르는 형태로 출제됩니다.
  According to the CEO, **she** has a plan to expand into the European Market.
  대표이사에 따르면, 그녀는 유럽 시장으로 진출할 계획이 있다.

3 소유격 인칭대명사: 명사 앞

- 소유격 인칭대명사는 다른 인칭대명사와 달리 반드시 뒤에 명사가 와야 합니다.
  Their computers will be replaced next month. 그들의 컴퓨터는 다음 달에 교체될 것이다.
  소유격   명사

- 소유격 인칭대명사와 명사 사이에 형용사가 올 수 있습니다.
  Their old computers will be replaced next month.
  소유격 형용사   명사
  그들의 오래된 컴퓨터는 다음 달에 교체될 것이다.

- '소유격 인칭대명사 + own' 뒤에도 명사가 올 수 있습니다.
  my own / your own / his own / her own / its own / our own / their own
  We train **our own** employees every six months.
  우리는 매 6개월마다 우리 직원들을 교육시킨다.

38 기적의 토익 RC

4 목적격 인칭대명사 vs. 소유대명사

· **목적격**은 타동사 뒤, 전치사 뒤에 씁니다.

I advised **them** to meet the manager personally.
　　<u>타동사</u>　<u>목적격</u>
나는 그들에게 개인적으로 매니저를 만나볼 것을 권했다.

The optician recommended a hard contact lens for **me**.
그 안경사는 나에게 하드 콘택트렌즈를 추천해 주었다.　　　　<u>전치사 목적격</u>

`800+`

· **소유대명사**는 '소유격 + 명사'를 대신하며 주어, 목적어, 보어 자리에 옵니다.

Mr. Kim's vacation request was approved, but **mine** is still under review.
　　　　　　　　　　　　　　　　　　　　　　　　<u>주어(mine=my request)</u>
Kim 씨의 휴가 요청은 승인되었으나 내 요청은 여전히 검토 중이다.

The contract has ended, but we'll extend **yours**.
　　　　　　　　　　　　<u>목적어(yours = your contract)</u>
계약은 끝났지만 우리는 당신의 것을 연장할 것이다.

출제 유형 2

재귀대명사

1 재귀대명사의 종류

인칭	수/성		재귀대명사
1인칭	단수		myself
	복수		ourselves
2인칭	단수		yourself
	복수		yourselves
3인칭	단수	남성	himself
		여성	herself
		사물	itself
	복수		themselves

2 재귀 용법

`800+`

· 주어=목적어일 때 **목적어 자리**에 재귀대명사를 씁니다.

Mr. Brown introduced **himself** to the audience. Brown 씨는 그 자신을 청중에게 소개했다.
　　　　　　　(himself=Mr. Brown)

· 전치사의 목적어가 가리키는 대상이 주어와 같으면 재귀대명사를 씁니다.

All <u>participants</u> are socializing among **themselves** in the reception.
리셉션에서 모든 참가자들은 그들끼리 서로 어울리고 있는 중이다.

· 재귀 용법으로 쓰인 재귀대명사는 문장에서 **생략할 수 없습니다.**

· 재귀대명사 숙어 표현

devote oneself to ~에 헌신하다	familiarize oneself to ~에 익숙하게 하다
commit oneself to ~에 전념하다	help oneself to ~을 마음껏 먹다
dedicate oneself to ~에 몰두하다, 헌신하다	distinguish oneself 두각을 나타내다

출제 포인트
보기에 소유대명사와 목적격 인칭대명사가 같이 주어지면 해석해서 정답을 선택합니다.

🔒 **확인 문제 ❸**

I received most team member's vacation requests except -------.

(A) you
(B) yours

✎ **적용 기술**

[기적의 필기노트] 93P
RC 기술 7

⚠️ **주의**
재귀대명사는 주격, 소유격 자리에는 올 수 없습니다.

출제 포인트
동사 뒤에 빈칸이 있고 보기에 재귀대명사가 있으면 주어=목적어인지 먼저 확인합니다.

🔒 **확인 문제 ❹**

They devoted ------- to keep the store clean and neat.

(A) them
(B) themselves

(B) ❹ (B) ❸ 정답

PART 5 문법 대명사 　39

확인 문제 ❺

Ms. Olson solved the issue by -------.

(A) herself
(B) her

800+

3 강조 용법

- 주어나 목적어가 한 행위를 강조할 때, 강조하는 명사 바로 뒤 또는 문장 맨 뒤에 재귀대명사를 씁니다.

  Ms. Keats **herself** painted the wooden fence. Keats 씨 자신이 그 나무 울타리를 칠했다.

  Managers resolved any customer problem **themselves**.
  매니저들은 어떤 고객 문제라도 그들 스스로 해결했다.

- 강조 용법으로 쓰인 재귀대명사는 대명사임에도 불구하고 주어/목적어/보어 역할이 아닌 부사처럼 사용되므로 재귀대명사를 빼고도 완전한 문장이 됩니다.

  Ms. Keats (**herself**) painted the wooden fence. Keats 씨 (자신이) 그 나무 울타리를 칠했다.

800+

4 재귀대명사 전치사구 관용 표현

by oneself(= alone, on one's own) 혼자서, 스스로	for oneself 혼자 힘으로
of itself 저절로	in itself 자체로, 본질적으로

- 문장 끝에 빈칸이 있고 빈칸 바로 앞에 by나 for가 있으면 무조건 재귀대명사가 정답입니다.

적용 기술

[기적의 필기노트] 94P
RC 기술 8

출제 유형 3

지시대명사

800+

1 that of / those of

- 주로 비교 구문에서 앞에 나온 명사를 대신할 때 that이나 those를 사용합니다.
- 앞에 나온 명사가 단수이면 that, 복수이면 those를 사용합니다.

  My office is much larger than **that** of my assistant.
  앞의 office를 대신함

  내 사무실은 내 비서 사무실보다 훨씬 더 크다.

  His communication skills are beyond **those** of others.
  앞의 communication skills를 대신함

  그의 의사소통 능력은 다른 사람들의 것(의사소통 능력)을 능가한다.

확인 문제 ❻

Our new car is more fuel-efficient than ------- of other car manufacturers.

(A) this
(B) that

출제 포인트

'those who + 복수 동사'는 'anyone who + 단수 동사'와 구분하여 알아두세요!

확인 문제 ❼

------- with one-year memberships will be sent weekly newsletters.

(A) Those
(B) That

---

2 those + who / p.p. / -ing / 전치사구: ~하는 사람들

- 지시대명사 those가 앞에 나온 특정 명사를 지칭하지 않을 경우, '~하는 사람들'이라는 의미의 대명사로 쓰입니다.
- those가 '~하는 사람들'의 뜻으로 쓰일 때는 뒤에 반드시 전치사구, 분사구, 관계대명사절 형태의 수식어가 위치합니다.

  Those at Green Apartment are required to dispose of home appliances properly.

  Those living at Green Apartment are required to dispose of home appliances properly. Green 아파트에 사는 사람들은 가전제품을 제대로 폐기해야 합니다.

- those 뒤에 관계대명사절이 올 경우, 전체 문장의 동사는 복수 형태가 되어야 합니다.

  Those who want to attend the event **are asked** to e-mail us.
  행사에 참가하고 싶은 사람들은 저희에게 이메일을 보내셔야 합니다.

정답 ❺ (A) ❻ (B) ❼ (A)

40 기적의 토익 RC

출제 유형 4　**부정대명사**

적용 기술

[기적의 필기노트] 96P
RC 기술 10

DAY 02

1　부정대명사의 종류

부정대명사	품사	수	뜻
one	형용사, 대명사	단수	(정해지지 않은) 하나의, 하나
another	형용사, 대명사	단수	(앞서 언급한 것을 제외한 정해지지 않은) 또 다른, 또 다른 하나
the other	형용사, 대명사	단수	나머지의, 나머지 하나
others	대명사	복수	(정해지지 않은) 다른 것들
the others	대명사	복수	(정해진) 나머지 것(사람)들 전부 다
other	형용사	–	다른
each other	대명사	–	(둘 사이에) 서로
one another	대명사	–	(셋 이상에서) 서로

⚠️ **주의**

each other와 one another는 주어 자리에 올 수 없어요.

2　부정대명사 구분

① **it/that** (대명사): 앞에 언급된 바로 그것(내 휴대폰 – 내 휴대폰)

　vs.

　one (대명사): 앞에 언급된 것과 같은 종류의 다른 것(내 휴대폰 – 내가 새로 살 휴대폰)

🔒 **확인 문제 ❽**

------- are supposed to move to a new office building.

(A) Another
(B) Some

② **another** (형용사/대명사)

　vs.

　the other (형용사/대명사)

　vs.

　the others (대명사)

　빈칸 앞뒤를 파악하여 품사를 먼저 걸러낸 후, 문맥상 의미가 적합한 것을 정답으로 선택합니다.

③ **any** (형용사/대명사): 부정문/의문문/조건문에 주로 쓰여요. 단, '어떤 ~라도'의 의미일 경우 긍정문에도 쓰입니다.

　vs.

　some (형용사/대명사): 주로 긍정문에 쓰여요.

출제 포인트

토익에서는 주로 none이 1년에 2-3회 정도 출제돼요. of 앞자리에 들어가는 none을 찾는 유형으로 가장 많이 출제됩니다. 이때 선택지로 none(대명사), no(형용사), not(부사)이 함께 제시돼요.

🔒 **확인 문제 ❾**

------- of the candidates are qualified.

(A) No
(B) None

`800+`

④ **no** (형용사) : 형용사이므로 명사 앞에 써야 합니다.

　vs.

　not (부사)

　vs.

　none (대명사): 단/복수 모두 가능해요. 주로 'none of the 복수 명사 + 복수[단수] 동사', 'none of 소유격 대명사 + 복수 명사 + 복수[단수] 동사'의 형태로 쓰여요.

None of the sales representatives are going to receive a monthly bonus.
영업사원들 중에 누구도 월간 보너스를 받지 못할 예정이다.

None of the information was available last week.
지난주에는 어떤 정보도 얻을 수 없었다.

(B) ❾ (B) ❽ **정답**

PART 5 문법 대명사　41

적용 기술

[기적의 필기노트] 95P
RC 기술 9

출제 포인트
전체 중 일부를 나타내는 대명사는 '대명사 + of + the/소유격/지시형용사 + 명사'의 형태로 출제됩니다.

🔒 확인 문제 ⑩

------- of the morning flights were cancelled due to inclement weather.

(A) Many
(B) Much

출제 유형 5

전체 중 일부를 나타내는 대명사

1 단수 취급하는 대명사

one of the + 복수 명사 ~중 하나
each of the + 복수 명사 ~중 각각
either of the + 복수 명사 ~중 (아무거나) 하나 } **+ 단수 동사**
neither of the + 복수 명사 ~중 어느 것도 아니다
much of the + 불가산 명사 ~중 많은 부분
little of the + 불가산 명사 ~중 거의 없음

One of the food vendors was open during the lunch time.
음식 노점상들 중 한 곳이 점심시간 동안 문을 열었다.

Neither of the candidates was qualified for the manager position.
지원자들 중 아무도 매니저 직책에 자격을 갖추지 못했다.

2 복수 취급하는 대명사

several of the + 복수 명사 ~중 여러의
both of the + 복수 명사 ~중 둘 다
many of the + 복수 명사 ~중 다수 } **+ 복수 동사**
few of the + 복수 명사 ~중 거의 없음
a few of the + 복수 명사 ~중 약간
fewer of the + 복수 명사 ~중 더 적음

Several of the employees are willing to transfer to the overseas branch.
직원들 중 여러 명이 해외 지사로 전근 갈 의향이 있다.

800+

3 단수·복수 둘다 가능한 대명사

→ of 뒤 명사에 수 일치 시켜야 합니다.

all of the + 명사 ~의 전부
most of the + 명사 ~의 대부분
some of the + 명사 ~중 일부 } **복수 명사 + 복수 동사**
any of the + 명사 ~중 어떤 것/아무 것   **불가산 명사 + 단수 동사**
half of the + 명사 ~중 절반
the rest of the + 명사 ~중 나머지

Half of the volunteers were college students from within Derby County.
자원봉사자들 중 절반이 더비 주에 있는 대학생들이었다.

정답 ⑩ (B)

42 기적의 토익 RC

풀이방법 대명사

DAY 02

1. All computer monitors will be replaced with the latest model except -------.

(A) I   (B) me   (C) my   (D) mine

내 것을 제외한 모든 컴퓨터 모니터가 최신 모델로 교체될 것이다.

> **이렇게 풀어요**
>
> 1. **선택지 보고 문법/어휘 문제 파악** 선택지가 모두 인칭대명사와 소유대명사로 구성되어 있으므로 인칭대명사의 격 또는 소유대명사 자리를 구분하는 문법 문제임을 파악할 수 있어요.
> 2. **빈칸 분석** 빈칸 앞에 전치사 except(~을 제외하고)가 있으므로 전치사의 목적어 역할을 할 수 있는 인칭대명사가 들어가야 함을 파악해요.
> 3. **정답 선택** 목적어 역할을 할 수 있는 목적격 (B)와 소유대명사 (D) 중에서 '내 것을 제외하고'라는 의미를 만들 수 있는 소유대명사 (D)를 정답으로 고릅니다.

2. The new manager will introduce ------- to the team members at the next weekly meeting.

(A) she   (B) her   (C) her own   (D) herself

신임 과장은 다음 주 주간 회의에서 자신을 팀원들에게 소개할 예정이다.

> **이렇게 풀어요**
>
> 1. **선택지 보고 문법/어휘 문제 파악** 선택지가 모두 인칭대명사와 재귀대명사로 구성되어 있으므로 인칭대명사의 격 또는 재귀대명사 자리를 구분하는 문법 문제임을 파악할 수 있어요.
> 2. **빈칸 분석** 빈칸 앞에 3형식 타동사 introduce(소개하다)가 있으므로 동사의 목적어 역할을 하는 인칭대명사가 들어갈 자리임을 파악해요.
> 3. **정답 선택** 목적어 역할을 할 수 있는 (C)와 재귀대명사 (D) 중, 주어와 목적어가 동일하므로 재귀대명사 (D)를 정답으로 고릅니다.

3. ------- who donate more than $1,000 at the fundraiser will be listed on Donors' Wall.

(A) Those   (B) They   (C) Them   (D) These

기금 모금 행사에서 1000달러 이상 기부하는 사람들은 Donor's Wall에 기록될 것이다.

> **이렇게 풀어요**
>
> 1. **선택지 보고 문법/어휘 문제 파악** 선택지가 모두 인칭대명사와 지시대명사로 구성되어 있으므로 문법 문제임을 파악할 수 있어요.
> 2. **빈칸 분석** 빈칸 뒤에 관계대명사 who가 있으므로, 선행사 역할을 하면서 본동사 will be listed의 주어가 될 수 있는 대명사가 들어가야 함을 파악해요.
> 3. **정답 선택** 주어 역할을 할 수 있는 지시대명사 (A)와 (D), 주격 인칭대명사 (B) 중에서 관계대명사절의 수식을 받을 수 있는 (A) those를 정답으로 고릅니다.

PART 5 문법 대명사   43

PART 5 어휘

명사 어휘 (2)

각 어휘와 함께 자주 쓰이는 표현을 통째로 외워두세요.

01 rate 비율, 요금, 속도

unemployment rate	실업률
at a discounted rate	할인된 가격에
group rate	단체 요금

02 phase 단계, 국면
`800+`

final phase	최종 단계
transitional phase	과도기

03 development 발달, 개발

under development	개발 중인
development in	~의 발전

04 access 입장, 접근
😺 빈출 토익 선생님 Pick!

have access to	~에 접근[출입]할 수 있다
gain[get] access to	~에 접근 권한을 갖게 되다
easy access	용이한 접근

05 needs 필요, 요구

meet one's needs	~의 요구를 충족시키다

06 admission 가입, 입장
😺 빈출 토익 선생님 Pick!

grant admission	입장[입학, 입회]을 허가하다
admission pass	입장권
admission fee	입장료
free admission	무료 입장

07 objection 반대

have no objection to	~에 이의가 없다

08 terms 조건

under the terms of agreement	합의 조건으로
terms of the contract	계약 조건
terms and conditions	조항 및 조건

09 reputation 평판, 명성

have a reputation as	~로서의 평판을 갖고 있다
earn a reputation	명성을 얻다
build a reputation	명성을 얻다

10 enthusiasm 열광, 열정
`800+`

greet with enthusiasm	열렬히 환영하다
show enthusiasm	열의를 보이다

11 expense 돈, 비용, 경비

reimburse for expenses	경비를 상환하다
cut expenses	경비를 삭감하다
operating expense	운영비
travel expense	여행 경비, 출장비

12 preparation 준비

in preparation for	~의 준비로
preparation needed to부정사	~하기 위해 필요한 준비

13 shortage 부족

shortage of	~의 부족
staffing shortage	직원 부족
parking shortage	주차 공간 부족

44 기적의 토익 RC

DAY 02

😺 빈출 토익 선생님 Pick!

14 assurance   보증, 보장

offer A assurance that   A에게 ~을 보장하다
an assurance of   ~의 보장

15 charge   요금, 책임, 담당

an additional charge   추가 요금
in charge of   ~을 맡아서, 담당해서
free of charge   무료로

`800+`
16 obligation   의무

acknowledge obligation to부정사   ~할 의무를 인정하다
have obligation   의무가 있다

17 reduction   감소, 할인

price reduction   가격 할인
budget reduction   예산 감소
a reduction in   ~의 감소

😺 빈출 토익 선생님 Pick!
18 modification   수정, 변경

make a modification to   ~에 수정을 하다
modifications are made   변경되다

19 exposure   노출

exposure to   ~에의 노출
give A wide exposure to   A가 널리 노출되게 하다

😺 빈출 토익 선생님 Pick!
20 policy   정책, 방침

comply with the policy   정책을 따르다, 준수하다
implement a policy   정책을 실행하다
insurance policy   보험 증권

`900+`
21 deliberation   숙고, 신중함

after much deliberation   심사숙고 후에
require considerable deliberation   상당한 숙고를 필요로 하다

`800+`
22 emphasis   강조, 주안점

emphasis on   ~에 대한 강조
place emphasis on   ~을 강조하다

23 compliance   준수, 따름

ensure compliance with   ~의 준수를 보장하다
in compliance with   ~에 따라

📢 풀이 방법

Until the end of this week, we will offer this round-trip ticket to Chicago at a discounted -------.

(A) policy   (B) attempt   (C) rate   (D) load

이번 주 말까지, 저희는 시카고까지의 이 왕복 티켓을 할인된 가격에 제공할 것입니다.

🎵 이렇게 풀어요

1. **선택지 보고 문법/어휘 문제 파악** 선택지가 서로 다른 명사 어휘로 구성되어 있으므로 어휘 문제임을 파악해요.
2. **빈칸 분석** 빈칸 앞에 있는 형용사 discounted(할인된)의 수식을 받아 적절한 의미를 이루는 명사가 들어가야 함을 파악해요.
3. **정답 선택** '가격'이라는 의미의 명사인 (C) rate를 정답으로 선택합니다.

PART 5 어휘 명사 어휘 (2)   45

따라 하면 문제가 풀리는

연습 문제

앞서 학습한 문제 풀이법을 적용하여 맞는 것에 ✔ 표시 하거나 괄호 안에
적절한 답을 쓰고 정답을 선택하세요.

01 ------- is dedicated to providing the best service possible.

(A) He
(B) His
(C) Him
(D) Himself

1. 선택지 보고 문법/어휘 문제 파악하기 ☐ 문법 문제 ☐ 어휘 문제
2. 빈칸 분석하기 빈칸 뒤에 있는 것 ☐ 명사 ☐ 동사 ☐ 부사
   → 빈칸에는 ☐ 주어 ☐ 목적어 역할을 할 수 있는 것이 들어가야 한다.
3. 정답 선택하기 정답 (   )

02 Today, ------- lunch menu is grilled salmon with a side of vegetables.

(A) we
(B) us
(C) our
(D) ourselves

1. 선택지 보고 문법/어휘 문제 파악하기 ☐ 문법 문제 ☐ 어휘 문제
2. 빈칸 분석하기 빈칸 뒤에 있는 것 ☐ 명사 ☐ 동사 ☐ 전치사
   → 빈칸에는 ☐ 목적격 대명사 ☐ 소유격 대명사가 들어가야 한다.
3. 정답 선택하기 정답 (   )

03 Although the old tablets are lighter, ------- has a longer battery life.

(A) myself
(B) me
(C) my
(D) mine

1. 선택지 보고 문법/어휘 문제 파악하기 ☐ 문법 문제 ☐ 어휘 문제
2. 빈칸 분석하기 빈칸 뒤에 있는 것 ☐ 명사 ☐ 동사 ☐ 부사
   → 빈칸에는 ☐ 주어 ☐ 목적어 역할을 할 수 있는 것이 들어가야 한다.
3. 정답 선택하기 정답 (   )

46 기적의 토익 RC

◯ 정답 및 해설 p.10

04 Ms. Sanders wanted to contact possible vendors -------.

(A) she
(B) her
(C) hers
(D) herself

1. 선택지 보고 문법/어휘 문제 파악하기 ☐문법 문제 ☐어휘 문제
2. 빈칸 분석하기 빈칸 앞에 있는 것 ☐완전한 문장 ☐불완전한 문장
   → 빈칸에는 ☐소유격 대명사 ☐재귀대명사가 들어가야 한다.
3. 정답 선택하기 정답 (   )

05 This seating area is reserved for ------- who purchased their tickets online in advance.

(A) nothing
(B) another
(C) themselves
(D) those

1. 선택지 보고 문법/어휘 문제 파악하기 ☐문법 문제 ☐어휘 문제
2. 빈칸 분석하기 빈칸 뒤에 있는 것 ☐명사 ☐관계대명사 ☐인칭대명사
   → 빈칸에는 ☐선행사 역할을 하는 것 ☐지시사 역할을 하는 것이 들어가야 한다.
3. 정답 선택하기 정답 (   )

06 The rear parking lot will not be available until further -------.

(A) notice
(B) cost
(C) attempt
(D) entry

1. 선택지 보고 문법/어휘 문제 파악하기 ☐문법 문제 ☐어휘 문제
2. 빈칸 분석하기 빈칸 앞 until further와 짝꿍 표현으로 어울려 쓰이는 명사가 정답이다.
3. 정답 선택하기 정답 (   )

PART 5 대명사 / 명사 어휘 (2)

DAY 01-02 누적 문제

제한시간 9분입니다! 시~작!

01. Stein Industries is looking to recruit ------- with a strong background in computer programming.

(A) them
(B) which
(C) whoever
(D) anyone

02. Featuring original family recipes, celebrity chef Peter Ware has announced the release of ------- cookbook for sale.

(A) his own
(B) him
(C) himself
(D) he

03. Many people who work downtown commute by bus, and the majority of ------- are in favor of adding a bus-only lane.

(A) their
(B) they
(C) them
(D) theirs

04. Whenever Ms. Walker is in Paris on business purposes, she will be accompanied by ------- interpreter.

(A) her
(B) she
(C) hers
(D) herself

05. You will have unlimited ------- to the indoor pool and fitness center during your stay.

(A) access
(B) rate
(C) policy
(D) charge

06. Mr. Miller ------- was allowed to choose a holiday reward from free products, paid day offs, or cash bonus.

(A) he
(B) his own
(C) him
(D) himself

07. UPhone smartphones, affordable by -------, are greatly discounted with long-time service plans.

(A) their own
(B) themselves
(C) them
(D) they

08. Fellow employees at Dustin Flooring agree that Sean Reynolds deserved the ------- to supervisor.

(A) promoting
(B) promotion
(C) promoter
(D) promote

09. Mr. Scott wanted to make a last-minute ------- to the office rental agreement.

(A) obligation
(B) admission
(C) application
(D) modification

10. Mr. McBride was named team leader for the project since ------- initially proposed the idea.

(A) him
(B) he
(C) his
(D) himself

11. Regardless of what topic the research papers are written about, ------- should be reviewed by a group of peers.

(A) other
(B) all
(C) both
(D) every

12. Body Ball can help ------- build muscle, burn fat, and tone your body with short and simple workouts.

(A) you
(B) yours
(C) yourself
(D) yourselves

48 기적의 토익 RC

13. Two teachers were recognized at the Local Leadership Awards for ------- volunteer work.

(A) them
(B) their
(C) they
(D) themselves

14. Café customers should check order numbers on the receipt before leaving to ensure that takeout order is -------.

(A) they
(B) their
(C) them
(D) theirs

15. Because he has the most sales experience, Mr. Rolle has decided to deal with the VIP client -------.

(A) he
(B) his
(C) him
(D) himself

16. Upcoming volunteer ------- in Carson City are posted on the city's Web site.

(A) active
(B) activate
(C) activities
(D) activation

17. ------- for the research grant can check their status on the research center's Web site.

(A) Application
(B) Applying
(C) Apply
(D) Applicants

18. The newly hired workers have opportunities to familiarize ------- with the computer software programs.

(A) they
(B) their
(C) themselves
(D) them

19. All related costs for parts will be covered by the manufacturer under the ------- of contract.

(A) needs
(B) terms
(C) series
(D) stretch

20. A friend of ------- will pick us up from Tokyo International Airport.

(A) I
(B) me
(C) my
(D) mine

21. Ms. Harris will update the company brochure in ------- for the upcoming trade fair.

(A) deliberation
(B) reduction
(C) preparation
(D) reputation

22. Employment contracts specify that coworkers may not discuss their salaries among -------.

(A) themselves
(B) theirs
(C) them
(D) they

23. The HR manager led the orientation for the new employees with ------- last month.

(A) enthusiasm
(B) expense
(C) objection
(D) assurance

24. The factory managers are required to tour the assembly line to ensure ------- with the new safety regulations.

(A) compliance
(B) shortage
(C) expense
(D) development

PART 5 대명사 / 명사 어휘 (2)

PART 6

뒤의 내용이 단서인 명사 어휘 `800+`

선택지가 서로 다른 명사 어휘로 이루어져 있으면 앞뒤 문맥을 파악합니다.

적용 기술

[기적의 필기노트] 158P
RC 기술 76

VOCA

priority 최우선 사항
strive to부정사 ~하려고 노력
하다
conduct 시행하다
on a rolling basis 수시로
focus group 포커스 그룹
(여론 조사를 위해 뽑힌 소수의
사람들로 이뤄진 그룹)
procedure 절차
fellow 동료
come up with ~을 생각해
내다
achieve 달성하다
goal 목표

 **풀이 방법** notice 해석 p.13

Here at Dole Tech, ------- is our number one priority. That is why our company
01.
strives to develop products that make our customers happy.

Surveys are conducted on a rolling basis, and focus groups are held monthly. The
results of each are posted in our weekly newsletter. We hope that this procedure
will help each of you, our fellow employees, to come up with innovative and popular
ideas for new products, designs, and features. You are all encouraged to submit
anything that could help ------- achieve that goal.

PART 5

01. (A) satisfaction
    (B) timeliness
    (C) safety
    (D) price

이렇게 풀어요

1. **선택지 보고 문법/어휘 문제 파악** 선택지가 서로 다른 명사 어휘로 이루어져 있으므로 어휘 문제임을 파악합니다.
   (A) 만족   (B) 시기적절함   (C) 안전   (D) 가격

2. **빈칸 분석** 어휘 문제이므로 문맥을 파악합니다. 'Dole Tech에서는 -------이 최우선입니다'라는 빈칸 문장 뒤에 그렇기 때문에 회사가 고객들을 행복하게 하는 제품을 개발하기 위해 노력한다는 내용이 있으므로 이와 자연스럽게 연결될 수 있는 어휘가 들어가야 함을 파악합니다.

3. **정답 선택** 빈칸 뒤의 내용을 단서로 하여 문맥상 가장 적절한 (A) satisfaction을 정답으로 선택합니다.

해설

빈칸은 타동사 help의 목적어 자리이므로 (C)와 (D)가 정답의 후보인데, 뒤에 목적격 보어로 온 동사 achieve의 의미상의 주어가 되어야 하므로 소유대명사인 (D)는 답이 될 수 없어요. 따라서 목적격인 (C) us가 정답입니다.

PART 5 문법 적용 문제

You are all encouraged to submit anything that could help ------- achieve that goal.

(A) we   (B) our   (C) us   (D) ours

50 기적의 토익 RC

따라 하면 문제가 풀리는

연습 문제

빈칸 뒤 내용에서 단서가 될 부분을 찾아 표시하세요.
표시한 것을 바탕으로 정답 어휘를 선택하세요.

🔾 정답 및 해설 p.13

DAY 02

01

Dear Mr. Jefferson,

I wanted to give you some details regarding your upcoming -------. You will take Golden Air to Seattle, and your flight will leave at 8 a.m. on Monday. A shuttle will take you from the airport to your hotel.

(A) travel　　　　　(B) show

02

Dear Ms. Moyer,

We received your complaint about the ------- of your last order. Because of the unexpected storm that severely hit one of our warehouses, we were not able to ship out your order on time. We are doing everything we can to complete your order as soon as possible.

(A) defect　　　　　(B) delay

03

Hattiesburg Daily (19 November) — Hattiesburg's mayor, Marilyn Ellis, has called for an ------- of the city's public transportation network. She believes that more buses and routes will help to decrease the number of drivers on the road, particularly during rush hour.

(A) obligation　　　　　(B) expansion

04

CARTERSVILLE — Local residents are excited about an upcoming change in ------- policy at Cartersville Pizzeria. Although the popular pizzeria hasn't officially hired any drivers, it has worked out a deal with Home Service, who will bring orders directly to your front door.

(A) delivery　　　　　(B) discounts

PART 6 뒤의 내용이 단서인 명사 어휘　51

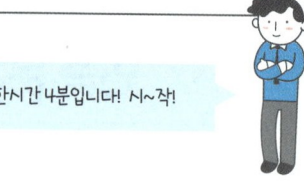

제한시간 4분입니다! 시~작!

Questions 01-04 refer to the following notice.

Rosa Industries is known for putting ------- first. Our management has decided to include the new
01.
medical insurance package that fully covers their spouse and children.

All insurance claims should be forwarded to the personnel department for approval. -------. We
02.
believe ------- our workers and their loved ones healthy will increase productivity at our company
03.
more and more as time goes on. All employees are ------- to maintain their health for the sake of
04.
themselves, their families, and the company.

유형 적용 문제

01. (A) customers
(B) employees
(C) donors
(D) faculties

03. (A) keep
(B) keeping
(C) kept
(D) will keep

02. (A) Certain medications and treatments may not be
available.
(B) A list of medical professionals can be found on
the company Web site.
(C) All employees are required to review the
insurance policy thoroughly before signing it.
(D) Once approved, the medical expenses will be
reimbursed on the first of the month.

04. (A) appealed
(B) rotated
(C) urged
(D) housed

52 기적의 토익 RC

📍 정답 및 해설 p.13

DAY 02

Questions 05-08 refer to the following announcement.

St. Louis Manufacturing puts a strong emphasis on efficiency at its main -------. The entire
05.
production process is designed to reduce wasted materials and time. However, there may be more
room for improvement, so employees should make recommendations if they think of them. -------
06.
with a line manager or use the suggestion box by the office to do so. -------. Its amount will be
07.
based on the effectiveness of the idea to improve conditions and productivity here at the plant.
-------, the employee's picture will be posted on the Wall of Brilliance in the lounge.
08.

유형 적용 문제

05. (A) market
   (B) store
   (C) office
   (D) factory

06. (A) To speak
   (B) Speaking
   (C) Speech
   (D) Speak

07. (A) Employees who do so are listed in the factory worker's handbook.
   (B) Management has plans to renovate the employee's break room.
   (C) Cutting edge technology is used on our assembly lines.
   (D) Employees with helpful ideas will receive a bonus at the end of each quarter.

08. (A) Hence
   (B) Also
   (C) Otherwise
   (D) Similarly

PART 6 뒤의 내용이 단서인 명사 어휘   53

PART 7

True · Not True 문제 / 추론 문제

질문과 보기의 표현이 지문에서는 다른 말로 바꾸어 표현되는 경우가 많으므로
패러프레이징 연습을 해 두세요.

적용 기술

[기적의 필기노트] 176P~178P
RC 기술 90, 91

출제 유형 1

True · Not True 문제

사실 파악 문제는 지문의 전반적인 내용을 제대로 이해하고 있는지를 묻습니다. 각 선택지 문장과 지문 내용을 대조하면서 정답과 오답을 추려내야 하므로 시간이 상당히 소요되며 집중력을 요구하는 유형입니다. 보통 6~9문제 정도가 출제돼요.

기출 표현 확인

패러프레이징 표현
· appetizers and drinks will be served → food will be provided
· nominated for the leaders awards → is in position of leadership

1 질문 유형

What is **true** about the new policy? 새로운 규정에 대해 사실인 것은?

What does the article **indicate** about Ms. Bravo? Bravo 씨에 대해 기사는 무엇을 언급하는가?

What is **NOT mentioned** in the advertisement? 광고에 언급되지 않은 것은?

What is **NOT true** about Star Inc.? Star 사에 대해 사실이 아닌 것은?

800+
2 핵심 전략

· mentioned in the letter, indicated in the advertisement와 같이 지문 전반에 대해 묻는 경우에는 먼저 선택지를 모두 읽은 후 지문을 읽으면 문제풀이 시간을 단축할 수 있습니다.
· 문제의 about 뒤에 편지/이메일의 수신인이나 발신인, 광고의 소재가 오는 경우도 지문 전반에 대해 묻는 유형이에요.
· 문제의 about 뒤에 특정 명사나 고유 명사(new policy, Tradefresh Market, Mr. Baron 등)가 올 경우 지문에서 해당 키워드가 언급된 곳 주변의 내용과 선택지를 대조해가며 정답을 찾습니다.

출제 유형 2

추론 문제

추론 문제는 간접적으로 제시된 여러 단서들을 종합하여 정답을 추론해야 하므로 고난도 문제에 속합니다. 자신의 주관적인 판단을 개입시키지 않고 명확한 근거를 확인하여 정답을 선택해야 해요.

기출 표현 확인

패러프레이징 표현
· renovations are nearly complete / should be open starting ~
→ currently closed

1 질문 유형

What is **implied[suggested]** about the apartments? 아파트에 대해 암시된 것은?

For whom is the Web page mainly **intended**? 웹페이지는 주로 누구를 대상으로 하는가?

Where would this notice most **likely be found**? 이 공지는 어디서 찾아볼 수 있겠는가?

800+
2 핵심 전략

· 대상을 묻는 문제(For whom ~, To whom ~)는 지문 초반부에서 단서를 찾을 수 있습니다.
· 출처를 묻는 문제(Where ~ likely be found)는 기사나 공지에서 자주 출제됩니다. 전반적인 내용을 파악한 후 어디에서 찾아볼 수 있는 지문인지 추론하면 됩니다.
· implied/suggested 등으로 묻는 문제는 지문 전반에 대해 묻는 경우에는 선택지를 먼저 읽어 두고, 키워드에 대해 물을 경우에는 해당 키워드가 언급된 주변에서 단서를 찾으세요.

54 기적의 토익 RC

True·Not True 문제

DAY 02

coupon

○ 해석 p.14

> Wright Hardware now carries Mason brand power tools! Present this coupon at any Wright Hardware location when purchasing Mason brand products to receive 10% off on them!
>
> *Does not apply to other brands.
> *Offer expires on 1 March.

Q. What is true about the coupon?

(A) It is valid through the month of March.
(B) It can be used when making online purchases.
(C) It can only be used on a certain brand.
(D) It only applies to one item per customer.

🔖 이렇게 풀어요

1. 문제 먼저 파악 true → 지문 전반에 대해 사실인 것을 묻는 문제임을 파악해요.

2. 각 선택지와 지문 내용 비교해가며 읽기

(A) valid through the month of March [X] → 3월 1일에 만료된다고 했어요.

(B) when making online purchases [X] → 어느 지점에서든 쿠폰을 제시하면 할인을 받는다고 했어요.

(C) used on a certain brand [O] → Mason 브랜드 제품을 구매할 때 쿠폰을 보여 주면 할인을 받는다고 했고, 다른 브랜드는 적용되지 않는다고 했어요.

(D) one item per customer [X] → 언급되지 않았어요.

핵심어 확인! Present this coupon, purchasing Mason brand products

3. 정답 선택 purchasing Mason brand products를 a certain brand로 표현한 (C)를 정답으로 선택합니다.

PART 7 True·Not True 문제 / 추론 문제   55

 **추론 문제**

e-mail   ○ 해석 p.14

To: m.jones@nmail.net
From: s.lowery@thelofts.org
Subject: Maintenance

Dear Resident,

The main parking lot for The Lofts is going to be repaved and repainted later this month. The work is scheduled to begin on Friday, August 15 and be completed on Sunday, August 17.

During that time, we ask that you either use street parking or use the lot across the street. Parking expenses incurred during the time of work will be deducted from your next month's rent if you submit all receipts to the management office.

We look forward to upgrading the facilities here at The Lofts.

Sharon Lowery

Q. Who most likely is Ms. Lowery?

(A) A construction worker
(B) A building manager
(C) A security guard
(D) A delivery driver

♩ **이렇게 풀어요**

1. **문제 먼저 파악** who most likely, Ms. Lowery → Lowery 씨가 누구인지(직업) 추론하는 문제임을 파악해요.

2. **문제의 핵심어구를 지문에서 찾아 주변 내용 파악** 먼저 질문의 핵심어구인 Ms. Lowery는 이메일을 쓴 사람임을 파악합니다. 지문의 핵심어들을 통해 Lowery 씨가 주민들에게 주차장 공사에 대해 알리고 있음을 알 수 있어요.

   핵심어 확인! Dear Resident, parking lot is going to be repaved and repainted, upgrading the facilities here

3. **정답 선택** 건물 시설에 대해 주민들에게 알리는 사람은 건물 관리자일 것이므로 (B)를 정답으로 선택합니다.

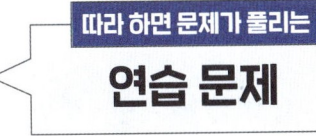

따라 하면 문제가 풀리는

연습 문제

먼저 문제의 키워드에 표시한 후,
지문에서 단서를 찾아 적절한 답을 고르세요.

♀ 정답 및 해설 p.15

DAY 02

01 online chat discussion

Luciano Romani (9:05 A.M.)	Hello, this is Luciano Romani, a technician for Tidwell Communications. I'm scheduled to visit your home today to install a high-speed Internet line. Will someone be there between 4 and 6 P.M.?
Theresa Harrison (9:08 A.M.)	Yes. Is there anything special I need to prepare?
Luciano Romani (9:09 A.M.)	Please just make sure that the furniture and other items are cleared away from the wall. Also, another technician will be with me. He's part of our on-the-job experience program for new hires.
Theresa Harrison (9:10 A.M.)	That's no problem.

Q. What is mentioned about Mr. Romani's coworker?

(A) He made a scheduling error.
(B) He is undergoing a training process.

02 article

Run for a Cure

8 May — Stockbridge College will host a special charity event later this month in order to raise money for cancer research. People who wish to participate in the event are asked to find sponsors to agree to make a donation for every mile they run. Sponsors can be business or individuals, including the participants themselves. Advance registration is encouraged, but those who show up ready to run on the day of the event will also be allowed to participate in the run. For more information, visit the event Web site at www.run4acure.com.

Q. What is NOT true about the event?

(A) Participants must find their own sponsors.
(B) Participants must register in advance.

PART 7 True·Not True 문제 / 추론 문제   57

토익에 나올
실전 문제

제한시간 10분입니다! 시~작!

Questions 01-02 refer to the following online advertisement.

Sparrow Messaging

Sparrow Messaging(SM) is a secure messenger software program that offers several benefits over other messenger services. Since SM performs a variety of functions, users don't need to clutter their work computer's desktop with shortcuts to multiple different programs. You will find that deleting all the unnecessary programs from your work computers will help them run more efficiently.

SM Functions: Simply connect to the Internet and

– Securely send and receive messages
– Transfer any sizes and types of files
– Connect to multi-party phone calls
– Participate in video conferences

Try SM now!

Trial version (FREE): click here

Download the SM installer program and enjoy the trial version of SM. But be aware that you are not allowed to use some functions in this version.

Full office version ($7.99 monthly): click here

You can enjoy every feature of SM. You will get free monthly software updates with increased security features.

---

01. What does Sparrow Messaging allow its users to do?

(A) Connect to the Internet quickly
(B) Delete unneeded software programs
(C) Save money on virus protection software
(D) Record and save video of online meetings

02. What is true about Sparrow Messaging?

(A) It is updated regularly.
(B) It has received positive reviews.
(C) It includes a satisfaction guarantee.
(D) It offers discounts for long-term contracts.

---

paraphrasing   주어진 어휘 또는 표현과 패러프레이징 될 수 있는 것을 연결하세요.

1. unnecessary •
2. run more efficiently •
3. get monthly updates •

• (a) perform better
• (b) updated regularly
• (c) unneeded

58 기적의 토익 RC

◉ 정답 및 해설 p.15

DAY 02

Questions 03-04 refer to the following form.

Cleveland Hotel: Event Hall Reservation Form

Thank you for choosing to hold your event at Cleveland Hotel! Please fill out this form so that we can best accommodate you and your group. We will e-mail an approximate estimate based on your request.

Contact Person: _____

e-mail: _____

Mobile: _____

Event Date(s): _____

Hall Preference: [   ] Diamond Ballroom   [   ] Crystal Hall   [   ] Flower Garden (outside)

Seating: [   ] Round Tables   [   ] Lecture   [   ] Wedding   [   ] Other: _____

Approximate Number of Guests: _____

Audio/Visual Equipment Rental: [   ] Yes   [   ] No

Rooms for guests: [   ] Yes, approximately _____   [   ] No

---

03. What will a Cleveland Hotel employee do?

(A) Send a price quote
(B) Videotape the entire event
(C) Repair audio and visual equipment
(D) Prepare meals for upcoming events

04. What is suggested about Cleveland Hotel?

(A) It recently opened.
(B) It hosts outdoor events.
(C) It offers some catering options.
(D) It gives discounts to large groups.

---

paraphrasing   주어진 어휘 또는 표현과 패러프레이징 될 수 있는 것을 연결하세요.

1. estimate •   • (a) outdoor

2. fill out •   • (b) complete

3. outside •   • (c) price quote

PART 7 True·Not True 문제 / 추론 문제   59

토익에 나올 실전 문제

Questions 05-07 refer to the following article.

PSD Presents Prestigious Award
by Carolyn Hewitt

February 15 — The Partnership for Sustainable Design (PSD) has selected Leah O'Donnell as this year's recipient of the Making a Difference Award. The award is given annually to an architect who is dedicated to sustainability. Ms. O'Donnell has been a shining example of the group's ideals, particularly in her latest project, the Jenkins Bank Tower, which won her the award. "The PSD believes that new buildings don't have to create new waste," said founder and PSD President Andre Cooper. The PSD has worked for two decades to minimize the construction industry's effect on the environment. For the past five years, the PSD has led the way in contributing financially to key studies and experiments focused on the development of new construction materials. One such project resulted in a unique form of insulation made from recycled plastic bottles. Ms. O'Donnell made use of this throughout the Jenkins Bank Tower building, and she even taught a Web-based class on sustainable building materials. This theme is expected to be repeated in her upcoming keynote address at May's industry conference in New York.

05. What is suggested about Ms. O'Donnell?
   (A) She signed up to be a judge for an event.
   (B) She has been a PSD member for several years.
   (C) She designed an environmentally friendly building.
   (D) She submitted a suggestion to Mr. Cooper.

06. What happened five years ago?
   (A) The PSD started investing in some research.
   (B) The PSD was founded by Mr. Cooper.
   (C) Ms. O'Donnell was given her first industry award.
   (D) Ms. O'Donnell was hired by Jenkins Bank.

07. What does Ms. O'Donnell plan to do in May?
   (A) Speak at an industry event
   (B) Start developing a new material
   (C) Raise funds for a project
   (D) Teach an online class

paraphrasing 주어진 어휘 또는 표현과 패러프레이징 될 수 있는 것을 연결하세요.

1. annually •   • (a) every year
2. contributing financially •   • (b) speak at an event
3. keynote address •   • (c) investing

60 기적의 토익 RC

DAY 02

Questions 08-10 refer to the following Web page.

http://www.longoriahotel.com

Room Service Now Available at Longoria Hotel

Guests staying at Longoria Hotel can now enjoy delicious dishes from our on-site restaurant, Indigo, from the comfort of their rooms. This service is available during the restaurant's regular hours of operation. For just $14.95, you can get our featured entrée with two side dishes, which is different every day. You can also order entrées, appetizers, and desserts individually.

Meals are charged to the room, so there is no need to prepare cash in advance. Please allow extra time to receive your food during busy periods. When you are finished with your meal, simply leave the tray and dishes outside the door in the hallway, and an Indigo employee will retrieve the items.

To place an order, dial #03 from your room's phone. If you have any food allergies or other dietary restrictions, you can find out more about what is in each dish by asking for the chef when you contact the restaurant.

---

08. What is indicated about Longoria Hotel's room service meals?

(A) They received favorable ratings.
(B) They are available around the clock.
(C) They include a daily special.
(D) They should be purchased with cash.

09. Who will collect used dishes from hotel guests?

(A) A hotel manager
(B) A front desk receptionist
(C) A housekeeping department worker
(D) A restaurant staff member

10. According to the Web page, how can guests get information about specific ingredients?

(A) By calling the front desk
(B) By speaking to a chef
(C) By reading an online menu
(D) By downloading a smartphone app

---

paraphrasing 주어진 어휘 또는 표현과 패러프레이징 될 수 있는 것을 연결하세요.

1. employee   •
2. retrieve   •
3. what is in each dish •

• (a) collect
• (b) staff member
• (c) ingredients

PART 7 True·Not True 문제 / 추론 문제   61

'멋진 당신, 오늘도 화이팅'

DAY
03

오늘의 학습 포인트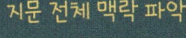

PART 5. 형용사

1. 형용사의 역할 – 명사 수식/보어 역할

2. 형용사의 형태 – 일반 형용사(-tive/-ful/-ous/-able 등)/ '-ly'로 끝나는 형용사/ 분사 형용사

3. 형용사의 구분 – successful vs. successive/impressive vs. impressed 등

4. 형용사 표현 – be aware of, be capable of 등

5. 수량 형용사 – 단수/복수/불가산 명사와 쓰이는 것 구분하기

PART 6. 앞 문장의 명사를 받는 인칭대명사

보기가 모두 대명사, 빈칸 앞에서 대신하는 명사 찾기

PART 7. 의도 파악 문제/문장 삽입 문제

앞뒤 문장과의 논리 파악

지문 전체 맥락 파악

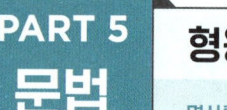

PART 5 문법

형용사

명사를 수식하는 역할의 형용사를 묻는 문제가 가장 많이 출제됩니다.

✎ 적용 기술

[기적의 필기노트] 97P
RC 기술 11

출제 포인트
명사를 수식하는 형용사 자리 문제는 매회 1~2문제씩 꾸준히 출제됩니다.

🔒 **확인 문제 ❶**

She is Mr. Kim's ------- supervisor.

(A) immediate
(B) immediately

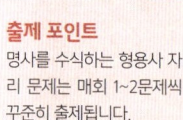

출제 포인트
토익에는 be, become이 가장 자주 출제돼요.

⚠️ **주의**
목적격 보어 역할을 하는 형용사를 고르는 문제는 우리말 해석에 의존할 경우, 부사를 선택하기 쉬워 오답율이 높은 유형입니다. 반드시 5형식 동사를 암기하고 있어야 해요.

🔒 **확인 문제 ❷**

The social event made the relationship -------.

(A) strong
(B) strongly

출제 유형1
형용사의 역할

1 명사 수식

- 형용사의 가장 기본적인 역할은 <u>명사 앞에서 명사를 수식</u>하는 것입니다. 단, 형용사 뒤 표현이 길어지면 명사를 뒤에서 수식합니다. 예) the person <u>responsible</u> for cleaning ~

- 관사 + <u>형용사</u> + 명사
  a **successful** entrepreneur 성공한 기업가   the **innovative** technology 혁신적인 기술

- 관사 + 부사 + <u>형용사</u> + 명사
  a highly **competitive** market 매우 경쟁이 심한 시장

- 소유격 + <u>형용사</u> + 명사
  Mr. Ben's **immediate** supervisor 벤 씨의 직속 상사
  their **creative** idea 그들의 창의적인 아이디어

- 한정사 + <u>형용사</u> + 명사 ＊한정사: this/that/these/those/some/any/every 등
  any **important** data 그 어떠한 중요한 자료라도   those **defective** items 그 결함이 있는 물품들

2 보어 역할

- **주격 보어**: 형용사는 주어를 보충 설명합니다.
  Tips for drawing oil paintings <u>are</u> **helpful**. 유화를 그리는 것에 대한 팁은 도움이 된다.
  (tips=helpful)

주격 보어를 갖는 2형식 동사	
be ~이다	remain/stay ~한 상태로 남다
become/grow/get ~이 되다	seem/look/appear ~한 상태로 보이다
prove ~한 상태임이 드러나다, 증명되다	

`800+`

- **목적격 보어**: 형용사는 목적어 뒤에서 목적어를 보충 설명합니다.
  Users of the RT9 Laptop <u>found</u> its long-lasting battery very **helpful**.
  (battery가 very helpful함)
  RT9 노트북 사용자들은 오래 지속되는 배터리가 매우 도움이 된다는 것을 알게 되었다.

목적격 보어를 갖는 5형식 동사	
make ~을 -한 상태로 만들다	keep ~을 -한 상태로 유지시키다
find ~을 -한 상태라고 생각하다	consider ~을 -한 상태로 간주하다
leave ~을 -한 상태로 남겨 놓다	deem ~을 -하다고 여기다, 간주하다

(A) ❷ (A) ❶ 정답

64 기적의 토익 RC

> 출제 유형 2 **형용사의 형태**

✎ 적용 기술

[기적의 필기노트] 97P, 138P
RC 기술 11, 53

DAY 03

1 일반 형용사

형용사 어미	예시	형용사 어미	예시
-tive/-sive	competitive 경쟁력 있는 extensive 넓은, 광범위한	-al	exceptional 우수한, 특출한 functional 실용적인
-ful	successful 성공적인 helpful 도움이 되는	-cial/-tial	beneficial 유익한, 이로운 substantial 풍부한
-ous	various 다양한 serious 심각한	-ic/-tic	specific 구체적인 dramatic 극적인
-able/-ible	affordable (가격이) 알맞은 accessible 이용 가능한	-ary	necessary 필수의 temporary 일시적인

⚠ 주의

형용사 어미를 갖고 있지만 명사 인 어휘에 주의하세요.
approval 승인
arrival 도착
appraisal 평가
alternative 대안
representative 직원

🔒 확인 문제 ❸

The monthly rent is -------.

(A) afford
(B) affordable

`800+`

2 '-ly'로 끝나는 형용사

• 형용사에 어미 '-ly'가 붙은 단어들은 대부분 부사이지만, 명사에 어미 '-ly'가 붙으면 형용사입니 다. 형태만 보고 형용사를 부사로 혼동하지 않도록 주의하세요.

likely ~할 것 같은 timely 시기적절한	friendly 친절한 leisurely 한가한	costly 값 비싼 orderly 질서정연한

in a **timely** manner 시기적절하게   be **likely** toV ~할 것 같다
in an **orderly** fashion 질서정연하게

• 기간을 나타내는 명사에 '-ly'가 붙은 단어는 형용사와 부사로 모두 사용됩니다.

daily 매일의, 매일 quarterly 분기의, 매 분기	weekly 주간의, 매주 yearly 한 해의, 매해	monthly 한 달의, 매달

daily work 일일 업무   **weekly** meeting 주간회의   **montly** rent 월 임대료
hold the event **yearly** 매해 행사를 개최하다

🔒 확인 문제 ❹

This product is made with environmentally ------- materials.

(A) friend
(B) friendly

3 형용사로 굳어진 분사 형태의 형용사

• 특정 현재분사(-ing)와 과거분사(p.p.)는 형용사로 사용되며, 토익에서는 현재분사와 과거분사를 구분하는 문제로 출제됩니다.

-ing	growing 증가하는 remaining 남아있는	missing 분실된 rewarding 보람 있는	promising 유망한 emerging 최근 생긴	leading 선도하는 inviting 매력적인
p.p.	impressed 감명받은 damaged 손상된 completed 완료된	informed 잘 아는 proposed 제안된 attached 첨부된	experienced 경험 많은 limited 제한된 informed 잘 아는	detailed 자세한 revised 수정된

IK Electronics has been a (**leading** / ~~led~~) company for the last 10 years.
IK 전자는 지난 10년 동안 선두 기업이었다.

🔒 확인 문제 ❺

She wanted to return a ------- item.

(A) damaged
(B) damaging

(A) ❸ (B) ❹ (B) ❺ `정답`

PART 5 문법 형용사   65

적용 기술

[기적의 필기노트] 98P, 101P
RC 기술 12, 15

출제 포인트

dependent와 reliant는 뒤에 전치사 on과 함께 쓰여요.

🔒 확인 문제 ❻

The company experienced
------- growth.

(A) considerate
(B) considerable

출제 포인트

be동사 뒤에 알맞은 형태를 고르는 문제는 명사/현재분사보다는 형용사/과거분사가 정답이 되는 경우가 많아요.

🔒 확인 문제 ❼

The room rates at Texas
Inn are -------.

(A) reasoned
(B) reasonable

출제 유형 3

형용사의 구분

`800+`

1 파생어 형용사

- 하나의 어휘에서 파생되어 형태가 비슷하지만 의미는 다른 형용사입니다. 두 형용사가 보기에 함께 주어지므로 반드시 의미를 구별할 수 있도록 암기해 두세요.

successful 성공적인 successive 연속적인	confident 확신하는 confidential 기밀의	favorite 가장 좋아하는 favorable 우호적인
dependent 의존적인 dependable 믿을 만한	extensive 광범위한 extended 연장된	various 다양한 variable 변동이 심한
reliable 믿을 수 있는 reliant 의지하는	comprehensive 종합적인 comprehensible 이해할 수 있는	understanding 이해심 있는 understandable 이해할 만한
considerate 배려하는 considerable 상당한	last 지난, 마지막의 lasting 지속하는	complete 완전한 completed 완료된
beneficial 유익한 beneficent 인정 많은	respectable 존경할만한 respective 각각의, 각자의	impressive 인상적인 impressed 감명받은

Mr. Walter is a (**successful** / ~~successive~~) business person.
Walter 씨는 성공한 사업가이다.

The company is (~~reliable~~ / **reliant**) on exportable products.
그 회사는 수출용 제품에 의존한다.

`800+`

2 be동사 뒤 문법 구분

- be동사 뒤에는 현재분사, 과거분사, 형용사, 명사가 올 수 있으므로 함께 선택지로 제시될 경우 용법을 구분할 수 있어야 합니다.
  - be동사 뒤에 형용사가 오면 형용사가 주어의 상태를 설명
  - be동사 뒤에 명사가 오면 주어와 동격 관계
  - be동사 뒤에 현재분사가 오면 주어와 능동 관계이고, 목적어 필요
  - be동사 뒤에 과거분사가 오면 주어와 수동 관계이고, 목적어 불필요

Our rates are (**competitive** / ~~competed~~ / ~~competing~~ / ~~competition~~).
우리의 요금은 경쟁력이 있다.

Individuals have the right to be (~~informing~~ / **informed** / ~~information~~ / ~~informative~~) about the use of their personal data.
개인들은 그들의 개인 정보의 사용에 대해 정보를 제공받을 권리가 있다.

(B) ❼ (B) ❻ 답장

66   기적의 토익 RC

출제 유형 4

형용사 표현

1 형용사 짝꿍 표현

· 뒤의 명사를 수식하는 **형용사 어휘**나 **품사 구분 문법** 문제로 출제돼요.

confidential information[document] 기밀 정보[문서]
considerable/significant/substantial increase 상당한 증가
broad/wide/diverse range 넓은 범위
convincing argument 설득력 있는 주장
defective product 결함 있는 제품
reasonable/affordable price[rate] 합리적인 가격[요금]
reliable product[service] 믿을만한 제품[서비스]
comprehensive knowledge 포괄적인 지식
steady sales 지속적인 판매
alphabetical order 알파벳 순서
commercial[residential] property 상업용[주거용] 건물
constructive feedback 건설적인 의견
extensive experience 많은 경험
generous amount 많은 양
collective effort 공동의 노력
protective equipment 보호 장비
perishable goods 상하기 쉬운 제품
particular area 특정 지역

🔒 **확인 문제 ❽**

Please transport the ------- goods safely in a refrigerator car.

(A) perishable
(B) generous

2 형용사 숙어(be + 형용사 + 전치사)

· 형용사와 뒤에 오는 전치사를 함께 암기하면, 형용사 어휘 부분이 빈칸으로 출제될 경우 쉽게 정답을 고를 수 있어요.

be aware of ~을 인식하다, 알다	be relevant to ~와 관련있다
be appreciative of ~에 감사하다	be capable of ~을 할 수 있다
be exempt from ~로부터 면제받다	be accessible to ~을 이용할 수 있다
be enthusiastic about ~에 열정적이다	be responsible for ~을 책임지다
be available for ~을 위해 이용 가능하다	be compatible with ~과 호환되다
be vulnerable to ~에 취약하다	be dependent/reliant on ~에 의존하다
be eligible for ~할 자격이 있는	be comparable to ~에 견줄 만하다
be optimistic about ~에 대해 낙관적인	be accountable to ~에 책임을 지다

🔒 **확인 문제 ❾**

The manager is ------- for conducting a survey.

(A) exempt
(B) responsible

· eligible은 전치사 for 또는 to부정사와 함께 사용돼요.
I'm **eligible for** a discount. 나는 할인받을 자격이 있다.

He **is eligible to get** a free item. 그는 무료 제품을 받을 자격이 있다.

· optimistic과 aware는 뒤에 that절이 오기도 합니다.
He **is aware that** the sales is decreasing. 그는 매출이 감소하고 있다는 것을 인식하고 있다.

(B) ❾ (A) ❽ 정답

PART 5 문법 형용사   67

적용 기술

[기적의 필기노트] 100P
RC 기술 14

⚠️ **주의**

every 뒤에 복수 명사가 오면
'~마다'라는 의미의 부사입니다.
every two days 이틀마다

🔒 **확인 문제 ⑩**

------ participants are
expected to attend the
local festival.

(A) Numerous
(B) Each

🔒 **확인 문제 ⑪**

The company decided
to spend ------ money in
advertising.

(A) less
(B) fewer

출제 유형 5

수량 형용사

빈칸 뒤의 명사를 보고 적절한 수량 형용사를 고르는 문제로 출제됩니다.

1 수량 형용사 + 단수 명사

each 각각의 every 모든 another 다른 a single 하나의	+ 단수 명사

Each worker removed their belongings to the new office.
각각의 직원들은 소지품을 새 사무실로 옮겼다.

Every employee should attend the meeting. 모든 직원들은 회의에 참석해야 한다.

2 수량 형용사 + 복수 명사

many 많은 fewer 더 적은 various 다양한 a number of 많은	a few 몇 개의 numerous 많은 a variety of 다양한 the number of ~의 수	few 거의 없는 both 둘 다의 several 여러 개의 a series of 일련의	+ 복수 명사

There are **several** managers in the meeting room. 회의실에 여러 명의 매니저들이 있다.

Various items will be discounted. 다양한 아이템들이 할인될 것이다.

- a number of와 the number of 뒤에는 모두 가산 복수 명사가 옵니다. 하지만 이 두 표현이 주어로 사용되면 'a number of + 복수 명사'는 복수 동사와, 'the number of + 복수 명사'는 단수 동사와 써야 합니다.

A number of mobile phone accessories are on sale.
많은 휴대폰 액세서리가 세일 중이다.

The number of tourists has been decreasing. 관광객의 수는 줄어들고 있다.

3 수량 형용사 + 불가산 명사

much 많은 a little 적은 little 거의 없는 less 더 적은 least 가장 적은 a great deal of 많은 a large amount of 많은	+ 불가산 명사

We have **little** time to finish the work. 우리는 그 일을 끝낼 시간이 거의 없다.

She spent **a great deal of** time studying for the test.
그녀는 시험 공부를 하느라 많은 시간을 썼다.

4 수량 형용사 + 가산 복수 명사/불가산 명사

보기에 가산 복수 명사와 불가산 명사가 모두 있을 경우 동사의 수를 확인해서 정답을 선택하세요. 단수 동사일 경우 불가산 명사가 정답입니다.

all 모든 other 다른 some 몇몇의 more 더 많은 most 대부분의 a lot of/lots of/plenty of 많은	+ 가산 복수/불가산 명사

정답 ⑩ (A) ⑪ (A)

68　기적의 토익 RC

형용사

1. The poor customer service will cause a ------- decrease in sales in the long run.

(A) signify   (B) signifies   (C) significant   (D) significantly

형편없는 고객 서비스는 장기적으로 매출에 있어서 상당한 감소를 야기할 것이다.

> **이렇게 풀어요**
>
> **1. 선택지 보고 문법/어휘 문제 파악** 선택지가 모두 동사 signify(의미하다)의 파생어로 구성되어 있으므로 문법 문제임을 파악할 수 있어요.
> **2. 빈칸 분석** 빈칸 앞에 부정관사 a가 있고 뒤에 명사 decrease(감소)가 있으므로 빈칸은 decrease와 함께 복합 명사를 완성할 명사 또는 명사를 수식하는 수식어가 필요한 자리임을 파악해요.
> **3. 정답 선택** 명사를 수식하는 기능을 하는 형용사 (C) significant(상당한)를 정답으로 고릅니다.

2. Please check if the shop is ------- by reading online testimonials.

(A) depend   (B) depends   (C) dependable   (D) dependent

온라인 추천글을 읽어서 그 가게가 신뢰할 만한지 확인하세요.

> **이렇게 풀어요**
>
> **1. 선택지 보고 문법/어휘 문제 파악** 선택지가 모두 동사 depend(신뢰하다, 의지하다)의 파생어로 구성되어 있으므로 문법 문제임을 파악할 수 있어요.
> **2. 빈칸 분석** 빈칸 앞에 주격 보어를 가지는 2형식 동사인 be동사 is가 있으므로 빈칸은 보어 자리임을 파악해요.
> **3. 정답 선택** 보어 역할을 하는 형용사 (C)와 (D) 중에서, '가게가 신뢰할 만한지'의 의미가 되는 것이 자연스러우므로 (C) dependable을 정답으로 고릅니다. dependent는 '의존적인'이라는 의미이므로 어울리지 않는다는 것을 알 수 있어요.

3. During the event, a reusable shopping bag will be given to ------- customer who spends $50 or more.

(A) most   (B) every   (C) some   (D) those

행사 기간 동안 50달러 이상을 소비하는 고객들에게는 재사용 가능한 쇼핑백이 제공될 것이다.

> **이렇게 풀어요**
>
> **1. 선택지 보고 문법/어휘 문제 파악** 선택지가 모두 수량 또는 지시형용사이므로 뒤의 명사의 수에 맞는 형용사를 고르는 문법 문제임을 파악할 수 있어요.
> **2. 빈칸 분석** 빈칸 앞에 전치사 to, 뒤에 명사 customer(고객)가 있으므로 빈칸은 customer와 함께 복합 명사를 완성할 명사 또는 customer를 수식할 형용사가 들어갈 자리임을 파악해요.
> **3. 정답 선택** 빈칸 뒤의 가산 단수 명사 customer와 쓰일 수 있는 수량 형용사 (B) every를 정답으로 고릅니다. 나머지 선택지는 가산 복수 명사를 수식해요.

PART 5 문법 형용사   69

PART 5 어휘

명사 어휘 (3)

각 어휘와 함께 자주 쓰이는 표현을 통째로 외워두세요.

01 clearance 정리

have a clearance sale 재고 정리 세일을 하다
customs clearance 통관

02 pace 속도

at one's own pace 자신만의 속도로
at a rapid pace 빠른 속도로

03 restriction 제한, 규제, 제약

restrictions on ~에 대한 규제
time restriction 시간 제한

800+ 🐾 빈출 토익 선생님 Pick!
04 alternative 대안

be an alternative to ~의 대안이다
alternative energy 대체 에너지

05 engagement 약속, 참여, 종사

prior engagement 선약
engagement in ~에 종사

🐾 빈출 토익 선생님 Pick!
06 qualification 자격, 조건

meet the qualifications 조건을 갖추다
qualifications for ~에 필요한 자격

07 restoration 복원, 복구

restoration of ~의 복원, 복구
restoration project 복원 사업

08 measure 조치

safety measure 안전 조치
take measures 조치를 취하다

09 industry 산업

fastest growing industry 가장 빠르게 성장하는 산업

10 approach 접근

approach to ~로의 접근
innovative[creative] approach 혁신적인[창의적인] 접근

🐾 빈출 토익 선생님 Pick!
11 process 과정, 절차

assembly process 조립 과정
in the process of ~의 과정에서

12 comparison 비교

in comparison to ~와 비교할 때
a comparison between A and B A와 B 간의 비교

13 range 다양성, 범위

offer a wide range of 다양한 ~을 제공하다

🐾 빈출 토익 선생님 Pick!
14 approval 승인, 찬성

receive approval from ~의 승인을 받다
obtain approval to부정사 ~하기 위한 승인을 얻다
formal[official] approval 공식적인 승인

70 기적의 토익 RC

15 order — 주문(품), 질서

out of order	고장이 난
in order of preference	선호도 순으로
in alphabetical order	알파벳 순으로
streamline the ordering process	주문 절차를 간소화하다

`800+`

16 objective — 목적, 목표

objectives to be achieved	달성해야 할 목표
career objective	경력 목표

17 payment — 지불, 지급, 납입

send payment for	~에 대한 대금을 보내다
make a payment	납부하다, 지불하다

18 term — 용어, 학기, 기간

read the contract terms	계약 조건을 읽다
long-term employment	장기 고용
short-term forecast	단기 예측

🐾 빈출 토익 선생님 Pick!

19 production — 생산

be in production	생산 중이다
production quota	생산 할당(량)
production capacity	생산 능력

20 personnel — 직원, 인사과

authorized personnel	허가된 직원, 관계자
personnel department	인사과

21 colleague — 동료

socialize with colleagues	동료들과 어울리다
long-time colleague	오랜 동료

22 variety — 여러 가지, 다양성

a variety of	여러 가지의

🐾 빈출 토익 선생님 Pick!

23 destination — 목적지, 도착지

tourist destination	관광지
final destination	최종 목적지
popular destination	인기 여행지

24 consultation — 상담, 자문, 진찰

brief consultation	간단한 진찰
get a consultation	상담을 받다

25 usage — 사용, 용법

water usage	물 사용
read the usage guidelines	사용 지침을 읽다

🧑‍🏫 풀이 방법

The report indicated that our sales declined significantly in ------- to the last quarter's.

(A) compliance　　(B) comparison　　(C) assurance　　(D) patience

보고서는 우리의 매출이 지난 분기의 매출과 비교하여 상당히 감소했음을 나타냈다.

> **이렇게 풀어요**
>
> **1. 선택지 보고 문법/어휘 문제 파악** 선택지가 서로 다른 명사 어휘로 구성되어 있으므로 어휘 문제임을 파악해요.
>
> **2. 빈칸 분석** 빈칸 앞뒤로 전치사 in과 to가 있으므로 이 전치사들과 함께 쓰이는 명사가 들어가야 함을 파악해요.
>
> **3. 정답 선택** in comparison to(~와 비교할 때)의 형태로 쓰일 수 있는 (B) comparison을 정답으로 선택합니다.

PART 5 어휘 명사 어휘 (3)

따라 하면 문제가 풀리는

연습 문제

앞서 학습한 문제 풀이법을 적용하여 맞는 것에 ✔ 표시 하거나 괄호 안에
적절한 답을 쓰고 정답을 선택하세요.

01 You can purchase any items at a ------- price.

(A) competed
(B) competitive
(C) competition
(D) competitors

1. 선택지 보고 문법/어휘 문제 파악하기 ☐ 문법 문제 ☐ 어휘 문제
2. 빈칸 분석하기 빈칸 뒤에 있는 것 ☐ 동사 ☐ 부사 ☐ 명사
   → 빈칸에는 ☐ 형용사 ☐ 동사가 들어가야 한다.
3. 정답 선택하기 정답 (   )

02 Trent Home Goods has become the country's ------- manufacturer of kitchen appliances.

(A) lead
(B) leading
(C) leads
(D) leader

1. 선택지 보고 문법/어휘 문제 파악하기 ☐ 문법 문제 ☐ 어휘 문제
2. 빈칸 분석하기 빈칸 앞에 있는 것 ☐ 명사의 소유격 ☐ 명사의 복수형
   빈칸 뒤에 있는 것 ☐ 동사 ☐ 부사 ☐ 명사
   → 빈칸에는 ☐ 형용사 ☐ 동사가 들어가야 한다.
3. 정답 선택하기 정답 (   )

03 All employees should obtain ------- from their supervisors to use a company car.

(A) usage
(B) process
(C) approval
(D) variety

1. 선택지 보고 문법/어휘 문제 파악하기 ☐ 문법 문제 ☐ 어휘 문제
2. 빈칸 분석하기 빈칸앞에 있는 동사 (   )
   동사의 의미 (   )
   → 이 동사와 어울려 쓸 수 있는 명사가 정답이다.
3. 정답 선택하기 정답 (   )

Q 정답 및 해설 p.18

DAY 03

04 Thanks to mass production methods, many household items are now ------- for the general public.

(A) affords
(B) afforded
(C) affording
(D) affordable

---
1. 선택지 보고 문법/어휘 문제 파악하기 ☐문법 문제 ☐어휘 문제
2. 빈칸 분석하기 빈칸 앞에 있는 것 ☐2형식 동사 ☐4형식 동사
  → 빈칸은 ☐목적어 ☐주격 보어 자리이다.
  → 따라서 ☐형용사 ☐동사가 와야 한다.
3. 정답 선택하기 정답 (   )
---

05 Professional athletes have to practice every day to keep their teamwork -------.

(A) strong
(B) strongly
(C) strength
(D) strengthen

---
1. 선택지 보고 문법/어휘 문제 파악하기 ☐문법 문제 ☐어휘 문제
2. 빈칸 분석하기 빈칸 앞에 있는 것 ☐2형식 동사 ☐5형식 동사
  → 빈칸은 ☐목적어 ☐목적격 보어 자리이다.
  → 따라서 ☐형용사 ☐부사가 와야 한다.
3. 정답 선택하기 정답 (   )
---

06 The amount of the cash bonus is ------- on their combined annual sales.

(A) depend
(B) dependent
(C) dependable
(D) depended

---
1. 선택지 보고 문법/어휘 문제 파악하기 ☐문법 문제 ☐어휘 문제
2. 빈칸 분석하기 빈칸 앞에 있는 것 ☐2형식 동사 ☐4형식 동사
  → 빈칸은 ☐목적어 ☐주격 보어 자리이다.
  → 빈칸은 ☐형용사 ☐동사가 와야 한다.
  → 정답이 될 수 있는 후보 (,   )
3. 정답 선택하기 정답 (   )

PART 5 형용사 / 명사 어휘 (3) 73

토익에 나올 실전 문제

DAY 01-03 누적 문제

제한시간 9분입니다! 시~작!

01. Lorenzo Marketing is credited with creating the ------- advertisement for this year's clothing line.

(A) innovate
(B) innovation
(C) innovative
(D) innovatively

02. Even though it was left in the drawer, the flash light is still -------.

(A) function
(B) functions
(C) functional
(D) functionally

03. Since seats are ------- to be sold out, Hayden Theater recommends reserving tickets to the show well in advance.

(A) likes
(B) likelihood
(C) liked
(D) likely

04. Guards patrol the facility every hour to check whether it is -------.

(A) secure
(B) secures
(C) security
(D) securing

05. Holiday bonus pay for Trujillo staff members is ------- on the year's profits.

(A) depended
(B) dependable
(C) dependent
(D) depends

06. The new independent study focuses on the ------- effects of a high-protein diet.

(A) benefit
(B) beneficial
(C) benefits
(D) beneficially

07. Mr. Baker wanted to become a freelancer because he would be able to work at his own -------.

(A) load
(B) entry
(C) pace
(D) cost

08. Wilkerson Café offers a special lunch menu to stay ------- with nearby restaurants.

(A) competes
(B) competitively
(C) competitor
(D) competitive

09. Taking passengers to a ------- range of destinations, Horizon Airlines has been voted number one for its service.

(A) wide
(B) widen
(C) widely
(D) widening

10. If you register for our membership, you are eligible to get a free ------- with our experts.

(A) usage
(B) comparison
(C) continuity
(D) consultation

11. The survey shows that customers are ------- of the new parking area for the handicapped people.

(A) appreciation
(B) appreciates
(C) appreciating
(D) appreciative

12. All magazines and newspapers are arranged in ------- order.

(A) chronicle
(B) chronology
(C) chronological
(D) chronologically

74   기적의 토익 RC

13. Alley Pizza is known for its ------- delivery service to any location.

(A) relied
(B) relies
(C) rely
(D) reliable

14. Mr. Bale was named Employee of the Month for his ------- performance.

(A) impress
(B) impressed
(C) impressing
(D) impressive

15. After undergoing ------- tests, the prototype will be approved for mass production.

(A) exhaust
(B) exhausted
(C) exhaustive
(D) exhaustion

16. Daniel's Builders demands that all construction workers follow safety ------- when entering the construction site.

(A) measures
(B) advances
(C) perspectives
(D) properties

17. Mr. Hoffmann has more field experience than most of ------- with similar educational backgrounds.

(A) this
(B) those
(C) these
(D) them

18. During the Fisherman's Cooking Contest, you can help ------- to samples of seafood.

(A) you
(B) your
(C) yours
(D) yourself

19. Only a few candidates possess all of the ------- our HR department requires.

(A) qualifications
(B) alternatives
(C) destinations
(D) engagements

20. The management team took time to review the ------- criticism given by customers.

(A) constructs
(B) constructive
(C) construction
(D) constructing

21. The board members decided to utilize an innovative ------- to boosting sales beginning next quarter.

(A) industry
(B) approach
(C) stretch
(D) phase

22. Mr. Wilkerson gave some ------- comments and personal tips about public speaking.

(A) value
(B) valuing
(C) valuable
(D) valuably

23. One of the primary ------- of this project is to successfully expand our presence into the European markets.

(A) payments
(B) objectives
(C) clearances
(D) restorations

24. Building management thanks all residents for your ------- effort to reduce garbage by 10% over the past month.

(A) collect
(B) collector
(C) collecting
(D) collective

PART 5 형용사 / 명사 어휘 (3)   75

PART 6

앞 문장의 명사를 받는 인칭대명사

보기가 모두 대명사로 이루어져 있으면 빈칸 앞의 어떤 명사를 대신하는지 파악합니다.

적용 기술

[기적의 필기노트] 159P
RC 기술 77

VOCA

tablet device 태블릿 기기
rely on ~에 의지하다
improve 개선시키다
token of appreciation 감사의 표시
valid 유효한

풀이 방법
e-mail
해석 p.21

Date: 15 June
To: Rebecca Wagner <r.wagner@hmail.com>
From: Customer Service <custserv@everbrite.com>
Subject: Thank you!

Dear Ms. Wagner,

This e-mail is to thank you for your giving a review of our EverBrite tablet device. Our company relies on customers like yourself who help us figure out what we are doing wrong and how we can improve our products and services.

Please accept the ------- coupon as a token of our appreciation. It is valid on any
PART 5
online or in-store purchase of EverBrite merchandise. You mentioned that your previous purchase was a gift. Now, you can go out and get a brand new EverBrite tablet at the special weekend sale event going on at ------- flagship store.
01.

Thanks again,

Service Department, EverBrite Electronics

---

01. (A) my
(B) our
(C) their
(D) his

핵심 포인트

<PART 6 빈출 인칭대명사>
소유격: my, our, your, his, her, its, their
목적격: me, us, you, him, her, it, them

이렇게 풀어요

1. **선택지 보고 문법/어휘 문제 파악** 선택지가 모두 소유격 대명사로 이루어져 있으므로 앞에 나오는 명사와 수와 인칭이 일치되는 대명사를 찾는 문법 문제임을 파악해요.

2. **빈칸 분석** 빈칸이 포함된 문장이 '플래그십 매장에서 진행되는 할인 행사에서 태블릿을 구입할 수 있다'라는 의미인데, 빈칸 앞 내용을 근거로 태블릿 기기를 파는 EverBrite 회사에서 작성한 이메일임을 파악해요.

3. **정답 선택** EverBrite의 플래그십 매장을 지칭해야 하므로 (B) our를 정답으로 선택합니다.

해설

빈칸 앞에 관사, 뒤에 명사가 있으므로 빈칸은 형용사 자리입니다. 형용사 역할을 하는 분사인 (A)와 (C) 중, '첨부된'이라는 수동의 의미가 되어야 하므로 과거분사 (A)가 정답입니다.

PART 5 문법 적용 문제

Please accept the ------- coupon as a token of our appreciation.

(A) attached　　　(B) attach　　　(C) attaching　　　(D) attaches

76　기적의 토익 RC

따라 하면 문제가 풀리는

연습 문제

빈칸 앞 내용에서 단서가 될 부분을 찾아 표시하세요.
표시한 것을 바탕으로 정답 어휘를 선택하세요.

🔍 정답 및 해설 p.21

DAY 03

01

Dear Ms. Bishop,

Thank you for providing feedback on the dining set you ordered from MoreHome.com. We are sorry to hear that some of the bowls were cracked upon arrival. We will replace ------- free of charge.

(A) hers　　　　　　(B) them

02

This letter is in regards to the rental contract I have for the apartment at 41 Cricket Lane. I will be moving out three months early. ------- company is transferring me to Detroit.

(A) My　　　　　　(B) Any

03

Dear Mr. Harris

This e-mail is to remind you of the summer vacation request that was due last Friday. All staff members except ------- submitted it on time.

(A) him　　　　　　(B) you

04

Both Vanessa Bosch and Christopher Wilde have announced their retirement at the end of the year. ------- have a combined 80 years of experience in Marketing.

(A) We　　　　　　(B) They

PART 6 앞 문장의 명사를 받는 인칭대명사　77

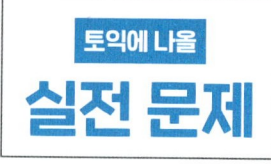 토익에 나올
실전 문제

계한시간 4분입니다! 시~작!

Questions 01-04 refer to the following e-mail.

Date: 29 May
To: Thomas Ackerman <tackerman@cmail.net>
From: Ruben Huntz <rhuntz@gavinappliance.net>
Subject: Product Defect

Dear Mr. Ackerman,

On behalf of Gavin Appliances, I would like to congratulate you on the recent ------- of a Gavin 46S
    01.
AC unit in your home. However, due to a product defect detected in some units coming from one of
our manufacturing plants, certain models will need a replacement part.

-------. To confirm if your unit is in need of replacement parts, please check the serial number
02.
beneath the plastic hood. If ------- starts with "ITV," your model will need replacements. Please call
            03.
and let us know when a technician can come to your house with the new parts. Gavin Appliances
will replace them absolutely ------- of charge.
            04.

We apologize for the inconvenience. Thank you in advance for your understanding and
cooperation.

Ruben Huntz
Customer Service Support Team, Gavin Appliances

01. (A) installation
    (B) review
    (C) content
    (D) reception

02. (A) Please fill out the satisfaction questionnaire on
        our Web site.
    (B) Gavin Appliances offers a warranty on all of its
        products.
    (C) Not all of the Gavin 46S model units contain this
        defect.
    (D) Certain older models may not have this feature.

유형 적용 문제

03. (A) ours
    (B) them
    (C) it
    (D) we

04. (A) ahead
    (B) prior
    (C) free
    (D) instead

78 기적의 토익 RC

○ 정답 및 해설 p.21

Questions 05-08 refer to the following letter.

Dear Eagle WiFi Subscriber,

------- November 1, some changes to your WiFi Internet service will be implemented. You are -------
   05.   **06.**

to use secure passwords, and to prove your age to access certain Web sites. These measures will

be put into place for the safety of all subscribers. Also, several IT specialists have been hired to

monitor and improve your network security. We hope that all subscribers like ------- enjoy more
                                                                 07.

secured and protected services. -------.
                                     08.

유형 적용 문제

05. (A) Effecting
    (B) Effected
    (C) Effects
    (D) Effective

07. (A) them
    (B) us
    (C) you
    (D) it

06. (A) required
    (B) attached
    (C) devoted
    (D) decided

08. (A) Our call center representatives are available every day around the clock.
    (B) More details about the new security measures can be found on our Web site.
    (C) There are several software programs you can use to keep your computer safe.
    (D) Please note that a service fee will be deducted from your account automatically.

PART 6 앞 문장의 명사를 받는 인칭대명사

PART 7

의도 파악 문제 / 문장 삽입 문제

의도 파악 문제는 문제의 표현을 지문에 표시해놓고 지문의 맥락을 파악하세요.
문장 삽입 문제는 빈칸 앞 문장과의 논리를 파악하는 것이 중요해요.

✎ 적용 기술

[기적의 필기노트] 182P
RC 기술 93

🔒 기출 표현 확인

따옴표 기출 문장
· You have a point.
· I wish I could.
· That won't work for me.
· Sounds good.
· Take your time.

✎ 적용 기술

[기적의 필기노트] 180P
RC 기술 92

출제 포인트
단서 없이 논리적 판단으로
해결해야 하는 경우가 가장
많이 출제돼요.

출제 유형 1

의도 파악 문제

의도 파악 문제는 따옴표 안에 제시된 문장을 직역하여 의미를 파악하는 것이 아니라 앞뒤 맥락과
함께 이해할 수 있는지 묻습니다. 문자 메시지와 온라인 채팅 지문에서 출제됩니다.

1 질문 유형

At + 시간, what does + 사람 이름 + most likely mean when she[he] writes, "-------"?
~시 -분에, ~ 씨가 "-------"라고 썼을 때 의미하는 바는 무엇인가?

`800+`
2 핵심 전략

· 보통 제시된 문장의 앞 → 뒤 → 전체적인 맥락의 순으로 단서가 제시됩니다. 따라서 어떤 상황에
서 문자 메시지나 채팅이 오가고 있는지 파악하는 것이 중요합니다.
· 업무에 대해 요청하고 해주겠다고 수락하는 상황, 일이 어떻게 진행되어 가고 있는지 확인하는
상황, 도움을 요청하고 수락하는 상황, 상대의 의견이나 제안에 동의하는 상황이 자주 출제돼요.

출제 유형 2

문장 삽입 문제

문장 삽입 문제는 특정 정보를 포함한 문장을 제시합니다. 논리적 흐름에 맞춰 해당 정보가 들어갈
위치를 찾아내야 하는 고난도 문제이므로, 제시된 문장에서 연결어, 지시어, 대명사 등의 단서를 찾는
것이 핵심입니다. 매회 2문제가 출제돼요.

1 질문 유형

In which of the positions marked [1], [2], [3], and [4] does the following
sentence best belong?
[1], [2], [3], 그리고 [4]로 표시된 곳 중 다음 문장이 들어가기에 가장 적절한 곳은?

`800+`
2 핵심 전략

· 주어진 문장에 연결어(However, Therefore, Also 등)가 있는 경우 앞 문장과의 인과 관계를
파악합니다.
· 주어진 문장에 지시어나 대명사(This, Those, It, They 등)가 있는 경우 그것이 가리키는 명사가
있는 곳을 찾아 그 뒤에 문장을 넣어 연결이 자연스러운지 확인합니다.
· 주어진 문장에 단서가 없는 경우 논리적 흐름이 어색한 곳을 골라내거나 또는 주어진 문장에서
사용된 특정 단어가 다시 사용된 문장을 찾습니다.

80 기적의 토익 RC

의도 파악 문제

DAY 03

text message chain

◯ 해석 p.23

Miles Bowen [5:18 P.M.]	Chad, are you in the office?
Chad Sellers [5:19 P.M.]	Yes. Did you forget something?
Miles Bowen [5:20 P.M.]	There's a document that I was supposed to send by courier service to our clients in Fairburn. Do you think you could handle that?
Chad Sellers [5:22 P.M.]	It shouldn't be a problem. Which document is it?
Miles Bowen [5:23 P.M.]	It's the file labeled Fairburn with today's date on it. It's in the file cabinet next to my desk.
Chad Sellers [5:25 P.M.]	There's a keypad lock on it.
Miles Bowen [5:26 P.M.]	Oh, you don't know the code? It's 5772.
Chad Sellers [5:28 P.M.]	Okay, I found it. Did you already ask the courier to come pick it up?
Miles Bowen [5:29 P.M.]	I just did. Thanks for your help.

Q. At 5:25 P.M., what does Mr. Sellers most likely mean when he writes, "There's a keypad lock on it"?

(A) He is in the wrong place.
(B) He needs some information.
(C) He has to visit the security department.
(D) He doesn't have the authority to access a file.

🖊 이렇게 풀어요

1. 문제 먼저 파악 Ms. Sellers most likely mean, "There's a keypad lock on it" → 의도 파악 문제임을 파악해요.

2. 따옴표 안에 있는 문장의 주변 문장을 읽고 맥락 파악
Miles Bowen이 택배 발송을 부탁하며 문서는 본인 책상 옆에 있는 파일 캐비닛에 있다고 하자, Chad Sellers가 "키패드 자물쇠가 달려 있다"고 했어요. 이는 캐비닛이 잠겨 있어서 열 수 없으니 암호를 알려 달라는 의미임을 알 수 있어요.

핵심어 확인! It's in the file cabinet next to my desk.

3. 정답 선택 Sellers 씨의 의도를 He needs some information으로 표현한 (B)를 정답으로 선택합니다.

PART 7 의도 파악 문제 / 문장 삽입 문제 81

문장 삽입 문제

press release   ⚲ 해석 p.23

READY FOR IMMEDIATE RELEASE

Contact: Diyah Shah, 555-6852

Palmdale (3 June) — Pacific Trucking is pleased to announce plans to expand its area of operations. — [1] —. While it originally only shipped goods across states in the Pacific and Mountain Time Zones, it will soon cover locations throughout the continental United States.

In order to meet the new demand, Pacific Trucking will begin hiring as early as next week. — [2] —. During the initial phase of expansion, the company will hire 100 full-time drivers.

Pacific Trucking is a successful and highly respected employer. — [3] —. All employees are given access to health and dental plans at affordable rates. If you already own a truck and would like to become a Pacific Trucking driver, you may be required to have it modified to meet the company's environmental standards. — [4] —. If yours is near its expiration date, you may be asked to renew it before being accepted. For more information, visit www.pacifictrucking.com/careers.

Q. In which of the positions marked [1], [2], [3], and [4] does the following sentence best belong?

"Only those with a valid commercial driver's license should apply for the driver position."

(A) [1]
(B) [2]
(C) [3]
(D) [4]

✔ 이렇게 풀어요

1. **주어진 문장 먼저 파악** Only those with a valid commercial driver's license should apply for the driver position → 운전기사직 지원 자격에 관한 내용으로 유효한 사업용 운전면허를 언급했습니다.

2. **문제의 핵심어구와 관련된 내용을 지문에서 파악** 마지막 단락 [4] 뒤에 "만기일이 가깝다면, 합격하기 전에 갱신하도록 요청을 받을 수 있습니다"라고 했습니다.

   핵심어 확인! If yours is near its expiration date, you may be asked to renew it

3. **정답 선택** [4] 뒤에 있는 문장에서 만기일이나 갱신은 사업용 운전면허에 대한 내용으로 보는 것이 적절하므로 (D)를 정답으로 선택합니다.

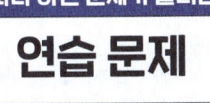 따라 하면 문제가 풀리는 **연습 문제**

먼저 문제의 키워드에 표시한 후,
지문에서 단서를 찾아 적절한 답을 고르세요.

◇ 정답 및 해설 p.23

DAY 03

---

01 text message chain

> **Makenna Lyons [3:18 P.M.]**
> Danny, we have a problem. I just heard from our seafood supplier. They said that due to an accident, they won't be able to bring any fresh fish to our restaurant today.
>
> **Danny Goodman [3:20 P.M.]**
> Seriously? But today is Friday. Our dinner special today is the fried fish platter.
>
> **Makenna Lyons [3:21 P.M.]**
> I know, and I don't want to disappoint them. Could you come up with a replacement special for today?
>
> **Danny Goodman [3:23 P.M.]**
> I'll check our freezer.
>
> **Makenna Lyons [3:34 P.M.]**
> Great. I'm counting on you!

Q. At 3:23 P.M., what does Mr. Goodman mean when he writes, "I'll check our freezer"?

(A) He will examine a device.
(B) He will create a new dish.

---

02 article

> The charity organization Backyard Ball has recently been gaining more and more attention. It was initially founded in an effort to encourage children to get outside and play for at least an hour a day. The group's sudden rise in popularity is most likely thanks to former basketball star Eric Banks. — [1] —. Since his first appearance as a casual coach at some games in his hometown of Detroit, Backyard Ball's membership has grown by over 500%. — [2] —.

Q. In which of the positions marked [1] and [2] does the following sentence best belong?

"Mr. Banks joined the program after retiring last year."

(A) [1]
(B) [2]

PART 7 의도 파악 문제 / 문장 삽입 문제   83

 토익에 나올
실전 문제

제한시간 13분입니다! 시~작!

Questions 01-02 refer to the following text message chain.

Irene Jones [10:03 A.M.]
How is the office move for Dawson Legal coming along?

Kevin Bradley [10:07 A.M.]
The office furniture is all loaded up, and we're on our way to their new location now.

Irene Jones [10:08 A.M.]
Already? I could actually use some help with the Covina move to Gordon Street.

Kevin Bradley [10:09 A.M.]
I'll get there as soon as I can, but we'll have some extra paperwork to finish up first.

Irene Jones [10:10 A.M.]
Did something go wrong?

Kevin Bradley [10:11 A.M.]
They requested extra packing materials and tape at the last minute, so I'll have to adjust their invoice.

Irene Jones [10:12 A.M.]
I see. Let me know when you finish up with that.

---

01. What kind of business does Mr. Bradley work for?

(A) A law firm
(B) A furniture store
(C) A moving company
(D) A real estate agency

02. At 10:08 A.M., what does Ms. Jones most likely mean when she writes, "Already"?

(A) She spoke with clients about an invoice.
(B) She expected a task to take longer.
(C) She has missed an appointment.
(D) She is unsure of a schedule.

---

paraphrasing 주어진 어휘 또는 표현과 패러프레이징 될 수 있는 것을 연결하세요.

1. use some help •

2. adjust •

3. invoice •

• (a) revise

• (b) get assistance

• (c) transactional statement

84 기적의 토익 RC

○ 정답 및 해설 p.24

Questions 03-05 refer to the following letter.

Melissa Alger
143 Richmond Street
MANCHESTER
M1 2PZ

Dear Ms. Alger,

We have received your application for the open position at Herrera. The images you submitted were impressive and artistic, and we believe that your skills could be a great addition to our team. —[1]—. We mainly provide contents for print and online marketing, though some projects include logo creation or artwork for smartphone applications. —[2]—.

In order to be hired for this position, you must demonstrate at least two years' experience in the field. Since you are a freelancer, this can be confirmed through the submission of letters of recommendation from three of your clients. The aim is to confirm your experience not only with various software programs, but also with delivering projects on time and to the requested specifications. —[3]—. Once everything we need is received, we will contact you again regarding possible interview times.

I look forward to hearing from you. —[4]—.

Sincerely,

Annie Joplin
Herrera

03. Why was the letter sent?

(A) To schedule a job interview
(B) To request proof of eligibility
(C) To offer a job to an applicant
(D) To provide an employee evaluation

04. What type of business most likely is Herrera?

(A) A software sales company
(B) A graphic design firm
(C) An art institute
(D) A computer programming service

05. In which of the positions marked [1], [2], [3], and [4] does the following sentence best belong?

"These references should include a description of your current or previous job duties."

(A) [1]
(B) [2]
(C) [3]
(D) [4]

paraphrasing 주어진 어휘 또는 표현과 패러프레이징 될 수 있는 것을 연결하세요.

1. submit •   • (a) proof of eligibility
2. logo creation or artwork •   • (b) turn in
3. letters of recommendation •   • (c) graphic design

PART 7 의도 파악 문제 / 문장 삽입 문제

 **실전 문제**

Questions 06-09 refer to the following online chat discussion.

Daksha Goyal [9:03 A.M.]	Don't forget that the employee lounge will be off limits today. Based on the staff survey that everyone filled out last month, we determined that most people thought the employee lounge was too dark, so it's going to be repainted.
Anke Bauer [9:04 A.M.]	I remember reading about that in the staff newsletter. A crew from Eureka Repairs is coming today at 11 A.M., right?
Daksha Goyal [9:05 A.M.]	That's right. But the room isn't ready yet. I'm moving the furniture out of it now.
Camelia Mazzi [9:05 A.M.]	Wasn't that supposed to be done yesterday afternoon?
Daksha Goyal [9:06 A.M.]	Yes, but we had some prospective investors visit the office yesterday, and Mr. Toscano showed them around the building. We didn't want a lot of furniture in the hallway because we thought it would make a bad impression.
Camelia Mazzi [9:07 A.M.]	That makes sense. Do you need any help?
Daksha Goyal [9:07 A.M.]	Well, there are a few items that I won't be able to lift without a cart. I think the building manager has one I can borrow, but I haven't been able to track him down.
Anke Bauer [9:08 A.M.]	I've got it covered.
Daksha Goyal [9:09 A.M.]	Thanks, Anke! That would be really helpful. Please bring it up to the 3rd floor as soon as you get it.
Camelia Mazzi [9:10 A.M.]	And we'd better make sure there is a place for the Eureka Repairs truck. I'll put up a sign an hour before they get here to hold a spot by the entrance.

06. What does Mr. Goyal suggest about the employee lounge?

(A) It needs a new lighting system.
(B) It can be used as a meeting room.
(C) It will receive some new furniture.
(D) Its wall color will be changed.

07. Why did a task get delayed yesterday?

(A) Because a budget had not been approved
(B) Because a shipment did not arrive
(C) Because some visitors were taking a tour
(D) Because employees disagreed about a budget

08. At 9:08 A.M., what does Ms. Bauer most likely mean when she writes, "I've got it covered"?

(A) She will collect some surveys.
(B) She will borrow some equipment.
(C) She will move some heavy items.
(D) She will e-mail a final report.

09. What will happen at ten o'clock?

(A) Some employees will attend a meeting.
(B) Some workers will arrive at the building.
(C) Mr. Goyal will contact a repair company.
(D) Ms. Mazzi will reserve a parking spot.

paraphrasing 주어진 어휘 또는 표현과 패러프레이징 될 수 있는 것을 연결하세요.

1. be repainted •
2. show them around the building •
3. hold a spot •

• (a) take a tour
• (b) color will be changed
• (c) reserve

86 기적의 토익 RC

Questions 10-13 refer to the following article.

Journalists to Gather for Annual Event
by Mandy Nadeau

VANCOUVER (April 29) — This weekend, Stroude Plaza will be filled with journalists as they attend the Canadian Correspondents Conference (CCC). —[1]—. Participants can enjoy two days of lectures from award-winning journalists such as Antoine Lawrence, workshops on writing skills, and networking opportunities. Donald Zimmerman, president of the Newspaper Writers Guild (NWG), first established the event ten years ago as a way to provide professional development opportunities to his club's members. —[2]—. Since that time, it has grown to include journalists throughout Canada, whether in traditional print journalism or in online-based news sites.

Event planner Louise Baxter is pleased with the interest in the event. —[3]—. "Over 90% of attendees return for the following year, demonstrating how useful the CCC is," Baxter said. The figure for newcomers is also rising steadily. Last year, 920 of the attendees attended the event for the first time. —[4]—.

Tickets are available for $75 for one day or $130 for both days. Attendees should note that, unlike last year, there will be no ticket sales at the door. For more information and a complete schedule of the activities, visit www.cancorcon.ca.

10. Who founded the Canadian Correspondents Conference?

(A) Ms. Nadeau
(B) Mr. Lawrence
(C) Mr. Zimmerman
(D) Ms. Baxter

11. What is mentioned about the journalists at the conference?

(A) Some of them will be presented with awards.
(B) They come from all over the world.
(C) Most of them are interested in the workshops.
(D) They write in a variety of formats.

12. What is suggested about conference tickets?

(A) They must be purchased in advance.
(B) They are sold to NWG members only.
(C) They can be acquired at group discounts.
(D) They are expected to sell out.

13. In which of the positions marked [1], [2], [3], and [4] does the following sentence best belong?

"This year, that number is expected to surpass one thousand."

(A) [1]
(B) [2]
(C) [3]
(D) [4]

paraphrasing 주어진 어휘 또는 표현과 패러프레이징 될 수 있는 것을 연결하세요.

1. rising steadily •   • (a) exceed

2. surpass •   • (b) shows steady growth

3. acquire •   • (c) purchase

'멋진 당신, 오늘도 화이팅'

DAY

04

오늘의 학습 포인트

PART 5. 부사 (1)

부사의 역할과 위치
- 동사 수식: 동사 앞, 동사와 동사 사이, 자동사 뒤, '타동사 + 목적어' 뒤, 수동태 뒤
- 형용사 수식: '형용사 + 명사' 앞에서 수식, 보어 수식
- to부정사 수식/동명사 수식: 주로 뒤에서 수식
- 분사 수식: 앞에서 수식, 분사구문의 경우 앞/뒤에서 수식

PART 6. 지시형용사 뒤 명사 어휘

빈칸 앞에 this, that 등이 있으면 앞 내용에서 지칭하는 것 찾기

PART 7. 이중 지문 연계 문제

보기가 모두 고유명사나 숫자로 되어 있을 경우 연계 문제 확률 ↑

PART 5
문법

부사 (1)

동사를 수식하는 부사 자리 문제가 가장 많이 출제됩니다.

적용 기술

[기적의 필가노트] 102~104P
RC 기술 16, 17, 18

출제 유형

부사의 역할과 위치

1 동사 수식

· 동사 앞(주어와 동사 사이)

부사는 동사 앞에서 동사를 수식합니다. 동사 앞 빈칸은 자동사든 타동사든 구분할 필요 없이 100% 부사가 정답입니다. → 시험에 자주 출제돼요!

The spokesperson **formally** announced Mr. Richard's retirement.
　　　　　　　　　　부사　　　동사

대변인은 Richard 씨의 사임을 공식적으로 발표했다.

| 기출 '부사 + 동사' 표현 |

actively seek 적극적으로 찾다　　　　　　　steadily rise 지속적으로 상승하다
promptly respond 즉시 응답하다　　　　　　assertively ask 단호하게 요청하다

· 동사와 동사 사이

진행형은 be동사와 -ing 사이, 수동태와 완료형은 be동사와 p.p. 사이, '조동사 + 동사원형'의 경우 조동사와 동사원형 사이에 부사가 위치합니다.

[be + ------ + V-ing]

The demand for the item is **steadily** rising. 그 제품에 대한 수요는 꾸준히 증가하고 있다.

[be + ------ + p.p.]

Professor Kennedy's research is **generously** funded.
Kennedy 교수의 연구는 후한 자금 지원을 받고 있다.

[have + ------ + p.p.]

Our company has **recently** relocated to Seoul. 우리 회사는 최근 서울로 이전했다.

[조동사 + ------ + 동사원형]

Security guards will **randomly** inspect passengers.
경비원들이 승객들을 무작위로 검사할 예정이다.

800+

· 자동사 뒤

부사는 자동사 뒤에 와서 자동사를 수식합니다. 자동사와 함께 자주 사용되는 전치사 바로 앞에 위치합니다.

China relies **heavily** on the exports. 중국은 수출에 상당히 의존한다.
　　　　자동사　　부사　　전치사

| 기출 '자동사 + 부사 + (전치사)' 표현 |

work closely with ~와 긴밀히 일하다　　　　work diligently 열심히 일하다
work remotely 재택 근무하다　　　　　　　work cooperatively 협력하여 일하다
progress smoothly 순조롭게 진행되다　　　function reliably 믿을만하게 기능하다
act professionally 전문가답게 행동하다　　　behave responsibly 책임감 있게 행동하다
listen carefully[attentively] 귀 기울여 듣다
drop[decrease] considerably 상당히 하락하다[감소하다]
rise[increase] significantly 상당히 상승하다[증가하다]

확인 문제 ❶

Our representatives ------ answer your calls.
(A) promptly
(B) prompt

확인 문제 ❷

The company has ------ expanded since its founding.
(A) steady
(B) steadily

확인 문제 ❸

Mr. Jade should work ------ with the new interns.
(A) close
(B) closely

정답 ❶ (A) ❷ (B) ❸ (B)

90　기적의 토익 RC

- **'타동사 + 목적어' 뒤**

  부사는 '타동사 + 목적어(대명사 또는 명사)' 뒤에 와서 동사를 수식합니다.

  Our certified mechanic will inspect your car thoroughly.
  　　　　　　　　　　　　　　　 타동사　　목적어

  당사의 공인 기술자가 귀하의 차량을 철저히 검사할 예정입니다.

  | 기출 '타동사 + 목적어 + 부사' 표현 |

review A carefully A를 주의 깊게 검토하다	resolve A swiftly[quickly] A를 신속히 해결하다
submit A separately A를 각각 제출하다	examine A closely A를 면밀히 검사하다
run A efficiently A를 효율적으로 운영하다	measure A carefully A를 신중히 측정하다
follow A precisely A를 정확하게 따르다	issue A separately A를 각각 따로 발행하다

- **수동태 동사 뒤**

  부사는 수동태 동사인 'be + p.p.'를 뒤에서 수식합니다.

  The products were transported quickly. 제품들은 빠르게 운반되었다.
  　　　　　 수동태 동사　　　　　 부사

  | 기출 'be + p.p. + 부사' 표현 |

be shared externally 외부와 공유되다	be owned independently 단독으로 소유되다
be shipped separately 각각 배송되다	be refunded directly 바로 환불되다

2 형용사 수식

- 부사는 '형용사 + 명사'를 앞에서 수식합니다.

  The new product line features unusually bright colors.
  　　　　　　　　　　　　　　　　　　 부사　　 형용사　 명사

  신제품 라인은 유난히 밝은 색상이 특징이다.

- '형용사 + 명사' 앞에는 부사 외에 형용사도 올 수 있습니다. 이때 형용사가 올지 부사가 올지는 문맥을 통해 판단합니다.

  | 기출 '부사 + 형용사' 표현 |

highly competitive 매우 경쟁력 있는	extremely popular 매우 인기 있는
remarkably high 상당히 높은	fairly optimistic 상당히 낙관하는
directly applicable 바로 적용할 수 있는	fully refundable 전액 환불 가능한
surprisingly short 매우 짧은	exceptionally positive 특히 긍정적인
markedly successful 두드러지게 성공적인	immediately available 즉시 이용 가능한

- 부사는 주격 보어인 형용사를 수식합니다. 'be/become + ------- + 형용사' 구조에서 빈칸은 부사 자리입니다.

  Deposits made in cash will be immediately available from your bank account.
  　　　　　　　　　　　　　　　 be　　　 부사　　 주격 보어(형용사)

  현금성 저축은 귀하의 계좌에서 즉시 사용 가능합니다.

- 부사는 목적격 보어인 형용사를 수식합니다. 'make/find/keep/consider + 목적어 + ------- + 형용사' 구조에서 빈칸은 부사 자리입니다.

  The increasing sales kept our management extremely optimistic about the new
  　　　　　　　　　　　 keep　　 목적어　　　　　 부사　　 목적격 보어(형용사)

  product lines. 매출 증가로 인해 우리 경영진은 신제품 라인에 대해 매우 낙관적이었다.

⚠ 주의

'5형식 동사(make, find, keep, consider) + 목적어' 뒤에는 목적격 보어 역할을 하는 형용사가 와야 합니다. 3형식 동사로 생각해서 부사를 고르면 오답이니 주의하세요.

We found it effective.
　　　　　　　effectively (×)

⚠ 주의

수동태 뒤 빈칸은 부사 자리입니다. 하지만 5형식 동사의 수동태 뒤 빈칸은 형용사 자리이므로 주의하세요.

The customer data are kept secure.
securely (×)

🔒 확인 문제 ❹

Please wrap it -------.

(A) separately
(B) separate

출제 포인트

be동사와 명사구 사이에서 명사구를 수식하는 부사를 찾는 문제가 출제돼요.

He was clearly the most qualified applicant.

🔒 확인 문제 ❺

He received ------- positive survey results.

(A) exceptional
(B) exceptionally

정답 ❹ (A) ❺ (B)

PART 5 문법 부사 (1)　91

800+
3 전치사구 수식

· 부사는 부사구 또는 형용사구 역할을 하는 전치사구를 앞에서 수식합니다.
We will ship your orders **directly** from the vendors.
우리는 당신의 주문품을 판매회사에서 바로 배송할 것입니다.

4 to부정사 수식

· to부정사를 수식하는 부사는 동사와 마찬가지로 주로 to부정사 뒤에 위치합니다.
Ms. Jones wanted to participate **actively** in the volunteer opportunities.
Jones 씨는 자원봉사 기회에 적극적으로 참여하기를 원했다.

The financial officer agreed to distribute funding **equally**.
재무 담당자는 자금을 균등하게 분배하는 것에 동의했다.

800+
· 부사는 to부정사를 to와 동사원형 사이에서 수식합니다. to부정사에서 to와 동사원형 사이에는 다른 품사는 들어갈 수 없으므로 100% 부사가 정답입니다.
The financial officer agreed to **equally** distribute funding.

800+
5 동명사 수식

· 동명사는 to부정사와 마찬가지로 동사에서 파생된 것으로 동사의 성격을 가지고 있어요. 따라서 부사가 동명사를 수식하며, 이때는 보통 동명사를 뒤에서 수식합니다.
One of the interns suggested introducing a free trial offer **quickly**.
인턴 가운데 한 명이 무료 시험 사용 서비스를 빨리 시작할 것을 제안했다.

Giselle Corporation is devoted to adhering **strictly** to toxic chemical disposal rules. Giselle Corporation은 유독성 화학 물질 처리 규칙을 엄격히 준수하는 데 전념하고 있습니다.

· 동명사가 전치사의 목적어 역할을 할 경우, 전치사와 동명사 사이에 부사가 위치할 수 있습니다.
King Buffet is known for **generously** donating to local charities.
King Buffet은 지역 자선 단체에 대한 아낌없는 기부로 잘 알려져 있다.

6 분사 수식

· 현재분사 또는 과거분사는 부사의 수식을 받으며, 이때 부사는 분사 앞에 위치합니다.
All tests should be taken under **carefully** controlled conditions.
모든 테스트는 신중하게 제어된 조건에서 수행되어야 한다.

· 명사를 뒤에서 수식하는 분사도 부사의 수식을 받는데, 이때는 주로 부사가 뒤에서 수식합니다.
We use organic vegetables and fruits grown **locally**.
우리는 지역에서 재배된 유기농 채소와 과일을 사용한다.

800+
· 문장 전체를 수식하는 분사구문의 경우 부사가 앞/뒤에서 수식할 수 있습니다.
Aggressively marketing the new delivery service, Big Burger expects to attract more customers.
신규 배달 서비스를 공격적으로 마케팅하면서 Big Burger는 더 많은 고객들을 유치할 것으로 기대하고 있다.

Designed **uniquely** by Adam Frasier, Henderson Tower is a must-see tourist attraction.
Adam Frasier에 의해 독특하게 디자인된 Henderson 타워는 꼭 봐야할 관광 명소이다.

🔒 **확인 문제 ⑥**

Mr. Peterson volunteered
to ------- offer his time.

(A) generous
(B) generously

🔒 **확인 문제 ⑦**

The company has
conducted regular surveys
for ------- improving its
customer service.

(A) consistently
(B) consistent

🔒 **확인 문제 ⑧**

------- placed beside the
cashiers, the display
counters have items on
sale.

(A) Strategy
(B) Strategically

정답 ⑥(B) ⑦(A) ⑧(B)

부사 (1)

1. When you stock ------- perishable items, they should be handled according to the guidelines.

(A) high   (B) higher   (C) highest   (D) highly

부패하기 매우 쉬운 물품들을 보관할 때는 지침에 따라 다루어져야 한다.

> **이렇게 풀어요**
>
> **1. 선택지 보고 문법/어휘 문제 파악** 선택지가 형용사 또는 부사인 high(높은, 높이, 많이)의 파생어로 구성되어 있으므로 문법 문제임을 파악할 수 있어요.
>
> **2. 빈칸 분석** 빈칸 뒤에 목적어 역할의 명사 items와 이를 수식하는 형용사 perishable이 있으므로 수식어가 필요한 자리임을 파악해요.
>
> **3. 정답 선택** 명사를 수식하는 형용사 앞에 올 수 있는 부사 (D) highly(매우)를 정답으로 고릅니다.

2. All sales representatives on duty should listen ------- to the customer's inquiries.

(A) attentive   (B) attention   (C) attended   (D) attentively

근무 중인 모든 영업 담당자들은 고객의 문의를 귀 기울여 들어야 한다.

> **이렇게 풀어요**
>
> **1. 선택지 보고 문법/어휘 문제 파악** 선택지가 동사 attend(참석하다, 주의를 기울이다)의 파생어로 구성되어 있으므로 문법 문제임을 파악할 수 있어요.
>
> **2. 빈칸 분석** 빈칸 앞에 자동사 listen이 있고 빈칸 뒤에 전치사 to가 있으므로 빈칸은 동사 또는 전치사구를 수식하는 수식어가 들어갈 자리임을 파악해요.
>
> **3. 정답 선택** 자동사와 전치사 사이에 위치하여 동사를 수식할 수 있는 부사 (D) attentively(귀 기울여, 신경 써서)를 정답으로 고릅니다.

3. Oslo Technology was hired to ------- design a new scheduling system for the clinic.

(A) specialty   (B) specialize   (C) specially   (D) specialist

Oslo Technology는 병원에 새로운 일정 관리 시스템을 특별히 고안하기 위해 고용되었다.

> **이렇게 풀어요**
>
> **1. 선택지 보고 문법/어휘 문제 파악** 선택지가 형용사 special(특별한)의 파생어로 구성되어 있으므로 문법 문제임을 파악할 수 있어요.
>
> **2. 빈칸 분석** 빈칸 앞에 to, 빈칸 뒤에 동사원형 design이 있으므로 빈칸은 동사원형을 수식하는 수식어가 들어갈 자리임을 파악해요.
>
> **3. 정답 선택** to부정사의 to와 동사원형 사이에서 수식할 수 있는 부사 (C) specially(특별히)를 정답으로 고릅니다.

PART 5 어휘
명사 어휘 (4)

각 어휘와 함께 자주 쓰이는 표현을 통째로 외워두세요.

01 performance — 실적, 성과, 공연

sales performance	매출 실적
performance appraisal	업무 평가
outstanding performance	뛰어난 성과

02 overview — 개관, 개요

an overview of the project	프로젝트에 대한 개요
provide a basic overview	기본적인 개요를 제공하다

🐾 빈출 토익 선생님 Pick!

03 demand — 요구, 수요

demand for	~에 대한 수요
in demand	수요가 많은
rising demand	증가하는 수요

04 operation — 영업, 작동

hours of operation	운영 시간
be in operation	가동 중이다

05 confidence — 신뢰, 자신감, 확신

have confidence in	~에 자신이 있다
lack confidence	자신감이 부족하다

06 agreement — 동의, 합의

agreement on	~에 관한 합의
long-term agreement	장기 협정
reach an agreement	합의에 도달하다

07 demonstration — 시범 설명

do a product demonstration	제품 시연을 하다
watch a demonstration	시범 설명을 보다

🐾 빈출 토익 선생님 Pick!

08 procedure — 절차, 방법

payment procedure	납부 절차, 지급 절차
proper procedure for	~을 위한 적절한 절차
follow a procedure	절차를 따르다

09 resource — 자원, 재원

resource allocation	자원 할당
renewable resource	재생 가능 자원

`800+`
10 accordance — 일치, 합의, 조화

in accordance with	~에 따라서

11 expectation — 예상, 기대

meet the expectations	기대에 부응하다
surpass one's expectation	~의 예상을 뛰어넘다
beyond one's expectation	~의 예상 외로

12 field — 지역, 분야, 현장

work in the field of	~ 분야에서 일하다
have experience in the field of	~ 분야에서 경력이 있다

🐾 빈출 토익 선생님 Pick!

13 improvement — 향상, 개선

improvement in	~의 향상, 개선
undergo improvement	개선되다
marked improvement	눈에 띄는 개선
room for improvement	개선의 여지

`800+`
14 flaw — 결함, 흠

technical flaw	기술적 결함
slight flaw	약간의 하자

94 기적의 토익 RC

15 atmosphere — 분위기, 대기

| pleasant atmosphere | 즐거운 분위기 |
| inviting atmosphere | 매혹적인 분위기 |

🐾 빈출 토익 선생님 Pick!
16 revenue — 수익, 세입

earn a revenue	수익을 올리다
increase revenues	수익이 증가하다
annual revenue	연간 수익

`900+`
17 assent — 승인, 찬성

| give formal assent | 공식 승인을 하다 |

18 intention — 의도, 목적

have (no) intention of	~할 의사가 있다(없다)
one's intention to	~하려는 의도
have every intention of -ing	기꺼이 ~할 의사가 있다

🐾 빈출 토익 선생님 Pick!
19 malfunction — 고장, 기능 불량

| equipment malfunction | 기기 고장 |
| experience a malfunction with | ~의 고장을 경험하다 |

20 negotiation — 협상, 교섭

| under negotiation | 교섭 중인 |
| contract negotiation | 계약 협상 |

🐾 빈출 토익 선생님 Pick!
21 shift — 근무조, 변화

day/overnight shift	낮/야간 근무조
closing shift	마감 근무조
shift in	~에 있어서의 변화

🐾 빈출 토익 선생님 Pick!
22 direction — 방향, 지시, 감독

| give directions to | ~로의 길[방향]을 알려주다 |
| under one's direction | ~의 감독하에 |

23 distance — 거리

| within walking distance | 걸어서 갈 수 있는 거리에 있는 |
| long-distance route | 장거리 노선 |

24 guideline — 가이드라인, 지침

| issue guidelines | 가이드라인을 발표하다 |
| clear guidelines | 분명한 지침 |

 풀이 방법

Industry experts reported that the ------- for pickup trucks in Europe will decrease next year.

(A) demand   (B) field   (C) agreement   (D) policy

업계 전문가들은 내년에 유럽에서 소형 트럭에 대한 수요가 감소할 것으로 보고했다.

이렇게 풀어요

1. **선택지 보고 문법/어휘 문제 파악** 선택지가 서로 다른 명사 어휘로 구성되어 있으므로 어휘 문제임을 파악해요.
2. **빈칸 분석** 빈칸 뒤에 for가 있으므로 for와 어울릴 수 있는 명사여야 하고, '소형 트럭에 대한 -------가 감소하다'라는 문맥이 되어야 함을 파악합니다.
3. **정답 선택** for와 함께 쓰여 '~에 대한 수요'라는 의미로 쓰이는 (A) demand를 정답으로 고릅니다.

PART 5 어휘 명사 어휘 (4)

따라 하면 문제가 풀리는

연습 문제

앞서 학습한 문제 풀이법을 적용하여 맞는 것에 ✔ 표시 하거나 괄호 안에
적절한 답을 쓰고 정답을 선택하세요.

01 The ------- popular event, Fireworks Over Fresno, will be held this Saturday night.

(A) extreme
(B) extremely
(C) extremes
(D) extremity

1. 선택지 보고 문법/어휘 문제 파악하기 ☐ 문법 문제 ☐ 어휘 문제
2. 빈칸 분석하기 빈칸 뒤에 있는 것 ☐ 동사 ☐ 형용사
　　　　　　　→ 빈칸은 ☐ 명사 ☐ 부사 자리이다.
3. 정답 선택하기 정답 (　　　)

02 Any purchase is ------- refundable with an original receipt.

(A) full
(B) fully
(C) fuller
(D) fullness

1. 선택지 보고 문법/어휘 문제 파악하기 ☐ 문법 문제 ☐ 어휘 문제
2. 빈칸 분석하기 빈칸 뒤에 있는 것 ☐ 주격 보어인 형용사 ☐ 동사
　　　　　　　→ 빈칸은 ☐ 명사 ☐ 부사 자리이다.
3. 정답 선택하기 정답 (　　　)

03 You should display this visitor's ID at all times for ------- reasons.

(A) failure
(B) training
(C) benefit
(D) security

1. 선택지 보고 문법/어휘 문제 파악하기 ☐ 문법 문제 ☐ 어휘 문제
2. 빈칸 분석하기 빈칸 앞에 있는 for 뒤에 있는 reasons와 짝꿍 표현으로 쓰이는 명사가 정답이다.
3. 정답 선택하기 정답 (　　　)

🔍 정답 및 해설 p.27

DAY 04

04 Test groups have responded ------- to Richie's new ice cream flavor.

(A) favor
(B) favorable
(C) favorably
(D) favored

1. 선택지 보고 문법/어휘 문제 파악하기 ☐문법 문제 ☐어휘 문제
2. 빈칸 분석하기 빈칸 앞에 있는 것 ☐자동사 ☐타동사
     → 빈칸은 ☐명사 ☐부사 자리이다.
3. 정답 선택하기 정답 (   )

05 The success is attributed to the employees who work ------- at Nashua Tech.

(A) diligently
(B) diligent
(C) diligence
(D) diligences

1. 선택지 보고 문법/어휘 문제 파악하기 ☐문법 문제 ☐어휘 문제
2. 빈칸 분석하기 빈칸 앞에 있는 것 ☐자동사 ☐타동사
     → 빈칸은 ☐명사 ☐부사 자리이다.
3. 정답 선택하기 정답 (   )

06 Some items are shipped ------- from our warehouse in Emerson City.

(A) direct
(B) direction
(C) directed
(D) directly

1. 선택지 보고 문법/어휘 문제 파악하기 ☐문법 문제 ☐어휘 문제
2. 빈칸 분석하기 빈칸 앞에 있는 것 ☐능동태 동사 ☐수동태 동사
     → 빈칸은 ☐명사 ☐부사 자리이다.
3. 정답 선택하기 정답 (   )

PART 5 부사 (1) / 명사 어휘 (4) 97

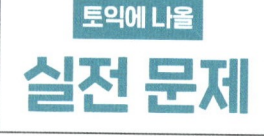

토익에 나올
실전 문제

DAY 01-04 누적 문제

제한시간 9분입니다! 시~작!

01. Global Geography's photographers -------
place cameras in habitats to capture natural
images of wildlife.

(A) strategy
(B) strategies
(C) strategically
(D) strategic

02. Kessler's automobiles are ------- designed to
reduce both emissions and fuel consumption.

(A) special
(B) specially
(C) specialize
(D) specialties

03. Service plans offered by Callahan Cable are
------- to those offered by its competitors.

(A) compares
(B) comparing
(C) comparison
(D) comparable

04. Ms. Donaldson had no ------- of transferring to
the Asian branch office.

(A) improvement
(B) intention
(C) malfunction
(D) training

05. We are ------- recruiting contract
photographers who have experience in filming
documentaries.

(A) acting
(B) action
(C) actively
(D) activated

06. Soother Patch helps those who ------- suffer
from lower back pain.

(A) many
(B) those
(C) sometimes
(D) whenever

07. Thanks to its latest clothing line, Bush
Fashion has expanded its customer base
-------.

(A) considered
(B) considering
(C) considerably
(D) consideration

08. Mr. Malone expected to receive his order
through express service, ------- by tomorrow.

(A) preferring
(B) preferably
(C) preference
(D) preferable

09. ------- situated next to a large parking garage,
Mooney's Steakhouse is a popular place for
lunch meetings.

(A) Convenient
(B) Convenience
(C) Conveniently
(D) Conveniences

10. Please review each of your answers -------
prior to turning in your test paper.

(A) cares
(B) careful
(C) cared
(D) carefully

11. *Fortune Magazine* listed George Nichols as
one of the most ------- gifted teenagers in
mathematics.

(A) excepted
(B) exception
(C) exceptional
(D) exceptionally

12. Since flammable liquids such as jet fuel
are ------- dangerous, special safety gear is
required when handling them.

(A) high
(B) height
(C) highly
(D) heighten

98 기적의 토익 RC

13. Any toxic materials should be disposed of properly under the supervisor's -------.

(A) security
(B) direction
(C) failure
(D) confidence

14. The workshop will feature several ------- sessions to build leadership skills.

(A) notably
(B) notable
(C) noting
(D) noted

15. After a series of debates, the labor union was ------- to the management's terms regarding working conditions.

(A) agree
(B) agreed
(C) agreeing
(D) agreeable

16. The CEO of Tucson Petrol ------- announced the relocation of its headquarters to Fresno.

(A) form
(B) formally
(C) formal
(D) formation

17. Once Ms. Cobb receives the budget for the renovation, ------- will recommend some décor options.

(A) her
(B) she
(C) hers
(D) herself

18. Ms. Janson's ------- is particularly helpful when selecting contracts.

(A) decide
(B) decisive
(C) decidedly
(D) decisiveness

19. The department managers are required to evaluate employee ------- according to the guidelines.

(A) performance
(B) resource
(C) inspection
(D) agreement

20. In only two years at Jo Pharmaceuticals, Dr. Lawson has ------- developed a new vaccine.

(A) successful
(B) successfully
(C) succeeded
(D) success

21. The manager reported that all assembly lines are in ------- as planned.

(A) shift
(B) benefit
(C) operation
(D) guideline

22. Ace Business Hotel always meets Ms. Twain's ------- with clean rooms and affordable rates.

(A) alternatives
(B) destinations
(C) objectives
(D) expectations

23. Beltran Furniture has a wide selection of ------- priced mattresses available on their Web site.

(A) reasonable
(B) reasonably
(C) reasoning
(D) reasons

24. All of the related parties involved in the environment issues finally come to an ------- at the final conference.

(A) agreement
(B) advance
(C) achievement
(D) admission

PART 5 부사 (1) / 명사 어휘 (4) 99

PART 6

지시형용사 뒤 명사 어휘 800+

빈칸 앞에 지시형용사가 있으면 앞 내용에서 지칭하는 게 무엇일지 찾습니다.

적용 기술

[기적의 필기노트] 159P
RC 기술 77

VOCA

as of ~부로
expand 확대되다
air 방영하다
partnership 협력, 제휴
provider 공급업체

풀이 방법

letter

○ 해석 p.30

Washington Streaming Services
79 Waterway Drive
Tacoma, WA 80314

Dear Streaming Service Customer,

Great news! As of February 1st, the library of shows and movies that you can watch with Washington Streaming Services will be expanded. For the same monthly price, you will now have access to dozens of television shows that aired as recently as last year. This ------- is thanks to a partnership with Wolf Broadcasting.
　　　　　　　　　　01.
Several of the network's popular TV series have been ------- listed on our
　　　　　　　　　　　　　　　　　　PART 5
homepage. Thank you for choosing WSS as an online entertainment provider.

Regards,

Customer Service Team
Washington Streaming Services

01. (A) addition
　　　(B) expense
　　　(C) contract
　　　(D) credit

핵심 포인트

<지시형용사>
단수: this, that
복수: these, those

이렇게 풀어요

1. **선택지 보고 문법/어휘 문제 파악** 선택지가 서로 다른 명사 어휘로 이루어져 있으므로 어휘 문제임을 파악할 수 있어요.
(A) 추가　(B) 비용　(C) 계약(서)　(D) 신뢰, 신용

2. **빈칸 분석** 빈칸 앞에 지시형용사 This가 있으므로 This가 지칭하는 것이 무엇인지 앞 내용에서 파악합니다. 앞 부분에 나온 2월 1일부터 방송과 영화 프로그램 종류가 확대될 것이라는 내용이 단서가 돼요.

3. **정답 선택** 방송과 영화 프로그램이 확대된 것은 콘텐츠가 '추가'되었다는 의미이므로 (A) addition을 정답으로 선택합니다.

해설

완료 시제 동사 구문(have been listed) 중간에 들어갈 수 있는 것은 부사이므로 (D)가 정답입니다.

PART 5 문법 적용 문제

Several of the network's popular TV series have been ------- listed on our homepage.

(A) completed　　(B) completing　　(C) complete　　(D) completely

100　기적의 토익 RC

따라 하면 문제가 풀리는

연습 문제

빈칸 앞 내용에서 단서가 될 부분을 찾아 표시하세요.
표시한 것을 바탕으로 정답 어휘를 선택하세요.

♀ 정답 및 해설 p.30

01

Scholarship Opportunities

April 12 — Students from around the country are rushing to put in their applications for one of the Extracurricular Leader scholarships. There are a number of different ones that vary in value from covering the cost of books to fully paying for tuition. These ------- are provided by business leaders in various fields.

(A) funds   (B) activities

02

Dear Ms. Barnes,

I am the owner of London's Sweet Tooth, a candy store chain in England. Rotterdam Chocolates has an outstanding reputation, and I would like to purchase your product in bulk for sale at my stores here in England. This ------- could be highly beneficial to both of our companies, so I look forward to hearing back from you soon.

(A) resource   (B) partnership

03

A group of local residents shared an idea to cover rooftops around the city with solar panels. This ------- would decrease the city's need to rely on outside sources for electric power.

(A) entry   (B) proposal

04

To: Sales Team
From: Melissa Franken, CEO
Subject: Quarterly Report

I am concerned about our most recent quarterly report. It seems that our sales have dropped by nearly 15% over the last few months. These ------- are unacceptable, and we need to make some major changes in order to meet our goal at the end of the year.

(A) numbers   (B) prices

PART 6 지시형용사 뒤 명사 어휘   **101**

Questions 01-04 refer to the following letter.

제한시간 4분입니다! 시~작!

Rosewood Cable Services
1111 College Avenue
Rosewood, OH 43070

Dear Rosewood Cable Customer,

This letter is ------- you that as of 1 May, the costs for certain services will be reduced. Our VIP
         01.
package will go from $50 to $43 per month, and our Special package will go from $40 to $35 per
month. These ------- are being offered to make us more competitive in the market. Please call today
         02.
if you would like to upgrade yours to one of the upper packages. -------. Also, your Internet speed
           03.
will be increased up to 500 Mbps, ------- you can enjoy twice faster downloads than your current
        04.
one.

---

01. (A) informed
    (B) information
    (C) to inform
    (D) informative

유형 적용 문제
02. (A) discounts
    (B) submissions
    (C) budgets
    (D) extensions

03. (A) The more people you refer to us, the bigger
        discounts you become eligible for.
    (B) You will have the most TV channels just with
        additional $5.
    (C) Visit our Web site for a full list of available
        channels and Internet options.
    (D) Rosewood Cable has been proudly serving this
        area for over a decade.

04. (A) then
    (B) so
    (C) that
    (D) after

Questions 05-08 refer to the following instructions.

Uses and Precautions: Delicious Dawn Toaster

The Delicious Dawn Toaster was ------- to be a safe and easy-to-use kitchen appliance. However,
                                    05.
there are certain uses of this toaster model that could be -------, causing damage to the appliance
                                                           06.
or even possibly starting a fire in your kitchen. Things such as butter, cheese, or jam could melt
and drip down into the heating wires of the appliance. These ------- are a common cause of toaster
                                                            07.
malfunctions. Another common problem comes from allowing the power cord to rest against the
side or over the top of the appliance. -------. Please be aware that the product's warranty does not
                                       08.
mention any of the situations listed above.

유형 적용 문제

05. (A) design
(B) designed
(C) designer
(D) designing

06. (A) hazardous
(B) seasoned
(C) effective
(D) settled

07. (A) ingredients
(B) devices
(C) chemicals
(D) tools

08. (A) In case of such an event, the wire can melt or
even catch fire.
(B) Damaged or faulty products should be returned to
the retailer.
(C) If the sensor detects metal, it automatically shuts
off the heat element.
(D) You can get some great recipe ideas to make
using your toaster.

PART 6 지시형용사 뒤 명사 어휘   103

PART 7 이중 지문 연계 문제

한 지문에 단서가 충분하지 않은 경우 다른 지문에서 추가적인 단서를 찾아 종합하여 정답을 찾는 유형입니다.

출제 유형

이중 지문 연계 문제

이중 지문에는 총 5문제가 주어지는데, 그중 1~2문제는 반드시 연계 문제로 출제됩니다. 선택지 4개가 모두 고유 명사나 시간 또는 장소로 구성된 경우 연계 문제일 확률이 높습니다.

1 자주 출제되는 이중 지문 유형

지문 1	지문 2	내용
이메일	이메일	· 예약 확인 또는 변경 요청 이메일 & 변경 사항, 오류 정정 안내 이메일 · 고객이 불만을 제기하는 이메일 & 해결 방법 안내 이메일
양식/웹사이트	이메일	· 일정표 & 일정에 대해 문의하는 이메일 · 주문 물품 목록 & 확인 또는 문의하는 이메일 · 기업이나 상품 소개 웹사이트 & 상품 주문 또는 문의 이메일
회람	이메일	· 회사 내 변경된 규정을 알리는 회람 & 변경 사항에 대해 문의하거나 요청하는 이메일 · 회사 내 행사를 공지하는 회람 & 행사 관련 업무를 요청하는 이메일
편지	이메일	· 직책을 제안하는 편지 & 제안을 수락하는 이메일
광고	이메일	· 구인 광고 & 자격 요건에 대해 문의하는 이메일 · 학원 프로그램 광고 & 신청되었음을 알리는 이메일
광고	양식	· 제품 광고 & 주문 양식
공지	이메일	· 행사 공지 & 세부사항에 대해 문의하는 이메일
기사	이메일	· 기업 관련 기사 & 문의 또는 정보 확인 이메일

출제 포인트

이중 지문에서는 이메일 지문이 가장 많이 출제됩니다. 함께 출제되는 지문으로는 이메일 & 양식이 가장 많이 출제되며 이중 지문의 65%이상을 차지합니다.

`800+`

2 핵심 전략

· 문제의 핵심 어구가 있는 지문에서 먼저 첫 단서를 찾고, 추가로 필요한 단서를 다른 지문에서 찾아 내용을 종합하여 답을 선택합니다.

· 선택지가 수치(시간, 날짜 등)로 구성되어 있을 경우 두 지문에서 해당 수치를 찾은 후 그 주변 내용을 파악하여 답을 선택합니다.

· 지출 내역서나 영수증과 같은 양식이 연계 지문으로 출제될 경우, 계산을 해서 풀어야 하는 문제가 출제될 수 있습니다. 이 경우, 나머지 한 개의 지문(이메일이나 편지 등)에서 환급이 제외되는 항목이 있거나 잘못 기입된 항목이 있다는 등의 내용이 언급되므로 이것을 적용하여 계산하면 비교적 쉽게 풀 수 있어요.

· 특정 인물에 대한 문제가 특히 자주 출제됩니다. 우선 문제에 언급된 이름이 나온 지문에서 인물에 대한 정보를 파악한 후, 다른 지문에서 그것과 유사한 내용이 나오는 부분을 찾으면 됩니다.

기출 표현 확인

<지문 1. 송장>
Item No: Z12P
Item: color printer
<지문 2. 이메일>
the printer was missing

Q. 이메일에서 아이템 Z12P에 대해 뭐라고 했는가?
A. not included in the shipment

이중 지문 연계 문제

e-mails

해석 p.32

To: Tyler Hawkins
From: Britney Krueger
Date: 27 October
Subject: Monitors

Dear Tyler,

As per your request, I looked into some options for new monitors for our office. I was able to find some good options for us from TechMate, and I narrowed them down to Clearview 20X, Crystal 9.7, ViewMaster 6, and Classic 45.

Among those four models, the Clearview 20X is the only one with a 5-star energy rating, which would help reduce our company's electric bill. The MagiScreen 500 also has a 5-star energy rating, but I didn't mention it because the cost would put us over budget. The Crystal 9.7 has an attractive display screen, but it has the lowest energy rating.

Feel free to browse product reviews yourself. When you're ready, let me know which model and how many you'd like me to place an order for.

Britney Krueger

To: Britney Krueger
From: Tyler Hawkins
Date: 28 October
Subject: Re: Monitors

Dear Britney,

Thanks for the info, it was very helpful. Let's go with the one with the 5-star energy rating that we can afford. Good call finding something that will reduce our operational expenses. The only thing is, I'm not sure if we should get them all at once. Let's try just getting one for your office as a start until we know exactly how many we'll need. Sometime next week HR will let us know exactly how many new employees will be joining our company.

Tyler Hawkins

PART 7 이중 지문 연계 문제　105

Q. Which monitor model does Mr. Hawkins have Ms. Krueger place an order for?

(A) Clearview 20X

(B) Crystal 9.7

(C) ViewMaster 6

(D) Classic 45

이렇게 풀어요

1. 문제 먼저 파악 선택지 4개가 모두 고유 명사 → 연계 문제일 가능성을 염두에 두고 선택지의 표현들을 지문에서 찾습니다.

2. 문제의 핵심 어구가 있는 지문에서 1차 단서 파악 Hawkins 씨가 쓴 이메일인 지문 2를 먼저 보면 도입부에 가격이 합리적이고 에너지 평가에서 별 다섯 개를 받은 제품으로 선택하자고 했습니다. 따라서 이것이 어떤 모니터인지를 지문 1에서 추가적으로 파악해야 해요.

3. 추가적인 단서를 나머지 지문에서 파악 5-star energy rating이 언급된 지문 1의 두 번째 단락에서 Clearview 20X는 유일하게 에너지 평가에서 별 다섯 개를 받았고 전기료를 줄이는 데 도움이 될 것이라고 했으므로 지문 2에서 Hawkins 씨가 언급한 조건과 일치합니다.

두 지문의 연결고리 확인! a 5-star energy rating, help reduce ~ electric bill, we can afford

4. 정답 선택 두 지문의 단서를 종합하여 (A) Clearview 20X를 정답으로 선택합니다.

따라 하면 문제가 풀리는

연습 문제

먼저 문제의 키워드에 표시한 후,
지문에서 단서를 찾아 적절한 답을 고르세요.

정답 및 해설 p.32

01 schedule and article

<Biology Lecture Series>
Free public lectures throughout January at the Kramer Institute

January 7: Stem Cells and Their Role in Therapies
January 14: Understanding Digestion
January 21: The Importance of Forest Conservation
January 28: The History of Genetics

All lectures will take place in room 100A. Seating is available on a first-come, first-served basis.

Distinguished biologist Dr. Paul Camacho has announced the debut screening of his new documentary, *Into the Lab*, which will be shown at the Logan Theater on February 25. The film follows Dr. Camacho and his team of researchers through an experiment step-by-step, from the planning stages to analyzing the results. The experiment provided new information about stem cells and how they can help and influence medical therapies, a topic that Dr. Camacho recently covered during the lecture at the Kramer Institute.

Q. When did Dr. Camacho most likely give a lecture at the Kramer Institute?

(A) January 7
(B) January 21

토익에 나올

실전 문제

계한시간 15분입니다! 시~작!

Questions 01-05 refer to the following memo and schedule.

To: All SoloCon Inc. Staff Members
From: Annie Knox
Subject: Upcoming changes
Sent: 12 September
Attachment: work schedule

The management has reviewed the most surveys of the staff working at our Lexington Tower location and agreed to renovate some spaces. Since you will not be able to work in the office on the day that work is being done in your section, a laptop will be issued to you on the day before your section is renovated. You will be expected to return it when you come in the day after your section is ready. Please follow standard office regulations when using the company laptop. Do not click on links or download material that are from sources that you do not trust.

Some more freedom will be given to each team. Each team will vote on where to place its furniture after returning to the office. For those teams that no longer need file cabinets since we digitized all client records, please note that we cannot simply throw them out as they do not belong to us. If you wish to get rid of them, I will inform the building manager.

SloCon Inc. Schedule

Date	Team(s)	Contact
23 Sept.	Personnel	Richard Moss
24 Sept.	Sales	Jessica Meyers
25 Sept.	Accounting, R&D	Bob Hager, Michelle White

108　기적의 토익 RC

📍정답 및 해설 p.32

01. Why did Ms. Knox send the memo to staff members?

(A) To introduce a new team member
(B) To announce some renovations
(C) To clarify a company policy
(D) To request their feedback

02. According to the memo, what will team members vote on?

(A) Where to relocate to
(B) Which furniture to replace
(C) When to start a project
(D) How to arrange office furniture

03. What is suggested about the file cabinets at SoloCon Inc.?

(A) They are the property of Lexington Tower.
(B) They were purchased earlier this year.
(C) They contain sensitive information about SoloCon Inc.
(D) They are not large enough.

04. When will laptops be issued to members of the personnel team?

(A) On 22 September
(B) On 23 September
(C) On 24 September
(D) On 25 September

05. What is indicated about the accounting team?

(A) It handles all of SoloCon Inc.'s transactions.
(B) It hosts weekly team meetings.
(C) It has fewer members that other teams.
(D) It shares an office space with another team.

---

paraphrasing 주어진 어휘 또는 표현과 패러프레이징 될 수 있는 것을 연결하세요.

1. place •   • (a) employees
2. review •   • (b) arrange
3. staff •   • (c) just
4. regulation •   • (d) go over
5. simply •   • (e) rule

PART 7 이중 지문 연계 문제 109

Questions 06-10 refer to the following Web site and announcement.

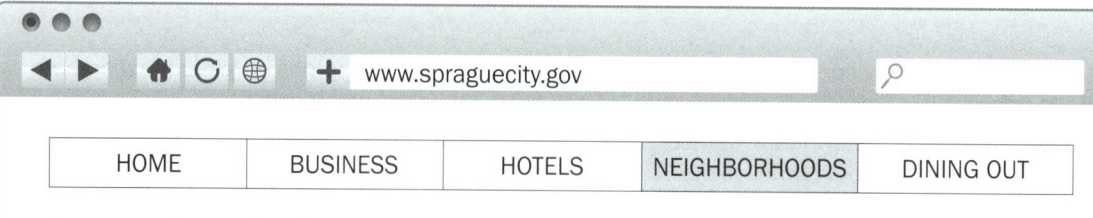

| HOME | BUSINESS | HOTELS | NEIGHBORHOODS | DINING OUT |

Neighborhoods in Sprague City

Segundo Heights, the heart of the city's shopping district, offers boutiques and specialty shops for everything under the sun. Street parking is free of charge Monday to Friday, and several bus stops make the neighborhood easy to reach by public transportation.

Hermon Hills brings together old and new with its historic buildings dotted among modern facilities. Gerhart Stadium is home to a number of events year-round, including sports competitions and Sprague City's Summer Concert Series.

Clarkwood is dominated by high-rise apartment buildings, but among these luxury dwellings you will find restaurants here and there, including the nationally renowned Pontiac Bistro. The path around Trisler Lake makes it an excellent place for a stroll.

Emerson Park is aptly named, due to its numerous green spaces, gardens, and a large golf course. This neighborhood is the perfect place to enjoy the outdoors.

Fundraiser for Fireworks Show a Success

Community organizations in Sprague City banded together to raise funding for the city's annual fireworks display, which was under threat of cancellation due to a lack of funding. Fortunately, through the help of Sprague Unity and Community Caretakers, and the generous support of locals, the show will go on.

Everyone is welcome to be a part of this exciting event, which is scheduled as the finale of the opening performance of the Summer Concert Series. Admission is free, but seats are expected to fill up quickly. There are also great viewing points around the neighborhood, marked on the neighborhood map here. Follow the link to download a copy for yourself. The approximate start time of the fireworks display is 9 P.M.

06. For whom was the Web site most likely written?

(A) Participants in an annual competition
(B) Tourists visiting Sprague City
(C) Candidates for a government position
(D) Business owners in Sprague City

07. According to the Web site, what is available in Segundo Heights?

(A) A subway station
(B) Fine-dining restaurants
(C) Daily free parking
(D) A wide variety of stores

08. What is NOT true about Clarkwood?

(A) It is near a body of water.
(B) It is primarily a residential area.
(C) It is a popular site for musicians.
(D) It is the home of a famous restaurant.

09. What is indicated about the fireworks show?

(A) It may be canceled due to bad weather.
(B) It is being held in Sprague City for the first time.
(C) It will raise funds for community projects.
(D) It will take place at Gerhart Stadium.

10. Why should Web site visitors click on the provided link?

(A) To view a schedule
(B) To share their feedback
(C) To reserve a seat
(D) To download a map

DAY 04

| paraphrasing | 주어진 어휘 또는 표현과 패러프레이징 될 수 있는 것을 연결하세요. |

1. easy to reach   •

2. dwellings   •

3. fundraiser   •

4. boutiques and specialty shops   •

5. dominated by apartment buildings   •

• (a) charity event

• (b) variety of stores

• (c) conveniently located

• (d) buildings

• (e) is a residential area

PART 7 이중 지문 연계 문제

Questions 11-15 refer to the following e-mail and voucher.

To: Patricia Lowry <p.lowry@scribnersolutions.com>

From: Tatsuhi Agano <tatsuhiagano@montrosehotel.com>

Date: November 6

Subject: Your Stay at Montrose Hotel

Attachment: montrose.voucher

Dear Ms. Lowry,

I would like to apologize for the negative experience you had at the Long Beach branch of Montrose Hotel. You indicated in your message that you had reserved a room with a seaside view from November 2 to November 4 but when you checked in, you were informed that all seaside rooms were already booked. It seems that one of our employees, who just started working here two weeks ago, did not complete the reservation form correctly when you called to book your room. As a result, you were placed in a garden-view room.

I've been informed that Tyrone Soto, the manager on duty, sent a complimentary bottle of wine to your room upon learning about the issue shortly after you checked in. In addition, I have attached a voucher for a free one-night stay at one of our California locations (Los Angeles, San Francisco, Fresno, or Long Beach). Please accept it with our compliments.

Sincerely,

Tatsuhi Agano
Director of Guest Relations, Montrose Hotel

Montrose Hotel: ONE-NIGHT VOUCHER   Number: 05485
Issued to: Patricia Lowry   Date: November 6

At Montrose Hotel, we appreciate that reliable service is essential to our guests, and we apologize that we did not meet your expectations. This voucher entitles the holder to one night's stay in a deluxe room at any of our California-based branches (see reverse side for addresses). No expiration date.

Issued by Montrose Hotel Guest Relations, Fresno, CA 93740. For questions or concerns, please call our hotline at 1-800-555-8338.

11. According to Mr. Agano, what caused a problem?

(A) An inexperienced employee
(B) An incorrect payment
(C) Some faulty software
(D) Some temporary closures

12. What happened at Montrose Hotel on November 2?

(A) Ms. Lowry met with Mr. Agano.
(B) Mr. Agano issued a room voucher.
(C) Mr. Soto took a booking by phone.
(D) Ms. Lowry received a free beverage.

13. What is suggested about Ms. Lowry?

(A) She was dissatisfied with the size of her room.
(B) She was not given the type of room she reserved.
(C) She made a complaint about the hotel's cleanliness.
(D) She thought the hotel's gardens would be open for visiting.

14. In the voucher, the word "appreciate" in paragraph 1, line 1, is closest in meaning to

(A) enhance
(B) praise
(C) understand
(D) admire

15. In what city does Mr. Agano most likely work?

(A) Los Angeles
(B) San Francisco
(C) Fresno
(D) Long Beach

---

paraphrasing 주어진 어휘 또는 표현과 패러프레이징 될 수 있는 것을 연결하세요.

1. reserve
2. just started working here two weeks ago
3. complimentary bottle of wine
4. issue
5. entitle

- (a) give the right
- (b) book
- (c) problem
- (d) free beverage
- (e) inexperienced

PART 7 이중 지문 연계 문제   113

'멋진 당신, 오늘도 화이팅'

DAY
05

오늘의 학습 포인트

PART 5. 부사 (2)

1. 부사의 종류
- 빈도 부사/부정 부사/시간 부사
- 숫자 표현과 사용되는 부사: approximately, almost 등
- 형태는 비슷하지만 의미가 다른 부사: high vs. highly/near vs. nearly 등
2. 빈출 부사의 구분 – just, ever, yet, well, still, so vs. very, enough vs. too
3. 접속부사 – however, therefore, then, nevertheless 등

↳ 접속사와 구분하기!

PART 6. 앞 문장의 내용을 요약하는 지시대명사

↳ 보기가 대명사이면 앞 문장을 대신할 수 있는 것 찾기

PART 7. 삼중 지문 연계 문제

↳ 가장 먼저 세 지문의 관계 파악할 것!

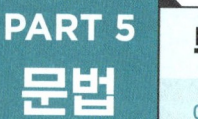

PART 5
문법
부사 (2)

여러 부사를 구분하는 문제가 출제되므로 쓰임을 확실히 알아두세요.

적용 기술

[기적의 필기노트] 106P
RC 기술 19

출제 포인트
부사 문제에서 선택지에 빈도 부사가 있고 문제의 동사가 현재 시제일 경우, 빈도 부사가 정답일 확률이 높습니다.

🔒 **확인 문제 ❶**

Houston Software -------
updates its products.

(A) regularly
(B) considerably

🔒 **확인 문제 ❷**

The product design
department ------- holds
client meetings on Monday
mornings.

(A) soon
(B) seldom

⚠ **주의**

recently와 lately는 과거 시제와 현재완료 시제 둘 다와 함께 사용할 수 있어요.

(B) ❷ (A) ❶ **정답**

출제 유형 1
부사의 종류

1 빈도 부사

- 빈도 부사는 어떤 일이나 행위가 **얼마나 자주 일어나는지 나타내는 부사**입니다.

always 항상	often 자주	sometimes 가끔	usually 보통
frequently 자주	occasionally 가끔	daily 매일	routinely 일상적으로
regularly 정기적으로	normally 보통	periodically 주기적으로	never 전혀 ~ 않다
typically 보통	rarely 거의 ~ 않다, 드물게		

- 빈도 부사는 반복되는 일반적인 사실을 나타내므로 **현재 시제 동사와 자주 출제**됩니다.

  Alice **usually** gets to work at 9 A.M. Alice는 보통 오전 9시에 출근한다.

`800+`

2 부정 부사

- 부정 부사는 그 자체로 부정의 의미를 가진 부사입니다.

hardly/rarely/seldom/scarcely/barely 거의 ~ 않다	never 결코 ~ 않다

- 부정 부사는 이미 부정의 의미를 가지고 있으므로 **not이나 no 등의 다른 부정어와 함께 쓸 수 없습니다.**

  Michael **seldom** asks questions when taking classes.
  Michael은 수업을 들을 때 거의 질문을 하지 않는다.

- 부정 부사가 문장 맨 앞에 나와 강조하는 역할을 하면 뒤에 주어와 동사가 도치됩니다.
  Ms. Smith **rarely** goes to the gym on Mondays.
  → **Rarely** does Ms. Smith go to the gym on Mondays.
  Smith 씨는 월요일에는 체육관에 거의 가지 않는다.

3 시간 부사

- 각 시제와 어울리는 부사를 알아두어야 합니다.

현재 또는 현재진행 시제와 출제되는 부사			
currently 현재	now 현재	presently 지금	still 여전히

This item is **currently** out of stock. 이 제품은 현재 재고가 없습니다.

과거 시제와 출제되는 부사				
once 한때	formerly 이전에	previously 이전에	recently/lately 최근에	ago ~ 전에

Chase was **once** one of the largest firms in North America.
Chase는 한때 북미에서 가장 큰 기업 중 하나였다.

116 기적의 토익 RC

|현재완료 시제와 출제되는 부사|

already 이미   recently/lately 최근에   so far 지금까지

Mr. Brown has **already** submitted his sales report.
Brown 씨는 판매 보고서를 이미 제출했다.

|미래 시제와 출제되는 부사|

soon 곧   shortly 곧

The clearance sale will be held **soon**. 재고 정리 세일이 곧 열릴 것이다.

4 숫자 표현과 사용되는 부사

· 숫자 표현 앞에 쓸 수 있는 부사는 정해져 있습니다.

approximately/about/around/roughly 대략	almost/nearly 거의
more than/over ~이상	at least 최소한
up to 최대한, ~까지	exactly 정확히

There are **over** 500 food trucks operating in New York City.
뉴욕시에는 500대 이상의 푸드 트럭이 운영되고 있다.

800+

5 형태는 비슷하지만 의미가 다른 부사

· 한 단어에서 파생되어 형태는 비슷하지만 완전히 다른 의미이므로 구분하여 알아두어야 합니다.

high 높게 – highly 매우	near 가까이 – nearly 거의
late 늦게 – lately 최근에	close 가깝게 – closely 자세히, 밀접하게
most 가장 많이 – mostly 대체로, 주로	hard 열심히, 힘들게 – hardly 거의 ~않다

I (high / **highly**) recommend him as a tour guide. 나는 그를 여행 가이드로 매우 추천한다.

Mr. Keller arrived (**late** / ~~lately~~) at the weekly meeting.
Keller 씨는 주간회의에 늦게 도착했다.

출제 유형 2

빈출 부사의 구분

800+

just	① 방금, 막 → 현재완료 시제와 쓰임
	The company has **just** released its new TV commercial.
	그 회사는 막 그들의 새로운 TV 광고를 공개했다.
	② 오직, 단지 → 강조하는 전치사구/명사구 바로 앞에 위치
	The position is **just** for an entry level accountant.
	그 직책은 입문 단계의 회계사만을 위한 것이다.
ever	① 부정문, 의문문, 조건문에 사용 / 긍정문 사용 불가
	② 예외) ~ than ever (before), the + 최상급 + ever

🔒 확인 문제 ❸

We will contact you ------- for the final interview.

(A) formerly
(B) shortly

🔒 확인 문제 ❹

You can save ------- 40% with our membership card.

(A) so
(B) up to

🔒 확인 문제 ❺

We have ------- redesigned our Web site.

(A) late
(B) lately

출제 포인트
highly, lately, closely, nearly가 정답 선택지로 자주 출제됩니다.

(B) ❺ (B) ❹ (B) ❸ 정답

PART 5 문법 부사 (2)

확인 문제 ❻

The design is ------
attractive that it will appeal
to the younger customers.

(A) so
(B) very

출제 포인트

so ~ that –can't/
couldn't: '너무 ~해서 –할
수 없다'
that절의 can't나 couldn't
를 단서로 하여 부사 so를
정답으로 선택하는 문제가
출제됩니다.

확인 문제 ❼

The deadline was
extended. ------, he didn't
submit the paper on time.

(A) Although
(B) Nevertheless

---

yet	① 부정문, 의문문에 주로 사용 / 긍정문 사용 불가
	② yet이 들어가는 위치
	· 부정어 뒤 not yet · 문장 뒤(맨 마지막) · have yet toV 아직 ~하지 못하다
well	① 잘 → good의 부사
	② 훨씬 → 전치사구를 강조
	well above/under/below 훨씬 웃도는/훨씬 못 미치는/훨씬 이하의
	well before/after 훨씬 전에/훨씬 후에
so vs. very	① 둘 다 '매우'를 의미
	② so는 that과 함께 쓰이지만 very는 that절과 함께 쓰일 수 없음
	so ~ that: 너무 ~해서 –하다
	Ms. Miller was **so** busy **that** she couldn't shop for groceries.
	밀러 씨는 너무 바빠서 장을 볼 수 없었다.
enough vs. too	① enough가 부사로 쓰일 경우 형용사를 뒤에서 수식
	형용사 + enough + to부정사: ~하기에 충분히 –한
	He is qualified **enough** to apply for the manager position.
	그는 매니저 직책에 지원하기에 충분히 자격을 갖추었다.
	② too는 형용사 또는 부사를 앞에서 수식
	too + 형용사/부사 + to부정사: 너무 ~해서 –할 수 없다 부정적 뉘앙스!
	The package is **too heavy** to move without someone's help.
	이 상자는 너무 무거워서 다른 사람의 도움 없이는 옮길 수 없다.

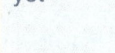

출제 유형 3 — 접속부사

· 접속부사는 앞뒤 두개의 문장을 연결해주는 부사입니다.

· 문장 2개를 각각 연결할 때는 콤마와 함께 두 번째 문장 앞에 쓰입니다.
The marketing proposal is not attractive. **Besides**, the cost seems too expensive.
그 마케팅 제안은 매력적이지 않다. 게다가, 비용이 너무 많이 드는 것 같다.

· 한 문장 안에서 두 개의 절을 연결할 때는 and나 but, 세미콜론과 함께 쓰입니다.
and therefore, and then, and also, and yet 등

· 접속부사는 반드시 접속사와 구분해야 합니다. → 중요!!

의미	접속부사	접속사
대조	however 하지만	but 하지만
결과	therefore/hence 그러므로 consequently 결과적으로	so 그래서
시간의 경과	meantime/meanwhile 그동안 afterwards 그 후에 then 그러고 나서 since then 그때 이후로	while ~하는 동안 after ~후에
첨가	also 또한 besides/moreover/furthermore/in addition 게다가	–
양보	nevertheless/nonetheless/notwithstanding 그럼에도 불구하고	although/though 비록 ~이지만 while ~한 반면에
조건	if so 그렇다면 otherwise 그렇지 않으면	if ~라면 unless ~가 아니라면

정답 ❻ (A) ❼ (B)

118 기적의 토익 RC

풀이 방법 부사 (2)

1. The merger negotiation between Indiana Energy and Northern Eco Company is ------- complete.

(A) near   (B) nearly   (C) nears   (D) neared

Indiana Energy와 Northern Eco Company 사이의 합병 협상이 거의 완료되었다.

DAY 05

> **이렇게 풀어요**
>
> **1. 선택지 보고 문법/어휘 문제 파악** 선택지가 near의 파생어로 구성되어 있으므로 문법 문제임을 파악할 수 있어요.
>
> **2. 빈칸 분석** 빈칸 앞에 is가 있고, 빈칸 뒤에 형용사 보어 complete가 있으므로 수식어가 들어갈 자리임을 파악해요.
>
> **3. 정답 선택** 형용사 주격 보어를 수식할 수 있는 부사인 (A)와 (B) 중에서 의미상 적합한 '거의'라는 뜻의 (B) nearly를 정답으로 고릅니다.

2. Ms. Mills' restaurant was not large ------- to accommodate all event participants.

(A) enough   (B) so   (C) just   (D) little

Mills 씨의 식당은 모든 행사 참가자들을 수용할 정도로 충분히 크지 않았다.

> **이렇게 풀어요**
>
> **1. 선택지 보고 문법/어휘 문제 파악** 선택지가 모두 부사로 쓰이는 어휘로 구성되어 있으므로 어휘 문제임을 파악할 수 있어요.
>
> **2. 빈칸 분석** 빈칸 뒤에 to부정사가 있다는 것을 파악해요.
>
> **3. 정답 선택** to부정사와 함께 쓰여 '~하기에 충분한'이라는 의미를 만들 수 있는 부사 (A) enough를 정답으로 고릅니다.

3. You are free to access most of the amenities in our hotel. -------, the sauna and spa will charge you some fees depending on what service you choose.

(A) Consequently   (B) Moreover   (C) However   (D) Additionally

당신은 우리 호텔의 대부분의 편의시설을 무료로 이용할 수 있습니다. 하지만, 사우나와 스파는 어떤 서비스를 선택하는지에 따라 비용이 부과될 것입니다.

> **이렇게 풀어요**
>
> **1. 선택지 보고 문법/어휘 문제 파악** 선택지가 다양한 부사 어휘로 구성되어 있으므로 어휘 문제임을 파악할 수 있어요.
>
> **2. 빈칸 분석** 빈칸 앞뒤 문장의 의미가 '무료로 사용할 수 있다'와 '사우나와 스파는 비용이 부과될 수 있다'로, 상반되는 내용임을 파악해요.
>
> **3. 정답 선택** '하지만'의 의미를 갖는 접속부사인 (C) However를 정답으로 고릅니다.

PART 5 문법 부사 (2)

PART 5 어휘

명사 어휘 (5)

각 어휘와 함께 자주 쓰이는 표현을 통째로 외워두세요.

01 aid 지원, 도움

| financial aid | 재정적 지원 |
| first aid | 응급 처치 |

02 benefit 혜택, 이득

housing benefit	주거 보조비
fringe benefit	부가 혜택
benefit of	~의 혜택
benefit to	~에게로의 혜택

🐾 빈출 토익 선생님 Pick!
03 exception 예외

| make an exception | 예외로 하다 |
| with the exception of | ~은 제외하고 |

04 cooperation 협동, 협력

| in cooperation with | ~와 협동하여 |
| cooperation among | ~ 간의 협동, 협력 |

05 constraint 제약

| budget constraints | 예산 제약 |
| unforeseen constraints | 예상하지 못한 제약 |

`800+`
06 crisis 위기

| face the energy crisis | 에너지 위기에 직면하다 |

🐾 빈출 토익 선생님 Pick!
07 inspection 검사, 점검

comprehensive inspection	포괄적인 조사
preliminary inspection	예비 점검
safety inspection	안전 점검
conduct inspection	검사를 실시하다

08 outcome 결과, 성과

| an expected outcome | 예상된 결과 |
| possible outcome | 가능성 있는 결과 |

09 proportion 부분, 비율

| a large proportion of | ~의 대부분 |
| in proportion to | ~에 비례하여 |

10 manual 설명서

| instruction manual | 취급 설명서 |
| translate the user's manual | 사용자 설명서를 번역하다 |

11 hazard 위험 (요소)

| workplace hazards | 직장 내 위험 요소 |
| potential hazards | 잠재적 위험 요소 |

12 assumption 추정

| make an assumption | 추정하다 |
| based on the assumption | 추정에 근거하여 |

13 stance 입장, 태도

| stance on | ~에 대한 입장 |

🐾 빈출 토익 선생님 Pick!
14 warranty 품질 보증서

be under warranty	보증 기간 중이다
come with a warranty	품질 보증이 된다
after a warranty period	보증 기간 후에
expired warranty	만료된 보증

120   기적의 토익 RC

800+ ☺ 빈출 토익 선생님 Pick!		
15 observance		준수, 기념
in observance of		~을 기념하여
observance of an agreement		계약의 준수

16 training		교육, 훈련
offer job training for		~에게 실무 교육을 제공하다
receive training		훈련을 받다
training session		교육 (과정)

☺ 빈출 토익 선생님 Pick!

17 restraint		규제, 통제
impose restraints on		~에 규제를 가하다

18 failure		실패, 고장
power failure		정전
cause of the failure		실패의 원인
failure to		~하지 못함

19 progress		진행, 진척
quarterly progress report		분기별 진행 보고서

20 adjustment		수정, 조정
make an adjustment		수정하다

☺ 빈출 토익 선생님 Pick!

21 appointment		예약, 약속, 임명
make an appointment		예약[약속]을 잡다
arrange an appointment		예약[약속]을 잡다
appointment of a new president		새로운 회장의 임명

22 awareness		인지, 의식
raise awareness of		~에 대한 인식을 높이다
increase public awareness		대중의 의식을 높이다

23 route		길, 경로
direct route to		~로 곧장 가는 경로
alternate route		대체 경로

900+		
24 vicinity		인근, 부근
in the vicinity of		~의 인근에

25 budget		예산
budget for		~을 위한 예산
annual budget		연간 예산
keep with a tight budget		빠듯한 예산으로 유지하다

DAY 05

🗣 풀이 방법

Most colleges offer a variety of financial ------- to international students.

(A) flaws   (B) shifts   (C) aid   (D) orders

대부분의 대학들은 외국인 학생들에게 다양한 재정적 지원을 제공한다.

> 🖊 이렇게 풀어요
>
> **1. 선택지 보고 문법/어휘 문제 파악**   선택지가 서로 다른 명사 어휘로 구성되어 있으므로 어휘 문제임을 파악해요.
> **2. 빈칸 분석**   빈칸 앞의 형용사 financial(재정적인)의 수식을 받아 자연스러운 의미를 만드는 명사가 들어가서, '재정적 -------을 학생들에게 제공하다'라는 문맥이 되어야 함을 파악합니다.
> **3. 정답 선택**   financial과 함께 쓰여 '재정적 지원'이라는 의미를 갖는 (C) aid를 정답으로 고릅니다.

PART 5 어휘 명사 어휘 (5)   121

따라 하면 문제가 풀리는

연습 문제

앞서 학습한 문제 풀이법을 적용하여 맞는 것에 ✔ 표시 하거나 괄호 안에
적절한 답을 쓰고 정답을 선택하세요.

01 The ------- efficient automated assembly line will increase production by at least 30%.

(A) high
(B) height
(C) highly
(D) heighten

> 1. 선택지 보고 문법/어휘 문제 파악하기 ☐문법 문제 ☐어휘 문제
> 2. 빈칸 분석하기 빈칸 뒤에 있는 것 ☐동사 ☐형용사 ☐부사
>   → 빈칸은 ☐명사 ☐부사 자리이다.
> 3. 정답 선택하기 정답 (   )

02 Ms. Garner ------- holds meetings to discuss strategies for improving sales figures.

(A) frequently
(B) significantly
(C) soundly
(D) reasonably

> 1. 선택지 보고 문법/어휘 문제 파악하기 ☐문법 문제 ☐어휘 문제
> 2. 빈칸 분석하기 빈칸 뒤에 있는 것 ☐현재 시제 ☐과거 시제 ☐미래 시제
>   빈칸 뒤 동사의 의미 (   )
>   → 동사의 시제와 의미에 어울리는 부사가 정답이다.
> 3. 정답 선택하기 정답 (   )

03 On March 20, Vincent Books will be closed in ------- of national holidays.

(A) observance
(B) restraint
(C) awareness
(D) exception

> 1. 선택지 보고 문법/어휘 문제 파악하기 ☐문법 문제 ☐어휘 문제
> 2. 빈칸 분석하기 빈칸 앞의 in, 빈칸 뒤의 of와 짝꿍으로 쓰이는 명사가 정답이다.
> 3. 정답 선택하기 정답 (   )

04 The merger will be approved -------, once the board members reach a final agreement.

(A) currently
(B) recently
(C) previously
(D) shortly

1. 선택지 보고 문법/어휘 문제 파악하기 ☐문법 문제 ☐어휘 문제
2. 빈칸 분석하기 빈칸 앞에 있는 것 ☐미래 시제 동사 ☐현재 시제 동사
3. 정답 선택하기 정답 (   )

05 ------- at the beginning of his internship, Mr. Singh performed above expectations.

(A) Even
(B) Much
(C) Rather
(D) Besides

1. 선택지 보고 문법/어휘 문제 파악하기 ☐문법 문제 ☐어휘 문제
2. 빈칸 분석하기 빈칸 뒤에 있는 것 ☐명사구 ☐전치사구
   → 빈칸은 ☐형용사 ☐부사 자리이다.
3. 정답 선택하기 정답 (   )

06 Chef Meyers suggests adding ------- one teaspoon of sugar when making fruit pies.

(A) intentionally
(B) eventually
(C) roughly
(D) definitely

1. 선택지 보고 문법/어휘 문제 파악하기 ☐문법 문제 ☐어휘 문제
2. 빈칸 분석하기 빈칸 뒤에 있는 것 ☐숫자 표현 ☐미래 시제 동사
3. 정답 선택하기 정답 (   )

PART 5 부사 (2) / 명사 어휘 (5)

DAY 01-05 누적 문제

제한시간 9분입니다! 시~작!

01. Gibson Manufacturing recorded a growth of ------- 15% over the last quarter alone.

(A) approximation
(B) approximately
(C) approximated
(D) approximate

02. ------- 600,000 passengers travel through Penn Station every weekday.

(A) Persistently
(B) Initially
(C) Roughly
(D) Casually

03. Be sure to submit your receipts to the accounting department as ------- as you return from business travel.

(A) far
(B) wide
(C) soon
(D) brightly

04. Mr. Holland wanted to get a part-time job within walking ------- of his apartment.

(A) stance
(B) distance
(C) proximity
(D) range

05. Lincoln Lane Pizza has received an increasing number of takeout orders -------.

(A) late
(B) lately
(C) later
(D) latest

06. Although professional food critics gave it poor reviews, Ronny's Diner ------- remains a favorite eatery among locals in Kingston.

(A) either
(B) moreover
(C) along
(D) nevertheless

07. With a large portion of meat and French fries piled high, the Steak Platter is big ------- for two hungry adults.

(A) full
(B) more
(C) enough
(D) firmly

08. This mobile app helps you arrange or reschedule ------- with our dental clinic more conveniently.

(A) intentions
(B) securities
(C) atmospheres
(D) appointments

09. Trucks by Manaford Auto are so sturdy that they ------- require maintenance.

(A) shortly
(B) easily
(C) seldom
(D) high

10. Please submit your ------- before the due date to avoid incurring any late charges.

(A) paid
(B) payable
(C) pays
(D) payment

11. ------- per quarter, Lawrence Construction gives overtime bonuses to its staff.

(A) Once
(B) Since
(C) After
(D) Along

12. Gentry Security ------- patrols areas that it has been hired to guard.

(A) additionally
(B) softly
(C) almost
(D) routinely

124 기적의 토익 RC

13. An intern has been assigned to Ms. Mullen's division, so she won't have to do this project by -------.
    (A) she
    (B) her
    (C) herself
    (D) hers

14. Mr. Tatum's study shows that most migratory birds' travel routes are ------- with the help of tracking technology.
    (A) predict
    (B) predicting
    (C) predictable
    (D) prediction

15. Since he hasn't completed his degree yet, Mr. Sanchez is ------- to apply for the position.
    (A) reluctantly
    (B) reluctant
    (C) reluctance
    (D) reluctancy

16. Due to the popularity of online shopping, Vincent Accessory will launch ------- online store.
    (A) of
    (B) if
    (C) its
    (D) beyond

17. When assigning team projects, Ms. Hines ------- divides employees into groups based on individual strengths.
    (A) noticeably
    (B) apparently
    (C) frequently
    (D) substantially

18. An ------- will be appointed to you, as you will need extra help with this assignment.
    (A) assistant
    (B) assistance
    (C) assisting
    (D) assist

19. The CEO requires full ------- across all related departments for the successful new product launch.
    (A) demonstration
    (B) cooperation
    (C) assurance
    (D) overview

20. Please consult the user's ------- before turning on your printer.
    (A) assent
    (B) route
    (C) manual
    (D) crisis

21. Highland Bank was founded in Edinburgh a little over a century -------.
    (A) ago
    (B) prior to
    (C) beginning
    (D) apart

22. Prof. Martins is looking for a town house in the ------- of Kansas University.
    (A) direction
    (B) hazard
    (C) vicinity
    (D) landmark

23. The anniversary sale at Salem Bedding will last ------- one week from today.
    (A) only
    (B) clearly
    (C) mostly
    (D) scarcely

24. After long negotiations, Ms. Stanford agreed with her landlord to make ------- to the current rental contract.
    (A) overviews
    (B) adjustments
    (C) benefits
    (D) objectives

PART 5 부사 (2) / 명사 어휘 (5)   125

PART 6

앞 문장의 내용을 요약하는 지시대명사 `800+`

빈칸 뒤에 동사가 있고 보기가 대명사로 이루어져 있으면 앞 문장을 대신할 수 있는 대명사를 선택하세요.

적용 기술

[기적의 필기노트] 160P
RC 기술 78

VOCA

provide A with B A에게 B를 제공하다
platform 플랫폼, 기반
trade 거래하다
sending party 발신자
wrap 포장하다
receiving party 수신자
package 포장하다
shipment 수송품
rely on ~에 의존하다
integrity 진실성
transaction 거래
considerably 상당히
maintain 유지하다

풀이 방법 | instructions

해석 p.39

Shipping items to other TradeNet customers:

We at TradeNet provide people with a platform to buy, sell, and trade goods. Therefore, it is the responsibility of the sending party to ------- wrap items before
PART 5
sending them to the receiving party. As a sender, it is in your best interest to package shipments well enough to avoid damage.

Please keep in mind that we operate on a strong feedback exchange system. ------- relies on the integrity of all involved in a transaction. TradeNet members are
01.
expected to leave an honest review of all transactions. People are considerably less likely to be willing to buy from someone with a bad reputation. In this way, we can maintain a high level of customer satisfaction.

01. (A) Either
(B) Some
(C) This
(D) Both

이렇게 풀어요

1. **선택지 보고 문법/어휘 문제 파악** 선택지가 다양한 품사로 구성되어 있으므로 문법 문제임을 파악해요.
   (A) 한정사, 대명사   (B) 한정사, 대명사   (C) 지시대명사   (D) 한정사, 대명사

2. **빈칸 분석** 빈칸 뒤에 동사 relies가 있으므로 빈칸에는 주어 역할을 할 수 있는 것이 들어가야 함을 파악합니다.

3. **정답 선택** 주어 자리에 올 수 있는, 대명사로 쓰이는 선택지 중 빈칸 앞 문장의 내용(강한 피드백 교환 시스템을 바탕으로 운영된다)을 대신할 수 있는 것은 this이므로 (C)를 정답으로 고릅니다.

핵심 포인트

<지시대명사의 종류>
this, that, those
→ 앞에 나온 내용을 대신합니다.

해설

to부정사(to wrap)의 to와 동사원형 사이에 들어갈 수 있는 것은 부사이므로 (D)가 정답입니다.

PART 5 문법 적용 문제

Therefore, it is the responsibility of the sending party to ------- wrap items before sending them to the receiving party.

(A) proper   (B) properness   (C) propriety   (D) properly

126 기적의 토익 RC

빈칸 앞 내용에서 단서가 될 부분을 찾아 표시하세요.
표시한 것을 바탕으로 정답 어휘를 선택하세요.

정답 및 해설 p.39

DAY 05

01

From now on, our bank's clients can access all of their accounts on their personal mobile devices. They can check their current balance, transfer funds to other accounts, and view their monthly statements. ------- is expected to increase customer satisfaction considerably.

(A) Some

(B) This

02

Santa Monica Condominium

Electronic Waste Disposal Policy

We will arrange an area to recycle any electronics right beside the recycling bins. Any small portable electronics can be disposed of for free. But larger ones such as refrigerators, laundry machines, dishwashers, and large ovens will incur a disposal fee. ------- will be implemented as of next month.

(A) This

(B) You

03

Thank you for purchasing a Crabtree Office Desk! As all of our products, it requires assembly, so please refer to the manual for instructions. Please be reminded that ------- makes our price so competitive in the market.

(A) another

(B) this

04

I ask you whether the order may arrive on July 7. My company plans to attend a trade fair in Chicago and there we will need to distribute the new brochures. If not, ------- will cause some changes in our schedule.

(A) one

(B) that

PART 6 앞 문장의 내용을 요약하는 지시대명사　127

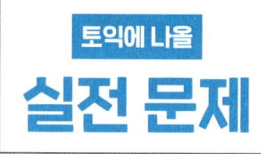

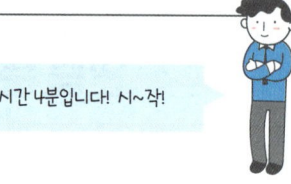

제한시간 4분입니다! 시~작!

Questions 01-04 refer to the following instructions.

Frankfurt Leather Shoes: Care and maintenance

Frankfurt Cobbler Company does its best to provide its customers with the highest quality hand-crafted leather shoes available. -------, even the highest quality items will lose their value if not
01.
cared for properly. Avoid ------- your shoes in a humid place, but also be sure not to leave them
02.
exposed to direct sunlight for extended periods. Also, clean them with a cloth if they become dirty.
------- should help to greatly extend the life of your shoes. Standard repairs such as new soles are
03.
covered under our standard 2-year warranty. -------. In such case, please visit one of our certified
04.
service centers.

유형 적용 문제

01. (A) Likewise
(B) Therefore
(C) Otherwise
(D) Nevertheless

03. (A) We
(B) Few
(C) These
(D) Ones

02. (A) storing
(B) store
(C) stores
(D) to store

04. (A) After that period, you will be charged for
maintenance services.
(B) If you haven't already, please leave a review on
our homepage.
(C) Please refer to your contract for more precise
details.
(D) Thank you for choosing Frankfurt Cobbler
Company.

정답 및 해설 p.39

Questions 05-08 refer to the following e-mail.

Date: 7 November
To: Emma Douglass <edouglass@lmail.net>
From: Henrietta White <hwite@fullertonmobile.net>
Subject: Mobile Phone

Dear Ms. Douglass,

I was happy to assist you with the activation of your FT4 mobile phone last week. Unfortunately, I have some bad news to report about your particular phone model. The manufacturer ------- some
05.
batteries swollen when it is overcharged. ------- could lead to overheating the circuitry, or worse,
06.
fire.

In order to determine ------- you have a faulty battery or not, remove the back cover of your phone
07.
and look for "Product ID Code." If the code ends in "PD2", we recommend bringing the battery into our store anytime. -------.
08.

Thank you,

Henrietta White
Supervisor, Fullerton Mobile

DAY 05

05. (A) found
(B) exchanged
(C) repaired
(D) produced

유형 적용 문제
06. (A) Some
(B) When
(C) This
(D) Hence

07. (A) so that
(B) whether
(C) although
(D) whose

08. (A) You will be sent a coupon book every month.
(B) Please complete the attached feedback form and send it back to us.
(C) We will dispose of yours and give you a new one for free.
(D) I'm very pleased to have you as a new member of our program.

PART 6 앞 문장의 내용을 요약하는 지시대명사   129

PART 7
삼중 지문 연계 문제

세 지문의 관계를 먼저 파악하고 문제를 풀면 빠르고 쉽게 해결할 수 있어요.

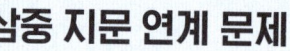

출제 유형
삼중 지문 연계 문제

삼중 지문에서 연계 문제는 1~2문제가 출제됩니다. 지문 2와 지문 3, 지문 3과 지문 1, 지문 1과 2를 연계하여 푸는 문제가 출제될 수 있습니다. 먼저 세 지문의 관계를 파악한 후 한 문제씩 풀어나가면 세 지문 전체를 읽지 않아도 문제를 풀 수 있어요.

1 자주 출제되는 삼중 지문 유형

출제 포인트
삼중 지문에서는 이중 지문보다 웹페이지의 출제 비중이 높습니다. 또한, 삼중 지문에 문자 메시지가 출제된 경우도 있으므로 다양한 종류의 지문 간 관계를 파악하는 연습을 해두세요.

지문 1	지문 2	지문 3	내용
광고	이메일	설명서	구인 광고 & 합격 안내 이메일 & 근무 설명서
공지	편지	일정표	행사 관련 공지 & 행사 참여 독려 편지 & 행사 일정표
기사	양식	이메일	시설을 소개하는 기사 & 시설 관련 신청 양식 & 시설 관련자에게 문의하거나 협조를 요청하는 이메일
기사	웹페이지	이메일	행사에 대해 소개하는 기사 & 행사 일정이 안내된 웹페이지 & 특정 행사에 참여 가능 여부를 알리는 이메일
기사	편지	이메일	공공장소에 적용될 정책 변화를 알리는 기사 & 정책 변화 관련하여 담당자에게 업무를 요청하는 편지 & 업무 요청에 대한 답신 이메일
웹페이지	이메일	이메일	기업의 홈페이지 & 주문 관련 문의 이메일 & 문의에 대한 답신 이메일

900+
2 핵심 전략

· 질문의 키워드를 통해 세 지문 중 먼저 확인할 지문을 정하세요. 해당 지문에서 단서를 찾고, 연관된 단서를 다른 지문에서 찾습니다. 두 개의 단서를 종합적으로 판단하여 정답을 고릅니다.

· 주로 세 번째~다섯 번째 문제가 연계 문제로 출제되는 경우가 많지만 첫 번째, 두 번째 문제도 연계 문제로 나올 수 있습니다.

· 세 지문 중 하나는 주로 표나 양식이지만 세 개 모두 일반 지문(이메일, 편지, 기사 등)으로 구성된 경우도 있습니다. 읽을 내용이 많으므로 어렵게 느껴질 수 있지만 각 지문의 길이는 길지 않으므로 끝까지 포기하지 않고 풀어 보세요.

· 다섯 문제 중 마지막 문제는 세 번째 지문에 직접적으로 단서가 등장하는 경우가 많으므로 시간이 부족할 경우 마지막 문제부터 푸세요.

삼중 지문 연계 문제

article, schedule, and letter

해석 p.41

DAY 05

Jacksonville to Replace Streetlights

(May 6) – Over the course of the next month, Zamora Lighting will be replacing streetlights around the downtown area of Jacksonville.

Detours will be designated so that the workers can install the lights without external delays or distractions. Each section of road will be worked on weekdays between 10 A.M. and 4 P.M. in order to avoid peak traffic times in the morning and evening. The schedule as well as its updates can be viewed on the city's Web site and will be published in local newspapers. If access to areas is required during the work period, people should contact a customer service manager of Zamora Lighting.

Streetlight Installment Schedule

Monday, May 14: Holiday – No Work
Tuesday, May 15: Division Street
Wednesday, May 16: Ridgewood Street
Thursday, May 17: Mayfield Lane
Friday, May 18: Edgewater Street

Once work is completed, the road will be reopened for traffic going both directions.

Dear Ms. Garrett,

We apologize for the inconvenience that the work will cause to your business on Wednesday, May 16. Please understand that foot traffic is still allowed on the roads, so your clients will still be able to access your agency. We recommend using street parking on Mayfield Lane on that day.

Randall Boone

PART 7 삼중 지문 연계 문제 131

Q. What is probably true about Ms. Garrett?

(A) She commutes to work by public transportation.
(B) She owns a business on Ridgewood Street.
(C) She usually parks on Mayfield Lane.
(D) She is currently away on vacation.

이렇게 풀어요

1. 문제 먼저 파악 문제에 언급된 사람 이름(Ms. Garrett)이 키워드 → 연계 문제임을 파악합니다.

2. 문제의 핵심 어구가 있는 지문에서 1차 단서 파악 Garrett이 언급된 지문 3에서 먼저 단서를 파악합니다. Garrett 씨에게 쓴 편지에서 '당신의 사업체에 5월 16일 수요일에 공사가 영향을 끼칠 것'이라고 했습니다.

3. 추가적인 단서를 또 다른 지문에서 파악 지문 2의 공사 일정에서 5월 16일 수요일에 Ridgewood 가에 가로등을 설치할 것임을 알 수 있습니다.

두 지문의 연결고리 확인! 지문 3 – your business on Wednesday, May 16

지문 2 – Wednesday, May 16: Ridgewood Street

4. 정답 선택 두 지문의 단서를 종합하여 Garrett 씨가 Ridgewood 가에 사업체를 소유하고 있다는 내용의 (B)를 정답으로 선택합니다.

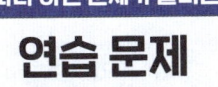

따라 하면 문제가 풀리는
연습 문제

먼저 문제의 키워드에 표시한 후,
지문에서 단서를 찾아 적절한 답을 고르세요.   ⦿ 정답 및 해설 p.41

01-02 advertisement, online review, and e-mail

Amethyst Spa Massage Treatments

We are pleased to offer the following options for 1-hour massages:
Thai Massage: $60
Swedish Massage: $70
Hot Stone Massage: $80
Sports Massage: $90

To book an appointment, call 555-6112. We are open daily from 7 A.M. to 9 P.M.

---

www.spa-reviews101.com

I recently visited Amethyst Spa for the first time, and it was an excellent experience. My one-hour massage was very relaxing — well worth the $80 that I paid for it. The entire staff at Amethyst Spa was friendly and professional. The receptionist even went above and beyond to help me. I asked for directions to a certain restaurant because I had left my phone at home. She printed out a map for me so that I wouldn't get lost! I definitely plan to become a regular customer.

— Stephanie Nicholson, Willow Lake

To: Stephanie Nicholson <nicholsons@inbox22.com>
From: Jasmine Rafferty <jasmine@amethystspa.com>
Date: July 9
Subject: Thanks!

Dear Ms. Nicholson,

Thank you for your recent review of our spa. We strive to provide the best spa treatments in town at an affordable price. I'm glad that Stacey was able to provide you with the information that you needed. Next month, we plan to launch a customer rewards program in which customers can earn points for each spa treatment they receive. We hope to see you again soon.

Warmest regards,

Jasmine Rafferty
Owner, Amethyst Spa

---

01. What service did Ms. Nicholson receive during her visit?

(A) Swedish massage
(B) Hot Stone massage

02. Who is Stacey?

(A) A receptionist
(B) A massage therapist

PART 7 삼중 지문 연계 문제   **133**

제한시간 15분입니다! 시~작!

Questions 01-05 refer to the following article, information, and form.

Colchester Going Green

March 23 — Auto parts manufacturer Colchester has announced plans to renovate its plants to make them more environmentally friendly. Company executives want to move to sustainable energy sources, as they believe that the popularity of gas-powered machines will soon pass. The project will include installing solar panels, adding a rainwater collection system, and improving the insulation of the walls. All employees at plants in Burlington, Langford, and Valleyview will be temporarily relocated while the work at their plant is being carried out. The work will begin at Colchester's largest plant in September, with the other two sites undergoing the modifications early next year.

"We are pleased to lead the way in practices that are beneficial to the environment," said John Lomas, foreman of the Valleyview plant. Company officials hope to keep production at the same level by adding additional shifts at the other sites.

Prestige Solar: Company Overview

If you are considering adding solar panels to your property, Prestige Solar can help you every step of the way.

Consultation: Our experienced technicians will advise you about the best placement for your panels to maximize their output.

Ongoing Help: Repairs during the warranty period are provided at no extra cost. In addition, we can take care of the regular removal of dust and grime buildup on the panels' surface to maximize efficiency.

Financing: Not ready to pay for your solar panels up front? You can pay your bill in installments, spreading out the cost of your solar panels over a period of up to five years.

Contact us to set up your free initial consultation. One of our staff members will visit your property on the assessment date, and the following day you will receive a report outlining the approximate costs.

○ 정답 및 해설 p.42

Prestige Solar
New Customer Booking Form

Company Name: Colchester

E-mail Address: n.lewis@colchestermfg.com

Proposed Installation Address: 4549 Carriage Lane, Langford

Company Representative: Nathaniel Lewis

Phone Number: 555-1039

Assessment Date: July 11

Requested Start Date of Work: September 5

Should you need to change or cancel the above booking, please contact us as soon as possible. Thank you for your interest in Prestige Solar!

DAY 05

01. In the article, the word "pass" in paragraph 1, line 4, is closest in meaning to

(A) adopt
(B) excel
(C) overtake
(D) end

02. What is implied about Mr. Lomas?

(A) He is the newest member of the management team.
(B) He will work at another site for a short time.
(C) He has a degree in environmental studies.
(D) He provided a strategy for improving production.

03. What is a service offered by Prestige Solar?

(A) Assisting with building permits
(B) Providing monthly output reports
(C) Cleaning the solar panels
(D) Seeking bank approval for financing

04. What is implied about the Langford plant?

(A) It is the company's largest facility.
(B) It was constructed within the last five years.
(C) Its goods required a safety recall.
(D) Its renovation work has been delayed.

05. What most likely will happen on July 12?

(A) Prestige Solar will be paid a deposit.
(B) Prestige Solar will begin an installation.
(C) Colchester will be visited by a technician.
(D) Colchester will receive an estimate.

---

paraphrasing 주어진 어휘 또는 표현과 패러프레이징 될 수 있는 것을 연결하세요.

1. be temporarily relocated •
2. removal of dust and grime buildup •
3. report outlining the approximate costs •

• (a) cleaning
• (b) work at another site for a short time
• (c) estimate

PART 7 삼중 지문 연계 문제   135

 **실전 문제**

Questions 06-10 refer to the following Web page, article, and review.

---

www.highlander.com/featuredproducts

| Home | Featured Products | Members | FAQs |

Highlander Camping Tent (2 Adults)

Features:

* Easy to set up

* Comes with 8 stakes

* Has optional support bars to help it withstand heavy wind and rain

* Double mesh lining keeps you dry and keeps bugs out

Price: $200

Come into our store to sign up for a membership and get 20% off your first purchase!

Highlander Does It Again

5 May — Highlander is known for being one of the best names in outdoor gear for activities such as hiking, camping, and fishing. For the third year in a row, it has been named Highest Quality Brand at the Annual Expo for Outdoor Enthusiasts (AEOE). This year, its most popular item was a tent designed for two adults.

"I'm so happy to be receiving this honor once again," said company CEO Scott McCulloch. "As always, we listen to what our customers ask for. That helps steer our development team in the right direction."

www.productbuzz.com/outdoors

Product: Highlander Camping Tent
Reviewer: Jorge Krauss

My best friend and I went on a camping trip in the Black Hills. To prepare for it, we purchased a Highlander Camping Tent with a 20% discount, and I'm glad that we did. The Highlander brand is known for its quality, and we were not disappointed. When we arrived at the campground, the staff there warned us of bad weather. After we set up the tent, we also used the optional support bars. Even though we heard the wind howl and rain come down all night, we stayed dry inside our tent. I highly recommend this product for any serious campers.

DAY 05

06. What is offered to new members?

(A) Extended product warranties
(B) Free express shipping
(C) Some camping gear
(D) A one-time discount

07. According to the article, what has Highlander recently done?

(A) Issued a product recall
(B) Changed its ownership
(C) Won an industry award
(D) Opened a new branch

08. In the article, the word "steer" in paragraph 2, line 3 is closest in meaning to

(A) attract
(B) guide
(C) purchase
(D) attempt

09. What is suggested about Mr. Krauss?

(A) He prefers going camping alone.
(B) He grew up in the Black Hills region.
(C) He went camping during a storm.
(D) He needed help from campground staff to set up his tent.

10. What does Mr. Krauss imply about his Highlander Camping Tent?

(A) It was the first item he purchased as a member.
(B) It is sturdy enough without the optional support.
(C) It was not large enough for 2 adults.
(D) It is not effective at keeping water out.

paraphrasing 주어진 어휘 또는 표현과 패러프레이징 될 수 있는 것을 연결하세요.

1. sign up for •

2. off •

3. for the third year in a row •

• (a) apply for

• (b) for three consecutive years

• (c) discount

PART 7 삼중 지문 연계 문제   137

 **실전 문제**

Questions 11-15 refer to the following e-mails and event information.

```
●  ●  ●                              E-mail
```

To:	Cody Gwinn
From:	Judith Franklin
Date:	April 14
Subject:	May 10 event

Hi Cody,

Thank you for agreeing to assist with purchasing the necessary supplies for the May 10 event. In addition to the items we already talked about, I think we should buy a bouquet of flowers for each category winner — so, four in total.

In addition, we will have representatives from various departments performing the on-stage activities. I believe that this will send a clear message that teamwork is highly valued at our company. Kimberly is currently working on the draft of the programs, so if you have any ideas for that, please let her know before she sends it to me.

Thanks!

Judith

Vergara Enterprises
Annual Company Banquet

Friday, May 10 Eagle Plaza (first-floor ballroom)

6:00 P.M.   Arrival and cocktails
6:30 P.M.   Buffet dinner
7:30 P.M.   Welcome address, Sales Manager Phil Neilson
7:45 P.M.   Speech, HR Manager Juan Silva
8:00 P.M.   Distribution of Annual Honors, IT Manager Naomi Fugere
            Ronnie Tavares – Best Creative Idea
            Kaumari Anagal – Top Annual Sales
            Muneto Sahaku – Welcome Award
            Edith Bannon – Lifetime Achievement Award

To: Kimberly Tolbert
From: Cody Gwinn
Date: April 15
Subject: Program draft

Hi Kimberly,

I've received the draft of the program that you sent. I think the schedule you devised will work well, with one exception. In my opinion, the Welcome Award should be given out first. Since this award is for someone who has joined our team in the last six months, it does not really match the level of achievement recognized by the other awards. We don't want to give it too much emphasis by putting it too late in the program order.

Other than that, I think the program looks great, and it is ready to be printed. Please use Yancy Printing as usual. Our company has an account with them. Although we do need to keep the budget in mind, please do not order the programs on flimsy paper, because this always looks very cheap. You'll have to check their options in person and choose something suitable.

Thanks for your help!

Cody

11. Who will receive some flowers on May 10?

(A) Mr. Neilson
(B) Mr. Silva
(C) Ms. Fugere
(D) Ms. Anagal

12. In the first e-mail, the word "clear" in paragraph 2, line 2, is closest in meaning to

(A) bright
(B) obvious
(C) empty
(D) open

13. What is true about the May 10 event?

(A) It includes a meal.
(B) It is for new employees only.
(C) Its attendees can bring guests.
(D) It finishes at 8:00 P.M.

14. What is indicated about Mr. Sahaku?

(A) He had the largest level of sales within the company last year.
(B) He does not want his part of the ceremony to be emphasized.
(C) He has worked for Vergara Enterprises for less than half a year.
(D) He plans to give a brief speech after Mr. Neilson.

15. What is Ms. Tolbert asked to do?

(A) Add some graphics to the design
(B) Look for a cheaper printer
(C) Select sturdy paper for the program
(D) Check the spelling of everyone's name

paraphrasing 주어진 어휘 또는 표현과 패러프레이징 될 수 있는 것을 연결하세요.

1. highly valued •
2. draft •
3. buffet dinner •

• (a) outline
• (b) very much regarded
• (c) meal

PART 7 삼중 지문 연계 문제 139

'멋진 당신, 오늘도 화이팅'

DAY
06

오늘의 학습 포인트

PART 5. 전치사 (1)
1. 전치사의 위치 - 명사(구) 앞/동명사 앞/명사절 앞
2. 시간 전치사 - 시점 전치사 vs. 기간 전치사 구분 중요!
3. 장소/위치/방향 전치사 - along, through, between, among 등
4. 이유/양보 전치사 - because of, due to, despite, in spite of 등
   → 접속사/접속부사와 구별하기!
5. '~에 관한'의 의미를 갖는 전치사 - about, on, regarding, concerning 등

PART 6. 알맞은 문장 고르기 - 선택지에 대명사
   → 보기 문장에 대명사, 앞에서 지칭하는 것 파악

PART 7. 문제 제기 이메일
   ↘ 출제 비중 ↑, 목적 문제 출제

PART 5
문법

전치사 (1)

쓰임에 맞는 전치사를 고르는 문제가 가장 많이 출제되므로 전치사의 종류와 의미를 구분하여 알아두세요.

✎ 적용 기술

[기적의 필기노트] 108P
RC 기술 21

출제 포인트
전치사 문제는 선택지에 파생어가 제시되는 다른 문법 문제와 달리 선택지에 부사, 접속사가 함께 제시되어 품사를 구분하는 문제로 출제돼요.

🔒 **확인 문제 ❶**

Our delivery is running late ------- an engine malfunction.

(A) because
(B) due to

🔒 **확인 문제 ❷**

You can participate in our contest ------- filling up the online form.

(A) by
(B) well

⚠ **주의**
that이 이끄는 명사절은 전치사 뒤에 올 수 없어요.

🔒 **확인 문제 ❸**

Customers want more details ------- what we offer on our Web site.

(A) additionally
(B) about

정답 ❶ (B) ❷ (A) ❸ (B)

출제 유형 1
전치사의 위치

1 명사(구) 앞

- 전치사는 명사(구)를 목적어로 취합니다. 따라서, **명사(구) 앞의 빈칸은 전치사 자리**입니다.
  We will hold the event **at** the city hall. 우리는 시청에서 행사를 개최할 것입니다.

- **전치사는 대명사 앞에 위치**할 수 있습니다. 이때, 목적격 대명사, 소유대명사, 재귀대명사가 전치사 뒤에 올 수 있습니다.
  Jane asked Clara to send an invitation **to** you.
  Jane이 Clara에게 당신에게 초대장을 보내 달라고 부탁했어요.

- '전치사 + 명사/대명사' 구조를 전치사구 또는 전명구라고 부르며, 명사(구)를 뒤에서 수식하거나 동사 또는 문장 전체를 수식하는 역할을 합니다.
  [동사를 수식하는 전치사구]
  She has lived **at** Pennington City. [앞의 동사 has lived 수식]
  그녀는 Pennington 시에 살았다.

  [문장 전체를 수식하는 전치사구]
  Prior to the board meeting, they rehearsed their presentation.
  이사회에 앞서 그들은 프레젠테이션 리허설을 했다.

2 동명사 앞

- 전치사는 명사구 역할을 할 수 있는 동명사를 목적어로 가질 수 있습니다. 따라서 **동명사 앞 빈칸은 전치사 자리**입니다.
  On arriving in Canada, we called him. 캐나다에 도착하자마자 우리는 그에게 전화했다.
  You can simply connect to the Internet **by** following these steps.
  여러분은 다음 단계에 따라 인터넷에 간단히 연결할 수 있습니다.

800+

3 명사절 앞

- 전치사는 명사 역할을 하는 명사절을 목적어로 가질 수 있습니다. 따라서 **명사절 앞의 빈칸은 전치사 자리**입니다. '전치사 + 명사절'은 문장 전체를 수식할 수 있어요.

- 명사절과 사용되는 전치사로 '~에 관하여'라는 의미의 **about, as to, regarding, concerning** 이 자주 출제됩니다.
  There might be a seminar **on** how business owners could increase work efficiency.
  사업주들이 업무 효율성을 높일 수 있는 방법에 대한 세미나가 있을 것입니다.

- 빈출 명사절 접속사: who, what, which, how, why, when, where, whose

출제 유형 2

시간 전치사

적용 기술

[기적의 필기노트] 109P, 110P
RC 기술 22, 23

1 at/on/in

· 시간 전치사 at, on, in은 뒤에 오는 시간 표현에 따라 구별하여 씁니다.

at	정확한 시각이나 시점	at 6 o'clock 6시 정각에 at 9 P.M. 오후 9시에 at noon 정오에 at midnight 자정에
on	날짜, 요일, 특정일	on October 25 10월 25일에 on Saturday 토요일에 on weekends 주말에
in	월, 년도, 계절, 세기, 오전/오후/저녁	in December 12월에 in 2019 2019년에 in summer 여름에 in the 21st century 21세기에

2 시점 전치사 vs. 기간 전치사

· 시점 전치사는 요일, 시각, 날짜와 같이 특정 시점 표현과 사용됩니다.

by ~까지 until ~까지 since ~이후로 from ~부터 before/prior to ~ 전에 after/following ~ 후에	+ 시점 표현

She has worked at this company **since** 2005.
그녀는 2005년 이래로 이 회사에서 근무해 왔다.

800+

· by와 until을 구분해야 합니다. by는 동작의 완료를 나타낼 때, until은 동작이나 상태의 지속을 나타낼 때 사용합니다.

by와 함께 쓰이는 동사 (완료 의미)	finish 끝내다 turn in 제출하다 deliver 배달하다	complete 완료하다 inform 알리다 arrive 도착하다	submit 제출하다 notify 알리다 cancel 취소하다
until과 함께 쓰이는 동사 (계속 의미)	wait 기다리다 last 지속하다 work 일하다	continue 계속하다 be open 열리다	stay 유지하다 postpone 지연되다

Please turn in your worked hours **on** this form by Friday.
금요일까지 이 양식에 근무 시간을 제출해 주세요.

The festival will continue **until** the end of the month. 축제는 이번 달 말까지 계속될 것이다.

· 기간 전치사는 시간(hours), 햇수(years), 주(weeks)와 같은 기간 표현과 사용됩니다.

for ~동안에 during ~동안에 over ~에 걸쳐서 within ~이내에 throughout ~(동안) 내내 around ~(동안) 내내 in ~후에/~만에	+ 기간 표현

Construction of Jefferson Mall is expected to be completed **in** a month.
Jefferson Mall의 건축은 한 달 뒤에 끝날 것이다.

· for와 during을 구분해야 합니다. for는 구체적인 숫자 기간 표현 앞에 쓰고 during은 기간을 나타내는 명사 앞에 씁니다.

Real estate values have increased significantly **for** the past decade.
지난 10년간 부동산의 가치는 엄청나게 증가했다.

Our customer appreciation event will take place **during** the month of May.
저희의 고객 감사 행사는 5월에 열릴 것입니다.

확인 문제 ❹

Most tourists visit our city ------- winter.

(A) at
(B) in

확인 문제 ❺

The client meeting will be delayed ------- January 31.

(A) within
(B) until

확인 문제 ❻

The stock price has increased ------- the past five years.

(A) for
(B) during

정답 ❹ (B) ❺ (B) ❻ (A)

PART 5 문법 전치사 (1)   143

적용 기술

[기적의 필기노트] 110P
RC 기술 23

🔒 확인 문제 ❼

Please leave your feedback ------- our Web site.

(A) in
(B) on

출제 포인트

under는 '~하에, ~중인'이라는 뜻으로도 자주 출제돼요.

under construction
under discussion
under negotiation

🔒 확인 문제 ❽

The sales are increasing ------- a new commercial.

(A) because
(B) thanks to

적용 기술

[기적의 필기노트] 111P
RC 기술 25

🔒 확인 문제 ❾

The details ------- the new coffee machine are written in the manual.

(A) regarding
(B) with

정답 ❼ (B) ❽ (B) ❾ (A)

출제 유형 3
장소/위치/방향 전치사

1 at/on/in

- 장소 전치사 at, on, in은 뒤에 오는 장소 표현에 따라 구별하여 씁니다.

at	구체적인 지점이나 장소	at the subway station 지하철역에서
on	표면에 붙어 있는 경우(층, 선반, 전시물 등), 도로, 국경 등	on the first floor 1층에 on the wall 벽에 on the street 거리에서
in	대륙, 나라, 주, 큰 도시, 공간의 내부	in the office 사무실에

2 위치/방향 전치사

to ~로   from ~에서, ~로부터   towards ~쪽으로, ~를 향해   along ~을 따라   near ~근처에
throughout ~의 전체의 걸쳐   across ~을 가로질러, ~전역에, ~의 건너편에
beside/next to ~ 옆에   above ~위에   below ~아래에   around ~ 주위에, ~ 전역에 걸쳐
through <장소/과정> ~을 거쳐/통과하여 = all over, across <수단> ~을 통해 <시간> ~내내
between ~사이에(둘 사이에) vs. among ~사이에(셋 이상 사이에)

출제 유형 4
이유/양보 전치사

- 이유/양보 전치사는 같은 의미의 접속사 및 접속부사와 구별할 수 있어야 합니다.

	전치사	접속사	접속부사
이유 (~때문에)	because of / due to / owing to / on account of / thanks to	because / since / as / now that / in that	for this reason / hence / therefore / consequently
양보 (~에도 불구하고)	despite / in spite of / notwithstanding	although / though / even though / even if / while	however / nevertheless / nonetheless

(**Despite** / ~~Although~~) the bad weather, many fans came.
악천후에도 불구하고 많은 팬들이 왔다.

출제 유형 5
'~에 관한'의 의미를 갖는 전치사

- '~에 관한'의 의미를 갖는 아래 전치사와 자주 출제되는 명사 어휘도 알아두세요.

about   on   regarding   concerning   pertaining to   as to
in[with] regard to   with respect to   with[in] reference to

- 함께 출제되는 명사 어휘: details 세부사항   information 정보   inquiries 문의사항
questions 질문   concerns 우려, 걱정
If you have inquiries **about** this job opening, feel free to contact Ms. Herald.
이 공석에 대해 문의사항이 있다면, Herald 씨에게 편하게 연락주세요.

144 기적의 토익 RC

풀이 방법 전치사 (1)

DAY 06

---

1. The new vending machine will be placed ------- the emergency exit.

(A) beside   (B) when   (C) away   (D) only

....

새 자판기는 비상구 옆에 놓일 것이다.

> **이렇게 풀어요**
>
> 1. **선택지 보고 문법/어휘 문제 파악** 선택지가 서로 다른 품사의 어휘로 구성되어 있으므로 문법 문제임을 파악할 수 있어요.
> 2. **빈칸 분석** 빈칸 앞의 동사가 수동태이므로 빈칸 뒤의 명사구 the emergency exit를 수식어로 만들어 줄 수 있는 역할을 하는 품사가 들어가야 함을 파악해요.
> 3. **정답 선택** 명사구를 수식어로 바꿔 줄 수 있는 역할을 하는 전치사 (A) beside를 정답으로 고릅니다.

---

2. Any items can be returned or exchanged ------- five days from the date of purchase.

(A) at   (B) before   (C) within   (D) of

....

모든 제품은 구입일로부터 5일 이내에 반품되거나 교환될 수 있습니다.

> **이렇게 풀어요**
>
> 1. **선택지 보고 문법/어휘 문제 파악** 선택지가 모두 전치사로 구성되어 있으므로 어휘 문제임을 파악할 수 있어요.
> 2. **빈칸 분석** 빈칸 뒤의 명사 five days를 수식어로 만들어 줄 알맞은 전치사가 들어가야 함을 파악해요.
> 3. **정답 선택** five days는 기간을 나타내는 표현이므로 '5일 이내에'라는 의미를 만들 수 있는 전치사 (C) within을 정답으로 고릅니다.

---

3. Ms. Bennett did not submit the report on time ------- a couple of deadline extensions.

(A) with   (B) although   (C) despite   (D) nonetheless

....

Bennett 씨는 몇 번의 마감기한 연장에도 불구하고 제시간에 보고서를 제출하지 않았다.

> **이렇게 풀어요**
>
> 1. **선택지 보고 문법/어휘 문제 파악** 선택지가 서로 다른 품사의 어휘로 구성되어 있으므로 문법 문제임을 파악할 수 있어요.
> 2. **빈칸 분석** 빈칸 뒤의 명사구 a couple of deadline extensions를 수식어로 만들 수 있는 알맞은 전치사가 들어가야 함을 파악해요.
> 3. **정답 선택** 빈칸 앞의 '제시간에 제출하지 않았다'와 빈칸 뒤의 '몇 번의 마감기한 연장'을 자연스럽게 이어줄 수 있는 전치사로 '~에도 불구하고'라는 의미인 (C) despite를 정답으로 고릅니다.

PART 5 문법 전치사 (1)

PART 5 어휘

형용사 어휘 (1)

각 어휘와 함께 자주 쓰이는 표현을 통째로 외워두세요.

---

01 local
지역의, 현지의

local ingredients	현지의 재료
local residents	지역 주민
local supplier	지역 공급업체

🐾 빈출 토익 선생님 Pick!

02 promising
유망한, 촉망되는

| promising location | 유망한 장소 |
| promising candidate | 유망한 후보 |

---

03 urgent
긴급한

require urgent attention	긴급한 주의를 요하다
in urgent need of	~이 긴급히 필요한
urgent matter	시급한 문제, 급한 일
urgent medical care	긴급한 치료

800+

04 ample
충분한

| ample space | 충분한 공간 |

---

05 critical
중요한, 비판적인

| it is critical that | ~는 중요하다 |
| be critical of | ~을 비평하다 |

---

06 diverse
다양한

a diverse range of	다양한 범위의
diverse attractions	다양한 볼거리
diverse line of products	다양한 제품 라인

800+

07 adequate
충분한, 적절한

| adequate for | ~에 적절한 |
| adequate funding | 충분한 자금 지원 |

🐾 빈출 토익 선생님 Pick!

08 outstanding
뛰어난, 중요한, 미지불된

outstanding employee/candidate	뛰어난 직원/후보
outstanding performance	뛰어난 실적
outstanding balance	미불 잔고

900+

09 concentrated
집중적인

| concentrated effort | 집중적인 노력 |

900+

10 bound
~할 것 같은, ~할 가능성이 큰

| be bound to부정사 | ~할 것 같다 |

🐾 빈출 토익 선생님 Pick!

11 eligible
자격이 있는, 적격의

| eligible to부정사 | ~할 자격이 있는 |
| eligible for | ~에 자격이 있는 |

---

12 harsh
가혹한, 혹독한

| harsh reviews | 가혹한 평가, 혹평 |

800+

13 collective
집단의, 공동의

| collective effort | 공동의 노력 |

---

14 steady
꾸준한, 안정된

steady progress	꾸준한 발전
steady growth	꾸준한 성장
remain steady	안정된 상태를 유지하다

---

15 exclusive
독점적인, 전용의

| exclusive use | 전용 |
| exclusive access | 독점적 사용 |

146 기적의 토익 RC

🐾 빈출 토익 선생님 Pick!

16 preferred 선호되는

one's preferred option	선호되는 옵션
preferred means of	선호되는 방법
preferred but not required	선호하지만 필수는 아닌

🐾 빈출 토익 선생님 Pick!

17 relevant 관련 있는, 적절한

information relevant to	~에 관련된 정보
have relevant experience	관련 경험이 있다
relevant terms	관련된 약관

18 routine 일상의, 정기적인

| routine inspection | 정기 점검 |
| routine visit | 정기 방문 |

19 comparable 비슷한, 비교할 만한

| comparable to | ~와 비교할 수 있는 |
| comparable with | ~와 견줄만한 |

20 continual 반복되는, 빈번한

| provide continual updates | 빈번한 업데이트를 제공하다 |

21 challenging 힘든, 도전적인

| challenging task/work | 도전적인 일/업무 |

22 accurate 정확한

| accurate inventory control | 정확한 재고 관리 |
| accurate information | 정확한 정보 |

🐾 빈출 토익 선생님 Pick!

23 extensive 대규모의, 폭넓은

| extensive experience | 폭넓은 경험 |
| extensive selection of | 광범위한 |

24 temporary 일시적인, 임시의

temporary inconvenience	일시적인 불편
temporary suspension	임시 중단
temporary job	임시직

25 common 흔한, 보통의, 공동의

| common goal | 공동의 목적 |
| common ground | 공통점 |

🐾 빈출 토익 선생님 Pick!

26 defective 결함이 있는

defective item	결함이 있는 품목
defective product	결함이 있는 제품
defective merchandise	결함이 있는 상품

DAY 06

🧑‍🏫 풀이 방법

An emergency response team is ready in case a guest needs ------- medical care.

(A) durable   (B) fluent   (C) similar   (D) urgent

손님에게 긴급한 치료가 필요한 경우에 대비하여 비상 대응 팀이 대기하고 있다.

> **🔖 이렇게 풀어요**
>
> **1. 선택지 보고 문법/어휘 문제 파악** 선택지가 서로 다른 형용사 어휘로 구성되어 있으므로 어휘 문제임을 파악해요.
> **2. 빈칸 분석** 빈칸 뒤의 medical care와 문맥상 어울릴 수 있는 형용사가 들어가야 함을 파악합니다.
> **3. 정답 선택** '긴급한 치료'라는 의미가 되는 것이 자연스러우므로 (D) urgent를 정답으로 고릅니다.

PART 5 어휘 형용사 어휘 (1) 147

따라 하면 문제가 풀리는

연습 문제

앞서 학습한 문제 풀이법을 적용하여 맞는 것에 ✔ 표시 하거나 괄호 안에
적절한 답을 쓰고 정답을 선택하세요.

01 You can return or exchange ------- merchandise within 7 business days of your purchase.

(A) routine
(B) exclusive
(C) diverse
(D) defective

1. 선택지 보고 문법/어휘 문제 파악하기 ☐ 문법 문제 ☐ 어휘 문제
2. 빈칸 분석하기　빈칸 앞에 있는 동사 exchange의 의미 (　　　)
　　　　　　　　 빈칸 뒤에 있는 명사 merchandise의 의미 (　　　)
　　　　　　　　 → 문맥상 위의 동사, 명사와 함께 쓰일 수 있는 형용사를 답으로 고른다.
3. 정답 선택하기　정답 (　　　)

02 All researchers should clear the security check ------- entering the lab.

(A) every
(B) before
(C) rather
(D) even

1. 선택지 보고 문법/어휘 문제 파악하기 ☐ 문법 문제 ☐ 어휘 문제
2. 빈칸 분석하기　빈칸 뒤에 있는 것 ☐ 동명사 ☐ 동사원형
　　　　　　　　 → 빈칸은 ☐ 부사 ☐ 전치사 자리이다.
3. 정답 선택하기　정답 (　　　)

03 Visitors can enjoy a panoramic city view ------- McCarthy Tower.

(A) during
(B) due to
(C) into
(D) at

1. 선택지 보고 문법/어휘 문제 파악하기 ☐ 문법 문제 ☐ 어휘 문제
2. 빈칸 분석하기　빈칸 뒤 명사가 의미하는 것 ☐ 구체적인 장소 ☐ 기간
3. 정답 선택하기　정답 (　　　)

정답 및 해설 p.45

04 ------- the rainy weather, the soccer match was held as scheduled.

(A) Regardless
(B) As well as
(C) Despite
(D) If only

1. 선택지 보고 문법/어휘 문제 파악하기 ☐문법 문제 ☐어휘 문제
2. 빈칸 분석하기 빈칸 뒤에 있는 것 ☐동사구 ☐명사구
   → 빈칸은 ☐부사 ☐전치사 자리이다.
3. 정답 선택하기 정답 (   )

05 All of the serving staff members are requested to work extra shifts ------- the peak season.

(A) beside
(B) during
(C) beyond
(D) for

1. 선택지 보고 문법/어휘 문제 파악하기 ☐문법 문제 ☐어휘 문제
2. 빈칸 분석하기 빈칸 앞뒤 문맥을 연결할 수 있는 의미 ☐~ 옆에 ☐~ 너머 ☐~ 동안
   → 정답의 후보 2개 (,   )
   → 빈칸 뒤 명사가 ☐확정된 기간을 나타내는 명사 ☐구체적인 숫자 표현으로 나타낸 기간이다.
3. 정답 선택하기 정답 (   )

06 The cheese products are located ------- the milk and meat sections.

(A) between
(B) upon
(C) for
(D) among

1. 선택지 보고 문법/어휘 문제 파악하기 ☐문법 문제 ☐어휘 문제
2. 빈칸 분석하기 빈칸 뒤에 있는 접속사 (   )
3. 정답 선택하기 정답 (   )

PART 5 전치사 (1) / 형용사 어휘 (1)   149

DAY 01-06 누적 문제

제한시간 9분입니다! 시~작!

01. ------ road work on Main Street, drivers are advised to take a detour along Forrest Lane.

(A) Due to
(B) As long as
(C) Whereas
(D) Even though

02. Some students at Dawson Academy complain that they are not given ------ time to complete tests.

(A) concentrated
(B) adequate
(C) continual
(D) bound

03. Mr. Todd passed around handouts ------ starting the weekly management meeting.

(A) so that
(B) before
(C) along
(D) therefore

04. Mr. Burke will lead the training workshop ------ Bronson Community Center.

(A) at
(B) to
(C) on
(D) from

05. Subscribers to *Innovations Monthly* can access the digital version of the magazine ------ registering online.

(A) inside
(B) about
(C) after
(D) onto

06. Please leave boxes or packages ------ the door if no one is present at the address.

(A) beside
(B) since
(C) in
(D) toward

07. The order delivery will not be made ------ the afternoon because one of our delivery trucks broke down.

(A) among
(B) until
(C) for
(D) into

08. Employees are invited to come to the award dinner ------ 6:30 tomorrow evening.

(A) by
(B) on
(C) from
(D) out

09. Here at Daytona Hotel, we strive to provide the best possible service to ------ guests.

(A) we
(B) us
(C) our
(D) ours

10. ------ the next academic year, history professors are expected to create a new curriculum.

(A) Over
(B) Every
(C) Responded
(D) Without

11. Mr. Hughes may not have much experience teaching children, but his background in education is ------.

(A) preferred
(B) harsh
(C) extensive
(D) challenging

12. Although currency values may vary ------ the day, Sydney Bank offers the best exchange rate within 24 hours.

(A) throughout
(B) concerning
(C) as for
(D) below

150   기적의 토익 RC

13. Dakota Livestock, which supplied ------- 75,000 tons of beef to clients last year, was acquired by a Canadian company yesterday.

(A) outside
(B) over
(C) for
(D) through

14. Due to a problem with its supplier, Jay's Italian Restaurant has not offered seafood dishes -------.

(A) greatly
(B) recently
(C) shortly
(D) willingly

15. The focus group indicated that most people have an ------- low interest in playing old-fashioned board games.

(A) extreme
(B) extremely
(C) extremes
(D) extremity

16. Stein Investments has now become ------- for its clients' losses.

(A) account
(B) accounts
(C) accounting
(D) accountable

17. Valdez Company's stock value has risen steadily ------- the past three quarters.

(A) for
(B) with
(C) on
(D) as

18. There has been a noticeable ------- in movie streaming service subscriptions in the past year.

(A) increases
(B) increased
(C) increasing
(D) increase

19. Thanks to paid training and tuition reimbursement programs, Vargas Tech is a ------- company to work for.

(A) missing
(B) promising
(C) following
(D) presiding

20. Hooper Industries hired Antwan Ray as a software engineer ------- his lack of experience.

(A) although
(B) as if
(C) since
(D) despite

21. If you have a bachelor's degree or higher, you are ------- to apply for the position.

(A) steady
(B) eligible
(C) exclusive
(D) common

22. Ms. Brandt will only answer questions that are ------- to the seminar topic during the press conference.

(A) routine
(B) relevant
(C) collective
(D) defective

23. Customers tend to compare prices online ------- placing an order.

(A) aside from
(B) in spite of
(C) prior to
(D) across from

24. Channel 7 News is known for giving ------- weather forecasts.

(A) comparable
(B) accurate
(C) temporary
(D) equal

PART 5 전치사 (1) / 형용사 어휘 (1)   151

PART 6

알맞은 문장 고르기 - 선택지에 대명사 [800+]

문장 고르기 문제는 선택지를 먼저 보고 대략적인 내용/특징을 파악합니다.

✎ 적용 기술

[기적의 필기노트] 165P
RC 기술 83

📖 VOCA

tool 도구
regular 일반적인, 보통의
blender 믹서기
feature 특징, 기능
handle 다루다
blade (칼·도구의) 날

🙋 풀이 방법 review

○ 해석 p.48

As a person who does a lot of cooking at home, the Mix o' Matic is a great kitchen tool. It is easier to use than a regular blender. It just has a single dial for speed! ------- that, it also has special features that make it safe even for a child to handle.
⚡ PART 5

For example, there is a sensor that stops the blade if your fingers get too close to them. -------. That is probably my favorite thing about the Mix o' Matic.
　　　　　01.

---

01. (A) I have been using my Mix o' Matic for a little over a year.
　　　(B) It took a long time to develop the safety features.
　　　(C) Many other customers have left reviews.
　　　(D) Most of all, it makes cleanup much easier.

✔ 이렇게 풀어요

1. 선택지 특징 파악 문장 고르기 문제이므로 선택지를 먼저 보고 대략적인 내용이나 특징을 파악합니다.
(A) 믹서기를 사용한 기간 언급
(B) 안전 기능을 개발하는 데 오래 걸림
(C) 고객들이 후기를 남겼음
(D) 훨씬 쉽게 세척할 수 있음

2. 빈칸 분석 빈칸 앞에 믹서기의 여러 장점이 나열되어 있고, 빈칸 뒤에 그것(빈칸)이 자신이 가장 좋아하는 점이라고 했으므로, 빈칸에도 장점 중 하나가 들어가야 함을 파악해요.

3. 정답 선택 선택지 중 장점에 관한 내용인 (D)를 정답으로 선택합니다.

○ 해설

빈칸 뒤에 명사 역할을 하는 대명사(that)가 있으므로 전치사가 들어가야 합니다. 따라서 유일한 전치사인 (D)가 정답입니다.

⚡ PART 5 문법 적용 문제

------- that, it also has special features that make it safe even for a child to handle.

(A) Although　　　(B) Because　　　(C) Nevertheless　　　(D) Despite

152　기적의 토익 RC

따라 하면 문제가 풀리는

연습 문제

빈칸 앞뒤 내용에서 단서가 될 부분을 찾아 표시하세요.
표시한 것을 바탕으로 정답 어휘를 선택하세요.

🔾 정답 및 해설 p.48

01

> The CEO of West Side Industries, Michelle Baker, held a press conference yesterday after a quarterly board meeting. -------. It would start by opening branches in Montreal and Toronto.

(A) She announced her intention of expanding the company internationally.
(B) The company is known for its high-quality products.

02

> Employees at Lucas Manufacturing have gone on strike. -------. Union leader Janet Bay is set to meet with the company's board members tomorrow afternoon.

(A) A 20% rise in profits was recorded last year.
(B) They are demanding a pay increase and health benefits.

03

> *News 5* has earned an outstanding reputation for its balanced reporting on important national events. -------. The ceremony will be held this Saturday at 8 P.M.

(A) A new reporting team is needed to cover international events.
(B) It has been selected for the Excellence in Journalism Award at the Annual TV Awards.

04

> As a member of the Sally's Seafood Shack team, you are expected to come to work in a clean uniform. -------. Just submit them to the manager's office.

(A) We will reimburse your dry cleaning expenses if you have receipts.
(B) There will be a special promotion running all next month.

PART 6 알맞은 문장 고르기-선택지에 대명사   153

 토익에 나올

실전 문제

제한시간 4분입니다! 시~작!

Questions 01-04 refer to the following article.

Festival of Light

The city of New Rochelle will be celebrating the new year with the Festival of Light. This annual event has attracted tourists from all around the region ever ------- it first started nearly 20 years ago.
01.
This year, Central Park will be adorned with strings of colorful lights. -------. With this new feature,
02.
more people are expected to visit after sundown. Couples, families, and friends all come together to admire the beautiful scenery and take pictures. Professional photographers also ------- the area,
03.
often offering to take pictures for people who come to the park. The city ------- this festival and
04.
admission is free for everyone, so pay a visit to Central Park in New Rochelle before the lights are taken down in January.

01. (A) over
   (B) since
   (C) from
   (D) for

유형 적용 문제
02. (A) Information about the festival will be distributed by the Department of Tourism.
   (B) Photos of last year's event have been posted on the city's Web site.
   (C) They will be turned on at sundown and remain lit until midnight.
   (D) Parking passes can be obtained from City Hall.

03. (A) would have frequent
   (B) frequent
   (C) will frequent
   (D) had been frequenting

04. (A) funds
   (B) guides
   (C) rents
   (D) transfers

Questions 05-08 refer to the following review.

Over That Hill is an exciting children's book that can also be ------- for adults. The main character is
05.
a snail. She is much faster than you would expect, though. -------. *Over That Hill* has some realistic
06.
situations that are easy for anyone to ------- to. I was easily able to understand how the main
07.
character felt. ------- the great story, the illustrations are absolutely beautiful. After reading this book,
08.
I bought a copy for each of my friends with young kids.

05. (A) enjoy
    (B) enjoying
    (C) enjoyed
    (D) enjoyable

유형 적용 문제
06. (A) Some children would be disappointed by the
        ending.
    (B) Unfortunately, the book can only be purchased
        online.
    (C) The author stated that the story was originally
        meant for adults.
    (D) She can outrun animals that she never could in
        the real world!

07. (A) read
    (B) greet
    (C) relate
    (D) overcome

08. (A) Far from
    (B) Close to
    (C) Ahead of
    (D) Aside from

PART 7

이메일 (1) 문제 제기 이메일

이메일은 싱글, 더블, 트리플 지문에서 모두 출제되므로 충분히 연습해 두어야 합니다.

✎ 적용 기술

[기적의 필기노트] 172P
RC 기술 88

이메일은 PART 7에서 가장 출제 비중이 높은 지문입니다. 지문 상단의 To, From, Subject 부분을 통해 수신자, 발신자, 제목을 우선적으로 확인하고 지문을 읽으면 내용을 수월하게 파악할 수 있습니다. 문제를 제기하는 이메일은 주로 배송 문제나 상품 결함, 일정 문제 등의 내용이 출제됩니다.

문제 제기 이메일에 자주 출제되는 어휘

문제 제기 이메일에서 자주 출제되는 문제

· 목적 문제
목적 문제의 답으로는 To file a complaint, To complain about으로 시작하는 선택지가 정답이 될 확률이 높아요.
What is the purpose of the e-mail?
→ To file a complaint 불만을 제기하기 위해서/ To complain about late delivery 늦은 배송에 대해 불평하기 위해서

1 주문/배송 관련 문제 제기

shipment	수송(품)	order	주문(품)
missing	분실한	incident	사건, 일
load	화물, 짐	back order	이월 주문(재고가 없어 미룬 주문)
overdue	지불 기한이 넘은	shipment	수송
courier	택배 회사, 배달원	contain	포함하다
resolve	해결하다	merchandise	물품, 상품
package	소포	receipt	영수증
mishandle	잘못 처리하다	overnight delivery	익일 배송
on one's behalf	~를 대신하여	refund	환불; 환불하다

2 상품 결함 관련 문제 제기

crack	결함, 틈; 금이 가다	visible	눈에 보이는
faulty	흠이 있는	primarily	주로
damage	손상, 훼손	malfunction	고장; 고장나다
acknowledge	인정하다	figure	수치
affect	영향을 미치다	inspect	점검하다
occasion	경우	regarding	~와 관련한
suitable	적합한	in bulk	대량으로
presumably	아마, 짐작건대	concern	우려
misprint	오타	complaint	불만
issue	(신문, 잡지 등의) 호	keep track of	~을 추적하다
be aware of	~을 알아차리다	expedite	신속히 처리하다
in-store	매장 내의	accompany	동반하다

156 기적의 토익 RC

풀이방법 문제 제기 이메일

e-mail
해석 p.50

To: cust.serv@primoauto.com
From: d.wade@bmail.com
Date: 9 August
Subject: Order #8784484

Dear Service Representative,

I was in your store looking for a new air filter for my car last week, but the staff there told me that the size I needed was gone and helped me place an order for one. He told me that I would have to pay shipping for the item since it's not normally in your store.

After receiving my order, I looked at the invoice. I was charged $3 for shipping and $7 for the filter, bringing the total to $10. However, your store's sale flyer for this week shows the exact same product I ordered on sale for $7. It seems that your staff made a mistake when I was there. Since I wasn't able to pick it up from your store, I think that you should refund the cost of shipping to me. Please let me know if you can do this.

Sincerely,

Devin Wade

---

01. The word "gone" in paragraph 1, line 2 is closest in meaning to

(A) missing
(B) finished
(C) unavailable
(D) replaceable

02. How much does Mr. Wade expect to be refunded?

(A) $3
(B) $7
(C) $10
(D) $20

이렇게 풀어요

01. 문단 두번째 줄의 단어 "gone"과 의미상 가장 가까운 것은

(A) 분실한
(B) 끝난
(C) 구입할 수 없는
(D) 교체 가능한

해설 지문에서 gone은 원하는 사이즈가 없다는 의미로 쓰였습니다. 따라서 '구입할 수 없는'이라는 의미의 unavailable과 의미가 가장 가까우므로 (C)가 정답입니다.

02. Wade 씨는 얼마나 환불받을 것으로 예상하는가?

(A) 3달러
(B) 7달러
(C) 10달러
(D) 20달러

해설 두 번째 단락 초반부에 I was charged $3 for shipping에서 배송비로 3달러를 청구받았다고 했는데 후반부에 you should refund the cost of shipping to me에서 배송비를 환불받아야 한다고 했으므로 (A)가 정답입니다.

PART 7 이메일 (1) 문제 제기 이메일   157

따라 하면 문제가 풀리는

연습 문제

먼저 문제의 키워드에 표시한 후,
지문에서 단서를 찾아 적절한 답을 고르세요.

01 e-mail

To: Paper Express <info@paper-express.net>
From: Crystal Cho <ccho@wendtinsurance.com>
Date: November 16
Subject: Order #49580

Dear Paper Express,

I recently placed a large order for paper for Wendt Insurance. It included standard white copy paper in both A3 and A4 sizes, pads of lined paper, and premium résumé paper. The order was supposed to arrive two days ago, but we still don't have it. Please look into this matter, as we will have to purchase our paper elsewhere if we do not receive the items within a few days.

Crystal Cho

Q. What is the purpose of the e-mail?

(A) To report a late delivery
(B) To add items to an order

02 e-mail

To: Serrano Apparel <customerservice@serranoapparel.com>
From: Roy Newman <roy_newman@victoriasales.com>
Date: March 28
Subject: Defective item

Dear Customer Service,

I purchased a denim jacket from your Web site last week (order #29805), but the seam on one of the sleeves is torn. Please let me know how I can get a replacement for this item. I'd like this matter to be taken care of as soon as possible, as I'm going on a trip to San Diego next week and would like to take the jacket with me. You can reach me by phone at 555-5490.

Roy Newman

Q. Why does Mr. Newman want a problem to be settled quickly?

(A) He wants to take advantage of a sale.
(B) He plans to go out of town soon.

03 e-mail

To: Patrick Webster <webster.p@montgomeryautos.com>
From: Roma Senhar <senhar.r@montgomeryautos.com>
Date: September 3
Subject: Mandatory training

Dear Mr. Webster,

I received your memo about the mandatory training session for staff on September 22. Unfortunately, my team has a scheduling conflict. We will be at the National Automotive Trade Fair for that entire week. Could you record the session? That way, my team can watch it on video when they get back. I think this is the best solution to avoid postponing the training. Please let me know what you think.

Roma Senhar

Q. What does Ms. Senhar ask Mr. Webster to do?

(A) Change the date of a training session
(B) Make a video of a training session

04 e-mail

To: Niagara Power Company <billing@npc.com>
From: Penelope Snowe <p.snowe@nmail.com>
Date: 3 July
Subject: Late fee

To Whom it May Concern,

I was out of town on business for several weeks last month. When I returned, I found my monthly electric bill from your company was already past due. I'll pay the $5 late fee this time, but I don't want to have this problem again. Please let me know what I need to do to have the amount of my electric bill directly taken from my checking account each month.

Sincerely,

Penelope Snowe

Q. What is true about Ms. Snowe?

(A) She wants to set up automatic payments.
(B) She recently interviewed for a new job.

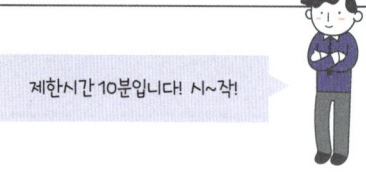

제한시간 10분입니다! 시~작!

Questions 01-02 refer to the following e-mail.

E-mail	
To:	Joseph Bader <baderjoseph@cedartech1.com>
From:	Riddell Inc. <orders@riddellinc.com>
Date:	October 11
Subject:	A message from Riddell Inc.

Dear Mr. Bader,

The leather armchair that you recently ordered from Riddell Inc. is out of stock. This was not indicated in our online catalog as it should have been. We will not be receiving a new shipment from the manufacturer for two weeks, so I'm afraid this item will arrive at your home much later than expected. If you do not want to wait, how about choosing chocolate brown instead of chestnut brown? It does not look very different, and it could be sent as early as tomorrow morning. You can visit your account page to make adjustments.

Thank you for your understanding, and we apologize for the inconvenience.

Charles Hart
Customer Service Agent, Riddell Inc.

01. What is the purpose of the e-mail?

(A) To thank a customer for providing feedback
(B) To confirm the receipt of a payment
(C) To inform a customer of a delivery delay
(D) To explain a change in shipping fees

02. What does Mr. Hart suggest doing?

(A) Selecting a different color
(B) Placing a rush order
(C) Checking with another branch
(D) Viewing an online catalog

---

paraphrasing 주어진 어휘 또는 표현과 패러프레이징 될 수 있는 것을 연결하세요.

1. choose • • (a) select
2. make adjustments • • (b) change
3. arrive much later than expected • • (c) be delayed

160 기적의 토익 RC

정답 및 해설 p.51

Questions 03-04 refer to the following e-mail.

To: Judy Yu
From: William Ponce
Date: 18 June
Subject: Your latest business trip

Dear Judy,

I got your e-mail reporting the expenses from your business trip last week. However, there seems to be a problem. When I tried to open the attachments, I got an error message saying that the files had been corrupted. I know that our company accepts electronic receipts now, but in this case, I'm going to need you to send me a proof of purchase for each of your business related expenses. The IT team has already been informed of this issue, but in the meantime, I can't process your reimbursement until you send me those documents.

Thanks in advance for your understanding!

- William Ponce

03. What problem does Mr. Ponce mention?

(A) Some clients rejected a contract.
(B) Some files could not be viewed.
(C) A business trip was postponed.
(D) A company policy has changed.

04. What should Ms. Yu send to Mr. Ponce?

(A) Emergency contact information
(B) A revised business contract
(C) Results of a client meeting
(D) Copies of receipts

---

paraphrasing 주어진 어휘 또는 표현과 패러프레이징 될 수 있는 것을 연결하세요.

1. problem •   • (a) receipts
2. attachments •   • (b) issue
3. proof of purchase •   • (c) files

PART 7 이메일 (1) 문제 제기 이메일   161

 실전 문제

Questions 05-07 refer to the following e-mail.

To: Abigail Ruiz <ruiza@caxtonltd.com>
From: Hua Cheng <chenghua@orlandns.org>
Date: June 30
Subject: Community Center

Dear Ms. Ruiz,

My name is Hua Cheng, and I am the president of the Orland Nature Society, a community group dedicated to environmental issues that affect Orland. I recently read about the city council's proposal to demolish a portion of Hutchinson Park in order to expand the local community center and its parking lot. I am worried that the current plans have not taken all factors into consideration. Although Hutchinson Park is not very popular among residents, it serves as an essential habitat for a number of rare bird species, as well as other small animals. It must be protected. I believe that building a multi-story parking lot for the community center could be the solution, as it would not take up any additional space. Some of my fellow society members and I will voice our support for this alternative at the upcoming city council meeting next week. I hope you and the rest of the council will take our comments under advisement.

Sincerely,

Hua Cheng

05. Why did Mr. Cheng send the e-mail?

(A) To invite Ms. Ruiz to join a club
(B) To volunteer for a community event
(C) To express concern about a project
(D) To plan a park cleanup day

06. What is suggested about Hutchinson Park?

(A) It is near Mr. Cheng's home.
(B) It is the largest park in the area.
(C) It is home to a variety of wildlife.
(D) It has a multi-story parking lot.

07. What does Mr. Cheng plan to do next week?

(A) Attend a public meeting
(B) Visit Ms. Ruiz's office
(C) Vote in an election
(D) Post some comments online

paraphrasing 주어진 어휘 또는 표현과 패러프레이징 될 수 있는 것을 연결하세요.

1. demolish •   • (a) destroy
2. expand •   • (b) home
3. habitat •   • (c) widen

162 기적의 토익 RC

Questions 08-10 refer to the following e-mail.

● ● ●

To: Maine Hardware <cust.serv@mainehardware.com>
From: Henry Barrera <h.barrera@rmail.com>
Date: 9 June
Subject: Order #HR2285544

To Whom It May Concern,

I ordered a Brickson power drill and some other tools from your online store last week. The package arrived today, and I was very disappointed to find that the drill has something wrong. I followed the instructions and even tried changing the battery, but it will not turn on. I need that power tool this weekend because I've been hired to build a deck. My client will not be happy if I have to postpone the project. It's important that you replace this drill as quickly as possible. Since I am a loyal customer, I expect that you will send me another Brickson power drill via express delivery service. I will go to the post office this afternoon to send back the original drill.

Sincerely,

Henry Barrera

08. What is the problem with an item in Mr. Barerra's order?

(A) It is the wrong brand.
(B) It is defective.
(C) It is missing a part.
(D) It did not arrive on time.

09. Why does Mr. Barrera request an item to be replaced urgently?

(A) He needs it to complete a job.
(B) He plans to move to a new address.
(C) He wants to give it as a gift.
(D) He is supposed to start a home project.

10. What does Mr. Barrera expect the company to do?

(A) Apologize for a mistake
(B) Waive a fee
(C) Issue a refund
(D) Use express shipping

---

paraphrasing 주어진 어휘 또는 표현과 패러프레이징 될 수 있는 것을 연결하세요.

1. instructions •
2. drill •
3. delivery •

• (a) shipping
• (b) tool
• (c) manual

PART 7 이메일 (1) 문제 제기 이메일 163

'멋진 당신, 오늘도 화이팅'

DAY

07

오늘의 학습 포인트

PART 5. 전치사 (2)

1. 분사 형태의 전치사 - following, including, given 등
2. 두 단어 이상으로 이루어진 전치사 - instead of, prior to, in charge of, as a result of 등
3. 동명사와 자주 쓰이는 전치사 - before, after, by, upon + -ing
4. 전치사 숙어 - 자동사 + 전치사/타동사 + 목적어 + 전치사/명사 + 전치사/ 형용사 + 전치사
5. 전치사 관용 표현 - until further notice, in one's absence, in advance 등

PART 6. 순서를 나타내는 형용사 어휘

보기가 initial, final, previous 등. 시간 표현 단서 찾기!

PART 7. 정보 전달 이메일

출제 비중 ↑. <목적 - 세부 내용 - 요청사항>의 순서로 지문 전개

PART 5 문법

전치사 (2)

특정 전치사와 쓰이는 숙어 표현이 출제되므로 동사와 전치사를 묶어서 암기하세요.

✎ **적용 기술**

[기적의 필기노트] 111P
RC 기술 25

출제 유형 1
분사 형태의 전치사

`800+`

· -ing 또는 p.p.로 끝나는 분사 형태의 전치사도 있다는 점을 알아두세요.

following ~ 후에	considering ~을 고려하여	given ~을 감안할 때
including ~을 포함하여	pending ~가 있을 때까지	excluding ~을 제외하고

Following the sessions, the reception will be held in the cafeteria.
그 시간 후에 카페테리아에서 리셉션이 열릴 것이다.

· following은 형용사로 '다음의'라는 의미로 출제되기도 합니다.
Mr. Kerrigan will present his proposal at the **following** board meeting.
Kerrigan 씨는 그의 제안서를 다음 이사회에서 발표할 것이다.

· considering은 부사절 접속사로도 쓰입니다. 동일한 의미의 전치사 given은 that과 함께 접속사로 사용돼요.
Considering[Given that] he has such a long work experience, Mr. Malcom is well qualified for this position.
그가 그토록 오랜 경력을 가지고 있는 것을 고려하면, Malcom 씨는 이 직책에 적임자이다.

출제 포인트

considering이 가장 자주 출제돼요.

🔒 **확인 문제 ❶**

------- her presentation, she answered questions from potential clients.

(A) Followed
(B) Following

출제 유형 2
두 단어 이상으로 이루어진 전치사

1 두 단어 전치사

instead of ~ 대신에	according to ~에 따르면	prior to ~ 이전에	ahead of ~에 앞서
along with ~와 함께	such as ~와 같은	as of + 시점 ~부로	regardless of ~와 관계없이

Many people make a payment by credit cards **instead of** cash.
많은 사람들이 현금 대신 신용카드로 지불한다.

`800+`

2 세 단어 이상 전치사

in response to ~에 응하여	in celebration of ~을 축하하여	in honor of ~을 기념하여
in terms of ~의 면에서	in charge of ~을 책임지는	in case of ~의 경우에
in observance of ~을 준수[기념]하여	in compliance with ~을 준수하여	in favor of ~을 찬성하여
in light of ~을 고려하여	on the basis of ~을 기반으로	as a result of ~의 결과로

He is **in charge of** the renovation project. 그는 그 개조 공사 프로젝트를 책임지고 있다.

I'm writing **in response to** your request. 귀하의 요청에 대해 답변 드립니다.

🔒 **확인 문제 ❷**

You have to submit your application form ------- the processing fee.

(A) such as
(B) along with

출제 포인트

세 단어 이상으로 구성된 전치사의 경우 명사 어휘 문제 또는 명사 앞뒤의 전치사를 묻는 문제로 주로 출제돼요.

정답 ❶ (B) ❷ (B)

166 기적의 토익 RC

출제 유형 3

동명사와 자주 쓰이는 전치사

· 동명사와 자주 쓰이는 빈출 전치사를 알아두세요.

before -ing ~하기 전에	after -ing ~한 후에
by -ing ~함으로써	for -ing ~하기 위해서
in -ing ~함에 있어	on/upon -ing ~하자마자
without -ing ~하지 않고	instead of -ing ~하는 것 대신에

Upon completing this course, a certificate will be issued.
이 과정을 수료하자마자, 증명서가 발급될 것입니다.

We can install your new carpet **without** disrupting your daily store operation.
당신의 가게 운영을 방해하지 않고 우리는 새로운 카펫을 설치할 수 있습니다.

The manager decided to replace the broken printer **instead of** repairing it.
매니저는 고장 난 프린터를 수리하는 대신에 교체하기로 결정했다.

🔒 **확인 문제 ❸**

Please wear a protective helmet ------- entering the construction site.

(A) with
(B) before

출제 유형 4

전치사 숙어

✎ **적용 기술**

[기적의 필기노트] 111P
RC 기술 24

1 자동사 + 전치사

· 전치사에 주의해서 동사를 암기하세요. 특히, 두 종류의 전치사를 쓰는 자동사에 주의하세요.

comply with ~을 따르다	benefit from ~에서 이득을 얻다
interfere with ~을 방해하다	specialize in ~을 전문으로 하다
depend on ~에 의존하다, ~에 달려 있다	rely upon ~에 의존하다
qualify for ~의 자격을 얻다	focus on ~에 집중하다
collaborate on[with] ~에 대해[~와] 협동하다	register for/enroll in ~에 등록하다
contribute to ~에 기여하다	appeal to ~의 관심을 끌다

Many researchers have come to **rely upon** artificial intelligence.
많은 연구자들이 인공 지능에 의존하게 되었다.

Business success **depends** heavily **on** advertising. 사업 성공은 광고에 크게 달려 있다.

🔒 **확인 문제 ❹**

You will qualify ------- a free item.

(A) for
(B) as

2 타동사 + 목적어 + 전치사

· 중간에 목적어가 온다는 점에 주의하여 암기하세요. 동사와 전치사 모두 빈칸으로 출제될 수 있습니다.

give A to B A를 B에게 주다	offer A to B A를 B에게 제공하다
send A to B A를 B에게 보내다	submit A to B A를 B에게 제출하다
issue A to B A를 B에게 발급하다	donate A to B A를 B에게 기부하다
extend A to B A를 B까지 연장하다	add A to B A를 B에 더하다
return A to B A를 B로 돌려보내다	import A from B A를 B로부터 수입하다
obtain A from B A를 B로부터 얻다	recommend A for B A를 B에게 추천하다
provide A with B A에게 B를 제공하다	share A with B A를 B와 공유하다
transform A into B A를 B로 변형시키다	transfer A to B A를 B로 옮기다
replace A with B A를 B로 대체하다	reward A with B A를 B로 보상하다

Ms. Cooper will **share** her ideas **with** her team members.
Cooper 씨는 그녀의 아이디어를 팀원들과 공유할 것이다.

🔒 **확인 문제 ❺**

He obtained permission ------- his supervisor.

(A) from
(B) to

(A) ❺ (A) ❹ (B) ❸ **정답**

PART 5 문법 전치사 (2) **167**

3 명사 + 전치사

- '명사 + 전치사' 관용어구는 명사와 전치사 모두 빈칸으로 출제될 수 있습니다.

access to ~에 대한 접근, 이용	addition to ~에 추가	admission to ~로의 입장
compliance with ~의 준수	emphasis on ~에 대한 강조	exposure to ~에 노출
interest in ~에 대한 관심	investment in ~에 대한 투자	objection to ~에 대한 반대
perspective on ~에 대한 관점	proximity to ~에 가까움	enthusiasm for ~에 대한 열정
problem with ~의 문제	demand for ~에 대한 수요	awareness of ~의 인식
standard for ~에 대한 기준	relationship between ~ 사이의 관계	increase in ~의 증가
decrease in ~의 감소	decline/drop in ~의 감소	approval for ~에 대한 승인

Demand for direct flights is drastically increasing.
직항 비행편에 대한 수요가 급격히 증가하고 있다.

Access to client information is restricted. 고객 정보에 대한 접근은 제한되어 있다.

4 형용사 + 전치사

- 전치사와 짝꿍으로 암기하세요. 'be + 형용사 + 전치사' 구문을 묻는 형태로도 출제됩니다.

responsible for ~에 책임이 있는	available for ~에게 가능한
appropriate for ~에 적합한	adequate for ~에 적합한
close to ~에 가까운	acceptable to ~가 받아들일 수 있는
relevant to ~와 관련 있는	dependent[reliant] on ~에 의존하는
aware of ~을 인식하는	compatible with ~와 호환이 되는
subject to ~될 수 있는	adjacent to ~에 인접한

This modified terms and conditions were **acceptable to** both parties.
수정된 조건들은 두 당사자가 받아들일 만했다.

출제 유형 5

전치사 관용 표현

- 전치사 부분이 빈칸으로 출제되거나 표현 전체가 문제로 출제될 수 있으므로 통째로 암기하세요.

until further notice 추후 공지가 있을 때까지	without delay 지체 없이
within city limits 시 경계 내에	with enthusiasm 열심히, 열중하여
under pressure 압박을 받는	in one's absence ~의 부재 시에
at one's own pace 자신만의 속도로	in production 생산 중인
at all times 항상	at one's convenience ~가 편리할 때에
in detail 자세히	under one's direction ~의 감독 하에
in advance 미리	without exception 예외 없이
in transit 운송 중인	with emphasis 강조하여

Her assistant will take care of vacation requests **in Ms. Cosby's absence.**
Cosby 씨가 부재 시에는 그녀의 비서가 휴가 요청을 처리할 것이다.

🔒 **확인 문제 ⑥**

Some residents have objection ------- the construction plan.

(A) to
(B) for

🔒 **확인 문제 ⑦**

This glass is vulnerable ------- heat.

(A) to
(B) for

🔒 **확인 문제 ⑧**

All workers are asked to display their security badge ------- all times.

(A) for
(B) at

정답 ⑥ (A) ⑦ (A) ⑧ (B)

168 기적의 토익 RC

풀이방법 전치사 (2)

1. New members get to enjoy benefits ------- free shipping and 15% off their first order.

(A) moreover   (B) including   (C) prior to   (D) against

신규 회원은 무료 배송과 첫 주문 시 15% 할인을 포함한 혜택들을 누릴 수 있습니다.

> **이렇게 풀어요**
>
> **1. 선택지 보고 문법/어휘 문제 파악** 선택지가 모두 전치사로 구성되어 있으므로 어휘 문제임을 파악할 수 있어요.
>
> **2. 빈칸 분석** 빈칸 뒤의 명사구 free shipping and 15% off를 수식어로 만들 수 있는 적절한 전치사가 들어가야 함을 파악해요.
>
> **3. 정답 선택** '무료 배송과 첫 주문 시 15% 할인을 포함한 혜택'이라는 의미를 만들 수 있는 전치사 (B)를 정답으로 고릅니다.

2. Oklahoma Communication will postpone the stockholders' meeting ------- further notice.

(A) above   (B) under   (C) near   (D) until

Oklahoma Communication은 추후 통지가 있을 때까지 주주 회의를 연기할 것이다.

> **이렇게 풀어요**
>
> **1. 선택지 보고 문법/어휘 문제 파악** 선택지가 모두 전치사로 구성되어 있으므로 어휘 문제임을 파악할 수 있어요.
>
> **2. 빈칸 분석** 빈칸 뒤의 명사구 further notice를 수식어로 만들 수 있는 적절한 전치사가 들어가야 함을 파악한다.
>
> **3. 정답 선택** '추후 통지가 있을 때까지'라는 의미의 관용구 until further notice를 만드는 전치사 (D) until을 정답으로 고릅니다.

3. We have provided the local residents ------- affordable housing options.

(A) with   (B) to   (C) in   (D) on

우리는 지역 주민들에게 합리적인 가격의 주택 옵션을 제공해왔습니다.

> **이렇게 풀어요**
>
> **1. 선택지 보고 문법/어휘 문제 파악** 선택지가 모두 전치사로 구성되어 있으므로 어휘 문제임을 파악할 수 있어요.
>
> **2. 빈칸 분석** 빈칸 앞의 동사 provide와 함께 쓰이는 전치사가 들어가야 함을 파악해요.
>
> **3. 정답 선택** provide는 'provide A with B'의 형태로 'A에게 B를 제공하다'라는 의미로 쓰이므로 (A) with를 정답으로 고릅니다.

PART 5 문법 전치사 (2)

PART 5 어휘

형용사 어휘 (2)

각 어휘와 함께 자주 쓰이는 표현을 통째로 외워두세요.

900+
01 pending
미결인, 임박한

status of pending orders	처리 중인 주문 상황
pending decision	미결 문제
pending issues	해결되지 않은 문제

800+
02 supplementary
보충의, 추가의

| supplementary battery | 보조 배터리 |
| supplementary materials | 보충 자료 |

🐾 빈출 토익 선생님 Pick!
03 potential
가능성이 있는, 잠재적인

| attract potential customer/client | 잠재 고객을 끌어모으다 |

04 additional
추가의

| additional cost/charge | 추가 경비/요금 |
| at no additional fee | 추가 요금 없이 |

05 essential
필수적인

| essential qualifications to | ~을 위해 필수적인 자격 요건 |
| it is essential that | ~은 필수적이다 |

🐾 빈출 토익 선생님 Pick!
06 available
이용할 수 있는, 시간이 있는

be available for	~을 위해 이용이 가능하다
be available at	(장소) ~에서/(가격) ~의 금액으로 구입할 수 있다
job openings available	채용 중인 일자리

07 accustomed
익숙한

| be accustomed to | ~에 익숙하다 |

08 opposite
반대의, 맞은편의

| in opposite directions | 반대 방향으로 |

🐾 빈출 토익 선생님 Pick!
09 clear
분명한, 확실한

need clear instruction	명확한 지시가 필요하다
make it clear that	~을 분명히 하다
clear understanding of	~의 확실한 이해

10 aware
알고 있는

| be aware of | ~을 알다 |
| be aware that | ~을 알다 |

11 delicate
섬세한, 민감한

| delicate issue | 민감한 문제 |
| delicate negotiation | 신중을 요하는 협상 |

12 sustainable
지속 가능한

| sustainable growth | 지속 가능한 성장 |
| sustainable resource | 지속 가능한 자원 |

900+
13 versatile
다재다능한, 다용도의

| versatile furniture | 다용도 가구 |
| versatile performer | 다재다능한 연기자[연주자] |

🐾 빈출 토익 선생님 Pick!
14 capable
할 수 있는, 유능한

| capable of | ~을 할 수 있는 |

800+
15 transparent
투명한

| transparent process | 투명한 절차 |

170 기적의 토익 RC

16 previous　　　　　　　　이전의

previous year	작년
previous commitment	선약
previous version	이전 버전

17 notable　　　　주목할 만한, 중요한, 유명한

| notable feature | 눈에 띄는 특징 |
| be notable for | ~로 유명하다 |

빈출 토익 선생님 Pick!
18 specific　　　　　구체적인, 특정한

specific feature	특정 기능
specific event	특정 사건
specific information	특정 정보

`800+`
19 enthusiastic　　　　　열정적인

| enthusiastic about | ~에 열정적인 |
| enthusiastic fans | 열정적인 팬들 |

20 ambitious　　　　　　야심 있는

| ambitious plan | 야심 찬 계획 |
| meet one's ambitious goal | ~의 야심찬 목표를 달성하다 |

빈출 토익 선생님 Pick!
21 primary　　　　　　주된, 주요한

primary concern	주된 관심사
primary goal	주된 목적
primary funding source	주된 자금 출처

22 initial　　　　　　처음의, 초기의

| initial investment | 초기 투자 |
| initial projections | 초기 예상 |

23 standard　　　　표준의, 일반적인

| standard price | 표준 가격 |
| standard business hours | 일반적인 영업시간 |

24 mandatory　　　　　　의무적인

| It is mandatory for A to부정사 | A는 ~을 해야 한다 |
| It is mandatory that | ~은 의무이다 |

빈출 토익 선생님 Pick!
25 upcoming　　　　다가오는, 곧 있을

upcoming year	내년, 다가올 해
upcoming event/seminar/holidays	곧 있을 행사/세미나/휴일
upcoming change in	~에 있어서의 곧 있을 변화

 풀이 방법

Robinson brand products are ------- at almost any auto supplies store.

(A) outstanding　　　　(B) available　　　　(C) diverse　　　　(D) transparent

Robinson 브랜드의 제품들은 거의 모든 자동차 용품점에서 구입할 수 있다.

> **이렇게 풀어요**
>
> **1. 선택지 보고 문법/어휘 문제 파악**　선택지가 서로 다른 형용사 어휘로 구성되어 있으므로 어휘 문제임을 파악해요.
>
> **2. 빈칸 분석**　빈칸 앞의 be동사(are), 빈칸 뒤의 전치사 at과 함께 쓰일 수 있는 형용사가 들어가야 함을 파악해요.
>
> **3. 정답 선택**　be available at의 형태로 쓰이는 (B) available을 정답으로 고릅니다.

PART 5 어휘 형용사 어휘 (2)　171

따라 하면 문제가 풀리는

연습 문제

앞서 학습한 문제 풀이법을 적용하여 맞는 것에 ✔ 표시 하거나 괄호 안에
적절한 답을 쓰고 정답을 선택하세요.

01 There were several complaints ------- long wait times at Benny's Bento Box.

(A) above
(B) concerning
(C) under
(D) by

1. 선택지 보고 문법/어휘 문제 파악하기 ☐문법 문제 ☐어휘 문제
2. 빈칸 분석하기 빈칸 앞 내용 ☐불만이 있다 ☐고객이 많다
　　　　　　　　빈칸 뒤 내용 ☐음식이 맛있다 ☐대기 시간이 길다 ☐주차 공간이 없다
3. 정답 선택하기 앞뒤 내용을 연결해 줄 수 있는 어휘 (　　　　)

02 Beans and nuts can be used as sources of protein ------- meat.

(A) prior to
(B) because of
(C) instead of
(D) except for

1. 선택지 보고 문법/어휘 문제 파악하기 ☐문법 문제 ☐어휘 문제
2. 빈칸 분석하기 빈칸 앞 내용 ☐콩류와 견과류의 쓰임 ☐콩류와 견과류의 종류
　　　　　　　　빈칸 뒤 내용 ☐장소 ☐식재료 ☐회사명
3. 정답 선택하기 앞뒤 내용을 연결해 줄 수 있는 어휘 (　　　　)

03 You will be able to process more orders faster ------- installing this upgraded software.

(A) due to
(B) to
(C) by
(D) at

1. 선택지 보고 문법/어휘 문제 파악하기 ☐문법 문제 ☐어휘 문제
2. 빈칸 분석하기 빈칸 뒤에 있는 것 ☐to부정사 ☐동명사
　　　　　　　　빈칸 앞뒤 문맥을 이어주는 의미 ☐~함으로써 ☐~하기 전에
3. 정답 선택하기 정답 (　　　)

172　기적의 토익 RC

♀ 정답 및 해설 p.54

04 Over the last three years, Tao Car Tuning has increased its revenues ------- Mr. Hudson's direction.

(A) on
(B) for
(C) in
(D) under

> 1. 선택지 보고 문법/어휘 문제 파악하기 ☐ 문법 문제 ☐ 어휘 문제
> 2. 빈칸 분석하기 빈칸 뒤의 명사구 (   )
> 　　　　　　　　이 명사구의 의미 (   )
> 3. 정답 선택하기 명사구와 함께 쓰여 관용어구를 만드는 전치사 (   )

05 This seminar features basic strategies to attract ------- clients to your business.

(A) opposite
(B) essential
(C) notable
(D) potential

> 1. 선택지 보고 문법/어휘 문제 파악하기 ☐ 문법 문제 ☐ 어휘 문제
> 2. 빈칸 분석하기 빈칸 앞에 있는 동사 attract의 의미 (   )
> 　　　　　　　　빈칸 뒤에 있는 명사 clients의 의미 (   )
> 　　　　　　　　→ 문맥상 위의 동사, 명사와 함께 쓰일 수 있는 형용사를 답으로 고른다.
> 3. 정답 선택하기 정답 (   )

06 With their proximity ------- water sources, factories are careful when disposing waste.

(A) in
(B) for
(C) on
(D) to

> 1. 선택지 보고 문법/어휘 문제 파악하기 ☐ 문법 문제 ☐ 어휘 문제
> 2. 빈칸 분석하기 빈칸 앞 명사 (   )
> 3. 정답 선택하기 위의 명사와 함께 쓰이는 전치사 (   )

PART 5 전치사 (2) / 형용사 어휘 (2)　173

토익에 나올 실전 문제

DAY 01-07 누적 문제

제한시간 9분입니다! 시~작!

01. The new CFO's seat was arranged ------- Mr. Pennington and Ms. Pratt at the awards ceremony.
(A) throughout
(B) between
(C) until
(D) before

02. Most of our inventory will be half off, ------- new arrivals for the summer season.
(A) included
(B) include
(C) to include
(D) including

03. Mr. Peyton was given an award ------- his dedication to community volunteer programs.
(A) for
(B) from
(C) as
(D) in

04. Cruz Hardware customers who are ------- to getting DIY tips from employees will have to refer to the company Web site instead.
(A) accustomed
(B) specific
(C) sustainable
(D) general

05. Orders should arrive in two business days, ------- merchandise shipped directly from the manufacturer.
(A) into
(B) however
(C) whereas
(D) except

06. Please keep this original copy of the signed contract ------- the cabinet with a digital lock.
(A) in
(B) by
(C) of
(D) for

07. ------- the contract, payments are to be made on the first of every month.
(A) According to
(B) Aside from
(C) Prior to
(D) Thanks to

08. The San Andrade solar plant is the region's ------- electricity source from reusable energy.
(A) primary
(B) previous
(C) diverse
(D) ample

09. Anyone who uses the cafeteria should clean it up, ------- of which position they hold in the company.
(A) partial
(B) aside
(C) regardless
(D) outside

10. In order to prepare for the new season quickly, shelf space should be cleared ------- the new shipment's arrival.
(A) ahead of
(B) alongside
(C) within
(D) almost

11. ------- being elected, Mayor Townsend released a proposal for the city beautification campaign.
(A) Upon
(B) Like
(C) At
(D) Into

12. Since there is some road repair on Stewart Drive, it will be blocked ------- October 20.
(A) until
(B) about
(C) through
(D) behind

174 기적의 토익 RC

13. Travelers ------- small children will be allowed to board the plane first.

(A) with
(B) after
(C) under
(D) beside

14. International students ------- all departments are encouraged to apply for the internship.

(A) after
(B) below
(C) across
(D) since

15. Even after she transferred to the Miami office, Ms. Stein ------- keeps in touch with her old coworkers in Boston.

(A) previous
(B) still
(C) but
(D) fully

16. Trisha Bowden, the most experienced worker at Hammond Bank, ------- lived in Australia for three years.

(A) additionally
(B) almost
(C) previously
(D) ever

17. Wendy Clay, Chief of Logistics, wants to inspect the fleet's new electric vehicles -------.

(A) her
(B) she
(C) hers
(D) herself

18. Mr. Deegan said that ------- wouldn't have completed the blueprint on time without an intern's assistance.

(A) himself
(B) him
(C) he
(D) his

19. Howe's Shipping's drivers are supposed to be ------- of any local road closures.

(A) clear
(B) opposite
(C) delicate
(D) aware

20. ------- an account manager, Ms. Shields is expected to give financial advice to clients.

(A) To
(B) As
(C) With
(D) Of

21. To avoid any accidents or injuries, wearing safety gear is ------- for everyone on the job site.

(A) notable
(B) mandatory
(C) disruptive
(D) ambiguous

22. To view the full list of ------- performances, please visit our theater's Web page.

(A) potential
(B) standard
(C) upcoming
(D) capable

23. The state council decided to build a reservoir ------- repeated heavy rains in summer and severe drought in winter.

(A) in order for
(B) as a result of
(C) apart from
(D) such as

24. If our company wants to expand its customer base, it is ------- that we launch an ad campaign.

(A) essential
(B) bound
(C) steady
(D) routine

PART 5 전치사 (2) / 형용사 어휘 (2)   175

PART 6

순서를 나타내는 형용사 어휘

보기에 순서를 나타내는 형용사가 있으면 지문에서 시간 표현을 찾으세요.

VOCA

informative 유익한
input 의견
fill out 작성하다
arrange 준비하다, 마련하다
inform 알리다

출제 포인트
<순서를 나타내는 형용사>
initial 처음의, 초기의
final 마지막의
previous 이전의

 **풀이 방법**   e-mail   ◯ 해석 p.57

To: Event Participants
From: Janet Wheeler <j.wheeler@bosem.org>
Date: 18 December
Subject: Business Owner Seminar
Attachment: Feedback Form

Dear Participants,

Thank you for coming to last week's Business Owner Seminar in Fillmore. I hope that it proved to be helpful and informative for you. Thanks to your support and participation, this year's ------- seminar was a huge success. We are currently
         01.
considering changing next year's lineup and would like to get your input on it. Please take a moment to fill out the attached feedback form and send it back to us. We want to know what we can do to better serve you and your business.

The next round of Business Owner Seminar will be held ------- Houston. Our
                                    🔖 **PART 5**
organization will arrange the schedule and keep you all informed.

Janet Wheeler
Senior Coordinator, Business Owner Seminar

01. (A) final
     (B) periodic
     (C) following
     (D) necessary

이렇게 풀어요

1. 선택지 보고 문법/어휘 문제 파악   선택지가 서로 다른 형용사 어휘로 이루어져 있으므로 어휘 문제임을 파악할 수 있어요.
(A) 마지막의   (B) 주기적인   (C) 그 다음의   (D) 필요한

2. 빈칸 분석   '올해의 ------- 세미나는 대성공이었습니다'
빈칸 앞에서 마지막 주 세미나라고 했고, 빈칸 뒤에서는 내년도의 라인업을 변경하는 것을 고려하고 있다고 했어요. 이메일이 쓰여진 날짜는 12월 18일임을 추가적으로 파악합니다.

3. 정답 선택   문맥상 올해의 '마지막' 세미나가 되어야 자연스러우므로 (A) final을 정답으로 고릅니다.

해설

빈칸 뒤에 장소(도시)를 나타내는 명사가 있으므로 장소 전치사 (C) in이 정답입니다.

🔖 **PART 5 문법 적용 문제**

The next round of Business Owner Seminar will be held ------- Houston.

(A) about   (B) for   (C) in   (D) to

176   기적의 토익 RC

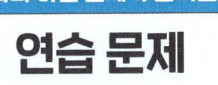

따라 하면 문제가 풀리는

연습 문제

지문 전반에서 단서가 될 부분을 찾아 표시하세요.
표시한 것을 바탕으로 정답 어휘를 선택하세요.

📍정답 및 해설 p.57

DAY 07

01

Dear Workshop Participants,

Thank you for attending the Leaders in Retail Workshop last weekend. In order to improve our ------- series of workshops, we would like to gather feedback from everyone who attended this one.

(A) next   (B) several

02

The Stanza Band will be doing a special acoustic performance at Turner Record Store on Saturday, May 18. Their manager has announced that the band will perform songs from their first album along with new songs off their album that is scheduled to be released on the day of the ------- show.

(A) upcoming   (B) first

03

We appreciate your purchase. The 15% discount coupon that you obtained from your ------- order has been successfully applied. You can expect to receive this shipment by Tuesday, August 7.

(A) following   (B) previous

04

Dear Mr. Connors,

This is your ------- notification to pay the parking ticket that was issued to you on 9 January. If you do not send a payment of $45 to San Jose Courthouse by 3 April, your driver's license will be suspended.

(A) final   (B) current

PART 6 순서를 나타내는 형용사 어휘   177

토익에 나올 실전 문제

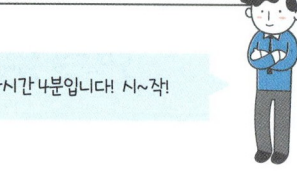

제한시간 4분입니다! 시~작!

Questions 01-04 refer to the following information.

Douglas Cain

Many people know Douglas Cain's name because of his successful basketball career. Since he officially retired as a basketball player, he ------- as a sports commentator on the nationwide sports
01.
TV channel. Here is another story you may find interesting. You are probably familiar with the name Christopher Douglass, which is the pen name of Mr. Cain. He chose not to use his real name because he was afraid his ------- success could influence his book sales. -------. Thanks to his pen
02.   **03.**
name, Mr. Cain can enjoy the fame of both star athlete and acclaimed author -------.
04.

01. (A) will serve
(B) has served
(C) served
(D) to serve

유형 적용 문제
02. (A) following
(B) unexpected
(C) former
(D) temporary

03. (A) His popular book series is based on his career as a professional athlete.
(B) Several of his teammates provided feedback on early drafts of his writing.
(C) It is proved by the fact that his book has been on the bestseller list.
(D) This allows him to be evaluated based on his writing alone.

04. (A) separation
(B) separated
(C) separate
(D) separately

178   기적의 토익 RC

정답 및 해설 p.58

Questions 05-08 refer to the following e-mail.

To: All Employees
From: Danielle Frost
Date: 8 August
Subject: Company picnic
Attachment: map

Attention Associates,

Our annual company picnic is scheduled for Friday, 21 August this year. ------- you are out sick or
05.
on vacation, you are expected to attend. We ------- the office together at 10:30 and take a chartered
06.
bus to Gardena Park. -------. We plan to cook corn on the cob, cheeseburgers, and hot dogs. If you
07.
have any dietary restrictions or food allergies, please inform me in advance. The ------- activity on
08.
the agenda is ultimate frisbee. The teams will be chosen by department heads once we arrive. I'm
sure we'll all have a great time again this year. See you there.

Sincerely,

Danielle Frost
Manager, Personnel Department

---

05. (A) Whereas
(B) Unless
(C) So much as
(D) When

06. (A) will depart
(B) departed
(C) departing
(D) have departed

07. (A) The event will be catered by Paulie's Pasta Palace.
(B) Thank you all for your hard work and effort all year.
(C) You will be reimbursed for parking once you submit your ticket.
(D) We have reserved a covered area and two barbecue pits for the day.

유형 적용 문제
08. (A) recurring
(B) annual
(C) timely
(D) first

PART 6 순서를 나타내는 형용사 어휘   179

PART 7

이메일 (2) 정보 전달 이메일

이메일은 주로 〈글을 쓴 목적 - 세부 내용 - 요청사항〉의 순서로 지문이 전개돼요.

정보를 전달하는 이메일은 사내에서 정보를 공유하는 내용 또는 기업에서 고객에게 정보를 전달하거나 확인을 요청하는 내용이 주로 출제됩니다. 첫 번째 단락에서 주제 또는 목적이 드러나는 경우가 많으므로 지문의 초반부 내용을 바탕으로 세부사항이나 구체적인 요청사항을 파악해 나가면 흐름을 쉽게 파악할 수 있습니다.

정보 전달 이메일에서 자주 출제되는 문제

진위파악 문제
What is stated/
indicated about 키워드?
→ 키워드는 수신인 또는 발신인 등 인물로 출제되거나 이메일의 주제와 관련된 어휘가 제시돼요.

요청 문제
What is 사람 asked to do?
→ 요청 문제의 90%는 마지막 단락의 if절, 명령문, please가 포함된 문장에 단서가 있어요.

정보 전달 이메일에 자주 출제되는 어휘

issue	문제; 발행물	attach	첨부하다
overdue	지불 기한이 지난	enclose	동봉하다
inform	알리다	workload	업무량, 작업량
relevant	관련 있는	scheduling conflict	일정의 겹침
approval	승인, 찬성	stop by	~에 들르다
fill in	다른 사람의 업무를 대신하다	arrange	준비하다, 배열하다
state	명시하다	advantage	장점
confirmation	확인	undertake	착수하다
represent	대표하다	dispose of	~을 없애다, 처리하다
facility	시설	expertise	전문지식
specification	설명	knowledgeable	아는 것이 많은
tentative	임시의	selected	엄선된
inquiry	질문, 문의	extend	연장하다
rescheduling	일정을 다시 잡는 것	process	처리하다; 과정
indicate	나타내다, 보여주다	at your earliest convenience	가급적 빨리
remind	상기시키다	announce	알리다
clarify	명확하게 하다, 분명히 말하다	exceed	넘어서다, 초과하다
stress	강조하다	periodic	주기적인
companion	동행, 동반자	electronically	컴퓨터로, 전자상으로

180 기적의 토익 RC

풀이방법 정보 전달 이메일

e-mail

해석 p.59

To: allstaff@cedarburg.net
From: c.martell@cedarburg.net
Date: Tuesday, August 3
Subject: Office Vents

Attention Associates,

As you know, there is a problem with the central air vents in our building. Work on them has been scheduled to begin tomorrow morning, but the technicians are not sure what time they will finish. Therefore, the management has decided it is best to have you all work from home tomorrow.

While working remotely, please stay logged into our instant messenger program and keep your phone handy. That way we can still contact each other just as efficiently as if we were in the office together.

I apologize for the inconvenience this may cause.

Sincerely,

Cindy Martell

DAY 07

01. What is stated about the office?
(A) It is a good place to host meetings.
(B) It has a ventilation problem.
(C) It was recently renovated.
(D) It will be relocated soon.

02. What are associates asked to do on Wednesday?
(A) Attend a meeting
(B) Come into work early
(C) Log into a messaging service
(D) Schedule appointments

이렇게 풀어요

01. 사무실에 대해 언급된 것은 무엇인가?
(A) 회의를 열기에 좋은 장소다.
(B) 환기 문제가 있다.
(C) 최근에 보수되었다.
(D) 곧 이전할 것이다.

해설 질문의 키워드 office가 지문에서 building으로 바뀌어 표현되었어요. building에 대해 언급된 첫 번째 단락에서 there is a problem with the central air vents in our building이라고 환기 문제를 언급했으므로 (B)가 정답입니다.

02. 동료들은 수요일에 무엇을 하도록 요청받는가?
(A) 회의에 참석하기
(B) 일찍 출근하기
(C) 메시지 서비스에 접속하기
(D) 약속을 잡기

해설 메일을 보낸 날이 화요일이므로 수요일은 내일입니다. 두 번째 단락에서 please stay logged into our instant messenger program이라며 메신저 프로그램에 접속할 것을 요청했으므로 (C)가 정답입니다.

PART 7 이메일 (2) 정보 전달 이메일　181

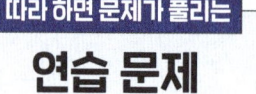

따라 하면 문제가 풀리는

연습 문제

먼저 문제의 키워드에 표시한 후,
지문에서 단서를 찾아 적절한 답을 고르세요.

01   e-mail

From: Fabian Vela <f_vela@brunsonconsulting.net>
To: All Employees <allstaff@brunsonconsulting.net>
Date: June 19
Subject: Parking resurfacing

Dear Staff,

From July 1 to July 5, our office parking lot will be off limits while it undergoes a resurfacing project. We have negotiated with the manager of the Faribault Building, and he has agreed to allow our employees to use their lot. If you wish to do so, you must pick up a pass from the HR office. Otherwise, their security team will not allow you to enter the lot.

Fabian Vela

Q. What is suggested about the Faribault Building?

(A) It will have repairs made to its parking lot.
(B) Its parking lot requires a pass.

02   e-mail

To: Roseway Jewelry Clerks <clerklist@rosewayjewelry.com>
From: Sierra Green <sgreen@rosewayjewelry.com>
Date: December 18
Subject: Information for store clerks

From the 1st of next month, Roseway Jewelry will no longer accept returns without a valid receipt, even if the item is in its original packaging. We have announced the change on our Web site and posted notices throughout the store. However, customers may still have questions about this change, so please direct them to a manager if you are unsure whether or not a return is allowed.

Sierra Green, Branch Manager

Q. What is the purpose of the e-mail?

(A) To explain a new policy
(B) To announce a jewelry sale

○ 정답 및 해설 p.59

03   e-mail

To: Priya Chetti <pchetti@alvareztransportation.com>
From: Miguel Guerrero <miguel.g@alvareztransportation.com>
Date: November 13
Subject: Re: Forgotten item

Dear Ms. Chetti,

I'm sorry to hear that you left one of your bags on our shuttle bus. All items that remain on the bus after the last stop are taken to my office, which is located at Terminal 4 of the airport. To investigate your inquiry further, I would need to know the size and color of the bag, along with any other details, such as the brand. Please e-mail me at your earliest convenience.

Sincerely,

Miguel Guerrero

Q. What is Ms. Chetti asked to do?

(A) Visit Mr. Guerrero's office
(B) Provide additional information

04   e-mail

To: All Employees <staff@phelpsltd.com>
From: Brady Patton <bpatton@phelpsltd.com>
Date: January 8
Subject: Lunchtime Lecture

In an effort to support the professional development of our staff, Phelps Ltd. will begin holding monthly lectures for employees each month. The first lecture will be held from noon to 1 P.M. on January 28 in the conference room. The topic will be "Technology Timesavers". If you would like to participate in this event, please sign up in the HR office, as a catered lunch will be provided. I hope that you will find the session informative.

Brady Patton

Q. What is NOT mentioned about the January 28 event?

(A) Its participants must register in advance.
(B) It is required for all employees.

PART 7 이메일 (2) 정보 전달 이메일   183

토익에 나올 실전 문제

제한시간 10분입니다! 시~작!

Questions 01-02 refer to the following e-mail.

To:	Sean Briggs
From:	Filmore Furniture
Date:	1 September
Subject:	Newsletter

Dear Mr. Briggs,

At Filmore Furniture, we have expanded our inventory of recliner armchairs. Based on your purchases, you may be interested in the Hopeland ReMax. It's an armchair with built-in cupholders, USB ports to charge your portable electronic devices, and a massage function with three different speeds. Visit our showroom to try one out!

As a reminder, now that you have been upgraded from a Silver to a Gold member, you now qualify for our full delivery service for free. That includes everything such as delivery, installation, and removal of old furniture.

Sincerely,

Dayana Hamilton
Sales Manager, Filmore Furniture

01. Why did Ms. Hamilton send the e-mail?

(A) To introduce a popular product
(B) To request feedback on a purchase
(C) To explain a company policy
(D) To report on the status of a delivery

02. What is indicated about Mr. Briggs' membership?

(A) It is about to expire.
(B) It was recently upgraded.
(C) It will be automatically renewed.
(D) It requires monthly payments.

paraphrasing 주어진 어휘 또는 표현과 패러프레이징 될 수 있는 것을 연결하세요.

1. removal •
2. expand •
3. function •

• (a) widen
• (b) disposal
• (c) capability

184 기적의 토익 RC

정답 및 해설 p.60

Questions 03-04 refer to the following e-mail.

To: Charlene Yee <yeechar@geosales.com>
From: Lexington Supermarket <info@lexingtonsuper.com>
Date: December 13
Subject: Don't miss it!

Dear Ms. Yee,

As one of the newest recipients of Lexington Supermarket Rewards Card (LSRC), you should be made aware of the options available to you. Most shoppers know that they can earn one point for every dollar spent at Lexington Supermarket. We also send out our monthly *Lexington Spotlight*, a list of brands that will earn you double points throughout the designated month.

However, if you're only using your LSRC membership benefits at Lexington Supermarket, you're not growing your points in the fastest way possible. Instead, you should take advantage of the point-earning opportunities offered by our partners, which include Western Rail, McGrath Apparel, Evergreen Cinemas, and more. Be sure to present your LSRC when you visit them to boost your points even more.

Thank you for shopping with us!

The LSRC Team

03. Why is Ms. Yee receiving the e-mail?
(A) She purchased a certain amount of groceries.
(B) She responded to a customer questionnaire.
(C) She downloaded some supermarket coupons.
(D) She recently signed up for a loyalty program.

04. What is Ms. Yee encouraged to do?
(A) Add her name to a mailing list
(B) Provide reviews of her favorite brands
(C) Use a membership card at other businesses
(D) Review the changes in the benefits policy

paraphrasing 주어진 어휘 또는 표현과 패러프레이징 될 수 있는 것을 연결하세요.

1. recipient   •   • (a) apply
2. take advantage of •   • (b) receiver
3. signed up for   •   • (c) use

PART 7 이메일 (2) 정보 전달 이메일 185

 실전 문제

Questions 05-07 refer to the following e-mail.

To:	Felicia Maldano <fmaldano@m1-solutions.net>
From:	Mickey Soto <mickey@tpcevent.org>
Date:	November 10
Subject:	Tax Professionals Conference

Dear Ms. Maldano,

I am really looking forward to hearing your talk on customer service tips for accountants at the upcoming Tax Professionals Conference. Thank you, once again, for covering Timothy Kramer's morning session, as he had to cancel at the last minute due to illness. His informative talk last year on selecting tax software was helpful to a lot of participants, so it will be a shame to miss out on his expertise this year. However, I've already heard a lot of positive comments about your selected topic, so I believe that it will be well received. Please remember that if you have any photos or graphics that will accompany your presentation, they should be sent to me by the end of tomorrow so that I can double-check their compatibility with our system. Also, on our Web site, we asked people to submit questions about the conference topics. I'll send those to you tomorrow to help you prepare for the Q&A session at the end.

Sincerely,

Mickey Soto

05. Why does Mr. Soto thank Ms. Maldano?

(A) She prepared some notes for Mr. Kramer.
(B) She suggested a topic for Mr. Soto's speech.
(C) She donated to a conference budget.
(D) She accepted a task on short notice.

06. What is suggested about Mr. Kramer?

(A) He was nominated for an award.
(B) He was a presenter at last year's event.
(C) He has started his own tax preparation company.
(D) He is Ms. Maldano's former colleague.

07. What does Mr. Soto plan to send tomorrow?

(A) A finalized schedule
(B) Images for the presentation slides
(C) A list of system requirements
(D) Questions from conference participants

paraphrasing 주어진 어휘 또는 표현과 패러프레이징 될 수 있는 것을 연결하세요.

1. photos or graphics •   • (a) materials
2. on short notice •   • (b) used to work together
3. former colleague •   • (c) unexpectedly

Questions 08-10 refer to the following e-mail.

To: <selmavernon@antonioco.com>
From: <randolphi@nbexpo.net>
Date: May 20
Subject: National Business Expo

Dear Ms. Vernon,

On behalf of the National Business Expo (NBE), I would like to thank you for registering for this year's event at Hopkins Plaza. Your registration for the 2-day VIP package is confirmed, and you will receive your welcome packet in the mail approximately one week before the expo begins on June 7.

All participants must wear an NBE-issued ID badge while on the premises. It seems that you did not upload a photograph of yourself on the registration page. Could you please e-mail one to me so that your badge can be made in time to send it with the welcome packet? If not, you may have difficulty at the entrance. Please note that due to Hopkins Plaza's downtown location, its parking lot is very small. If you are visiting from out of town, we recommend taking a bus or taxi from your hotel.

Warmest regards,

Ivan Randolph

08. Who most likely is Mr. Randolph?

(A) A hotel owner
(B) A business professor
(C) An event planner
(D) A print shop worker

09. What does Mr. Randolph ask Ms. Vernon to do?

(A) Submit a photograph
(B) Upgrade to a VIP package
(C) Choose a designated seat
(D) Sign a registration form

10. What is mentioned about Hopkins Plaza?

(A) It was the site of last year's expo.
(B) It has limited space for vehicles.
(C) It operates a shuttle service.
(D) It is completely booked for June 7.

---

paraphrasing 주어진 어휘 또는 표현과 패러프레이징 될 수 있는 것을 연결하세요.

1. operates a shuttle service •
2. completely booked •
3. parking lot is very small •

• (a) limited space for vehicles
• (b) not available
• (c) offers transportation

PART 7 이메일 (2) 정보 전달 이메일   187

'멋진 당신, 오늘도 화이팅'

DAY

08

오늘의 학습 포인트

PART 5. 동사의 형태 변화와 종류

1. 동사의 형태 – 기본형/과거형/3인칭 단수 현재형/과거분사형/현재분사형

> 동사 자리에 단독으로 위치

> be동사와 함께.
> be + -ing, be + p.p.

2. 반드시 동사원형을 쓰는 경우 – 조동사 뒤/명령문

3. 동사의 종류
- 1형식: 뒤에 전치사구/부사. go, come, arrive, wait, work 등 ┐
- 2형식: 주격 보어 갖는 동사. be, become, remain, prove 등 ┘ 자동사
- 3형식: 목적어 갖는 동사. explain, attend, handle 등 ┐
- 4형식: 목적어 2개 갖는 동사(간·목/직·목). give, offer, send 등 │ 타동사
- 5형식: 목적어와 목적격 보어 갖는 동사. make, find, appoint 등 ┘

PART 6. 앞의 내용이 단서인 동사 어휘

> 보기가 동사 어휘. 문맥 파악하기!

PART 7. 편지

> 출제 비중 ↑. 발신자/수신자/소속 확인하기

PART 5
문법
동사의 형태 변화와 종류

1형식~5형식 동사의 특징을 알아두면 동사 문제를 빠르게 풀 수 있어요.

출제 유형 1
동사의 형태

🔒 **확인 문제 ❶**

Ms. Moore ------- an e-mail to her employees.

(A) sending
(B) sent

- 하나의 동사는 기본형, 과거형, 과거분사형, 현재분사형, 3인칭 단수 현재형의 총 5가지 형태를 가지고 있습니다.

기본형	과거형	과거분사형	현재분사형	3인칭 단수 현재형
send	sent	sent	sending	sends
offer	offered	offered	offering	offers

- 동사 자리에 단독으로 위치할 수 있는 형태는 기본형, 과거형, 3인칭 단수 현재형입니다.

- 현재분사형은 단독으로는 동사 자리에 위치할 수 없고, be동사와 함께 쓰여 진행형(be + -ing)이 되어야 동사 자리에 올 수 있습니다.
  The manager **is talking** to his customer. 관리자가 그의 고객과 이야기하고 있다.

- 과거분사형 또한 단독으로 동사 자리에 위치할 수 없고, be동사와 함께 쓰여 수동형(be + p.p.)이 되거나, have동사와 함께 쓰여 완료형이 되어야 동사 자리에 올 수 있습니다.
  The subject of the talk **was announced** last week. 강연 주제가 지난주에 발표되었다.
  The board of directors **has approved** the plan. 이사회는 그 계획을 승인했다.

출제 유형 2
반드시 동사원형을 쓰는 경우

1 조동사 + 동사원형

🔒 **확인 문제 ❷**

The order will ------- tomorrow.

(A) arrive
(B) arrived

- 조동사는 동사 앞에 위치하여 의미를 보충하거나 문법적 기능을 나타냅니다. 조동사 뒤에는 반드시 동사원형이 와야 해요.

<조동사> will/would ~일 것이다　can/could ~할 수 있다　shall/should ~해야 한다
must ~해야 한다　may/might ~일지도 모른다
<조동사처럼 쓰는 표현> would like to ~하고 싶다　be going to ~할 것이다
have to ~해야 한다　ought to ~해야 한다

　　　　　　+ 동사원형

All hopeful attendees <u>must</u> **register** in advance to ensure a seat.
참석을 희망하는 모든 이들은 사전에 등록하여 좌석을 확보해야 합니다.

We <u>have to</u> **consider** our budget. 우리는 예산을 고려해야 한다.

정답 ❶ (B) ❷ (A)

190　기적의 토익 RC

2 명령문

- 명령문은 주어 없이 **동사원형으로 시작**합니다.
  Fill out this registration form. 이 등록 양식을 작성하세요.

- 동사원형 앞에 부사 please가 위치할 수 있습니다.
  Please **fill** out this registration form. 이 등록 양식을 작성해주시기 바랍니다.

- 명령문 앞에 전치사구, to부정사구, 또는 조건/시간 부사절이 위치할 수 있습니다.
  In order to get a discount, **join** our membership program now.
  할인을 받기 위해서, 우리의 멤버십 프로그램에 지금 가입하세요.

출제 유형 3 동사의 종류

1 1형식 동사: 자동사

- 1형식 동사는 완전 자동사로 **바로 뒤에 전치사구 또는 부사가** 위치합니다.
  Several clients will **come** to our office tomorrow.
  몇몇 고객들이 내일 우리 사무실에 올 것이다.

- 동사 어휘 문제에서 자동사와 타동사를 구분하는 문제가 출제됩니다.

|빈출 1형식 자동사|

go 가다	come 오다	arrive 도착하다	depart 출발하다
happen 발생하다	occur 발생하다	wait 기다리다	talk 이야기하다
rise 오르다	work 일하다	vary 다르다	commence 시작하다

|특정 전치사와 쓰이는 빈출 자동사|

comply with ~을 준수하다	respond to ~에 응답하다	depend on ~에 의존하다, ~에 달려 있다
rely on ~에 의존하다	interfere with ~을 방해하다	object to ~에 반대하다
account for ~을 설명하다	appeal to ~에 호소하다	lead to ~로 이어지다
proceed to ~로 가다	reply to ~에 답하다	consist of ~로 구성되다

2 2형식 동사: 자동사

- 2형식 동사는 주어를 보충 설명하는 **주격 보어를 갖는 동사**입니다.
  – 형용사 주격 보어: All of Maria Montel's films **were** highly <u>successful</u>.
      Maria Montel의 모든 영화들은 매우 성공적이었다.
  – 명사 주격 보어: The Former chef at Carton Hotel **has become** <u>the owner</u> of a
      restaurant chain.
      Carton Hotel의 전 주방장은 레스토랑 체인의 소유주가 되었다.

|빈출 2형식 동사|

be ~이다	become ~이 되다	remain 여전히 ~이다	stay ~로 남다
prove ~을 증명하다	appear ~인 것 같다	seem ~같아 보이다	feel 느끼다
look ~을 보다	sound ~처럼 들리다		

출제 포인트
명령문은 부사 simply가 빈칸 앞에 주어지는 경우가 자주 출제돼요.

🔒 확인 문제 ❸

Simply ------- our Web site to get more information.

(A) visiting
(B) visit

✎ 적용 기술

[기적의 필기노트] 113P
RC 기술 26

🔒 확인 문제 ❹

Mr. Long ------- with the building codes.

(A) observed
(B) complied

출제 포인트
명사 보어 문제는 동사 be, become, remain이 출제되는데, 이 동사들이 빈칸으로 출제되는 경우가 많아요.

🔒 확인 문제 ❺

Emerson Chemical has ------- a leading company.

(A) become
(B) arrived

정답 ❸ (B) ❹ (B) ❺ (A)

PART 5 문법 동사의 형태 변화와 종류 191

3 3형식 동사: 타동사

- 3형식 동사는 **목적어를 갖는 동사**입니다. 명사, 대명사, to부정사, 동명사, 명사절이 목적어 자리에 옵니다.

A group of professors will **develop** a new curriculum for online classes.
한 그룹의 교수들이 온라인 수업을 위한 새로운 교육 과정을 개발할 것이다.

| 빈출 3형식 타동사 |

answer 답하다	explain 설명하다	attract 끌어들이다	exceed 초과하다
anticipate 예상하다	oppose 반대하다	join 합류하다	attend 참석하다
reach 도달하다	await 기다리다	handle 다루다, 처리하다	discuss 논의하다

- 동명사/to부정사/명사절을 목적어로 갖는 동사는 구분하여 암기해 두세요.

| 동명사를 목적어로 갖는 3형식 타동사 |

recommend 추천하다	finish 끝내다	consider 고려하다	suggest 제안하다	include 포함하다

| to부정사를 목적어로 갖는 3형식 타동사 |

want 원하다	decide 결정하다	plan 계획하다	agree 동의하다
strive 노력하다	wish 원하다	hope 희망하다	tend ~하는 경향이 있다

`800+`

| 명사절을 목적어로 갖는 3형식 타동사 |

announce 알리다	mention 언급하다	explain 설명하다	state 명시하다
suggest 제안하다	agree 동의하다	ensure 보장하다	indicate 나타내다

4 4형식 동사: 타동사

- 4형식 동사는 뒤에 '~에게'라는 간접 목적어와 '~을'이라는 직접 목적어를 필요로 하는 동사입니다. 주로 '주다'라는 의미를 가진 동사들이 이에 해당해요.

The CEO's assistant **sent** them a reminder. 그 최고 경영자의 비서는 그들에게 메모를 보냈다.

| 빈출 4형식 타동사 |

give 주다	offer 제공하다	send 보내다	grant 수여하다
award 수여하다	bring 가져오다	forward 보내다	assign 할당하다

5 5형식 동사: 타동사

- 5형식 동사는 뒤에 목적어와 목적격 보어(목적어를 보충하는 말)를 갖는 타동사입니다.

형용사 목적격 보어: Marshall **found** the coursework difficult.
　　　　　　　　　　Marshall은 그 과제가 어렵다고 느꼈다.

명사 목적격 보어: The shareholders **elected** Mr. Burns the new Finance Manager.
　　　　　　　　　주주들은 Burns 씨를 새 재무부장으로 임명했다.

`800+`

| 빈출 5형식 타동사 |

make ~하게 하다	find ~임을 알아내다, ~라고 생각하다	keep ~하게 두다, 유지하다
appoint ~로 임명하다	name ~로 명명하다	call ~라고 부르다
consider ~라고 생각하다	get (어떤 상태로) 되게 하다	

⚠️ **주의**
모든 타동사가 명사와 대명사를 목적어로 가질 수 있지만, 동명사/to부정사/명사절을 목적어로 갖는 동사는 정해져 있습니다.

🔒 **확인 문제 ❻**

Mr. Wilkinson ------- that the project deadline should be extended.

(A) agreed
(B) planned

출제 포인트
announce, inform, notify를 구별하는 문제가 출제되므로 각 동사가 쓰이는 구조를 알아두세요.
announce + (to 사람) + that절
inform/notify + 간·목 + that절
She (~~announced~~ / **notified**) me that my request will be processed.

🔒 **확인 문제 ❼**

Ms. Miller has ------- her computer secure.

(A) given
(B) kept

정답 ❻ (A) ❼ (B)

192　기적의 토익 RC

풀이 방법

동사의 형태 변화와 종류

1. To secure a seat at the live show, you should ------- tickets as soon as possible.

(A) purchase   (B) purchases   (C) purchasing   (D) purchased

라이브 공연에서 좌석을 확보하기 위해서는, 티켓을 가능한 한 빨리 구입하셔야 합니다.

이렇게 풀어요

1. **선택지 보고 문법/어휘 문제 파악** 선택지가 모두 동사 purchase(구입하다)의 파생어로 구성되어 있으므로 문법 문제임을 파악할 수 있어요.
2. **빈칸 분석** 빈칸 앞에 조동사 should가 있다는 것을 파악해요.
3. **정답 선택** 조동사 뒤에는 동사원형이 와야 하므로 (A) purchase를 정답으로 고릅니다.

2. Brightville Adventures has ------- one of the most popular attractions in the region.

(A) recommended   (B) searched   (C) remained   (D) trusted

Brightville Adventures는 그 지역에서 가장 인기 있는 명소 중 하나로 남아 있다.

이렇게 풀어요

1. **선택지 보고 문법/어휘 문제 파악** 선택지가 모두 동사로 구성되어 있으므로 어휘 문제임을 파악할 수 있어요.
2. **빈칸 분석** 빈칸 앞의 주어 Brightville Adventures와 빈칸 뒤의 명사구 one of the most popular attractions가 동격임을 파악해요.
3. **정답 선택** 명사 주격 보어를 가질 수 있는 2형식 동사 (C) remained를 정답으로 고릅니다.

3. Over 50% of the survey participants ------- the new package design appealing.

(A) bring   (B) find   (C) like   (D) raise

설문 참가자들의 50퍼센트 이상이 새 포장 디자인이 매력적이라고 생각한다.

이렇게 풀어요

1. **선택지 보고 문법/어휘 문제 파악** 선택지가 모두 동사로 구성되어 있으므로 어휘 문제임을 파악할 수 있어요.
2. **빈칸 분석** 빈칸 뒤에 명사구 the new package design과 형용사 보어 appealing이 있으므로 5형식 타동사가 들어갈 자리임을 파악해요.
3. **정답 선택** 목적어와 목적격 보어를 가질 수 있는 5형식 타동사 (B) find를 정답으로 고릅니다.

PART 5 어휘

형용사 어휘 (3)

각 어휘와 함께 자주 쓰이는 표현을 통째로 외워두세요.

---

01 responsive 즉각 대응하는, 열의를 보이는

responsive to ~에 빠른 반응을 보이는

---

02 helpful 도움이 되는

helpful advice 유익한 조언
helpful in -ing ~하는 데 도움이 되는
it is helpful for A to부정사 A가 ~하는 것은 도움이 되다

`800+`
03 collaborative 공동의

collaborative effort 공동의 노력

☀ 빈출 토익 선생님 Pick!
04 leading 선도적인, 주요한

leading competitor 주요 경쟁자
leading supplier 선도적인 공급 회사
play a leading role 주도적 역할을 하다

---

05 distinct 뚜렷이 다른, 분명한

distinct from ~와 완전히 다른
distinct advantage 뚜렷한 이점
distinct brands 별개의 브랜드

`800+`
06 consecutive 연속적인, 계속되는

for + 숫자 + consecutive days[years/months]
~일[년/달] 연속으로

☀ 빈출 토익 선생님 Pick!
07 affordable (가격이) 알맞은, 감당할 수 있는

at affordable prices 알맞은 가격에, 저렴한 가격에
affordable rate 저렴한 요금
affordable housing 알맞은 가격의 주택
affordable to ~가 감당할 수 있는

`900+`
08 vulnerable 연약한, 취약한

be vulnerable to ~에 취약하다

---

09 significant 상당한, 중요한

significant growth 상당한 증가
significant contribution 주요한 공헌

---

10 innovative 혁신적인

innovative approach 혁신적인 접근
innovative design 혁신적인 디자인
innovative system 혁신적인 시스템

---

11 normal 보통의, 평범한, 정상적인

in normal circumstances 일반적인 상황에서
in normal ways 보통의 방법으로

☀ 빈출 토익 선생님 Pick!
12 secure 안전한, 확실한

secure place[location] 안전한 장소
secure site 안전한 사이트
secure environment 안전한 환경
keep A secure A를 안전하게 보관하다

---

13 certain 확실한, 특정한

to a certain extent 얼마간, 어느 정도까지
for certain reasons 특정 이유로
be certain of ~을 확신하다

`900+`
14 perishable 잘 상하는, 썩기 쉬운

perishable goods[product/item/food]
잘 상하는 상품[제품/품목/식품]

194 기적의 토익 RC

15 exemplary　　모범적인

exemplary service　　모범적인 서비스
exemplary performance　　모범적인 성과

빈출 토익 선생님 Pick!
16 remarkable　　놀랄 만한, 주목할 만한

remarkable achievement　　놀랄 만한 업적
remarkable progress　　현저한 진보
be remarkable for　　~로 주목할 만하다

---

17 thorough　　빈틈없는, 철저한

thorough inspection　　철저한 검사
thorough understanding　　철저한 이해

빈출 토익 선생님 Pick!
18 valid　　유효한, 정당한

valid receipt　　유효한 영수증
be valid for　　~ 동안 유효하다

빈출 토익 선생님 Pick!
19 immediate　　즉각적인, 가까운

immediate attention　　즉각적인 관심
immediate supervisor　　직속 상사
immediate vicinity of　　매우 가까운 지역의

---

20 noteworthy　　주목할 만한

noteworthy differences　　주목할 만한 차이
noteworthy achievement　　주목할 만한 업적

---

21 compatible　　호환이 되는, 양립될 수 있는

be compatible with　　~와 호환되다

---

22 suitable　　적절한, 알맞은

be suitable for　　~에 알맞다
suitable candidate[employee]　　적합한 후보[직원]

---

23 sufficient　　충분한

sufficient to　　~에 충분한
sufficient time　　충분한 시간
sufficient inventory　　충분한 재고

800+ **빈출** 토익 선생님 Pick!
24 subsequent　　그 다음의, 차후의

subsequent to　　~ 다음에
in subsequent months[years]　　차후 몇 달[년]간
subsequent events　　후속 사건

DAY 08

 풀이 방법

Bautista University is dedicated to making its tuition ------- to students of all income levels.

(A) affordable　　(B) permitted　　(C) distinct　　(D) thorough

Bautista 대학은 모든 소득 수준의 학생들이 감당할 수 있는 수업료를 책정하는 것에 전념한다.

> 이렇게 풀어요
>
> 1. **선택지 보고 문법/어휘 문제 파악** 선택지가 서로 다른 형용사 어휘로 구성되어 있으므로 어휘 문제임을 파악해요.
> 2. **빈칸 분석** 빈칸 뒤의 전치사 to와 어울려 쓰일 수 있는 것이어야 하고, '모든 소득 수준의 학생들에게 -------한 수업료'라는 문맥에 적절한 형용사가 들어가야 함을 파악해요.
> 3. **정답 선택** '(가격이) 알맞은, 감당할 수 있는'이라는 의미를 가진 (A) affordable을 정답으로 고릅니다.

PART 5 어휘 형용사 어휘 (3)　195

따라 하면 문제가 풀리는

연습 문제

앞서 학습한 문제 풀이법을 적용하여 맞는 것에 ✔ 표시 하거나 괄호 안에 적절한 답을 쓰고 정답을 선택하세요.

01 Citizens of Elkton have ------- over $100,000 to save their public library.

(A) donate
(B) donating
(C) donated
(D) donates

1. 선택지 보고 문법/어휘 문제 파악하기 ☐ 문법 문제 ☐ 어휘 문제
2. 빈칸 분석하기 문장에 없는 요소 ☐ 주어 ☐ 동사
   → 빈칸은 ☐ 주어 형태 ☐ 동사 형태를 완성할 자리이다.
3. 정답 선택하기 정답 (   )

02 One of these water purifiers can ------- enough drinking water for a small village.

(A) provide
(B) provides
(C) providing
(D) provision

1. 선택지 보고 문법/어휘 문제 파악하기 ☐ 문법 문제 ☐ 어휘 문제
2. 빈칸 분석하기 빈칸 앞에 있는 것 ☐ 전치사 ☐ 조동사 ☐ 부사
   → 빈칸은 ☐ 동사원형 ☐ 명사 자리이다.
3. 정답 선택하기 정답 (   )

03 This hotel room is ------- for a family that travels with more than four people.

(A) normal
(B) exemplary
(C) suitable
(D) current

1. 선택지 보고 문법/어휘 문제 파악하기 ☐ 문법 문제 ☐ 어휘 문제
2. 빈칸 분석하기 빈칸 앞의 be동사, 빈칸 뒤의 전치사 for와 함께 짝꿍으로 쓰이는 형용사가 정답이다.
3. 정답 선택하기 정답 (   )

196 기적의 토익 RC

♀ 정답 및 해설 p.63

04 Thousands of people ------- in the annual Mason City Marathon each year.

(A) attend
(B) join
(C) participate
(D) follow

1. 선택지 보고 문법/어휘 문제 파악하기 ☐ 문법 문제 ☐ 어휘 문제
2. 빈칸 분석하기 빈칸 뒤에 있는 전치사 (   )
3. 정답 선택하기 함께 쓰이는 동사가 정답 (   )

05 Benjamin Jones ------- that he will run for mayor of Whitestone next year.

(A) invited
(B) announced
(C) supported
(D) acquired

1. 선택지 보고 문법/어휘 문제 파악하기 ☐ 문법 문제 ☐ 어휘 문제
2. 빈칸 분석하기 빈칸 뒤에 있는 것 주격 ☐ 보어 ☐ 명사절
            → 빈칸은 ☐ 2형식 동사 ☐ 3형식 동사 자리이다.
3. 정답 선택하기 정답 (   )

06 Gourmet Market ------- store members an additional discount.

(A) supplies
(B) offers
(C) registers
(D) assists

1. 선택지 보고 문법/어휘 문제 파악하기 ☐ 문법 문제 ☐ 어휘 문제
2. 빈칸 분석하기 빈칸 뒤에 있는 것 ☐ 명사구 + 명사구 ☐ 명사구 + 형용사 보어
            → 빈칸은 ☐ 4형식 동사 ☐ 5형식 동사 자리이다.
3. 정답 선택하기 정답 (   )

PART 5 동사의 형태 변화와 종류 / 형용사 어휘 (3)   197

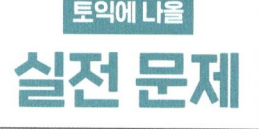 DAY 01-08 누적 문제

제한시간 9분입니다! 시~작!

01. Rose Weiss, a professional financial advisor, ------- global currency markets on a daily basis.

(A) evaluation
(B) evaluator
(C) evaluating
(D) evaluates

02. Medical emergency professionals are ------- to remain calm in any kind of situation.

(A) instruct
(B) instructed
(C) instructor
(D) instructs

03. DeRosa Bank offers its VIP clients access to vault space that is completely ------- and guarded around the clock.

(A) accustomed
(B) secure
(C) additional
(D) relevant

04. Supervisors at Deacon Manufacturing ------- to include a new lounge room and café in the renovation plan.

(A) deciding
(B) have decided
(C) decision
(D) to decide

05. Ticket sales for Lawson County Fair ------- what event planners had predicted.

(A) exceeding
(B) excessive
(C) exceeded
(D) being exceeded

06. Franco Home's silverware is affordable but ------- to rust if not handled carefully.

(A) remarkable
(B) vulnerable
(C) exemplary
(D) subsequent

07. In order to prevent damage from the elements, ------- weather resistant paint on the outside of your home.

(A) to use
(B) usage
(C) use
(D) using

08. A supervisor's approval is ------- before taking leave at Lucian, Inc.

(A) require
(B) to require
(C) required
(D) requires

09. Since direct sunlight can ------- paintings, those artworks are displayed in the museum's basement.

(A) damaged
(B) damages
(C) damage
(D) damaging

10. Digitizing all of the client files is ------- to be an enormous task.

(A) seeking
(B) proving
(C) meeting
(D) placing

11. Perfect Fit ------- an indoor swimming pool and 400-meter track in its basement.

(A) arrives
(B) competes
(C) refers
(D) features

12. Your colleagues will ------- you with any other details that are specific to your position here.

(A) describe
(B) search
(C) provide
(D) schedule

13. The stage director estimated that $500 would be ------- to acquire the props needed for the performance.

(A) sufficient
(B) flexible
(C) capable
(D) calculating

14. The personnel department ------- to hold a series of workshops next month.

(A) supplies
(B) plans
(C) revises
(D) suggests

15. A recent survey reports that most online customers ------- the quick check-out very convenient to use.

(A) take
(B) place
(C) join
(D) find

16. A tour of the main production facility is ------- the itinerary for Mr. Massey's business trip.

(A) on
(B) as
(C) for
(D) around

17. Mr. Randall is known for recruiting employees who are ------- competent.

(A) exceptionally
(B) exceptions
(C) excepting
(D) excepted

18. Developers are trying to increase the battery life of the AirLite Tablet without reducing -------.

(A) functioned
(B) functionally
(C) functional
(D) functionality

19. Ms. Collins has developed ------- computer software programs that predict stock values and markets.

(A) possible
(B) severe
(C) normal
(D) innovative

20. The management has ------- to reduce individual workloads by hiring more staff.

(A) promise
(B) promised
(C) promises
(D) promising

21. In order to receive their 20% discount on university clothing, students must show a ------- student ID.

(A) clear
(B) steady
(C) common
(D) valid

22. During the press conference, Mr. Whitman officially ------- that his company will acquire HB Industries.

(A) told
(B) remained
(C) announced
(D) outlined

23. To keep all ------- items fresh for as long as possible, Mullins Shipping uses a shrink-wrapping machine.

(A) mandatory
(B) noteworthy
(C) perishable
(D) thorough

24. Residents argued that the original Newton Library building ------- as a museum instead of being demolished.

(A) to restore
(B) restoring
(C) that restores
(D) should be restored

PART 5 동사의 형태 변화와 종류 / 형용사 어휘 (3)   199

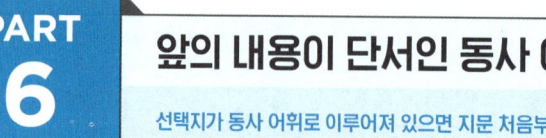

PART 6 앞의 내용이 단서인 동사 어휘

선택지가 동사 어휘로 이루어져 있으면 지문 처음부터 읽으면서 문맥을 파악하세요.

✎ 적용 기술

[기적의 필기노트] 158P
RC 기술 76

📖 VOCA

business 사업체
access 접근 가능함
job opening 채용 공고
field 분야
expertise 전문 지식

🔒 기출 표현 확인

<정답 동사> join
<지문 단서> meet, colleague, meeting

👨 풀이 방법 · e-mail

🔎 해석 p.66

To: Richard Saldana <rsaldana@rmail.net>
From: Member Services <mserv@joblink.net>
Date: 15 September
Subject: Status Upgrade

Dear Member,

This e-mail is to confirm that you upgraded your membership with Job Link to the Gold Package. Your business now has access to a variety of features. You may ------- job openings, access profiles, and search by fields of experience or expertise.
01.

Feel free to do so by logging into our Web site at www.joblink.net/login at your convenience.

Please ------- that we here at Job Link respect your company's privacy. Only
🔗 **PART 5**

company details that you request to be posted can be viewed.

Sincerely,

Job Link Member Services

01. (A) apply
(B) post
(C) receive
(D) attract

🔖 이렇게 풀어요

1. 선택지 보고 문법/어휘 문제 파악 선택지가 서로 다른 동사 어휘로 구성되어 있으므로 어휘 문제임을 파악합니다.
(A) 적용하다, 신청하다　(B) 게시하다　(C) 받다　(D) 끌어들이다

2. 빈칸 분석 빈칸 앞에서 멤버십이 업그레이드되어 다양한 기능에 접근할 수 있다고 알리고 있어요. 이와 관련해서 '채용 공고'와 어울릴 수 있는 동사를 골라야 함을 파악해요.

3. 정답 선택 사업체가 채용 공고를 '게시할' 수 있으므로 (B) post를 정답으로 선택합니다.

🔎 해설

빈칸 앞에 Please가 있고 문장의 주어가 없으므로 명령문입니다. 따라서 동사원형이 와야 하므로 (B)가 정답입니다.

🔗 PART 5 문법 적용 문제

Please ------- that we here at Job Link respect your company's privacy.

(A) notable　(B) note　(C) to note　(D) noted

200　기적의 토익 RC

따라 하면 문제가 풀리는

연습 문제

빈칸 앞 내용에서 단서가 될 부분을 찾아 표시하세요.
표시한 것을 바탕으로 정답 어휘를 선택하세요.

○ 정답 및 해설 p.66

01

How was your experience today? Lily's Garden wants to hear what you have to say about our restaurant, so please take a moment to fill out a survey. If you do, you'll receive a coupon for 10% off the next time you ------- here!

(A) dine   (B) negotiate

02

The National Arbor Group (NAG) is dedicated to restoring forests across the country. To date, we have ------- over 5,000 square miles of trees.

(A) planted   (B) logged

03

Rochester Roofing was founded five years ago with only a few employees, but quickly gained an outstanding reputation. To keep up with demand, founder Kelly Moss ------- 20 more employees.

(A) posted   (B) hired

04

The renovation project will expand the kitchen area and add a drive-through window. This will ------- the number of customers we can serve.

(A) reduce   (B) maximize

DAY 08

PART 6 앞의 내용이 단서인 동사 어휘   201

제한시간 4분입니다! 시~작!

Questions 01-04 refer to the following e-mail.

To: t.jensen@rmail.net
From: custserv@borneo.net
Date: 7 October
Subject: Borneo Account

Dear Customer,

For being a frequent customer, we at Borneo.net have rewarded you with a credit of $10. -------
01.
credit can be used toward any item on our Web site. Keep in mind that it does not ------- to shipping
02.
fees. Next time you log into www.borneo.net, check the My Account page. To use the credit, simply
click the "My Credit" button ------- you check out.
03.

Feel free to contact our service department at any time with any questions you may have. -------.
04.

Sincerely,

Borneo Online Outlet Service Team

---

01. (A) Other
    (B) This
    (C) Some
    (D) Another

유형 적용 문제
02. (A) accrue
    (B) apply
    (C) direct
    (D) send

03. (A) around
    (B) within
    (C) whereas
    (D) before

04. (A) Thank you again for your recent visit to our store.
    (B) Please take a moment to fill out an online questionnaire.
    (C) Please note that special offers are only available for a limited time.
    (D) We have service representatives online 24 hours a day, 7 days a week.

Questions 05-08 refer to the following e-mail.

To: Howard Foley <h.foley@fmail.net>
From: Customer Service Team <service@wildwheelsmag.net>
Date: 2 February
Subject: Cancellation

Dear Subscriber,

This e-mail is being sent ------- you cancelled your subscription to *Wild Wheels Magazine*. If you
                              05.
clicked "unsubscribe" accidentally, please contact us. We can ------- your subscription immediately.
                                                              06.
-------. Please use that in correspondence with our service representatives.
07.

Keep in mind that there are still two months remaining on your 1-year subscription. You will
continue ------- our magazine until that expires.
         08.

Sincerely,

Wild Wheels Magazine

---

05. (A) due to
　　　(B) if
　　　(C) because
　　　(D) then

유형 적용 문제
06. (A) report
　　　(B) restore
　　　(C) transfer
　　　(D) collect

07. (A) Please do not respond to this e-mail.
　　　(B) It will renew itself automatically after that time.
　　　(C) For questions or concerns, please contact
　　　　　customer service.
　　　(D) Your cancellation code is HF9241.

08. (A) receivable
　　　(B) receipts
　　　(C) received
　　　(D) receiving

PART 7

편지

편지 지문은 문제를 풀기 전, 발신자와 수신자의 이름과 소속(회사/기관)을 먼저 확인하세요.

 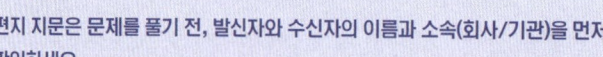

편지는 이메일과 함께 PART 7에서 출제 비중이 높은 지문 중 하나입니다. 개인과 회사 또는 회사 간에 주고받는 편지가 출제돼요. 이메일과 달리 상단에 발신인의 회사명이 명시됩니다. 수신인이 요청한 업무가 완료되었다고 알리거나 문제가 해결되었다고 알리는 내용, 또는 업무상 정보를 주고받는 내용이 주로 출제됩니다.

편지에서 자주 출제되는 문제

· 세부사항 문제
세부사항 문제가 지문당 2개가 나오는 경우도 있어요. 수신자/발신자에 관한 문제일 경우 이름이나 your와 같은 대명사가 언급된 부분에서 단서를 파악할 수 있습니다. 일반 명사가 키워드로 제시될 경우 해당 키워드를 지문에서 빠르게 찾는 것이 중요해요.

🔒 **기출 확인**

특정 문제가 해결되었음을 알리는 편지일 경우, 목적 문제에 대한 정답으로는 To announce approval 등과 같이 승인 여부나 문제 해결 여부를 알리는 선택지가 자주 출제돼요.

편지에 자주 출제되는 어휘

compensate	보상하다	resolve	해결하다
renovate	보수[개조]하다	finalize	마무리하다
correct	수정하다	reimburse	배상[변제]하다
follow up on	~에 대해 후속 조치하다	handle	처리[해결]하다
convert	전환하다	approve	승인하다
deduct	공제하다	address	해결하다, 처리하다
fulfill	이행하다	convince	확신시키다
meet one's need	필요를 충족시키다	cooperate	협력하다
strengthen	강화하다	satisfy	만족시키다
implement	실행하다	accomplish	완수하다
compromise	타협하다	mediate	중재하다, 조정하다
negotiate	협상하다, 교섭하다	revise	수정하다, 변경하다
evaluate	평가하다	assume	가정하다
critical	중요한	facilitate	촉진하다, 용이하게 하다
expert	전문가, 전문적인	certify	증명하다
by far	훨씬, 단연코	forward	보내다
affair	사안, 일	record	기록, 기록하다
inadvertently	부주의로 인하여	invaluable	귀중한
adequately	적절히	prompt	신속한
illustrate	설명하다	consent form	동의서
enterprise	기업, 회사	work ethic	직업 윤리

 **편지**

letter
〇 해석 p.67

Blackwell Shop
2963 Geary Blvd
San Francisco CA 94118

Dear Mr. Edwards,

The work on your car is complete and it is now ready for pickup.

The fan belt was worn out and needed to be completely replaced. As discussed over the phone, the brake pads were also in poor condition, so we replaced those as well. The tires were rotated free of charge, and we changed the oil and refilled the antifreeze. The full invoice for the work performed has been printed and is waiting for you at our reception desk. We are open from 8 A.M. to 7 P.M. throughout the week.

We would like to thank you for choosing Blackwell Shop. After picking up your vehicle, please go to our Web site and leave a comment about our service. Also, be sure to follow us on social media for updates on services and promotions.

Annie Moore
Customer Service Representative

---

01. What kind of service did Mr. Edwards receive?
(A) Package delivery
(B) Automobile repair
(C) Appliance installation
(D) Web site maintenance

02. What is Mr. Edwards asked to do on a Web site?
(A) Make an appointment
(B) Browse a listing
(C) Write a review
(D) Pay a bill

▼ 이렇게 풀어요

01. Edwards 씨는 어떤 종류의 서비스를 받았는가?
(A) 소포 배달
(B) 자동차 수리
(C) 기기 설치
(D) 웹사이트 유지 관리

해설 지문에 제시된 car와 차량 부품인 fan belt, brake pads, tire, oil, antifreeze 등을 단서로 자동차 수리 서비스를 받았음을 알 수 있으므로 (B)가 정답입니다.

02. Edwards 씨는 웹사이트에서 무엇을 하도록 요청 받는가?
(A) 예약하기
(B) 목록을 둘러보기
(C) 후기를 작성하기
(D) 청구 금액을 지불하기

해설 Web site가 언급된 마지막 단락에서 please go to our Web site and leave a comment about our service라며 웹사이트에 서비스에 대한 의견을 남겨 달라고 했으므로 (C)가 정답입니다.

PART 7 편지 205

따라 하면 문제가 풀리는

연습 문제

먼저 문제의 키워드에 표시한 후,
지문에서 단서를 찾아 적절한 답을 고르세요.

01 letter

Dear Ms. Vaughn,

Due to a glitch in our software system, some bank transfers made on October 3 had duplicate entries in customers' accounts. As a result, you were issued two payments of $231.22 each from BTN Incorporated. The second payment should not have been deposited into your account, so we have deducted $231.22 to correct the error. If you have any questions about this transfer, please feel free to call me at 555-4630. I apologize for any inconvenience caused.

Dean Abbott
Accounts Manager, Warren Bank

Q. Why should Ms. Vaughn contact Mr. Abbott?

(A) To make an inquiry
(B) To confirm a transfer

02 letter

Sandra Manning
1820 Mulvey Avenue
Winnipeg, MB R3M 2A6

Dear Ms. Manning,

Thank you for purchasing a custom oak cabinet from Riverview Furniture. We have completed the production stage of your item, and it is now ready to be shipped. The item is scheduled to leave our warehouse on April 4 and be delivered between 1 P.M. and 5 P.M. on April 7. We have received your payment in full. We hope to serve you again soon.

Sincerely,

Ken Tetreault
Customer Service Agent, Riverview Furniture

Q. What is the purpose of the letter?

(A) To confirm the status of an order
(B) To apologize for a shipping delay

○ 정답 및 해설 p.68

03   letter

> Dear Mr. Burris,
>
> On behalf of the National Science Association, I would like to inform you that your membership will expire soon, on November 30. —[1]—. As you know, member benefits include attendance at science events and workshops, discounts on science-related books, and exclusive access to the content on our Web site. —[2]—. Please complete it and mail it back if you wish to continue receiving your membership benefits. We hope you will remain part of our special group!
>
> Kieran Foster

Q. In which of the positions marked [1] and [2] does the following sentence best belong?

"Enclosed you will find a membership renewal form."

(A) [1]
(B) [2]

04   letter

> HR Director Latonia Decaro
> Roanoke Incorporated
> 611 Hill Street
> Dallas, TX 75204
>
> Dear Ms. Decaro,
>
> I am writing on behalf of Suzanne Kessler, who has applied for a marketing assistant position at your company. During her three years at GPL Enterprises, Ms. Kessler has worked on numerous advertising campaigns. I have always been impressed with her unique perspective and innovate ideas. She would make an excellent addition to your team. I am happy to cooperate further with your recruitment process if you have detailed questions.
>
> Jack Collins
> Marketing Director, GPL Enterprises

Q. What does Mr. Collins mention about Ms. Kessler?

(A) She has creative ideas.
(B) She has a cooperative attitude.

PART 7 편지   207

토익에 나올 실전 문제

제한시간 11분입니다! 시~작!

Questions 01-03 refer to the following letter.

Penny Dumont
875 Strand Avenue
Houston, TX 77032

Dear Ms. Dumont,

Thank you for considering Gemini Co. for your upcoming project. —[1]—. Now that I have visited the property in person, I can offer you a detailed pricing breakdown (enclosed). The total cost of replacing your entire rooftop with slate tiles will be $18,500. This includes labor and all materials. —[2]—. If you do not schedule the work within that time period, we would most likely need to assess your property again.—[3]—.

We hope you will select Gemini Co. due to its experienced employees and high standards. —[4]—. Should you wish to find out what our past clients thought about our work, please visit the "Testimonials" page on our Web site. To book the work, please call 555-3776.

I hope to hear from you soon,

Nick Sussex
Technician, Gemini Co.

---

01. What kind of business most likely is Gemini Co.?

(A) A roofing company
(B) A courier service
(C) An equipment repair shop
(D) A real estate agency

02. Why should Ms. Dumont visit a Web site?

(A) To confirm the start date of a project
(B) To sign up for a company newsletter
(C) To browse a photo gallery of work
(D) To read the opinions of other customers

03. In which of the positions marked [1], [2], [3], and [4] does the following sentence best belong?

"The quoted price is valid for six months."

(A) [1]
(B) [2]
(C) [3]
(D) [4]

---

paraphrasing 주어진 어휘 또는 표현과 패러프레이징 될 수 있는 것을 연결하세요.

1. property •

2. replacing your entire roof •

3. what our past clients thought •

• (a) building

• (b) roofing

• (c) opinions of other customers

208 기적의 토익 RC

정답 및 해설 p.69

Questions 04-06 refer to the following letter.

Daisy Tyler
177 Southlands Road
Toronto, ON
M5V 2L6

Dear Ms. Tyler,

I regret to inform you that there is an issue with the rental property on Gallivan Drive. I know you were planning on moving your travel agency's offices there on August 1. Unfortunately, we are having difficulty evicting the current tenant, so the new move-in date would be August 8.

I realize that your current lease expires on July 31, so this creates a serious problem for you. Fortunately, there are two solutions I can offer. First, there is a space available on Paloma Avenue in the Fordham Building. The monthly rent would be the same, and it has the added benefit of being a very short walk from a subway station and two bus stops. Alternatively, my company can cover the cost of renting a temporary storage unit for all of your office furniture and other items so that you can still leave your current site on time. Please contact me to discuss these options further.

Sincerely,

Alex Wright
Ace Realty

DAY 08

04. What does Ms. Tyler plan to do in August?

(A) Hire another employee
(B) Renew a rental agreement
(C) Take a vacation
(D) Relocate her business

05. What is indicated about the Fordham Building?

(A) It has a modern design.
(B) It is located on Gallivan Drive.
(C) It is near public transportation.
(D) It is temporarily unavailable.

06. What does Mr. Wright offer to pay for?

(A) Storing some items
(B) Redecorating a room
(C) Advertising job openings
(D) Replacing damaged furniture

paraphrasing 주어진 어휘 또는 표현과 패러프레이징 될 수 있는 것을 연결하세요.

1. moving	(a) public transportation
2. a very short talk from	(b) relocate
3. a subway station and two bus stops	(c) near

PART 7 편지 209

Questions 07-11 refer to the following e-mail and letter.

To: Chapman Public Library <contact@chapmanlibrary.org>
From: Jackie Hannan <jhannon@ctwmailbox.com>
Date: February 4
Subject: Library Classes

To Whom It May Concern:

I am a regular patron of the library, and I have noticed that the majority of the classes you offer are geared toward children and young adults. While I believe that it is important to get young people interested in library activities, you must not forget about your elderly patrons. Would it be possible to open some classes specifically designed for senior citizens? I know that many people at my age, including myself, would like to learn more about technology.

Other than that, I have no complaints about the library's services. I usually visit the library at least once a week, and I'm always impressed with how experienced and well-informed your employees are. They have helped me with complex research on multiple occasions.

Thank you for your consideration.

Jackie Hannan

3976 Brookview Road, Chapman, Kansas 67431

Jackie Hannan
3976 Brookview Road
Chapman, KS 67431

Dear Ms. Hannan,

Thank you for contacting Chapman Public Library. We value the opinions of our patrons, so we appreciate your taking the time to get in touch. You'll be pleased to learn that we have several new classes starting next month, so I hope that you will find something of interest to you.

Storyworld	Basic reading class for early readers, age 5 to 7	Mondays 4:30 P.M.
Book Explorers	Book club for teens interested in Sci-Fi	1st Wednesday of the month, 7:00 P.M.
Lab Leaders	Meet in our computer lab to learn how to browse the Internet, use tablet PCs, and download smartphone apps	Thursdays 2:30 P.M.
Career Success	Take your job to the next level by strengthening your skills in public speaking, giving presentations, and negotiating	Tuesdays 7:30 P.M.

210　기적의 토익 RC

You can register for any of the above classes by visiting the library's check-out desk. We are also asking patrons to contribute markers, colored paper, glue, and more for our morning children's activities. If you are interested in doing so, please e-mail Spencer Cobb at s.cobb@chapmanlibrary. org.

We hope to see you soon at the library!

Marie Devon
Head Librarian, Chapman Public Library

07. Which class would Ms. Hannan most likely be interested in?

(A) Storyworld
(B) Book Explorers
(C) Lab Leaders
(D) Career Success

08. What does Ms. Hannan like about the library?

(A) The selection of modern books
(B) The wide range of classes
(C) The knowledgeable staff
(D) The convenient hours

09. In the letter, the word "value" in paragraph 1, line 1, is closest in meaning to

(A) care about
(B) estimate
(C) agree with
(D) cost

10. What is indicated about Book Explorers?

(A) It includes writing practice.
(B) It is the library's most popular class.
(C) It is designed for all ages.
(D) It meets once a month.

11. Why should library patrons contact Mr. Cobb?

(A) To donate some supplies
(B) To sign up for a class
(C) To volunteer to be an instructor
(D) To make suggestions for classes

---

paraphrasing 주어진 어휘 또는 표현과 패러프레이징 될 수 있는 것을 연결하세요.

1. patron •
2. designed for •
3. well-informed •
4. contribute •
5. make suggestions •

• (a) knowledgeable
• (b) deliver opinions
• (c) customer
• (d) prepared for
• (e) donate

PART 7 편지 211

'멋진 당신, 오늘도 화이팅'

DAY
09

오늘의 학습 포인트

PART 5. 주어와 동사의 수 일치
1. 단수 취급하는 주어 - 불가산 명사/고유 명사/the number of/each + 명사 등
2. 복수 취급하는 주어 - Both A and B/many + 복수 명사/a number of 등
3. 주격 관계절의 수 일치 - 선행사의 수에 따라 동사 수 일치
4. 부분/전체 표현의 수 일치 - '부분/전체 표현 + of + 명사'가 주어일 때 of 뒤 명사에 수 일치
5. there 구문의 수 일치 - there 뒤 명사에 수 일치
6. 수 일치의 예외 - 의무/명령/요청/제안을 나타내는 동사의 that절에는 무조건 동사원형
   - 'It ~ that' 구문에서 의무 형용사가 쓰이면 that절에는 무조건 동사원형

PART 6. 뒤의 내용이 단서인 동사 어휘
보기가 동사 어휘. 문맥 파악하기!

PART 7. 제품/서비스 광고
난이도 낮은 지문, 제품 특징/혜택 문제 출제

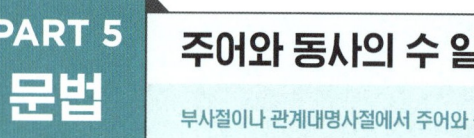

PART 5
문법
주어와 동사의 수 일치

부사절이나 관계대명사절에서 주어와 동사의 파악이 까다로울 수 있으므로 수 일치에 주의하세요.

✎ 적용 기술

[기적의 필기노트] 114P, 115P
RC 기술 27, 29

🔒 확인 문제 ❶

Mario Pizzas ------- its menu every three months.

(A) update
(B) updates

⚠ 주의

the number of(~의 수)와 a number of(많은)를 혼동하지 않도록 구분해 두세요.

출제 유형 1

단수 주어 + 단수 동사 / 복수 주어 + 복수 동사

1 단수 취급하는 주어

- **가산 단수 명사**: A customer service manager **handles** customer complaints.
  고객 서비스 매니저는 고객 불만을 처리한다.

- **단수 대명사**: She **comes** to the office before 7 a.m.
  그녀는 오전 7시 전에 사무실에 온다.

- **불가산 명사**: Written permission **is** necessary before using a company car.
  회사 차량을 이용하기 전에 먼저 서면 허가가 필요합니다.

- **고유 명사**: Jason's Place **offers** various kinds of coffee and tea.
  Jason's Place는 다양한 종류의 커피와 차를 제공한다.

`800+`
- **동명사**: Offering order tracking online **reduces** the number of e-mail inquiries.
  주문 추적을 온라인으로 제공하는 것은 이메일 문의 수를 줄인다.

`900+`
- **명사절**: What venue we will reserve **depends** on the budget.
  우리가 어떤 장소를 예약할지는 예산에 달려 있다.

- **one/every/each + 단수 명사** 하나의/모든/각각의
  Each class **consists** of 15 students. 각 수업은 15명의 학생들로 구성됩니다.

- **every/any/some/no + -thing/-body/-one** (everything, anybody, someone, no one 등)

`800+`
- **the number of + 복수 명사** ~의 수
  The number of corporate accounts **has decreased** significantly.
  기업 거래처의 수가 상당히 감소했다.

2 복수 취급하는 주어

- **가산 복수 명사**
- **'A and B', 'Both A and B'의 구조로 쓰인 주어**
  Both the chief editor and her assistant **are reviewing** the final draft.
  편집장과 그녀의 비서 둘 다 최종본을 검토하고 있다.

- **many/several/few/a few/both + 복수 명사**
- **a variety of/a range of + 복수 명사** 다양한
- **a series of + 복수 명사** 일련의
- **a number of + 복수 명사** 많은
  A number of on-the-job training sessions **are** designed for the existing accountants.
  현직 회계사들을 위한 많은 현장 연수 교육이 기획되어 있다.

🔒 확인 문제 ❷

A number of applicants ------- waiting in a lobby.

(A) is
(B) are

(B) ❷ (B) ❶ 정답

214 기적의 토익 RC

3 주어와 동사 사이의 수식어구는 수 일치에 영향을 주지 않음

- 전치사구: Machines [in the assembly line] **are** inspected every morning.
  복수 주어 ――――――――――――――― 복수 동사
  조립 라인의 기계들은 매일 아침 점검된다.

- to부정사구: The proposal [to build new apartments] **was** rejected by the city
  단수 주어 ――――――――――――― 단수 동사
  council.
  새 아파트를 짓자는 제안은 시의회에 의해 거부되었다.

- 현재분사구: The board members [attending the trade fair] **were** invited to the
  복수 주어 ――――――――――――― 복수 동사
  reception.
  무역박람회에 참가하는 이사진들은 리셉션에 초대되었다.

- 과거분사구: The manuscript [edited by editorial members] **was** published last
  단수 주어 ――――――――――――― 단수 동사
  week.
  편집자들이 편집한 원고는 지난주에 출간되었다.

- 관계절: The employees [who should be in the meeting] **are** listed on the board.
  복수 주어 ――――――――――――――――― 복수 동사
  회의에 와야 하는 직원들은 게시판에 명단이 기재되어 있다.

출제 유형 2

주격 관계절의 수 일치

800+

- 주격 관계대명사 뒤에는 동사가 바로 이어서 나오는데, 이때 **동사의 수는 관계절이 수식하는 명사인 선행사의 수가 단수인지 복수인지에 따라 결정**됩니다.

  We will give a contract to a company [that **covers** Wyoming and the adjoining
  단수 선행사 ――― 단수 동사
  states.]
  우리는 Wyoming주와 그 인접 주들을 커버하는 회사와 계약할 것이다.

  Any members [who **renew** their membership by the end of this month] get an
  복수 선행사 ――― 복수 동사
  extra 10% off.
  이달 말까지 회원권을 갱신하는 모든 회원들께 추가 10% 할인이 제공됩니다.

⚠ 주의

수식어구인 to부정사와 현재분사구는 동사와 구분이 비교적 쉽지만, 과거분사구의 경우 동사와 혼동하기 쉬우므로 주의하세요.

🔒 확인 문제 ❸

The meeting room which I reserved online ------- by someone else.

(A) is occupied
(B) are occupied

DAY 09

✎ 적용 기술

[기적의 필기노트] 116P
RC 기술 30

🔒 확인 문제 ❹

He won the tennis game that ------- last week.

(A) were held
(B) was held

정답 ❸ (A) ❹ (B)

PART 5 문법 주어와 동사의 수 일치 **215**

확인 문제 ❺

Some of the information
------- outdated.

(A) were
(B) was

출제 유형 3

부분/전체를 나타내는 표현의 수 일치

`800+`

- '부분/전체를 나타내는 표현 + of + 명사'가 주어로 쓰이면 of 뒤의 명사에 동사의 수를 일치시킵니다.

- all/most/any/some/half + of the 단수 명사 + 단수 동사
  + of the 불가산 명사 + 단수 동사
  + of the 복수 명사 + 복수 동사

- the rest/percent/the bulk/분수 + of the 단수 명사 + 단수 동사
  나머지   대부분   + of the 불가산 명사 + 단수 동사
  + of the 복수 명사 + 복수 동사

Most of the protective equipment **is inspected** every quarter.
불가산 명사   단수 동사
대부분의 보호 장비는 매 분기마다 점검을 받는다.

All of the speakers **have joined** the panel discussion.
복수 명사   복수 동사
모든 강연자들은 패널 토의에 참가했다.

적용 기술

[기적의 필기노트] 115P
RC 기술 28

⚠ 주의

There 구문은 1형식 문장이므로 be동사 뒤에 현재분사/과거분사/형용사가 올 수 없어요.
There are (limited / **limitations**) on use of funds.

출제 유형 4

there 구문의 수 일치

`900+`

- there 구문에서는 동사 뒤에 있는 명사가 주어입니다. 따라서 뒤에 있는 명사를 보고 앞의 동사를 수 일치시킵니다.

- there 구문에서 자주 쓰이는 동사: be동사, exist, remain
  There **remain** seven office desk sets in the warehouse.
  창고에 7개의 사무용 책상 세트가 남아 있다.

출제 유형 5

수 일치의 예외

`800+`

- 의무/명령/요청/제안을 나타내는 동사의 that절에는 주어의 인칭/수에 관계없이 동사원형을 씁니다.

| 빈출 의무/명령/요청/제안 동사 |

require/request/ask 요구하다   suggest/propose/recommend 제안하다
mandate 명령하다   insist 주장하다   order 명령하다   demand 요구하다

The new policy mandates that the manager on duty **approve** all return requests.
새 정책은 당직 관리자가 모든 반품 요청에 대해 승인하도록 규정하고 있다.

- 'It ~ that'의 가주어/진주어 구문에서 의무를 나타내는 형용사가 쓰이면 that절에는 주어의 인칭/수에 관계없이 동사원형을 씁니다.

| 빈출 의무 형용사 |

important 중요한   necessary 필요한   imperative 반드시 해야 하는
essential 필수적인   vital 필수적인   mandatory 의무적인   advisable 권장되는

확인 문제 ❻

The tenant insisted that the bath tub ------- for free.

(A) is repaired
(B) be repaired

(B) ❻ (B) ❺ **정답**

216 기적의 토익 RC

주어와 동사의 수 일치

1. Various tax preparation services offered by Carson Software ------- your time and money.

(A) save   (B) saving   (C) saves   (D) to save

Carson Software에서 제공되는 다양한 세금 준비 서비스는 당신의 시간과 돈을 절약해 준다.

> **이렇게 풀어요**
>
> **1. 선택지 보고 문법/어휘 문제 파악** 선택지가 모두 동사 save(절약하다)의 파생어로 구성되어 있으므로 문법 문제임을 파악해요.
> **2. 빈칸 분석** 주어 Various tax preparation services 뒤에 동사가 없으므로 빈칸에는 동사가 들어가야 함을 파악해요.
> **3. 정답 선택** 주어 Various tax preparation services가 복수이므로 유일한 복수 동사인 (A) save를 정답으로 고릅니다.

2. The project will be given to a company which ------- extensive knowledge of the texture industry.

(A) possession   (B) possesses   (C) are possessed   (D) possess

그 프로젝트는 직물 산업에 대한 폭넓은 지식을 가지고 있는 기업에게 주어질 것이다.

> **이렇게 풀어요**
>
> **1. 선택지 보고 문법/어휘 문제 파악** 선택지가 모두 동사 possess(가지다)의 여러 형태와 파생어로 구성되어 있으므로 문법 문제임을 파악해요.
> **2. 빈칸 분석** 관계대명사 which 뒤에 동사가 없으므로 빈칸에는 동사가 들어가야 함을 파악해요.
> **3. 정답 선택** 주격 관계대명사 which 앞의 선행사 a company가 단수이므로 단수 동사 (B) possesses를 정답으로 고릅니다.

3. The guidelines for online security require that every staff member ------- their passwords every quarter.

(A) changing   (B) changes   (C) to change   (D) change

온라인 보안 지침은 모든 직원들이 매 분기 마다 비밀번호를 변경하도록 요구한다.

> **이렇게 풀어요**
>
> **1. 선택지 보고 문법/어휘 문제 파악** 선택지가 모두 동사 change(바꾸다)의 파생어로 구성되어 있으므로 문법 문제임을 파악해요.
> **2. 빈칸 분석** 목적어 역할을 하는 that 절의 주어 every staff member 뒤에 동사가 없으므로 동사가 들어갈 자리임을 파악해요.
> **3. 정답 선택** 동사 recommend는 제안을 나타내는 동사이므로 목적어로 쓰인 that절 내의 동사는 동사원형이 되어야 합니다. 따라서 (D) change를 정답으로 고릅니다.

PART 5 어휘

형용사 어휘 (4)

각 어휘와 함께 자주 쓰이는 표현을 통째로 외워두세요.

800+

01 complex 복잡한, 복합적인

complex issues 복잡한 문제들

02 prior 사전의, 우선하는

prior experience 사전 경험
prior to -ing ~에 앞서

🐝 빈출 토익 선생님 Pick!

03 accessible 접근 가능한, 이용 가능한

publicly accessible 공개적으로 접근 가능한
easily accessible 쉽게 접근할 수 있는
be accessible to ~가 접근할 수 있다

04 confidential 비밀의, 기밀의

strictly confidential 극비의
confidential information 기밀 정보
remain confidential 비밀로 유지되다

05 former 예전의, 이전의

former staff members 예전 직원들
former position 이전 직책
former colleague 전 동료

800+

06 contemporary 현대의, 동시대의

contemporary artworks 현대 미술
contemporary design 현대 디자인

🐝 빈출 토익 선생님 Pick!

07 reliable 믿을 수 있는, 신뢰할 수 있는

reliable product 믿을 수 있는 제품
provide reliable service 신뢰할 수 있는 서비스를 제공하다
prove to be reliable 믿을 수 있는 것으로 판명 나다

---

08 substantial 상당한

substantial amount of 상당한 양의
substantial impact on ~에 미치는 상당한 영향
substantial sales increase 상당한 판매 증가

09 overwhelming 엄청난, 압도적인

overwhelming demand for ~에 대한 엄청난 요구
receive an overwhelming response 압도적인 반응을 얻다
overwhelming attendance 엄청난 참석률

800+

10 unforeseen 예측하지 못한, 뜻밖의

unforeseen circumstances 예측하지 못한 상황
unforeseen events 뜻밖의 사건들
unforeseen problems 예측하지 못한 문제들

11 competent 능력 있는, 능숙한

highly competent employees 대단히 유능한 직원들
competent candidate 능력 있는 후보자

800+

12 equivalent 동등한, 맞먹는

be equivalent to ~와 맞먹다

🐝 빈출 토익 선생님 Pick!

13 prominent 중요한, 유명한, 현저한

play a prominent role 중요한 역할을 하다
prominent firm 유명한 회사
prominent manufacturer 유명한 제조사

14 rewarding 보람 있는

rewarding experience 보람 있는 경험
rewarding career 보람 있는 직업
find A rewarding ~가 보람 있다고 생각하다

218 기적의 토익 RC

15 drastic
과감한, 급격한

drastic change	급격한 변화
take drastic measures	과감한 조치를 취하다

16 reluctant
꺼리는, 마지못한

be reluctant to부정사	~하기를 꺼리다, 주저하다

17 prompt
즉각적인, 지체 없는

prompt response	신속한 대응
prompt reply	신속한 답변

🐾 빈출 토익 선생님 Pick!
18 exceptional
이례적인, 뛰어난

exceptional promotion	이례적인 승진
exceptional fuel efficiency	뛰어난 연비

800+
19 obsolete
구식의, 한물간

become obsolete	구식이 되다
obsolete technology	한물간 기술

20 ongoing
진행 중인

ongoing research	진행 중인 연구
ongoing effort to부정사	~하려는 지속적인 노력

21 generous
후한, 너그러운

generous donation	후한 기부
generous funding	후한 자금 지원
give a generous amount of time	시간을 충분히 주다

🐾 빈출 토익 선생님 Pick!
22 reasonable
합리적인, 적당한

at a reasonable price	적당한 가격에
at reasonable rates	적당한 비율로
reasonable financial goal	합리적인 재정 목표

800+
23 feasible
실현 가능한

feasible plan	실현 가능한 계획
feasible solution	실현 가능한 해결책
feasible alternative to	~에 대해 실현 가능한 대안

🐾 빈출 토익 선생님 Pick!
24 prevalent
일반적인, 널리 퍼진

be prevalent among[in]	~에 널리 퍼져 있다
prevalent trends	널리 퍼진 추세
prevalent disease	널리 퍼진 질병

25 apparent
분명한, 명백한

apparent to	~에게 명백한
for no apparent reason	명백한 이유 없이
it is apparent that	~은 분명하다

DAY 09

🧑‍🏫 풀이 방법

Public facilities should be more easily ------- to local residents.

(A) prominent   (B) accessible   (C) generous   (D) prompt

공공 시설들은 지역 주민들이 더 쉽게 접근할 수 있어야 한다.

> **이렇게 풀어요**
>
> 1. **선택지 보고 문법/어휘 문제 파악** 선택지가 서로 다른 형용사 어휘로 구성되어 있으므로 어휘 문제임을 파악해요.
> 2. **빈칸 분석** 빈칸 뒤의 전치사 to와 어울려 쓰일 수 있어야 하고, '공공 시설들에 지역 주민들이 쉽게 -------'라는 문맥에 적절한 형용사가 들어가야 함을 파악해요.
> 3. **정답 선택** '접근 가능한, 이용 가능한'이라는 의미를 가진 (B) accessible을 정답으로 고릅니다.

PART 5 어휘 형용사 어휘 (4)   219

따라 하면 문제가 풀리는

연습 문제

앞서 학습한 문제 풀이법을 적용하여 맞는 것에 ✓ 표시 하거나 괄호 안에 적절한 답을 쓰고 정답을 선택하세요.

01 Rockaway Industrial ------- solar panels to countries around the world.

(A) provide
(B) provides
(C) providing
(D) provision

1. 선택지 보고 문법/어휘 문제 파악하기 ☐문법 문제 ☐어휘 문제
2. 빈칸 분석하기 빈칸 앞에 있는 문장의 주어 ☐단수 주어 ☐복수 주어
   → 빈칸은 ☐단수 동사 ☐복수 동사 자리이다.
3. 정답 선택하기 정답 (   )

02 Officials from the government ------- our main facility every quarter.

(A) inspector
(B) inspection
(C) inspect
(D) inspects

1. 선택지 보고 문법/어휘 문제 파악하기 ☐문법 문제 ☐어휘 문제
2. 빈칸 분석하기 빈칸 앞에 있는 문장의 주어 (   )
   → ☐단수 주어 ☐복수 주어
   → 빈칸은 ☐단수 동사 ☐복수 동사 자리이다.
3. 정답 선택하기 정답 (   )

03 I was not able to attend the meeting due to the ------- engagement with a supervisor.

(A) formal
(B) prior
(C) drastic
(D) prompt

1. 선택지 보고 문법/어휘 문제 파악하기 ☐문법 문제 ☐어휘 문제
2. 빈칸 분석하기 빈칸 앞 전치사 due to의 의미 (   )
   → 빈칸 뒤에는 회의에 참석하지 못한 ☐결과 ☐이유가 이어져야 한다.
3. 정답 선택하기 정답 (   )

04 This is an update to the security policy which ------- last month.

(A) have been implemented
(B) was implemented
(C) were implemented
(D) be implemented

> 1. 선택지 보고 문법/어휘 문제 파악하기 ☐ 문법 문제 ☐ 어휘 문제
>
> 2. 빈칸 분석하기 빈칸 앞 which가 수식하는 선행사 (   )
>   → 선행사가 ☐ 단수 ☐ 복수이다.
>   → 빈칸은 ☐ 단수 동사 ☐ 복수 동사 자리이다.
>
> 3. 정답 선택하기 정답 (   )

05 One of the senior accountants ------- training sessions at Seymour Financial.

(A) leading
(B) lead
(C) leads
(D) have led

> 1. 선택지 보고 문법/어휘 문제 파악하기 ☐ 문법 문제 ☐ 어휘 문제
>
> 2. 빈칸 분석하기 빈칸 앞에 있는 문장의 주어 (   )
>   → 주어가 ☐ 단수 ☐ 복수이다.
>   → 빈칸은 ☐ 단수 동사 ☐ 복수 동사 자리이다.
>
> 3. 정답 선택하기 정답 (   )

06 Anyone who ------- to apply for a transfer should contact a Personnel representative.

(A) wanting
(B) want
(C) are wanting
(D) wants

> 1. 선택지 보고 문법/어휘 문제 파악하기 ☐ 문법 문제 ☐ 어휘 문제
>
> 2. 빈칸 분석하기 빈칸 앞 who가 수식하는 선행사 (   )
>   → 선행사가 ☐ 단수 ☐ 복수이다.
>   → 빈칸은 ☐ 단수 동사 ☐ 복수 동사 자리이다.
>
> 3. 정답 선택하기 정답 (   )

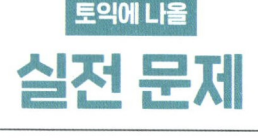

토익에 나올 실전 문제

DAY 01-09 누적 문제

제한시간 9분입니다! 시~작!

01. Since Mr. Jordan ------- to the Rome branch already, a new training supervisor is needed at headquarters.
(A) relocate
(B) relocating
(C) has relocated
(D) being relocated

02. Everwood Landscaping was chosen because they promised to fulfill all of the service requirements at a ------- price.
(A) informative
(B) unforeseen
(C) reasonable
(D) former

03. To meet rush orders, Donna's Fabric ------- temporary warehouse workers for its packaging lines.
(A) is hiring
(B) hiring
(C) hire
(D) have hired

04. Most medical doctors recommend that a patient with diabetes ------ their eating and exercise daily.
(A) record
(B) recorded
(C) to record
(D) has recorded

05. Anyone who ------ their contact information will receive a free shipping code.
(A) update
(B) updates
(C) to update
(D) updating

06. Anderson Farm in Louisiana ------- hardships due to flooding.
(A) experience
(B) experienced
(C) experiencing
(D) experiential

07. The delivery date of your shipment ------- on the time the order is placed.
(A) depend
(B) depends
(C) depending
(D) dependent

08. Estrada Manufacturing supplies ------- auto parts for several major car companies.
(A) vulnerable
(B) reliable
(C) previous
(D) immediate

09. When she worked as a news reporter, Ms. Graves ------- many leading business owners in the city.
(A) interviewer
(B) interviewing
(C) interviewed
(D) were interviewing

10. Ms. Edwards ------- any questions regarding the new project at the weekly meeting.
(A) have answered
(B) answering
(C) will answer
(D) answer

11. Feedback forms ------- from nearly every member who attended the convention.
(A) were collected
(B) are collecting
(C) collectables
(D) to collect

12. Waiving trash collection fees ------- people to recycle their waste properly.
(A) encourage
(B) have encouraged
(C) to encourage
(D) can encourage

222   기적의 토익 RC

13. People entering an active job site ------- to wear safety gear such as boots and a hardhat.

(A) forces
(B) forcing
(C) are forced
(D) forceful

14. All of the open positions ------- candidates to have a minimum of a bachelor's degree in order to be considered.

(A) expose
(B) require
(C) obtain
(D) call

15. James Holt and Rebecca Smith ------- on another book that focuses on the British royal family.

(A) initiated
(B) explained
(C) collaborated
(D) gathered

16. After transferring from the headquarter office, Mr. Clay is ------- supervising the sales department in the Boston branch.

(A) now
(B) well
(C) otherwise
(D) fairly

17. Many companies are looking ------- talented software developers.

(A) over
(B) for
(C) upon
(D) throughout

18. Ms. Bannon made it ------- that she is not available to work this Saturday.

(A) clear
(B) cleared
(C) clearly
(D) clears

19. Richmond Real Estate received a local business award for its ------- customer service.

(A) feasible
(B) complex
(C) drastic
(D) exceptional

20. Customers ------- positively to the new self-checkout counters.

(A) responded
(B) responding
(C) response
(D) responds

21. Due to his fear of heights, Mr. Freeman was ------- to join his colleagues on a mountain hiking trip.

(A) remarkable
(B) confidential
(C) accessible
(D) reluctant

22. The department ------- Mr. Ingram's promotion by going out to lunch tomorrow.

(A) will be celebrating
(B) are celebrating
(C) have celebrated
(D) celebrate

23. The entire garden of Frazier Mansion, an ------- area of 5 football fields, has been converted into a public park.

(A) equivalent
(B) exemplary
(C) apparent
(D) enthusiastic

24. The ongoing drought is having a ------- effect on both farmers and food prices.

(A) competent
(B) substantial
(C) suitable
(D) confidential

PART 5 주어와 동사의 수 일치 / 형용사 어휘 (4)   223

PART 6

뒤의 내용이 단서인 동사 어휘 `800+`

빈칸이 지문 초반에 있고 선택지가 동사 어휘로 이루어져 있으면 빈칸 뒤 내용을 파악하세요.

적용 기술

[기적의 필기노트] 158P
RC 기술 76

📘 VOCA

allow A to부정사 A가 ~할 수 있게 하다
coffee ground 커피 가루
brew timer 끓이는 시간을 설정하는 타이머
enter 입력하다
arrow 화살표
custom setting 사용자 지정 설정

👨 풀이 방법 · instructions   해석 p.75

Instructions: Programming your Morning Mate Coffee Maker

The Morning Mate Coffee Maker allows you to have a freshly brewed cup of coffee waiting for you as soon as you get out of bed in the morning. All you have to do is put in coffee grounds and ------- the brew timer.
01.

With the push of a button, you can simply enter the time that you ------- your coffee
🔧 PART 5

to be ready.

The digital interface will show a series of options. You can set a different time for each day of the week. Just use the arrow buttons to navigate through the list.

After entering your custom settings, be sure to press Save.

01. (A) reset
(B) program
(C) pause
(D) hold

🖊 이렇게 풀어요

1. 선택지 보고 문법/어휘 문제 파악 선택지가 서로 다른 동사 어휘로 구성되어 있으므로 어휘 문제임을 파악합니다.

    (A) (기기의 시간, 숫자 등을) 다시 맞추다   (B) 설정하다   (C) 정지시키다   (D) 들다, 잡다

2. 빈칸 분석 커피 메이커 사용 설명서이고, 빈칸이 포함된 문장에서 '당신은 커피 가루를 넣고 타이머를 -------하기만 하면 된다'고 했으므로 '타이머'와 어울릴 수 있는 동사를 골라야 함을 파악해요.

3. 정답 선택 기기 작동 전에 할 수 있는 동작으로 적절한 것은 기기를 '설정하는' 것이므로 (B) program을 정답으로 선택합니다.

💡 해설

빈칸은 that절의 주어(you) 뒤의 동사 자리입니다. (A), (B)는 동사가 아니므로 정답에서 제외시키고 (C)와 (D) 중 주어 you와 수 일치하는 (D)가 정답입니다.

🔧 PART 5 문법 적용 문제

With the push of a button, you can simply enter the time that you ------- your coffee to be ready.

(A) to want   (B) wanting   (C) wants   (D) want

따라 하면 문제가 풀리는

연습 문제

빈칸 뒤 내용에서 단서가 될 부분을 찾아 표시하세요.
표시한 것을 바탕으로 정답 어휘를 선택하세요.

정답 및 해설 p.75

01

Dear Account Holder,

Thank you for opening a checking account with Wilson Bank! Please don't forget to ------- your bank card before its first use. You can do so by calling the number on the sticker attached to the new card.

(A) activate   (B) state

02

A new senior judge has been ------- to Bensonville Courthouse. Judge Adams was selected for the position thanks to her history of compassionately hearing out legal battles.

(A) retired   (B) appointed

DAY 09

03

Our marketing team will promote our new policy to ------- our products. Market analysts have recently reported that most consumers highly evaluate companies that implement environmentally friendly practices.

(A) return   (B) recycle

04

Please take a number if you would like to ------- a car insurance policy for the first time. New policy buyers are required to present their driver's license and car registration.

(A) purchase   (B) access

PART 6 뒤의 내용이 단서인 동사 어휘   225

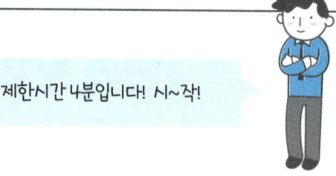

제한시간 4분입니다! 시~작!

Questions 01-04 refer to the following instructions.

Programming your LM all-purpose remote control: Instructions

Program your LM all-purpose remote to control your TV, DVD player, surround sound system, and more. This will ------- space on your coffee table by getting rid of other remotes that clutter up your
01.
living room.

First, ------- press "Program Device" while pointing at the receptor.
02.

------- the light on the remote flashes three times, it has connected to the device. Depending on the
03.
device, different buttons may have different functions. -------.
04.

You can view a list of connected devices on the screen at the top of your remote.

유형 적용 문제

01. (A) reform
(B) save
(C) contribute
(D) divide

02. (A) gentle
(B) gentleness
(C) gently
(D) gentlest

03. (A) For
(B) During
(C) When
(D) Even

04. (A) You may have to consult the instructions for the device.
(B) Please report any device that does not connect to our product.
(C) This all-purpose remote will make your life easier.
(D) Only use approved batteries for your remote.

♀ 정답 및 해설 p.75

Questions 05-08 refer to the following e-mail.

From: Gold House Investments
To: Justin Lewis
Date: 18 September
Subject: Office work

Hello, this is David from Gold House Investments. I'm pleased to let you know that we have chosen your company to ------- our office. My associates and I have read the reviews of your company's
05.
work, and we all look forward to having you work on our office remodeling.

-------. For example, since we want to have the work completed as fast as possible, there may be
06.
extra fees. -------, we have a strict budget to adhere to. I believe that it would be best ------- face-to-
07.   08.
face to work out such details.

Thank you,

Henrietta White
Supervisor, Gold House Investmets

유형 적용 문제

05. (A) renovate
(B) move
(C) replace
(D) build

06. (A) We would like to expand the customer waiting area.
(B) There are some issues we would like to discuss in person.
(C) Please contact either me or my secretary to schedule a meeting.
(D) The pictures of previous work on your Web site are very impressive.

07. (A) Therefore
(B) At the same time
(C) As much as
(D) In return

08. (A) meeting
(B) to meet
(C) met
(D) meets

PART 6 뒤의 내용이 단서인 동사 어휘 **227**

PART 7

광고 (1) 제품 및 서비스 광고

광고 지문은 글의 흐름이 단순한 편이므로 난이도가 낮은 유형이에요.

적용 기술

[기적의 필기노트] 188P
RC 기술 96

제품/서비스 광고는 지문 초반부에서 광고되는 제품/서비스의 종류를 파악한 후 세부사항을 확인해야 합니다. 광고는 대개 <제목(업종 또는 광고 제품) – 제품의 특징 및 장점 – 관련 정보 및 혜택 – 구매 방법/연락처>의 구조로 내용이 전개돼요.

제품 및 서비스 광고에 자주 출제되는 어휘

제품/서비스 광고에서 자주 출제되는 문제

무엇을 광고하는지 묻는 문제
What is being advertised?
→ 제목이나 지문 초반부에서 광고되는 것을 파악할 수 있어요.

특징/혜택에 대해 사실 여부를 묻는 문제
What is (NOT) stated about ~?
→ 보통 2~3번째 단락에 단서가 자주 등장하는데 혜택 관련 어구, 비교 구문, 항목별 특징이 제시된 부분에 단서가 자주 언급돼요.

---

1 신제품 출시

newly	새롭게	exclusive	독점적인
description	설명	feature	특징; 특징으로 하다
a wide range of	다양한	latest trend	최신 유행
extensive	광범위한	release	출시; 출시하다
launch	출시하다	try out	~해보다
top-of-the-line	최고급	trial period	체험 기간
boast	자랑할 만한 ~을 갖고 있다	take advantage of	~을 이용하다

2 할인/프로모션

a special offer	특가 제공	purchase	구매; 구매하다
inclusive	일체의 경비가 포함된	serve	제공하다
proudly	자랑스럽게	competitor	경쟁사
save	절약하다	cover	다루다
valid	유효한	discounted rate	할인된 가격
receive	받다	budget	예산
open to public	대중에게 개방된	payment	지불

3 부동산 광고

lease	임대; 임대하다	unit	한 가구
real estate	부동산, 토지	spacious	넓은
conveniently	편리하게	housing	주택
landlord	집주인	tenant	세입자
property	부동산	premise	부지
cozy	아늑한	furnished	가구가 딸려 있는
garage	주차장	deposit	보증금

풀이 방법

제품 및 서비스 광고

advertisement

⚲ 해석 p.76

Item: RZ-7 Circular Saw
From the award-winning LumberJack brand!
Asking price: $100
Location: Wayzata, MN

Description:
– Purchased new last year. Original price was $195.
– Adjustable for 6", 8", or 10" blades.
– Power cord is optional. Battery can last a full work day.

Contact information: Jessica at 555-7623. Will post images of saw upon request.

---

01. What is NOT stated about the saw?

(A) Its brand has won several awards.
(B) Its battery lasts a long time.
(C) It was originally bought a year ago.
(D) It comes with an extra set of blades.

02. According to the advertisement, what is the owner willing to do?

(A) Accept a different price
(B) Ship the item to the buyer
(C) Post pictures of the item
(D) Reserve the item

이렇게 풀어요

01. 톱에 대해 언급되지 않은 것은 무엇인가?

(A) 해당 브랜드는 여러 개의 상을 수상하였다.
(B) 배터리가 오래 지속된다.
(C) 원래 1년 전에 구입했다.
(D) 추가 톱날 세트가 함께 제공된다.

해설 지문의 award-winning LumberJack brand은 (A), Battery can last a full work day는 (B), Purchased new last year는 (C)에 해당합니다. 추가 톱날 세트 관련 내용은 언급되지 않았으므로 (D)가 정답입니다.

02. 광고에 따르면 소유자가 기꺼이 하려는 것은 무엇인가?

(A) 다른 가격을 수용하기
(B) 구매자에게 아이템을 배송하기
(C) 아이템 사진을 게시하기
(D) 아이템을 예약하기

해설 Contact information 마지막 부분에서 요청 시 톱의 사진을 올려 준다고(Will post images of saw upon request) 했으므로 (C)가 정답입니다.

PART 7 광고 (1) 제품 및 서비스 광고 229

따라 하면 문제가 풀리는

연습 문제

먼저 문제의 키워드에 표시한 후,
지문에서 단서를 찾아 적절한 답을 고르세요.

01 advertisement

O'Connell Paints Employee Appreciation Event

Employees get extra discounts on all products!
One day only (Wednesday, 5 November)

Enjoy special savings such as:
60% off paint rollers
55% off outdoor paints
50% off paint brushes
45% off painting stencils

Our store will only be open to our employees on the day of the event. We will return to normal operations on the following day.

Q. When will O'Connell Paints reopen to the public?

(A) On 6 November
(B) On 5 November

02 advertisement

Bromley Culinary Institute

For the past two decades, the Bromley Culinary Institute has been providing top-class cooking lessons for prospective chefs. You won't want to miss what we have to offer.
• Small class sizes taught by experienced instructors
• Opportunities to cook food from around the world
• A flexible schedule to accommodate working students

Thanks to our vast network of restaurants and catering companies, our job placement assistance program is one of the best in the country. Call us today at 555-4416.

Q. What is indicated about the Bromley Culinary Institute?

(A) It has professional connections to dining establishments.
(B) Its instructors come from many different countries.

○ 정답 및 해설 p.77

03   advertisement

Bee Healthy Wraps
Pack of 6: $24.99

Features
• Can seal food in containers just like plastic wrap
• Made from 100% beeswax, so they're nontoxic
• Water resistant and able to be used up to ten times
• Do not lose grip in refrigerator or freezer
• Fully biodegradable and can even be disposed of with food waste

Each pack of Bee Healthy Wraps comes with six 30 cm x 30 cm wraps in six different colorful patterns. Keep plastic waste out of your kitchen! Order today at www.beehealthywraps.com.

Q. What benefit of the product is mentioned?

(A) It can be reused.
(B) It is lightweight.

04   advertisement

Bluebell Cleaners can make your home shine!
555-0336 ◆ www.bluebellcleaners.com

We have experienced and professional cleaning crews ready to help your home look its best. No job is too big or too small! We will supply our own equipment and cleaning products. All you need to do is tell our friendly staff exactly what you need. We're available Monday through Saturday, even on short notice. Call today for an estimate or to book an appointment.

Q. What is true about Bluebell Cleaners?

(A) It offers cleaning products for sale.
(B) It can handle projects of any size.

PART 7 광고 (1) 제품 및 서비스 광고   231

제한시간 10분입니다! 시~작!

Questions 01-02 refer to the following advertisement.

Having trouble selecting a gift? The SmartShop card is the perfect solution! Our gift card can be used in hundreds of popular retail stores across the country, and you can purchase the card in values ranging from $10 to $500. You'll also love the fact that, unlike most gift cards, there is no expiration date for the balance on the card. With the SmartShop card, your friends and family can have fun shopping in person at the stores they love. Visit our Web site at www.smartshopcard.net to order yours today. There, you can also choose among designs suitable for a wide range of special occasions.

01. What is mentioned about the SmartShop card?

(A) Its credit does not expire.
(B) It is easy to replace if lost.
(C) It can be used online.
(D) It is valid in several countries.

02. According to the advertisement, what can customers do on the Web site?

(A) Receive gift recommendations
(B) Select a card design
(C) Request gift wrapping
(D) Browse a list of stores

paraphrasing 주어진 어휘 또는 표현과 패러프레이징 될 수 있는 것을 연결하세요.

1. purchase •
2. there is no expiration date •
3. suitable •
4. choose •
5. occasion •

• (a) select
• (b) event
• (c) does not expire
• (d) appropriate
• (e) buy

정답 및 해설 p.78

Questions 03-04 refer to the following advertisement.

Introducing the **Flowlex Yoga Mat** by Lavender Inc.
Take your yoga to the next level!
$74.99

- Dimensions: 75 inches long x 27 inches wide, giving you more space for your yoga practice
- Thickness: 0.25 inches
- Material: Biodegradable nano-elastic material draws moisture away from the outer layer
- Pose Markings: Guidance to help you get the perfect alignment every time
- Accessories: Mesh bag with strap for easy transport
- Environmental Responsibility: Exclusive use of non-toxic materials that are odor-free, and fully recyclable packaging

DAY 09

03. What does the nano-elastic feature of the Flowlex Mat do?

(A) It prevents the mat from curling up.
(B) It regulates the mat's temperature.
(C) It keeps the mat's surface dry.
(D) It releases a pleasant scent.

04. What is true about the Flowlex Mat?

(A) It comes with a separate carrying container.
(B) It is available in a variety of sizes.
(C) It has been designed in numerous colors.
(D) It is sold with a video of yoga poses.

---

paraphrasing 주어진 어휘 또는 표현과 패러프레이징 될 수 있는 것을 연결하세요.

1. guidance •
2. odor-free •
3. regulate •
4. draws moisture away •
5. comes with •

• (a) explanations
• (b) is included
• (c) keeps dry
• (d) control
• (e) does not smell

PART 7 광고 (1) 제품 및 서비스 광고   233

 **실전 문제**

Questions 05-07 refer to the following Web site advertisement.

http://www.cuevassolutions.net

● ● ●

Cuevas Solutions

A home is a major investment, but many people focus on the interior of their home while neglecting their outdoor areas. Cuevas Solutions can help you transform your yard into an inviting and accessible space.

We offer a free initial consultation to all prospective customers. During the consultation, one of our garden design specialists will:
- Speak with you about your favored options, taking notes on the details
- Make suggestions for plants that would grow well in your lighting conditions
- Measure the dimensions of your yard and the available space
- Give you a quote for the expected cost of the work

Call us at 555-0671 to set up an appointment. We are currently based in Chesterfield, but we will soon be sending crews from a branch in Oakmont once it is in operation.

05. What is the advertisement promoting?

(A) Real estate services
(B) An interior design firm
(C) Landscaping services
(D) Gardening tools for sale

06. What is NOT included in the initial consultation?

(A) Showing images of past projects
(B) Taking measurements
(C) Recording customer preferences
(D) Providing pricing estimates

07. What is suggested about Cuevas Solutions?

(A) Its owner handles all inquiries.
(B) It provides a money-back guarantee.
(C) It plans to open a new branch.
(D) It is the top-rated company of its kind.

paraphrasing 주어진 어휘 또는 표현과 패러프레이징 될 수 있는 것을 연결하세요.

1. transform •
2. initial •
3. make suggestions •
4. quote •
5. based in •

• (a) recommend
• (b) headquartered in
• (c) first
• (d) pricing estimate
• (e) change

234 기적의 토익 RC

Questions 08-10 refer to the following advertisement.

Don't miss the new washing machine from Siebert Appliances!

For the past five years, Siebert Appliances has been the top-selling brand for home appliances, and we're pleased to bring you our latest creation, the Najera-9 washing machine. —[1]—. It has the same high level of quality you've come to expect from our goods, which we have maintained since opening two decades ago.

The Najera-9 offers 5.5 cubic feet of space, much more than most other brands. —[2]—. Its stabilizing technology ensures that it hardly makes a sound while in use, meaning you can do laundry late at night without disturbing others. Unlike conventional washing machines, the Najera-9 has unique technology that can detect the weight of each load. —[3]—. It also has a timer that allows you to load the machine and then set it to start up to twelve hours in advance.

The Najera-9 comes with a ten-year warranty on all parts and labor. —[4]—. Order yours today at www.siebertapp.com, or stop by one of our branches.

DAY 09

08. How long has Siebert Appliances been in business?

(A) Two years
(B) Five years
(C) Ten years
(D) Twenty years

09. What is NOT indicated as a feature of the Najera-9 washing machine?

(A) A programmable timer
(B) A large capacity
(C) Energy efficiency
(D) Quiet operation

10. In which of the positions marked [1], [2], [3], and [4] does the following sentence best belong?

"Thanks to this sensor system, up to 40 percent less water is used."

(A) [1]
(B) [2]
(C) [3]
(D) [4]

---

paraphrasing 주어진 어휘 또는 표현과 패러프레이징 될 수 있는 것을 연결하세요.

1. latest creation   •   • (a) quiet operation
2. two decades   •   • (b) new product
3. ensure   •   • (c) operating
4. in business   •   • (d) guarantee
5. hardly makes a sound while in use •   • (e) twenty years

PART 7 광고 (1) 제품 및 서비스 광고   235

'멋진 당신, 오늘도 화이팅'

DAY
10

오늘의 학습 포인트

PART 5. 능동태와 수동태

1. 능동태와 수동태의 형태 구분 – 수동태: be + p.p.

2. 자동사의 태 – 자동사는 목적어 X → 수동태 불가/'자동사 + 전치사'는 수동태 가능
   deal with → be dealt with

3. 3형식 동사의 수동태 – 빈칸 뒤 목적어 O → 능동태/목적어 X → 수동태

4. 4형식 동사의 수동태 – 능·수동태 모두 뒤에 목적어 → 해석으로 구분

5. 5형식 동사의 수동태 – 수동태 뒤에 형용사/명사/to부정사가 올 수 있음

6. 감정 동사의 수동태 – 주어가 감정의 원인이면 능동태/감정을 느끼면 수동태
   interest, delight, please 등

7. 수동태 숙어 – be equipped with, be interested in, be accustomed to 등

PART 6. 앞의 내용이 단서인 동사 시제

지문에서 날짜 표현/시제 파악하기

PART 7. 구인 광고

지원자에게 요구되는 자격 요건 등 파악하기

PART 5
문법

능동태와 수동태

수동태는 3형식 타동사의 출제 비중이 가장 높으므로 동사를 보고 자동사인지 타동사인지 구분할 수 있어야 해요.

출제 유형 1

능동태와 수동태의 형태 구분

🔒 **확인 문제 ❶**

The application form ------- by July 31.

(A) should be submitted
(B) submitting

출제 포인트
보기에 능동태와 수동태 동사가 함께 제시되었을 때 태/시제를 바로 파악할 수 있어야 해요.

✎ **적용 기술**

[기적의 필기노트] 118P
RC 기술 32

- 수동태 동사의 기본 형태는 'be + p.p.(과거분사)'입니다.
  수동태 문장: <u>Spelling errors</u> **were corrected** <u>by the editors</u>.
  　　　　　　　　주어　　　　　　동사(수동)　　　　by + 주체

- 수동태 동사는 주어의 수에 따라 be동사가 변화합니다.
  sends [단수 능동태] – is sent [단수 수동태]
  send [복수 능동태] – are sent [복수 수동태]

- 수동태 동사는 시제에 따라 be동사가 변화합니다.
  sent [단순 과거 능동태] – was/were sent [단순 과거 수동태]
  has/have sent [현재완료 능동태] – has/have been sent [현재완료 수동태]
  will send [단순 미래 능동태] – will be sent [단순 미래 수동태]

출제 유형 2

자동사(1, 2형식 동사)의 태

`800+`

1 자동사는 수동태 불가

- 자동사는 목적어를 취하지 않으므로 수동태로 쓸 수 없습니다.

rise 오르다	appear 나타나다	exist 존재하다	remain 남아 있다	consist 구성되다
work 일하다	depart 떠나다	proceed 진행하다	arrive 도착하다	participate 참석하다
occur/happen/take place 발생하다		last 지속되다		

`900+`

2 '자동사 + 전치사'는 수동태 가능

- '자동사 + 전치사'는 뒤에 목적어가 올 수 있으므로 수동태로 쓸 수 있습니다.

deal with ~을 다루다, 처리하다 → be dealt with
account for ~을 설명하다 → be accounted for
refer to ~을 언급하다, ~을 참조하다 → be referred to
carry out ~을 실행하다 → be carried out
take care of ~을 돌보다, ~을 담당하다 → be taken care of

🔒 **확인 문제 ❷**

With this all-day pass, you ------- in any seminars you want.

(A) are participated
(B) can participate

정답 ❶ (A) ❷ (B)

238　기적의 토익 RC

출제 유형 3
3형식 동사의 수동태

- 3형식 동사의 수동태는 뒤에 목적어가 없습니다. 따라서 보기가 3형식 동사일 경우, **빈칸 뒤에 목적어가 있으면 능동태, 없으면 수동태**가 정답입니다. → 3형식 동사: p.193 참고

| Emily | contacted | the customer |. Emily는 고객에게 연락했다.

| The customer | was contacted | (by Emily) |. 수동태 동사 뒤 목적어 없음

출제 유형 4
4형식 동사의 수동태

`800+`
- **4형식 동사는 능동태와 수동태 모두 뒤에 목적어가 나오므로 해석으로 구분해야 합니다.**

| The security department | issued | Mr. Willis | a temporary pass |
→4형식 동사: p.193 참고
간접목적어(~에게)　직접목적어(~을)
보안 부서에서 Willis 씨에게 임시 출입증을 발급했다.

| Mr. Willis | was issued | a temporary pass |.
직접목적어(a temporary pass)가 수동태 동사 뒤에 남음

Willis 씨는 임시 출입증을 발급받았다.

출제 유형 5
5형식 동사의 수동태

`800+`
1 수동태 동사 뒤에 형용사가 오는 경우

| The company | will keep | the prices | reasonable |.
회사는 가격을 합리적으로 유지할 것이다.

| The prices | will be kept | reasonable |. 가격은 합리적으로 유지될 것이다.
형용사 reasonable이 뒤에 남음

| **목적격 보어 자리에 형용사를 취하는 5형식 동사** |

| make 만들다 | keep 유지하다 | find 알게 되다 | consider 여기다 | deem 여기다 |

`900+`
2 수동태 동사 뒤에 명사가 오는 경우

| The city council | appointed | Mr. Reid | a new chairperson |.
시의회는 Reid 씨를 새 의장으로 임명했다.

| Mr. Reid | was appointed | a new chairperson |. Reid 씨는 새 의장으로 임명되었다.
명사 a new chairperson이 뒤에 남음

| **목적격 보어 자리에 명사를 취하는 5형식 동사** |

elect A B A를 B로 선출하다　　name A B A를 B로 임명하다, 이름짓다　　appoint A B A를 B로 임명하다
call A B A를 B로 부르다　　consider A B A를 B로 여기다, 간주하다

✎ 적용 기술

[기적의 필기노트] 117P
RC 기술 31

🔒 확인 문제 ❸

The software -------
tomorrow morning.

(A) will upgrade
(B) will be upgraded

⚠ 주의

수동태 문장임에도 'by + 명사'가 없는 경우가 더 많이 출제돼요. 따라서 'by + 주어'를 능/수동태 구분의 기준으로 삼아서는 안 돼요.

✎ 적용 기술

[기적의 필기노트] 119P
RC 기술 33

✎ 적용 기술

[기적의 필기노트] 120P
RC 기술 35

🔒 확인 문제 ❹

Ms. Garfield ------- them a pie.

(A) sent
(B) was sent

출제 포인트
동사 keep이 5형식으로 쓰여 형용사 보어와 함께 능/수동태를 묻는 유형으로 자주 출제돼요.

(A) ❸ (B) ❹ 정답

PART 5 문법 능동태와 수동태　239

3 수동태 동사 뒤에 to부정사가 오는 경우

He | allowed | me | to download the files . 그는 내가 파일을 다운로드하는 것을 허락했다.

I | was allowed | to download the files . to부정사 to download가 뒤에 남음

|목적격 보어 자리에 to부정사를 취하는 5형식 동사|

allow A toV A가 ~하도록 허락하다
encourage A toV A가 ~하도록 권장하다
ask/invite A toV A가 ~하도록 요청하다
advise A toV A가 ~하도록 조언하다

permit A toV A가 ~하도록 허가하다
expect A toV A가 ~하도록 기대하다
instruct A toV A가 ~하도록 지시하다

🔒 확인 문제 ❺

Mr. Bae ------- to join the weekly meeting.

(A) was invited
(B) invited

✎ 적용 기술

[기적의 필기노트] 120P
RC 기술 34

🔒 확인 문제 ❻

Ms. Donovan ------- about the tight deadline.

(A) concerned
(B) is concerned

출제 유형 6
감정 동사의 수동태

· 주어가 감정의 원인이면 능동태, 감정을 느끼면 수동태를 씁니다.

The free return service **satisfied** most customers.
주어(반품 서비스) · 만족의 원인
무료 반품 서비스는 대부분의 고객들을 만족시켰다.

Most customers **were satisfied** with the free return service.
주어(고객) · 만족을 느낌
대부분의 고객들은 무료 반품 서비스에 대해 만족했다.

|빈출 감정 동사|

interest 흥미를 일으키다	excite 흥분시키다	concern 걱정스럽게 하다	delight 기쁘게 하다
satisfy 만족시키다	please 기쁘게 하다	disappoint 실망시키다	surprise 놀라게 하다
amuse 기쁘게 하다	tire 피곤하게 하다	fascinate 매료시키다	

출제 유형 7
수동태 숙어

🔒 확인 문제 ❼

This office ------- with the climate control.

(A) equips
(B) is equipped

---

be + p.p. + with	be pleased with ~에 기뻐하다 be associated with ~와 연관되다 be covered with ~로 덮이다	be equipped with ~을 갖추다 be acquainted with ~을 알게 되다
be + p.p. + to	be committed/dedicated/devoted to ~에 헌신하다 be accustomed to ~에 익숙해지다 be attached to ~에 첨부되다	be opposed to ~에 반대하다
be + p.p. + in	be interested in ~에 관심이 있다 be engaged in ~에 종사하다	be involved in ~에 관계되다
be + p.p. + on	be based on ~에 근거/토대를 두다	be focused on ~에 중점을 두다
be + p.p. + about	be concerned about ~에 대해 걱정하다	

(B) ❼ (B) ❻ (A) ❺ 정답

240 기적의 토익 RC

능동태와 수동태

1. The road repair work on Bloomington Expressway ------- due to unfavorable weather conditions.

(A) delayed   (B) has been delayed   (C) will delay   (D) delay

Bloomington 고속도로의 도로 보수 공사는 악천후로 인해 지연되었다.

이렇게 풀어요

1. **선택지 보고 문법/어휘 문제 파악** 선택지가 3형식 동사 delay(지연시키다)의 다양한 동사 형태로 구성되어 있으므로 문법 문제임을 파악해요.
2. **빈칸 분석** 주어 The road repair work 뒤에 동사가 없으므로 빈칸에는 동사가 들어가야 함을 파악해요. 또한 빈칸 뒤에 목적어가 없이 전치사 due to가 있으므로 수동태 동사가 들어가야 함을 파악합니다.
3. **정답 선택** 수동태 동사인 (B) has been delayed를 정답으로 고릅니다.

2. All kitchen tools ------- clean and tidy in their labeled containers.

(A) to keep   (B) is keeping   (C) should be kept   (D) would have kept

모든 주방 도구는 라벨이 부착된 용기에 깨끗하고 정돈된 상태로 보관되어야 합니다.

이렇게 풀어요

1. **선택지 보고 문법/어휘 문제 파악** 선택지가 5형식 동사 keep의 다양한 형태로 구성되어 있으므로 문법 문제임을 파악해요.
2. **빈칸 분석** 주어 All kitchen tools 뒤에 동사가 없으므로 빈칸에는 동사가 들어가야 함을 파악해요. 또한 빈칸 뒤에 목적어가 없이 보어 역할을 하는 clean and tidy만 있으므로 수동태 동사가 들어가야 함을 파악합니다.
3. **정답 선택** 수동태 동사인 (C) should be kept를 정답으로 고릅니다.

3. Danielson Used Cars' customers ------- with various payment options.

(A) satisfying   (B) have satisfied   (C) satisfied   (D) are satisfied

Danielson 중고 차량의 고객들은 다양한 지불 옵션에 만족해한다.

이렇게 풀어요

1. **선택지 보고 문법/어휘 문제 파악** 선택지가 3형식 동사 satisfy(만족시키다)의 다양한 형태로 구성되어 있으므로 문법 문제임을 파악해요.
2. **빈칸 분석** 주어 Danielson Used Cars' customers 뒤에 동사가 없으므로 빈칸에는 동사가 들어가야 함을 파악해요. 또한 빈칸 뒤에 목적어 없이 전치사 with가 왔으므로 수동태 동사가 들어가야 함을 파악합니다.
3. **정답 선택** 수동태 동사인 (D) are satisfied를 정답으로 고릅니다.

PART 5 문법 능동태와 수동태   241

PART 5 어휘

형용사 어휘 (5)

각 어휘와 함께 자주 쓰이는 표현을 통째로 외워두세요.

01 selective   까다로운, 조심해서 고르는

selective about[in]   ~에 있어 까다로운

02 renowned   유명한

renowned as[for]   ~로 유명한
renowned writer/painter   유명한 작가/화가

03 appropriate   적절한

appropriate for   ~에 적절한

04 detailed   자세한

detailed descriptions   자세한 묘사

05 applicable   해당되는, 적용되는

applicable regulations   해당 규정
applicable experience   실무 경력
if applicable   가능하다면, 해당된다면

🐾 빈출 토익 선생님 Pick!
06 respective   각각의, 각자의

respective holders   각각의 소유자들
respective supervisors   각자의 상사들

07 optimal   최선의, 최상의

optimal performance   최상의 성능
in optimal condition   최적의 조건에서

08 decisive   결정적인, 결단력 있는

decisive evidence   결정적인 증거
decisive measures   결정적인 조치

09 partial   부분적인

partial payment   부분적인 비용 지불

🐾 빈출 토익 선생님 Pick!
10 tentative   임시의, 잠정적인

tentative schedule/itinerary   임시 일정/여행 일정
tentative agreement   잠정적 합의
tentative projection   잠정적 추정치

11 rare   드문, 희귀한

on rare occasions   드문 상황에서는
rare item   희귀한 제품

🐾 빈출 토익 선생님 Pick!
12 considerable   상당한

considerable increase in demand   수요에 있어서의 상당한 증가
have considerable market share   상당한 시장 점유율을 가지다
considerable amount of work   상당한 업무량

13 comprehensive   포괄적인, 전반적인

comprehensive range of products   매우 다양한 제품
comprehensive travel itinerary   전반적인 여행 일정
comprehensive inspection   종합적인 검사

14 impermissible   허용할 수 없는

impermissible behavior   허용할 수 없는 행위
impermissible approach   허용할 수 없는 접근
impermissible invasion   용납할 수 없는 침해

15 eager   간절히 바라는

be eager to부정사   ~하기를 간절히 바라다

242   기적의 토익 RC

16 lucrative　　　　　　　　　수익성 있는, 유리한

lucrative business　　　　　　수익성 있는 사업
lucrative contract　　　　　　유리한 계약

17 financial　　　　　　　　　　　　금융의

financial crisis　　　　　　　금융 위기
financial incentives　　　　　금전적 장려책
financial support　　　　　　금전적 지원

18 cautious　　　　　　　　　조심하는, 신중한

be cautious not to부정사　　　~하지 않으려고 조심하다
financially cautious　　　　　재정적으로 신중한

19 regular　　　　　　　　　　　정기적인

regular customer　　　　　　단골 고객
regular maintenance　　　　　정기 보수
at regular intervals　　　　　정기적으로

20 preliminary　　　　　　　　　사전의

preliminary plans　　　　　　사전 계획
preliminary research　　　　　사전 조사
preliminary questions　　　　사전 질문

🐾 빈출 토익 선생님 Pick!
21 flexible　　　　　　　융통성 있는, 탄력적인

flexible working hours　　　탄력적 근무 시간
flexible shifts　　　　　　　탄력적 교대 근무
flexible schedule　　　　　　변경 가능한 일정

22 skilled　　　　　　　　숙련된, 기술이 좋은

highly skilled　　　　　　　매우 숙련된
be skilled in[at]　　　　　　~에 노련하다

23 subtle　　　　　　　　　　　미묘한

subtle differences between　~ 간의 미묘한 차이

24 dependent　　　　　　의지하는, 좌우되는

be dependent on　　　~에 의지하다, ~에 좌우되다

🐾 빈출 토익 선생님 Pick!
25 lasting　　　　　　　　　　지속적인

make a lasting effort　　　지속적으로 노력하다
lasting effect　　　　　　　지속적인 효과

26 durable　　　　　　　　　내구성 있는

durable material　　　　　내구성 좋은 재료
durable goods　　　　　　내구성 좋은 제품

DAY 10

 풀이 방법

The amount of the fine for traffic violations is ------- on several different factors.

(A) dependent　　　　　(B) partial　　　　　(C) optimal　　　　　(D) respective

교통 위반에 대한 벌금의 액수는 여러 요인에 좌우된다.

✓ 이렇게 풀어요

1. **선택지 보고 문법/어휘 문제 파악**　선택지가 서로 다른 형용사 어휘로 구성되어 있으므로 어휘 문제임을 파악해요.
2. **빈칸 분석**　빈칸 뒤에 전치사 on이 있으므로 on과 함께 쓰일 수 있는 형용사가 들어가야 함을 파악해요.
3. **정답 선택**　be dependent on(~에 의존하다, ~에 좌우되다)의 형태로 쓰이는 (A) dependent를 정답으로 고릅니다.

PART 5 어휘 형용사 어휘 (5)　**243**

따라 하면 문제가 풀리는
연습 문제

앞서 학습한 문제 풀이법을 적용하여 맞는 것에 ✓ 표시 하거나 괄호 안에 적절한 답을 쓰고 정답을 선택하세요.

01 A shipment of fresh seafood ------- to Captain's Cabin every morning.

(A) delivers
(B) is delivered
(C) delivery
(D) delivering

1. 선택지 보고 문법/어휘 문제 파악하기 ☐ 문법 문제 ☐ 어휘 문제
2. 빈칸 분석하기 빈칸 앞에 있는 것 ☐ 주어 ☐ 동사
   → 빈칸은 ☐ 동사 ☐ 목적어 자리이다.
   → 빈칸 뒤에 목적어가 ☐ 있으므로 ☐ 없으므로 ☐ 능동태 동사 ☐ 수동태 동사 자리이다.
3. 정답 선택하기 정답 (   )

02 All of the crates ------- once the ship arrived in Chesapeake Bay.

(A) inspect
(B) inspected
(C) were inspected
(D) have inspected

1. 선택지 보고 문법/어휘 문제 파악하기 ☐ 문법 문제 ☐ 어휘 문제
2. 빈칸 분석하기 빈칸 앞에 있는 것 ☐ 주어 ☐ 동사
   → 빈칸은 ☐ 동사 ☐ 목적어 자리이다.
   → 빈칸 뒤에 목적어가 ☐ 있으므로 ☐ 없으므로 ☐ 능동태 동사 ☐ 수동태 동사 자리이다.
3. 정답 선택하기 정답 (   )

03 Your bank login ID and password should ------- safe at all times.

(A) be kept
(B) keep
(C) have kept
(D) keeping

1. 선택지 보고 문법/어휘 문제 파악하기 ☐ 문법 문제 ☐ 어휘 문제
2. 빈칸 분석하기 should를 제외하고 빈칸 앞에 있는 것 ☐ 주어 ☐ 동사
   → 빈칸은 ☐ 동사 ☐ 목적어 자리이다.
   → 빈칸 뒤에 목적어가 ☐ 있으므로 ☐ 없으므로 ☐ 능동태 동사 ☐ 수동태 동사 자리이다.
3. 정답 선택하기 정답 (   )

244 기적의 토익 RC

🔍 정답 및 해설 p.80

04 I attached the ------- schedule of the upcoming Fall Festival.

(A) renowned
(B) optimal
(C) tentative
(D) subtle

> 1. 선택지 보고 문법/어휘 문제 파악하기 ☐ 문법 문제 ☐ 어휘 문제
> 2. 빈칸 분석하기 빈칸 뒤의 명사 (   )
>   → 의미 (   )
>   → 이 명사의 의미를 꾸며주면서 함께 쓰일 수 있는 형용사가 정답이다.
> 3. 정답 선택하기 정답 (   )

05 Kelly Marx ------- Salesperson of the Year at Houston Auto.

(A) named
(B) has named
(C) is naming
(D) was named

> 1. 선택지 보고 문법/어휘 문제 파악하기 ☐ 문법 문제 ☐ 어휘 문제
> 2. 빈칸 분석하기 빈칸 앞에 있는 것 ☐ 주어 ☐ 동사
>   → 빈칸은 ☐ 동사 ☐ 목적어 자리이다.
>   → 빈칸 뒤에 목적어와 보어가 나란히 나오지 않았으므로 ☐ 능동태 동사 ☐ 수동태 동사 자리이다.
> 3. 정답 선택하기 정답 (   )

06 According to the survey results, many customers ------- in our extended warranty program.

(A) interest
(B) are interested
(C) interested
(D) have interested

> 1. 선택지 보고 문법/어휘 문제 파악하기 ☐ 문법 문제 ☐ 어휘 문제
> 2. 빈칸 분석하기 빈칸 앞에 있는 것 ☐ 주어 ☐ 동사
>   → 빈칸은 ☐ 동사 ☐ 목적어 자리이다.
>   → 빈칸 뒤에 목적어가 ☐ 있으므로 ☐ 없으므로 ☐ 능동태 동사 ☐ 수동태 동사 자리이다.
> 3. 정답 선택하기 정답 (   )

PART 5 능동태와 수동태 / 형용사 어휘 (5)   245

토익에 나올
실전 문제

DAY 01-10 누적 문제

제한시간 9분입니다! 시~작!

01. Ms. Joyce ------- the training session with an introduction and welcoming speech.

(A) starting
(B) will start
(C) to be started
(D) is started

02. All terms of contracts should be specifically -------, avoiding disputes in the future.

(A) settle
(B) settlement
(C) settled
(D) settling

03. The new findings from the customer survey are ------- to the new marketing campaign.

(A) tentative
(B) extensive
(C) urgent
(D) applicable

04. As per the law passed last year, all construction sites ------- by strict environmental guidelines.

(A) have been regulated
(B) were regulating
(C) had regulated
(D) will be regulating

05. Even though meteorologists ------- a massive snowstorm, Schenectady's public school classes have not been cancelled.

(A) predictable
(B) are predicted
(C) predict
(D) prediction

06. As of yesterday, all of the employees ------- of the new sales incentive program.

(A) have been informed
(B) will be informing
(C) had informed
(D) informative

07. Roswell Bank ------- new security measures to protect its clients from identity theft and account hacking.

(A) implementing
(B) has implemented
(C) is being implemented
(D) had been implemented

08. Following the acquisition of several regional trucking businesses, Silk Road Trucking ------- its service area.

(A) is expanded
(B) has been expanded
(C) will be expanding
(D) being expanded

09. The BlasTalk social networking app that ------- to the Asian countries has attracted nearly a million users.

(A) will introduce
(B) is introducing
(C) was introduced
(D) introduces

10. A ------- material should be chosen to cover the tops of stall tents at the flea market.

(A) cautious
(B) durable
(C) eager
(D) decisive

11. Hartford, Inc. ------- employee responsibilities in "Hartford, Inc.: Employee Guidebook."

(A) describing
(B) describes
(C) to describe
(D) had been described

12. All formal statements regarding the product should be made on ------- platforms.

(A) lucrative
(B) appropriate
(C) impermissible
(D) exceptional

246   기적의 토익 RC

13. The board members of Maxwell Manufacturing are ------- moving its factory abroad to reduce production costs.

(A) consider
(B) considering
(C) consideration
(D) being considered

14. The sales manager ------- that the company set a new record for profits.

(A) announce
(B) announcing
(C) announced
(D) to announce

15. Before it expanded into Canada, Tofu Table only ------- vegetarian dishes.

(A) offer
(B) to offer
(C) offered
(D) offering

16. Service charges may ------- from month to month based on data usage and in-app purchases.

(A) vary
(B) form
(C) supply
(D) present

17. A notification ------- a scheduled blackout for electricity work will be sent to the local residents.

(A) from
(B) with
(C) regarding
(D) according to

18. Ms. Moss has proven ------- to be capable of working effectively under extreme pressure.

(A) she
(B) herself
(C) hers
(D) her

19. The IT department announced that the new software ------- on all workstations on Friday.

(A) installs
(B) is installing
(C) will be installed
(D) to be installing

20. For ------- instructions on how to assemble your furniture, please refer to the owner's manual.

(A) lasting
(B) challenging
(C) detailed
(D) concentrated

21. Ivory Academy ------- detailed academic records of all of its current attendees.

(A) has been kept
(B) keeps
(C) keep
(D) was kept

22. Adkins Auto Rental predicts a ------- increase in demand for the duration of the summer.

(A) flexible
(B) comprehensive
(C) preliminary
(D) considerable

23. Hailey Brown's poetry collection ------- illustrations by Lucy Steele.

(A) will include
(B) is included
(C) inclusive
(D) including

24. Reporters for *Beltran Times Newspaper* are not ------- about the stories they cover.

(A) noteworthy
(B) overwhelming
(C) selective
(D) prominent

PART 6

앞의 내용이 단서인 동사 시제

선택지가 다양한 동사 시제로 이루어져 있으면 지문에서 날짜 표현이나 시제를 파악하세요.

적용 기술

[기적의 필기노트] 161P
RC 기술 79

VOCA

complaint 불만
tenant 세입자
regarding ~에 관한
poor 좋지 않은
completion 완료
contractor 계약자, 하청업자
off-limit 출입금지구역
resident 주민
lot 부지
reimburse 상환하다
expense 비용

 **풀이 방법** e-mail ◯ 해석 p.83

From: Building Management
To: All Residents
Subject: Parking Lot Maintenance
Date: 16 July

Over the past several months, we ------- complaints from tenants regarding the poor
                    PART 5
condition of our building's parking lot. Dozer Construction was selected to do the
renovation project because their expected completion time was considerably shorter
than other contractors.

The work will take place from 24 to 26 July, during which time our building's parking
lot will be off-limits. Therefore, residents with cars will have to find street parking or
use a different lot. The management office ------- alternative parking expenses
                                               01.
during that time. Please keep your parking receipts during these dates.

Vanessa Lohan
Oakland Tower Building Manager

01. (A) is reimbursing
     (B) will reimburse
     (C) had reimbursed
     (D) reimburse

이렇게 풀어요

1. **선택지 보고 문법/어휘 문제 파악** 선택지가 동사 reimburse(상환하다, 변제하다)의 다양한 형태로 구성되어 있으므로 문법 문제임을 파악합니다.

2. **빈칸 분석** 빈칸 앞은 건물의 주차장 공사가 진행될 예정이라는 앞으로의 계획에 대해 알리는 내용입니다.

3. **정답 선택** 공사가 진행될 동안 발생할 비용에 대해서 상환해 줄 것이라는 의미가 되어 앞으로의 일을 나타내야 해요. 따라서 미래 시제가 되어야 하므로 (B) will reimburse를 정답으로 선택합니다.

해설

빈칸 앞에 주어가 있고 뒤에 목적어가 있으므로 능동태 동사가 들어가야 합니다. 따라서 (B)가 정답입니다.

PART 5 문법 적용 문제

Over the past several months, we ------- complaints from tenants regarding the poor
condition of our building's parking lot.

(A) are received   (B) have received   (C) were received   (D) have been received

248 기적의 토익 RC

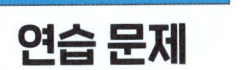 **연습 문제**

따라 하면 문제가 풀리는

빈칸 앞 내용에서 단서가 될 부분을 찾아 표시하세요.
표시한 것을 바탕으로 정답 어휘를 선택하세요.

정답 및 해설 p.84

01

Please take a moment to proceed to Barbeque Town's Web site and fill out our online survey. Upon submitting it, you ------- a coupon for 15% off.

(A) have been issued　　(B) will be issued

02

Dear Mr. Patel

Thank you for signing up for the upcoming career development seminar, scheduled for July 7. According to your form, you ------- the tourist bag as a gift.

(A) choose　　(B) chose

03

This letter is to confirm that we received your application for the senior accountant position at Lexington Corporation. It normally takes two weeks for us to process applications. A representative ------- you in that time.

(A) will contact　　(B) had contacted

04

To: Samuel Dent <samueldent@aoo.com>
From: Customer Service <cs@passionapparel.com>
Date: May 11
Re: Return request

Dear Mr. Dent,

On May 9, we ------- the sweater that you sent back to us as a return. I would like to remind you that it is our store's policy to not refund shipping fees. Thus, we will credit your account in the amount of $17.99, the full amount that you paid for the item, in five business days.

(A) will receive　　(B) received

PART 6 앞의 내용이 단서인 동사 시제　249

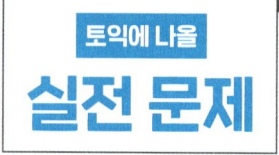

토익에 나올
실전 문제

제한시간 4분입니다! 시~작!

Questions 01-04 refer to the following e-mail.

From: Personnel
To: All Employees
Date: 9 March
Subject: Office Relocation

Our CEO officially announced the acquisition of Downy Travel in the press conference last week.
He ------- that our current office is too small to accommodate all new employees. As of Monday, 14
01.
March, we will be moving to a more ------- office located at 481 Broadway Avenue.
02.

A moving company will bring all of our office equipment and furniture to our new office. They will be
moving everything on Saturday, 12 March, so please box up your belongings before leaving the
office on Friday evening. -------, we ask that you clean up around your work area. The movers will
03.
charge a fee if they have to provide cleaning service as well.

One more thing, your boxes will be put on your new desks. -------. That will let us start our daily
04.
work without any delay.

Yulia Franco

유형 적용 문제

01. (A) will admit
(B) admitted
(C) to admit
(D) admits

02. (A) spacious
(B) luminous
(C) traditional
(D) expensive

03. (A) Regardless
(B) In addition
(C) As such
(D) Somehow

04. (A) Packing labels will be made available in the HR
office.
(B) You will have a chance to meet the employees of
Downy Travel next week.
(C) The moving company has received awards for its
good service.
(D) I ask you to arrive a little early on Monday to
unpack your things.

250   기적의 토익 RC

정답 및 해설 p.84

Questions 05-08 refer to the following instructions.

How to set up your DVR

Set up your Rockwell DVR so that you never have to miss your favorite shows again. You can even
------- to your favorite parts by rewinding or fast-forwarding.
  05.

Start by ------- selecting a time and channel.
      06.

-------. To view something you have recorded, choose it from the "My Recordings" list. Shows -------
 07.   **08.**
in chronological order by the original date and time of broadcast.

The DVR cannot detect if a show has already been recorded. Keep in mind that reruns may appear
multiple times in your recordings list.

05. (A) reset
    (B) skip
    (C) look
    (D) inquire

06. (A) specify
    (B) specification
    (C) specifically
    (D) specific

07. (A) Your Rockwell DVR can store up to 500 hours of shows or movies.
    (B) Use the "Parental Controls" option to lock certain shows with a password.
    (C) Be sure to read the instructions carefully before recording anything.
    (D) A dropdown screen with personal settings will appear.

유형 적용 문제
08. (A) were listed
    (B) will be listed
    (C) have been listed
    (D) will have been listed

PART 6 앞의 내용이 단서인 동사 시제

PART 7

광고 (2) 구인 광고

구인 광고는 지문 구조가 정형화되어 있으므로 이를 파악해 두면 문제 푸는 시간을 단축할 수 있어요.

특정 직업이나 직위의 사람을 모집하는 광고입니다. 구인 광고는 <제목(광고하는 직책) – 구인 직종 및 담당 업무 설명 – 지원자의 자격 요건 및 우대 조건 – 지원 방법>의 순서로 전개됩니다. 문제 유형에 따라 단서를 파악해야 하는 위치를 바로 찾는 연습을 하면 쉽게 풀 수 있는 유형 중 하나입니다. 단, 지문에 언급된 지원자의 자격 요건이 필수 사항인지 우대 사항인지 구별하는 게 중요합니다.

- 필수 사항을 나타내는 표현: must, should, mandatory, required
- 우대 사항을 나타내는 표현: preferred, a plus, desirable

적용 기술

[기적의 필기노트] 190P
RC 기술 97

구인 광고에서 자주 출제되는 문제

· 광고하는 직책 문제
What position is being advertised?
→ 지문의 제목에서 바로 언급되는 경우도 있고, 주로 첫 단락의 looking for/hiring/recruiting/have an opening at 등의 표현 뒤에 단서가 제시돼요.

구인 광고에 자주 출제되는 어휘

application	(입사) 지원서	apply for	~에 지원하다
successful applicant [successful candidate]	합격자	bilingual	2개 국어를 할 줄 아는
now hiring	현재 채용 중인	conduct an interview	면접을 실시하다
candidate	지원자, 후보자	associate	동료
division	(회사) 부서	ideal	이상적인
temporary	임시의	in person	(본인이) 직접
look for	~을 찾다, 구하다	on behalf of	~를 대신하여
opening	공석	review	검토하다
qualification	자격 조건	fluency	능통함, 유창함
forward	보내다, 발송하다	recommend	추천하다
register for	~에 등록하다	sign up for	~에 등록하다
be preferred	우대되다	seek	찾다, 구하다
receptionist	접수 담당자	full-time	정규직의
step down	은퇴하다	applicant	지원자
previous experience	이전 경력	degree	학위
duties[responsibilities]	직무, 책무	relevant	관련 있는
flexible hours	유동적 근무시간	arrange	정하다
field of expertise	전문 분야	specialize in	~을 전공하다
reference	추천서	résumé	이력서

구인 광고

advertisement   💡해석 p.85

Daytona Digital is Recruiting

Daytona Digital, the country's fastest growing digital graphics design agency, is preparing to expand once again. It's new office will be located in Los Angeles. While it is company policy to fill senior positions with current Daytona Digital employees, more graphic designers will be needed.

The requirements for the position of Graphic Designer at Daytona Digital are as follows:

– A 2- or 4-year college degree (preferably but not necessarily in graphic design)
– 12 months or more working in a similar position
– A current Digital Graphic Design certificate
– Familiarity with most graphic design software and tools

01. What is mentioned about Daytona Digital?

    (A) It promotes from within the company.
    (B) It is currently based in Los Angeles.
    (C) It has plans to expand internationally.
    (D) It employs more graphic designers than any other company.

02. What is NOT a requirement for a qualified candidate?

    (A) Certification in graphic design
    (B) One year of relative experience
    (C) A degree in graphic design
    (D) Proficiency in certain software

DAY 10

이렇게 풀어요

01. Daytona Digital에 대해 언급된 것은 무엇인가?

    (A) 회사 내부에서 승진시킨다.
    (B) 현재 로스앤젤리스에 본사를 두고 있다.
    (C) 국제적으로 확장할 계획이다.
    (D) 그래픽 디자이너를 다른 어떤 회사보다 더 많이 채용한다.

해설 첫 단락에 고위 직군은 현 Daytona Digital 직원으로 채우는 것이 회사 방침이라고(company policy to fill senior positions with current Daytona Digital employees) 했으므로 (A)가 정답입니다.

02. 후보 자격 요건이 아닌 것은 무엇인가?

    (A) 그래픽 디자인 자격증
    (B) 1년의 관련 경험
    (C) 그래픽 디자인 학위
    (D) 특성 소프트웨어에 대한 숙련도

해설 ((A)는 A current Digital Graphic Design certificate, (B)는 12 months or more working in a similar position, (D)는 Familiarity with most graphic design software and tools에 언급되었습니다. 그러나 대학 학위는 우대하나 필수적이지는 않다고 (preferably but not necessarily in graphic design) 했으므로 (C)가 정답입니다.

PART 7 광고 (2) 구인 광고   253

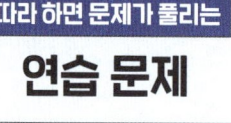

따라 하면 문제가 풀리는

연습 문제

먼저 문제의 키워드에 표시한 후,
지문에서 단서를 찾아 적절한 답을 고르세요.

01 job advertisement

Assistant Cook Needed

Oakland Steakhouse is seeking an assistant cook for its downtown location. Duties include preparing ingredients, plating food, organizing supplies, and keeping the kitchen clean. The ideal candidate will have a hard-working attitude and the ability to work in a fast-paced environment. We are willing to train the right person, but the selected applicant must hold a valid health and food-handling certificate issued by the state of California. To download an application, visit www.oaklandsteakhouse.com.

Q. What is one requirement of the job?

(A) State health certification
(B) Previous experience in the field

02 job advertisement

Mays Publishing Seeks Graphic Designers

Mays Publishing is responsible for a wide variety of hobby magazines, including popular titles such as *Garden Art Monthly* and *Dog World*. We are currently expanding our graphic design team. The positions are full-time, but employees are permitted to work from home two of the five days. The ideal candidate has at least three years of graphic design experience or a bachelor's degree in a related field. To apply, send a résumé and sample portfolio to hr@mayspublishing.com.

Q. What is indicated about Mays Publishing's graphic designers?

(A) They must hold a bachelor's degree.
(B) They can work remotely part-time.

254   기적의 토익 RC

03 job advertisement

SUP Shipping - Now Hiring Distribution Associates

Motivated and energetic applicants needed to fill several positions in the SUP Shipping distribution center at 200 Clemont Street in Elgin, IA. First shift is from 4 until 8 A.M. Distribution associates pull boxes from the conveyor belts and arrange them in delivery trucks based on where they are going in order to facilitate the drivers' routes. Regular lifting of packages up to 50 lbs. should be expected. Competitive salary also gives limited access to health care. Apply in person or online at www.sup.com/openings.

Q. What is a duty of the distribution associate?

(A) Sorting packages by destination

(B) Delivering packages to customers

04 job advertisement

Warehouse Distribution Manager Needed

Enjoy an exciting and successful career with Leeson Cosmetics. We are one of the largest suppliers of cosmetics in the country, and we are currently in need of a warehouse distribution manager at our Atlanta branch. Duties include ensuring the on-time delivery of goods through monitoring stock levels carefully. Applicants must have at least two years' experience in a management role. Applications will be accepted until June 1, and references will be checked after the interview stage.

Q. What information is NOT provided in the job advertisement?

(A) The interview dates

(B) The required experience

토익에 나올
실전 문제

제한시간 10분입니다! 시~작!

Questions 01-02 refer to the following advertisement.

Emberton National Park is currently seeking hiking guides for the summer season. Previously open to the public for just six months of the year, the park is now continuously accessible.

To accommodate overseas visitors, you must be fluent in English and one of the following languages: Spanish, French, or Mandarin. We will provide detailed maps and training, but you must be fit enough to handle hikes of up to 20 miles per day.

To apply for a position, visit www.emberton.gov. Successful applicants must be free to work anytime, as work shifts are assigned for both weekdays and weekends.

01. What has recently changed at Emberton National Park?
(A) It offers maps on its Web site.
(B) It is now open year-round.
(C) It has free admission in the summer.
(D) It has constructed new hiking trails.

02. What is NOT indicated as a requirement for the position?
(A) Ability to work a flexible schedule
(B) Fluency in two languages
(C) A high level of physical fitness
(D) Knowledge of the park's trail system

---

paraphrasing 주어진 어휘 또는 표현과 패러프레이징 될 수 있는 것을 연결하세요.

1. currently seeking •
2. continuously accessible •
3. overseas visitors •
4. be free to work anytime •
5. work shifts are assigned •

• (a) ability to work a flexible schedule
• (b) required to work
• (c) people from other countries
• (d) now looking for
• (e) open year-round

256   기적의 토익 RC

🔍 정답 및 해설 p.86

Questions 03-05 refer to the following job announcement.

LOAN OFFICER NEEDED

Sutter Bank is looking for a full-time loan officer who is very well organized for its branch in Grand Rapids. The position involves assessing potential borrowers to determine the eligibility and to recommend loan products that meet their needs. As Sutter Bank is a fast-paced environment, you must be able to multitask while keeping a high degree of accuracy. At least 2 years' experience working at a bank or credit union is required.

Loan officers work 40 hours a week during our opening hours, Monday to Friday, 9 A.M. to 6 P.M. We have a friendly and welcoming staff, and employees can take advantage of the convenient on-site cafeteria and free underground parking. Sutter Bank offers competitive wages, medical insurance, and paid overtime. In addition, employees earn generous bonus payments for meeting their quarterly targets.

To apply for the position, please e-mail a résumé and cover letter to hr@sutterbank.com with "Job #0927" in the subject line.

DAY 10

03. What is NOT indicated as a preferred qualification for the job?
(A) Ability to perform multiple tasks simultaneously
(B) Previous work at a financial institution
(C) A university degree in finance or accounting
(D) Strong organizational skills

04. What is suggested about Sutter Bank?
(A) It pays the highest wages in the field.
(B) It is closed on the weekend.
(C) It recently opened a new branch.
(D) It provides loans exclusively to businesses.

05. What benefit of the position is mentioned?
(A) Paid vacation
(B) Quarterly staff parties
(C) Free cafeteria meals
(D) Performance bonuses

paraphrasing 주어진 어휘 또는 표현과 패러프레이징 될 수 있는 것을 연결하세요.

1. the position involves	(a) closed on the weekend
2. meet their needs	(b) performance bonuses
3. opening hours, Monday to Friday	(c) the duty includes
4. bonus payments for meeting their quarterly targets	(d) satisfy them
5. be able to multitask	(e) ability to perform multiple tasks simultaneously

PART 7 광고 (2) 구인 광고   257

Questions 06-10 refer to the following e-mail, advertisement, and schedule.

To:	Josephine Greer <j.greer@coretech.com>
From:	Calvin Bauer <c.bauer@coretech.com>
Date:	21 May
Subject:	Recruitment

Hi Josephine,

I need your help advertising job openings at our company. As you know, it's the end of the semester, and a lot of young people with a lot of potential will be graduating. That's why we need to act quickly. I apologize for the short notice, but please understand that my department has been extremely busy with the launch of the CT Tablet. When making the post, don't forget to include information like the location, initial salary, position responsibilities, and shifts that we're hiring for. Thanks in advance.

Sincerely,

Calvin Bauer
R&D Manager, Core Tech

Become a core member of Core Tech!

The popular electronics manufacturer Core Tech is looking for enthusiastic people to fill some entry level positions. We are currently hiring standard shift (Monday through Friday, 9-5) only. All of the following positions are located at our main headquarters building in Semmes, AL.

Job openings:

– HR Staff: Assist with the planning of regular training sessions for staff; Handle confidential paperwork regarding other employees; Assist staff with issues regarding pay or work environment. Must pass a background check.

– Product Design: Join our innovative product designers to develop and upgrade electronic products. A strong sense of creativity is a must for this position.

– Quality Control: Conduct thorough tests of all Core Tech products before they are unveiled to the public. This position requires very precise attention to detail.

To apply for any of these positions, visit Core Tech's Web site and fill out an initial application. After the initial review period, those who pass will be asked to do an initial interview via video conference.

Core Tech New Employee Orientation: July 9

Core Tech Headquarters Office: 8554 Tunbridge Road, Semmes, AL 36575

Department	New Members	Notes
HR Staff	Natalie Phelps Eric Bradley	Background checks will begin
Product Design	Liam Glenn Ashley Byrd	Share ideas on innovative technology
Quality Control	Simone Lowery Audrey Blackwell	Participate in competitive exercises

06. Why does Mr. Bauer ask Ms. Greer to do a task quickly?

(A) The company's busy season will begin soon.
(B) More workers are needed for a product launch.
(C) Many students will graduate college soon.
(D) Some employees joined a competitor.

07. What information requested by Mr. Bauer was NOT included in the advertisement?

(A) The available shifts
(B) The starting wage
(C) The job duties
(D) The work location

08. How can candidates apply for a job at Core Tech?

(A) By contacting an HR representative
(B) By mailing an application to its headquarters
(C) By completing an online application
(D) By attending an interview event

09. What is implied about Ms. Byrd?

(A) She may be up for promotion soon.
(B) She is very creative.
(C) She is attentive to details.
(D) She passed a background check.

10. What is indicated about the Quality Control team members at the July 9 event?

(A) They will meet via video conference.
(B) They will take part in a competition.
(C) They will submit documents for a background check.
(D) They will discuss their thoughts on new technology.

DAY 10

---

paraphrasing 주어진 어휘 또는 표현과 패러프레이징 될 수 있는 것을 연결하세요.

1. notice   •

2. entry   •

3. competitive exercises   •

• (a) alert

• (b) beginner

• (c) competition

PART 7 광고 (2) 구인 광고   259

'멋진 당신, 오늘도 화이팅'

DAY
11

오늘의 학습 포인트

PART 5. 시제

1. 단순 시제
현재 – 시간/조건 부사절에서 미래를 나타낼 때 현재 시제 사용 가능

미래 – as of/starting + 미래 시점, upcoming/following + 명사 등과 함께 출제

과거 – 시간 표현 + ago/last + 시간 표현 등과 함께 출제

2. 완료 시제
현재완료 have/has p.p. – 완료/계속/경험

과거완료 had p.p. – 기준이 되는 과거 동사 반드시 필요

미래완료 will have p.p. – 'By the time + 주어 + 현재 동사, 주어 + 미래완료'

3. 진행 시제 – 현재 진행은 미래 시제 대신 사용 가능

PART 6. 뒤의 내용이 단서인 동사 시제
지문에서 날짜 표현/시제 파악하기

PART 7. 사내 공지
목적 문제 자주 출제. 지문 초반부 확인하기

PART 5
문법

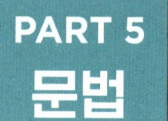

시제

문맥에 맞는 동사의 시제를 선택할 수 있어야 합니다. 미래 시제의 출제 비중이 가장 높아요.

✎ 적용 기술

[기적의 필기노트] 122P, 123P, 125P
RC 기술 36, 37, 39

출제 포인트
빈도 부사를 단서로 하여 현재 시제를 찾는 문제가 자주 출제돼요.

🔒 확인 문제 ❶

They usually ------ the meeting on Tuesdays.

(A) will hold
(B) hold

🔒 확인 문제 ❷

The promotional event ------ next week.

(A) will be held
(B) is held

> **출제 유형 1**
> ## 단순 시제

1 현재 시제

- 현재 시제의 동사 형태는 동사의 기본형 또는 3인칭 단수 현재형입니다.

- 현재 시제의 단서가 되는 표현을 문장에서 빠르게 찾아야 해요.

currently 현재	usually 주로, 보통	frequently 자주	often 종종 · still 여전히
every day/each day 매일		every week/each week 매주	
every month/each month 매달		every year/each year 매해	

Coops grocery store <u>currently</u> **accepts** payment by credit card.
Coops 식료품점은 현재 신용카드로 결제가 가능하다.

> **800+**
- 시간/조건의 부사절에서 미래를 나타낼 때 미래 시제 대신 현재 시제를 사용합니다.

시간 부사절 접속사	when ~일 때	before ~ 전에	after ~ 후에	as soon as ~하자마자
	by the time ~할 때쯤	once 일단 ~하면	while ~하는 동안	
조건 부사절 접속사	if ~라면	unless ~하지 않는다면		as long as ~하는 한
	provided/providing (that) ~인 경우에 = if			

Ms. Grandson will buy new furniture <u>when</u> she **moves** to a larger office next month.
_{will move (x)}
Grandson 씨는 다음 주 더 큰 사무실로 이사할 때 새 가구를 구입할 것이다.

<u>If</u> you **register** for membership, you will get additional discounts.
will register (X)
당신이 멤버십에 등록하면, 추가 할인을 받을 것입니다.

2 미래 시제

- 미래 시제의 동사 형태는 'will + 동사원형' 또는 'is/are going to부정사'입니다.

- 미래 시제의 단서가 되는 표현을 문장에서 빠르게 찾아야 해요.

tomorrow 내일	shortly/soon 곧	next + 시간 표현 다음 ~에
as of/effective of + 미래 시점 ~부로		
starting/beginning + 미래 시점 ~부터		
upcoming/following + 명사 다가오는/다음의 '명사'		

As of next week, the new dress code **will be implemented**.
다음 주부터 새로운 복장 규정이 시행될 것입니다.

정답 ❶ (B) ❷ (A)

262 기적의 토익 RC

3 과거 시제

- 과거 시제의 동사 형태는 '동사원형 + (e)d' 또는 불규칙 동사(spend-spent 등)의 경우 해당 과거형입니다.

- 과거 시제의 단서가 되는 표현을 문장에서 빠르게 찾아야 해요.

| yesterday 어제 | recently 최근에 | once 한때 |
| 시간 표현 + ago ~ 전에 | last + 시간 표현 지난 ~ | in + 지난 연도/과거 시점 ~에 |

- 문장에 과거 시제 단서 표현이 없는 경우, 이미 끝나버린 상황인지 해석을 통해 판단하거나 'since절'인지 확인합니다. → 'since + 주어 + 과거 시제 동사, 주어 + 현재완료 동사'
Since Lux, Inc. **launched** a new application, profits have risen considerably.
Lux 사가 새 어플리케이션을 출시한 이래로, 수익이 상당히 증가했다.

출제 유형 2
완료 시제

1 현재완료: have/has p.p.

- 완료의 의미: ~했다

|완료의 의미일 때 함께 쓰이는 표현|

| just 막 | already 이미 | now 지금 |

Mr. Dewitt has **already completed** the sales report.
Dewitt 씨는 이미 판매 보고서를 완료했다.

- 계속의 의미: ~해 왔다

|계속의 의미일 때 함께 쓰이는 표현|

| for + 기간 ~동안 | during/for/over/in + the last[past] + 기간 지난 ~동안 |
| always 항상 | since + 주어 + 과거 동사/since + 과거 시점 ~ 이래로 |

They **have offered** a delivery service for two years.
그들은 2년 동안 배달 서비스를 제공하고 있다.

- 경험의 의미: ~해 본 적이 있다

|경험의 의미일 때 함께 쓰이는 표현|

| ever ~해 본 적이 있다 | never ~해 본 적이 없다 | recently 최근에 | lately 최근에 |

Ms. Arroyo **has never made** an online purchase. Arroyo 씨는 온라인 구매를 해본 적이 없다.

2 과거완료: had p.p.

- 과거보다 더 앞서 일어난 일을 나타낼 때 사용합니다.

- 과거완료 시제가 사용되기 위해서는 반드시 기준이 되는 과거 동사가 있어야 합니다.
The clients **had** already **left** before I arrived. 내가 도착하기 전에 고객들은 이미 떠났다.
→ 도착한(arrived) 것보다 떠난(left) 것이 더 과거의 일이므로 과거완료 시제(had left)를 써요.

⚠ 주의

recently는 현재완료 시제와 사용되기도 해요.
The sales **have** recently **increased**.

🔒 확인 문제 ❸

She ------- the branch office last month.

(A) visited
(B) visits

✎ 적용 기술

[기적의 필기노트] 124P
RC 기술 38

🔒 확인 문제 ❹

Claire ------- as a department head since 2015.

(A) had worked
(B) has worked

⚠ 주의

since가 이유를 나타내는 부사절 접속사로 쓰이면 주절에 다양한 시제가 올 수 있어요.
He **was** late since he missed the bus.

🔒 확인 문제 ❺

Morris Company ------- the order before she called to cancel it.

(A) had shipped
(B) will ship

정답 ❸ (A) ❹ (B) ❺ (A)

PART 5 문법 시제 263

- 'By the time + 주어 + 과거 동사, 주어 + 과거완료' ~했었을 때쯤에는, (이미) ~했었다
  By the time my order **was delivered**, I **had left** for my business trip.
  내 주문품이 도착했을 때, 나는 출장을 떠난 뒤였다.

`800+`

3 미래완료: will have p.p.

- 미래완료 시제는 미래의 한 시점에서 행동이나 현상이 완료될 것임을 나타냅니다.

- 'By the time + 주어 + 현재 동사, 주어 + 미래완료' ~했을 때쯤이면, ~할 것이다
  By the time the manager **comes** back, James **will have finished** the assignment. 관리자가 돌아올 때쯤이면, 제임스는 업무를 끝냈을 것이다.

출제 유형 3   진행 시제

1 현재 진행/과거 진행/미래 진행

- 현재 진행 시제는 가까운 미래의 일을 나타낼 때 미래 시제 대신 사용할 수 있어요.
  We **are relocating** to a new office building tomorrow.
  미래 시점 표현이 있는데 보기에 미래 시제 동사가 없으면 현재 진행 선택!
  우리는 내일 새 사무실 건물로 이전한다.

- 과거 진행 시제는 특정 과거 시점에 진행되고 있던 일을 나타냅니다.
  He **was driving** a company car yesterday at two o'clock.
  그는 어제 오후 2시에 회사 차를 운전하는 중이었다.

`800+`

- 미래 진행은 특정 미래 시점에 진행되고 있을 일을 나타냅니다.
  The spokesperson **will be announcing** the merger next Monday.
  대변인은 다음 주 월요일에 합병을 발표할 것이다.

2 진행 시제로 쓸 수 없는 동사

감정 동사	prefer 선호하다 surprise 놀라다 please 기쁘게 하다, 만족시키다 like 좋아하다
상태 동사	consist 구성되다 exist 존재하다 include 포함하다 know 알다
소유 동사	have 갖다 possess 소지하다 own 소유하다 belong to ~에 속하다

Mr. Parker **is being pleased** with the product he purchased.
(X)
→ is pleased
Parker 씨는 그가 구입한 물건에 만족한다.

🔒 **확인 문제 ❻**

Mr. Lee ------- the awards at the upcoming job fair.

(A) will be presented
(B) is presenting

정답 ❻ (B)

264   기적의 토익 RC

시제

1. For the last three quarters, complaints about a late delivery ------- considerably.

(A) decline   (B) declining   (C) have declined   (D) will decline

지난 3분기 동안, 늦은 배송에 대한 불만은 상당히 감소했다.

> ✔ 이렇게 풀어요
>
> 1. **선택지 보고 문법/어휘 문제 파악** 선택지가 동사 decline(감소하다)의 다양한 형태로 구성되어 있으므로 문법 문제임을 파악해요.
> 2. **빈칸 분석** 주어 complaints와 전치사구 about a late delivery 뒤에 동사가 없으므로 빈칸에는 동사가 들어가야 함을 파악합니다.
> 3. **정답 선택** 시제를 결정하는 시간 표현인 For the last three quarters(지난 3분기 동안)를 단서로 하여 현재완료 시제인 (C) have declined를 정답으로 고릅니다.

2. When an expense reimbursement request --------, the accounting department will deposit a payment to a designated bank account.

(A) to approve   (B) approved   (C) is approved   (D) will be approved

비용 상환 요청이 승인되면, 회계팀은 지정된 은행 계좌에 입금을 할 것이다.

> ✔ 이렇게 풀어요
>
> 1. **선택지 보고 문법/어휘 문제 파악** 선택지가 동사 approve(승인하다)의 다양한 형태로 구성되어 있으므로 문법 문제임을 파악해요.
> 2. **빈칸 분석** 시간 부사절의 주어 an expense reimbursement request 뒤에 동사가 없으므로 빈칸에는 동사가 들어가야 함을 파악해요.
> 3. **정답 선택** 주절의 동사가 will deposit으로 미래 시제이므로, 시간 부사절의 시제는 현재가 되어야 하므로 (C) is approved를 정답으로 고릅니다.

3. The job fair ------- place at Dolton Hall at the beginning of next month.

(A) took   (B) has taken   (C) is taking   (D) had taken

채용박람회는 다음 달 초에 Dolton Hall에서 열릴 것이다.

> ✔ 이렇게 풀어요
>
> 1. **선택지 보고 문법/어휘 문제 파악** 선택지가 동사 take의 다양한 형태로 구성되어 있으므로 문법 문제임을 파악해요.
> 2. **빈칸 분석** 주어 The job fair 뒤에 동사가 없으므로 빈칸에는 동사가 들어가야 함을 파악해요.
> 3. **정답 선택** 시제를 결정하는 시간 표현인 next month(다음 달)를 단서로 하여 미래 시제를 대신할 수 있는 현재진행 시제인 (C) is taking을 정답으로 고릅니다.

PART 5
어휘

동사 어휘 (1)

각 어휘와 함께 자주 쓰이는 표현을 통째로 외워두세요.

01 rely   의지하다, 신뢰하다

rely on[upon]	~에 의지하다, 의존하다

🐾 빈출 토익 선생님 Pick!

02 earn   벌다, 얻다

earn reputation	평판을 얻다, 명성을 쌓다
earn one's degree	학위를 따다
earn money/profits/wages	돈/이윤/임금을 벌다

🐾 빈출 토익 선생님 Pick!

03 complete   완료하다, 끝마치다, 작성하다

complete the service	서비스를 완료하다
complete the form/survey	서식/설문지를 작성하다
be completed	완성되다

04 establish   설립하다, 수립하다

establish expectations	기대치를 설정하다
establish a sense of trust	신뢰감을 형성하다
establish oneself as	~로서 자리를 잡다

05 deliver   배달하다, (강연, 연설을) 하다

deliver A to B	A를 B에 배달하다
deliver a speech	연설하다
program is delivered	프로그램이 제공되다

06 enable   할 수 있게 하다

enable A to부정사	A가 ~을 할 수 있게 하다

07 authorize   재가하다, 인가하다

authorize A to부정사	A에게 ~할 수 있는 권한을 부여하다
authorize bank transactions	은행 거래를 허가하다
authorize payment for	~의 지불을 허가하다

08 fall   떨어지다, 줄다

fall within (= belong to)	~에 포함되다
fall behind	뒤처지다
fall short of expectations	기대에 미치지 못하다

09 review   검토하다, 평가하다

review thoroughly	철저히 검토하다
review the proposal/report	제안서/보고서를 검토하다

10 lead   (어떤 결과로) 이르게 하다, 이끌다

lead to + 동명사/명사	~하는 결과를 낳다
lead A to부정사	A가 ~하도록 이끌다

11 gain   얻다, 쌓다

gain knowledge	지식을 얻다
gain experience	경험을 얻다
gain recognition	인정받다

12 differ   다르다

differ greatly/significantly	크게/상당히 다르다

🐾 빈출 토익 선생님 Pick!

13 implement   시행하다

implement procedure	절차를 시행하다
implement a policy	정책을 시행하다
implement the strategy	전략을 시행하다

14 encounter   맞닥뜨리다, 만나다

encounter difficulties	곤란에 직면하다
encounter similar cases	비슷한 사건에 직면하다
encounter + 사람	~을 만나다

15 require 필요하다, 요구하다

require that	~을 해야 한다
require A to부정사	A에게 ~할 것을 요구하다
be required to부정사	~하는 것이 요구된다

16 remove 없애다, 제거하다

remove A from B	B에서 A를 없애다

17 maintain 유지하다, 주장하다

maintain relationship	관계를 유지하다
maintain steady sales	꾸준한 판매를 유지하다
maintain that	~라고 주장하다

18 view 보다, 여기다

view A as B	A를 B로 여기다

19 oversee 감독하다

oversee the employees	직원들을 감독하다
oversee daily operations	일일 작업을 감독하다

`800+` 🐾 빈출 토익 선생님 Pick!
20 defer 미루다, 연기하다

be deferred until	~까지 연기되다
defer a payment	지불을 연기하다

21 launch 시작하다, 출시하다

launch a campaign	캠페인을 시작하다
launch a new line of products	신제품을 출시하다

`800+`
22 emphasize 강조하다

emphasize the importance of	~의 중요성을 강조하다
emphasize A over B	A를 B보다 강조하다

🐾 빈출 토익 선생님 Pick!
23 enforce 시행하다, 강요하다

enforce guidelines	가이드라인을 시행하다
enforce a new policy	새로운 정책을 시행하다
strictly enforce	엄격히 시행하다

24 register 등록하다

register for	~에 등록하다
register in advance	미리 등록하다

25 issue 발급하다, 발행하다

issue a permit	허가증을 발행하다
issue a full refund	전액 환불하다

26 tend 경향이 있다

tend to부정사	~하는 경향이 있다

DAY 11

 풀이 방법

Don't forget to ------- the day's lesson materials thoroughly before attending each lecture.

(A) maintain　　　　(B) launch　　　　(C) review　　　　(D) defer

각 강의에 출석하기 전에 그 날의 수업 자료를 철저히 검토하는 것을 잊지 마세요.

> 🔖 이렇게 풀어요
>
> **1. 선택지 보고 문법/어휘 문제 파악** 선택지가 서로 다른 동사 어휘로 구성되어 있으므로 어휘 문제임을 파악해요.
> **2. 빈칸 분석** 빈칸 뒤의 materials(자료), thoroughly(철저히)와 문맥상 어울릴 수 있는 동사가 들어가야 함을 파악해요.
> **3. 정답 선택** review thoroughly(철저히 검토하다)의 형태로 자주 쓰이는 (C) review를 정답으로 고릅니다.

PART 5 어휘 동사 어휘 (1)　267

따라 하면 문제가 풀리는

연습 문제

앞서 학습한 문제 풀이법을 적용하여 맞는 것에 ✔ 표시 하거나 괄호 안에
적절한 답을 쓰고 정답을 선택하세요.

01 The assistant professor normally ------- the writing assignments that students turn in.

(A) checks
(B) will check
(C) to check
(D) has checked

1. 선택지 보고 문법/어휘 문제 파악하기 ☐문법 문제 ☐어휘 문제
2. 빈칸 분석하기 빈칸 앞에 있는 것 ☐주어 + 부사 ☐동사 + 부사
   → 빈칸은 ☐동사 ☐목적어 자리이다.
   → normally와 어울려 쓰일 수 있는 ☐미래 시제 동사 ☐현재 시제 동사가 들어가야 한다.
3. 정답 선택하기 정답 (   )

02 Pelham Electronics ------- three years ago by the inventor William Tanner.

(A) will be founded
(B) is founded
(C) was founded
(D) has been founded

1. 선택지 보고 문법/어휘 문제 파악하기 ☐문법 문제 ☐어휘 문제
2. 빈칸 분석하기 빈칸 뒤에 있는 것 ☐과거 시제 표현 ☐미래 시제 표현
   → 빈칸은 ☐과거 시제 동사 ☐미래 시제 동사 자리이다.
3. 정답 선택하기 정답 (   )

03 Personal banking classes ------- at the Landry Community Center next week.

(A) was held
(B) will be held
(C) have been held
(D) had been held

1. 선택지 보고 문법/어휘 문제 파악하기 ☐문법 문제 ☐어휘 문제
2. 빈칸 분석하기 빈칸 뒤에 있는 것 ☐과거 시제 표현 ☐미래 시제 표현
   → 빈칸은 ☐과거 시제 동사 ☐미래 시제 동사 자리이다.
3. 정답 선택하기 정답 (   )

⚲ 정답 및 해설 p.89

04 Mr. Greene ------- his own bakery shop over the last five years.

(A) operates
(B) will operate
(C) operated
(D) has operated

1. 선택지 보고 문법/어휘 문제 파악하기 ☐ 문법 문제 ☐ 어휘 문제
2. 빈칸 분석하기 빈칸 뒤에 있는 시간 표현 (   )
   → 빈칸은 ☐ 현재완료 시제 동사 ☐ 미래 시제 동사 자리이다.
3. 정답 선택하기 정답 (   )

05 When her transfer application -------, Alicia Wise will join our department.

(A) was approved
(B) is approved
(C) will be approved
(D) to be approved

1. 선택지 보고 문법/어휘 문제 파악하기 ☐ 문법 문제 ☐ 어휘 문제
2. 빈칸 분석하기 빈칸 앞에 있는 것 ☐ 시간 부사절의 주어 ☐ 시간 부사절의 동사
   → 빈칸은 ☐ 목적어 ☐ 동사 자리이다.
   주절의 동사의 시제 ☐ 현재 시제 ☐ 미래 시제
   → 빈칸에는 ☐ 현재 시제 동사 ☐ 미래 시제 동사가 들어가야 한다.
3. 정답 선택하기 정답 (   )

06 Manorville Flower ------- its variety of flower baskets to addresses within the city limits.

(A) delivers
(B) establishes
(C) earns
(D) oversees

1. 선택지 보고 문법/어휘 문제 파악하기 ☐ 문법 문제 ☐ 어휘 문제
2. 빈칸 분석하기 빈칸 뒤 목적어 (   )
   목적어 뒤에 나오는 전치사 (   )
   → 위의 전치사와 함께 쓰이는 동사가 답이다.
3. 정답 선택하기 정답 (   )

PART 5 시제 / 동사 어휘 (1)   **269**

DAY 01-11 누적 문제

제한시간 9분입니다! 시~작!

01. During the next few weeks, all of the employees ------- the online training course.

(A) to complete
(B) will complete
(C) completed
(D) completing

02. Ms. Cervantes ------- her idea for a new business with a market analyst last week.

(A) discussion
(B) is discussing
(C) discussed
(D) to discuss

03. More maintenance workers ------- at the new apartment complex in Lakeville this coming autumn.

(A) will be hired
(B) had been hired
(C) hiring
(D) to hire

04. Ever since it opened for business in 2006, Mercado Company ------- employee performance in November.

(A) will be evaluating
(B) are evaluating
(C) has evaluated
(D) evaluates

05. Ms. Logan ------- as a paid intern at Inno Tech for the last three months.

(A) has been working
(B) will be working
(C) is working
(D) should have been working

06. Mr. Jansen will report to the factory manager after he ------- the thorough inspection tomorrow.

(A) finishing
(B) will finish
(C) finishes
(D) to finish

07. If the weather is favorable, the grand opening of Duchess Heights Mall ------- outside as scheduled.

(A) had been held
(B) will have been held
(C) was held
(D) will be held

08. Ms. Lutz called a special management meeting last Monday and she ------- for the recent rise in customer complaints.

(A) apologizing
(B) apologizes
(C) apologized
(D) apology

09. Clara Grill ------ a catering service at Canada Investment's upcoming banquet.

(A) will offer
(B) had offered
(C) was offering
(D) offering

10. Over the past three months, Balatas Country Club ------- its clubhouse and spa facility.

(A) renovating
(B) has renovated
(C) renovates
(D) renovation

11. Since last October, sales of antifreeze ------- at Tony's Auto Supplies.

(A) increasing
(B) increasingly
(C) will increase
(D) have increased

12. When Stanford, Inc. announced a job opening, applicants ------- submitting their résumés.

(A) beginning
(B) began
(C) begin
(D) had begun

270 기적의 토익 RC

정답 및 해설 p.90

13. The parking lot will be closed temporarily while the resurfacing work -------.

(A) had been carried out
(B) is being carried out
(C) carrying out
(D) was carried out

14. If a client ------- to change service plans, the branch manager must approve any contract changes.

(A) wants
(B) wanted
(C) wanting
(D) will want

15. In order to get a smoothly finished surface, any original paint layers ------- before applying the new paint.

(A) were removing
(B) must be removed
(C) to remove
(D) have removed

16. Students participating ------- any charity events this week are eligible for free items contributed from the local businesses.

(A) in
(B) at
(C) from
(D) toward

17. Golden Airlines serves gourmet meals ------- its passengers on international flights.

(A) to
(B) at
(C) as
(D) on

18. After only a month with the new supplier, there have ------- been two incomplete shipments.

(A) reasonably
(B) moreover
(C) already
(D) some

19. New zoning laws have ------- Parker's Pizza to open a branch in a residential area.

(A) emphasized
(B) delivered
(C) implemented
(D) enabled

20. At Wilson Department Store, sales associates can work in other departments once they have ------- the online training.

(A) completed
(B) deferred
(C) encountered
(D) earned

21. Produce prices will ------- depending on crop yield sizes and what is currently in season.

(A) view
(B) differ
(C) lead
(D) rely

22. Mr. Hurst expects his employees to share the experience they ------- from attending the workshop.

(A) gained
(B) completed
(C) removed
(D) required

23. The Pacific Weather Advisory ------- an evacuation alert when tsunamis are expected to hit Hawaii.

(A) enforces
(B) launches
(C) issues
(D) registers

24. This month, Farrell Consulting ------- an official set of guidelines for dealing with first-time clients and small businesses.

(A) encountered
(B) oversaw
(C) differed
(D) implemented

PART 5 시제 / 동사 어휘 (1)   271

PART 6

뒤의 내용이 단서인 동사 시제 800+

선택지가 다양한 동사 시제로 이루어져 있으면 지문에서 날짜 표현이나 시제를 파악하세요.

적용 기술

[기적의 필기노트] 161P
RC 기술 79

VOCA

press conference 기자 회견
overseas 해외의
manage 관리하다
to date 지금까지
houseware 가정용품
domestic 국내의

 **풀이 방법** ▸ article ♀ 해석 p.92

HARTFORD (17 March) — Designs by Diaz has announced at a press conference that it ------- into the international market. Their first overseas branch will open later
01.
this year. It plans to send recently promoted staff to manage the new branch in Madrid. To date, the houseware supply company has 27 branches across the country. Each one has excellent customer satisfaction ratings. The CEO, Marcus Diaz, ------- to keep that trend going. He said that if the Madrid branch is as
🔖 **PART 5**
successful as the domestic ones, he would like to open another one in Barcelona sometime next year.

01. (A) has been expanding
　　(B) will be expanding
　　(C) has expanded
　　(D) is expanded

🖋 **이렇게 풀어요**

1. **선택지 보고 문법/어휘 문제 파악** 선택지가 동사 expand(확장하다)의 다양한 형태로 구성되어 있으므로 문법 문제임을 파악합니다.

2. **빈칸 분석** 빈칸 뒤의 올해 말에 첫 해외 지사를 열 것이라는 내용을 파악합니다.

3. **정답 선택** 미래 시제인 (B) will be expanding을 정답으로 선택합니다.

해설

앞에서 회사의 현재 상황(지점 수, 고객 평가)에 대해 설명하고 있으므로, 빈칸이 포함된 문장도 현재의 추세가 계속되길 '바란다'는 의미가 되도록 현재 시제로 이어지는 것이 자연스러워요. 따라서 (A)가 정답입니다.

🔖 **PART 5 문법 적용 문제**

The CEO, Marcus Diaz, ------- to keep that trend going.

(A) hopes　　　　(B) has hoped　　　　(C) will hope　　　　(D) hoped

272 기적의 토익 RC

연습 문제

따라 하면 문제가 풀리는

빈칸 뒤 내용에서 단서가 될 부분을 찾아 표시하세요.
표시한 것을 바탕으로 정답 어휘를 선택하세요.

정답 및 해설 p.92

01

Meredith Black, artist native to the Portland area, announced that she ------- 10 sculptures to the Portland Community Center. The event is scheduled to take place next summer for one month from 19 July.

(A) will present

(B) has presented

02

Dear Ms. Greene,

Thank you for the feedback you provided about your dining experience at our restaurant. As you already know, we ------- a new policy that our restaurant's staff members are required to keep their cell phones off. Since introducing it, customer reviews have already improved by a full star!

(A) will implement

(B) implemented

DAY 11

03

Kelly Construction Company won the contract and ------- Carson Theater. Work is scheduled to begin on 7 May and be completed no later than 12 June. This renovation will enable it to accommodate larger audiences.

(A) will renovate

(B) renovated

04

Our company ------- its image through a series of changes. We have begun donating to local charities, and as of next week, uniforms featuring our new logo will be distributed.

(A) is upgrading

(B) had upgraded

PART 6 뒤의 내용이 단서인 동사 시제 273

제한시간 4분입니다! 시~작!

Questions 01-04 refer to the following press release.

Snowbird Bakery is well known for offering the finest bread, cakes, and cookies, all baked fresh every morning. We have been named "the Finest Bakery in Salt Lake City" for three ------- years.
01.
Nevertheless, Emily Donahue, owner of Snowbird Bakery, ------- to make the changes to our
02.
operation. From the beginning of this month, we are offering an exciting new service. Contact us in advance to make a custom cake for your special ------- such as weddings or other celebrations.
03.
Choose a flavor and design and we can make it for you. -------. This is available only to customers
04.
within the city limits of Salt Lake City.

01. (A) occasional
(B) precise
(C) initial
(D) consecutive

유형 적용 문제
02. (A) will decide
(B) to decide
(C) decided
(D) decides

03. (A) deals
(B) appreciation
(C) promotions
(D) occasions

04. (A) In addition, we will even deliver it to your event free of charge.
(B) Our store is going to close temporarily for a renovation project.
(C) Thank you to all our customers for your continuous loyal support.
(D) The nutritional values of each of our goods are posted on our Web site.

○ 정답 및 해설 p.93

Questions 05-08 refer to the following article.

Tour Games (9 December) — The mayors of two neighboring towns, Pottsville and Eagleton, ------- **05.** in a friendly competition. Starting next month, the town which will attract the most tourists wins. The contest will be decided by the number of people who collect all of the stamps on the city passport. -------. To promote this competition, city passports are designed to ------- as a discount pass that **06.** **07.** can be used at the stores and restaurants near the chosen attractions. The winning town will have to get a grant for the renovation of the winner's city library. ------- town wins, both are sure to benefit **08.** from their attempts to increase tourism.

유형 적용 문제

05. (A) have partaken
(B) will partake
(C) were partaking
(D) partake

07. (A) observe
(B) receive
(C) buy
(D) serve

06. (A) Many restaurants and stores want to join in this competition.
(B) Pottsville normally has more visitors than Eagleton around this time of year.
(C) Each city has picked 10 famous attractions to give them out.
(D) Discounts on public transportation will be available for anyone visiting either town.

08. (A) Whenever
(B) Whomever
(C) Whichever
(D) Whatever

DAY 11

PART 6 뒤의 내용이 단서인 동사 시제 275

PART 7

공지 (1) 사내 공지

사내 공지는 PART 7 문제 전반부에 싱글 지문으로 출제되거나 이중/삼중 지문으로도 출제돼요.

사내 공지는 직원들을 대상으로 인사 이동 공지, 규정 변경 공지, 업무 협조 요청 등을 하는 내용이 출제돼요. 주로 <공지의 제목 – 공지 목적 또는 주제 언급 – 구체적인 정보 설명 – 기타 정보(관련 담당자 등)>의 순서로 지문이 전개됩니다.

사내 공지에서 자주 출제되는 문제

목적 문제
What is the purpose of the notice?
→ 지문 초반에서 welcome, policy, introduce 등의 키워드 주위에서 단서가 제시돼요.

새로 온 인물의 경력, 업적에 관한 문제
In what field does Mr. Winston work?
→ 주로 인물을 소개하는 단락 내의 respected people in, dedicated in 같은 표현 주위에서 단서가 제시돼요.

사내 공지에 자주 출제되는 어휘

transfer	전근시키다	retire	퇴직하다, 퇴임하다
qualified	적임의, 자격 있는	replacement	후임자
be in charge of	~을 담당하다	lay off	해고하다
temporary position	임시직	evaluate	평가하다
performance	성과, 실적	nomination	임명, 지명
promote	승진하다	dismissal	해고
appoint	임명하다	assignment	임무, 맡은 일
HR department	인사부서	retirement allowance	퇴직금
undertake	담당하다	job performance	직무 수행
exceptional	특출한	representative	대표, 대표자
resignation	사임, 사직	take on	~을 떠맡다
opportunity	기회	prestigious	명성 있는
career	직업 (경력)	in excess of	~을 초과하여, ~보다 많이
advancement	발전	relinquish	(직위를) 내주다
transition	변화	considerable	상당한
manage	관리하다	appointee	임명된 사람
persuade	설득하다	competent	유능한
propose	제안하다	field	분야
undertake	(일, 책임을) 맡다	turn out	모습을 드러내다, 나타나다
growth	성장, 증가	gratitude	감사, 고마움
discard	버리다, 폐기하다	break room	휴게실

276　기적의 토익 RC

풀이방법 사내 공지

notice

해석 p.94

Announcement: Globalization Major

As the president of this Columbine University, it is my honor to welcome Professor William Collins. He will be the head of our Globalization Department. A decade ago, he completed his thesis on international trade relations and has been one of the most respected people in his field since then. Adding him to our staff will certainly improve the reputation of our school and attract even more students who are interested in business, marketing, trade, and international relations.

Globalization will be available to our students as either a major or a minor as of the fall semester. Professor Collins will make a presentation about the major in Kennedy Lecture Hall from 2-3 p.m. this coming Tuesday.

---

01. What is the main purpose of the announcement?

(A) To announce a presidential election
(B) To specify the requirements of a major
(C) To promote a study abroad program
(D) To introduce a professor to a university

02. What is indicated about Professor Collins?

(A) He graduated from Columbine University.
(B) He completed his thesis two years ago.
(C) He is scheduled to give a speech.
(D) He majored in Economics.

DAY 11

이렇게 풀어요

01. 공지의 주요 목적은 무엇인가?

(A) 총장 선거를 알리기 위해서
(B) 전공 필수 과목을 명시하기 위해서
(C) 유학 프로그램을 홍보하기 위해서
(D) 교수를 대학에 소개하기 위해서

해설 첫 문장에서 it is my honor to welcome Professor William Collins라고 했으므로 (D)가 정답입니다.

02. Collins 교수에 대해 언급된 것은 무엇인가?

(A) Columbine 대학을 졸업했다.
(B) 2년 전에 논문을 완성했다.
(C) 연설할 예정이다.
(D) 경제학을 전공했다.

해설 마지막 단락에서 Professor Collins will make a presentation 이라고 했으므로 make a presentation을 give a speech로 패러프레이징한 (C)가 정답입니다.

PART 7 공지 (1) 사내 공지

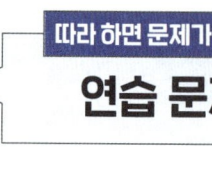

따라 하면 문제가 풀리는

연습 문제

먼저 문제의 키워드에 표시한 후,
지문에서 단서를 찾아 적절한 답을 고르세요.

01 notice

This is a reminder that Parking Lot A will be closed for renovation for two weeks from next Monday. Even though Parking lot B will be open, it will be reserved for our clients and company cars only. During this time, all employees are encouraged to commute by bus or subway. We are just two blocks away from Central Station. If you need to bring your car, you should use street parking at your expense.

I apologize for any inconvenience this may cause and thank you for patience.

General Manager
Atlanta Cable & Internet

Q. What is suggested about Atlanta Cable & Internet?

(A) It is located close to public transportation.
(B) It will reimburse parking expenses.

02 notice

I'm pleased to announce that we will have a much safer and more secure working environment. As of March 1, all PIN-access doors will be replaced with ones accessed by your biometric data, or fingerprint. This is because some of the PIN numbers were released to unauthorized people such as pizza delivery men or couriers. Therefore, please come to the security office, enter your fingerprint into our security data system, and sign an agreement form by the end of this week. I guarantee you that it will only be used for security purposes.

Q. What should the employees do by the end of this week?

(A) Reissue new PIN numbers
(B) Register their biometric information

정답 및 해설 p.94

03 notice

As the summer season is the busiest time for our golf resort, we will begin restricting the number of vacation days that employees can take during this period. We hope it will help to maintain our level of service by making sure we have enough staff members working each shift. From June 1, you will only be allowed to take three vacation days in a row. For more information, please speak to an HR representative.

Q. What is the purpose of the notice?

    (A) To ask for volunteers to cover shifts
    (B) To update a vacation policy

04 announcement

Attention, staff! I would like to take this opportunity to introduce myself. My name is Tabitha Conley, and I am the new building manager. My aim for the next month is to adapt our building to make it comply with the latest fire safety requirements issued by the government. This will involve installing new equipment such as automatic sprinklers. Later this week, I will e-mail the details about the rules we are required to follow. Please let me know if you have any questions.

Q. What does Ms. Conley say she will do?

    (A) Distribute information about regulations
    (B) Teach employees how to use new equipment

PART 7 공지 (1) 사내 공지　279

토익에 나올 실전 문제

제한시간 10분입니다! 시~작!

Questions 01-02 refer to the following announcement.

Announcement: Changes at Lowe, Cortese & Associates

Following an exhaustive search for a job candidate with the unique set of qualifications required by our firm, we are delighted to introduce Marie Katz as the newest member of the Lowe, Cortese & Associates team. She will be taking on the role of senior associate, focusing on property law. Her previous work experience includes handling real estate cases at Dwight, Webster, and Gilbert. Along with her expertise and impressive communication skills, she brings with her a large network of professional contacts and loyal customers. We believe that we will be able to reach our goal of expanding our property law department with the help of Ms. Katz. Everyone on staff will have a chance to get to know more about her background and her approach to dealing with clients next week, as she will give a brief presentation at the beginning of the weekly meeting.

01. What is the purpose of the announcement?

(A) To notify clients of changes in legal fees
(B) To welcome a lawyer to a business
(C) To promote a job opening at a law firm
(D) To introduce a new legal regulation

02. What is true about Ms. Katz?

(A) She will give a talk to her coworkers.
(B) She will lead a communication workshop.
(C) She will handle all new clients.
(D) She will be absent from a weekly meeting.

paraphrasing 주어진 어휘 또는 표현과 패러프레이징 될 수 있는 것을 연결하세요.

1. take on the role of •   • (a) rule
2. deal with clients •   • (b) give a talk
3. give a brief presentation •   • (c) not attend
4. regulation •   • (d) manage patrons
5. be absent from •   • (e) be in charge of

280   기적의 토익 RC

🔍 정답 및 해설 p.95

Questions 03-04 refer to the following announcement.

Honoring Dedicated Service

The management team at the Brentwood Community Center would like to show our deepest appreciation for Ms. Shirley Galloway. Ms. Galloway moved to Brentwood 25 years ago, and since that time she has dedicated her free time to worthwhile projects. For example, she founded a series of English classes for non-native speakers as a volunteer at Brentwood Library, and these have been running for the past 15 years. As a member of several community groups, such as the Brentwood Readers Club and the Backyard Garden Association, Ms. Galloway has gotten to know many residents of our city. Before joining our team 10 years ago, Ms. Galloway traveled throughout the region to learn about the best methods for taking action toward resolving a number of social issues.

We are holding a farewell reception for Ms. Galloway on Friday, April 20, at 3 P.M. at the Brentwood Community Center. Members of the public are encouraged to attend the event.

DAY 11

03. According to the announcement, how has Ms. Galloway helped the community?

(A) By founding a gardening club
(B) By starting a language education program
(C) By making financial contributions to the library
(D) By running for political office

04. For how long has Ms. Galloway worked at the Brentwood Community Center?

(A) 25 years
(B) 15 years
(C) 10 years
(D) 5 years

---

paraphrasing 주어진 어휘 또는 표현과 패러프레이징 될 수 있는 것을 연결하세요.

1. show appreciation •
2. found •
3. a series of English classes •
4. resolve •
5. make financial contributions •

• (a) language education program
• (b) donate
• (c) create
• (d) find solutions
• (e) thank

PART 7 공지 (1) 사내 공지 281

 **실전 문제**

Questions 05-07 refer to the following notice.

The success of Tetreault Consulting is heavily dependent on the dedication and professionalism of our staff. We are committed to a policy of giving our staff members increasing levels of responsibility to help them hone their skills and progress in their careers. In light of this, we are pleased to announce that Assistant PR Director Ron Marchant will become the new PR Director as of September 1.

Over the past few years, Mr. Marchant has worked hard to manage the perception of our company. His talent has been recognized by others in the field, as he has been nominated for the prestigious Mela-Amaya Prize four times, finally taking it home last fall. Through the News Network program he developed, he greatly improved the dialog between our company and newspapers, magazines, and blogs.

Mr. Marchant will replace Suzanne Barron, who will leave our Vancouver branch in Canada next month to head up the PR department in our Dublin branch in Ireland. We wish both Mr. Marchant and Ms. Barron all the best in their new roles.

05. What is the notice mainly about?
(A) A change in a policy
(B) A staff member's promotion
(C) The new location of a company
(D) A company's achievement

06. What is mentioned about Mr. Marchant?
(A) He graduated from a prestigious university.
(B) He recruited several new clients for the business.
(C) He won an industry award several times.
(D) He improved communication with media outlets.

07. What will Ms. Barron do next month?
(A) Transfer overseas
(B) Go into retirement
(C) Be interviewed by a newspaper
(D) Search for her replacement

paraphrasing 주어진 어휘 또는 표현과 패러프레이징 될 수 있는 것을 연결하세요.

1. be recognized
2. replace
3. dialog between our company and newspapers, magazines, and blogs
4. role
5. transfer overseas

(a) duty
(b) relocate
(c) be appreciated
(d) take over
(e) communication with media outlets

282　기적의 토익 RC

Questions 08-10 refer to the following notice.

Notice to Employees:

Bachman Accounting is currently recruiting new employees in a number of positions to facilitate our company expansion. Over the past few months, our customer base has grown significantly, as both individual and corporate clients were forced to seek new accounting assistance after Kembery Inc. — previously the largest accounting firm in the area — went out of business.

To address the need for a larger staff, we have uploaded job descriptions on career Web sites and advertised in the local newspaper. Several of our HR staff members also operated a booth at the Miller City Career Fair to get the word out. However, despite all of this hard work, we still need your help. If you know of anyone who might be a good fit for our team, please let them know about the open positions. We will give special attention to anyone who is personally recommended by a staff member, so if someone you know has applied, please send the person's name, phone number, and e-mail address to Rosario Conner at r_conner@bachmanacc.com by March 31.

08. According to the notice, what has assisted with Bachman Accounting's growth?
(A) Months of heavy advertising
(B) Investment in employee training
(C) The closure of a major competitor
(D) The launch of a new service

09. What is NOT mentioned as a recruitment method used by Bachman Accounting?
(A) Posting job listings online
(B) Attending a job fair
(C) Hiring a recruitment firm
(D) Placing newspaper advertisements

10. What are employees asked to do by March 31?
(A) Review the job duties for open positions
(B) Submit contact information for job candidates
(C) Sign up for a group training session
(D) Suggest a business for a partnership

---

paraphrasing 주어진 어휘 또는 표현과 패러프레이징 될 수 있는 것을 연결하세요.

1. currently recruiting •
2. went out of business •
3. address •
4. open positions •
5. person's name, phone number, and e-mail address •

• (a) deal with
• (b) contact information
• (c) now hiring
• (d) job opening
• (e) closure

PART 7 공지 (1) 사내 공지   283

'멋진 당신, 오늘도 화이팅'

DAY

12

오늘의 학습 포인트

PART 5. to부정사

1. to부정사의 역할 – 명사/형용사/부사 역할
2. to부정사의 태 – 수동태: to be p.p.
   – to뒤의 동사가 자동사이면 능동, 타동사이면 빈칸 뒤 목적어 유무 따지기
3. to부정사의 의미상의 주어 – 'for + 명사/대명사'
4. to부정사 관용 표현 – eligible toV, attempt toV, expect A toV 등
5. 준사역동사 help – help + 사람 목적어 + to부정사/동사원형

PART 6. 일반적인 사실을 나타내는 현재 시제

보기가 다양한 동사 시제. 지문의 시제 파악하기

PART 7. 공공장소에서의 공지

제목과 초반부 꼭 읽기

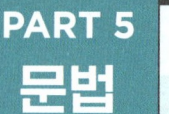

PART 5
문법

to부정사

명사 역할과 부사 역할의 출제 비중이 높고, to부정사와 사용되는 동사/명사/형용사 어휘도 자주 나와요.

⚠️ **주의**

to부정사는 동사의 성격을 갖고 있지만 전치사의 목적어 자리에는 올 수 없어요.

🔒 **확인 문제 ❶**

Most parents encourage their children ------- extracurricular activities.

(A) join
(B) to join

출제 포인트

토익에는 주격 보어보다 목적격 보어로서의 to부정사가 더 자주 출제돼요.

🔒 **확인 문제 ❷**

The city of Yorkshire has a plan ------- a new parking garage in downtown.

(A) to build
(B) building

출제 유형 1
to부정사의 역할

1 명사 역할

- to부정사는 **타동사의 목적어 자리**에 올 수 있습니다. 단, 모든 타동사가 to부정사를 목적어로 가질 수 있는 것은 아니므로 해당 동사를 암기해 두어야 합니다. → p.288 '3형식 동사 + to부정사' 참고

  Susan decided **to cancel** the upcoming workshop.
  　　　　　　　　목적어
  Susan은 곧 있을 워크샵을 취소하기로 결정했다.

  800+
- to부정사는 **주어 자리**에 올 수 있습니다. to부정사 주어는 **단수** 취급합니다.

  To cooperate with other departments is fundamental to success.
  　주어　　　　　　　　　　　　　　　　　　　동사
  다른 부서와 협업하는 것은 성공을 위해 중요하다.

- to부정사가 쓰인 주어가 길면 가주어 It을 주어 자리에 쓰고 to부정사를 뒤로 보냅니다.(가주어/진주어 구문)

  It is important **to comply** with all safety procedures.
  　　　　　　　　　목적어
  모든 안전 절차를 준수하는 것이 중요합니다.

- to부정사는 **주격 보어, 목적격 보어 자리**에 올 수 있습니다. 주격 보어 자리에 올 때는 주로 be동사, appear, seem, remain과 함께 쓰입니다. to부정사를 목적격 보어로 취하는 동사는 별도로 암기해 두세요. → p.288 '5형식 동사 + 목적어 + to부정사' 참고

  Some of the machines appear **to be broken**. 몇몇 기기들이 고장 난 것처럼 보인다.
  　　　　　　　　　　　　　　주격 보어

  The HR Department asked the new interns **to update** their contact information.
  　　　　　　　　　　　　　　　　　　　　　목적격 보어
  인사부에서 신입 인턴들에게 연락처를 업데이트 해달라고 요청했다.

2 형용사 역할

- to부정사가 형용사 역할을 하여 명사를 수식할 때는 **명사 뒤에서 수식**하며, '~할/ ~하는'이라는 의미를 나타냅니다.

  The product developers are looking for a way **to improve** the battery life.
  제품 개발자들은 배터리 수명을 개선할 방법을 찾고 있다.　　　　　　way 수식

- to부정사의 수식을 받는 명사를 암기해 두세요. → p.288 '명사 + to부정사' 참고

정답 ❶ (B) ❷ (A)

286 기적의 토익 RC

3 부사 역할

- to부정사가 동사 또는 문장 전체를 부사처럼 수식할 경우 목적, 원인, 결과를 의미하며, '~하기 위해서'라는 의미로 쓰이는 목적의 출제 비중이 가장 높습니다.

  To accomplish this project, we will hire more workers.
  이번 프로젝트를 완수하기 위해 우리는 직원들을 더 채용할 것이다.

- 부사 역할로 쓰인 to부정사는 문장 맨 앞 또는 문장 끝에 위치합니다.

  Several musicians held a joint concert **to raise money**.
  여러 음악인들이 돈을 모으기 위해 합동 콘서트를 열었다.

- to부정사가 목적을 의미할 때는 in order to, so as to(~하기 위해서)로도 쓸 수 있습니다.

  In order to make room for new arrivals, the store holds a clearance sale.
  신제품을 위한 공간을 마련하기 위해, 그 상점은 재고 정리 세일을 연다.

출제 유형 2

to부정사의 태/to부정사의 의미상의 주어

`800+`
1 to부정사의 태 일치

- to부정사의 능동태(to + 동사원형)와 수동태(to be p.p.)를 구별하는 문제가 출제됩니다.

- to부정사의 동사가 자동사이면 능동, 타동사이면 빈칸 뒤에 목적어가 있는지 여부를 따져 능동인지 수동인지 구분합니다.

  　　　　　　　　　　　　　　　　　　　　　　　자동사
  The manager encouraged his team members (**to participate** / ~~to be participated~~) in the charity event. 매니저는 그의 팀원들에게 자선 행사에 참석하라고 권장했다.

  The customer wanted his order (~~to deliver~~ / **to be delivered**) tomorrow.
  고객은 그의 주문이 내일 배달되기를 원했다. 　목적어 없으므로 수동태

`900+`
2 to부정사의 의미상의 주어

- to부정사는 동사원형을 포함하고 있으므로 동사가 나타내는 행위 또는 상태의 주체를 표시할 필요가 있을 때 to부정사 앞에 의미상의 주어 'for + 명사/대명사'를 씁니다.

  It is difficult **for him** to analyze the data. 그가 자료를 분석하기는 어렵다.

출제 유형 3

to부정사 관용 표현

---

1 형용사 + to부정사

(un)able toV ~할 수 있다(~할 수 없다)	eligible toV ~할 자격이 있다
(un)likely toV ~할 것 같다(~할 것 같지 않다)	eager toV ~하기를 갈망하다
pleased toV ~하는 것을 기뻐하다	(un)willing toV 기꺼이 ~하다(~하기를 꺼리다)
hesitant toV ~하기를 주저하다	reluctant toV ~하기를 꺼려하다
apt/prone toV ~하기 쉽다	

🔒 **확인 문제 ❸**

------- your seat at the workshop, please book it in advance.

(A) To secure
(B) Security

출제 포인트
in order to의 경우 to부정사 부분보다는 in order to 표현 자체를 묻는 문제가 더 자주 나와요.

🔒 **확인 문제 ❹**

Ms. Lee was asked ------- the interview.

(A) to be conducted
(B) to conduct

출제 포인트
to부정사의 의미상의 주어 관련 문제는 전치사 for를 묻는 문제가 출제돼요.

✎ **적용 기술**

[기적의 필기노트] 127P~130P
RC 기술 41, 42, 44, 45

🔒 **확인 문제 ❺**

All subscribers are eligible to ------- a free item.

(A) receiving
(B) receive

정답 ❸ (A) ❹ (B) ❺ (B)

PART 5 문법 to부정사　287

2 명사 + to부정사

ability toV ~하는 능력	opportunity toV ~할 기회	chance toV ~할 기회
effort toV ~하려는 노력	attempt toV ~하려는 시도	way toV ~할 방법
plan toV ~할 계획	need toV ~할 필요	offer toV ~하겠다는 제안
decision toV ~하겠다는 결정	right toV ~할 권리	means toV ~하려는 조치

3 3형식 동사 + to부정사

⚠ **주의**

전치사 to를 동반하는 관용 표현과 구분하세요.
· be accustomed to -ing/N
· be used to -ing/N
· object to -ing/N
· be opposed to -ing/N
· be committed/dedicated/devoted to -ing/N

want toV 원하다	need toV 필요로 하다	wish toV 바라다	hope toV 바라다
expect toV 기대하다	plan toV 계획하다	decide toV 결정하다	ask toV 요청하다
promise toV 약속하다	refuse toV 거절하다	fail toV ~하지 못하다	afford toV 여유가 있다
strive toV 노력하다			

4 5형식 동사 + 목적어 + to부정사

<능동태> 동사 + 목적어(A) + to부정사	<수동태> 목적어 + be p.p. + to부정사
expect A toV A가 ~할 것을 기대하다, 예상하다	be expected toV ~할 것으로 기대되다, 예상되다
invite A toV A가 ~하도록 제안하다	be invited to V ~하라고 제안받다
ask A toV A가 ~하는 것을 요청하다	be asked toV ~하라고 요청받다
require A toV A가 ~하는 것을 요청하다	be required toV ~하라고 요청받다
request A toV A가 ~하는 것을 요청하다	be requested toV ~하라고 요청받다
allow/permit A toV A가 ~하는 것을 허락하다	be allowed/permitted toV ~하도록 허락받다
advise A toV A가 ~하는 것을 권장하다	be advised toV ~하라고 권장받다
remind A toV A가 ~하라고 상기시켜주다	be reminded toV ~할 것을 상기하게 되다
encourage A toV A가 ~하도록 권장하다	be encouraged toV ~할 것을 권장받다
persuade A toV A가 ~하도록 설득하다	be persuaded toV ~하라고 설득되다
enable A toV A가 ~할 수 있게 하다	be enabled toV ~할 수 있게 되다

🔒 **확인 문제 ❻**

This mobile app helps you
------- available property.

(A) find
(B) finding

출제 유형 4

준사역동사 help

· help는 'help + 사람 목적어 + to부정사/동사원형'의 형태로 쓰입니다.
The new accounting software **helps you to sort/sort** all transactions more easily. 새로운 회계 소프트웨어는 당신이 모든 거래를 더 쉽게 분류하도록 도와준다.

800+

· 목적어를 생략하고 to부정사/동사원형을 바로 쓰기도 합니다.
The new accounting software **helps to sort/sort** all transactions more easily.
→ 목적어가 생략될 경우 동사 2개가 나란히 오는 특이한 형태의 구문이 되므로 주의하세요.

정답 ❻ (A)

288 기적의 토익 RC

to부정사

1. A customer service manager plans ------- our exchange and refund policy.

(A) update   (B) updates   (C) updating   (D) to update

고객 서비스 매니저는 우리의 교환 및 환불 정책을 업데이트할 계획이다.

> **✔ 이렇게 풀어요**
>
> **1. 선택지 보고 문법/어휘 문제 파악**   선택지가 동사 update(업데이트하다)의 다양한 형태로 구성되어 있으므로 문법 문제임을 파악할 수 있어요.
>
> **2. 빈칸 분석**   동사 plans 뒤에서 명사구 our exchange and refund policy를 취할 수 있는 문법 요소가 들어가야 함을 파악합니다.
>
> **3. 정답 선택**   동사 plans의 목적어 역할을 함과 동시에 빈칸 뒤의 명사구를 목적어로 취할 수 있는 to부정사 (D) to update를 정답으로 고릅니다.

2. The restaurant manager rearranged the tables ------- more diners on the patio.

(A) to accommodate   (B) accommodated   (C) can accommodate   (D) accommodates

레스토랑 매니저는 테라스에 더 많은 손님들을 수용하기 위해 테이블을 재배치했다.

> **✔ 이렇게 풀어요**
>
> **1. 선택지 보고 문법/어휘 문제 파악**   선택지가 동사 accommodate(수용하다)의 다양한 형태로 구성되어 있으므로 문법 문제임을 파악해요.
>
> **2. 빈칸 분석**   빈칸 앞에 완전한 문장이 있고, 빈칸 뒤의 명사구 more diners를 취할 수 있는 문법 요소가 들어가야 함을 파악해요.
>
> **3. 정답 선택**   '~하기 위해서'라는 의미로 쓰일 수 있는 to부정사 (A) to accommodate를 정답으로 고릅니다.

3. The new file management software will help researchers ------- the processing of field data.

(A) expedite   (B) expediting   (C) expedites   (D) expedited

새로운 파일 관리 소프트웨어는 연구원들이 현장 자료의 처리를 신속하게 하도록 도울 것이다.

> **✔ 이렇게 풀어요**
>
> **1. 선택지 보고 문법/어휘 문제 파악**   선택지가 동사 expedite(신속히 처리하다)의 다양한 형태로 구성되어 있으므로 문법 문제임을 파악해요.
>
> **2. 빈칸 분석**   빈칸 앞에 동사 help와 사람 목적어(researchers)가 있음을 파악합니다..
>
> **3. 정답 선택**   준사역동사 help가 쓰인 5형식 구문에서 목적격 보어 자리에 올 수 있는 형태인 동사원형 (A) expedite를 정답으로 고릅니다.

PART 5 문법 to부정사

PART 5 어휘

동사 어휘 (2)

각 어휘와 함께 자주 쓰이는 표현을 통째로 외워두세요.

01 communicate — 연락하다, 의사소통하다

communicate with	~와 연락하다
communicate effectively	효과적으로 의사소통하다

02 recruit — 모집하다

recruit director	감독을 모집하다
recruit additional employee	추가 직원을 모집하다

03 deduct — 빼다, 공제하다

deduct A from B	B에서 A를 빼다, 공제하다

🐾 빈출 토익 선생님 Pick!
04 accommodate — 공간을 제공하다, 수용하다

accommodate + 인원 수	~명을 수용하다
accommodate one's needs	~의 요구를 수용하다

05 serve — 제공하다, 도움이 되다

serve A to B	A를 B에게 제공하다
serve 사람	~를 응대하다, 돕다
serve as	~로 일하다, ~로 유용하다

06 improve — 개선하다, 향상시키다

improve productivity	생산성을 높이다
be noticeably/remarkably improved	크게 향상되다

800+
07 compile — 엮다, 편집하다

compile research data	연구 자료를 편집하다
compile the financial records	재무 기록을 편집하다

08 initiate — 시작하다, 착수하다

initiate the process	절차를 시작하다
initiate the request	요청사항에 착수하다

09 unveil — 밝히다, 발표하다

unveil plans	계획을 밝히다
unveil new product	신제품을 발표하다
be unveiled on 시점	~에 밝혀지다

10 finance — 자금을 대다

finance one's own business	자기 사업에 자금을 대다
be financed by	~에게 재정 지원을 받다

800+
11 emerge — 나오다, 드러나다

emerge as	~로 부각되다
emerge from	~에서 나오다

🐾 빈출 토익 선생님 Pick!
12 submit — 제출하다

submit an application	신청서를 제출하다
submit the proposal/report	제안서/보고서를 제출하다
submit A to B	A를 B에게 제출하다

13 attract — 끌다, 끌어모으다

attract 사람 to	~을 -로 끌어모으다
attract buyers/tourists	구매자들/관광객들을 끌어모으다
attract attention	주목을 끌다

800+
14 expedite — 신속히 처리하다, 촉진시키다

expedite the process	과정을 촉진시키다
expedite one's order	주문을 신속히 처리하다

☘ 빈출 토익 선생님 Pick!

15 relocate 이전시키다, 전근하다

　relocate A to B　　　　　　A를 B로 이전시키다

800+

16 evolve 발달하다, 진전시키다

　evolve from A to B　　　　A에서 B로 발달하다

17 respond 대답하다, 대응하다

　respond to　　　　　　　~에 대응하다
　respond immediately　　　즉시 대응하다

18 enter 들어가다, 입력하다

　enter A into B　　　A를 B에 기입하다, 입력하다
　enter a contest　　　대회에 참가하다

800+

19 transform 변형시키다

　transform A into B　　　A를 B로 변형시키다

20 provide 제공하다

　provide A with B　　　A에게 B를 제공하다
　provide B to A　　　　B를 A에게 제공하다
　provide an explanation　해명을 하다

21 recommend 추천하다, 권고하다

　recommend A (highly) for B　B에 대해 A를 (매우) 추천하다
　recommend that　　　　　~하기를 권하다

☘ 빈출 토익 선생님 Pick!

22 handle 다루다, 처리하다

　handle complaints/requests　불만/요청을 처리하다
　handle A with care　　　　A를 조심스럽게 다루다

23 engrave 새기다

　engrave A on B　　　　A를 B에 새기다
　be engraved with　　　~가 새겨져 있다

24 resolve 해결하다

　resolve conflicts/issues　갈등/문제를 해결하다

800+

25 delegate 위임하다, 선정하다

　delegate A to 사람　　　　　　　A를 ~에게 위임하다
　plans has been delegated to 사람 계획이 ~에게 위임되었다
　delegate the task to 사람　　　업무를 ~에게 위임하다

☘ 빈출 토익 선생님 Pick!

26 ensure 반드시 ~하게 하다, 보장하다

　ensure the safety of　　　~의 안전을 보장하다
　ensure that　　　　　　반드시 ~하게 하다

DAY 12

👨‍🏫 **풀이 방법**

The branch manager ------- Zhang Technologies for the company's mobile service.

(A) deducted　　　(B) compiled　　　(C) financed　　　(D) recommended

지점장은 회사의 모바일 서비스를 위해 Zhang Technologies를 추천했다.

↶ 이렇게 풀어요

1. **선택지 보고 문법/어휘 문제 파악**　선택지가 서로 다른 동사 어휘로 구성되어 있으므로 어휘 문제임을 파악해요.

2. **빈칸 분석**　빈칸 뒤에 전치사 for가 있으므로 for와 함께 쓰이는 동사가 들어가야 함을 파악해요.

3. **정답 선택**　recommend A for B의 형태로 쓰이는 (D) recommended를 정답으로 고릅니다.

PART 5 어휘 동사 어휘 (2)　291

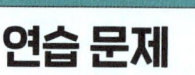
따라 하면 문제가 풀리는
연습 문제

앞서 학습한 문제 풀이법을 적용하여 맞는 것에 ✔ 표시 하거나 괄호 안에 적절한 답을 쓰고 정답을 선택하세요.

01 The store manager is required to ------- immediately to any customer complaints.

(A) initiate
(B) recruit
(C) respond
(D) submit

> 1. 선택지 보고 문법/어휘 문제 파악하기 ☐문법 문제 ☐어휘 문제
> 2. 빈칸 분석하기 빈칸 앞 문장의 주어 (   )
>   주어가 '고객 불만에 즉시 -------해야 한다'는 문맥을 완성하는 동사가 정답이다.
> 3. 정답 선택하기 정답 (   )

02 Mr. Fuller's supervisors asked him ------- the building's interior floor plan.

(A) designer
(B) to design
(C) designed
(D) designs

> 1. 선택지 보고 문법/어휘 문제 파악하기 ☐문법 문제 ☐어휘 문제
> 2. 빈칸 분석하기 빈칸 앞에 있는 동사 (   )
>   빈칸 앞의 동사가 취하는 목적격 보어의 형태 ☐to부정사 ☐동명사
> 3. 정답 선택하기 정답 (   )

03 In an effort ------- sales, Galvan Hardware started running ad campaigns.

(A) increase
(B) increased
(C) to increase
(D) increasing

> 1. 선택지 보고 문법/어휘 문제 파악하기 ☐문법 문제 ☐어휘 문제
> 2. 빈칸 분석하기 빈칸 앞에 있는 명사 (   )
>   빈칸 앞의 명사를 수식할 수 있는 형태 ☐동명사 ☐to부정사
> 3. 정답 선택하기 정답 (   )

○ 정답 및 해설 p.98

04 Fowler Supermarket began offering membership discounts ------- more customers.

(A) attracting
(B) to attract
(C) attraction
(D) attracted

1. 선택지 보고 문법/어휘 문제 파악하기 ☐ 문법 문제 ☐ 어휘 문제
2. 빈칸 분석하기 빈칸 앞에 있는 것 ☐ 완전한 문장 ☐ 불완전한 문장
   → 빈칸에는 ☐ 동사 역할 ☐ 부사 역할을 하는 것이 와야 한다.
3. 정답 선택하기 정답 (   )

05 A rewards program will help you ------- up a regular customer base.

(A) building
(B) builds
(C) built
(D) build

1. 선택지 보고 문법/어휘 문제 파악하기 ☐ 문법 문제 ☐ 어휘 문제
2. 빈칸 분석하기 빈칸 앞에 있는 동사 (   )
   빈칸 앞의 동사가 취하는 목적격 보어의 형태 ☐ 동사원형 ☐ 동명사
3. 정답 선택하기 정답 (   )

06 Guerra Industries is eager ------- its latest tablet device to the public.

(A) to introduce
(B) introducing
(C) introduce
(D) introduction

1. 선택지 보고 문법/어휘 문제 파악하기 ☐ 문법 문제 ☐ 어휘 문제
2. 빈칸 분석하기 빈칸 앞에 있는 형용사 (   )
   빈칸 앞의 형용사를 수식할 수 있는 형태 ☐ 동사원형 ☐ to부정사
3. 정답 선택하기 정답 (   )

PART 5 to부정사 / 동사 어휘 (2)   293

DAY 01-12 누적 문제

제한시간 9분입니다! 시~작!

01. This mobile application can allow you ------- your order whenever you want.

(A) are tracked
(B) to track
(C) tracks
(D) has tracked

02. Gong Law and Associates was able ------- its operational expenses.

(A) reduction
(B) reduces
(C) reduced
(D) to reduce

03. The professor encourages all students ------- their work prior to the deadline.

(A) will submit
(B) submitted
(C) submission
(D) to submit

04. Since the current contract with Sullivan Cable is set ------- next month, the company is considering switching providers.

(A) expires
(B) had expired
(C) to expire
(D) be expiring

05. Goodlettsville Library wishes ------- enough funds to upgrade its computers and other equipment.

(A) to raise
(B) had raised
(C) is raising
(D) raised

06. ------- renew your magazine subscription, simply call and speak with a representative.

(A) To
(B) In
(C) Of
(D) At

07. The customer service managers strive ------- the response time to calls from customers.

(A) reduced
(B) to reduce
(C) will reduce
(D) reduction

08. The games' opening ceremony is to ------- promptly at 9:00 A.M. on Monday.

(A) commencing
(B) commenced
(C) commence
(D) commencement

09. Windmills in this area are expected ------- sufficient electricity for every home in the town.

(A) generation
(B) are generating
(C) will generate
(D) to generate

10. Billy's Fashion's customers are asked ------- the store's Web site and give feedback.

(A) visited
(B) visiting
(C) to visit
(D) visitors

11. Endorsing local celebrities is an effective way ------- a brand's presence in a new market.

(A) to establish
(B) establishing
(C) establishment
(D) establishes

12. In an effort ------- employee productivity, Creep Paper introduced flexible working hours.

(A) improved
(B) to improve
(C) improving
(D) improvement

294 기적의 토익 RC

13. Most local restaurants tend ------- locally grown produce, meats, and fruits.

(A) using
(B) to use
(C) usage
(D) useful

14. ------- expedite shipping during the winter holidays, Antonio's Tea Factory is hiring part-time warehouse workers.

(A) For
(B) Because of
(C) So that
(D) In order to

15. Last quarter, Decker Furniture sold more chairs than it ------- during the previous year.

(A) is doing
(B) does
(C) did
(D) will have done

16. Ms. Peterson ------- that the hospitality industry would be booming in Colorado next quarter.

(A) predict
(B) predicted
(C) predictable
(D) prediction

17. The number of international applicants for this position ------- since it offers experience in working abroad.

(A) double
(B) are double
(C) has doubled
(D) doubly

18. Neither of the ------- was reluctant to handle the old model of truck.

(A) technical
(B) technicians
(C) technically
(D) technologies

19. Having a degree in computer science ------- the chance of promotion at Louisville Designs.

(A) recruits
(B) improves
(C) unveils
(D) submits

20. The board members believe that the new ad campaign will ------- more customers to their stores.

(A) resolve
(B) provide
(C) attract
(D) evolve

21. With this upgraded teleconferencing system, employees of Bishop Industries can ------- with those working overseas.

(A) initiate
(B) communicate
(C) encounter
(D) emphasize

22. If you would like to ------- your international shipment, you should select the Customs Bypass option.

(A) implement
(B) enforce
(C) expedite
(D) relocate

23. Hahn's Financial will be relocating to a larger office space next month to ------- its new accountants.

(A) ensure
(B) accommodate
(C) respond
(D) issue

24. Alexander Hunt ------- as the winner of the 18th Annual Monterey Golf Tournament.

(A) emerged
(B) established
(C) relied
(D) delegated

PART 6
일반적인 사실을 나타내는 현재 시제 800+

선택지가 다양한 동사 시제로 이루어져 있으면 지문에서 날짜 표현이나 시제를 파악하세요.

적용 기술

[기적의 필기노트] 162P
RC 기술 80

VOCA

benefit 혜택
come along with ~와 함께 따라 오다
serve 제공하다
rest 쉬다, 휴식을 취하다

 **풀이 방법** card   해석 p.100

Congratulations on joining the VIP Sky Club! There are many benefits that come along with your membership.

You now have access to our airport lounges, which each ------- high-speed Internet access, comfortable lounge chairs, and a shower room. **01.**

Our airport lounges also offer a free snack and beverage bar, along with a mini-deli that serves soup and sandwiches. You do have to pay for anything you get from there, though.

We are pleased ------- you with a comfortable place to rest while you travel.
PART 5

01. (A) to feature
(B) featuring
(C) has featured
(D) features

이렇게 풀어요

1. **선택지 보고 문법/어휘 문제 파악** 선택지가 동사 feature(특징으로 삼다)의 다양한 형태로 구성되어 있으므로 문법 문제임을 파악합니다.

2. **빈칸 분석** 빈칸은 동사 자리이므로 준동사인 (A)와 (B)는 먼저 제외시킵니다. 빈칸 앞 내용은 회원으로 가입함으로써 제공되는 혜택에 관한 것이므로 빈칸에도 일반적인 사실(혜택)을 나타낼 때 사용할 수 있는 동사 시제가 들어가야 함을 파악해요.

3. **정답 선택** 현재 시제인 (D) features를 정답으로 선택합니다.

해설

빈칸 앞의 형용사 pleased는 to 부정사를 취하므로 (B)가 정답입니다.

PART 5 문법 적용 문제

We are pleased ------- you with a comfortable place to rest while you travel.

(A) providing   (B) to provide   (C) should provide   (D) provide

296 기적의 토익 RC

 따라 하면 문제가 풀리는

연습 문제

지문 전반에서 단서가 될 부분을 찾아 표시하세요.
표시한 것을 바탕으로 정답 어휘를 선택하세요.

정답 및 해설 p.100

01

Prequel Rocks Box Office
by Barry Sherman

MONTREAL (JUNE 2) — The long-awaited prequel to the 2010 hit movie *Cop Chase* was released in theaters yesterday, and it broke a record in ticket sales. The movie ------- cameos from the original film's cast, but mainly focuses on a young new protagonist.

(A) features   (B) will feature

02

Thank you for staying at Little Rock B&B. Please indicate your meal preference for breakfast. Every breakfast option ------- with your choice of Vietnamese style coffee and a fruit basket. Return this card to a staff member.

(A) came   (B) comes

03

Established as a regional bed and breakfast two decades ago, Paradise Resort has become a nationwide resort chain. We ------- a variety of accommodation options such as a hotel, lodge, and private condo. You will not be disappointed at Paradise Resort.

(A) feature   (B) had featured

04

Dear Ms. Willis,

This letter is a reminder that your subscription to *Today's Style* will expire on April 17. We ------- reminders two weeks before the expiration date. You can renew your membership by either responding to this letter, calling our service center, or visiting our Web site.

(A) send   (B) will send

PART 6 일반적인 사실을 나타내는 현재 시제 297

토익에 나올
실전 문제

제한시간 4분입니다! 시~작!

Questions 01-04 refer to the following review.

Rolling Thunder is an ------- musical for all ages. I watched it with my family. We all thought it was
01.
much funnier than most other musicals. We were laughing from start to -------! It comes no surprise
02.
that the script and score were written by a famous comedian. Also, *Rolling Thunder* ------- a cast of
03.
famous movie actors who are easy to recognize. -------. Overall, I give a rating of five stars and two
04.
thumbs up to this performance.

유형 적용 문제

01. (A) entertainment
 (B) entertaining
 (C) entertains
 (D) entertained

03. (A) will feature
 (B) would have featured
 (C) features
 (D) had featured

02. (A) finish
 (B) part
 (C) search
 (D) decline

04. (A) I found the ticket refund and exchange policy very
  complicated.
 (B) They looked exactly like they do on screen.
 (C) It was hard to see the stage from where we were
  sitting.
 (D) For a limited time, there is also a discount for
  groups.

정답 및 해설 p.101

Questions 05-08 refer to the following voucher.

Discount Voucher

Happy birthday from everyone at MB Parker's! Please accept this coupon as a token of our -------
                                                                                          05.

of your loyalty. You are eligible ------- it for any purchase of $50 in our store! Just present it to the
                                   06.

cashier. -------. The code is written on the back side of this card, so enter it when you check out.
        07.

This special offer ------- clearance merchandise. Valid until December 31.
                   08.

---

05. (A) donation
    (B) appreciation
    (C) satisfaction
    (D) attachment

06. (A) using
    (B) use
    (C) to use
    (D) used

07. (A) Thank you for joining MB Parker's membership program.
    (B) We hope you enjoy your special day at our store.
    (C) Check our store locations on our Web site, www. mbparkers.com.
    (D) This can even be applied to your online purchases.

유형 적용 문제

08. (A) exempt
    (B) exempts
    (C) exempted
    (D) had exempted

DAY 12

PART 7 공지 (2) 공공장소에서의 공지

공지는 싱글 지문에서 출제 비중이 높은 편입니다.

역, 도서관 같은 공공장소에서의 공지는 변경 사항을 알리거나 시설 이용 시 주의 사항을 안내하는 내용이 출제됩니다. 매 시험 1지문 정도 출제돼요. 공지는 지문의 제목과 초반부를 꼭 읽어야 합니다. 공지의 목적이나 대상은 대부분 제목이나 지문의 첫 부분에 나와 있어요. 특히 제목에 단서가 있는 경우가 많으므로 반드시 제목을 읽습니다.

공공장소의 공지에서 자주 출제되는 문제

· 의문사 + contact 문제
How/Why + contact?
유형의 연락 정보 문제는 지문 후반부에 단서가 있으므로 해석하지 말고 지문 후반부에서 연락 정보를 찾은 후 선택지와 대조하여 답을 고릅니다.

🔒 **기출 표현 확인**

<공지 내용>
· access to the library will be difficult
· we are moving to a new location

공공장소에서의 공지에 자주 출제되는 어휘

improve	개선하다, 향상시키다	admission fee	입장료
institute	협회	auditorium	강당
banquet room	연회실	opening address	개회사
business district	상업 지구	cafeteria	구내식당
current	현재의	donation	기부
multiple	다수의	proceeds	수익금
associate	참가시키다	arrangement	조정, 준비
convene a meeting	회의를 소집하다	adjourn	연기하다
initiative	계획	conclude	끝나다
adjustment	조정	prohibit	금지하다
upcoming	다가오는	host	주최하다
installation	설치	in session	개회 중인
organization	단체, 조직	attendee	참석자
preview	시사회	registration form	등록 신청서
extend	연장하다	resume	재개하다
cooperation	협조	make an arrangement	일정을 잡다
tentative	임시의, 잠정적인	restriction	제한
volunteer	자원해서 일하다	undertake	담당하다
ensure	확실히 하다	supervise	감독하다, 지도하다
in violation of	~을 위반하여	obey	따르다, 준수하다

300 기적의 토익 RC

공공장소에서의 공지

notice

해석 p.102

Passengers Using Buffalo Train Station

Please be aware that the recent storm severely damaged certain portions of the tracks for the east-bound trains. In order to perform repairs, the number of trains between Buffalo and Albany will be greatly reduced from September 7 through 21.

If you already purchased tickets for a train that has been cancelled, please see Louis Sinclair in our customer service department to have them changed to the closest available train. We apologize in advance for any inconvenience this may cause.

---

01. What is mentioned about the east-bound train tracks?

(A) They were damaged by severe weather.

(B) They allow for faster trains.

(C) They are currently undergoing inspection.

(D) They have opened before schedule.

02. Why should people contact Mr. Sinclair?

(A) To file a complaint

(B) To exchange a ticket

(C) To upgrade a seat

(D) To request a refund

DAY 12

이렇게 풀어요

01. 동쪽으로 가는 기차의 선로에 대해 언급된 것은 무엇인가?

(A) 악천후로 인해 피해를 입었다.

(B) 더 빠른 기차가 다니게 한다.

(C) 현재 점검이 진행되고 있다.

(D) 예정된 것보다 앞서 개통했다.

해설 문제의 키워드인 east-bound train tracks가 바꾸어 표현된 지문의 tracks for the east-bound trains가 언급된 첫 문장에서 the recent storm severely damaged certain portions of the tracks for the east-bound trains라고 했으므로 (A)가 정답입니다.

02. 사람들은 왜 Sinclair 씨에게 연락해야 하는가?

(A) 불만을 제기하기 위해

(B) 표를 교환하기 위해

(C) 좌석 등급을 올리기 위해

(D) 환불을 요청하기 위해

해설 문제의 키워드인 Mr. Sinclair가 Louis Sinclair로 언급된 지문 후반부에서 If you already purchased tickets ~ please see Louis Sinclair in our customer service department to have them changed ~라고 했으므로 (B)가 정답입니다.

PART 7 공지 (2) 공공장소에서의 공지 301

따라 하면 문제가 풀리는

연습 문제

먼저 문제의 키워드에 표시한 후,
지문에서 단서를 찾아 적절한 답을 고르세요.

---

01 notice

> Notice to Camden Bank Customers
>
> The Camden Bank branch at 942 Austin Street will be closed July 8–9 for a staff training exercise. Many services, such as making withdrawals and paying bills, will still be able to be accessed through the ATMs located outside the building near the main entrance. Customers are also encouraged to carry out transactions online. Alternatively, our branch at 1356 Lewbow Lane will remain open during this time. We apologize for any inconvenience this may cause.

Q. What is the purpose of the notice?

(A) To announce a temporary closure
(B) To promote a new service

---

02 notice

> Attention Dream Restaurant Customers
>
> Please note that the table near our ordering counter is for customers to wait only, not for dining. All food must be ordered as takeout and removed from the premises. We do not have employees on hand to clean up after meals eaten within the business. We have chosen to rent such a small space for our restaurant in order to keep operating costs down. These savings are passed on to customers in the form of low prices. Thank you for your understanding.

Q. What does Dream Restaurant do to reduce costs?

(A) Offer short hours of operation
(B) Run the business from a small site

03 notice

The Department of Transportation will be resurfacing Kenner Street from Friday, May 10, to Wednesday, May 15. The main entrance to Prospect Business Complex (PBC) will be locked during this time, as both the roadway and the sidewalk will be inaccessible. The side entrance on 18th Avenue will still be in use, and there will be no effect on the building's parking situation. For questions or concerns, please contact PBC Building Manager Judith Timms at 555-3697.

Q. What is suggested about PBC?

(A) It houses the Department of Transportation's office.
(B) Its main entrance is accessed from Kenner Street.

04 notice

Notice to Harrisburg Public Library Visitors

The Harrisburg Public Library is pleased to be hosting its second annual Summer Literary Festival from August 1 to August 7. Throughout the festival, we will be featuring lectures from talented authors such as Wanda Girard, Dawn Matz, and Francis Kline. Participants will also have the opportunity to purchase *Sunflower Days*, the latest book from Wanda Girard, which was called "a must-read that will move your heart" by literary critic Danielle Jordison of the *National Express Magazine*.

Q. Who is Mr. Kline?

(A) An author
(B) A literary critic

 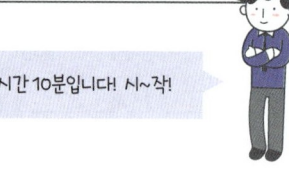

토익에 나올 실전 문제

제한시간 10분입니다! 시~작!

Questions 01-02 refer to the following online notice.

---

http://www.oaklandlibrary.org

Oakland Library Members!

We realize that most research is conducted online rather than using printed media these days. Therefore, we have decided to cancel some of our print magazine subscriptions and increase the size of our computer lab area.

The area that was formerly used to store print magazines is being renovated to make room for an additional 10 computers. If you need to find an original print copy of a magazine, please contact me with the magazine title and date of issue. I will contact the magazine to provide one if necessary.

Thanks,

Larry Templeton
Senior Librarian, Oakland Library
555-8712

---

01. What is mentioned about Oakland Library?
   (A) It will start holding classes for local residents.
   (B) It will provide more computer stations.
   (C) It will offer online research assistance.
   (D) It will relocate to a larger building.

02. According to the notice, why should readers contact Mr. Templeton?
   (A) To request periodicals in print
   (B) To subscribe to a publication
   (C) To submit a formal complaint
   (D) To place a bid for a renovation

---

paraphrasing 주어진 어휘 또는 표현과 패러프레이징 될 수 있는 것을 연결하세요.

1. research is conducted online   •
2. store print magazines   •
3. make room for an additional 10 computers   •
4. original print copy of a magazine   •
5. relocate to a larger building   •

• (a) move to a bigger space
• (b) provide more computer stations
• (c) keep printed materials
• (d) periodicals in print
• (e) looking for the information online

304   기적의 토익 RC

정답 및 해설 p.103

Questions 03-04 refer to the following notice.

Attention Tampa Residents,

City Council has voted to convert city bus engines to hybrid ones. This change will reduce harmful emissions by up to 70%. Also, all the bus stations will be fitted with solar panels to partially power themselves and reduce electricity usage at night.

The proposal was put forward by Emma Stanton, a senior official in the city's Parks Department. Her office has a hotline that is used to gather ideas from the public on how to help reduce our impact on the environment. Residents are urged to call it at 555-7234 to share their thoughts.

03. What is mentioned about city buses in Tampa?
 (A) They will have more seating for passengers.
 (B) They will run less frequently at night time.
 (C) They will only use renewable energy.
 (D) They will soon cause less pollution.

04. Why might readers contact Ms. Stanton?
 (A) To recommend environmentally friendly changes
 (B) To express concerns about public parks
 (C) To volunteer as a campaign assistant
 (D) To cast a vote on public issues

DAY 12

---

paraphrasing 주어진 어휘 또는 표현과 패러프레이징 될 수 있는 것을 연결하세요.

1. convert •
2. reduce harmful emissions •
3. put forward •
4. gather ideas from the public •
5. impact •

• (a) propose
• (b) cause less pollution
• (c) switch
• (d) effect
• (e) hear the opinions

PART 7 공지 (2) 공공장소에서의 공지   305

Questions 05-07 refer to the following notice.

2nd Annual Penfield Community Art Show

The 2nd Annual Penfield Community Art Show is scheduled for Saturday, October 11. Whether you are working as a professional artist or just getting started, we'd love to see your work! Registration forms are available online at www.penfieldart.com. Items should be dropped off at the Ellsworth Art Institute, or at the site of the show, the Penfield Public Library, on or before October 8.

Staff members from the Broyles Gallery, a commercial gallery located downtown, have generously volunteered to help with the set-up of the artwork, sharing their expertise on lighting and arranging the pieces. During the event, there will be an auction for several pre-selected pieces. In addition, judges will assess the art and give away prizes in several categories.

To make the event a success, we need volunteers to assist with set-up/take-down, welcoming visitors, and working at the concession stand. If you are able to share your time, please contact Noreen Austin at 555-7931.

05. Where will an art show be held?

(A) At a community center
(B) At a commercial gallery
(C) At a public library
(D) At an art institute

06. What will visitors have the opportunity to do at the event?

(A) Listen to a talk from an artist
(B) Vote on their favorite paintings
(C) Register for a prize drawing
(D) Bid on some artwork

07. Who most likely is Ms. Austin?

(A) An event planner
(B) An art critic
(C) A gallery owner
(D) A local reporter

---

paraphrasing 주어진 어휘 또는 표현과 패러프레이징 될 수 있는 것을 연결하세요.

1. items should be dropped off at ·
2. have generously volunteered to help ·
3. auction for several pre-selected pieces ·
4. assess ·
5. give away prizes ·

· (a) expressed the willingness to help
· (b) evaluate
· (c) award
· (d) submit the work to
· (e) bid on some artwork

306   기적의 토익 RC

Questions 08-10 refer to the following notice.

Notice Regarding Cessna Boulevard

The Department of Transportation (DOT) has finalized plans for changes to Cessna Boulevard. Beginning March 20, roadwork will begin on the entire length of the thoroughfare to build an additional lane in each direction. As a result, there will be partial road closures on and off for the next six months. The work is being carried out using surplus funds redirected from Plymouth Bridge. The bridge recently underwent a safety assessment, and since no repairs were needed, the resources that had been allocated for the expected repairs were added to the Cessna Boulevard budget. The bridge was supposed to be repainted this month, but that work has been postponed to early January.

Traffic congestion is expected to be an issue in the Valena neighborhood while the work is being carried out. Residents and visitors alike are encouraged to carpool whenever they can in order to cut down on the number of vehicles on the road.

---

08. What is one purpose of the notice?

(A) To announce changes to a repair schedule
(B) To give details about a construction project
(C) To request feedback about a roadway
(D) To warn drivers about safety issues

09. What is mentioned about Plymouth Bridge?

(A) It is an alternative route to Cessna Boulevard.
(B) It failed to pass a safety inspection.
(C) It will not be repainted until next year.
(D) It was open to traffic last year.

10. What are local residents encouraged to do?

(A) Share rides when possible
(B) Check for closures online
(C) Use public transportation
(D) Report problems to the DOT

DAY 12

---

paraphrasing 주어진 어휘 또는 표현과 패러프레이징 될 수 있는 것을 연결하세요.

1. build an additional lane •
2. there will be partial road closures •
3. has been postponed to early January •
4. postpone •
5. carpool •

• (a) share rides
• (b) widen the road
• (c) some roads will be closed
• (d) not be painted until next year
• (e) delay

PART 7 공지 (2) 공공장소에서의 공지 307

'멋진 당신, 오늘도 화이팅'

DAY

13

오늘의 학습 포인트

PART 5. 동명사

1. 동명사의 역할 – 주어/타동사의 목적어/전치사의 목적어
2. 동명사 vs. 명사 – 빈칸 뒤 보어나 목적어 → 동명사

   – 빈칸 앞 관사 → 명사

   – 형용사가 수식 → 명사/부사가 수식 → 동명사
3. 동명사의 태 – 수동태: being p.p./동사가 자동사이면 능동, 타동사이면

   빈칸 뒤 목적어 유무 따지기
4. 동명사의 의미상의 주어 – 동명사 앞에 명사/대명사의 소유격
5. 전치사 to vs. to부정사의 to – 전치사 to + 명사/동명사

   – 부정사 to + 동사원형
6. -ing형 명사 vs. 일반 명사 – planning vs. plan/staffing vs. staff 등

PART 6. Thank you for/apologize for + 명사

빈칸 앞에 thank you for/apologize for, 앞뒤 문장 문맥 파악하기

PART 7. 회람

회사 내에서 정보 공지. 제목(Subject, Re) 읽기!

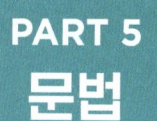

PART 5
문법

동명사

전체적인 출제빈도는 높지 않지만 동명사가 들어가는 자리 및 동명사 숙어 표현이 주로 출제됩니다.

＼ 적용 기술

[기적의 필기노트] 132P, 133P
RC 기술 46, 47

🔒 확인 문제 ❶

------- this survey form only takes a couple of minutes.

(A) Completed
(B) Completing

🔒 확인 문제 ❷

The financial advisor recommended ------- extra money in the stock market.

(A) investment
(B) investing

출제 포인트
동명사 자리를 묻는 문법 문제 중에서 전치사의 목적어 자리 문제가 가장 많이 출제돼요.

🔒 확인 문제 ❸

There was a harsh debate on ------- the old theater.

(A) conserving
(B) conservation

출제 유형 1
동명사의 역할

`800+`

1 주어 역할

· 동명사 주어는 **단수 취급**하며, 과거분사 형용사와 구분하는 문제가 출제됩니다. 형용사일 경우 뒤의 명사를 수식해야 하는데 이 경우 동사와의 수 일치를 확인합니다.
   (**Upgrading** / ~~Upgraded~~) your computers enhances your work efficiency.
   컴퓨터를 업그레이드하는 것은 여러분의 업무 효율성을 향상시킵니다.

   → 과거분사 형용사 Upgraded가 올 경우 주어가 복수인 computers이므로 단수 동사 enhances와 수가 일치하지 않기 때문에 동명사 Upgrading이 정답입니다.

2 타동사의 목적어 역할

· 동명사는 **3형식 타동사의 목적어** 역할을 할 수 있습니다.
   The new manager considered **holding** a videoconference.
   새 매니저는 화상 회의를 여는 것을 고려했다.

· 모든 타동사가 동명사를 목적어로 가질 수 있는 것은 아니므로 **동명사를 목적어로 가지는 특정 동사**를 암기해야 합니다.

동명사를 목적어로 취하는 동사

recommend -ing ~하는 것을 추천하다, 권장하다	consider -ing ~하는 것을 고려하다
suggest -ing ~하는 것을 제안하다	avoid -ing ~하는 것을 피하다
finish -ing ~하는 것을 끝내다	enjoy -ing ~하는 것을 즐기다

3 전치사의 목적어 역할

· 동명사는 전치사의 목적어 역할을 할 수 있습니다.
   Guests will get a discount coupon by **offering** their feedback.
   투숙객은 피드백을 제공함으로써 할인 쿠폰을 받을 것이다.

· 동명사와 함께 자주 출제되는 전치사로는 for, by, in이 있어요. for -ing는 '~하기 위해서', by -ing는 '~함으로써', in -ing는 '~함에 있어서'라는 의미입니다.

정답 ❶ (B) ❷ (B) ❸ (A)

310 기적의 토익 RC

출제 유형 2

동명사 vs. 명사

적용 기술

[기적의 필기노트] 133P
RC 기술 48

1 빈칸 뒤에 보어나 목적어가 있으면 동명사

The Department of Transportation suggested (**using** / ~~usage~~) the bus or
subway during the festival.
　　　　　　　　　　　　　　　　　　　　　목적어
교통부는 축제 기간 동안 버스나 지하철을 이용하는 것을 제안했다.

→ 동사 suggest의 목적어로 동명사와 명사가 모두 올 수 있으나 뒤에 목적어가 바로 이어지므로 동명사인 using이 정답입니다.

2 빈칸 앞에 관사(a/an/the)가 있으면 명사

The board members made the (~~deciding~~ / **decision**) to open a new office in
Sweden.　　　　　　　　　　　　　관사
이사진들은 스웨덴에 새 사무실을 열기로 결정했다.

확인 문제 ❹

Ms. Wong specialized in
------- an online security
system.

(A) developing
(B) development

`800+`
3 형용사가 수식하면 명사, 부사가 수식하면 동명사

You can stay safe on the road by thoroughly (**inspecting** / ~~inspection~~) your
delivery truck.　　　　　　　　　　부사
배달 트럭을 철저히 점검함으로써 도로에서 안전할 수 있다.

출제 유형 3

동명사의 태/동명사의 의미상의 주어

확인 문제 ❺

She is responsible for
------- the daily report.

(A) submitting
(B) being submitted

`900+`
1 동명사의 태 일치

· 동명사의 수동태는 'being p.p.'입니다.

· 동명사의 능동태와 수동태를 구별하는 문제는 동명사로 제시된 **동사가 자동사이면 능동, 타동사
이면 빈칸 뒤의 목적어 여부를 따져 능/수동**을 가립니다.
His latest novel became more popular by (~~translating~~ / **being translated**) into
English. 그의 최근 소설은 영어로 번역됨으로써 인기가 더 많아졌다.

→ 타동사 translate 뒤에 목적어 없이 전치사구가 있으므로 수동태인 being translated가 정답입니다.

`900+`
2 동명사의 의미상의 주어

· **동명사 앞에 명사의 소유격 또는 대명사의 소유격** 써서 동사의 행위 주체를 나타냅니다.
I appreciate **your** filling in for me this afternoon.
오늘 오후에 당신이 저를 대신해 업무를 해주어서 감사합니다.

(A) ❺ (A) ❹ 답정

PART 5 문법 동명사 311

적용 기술

[기적의 필기노트] 134P
RC 기술 49

🔒 확인 문제 ➏

Ms. Bell spent most of her free time ------- a novel.

(A) write
(B) writing

적용 기술

[기적의 필기노트] 135P
RC 기술 50

🔒 확인 문제 ➐

I am used to ------- up at 5 in the morning.

(A) wake
(B) waking

출제 포인트

-ing형 명사 opening의 출제 빈도가 가장 높으며, '공석'이라는 의미와 '개장, 개회'라는 의미 두 가지 모두 자주 출제돼요.

🔒 확인 문제 ➑

The ------- of Harrison Mall will be scheduled for next week.

(A) opening
(B) open

출제 유형 4
동명사 숙어 표현

- -ing 앞에 있는 어휘나 표현이 정답을 고르는 단서가 되므로 통째로 암기해 두세요.

on/upon -ing ~하자마자	be worth -ing ~할 가치가 있다
spend + 시간/돈 + -ing ~하는 데 시간/돈을 쓰다	be busy (in) -ing ~하느라 바쁘다
cannot help -ing ~하지 않을 수 없다	keep -ing 계속해서 ~하다
have difficulty -ing ~하는 것이 어렵다	have a problem -ing ~하는 데 문제가 있다
go -ing ~하러 가다	feel like -ing ~하고 싶다

출제 유형 5
전치사 to vs. to부정사의 to

800+

- 전치사 to 뒤에는 명사나 동명사를 써야 하고, 부정사 to 뒤에는 동사원형을 써야 합니다. 이를 구별하는 특별한 방법은 없으므로 중요 표현을 반드시 암기해 두어야 합니다.

| 전치사 to와 함께 사용되는 숙어 표현 |

look forward to 명사/-ing ~하기를 고대하다	object to 명사/-ing ~에 반대하다
be used to 명사/-ing ~에 익숙하다	when it comes to 명사/-ing ~에 대해서라면
be committed to 명사/-ing ~하는 것에 전념하다	
be devoted/dedicated to 명사/-ing ~하는 것에 헌신하다	

출제 유형 6
-ing형 명사 vs. 일반 명사

800+

- 동사의 성격 없이 명사로 굳어진 -ing형 명사와 일반 명사가 함께 선택지로 제시될 때는 문맥상 알맞은 것을 골라야 합니다.

As (**seating** / ~~seat~~) is limited, please sign up for the event in advance.
좌석이 제한되어 있으므로 사전에 행사에 등록해주세요.

| -ing형 명사와 일반 명사의 구분 |

opening 공석, 개회 - open 야외, 옥외	cleaning 청소 - clean 손질
accounting 회계 업무 - account 계좌, 계정	marketing 마케팅 - market 시장
advertising 광고업 - advertisement 광고	funding 자금 조달 - fund 자금
seating 좌석 배치, 수용력 - seat 자리	spending 지출 - spend 지출(액)/비용
pricing 가격 책정 - price 가격	planning 계획 수립 - plan 계획
housing 주택/주택 공급 - house 집	staffing 직원 배치 - staff 직원

- -ing형 명사는 불가산 명사인 경우가 많으며, 가산 단수 명사와 구별하는 문제가 주로 출제됩니다.

The Central Animal Shelter was granted ample (~~fund~~ / **funding**) from the city council.
Central 동물 보호소는 시의회로부터 많은 자금 조달을 받았다.

(A) ➏ (B) ➐ (B) ➑ 답정

312 기적의 토익 RC

 **동명사**

1. By ------- its printers, Dawson Printing can produce larger banners than before.

(A) upgrade   (B) upgrades   (C) upgrading   (D) upgraded

프린터들을 업그레이드함으로써 Dawson Printing은 전보다 더 큰 배너를 제작할 수 있다.

> **이렇게 풀어요**
>
> **1. 선택지 보고 문법/어휘 문제 파악** 선택지가 명사이자 동사인 upgrade의 다양한 형태로 구성되어 있으므로 문법 문제임을 파악해요.
>
> **2. 빈칸 분석** 빈칸은 전치사 by의 목적어 역할을 함과 동시에, 빈칸 뒤 '소유격 + 명사' 형태의 its printers를 목적어로 취할 수 있는 준동사가 들어가야 함을 파악합니다.
>
> **3. 정답 선택** 전치사의 목적어 역할을 할 수 있는 동명사 (C) upgrading을 정답으로 고릅니다.

2. Mr. Wood suggested ------- more payment options for those who purchase over $1,000.

(A) being introduced   (B) introduced   (C) introducing   (D) introduces

Wood 씨는 1,000달러 이상 구입하는 사람들에게 더 많은 결제 옵션을 도입하는 것을 제안했다.

> **이렇게 풀어요**
>
> **1. 선택지 보고 문법/어휘 문제 파악** 선택지가 동사 introduce(도입하다)의 다양한 형태로 구성되어 있으므로 문법 문제임을 파악해요.
>
> **2. 빈칸 분석** 빈칸 앞 동사 suggest의 목적어이면서, 빈칸 뒤 명사구 more payment options를 목적어로 취할 수 있는 준동사가 들어가야 함을 파악합니다.
>
> **3. 정답 선택** 동명사 형태인 (A)와 (C) 중에서 목적어를 가질 수 있는 능동태인 (C) introducing을 정답으로 고릅니다.

3. We at Emily's Kitchen are looking forward to ------- you soon.

(A) serve   (B) served   (C) serving   (D) service

저희 Emily's Kitchen은 당신을 곧 대접하기를 고대하고 있습니다.

> **이렇게 풀어요**
>
> **1. 선택지 보고 문법/어휘 문제 파악** 선택지가 동사 serve(대접하다, 제공하다)의 다양한 형태로 구성되어 있으므로 문법 문제임을 파악해요.
>
> **2. 빈칸 분석** 빈칸 앞에 to가 있는데, 여기서 to는 전치사임을 파악합니다.
>
> **3. 정답 선택** 전치사 to 뒤에는 동명사가 와야 하므로 (C) serving을 정답으로 고릅니다.

PART 5 문법 동명사   313

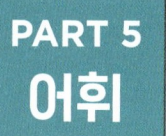

PART 5 어휘

동사 어휘 (3)

각 어휘와 함께 자주 쓰이는 표현을 통째로 외워두세요.

01 transfer — 옮기다, 이동하다
transfer from A to B — A에서 B로 옮겨지다
transfer 사람 to — ~를 …로 전근시키다

02 aim — 목표하다
aim to — ~을 목표로 하다
be aimed at — ~을 목표로 삼다

03 replace — 대신하다, 교체하다
replace A with B — A를 B로 대체하다
replace the defective part — 불량 부품을 교체하다

04 anticipate — 예상하다, 기대하다
highly anticipate — 크게 기대하다
anticipate increase in sales — 판매 증가를 예상하다

05 grant — 주다, 승인하다
grant permission — 허가하다
grant 사람 access to — ~에게 접근 권한을 부여하다

🐾 빈출 토익 선생님 Pick!
06 arrange — 마련하다, 처리하다
arrange transportation — 차편을 마련하다
arrange a meeting — 만남을 주선하다
arrange A for 사람 — ~를 위해 A를 준비하다

07 prohibit — 금지하다
prohibit A from -ing — A가 ~하는 것을 금하다
A is prohibited — A가 금지되다

08 specialize — 전공하다, 전문으로 하다
specialize in — ~을 전문으로 하다

09 remind — 상기시키다, 다시 알려 주다
remind 사람 of — ~에게 …을 상기시키다
remind 사람 to부정사 — ~에 …하도록 상기시키다

10 notify — 알리다, 통지하다
notify 사람 of/that — ~에게 …를 알리다
notify in advance — 미리 알리다
notify immediately — 즉시 알리다

🐾 빈출 토익 선생님 Pick!
12 perform — 수행하다, 실시하다
be performed on a monthly basis — 월 단위로 실시되다
perform well — 솜씨가[실적이] 좋다

800+
13 stimulate — 자극하다, 활발하게 하다
stimulate growth — 성장을 촉진하다
stimulate the economy — 경기를 부양시키다

14 cover — 다루다, 보상하다, 덮다
cover the damages — 손해를 보상하다
cover the topic — 그 주제를 다루다

15 express — 나타내다, 표현하다
express concerns — 우려를 나타내다
express interests — 관심을 보이다

16 occupy — 차지하다

| occupy the seats | 자리를 차지하다 |
| occupy the parking area | 주차 구역을 차지하다 |

800+

17 conclude — 결론을 내리다, 끝내다

conclude that	~라고 결론을 내리다
conclude with	~로 마무리 짓다
conclude the meeting	회의를 끝내다

🐾 빈출 토익 선생님 Pick!
18 demonstrate — 증명하다, 설명하다

demonstrate a new product	신제품을 설명하다
demonstrate the capabilities of	~의 역량을 보이다
demonstrate the ability to부정사	~할 수 있는 능력을 입증하다

19 expect — 기대하다, 예상하다

expect to부정사	~할 것을 기대하다
expect 사람 to부정사	~가 …할 것을 기대하다
be expected to부정사	~할 것으로 기대되다

20 prevent — 막다, 방지하다

| prevent A from -ing | A가 ~하는 것을 막다 |
| prevent damage | 손상을 방지하다 |

21 describe — 묘사하다, 설명하다

describe A as B	A를 B라고 설명하다
describe in detail	자세히 묘사/설명하다
clearly describe	명확히 묘사/설명하다

22 recover — 회복하다

| recover from | ~에서 회복하다 |

23 follow — 따르다, 따라가다, 뒤따르다

| follow the instructions | 지시를 따르다 |
| follow directions | 지시를 따르다 |

24 reveal — 드러내다, 밝히다

| reveal information | 정보를 밝히다 |
| reveal the policy | 정책을 밝히다 |

25 operate — 작동하다, 가동하다

| operate the system/machine | 시스템/기계를 작동하다 |
| easy to operate | 작동이 쉬운 |

🐾 빈출 토익 선생님 Pick!
26 seek — 찾다, 구하다

| seek staff/workers | 직원을 구하다 |
| seek advice/help | 조언/도움을 구하다 |

DAY 13

 풀이 방법

Every Monday the sales team of Harrington Cosmetics meets to ------- upcoming promotions.

(A) expect   (B) recover   (C) discuss   (D) occupy

매주 월요일에 Harrington 화장품의 영업팀은 다가오는 홍보에 대해 논의하기 위해 만난다.

> **이렇게 풀어요**
>
> **1. 선택지 보고 문법/어휘 문제 파악**   선택지가 서로 다른 동사 어휘로 구성되어 있으므로 어휘 문제임을 파악해요.
> **2. 빈칸 분석**   '다가오는 홍보를 -------하기 위해 만난다'라는 문맥에 어울릴 수 있는 동사가 들어가야 함을 파악합니다.
> **3. 정답 선택**   영업팀이 홍보에 대해 '논의하기' 위해 만난다는 문맥이 되는 것이 자연스러우므로 (C) discuss를 정답으로 고릅니다.

PART 5 어휘 동사 어휘 (3)   315

따라 하면 문제가 풀리는

연습 문제

앞서 학습한 문제 풀이법을 적용하여 맞는 것에 ✔ 표시 하거나 괄호 안에
적절한 답을 쓰고 정답을 선택하세요.

01 People generally recommend ------- a table when dining at Bay Shore Restaurant.

(A) reserving
(B) reservation
(C) to reserve
(D) reserved

1. 선택지 보고 문법/어휘 문제 파악하기 ☐ 문법 문제 ☐ 어휘 문제
2. 빈칸 분석하기 빈칸 앞에 있는 것 ☐ 타동사 ☐ 자동사
   → 빈칸은 ☐ 목적어 ☐ 보어 자리이다.
   → 정답 후보 2개 (,   )
   → 빈칸 바로 뒤에 ☐ 명사 ☐ 전치사가 있다.
3. 정답 선택하기 정답 (   )

02 By ------- its age restriction, Bristol Amusement Park increased attendance by 15 percent.

(A) remove
(B) removed
(C) removing
(D) removal

1. 선택지 보고 문법/어휘 문제 파악하기 ☐ 문법 문제 ☐ 어휘 문제
2. 빈칸 분석하기 빈칸 앞에 있는 것 ☐ 명사 ☐ 전치사
   → 빈칸에는 ☐ 동사 ☐ 동명사가 들어가야 한다.
3. 정답 선택하기 정답 (   )

03 Please avoid ------- on any wires or hoses during this tour of the factory.

(A) steps
(B) stepping
(C) stepped
(D) to step

1. 선택지 보고 문법/어휘 문제 파악하기 ☐ 문법 문제 ☐ 어휘 문제
2. 빈칸 분석하기 빈칸 앞에 있는 것 ☐ 타동사 ☐ 자동사
   → 빈칸은 ☐ 주어 ☐ 목적어 자리이다.
3. 정답 선택하기 정답 (   )

04 Just keep ------- the detour signs to get onto Billy Avenue.

(A) follow
(B) to follow
(C) followed
(D) following

1. 선택지 보고 문법/어휘 문제 파악하기 ☐ 문법 문제 ☐ 어휘 문제
2. 빈칸 분석하기 빈칸 앞에 있는 동사 (   )
　　　　　　　 → ☐ 동명사 ☐ to부정사와 함께 쓰인다.
3. 정답 선택하기 정답 (   )

05 Mr. Concord at Chester Bank ------- in mortgages and business loans.

(A) arranges
(B) replaces
(C) anticipates
(D) specializes

1. 선택지 보고 문법/어휘 문제 파악하기 ☐ 문법 문제 ☐ 어휘 문제
2. 빈칸 분석하기 빈칸 뒤에 있는 전치사 (   )
　　　　　　　 → 이 전치사와 함께 쓰이는 동사가 정답이다.
3. 정답 선택하기 정답 (   )

06 Residents in Portland are looking forward to ------- the newly renovated library.

(A) visit
(B) visited
(C) visiting
(D) visits

1. 선택지 보고 문법/어휘 문제 파악하기 ☐ 문법 문제 ☐ 어휘 문제
2. 빈칸 분석하기 빈칸 앞에 있는 것 ☐ 부정사 to ☐ 전치사 to
　　　　　　　 → 빈칸에는 ☐ 동사원형 ☐ 동명사가 들어가야 한다.
3. 정답 선택하기 정답 (   )

PART 5 동명사 / 동사 어휘 (3)

실전 문제

DAY 01-13 누적 문제

제한시간 9분입니다! 시~작!

01. After ------- an oil crisis, Farrell Auto has now developed electric cars.

(A) face
(B) faces
(C) facing
(D) faced

02. Comedian Johnny Orwell was hired ------- the next season of the once-popular TV show *My Friends*.

(A) writes
(B) to write
(C) had written
(D) to be written

03. The management is considering ------- the recruiting tasks to an outside agency.

(A) delegates
(B) delegating
(C) to delegate
(D) delegation

04. Callahan's has become the most popular home improvement store in the region by ------- huge reward points.

(A) to offer
(B) offering
(C) offers
(D) offer

05. After he inspected the engine, the mechanic suggested ------- the car with a new one.

(A) replace
(B) replaced
(C) replacing
(D) replacement

06. ------- the contract to renovate Holder's Bank's office was Ms. Harman's first accomplishment in our agency.

(A) Secure
(B) Secured
(C) Security
(D) Securing

07. ------- a clean and healthy work environment is one of HR's main responsibilities.

(A) Being maintained
(B) Will maintain
(C) Maintaining
(D) Maintains

08. The new model of forklift, Titan 2000, proved itself capable of ------- up to 4 tons of load at once.

(A) handles
(B) handler
(C) handling
(D) to handle

09. Ms. Bolton and her team members finished ------- the terms and conditions of car rental contract.

(A) revise
(B) revisions
(C) revising
(D) revised

10. Stockroom employees are responsible for ------- all inventory items in the store.

(A) manages
(B) managing
(C) to manage
(D) managed

11. The user's manual recommends ------- the hand mixer right after use.

(A) clean
(B) to clean
(C) cleaner
(D) cleaning

12. ------- automated teller machines at every corner has made British Star Bank' customers feel very convenient.

(A) Being installed
(B) Installation
(C) Installed
(D) Installing

13. All sales representatives were busy ------- the store display layout over the weekend.
(A) changing
(B) changed
(C) to change
(D) changes

14. We are looking forward to ------- business with you in the near future.
(A) do
(B) did
(C) doing
(D) does

15. Atlantic Airways has specialized in ------- perishable goods internationally.
(A) transporting
(B) to transport
(C) was transported
(D) transportation

16. The government proposed a series of tax exemptions for small businesses ------- the local economy.
(A) to improve
(B) improve
(C) improvement
(D) will improve

17. Ms. Bauer, who ------- works as an intern, is going to be hired as a full-time employee next month.
(A) currently
(B) formerly
(C) shortly
(D) originally

18. Due to a decrease in demand, Blanchard Auto will manufacture ------- cars than in previous years.
(A) fewer
(B) some
(C) all
(D) both

19. The employment contract ------- daily responsibilities of the job and financial compensation.
(A) reminds
(B) transfers
(C) prohibits
(D) covers

20. Shift supervisors ------- how to use new equipment on the assembly line at Sutton Manufacturing.
(A) specialize
(B) demonstrate
(C) recover
(D) stimulate

21. All food containers should be sealed properly to ------- contents from spoiling while in transit.
(A) prevent
(B) grant
(C) replace
(D) perform

22. To accommodate the new staff members, Rios Marketing is ------- a larger office near the downtown area of Scranton.
(A) concluding
(B) aiming
(C) seeking
(D) following

23. Most passengers ------- frustration about the decreased leg room in the Sonic Airlines planes.
(A) ensured
(B) entered
(C) resolved
(D) expressed

24. Although most souvenir shops in Victoria ------- throughout the year, some shut down for the winter.
(A) engrave
(B) operate
(C) initiate
(D) compile

PART 6

Thank you for/apologize for + 명사

빈칸 앞에 thank you for/apologize for가 있으면 바로 앞뒤 문장의 문맥을 파악합니다.

VOCA

accept 받아들이다
proceed to ~로 가다
fill out 작성하다
initial 처음의
in addition to ~에 더해
facility 시설

 **풀이 방법**　e-mail　　　　　　　　　　　　　　　 해석 p.109

To: Linda Groves
From: Jessica Curry
Date: 12 May
Subject: Your first day!

Dear Ms. Groves,

You have been accepted as an intern! Thank you for ------- this program here at
01.
Sugar Land. It will be a pleasure to have you on our team for the next few months.
When you arrive on 1 June, please bring a printed copy of this acceptance e-mail
and a photo ID. The security team will assist you with ------- a security badge. Then,
PART 5
you should proceed to the Personnel office where you should report to Anita Park.
She will help you fill out your initial paperwork in addition to give you a tour of the
facilities. Feel free to contact me or Ms. Park if you have any questions or concerns.

Jessica Curry
Personnel Manager, Sugar Land Corporation

01. (A) accounting
(B) joining
(C) adding
(D) training

이렇게 풀어요

1. **선택지 보고 문법/어휘 문제 파악**　선택지가 다양한 동명사 어휘로 이루어져 있으므로 어휘 문제임을 파악해요.
(A) 설명하다　(B) 합류하다　(C) 추가하다　(D) 교육시키다

2. **빈칸 분석**　빈칸 앞에 인턴으로 선정되었다는 내용이 있고, 빈칸 뒤에는 팀에서 함께하게 되어 기쁘다는 내용이 있음을 파악합니다.

3. **정답 선택**　앞뒤 문맥과 어울리는 (B) joining을 정답으로 선택합니다.

해설

빈칸 앞에 전치사 with가 있으므로 빈칸에는 명사 역할을 하는 것이 들어가야 해요. (A)와 (C)가 정답 후보인데, 빈칸 뒤에 목적어가 있으므로 (C)는 답이 될 수 없습니다. 따라서 (A)가 정답입니다.

PART 5 문법 적용 문제

The security team will assist you with ------- a security badge.

(A) creating　　　　(B) create　　　　(C) creation　　　　(D) to create

320　기적의 토익 RC

따라 하면 문제가 풀리는

연습 문제

지문에서 단서가 될 부분을 찾아 표시하세요.
표시한 것을 바탕으로 정답 어휘를 선택하세요.

◉ 정답 및 해설 p.109

01

Thank you for the ------- that you provided about your last visit to Delta Hair Salon. We are always eager to hear out our customers.

(A) purchase

(B) feedback

02

Dear Mr. Johnson,

We have reviewed your complaint, and concluded that you were sent the Sky Blue instead of the Baby Blue that you ordered. We apologize for the -------. Please let us know how you would like to resolve this issue.

(A) error

(B) delay

03

Dear Ms. Harper,

Thank you for your ------- to the Highland Scholarship Program. Every contribution helps students pay for their books and tuition.

(A) donation

(B) volunteering

DAY 13

04

Dear residents,

The trash disposal area for our apartment complex has been moved to the back of the parking lot. We apologize for any ------- this may cause.

(A) confusion

(B) promotion

PART 6 Thank you for/apologize for + 명사   321

토익에 나올
실전 문제

제한시간 4분입니다! 시~작!

Questions 01-04 refer to the following e-mail.

To: j.archer@jfob.net
From: l.watts@gymbarn.net
Date: 7 April
Subject: Welcome

Dear Mr. Archer,

Welcome to Barn Gym. This e-mail ------- to you under your agreement. We are open 24/7, so you
01.
can come and work out anytime. -------. We are very proud of it because Barn Gym is the only place
02.
to do that.

There is one more thing. We totally understand every challenge and obstacle you ------- at the
03.
beginning of or during the workout. Just come to the desk or ask one of our staff around you. All of
our staff are certified trainers and are willing to help you lose weight and get in the best shape of
your life.

Thank you again for ------- a member of Barn Gym.
04.

Sincerely,

Loretta Watts

---

01. (A) was sending
    (B) sends
    (C) will send
    (D) has been sent

02. (A) More details are posted on our Web site.
    (B) This is why we have the most memberships in this area.
    (C) Thank you for your interest in Barn Gym.
    (D) There will be a $5 service fee for a locker key replacement.

03. (A) meet
    (B) face
    (C) guide
    (D) follow

유형 적용 문제
04. (A) arranging
    (B) becoming
    (C) cooperating
    (D) returning

322 기적의 토익 RC

📍정답 및 해설 p.109

Questions 05-08 refer to the following letter.

Dear Mr. Simmons,

Last Tuesday, October 29, you made a complaint that you were not able to access the Internet during the afternoon. There were a lot of reports from the subscribers who ------- at Riverfront
05.

Palace Apartment. -------. Unfortunately, it was not fully back to service until 6:30 P.M. After an
06.

investigation, we found the outage was caused by a cut in the main line while construction workers were inspecting and changing the old gas pipe to your apartment. One worker accidentally cut our Internet line while ------- the pipe.
07.

We apologize for the -------. We will compensate it with a deduction of the amount of a day of
08.

service. It is $1.25 and will be reflected on your next bill. For more information on this issue, please feel free to call our customer service center or visit our Web site.

Regards,

Fernando Gomez
Director of Customer Service

---

05. (A) reside
(B) resides
(C) will have resided
(D) will reside

06. (A) The repair work was originally scheduled for next Monday.
(B) We expected some hardware maintenance work to only last briefly.
(C) Most residents in the building subscribe our Basic Internet Service.
(D) We send this reminder that your contract will expire next month.

07. (A) to replace
(B) replacing
(C) will replace
(D) replacements

유형 적용 문제

08. (A) malfunction
(B) cancellation
(C) delay
(D) disruption

PART 6 Thank you for/apologize for + 명사　323

PART 7

회람

회람은 회사가 전 직원이나 특정 부서 직원들에게 보내는 글이므로 목적이 명료하고 세부 정보가 나열되는 경우가 많아요.

회람은 회사 내에서 새로운 정보나 변경 사항을 공지하는 지문입니다. 지문 상단에 수신자(To), 발신자(From), 제목(Subject, Re)이 제시되는데, 이 부분의 내용을 파악해두면 지문 내용을 미리 예상하고 읽을 수 있습니다.

회람에서 자주 출제되는 문제

· 목적 문제
What is the purpose of the memo?
→ 변경 사항을 공지하는 회람의 목적을 묻는 문제에 대한 답으로는 'To inform employees [staff] of ~' 형태의 선택지가 출제돼요.

🔒 **기출 표현 확인**

<회람 제목으로 출제된 것>
· paper usage
· important information
· global videoconference

회람에 자주 출제되는 어휘

merger	합병하다	comply with	~을 준수하다
downsize	규모를 줄이다	official	공식적인
reliability	신뢰도	matter	사안
scale down	규모를 축소하다	aspect	측면
adopt	채택하다	essential	필수적인
restriction	제한, 규제	modify	수정하다, 변경하다
policy	정책, 규정	cost-efficient	비용 효율이 높은
innovation	혁신	partnership	협력, 제휴
mediate	중재하다, 조정하다	incur	초래하다, 발생하다
conform to	~을 지키다, 따르다	deficit	부족
follow	따르다	streamline	간소화하다
observe	관찰하다, 지키다	install	설치하다
immediately	즉시	entitled to	~할 권리가 있는
vacate	비우다	take effect	효력이 발생하다
telecommute	재택근무하다	specific	특정한, 구체적인
immediate supervisor	직속 상사	occasional	가끔, 가끔의
instead of	~ 대신에	periodic	주기적인
analysis	분석	glitch	작은 문제
allocate	할당하다	company-wide	회사 전반의
workforce	직원, 노동력	handout	유인물, 인쇄물

 풀이 방법 회람

memo   해석 p.110

> To: Windrose Tower Branch Staff
> From: Serena Carrillo
> Subject: Parking
> Date: 16 January
>
> Attention Staff Members,
>
> This weekend, Windrose Tower will install a sentry booth and tollgate at the entrance to the building's parking lot. Anyone without a pass will have to pay a fee of $5 per hour. You will have a one-week grace period to obtain one from the HR department.
>
> In order to receive your pass, you must register your vehicle with HR. Bring your driver's license, a copy of your state registration, and proof that your vehicle is insured. Parking passes take a full day to be issued, so please be sure to do so before you have to pay a parking fee.
>
> Building management explains the change is due to complaints about non-employees taking up all of the parking spaces since it was free. This should make it easier for building employees to find parking.

01. What is the main purpose of the memo?
(A) To welcome new staff
(B) To announce a new policy
(C) To propose a construction project
(D) To give directions to a parking area

02. What is a requirement to get an employee parking pass?
(A) Toll road ticket
(B) A $5 processing fee
(C) Approval from the security team
(D) An insurance statement

DAY 13

이렇게 풀어요

01. 회람의 주요 목적은 무엇인가?
(A) 신입 직원을 환영하기 위해서
(B) 새 정책을 알리기 위해서
(C) 건설 공사를 제안하기 위해서
(D) 주차장으로 가는 길을 알려주기 위해서

해설 첫 번째 단락에서 will install booth and tollgate, Anyone without a pass will have to pay a fee, a one-week grace period to obtain one 등을 언급하며 주차 관리에 대한 새로운 정책을 알리고 있으므로 (B)가 정답입니다.

02. 직원 주차증을 받기 위해 요구되는 것은 무엇인가?
(A) 고속도로 통행권
(B) 처리비 5달러
(C) 보안팀으로부터의 승인
(D) 보험증서

해설 문제의 키워드 get an employee parking pass에 해당하는 지문의 두 번째 단락의 receive your pass 이후 부분에서 Bring your driver's license, a copy of your state registration, and proof that your vehicle is insured라고 했으므로 (D)가 정답입니다.

PART 7 회람   325

따라 하면 문제가 풀리는
연습 문제

먼저 문제의 키워드에 표시한 후,
지문에서 단서를 찾아 적절한 답을 고르세요.

01 memo

> To: All Staff Members
> From: Miles Lopez
> Subject: Community volunteers
> Date: 16 April
>
> This coming weekend there will be a special volunteer event to remove trash from McMahon Park. The park is located directly across from our office building, and by helping it look better, we also improve our image for clients who visit our office. Those of you who volunteer during the morning or afternoon shift will be given a half-day off the following Monday morning.

Q. What are staff members asked to do?

(A) Work remotely on Monday
(B) Join a park cleanup event

02 memo

> To: Lauria Enterprise Staff
> From: Bryce Zwick
> Date: January 10
> Re: Please read
>
> Following the successful negotiation of our first overseas partnership in Indonesia, along with many years of dedicated service, Business Development Manager Marshall Doughty plans to step down from his position at the end of this month. All employees are welcome to attend a farewell reception for Mr. Doughty on Thursday, January 31, at 4 P.M. in the conference room. Mr. Doughty's replacement will begin work the following week. Her name is Michelle Howard, and we are pleased to have her on board.

Q. What is the memo announcing?

(A) An upcoming business merger
(B) A change in personnel

정답 및 해설 p.111

03 memo

To: All Shine Theater Employees
From: Fiona Wells
Subject: Seating policy
Date: April 16

It is important that you explain the upcoming change in our seating policy to customers at the time of ticket purchase. Currently, when audience members arrive late, an usher takes them to their seats right away. From May 1, latecomers will have to wait until a break in the performance in order to enter the auditorium. We hope this will help to cut down on distractions for both the performers and the other audience members.

Q. Why does Ms. Wells plan to change a policy?

(A) To avoid disrupting performances
(B) To increase the number of ticket sales

04 memo

To: All Norfolk Finance Employees
From: Ashia Havaldar
Date: July 2
Re: Negotiations finalized

I am pleased to report that the negotiations with GP International were successful. We will finalize the merger of the two companies over the next few weeks and will begin operating under the name Norfolk-GP from August 1. Norfolk's current CEO, Avery Madera, will continue to oversee operations at all levels, as GP's CEO plans to go into retirement. There may be some restructuring in the upcoming months, but our plans do not include any layoffs.

Q. According to the memo, what will happen in August?

(A) A company's name will be changed.
(B) A new CEO will be introduced.

PART 7 회람 327

토익에 나올
실전 문제

제한시간 10분입니다! 시~작!

Questions 01-02 refer to the following memo.

Attn: All Evanston Inc. Employees
Subject: Office Hour Policy
Date: 18 August

It has come to the attention of the management that the majority of the employees in our office have school-age children, and sometimes a 9 to 5 work schedule is difficult for them to follow. In order to accommodate them, we have decided to initiate a new policy.

The time that you spend in the office is officially measured by the time clock at the entrance to the office. Our CEO has agreed to allow for more flexible hours. So long as you are at the office between the hours of 10 A.M. and 2 P.M., you are free to fill the remainder of your 40 hour workweek according to your own schedule. This will allow you to go to your kids' afterschool events without having to use personal time off. If you have questions about this policy, please direct them to the HR office.

01. What is indicated about the employees at Evanston Inc.?

(A) They are required to fill out weekly time sheets.
(B) Some of them submitted suggestion cards.
(C) Most of them have kids in school.
(D) A few of them only work remotely.

02. According to the memo, what does the new policy allow employees to do?

(A) Lead more social lives
(B) Attend school events
(C) Take night classes
(D) Work from home

---

paraphrasing   주어진 어휘 또는 표현과 패러프레이징 될 수 있는 것을 연결하세요.

1. have school-age children   •

2. follow   •

3. initiate   •

4. allow for more flexible hours   •

5. go to your kids' afterschool events   •

• (a) adhere to

• (b) attend school events

• (c) have kids in school

• (d) introduce

• (e) permit to work according to one's own schedule

328   기적의 토익 RC

🔎 정답 및 해설 p.112

Questions 03-05 refer to the following memo.

Date: November 30
To: All Employees
From: Leslie Carone
Subject: Employee lounge

Employees are asked to keep in mind that shared areas should be treated with extra care. After using the appliances in the employee lounge, such as the microwave or refrigerator, be sure to leave the item like you found it. Spills should be cleaned up right away, and old food should be thrown out.

The management team is taking action in this matter based on your comments in last month's staff survey. A lot of people complained that the lounge was not a suitable place to spend time and relax due to cleanliness issues. We are working toward addressing this and other issues brought to our attention.

We would also like to remind team leaders that the lounge is not to be used for team meetings. Some of you have been meeting there when our other conference rooms are booked, especially since two of them are not available this month while undergoing renovations. If you cannot find an open room in our office, please go to a nearby café. Team funds can be used to purchase beverages for team members in this case. Please speak to the finance department if you have any questions about the budget limit.

03. What is mainly being discussed?

(A) Installation of new appliances
(B) Nominations for team leaders
(C) Instructions for reserving rooms
(D) Guidelines for break room use

04. What did the company do last month?

(A) Gathered feedback from employees
(B) Purchased some new equipment
(C) Relocated to a smaller building
(D) Changed the staff's working hours

05. What will some teams most likely do this month?

(A) Review their employees' performance
(B) Submit requests for renovation work
(C) Hold some of their meetings off-site
(D) Attend an industry conference

DAY 13

---

paraphrasing | 주어진 어휘 또는 표현과 패러프레이징 될 수 있는 것을 연결하세요.

1. matter   •   • (a) issue

2. staff survey   •   • (b) off-site

3. go to a nearby café   •   • (c) vacant room

4. open room   •   • (d) gathered feedback from employees

5. budget limit   •   • (e) amount of money that can be spent

PART 7 회람   329

 **실전 문제**

Questions 06-10 refer to the following memo and form.

To: All Acre Travel Agency Employees
From: Connie Kirk, Office Manager
Date: January 6
Re: Staff uniforms

I am writing to inform you about a change in our dress code policy. From next month, all employees will be required to wear uniforms rather than their own business attire. As you all know, we have recently changed our business's name and logo. Adding uniforms was recommended by our consultant as a way to help our clients get used to the transition more easily.

The new logo is purple and sky blue, so managers will wear purple uniforms whereas the rest of the staff will wear sky blue ones. Each uniform set comes with a pair of trousers and a short-sleeved, button-up shirt. Employees are eligible to receive up to four sets of free uniforms. There is also an optional sweater available in gray. Those wishing to order one or more of these should pay for half the cost of the item ($18), and the company will cover the cost of the other half.

Please complete the Uniform Request Form by the end of the week. The uniforms will arrive on January 27, and employees should start wearing them from February 1. Thank you for your cooperation.

Uniform Request Form

Please note that samples of each uniform item in various sizes are available in the HR department. If you elect to order the size without checking in advance and it is too small or large, you will be responsible for the cost of the replacement.

Employee Name: Lyle Ramos   **Size:** Large
Number of Sets Requested: 3   **Number of Sweaters Requested:** 0
Color Needed: [✔] Purple [   ] Sky Blue
Logo Position: [   ] Front Right   [   ] Front Left   [   ] Back Center   [✔] Any Available

06. What benefit of the uniforms does Ms. Kirk mention?

(A) They will help customers adjust to a rebranding.
(B) They will improve the sense of teamwork.
(C) They will make employees more comfortable.
(D) They will increase the level of professionalism.

07. What is indicated about the sweater?

(A) It will be partially paid for by the company.
(B) It is required for all employees to wear.
(C) It is available in four sizes.
(D) It has a row of buttons.

08. What is implied about Mr. Ramos?

(A) He will receive his uniform on February 1.
(B) He ordered the maximum number of sets.
(C) He works as a manager at Acre Travel Agency.
(D) He needs two different sizes of clothing.

09. In the form, the word "elect" in paragraph 1, line 2, is closest in meaning to

(A) return
(B) choose
(C) vote
(D) refuse

10. What is suggested on the order form?

(A) The HR team will measure employees for their uniforms.
(B) The number of large uniforms may run out.
(C) Mr. Ramos has checked out some sizes in person.
(D) Mr. Ramos has no preference for the logo placement.

DAY 13

---

paraphrasing 주어진 어휘 또는 표현과 패러프레이징 될 수 있는 것을 연결하세요.

1. changed our business's name and logo   •   • (a) rebranding
2. get used to the transition   •   • (b) choose
3. eligible to receive   •   • (c) be partially paid for by the company
4. the company will cover the cost of the other half •   • (d) can get
5. elect   •   • (e) adjust to the change

PART 7 회람   331

'멋진 당신, 오늘도 화이팅'

DAY
14

오늘의 학습 포인트

PART 5. 분사

1. 분사의 역할 - 명사 수식/보어 역할
2. 현재분사(-ing) vs. 과거분사(p.p.) - 명사와 분사가 능동 → 현재분사/
   수동 → 과거분사
3. 감정동사의 분사 - 분사가 수식하는 명사가 감정의 원인 → 현재분사/
   감정을 느끼는 주체 → 과거분사(surprising-surprised 등)
4. 분사구문 - 부사절 역할/주어와 분사구문이 능동 → 현재분사/수동 → 과거분사

PART 6. 시간 표현이 없는 현재완료 시제

빈칸이 동사 자리. 앞뒤 해석을 통해 시제 파악하기

PART 7. 비즈니스 기사

난이도 ↑, 길이가 긴 싱글 지문으로 주로 출제

PART 5 문법

분사

명사를 수식하는 현재분사와 과거분사가 자주 출제되므로 각 형태가 정답이 되는 경우를 구분하여 학습하세요.

✎ 적용 기술

[기적의 필기노트] 136P
RC 기술 51

출제 포인트

· 현재분사 + 명사:
  명사가 ~하다
· 과거분사 + 명사:
  명사가 ~되다
· 명사 + 과거분사:
  명사가 ~되다
· 명사 1 + 현재분사 + 명사 2: 명사 1이 ~하다

🔒 확인 문제 ❶

The carpet looked ------
due to the water leak.

(A) damage
(B) damaged

🔒 확인 문제 ❷

All IT companies should
keep their customers -------
with their service.

(A) satisfied
(B) satisfaction

출제 유형 1
분사의 역할

1 명사 수식

· 분사는 형용사처럼 명사를 앞이나 뒤에서 수식할 수 있습니다.

Jennifer Holden is one of the most **leading** <u>fashion designers</u>.
Jennifer Holden은 가장 선도적인 패션 디자이너 중 한 명이다.

Any <u>issues</u> **caused** by this change should be reported to the HR Department.
이 변경으로 인해 발생한 모든 문제는 인사부에 보고되어야 합니다.

2 보어 역할

· 현재분사(-ing)와 과거분사(p.p.)는 형용사로 사용될 수 있으므로 2형식 동사의 주격 보어, 5형식 동사의 목적격 보어 역할을 합니다.

Our payment options <u>are</u> very **limited**, but you can choose any of them.
저희의 대금 지불 방식은 매우 제한적이지만, 그중 어떤 것도 선택하실 수 있습니다.

After he had obtained the certificate, he <u>became</u> **qualified** for the position.
자격증을 취득한 이후에, 그는 그 직책에 맞는 자격을 갖추었다.

`800+`

· 5형식 동사 뒤에 오는 목적어와 목적격 보어가 능동 또는 진행의 의미 관계일 때 현재분사 형태의 목적격 보어를 씁니다.

Frequent cleaning will <u>make</u> your coffee machine **functioning** well.
　　　　　　　　　　　　　　 목적어　　　　　　목적격 보어
자주 세척을 하면 당신의 커피 머신이 잘 작동할 것입니다.

· 5형식 동사 뒤에 오는 목적어와 목적격 보어가 수동 또는 완료의 의미 관계일 때 과거분사 형태의 목적격 보어를 씁니다.

Mr. Cosby <u>found</u> his wallet **missing** when he paid for the pizzas.
　　　　　　　　　　 목적어　　　 목적격 보어
Cosby 씨는 피자 값을 지불할 때 지갑이 없어진 것을 발견했다.

정답 ❶ (B) ❷ (A)

334　기적의 토익 RC

출제 유형 2

현재분사(-ing) vs. 과거분사(p.p.)

1 현재분사

- 수식받는 명사와 분사가 **능동** 관계이면 현재분사를 씁니다.

- 주어와 보어 또는 목적어와 보어가 **능동** 관계이면 현재분사를 씁니다.

| 빈출 현재분사 |

leading 선도하는	promising 유망한	missing 분실한	inviting 매력적인
entertaining 흥미로운	challenging 도전적인	convincing 설득력 있는	rewarding 가치 있는
surrounding 인근의, 주의의	demanding 까다로운	encouraging 고무적인	outstanding 뛰어난

Heiman Market is one of the (**leading** / ~~led~~) companies in the retail industry.
회사가 선도하다

Heiman Market은 유통업계에서 선도 기업들 중 하나이다.

2 과거분사

- 수식받는 명사와 분사가 **수동** 관계이면 과거분사를 씁니다.

- 주어와 보어 또는 목적어와 보어가 **수동** 관계이면 과거분사를 씁니다.

| 빈출 과거분사 |

attached 첨부된	enclosed 동봉된	damaged 손상된	limited 제한된, 한정된
detailed 상세한	revised 수정된	reserved 예약된	updated 업데이트된
designated 지정된	reduced 감소된	renovated 개조된	qualified 자격을 갖춘
skilled 능숙한	experienced 경험 많은	preferred 선호하는	

This special promotion is offered only for a (**limited** / ~~limiting~~) time.
본 특별 홍보 행사는 한정된 기간 동안만 제공됩니다.   시간이 한정되다

출제 유형 3

감정동사의 분사

1 감정동사의 분사 구분

- 감정 동사에서 파생된 분사의 수식을 받는 **명사가 감정의 원인이면 현재분사, 감정을 느끼는 주체이면 과거분사**를 씁니다.

The board members were gathered to discuss the (**disappointing** / ~~disappointed~~) sales figures.   실적이 실망스러움을 느끼게 하는 원인

이사들은 실망스런 판매 실적에 대해 논의하기 위해 모였다.

- 감정 동사에서 파생된 분사가 주격/목적격 보어로 사용될 경우, **주어/목적어가 감정의 원인이면 현재분사, 감정을 느끼는 주체이면 과거분사**를 씁니다.

Most of the audience felt Prof. Kang's lecture (**interesting** / ~~interested~~).
강의가 흥미로움을 느끼게 하는 원인

대부분의 청중들은 Kang 교수의 강의를 흥미롭다고 느꼈다.

적용 기술

[기적의 필기노트] 137P
RC 기술 52

⚠️ **주의**

자동사는 현재분사로만 쓰입니다 (수동태가 없으므로).
예) rising 상승하는, remaining 남아 있는, participating 참가하는, lasting 지속되는, existing 기존의, emerging 새로 생긴/떠오르는, growing 증가하는

🔒 **확인 문제 ❸**

Please refer to the -------
file in the e-mail.

(A) attaching
(B) attached

적용 기술

[기적의 필기노트] 139P
RC 기술 54

🔒 **확인 문제 ❹**

Anyone ------- in learning a foreign language contacts us.

(A) interesting
(B) interested

정답 ❸ (B) ❹ (B)

PART 5 문법 분사   335

출제 포인트
주어가 사물이면 현재분사, 주어가 사람이면 과거분사를 고르는 유형으로 주로 출제돼요.

2 감정 동사에서 파생된 빈출 현재분사/과거분사

satisfy 만족시키다 – satisfying 만족스러운 – satisfied 만족한
surprise 놀라게 하다 – surprising 놀라운 – surprised 놀란
excite 들뜨게 하다 – exciting 흥미로운 – excited 신이 난
tire 피곤하게 하다 – tiring 피곤하게 하는 – tired 피곤한
interest 흥미를 끌다 – interesting 흥미로운 – interested 들뜬, 신이 난
disappoint 실망시키다 – disappointing 실망스러운 – disappointed 실망한
annoy 짜증나게 하다 – annoying 짜증나게 하는 – annoyed 짜증난

✎ 적용 기술
[기적의 필기노트] 139P
RC 기술 55

출제 유형 4
분사구문

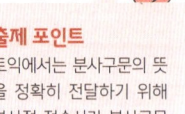

출제 포인트
토익에서는 분사구문의 뜻을 정확히 전달하기 위해 부사절 접속사가 분사구문 앞에 그대로 쓰인 형태가 더 자주 출제됩니다.

`800+`

1 분사구문

· 분사구문은 '접속사 + 주어 + 동사'의 부사절을 분사를 이용해 부사구로 바꾼 구문으로, 시간/조건/양보/이유 등을 나타내는 **부사절** 역할을 합니다.
Because I missed the bus, I was late for the weekly manager meeting.
= **Missing the bus**, I was late for the weekly manager meeting.
버스를 놓쳤기 때문에 주간 매니저 회의에 늦었다.

· 주절의 주어와 분사구문이 능동 관계면 현재분사, 수동 관계면 과거분사를 쓴다.
Placing the online order, he got a confirmation e-mail.
온라인 주문을 한 후에 그는 확인 이메일을 받았다.

Located in the old building, the restaurant has a lack of parking space.
오래된 건물에 위치한 이 식당은 주차 공간이 부족합니다.

`900+`

2 현재분사/과거분사 중 한가지 구문으로만 출제되는 표현

| 현재분사 구문으로만 출제되는 표현 |

beginning/starting ~부터, ~에 시작하여	preferring toV ~하는 것을 선호하면서
allowing A toV A가 ~하는 것을 가능하게 하면서	ensuring that 주어 + 동사 ~을 확실히 하면서

Copy Heaven installed new printers, **allowing** it to produce posters of various sizes. Copy Heaven은 다양한 크기의 포스터를 제작하는 것을 가능하게 하는 새 프린터를 설치했다.

| 과거분사 구문으로만 출제되는 표현 |

compared to ~와 비교했을 때	unless otherwise p.p. 달리 ~되어 있지 않다면
as p.p. ~된 바와 같이 → as discussed 논의된 대로, as mentioned 언급된 대로, as stated 명시된 대로	

Unless otherwise stated, you can check out only two books.
달리 명시되어 있지 않다면, 당신은 두 권의 책만 대출할 수 있습니다.

🔒 확인 문제 ❺
When ------- our plant, you are not allowed to take pictures.
(A) touring
(B) toured

🔒 확인 문제 ❻
As ------- on the form, we reserve all rights.
(A) indicating
(B) indicated

정답 ❺ (A) ❻ (B)

336 기적의 토익 RC

분사

1. After only three years since its establishment, Edmond Tour became one of the most ------- travel agencies.

(A) promise   (B) promising   (C) promises   (D) promised

설립한 지 겨우 3년 만에 Edmond 투어는 가장 유망한 여행사 중 하나가 되었다.

> 이렇게 풀어요
>
> 1. 선택지 보고 문법/어휘 문제 파악 선택지가 명사이자 동사인 promise(장래성; 가망이 있다)의 다양한 형태로 구성되어 있으므로 문법 문제임을 파악해요.
> 2. 빈칸 분석 빈칸 뒤에 명사 travel agencies가 있으므로 빈칸에는 명사를 수식하는 형용사가 들어가야 함을 파악합니다.
> 3. 정답 선택 형용사로 사용될 수 있는 현재분사 형용사 (B) promising을 정답으로 고릅니다.

2. According to the screening schedule at the movie festival, it is full of ------- films submitted from student directors.

(A) excite   (B) exciting   (C) excited   (D) excitement

상영 일정에 따르면 본 영화제는 학생 감독들이 제출한 신나는 영화들로 가득합니다.

> 이렇게 풀어요
>
> 1. 선택지 보고 문법/어휘 문제 파악 선택지가 감정 동사 excite(신나게 하다)의 다양한 형태로 구성되어 있으므로 문법 문제임을 파악해요.
> 2. 빈칸 분석 빈칸 뒤에 명사 films가 있으므로 빈칸에는 형용사가 들어가야 함을 파악해요.
> 3. 정답 선택 film(영화)가 감정의 원인이므로 현재분사 (B) exciting을 정답으로 고릅니다.

3. Evergreen Furniture will sign a contract with Emerson Shipping, ------ its customers to have more delivery options.

(A) allow   (B) allows   (C) allowing   (D) allowed

Evergreen Furniture는 Emerson Shipping과 계약을 체결하여 고객들에게 더 많은 배송 옵션을 제공할 예정이다.

> 이렇게 풀어요
>
> 1. 선택지 보고 문법/어휘 문제 파악 선택지가 동사 allow(허용하다)의 다양한 형태로 구성되어 있으므로 문법 문제임을 파악해요.
> 2. 빈칸 분석 콤마 앞에 이미 완전한 문장이 있으므로, 빈칸 뒤 명사 its customers 이하를 수식어로 만들 수 있는 문법 요소가 들어가야 함을 파악해요.
> 3. 정답 선택 (C)와 (D) 중 '고객들이 더 많은 배송 옵션을 가질 수 있도록'이라는 의미의 분사구문을 만들 수 있는 (C) allowing을 정답으로 고릅니다.

PART 5 문법 분사 337

PART 5 어휘
동사 어휘 (4)

각 어휘와 함께 자주 쓰이는 표현을 통째로 외워두세요.

---

01 attach 붙이다, 첨부하다

attach A to B	A를 B에 붙이다
be attached to	~에 첨부되다

02 succeed 성공하다

succeed in -ing	~하는 데 성공하다

03 expand 확대하다, 확장하다

expand one's customer base	고객층을 확대하다
expand one's business	사업을 확장하다
expand into	~로 확대하다

`800+`
04 force 강요하다

be forced to부정사	~하도록 강요당하다
force A(사람) to부정사	A에게 ~할 것을 강요하다

05 indicate 나타내다, 보여 주다

clearly indicate	명백히 나타내다
indicate the preference	선호도를 나타내다

🐾 빈출 토익 선생님 Pick!
06 promote 승진시키다, 홍보하다

be promoted to 직책/직위	~로 승진되다
promote a product	제품을 홍보하다

07 address 연설하다, 다루다

address an issue/a problem	문제를 다루다
address the concern	우려에 대해 고심하다

🐾 빈출 토익 선생님 Pick!
08 conduct 실시하다, 수행하다

conduct a customer survey	고객 여론 조사를 실시하다
conduct research	연구하다, 조사하다

09 determine 결정하다, 밝히다

determine the cause of	~의 원인을 밝히다
determine whether	~ 여부를 결정하다

10 extend 연장하다, 보내다

extend a deadline	마감을 연장하다
extend an invitation	초대장을 보내다

11 feature 특징으로 삼다

be featured in a magazine	잡지에 특집으로 실리다

12 file 제기하다, 보관하다

file a complaint	항의를 제기하다
file income tax returns	소득세 신고서를 제출하다

13 revise 수정하다, 개정하다

revise a budget proposal	예산 제안서를 수정하다
revise the sales goals	판매 목표를 수정하다

🐾 빈출 토익 선생님 Pick!
14 contribute 기부하다, 기증하다

contribute A to B	A를 B에게 기부하다
contribute financially	금전적으로 기여하다

`800+`
15 assume (책임을) 맡다, 추정하다

assume the responsibility	책임을 맡다
assume + 직책	~을 맡다

338 기적의 토익 RC

16 distribute 나누어 주다, 배포하다

be distributed to	~에게 배포되다
distribute A to B	A를 B에게 나누어 주다

빈출 토익 선생님 Pick!
17 exceed 넘다, 초과하다

exceed a budget	예산을 초과하다
exceed one's expectation	예상을 뛰어넘다

18 raise 올리다, 모으다

raise money	돈을 마련하다
raise funds	기금을 모으다, 자금을 조달하다

800+
19 claim 주장하다, 요구하다

claim the right	권리를 주장하다

20 accept 받아들이다, 수락하다

accept an invitation	초대에 응하다
accept the offer	제안을 받아들이다
accept the position	직책을 수락하다

21 expire 만료되다

be set to expire	만료될 예정이다

22 adjust 조정하다, 조절하다

adjust the schedule/price	일정/가격을 조정하다
adjust to a new environment	새 환경에 적응하다

23 reserve 예약하다

be reserved for	~을 위해 따로 잡아 두다
reserve a room/flight	방/항공편을 예약하다

24 combine 결합하다

combine A with B	A를 B와 결합하다
combine one's efforts	~의 노력을 모으다

빈출 토익 선생님 Pick!
25 enhance 높이다, 향상시키다

enhance reputation	명성을 높이다
enhance the customer experience	고객 경험을 높이다
enhance the productivity/efficiency	생산성/효율성을 높이다

26 divide 나뉘다, 갈라지다

divide A into B	A를 B로 나누다
be divided equally	동등하게 나뉘다

풀이 방법

To ------- its clothing lines, Ridgefield Fashion runs new ads throughout the city.

(A) attach　　　　(B) conduct　　　　(C) reserve　　　　(D) promote

자사의 의류 라인을 홍보하기 위해, Ridgefield 패션은 시 전역에 걸쳐 새 광고를 내보낸다.

이렇게 풀어요

1. **선택지 보고 문법/어휘 문제 파악** 선택지가 서로 다른 동사 어휘로 구성되어 있으므로 어휘 문제임을 파악해요.
2. **빈칸 분석** 빈칸 뒤에 일종의 '제품'을 의미하는 clothing lines가 있고 그 뒤에 광고를 내보낸다는 내용이 있으므로 제품을 어떻게 하기 위해 광고를 하는지 나타내 줄 동사가 들어가야 함을 파악합니다.
3. **정답 선택** 의류 라인을 '홍보하기' 위해 광고를 내보낸다는 문맥이 가장 자연스러우므로 (D) promote를 정답으로 고릅니다.

PART 5 어휘 동사 어휘 (4)

따라 하면 문제가 풀리는

연습 문제

앞서 학습한 문제 풀이법을 적용하여 맞는 것에 ✔ 표시 하거나 괄호 안에
적절한 답을 쓰고 정답을 선택하세요.

---

01 Please refer to the ------- manual in the package.

(A) enclose
(B) enclosed
(C) to enclose
(D) enclosure

1. 선택지 보고 문법/어휘 문제 파악하기 ☐ 문법 문제 ☐ 어휘 문제
2. 빈칸 분석하기 빈칸 앞에 있는 것 ☐ 형용사 ☐ 관사
   빈칸 뒤에 있는 것 ☐ 명사 ☐ 동사
   → 빈칸에는 ☐ 형용사 역할을 하는 것 ☐ 동사 역할을 하는 것이 들어가야 한다.
3. 정답 선택하기 정답 (   )

---

02 Thanks to the workshop, all employees have become ------- at operating the lifts.

(A) skill
(B) skilling
(C) skilled
(D) skills

1. 선택지 보고 문법/어휘 문제 파악하기 ☐ 문법 문제 ☐ 어휘 문제
2. 빈칸 분석하기 빈칸 앞에 있는 것 ☐ 2형식 동사 ☐ 5형식 동사
   → 빈칸에는 ☐ 보어 ☐ 목적어가 들어가야 한다.
3. 정답 선택하기 정답 (   )

---

03 The panel members will ------- the issues on ocean conservation.

(A) expand
(B) address
(C) conduct
(D) force

1. 선택지 보고 문법/어휘 문제 파악하기 ☐ 문법 문제 ☐ 어휘 문제
2. 빈칸 분석하기 빈칸 뒤에 있는 있는 목적어 (   )
   → 이 목적어와 짝꿍 표현으로 쓰이는 동사가 정답이다.
3. 정답 선택하기 정답 (   )

◉ 정답 및 해설 p.114

04 The ------- sales of Xenon-8 have led to its product line change.

(A) disappointing
(B) disappointed
(C) disappointment
(D) to disappoint

> 1. 선택지 보고 문법/어휘 문제 파악하기 ☐문법 문제 ☐어휘 문제
> 2. 빈칸 분석하기 빈칸 앞에 있는 것 ☐전치사 ☐관사 빈칸 뒤에 있는 것 ☐명사 ☐동사
>   → 빈칸에는 ☐명사 ☐형용사 들어가야 한다. → 정답 후보 2개 (,   )
>   → sales와의 의미 관계 ☐감정의 원인 ☐감정을 느끼는 주체
> 3. 정답 선택하기 정답 (   )

05 Please park your vehicle in the parking lot ------- only for hotel guests.

(A) designate
(B) designated
(C) designating
(D) designation

> 1. 선택지 보고 문법/어휘 문제 파악하기 ☐문법 문제 ☐어휘 문제
> 2. 빈칸 분석하기 빈칸 앞에 있는 것 ☐완전한 절 ☐불완전한 절
>   → 빈칸에는 ☐문장의 필수 성분 ☐수식어 역할을 하는 것이 들어가야 한다.
>   → 정답의 후보 2개 (,   ) → parking lot과의 의미 관계 ☐능동 ☐수동
> 3. 정답 선택하기 정답 (   )

DAY 14

06 When ------- for a permit, you should include your current mailing address.

(A) apply
(B) applied
(C) applicant
(D) applying

> 1. 선택지 보고 문법/어휘 문제 파악하기 ☐문법 문제 ☐어휘 문제
> 2. 빈칸 분석하기 빈칸 앞에 있는 것 ☐접속사 ☐전치사
>   → 빈칸이 포함된 절에 동사가 없으므로 ☐명사 ☐분사가 들어가야 한다.
>   → 정답의 후보 2개 (,   ) → 주절의 주어 you와의 의미 관계 ☐능동 ☐수동
> 3. 정답 선택하기 정답 (   )

PART 5 분사 / 동사 어휘 (4)   341

토익에 나올 실전 문제

DAY 01~14 누적 문제

제한시간 9분입니다! 시~작!

01. Some of the ------- venues are not suitable for holding more than 10 sessions at the same time.
(A) suggest
(B) suggests
(C) suggested
(D) suggestion

02. All of the ------- materials have been brought to the job site, so construction of Manning Tower can finally begin.
(A) require
(B) requiring
(C) required
(D) requirement

03. Due to the rapidly ------- deadline, almost all team members are required to work extra next week.
(A) approaching
(B) approach
(C) approached
(D) to approach

04. Mr. Wenger had trouble choosing an intern, as all of the applicants were -------.
(A) qualify
(B) qualification
(C) qualifies
(D) qualified

05. The study will focus on the ------- effect of the plastic products on the sea ecosystem.
(A) lasts
(B) lasting
(C) lasted
(D) last

06. Please arrive at the theater at least 30 minutes prior to your ------- show time.
(A) schedule
(B) schedules
(C) scheduled
(D) scheduling

07. Timmy Buck's clients are almost always ------- with his custom-made furniture.
(A) to satisfy
(B) satisfying
(C) satisfied
(D) satisfactory

08. All toys and clothing ------- from the local residents will be donated to charities such as Open Arms Society.
(A) collecting
(B) have collected
(C) collects
(D) collected

09. When -------- your new office chair set, please consult the manual.
(A) had assembled
(B) to assemble
(C) assembling
(D) assembled

10. Camacho Department Store will offer free makeup classes ------- on Saturday, August 5.
(A) beginning
(B) will begin
(C) beginner
(D) begin

11. With a lack of office space, Hammington Law will relocate to the newly ------- office building.
(A) remodeling
(B) remodeled
(C) being remodeled
(D) remodel

12. Chemical pesticides ------- by Hancock Farms have been found in the drinking water.
(A) using
(B) used
(C) usefully
(D) usage

정답 및 해설 p.115

13. The ------- floor plan for the new headquarters office must be submitted tomorrow.

(A) proposal
(B) proposing
(C) proposed
(D) proposes

14. Our staff members would be ------- to assist you whenever you need help in our hotel.

(A) to delight
(B) delighting
(C) delighted
(D) delights

15. Most business owners reported that ------- approval for a business loan from a bank is the most stressful task.

(A) obtain
(B) obtains
(C) obtained
(D) obtaining

16. The actors starring in the next production plan ------- rehearsing next week.

(A) begin
(B) to begin
(C) began
(D) will begin

17. Northern Marketing ------- twice as many clients by the beginning of next year.

(A) would have had
(B) will have
(C) had
(D) has

18. Grisham Consulting put a large amount of funding ------- renovating its office.

(A) around
(B) into
(C) over
(D) for

19. The latest Washington truck model ------- an attached tow cable.

(A) features
(B) conducts
(C) addresses
(D) forces

20. During Kenosha's Citizen Recognition Day, Julia Wings ------- an award for her participation in charity events.

(A) revised
(B) contributed
(C) accepted
(D) assumed

21. Mr. Pham ------- 10 seats for the upcoming Boston Leadership Seminar.

(A) divided
(B) raised
(C) indicated
(D) reserved

22. Cindy Bauer's Beauty Salon does everything it can to ------- its services for clients.

(A) distribute
(B) enhance
(C) claim
(D) combine

23. Ms. Nishida is on pace to ------- her quarterly sales quota by the end of the week.

(A) determine
(B) succeed
(C) exceed
(D) reveal

24. Cox Real Estate ------- invitations to the open house via e-mail last week.

(A) extended
(B) recovered
(C) notified
(D) performed

DAY 14

PART 5 분사 / 동사 어휘 (4)   343

PART 6

시간 표현이 없는 현재완료 시제 ▮900+

빈칸이 동사 자리일 경우 앞뒤 문장 해석을 통해 어느 시점인지 시제를 파악합니다.

📖 VOCA

fundraising 기금 모금
celebrity 유명인사
entire 전체의
valuable 가치 있는
fund 기금, 자금
throughout ~의 전체에 걸쳐
appeal 호소, 간청
approve 승인하다
outdated 구식의

 **풀이 방법**   article   ♀ 해석 p.117

Medina Makes a Mark

The singer Alex Medina ------- to the community by leading a fundraising project for
01.
local schools. "Thanks to a celebrity being at the front of this fundraiser," said Tina
Sharpton, principal of Troy High School, "this entire project was a huge success by
not only raising the money our schools need, but also giving the students valuable
experience."

The funds ------- during the project will be used to update computer labs throughout
    🔩 PART 5
the Troy school district. Despite several appeals to government officials, funding
had not been approved over 8 years. Students have expressed excitement and
enthusiasm about the upgrade. They are eager to use current technology instead of
the outdated equipment that they had before.

01. (A) contribute
      (B) contribution
      (C) has contributed
      (D) will contribute

🌱 이렇게 풀어요

1. **선택지 보고 문법/어휘 문제 파악** 선택지가 동사 contribute(기여하다)의 다양한 형태로 구성되어 있으므로 문법 문제임을 파악해요.

2. **빈칸 분석** 빈칸 앞에 주어가 있으므로 빈칸에는 동사가 들어가야 합니다. 빈칸 뒤 내용을 보면 Alex Medina가 기금 모금 프로젝트와 관련이 되어 있고, Tina Sharpton의 말에 따르면 그녀 덕분에 이 프로젝트가 성공적이었다고 과거 시제로 말하고 있습니다.

3. **정답 선택** Alex Medina가 지역사회에 '기여했다'고 과거에 완료된 일을 나타내는 것이 적절하므로 현재완료 시제 (C)가 정답입니다.

♀ 해설

빈칸부터 project까지가 앞에 나온 주어 funds를 수식하는 역할을 합니다. 분사인 (C)와 (D) 중, funds와 raise가 '기금이 모이다'라는 수동 관계가 되어야 하므로 (C)가 정답입니다.

🔩 PART 5 문법 적용 문제

The funds ------- during the project will be used to update computer labs throughout the
Troy school district.

(A) raise   (B) are raised   (C) raised   (D) raising

344 기적의 토익 RC

따라 하면 문제가 풀리는

연습 문제

빈칸 앞뒤 내용에서 단서가 될 부분을 찾아 표시하세요.
표시한 것을 바탕으로 정답 어휘를 선택하세요.

○ 정답 및 해설 p.117

01

Beach Burgers ------- another branch in Los Angeles, which means that it is now the most popular fast food chain in southern California. It started as a small, family-run food truck around the downtown area of San Diego.

(A) has opened

(B) will open

02

Real estate developers are calling for the demolishment of Centerville Theater. Many locals are against the idea because the venue ------- the only place to provide live entertainment to such a small town.

(A) will remain

(B) has remained

03

Dear Ms. Bowen,

Upon reviewing your order, we agree that you were overcharged. The difference of $19.93 was refunded to your account. You can see that it ------- on your credit card.

(A) will have been reflected

(B) has been reflected

04

Dear Ms. Michaels,

We regret to inform you that the company ------- your application to transfer to the Jakarta branch. Unfortunately, there are no openings there at this time, but we encourage you to apply again when one opens up.

(A) will decline

(B) has declined

PART 6 시간 표현이 없는 현재완료 시제   345

 **토익에 나올**

실전 문제

제한시간 4분입니다! 시~작!

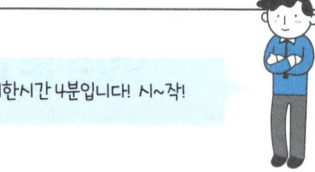

Questions 01-04 refer to the following article.

Dino Diner

A new restaurant themed after the famous film series *Dinosaur District* ------- here in Covington.
                                                                                    01.

The owner, Travis Short, claims that using the theme of a movie helps with marketing. "Sure, I have to pay royalties to the studio. But that's less than what most restaurants have to spend on commercials and branding," he said in an interview.

Since the restaurant's grand opening last weekend, it has ------- a considerable deal of attention.
                                                                              02.

-------. "Our kids love the *Dinosaur District* movies, so it's worth the wait," said one parent regarding
03.

the restaurant. It seems like Dino Diner will ------- become known as a landmark of Covington.
                                                              04.

유형 적용 문제

01. (A) opens
     (B) opening
     (C) has opened
     (D) will open

02. (A) awarded
     (B) received
     (C) completed
     (D) delivered

03. (A) Delivery drivers are wanted for lunch and dinner shifts.
     (B) Families waited in line for up to two hours to be seated.
     (C) The restaurant's menu is posted on its Web site.
     (D) A takeout window will be installed soon.

04. (A) soon
     (B) ago
     (C) recently
     (D) once

정답 및 해설 p.118

Questions 05-08 refer to the following e-mail.

To: William McBride
From: Melissa Frey
Date: 9 November
Subject: Welcome to Hanover Labs!

Dear Ms. McBride,

We at Hanover Labs ------- your application for the Junior Researcher position with Team A. You
05.
were chosen among many candidates. Our HR and management think you are very well qualified

and ready to ------- a wide range of tasks. Your first day will be Monday, 14 November. Please go to
06.
the reception desk in the main lobby and ask for Dominick Arias. He is one of our junior researchers

who you will work with. He knows everything ------- for your first day. He will escort you to the
07.
security department to take a photo for your badge. -------. You will obtain a temporary one there.
08.
An orientation and welcoming reception will follow.

If you have any questions, feel free to let me know.

Sincerely,

Melissa Frey
HR Manager, Hanover Labs

유형 적용 문제

05. (A) have accepted
(B) will accepted
(C) accept
(D) were accepting

07. (A) need
(B) needs
(C) needed
(D) needing

06. (A) train
(B) perform
(C) request
(D) cancel

08. (A) You are required to pay $5 for reissuing your badge.
(B) You may have difficulty navigating our facilities at first.
(C) Feel free to download one from the company's homepage.
(D) It will take a couple of days for it to be issued.

PART 6 시간 표현이 없는 현재완료 시제 347

PART 7

기사 (1) 비즈니스 기사 `800+`

기사는 매회 2~3개의 지문이 출제됩니다. 가장 난이도가 높은 유형이므로 마지막에 푸는 것이 효율적입니다.

기업/인물/비즈니스에 관련된 기사는 길이가 긴 싱글 지문으로 자주 출제되고 생소한 어휘가 포함되어 있는 경우가 많으므로 비교적 난이도가 높은 유형입니다. 문제를 먼저 읽고 필요한 정보만 지문에서 파악하는 것이 문제 풀이 시간을 줄이는 데 도움이 돼요. 또한, 문제의 순서와 지문의 전개 순서가 같은 경우가 많으므로 문제의 순서대로 지문에서 단서를 찾으세요.

비즈니스 기사에서 자주 출제되는 문제

· 문장 삽입 문제
기업의 사업 진행 상황이나 사업가의 경력에 대한 세부적인 내용이 삽입할 문장으로 주어집니다. 문장에 연결어, 지시어, 시간, 대명사가 포함되어 있는 경우가 많으므로 앞뒤 문맥 관계를 파악하는 것이 핵심입니다.

비즈니스 기사에 자주 출제되는 어휘

owner	소유주, 사장	adjacent to	~에 인접한
formerly	이전에	found	설립하다
manufacturer	제조업체	conglomerate	복합 기업, 대기업
entrepreneur	기업가	board of directors	이사회
go out of business	파산하다	head office	본사
subsidiary	자회사	boost	증대시키다
forgery	위조, 허위	union	노조
summit	정상회담	niche	틈새시장
enhance	(품질을) 높이다	file for bankruptcy	파산 신청을 하다
consolidate	통합하다	on the market	시판되는
takeover	인수, 취득	arbitrate	중재하다
go on strike	파업하다	diversify	다각화하다
feasibility	타당성, 실행가능성	produce	생산하다
top-selling	가장 잘 팔리는	consistently	지속적으로
rise	상승하다, 증가하다	press conference	기자회견
shut down	문을 닫다, 폐쇄하다	maximize	최대화하다
distributor	유통업자, 배급업자	unforeseen	예측할 수 없는
spokesperson	대변인	set forth	제시하다
converge	모여들다	region	지역

비즈니스 기사

article

◯ 해석 p.119

Another Mobile Hit by Helena Saunders

The developer Helena Saunders has launched yet another mobile app that is being downloaded and used by millions of people. —[1]—. Although Ms. Saunders has an educational background in the fashion business and tried to start her career at a fashion design agency, she decided to give up on those hopes when her self-taught hobby of developing mobile apps proved to be considerably more promising.

It seems that the brilliance of her apps lies in their simplicity. —[2]—. Most people want to use apps that don't require their full attention.

Her first app simply involved swiping left or right on outfits. It would remember preferences and recommend similar styles based on them. —[3]—. Retail companies were quick to fund that app. This time, she created an app to find friends based on their location and clothing preferences. —[4]—. In the first month alone, it was downloaded by over three million mobile users, which grows by the day.

---

01. What is suggested about Ms. Saunders?
(A) She founded her own fashion design company.
(B) She did not receive formal training in mobile development.
(C) She believes that new outfits should be displayed at fashion shows.
(D) She started working at a software development company two years ago.

02. In which of the positions marked [1], [2], [3], and [4] does the following sentence best belong?

"The apps developed by Ms. Saunders normally require only one hand to use."

(A) [1]
(B) [2]
(C) [3]
(D) [4]

🔖 이렇게 풀어요

01. Saunders 씨에 대해 암시되는 것은 무엇인가?
(A) 자신의 패션 디자인 회사를 설립했다.
(B) 모바일 개발에 관한 정식 교육을 받지 않았다.
(C) 새로운 의상을 패션쇼에서 선보여야 한다고 생각한다.
(D) 2년 전에 소프트웨어 개발 회사에서 일을 시작했다.

해설 문제의 키워드인 Ms. Saunders가 Helena Saunders로 언급되어 있는 첫 단락에서 her self-taught hobby of developing mobile apps라고 했으므로 그녀는 모바일 개발에 관한 정식 교육을 받지 않았음을 알 수 있습니다. 따라서 (B)가 정답입니다.

02. [1], [2], [3] 그리고 [4]로 표시된 위치 중 다음 문장이 들어가기에 가장 적절한 곳은 어디인가?

"Saunders 씨에 의해 개발된 앱은 작동시키는 데 보통 한 손만 필요하다."

해설 주어진 문장은 앱을 한 손만으로 작동할 수 있다는 편리함에 대한 내용입니다. 따라서 흐름상 편리함에 관련된 문장 앞 또는 뒤에 와야 해요. 두 번째 단락의 [2] 앞에 simplicity가 언급되었고, [2] 뒤에는 사람들이 전적으로 주의를 쏟지 않아도 되는 앱을 쓰고 싶어 한다는 내용이 있으므로 문장이 [2]에 들어가는 것이 논리적으로 알맞습니다. 따라서 (B)가 정답입니다.

PART 7 기사 (1) 비즈니스 기사   349

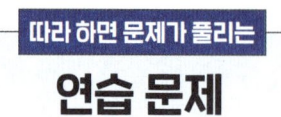

따라 하면 문제가 풀리는
연습 문제

먼저 문제의 키워드에 표시한 후,
지문에서 단서를 찾아 적절한 답을 고르세요.

01 article

Leave Room for Dessert

Timber Grill owner and chef Lloyd Merrit wanted to offer more than just steaks. —[1]—. He
worked to create a sweet dessert dish that would stay within the theme of the restaurant:
foods on the grill. After months of experimentation, he finally settled on his signature dish,
Grilled Peaches. Merrit soaks the peaches overnight in a juice blend, then sprinkles them with
a mix of cinnamon and other spices. —[2]—. With a full dining room every night, it's clear that
Merrit's hard work has paid off.

Q. In which of the positions marked [1] and [2] does the following sentence best belong?

"The finished product is a tasty treat that keeps customers coming back for more."

(A) [1]
(B) [2]

02 article

(December 7) — Andrew Logan, the famous real estate developer, worked hard to get to
where he is now. When he first got into the field of real estate development in Arizona, he
noticed that there was one major problem. "I needed people who already had the skills
necessary to build houses, but they were so hard to find," Mr. Logan said in an interview.
"The people who were already trained often went to other places." That's why he started
putting his employees first. "Once I found someone who was good, I made sure that they were
happy working for me."

Q. What problem did Mr. Logan have with his business?

(A) There were not enough skilled employees.
(B) There was no affordable real estate.

03 article

May 10 — The city council of Munford agreed to fund a large-scale art project in its downtown area. It will work in collaboration with the Munford Academy of Modern Art to paint murals on the walls of the buildings in the city's shopping district. This will be a great way for young artists to get some exposure while also attract the attention of visitors. Councilman Joe Rogers says that the project will pay for itself within a year. "We'll have tons of tourists coming here to get their pictures in front of the murals," he said before the council voted on the issue. "After Sebring did something similar, it started to bring in 20% more tourists every year."

Q. What benefit of the project is mentioned?

(A) It will increase tourism in Munford.
(B) It will draw attention to Munford's art museum.

04 article

The Sound of Silence

TOLEDO — Step into Lammar Café, and you'll be welcomed by American 50s-style décor. With classic menu items like hamburgers and milkshakes, and vintage uniforms for the wait staff, you'll think you've gone back in time. —[1]—. The restaurant is going the extra mile to keep the restaurant authentic — cell phones are not allowed. The policy is strictly followed, and anyone seen using a cell phone is asked to take the call outside. —[2]—. However, most patrons enjoy the experience of being present in the moment without constantly checking their phones.

Q. In which of the positions marked [1] and [2] does the following sentence best belong?

"Some customers admit difficulty adjusting to the rule."

(A) [1]
(B) [2]

 토익에 나올
실전 문제

제한시간 13분입니다! 시~작!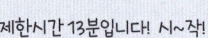

Questions 01-03 refer to the following article.

Oklahoma City (19 March) — Lisette Inc. recently announced its business takeover of Belford Logging. This will help reduce the company's overall operation expenses, considering that the majority of wood that it uses was supplied by Belford Logging.

Lisette Inc. started out as a custom furniture design company, but within a few short years, turned into a major mass-producer of assembly line furniture. A hand-crafted chair or table could take weeks to make, but their facility here in Oklahoma City can finish dozens every day.

Lisette Inc. was founded by Lisette Medina, who learned carpentry as an apprentice after finishing high school. "Although I first learned the importance of traditional woodworking," she said in an interview, "I believe that as a business, you have to crank out products quickly to make a profit and not just do it as a hobby."

When asked about the takeover of Belford Logging, Ms. Medina shared her hopes for her company. "My goal is to have the Lisette Inc. brand in every household across the country. I don't plan to stop growing until I achieve that," she said.

Lisette Inc. currently employs 12,000 workers, and intends to hire more for another production facility that will open in October of this year.

01. What is the main topic of the article?

(A) Lisette Inc. is offering a new line of custom products.
(B) Lisette Inc. has acquired one of its suppliers.
(C) Lisette Inc. is the leading employer in its field.
(D) Lisette Inc. has grown internationally.

02. What does Lisette Inc. produce?

(A) Quickly assembled furniture
(B) Wooden cooking utensils
(C) Woodworking tools
(D) Garden decorations

03. What is stated about Ms. Medina?

(A) She is originally from Oklahoma City.
(B) She will step down as CEO in October.
(C) She wants to continue expanding her company.
(D) She still practices traditional woodworking as a hobby.

---

paraphrasing 주어진 어휘 또는 표현과 패러프레이징 될 수 있는 것을 연결하세요.

1. business takeover   •   • (a) has acquired
2. make a profit   •   • (b) earn money
3. don't plan to stop growing •   • (c) plans to employ additional workers

352 기적의 토익 RC

Questions 04-06 refer to the following article.

Changing the Meaning of "Office"

May 19 — At Richland Designs, the word "office" is becoming more of a concept than a physical place. —[1]—. The company has launched its Remote Employment Program, or *REP*, as it is more commonly known by employees. The program supplies employees with the tools they need to work from home. Timothy Wilhelm, the president of Richland Designs, adopted the change in an effort to make the company more desirable to potential job candidates. —[2]—. "In order to bring in the best talent, you have to offer the best working conditions," Wilhelm said. "In a highly competitive industry like ours, having the right team members is the only way to succeed. —[3]—."

Employees who opt into REP can select up to four days of the week to work remotely. In addition to having a change of scenery that may boost creativity, the practice also eliminates the need for a long and stressful commute. According to a recent survey, the average employee spends over an hour commuting each weekday. —[4]—. Supporters of REP hope to combat this issue.

04. According to the article, why has Richland Designs changed a policy?

(A) To increase the staff's productivity level
(B) To respond to some customer complaints
(C) To attract more highly qualified workers
(D) To follow a competitor's actions

05. What is suggested about REP?

(A) Its participation is voluntary.
(B) Its designer provides training.
(C) It is opposed by Mr. Wilhelm.
(D) It requires extensive experience.

06. In which of the positions marked [1], [2], [3], and [4] does the following sentence best belong?

"It can leave them overly tired, contributing to inefficiency."

(A) [1]
(B) [2]
(C) [3]
(D) [4]

---

paraphrasing 주어진 어휘 또는 표현과 패러프레이징 될 수 있는 것을 연결하세요.

1. launched •
2. bring in the best talent •
3. opt into •

• (a) voluntary
• (b) introduced
• (c) attract more highly qualified workers

 **실전 문제**

Questions 07-09 refer to the following article.

Dining in the Heart of New Orleans: Hillview Café

by Lorraine Ferguson

March 12 — After twenty-five years in business, Hillview Café began a new phase. The restaurant was sold to Tyrone Manning last month, and he is working hard to continue the dining establishment's standard of excellence. I sat down with Mr. Manning earlier this week.

LF: In a recent review in *Dining Daily*, Casey Rigsby called her dining experience "a delight for the senses". What have you done to achieve such high praise?

TM: Our head chef, Scott Cobos, has created an extensive menu with dishes that appeal to a wide variety of tastes. After ten years of working at Hillview Café, he has perfected some of the diners' favorites. He's also willing to try new things.

LF: Even though it has the word "café" in its name, your restaurant is often classified as "fine dining." How would you describe the atmosphere you are trying to create?

TM: Along with amazing food, we strive to provide top-notch service. At the same time, we don't take ourselves too seriously. The mood at lunchtime is serious, with many people meeting there on business. In the afternoon, it takes on a more relaxed quality. Then in the evening, we energize the space with live music and colorful lights.

07. What is the purpose of the article?

(A) To promote a restaurant's anniversary party
(B) To introduce new items on a menu
(C) To highlight a business's change in ownership
(D) To provide cooking tips from a professional chef

08. Who most likely is Ms. Rigsby?

(A) A magazine salesperson
(B) A restaurant manager
(C) A professional chef
(D) A food critic

09. What is mentioned about Hillview Café's atmosphere?

(A) It changes depending on the time of day.
(B) It promotes conversations between dining parties.
(C) It received poor reviews from some customers.
(D) It has been improved with new decorations.

paraphrasing 주어진 어휘 또는 표현과 패러프레이징 될 수 있는 것을 연결하세요.

1. The restaurant was sold to Tyrone Manning •
2. achieve high praise •
3. classified •

• (a) categorized
• (b) business's change in ownership
• (c) highly acclaimed

354 기적의 토익 RC

Questions 10-13 refer to the following article.

ZoomCore to join Technology Expo

MEDFORD (10 Nov.) — Computer manufacturer ZoomCore has announced that it will be joining the 2-week Medford Technology Expo for the first time next month. —[1]—.

Showing new products at the expo is generally considered a risky chance for young electronics companies such as ZoomCore. Most of them either lose all of their support or gain considerable attention and funding from investors. —[2]—.

Computers released by ZoomCore have been extremely popular among online gamers. "Few things are more frustrating than a slow computer when trying to relax," said CEO Gordon Willis. —[3]—. "We made some custom modifications to bring in our best gaming computers yet and give people a new and exciting gaming experience."

—[4]—. Mr. Willis said that the display his company plans to set up will make people feel like they are among pro gamers. "It's going to be an experience, the likes of which you have never seen," he said in a press release. "For those who are unable to attend, you can see what we are doing at the expo through our company Web site."

---

10. The word "considerable" in paragraph 2, line 2, is closest in meaning to

(A) persistent
(B) substantial
(C) thoughtful
(D) conscious

11. According to the article, what does ZoomCore intend to unveil at the expo?

(A) Some newly developed games
(B) Revolutionary computer designs
(C) Top-of-the-line graphics and sound cards
(D) Computers with customized changes

12. What does ZoomCore plan to do at the expo?

(A) It will hire a professional gamer spokesperson.
(B) It will offer some products at discounted prices.
(C) It will be broadcasted online.
(D) It will demonstrate how to select personalized settings.

13. In which of the positions marked [1], [2], [3], and [4] does the following sentence best belong?

"Given ZoomCore's rising popularity, analysts expect it to attract lots of backing."

(A) [1]
(B) [2]
(C) [3]
(D) [4]

---

paraphrasing 주어진 어휘 또는 표현과 패러프레이징 될 수 있는 것을 연결하세요.

1. gain attention •   • (a) attract people
2. release •   • (b) customized changes
3. custom modifications •   • (c) unveil

PART 7 기사 (1) 비즈니스 기사   355

'멋진 당신, 오늘도 화이팅'

DAY

15

오늘의 학습 포인트

PART 5. 등위접속사와 상관접속사
1. 등위접속사 - and/or/but/so
2. 상관접속사 - both A and B/either A or B/neither A nor B/
   not A but B/not only A but (also) B

PART 6. 접속부사 - 첨가

↳ 보기가 besides, moreover, furthermore 등

PART 7. 문화/예술/지역사회 관련 기사

매회 1~2지문. 기사는 마지막에 풀기

PART 5 문법 — 등위접속사와 상관접속사

문맥에 맞는 알맞은 등위접속사를 선택하는 문제, 상관접속사의 짝을 선택하는 문제가 주로 출제됩니다.

◈ 적용 기술

[기적의 필기노트] 141P
RC 기술 57

🔒 확인 문제 ❶

This training is intended for interns ------ new hires.

(A) to
(B) and

🔒 확인 문제 ❷

This item is temporarily out of stock ------ will be restocked in the afternoon.

(A) because
(B) but

출제 유형1 등위접속사

1 등위접속사 and/or

· 등위접속사 and와 or는 단어와 단어, 구와 구, 절과 절을 연결할 수 있습니다.
The new guidelines are <u>simple</u> **and** <u>easy</u> to follow. 새로운 지침은 간단하고 따르기 쉽다.

You can wait <u>for him now</u> **or** <u>come back tomorrow.</u>
당신은 그를 지금 기다리거나 내일 다시 오시면 됩니다.

2 등위접속사 but

· but은 완전한 2개의 절을 연결할 수 있습니다.
<u>Mr. Clint submitted his loan application last week,</u> **but** <u>it was not processed yet.</u>
Clint 씨는 지난주에 대출 신청서를 제출했으나 아직 처리되지 않았다.

· but이 연결하는 동사 이하의 절 또는 완전한 2개의 절의 경우 반드시 그 내용이 서로 반대의 의미가 되어야 하며, 각각의 절에서 반대의 의미를 나타내는 단서 어휘를 찾아야 합니다.
→ 위의 첫 번째 예문에서는 형용사 simple과 hard, 두 번째 예문에서는 was representing과 returned가 단서가 됩니다.

800+

· but은 동사 이하의 절을 연결할 수 있습니다.
Some test questions <u>looked simple</u> **but** <u>were hard to solve.</u>
몇몇 시험 문제들은 단순해 보였지만 풀기에 어려웠다.

정답 ❶ (B) ❷ (B)

358 기적의 토익 RC

3 등위접속사 so

- so는 완전한 절과 절을 연결하는 문제로 출제됩니다.
  Ms. Patel missed the train, **so** she was unable to attend the weekly meeting.
  Patel 씨는 기차를 놓쳐서 주간 회의에 참석할 수 없었다.

- so가 연결하는 두 절의 관계는 앞의 절이 원인, 뒤의 절이 결과가 되어야 합니다. 위의 예문에서도 열차를 놓친 것이 회의에 참석할 수 없는 이유가 됩니다.

- so는 단어나 구는 연결할 수 없습니다.

4 등위접속사 so vs. 부사절 접속사 because

- 등위접속사 so와 부사절 접속사 because는 둘 다 연결하는 두 절의 내용이 인과 관계를 나타냅니다. 하지만 원인과 결과를 의미하는 절의 위치가 다르기 때문에 이를 구분하는 문제가 출제됩니다.

- 등위접속사 so는 앞절에 원인, 뒷절에 결과가 위치합니다.
  Her flight was delayed for two hours, **so** Ms. Turner was not able to make it to
  <u>원인</u>   <u>결과</u>
  the conference in time.
  비행기가 2시간 동안 지연되어서, Turner 씨는 학회에 제시간에 도착할 수 없었다.

- 부사절 접속사 because는 because가 이끄는 부사절의 내용이 원인, 주절에 결과가 위치합니다.
  Ms. Turner was not able to make it to the conference in time **because** her flight
  <u>결과</u>   <u>원인</u>
  was delayed for two hours.
  Turner 씨는 학회에 제시간에 도착할 수 없었는데, 비행기가 2시간 동안 지연되었기 때문이다.

- because가 이끄는 부사절은 주절 앞/뒤에 모두 위치할 수 있지만, 등위접속사 so가 이끄는 절은 주절 뒤에만 올 수 있습니다.

🔒 **확인 문제 ❸**

You are a current member,
------- you will be eligible
for this free item.

(A) so
(B) when

🔒 **확인 문제 ❹**

The company cut the
travel budget, ------- we
have to rent a compact
car.

(A) because
(B) so

정답 ❸ (A) ❹ (B)

PART 5 문법 등위접속사와 상관접속사　359

적용 기술

[기적의 필기노트] 141P
RC 기술 56

출제 포인트

상관접속사 both A and B와 전치사구 between A and B를 구분하는 문제가 출제되며, between A and B는 전치사 구문임을 명심해야 합니다.

🔒 확인 문제 ❺

He accessed his e-mail account neither from his computer in the office ------ his mobile devices.

(A) or
(B) nor

(정답) ❺ 정답 (B)

출제 유형 2

상관접속사

1 상관접속사의 종류

· 상관접속사는 항상 서로 알맞은 짝을 찾는 문제로 출제되므로 **짝을 맞춰 암기**해야 합니다.

· 상관접속사에서 **A와 B는 대등한 구조**여야 합니다.

| 상관접속사의 종류 |

both A and B A와 B 모두	either A or B A 또는 B 중 하나
neither A nor B A도 B도 아닌	not A but B A가 아닌 B
not only A but (also) B = B as well as A A뿐만 아니라 B도	

Ms. Ann is teaching yoga classes for **both** beginner **and** intermediate students.
Ann 씨는 초급과 중급 학생들을 모두를 위한 요가 수업을 가르치고 있다.

You can reserve **either** Meeting Room A **or** Main Conference Room for the client meeting. 클라이언트 미팅을 위해 A 회의실 또는 메인 컨퍼런스룸을 예약할 수 있습니다.

· not only A but also B의 구문에서 also는 생략할 수 있습니다.
Mr. Harley organized **not only** the opening ceremony **but (also)** the panel discussion. Harley 씨는 개회식뿐만 아니라 패널 토론도 기획했다.

900+

2 상관접속사의 수 일치

· both A and B + 복수 동사
· either A or B → B에 수 일치
· neither A nor B → B에 수 일치
· not only A but (also) B → B에 수 일치
· B as well as A → B에 수 일치
· not A but B → B에 수 일치

등위접속사와 상관접속사

1. There was very high volume of survey data collected, ------- Mr. Harris hired additional assistants.

(A) where (B) here (C) nor (D) so

수집한 설문조사 자료가 너무 많아서, Harris 씨는 조수를 추가로 고용했다.

> **✔ 이렇게 풀어요**
>
> **1. 선택지 보고 문법/어휘 문제 파악** 선택지가 다양한 품사의 어휘로 구성되어 있으므로 문법 문제임을 파악해요.
> **2. 빈칸 분석** 빈칸 앞뒤에 완전한 절이 있으므로 빈칸에는 접속사가 들어가야 함을 파악합니다.
> **3. 정답 선택** 빈칸 앞 절의 내용이 원인, 뒤의 절의 내용이 결과이므로 인과 관계를 나타내는 등위접속사 (D) so를 정답으로 고릅니다.

2. ------- Ms. Cleveland and her team members are required to participate in the on-the-job training.

(A) Both (B) Either (C) Neither (D) Not only

Cleveland 씨와 그녀의 팀원들 모두 현장 실습 트레이닝에 참가해야 합니다.

> **✔ 이렇게 풀어요**
>
> **1. 선택지 보고 문법/어휘 문제 파악** 선택지가 다양한 품사의 어휘로 구성되어 있으므로 문법 문제임을 파악해요.
> **2. 빈칸 분석** 빈칸 뒤에 A and B의 구조가 있음을 파악합니다.
> **3. 정답 선택** 상관접속사 both A and B를 완성하는 (A) Both를 정답으로 고릅니다.

3. The new printer is connected to the company network, so it can be controlled either manually or -------.

(A) remote (B) remotely (C) remoteness (D) remotes

새 프린터가 회사 네트워크에 연결되었으니, 수동으로 또는 원격으로 조정할 수 있습니다.

> **✔ 이렇게 풀어요**
>
> **1. 선택지 보고 문법/어휘 문제 파악** 선택지가 형용사/명사인 remote의 파생어로 구성되어 있으므로 문법 문제임을 파악해요.
> **2. 빈칸 분석** 빈칸 앞에 either와 or가 있으므로 either A or B의 구조를 완성시켜야 함을 파악합니다.
> **3. 정답 선택** or 앞에 부사 manually가 있으므로 이와 같은 품사인 부사 (B) remotely를 정답으로 고릅니다.

PART 5 문법 등위접속사와 상관접속사

PART 5 어휘

부사 어휘 (1)

각 어휘와 함께 자주 쓰이는 표현을 통째로 외워두세요.

01 fully — 완전히, 충분히

- fully refundable — 전액 환불이 가능한
- fully equipped — 완전히 갖춰진
- fully furnished — 가구가 완비된

02 separately — 따로따로, 별도로

- separately from — ~와는 별도로
- be paid separately — 별도로 지불되다

03 largely — 주로

- largely due to — 주로 ~ 때문에
- consist largely of — 주로 ~로 이루어지다

04 quarterly — 분기별로

- change quarterly — 분기별로 바뀌다
- quarterly report — 분기별 보고서
- quarterly sales — 분기별 매출

800+ 🐾빈출 토익 선생님 Pick!
05 potentially — 잠재적으로

- potentially hazardous/dangerous — 잠재적으로 위험한

06 promptly — 지체 없이, 즉시

- handle promptly — 즉시 처리하다
- respond promptly to — ~에 즉시 대응하다

07 widely — 널리, 폭넓게

- widely used — 널리 사용되는
- widely known/acknowledged — 널리 알려진/인정받은

🐾빈출 토익 선생님 Pick!
08 primarily — 주로

- made primarily of — 주로 ~로 만든
- primarily focus on — 주로 ~에 초점을 맞추다

🐾빈출 토익 선생님 Pick!
09 steadily — 꾸준히

- steadily decrease/increase — 꾸준히 감소하다/증가하다
- proceed steadily — 꾸준히 진행하다
- grow/rise steadily — 꾸준히 성장하다/오르다

10 regularly — 정기적으로, 규칙적으로

- meet regularly (with) — (~을) 정기적으로 만나다
- regularly check — 정기적으로 점검하다

11 quickly — 빠르게

- react quickly to — ~에 빠르게 반응하다
- respond quickly to — ~에 빠르게 대응하다

800+
12 traditionally — 전통적으로

- traditionally held — 전통적으로 열리는
- traditionally known as — 전통적으로 ~로 알려진

🐾빈출 토익 선생님 Pick!
13 markedly — 현저하게, 두드러지게

- become markedly better — 현저히 좋아지다
- markedly successful — 현저하게 성공한

14 mutually — 서로, 상호 간에

- mutually beneficial — 서로에게 득이 되는
- mutually acceptable — 상호 간에 용인되는
- mutually agreed — 상호 합의된

362 기적의 토익 RC

15 precisely
바로, 정확히

precisely at 시각   ~시 정각에
follow the instructions precisely   지시를 정확히 따르다

16 efficiently
능률적으로, 효율적으로

work efficiently   능률적으로 일하다
function efficiently   능률적으로 작동하다

🐾 빈출 토익 선생님 Pick!
17 highly
대단히, 매우

speak highly of   ~을 대단히 칭찬하다
highly efficient   고성능의, 매우 효율적인
highly qualified   자격을 충분히 갖춘
highly recommended   매우 추천되는

18 formally
공식적으로, 형식적으로

dress formally   정장을 차려입다
formally announced   공식적으로 발표된
formally appointed   공식적으로 임명된

19 exclusively
독점적으로

be available exclusively to   ~만 독점적으로 이용이 가능한
work exclusively with   ~와만 일하다

20 heavily
심하게, 아주 많이

rain heavily   비가 많이 오다
heavily damaged   크게 손상된
rely heavily on   ~에 크게 의존하다

🐾 빈출 토익 선생님 Pick!
21 conveniently
편리하게, 알맞게

conveniently located   편리한 위치에 있는
conveniently situated   편리한 위치에 있는
reach 장소 more conveniently   ~에 더 편리하게 도달하다

`800+`
22 readily
손쉽게, 순조롭게

readily available   쉽게 이용할 수 있는
readily agreed   흔쾌히 수락한
readily accessible   쉽게 접근할 수 있는, 쉽게 입수 가능한

23 easily
쉽게

easily find the information   쉽게 정보를 찾다
easily accessible   쉽게 접근 가능한
be easily seen   쉽게 보이다

`800+`
24 partly
부분적으로, 어느 정도

partly responsible for   ~에 부분적으로 책임이 있는
partly the result of   부분적으로 ~의 결과

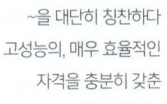 **풀이 방법**

The vegetarian dish at Grover's Diner is ------- recommended by local food critics.

(A) quickly   (B) highly   (C) promptly   (D) separately

Grover's Diner의 채식주의자를 위한 요리는 지역의 음식 평론가들에 의해 매우 추천된다.

> 💧 이렇게 풀어요
>
> **1. 선택지 보고 문법/어휘 문제 파악** 선택지가 서로 다른 부사 어휘로 구성되어 있으므로 어휘 문제임을 파악해요.
> **2. 빈칸 분석** 빈칸 뒤의 recommended와 문맥상 잘 어울리는 동사가 들어가야 함을 파악합니다.
> **3. 정답 선택** be highly recommended의 형태로 자주 쓰이는 (B) highly를 정답으로 고릅니다.

PART 5 어휘 부사 어휘 (1)   363

따라 하면 문제가 풀리는

연습 문제

앞서 학습한 문제 풀이법을 적용하여 맞는 것에 ✔ 표시 하거나 괄호 안에
적절한 답을 쓰고 정답을 선택하세요.

01 My order was shipped out late ------- arrived on the expected date.

(A) despite
(B) but
(C) even
(D) nearly

1. 선택지 보고 문법/어휘 문제 파악하기 ☐문법 문제 ☐어휘 문제
2. 빈칸 분석하기　빈칸 앞에 있는 것 ☐완전한 절 ☐불완전한 절
　　　　　　　　빈칸 뒤에 있는 것 ☐부사 ☐동사
　　　　　　　　→ 빈칸에는 ☐전치사 ☐부사 ☐접속사가 들어가야 한다.
3. 정답 선택하기　정답 (　　　)

02 Mr. Singleton is going on vacation, ------- Ms. Jensen will cover for him.

(A) because
(B) so
(C) to
(D) before

1. 선택지 보고 문법/어휘 문제 파악하기 ☐문법 문제 ☐어휘 문제
2. 빈칸 분석하기　빈칸 앞에 있는 것 ☐완전한 절 ☐불완전한 절
　　　　　　　　빈칸 뒤에 있는 것 ☐완전한 절 ☐불완전한 절
　　　　　　　　→ 빈칸에는 ☐전치사 ☐접속사가 들어가야 한다.
　　　　　　　　→ 빈칸 앞뒤 내용의 관계 ☐원인과 결과 ☐상반되는 내용
3. 정답 선택하기　정답 (　　　)

03 You can contact us by ------- sending an e-mail or calling our 24-7 hotline.

(A) almost
(B) and
(C) either
(D) which

1. 선택지 보고 문법/어휘 문제 파악하기 ☐문법 문제 ☐어휘 문제
2. 빈칸 분석하기　빈칸 뒤에 있는 접속사 (　　　)
　　　　　　　　→ 위의 것과 짝을 이루어 상관접속사를 완성하는 것이 정답
3. 정답 선택하기　정답 (　　　)

♀ 정답 및 해설 p.124

04 Due to construction, neither the Main Street ------- the Houston Avenue entrances are accessible.

(A) nor
(B) and
(C) or
(D) but

1. 선택지 보고 문법/어휘 문제 파악하기 ☐문법 문제 ☐어휘 문제

2. 빈칸 분석하기 빈칸 앞에 있는 상관접속사의 일부 표현 (   )
　　　　　　　　→ 위의 것과 짝을 이루어 상관접속사를 완성하는 것이 정답이다.

3. 정답 선택하기 정답 (   )

05 The new office building is ------- located close to the subway station.

(A) mutually
(B) readily
(C) conveniently
(D) exclusively

1. 선택지 보고 문법/어휘 문제 파악하기 ☐문법 문제 ☐어휘 문제

2. 빈칸 분석하기 빈칸 뒤에 있는 동사 (   )
　　　　　　　　→ 의미 (   )
　　　　　　　　→ 이 동사와 함께 쓰이는 부사가 정답이다.

3. 정답 선택하기 정답 (   )

06 Travel Trunk's suitcases are known for being durable and ------- to carry.

(A) light
(B) lightly
(C) lights
(D) lighting

1. 선택지 보고 문법/어휘 문제 파악하기 ☐문법 문제 ☐어휘 문제

2. 빈칸 분석하기 and 앞에 있는 단어의 품사 ☐명사 ☐형용사
　　　　　　　　→ 빈칸에는 ☐부사 ☐형용사가 들어가야 한다.

3. 정답 선택하기 정답 (   )

PART 5 등위접속사와 상관접속사 / 부사 어휘 (1)　365

DAY 01~15 누적 문제

제한시간 9분입니다! 시~작!

01. Ms. Carr has an impressive educational
background, ------- she would be a great asset
to the Research Division.
(A) in
(B) so
(C) when
(D) regarding

02. To make up for the inconvenience, we offer
you ------- free shipping or 15% off your next
order.
(A) some
(B) either
(C) as
(D) toward

03. The ideal candidate would have at least
three years of experience ------- excellent
communication skills.
(A) therefore
(B) nor
(C) as well
(D) and

04. Hopewell Auto Manufacturing's stock value is
expected to continue rising -------.
(A) steadily
(B) exclusively
(C) partly
(D) formally

05. Many colleagues find Nick Gruber's
leadership to be ------- and passionate.
(A) strong
(B) strongly
(C) strength
(D) strongest

06. All of the meals on the menu at Maison de
Marseille are served with ------- soup and
salad.
(A) also
(B) unless
(C) both
(D) neither

07. Anyone with a degree in finance ------- a
related field is encouraged to apply for the job.
(A) at
(B) or
(C) for
(D) until

08. During the upcoming marathon race,
neither buses ------- trams will operate in the
downtown area.
(A) nor
(B) but
(C) and
(D) or

09. Qualified candidates are encouraged to
submit their applications ------- so as not to
miss the deadline.
(A) fully
(B) separately
(C) promptly
(D) primarily

10. All applications ------- for the job opening at
Bartlett Legal will be personally reviewed by
Jen Bartlett.
(A) submitting
(B) to submit
(C) submitted
(D) submission

11. Steward Tech removed unnecessary security
measures, ------- to let its employees work
more efficiently.
(A) prefers
(B) to prefer
(C) preference
(D) preferring

12. Upon ------- your advanced carpentry courses,
the certificate will be issued.
(A) complete
(B) completed
(C) completing
(D) completion

366   기적의 토익 RC

13. Most residents objected to ------- an additional power plant on the outskirts of Cunningham.

(A) construct
(B) construction
(C) constructed
(D) constructing

14. For more testimonials from former seminar attendees or ------- for the next workshop, please visit our training center's Web page.

(A) registering
(B) to register
(C) register
(D) registered

15. After she reviews all of the applicants' résumés, Ms. Estes ------- which people to interview.

(A) had decided
(B) will decide
(C) decided
(D) decides

16. The mayor of Harrington suggested planting trees ------- Sunset Highway.

(A) along
(B) inside
(C) through
(D) forward

17. People are afraid of getting injured on a ride at Louisville Theme Park, but it only happened -------.

(A) once
(B) for
(C) at
(D) ever

18. Please use the tablet at your table, instead of calling a server, if ------- are ready to order.

(A) your
(B) yours
(C) yourself
(D) you

19. Employees will receive overtime compensation in the form of a check that is issued -------.

(A) quarterly
(B) conveniently
(C) typically
(D) largely

20. The Management Skills Workshop includes not only lectures ------- hands-on exercises.

(A) as if
(B) aside from
(C) on top of
(D) but also

21. Willingboro Industries ------- holds focus group sessions, so their products are reviewed by customers before being mass produced.

(A) mutually
(B) readily
(C) abruptly
(D) regularly

22. It is important to follow application guidelines ------- to avoid being disqualified.

(A) potentially
(B) precisely
(C) efficiently
(D) traditionally

23. Mr. Henderson will be working at our office from now on, ------- please help him feel welcome here.

(A) so
(B) then
(C) once
(D) ever

24. The company's new marketing strategy is ------- different from what it had been in the past.

(A) separately
(B) mutually
(C) securely
(D) markedly

PART 6

접속부사 - 첨가

보기에 전치사, 부사, 접속사가 같이 나오면 우선 문장 구조 분석을 통해 적절한 것을 골라낸 후, 앞뒤 문맥을 파악합니다.

✎ 적용 기술

[기적의 필기노트] 163P
RC 기술 81

🗂 VOCA

convenience store 편의점
a good deal of 많은
concern 우려
eating habit 식습관
reduce 줄이다
latest 최신의

 풀이 방법   press release   ♀ 해석 p.127

We here at Donut Delight have always been known for making delicious donuts. They are available in ------- major supermarkets and most convenience stores
                                    🔩 PART 5
across the country. However, this coming April, we are going to introduce some healthier food options. There has been a good deal of concern about the eating habits of our culture. As a company that truly cares about its customers, Donut Delight will now offer healthy foods such as whole grain muffins. -------, we have
                                                                            01.
changed our original recipe to reduce the amount of fat and sugar in our donuts by 10%. Now you can feel better about enjoying our products. Visit your local supermarket today to experience our latest flavors!

01.　(A) Moreover
　　　(B) Instead
　　　(C) Unless
　　　(D) Despite

핵심 포인트
첨가의 의미를 갖는 접속부사
besides 게다가
moreover 게다가
furthermore 더욱이
in addition 게다가
also 또한

📎 이렇게 풀어요

1. **선택지 보고 문법/어휘 문제 파악** 선택지가 부사, 접속사, 전치사로 구성되어 있으므로 문법 문제임을 파악해요.

2. **빈칸 분석** 빈칸 뒤에 콤마가 있고, 그 뒤에 완전한 절이 있으므로 접속사인 (C)와 전치사인 (D)는 답에서 제외시킵니다. 앞 내용에서 Donut Delight가 건강한 음식을 제공할 것이라고 했고, 빈칸 뒤에서 지방과 설탕의 양을 줄이기 위해 레시피를 변경했다고 했으므로 건강한 음식을 제공하는 것의 연장선상에서 행한 일임을 파악합니다.

3. **정답 선택** 내용을 추가할 때 쓰이는 접속부사인 (A) Moreover(게다가)를 정답으로 고릅니다.

♀ 해설

빈칸 뒤에 and가 있으므로 and와 함께 both A and B 구조로 쓰이는 (B)가 정답입니다.

🔩 PART 5 문법 적용 문제

They are available in ------- major supermarkets and most convenience stores across the country.

(A) either　　　　(B) both　　　　(C) neither　　　　(D) not only

368   기적의 토익 RC

따라 하면 문제가 풀리는
연습 문제

빈칸 앞뒤 내용에서 단서가 될 부분을 찾아 표시하세요.
표시한 것을 바탕으로 정답 어휘를 선택하세요.

◯ 정답 및 해설 p.127

01

Welcome to the Hopewell Insurance family! As a premium member, any medical prescriptions you need will be completely covered. -------, 90% of hospital fees will be covered, including overnight stays.

(A) On the other hand　　(B) Moreover

02

The Milford Job Fair will be held at the Milford Community Center from 10 A.M. to 4 P.M. on Saturday, July 3. Job seekers are required to bring multiple copies of their résumés in preparation for on-site interviews. -------, they are encouraged to present any types of references to help appeal to future employers.

(A) Instead　　(B) Furthermore

03

We ask all employees to box up their belongings so that the moving company can bring them to our new office. -------, please assist with cleaning the areas around your workspaces.

(A) However　　(B) In addition

04

Gold Class members receive discounts at airports and select hotels around the country. -------, they get double reward miles when purchasing domestic flight tickets.

(A) Also　　(B) Rather

DAY 15

PART 6 접속부사-첨가　369

토익에 나올
실전 문제

제한시간 4분입니다! 시~작!

Questions 01-04 refer to the following e-mail.

To: Marcus Hill <mhill@eronmail.com>
From: Bull Mountain Hotel
Date: 7 February
Subject: Your stay
Attachment: Facilities

Dear Guest,

We look forward to having you stay here at our hotel next week. There are ------- recent changes to
                                                                              01.
hour hotel we would like to let you know about. The renovation project on our indoor pool is
completed, and it now has a Jacuzzi and a children's pool. It is open from 6 A.M. through 10 P.M.
-------.
02.

-------, our newly added business center is available all day if you stay for any business purposes.
03.
You can use a photocopier, printer, and fax at a ------- fee.
                                                  04.

Thank you in advance for choosing Bull Mountain Hotel. See you next week.

Sincerely,

Bull Mountain Hotel Service Team

유형 적용 문제

01. (A) each
    (B) a few
    (C) much
    (D) another

03. (A) After all
    (B) Without
    (C) Unless
    (D) Also

02. (A) Extra towels are available at the front desk.
    (B) There is an opening for a lifeguard position.
    (C) Catalogues can be accessed online.
    (D) The construction team can only work during the
        day.

04. (A) occasional
    (B) precise
    (C) initial
    (D) nominal

○ 정답 및 해설 p.127

Questions 05-08 refer to the following article.

Air travel just got a little more comfortable thanks to Red Jet Airlines. -------. This allows an extra
05.

two inches of leg room for all passengers. It may not ------- like much, but a little space goes a long
06.

way. It will help to reduce instances when passengers accidentally kick the seat in front of them.

-------, all of the seats have been refitted with soft microfiber cushions to help passengers relax and
07.

fall asleep. Since Red Jet Airlines has expanded its -------, more people will be able to fly in comfort
08.

even in economy class.

유형 적용 문제

05. (A) Air fares have been reduced for the upcoming
holiday season.
(B) Red Jet has removed three rows of seats from
each of its planes.
(C) A flight attendant will demonstrate how to use the
seatbelt.
(D) The safety of our passengers is our top priority.

07. (A) For example
(B) Therefore
(C) Nevertheless
(D) In addition

06. (A) seem
(B) to seem
(C) seeming
(D) had seemed

08. (A) staff
(B) hours
(C) customers
(D) seating

DAY 15

PART 6 접속부사-첨가 371

PART 7

기사 (2) 문화/예술/지역사회 관련 기사 `800+`

기사는 매회 2~3개의 지문이 출제됩니다. 가장 난이도가 높은 유형이므로 마지막에 푸는 것이 효율적입니다.

문화/예술/지역사회에 관련된 기사는 음악, 문학, 미술, 환경 등 다양한 주제로 출제됩니다. 수상 작품 및 작가에 대한 내용이나 지역사회 발전을 위한 프로젝트 등에 관련된 내용이 자주 나옵니다.

문화/예술/지역사회 관련 기사에 자주 출제되는 어휘

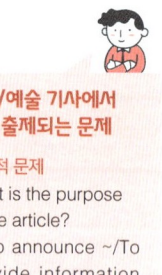

문화/예술 기사에서 자주 출제되는 문제

· 목적 문제
What is the purpose of the article?
→ To announce ~/To provide information ~과 같이 정보를 전달하기 위한 기사와 To encourage people to attend ~와 같이 독자들의 참여를 유도하는 기사가 자주 출제돼요.

1 문화/예술

attraction	관광명소	culinary	요리의
banquet room	연회실	novice	초보자
charity	자선 [단체]	critic	평론가
recognize	인정하다	curator	관장
permanent	영구적인	entry	참가, 출품작
accommodation	숙박시설	perspective	관점
gain popularity	인기를 얻다	winner	수상자
acclaimed	호평받는	diverse	다양한
fiction	소설, 허구	literature	문학
production	(영화, 연극의) 제작	reputation	명성
run	상영; 상영하다	pursue	추구하다

2 지역사회(교통, 건설, 환경 등)

pedestrian	보행자	material	재료
conserve	보호하다, 보존하다	overpass	고가도로
lane	차로	direction	방향
intersection	교차로	highway	고속도로
suburban	교외의	entrance	진입로
congestion	혼잡, 정체	traffic jam	교통 체증
vehicle	차량	speeding	과속
overlook	내려다보다	architect	건축가
hallway	복도, 현관	disruption	붕괴, 중단
landscape	풍경	convert A into B	A를 B로 개조하다
structure	구조물	harmonize	조화를 이루다

문화/예술/지역사회 관련 기사

article

◯ 해석 p.128

Entertainment News

LIVONIA (Sept. 7) — The popular rock group Thunder Head has announced that it is getting back together after they broke up 10 years ago, and will return to the stage with a nationwide tour.

Thunder Head started out 15 years ago and became famous immediately. Their concerts were sold out and two of the albums that they released went triple platinum. However, according to the group's manager, Tim Dawkins, the sudden fame was too much for the musicians to handle.

"All the sudden media attention was too much for them at the time," said Dawkins. "Now that they've worked out problems with each other and had some time to pursue individual studies, they're ready to get back on the road. I'm pleased to announce that they will go back on tour from March to August."

Show tickets will be available on the group's fan page.

01. What is the main purpose of the article?
(A) To summarize a composer's career
(B) To announce a group's reunion
(C) To promote some new songs
(D) To describe a music style

02. According to Mr. Dawkins, what will happen in March?
(A) A group member will get married.
(B) A new album will be released.
(C) A musical tour will start.
(D) Tickets will go on sale.

DAY 15

이렇게 풀어요

01. 기사의 주요 목적은 무엇인가?
(A) 작곡가의 경력을 요약하기 위해서
(B) 그룹의 재결성을 알리기 위해서
(C) 신곡을 홍보하기 위해서
(D) 음악 스타일을 설명하기 위해서

해설 첫 번째 단락에서 The popular rock group ~ announced that it is getting back together라고 했으므로 getting back together를 group's reunion으로 패러프레이징한 (B)가 정답입니다.

02. Dawkins 씨에 따르면, 3월에 무슨 일이 일어날 것인가?
(A) 한 그룹 멤버가 결혼할 것이다.
(B) 새 앨범이 발매될 것이다.
(C) 음악 투어를 시작할 것이다.
(D) 티켓이 판매에 들어갈 것이다.

해설 지문의 키워드 March가 언급된 세 번째 단락에서 tour from March to August라고 했으므로 3월에 투어가 시작할 것임을 알 수 있어요. 따라서 (C)가 정답입니다.

PART 7 기사 (2) 문화/예술/지역사회 관련 기사　373

먼저 문제의 키워드에 표시한 후,
지문에서 단서를 찾아 적절한 답을 고르세요.

01 article

The Leverton Museum of Modern Art has announced plans to postpone the closing date for "Shadows of Time," an exhibition by sculptor Teresa Ashton. —[1]—. It was originally scheduled to run only until February 28 but will now be open to the public for an additional three weeks. The exhibit got off to a slow start, with only 21 people attending the exhibit on the opening day. —[2]—. Local residents, however, soon gained interest in Ashton's sculptures when word spread about her unique sculpting process.

Q. In which of the positions marked [1] and [2] does the following sentence best belong?

"Critics had also written unfavorable reviews about the work."

(A) [1]
(B) [2]

02 article

Concert Hall Renovations Back on Track

Plans to renovate the main auditorium of Platinum Concert Hall are once again underway. —[1]—. Now, thanks to a generous donation from local entrepreneur Andre Desmond, the project can move forward. "We were concerned that we would have to cancel the project altogether," said the hall's manager, Vivian Ross. "Through Mr. Desmond's help, we can make the improvements that we desperately need." —[2]—. The renovations will include replacing worn seats, restoring old woodwork, and adding additional lighting.

Q. In which of the positions marked [1] and [2] does the following sentence best belong?

"The work had been temporarily halted due to a lack of funding."

(A) [1]
(B) [2]

03 article

June 10 — At a ceremony held last night, Chester Burgess accepted the Lifetime Achievement Award from the Hartford Artistic Association (HAA). The award is given every year to an artist, performer, or theater-related worker who is living in Hartford and contributing to the art community. Mr. Burgess is known for his work in costume design, preparing items for Sheridan Theater and other groups for over thirty years. Examples of his work can be found on the HAA Web site at www.haa1.org.

Q. What is suggested about Mr. Burgess?

(A) He is the owner of a theater.
(B) He is a resident of Hartford.

04 article

Westview Port Quarterly Review
April 4

The Port Commissioner has released its quarterly review of Westview Port, and it indicates significant growth. The number of cargo ships using the port has increased by 12% compared to the same time period last year. These ships carry everything from coal and iron to furniture and luxury items. Owing to the growth, Westview Port is on track to become the area's largest source of employment by the end of next year.

Q. What is mentioned about Westview Port in the article?

(A) It is used to transport a variety of goods.
(B) It is located near some train tracks.

토익에 나올 실전 문제

제한시간 12분입니다! 시~작!

Questions 01-04 refer to the following article.

BROOKSVILLE (18 September) — The composer Mary Cornwall and playwright Bob Ballard have come together to create a new show that is taking Brooksville by storm. The musical *Alongside Me* has been such a hit that tickets have already sold out until the end of the show's projected running time in mid-December. —[1]—.

Every good show needs a good stage, and no shortcuts were taken in the preparation of this one. —[2]—. The interior designer Lily O'Hare was hired to design the multiple sets that make up the background. The entire stage was designed to rotate in order to provide seamless transitions between scenes.

The lead role is played by Suzanne Coeur in her debut performance. —[3]—. Her acting and singing ranges are so impressive that she rivals any experienced actress. Several film producers are competing to get her to join their studios.

"I've done my best, and I'm really humbled by how much everyone loves the show," said Ms. Coeur in an interview. "I really look forward to auctioning the things we used on stage for charity on December 23."

A second season of the show is sure to come soon. —[4]—. Once it is announced, expect tickets to sell out quickly.

01. Why was the article written?

(A) To promote a theater
(B) To complain about tickets
(C) To profile a young playwright
(D) To discuss a theatrical performance

02. What is true about *Alongside Me*?

(A) It is a solo performance.
(B) It features rotating sets.
(C) It has won several awards.
(D) It stars an experienced actress.

03. According to the article, what is scheduled to take place on December 23?

(A) The second season of *Alongside Me* will begin.
(B) Some cast members will sign autographs.
(C) Stage props will be auctioned off.
(D) A director will give a speech.

04. In which of the positions marked [1], [2], [3], and [4] does the following sentence best belong?

"This comes as a shock to anyone who has seen the show."

(A) [1]
(B) [2]
(C) [3]
(D) [4]

---

paraphrasing 주어진 어휘 또는 표현과 패러프레이징 될 수 있는 것을 연결하세요.

1. musical ·   · (a) stage props
2. experienced ·   · (b) professional
3. the things we used on stage ·   · (c) theatrical performance

376   기적의 토익 RC

Questions 05-07 refer to the following article.

A Celebration of Creativity in Southfield

May 3 — Topping the work of over one hundred other entries, *Summer Winds*, a poem by Theresa Suarez, took home first place in the 5th Annual Southfield Poetry Contest on Friday. Amateur poets from Southfield submitted their work to the Southfield Public Library throughout April. The entries have been on display at the library for two weeks, and the event culminated in an awards ceremony where the top five winners gave a live reading of their poems, and trophies were distributed. This year, poets were directed to make their creations on the theme of "Nature," whereas previous years did not put any restrictions on the subject matter. Nolan Becker and Altea Santana were awarded second and third place with their submissions *The Blackbird Cries and Sweet River*, respectively.

As this was the fifth year of the event, organizers decided to include the winning poems from the past five years, and those receiving the "Honorable Mention" designation, in a collection of poetry called *Springfield Voices*. This is the first volume in what is expected to be an ongoing series. It will be printed locally and available for sale at the library next month. All proceeds will go toward funding community projects in Southfield.For more information about future activities in the area, visit www.gosouthfield.com/events.

05. What kind of event is discussed in the article?

(A) A writing competition
(B) An annual fundraiser
(C) An art festival
(D) An anniversary party

06. According to the article, what most likely did Ms. Suarez do on Friday evening?

(A) Accepted a cash prize
(B) Read a composition aloud
(C) Assessed the work of others
(D) Participated in an interview

07. What is indicated about *Springfield Voices*?

(A) It was first published five years ago.
(B) It was solely created by Mr. Becker.
(C) It has become a best-seller.
(D) It will be sold starting in June.

---

paraphrasing 주어진 어휘 또는 표현과 패러프레이징 될 수 있는 것을 연결하세요.

1. poetry contest   •
2. gave a live reading of their poems   •
3. available for sale   •

• (a) be sold
• (b) read a composition aloud
• (c) writing competition

 **실전 문제**

Questions 08-12 refer to the following invitation, article, and text message.

The owners and staff of The Lund cordially invite you to

**The Lund Extravaganza
a Ribbon-Cutting Ceremony
on Thursday, May 13, at 3 P.M.**

We are pleased to open our doors and provide luxury accommodations to business travelers.

3 P.M. Cocktail reception at Mountainview Terrace*.
Please present this card, as the event is by invitation only.

4 P.M. Ribbon-Cutting Ceremony and entertainment in the
Crystal Ballroom. Refreshments will be served.

The Lund is located at 5700 Sherman Avenue.
Free parking is available.

*In case of poor weather, the reception
will be moved to the Rose Lounge.

The Lund Keeps Entertainer's Name Under Wraps

MAY 11 — The Lund Extravaganza will take place in just a few days, and while the entertainer for the main performing act is settled, information about who it is has been a heavily guarded secret. "We thought that keeping the name undisclosed would be a way to build interest and intrigue in our event," said The Lund Manager Stefan Berg. "But we are sure that everyone will be delighted by what we have to offer."

Natalie Palmero, the owner of The Lund, has close family ties to singer Adelaide Sagese, so many speculate that she will be the mystery guest. As the guest list is restricted to invitees only, it would not be surprising if the venue showcased a major star. In addition, comedian Jerry Dunston is in town for a number of gigs but has nothing listed on his Web site for Thursday evening. His quirky humor might be the right fit for the young business professionals that The Lund seeks to attract. DJ Raghu Nayar was also spotted in the neighborhood earlier today.

The Lund is taking bookings online, and the occupancy rate is already very high. It's likely that people not only want to see what this new facility has to offer — including its expertly manicured gardens and fine dining restaurants — but also they want to take advantage of the introductory rate of just $125 per night.

Thursday, May 15, 9:05 A.M.
To: Yun Mao
From: Stefan Berg

It has already started drizzling, and heavier rains are expected later today. We have no choice but to move the reception to our backup site. The main performer is setting up the sound equipment now. I've heard some of the material, and it's hilarious. I think our guests will love this special surprise.

08. What kind of event is scheduled for May 13?

(A) A training seminar
(B) An awards ceremony
(C) A community fundraiser
(D) A grand opening

09. In the article, the word "settled" in paragraph 1, line 2, is closest in meaning to

(A) achieved
(B) finalized
(C) rested
(D) rewarded

10. What is indicated about The Lund?

(A) It was designed by a famous architect.
(B) It is part of a chain of businesses.
(C) It has a well-kept outdoor space.
(D) It is located in the city center.

11. Where will drinks be served initially?

(A) In the Main Lobby
(B) In the Crystal Ballroom
(C) In the Rose Lounge
(D) On the Mountainview Terrace

12. Who most likely will be the special performer at the event?

(A) Natalie Palmero
(B) Adelaide Sagese
(C) Jerry Dunston
(D) Raghu Nayar

---

paraphrasing 주어진 어휘 또는 표현과 패러프레이징 될 수 있는 것을 연결하세요.

1. ribbon-cutting ceremony •
2. has been a heavily guarded secret •
3. expertly manicured gardens •

• (a) has not revealed
• (b) grand opening
• (c) well-kept outdoor space

PART 7 기사 (2) 문화/예술/지역사회 관련 기사   379

'멋진 당신, 오늘도 화이팅'

DAY
16

오늘의 학습 포인트

PART 5. 명사절 접속사
1. 명사절의 역할 – 주어/타동사의 목적어/전치사의 목적어/보어
2. 명사절 접속사의 종류 – that/whether/if/의문사
3. 복합관계대명사 – whoever/whomever/whatever/whichever

PART 6. 접속부사 –인과
보기가 hence, therefore, consequently 등

PART 7. 문자 메시지

2~3 지문 출제. 의도 파악 문제 출제

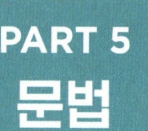

PART 5 문법

명사절 접속사

토익에서 명사절 관련 문제는 빈칸에 알맞은 접속사(that/what/whether 등)를 찾는 문제로 주로 출제돼요.

출제 유형 1
명사절의 역할

⚠ **주의**

명사절 주어는 단수 취급하므로 단수 동사와 쓰여요.

🔒 **확인 문제 ❶**

------- we discussed in the meeting will be sent to you.

(A) Because
(B) What

900+

1 주어 역할

· 명사절은 '명사절 접속사 + 주어 + 동사' 구조이며, 문장에서 명사 역할을 합니다.

· 명사절은 명사와 마찬가지로 **문장의 주어 역할**을 합니다.
What I received from the manager is the tentative schedule for the upcoming
　　명사절 접속사　　　　　　　　　　　　　　　　　　 동사
event. 내가 매니저로부터 받은 것은 다가올 행사에 대한 잠정적인 일정이다.

2 타동사의 목적어/전치사의 목적어 역할

· 명사절은 명사와 마찬가지로 **타동사의 목적어 역할/전치사의 목적어 역할**을 합니다.
The marketing department <u>announced</u> **that the new product will be launched**
　　　　　　　　　　　　　　 타동사
as scheduled.
마케팅 부서에서 신상품이 일정대로 출시될 것이라고 발표했다.

The fees that you have to pay monthly depends <u>on</u> **what service plan you choose.**
　　　　　　　　　　　　　　　　　　　　　　　 전치사
당신이 매달 내야 하는 요금은 어떤 요금제를 선택하느냐에 따라 다르다.

출제 포인트

명사절을 목적어로 갖는 대표 타동사: say, state, announce, mention, explain, report, request, suggest, recommend, propose, expect, predict, specify, know, notice 등

900+

3 보어 역할

· 명사가 보어 역할을 할 수 있듯이 명사절 또한 **주격 보어 역할**을 합니다.
My recommendation is **that the company should reduce the expense for office**
　　　　　　　　　　 be동사
supplies. 제가 권고하는 것은 회사가 사무용품에 대한 지출을 줄여야 한다는 것입니다.

✎ **적용 기술**

[기적의 필기노트] 142P~144P
RC 기술 58, 59, 60

출제 유형 2
명사절 접속사의 종류

🔒 **확인 문제 ❷**

The CEO anticipated ------- the sales will improve next quarter.

(A) and
(B) that

1 명사절 접속사 that

· that이 명사절 접속사로 사용될 경우 **뒤에 완전한 절**이 옵니다.
The company announced **that** the city council approved its proposal.
　　　　　　　　　　　　　　　 주어(the city council)와 목적어(its proposal)를 모두 갖춘 완전한 절
회사는 시 의회가 회사의 제안을 승인했다고 발표했다.

· **목적어 역할**을 하는 명사절을 이끄는 접속사 that은 생략할 수 있습니다.

(B) ❷ (B) ❶ 답정

382　기적의 토익 RC

- 동격 접속사 that으로 사용됩니다.

He realized the fact **that** he was being selfish.

그는 그가 이기적으로 행동하고 있었다는 사실을 깨달았다.

– 동격의 that절을 이끄는 명사: fact, chance, idea, news, possibility, report 등

`800+`

- that절을 취하는 형용사를 알아두세요. → 형용사 또는 that이 빈칸으로 출제돼요.

be aware that ~을 알고 있다	be sorry that ~해서 유감이다	be afraid that ~라니 걱정이다

be certain/convinced/confident/sure that ~을 확신하다

be glad/happy/delighted/pleased that ~라니 기쁘다

- 명사절 접속사 what과 구분하는 문제가 출제되는데, 빈칸 뒤 문장 구조를 분석하여 구분해야 합니다. 'what + 불완전한 절', 'that + 완전한 절'의 문장 구조로 쓰입니다.

The good news is (**that** / ~~what~~) all sales representatives will receive a cash bonus. → 뒤에 완전한 절이 있으므로 that을 써야 합니다.

좋은 소식은 모든 영업사원들이 현금 보너스를 받게 될 것이라는 것이다.

2 명사절 접속사 whether/if

- 명사절 접속사 whether/if가 이끄는 절은 '~인지 (아닌지)'의 의미입니다.

- whether가 이끄는 명사절은 주어, 타동사의 목적어, 전치사의 목적어, 보어 자리에 올 수 있습니다.

- whether가 명사절 접속사로 사용될 경우 뒤에 완전한 절이 옵니다.

The designers will conduct a survey as to **whether** customers are satisfied with
 완전한 절

the new product.

디자이너들은 고객들이 신제품에 만족하는지 그렇지 않은지에 대해 설문조사를 시행할 것이다.

- whether는 or와 함께 'whether A or B(A든지 B든지)', 'whether or not(~할지 말지, ~인지 아닌지)'의 형태로 쓰입니다.

They need to decide **whether** they will renew the rental contract **or** move to a larger office. 그들은 임대 계약을 갱신할지 더 큰 사무실로 이사를 갈지 결정해야 한다.

`800+`

- whether는 'whether to부정사' 또는 'whether or not to부정사' 구조로도 출제됩니다.

I will decide **whether to purchase it or not**. = I will decide **whether or not to purchase it**. 나는 그것을 살지 말지 결정할 것이다.

- 명사절 접속사 if는 타동사의 목적어 자리에만 올 수 있습니다. if는 부사절 접속사로 더 자주 출제돼요.

⚠️ **주의**

that이 이끄는 명사절은 주어, 동사의 목적어, 보어 역할을 하지만, 전치사의 목적어로 쓰일 수는 없어요.

He will share some thoughts on (~~that~~ / **whether**) investing in the stock market is profitable.

🔒 **확인 문제 ❸**

This booklet specifies ------- each staff member should do during the emergency.

(A) that
(B) what

🔒 **확인 문제 ❹**

Mr. Miller is concerned about ------- his department will be reorganized or not.

(A) that
(B) whether

출제 포인트

부사절 접속사 whether와 구분하기

· whether: 명사절 접속사로만 쓰임

· whether ~ or not, whether A or B: 명사절/부사절 접속사로 모두 쓰임

정답 ❸ (B) ❹ (B)

PART 5 문법 명사절 접속사 383

3 의문사

- 명사절 접속사로 쓰이는 의문사는 의문대명사, 의문형용사, 의문부사로 나뉩니다.

의문대명사	who / whom / what / which + 불완전한 절
의문형용사	what / which / whose + 명사 + 불완전한 절
의문부사	when / where / how / why + 완전한 절

Ms. Holland will decide **which** is more appropriate for her client.

→ which가 명사절의 주어 역할을 하므로 뒤에 주어가 생략된 불완전한 절이 와요.

Holland 씨는 그녀의 고객에게 어떤 것이 더 적합한지 결정할 것이다.

The department members will discuss **whose proposal** they will choose.

→ whose proposal이 타동사 choose의 목적어 역할을 하므로 뒤에 목적어가 생략된 불완전한 절이 와요.

부서 구성원들은 누구의 제안서를 선택할지 논의할 것이다.

This document explains **how** the return request should be processed.

→ 의문부사는 주어/목적어/보어와 같은 문장성분이 될 수 없으므로 뒤에 완전한 절이 와요.

이 문서는 반품 요청이 어떻게 처리되어야 하는지를 설명하고 있다.

`800+`

- '의문사 + to부정사'의 형태로 쓰일 수 있습니다.

Employees will learn **how to operate** this system.

직원들은 이 시스템을 어떻게 작동시키는지 배울 것이다.

`출제 유형 3`
복합관계대명사

`900+`
1 복합관계대명사의 종류

whoever(= anyone who) 누구든 간에	whomever(= anyone whom) 누구든 간에
whatever(= anything that) 무엇이든 간에	whichever(= any 명사 that) 어느 것이든 간에

`900+`
2 복합관계대명사의 쓰임

- 복합관계대명사는 명사절 접속사이자 대명사 역할을 하므로 뒤에 불완전한 절이 옵니다.
Whoever wants to attend the retirement party should send an e-mail to my assistant. → Whoever가 동사 wants의 주어 역할을 하므로 뒤에 불완전한 절이 옵니다.

은퇴 파티에 참석하고 싶은 사람은 누구든 간에 내 비서에게 이메일을 보내야 한다.

- **whatever**와 **whichever**는 뒤에 명사가 올 경우 명사를 꾸며주는 **복합관계형용사**로도 쓰입니다.
We will hold a meeting at **whichever** conference room available.

우리는 이용할 수 있는 어느 회의실에서든 회의를 열 것이다.

🔒 확인 문제 ❶

She forgot ------- she started subscribing the *Bahamas Post*.

(A) what
(B) when

⚠️ 주의

복합관계대명사는 '선행사 + 관계대명사'이므로 앞에 선행사가 올 수 없어요.

🔒 확인 문제 ❷

This voucher will be given to ------- is interested in our service.

(A) how
(B) whoever

(B) ❷ (B) ❶ 정답

384 기적의 토익 RC

명사절 접속사

1. During the job fair, you can figure out ------- job seekers prefer your company or not.

(A) both   (B) that   (C) after   (D) whether

취업 박람회 동안, 당신은 구직자들이 당신의 회사를 선호하는지 그렇지 않은지 알 수 있다.

이렇게 풀어요

1. **선택지 보고 문법/어휘 문제 파악** 선택지가 다양한 품사로 구성되어 있으므로 문법 문제임을 파악해요.
2. **빈칸 분석** 빈칸 뒤에 주어와 동사를 갖춘 절이 있으므로 빈칸에는 접속사가 들어가야 함을 파악합니다.
3. **정답 선택** 빈칸부터 문장 끝까지가 본동사이자 타동사인 figure out의 목적어 역할을 하는 명사절이 되어야 하므로 명사절 접속사 역할을 할 수 있는 (B)와 (D) 중에서 정답을 골라야 하는데, 문장 끝의 or not을 단서로 하여 (D) whether를 정답으로 고릅니다.

2. The art director will determine ------- has to be prepared before the stage rehearsal.

(A) what   (B) that   (C) this   (D) for

미술 감독은 무대 리허설 전에 어떤 것이 준비되어야 하는지 결정할 것이다.

이렇게 풀어요

1. **선택지 보고 문법/어휘 문제 파악** 선택지가 다양한 품사로 구성되어 있으므로 문법 문제임을 파악해요.
2. **빈칸 분석** 빈칸 앞에 동사 determine이 있고 뒤에 동사 has to be prepared가 있으므로 빈칸에는 동사 determine의 목적어 역할을 하는 명사절 접속사가 들어가야 함을 파악합니다.
3. **정답 선택** 명사절 접속사로 쓰이는 (A)와 (B) 중에서 빈칸 뒤에 주어가 없는 불완전한 절이 있으므로 (A) what을 정답으로 고릅니다.

3. The marketing manager will choose ------- will work at the company booth.

(A) many   (B) who   (C) anything   (D) whether

마케팅 부장은 회사 부스에서 누가 일할지 선택할 것이다.

이렇게 풀어요

1. **선택지 보고 문법/어휘 문제 파악** 선택지가 다양한 품사로 구성되어 있으므로 문법 문제임을 파악해요.
2. **빈칸 분석** 빈칸 앞에 본동사 will choose가 있고 빈칸 뒤에 동사 will work를 가진 절이 있으므로 빈칸에는 동사의 목적어 역할을 하는 명사절 접속사가 들어가야 함을 파악합니다.
3. **정답 선택** 명사절 접속사로 쓰이는 (B)와 (D) 중에서 명사절 접속사 역할을 함과 동시에 will work의 주어 역할을 할 수 있는 의문대명사 (B) who를 정답으로 고릅니다.

PART 5 문법 명사절 접속사   385

PART 5 어휘

부사 어휘 (2)

각 어휘와 함께 자주 쓰이는 표현을 통째로 외워두세요.

01 actively   적극적으로, 활발히

actively seeking	적극적으로 찾는
actively involved in	적극적으로 참여하는
participate actively	적극적으로 참가하다

02 newly   새로, 새롭게

newly constructed	새롭게 건축된
newly hired	새로 고용된
newly released	새롭게 출시된

03 permanently   영구적으로

permanently damaged by	~에 의해 영구적으로 손상된
permanently out of stock	영구적으로 품절된

04 closely   면밀히, 밀접하게

examine (more) closely	(더) 면밀히 조사하다
be closely related	밀접하게 연관되어 있다

`800+` 😺 빈출 토익 선생님 Pick!

05 exceptionally   매우, 특별히

exceptionally talented	특별히 재능이 있는
work exceptionally well	매우 효과가 있다

`800+`

06 professionally   직업적으로, 전문적으로

act professionally	전문적으로 연기하다

😺 빈출 토익 선생님 Pick!

07 significantly   상당히, 크게

prices are significantly lower than	~보다 가격이 훨씬 낮다
differ significantly	상당히 다르다

08 generally   일반적으로, 보통

generally prefer	일반적으로 선호하다

09 forcefully   격렬하게

argue forcefully about	~에 대해 격렬히 논쟁하다

10 recently   최근에

recently purchased	최근에 구입된
recently renovated	최근에 수리된
the most recently hired employee	가장 최근에 고용된 직원

11 considerably   많이, 상당히

be reorganized considerably	크게 재편성되다
considerably higher than	~보다 상당히 높은

😺 빈출 토익 선생님 Pick!

12 remarkably   현저히, 매우

remarkably stylish	매우 멋진
remarkably well	대단히 잘

13 diligently   부지런히, 열심히

work diligently	열심히 일하다

14 roughly   대략, 거의

roughly 숫자 people	약 ~명의 사람들

`900+`

15 reportedly   소문에 의하면

be reportedly sold for	소문에 의하면 ~에 팔리다
reportedly due to	소문에 의하면 ~ 때문에

386   기적의 토익 RC

16 finally
마침내

finally solved
마침내 해결된
finally won the contract
마침내 계약을 체결한

17 assertively
단정적으로, 단호히

assertively ask A to부정사
A에게 ~할 것을 단호히 요청하다

18 aggressively
공격적으로

pursue aggressively
공격적으로 추구하다
aggressively searching for employment
활발히 구직 활동을 하다
expand one's business aggressively
사업을 공격적으로 확장하다

❤ 빈출 토익 선생님 Pick!
19 nearly
거의

nearly doubled
거의 두 배가 된
nearly completed
거의 완성된

20 consistently
지속적으로, 끊임없이

address concerns consistently
우려를 끊임없이 제기하다
be consistently late for work
지속적으로 직장에 늦다

21 mistakenly
잘못하여, 실수로

mistakenly deleted
실수로 삭제된

❤ 빈출 토익 선생님 Pick!
22 reasonably
합리적으로

reasonably priced
적절하게 가격이 매겨진

23 smoothly
부드럽게, 순조롭게

be progressing smoothly
순조롭게 진행되고 있다
go smoothly
순탄하게 진행되다

24 specially
특별히, 특히

be specially designed for
~을 위해 특별히 설계되다
focus specially on
~에 특히 중점을 두다

25 randomly
무작위로, 임의로

randomly select
무작위로 선택하다
randomly draw
무작위로 추첨하다

26 greatly
대단히, 크게

differ greatly
크게 다르다
greatly enhance the system
시스템을 크게 향상시키다
benefit greatly from
~에서 크게 이익을 얻다

풀이 방법

Students can now enjoy a variety of afterschool programs thanks to the ------- acquired funding.

(A) newly　　　　(B) highly　　　　(C) roughly　　　　(D) closely

새로 획득한 자금 덕분에 학생들은 이제 다양한 방과 후 프로그램을 즐길 수 있다.

> 이렇게 풀어요
>
> 1. **선택지 보고 문법/어휘 문제 파악** 선택지가 서로 다른 부사 어휘로 구성되어 있으므로 어휘 문제임을 파악해요.
> 2. **빈칸 분석** 빈칸 앞 내용이 '~ 덕분에 이제 방과 후 프로그램을 즐길 수 있다'라는 문맥이므로 빈칸부터 funding까지가 원인에 해당함을 파악합니다.
> 3. **정답 선택** '새로 획득한 자금'이라는 의미가 되는 것이 자연스러우므로 (A) newly를 정답으로 고릅니다.

PART 5 어휘 부사 어휘 (2)

따라 하면 문제가 풀리는

연습 문제

앞서 학습한 문제 풀이법을 적용하여 맞는 것에 ✔ 표시 하거나 괄호 안에
적절한 답을 쓰고 정답을 선택하세요.

01 ------- you need to bring is a recording or note taking device.

(A) After
(B) What
(C) With
(D) Even

> 1. 선택지 보고 문법/어휘 문제 파악하기 ☐ 문법 문제 ☐ 어휘 문제
> 2. 빈칸 분석하기 문장의 본동사 (   ) → 본동사 앞에 동사 need를 가진 절이 있다.
>   → 빈칸에는 ☐ 전치사 ☐ 접속사가 들어가야 한다.
> 3. 정답 선택하기 정답 (   )

02 Mr. Solomon explained ------- the marketing team needs more resources to operate effectively.

(A) around
(B) before
(C) that
(D) much

> 1. 선택지 보고 문법/어휘 문제 파악하기 ☐ 문법 문제 ☐ 어휘 문제
> 2. 빈칸 분석하기 문장의 본동사 (   )
>   빈칸 뒤에 있는 것 ☐ 완전한 절 ☐ 불완전한 절
>   → 빈칸에는 ☐ 전치사 ☐ 접속사가 들어가야 한다.
>   → 빈칸부터 문장 끝까지가 동사의 목적어 역할을 하므로 ☐ 명사절 접속사 ☐ 부사절 접속사가 들어가야 한다.
> 3. 정답 선택하기 정답 (   )

03 Ms. Smith's strength is ------- she has extensive experience working overseas.

(A) some
(B) that
(C) until
(D) only

> 1. 선택지 보고 문법/어휘 문제 파악하기 ☐ 문법 문제 ☐ 어휘 문제
> 2. 빈칸 분석하기 문장의 본동사 (   )
>   빈칸 뒤에 있는 것 ☐ 완전한 절 ☐ 불완전한 절
>   → 빈칸에는 ☐ 전치사 ☐ 접속사가 들어가야 한다.
>   → 빈칸부터 문장 끝까지가 be동사의 보어 역할을 하므로 ☐ 명사절 접속사 ☐ 부사절 접속사가 들어가야 한다.
> 3. 정답 선택하기 정답 (   )

♀ 정답 및 해설 p.133

04 Prof. Duffy will share some thoughts on ------- investing in the stock market is profitable.

(A) since
(B) whether
(C) regarding
(D) though

> 1. 선택지 보고 문법/어휘 문제 파악하기 ☐ 문법 문제 ☐ 어휘 문제
> 2. 빈칸 분석하기 빈칸 앞에 있는 것 ☐ 전치사 ☐ 부사
>   빈칸 뒤에 있는 것 ☐ 완전한 절 ☐ 불완전한 절
>   → 빈칸에는 ☐ 전치사 ☐ 접속사가 들어가야 한다.
>   → 빈칸부터 문장 끝까지가 전치사의 목적어 역할을 하므로 ☐ 명사절 접속사 ☐ 부사절 접속사가 들어가야 한다.
> 3. 정답 선택하기 정답 (   )

05 Caesar's Car Dealer is well known for having ------- priced cars in stock.

(A) remarkably
(B) nearly
(C) smoothly
(D) reasonably

> 1. 선택지 보고 문법/어휘 문제 파악하기 ☐ 문법 문제 ☐ 어휘 문제
> 2. 빈칸 분석하기 빈칸 뒤에 있는 과거분사 (   )
>   → 의미 (   )
>   → 이 과거분사와 짝꿍 표현으로 쓰이는 부사가 정답이다.
> 3. 정답 선택하기 정답 (   )

06 Please indicate ------- you want to work.

(A) what
(B) which
(C) whichever
(D) where

> 1. 선택지 보고 문법/어휘 문제 파악하기 ☐ 문법 문제 ☐ 어휘 문제
> 2. 빈칸 분석하기 문장의 본동사 (   )
>   빈칸 뒤에 있는 것 ☐ 완전한 절 ☐ 불완전한 절
>   → 빈칸에는 ☐ 의문대명사 ☐ 복합관계대명사 ☐ 의문부사가 들어가야 한다.
> 3. 정답 선택하기 정답 (   )

PART 5 명사절 접속사 / 부사 어휘 (2)   389

DAY 01-16 누적 문제

제한시간 9분입니다! 시~작!

01. ------- the Pro Laptop X series will be discontinued or not depends on this year's sales.

(A) Whether
(B) Although
(C) However
(D) Nearly

02. At the meeting tomorrow, our department director will announce ------- will lead this new project.

(A) who
(B) something
(C) when
(D) those

03. Thanks to the use of power tools, production at Dunlap Industrial became ------- faster.

(A) exclusively
(B) potentially
(C) professionally
(D) considerably

04. Temporary workers at the loading zone are allowed to wear ------- they want instead of the company uniforms.

(A) many
(B) whatever
(C) theirs
(D) both

05. ------- should be revised in the book cover is the misspelled name of the writer.

(A) Where
(B) Whoever
(C) Which
(D) What

06. Nikita's Interior Designs is so popular because it understands ------- to keep its clients satisfied.

(A) what
(B) how
(C) behind
(D) until

07. The discussion will be about ------- product is supposed to be advertised first.

(A) anyone
(B) neither
(C) which
(D) every

08. Ms. Fowler is in charge of deciding ------- employees' travel expense reimbursement requests should be approved.

(A) ever
(B) after
(C) during
(D) whether

09. ------- opens the store first should shut off the security alarm and turn on the cash registers.

(A) Whoever
(B) Anyone
(C) Most
(D) They

10. Among the many business banking options available, it is not easy to determine ------- would serve you best.

(A) where
(B) which
(C) how
(D) why

11. Merrimack Flooring works ------- with local suppliers to provide the best recommendations to their customers.

(A) finally
(B) abruptly
(C) closely
(D) heavily

12. Based on ------- a server has worked extra hours, the amount of the end-of-month bonus may vary.

(A) only
(B) following
(C) despite
(D) whether

13. Due to a scheduled regular inspection of company laptops, please bring back ------- ones you checked out by tomorrow.

(A) whichever
(B) whoever
(C) that
(D) as

14. Economists are trying to figure out ------- influenced the drop of the Asian stock market.

(A) then
(B) what
(C) whom
(D) that

15. Horton & Associates will hold its annual awards ceremony at ------- venue can accommodate more than 1,500 people.

(A) some
(B) every
(C) their
(D) whichever

16. A proper research paper should include coauthors' names ------- references to all sources cited in it.

(A) unless
(B) despite
(C) as well as
(D) in advance

17. The sharp rise in the cost of meat ------- Burger Baron to charge more for most of its menu options.

(A) causing
(B) was caused
(C) caused
(D) to cause

18. The itemized table of company spending showed ------- where cuts needed to be made.

(A) exact
(B) exactly
(C) exactness
(D) exacted

19. Lansdale Footwear is ------- seeking competent sales representatives who are willing to work on weekends.

(A) recently
(B) nearly
(C) randomly
(D) actively

20. Mr. Godfrey is wondering ------- Mr. Lang decided to switch suppliers.

(A) why
(B) whom
(C) which
(D) whenever

21. The non-paid interns at Acosta Legal ------- handle office tasks such as typing and photocopying documents.

(A) generally
(B) precisely
(C) suddenly
(D) reasonably

22. The first Monday of each month is ------- the utility bills are sent to customers.

(A) which
(B) why
(C) when
(D) who

23. ------- half of the people who saw *Burning Bridges* say that it was a boring movie.

(A) Smoothly
(B) Newly
(C) Roughly
(D) Specially

24. Some panel members in the public hearing argued ------- about the plan to develop the waterfront area.

(A) mistakenly
(B) forcefully
(C) permanently
(D) traditionally

PART 5 명사절 접속사 / 부사 어휘 (2)   391

PART 6

접속부사 - 인과

보기가 다양한 접속부사 어휘로 구성되어 있으면 앞뒤 문맥을 파악합니다.

적용 기술

[기적의 필기노트] 163P
RC 기술 81

VOCA

transaction 거래
conclude 결론짓다, 판단을 내리다
charge 청구하다
by mistake 실수로
remove 없애다, 제거하다
balance 잔고, 지불 잔액
freeze 동결하다

풀이 방법   letter   해석 p.136

Dear Mr. McBee,

We have reviewed the two transactions of $28.73 on your card that posted on December 9, as you requested, and have concluded that you were mistakenly charged twice by mistake. ------, we have cancelled the second one. Also, we
01.

removed the amount of $28.73 from your balance. That is not all. Also, in order to apologize, we have decided to freeze interest on your balance until March. We hope ------ you find this action satisfactory. Our credit company is glad to have you
PART 5

as a customer and looks forward to continuing doing business with you.

Sincerely,

Southfield Credit Customer Service

---

01. (A) Unfortunately
(B) Nevertheless
(C) Hence
(D) Furthermore

핵심 포인트

인과를 나타내는 접속부사
hence 그러므로
therefore/thus 그러므로
consequently 결과적으로
accordingly 그에 따라
as a result 그 결과

이렇게 풀어요

1. **선택지 특징 파악** 선택지가 다양한 접속부사 어휘로 이루어져 있으므로 어휘 문제임을 파악해요.
   (A) 안타깝게도   (B) 그럼에도 불구하고   (C) 그러므로   (D) 게다가

2. **빈칸 분석** '실수로 귀하에게 두 번 청구된 것으로 결론지었습니다. ------, 저희는 두 번째 것을 취소했습니다'
   빈칸 앞에 카드 대금이 두 번 청구되었다는 내용이 있고, 빈칸 뒤에 두 번째 것을 취소했다는 내용이 있으므로 인과 관계를 나타내는 말이 들어가야 함을 파악합니다.

3. **정답 선택** '그러므로'라는 의미의 (C) Hence를 정답으로 선택합니다.

해설

빈칸 뒤에 완전한 절이 있으므로 (A)와 (D)는 답이 될 수 없어요. (C) whether는 문맥상 적절하지 않으므로 (B) that이 정답입니다.

PART 5 문법 적용 문제

We hope ------ you find this action satisfactory.

(A) what   (B) that   (C) whether   (D) even

392   기적의 토익 RC

따라 하면 문제가 풀리는

연습 문제

빈칸 앞뒤 내용에서 단서가 될 부분을 찾아 표시하세요.
표시한 것을 바탕으로 정답 어휘를 선택하세요.

📍 정답 및 해설 p.136

01

Due to a lack of registration, the class ES201 that you signed up for will not be taught this semester. -------, to maintain your full time student status, you must select another 3-credit course.

(A) In contrast

(B) Consequently

02

Some of the artwork that will be sold at the auction is valued at over a million dollars per piece. -------, the most reliable private security has been hired for the event.

(A) For this reason

(B) Additionally

03

The international film festival has drawn more global attention this year than ever before. -------, we highly recommend you book a hotel room in our city in advance.

(A) Therefore

(B) However

04

The mayor of Lorton, Tommy Savage, has announced that the city will be significantly reducing business regulations in the city. -------, several national chains have expressed interest in opening branches in Lorton within the next several months.

(A) As a result

(B) On the contrary

DAY 16

PART 6 접속부사-인과　393

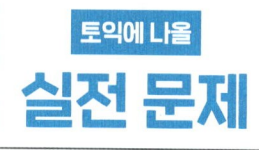

제한시간 4분입니다! 시~작!

Questions 01-04 refer to the following letter.

Houston Home Appliances
3665 Davisson Street
Connersville, IN 47331

30 June

Brianne Wallace
1875 Deer Haven Drive
Greenville, SC 29601

Dear Ms. Wallace,

We regret to inform you that the Swisher 7 model dishwasher has a ------- part in it. We found the
01.
drain hose prone to leaking despite short use. -------, it must be replaced before causing water
02.
damage in your home. All you need to do is contact our service center at 555-1320 to set up an
appointment. We will send a technician to your house at your convenience. -------. We apologize for
03.
this inconvenience. After the technician ------- the work, please visit our Web site to fill out a
04.
customer satisfaction survey. Thank you in advance.

Sincerely,

Houston Home Appliances

---

01. (A) discounted
(B) new
(C) faulty
(D) changeable

유형 적용 문제
02. (A) Apart from
(B) Therefore
(C) Regardless
(D) Still

03. (A) There will be no charge for the installation of the
new hose.
(B) Please return your appliance to the nearest retail
location.
(C) We've scheduled you for the first week of July.
(D) Our products' features are posted on our Web
site.

04. (A) will have completed
(B) is completing
(C) completed
(D) completes

394 기적의 토익 RC

Questions 05-08 refer to the following letter.

December 23

Barry Harper
4160 Pollock Lane
Omaha, NE 68102

Dear Mr. Harper,

Thank you for subscribing to *Airplane Planet* magazine. We ------- to providing the most up-to-date
05.
information about airplanes and aviation. -------. Their experience helps them analyze and
06.
understand new developments in the field of flight. -------, their articles and commentary are all
07.
reliable. If you are interested in ------- to our magazine, please be sure to include your credentials
08.
and any relevant references.

Sincerely,

Airplane Planet Subscription Management

유형 적용 문제

05. (A) commit
    (B) are committed
    (C) have committed
    (D) will commit

07. (A) Despite that
    (B) For this reason
    (C) In part
    (D) Conversely

06. (A) You can renew your subscription by the end of
       this year.
    (B) Please read the membership terms and conditions
       included with this letter.
    (C) All of our contents are written only by current or
       former pilots and airplane designers.
    (D) Your subscription includes access to the digital
       version of our magazine as well.

08. (A) contributing
    (B) contribution
    (C) to contribute
    (D) contributed

PART 6 접속부사-인과   395

PART 7

문자 메시지 `800+`

문자 메시지는 전체적인 지문의 흐름을 파악하며 읽어야 정답 단서를 찾을 수 있어요.

문자 메시지는 급한 상황이나 문제가 발생한 상황에서 부탁을 하거나 업무를 요청하는 내용이 자주 출제됩니다. 토익 1회당 2지문 정도 출제되며 의도 파악 문제가 함께 나옵니다. 지문의 특성상 짧은 구어체 표현들이 많이 포함되어 있습니다.

문자 메시지에서 자주 출제되는 문제

· 의도 파악 문제
→ 주로 업무 요청에 대해 수락 또는 거절하거나 추가 정보를 묻는 문장이 문제로 출제돼요. 정답 선택지에 출제된 아래 표현들을 익혀두세요. have agreed to/accepts/are willing to/will check/contact

문자 메시지에서 자주 출제되는 어휘

still	여전히, 아직	input	의견
almost done	거의 다 한	headquarters	본사
hectic	정신없이 바쁜	head	~로 향하다
be in time	제시간에 도착하다	run out of	~이 다 떨어지다
suitable	적당한	storehouse	창고
Got it.	알겠어요.	reluctant	꺼리는
Certainly.	물론이죠.	figure out	알아보다
in a rush	급하게	exception	예외
manage to부정사	가까스로 ~하다	interest	관심, 흥미
afterward	이후에	reach	연락하다
company newsletter	사보	in-house	사내의
assistance	도움, 보조	timetable	일정표
reschedule	일정을 변경하다	board of directors	이사회
unexpectedly	갑자기	get together	모이다
That's a relief.	다행이네요.	organizing committee	조직 위원회
at short notice	예고 없이, 촉박하게	stop by	~에 들르다
based on	~에 기반하여	run late	늦어지다
business day	영업일	rating	평가, 등급
expire	만료되다	waive	면제하다
workflow	작업 흐름, 작업 속도	slot	자리

396 기적의 토익 RC

문자 메시지

text message chain

○ 해석 p.138

Howard Ball [9:39 A.M.]	Kelly, what's the status of the pamphlets for Fulbright Travel?
Kelly Banks [9:40 A.M.]	They needed two thousand 3-fold ones in black and white, right? We should be done with them by tomorrow morning.
Howard Ball [9:41 A.M.]	They just called and said that they want them in color, not black and white.
Kelly Banks [9:42 A.M.]	Really? We'll have to bring Aaron in on this, then.
Kelly Banks [9:43 A.M.]	Aaron, can your printers complete an order of two thousand 3-folds in color by tomorrow?
Aaron Foster [9:44 A.M.]	I would have to get started on them right away, but yes.
Howard Ball [9:45 A.M.]	Very well. I'll let them know that.

01. What does a client want to do?

(A) Alter a print order

(B) Change an address

(C) Get a partial refund

(D) Upgrade to express shipping

02. At 9:45 A.M., what does Mr. Ball most likely mean when he writes, "Very well"?

(A) He is feeling in good health.

(B) Ms. Banks' application was approved.

(C) A client will be satisfied with a work schedule.

(D) Mr. Foster deserves a promotion for his hard work.

이렇게 풀어요

01. 고객이 원하는 것은 무엇인가?

(A) 인쇄 주문을 변경하는 것

(B) 주소를 변경하는 것

(C) 부분 환불을 받는 것

(D) 특급 배송으로 업그레이드하는 것

해설 Howard Ball의 첫 메시지를 통해 Fulbright Travel이 고객임을 알 수 있습니다. 9시 41분 Howard Ball의 메시지에서 They just called and said that they want them in color, not black and white라고 했으므로 고객이 인쇄 주문 사항을 변경하고 싶어한다는 것을 파악할 수 있어요. 따라서 (A)가 정답입니다.

02. 오전 9시 45분에, Ball 씨가 "Very well"이라고 썼을 때 의도한 바는 무엇일 것 같은가?

(A) 그는 건강함을 느낀다.

(B) Banks 씨의 신청서가 승인되었다.

(C) 고객은 작업 일정에 만족할 것이다.

(D) Foster 씨는 일을 열심히 해서 승진할 만하다.

해설 9시 41분 Howard Ball의 메시지부터 순서대로 확인해 보면, 고객의 주문 변경 요청에 대해 인쇄소의 Aaron에게 가능 여부를 문의했고, Aaron이 가능하다고 했습니다. 따라서 Howard Ball이 "아주 좋아요"라고 한 것은 고객 요청대로 이루어져 고객이 만족할 것이라는 의도를 담고 있으므로 (C)가 정답입니다.

PART 7 문자 메시지 **397**

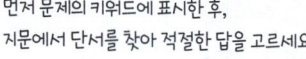

01 text message chain

Earl Ledezma [10:15 A.M.]
We still need one more presenter for the science convention. Any ideas?

Georgia Behrens [10:16 A.M.]
I saw a really interesting talk online by Dr. Jeremiah Otis of Springfield University. He would make a great addition to the schedule. I'm not sure whether he is free on that day, though.

Earl Ledezma [10:17 A.M.]
I'll check on it.

Georgia Behrens [10:18 A.M.]
Thanks. Let's meet later this week to discuss this further.

Q. At 10:17 A.M., what does Mr. Ledezma mean when he writes, "I'll check on it"?

(A) He will try to reserve space for an event at Springfield University.

(B) He will find out whether Dr. Otis is available.

02 text message chain

[1:02 P.M.] Kasumi Yamaoka
Are you back from lunch yet?

[1:03 P.M.] Adam Emerson
Yes, I just got back. Why?

[1:04 P.M.] Kasumi Yamaoka
I need to download and print some studies from the database for this afternoon's meeting, but something is wrong with my password. I keep getting an error message when I type it in.

[1:05 P.M.] Adam Emerson
You can come to my office and use my account in the meantime.

[1:06 P.M.] Kasumi Yamaoka
Thanks! I'll see you soon.

Q. What problem does Ms. Yamaoka mention?

(A) Her password is not working.

(B) The printer is out of ink.

정답 및 해설 p.138

03 text message chain

David Chung [3:09 P.M.]
Have you placed the order for our banners yet?

Corrine Burcham [3:10 P.M.]
Not yet. I just got to the print shop. Traffic is really congested in the downtown area.

David Chung [3:11 P.M.]
Oh, how lucky! I just found out that Ms. Kaster wants to hang banners at all entrances, so we need three of them instead of one.

Corrine Burcham [3:12 P.M.]
I can take care of that. They should all be the same, right?

David Chung [3:13 P.M.]
Yes, that's right. Thanks!

Q. At 3:11 P.M., what does Mr. Chung most likely mean when he writes, "Oh, how lucky"?

(A) He found a better way to avoid the traffic.
(B) He did not miss his opportunity to request a change.

04 text message chain

Giorgio Pirozzi [11:43 A.M.]
I'm here at the Goldcliff Conference Hall. Unfortunately, their ballroom is booked for the day that we went to hold the awards dinner.

Wooseok Lee [11:47 A.M.]
Are there any other rooms available?

Giorgio Pirozzi [11:48 A.M.]
Yes, a small room that can hold about two hundred people. It isn't recently remodeled like the other one, though. Can you come and take a look?

Wooseok Lee [11:49 A.M.]
I'm wrapping things up with Lara Kennedy, our new client, at her office now. I'll be there shortly.

Q. Where does Mr. Lee plan to meet Mr. Pirozzi?

(A) At a conference venue
(B) At a new client's office

PART 7 문자 메시지

토익에 나올

실전 문제

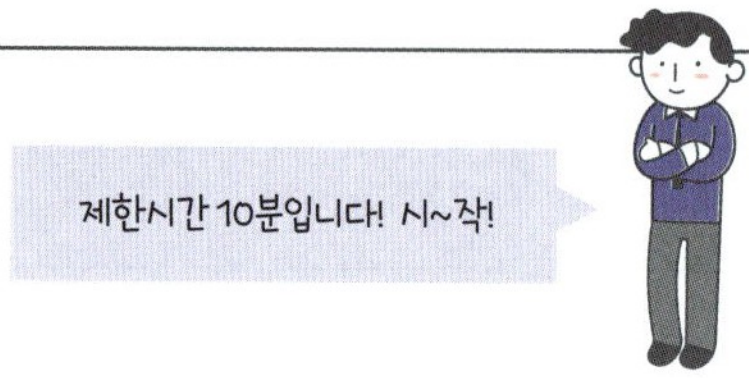

제한시간 10분입니다! 시~작!

Questions 01-02 refer to the following text message chain.

Gary Johnson [4:07 P.M.]
My computer can't connect to the network again. Could you come and have a look at it?

Rachel Morrow [4:08 P.M.]
Sorry, I already left for the training. I won't come back today. I think Vanessa Reynolds should still be in the office, though.

Gary Johnson [4:09 P.M.]
Okay. I'll try getting in touch with her.

Rachel Morrow [4:10 P.M.]
By the way, I heard that everyone on your floor will get new computers soon.

Gary Johnson [4:11 P.M.]
It's about time! Thanks for the good news!

01. What is most likely true about Ms. Morrow?

(A) She works in the IT department.
(B) She normally finishes work at 4 P.M.
(C) She recently installed new equipment.
(D) She is in charge of purchasing office supplies.

02. At 4:11 P.M., what does Mr. Johnson most likely mean when he writes, "It's about time"?

(A) He restored his network connection.
(B) He has been wanting an equipment upgrade.
(C) Ms. Reynolds said that she has no time to meet.
(D) Ms. Morrow is taking too long to respond to a request.

paraphrasing 주어진 어휘 또는 표현과 패러프레이징 될 수 있는 것을 연결하세요.

1. won't come back today •   • (a) available some other day
2. get in touch with •   • (b) set up
3. install •   • (c) contact

400   기적의 토익 RC

◯ 정답 및 해설 p.139

Questions 03-04 refer to the following text message chain.

To: Haley Pearson
From: Clark Rhodes
Sent: Tuesday, 1:32 P.M.

Traffic is congested coming back from my business lunch with Ms. Meyers. I'm in my car now, but I might be a bit late for the group interview for the sales position. Could you greet everyone in the lobby and direct them to Conference Room C? Thanks!

03. What most likely did Mr. Rhodes do at lunchtime?

(A) Sent an e-mail to his colleague
(B) Attended a medical appointment
(C) Got his car fixed
(D) Met with a client

04. What does Mr. Rhodes ask Ms. Pearson to do?

(A) Reschedule a meeting
(B) Speak to a director
(C) Welcome some job candidates
(D) Reserve a conference room

DAY 16

paraphrasing 주어진 어휘 또는 표현과 패러프레이징 될 수 있는 것을 연결하세요.

1. traffic is congested   •   • (a) welcome
2. business lunch with   •   • (b) met with a client
3. greet   •   • (c) there are lots of traffic on the road

PART 7 문자 메시지   401

 **실전 문제**

Questions 05-07 refer to the following text message chain.

Ashley McHale [9:43 A.M.]
Hi, Darrell. Could you do me a favor?

Darrell Lawson [9:46 A.M.] What's up?

Ashley McHale [9:47 A.M.]
I'm showing a group of prospective customers around the gym today at 1 P.M., but I just realized I'm supposed to teach a kickboxing class.

Darrell Lawson [9:53 A.M.]
I'm looking to pick up some extra shifts. What level is it?

Ashley McHale [9:54 A.M.]
Intermediate, and it runs from 1:30 P.M. to 2:30 P.M.

Darrell Lawson [9:55 A.M.] I'm on it.

Ashley McHale [9:56 A.M.] Thanks! I really appreciate it.

Darrell Lawson [9:57 A.M.]
Would it be possible to find out in advance the names of the members who will be in attendance?

Ashley McHale [9:58 A.M.]
Of course. Would you like that e-mailed to you, or should I print out a hard copy?

Darrell Lawson [9:59 A.M.] Whatever is easier for you.

05. Who will take a tour with Ms. McHale today?

(A) Potential members
(B) Corporate investors
(C) Job applicants
(D) Fitness instructors

06. At 9:55 A.M., what does Mr. Lawson most likely mean when he writes, "I'm on it"?

(A) He will review a schedule of work shifts.
(B) He will find some information for Ms. McHale.
(C) He is available to teach an exercise class.
(D) He can confirm that a level is correct.

07. What does Mr. Lawson ask Ms. McHale to do?

(A) Approve an additional payment
(B) Speak to a colleague about a plan
(C) Prepare some promotional materials
(D) Provide information about participants

paraphrasing 주어진 어휘 또는 표현과 패러프레이징 될 수 있는 것을 연결하세요.

1. prospective customers •   • (a) information about participants
2. pick up some extra shifts •   • (b) potential members
3. the names of the members who will be in attendance •   • (c) do more work

402   기적의 토익 RC

Questions 08-10 refer to the following text message chain.

William Emery [11:03 A.M.]
Susan, have you been having any trouble with the database today?

Susan Vaca [11:04 A.M.]
No, it seems to be behaving normally to me. Why do you ask?

William Emery [11:05 A.M.]
I'm trying to finish up the analysis of the footwear market for my summary report. However, when I try to sign in, I keep getting an error message. I know I'm using the correct log-in details and password. I just need to download a copy of files that have the demographics breakdown for our region for the past three years.

Susan Vaca [11:06 A.M.]
I can handle that.

William Emery [11:07 A.M.]
Thanks a lot! That's a big help to me.

Susan Vaca [11:10 A.M.]
Would you like me to send them to you by e-mail?

William Emery [11:11 A.M.]
Actually, I think the file sizes will be far too big for that. I'll just stop by your office with an external hard drive shortly.

---

08. What kind of project is Mr. Emery working on?

(A) A footwear design
(B) A database upgrade
(C) An employee evaluation
(D) A research document

09. At 11:06 A.M., what does Ms. Vaca agree to do when she writes, "I can handle that"?

(A) She will reset Mr. Emery's password.
(B) She will print copies of a contract.
(C) She will download some files.
(D) She will contact the IT department.

10. What does Mr. Emery plan to do soon?

(A) Get his computer checked
(B) Give a presentation
(C) Read an e-mail from Ms. Vaca
(D) Visit Ms. Vaca in person

---

paraphrasing 주어진 어휘 또는 표현과 패러프레이징 될 수 있는 것을 연결하세요.

1. handle •   • (a) deal with
2. stop by your office •   • (b) soon
3. shortly •   • (c) visit in person

PART 7 문자 메시지 403

'멋진 당신, 오늘도 화이팅'

DAY
17

오늘의 학습 포인트

PART 5. 형용사절 접속사
1. 관계대명사의 역할과 종류 - who/whom/which/whose 등
2. 관계대명사 that의 특징 - 콤마나 전치사 뒤에 X, 뒤에 불완전한 절
3. 관계대명사의 쓰임 - 전치사 + 관계대명사/수량 표현 + of + 관계대명사
4. 관계부사 - when/where/why/how + 완전한 절

PART 6. 접속부사 -역접
보기가 nevertheless, however, nonetheless 등

PART 7. 온라인 채팅
2지문 가량 출제. 의도 파악 문제 출제

PART 5 문법

형용사절 접속사

각 관계대명사가 들어가는 자리를 알아두세요. 소유격 관계대명사가 자주 출제돼요.

✎ 적용 기술

[기적의 필기노트] 145P~146P
RC 기술 61, 62, 63

출제 유형 1

관계대명사의 역할과 종류

1 선행사에 따른 관계대명사의 종류

선행사 \ 격	주격	목적격	소유격
사람	who	whom/who	whose
사물	which	which	whose
사람/사물	that	that	whose

⚠ 주의

빈칸 뒤에 오는 절이 목적어가 없는 불완전한 절인지 여부를 판단하기 위해서는 동사가 타동사인지 아닌지 판단할 수 있어야 해요.

- **주격 관계대명사** 뒤에는 주어가 없는 **불완전한 절**이 옵니다.
  Ms. Abbot is a new graphic designer **who** will work at the company booth.
  Abbot 씨는 회사 부스에서 일하게 될 새 그래픽 디자이너입니다.

- **목적격 관계대명사** 뒤에는 목적어가 없는 **불완전한 절**이 옵니다.
  Mr. Byron is an award-winning fashion designer **whom** I invited as a keynote speaker.
  Byron 씨는 제가 기조 연설자로 초대한 수상경력이 있는 패션 디자이너입니다.

- **소유격 관계대명사**는 형용사절 접속사 역할과 동시에 소유격 역할을 하기 때문에 반드시 **뒤에 명사**가 와야 합니다.
  She met Paul Jenson **whose** old painting she purchased on a flea market.
  그녀는 Paul Jenson을 만났는데 그녀는 그의 오래된 그림을 벼룩시장에서 구입했다.

2 관계대명사의 생략

- **목적격** 관계대명사는 **생략**할 수 있습니다.
  Mr. Hampton is one of the clients **(whom)** I met in Tokyo last month.

- **'주격 관계대명사 + be동사'**는 **생략**할 수 있습니다. 이 경우 선행사 뒤에 바로 형용사나 분사가 옵니다.
  Maria finally received her order **(which was)** placed last month.
  Maria는 마침내 지난달 주문했던 상품을 수령했다.

🔒 확인 문제 ❶

She downloaded a computer software ------- serial numbers she received by e-mail.

(A) which
(B) whose

(B) ❶ 정답

406 기적의 토익 RC

출제 유형 2

관계대명사 that의 특징

`800+`

· 관계대명사 that은 **콤마**나 **전치사** 뒤에 올 수 없습니다.
Ms. Cumberland owns a seafood restaurant, (~~that~~ / **which**) is popular among local residents. Cumberland 씨는 지역 주민들 사이에서 인기 있는 해산물 식당을 소유하고 있다.

Event participants are asked to visit the reception desk at (~~that~~ / **which**) their parking gets validated. 행사 참가자들은 접수 데스크에서 주차 확인을 받아야 합니다.

· who, whom, which 대신 that을 쓸 수 있습니다. 단, whose를 대신해서는 쓸 수 없어요.

· 명사절 접속사 that 뒤에는 완전한 절이 오지만, 관계대명사 that 뒤에는 불완전한 절이 옵니다.
The manager announced **that** the meeting was canceled.
　　　　　　　　　　　　명사절 접속사　　　　　완전한 절
매니저는 회의가 취소되었다고 알렸다.

The manager approved the proposal **that** I submitted.
　　　　　　　　　　　　　　　　관계대명사　불완전한 절
매니저는 내가 제출한 제안서를 승인했다.

출제 유형 3

관계대명사의 쓰임

`800+`

1 전치사 + 관계대명사

· 결합하는 두 문장의 공통 명사가 뒷문장에서는 전치사의 목적어로 쓰였을 때 '전치사 + 관계대명사' 형태로 두 문장을 연결할 수 있습니다.
I found **the box**. + I had put some documents in **the box**.
나는 상자를 찾았다. + 나는 몇몇 서류를 상자 안에 넣어두었다.
→ I found the box **which** I had put some documents **in**.
→ I found the box **in which** I put some documents.
나는 몇몇 서류를 넣어두었던 상자를 찾았다.

· '전치사 + 관계대명사' 뒤에는 완전한 절이 옵니다.

`900+`

2 수량 표현 + of + 관계대명사

· '수량 표현 + of' 뒤에 관계대명사가 위치하기 위해서는 반드시 절이 2개 이상 있고, 접속사가 없어야 합니다.
We have 20 members, all of (**whom** / ~~them~~) are interested in investing in the project. 우리는 20명의 구성원들이 있고, 그들 모두 그 프로젝트에 투자하는 것에 관심이 있다.
　→ 절이 2개 있고 접속사가 없기 때문에 대명사 them은 올 수 없어요. 따라서 앞의 members를 선행사로 하는 관계대명사 whom이 정답입니다.

· '수량 표현 + of' 뒤에 오는 관계대명사는 수량 표현 앞 선행사가 사람이면 whom, 사물이면 which를 씁니다.

선행사, + all/most/some/any/half/many + of + whom 또는 which

적용 기술

[기적의 필기노트] 147P
RC 기술 64

🔒 **확인 문제 ❷**

Terry is one of the applicants, ------- worked as an intern two years ago.

(A) who
(B) that

출제 포인트
관계대명사 앞에 들어갈 전치사를 묻거나, 전치사 뒤에 들어갈 관계대명사를 묻는 형태로 출제돼요.

🔒 **확인 문제 ❸**

He is searching a commercial property ------- he will open a new restaurant.

(A) that
(B) at which

🔒 **확인 문제 ❹**

I reviewed five proposals, two of ------- meet our need.

(A) them
(B) which

정답 ❷ (A) ❸ (B) ❹ (B)

DAY 17

PART 5 문법 형용사절 접속사　407

적용 기술

[기적의 필기노트] 148P
RC 기술 65

⚠ 주의

관계부사 how는 선행사 the way와 함께 쓸 수 없어요.

🔒 확인 문제 ⑤

The charity party ------- Mr. Smith hosted was quite successful.

(A) which
(B) where

출제 유형 4
관계부사

1️⃣ 선행사에 따른 관계부사의 종류

선행사	관계부사
시간을 나타내는 명사(the time, the day 등)	when
장소를 나타내는 명사(the place, the building 등)	where
이유를 나타내는 명사(the reason)	why
방법을 나타내는 명사(the way)	how

· 관계부사는 형용사절 접속사 역할과 동시에 부사 역할을 하므로 **뒤에 완전한 절**이 옵니다.
  Diana explained the reason **why** <u>she needs to transfer to the Boston branch</u>.
  완전한 절

  Diana는 자신이 보스턴 지점으로 전근해야 하는 이유를 설명했다.

· 관계부사는 '전치사 + 관계대명사'로 쓸 수 있습니다.

  장소를 나타내는 명사 + where = in/at/on/to which
  시간을 나타내는 명사 + when = in/on/at which
  이유를 나타내는 명사 + why = for which
  방법을 나타내는 명사 + how = in which

`800+`

2️⃣ 관계대명사와 관계부사의 구별

· 관계대명사 뒤에는 주어/목적어/보어가 없는 불완전한 절이 오고, 관계부사 뒤에는 완전한 절이 옵니다.
  Ms. Evans became the department manager (**who** / ~~where~~) <u>is responsible for training new employees</u>.
  주어가 없는 불완전한 절

  Evans 씨는 신입 사원들을 교육하는 것을 담당하는 부서장이 되었다.

  We need to reserve a larger ballroom (~~which~~ / **where**) <u>it accommodates more than 200 people</u>.
  완전한 절

  우리는 200명 이상을 수용하는 더 큰 연회장을 예약해야 한다.

(A) ⑤ 답정

408 기적의 토익 RC

형용사절 접속사

1. The restaurant owner will visit the branches ------- sales have decreased for the last two quarters.

(A) his   (B) which   (C) whose   (D) more

그 식당 소유주는 지난 2분기 동안 매출이 감소한 지점을 방문할 것이다.

> **이렇게 풀어요**
>
> **1. 선택지 보고 문법/어휘 문제 파악** 선택지가 다양한 품사로 구성되어 있으므로 문법 문제임을 파악해요.
> **2. 빈칸 분석** 빈칸 앞에 본동사 will visit와 목적어 the branches가 있고, 뒤에 동사 have decreased가 있으므로 빈칸에는 접속사 역할이 가능한 단어가 들어가야 함을 파악합니다.
> **3. 정답 선택** 빈칸부터 문장 끝까지가 명사 the branches를 수식하는 형용사절이 되어야 하므로 (B)와 (C) 중에서 명사 sales앞에 올 수 있는 소유격 관계대명사 (C) whose를 정답으로 고릅니다.

2. The intersection ------- a chain collision occurred last week will be blocked for the investigation.

(A) who   (B) at which   (C) that   (D) whose

지난주에 연쇄 추돌이 발생한 교차로는 조사를 위해 폐쇄될 것이다.

> **이렇게 풀어요**
>
> **1. 선택지 보고 문법/어휘 문제 파악** 선택지가 모두 관계대명사로 구성되어 있으므로 문법 문제임을 파악해요.
> **2. 빈칸 분석** 빈칸 뒤에 완전한 절(a chain ~ week)이 있음을 파악합니다.
> **3. 정답 선택** 완전한 절 앞에 올 수 있는 '전치사 + 관계대명사' 형태인 (B) at which를 정답으로 고릅니다.

3. Malcom Network will relocate to the Orlando commercial district ------- many online businesses concentrate.

(A) which   (B) that   (C) where   (D) whose

Malcom Network는 많은 온라인 사업체들이 모이는 올랜도 상업 지구로 이전할 것이다.

> **이렇게 풀어요**
>
> **1. 선택지 보고 문법/어휘 문제 파악** 선택지가 관계대명사와 관계부사로 구성되어 있으므로 문법 문제임을 파악해요.
> **2. 빈칸 분석** 빈칸 뒤에 완전한 절이 있음을 파악합니다.
> **3. 정답 선택** 완전한 절 앞에 올 수 있는 관계부사 (C) where를 정답으로 고릅니다.

PART 5 어휘
부사 어휘 (3)

각 어휘와 함께 자주 쓰이는 표현을 통째로 외워두세요.

01 firmly — 단호히, 확고히

firmly believe — 확고히 믿다
be firmly established — 확고히 자리를 잡다

02 initially — 처음에, 초기에

initially believed to be — 처음에 ~로 알려진
initially proposed plan — 처음에 제안된 계획

😺 빈출 토익 선생님 Pick!
03 dramatically — 극적으로

dramatically increase/rise — 극적으로 오르다
dramatically fall/drop — 극적으로 감소하다

04 carefully — 주의하여, 신중히

carefully inspect — 주의 깊게 검사하다
carefully review — 신중히 검토하다
carefully examine — 신중히 조사하다

`800+`
05 enthusiastically — 열광적으로, 열심히

applaud enthusiastically — 열광적으로 박수를 치다

😺 빈출 토익 선생님 Pick!
06 completely — 완전히

completely free of charge — 완전히 무료인
completely forget to부정사 — ~하는 것을 완전히 잊다

07 fairly — 상당히, 꽤

fairly expensive — 상당히 비싼
fairly complicated — 상당히 복잡한

`800+`
08 voluntarily — 자발적으로

voluntarily recall — 자발적으로 회수하다
voluntarily undertake — 자발적으로 착수하다

09 directly — 곧장, 직접

report directly to — ~에게 직접 보고하다
go/proceed directly to — ~로 곧장 가다
respond directly — 직접 대답하다

`800+`
10 intentionally — 의도적으로, 고의로

intentionally designed for — ~을 위해 의도적으로 설계된
intentionally leak the news — 일부러 그 소식을 흘리다

😺 빈출 토익 선생님 Pick!
11 accidentally — 우연히, 뜻하지 않게

accidentally dropped — 실수로 떨어뜨린
accidentally deleted — 실수로 지운

12 clearly — 분명히, 또렷하게

be clearly stated — 분명히 언급되다
speak clearly — 분명히 말하다
clearly visible — 또렷하게 보이는

`800+`
13 generously — 관대하게, 후하게

generously offer to부정사 — ~할 것을 관대하게 제안하다
generously extend the deadline — 마감 기한을 넉넉하게 연장하다

14 originally — 원래, 본래

originally scheduled for 시간/날짜 — 원래 ~로 예정된
originally intended as — 원래 ~로 의도된

15 particularly
특히, 특별히

particularly good at 특히 ~을 잘하는
particularly distinctive candidate 특히 두드러지는 후보

800+
16 tentatively
임시로, 시험적으로

tentatively scheduled for 시간/날짜 임시로 ~로 예정된
tentatively scheduled to부정사 ~하기로 임시로 예정된

17 unusually
대단히, 평소와 달리

unusually high demand 대단히 높은 수요
unusually cold weather 유난히 추운 날씨

18 briefly
잠시, 간단히

briefly expressed 간략히 표현된
speak briefly 간략히 말하다
briefly visit 짧게 방문하다

🐾 빈출 토익 선생님 Pick!
19 properly
제대로, 적절히

function properly 제대로 기능하다
operate properly 제대로 작동하다

🐾 빈출 토익 선생님 Pick!
20 relatively
비교적

remain relatively stable 비교적 안정되어 있다
relatively expensive 비교적 비싼

21 cordially
다정하게, 진심으로

cordially invite to부정사 ~하기를 진심으로 청하다

🐾 빈출 토익 선생님 Pick!
22 accordingly
그에 따라서

adjust accordingly 그에 따라 조정하다
act accordingly 그에 따라 행동하다
award a bonus accordingly 상황에 맞게 보너스를 주다

900+
23 undoubtedly
의심할 여지 없이, 확실히

will undoubtedly be promoted 틀림없이 승진할 것이다
undoubtedly the best place to부정사
의심할 여지 없이 ~하기에 최고의 장소

24 strategically
전략적으로

be located strategically 전략적으로 위치하다
compete strategically 전략적으로 경쟁하다

 풀이 방법

Once you land in Los Angeles, you will go ------- to the luggage claim area before your customs inspection.

(A) firmly   (B) fairly   (C) directly   (D) greatly

로스엔젤레스에 착륙하면 세관 검사 전에 수하물 찾는 곳으로 곧장 가실 것입니다.

> 🖌 이렇게 풀어요
>
> 1. **선택지 보고 문법/어휘 문제 파악** 선택지가 서로 다른 부사 어휘로 구성되어 있으므로 어휘 문제임을 파악해요.
> 2. **빈칸 분석** 빈칸 앞에 동사 go가 있고, 뒤에 전치사 to가 있으므로 '~로 ------- 가다'라는 문맥이 되어야 함을 파악합니다.
> 3. **정답 선택** '수하물 찾는 곳으로 곧장 가다'라는 문맥이 가장 자연스러우므로 (C) directly를 정답으로 고릅니다.

PART 5 어휘 부사 어휘 (3)   411

따라 하면 문제가 풀리는

연습 문제

앞서 학습한 문제 풀이법을 적용하여 맞는 것에 ✔ 표시 하거나 괄호 안에
적절한 답을 쓰고 정답을 선택하세요.

01 Studio 83's new film ------- will be released on September 10 is directed by Betty Abbott.

(A) and
(B) which
(C) what
(D) of

1. 선택지 보고 문법/어휘 문제 파악하기 ☐ 문법 문제 ☐ 어휘 문제
2. 빈칸 분석하기 문장의 본동사 ( )
   빈칸 뒤에 있는 것 ☐ 동사 ☐ 부사
   → 빈칸에는 ☐ 전치사 ☐ 접속사가 들어가야 한다.
   → 빈칸부터 September 10까지가 주어인 new film을 뒤에서 수식하므로 ☐ 명사절 접속사 ☐ 형용사절 접속사가
     들어가야 한다.
3. 정답 선택하기 정답 ( )

02 Your speech was ------- scheduled for 10 A.M but was postponed to a later time.

(A) originally
(B) relatively
(C) greatly
(D) firmly

1. 선택지 보고 문법/어휘 문제 파악하기 ☐ 문법 문제 ☐ 어휘 문제
2. 빈칸 분석하기 빈칸 뒤에 있는 동사 ( ) 빈칸 뒤에 있는 접속사 ( )
   → 문맥상 ☐ 원인과 결과 ☐ 반대되는 내용이 되어야 함을 파악한다.
3. 정답 선택하기 정답 ( )

03 Amanda Burke, ------- paintings will be exhibited, will appear on the local news.

(A) who
(B) much
(C) whose
(D) her

1. 선택지 보고 문법/어휘 문제 파악하기 ☐ 문법 문제 ☐ 어휘 문제
2. 빈칸 분석하기 문장의 주어 ( ) 문장의 본동사 ( )
   → 빈칸에는 ☐ 대명사 ☐ 접속사가 들어가야 한다.
   → 정답이 될 수 있는 후보 2개 (,)
   → 빈칸부터 will be exhibited까지가 주어인 Amanda Burke를 수식하는데, 빈칸 바로 뒤에 ☐ 명사 ☐ 형용사가 있다.
3. 정답 선택하기 정답 ( )

412 기적의 토익 RC

♀ 정답 및 해설 p.141

04 The new apartment, ------- is furnished with chairs and tables, feels very cramped.

(A) which
(B) who
(C) that
(D) whom

> 1. 선택지 보고 문법/어휘 문제 파악하기 ☐문법 문제 ☐어휘 문제
>
> 2. 빈칸 분석하기 문장의 주어 (   )
>   문장의 본동사 (   )
>   → 빈칸 바로 뒤에 ☐동사 ☐부사가 있고 선행사가 ☐사람 ☐사물임을 파악한다.
>
> 3. 정답 선택하기 정답 (   )

05 Please make use of the business center ------- you can print color copies.

(A) which
(B) where
(C) why
(D) who

> 1. 선택지 보고 문법/어휘 문제 파악하기 ☐문법 문제 ☐어휘 문제
>
> 2. 빈칸 분석하기 빈칸 뒤에 있는 것 ☐완전한 절 ☐불완전한 절
>   → 빈칸에는 ☐관계대명사 ☐관계부사가 들어가야 한다.
>   → 정답이 될 수 있는 후보 2개 (,   )
>   → 선행사가 ☐장소 ☐이유를 나타낸다.
>
> 3. 정답 선택하기 정답 (   )

06 We interviewed about 30 applicants, all of ------- seemed enthusiastic.

(A) which
(B) how
(C) whom
(D) them

> 1. 선택지 보고 문법/어휘 문제 파악하기 ☐문법 문제 ☐어휘 문제
>
> 2. 빈칸 분석하기 빈칸 앞 콤마(,) 앞에 있는 것 ☐완전한 절 ☐불완전한 절
>   빈칸 뒤에 있는 것 ☐동사 ☐부사
>   → 빈칸에는 ☐대명사 ☐접속사가 들어가야 한다.
>   → most of 앞의 선행사가 ☐사람 ☐사물이다.
>
> 3. 정답 선택하기 정답 (   )

PART 5 형용사절 접속사 / 부사 어휘 (3) 413

토익에 나올 실전 문제

DAY 01-17 누적 문제

제한시간 9분입니다! 시~작!

01. Mr. Bryant, ------- is in charge of training, is planning to hold a workshop next month.
(A) who
(B) until
(C) despite
(D) even

02. Ms. Fowler decided to take a bypass ------- avoids areas with heavy traffic.
(A) who
(B) that
(C) while
(D) then

03. Ms. Cuddy sent the survey result to her manager ------- presentation is tomorrow.
(A) who
(B) that
(C) whose
(D) which

04. Galloway, ------- donated his old books, volunteered to work at the library during the book sales.
(A) he
(B) who
(C) that
(D) how

05. A new turbine ------- generates energy more efficiently is being developed.
(A) if
(B) where
(C) that
(D) some

06. 25% of the customers ------- purchased any of Min's Kitchen meal kits signed up for its regular delivery service.
(A) if
(B) who
(C) them
(D) what

07. Scientists claim that employees ------- take a nap during the day are more productive at work.
(A) when
(B) which
(C) who
(D) how

08. This daily bus pass is very useful for tourists ------- hotels are located in the cultural district.
(A) that
(B) there
(C) whose
(D) who

09. The blades of your Hodges lawnmower should be cleaned and sharpened regularly to keep it working -------.
(A) formally
(B) typically
(C) specially
(D) properly

10. Several film awards, one of ------- was for Movie of the Year, went to *High Tide*.
(A) which
(B) how
(C) them
(D) so

11. Most of the hotels around the convention center have a business lounge ------- guests can print out or send a fax.
(A) why
(B) where
(C) unless
(D) those

12. The picnic ------- employees' family members are invited has been postponed because stormy weather was predicted.
(A) who
(B) to which
(C) them
(D) that

414   기적의 토익 RC

13. The delivery person asked ------- she should put the package.

(A) which
(B) where
(C) what
(D) whichever

14. Researchers at Newark Labs are reviewing all clinical test results ------- to develop a better flu vaccine.

(A) undoubtedly
(B) carefully
(C) relatively
(D) accordingly

15. There was a harsh debate about ------- the new mobile phone should be released.

(A) those
(B) that
(C) when
(D) whose

16. Mr. Holloway gave a ------- speech about the need for an online marketing strategy.

(A) convincingly
(B) to convince
(C) convincing
(D) convinced

17. All of the financial advisors recommend ------- the company departments to remove overlapping jobs.

(A) to reorganize
(B) reorganized
(C) reorganization
(D) reorganizing

18. Based on Mr. Clooney's -------, six additional workers would be needed to finish the construction on time.

(A) calculator
(B) to calculator
(C) calculations
(D) had calculated

19. The train station in Mocksville will be ------- operational by August.

(A) voluntarily
(B) completely
(C) generously
(D) relatively

20. We will pause the meeting ------- to get some more coffee.

(A) briefly
(B) cordially
(C) randomly
(D) nearly

21. A large group of volunteers showed up for the event, ------- were government employees.

(A) so much as
(B) as long as
(C) most of whom
(D) as for them

22. The responsibilities of the branch manager are quite ------- defined in the company's handbook.

(A) promptly
(B) unusually
(C) clearly
(D) widely

23. ------- needs to be discussed with potential clients will be determined at the manager's meeting.

(A) That
(B) What
(C) When
(D) How

24. Only those who ------- started as an intern are eligible to apply for the PR Representative position.

(A) compulsorily
(B) accidentally
(C) initially
(D) strategically

PART 5 형용사절 접속사 / 부사 어휘 (3)

PART 6

접속부사 – 역접

보기가 다양한 접속부사 어휘로 구성되어 있으면 앞뒤 문맥을 파악합니다.

✎ 적용 기술

[기적의 필기노트] 163P
RC 기술 81

🗂 VOCA

award-winning 수상 경력이 있는
renowned for ~로 명성 있는
represent 대변하다, 변호하다
court 법정
expertise 전문 지식
acknowledge 인정하다
fellow 동료
reputation 명성
settlement 협의
step down 물러나다
advisor 조언자

👨‍🏫 풀이 방법　article
○ 해석 p.144

Henry Martin's Law Firm

Henry Martin's Law Firm, ------- is an award-winning organization, has become
　　　　　　　　　　　　　　　　⚭ PART 5
renowned for winning court cases. The head lawyer, Mr. Martin, has represented
over 500 individual clients in court since 2001. His charisma and expertise are
acknowledged and respected by fellow lawyers and court officials alike. He
developed a reputation as one of the greatest court lawyers in history. As a result,
many lawyers who would have had to face him in court encouraged their clients to
agree to a settlement instead. -------, he has decided to step down from directly
　　　　　　　　　　　　　　　　　　01.
representing clients and simply act as an advisor to the other lawyers at his firm.

01. (A) Therefore
　　　(B) Nevertheless
　　　(C) Incidentally
　　　(D) Specifically

핵심 포인트
역접을 나타내는 접속부사
nevertheless 그럼에도 불구하고
nonetheless 그럼에도 불구하고
however 그러나
otherwise 그렇지 않으면

⚓ 이렇게 풀어요

1. 선택지 보고 문법/어휘 문제 파악　선택지가 다양한 접속부사 어휘로 이루어져 있으므로 어휘 문제임을 파악해요.

　(A) 그러므로　　(B) 그럼에도 불구하고　　(C) 그건 그렇고　　(D) 구체적으로 말하면

2. 빈칸 분석　'그를 법정에서 맞닥뜨려야 했던 많은 변호사들은 고객들에게 합의에 동의할 것을 권했다.
　------, 그는 직접 고객들을 대변하는 일에서 물러나기로 결심했다'
　빈칸 앞에서 Henry Martin 씨가 변호사로서 승승장구했던 이력을 열거하고, 빈칸 뒤에는 그가 고객들의 소송을 직접 맡지 않고 다른 변호사들에게 자문만 해주기로 했다는 내용을 전하고 있으므로 빈칸에는 역접 관계를 나타내는 말이 들어가야 함을 파악합니다.

3. 정답 선택　'그럼에도 불구하고'라는 의미의 (B) Nevertheless를 정답으로 선택합니다.

○ 해설

빈칸은 앞의 명사 Law Firm을 수식하는 형용사절의 주어 자리입니다. 콤마 뒤에는 that을 쓸 수 없으므로 (D)가 정답입니다.

⚭ PART 5 문법 적용 문제

Henry Martin's Law Firm, ------- is an award-winning organization, has become renowned for winning court cases.

(A) that　　　　　(B) whos　　　　　(C) whom　　　　　(D) which

416　기적의 토익 RC

따라 하면 문제가 풀리는

연습 문제

빈칸 앞뒤 내용에서 단서가 될 부분을 찾아 표시하세요.
표시한 것을 바탕으로 정답 어휘를 선택하세요.

정답 및 해설 p.144

01

Our office will be closed on Wednesday this week due to some scheduled electronic maintenance. -------, employees are still expected to work from a remote location from 9 to 5 on that day.

(A) Moreover

(B) However

02

You are authorized to access the company network to upload or download files. -------, for security purposes, it is inaccessible to anyone outside of the building.

(A) Unfortunately

(B) Similarly

03

I apologize to hear about the problem with your last order. As per store policy, I can offer a store credit of equal value. -------, we can send a new one to your address if you still want this item.

(A) Otherwise

(B) Therefore

04

Due to inclement weather, my crew was not able to get any work done on the construction site today. -------, we should still be able to meet the deadline since we were ahead of schedule.

(A) Likewise

(B) Nevertheless

DAY 17

PART 6 접속부사-역접   417

토익에 나올

실전 문제

제한시간 4분입니다! 시~작!

Questions 01-04 refer to the following article.

NEW BRUNSWICK (7 June) — A local favorite for ice cream and snacks will soon be closing for good. Jim Brady, owner of Cold Cones, has announced his plan -------. After this summer, the
01.
once-popular ice cream store will be renovated into a coffee shop. -------. She chose to pursue a
02.
career in advertising instead. She currently works at Finesse Fashion where she has been -------
03.
with creating the catchy slogan "Finesse is the finest."

-------, New Brunswick will not be completely out of delicious treats. The coffee shop that will
04.
replace it is going to feature a full dessert menu with various flavors of ice cream.

---

01. (A) retire
(B) to retire
(C) retiring
(D) retired

02. (A) Reservations are being taken for the last day of business.
(B) Mr. Brady will be offering special deals for the rest of the season.
(C) Mr. Brady hoped that his daughter would take over the family business.
(D) Customers will soon be able to place delivery orders via the restaurant's Web site.

03. (A) proposed
(B) increased
(C) credited
(D) designed

유형 적용 문제

04. (A) Hence
(B) Meantime
(C) Accordingly
(D) Nevertheless

418   기적의 토익 RC

♀ 정답 및 해설 p.145

Questions 05-08 refer to the following information.

Marissa Barnes

Marissa Barnes has proven ------- again and again as an expert in investing. For over a decade,
05.
she has continuously earned at least 15% on her investment choices. -------. They have been
06.
satisfied with higher earnings with her than from any other investments. She graduated from Wilson
University with a degree in business administration in 2005. After a short internship at Goldberg
Bank, she was recruited by Knox Financial to work as a market analyst. -------, she was quickly
07.
transferred to the client service department where she truly began to shine. Ms. Barnes -------
08.
known as one of the most famous investors in history.

유형 적용 문제

05. (A) she
  (B) hers
  (C) herself
  (D) her

07. (A) Although
  (B) However
  (C) Specifically
  (D) Therefore

06. (A) Many celebrities and business owners have
    entrusted their fortunes to her.
  (B) Contact Knox Financial to schedule an
    appointment with Ms. Barnes.
  (C) This is the perfect time to start investing in startup
    companies.
  (D) Financial advice services are available online.

08. (A) becomes
  (B) has become
  (C) had to become
  (D) would have become

DAY 17

PART 6 접속부사-역접   419

PART 7

온라인 채팅 800+

개인간의 채팅뿐만 아니라 업체와 개인간 대화 지문도 출제돼요.

온라인 채팅은 진행되는 일의 상황을 실시간으로 주고받으며 정보를 공유하는 지문입니다. 따라서 등장인물 간의 관계, 직업, 담당 업무 등을 확인해야 합니다. 주로 <채팅을 시작한 목적 – 일의 진행 상황 공유 또는 문제점에 대한 해결책 논의 – 요청/제안 또는 다음에 할 일 논의>의 흐름으로 지문이 전개됩니다.

온라인 채팅에서 자주 출제되는 문제

· 의도 파악 문제
→ 업무 진행 상황에 대해 구체적인 정보를 문의하는 문장이나 "확인해보겠다" 는 뉘앙스의 문장이 자주 출제돼요.

🔒 **기출 표현 확인**

· That won't work for me.
· It's been a challenge.

온라인 채팅 지문에서 자주 출제되는 어휘

arrange	준비하다	come up with	~을 생각해내다
make copies	복사하다	drop by	잠깐 들르다
wonder	궁금해하다	optional	선택적인
make sure	확실하게 하다	be about to**부정사**	지금 막 ~하려 하다
turn down	거절하다	status	(진행 과정의) 상황
call off	취소하다	double check	재확인하다
give a ride	(차를) 태워주다	deadline	마감일
need a ride	교통편이 필요하다	get in touch with	~와 연락하다
have trouble with	~에 문제가 있다	disappointing	실망스러운
be supposed to**부정사**	~하기로 되어 있다	hold off	보류하다
get off the phone	전화 통화를 끝내다	give an update	새로운 상황을 알리다
just in case	만약을 대비하여	take care of	~을 처리하다
Sure thing.	물론이죠.	cutting it close	시간이 촉박한
I doubt it.	아닌 것 같아요.	Go ahead.	그렇게 하세요.
(I'm) on my way.	가는 중이에요.	place an order	주문하다
incur a fee	비용을 발생시키다	get A down	A를 실망시키다
with regard to	~와 관련하여	preparation	준비
switch	바꾸다, 변경하다	relationship	관계
interrupt	방해하다	appear	나타나다, ~인 것 같다
run-through	예행연습, 리허설	holdup	중지

420 기적의 토익 RC

풀이방법 온라인 채팅

online chat discussion

💡해석 p.146

Virgil Dyer [10:24 A.M.] Is everything going well with the new exhibit? Has the contract with the gallery been finalized?

Melody Kim [10:25 A.M.] Yes, it has. They'll be sending us 30 sculptures in February.

Virgil Dyer [10:26 A.M.] Great! In that case, this would be a good time to get some brochures ready.

Melody Kim [10:27 A.M.] Robert already got started on that.

Virgil Dyer [10:28 A.M.] This exhibit will probably attract a lot of foreign tourists, so I want to provide several languages.

Robert Fennell [10:29 A.M.] I'm almost done, it's mostly pictures. I could print out a sample.

Melody Kim [10:30 A.M.] Before you do, we may need to make some changes.

Robert Fennell [10:31 A.M.] Okay, like what?

Melody Kim [10:32 A.M.] I want to reduce the picture sizes a bit so that we can include the captions in Spanish as well.

Robert Fennell [10:33 A.M.] I suppose I could do that.

---

01. What kind of business do the chat participants most likely work at?

(A) A stationery store
(B) A travel agency
(C) A museum
(D) A language school

02. At 10:31 A.M., what does Mr. Fennell most likely mean when he writes, "like what"?

(A) He likes the new exhibit.
(B) He will contact a print shop.
(C) He wants to know Ms. Kim's preference.
(D) He needs more detailed instructions to proceed.

이렇게 풀어요

01. 채팅 참여자들은 어떤 업종에서 일하겠는가?

(A) 문구점
(B) 여행사
(C) 박물관
(D) 어학원

해설 Virgil Dyer의 첫 번째 대사의 new exhibit, gallery 같은 어휘를 통해 이들이 박물관이나 미술관에서 일하고 있음을 유추할 수 있습니다. 따라서 (C)가 정답입니다.

02. 오전 10시 31분에, Fennell 씨가 "like what"라고 썼을 때 의도한 바는 무엇일 것 같은가?

(A) 그는 새 전시회를 좋아한다.
(B) 그는 인쇄소에 연락할 것이다.
(C) 그는 Kim 씨의 선호도를 알고 싶어한다.
(D) 그는 진행하기 위해 더 자세한 설명을 필요로 한다.

해설 앞서 Kim 씨가 인쇄하기 전에 몇 가지를 수정하고 싶다고 했고, 이에 Fennell 씨가 "like what?"이라고 묻자 다시 Kim 씨가 스페인어로도 설명을 넣을 수 있도록 사진 크기를 좀 줄이고 싶다고 했습니다. 이로 보아 작업 진행을 위한 상세한 지침이 필요하다는 의미로 주어진 표현을 썼음을 알 수 있으므로 (D)가 정답입니다.

DAY 17

PART 7 온라인 채팅　421

따라 하면 문제가 풀리는

먼저 문제의 키워드에 표시한 후,
지문에서 단서를 찾아 적절한 답을 고르세요.

01 online chat discussion

Jeanne Abbott [10:50 A.M.]
How are things coming along with Mr. Bedford's move?

Warren Delarosa [10:53 A.M.]
We moved the furniture in the first truckload. Now we're just unloading his boxed-up belongings at the new property.

Jeanne Abbott [10:54 A.M.]
Is that all? If you're almost finished, we could use some help at Ms. Kaminski's place. There are a lot of large items. It's at 560 Dwyer Street.

Warren Delarosa [10:55 A.M.]
My crew can head that way in about fifteen minutes.

Q. At 10:54 A.M., what does Ms. Abbott most likely mean when she writes, "Is that all"?

(A) She is worried that some items are missing.
(B) She wants to check whether a task is completed.

02 online chat discussion

Luiz Pereira [2:25 P.M.]
How are preparations going for the event on June 30?

Irene Tillis [2:26 P.M.]
We've finalized Alliance Park as the location for the food festival. I just received the paperwork from the city this morning.

Kieran Byrne [2:27 P.M.]
That's wonderful! Then I can get started on designing the flyers. I want to emphasize the cooking demonstrations and the wide variety of booths.

Luiz Pereira [2:28 P.M.]
Great job, Irene. And, Kieran, please try to get a draft ready to bring to the meeting on Friday.

Q. What are the writers discussing?

(A) An outdoor festival
(B) A cooking competition

♀ 정답 및 해설 p.146

03 online chat discussion

Mattie Worden [9:44 A.M.]

What's the status of the wooden cabinets that were on backorder? Mr. Kirk, one of our regular clients, is still waiting for them.

Stefan Baier [9:49 A.M.]

They're back in stock as of this morning. Did you want to call him to tell him they're ready?

Mattie Worden [9:50 A.M.]

Not until I can report the exact delivery details.

Demi Elliot [9:51 A.M.]

He's right here in town, at 3828 Elsie Drive, so my team can deliver them today between four and five o'clock.

Mattie Worden [9:52 A.M.]

Thanks, I'll let him know.

Q. What will Ms. Worden most likely do next?

(A) Update a delivery address
(B) Contact a customer

04 online chat discussion

Sharon Wynn [3:11 P.M.]

The sales pitch with Ocello Industries is just two days away. Are the slides finished?

Thomas Ventura [3:12 P.M.]

Yes, I've added all of the graphics and the latest figures. I've even practiced it with Ms. Bajpai a few times, so we have the timings down.

Sharon Wynn [3:14 P.M.]

I'm glad to hear that.

Mina Bajpai [3:15 P.M.]

I'll get the handouts done today. I'm going to instruct the printer to use full color and thick paper so that they look impressive.

Sharon Wynn [3:16 P.M.]

Seems like it's all set.

Q. At 3:16 P.M., what does Ms. Wynn most likely mean when she writes, "Seems like it's all set"?

(A) She thinks the group is ready for a presentation.
(B) She has already set up some equipment.

PART 7 온라인 채팅 423

토익에 나올 실전 문제

제한시간 10분입니다! 시~작!

Questions 01-03 refer to the following online chat discussion.

Juliette Buckley [2:19 P.M.]
At our last meeting, everything was almost ready to launch the campaign for Wilson Construction. Where do we stand now?

Rory Palmer [2:20 P.M.]
Actually, they said that they want to use a different logo in the commercials. We had to go back to the initial design phase.

Juliette Buckley [2:21 P.M.]
Will you still be able to meet the original deadline?

Jeff Cummings [2:22 P.M.]
I can send someone from my team to help. You're going to need it. Haven't any of you worked with them before?

Ingrid Hamill [2:23 P.M.]
I have, but I didn't have any problems when I did.

Rory Palmer [2:24 P.M.]
If Jeff is sending someone to help, then I'm sure my team can pull it off.

Juliette Buckley [2:25 P.M.]
Okay, good. Thanks again, Jeff.

---

01. What kind of problem are they talking about?

(A) A client requested a change.
(B) A space will not be sufficient.
(C) A task is too complicated.
(D) A file was deleted.

02. What does Mr. Cummings say he will do?

(A) Assist with a task personally
(B) Grant a deadline extension
(C) Negotiate with a client
(D) Reassign an employee

03. At 2:22 P.M., what does Mr. Cummings most likely mean when he writes, "Haven't any of you worked with them before"?

(A) He wants to take charge of the project.
(B) He is concerned about inexperienced coworkers.
(C) He needs more information about a client.
(D) He was left out of a series of contract negotiations.

---

paraphrasing 주어진 어휘 또는 표현과 패러프레이징 될 수 있는 것을 연결하세요.

1. launch •   • (a) reassign an employee
2. use a different logo •   • (b) start
3. send someone •   • (c) manage
4. pull off •   • (d) worried
5. concerned •   • (e) change the logo

◎ 정답 및 해설 p.148

Questions 04-06 refer to the following online chat discussion.

Rebecca Stone (2:35 P.M.)	How are the office preparations for Denzel Legal coming along?
Carson Guerrero (2:36 P.M.)	I'm done installing the new flooring. The electricity took a little longer than I expected, though.
Rebecca Stone (2:37 P.M.)	I just want to make sure their company can move into the office as scheduled. I don't want to have to change their lease contract at the last minute.
Carson Guerrero (2:38 P.M.)	I don't think that will be necessary.
Nathan Hayes (2:39 P.M.)	The walls are insulated and my crew has already finished the first coat of paint on them.
Carson Guerrero (2:39 P.M.)	Don't you normally put at least two coats on?
Nathan Hayes (2:40 P.M.)	Yes, we plan on doing that tomorrow so that the first coat can finish drying.
Rebecca Stone (2:41 P.M.)	Okay, so everything will be taken care of?
Nathan Hayes (2:42 P.M.)	Yes, you have nothing to worry about.
Rebecca Stone (2:43 P.M.)	Perfect. Sounds like we're all set, then.

04. What is implied about Denzel Legal?

(A) It has an excellent reputation.
(B) It is moving into a new office.
(C) It recently underwent renovations.
(D) It plans to recruit more employees.

05. What does Mr. Hayes still have to do?

(A) Install some flooring
(B) Update a client contract
(C) Connect an electric circuit
(D) Paint the walls a second time

06. At 2:43 P.M., what does Ms. Stone most likely mean when she writes, "Sounds like we're all set, then"?

(A) An office is conveniently located.
(B) An office will be prepared on time.
(C) A shipment has already arrived.
(D) A client requested an update.

DAY 17

paraphrasing 주어진 어휘 또는 표현과 패러프레이징 될 수 있는 것을 연결하세요.

1. as scheduled •
2. underwent renovations •
3. recruit more employees •
4. update •
5. prepared •

• (a) ready to use
• (b) hire additional workers
• (c) revise
• (d) remodeled
• (e) without delay

PART 7 온라인 채팅 425

 **실전 문제**

Questions 07-10 refer to the following online chat discussion.

Alex Bowen [1:17 P.M.]		Is everyone ready for the Wilber Tech Services banquet tonight?
Bailey Delacruz [1:18 P.M.]		I spoke with Ms. Sanders yesterday, but she still hasn't called me back with a final head count yet.
Alex Bowen [1:19 P.M.]		We have to start preparing the food any minute now. What if we don't provide enough for their event?
Rosa Faulkner [1:20 P.M.]		I already told our supplier that we'll make 50 servings.
Alex Bowen [1:21 P.M.]		But they said between 50 and 80. What if we didn't order enough ingredients?
Rosa Faulkner [1:22 P.M.]		They should be able to make a last-minute delivery. I'll ask.
Alex Bowen [1:23 P.M.]		Bailey, I need you to call Ms. Sanders and get a final answer.
Rosa Faulkner [1:24 P.M.]		They haven't sent their truck out yet, so we have time to make a change.
Bailey Delacruz [1:25 P.M.]		Actually, Mr. Jones just called. He said that there will be 80 people at their banquet tonight.
Alex Bowen [1:26 P.M.]		Well, that was close. I'll see you at the prep area in a bit.

SEND

426   기적의 토익 RC

07. What field do the writers most likely work in?

(A) Technical support
(B) Entertainment
(C) Food catering
(D) Tourism

08. At 1:22 P.M., what does Ms. Faulkner most likely mean when she writes, "I'll ask"?

(A) She will check on an express service.
(B) She will order more ingredients.
(C) She wants to inquire about attendance.
(D) She agrees that the delivery date should be rescheduled.

09. What information is provided by Mr. Jones?

(A) Why a venue was selected
(B) Where to deliver products
(C) What time an event will begin
(D) How many people will attend an event

10. What will Ms. Faulkner most likely do next?

(A) Increase an order
(B) Take a meal break
(C) Change a menu
(D) Greet a client

DAY 17

paraphrasing 주어진 어휘 또는 표현과 패러프레이징 될 수 있는 것을 연결하세요.

1. head count •
2. provide •
3. servings •
4. banquet •
5. increase •

• (a) event
• (b) add
• (c) portion
• (d) how many people will attend
• (e) cater

PART 7 온라인 채팅 427

'멋진 당신, 오늘도 화이팅'

DAY

18

오늘의 학습 포인트

PART 5. 부사절 접속사

1. 접속사 vs. 전치사 vs. 부사의 구분
+주어+동사 → +명사 → 수식하는 역할

2. 부사절 접속사의 종류
- 시간(when, after, before, until 등)/이유(because, since, as 등)
  양보(although, even if, even though 등)/조건(if, unless 등)
  목적(so that, in order that)/결과(so ~ that, such ~ that)

3. 부사절 접속사 + -ing/p.p. - when + -ing/p.p., while + -ing/p.p. 등

4. 복합관계부사 - whenever/wherever/however + 완전한 절

PART 6. 알맞은 문장 고르기 - 선택지에 접속부사
문맥 파악!

PART 7. 양식 - 일정표/초대장/영수증 등
문제 먼저 읽고 관련 정보를 지문에서 찾기!

PART 5
문법
부사절 접속사

부사절 접속사와 전치사, 부사를 구분하는 문제가 가장 많이 출제돼요.

✎ 적용 기술

[기적의 필기노트] 150P
RC 기술 67

🔒 확인 문제 ❶

------- he earned the certificate, he was able to apply for the position.

(A) Because
(B) Due to

출제 유형 1
접속사 vs. 전치사 vs. 부사의 구분

1 쓰이는 구조

- 접속사 + 주어 + 동사, 주어 + 동사~ / 주어 + 동사 ~ 접속사 + 주어 + 동사
- 전치사 + 명사/동명사/명사절
- 부사: 수식하는 역할만 가능, 문장을 연결할 수 없습니다.
- 주어 + 동사. 접속부사, 주어 + 동사

2 의미가 비슷한 접속사와 전치사

	접속사	전치사
시간	when/as ~하는 동안, ~할 때 while ~하는 동안 as soon as ~하자마자 once 일단 ~하면 by the time ~할 때쯤에	during ~동안 by ~까지 following ~한 후에 prior to ~전에
이유	because/since/now that/as ~이기 때문에	because of/due to/owing to/ on account of ~때문에 thanks to ~덕분에
조건	provided[providing] (that)/assuming (that)/ supposing (that) / if ~한다면 unless ~가 아니라면 as long as ~하는 한 only if ~하는 경우에만	without ~없이 in case of ~의 경우에 in the event of ~의 경우에
양보	although/though/even if/even though ~에도 불구하고 while/whereas ~인 반면에	despite / in spite of / notwithstanding ~에도 불구하고

(When / ~~Following~~) he invested in Bite Telecom, the stock price dropped.
주어 동사
→ 뒤에 '주어 + 동사'가 있으므로 접속사인 When이 정답입니다.
그가 Bite Telecom에 투자했을 때, 주가가 하락했다.

3 접속사와 전치사로 모두 사용되는 어휘

접속사/전치사일 때 의미가 같은 단어	접속사/전치사일 때 의미가 다른 단어
before ~전에 after ~후에 until ~까지 like ~처럼	since [접속사] ~한 이래로, ~이기 때문에 　　　 [전치사] (과거 시점) 이래로 as 　 [접속사] ~이기 때문에, ~할 때, ~함에 따라, ~처럼 　　 [전치사] ~로서 for 　 [접속사] ~이기 때문에(문장 사이에 쓰일 때) 　　 [전치사] ~을 위하여, ~에 대하여

(∀) ❶ 답정

430　기적의 토익 RC

출제 유형 2

부사절 접속사의 종류

적용 기술

[기적의 필기노트] 151P
RC 기술 68

1 시간 접속사

when ~할 때	after ~한 후에	before ~하기 전에
as soon as ~하자마자	once 일단 ~하면	while ~하는 동안
until ~할 때까지	as ~할 때, ~함에 따라	since ~한 이래로
by the time ~할 때쯤이면		

2 이유 접속사

because ~ 때문에   since ~ 때문에   as ~ 때문에   now that ~이므로

3 양보 접속사

although 비록 ~이지만	though 비록 ~이지만	even if 비록 ~이지만
even though 비록 ~이지만	whereas ~한 반면에	while ~한 반면에

- 양보 부사절과 주절의 내용은 항상 반대되는 내용이어야 합니다.
Although this product is newly introduced, it is quite similar with the old version.
이 제품은 새로 출시되었지만 이전 버전과 매우 비슷하다.

출제 포인트

since가 시간 접속사로 사용되면 시간 부사절에는 과거 시제, 주절에는 현재 완료 시제를 사용합니다. since가 이유 접속사로 사용될 경우에는 주절과 부사절의 시제는 다양하게 쓰일 수 있습니다.

4 조건 접속사

if ~라면   providing/provided (that) ~라면   supposing (that) ~라면   assuming (that) ~라면
as long as ~하는 경우에만   unless ~이 아니라면

- 조건을 나타내는 부사절과 주절이 모두 미래의 일을 의미할 경우 부사절에는 현재 시제, 주절에는 미래 시제를 씁니다.
I will contact you immediately if I find any errors in the document.
문서에서 어떠한 오류라도 발견하면 당신에게 즉시 연락하겠습니다.

5 목적 접속사

so that ~하기 위해서   in order that ~하기 위해서

- so that이 이끄는 절은 보통 주절 뒤에 오며, 조동사 can/could와 함께 쓰입니다.
Betty goes to the gym every morning **so that** she **can** stay healthy.
Betty는 건강을 유지할 수 있도록 매일 아침 체육관에 간다.

확인 문제 ❷

Mr. Aaron missed the meeting ------- his car was broken on the road.

(A) since
(B) so

정답 ❷ (A)

DAY 18

PART 5 문법 부사절 접속사   431

6 결과 접속사

> so 형용사/부사 that 매우 ~해서 that절 하게 되다
> such 명사 that 매우 ~이어서 그 결과 that절 하게 되다

The letters were **so** small **that** I needed a magnifier.
글씨가 매우 작아서 나는 돋보기가 필요했다.

The new TV has **such** a wide screen **that** it is the most expensive on the market. 새 TV는 매우 큰 화면을 가지고 있어서 시장에서 가장 비싸다.

출제 유형 3

부사절 접속사 + -ing/p.p.

800+

· 부사절 접속사 뒤에 절이 아닌 현재분사 또는 과거분사 구문이 올 수 있습니다.

| 분사구문 앞에 자주 오는 부사절 접속사 |

> When + -ing/p.p. ~할 때
> While + -ing/p.p. ~하는 동안
> Before/After/Since + -ing/being p.p. ~하기 전에/후에/이래로
> as/ if/once/unless/though/although/even though/even if + p.p.
> ~한 대로/~라면/일단 ~하면/~하지 않는 이상/~임에도 불구하고

When purchasing a used car, please check its car history.
중고차를 구매할 때는 차량 이력을 확인하세요.

As mentioned earlier, this work was difficult. 전에 말했듯이, 이 작업은 힘들었다.

출제 유형 4

복합관계부사

900+

> whenever(= no matter when) 언제 ~하더라도
> wherever(= no matter where) 어디에서 ~하더라도 **+ 완전한 절**
> however(= no matter how) 아무리 ~할지라도

· however 뒤에는 형용사/부사가 바로 이어 나올 수 있습니다.
We will rent a minivan **however** expensive it is.
얼마나 비싸든 간에, 우리는 미니밴을 빌릴 것이다.

· however는 주로 '그러나'라는 의미의 접속부사로 출제되는 경우가 더 많아요.

확인 문제 ❸

The internet connection was ------- unstable that the company changed its Internet service provider.

(A) so
(B) such

적용 기술

[기적의 필기노트] 152P
RC 기술 69

확인 문제 ❹

All inquiry e-mails should be directed to Ms. Wilson ------- otherwise indicated.

(A) for
(B) unless

적용 기술

[기적의 필기노트] 153P
RC 기술 70

출제 포인트

복합관계부사 중에서는 whenever가 가장 자주 출제돼요.

정답 ❸ (A) ❹ (B)

432 기적의 토익 RC

부사절 접속사

1. You are asked to contact your real estate agent ------- you visit the property.

(A) from   (B) with   (C) before   (D) along

당신은 건물을 방문하기 전에 부동산 중개인에게 연락해야 합니다.

> **이렇게 풀어요**
>
> 1. **선택지 보고 문법/어휘 문제 파악** 선택지가 다양한 품사로 구성되어 있으므로 문법 문제임을 파악해요.
> 2. **빈칸 분석** 빈칸 앞과 뒤에 절이 있으므로 빈칸에는 접속사가 들어가야 함을 파악합니다.
> 3. **정답 선택** '건물을 방문하기 전에 연락해야 한다'라는 의미를 만들 수 있는 접속사 (C) before를 정답으로 고릅니다.

2. ------- mobile phones feature new and innovative functions, people tend to use only the ones familiar to them.

(A) Since   (B) Although   (C) As soon as   (D) Rather than

비록 휴대전화들이 새롭고 혁신적인 기능을 특징으로 하지만, 사람들은 그들에게 익숙한 것들만 사용하는 경향이 있다.

> **이렇게 풀어요**
>
> 1. **선택지 보고 문법/어휘 문제 파악** 선택지가 모두 접속사로 구성되어 있으므로 어휘 문제임을 파악해요.
> 2. **빈칸 분석** 빈칸 뒤 두 문장의 문맥이 '새로운 기능이 있지만 익숙한 것만 사용한다'라는 대조되는 내용이 되어야 함을 파악합니다.
> 3. **정답 선택** '비록 ~이지만'이라는 의미의 (B) Although를 정답으로 고릅니다.

3. Any package will be returned to the sender ------- we fail to make a delivery after three attempts.

(A) if   (B) or   (C) while   (D) that

세 번의 시도에도 배달이 되지 않으면 어떠한 소포라도 보낸 사람에게 돌려보내질 것이다.

> **이렇게 풀어요**
>
> 1. **선택지 보고 문법/어휘 문제 파악** 선택지가 모두 접속사로 구성되어 있으므로 어휘 문제임을 파악해요.
> 2. **빈칸 분석** 빈칸 앞뒤 문장의 문맥으로 보아 '세 번의 시도에도 배달이 되지 않으면'이라는 의미가 되어야 함을 파악합니다.
> 3. **정답 선택** '~라면'이라는 의미의 (A) if를 정답으로 고릅니다.

PART 5 어휘

부사 어휘 (4)

각 어휘와 함께 자주 쓰이는 표현을 통째로 외워두세요.

01 severely — 심하게, 엄격하게
- severely damaged — 심한 피해를 입은
- severely affected by — ~의 영향을 심하게 받은

02 securely — 단단히, 안전하게
- securely fastened — 단단히 고정된
- wrapped securely — 안전하게 포장된

🐾 빈출 토익 선생님 Pick!
03 appropriately — 적절히, 알맞게
- respond appropriately — 적절히 대응하다
- be appropriately dressed — 적절히 차려입다

04 accurately — 정확히, 정밀하게
- predict accurately — 정확히 예측하다
- accurate record the expenditures — 지출을 정확히 기록하다

05 eagerly — 열심히, 간절히
- eagerly await — 간절히 기다리다
- eagerly anticipated — 간절히 고대했던

06 collaboratively — 협력하여
- work collaboratively with — ~와 협력하여 일하다

07 commonly — 보통, 흔히
- commonly known as — 보통 ~로 알려진
- commonly used strategy — 흔히 사용되는 전략

08 individually — 개별적으로, 각각 따로
- be individually wrapped — 개별 포장이 되어 있다

🐾 빈출 토익 선생님 Pick!
09 substantially — 상당히, 많이
- increase/rise substantially — 상당히 오르다
- decrease/fall substantially — 상당히 감소하다

10 beforehand — 사전에, 미리
- register beforehand — 사전에 등록하다
- arrange a meeting beforehand — 사전에 회의를 주선하다

11 casually — (복장이) 약식으로
- dress casually — 평상복 차림을 하다
- wear casually — 편하게 입다

12 merely — 그저, 단지
- be merely an estimate — 단지 추정일 뿐이다

13 momentarily — 잠깐, 잠시, 곧
- be halted momentarily — 잠시 중단되다
- will resume momentarily — 곧 재개될 것이다

14 enormously — 엄청나게, 대단히
- vary enormously — 엄청나게 다르다
- benefit enormously from — ~에서 크게 이익을 얻다

🐾 빈출 토익 선생님 Pick!
15 frequently — 자주, 빈번히
- frequently visited — 자주 방문되는
- occur frequently — 자주 발생하다
- meet frequently — 자주 만나다

16 broadly
대략, 폭넓게, 널리

broadly defined — 폭넓게 정의되는
be used broadly — 널리 쓰이다

17 clearly
또렷하게, 분명히

clearly explain — 분명하게 설명하다
clearly defined — 명료하게 규정된

👣 빈출 토익 선생님 Pick!
18 thoroughly
완전히, 철저히

thoroughly inspected/researched — 철저히 검사된/조사된
read guidelines thoroughly — 가이드라인을 꼼꼼히 읽다
thoroughly impressed with — ~에 깊은 감명을 받은

19 deeply
깊이, 크게

think deeply — 깊이 생각하다
deeply concerned — 깊이 염려하는

`900+`
20 impartially
공평하게, 편견 없이

be distributed impartially — 공평하게 분배되다
rule impartially on — ~을 편견 없이 판결하다
evaluate impartially — 공정하게 평가하다

`800+`
21 attentively
주의 깊게, 신경써서

handle customer suggestions attentively
고객의 제안을 주의 깊게 다루다
examine the trends attentively — 동향을 주의 깊게 검토하다
listen attentively to — ~을 귀 기울여 듣다

`800+`
22 rigidly
엄격히, 완고하게

rigidly follow — 엄격히 따르다
rigidly enforced — 엄격히 시행된

23 equally
똑같이, 동등하게

distribute equally — 동등하게 배분하다
equally important — 똑같이 중요한

24 exactly
정확히

remain exactly the same — 정확히 똑같다

25 approximately
거의, 약, 대략

last approximately 시간 표현 — 약 ~ 동안 지속되다

26 personally
직접, 개인적으로

personally respond to — ~에 직접 응답하다
personally recommended — 직접 추천된

🧑 풀이 방법

To ensure their satisfaction, Ms. Yates ------- calls customers during the first month after they purchase a vehicle.

(A) severely   (B) frequently   (C) accurately   (D) rigidly

그들의 만족을 보장하기 위해, Yates 씨는 고객들이 차를 구입한 후 첫 달 동안 자주 그들에게 전화를 한다.

> 🖊 이렇게 풀어요
>
> 1. **선택지 보고 문법/어휘 문제 파악** 선택지가 서로 다른 부사 어휘로 구성되어 있으므로 어휘 문제임을 파악해요.
> 2. **빈칸 분석** 빈칸 앞에 to부정사구가 있으므로 '~을 위해 Yates 씨는 고객들에게 ------- 전화한다'라는 문맥이 되어야 함을 파악합니다.
> 3. **정답 선택** '만족을 보장하기 위해 자주 전화한다'라는 문맥이 되는 것이 가장 자연스러우므로 (B) frequently를 정답으로 고릅니다.

PART 5 어휘 부사 어휘 (4) 435

DAY 18

따라 하면 문제가 풀리는

연습 문제

앞서 학습한 문제 풀이법을 적용하여 맞는 것에 ✔ 표시 하거나 괄호 안에
적절한 답을 쓰고 정답을 선택하세요.

---

01 ------- Ms. Nixon is unable to attend the meeting, Mr. Tyler will fill in for her.

(A) About
(B) Only
(C) If
(D) Other

> 1. 선택지 보고 문법/어휘 문제 파악하기 ☐ 문법 문제 ☐ 어휘 문제
>
> 2. 빈칸 분석하기 빈칸 뒤에 있는 것 ☐ 완전한 절 2개 ☐ 불완전한 절 1개와 완전한 절 1개
>
>   → 빈칸에는 ☐ 접속사 ☐ 전치사가 들어가야 한다.
>
> 3. 정답 선택하기 정답 (   )

---

02 Our chocolate-dipped cookies are ------- wrapped for protection.

(A) severely
(B) individually
(C) eagerly
(D) broadly

> 1. 선택지 보고 문법/어휘 문제 파악하기 ☐ 문법 문제 ☐ 어휘 문제
>
> 2. 빈칸 분석하기 빈칸 뒤에 있는 동사 (   )
>
>   → '보호를 위해 ------- 포장되어 있다'는 문맥에 어울리는 부사가 들어가야 한다.
>
> 3. 정답 선택하기 정답 (   )

---

03 Mr. Peck decided to open his business ------- the economy is in recession.

(A) because
(B) so that
(C) until
(D) although

> 1. 선택지 보고 문법/어휘 문제 파악하기 ☐ 문법 문제 ☐ 어휘 문제
>
> 2. 빈칸 분석하기 빈칸 앞 내용과 뒤 내용의 의미 관계가 ☐ 대조되는 내용 ☐ 목적을 나타내는 내용이 되는 것이 자연스럽다.
>
> 3. 정답 선택하기 정답 (   )

🔍 정답 및 해설 p.150

04 ------- Ms. Hanson is retiring, the personnel department is seeking a replacement.

(A) Though
(B) Because
(C) While
(D) Until

1. 선택지 보고 문법/어휘 문제 파악하기 ☐ 문법 문제 ☐ 어휘 문제
2. 빈칸 분석하기 빈칸 뒤에 있는 2개의 문장의 의미 관계가 ☐ 대조되는 내용 ☐ 이유를 나타내는 내용이 되는 것이 자연스럽다.
3. 정답 선택하기 정답 (   )

05 Ms. White renewed her license ------- she can qualify for the position.

(A) so that
(B) after
(C) since
(D) because

1. 선택지 보고 문법/어휘 문제 파악하기 ☐ 문법 문제 ☐ 어휘 문제
2. 빈칸 분석하기 빈칸 앞뒤 문장의 의미 관계가 ☐ 목적을 나타내는 내용 ☐ 대조되는 내용이 되는 것이 자연스럽다.
3. 정답 선택하기 정답 (   )

06 ------- farmland areas experience flooding, the average price of produce goes up significantly.

(A) Whenever
(B) Due to
(C) Following
(D) Besides

1. 선택지 보고 문법/어휘 문제 파악하기 ☐ 문법 문제 ☐ 어휘 문제
2. 빈칸 분석하기 빈칸 뒤에 있는 것 ☐ 완전한 절 2개 ☐ 불완전한 절 1개와 완전한 절 1개
   → 빈칸에는 ☐ 접속사 ☐ 전치사가 들어가야 한다.
3. 정답 선택하기 정답 (   )

PART 5 부사절 접속사 / 부사 어휘 (4)   437

DAY 01-18 누적 문제

제한시간 9분입니다! 시~작!

01. ------- everyone on the list arrived, Mr. Glover came out from backstage to give a welcoming speech.
(A) After
(B) About
(C) Last
(D) Only

02. Since they worked on the project together, both team members' bonuses were distributed -------.
(A) equally
(B) commonly
(C) eagerly
(D) particularly

03. ------- you have questions about your reservation, please e-mail our service team.
(A) For
(B) If
(C) Then
(D) And

04. ------- she had to take a detour, Ms. Wallace made it to the open house event early.
(A) Although
(B) Unless
(C) Since
(D) So that

05. ------- she attends classes in the morning, Ms. Dunlap only works later shifts.
(A) Due to
(B) Because
(C) Until
(D) Consequently

06. Lawrence High School bans the use of smartphones ------- students can concentrate on printed materials.
(A) such as
(B) so that
(C) ahead of
(D) while

07. Get free shipping ------- you place an order for $50 or more on jennyscloset.com.
(A) in that
(B) though
(C) whenever
(D) as much as

08. All passengers' luggage must be inspected at the customs area, ------- it was checked by security prior to boarding.
(A) with
(B) since
(C) among
(D) even if

09. Contest finalists will be notified ------- they have been selected by the panel.
(A) from
(B) once
(C) because
(D) against

10. ------- there are unexpected delays, orders will normally be delivered in two business days.
(A) Especially
(B) How
(C) Unless
(D) That

11. Lainey Corporation is recruiting people ------- have a background in customer service.
(A) who
(B) when
(C) whose
(D) wherever

12. Cummings Insurance will be moving to a larger office ------- it plans to hire several additional staff members.
(A) moreover
(B) while
(C) because of
(D) since

438   기적의 토익 RC

13. Residents are ------- concerned about possible flooding in St. Louis from another storm.

(A) rigidly
(B) firmly
(C) deeply
(D) newly

14. The Pottsdale Community Center organizes an awards ceremony ------- recognizes locals for their volunteering work.

(A) from
(B) which
(C) they
(D) if

15. Gold Members are given free investment advice and counseling, ------- other bank clients have to pay for such services.

(A) such
(B) around
(C) either
(D) whereas

16. Ms. Serrano must submit the daily report before she ------- the laboratory.

(A) left
(B) leaves
(C) had left
(D) is leaving

17. The spike in Pierson Electronics' stock value can ------- to the success of their mobile devices.

(A) be attributed
(B) attributes
(C) attributed
(D) attributing

18. ------- complaints from local residents, Stark Construction continued working at night to remain on schedule.

(A) In spite of
(B) Thanks to
(C) Apart from
(D) Including

19. Please make sure that your seatbelt is ------- fastened before takeoff.

(A) broadly
(B) exactly
(C) merely
(D) securely

20. The winners will be announced ------- the panel judges reach a final decision.

(A) upon
(B) nearly
(C) as soon as
(D) moreover

21. The owner of Rossville Used Cars ------- inspects all vehicles that customers want to trade in for credit.

(A) aggressively
(B) exceptionally
(C) personally
(D) relatively

22. All products are tested ------- before being shipped out from the warehouse at the end of each day.

(A) casually
(B) thoroughly
(C) impartially
(D) approximately

23. The training session has been postponed ------- all employees return from vacation.

(A) to
(B) into
(C) until
(D) upon

24. The children listened ------- to the presentation the museum tour guide gave.

(A) attentively
(B) enormously
(C) individually
(D) definitely

PART 5 부사절 접속사 / 부사 어휘 (4) 439

PART 6

알맞은 문장 고르기 – 선택지에 접속부사

선택지 문장에 접속부사가 있을 경우 앞뒤 문맥을 정확히 파악하는 것이 중요해요.

적용 기술

[기적의 필기노트] 164P
RC 기술 82

VOCA

refer to ~을 참고하다
handbook 안내서
procedural 절차의
precise 정확한
record 기록
transaction 거래
ensure 보장하다
account 계정
measure 조치

풀이 방법 — excerpt from a manual

해석 p.153

Refer to this handbook to review procedural or policy rules ------- you are working
 PART 5
here at Bryant Accounting. Our business has thousands of clients, and it is
important that we keep precise records of all transactions. Only thanks to our cyber
security team are we able to ensure the safety and privacy of our client accounts.
They do an excellent job of preventing our network from being hacked into. -------.
 01.

For example, you are all required to use a secure password that is to be changed
every other month.

01. (A) Therefore, be sure to use the proper format.
   (B) Besides, cyber threats are more serious than ever these days.
   (C) If you have a question, ask your immediate supervisor right away.
   (D) Nonetheless, some security measures must be followed by all
      employees.

이렇게 풀어요

1. 선택지 보고 문법/어휘 문제 파악 문장 고르기 문제이므로 각 선택지를 먼저 보고 대략적인 내용이나 특징을 파악합니다.
  (A) 그러므로, 적합한 양식을 사용하라고 안내함
  (B) 게다가, 사이버 폭력이 요즘 심각함
  (C) 질문이 있을 경우 상사에게 물어보라고 함
  (D) 그럼에도 불구하고, 몇몇 안전 조치들은 반드시 준수해야 함

2. 빈칸 분석 빈칸 앞 내용은 사이버 보안 팀이 네트워크가 해킹당하지 않도록 막는 일을 잘해내고 있다는 내용이고, 빈칸 뒤에는 모든 직원들에게 보안 비밀번호를 사용해야 한다는 예시를 들고 있어요.

3. 정답 선택 사이버 보안 팀이 업무를 잘해내고 있지만 그래도 여전히 안전 조치를 지켜야 하고, 그 예로 보안 비밀번호를 사용해야 한다는 흐름이 되는 것이 자연스러우므로 (D)를 정답으로 고릅니다.

해설

빈칸 앞의 안내서를 참고하는 것과 빈칸 뒤의 이곳에서 일하는 동작이 동시에 이루어지는 상황이므로 시간 부사절을 이끄는 접속사 (B)가 정답입니다.

PART 5 문법 적용 문제

Refer to this handbook to review procedural or policy rules ------- you are working here
at Bryant Accounting.

(A) except   (B) while   (C) how   (D) where

440 기적의 토익 RC

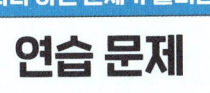

따라 하면 문제가 풀리는

연습 문제

빈칸 앞뒤 내용에서 단서가 될 부분을 찾아 표시하세요.
표시한 것을 바탕으로 정답 어휘를 선택하세요.

정답 및 해설 p.153

01

Your store's policy clearly states that items should be returned within one week in order to get a full refund. -------. I was out of town on business when my order arrived. By the time I found it was defective, I had already missed that window. I look forward to finding out whether you can help me or not.

(A) Also, your Web site mentions that your policy has changed.
(B) However, I hope that you can make an exception in this case.

02

A construction crew will be renovating several areas of our grocery store next month. They said that most of the work will be performed outside of our regular business hours. -------. We apologize for the inconvenience and possible noise in advance.

(A) Nevertheless, some work needs to be done while our store is open.
(B) It is the most highly rated construction company in the region.

03

The Frequent Flyer Club members will receive double points during this promotion. -------. So please hurry to log into our Web site to book your flight for this summer vacation.

(A) Therefore, it will last for two weeks from today.
(B) In addition, you automatically enter the lottery to win a free seat upgrade.

04

You're all aware that competition for government research grants is very intense these days. In order to win one of them, all required documents should be well prepared in a timely manner. -------. You can see what your department needs to prepare according to the timeline.

(A) A $50,000 grant was awarded to Camden Research Group last year.
(B) Therefore, I will distribute a checklist to you.

DAY 18

PART 6 알맞은 문장 고르기-선택지에 접속부사 441

토익에 나올
실전 문제

제한시간 4분입니다! 시~작!

Questions 01-04 refer to the following instructions.

Return and exchange procedure

In this part, you can find a simple solution for customer service ------. We understand it is not easy
01.
to handle all return and exchange requests. Some customers can just change their mind, or others
are very upset with our products. Here at Fashion de Florence, we value our customers the most.
------. If they bring in an item to return or exchange it, do not question them. Simply use the register
02.
to ------ the transaction. Thanks to this policy, our store ------ its reputation as the most customer-
03.   **04.**
friendly retail store in the region.

---

01. (A) issues
 (B) months
 (C) settings
 (D) reasons

03. (A) restart
 (B) replace
 (C) produce
 (D) process

유형 적용 문제

02. (A) If there is no supervisor nearby, use the phone by
  the register.
 (B) Enter the number on the price tag using the touch
  screen.
 (C) Discounted prices may not be applied to certain
  merchandise.
 (D) Hence, we have a motto that the customer is
  always right.

04. (A) can maintain
 (B) maintaining
 (C) had been maintaining
 (D) should have maintained

Questions 05-08 refer to the following memo.

From: Factory manager
To: Production workers
Date: March 19
Subject: Safety

Dear my colleagues,

Always keep safety in mind while on job sites. Because we use various toxic chemicals as raw materials, we may face hazardous situations while doing daily tasks. -------. If you see any potential
05.
hazards like this, report them to your supervisor immediately. They will take ------- to secure the
06.
hazard and put up appropriate signs. Never take shortcuts if it means ignoring ------- regulations.
07.
Please consult the checklist of what you have to follow when that particular situation happens.
Employees should never resume their work if any dangerous situations have not been -------.
08.
Thanks.

유형 적용 문제

05. (A) Please refer to the symbols on the chart in the manual book.
(B) For example, oils or liquid chemicals are spilt on the floor.
(C) We have a contract with an outside company.
(D) All production workers are required to join the on-the-job training.

06. (A) measures
(B) accounts
(C) opportunities
(D) options

07. (A) safety
(B) safely
(C) safe
(D) safes

08. (A) clearly
(B) cleared
(C) clearance
(D) clearing

PART 6 알맞은 문장 고르기–선택지에 접속부사 443

PART 7

양식 – 일정표/초대장/영수증 등

표가 제시되는 양식은 문제를 먼저 읽고 키워드를 기억해서 관련된 정보를 지문에서 찾으세요.

양식은 일정표(schedule), 초대장(invitation), 영수증(receipt), 송장(invoice), 전단지(flyer) 등 다양한 지문이 출제됩니다. 대부분의 지문에 시간, 날짜, 장소, 일정, 대상이 언급되는데 이러한 정보들이 문제로 출제되므로 모두 파악해 두어야 합니다.

여러 양식 지문에서 자주 출제되는 어휘

양식 지문에서 자주 출제되는 문제

· 세부 정보 문제
What is (NOT) indicated/stated in the invoice?
→ 반드시 선택지를 먼저 읽고 키워드를 기억한 후 지문에서 해당 정보가 있는지 없는지 빠르게 찾아 정답을 고릅니다.

1 영수증(receipt)/송장(invoice)

item	품목	quantity(Qty)	수량
unit price	단가	amount	총액
balance due	잔금, 미불액	billing address	청구 주소
paid by	~로 지불된	shipping address	배송 주소
transaction	거래	make a payment	결제하다
paper receipt	종이 영수증	subtotal	소계
summary	요약	recipient	받는 사람
proceed	진행하다	tax	세금; 세금을 부과하다

⚠️ **주의**

송장이나 주문서 지문에서는 비용을 지급한 날짜도 확인해야 해요.

2 전단지(flyer)/쿠폰(coupon, voucher)

present	제시하다	apply to	~에게 적용되다
be good for	~에게 유효하다	save	절약하다
cost	비용	tentative	임시적인
vendor	판매 회사, 행상인	economical	경제적인, 실속있는
reflect	반영하다	top seller	가장 잘 팔리는 것

🔒 **기출 확인**

초대장에서 자주 나오는 행사
banquet 연회
reception 환영/축하 행사
awards ceremony 시상식
charity 자선 행사
gala 경축 행사

3 초대장(invitation)

invite	초대하다	attendance	참석
formal	공식적인, 형식적인	rain date	우천시 행사 변경일
donate	기부하다	in the event of	~할 경우에는
reception	환영(회)	annual	연례의
book signing	책 사인회	presence	참석

양식 – 일정표/초대장/영수증 등

invoice

○ 해석 p.155

Riverside Inc. Invoice

Bill To: Golden Horizon Travels
ATTN: Cecil Fulton, Operations Manager
Delivery Location: 419 Celtic Way, Glenville

Item/Service	Unit Price	Quantity	Amount
A4 Paper	$15.00	4	$60.00
A3 Paper	$20.00	2	$80.00
Toner (X model series)	$17.00	2	$34.00
Toner (AZ model series)	$35.00	1	$35.00
*USB stick	$40.00	1	$40.00
Total			$249.00

*able to be connected to any computer models

Thank you for choosing Riverside Inc.! If you have any problems or questions, or would like to provide feedback about your experience with us, please contact Alissa Gill at a.gill@riversideinc.com.

01. What kind of business is Riverside Inc.?

(A) An airline
(B) A travel agency
(C) A stationery store
(D) A paper manufacturer

02. What is NOT indicated in the invoice?

(A) Where to send the shipment
(B) Which item is compatible
(C) Whom to contact at Riverside Inc.
(D) When the delivery was made

이렇게 풀어요

01. Riverside 사는 어떤 종류의 사업체인가?

(A) 항공사
(B) 여행사
(C) 문구점
(D) 종이 제조업체

해설 주문 내역 표의 paper, toner, USB stick을 통해 문구류를 취급하는 업체라는 것을 알 수 있으므로 (C)가 정답입니다.

02. 송장에서 언급되지 않은 것은 무엇인가?

(A) 어디로 배송해야 하는지
(B) 어떤 모델이 호환이 되는지
(C) Riverside 사의 누구에게 연락할지
(D) 언제 배송이 되었는지

해설 표 위의 Delivery Location에서 (A)를 확인할 수 있고 별표 (*)로 표시된 USB stick에 대한 설명 able to be connected ~ models를 통해 (B)를 확인할 수 있습니다. 또한 지문 마지막의 please contact Alissa를 통해 (C)도 확인 가능합니다. 배송이 언제 되었는지는 알 수 없으므로 (D)가 정답입니다.

PART 7 양식-일정표/초대장/영수증 등 445

따라 하면 문제가 풀리는

연습 문제

먼저 문제의 키워드에 표시한 후,
지문에서 단서를 찾아 적절한 답을 고르세요.

---

01 receipt

RECEIPT OF CASH PAYMENT

DATE: November 2
EMPLOYEE NAME: Isabelle Dunbar
DEPARTMENT: Sales

DESCRIPTION OF PAYMENT	AMOUNT
Cash received for taxi fares to and from the airport and all meals during a business trip to Montreal, where I will take part in a workshop designed for sales managers. Departing from Toronto to Montreal on November 5 and returning November 8.	$300.00

Payment issued by: Nicholas Mitchell
Payment received by: Isabelle Dunbar
Signature: *Isabelle Dunbar*

Q. What does Ms. Dunbar plan to do in Montreal?

(A) Attend a training session
(B) Sign a business contract

---

02 voucher

Castillo Hotel: Customer Voucher

Issued to: Bethany Namara

The voucher entitles the holder to one complimentary one-hour massage of their choice. It can be used at any Castillo Hotel site that offers an on-site spa: Castillo Hotel Seattle, Castillo Hotel Portland, or Castillo Hotel Sacramento.

This voucher cannot be combined with any other offer, and it has no cash value. Please inform the receptionist at the time of booking that a voucher will be presented.

Date of issue: January 10   Authorized by: Carl Turner

Q. What is NOT indicated on the voucher?

(A) When it will expire
(B) Where it is valid

03 invitation

Lander Dance Studio
cordially invites you to

Garden of Wonders
Saturday, July 12, 7 P.M.

Enjoy a five-course banquet at Nova Plaza while being entertained by professional and amateur dance performances. All proceeds from ticket sales for the event will go directly to Lander Dance Studio, the city's only non-profit studio for dance students.

Valet parking is available on-site, and the dress code for this event is formal.
We look forward to seeing you!

Q. What kind of event is Garden of Wonders?

(A) A dance contest
(B) A fundraising dinner

04 schedule of events

Regional Photography Conference
October 8–10 · Finnegan Convention Center

Schedule for Friday, October 10

Vendor Booths	**9:00 A.M.–Noon**
Camera accessories and equipment will be on sale in the main hall.	
Networking Luncheon	**Noon–1:30 P.M.**
Enjoy a catered lunch while networking with other professionals in the field.	
"Bringing Nature to Life"	**1:30 P.M.–3:00 P.M.**
Nature photographer Craig Mahmood gives a talk on capturing the beauty of nature in your photography.	
"Seven Elements of Design"	**3:30 P.M.–5:00 P.M.**
Vera Bradley, editor of *Images Magazine*, presents this talk on the key elements in good composition.	

Q. What is suggested about the final day of the Regional Photography Conference?

(A) It will include a closing ceremony.
(B) It does not have any talks in the morning.

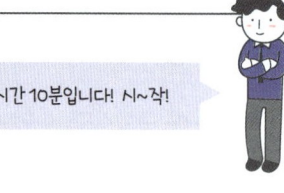

제한시간 10분입니다! 시~작!

Questions 01-02 refer to the following form.

Jocelyn's Gardening & Landscaping Services
Service Order Form

Requested date(s): August 25

Location: Goodwin University (Newly Acquired Western Plot)

Client name: Brenna Cruz

Mobile phone: 555-4323

Contract #: GH32354354

Estimated time: 6 hours

Tasks: Clear overgrown area, Remove weeds, Plant trees around edges of area

Required plants: 38 pine trees (medium)

Vehicle access: No

Water source: Yes

Other details / Specific requests: Students will begin moving in on 10 August. All work must be completed before that date.

01. What is implied about Goodwin University?

    (A) It has multiple campuses throughout Goodwin.
    (B) It is known for its agricultural programs.
    (C) It recently purchased some land.
    (D) It offers scholarships to locals.

02. What is suggested about the job site?

    (A) It is required to be accessed by foot.
    (B) It will be used to host events.
    (C) It is located next to a dormitory.
    (D) It features a beautiful flower bed.

paraphrasing 주어진 어휘 또는 표현과 패러프레이징 될 수 있는 것을 연결하세요.

1. newly acquired •	• (a) financial aid
2. task •	• (b) work list
3. remove •	• (c) hold
4. scholarship •	• (d) recently purchased
5. host •	• (e) get rid of

448 기적의 토익 RC

📍정답 및 해설 p.156

Questions 03-05 refer to the following invoice.

Margot Supplies Customer Invoice

Customer Name: Justine Goetz

Shipping Address: 392 Stark St.,Lombard, IL 60148

Payment: Credit Card XXXX-XXXX-XXXX-6798

Phone: 733-555-7901

Address Type: [X] Commercial   [ ] Residential

Order Date: July 29

Item #	Brand / Description	Unit Price	Quantity	Total
G0944	Stylz / Volumizing Shampoo	$12.99	15	$194.85
L7406	Fay / Deep Conditioning Treatment	$19.99	8	$159.92
S3185	Dario / Extra Strong Hair Gel	$5.99	20	$119.80
Z8520	Nolette / All-Day Anti-Frizz Serum	$24.99	12	$299.88
Coupon Applied: Discount code FAYSUMMER, 15% off all Fay products. All orders are shipped by overnight delivery absolutely free!		Subtotal		$774.45
		Discount		-$23.99
		Tax		$46.47
Thank you for being a Margot Supplies customer!		**Total**		**$796.93**

03. Where most likely does Ms. Goetz work?

(A) At a hardware store
(B) At a hair salon
(C) At a coffee shop
(D) At a delivery company

04. For which product did Ms. Goetz receive a discount?

(A) G0944
(B) L7406
(C) S3185
(D) Z8520

05. What is suggested by the invoice?

(A) The goods are expected to arrive on July 30.
(B) Ms. Goetz is a regular customer of Margot Supplies.
(C) Shipping fees will be charged for the order.
(D) Ms. Goetz used some store credit toward the purchase.

---

paraphrasing   주어진 어휘 또는 표현과 패러프레이징 될 수 있는 것을 연결하세요.

1. free •   • (a) use
2. delivery •   • (b) items
3. goods •   • (c) shipping
4. regular customer •   • (d) doesn't charge
5. apply •   • (e) purchases regularly

DAY 18

PART 7 양식-일정표/초대장/영수증 등   449

Questions 06-10 refer to the following advertisement and form.

Take your career to the next level with help from the Bertram Institute!

The Bertram Institute is partnering with the Regional Business Elite Association (RBEA) to provide its third annual Intensive Workshop to help business professionals improve their skills. For the first time, we are filming the proceedings so that participants can view the video later as a way to review the topics that were covered. The session will last from 9 A.M. to 5 P.M., with a one-hour lunch break (please bring a sack lunch or visit one of the nearby cafés). RBEA members can get an exclusive 20% discount on the fees. Register online at www.bertraminst.com.

This year's sessions:
"Harnessing Productivity: Making the Most of Your Time" – Presenter: Celina Enriquez
"Accounting Practices for the Tech-Savvy" – Presenter: Larry Bluhm
"The Do's and Don'ts of Supervising Your Team" – Presenter: Jasmine Mata

If you are traveling from out of town to attend the workshop, we have arranged a special discount at Carriage Hotel. Contact Nicole Montford at 555-0978 for more information about that facility and how to receive the discount.

Thank you for providing feedback about the classes and workshop at the Bertram Institute. We value your opinions, and we will use them to improve future activities.

Name: Beth Knutson   Class/Workshop: Intensive Workshop

1. How likely are you to recommend the Bertram Institute to a friend? Very likely
2. How satisfied were you with the overall class/workshop? Mostly satisfied
3. How satisfied were you with the building and facilities? Very satisfied
4. What was your favorite part of the class/workshop? The session taught by Ms. Mata was extremely helpful because it fits perfectly with my current role. I loved her real-life examples, which made the content more relatable.
5. How could we improve this class/workshop for next time? Even though it was an intensive workshop, I was surprised that lunch was the only time we were not in session. I think people would absorb the information better if there were short rest times in mid-morning and mid-afternoon.

06. What has changed about the workshop compared to last year?

(A) It will be recorded for future use.
(B) It will start earlier in the day.
(C) It will feature multiple presenters.
(D) It will be held at a different location.

07. What is indicated about the workshop participants?

(A) They must be Regional Business Elite Association members.
(B) They will receive a certificate of completion after the workshop.
(C) They are required to make their own arrangements for a meal.
(D) They can pay their registration fee at the door.

08. According to the advertisement, why should people contact Ms. Montford?

(A) To schedule a private session
(B) To register for the workshop
(C) To report problems with a Web site
(D) To inquire about accommodations

09. What is suggested about Ms. Knutson?

(A) She enjoys working with technology.
(B) She has problems with being productive.
(C) She is visiting from out of town.
(D) She oversees other employees.

10. What change would Ms. Knutson most likely be in favor of?

(A) Using a quieter room
(B) Adding more breaks
(C) Modernizing the building
(D) Offering the class online

---

paraphrasing 주어진 어휘 또는 표현과 패러프레이징 될 수 있는 것을 연결하세요.

1. filming •
2. topics that were covered •
3. bring a sack lunch •
4. helpful •
5. rest times •

• (a) be recorded
• (b) informative
• (c) breaks
• (d) subjects that were dealt with
• (e) make their own arrangements for a meal

PART 7 양식-일정표/초대장/영수증 등   451

DAY 18

'멋진 당신, 오늘도 화이팅'

DAY
19

오늘의 학습 포인트

PART 5. 비교 구문
1. 원급 비교 - as 형용사/부사의 원급 as
2. 비교급 비교 - 형용사/부사의 -er + than
   - more 형용사/부사 than
3. 최상급 비교 - the/소유격 + 형용사/부사의 -est
   - the/소유격 + most + 형용사/부사
4. 비교급/최상급 관용 표현 - no later than, A rather than B, at least 등

PART 6. 알맞은 문장 고르기 - 빈칸 뒤에 접속부사
접속부사 의미 먼저 파악하기

PART 7. 후기/설문조사
진위 확인 문제 출제

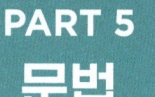

PART 5
문법

비교 구문

비교급이나 최상급 구문을 완성하는 문제가 주로 출제되며 평균 1문제 정도 나와요.

✏️ 적용 기술

[기적의 필기노트] 154P
RC 기술 71

🔒 확인 문제 ❶

This color printer can
produce as fast ------- the
black-and-white one.

(A) than
(B) as

출제 포인트
as many와 as much가
함께 선택지에 제시되므로
이 둘을 구분할 수 있어야
합니다.

출제 유형 1
원급 비교

1 원급 비교의 형태

> as 형용사/부사의 원급 as: ~만큼 –한/-하게
> not as 형용사/부사의 원급 as: ~만큼 –하지 않은/하지 않게

- 앞에 보어가 없는 불완전한 절이 있으면 'as ~ as' 사이에 형용사가 옵니다.
  The Q&A session was **as brief as** it was advertised.
  질문과 답변 시간은 안내된 만큼 짧았다.
  → as 앞에 있는 2형식 동사 was의 보어 역할을 해야 하므로 'as ~ as' 사이에 형용사 brief가 왔어요.

- 앞에 완전한 절이 있으면 'as ~ as' 사이에 부사가 옵니다.
  The transition to the new accounting system proceeded **as smoothly as**
  planned. 새 회계 시스템으로의 전환은 계획된 만큼 순조롭게 진행되었다.
  → as 앞에 자동사 proceeded로 끝나는 완전한 절이 있으므로 'as ~ as' 사이에 부사 smoothly가 왔어요.

`800+`
- 'as ~ as' 사이에 명사가 올 수 있습니다. 이때는 반드시 수량형용사가 함께 쓰입니다.

as many + 복수 명사 + as as much + 불가산 명사 + as	~만큼 많은 '명사'
as few + 복수 명사 + as as little + 불가산 명사 + as	~만큼 적은 '명사'

During the charity dinner, we must raise **as much** <u>funds</u> **as** we did last year.
자선 만찬 동안에 우리는 작년에 그랬던 것만큼 많은 기금을 모아야 한다.

`800+`
2 원급을 수식하는 부사

- 원급을 수식하는 부사는 'as ~ as' 앞에 위치합니다.

nearly 거의	almost 거의	just 딱, 꼭

The new laptop model is **just** <u>as light as</u> the existing one.
새 노트북 모델은 딱 기존의 것만큼 가볍다.

(B) ❶ 답정

454 기적의 토익 RC

출제 유형 2

비교급 비교

1 비교급의 형태

[1음절 단어] 형용사/부사의 -er + than: ~보다 더 -한/더 -하게
[2음절 이상의 단어] more 형용사/부사 than: ~보다 더 -한/더 -하게
less 형용사 than: ~보다 덜 -한/-하게

- 앞에 보어가 없는 불완전한 절이 있으면 'more ~ than' 사이에 형용사가 옵니다.
  Mobile shopping apps are **more popular than** online shopping.
  모바일 쇼핑앱은 온라인 쇼핑보다 더 인기있다.
  → more 앞의 2형식 동사 are의 보어 역할을 해야 하므로 'more ~ than' 사이에 형용사 popular가 왔어요.

- 앞에 완전한 절이 있으면 'more ~ than' 사이에 부사가 옵니다.
  With this checklist, you can spend your time **more productively than** other
  people. 이 체크리스트를 사용하면 다른 사람보다 시간을 더 생산적으로 보낼 수 있습니다.
  → more 앞에 완전한 절이 있으므로 'more ~ than' 사이에 부사 productively가 왔어요.

  `800+`
- 비교급 뒤에 명사가 올 경우, 'more/fewer/less + 명사 + than'의 형태로 쓰입니다. 이때
  more/fewer/less 앞에는 불완전한 절이 옵니다.

  불완전한 절 + more + 가산 복수/불가산 명사 + than 더 많은 '명사'
  불완전한 절 + fewer + 가산 복수 명사 + than 더 적은 '명사'
  불완전한 절 + less + 불가산 명사 + than 더 적은 '명사'

2 비교급 강조 표현

- 비교급을 수식하는 표현은 비교급 앞에 위치합니다.

  much/even/still/far/a lot/by far 훨씬

  The European market is **much** more competitive than the Asian one.
  유럽 시장은 아시아 시장보다 더 경쟁이 치열하다.

  `900+`
3 라틴어 비교급

- 라틴어 비교급은 -or로 끝나며 than 대신 to를 씁니다.

  prior to ~보다 먼저   superior to ~보다 우수한   inferior to ~보다 열등한

  The quality of our jacket is **superior to** that of other brands.
  우리 재킷의 품질은 다른 브랜드들의 것보다 더 우수하다.

적용 기술

[기적의 필기노트] 155P
RC 기술 72, 73

확인 문제 ❷

This apartment looks more
------- than mine.

(A) spacious
(B) spaciously

출제 포인트
비교급 강조 표현은 much
와 even이 가장 자주 출제
돼요.

확인 문제 ❸

Our new ice cream flavor
is ------- more popular than
existing ones.

(A) too
(B) even

정답 ❷ (A) ❸ (B)

DAY 19

PART 5 문법 비교 구문 455

적용 기술

[기적의 필기노트] 156P
RC 기술 74

🔒 확인 문제 ❹

These solar panels are the
most ------ of our products.

(A) efficient
(B) efficiently

⚠ 주의

부사의 최상급에는 the를 쓰지 않
아요.

출제 유형 3
최상급 비교

1 최상급의 형태

[1음절 단어] the/소유격 + 형용사/부사의 -est: 가장 ~한/가장 ~하게
[2음절 이상의 단어] the/소유격 + most + 형용사/부사: 가장 ~한/가장 ~하게
the/소유격 + least + 형용사/부사: 가장 덜 ~한/가장 덜 ~하게

- 앞에 보어가 없는 **불완전한 절**이 있으면 the/소유격 뒤에 **형용사**, 완전한 절이 있으면 **부사**를 씁니다.
  Regency Room is **the most spacious of** the banquet rooms.
  Regency Room은 연회실 중 가장 넓다.

- 최상급은 반드시 최상급이 속한 범위나 범주와 함께 사용해야 합니다.

among ~사이에서	out of ~중에서	of all 모든 ~중에서
in ~에서	ever 지금까지 가장 ~한	

Hudson Irvine is working **the most cooperatively among** the team members.
팀원들 가운데 Hudson Irvine이 가장 협조적으로 일하고 있습니다.

900+

2 최상급 강조 표현

- 아래 강조 부사는 **최상급 앞에** 위치합니다.

  by far/very/quite/much/even 단연코

- 아래 강조 표현은 **최상급 뒤에** 위치합니다.

the 최상급 ever 지금까지 가장 ~한	the 최상급 possible 가능한 가장 ~한

적용 기술

[기적의 필기노트] 157P
RC 기술 75

🔒 확인 문제 ❺

You are required to submit
the report no ------- than
Wednesday.

(A) late
(B) later

출제 유형 4
비교급/최상급 관용 표현

1 비교급 관용 표현

no later than 늦어도 ~까지 =by + 시점	than ever 전보다
more than + 숫자/시간 표현 ~ 이상	other than ~ 이외에
A rather than B B보다는 A	no longer 더 이상 ~ 하지 않는
no sooner A than B A하자마자 B하다	

800+

2 최상급 관용 표현

at least 적어도	at the latest 늦어도	at the earliest 빨라도
at your earliest convenience 가급적 빨리		

정답 ❹ (A) ❺ (B)

456 기적의 토익 RC

풀이방법 비교 구문

1. Ms. Scott suggested an alternate design to convey the message of the advertisement more ------- than before.

(A) effected   (B) effective   (C) effectively   (D) effect

Scott 씨는 광고의 메시지를 전보다 더 효과적으로 전달하기 위한 대안이 되는 디자인을 제안했다.

> **이렇게 풀어요**
>
> **1. 선택지 보고 문법/어휘 문제 파악** 선택지가 명사 또는 동사로 쓰이는 effect의 파생어로 구성되어 있으므로 문법 문제임을 파악해요.
> **2. 빈칸 분석** 빈칸 앞뒤에 각각 more와 than이 있으므로 비교급 관련 문제임을 파악합니다.
> **3. 정답 선택** 빈칸 앞에 완전한 문장이 있으므로 빈칸에는 동사 convey를 수식할 부사가 들어가야 합니다. 따라서 (C) effectively를 정답으로 고릅니다.

2. The environmentally friendly products are ------- more profitable than it was expected.

(A) even   (B) nearly   (C) very   (D) ever

친환경 제품들은 기대했던 것보다 훨씬 더 수익성이 좋다.

> **이렇게 풀어요**
>
> **1. 선택지 보고 문법/어휘 문제 파악** 선택지가 다양한 부사 어휘로 구성되어 있음을 파악해요.
> **2. 빈칸 분석** 빈칸 뒤에 비교급이 있으므로 이를 수식하는 부사가 들어가야 함을 파악합니다.
> **3. 정답 선택** 비교급을 강조할 수 있는 (A) even을 정답으로 고릅니다.

3. It will take ------- five business days to receive your order by ground shipping.

(A) much too   (B) even as   (C) as though   (D) at least

귀하의 주문 상품을 육로 배송으로 받는 데 영업일 기준으로 최소 5일이 소요됩니다.

> **이렇게 풀어요**
>
> **1. 선택지 보고 문법/어휘 문제 파악** 선택지가 다양한 품사의 어휘로 구성되어 있으므로 문법 문제임을 파악해요.
> **2. 빈칸 분석** 빈칸 뒤의 five business days를 수식할 수 있는 부사가 들어가야 함을 파악합니다.
> **3. 정답 선택** 숫자 표현 five와 함께 '적어도 5일의 영업일'이라는 의미를 만들 수 있는 (D) at least를 정답으로 고릅니다.

PART 5 문법 비교 구문

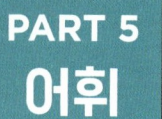

PART 5
어휘
빈출 숙어 (1)

숙어의 의미를 예문을 통해 효과적으로 암기하세요.

---

01 go through ~을 겪다, 거치다

New employees are required to **go through** an intense training program.
신입 직원들은 집중 교육 프로그램을 거치도록 요구된다.

02 fill in for ~의 일·직책을 대신하다

Some volunteers are needed to **fill in for** the employees who are taking leave next month.
다음 달에 휴가를 가는 직원들을 대신하기 위해 자발적으로 일할 사람들이 몇몇 필요하다.

☻ 빈출 토익 선생님 Pick!
03 carry out 시행하다, 실시하다

Deacon Marketing has been contracted to **carry out** a promotional campaign for us.
Deacon 마케팅 사는 우리의 홍보 캠페인을 시행하기로 계약을 맺었다.

900+
04 run the risk of ~의 위험을 감수하다

Medical staff members who do not use proper protection **run the risk of** becoming infected by patients. 적절한 보호물을 사용하지 않는 의료진들은 환자들에 의해 감염될 위험을 감수한다.

05 take place 개최되다, 열리다

Hometown Band's next performance will **take place** at Jones Beach. 이미 매진된 Hometown 밴드의 다음 공연은 Jones 해변에서 열릴 것이다.

☻ 빈출 토익 선생님 Pick!
06 compensate for ~에 대해 보상하다

Our company has no obligation to **compensate for** the outage. 우리 회사는 정전에 대해 보상할 의무가 없습니다.

800+ ☻ 빈출 토익 선생님 Pick!
07 attribute A to B A를 B의 덕분으로 보다

Werner Academy **attributes** its success **to** professionals who have a thirst for knowledge.
Werner 학회는 그들의 성공을 지식에 대한 열망이 있는 전문가들의 덕분으로 본다.

08 play a role 한몫을 하다, 역할을 맡다

The rising cost of fuel **played a role** in Ms. White's decision to sell her truck. 상승하는 연료비는 White 씨가 그녀의 트럭을 팔기로 결정하는 데 한몫을 했다.

09 turn down 거절하다

Mr. Hong **turned down** the job offer from Oakland Industries because he was unwilling to relocate.
Hong 씨는 이사하기가 싫었기 때문에 Oakland 산업의 일자리 제안을 거절했다.

☻ 빈출 토익 선생님 Pick!
10 pay off ~을 완전히 갚다, 성과를 거두다

Tomlin Law Firm offers assistance with **paying off** student loans to its employees. Tomlin 법률 사무소는 직원들에게 학자금 대출금을 완전히 갚아주는 것으로 도움을 준다.

800+
11 cope with ~에 대처하다

Pets such as dogs and cats often help people **cope with** stress in their lives. 개와 고양이 같은 애완동물들은 사람들이 삶의 스트레스에 대처하는 것을 종종 돕는다.

12 get along with ~와 잘 지내다

Part of being a competitive salesperson is the ability to **get along with** anyone. 경쟁력 있는 영업 사원이 되기 위한 조건 중 하나는 누구와도 잘 지내는 능력이다.

13 count on
~에 의지하다

Clients of Westbrook Insurance Company can **count on** friendly customer service around the clock. Westbrook 보험사의 고객들은 24시간 내내 친절한 고객 서비스에 의지할 수 있다.

빈출 토익 선생님 Pick!
14 fill out
작성하다, 기입하다

Fill out the customer survey to get 15% off your next purchase.
다음 구매 시 15퍼센트 할인을 받기 위해 고객 설문지를 작성하세요.

15 make up for
~을 벌충하다, 만회하다

Nikki's Bakery increased its prices to **make up for** the rise in the cost of flour. Nikki's 베이커리는 밀가루 가격의 상승을 벌충하기 위해 가격을 인상했다.

800+
16 run out of
~을 다 써버리다

Sarah's Café will **run out of** takeout cups if the daily shipment doesn't arrive soon. Sarah's 카페는 일일 배송품이 곧 도착하지 않으면 일회용 컵을 다 써버릴 것이다.

빈출 토익 선생님 Pick!
17 take over
~을 인계받다, 인수하다

Kate Marshall will **take over** the trade business after Mr. Bay's retirement.
Bay 씨의 은퇴 후에 Kate Marshall이 무역 사업을 인계받을 것이다.

18 call for
~을 필요로 하다, 요구하다

Employees on strike at Marcus Manufacturing are **calling for** a salary increase and paid leave. Marcus 제조사에서 파업 중인 직원들은 급여 인상과 유급 휴가를 요구하고 있다.

19 name after
~의 이름을 따서 명명하다

The latest invention by Future Tech was **named after** Mark Sellers, the company's first CEO.
Future Tech의 최신 발명품은 회사의 첫 번째 CEO인 Mark Sellers의 이름을 따서 명명했다.

800+
20 set forth
제시하다

The mayor of Wattsville **set forth** a plan to increase jobs in the public sector.
Wattsville의 시장은 공공 부문의 일자리를 늘리기 위한 계획을 제시했다.

풀이 방법

The city council will ------- its plan to renovate the local community center after agreeing on an appropriate budget.

(A) carry out   (B) take place   (C) give out   (D) pay off

시의회는 적절한 예산에 대해 협의한 후 지역 주민 센터를 보수하는 계획을 시행할 것이다.

이렇게 풀어요

1. **선택지 보고 문법/어휘 문제 파악** 선택지가 서로 다른 숙어 표현으로 구성되어 있으므로 어휘 문제임을 파악해요.
2. **빈칸 분석** 빈칸 뒤의 its plan(계획)과 함께 쓰일 수 있는 표현이 들어가야 함을 파악합니다.
3. **정답 선택** '시행하다, 실시하다'라는 의미의 (A) carry out을 정답으로 고릅니다.

PART 5 어휘 빈출 숙어 (1)   459

따라 하면 문제가 풀리는

연습 문제

앞서 학습한 문제 풀이법을 적용하여 맞는 것에 ✔ 표시 하거나 괄호 안에
적절한 답을 쓰고 정답을 선택하세요.

01 Please submit a recommendation for the position as ------- as you can.

(A) prompt
(B) prompted
(C) promptness
(D) promptly

1. 선택지 보고 문법/어휘 문제 파악하기 ☐ 문법 문제 ☐ 어휘 문제
2. 빈칸 분석하기 빈칸 앞과 뒤에 as가 있다. → ☐ 원급 구문 ☐ 최상급 구문
   → 빈칸 앞 as 앞에 ☐ 완전한 절 ☐ 불완전한 절이 있다.
   → 빈칸에는 ☐ 형용사 ☐ 부사가 들어가야 한다.
3. 정답 선택하기 정답 (   )

02 Keystone Cookware utensils are more ------- than those of other brands.

(A) expense
(B) expensive
(C) expensively
(D) expenses

1. 선택지 보고 문법/어휘 문제 파악하기 ☐ 문법 문제 ☐ 어휘 문제
2. 빈칸 분석하기 빈칸 앞에 more, 빈칸 뒤에 than이 있다. → ☐ 비교급 구문 ☐ 최상급 구문
   → 빈칸 앞 more 앞에 ☐ 완전한 절 ☐ 불완전한 절이 있다.
   → 빈칸에는 ☐ 형용사 ☐ 부사가 들어가야 한다.
3. 정답 선택하기 정답 (   )

03 Most airline passengers want more ------- for their bags than they are given.

(A) space
(B) spacious
(C) spaciously
(D) spacing

1. 선택지 보고 문법/어휘 문제 파악하기 ☐ 문법 문제 ☐ 어휘 문제
2. 빈칸 분석하기 빈칸 앞에 more, 빈칸 뒤에 ☐ 전치사 ☐ 부사가 있다.
   → 빈칸에는 ☐ 명사 ☐ 형용사가 들어가야 한다.
3. 정답 선택하기 정답 (   )

460 기적의 토익 RC

🔎 정답 및 해설 p.159

04 Sparkle Spark is one of the most ------- cleaners on the market.

(A) effect
(B) effects
(C) effective
(D) effectively

> 1. 선택지 보고 문법/어휘 문제 파악하기 ☐ 문법 문제 ☐ 어휘 문제
> 2. 빈칸 분석하기 빈칸 앞에 the most가 있다. → ☐ 비교급 구문 ☐ 최상급 구문
>   → 빈칸 앞 be동사 is의 보어 역할을 하는 것이 들어가야 한다.
>   → 빈칸에는 ☐ 형용사 ☐ 부사가 들어가야 한다.
> 3. 정답 선택하기 정답 (   )

05 Hydroelectric energy turned out to be ------- more profitable than originally predicted.

(A) very
(B) even
(C) clearly
(D) about

> 1. 선택지 보고 문법/어휘 문제 파악하기 ☐ 문법 문제 ☐ 어휘 문제
> 2. 빈칸 분석하기 빈칸 뒤에 있는 것 → ☐ 비교급 구문 ☐ 최상급 구문
>   → 빈칸 뒤 구문을 강조할 수 있는 부사가 정답이다.
> 3. 정답 선택하기 정답 (   )

06 The restaurant will ------- your extra work with an end-of-month bonus.

(A) compensate for
(B) give up
(C) name after
(D) turn down

> 1. 선택지 보고 문법/어휘 문제 파악하기 ☐ 문법 문제 ☐ 어휘 문제
> 2. 빈칸 분석하기 빈칸 뒤에 있는 명사구 (   )
>   명사구의 의미 (   )
>   → 이것을 '월말 보너스로 ------할 것이다'라는 문맥에 어울리는 동사가 정답이다.
> 3. 정답 선택하기 정답 (   )

DAY 19

PART 5 비교 구문 / 빈출 숙어 (1)   461

DAY 01~19 누적 문제

제한시간 9분입니다! 시~작!

01. All tasks on the job site should be carried out as ------- as possible to avoid any accidents or injuries.

(A) safe
(B) safest
(C) safety
(D) safely

02. Any customer complaints at Nielsen Grocery Store should be resolved more ------- than before.

(A) prompt
(B) promptly
(C) prompting
(D) prompted

03. Ms. Collins has more certifications ------- the other applicants do.

(A) than
(B) when
(C) as
(D) for

04. Please follow provided directions carefully when you ------- your Tony Digital Entertainment System.

(A) make sense
(B) cope with
(C) name after
(D) set up

05. Ms. Morris and Mr. Kemp ------- to Paris to cover the Fashion Week.

(A) travels
(B) was traveling
(C) traveled
(D) traveling

06. Critics agree that the second sequel was the most ------- of the trilogy.

(A) to impress
(B) impression
(C) impressively
(D) impressive

07. Thanks to automated equipment, the assembly line is capable of producing goods ------- faster.

(A) ever
(B) seldom
(C) a lot
(D) in order to

08. The energy generating water pipe turbine invented by Ayden Cooke is considered his most ------- idea yet.

(A) innovation
(B) innovates
(C) innovative
(D) innovatively

09. You should arrive ------- 15 minutes early to go through the security checkpoint.

(A) as much
(B) rather than
(C) at least
(D) very enough

10. No car repair shops in Erie are as ------- to its loyal customers as Bird Auto is.

(A) response
(B) responsive
(C) respond
(D) responsively

11. Saunders Engineering has built an engine that is more ------- than others on the market.

(A) efficient
(B) efficiency
(C) efficiently
(D) efficiencies

12. Zavala Home Online rearranged its main warehouse so that it can locate merchandise for orders more -------.

(A) quickest
(B) quicker
(C) quickly
(D) quick

462   기적의 토익 RC

13. *Nashville Monthly Update* is the ------- subscribed magazine about country music in Tennessee.

(A) most widely
(B) more widely
(C) widening
(D) wide

14. Participating in ------- volunteer programs as possible is difficult but usually very rewarding.

(A) as much
(B) as many
(C) much too
(D) too many

15. ------- coffee shops started charging $1 for a plastic cup, the amount of trash generated has decreased significantly.

(A) Since
(B) Due to
(C) Whereas
(D) As long as

16. Daily operation with new cash registers will go smoothly ------- clerks complete the training.

(A) if so
(B) without
(C) as long as
(D) prior to

17. Rachel Cain, the head of human resources, reviews all applications more ------- than any other department heads.

(A) closely
(B) close
(C) closing
(D) closer

18. Duncan Marketing offers ------- different service plans for businesses.

(A) many
(B) less
(C) near
(D) plenty

19. In his acceptance speech at the awards ceremony, Mr. Warwick ------- his success to his family's support.

(A) collected
(B) attributed
(C) reached
(D) achieved

20. While waiting for photo-taking, all new employees are asked to ------- paperwork for the security badge.

(A) turn down
(B) take over
(C) give up
(D) fill out

21. Russo Appliances is offering free shipping to become more ------- than its competitors.

(A) competed
(B) competitive
(C) competition
(D) competitively

22. Glimmerglass Manufacturing asked its factory workers to apply for extra shifts to ------- up for a delay in production.

(A) save
(B) place
(C) make
(D) do

23. Customers at Oliver's Kitchen can count ------- quick delivery service, along with high quality menu options.

(A) for
(B) on
(C) from
(D) against

24. Students who ------- part in volunteer activities are likely to get accepted to Mason University.

(A) reach
(B) put
(C) set
(D) take

PART 5 비교 구문 / 빈출 숙어 (1)   463

PART 6

알맞은 문장 고르기 – 빈칸 뒤에 접속부사

빈칸 뒤에 있는 접속부사의 의미를 먼저 파악하는 것이 중요해요.

╲ 적용 기술

[기적의 필기노트] 164P
RC 기술 82

🗋 VOCA

provider 공급자
access 접근; 접근하다
preference 선호도
analyze 분석하다
up to ~까지
at one's leisure 시간 날 때

🧑‍🏫 풀이 방법   e-mail   📍해석 p.162

To: Jeffrey Longino
From: customerservice@ezebookz.com
Date: 12 May
Subject: Successful Registration

Dear Mr. Longino,

Thank you for becoming a member of E-Z E-books, the leading provider of access to digital versions of all kinds of books and magazines. Your reading preferences have been analyzed and logged in our database. In this way, we can make book recommendations ------- to you than any of our competitors can.
                    ⑧ PART 5
-------. Therefore, you can access up to three books per week. E-books can be
 01.
downloaded from our Web site or via our mobile app.

Once again, thank you for joining E-Z E-books.

E-Z E-books Service Team

---

01. (A) You are currently a Silver Star member.
(B) Our library can be downloaded to any electronic device.
(C) We will e-mail you when we make additions to our library.
(D) Browse the personalized recommendation system at your leisure.

⒥ 이렇게 풀어요

1. 선택지 보고 문법/어휘 문제 파악 각 선택지를 먼저 보고 대략적인 내용이나 특징을 파악합니다.

(A) 당신은 현재 Silver Star 회원이라고 회원 등급을 알림

(B) 책 목록이 전자기기에 다운로드 될 수 있다고 알림

(C) 책이 추가되면 이메일로 알려주겠다고 함

(D) 시간 날 때 개인 추천 시스템을 둘러보라고 함

2. 빈칸 분석 빈칸 앞 단락에서 e-book 업체의 회원이 된 것을 환영하고 있고, 빈칸 뒤에 '그러므로' 당신은 책을 일주일에 세 권까지 볼 수 있다고 안내하고 있습니다.

3. 정답 선택 회원 등급을 알려주고 그에 따른 책 열람 권수를 안내하는 것이 자연스러우므로 (A)를 정답으로 고릅니다.

📍 해설

빈칸에는 앞의 명사구 book recommendations를 수식하는 표현이 들어가야 하는데, 뒤에 than과 함께 비교 대상이 제시되어 있으므로 선택지 중 유일한 비교급 표현인 (C)가 정답입니다.

⑧ PART 5 문법 적용 문제

In this way, we can make book recommendations ------- to you than any of our competitors can.

(A) suitable   (B) suitably   (C) more suitable   (D) most suitable

464   기적의 토익 RC

따라 하면 문제가 풀리는

연습 문제

빈칸 앞뒤 내용에서 단서가 될 부분을 찾아 표시하세요.
표시한 것을 바탕으로 정답 어휘를 선택하세요.

정답 및 해설 p.162

01

We conduct a customer survey every quarter. The survey results for the third quarter have come out. -------. Therefore, the personnel department will be conducting a series of training sessions over the next month.

(A) Many customers complained that our salespeople are unfamiliar with our products.
(B) Please take a minute to look over the results of our latest customer survey.

02

-------. Moreover, the associate with the highest number at the end of each month will receive a special prize.

(A) Please be sure to greet all of the customers in our store with a friendly smile.
(B) Associates will get an incentive of $5 when a customer who you assist opens a credit card.

03

The expense reports for the last quarter are available. -------. Consequently, the company will no longer refund first class flights, business class flights, or 5-star hotels.

(A) According to the budget team, our travel expenses are too high.
(B) The board of directors understands that some of you have to travel for work.

04

-------. In addition, you may be asked to provide presentations on potentially profitable investments.

(A) This renowned institution has some of the world's richest clients.
(B) The position's main responsibility will be analyzing stock market trends.

DAY 19

PART 6 알맞은 문장 고르기-빈칸 뒤에 접속부사   465

토익에 나올 실전 문제

제한시간 4분입니다! 시~작!

Questions 01-04 refer to the following e-mail.

To: Emily Porter
From: custserv@northstarair.net
Date: 7 November
Subject: NSA Mileage Rewards

Dear Ms. Porter,

Congratulations on joining the North Star Airlines mileage rewards program! -------. Accordingly, you
                                       01.

now have enough miles to qualify for an upgrade to first class! If you ------- to upgrade this flight,
                                     02.

just let our service team know in advance. The offer is good until all first class seats on that flight
are reserved.

You can also choose to save your points to upgrade a flight with ------- in the future.
                        03.

We are ------- that you have many airline options, and thank you for choosing North Star Airlines.
      04.

Sincerely,

NSA Customer Service

유형 적용 문제

01. (A) You can find a list and map of airport facilities on the Web site.
    (B) We regret to inform you that your flight has been cancelled.
    (C) Please check the departure and arrival boards for updates.
    (D) The flight you just reserved earns double mileage points.

02. (A) had liked
    (B) are liking
    (C) would like
    (D) will have liked

03. (A) us
    (B) you
    (C) him
    (D) them

04. (A) necessary
    (B) obvious
    (C) responsible
    (D) aware

정답 및 해설 p.163

Questions 05-08 refer to the following letter.

Dear Mr. Burns,

We have processed your application, and you are now a VIP member of Seven Flags Amusement Park! You can now access the park at any time ------- the year. -------. That is, you can skip ahead in
05. **06.**
line for rides by simply showing it to the guard. Please note that there may be a line of VIP members with the fast pass for popular rides at ------- times.
07.

Since you are on our mailing list, you will receive updates about any changes here at Seven Flags. We look forward to ------- you at our park soon!
08.

Sincerely,

Seven Flags Amusement Park

---

05. (A) throughout
　　 (B) until
　　 (C) from
　　 (D) after

유형 적용 문제
06. (A) Our peak season is right around the corner.
　　 (B) Check out videos of our exciting rides on our Web site.
　　 (C) We are open every day of the week from the start of May to the end of September.
　　 (D) Enclosed is a fast pass so that you can reduce your wait time.

07. (A) summer
　　 (B) peak
　　 (C) lunch
　　 (D) opening

08. (A) having
　　 (B) speaking
　　 (C) knowing
　　 (D) visiting

PART 6 알맞은 문장 고르기-빈칸 뒤에 접속부사　467

PART 7

후기/설문조사

후기/설문조사의 작성자가 좋게 평가한 부분과 개선점으로 건의한 부분이 문제로 출제돼요.

후기/피드백은 식당과 같은 특정 장소를 방문하거나 물건을 사용한 후 이에 대한 본인의 의견을 작성한 지문입니다. 설문조사는 주로 업체 측에서 고객에게 평가를 받기 위한 지문으로, 만족도를 표시한 형태로 제시됩니다. 진위 확인 문제가 자주 출제돼요.

후기/설문조사에서 자주 출제되는 어휘

후기/설문조사에서 자주 출제되는 문제

· 진위 확인 문제
What is mentioned/ indicated/stated/ true about + 키워드?
→ 글쓴이가 구입한 물건이나 이용한 시설에 대한 진위 파악 문제가 출제돼요.

feedback form	설문 양식, 설문지	complete	작성하다
collect	모으다, 수집하다	comfortable	편안한
courteous	공손한, 정중한	rate	평가하다
accurate	정확한	sufficiently	충분히
reasonable	(가격이) 적정한, 합리적인	quite	꽤
be known for	~로 유명하다	opinion	의견
unsatisfactory	불만족스러운	convenient	편리한
experience	경험	leading	선두의
advantage	장점	compared to	~에 비해
disadvantage	단점	happily	기꺼이
personal	개인적인	so far	지금까지는
worthy	가치 있는	minor	사소한
value	가치, 값을 매기다	correct	정정하다
product	제품	drawback	단점
previous	이전의	outstanding	뛰어난
accessible	접근할 수 있는	content	내용
clearly	명확하게	general public	일반 대중
positive	긍정적인	effort	노력
find out	~를 알게 되다	upon request	요청에 따라
end up -ing	결국 ~하게 되다	cleanliness	청결도
leave	남기다, 떠나다	former	이전의
occasion	경우, 때	routine	정기적인, 일상의

468 기적의 토익 RC

풀이방법 후기/설문조사

review

해석 p.164

Posted by: Bianca Wade

I recently stopped at the Conway Rest Area on a road trip along I-81 and tried some food at Kessler Deli while I was there. The employees were cheerful and energetic despite being so busy making sandwiches. Since it was my first time, I was confused as to which line I should go to, but they helped me by directing me which way to go. Everything on the menu looked delicious, and I ordered the Clubber Combo, which is a club sandwich with a special sauce, a side of baked potato chips, and a beverage.

Although everything was delicious, the sauce got all over my hands while eating it. I used the regular dry napkins they gave me, but my hands still felt sticky afterwards and I had to wash them right away.

Overall I would say this is a great place to eat and I would certainly come again the next time I pass through the area.

01. What does Ms. Wade mention about Kessler Deli?

(A) It has multiple wait lines.
(B) It is located in a bus terminal.
(C) It should hire more employees.
(D) It caters for large special events.

02. According to the review, what does Ms. Wade want the deli to do?

(A) Offer more drink options
(B) Increase its portion sizes
(C) Open another branch
(D) Provide wet napkins

이렇게 풀어요

01. Wade 씨가 Kessler Deli에 대해 언급한 것은 무엇인가?

(A) 대기 줄이 많다.
(B) 버스 터미널에 위치해 있다.
(C) 더 많은 직원을 고용해야 한다.
(D) 대형 특별 행사에 음식을 공급한다.

해설 첫 번째 단락에서 I was confused as to which line I should go to라고 했으므로 기다리는 줄이 많아 어느 줄에 서야 할지 몰랐다는 것을 알 수 있습니다. 따라서 (A)가 정답입니다.

02. 후기에 따르면, Wade 씨가 식당에 원하는 것은 무엇인가?

(A) 더 다양한 음료를 선택할 수 있게 하는 것
(B) 양을 늘리는 것
(C) 또 다른 지점을 여는 것
(D) 젖은 냅킨을 제공하는 것

해설 두 번째 단락에서 I used the regular dry napkins they gave me, but my hands still felt sticky라고 했으므로 그녀는 젖은 냅킨을 제공하기를 원한다는 것을 유추할 수 있습니다. 따라서 (D)가 정답입니다.

PART 7 후기/설문조사

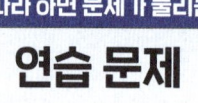

따라 하면 문제가 풀리는

연습 문제

먼저 문제의 키워드에 표시한 후,
지문에서 단서를 찾아 적절한 답을 고르세요.

01 review

> Vernon Hotel – Concord, NH
>
> "Great value for the price!"
>
> I recently stayed at Vernon Hotel for the first time, and I found the price for a single room to be very reasonable. Since I took a flight to Concord, I needed to use the hotel's airport shuttle. I couldn't believe that it departs every fifteen minutes from the airport, which was really convenient. It was also clean and comfortable. My only complaint is that the hotel's on-site restaurant has a very limited menu. However, this was only a minor issue.

Q. What impressed the reviewer about the hotel?

(A) Its dining options
(B) Its transportation service

02 survey

> **Abner Hotel Customer Survey**
> We value your opinions! Please tell us about your recent stay at our facility.
>
> How would you rate the following categories on a scale of 1 (Poor) to 10 (Excellent)? Please write N/A (not applicable) for any amenities you did not use.
>
> Reservation Process: _10_   Staff: _10_
> Room Size: _9_   Restaurant: _9_
> Room Cleanliness: _10_   On-Site Gym: _N/A_
>
> If you would like to be sent occasional coupons and special deals to your inbox, please add your name and contact information below.
>
> Name: _Noah Thorpe_   E-mail: _n.thorpe@winifredexpress.com_

Q. What is suggested about Mr. Thorpe?

(A) He would like to receive offers by e-mail.
(B) He was dissatisfied with the hotel's gym.

03 review

Reviewed by Crystal Rhodes

I've been using the Gilroy-90 for about three weeks now, and I am mostly pleased with the results. It gets my clothing very clean, and it doesn't make much noise when it's running. I can also program the machine to start at a later time, which is convenient for my busy schedule. It has several cycles to choose from, but, unfortunately, none of them have a water-saving feature. That is the only thing I would change if I could.

Q. What does Ms. Rhodes indicate about the washing machine?

(A) It does not use much water.
(B) It operates quietly.

04 review

Wellbright Electrics Feedback Form

Thank you for choosing Wellbright Electrics. Please take a moment to share your feedback.

Customer: Connie Sandford   Address: 972 Cheshire Road

Comments: I recently needed to have an entire property rewired. I wanted to make sure everything was done in time for summer vacation. The crew members who worked on my home answered all of my questions, and they made sure to vacuum up any dust and debris at the completion of the project. I would definitely recommend this company to my friends and family.

Q. What does Ms. Sandford mention about the work crew?

(A) They arrived for the project on time.
(B) They cleaned up after themselves.

토익에 나올

실전 문제

제한시간 10분입니다! 시~작!

Questions 01-02 refer to the following book review.

Into the Mountains

Katie Kramer has landed another huge success with *Into the Mountains*. It follows the chief of a tribe who has been forced to lead his people from their homelands in the plains and up into the nearby mountains to seek shelter from a series of storms.

Although Kramer takes leave of the characters in her *Water Ways* series, the main characters in this book are similarly easy to relate to. Like *Water Ways*, the characters are faced with trying to come up with ways to survive in what seems to be a dangerous and dying world.

01. What type of book is *Into the Mountains*?

(A) A historical textbook
(B) An adventure fiction
(C) A personal memoir
(D) A tour guide

02. What is implied about Katie Kramer?

(A) She has published a series of similar books.
(B) She directed a movie based on *Water Ways*.
(C) She goes mountain climbing in her spare time.
(D) She took lessons on wilderness survival tactics.

paraphrasing 주어진 어휘 또는 표현과 패러프레이징 될 수 있는 것을 연결하세요.

1. seek •

2. be faced with •

3. fiction •

• (a) run into

• (b) not a true story

• (c) look for

472 기적의 토익 RC

Questions 03-05 refer to the following survey.

Murphy Rentals

Thank you for your recent patronage of Murphy Rentals. We strive to provide affordable cleaning supplies and equipment to our customers. We would appreciate you sharing your feedback on the form below. All customers who submit their answers will be mailed a voucher for ten percent off their next purchase.

Customer: Lori Elliot   **Date:** March 17   **Mailing Address:** 152 Fox St., Fresno, CA 93724
Product(s) Used: Primeway Steam Carpet Cleaner **Drop-off/Pick-up Dates:** March 4/March 7

Please rate the following statements on a scale of 1 (Strongly Disagree) to 5 (Strongly Agree). If you did not use a service, please leave the item blank.

Web site
– I was able to find what I needed quickly.   _5_
– I thought the Web site had a state-of-the-art appearance.   _2_
– I was comfortable providing payment information on the Web site.   _4_

Staff
– The customer service agents on the helpline were friendly and knowledgeable.   ____
– The employee who dropped off my device was punctual.   _3_
– The employee who picked up my device was punctual.   _5_

Additional Comments: The delivery of the device was late, but I was impressed with the technician who picked up the device. He thoroughly wrapped it in plastic so that it would not drip any water or solution on my newly cleaned carpets as he carried it through the house.

---

03. How will Murphy Rentals show appreciation to customers who complete the survey?

(A) By issuing credit to an account
(B) By entering them in a prize drawing
(C) By sending them a discount coupon
(D) By providing free cleaning supplies

04. What did Ms. Elliot indicate about the company's Web site?

(A) She thought it looked modern.
(B) She plans to visit it again.
(C) It did not accept her payment.
(D) It was easy to navigate.

05. What did Ms. Elliot indicate about the staff member who provided a service on March 7?

(A) He answered questions about a device.
(B) He was careful not to make a mess.
(C) He helped Ms. Elliot to move some furniture.
(D) He failed to arrive on time.

---

paraphrasing 주어진 어휘 또는 표현과 패러프레이징 될 수 있는 것을 연결하세요.

1. affordable   •   • (a) a discount coupon
2. a voucher for ten percent off •   • (b) evaluate
3. rate   •   • (c) inexpensive

PART 7 후기/설문조사   473

Questions 06-10 refer to the following article, e-mail, and online review.

Grayburg Local News

February 5 — Plans have been approved for the construction of Grayburg Adventures, a water park in the northern part of Grayburg. The complex will include three water slides, a wading pool, and an Olympic-sized swimming pool. The work will begin in late March and is expected to be completed by the end of the year.

Supporters of the water park believe it will attract more tourists to the area. As tourism accounts for about fifteen percent of the local economy, bringing in more visitors would have a positive effect, especially for hotels, restaurants, and shops. The town has made a bid to host the State Junior Swim Meet at the water park early next year, and it has a good chance of being selected thanks to the modern facilities that can be offered.

Vitella Inc., which will perform the work, provided a discount because the site will be for community use. City officials said they would grant future contracts to the business if the water park is completed on time and to a high standard.

To: Gregory Duvall <g.duvall@vitellainc.com>
From: Heather Phillips <h.phillips@vitellainc.com>
Date: December 17
Subject: Grayburg Adventures

Dear Gregory,

I'd like to thank you for the hard work you and your team put into completing Grayburg Adventures. I've just spoken to Jill Berry of the city council, and she is extremely pleased, eagerly complimenting the overall quality of the work. Great job!

Heather

www.wayside-hotel.net/testimonials

| HOME | BOOK A ROOM | PHOTO GALLERY | **TESTIMONIALS** | CONTACT |

Wayside Hotel Customer Testimonials

Posted 6 days ago by Carmen Bailey

I will definitely be recommending Wayside Hotel to all of my friends and family. I recently visited Grayburg because I was invited to be a timer at the State Junior Swim Meet. As a member of the Southwest Swimming Association, I travel frequently to attend events, so I have stayed in numerous hotels throughout the region. The Wayside Hotel is definitely the best value I've seen. It has clean, spacious rooms and a friendly staff. I had never even heard of the hotel before. Little did I know that when I clicked that online banner by chance that I'd find such a great little gem.

06. What is the purpose of the article?

(A) To discuss an upcoming vote on city funding
(B) To promote local businesses in Grayburg
(C) To report on the winners of a competition
(D) To announce plans for a construction project

07. In the article, the phrase "accounts for" in paragraph 2, line 2, is closest in meaning to

(A) calculates
(B) represents
(C) justifies
(D) reports

08. What is implied about Vitella Inc.?

(A) It is owned by a member of the city council.
(B) It came in under budget for a venture.
(C) It will be offered future work in Grayburg.
(D) It began working on a task in February.

09. What most likely is true about Ms. Bailey?

(A) She grew up in Grayburg.
(B) She is a professional swim coach.
(C) She had a meeting with Ms. Phillips.
(D) She has been to Grayburg Adventures.

10. How did Ms. Bailey find out about the hotel?

(A) Through an online advertisement
(B) Through a friend's recommendation
(C) Through an association newsletter
(D) Through a newspaper article

---

paraphrasing 주어진 어휘 또는 표현과 패러프레이징 될 수 있는 것을 연결하세요.

1. grant •
2. compliment •
3. online banner •

• (a) praise
• (b) approve
• (c) online advertisement

DAY 19

PART 7 후기/설문조사 475

'멋진 당신, 오늘도 화이팅'

DAY
20

오늘의 학습 포인트

PART 5. 가정법/도치
1. 가정법 – 가정법 과거완료만 주로 출제
2. 도치 – 가정법 과거완료/가정법 미래 도치

      had가 앞으로   should가 앞으로

   – 부정어(never, seldom 등) 도치

PART 6. 알맞은 문장 고르기 – 선택지의 시제

      보기 문장이 다양한 시제. 문맥 파악하기!

PART 7. 웹페이지

      공지, 광고 등이 웹페이지 형태로 제시

PART 5 문법

가정법/도치

출제 빈도가 가장 낮은 유형이므로, 도치 구문만 알아도 토익에 대비할 수 있어요.

적용 기술

[기적의 필기노트] 167P
RC 기술 85

출제 포인트

토익에서는 if절과 주절의 동사 형태를 맞추는 문제로 출제돼요.

🔒 **확인 문제 ❶**

If he ------- a taxi, he would have arrived on time at the meeting.

(A) had taken
(B) has taken

 출제 유형1

가정법

`800+`

1 가정법 과거완료

· 가정법 과거완료는 '~했다면, …했을 텐데'라는 의미로 과거의 일과 반대되는 상황을 가정하고, 그에 따른 결과 또한 가정하는 문장 형태입니다.

If + 주어 + had p.p. ~, 주어 + would/could/should/might + have p.p.

If Ms. Evans **had left** the office 10 minutes earlier, she **would have arrived** on time. Evans 씨가 10분 일찍 회사에서 나갔다면, 그녀는 제시간에 도착할 수 있었을 텐데.

`900+`

2 가정법 미래

· 가정법 미래는 '만약 ~하면, …할 것이다'라는 의미로 **가능성이 희박한 미래의 일**을 표현할 때 사용합니다.

If + 주어 + should + 동사원형 ~, 주어 + will/can/may + 동사원형 또는 명령문

If you **should need** any assistance, you **can visit** our information desk.
어떠한 도움이라도 필요하시면, 저희의 안내 데스크를 방문하세요.

정답 ❶ (A)

478 기적의 토익 RC

출제 유형 2 **도치 구문**

적용 기술

[기적의 필기노트] 167P
RC 기술 85

900+

1 가정법 과거완료 도치

· 가정법 과거완료 문장에서 if절의 if가 생략되고 **had와 주어의 자리를 바꿔** 도치시킵니다.
[가정법 과거완료] **If you had spent** more time preparing for the proposal, you would have been granted the funds.
[가정법 과거완료 도치] **Had you spent** more time preparing for the proposal, you would have been granted the funds.
당신이 제안서를 준비하는 데 시간을 더 썼다면, 자금을 받을 수 있었을 텐데.

· 가정법 관련 도치는 항상 if절에서만 일어납니다. 도치되어 문장 맨 앞에 위치한 Had가 주로 빈칸으로 출제돼요.

확인 문제 ❷

------- you reviewed the manual thoroughly, you would have assembled it quickly.

(A) Are
(B) Had

900+

2 가정법 미래 도치

· 가정법 미래 문장에서 if절의 if가 생략되고 **조동사 should와 주어의 자리를 바꿔** 도치시킵니다.
[가정법 미래] **If you should need any assistance**, you can visit our information desk.
[가정법 미래 도치] **Should you need any assistance**, you can visit our information desk.
어떠한 도움이라도 필요하시면, 저희의 안내 데스크를 방문하세요.

확인 문제 ❸

------- you need more information, please e-mail me.

(A) Have
(B) Should

900+

3 부정어 도치

· 문장을 강조하기 위해 **부정어가 문장 맨 앞으로 나가면**, 뒤에 있는 **주어와 동사가 도치**됩니다.

|부정어|

never	hardly	seldom	rarely	scarcely	little

He **seldom** <u>went</u> to the gym after he was assigned to the morning shift.
→ **Seldom** <u>did he go</u> to the gym after he was assigned to the morning shift.
그가 오전 근무조에 배정된 후로 그는 체육관에 거의 가지 못했다.
→ 부정어 seldom이 맨 앞으로 이동한 문장에서 주어와 동사가 도치되어야 하지만 일반동사(went)만 있을 경우에는 동사의 시제를 반영한 do동사가 부정어와 주어 사이에 오고, 동사는 동사원형(go)이 돼요.

출제 포인트
부정어 도치 문제는 도치를 일으킬 수 있는 부정어를 찾는 문제 또는 동사 자리에 들어갈 알맞은 동사 형태를 고르는 문제가 출제돼요.

(B) ❸ (B) ❷ 답장

PART 5 문법 가정법/도치　479

DAY 20

4 'only + 전치사구/부사절' 도치

· 강조 역할을 하는 부사 only가 수식하는 전치사구 또는 부사절이 강조를 위해 문장 앞으로 이동하면 주어와 동사가 도치됩니다.

You can access your e-mail account **only through this computer**.
→ **Only through this computer** can you access your e-mail account.
이 컴퓨터를 통해서만 당신의 이메일 계정에 접속할 수 있습니다.

5 so/neither 도치

· '~도 또한 그러하다/그렇지 않다'라는 의미의 so, neither가 절의 맨 앞으로 이동하면 'so/neither + (조)동사 + 주어'의 형태로 도치됩니다. so는 긍정문에, neither는 부정문에 사용합니다.

Mr. Rialto went to Roger's retirement party, and **so** did I.
Rialto 씨는 Roger의 퇴직 파티에 갔고, 나도 그랬다(퇴직 파티에 갔다).
→ and 뒤의 I did so에서 강조를 위해 so가 앞으로 나가고 주어 I와 동사 did가 도치되었어요.

Andre Lee didn't work at the branch office, and **neither** did Mr. McFly.
Andre Lee는 지사에서 근무하지 않았고, McFly 씨도 그랬다(근무하지 않았다).
→ and 뒤의 Mr. McFly did neither에서 강조를 위해 neither가 앞으로 나가고 주어 Mr. McFly와 동사 did가 도치되었어요.

🔒 **확인 문제 ④**

Only in the reserved parking lot ------- the employees park their car.

(A) do
(B) are

🔒 **확인 문제 ⑤**

I attended the training last quarter and ------- did Mr. Min.

(A) only
(B) so

정답 ④ (A) ⑤ (B)

480   기적의 토익 RC

가정법/도치

1. ------- Mr. Watson been reminded of the payment due date, he would not have paid the late fee.

(A) Has   (B) Were   (C) Can   (D) Had

Watson 씨가 지급일에 대해 다시 알림을 받았었다면, 그는 연체료를 내지 않았을 텐데.

> ✔ 이렇게 풀어요
>
> **1. 선택지 보고 문법/어휘 문제 파악** 선택지가 be동사와 조동사로 구성되어 있으므로 문법 문제임을 파악해요.
> **2. 빈칸 분석** 빈칸 뒤에 주어와 be동사의 과거완료 been이 있으므로 빈칸에는 도치 구문을 만들 수 있는 동사 형태가 들어가야 함을 파악합니다.
> **3. 정답 선택** 뒤에 있는 주절의 동사 would not have paid를 단서로, 가정법 과거완료 구문이 도치된 형태가 되어야 함을 알 수 있습니다. 따라서 (D) Had를 정답으로 고릅니다.

2. ------- you have any questions about your order, feel free to contact us at 214-9212.

(A) Will   (B) Can   (C) Should   (D) May

당신의 주문에 대해 어떠한 질문이라도 있으시면, 214-9212로 연락주세요.

> ✔ 이렇게 풀어요
>
> **1. 선택지 보고 문법/어휘 문제 파악** 선택지가 모두 조동사로 구성되어 있으므로 문법 문제임을 파악해요.
> **2. 빈칸 분석** 빈칸 뒤에 주어와 동사원형이 있으므로 도치 구문임을 파악합니다.
> **3. 정답 선택** 절이 2개 있지만 접속사가 없고, 선택지가 모두 조동사이므로 도치 구조임을 파악합니다. 선택지 중에서 도치 구문을 이끌 수 있는 (C) Should를 정답으로 고릅니다.

3. ------- does Ms. Parker miss the project deadline.

(A) If   (B) Seldom   (C) Both   (D) Before

Parker 씨는 프로젝트 마감일을 거의 놓치지 않는다.

> ✔ 이렇게 풀어요
>
> **1. 선택지 보고 문법/어휘 문제 파악** 선택지가 다양한 품사의 어휘로 구성되어 있으므로 문법 문제임을 파악해요.
> **2. 빈칸 분석** 빈칸 뒤에 이어진 주어와 동사의 도치 구문을 이끌 수 있는 어휘가 들어가야 함을 파악합니다.
> **3. 정답 선택** 빈칸 뒤가 'does + 주어 + 동사원형'의 구조로 도치가 되어 있으므로 도치 구문을 이끌 수 있는 부정어 표현 (B) Seldom을 정답으로 고릅니다.

PART 5 문법 가정법/도치   481

DAY 20

PART 5 어휘

빈출 숙어 (2)

숙어의 의미를 예문을 통해 효과적으로 암기하세요.

---

01 work out 운동하다, 결과가 나오다

A study recommends **working out** for 20 minutes daily to stay healthy.
연구는 건강을 유지하기 위해 매일 20분간 운동할 것을 권장한다.

---

02 show off 자랑하다, 과시하다

Actor Billy Taylor **shows off** his driving skills by performing his own stunts in movies. 배우인 Billy Taylor 는 영화에서 고난도 연기를 직접 함으로써 그의 운전 기술을 과시한다.

---

03 stop by ~에 들르다

Stop by Lexington Hardware during our anniversary sale for savings on our entire inventory. 연간 할인 기간에 Lexington 철물점에 들르셔서 전체 물품에 대해 할인을 받으세요.

800+ 🐾 빈출 토익 선생님 Pick!

04 keep up with ~을 따라잡다, ~에 뒤지지 않다

In order to **keep up with** demand, the factory started operating around the clock.
수요를 따라잡기 위해 공장은 24시간 내내 가동하기 시작했다.

🐾 빈출 토익 선생님 Pick!

05 look over 검토하다

Ms. Jones usually **looks over** office supply requests before sending them to the company's supplier. Jones 씨는 회사의 공급업체에 보내기 전에 사무용품 요청사항들을 검토한다.

---

06 take care of ~를 돌보다, 신경을 쓰다

Our division **takes care of** resolving customer complaints.
우리 부서는 고객들의 불만을 해결하는 것에 신경을 쓴다.

🐾 빈출 토익 선생님 Pick!

07 figure out ~을 알아내다, 이해하다

Despite years of research, scientists still cannot **figure out** exactly why dinosaurs became extinct.
몇 년간의 조사에도 불구하고, 과학자들은 공룡들이 멸종한 이유에 대해 정확히 알아내지 못한다.

---

08 break down 고장나다

This morning's shipment was delayed because the delivery truck **broke down** on its way here. 배달 트럭 이 여기로 오는 중에 고장이 났기 때문에 오늘 아침의 배송이 지연되었다.

---

09 keep in mind 명심하다

Keep in mind that the oil should be changed every 6 months or 5,000 miles.
연료는 6개월 또는 5천 마일마다 교체되어야 한다는 것을 명심하세요.

900+

10 lag behind 뒤처지다

Despite the predictions of most sportscasters, Sam Grey **lagged behind** early in the marathon race.
대부분의 스포츠 캐스터들의 예상에도 불구하고, Sam Grey는 마라톤 경주에서 일찍 뒤처졌다.

---

11 make a difference 변화를 일으키다

The One America Charity strives to **make a difference** by helping to educate the poor.
One America 자선단체는 가난한 사람들을 교육시키는 것을 도움으로써 변화를 일으키고자 애쓴다.

800+ 🐾 빈출 토익 선생님 Pick!

12 call off 취소하다

The concert was **called off** because the band's lead singer was injured in an accident. 밴드의 리드 싱어 가 사고에서 부상을 입었기 때문에 콘서트는 취소되었다.

---

482 기적의 토익 RC

13 keep track of
~에 대해 계속 알고 있다, 파악하다

Many people who exercise use their cell phones to **keep track of** their workouts. 운동을 하는 많은 사람들은 그들의 운동에 대해 계속 파악하기 위해 휴대전화를 활용한다.

800+ 🐾 빈출 토익 선생님 Pick!
14 take A into account
A를 고려하다

Lucas forgot to **take** meal expenses **into account** when planning his business trip's budget.
Lucas는 그의 출장 예산을 짤 때 식사 비용을 고려하는 것을 잊었다.

🐾 빈출 토익 선생님 Pick!
15 get rid of
~을 처리하다, 없애다

Officials are trying to find a way to **get rid of** waste without causing pollution. 공무원들은 오염을 야기하지 않고 쓰레기를 처리하는 방안을 찾으려고 노력 중이다.

800+
16 to some extent
어느 정도는, 다소

To some extent, the new employee training manual reduced the time recruits spent in training. 새로운 직원 교육 매뉴얼은 신입 사원들이 교육에 쓰는 시간을 어느 정도는 줄였다.

---

17 in a row
연속으로

For 3 years **in a row**, the Oregon Trailblazers won the national volleyball championship. 3년 연속으로, Oregon Trailblazers는 전국 배구 대회에서 우승했다.

---

18 on behalf of
~을 대신하여

On behalf of the board of directors, I am honored to present this award to you.
이사회를 대신하여, 이 상을 당신에게 수여할 수 있어 영광입니다.

800+
19 come to an end
끝나다

The Houston Giants' winning streak **came to an end** with their loss in Yonkers yesterday. Houston Giants의 연승은 어제 Yonkers에게 패배함으로써 끝났다.

---

20 look into
~을 조사하다

Scientists are **looking into** the possibility of using biological energy sources. 과학자들은 생물 에너지 자원을 사용하는 것의 가능성을 조사하고 있다.

 풀이 방법

Employees are asked to ------- Mr. Banks' office when they arrive to receive their new name badges.

(A) work out   (B) drag on   (C) show off   (D) stop by

직원들은 새로운 명찰을 받기 위해 도착하면 Banks 씨의 사무실에 들르도록 요구된다.

> 🗸 이렇게 풀어요
>
> 1. **선택지 보고 문법/어휘 문제 파악** 선택지가 서로 다른 숙어 표현으로 구성되어 있으므로 어휘 문제임을 파악해요.
> 2. **빈칸 분석** 빈칸 뒤에 장소 표현이 있으므로 장소와 함께 쓰일 수 있는 표현이 들어가야 함을 파악합니다.
> 3. **정답 선택** '~에 들르다'라는 의미의 (D) stop by를 정답으로 고릅니다.

PART 5 어휘 빈출 숙어 (2)   483

따라 하면 문제가 풀리는

연습 문제

앞서 학습한 문제 풀이법을 적용하여 맞는 것에 ✓ 표시 하거나 괄호 안에
적절한 답을 쓰고 정답을 선택하세요.

01 If she ------- the contract, she would have hired a personal assistant.

(A) will win
(B) had won
(C) wins
(D) will have won

1. 선택지 보고 문법/어휘 문제 파악하기 ☐ 문법 문제 ☐ 어휘 문제
2. 빈칸 분석하기 주절의 동사 would have hired
    → ☐ 가정법 과거완료 ☐ 가정법 미래 문장임을 알 수 있다.
3. 정답 선택하기 정답 (   )

02 ------- you need more information, visit us online or call our hotline.

(A) Will
(B) Are
(C) Should
(D) Have

1. 선택지 보고 문법/어휘 문제 파악하기 ☐ 문법 문제 ☐ 어휘 문제
2. 빈칸 분석하기 빈칸 뒤에 완전한 절이 2개 있지만 ☐ 접속사 ☐ 전치사가 없으므로 도치 구문이다.
          → 도치 구문을 이끌 수 있는 조동사가 정답이다.
3. 정답 선택하기 정답 (   )

03 ------- it been held at a larger venue, more people could have attended the concert.

(A) Had
(B) Should
(C) Can
(D) Is

1. 선택지 보고 문법/어휘 문제 파악하기 ☐ 문법 문제 ☐ 어휘 문제
2. 빈칸 분석하기 빈칸 뒤에 완전한 절이 2개 있지만 ☐ 접속사 ☐ 전치사가 없으므로 도치 구문이다.
          → 주절의 동사 could have attended
          → ☐ 가정법 과거완료 ☐ 가정법 미래 도치이다.
3. 정답 선택하기 정답 (   )

484 기적의 토익 RC

♀정답 및 해설 p.168

04 Scarcely does she ------- photos of herself to her friends by her phone.

(A) sent
(B) sending
(C) to send
(D) send

> 1. 선택지 보고 문법/어휘 문제 파악하기 ☐ 문법 문제 ☐ 어휘 문제
> 2. 빈칸 분석하기 빈칸 앞에 'do동사 + 주어'가 있으므로 scarcely가 문장 맨 앞으로 나가 도치된 구문임을 알 수 있다.
> → 동사 자리에는 ☐ 동사원형 ☐ 과거분사 형태가 들어가야 한다.
> 3. 정답 선택하기 정답 (   )

05 ------- with a valid ID can people rent a car from the airport.

(A) Only
(B) When
(C) That
(D) Present

> 1. 선택지 보고 문법/어휘 문제 파악하기 ☐ 문법 문제 ☐ 어휘 문제
> 2. 빈칸 분석하기 빈칸 뒤에 있는 것 ☐ 부사구 + 주어 + 동사 ☐ 전치사구 + 조동사 + 주어 + 동사원형
> → 도치 구문을 이끌 수 있는 것을 골라야 한다.
> 3. 정답 선택하기 정답 (   )

06 The department manager should ------- vacation requests before approving them.

(A) carry on
(B) look over
(C) run for
(D) stand by

> 1. 선택지 보고 문법/어휘 문제 파악하기 ☐ 문법 문제 ☐ 어휘 문제
> 2. 빈칸 분석하기 빈칸 뒤에 있는 명사구 (   )
>   명사구의 의미 (   )
> → '승인하기 전에 -------해야 한다'라는 문맥에 어울리는 동사가 정답이다.
> 3. 정답 선택하기 정답 (   )

PART 5 가정법/도치 / 빈출 숙어 (2)

토익에 나올 실전 문제

DAY 01-20 누적 문제

제한시간 9분입니다! 시~작!

01. ------- you be unable to come in for your shift, contact Mr. Denver, and he will find someone to cover for you.

(A) If
(B) When
(C) Should
(D) Anytime

02. One of Mr. Smith's coworkers changed her mobile phone plan to a less expensive one and ------- did he.

(A) either
(B) so
(C) very
(D) well

03. This month's production quota would have been met last week if all raw materials ------- as scheduled.

(A) are shipped
(B) have been shipped
(C) had been shipped
(D) will be shipped

04. The development team is trying to ------- a way to extend battery life without making the device larger.

(A) carry on
(B) lag behind
(C) figure out
(D) call off

05. ------- did Mr. Choi visit the community center after he moved to a townhouse in Northside.

(A) When
(B) Rarely
(C) About
(D) One

06. Only with a valid driver's license ------- you able to rent a car from GRS Car Rental.

(A) can
(B) have
(C) do
(D) are

07. ------- Mr. Kelly repaired his left headlight, he would have avoid the fine from the police.

(A) Could
(B) Should
(C) Had
(D) Are

08. A new software system was introduced at Barney's Grocery to keep ------- of inventory.

(A) diary
(B) function
(C) report
(D) track

09. Mr. Carlson, the head coach, decided not to join the professional baseball team and ------- did some players.

(A) all
(B) neither
(C) clearly
(D) both

10. This past year has recorded the ------- drop in diesel vehicle sales in over a decade.

(A) sharper
(B) sharpen
(C) sharpest
(D) sharply

11. Wade Fashion's prices are significantly ------- in the summer than in other seasons.

(A) high
(B) higher
(C) highest
(D) highly

12. Any merchandise from Ritter Outlet can be returned ------- it was purchased on seasonal clearance sale.

(A) regardless
(B) so that
(C) unless
(D) since

486 기적의 토익 RC

13. Ms. Ray is in charge of planning the retirement dinner, ------- is supposed to be held in Ballroom B.

(A) which
(B) where
(C) when
(D) what

14. There will be a thorough investigation as to ------- is responsible for the car crash.

(A) that
(B) who
(C) whom
(D) whether

15. The recently ------- Secretary of Internal Affairs will be holding a press conference tomorrow at Huntington City Hall.

(A) appoint
(B) appointing
(C) appointment
(D) appointed

16. ------- make up for poor first quarter sales, Bailey Auto has decided to create special promotions.

(A) For those
(B) In order to
(C) As a result of
(D) At the time of

17. Almost all of the designers prepared colorful wardrobes for the fashion show, while ------- presented an all-black clothing line.

(A) one
(B) either
(C) each other
(D) the majority

18. Duncan Academy is in need of an academic ------- to coordinate class schedules.

(A) administrate
(B) administers
(C) administrator
(D) administrational

19. Most restaurant owners ------- to raise menu prices to maintain profits every year.

(A) tend
(B) call
(C) stand
(D) leave

20. All employees are expected to ------- themselves with the new sales policy by reviewing the attached slideshow file.

(A) contribute
(B) familiarize
(C) recognize
(D) advertise

21. ------- in mind that all expense reimbursement requests must be submitted along with original receipts by this Friday.

(A) Look
(B) Keep
(C) Work
(D) Give

22. Our sales representative will send you a copy of our brochure ------- you be interested in our products.

(A) will
(B) should
(C) which
(D) with

23. When opening a new business, the owner must take all factors into -------, including building accessibility and overhead costs.

(A) value
(B) amount
(C) account
(D) number

24. ------- did he invest in the stock market after he lost more than $10,000.

(A) Normally
(B) Approximately
(C) Scarcely
(D) Frequently

PART 6

알맞은 문장 고르기 – 선택지의 시제 [800+]

선택지 문장의 시제가 여러가지인 경우, 빈칸 앞 내용의 문맥을 파악하여 적절한 시제를 고릅니다.

VOCA

branch 지점
be aware of ~을 알다
temporarily 일시적으로
client base 고객층
floor plan 도면
release 출시, 출시하다
outweigh 능가하다
appeal to ~의 관심을 끌다

 memo   ◎ 해석 p.171

From: Joseph Swanson
To: Branch Managers
Subject: Bloomers' Fashion
Date: 18 February

Attention Branch Managers,

I'm sure that you are all aware of the decision to renovate the interior of three of our Bloomers' Fashion branches. Our plan is to close them temporarily until the renovation work is completely finished. Those branches that were chosen have very old interiors. Surveys show that our largest client base is teenagers. -------.
                                                                      01.

Attached are an approved floor plan and a renovation schedule. ------- you have any
                                                                      ⚑ PART 5
questions about it, feel free to contact Ms. Bolton anytime.

Joseph Swanson
CEO, Bloomers' Fashion

01. (A) It's just in time for the release of a new clothing line.
(B) The benefits outweigh the cost of construction.
(C) For the last few months, all of our branches have been successful in business.
(D) This change will help our business continue appealing to young customers.

이렇게 풀어요

1. 선택지 보고 문법/어휘 문제 파악 문장 고르기 문제이므로 각 선택지를 먼저 보고 대략적인 내용이나 특징을 파악합니다.
(A) 새 의류 라인을 출시할 때입니다.
(B) 혜택은 건설 비용을 능가합니다.
(C) 지난 몇 달 동안, 우리의 모든 지점들은 사업에서 성공적이었습니다.
(D) 이 변화는 우리가 젊은 고객들의 관심을 계속 끄는 데 도움이 될 것입니다.

2. 빈칸 분석 빈칸 앞 내용에서 회사가 세 지점의 인테리어를 보수할 것이라는 계획을 말하고 있습니다.

3. 정답 선택 인테리어 보수에 따른 변화가 가지고 올 효과에 대해 미래 시제로 쓰인 문장이 들어가는 것이 적절하므로 (D)를 정답으로 고릅니다.

해설

빈칸 뒤에 주어(you) 와 동사 (have)가 있으므로 빈칸에 접속사가 필요하지만 선택지에 접속사가 없으므로 도치 구문임을 파악할 수 있어야 합니다. 가정법 미래 도치 구문을 이끌 수 있는 (C) Should가 정답입니다.

⚑ PART 5 문법 적용 문제

------- you have any questions about it, feel free to contact Ms. Bolton anytime.

(A) To   (B) Will   (C) Should   (D) Can

488 기적의 토익 RC

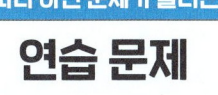

따라 하면 문제가 풀리는

연습 문제

빈칸 앞뒤 내용에서 단서가 될 부분을 찾아 표시하세요.
표시한 것을 바탕으로 정답 어휘를 선택하세요.

◉ 정답 및 해설 p.171

01

Julia Stark is set to win the Album of the Year award at this weekend's music awards ceremony. -------.

(A) It will be her fifth time and third year in a row.
(B) Tickets to the concert sold out in record time.

02

Due to drastic decrease in the copper supplies, most of the electric wire manufacturers have suffered from it over the past two quarter. With more than four decades of the company history, we experienced it a couple of times before and prepared for it. -------.

(A) We will not be able to meet our quota this month.
(B) We diversified the vendors all over the world.

03

We apologize for the inconvenience, but our café is currently closed for renovations. We received many complaints about insufficient dining area. -------.

(A) We do not take any reservation on weekends.
(B) There was a long waiting line during the peak time.

04

-------. Our chefs are developing recipes for new dishes based on recommendations given during our latest round of customer surveys. You can taste them starting next month.

(A) A secret BBQ sauce flavor was already sold in bottles at our restaurant.
(B) Our restaurant's menu will feature a variety of vegetarian options.

PART 6 알맞은 문장 고르기–선택지의 시제   489

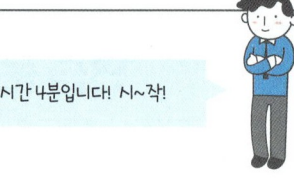

제한시간 4분입니다! 시~작!

Questions 01-04 refer to the following memo.

From: Erica West
To: All Staff
Subject: Office relocation
Date: 23 August

Next week, we will be moving to a new office located at 527 Elm Street. ------- of you should use
                                                                            01.
Friday afternoon to pack your things into boxes for the movers. -------. Monday will be our first day,
                                                                 02.
so the morning will be dedicated to ------- and setting up our workstations. We ------- regular
                                      03.   **04.**
operations after lunch on Monday.

Sincerely,

Erica West
Manager, Personnel Department

---

01. (A) Both
    (B) All
    (C) Some
    (D) Few

유형 적용 문제

02. (A) We were able to negotiate an affordable price.
    (B) Customers have complained about our location.
    (C) They will move everything to the new office on Saturday.
    (D) There are not many options for professional movers in this area.

03. (A) folding
    (B) unpacking
    (C) purchasing
    (D) attaching

04. (A) have been resumed
    (B) were resuming
    (C) had resumed
    (D) will resume

Questions 05-08 refer to the following e-mail.

From: Toby Fischer
To: Kelly Lloyd
Subject: Performance evaluations
Date: December 18

Ms. Lloyd,

I send this e-mail as a reminder that the performance evaluation reports for your employees were
------- on 15 December. -------. We understand you were very busy organizing the company booth at
  05.   **06.**
the St. Louise Trade Fair. ------- we will extend the deadline, so they should be submitted by the
               07.
end of this week.

All reports ------- through our Intranet, but now the Web page is not available anymore. So, please
      08.
submit them in person to the personnel department. If you have any questions or need help, please
contact Ms. Moorland.

Sincerely,

Toby Fischer

---

05. (A) posted
    (B) located
    (C) due
    (D) performed

유형 적용 문제
06. (A) Based on the evaluation results, cash bonus will
        be granted.
    (B) They should be placed in my inbox before lunch
        on January 2.
    (C) We have received them from all other
        departments except yours.
    (D) Some of our employees will start working here on
        January 2.

07. (A) Therefore
    (B) Additionally
    (C) However
    (D) For example

08. (A) were collected
    (B) collection
    (C) have collected
    (D) to collected

PART 7

웹페이지

웹페이지는 주로 기업이나 기관의 홈페이지가 출제돼요.

웹페이지는 형태상으로 온라인에서 보여지는 모습을 갖춘 지문으로, 내용은 공지나 광고가 주로 출제됩니다. 또한 다른 지문과 연계하여 이중 지문이나 삼중 지문으로 자주 출제됩니다.

웹페이지에서 자주 출제되는 문제

· 인물 파악 문제
Who most likely is 이름?
→ 인물의 직업을 묻는 문제는 지문에서 해당 이름이 언급된 곳 주변에 단서가 있어요. 단서가 1-2개 정도 제시되므로 이것을 조합하여 직종을 파악할 수 있어야 합니다.

웹페이지 지문에서 자주 출제되는 어휘

account	계정	listing	목록
sign up	가입하다	feature	특징
access	접속하다, 접속	personalized	개인이 원하는 대로 할 수 있는
demonstration	시연	check out	확인하다
capacity	용량	last updated	마지막으로 업데이트된
inquiry form	질문 양식	customer comments	고객 의견
up-to-the-minute	가장 최근의	subscriber	구독자
press release	보도 자료	coordinator	담당자
sophisticated	복잡한, 정교한	chance to부정사	~할 기회
register	등록하다	proceed to부정사	계속해서 ~하다
benefit	혜택	renewal	갱신
procedure	절차	approximately	거의
view	보다	through	~을 통해
per-person rate	1인당 요금	transaction	거래
up-to-date	최신의	be aimed at	~을 목표로 하다
category	부문, 범주	standard	표준의
wrap up	끝나다	browse	구경하다
rule	규칙	brief	간략한
testimonial	추천의 글	accurate	정확한
verified	확인된	supportive	지원하는, 도와주는

웹페이지

Web page

○ 해석 p.173

Sahara.com

Home	FAQs	**My Account**

Congratulations, Vanessa Graham! You have upgraded to Sahara Business Premium! Now you can enjoy special savings and discounts on all of bulk purchases for your restaurant through sahara.com.

Here are just a few benefits to enjoy with your account upgrade:
* Additional inventory search filter options
* cooking recipes from renowned chefs
* FREE Standard shipping for all orders
* 24-7 online chat or phone customer support

---

01. Who most likely is Ms. Graham?

(A) A real estate agent
(B) A software engineer
(C) A consultant
(D) A store owner

02. What is NOT a newly accessible feature?

(A) Round-the-clock support
(B) More ways to browse inventory
(C) Free express shipping on orders
(D) Cooking tips from professionals

이렇게 풀어요

01. Graham 씨는 누구일 것 같은가?

(A) 부동산 중개업자
(B) 소프트웨어 기술자
(C) 상담사
(D) 매장 주인

해설 Graham이 언급된 첫 번째 단락에서 Now you can enjoy ~ all of bulk purchases for your restaurant라고 했으므로 레스토랑의 주인임을 유추할 수 있습니다. 따라서 restaurant를 store로 표현한 (D)가 정답입니다.

02. 새로 이용 가능한 기능이 아닌 것은 무엇인가?

(A) 24시간 내내 지원
(B) 재고를 검색할 수 있는 더 많은 방법
(C) 주문에 대해 무료 특급 배송
(D) 전문가들로부터의 요리 팁

해설 업그레이드됨으로써 받을 수 있는 혜택 사항이 나열된 두 번째 단락에서 모든 주문에 대한 일반 배송이 무료라고 했지 특급 배송이라고는 하지 않았으므로 (C)가 정답입니다.

PART 7 웹페이지 493

따라 하면 문제가 풀리는

연습 문제

먼저 문제의 키워드에 표시한 후,
지문에서 단서를 찾아 적절한 답을 고르세요.

01 Web page

[My Account]

Welcome back, Beverly Nolin! You have successfully logged in. Your last login was at 3:52 P.M. on September 4. We have recently upgraded our Web site. Please note the following changes to your online account:

New features:
- Top up your cell phone credit quickly and easily
- Check your data usage in real time
- Pay your monthly bill as a one-time payment or set up a direct debit
- View warranty information and safety recalls that may apply to your purchase

Q. Who most likely is Ms. Nolan?

(A) A cell phone customer
(B) A cell phone technician

02 Web page

HOME	DEPARTMENTS	NEWS	CONTACT

At Jarvis Ltd., we understand that renting your property can be a stressful experience. You may have difficulty with tenants or be unsure about how to comply with the ever-changing regulations. By having us manage your property, you can save time as well as hassle. We will perform background checks on tenants, make arrangements for repairs, and collect rental payments. In addition, we have lawyers on staff who can counsel you anytime you need. Contact us today to find out how we can serve you.

Q. What is mentioned as a benefit of using Jarvis Ltd.?

(A) Consultations with legal professionals
(B) Discounts on repair work

03 Web page

www.communitylink.com.au/award

Community Link is a non-profit organization dedicated to reaching out to vulnerable people in the town of Busselton. We present the Community Link Awards every year to recognize those who are working to make a difference locally. Previous winners have contributed to a number of projects including opening a homeless shelter, teaching adult reading classes, cleaning up public spaces, and more. If you know someone whom you would like to nominate for this award, please e-mail Eliza Sinclair at e.sincliar@communitylink.com.au.

Q. Why should Web site visitors contact Ms. Sinclair?

(A) To suggest a person for an award
(B) To buy tickets for an awards show

04 Web page

Home	Hiking	Photo Gallery	**Notices**	Contact

Posted March 7

Dalgarno National Park is a popular vacation spot for nature lovers from around the world. We have over three hundred miles of hiking trails throughout the park. Tourist Web sites such as www.hikingdestination.net are currently selling maps of the hiking trails in the park. However, visitors should note that these maps are available without cost. To download one, simply click the "Hiking" tab above, select the trail by name or number, and print it on your home computer.

Q. What does the Web page include?

(A) Recommendations for the best hiking trails
(B) Instructions for acquiring free maps

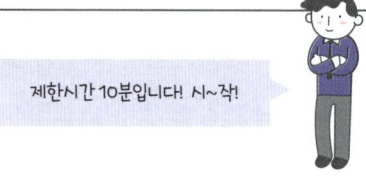

제한시간 10분입니다! 시~작!

Questions 01-02 refer to the following Web page.

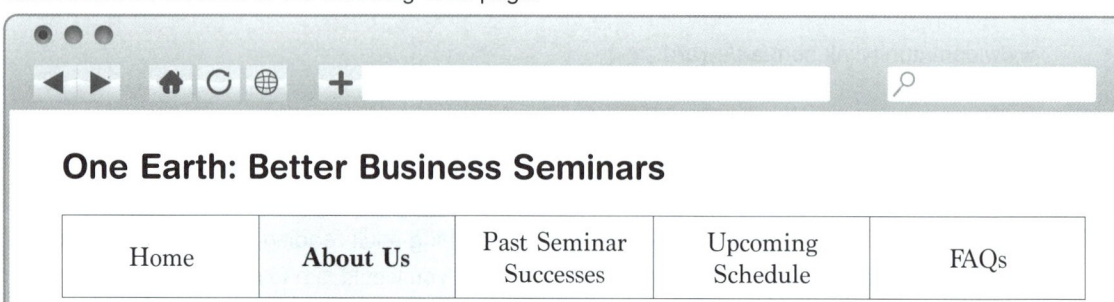

One Earth: Better Business Seminars

Home	**About Us**	Past Seminar Successes	Upcoming Schedule	FAQs

At One Earth, we have faith that all people can learn to work together regardless of economic, national, or social backgrounds.

Each speaker that we allow to take the stage speaks from personal experiences. Only after having worked a variety of jobs in different places around the world can you truly learn how to overcome all obstacles and work together with those who you once thought different from yourself.

By attending a One Earth: Better Business Seminar, you and your employees can learn how to cooperate more effectively with businesses in other countries. That is what we and our volunteer speakers want you to take away from our lessons.

01. What is indicated about One Earth's speakers?

(A) They are experts in their respective fields.
(B) They each speak multiple languages.
(C) They have diverse work experience.
(D) They do volunteer work regularly.

02. What is one goal of One Earth: Better Business Seminars?

(A) Providing work visas
(B) Encouraging volunteer work
(C) Facilitating international trade
(D) Improving international teamwork

paraphrasing 주어진 어휘 또는 표현과 패러프레이징 될 수 있는 것을 연결하세요.

1. having worked a variety of jobs •
2. cooperate more effectively •
3. businesses in other countries •

• (a) improve teamwork
• (b) diverse work experience
• (c) international corporations

정답 및 해설 p.174

Questions 03-05 refer to the following information on a Web page.

---

http://www.seymourcity.gov

| Home | Parks Department | **Chamber of Commerce** | Meet Your Representatives | Contact |

The Seymour City Chamber of Commerce (SCCC) represents over 50 local companies, covering nearly all industries. Anyone operating in the private sector can join the SCCC to help boost their profits and stability.

"The Seymour City Chamber of Commerce is a vital strategic partner to my accounting firm. The valuable tools it provides cannot be duplicated anywhere else!" —Tammy Ness, Ness Accounting

We accept new members on an ongoing basis, and you can start taking advantage of everything that SCCC has to offer as soon as you sign up. Members can attend free leadership development workshops throughout the year, taught by experts in the field. We also hold a members-only annual gala, which provides a platform for meeting and talking to other professionals. You can also get basic tax and regulation questions answered by our team of experienced lawyers.

Click here to download the membership application form. Fees range from $360 to $2,150 and are determined by the number of employees at the company. Please direct all inquiries to Reginald Vanhorne at 555-0733 or at r.vanhorne@seymourccc.com.

---

03. Who would be most interested in this information?

(A) Tourists to Seymour City
(B) Business owners
(C) Charity managers
(D) Property investors

04. What is NOT mentioned as a benefit of SCCC?

(A) Fundraising sponsorship
(B) Educational courses
(C) Legal assistance
(D) Networking opportunities

05. What is mentioned about SCCC's membership fees?

(A) They can be paid by direct debit.
(B) They are temporarily offered at a discount.
(C) They are charged on a monthly basis.
(D) They vary depending on the organization's size.

---

paraphrasing 주어진 어휘 또는 표현과 패러프레이징 될 수 있는 것을 연결하세요.

1. on an ongoing basis   •   • (a) continuously
2. be determined by   •   • (b) organization's size
3. the number of employees at the company •   • (c) vary depending on

PART 7 웹페이지 497

DAY 20

Questions 06-10 refer to the following Web page, form, and forum post.

National Birdwatchers Society Forum

The National Birdwatchers Society has created this space for bird lovers of all ages to share knowledge about bird habitats, nesting, feeding, etc. Please help us keep this forum organized and useful by adhering to the following guidelines:

1. Posts should not exceed twenty lines of text. Any bird-related topic is welcome, but we ask that you review former posts to see if it is better to start a new thread or to contribute to an existing one.
2. Advertising is not permitted. Although we do allow recommendations of brands for products related to bird-watching, repeated messages promoting a business or product will be deleted by the managers.
3. List where you live or where you spotted the bird in the subject line. This makes posts easier to search.
4. Include photos whenever possible. This is especially helpful for identification purposes.

National Birdwatchers Society Forum: Registration

Please complete the fi elds below to sign up for a free membership.

Name: Joel Buchanan E-mail   **Address:** jbuchanan@kentwoodl.com
User Name: jaybird.joel   **Registration Date:** February 3

Birding Experience: I have been studying birds on my own through books and videos.

NOTE: Membership accounts that are not used for a period of 12 months will be automatically deleted at the end of the 12th month. The activity period is reset if you take any of the following actions: posting, replying to comments, completing survey requests, or voting on forum issues.

National Birdwatchers Society Forum

Most Recent Post

Subject: Hummingbird visitors   **Posted by:** jaybird.joel   **Date:** April 4

Since I registered for the forum, I have noticed the same incorrect information posted again and again. A lot of people believe that hummingbirds are not attracted to beet sugar. They argue that only a commercial feeding solution, such as Grant Farm's Hummingbird Food, will work. I've been successfully using beet sugar dissolved in water for years, and I captured some great pictures of a hummingbird at my feeder just this morning (attached).

Photo attachment(s): hummingbird1jpeg, hummingbird2.jpeg

---

06. What is indicated about the National Birdwatchers Society?

(A) It is currently looking for more photographers.
(B) It has no age restrictions on its forums.
(C) Its membership size is growing steadily.
(D) It sells some products with its own brand.

07. What does the form mention about membership?

(A) It must be approved by a current member.
(B) It requires activity at least once a year.
(C) Its price may go up in the future.
(D) Its account password can be reset.

08. What is the purpose of Mr. Buchanan's post?

(A) To inquire about attracting a certain bird
(B) To correct a common misconception
(C) To invite forum members to an event
(D) To apologize for a previous post that he wrote

09. How did Mr. Buchanan's post fail to follow the guidelines?

(A) It did not indicate the location.
(B) It mentioned a brand name.
(C) It included multiple photos.
(D) It did not have an identification code.

10. What is implied about Mr. Buchanan?

(A) He studied birds formally at university.
(B) He has posted a video of a bird.
(C) He used to work at Grant Farm.
(D) He noticed a problem two months ago.

---

paraphrasing   주어진 어휘 또는 표현과 패러프레이징 될 수 있는 것을 연결하세요.

1. for all ages   •
2. guidelines   •
3. should not exceed   •

• (a) instructions
• (b) have limitations
• (c) no age restrictions

PART 7 웹페이지

MEMO

MEMO

MEMO

전국 조류 관찰자 협회 포럼: 등록
무료 멤버십 신청을 위해 아래의 항목들을 작성해 주시기 바랍니다.

성명: Joel Buchanan
이메일 주소: jbuchanan@kentwood1.com
사용자 이름: jaybird.joel
[10]등록 날짜: 2월 3일
새 관찰 경험: 저는 책과 동영상을 통해 혼자 새를 연구해 왔습니다.
주의: [07]12개월 동안 사용되지 않은 회원 계정은 12개월이 되는 시점에 자동으로 삭제될 것입니다. 다음 중 어느 조치든 취하실 경우에는 활동 기간이 재설정됩니다: 게시물 올리기, 의견에 답변하기, 설문 조사 요청서 작성하기, 또는 포럼 관련 문제에 대해 투표하기

registration 등록 field 항목, 영역 on one's own 혼자, 스스로 account 계정, 계좌 take actions 조치를 취하다 reply to ~에 답변하다 vote on ~에 대해 투표하다

전국 조류 관찰자 협회 포럼
가장 최근 게시물

[09]제목: 벌새 방문객   게시자: jaybird.joel   [10]날짜: 4월 4일
[08, 10]제가 이 포럼에 등록한 이후로, 부정확한 동일 정보가 계속해서 게시되고 있다는 것을 알게 되었습니다. 많은 분들이 벌새가 사탕무에서 얻은 설탕으로는 유인되지 않는다고 생각하고 있습니다. 이분들은 오직 Grant Farm의 Hummingbird Food과 같은 상업용 먹이를 이용한 해결책만이 효과가 있다고 주장하고 있습니다. [08]저는 사탕무에서 얻은 설탕을 수년 동안 물에 녹여 성공적으로 사용해 왔으며, 오늘 아침에 막 제 먹이통에 찾아온 벌새 한 마리를 몇몇 아주 멋진 사진으로 담아 냈습니다(첨부됨).

첨부된 사진: 벌새1.jpeg, 벌새2.jpeg

incorrect 부정확한 beet sugar 사탕무에서 얻는 설탕 commercial 상업의 work 효과가 있다 dissolved in ~에 녹인 capture (사진 등으로) ~을 담아 내다, 포착하다 feeder 먹이통

06. True 문제

전국 조류 관찰자 협회에 관해 언급된 것은 무엇인가?
(A) 현재 추가 사진사를 찾는 중이다.
(B) 포럼에 연령 제한이 없다.
(C) 회원 규모가 지속적으로 커지고 있다.
(D) 자체 브랜드로 된 일부 제품을 판매하고 있다.

[해설] 전국 조류 관찰자 협회의 포럼에 관한 설명이 제시된 첫 지문 시작 부분에, 새를 사랑하는 모든 연령대의 사람들을 위해 만든 공간이라고(has created this space for bird lovers of all ages) 쓰여 있으므로 (B)가 정답이다.

paraphrasing for bird lovers of all ages 새를 사랑하는 모든 연령대의 사람들을 위해 → no age restrictions 연령 제한이 없음

[어휘] look for ~을 찾다 restriction 제한, 제약 grow 늘어나다, 증가하다 steadily 지속적으로 one's own brand 자체 브랜드

07. True 문제

양식에서 멤버십에 관해 언급하는 것은 무엇인가?
(A) 반드시 현 회원에 의해 승인받아야 한다.
(B) 최소한 일 년에 한 번은 활동을 요구한다.
(C) 가입비가 향후에 오를 수 있다.
(D) 계정 비밀번호가 재설정될 수 있다.

[해설] 포럼 가입 신청서인 두 번째 지문 마지막에, 12개월 동안 사용하지 않으면 그 계정이 자동으로 삭제된다고(Membership accounts that are not used for a period of 12 months will be automatically deleted at the end of the 12th month) 나타나 있는데, 이는 일 년 중에 최소 한 번은 활동을 해야 한다는 말과 같으므로 (B)가 정답이다.

[어휘] approve ~을 승인하다 current 현재의 go up 오르다

08. 목적 문제

Buchanan 씨가 쓴 게시물의 목적은 무엇인가?
(A) 특정 새를 유인하는 일에 관해 문의하는 것
(B) 흔한 오해를 바로잡아 주는 것
(C) 포럼 회원들을 행사에 초대하는 것
(D) 자신이 쓴 이전 게시물에 대해 사과하는 것

[해설] Buchanan 씨가 쓴 게시물인 마지막 지문에 부정확한 정보가 계속 보인다는(I have noticed the same incorrect information) 말과 함께 벌새가 사탕무에서 얻은 설탕으로 유인되지 않는다고 사람들이 생각하는 것과 달리 자신은 그 설탕을 이용해(I've been successfully using beet sugar dissolved in water for years) 벌새를 유인한 사실을 사진과 함께 입증하고 있으므로 흔한 오해를 바로 잡기 위해 쓴 게시물임을 알 수 있다. 따라서 (B)가 정답이다.

[어휘] correct ~을 바로 잡다, 고치다 common 흔한 misconception 오해 previous 이전의, 과거의

09. 세부사항 문제 - 연계 문제

Buchanan 씨가 쓴 게시물은 어떤 점에서 가이드라인을 따르지 못했는가?
(A) 위치를 표기하지 않았다.
(B) 브랜드 명칭을 언급했다.
(C) 여러 장의 사진을 포함했다.
(D) 식별 코드가 들어 있지 않았다.

[해설] 첫 지문의 3번 항목을 보면, 제목 칸에 거주하는 곳이나 새를 목격한 곳을 기재해 달라고(List where you live or where you spotted the bird in the subject line) 쓰여 있는데, Buchanan 씨가 쓴 게시물인 세 번째 지문에는 제목에 새 이름만 쓰여 있으므로(Subject: Hummingbird visitors) 위치 관련 정보가 포함되어 있지 않다는 것을 알 수 있다. 따라서 (A)가 정답이다.

[어휘] indicate ~을 표기하다, 나타내다

10. 추론 문제 - 연계 문제

Buchanan 씨에 관해 암시된 것은 무엇인가?
(A) 대학교에서 정식으로 새에 관해 공부했다.
(B) 새를 담은 동영상을 게시했다.
(C) 한때 Grants Farm에서 일했었다.
(D) 두 달 전에 문제점을 알아차렸다.

[해설] 마지막 지문에 Buchanan 씨는 자신이 포럼에 등록한 이후로 부정확한 정보가 계속 올라오는 것을 봤다고(Since I registered for the forum, I have noticed the same incorrect information posted again and again) 알리고 있으며, 바로 위에 이 게시물의 날짜가 4월 4일로(Date: April 4) 쓰여 있다. 그런데 Buchanan 씨의 가입 신청서인 두 번째 지문에 가입 등록 날짜가 2월 3일로(Registration Date: February 3) 되어 있으므로 Buchanan 씨는 두 달 동안 그 부정확한 정보를 확인했음을 알 수 있다. 따라서 (D)가 정답이다.

paraphrasing 정답 1. (c) 2. (a) 3. (b)

신 분이라면 누구든지 수익과 안정성을 촉진시키는 데 도움이 될 수 있도록 SCCC에 가입하실 수 있습니다.

"세이모어 시티 상공회의소는 저희 회계 법인에 필수적인 전략적 파트너입니다. 이곳에서 제공하는 아주 소중한 수단들은 다른 어느 곳에서도 모방할 수 없는 것입니다!" – Tammy Ness, Ness Accounting

저희는 지속적으로 신규 회원을 받고 있으며, 가입 신청을 하시는 대로 저희 SCCC가 제공해 드리는 모든 것을 누리기 시작하실 수 있습니다. 회원들께서는 일년 내내 분야별 전문가들께서 가르치는 04(B)무료 리더십 개발 워크숍에 참석하실 수 있습니다. 저희는 또한 04(D)다른 전문가들과 만나고 이야기하실 수 있는 발판을 제공해 드리는 회원 전용 연례 행사도 개최하고 있습니다. 04(C)여러분께서는 또한 경험 많은 저희 변호사 팀을 통해 기본적인 세금과 규정 관련 질문에 대해 답변을 들으실 수도 있습니다.

여기를 클릭하셔서 회원 가입 신청서를 다운로드하시기 바랍니다. 05비용은 306달러에서 2,150달러의 범위에 이르며, 회사에 소속된 직원들의 수에 따라 결정됩니다. 모든 문의 사항은 555-0733 또는 r.vanhorne@seymourccc.com으로 Reginald Vanhorne 씨께 보내 주시기 바랍니다.

parks department 공원 관리부 chamber of commerce 상공회의소 Representative 국회 의원, 하원 의원 represent ~을 대표하다 cover ~을 포함하다 nearly 거의 industry 분야, 업계 operate 활동하다, 운영되다 private sector 민간 부문 profit 수익 stability 안정(성) vital 필수적인 strategic 전략적인 valuable 소중한 tool 수단, 도구 duplicate ~을 모방하다 accept ~을 받아들이다 on an ongoing basis 지속적으로 take advantage of ~을 이용하다 expert 전문가 field 분야 regulation 규정, 규제 range from A to B A에서 B의 범위에 이르다 determine ~을 결정하다

03. 주제 문제

이 정보에 누가 가장 관심 있어 할 것 같은가?
(A) 세이모어 시티에 오는 관광객들
(B) 사업가들
(C) 자선 단체 관리자들
(D) 부동산 투자자들

[해설] 첫 단락에 Seymour City Chamber of Commerce(SCCC)가 거의 모든 분야를 포함하는 50곳이 넘는 지역 기업들을 대표한다는 말과 함께 민간 부문에 속한 사람들은 누구나 가입할 수 있다고 (~ represents over 50 local companies, covering nearly all industries. Anyone operating in the private sector can join the SCCC ~) 알리고 있는데, 이는 일반 사업체를 운영하는 사람들을 가리키는 것이므로 (B)가 정답이다.

[어휘] charity 자선 단체, 자선 활동 property 부동산, 건물 investor 투자자

04. Not True 문제

SCCC의 혜택으로 언급되지 않은 것은 무엇인가?
(A) 기금 마련 행사 협찬
(B) 교육 과정
(C) 법률 관련 도움
(D) 인맥을 쌓을 수 있는 기회

[해설] 두 번째 단락의 Members can attend free leadership development workshops 부분에서 '교육 과정'을 뜻하는 (B)를, 그 뒤에 이어지는 a platform for meeting and talking to other professionals에서 '인맥을 쌓을 수 있는 기회'를 의미하는 (D)를, 그리고 바로 다음에 나오는 You can also get basic tax and regulation questions answered by our team of experienced lawyers에서 '법률 관련 도움'을 뜻하는 (C)를 확인할 수 있다. 하지만 특정 행사에 대한 협찬은 언급되어 있지 않으므로 (A)가 정답이다.

[어휘] fundraising 기금 마련 행사 sponsorship 협찬, 후원 legal 법률의 assistance 도움 networking 인적 관계 형성

05. True 문제

SCCC의 회비에 관해 언급된 것은 무엇인가?
(A) 자동 이체로 지불될 수 있다.
(B) 일시적으로 할인해 주고 있다.
(C) 한 달 단위로 청구된다.
(D) 단체의 규모에 따라 다르다.

[해설] 회비 관련 정보가 언급된 마지막 단락에, 가입비가 회사에 소속된 직원들의 수에 따라 결정된다는(Fees ~ are determined by the number of employees at the company) 말이 있으므로 이와 같은 규모의 다양성이 언급된 (D)가 정답이다.

paraphrasing are determined by the number of employees at the company 회사에 소속된 직원들의 수에 따라 결정된다 → vary depending on the organization's size 단체의 규모에 따라 다양하다

[어휘] direct debit 자동 이체 temporarily 일시적으로 on a monthly basis 한 달 단위로 vary 다르다, 다양하다 depending on ~에 따라, ~에 달려 있는

paraphrasing 정답 1. (a) 2. (c) 3. (b)

06-10은 다음 웹페이지와 양식 그리고 포럼 게시물을 참조하시오.

전국 조류 관찰자 협회 포럼

06전국 조류 관찰자 협회는 새를 사랑하는 모든 연령대의 분들께서 새 서식지와 둥지를 트는 것, 그리고 먹이 활동 등에 관한 지식을 공유하실 수 있도록 해 드리기 위해 이 공간을 마련했습니다. 다음 가이드라인을 준수하셔서 이 포럼을 체계적이고 유용한 곳으로 유지할 수 있도록 도와 주시기 바랍니다.

1. 게시물은 20줄을 초과할 수 없습니다. 새와 관련된 어떤 주제도 환영하지만, 새로운 주제란을 시작하시는 것이 더 좋은지, 또는 기존의 주제란에 글을 쓰시는 것이 더 나은지 확인해 보실 수 있도록 앞서 게시된 글들을 검토해 보시기를 요청 드립니다.
2. 광고는 허용되지 않습니다. 저희가 새 관찰과 관련된 제품 브랜드의 추천을 허용하기는 하지만, 한 업체나 제품을 홍보하는 반복적인 메시지는 관리자에 의해 삭제될 것입니다.
3. 09제목 칸에 거주하시는 곳이나 새를 목격하신 곳을 기재해 주시기 바랍니다. 이는 게시물을 더욱 쉽게 검색할 수 있게 해줍니다.
4. 가능하실 때 언제라도 사진을 포함시켜 주십시오. 이는 특히 식별 목적으로 사용하기에 유용합니다.

habitat 서식지 nest 둥지를 틀다 feeding 먹이 (활동) adhere to ~을 준수하다 exceed ~을 초과하다 former 이전의 thread 스레드(한 주제에 대한 집중 토론이 가능하도록 특정 게시물과 답장들을 모아 놓은 것) contribute to ~에 기고하다 existing 기존의 related to ~와 관련된 spot ~을 목격하다, 발견하다 subject line 제목 칸 identification 식별

Q. 웹사이트 방문자들은 왜 Sinclair 씨에게 연락해야 하는가?
(A) 상을 받을 사람을 추천하기 위해
(B) 시상식 행사 입장권을 구입하기 위해

[문제 키워드] Why / Web site visitors / contact / Ms. Sinclair
[해설] 키워드 Ms. Sinclair가 제시되는 부분에서 단서를 찾아야 한다. 이 이름이 제시되는 마지막 부분에 수상 후보자로 지명할 사람이 있으면 Sinclair 씨에게 이메일을 보내라고(If you know someone whom you would like to nominate for this award, please e-mail Eliza Sinclair ~) 알리고 있으므로 (A)가 정답이다.

04.

| 홈 | 하이킹 | 사진 갤러리 | **공지** | 연락처 |

3월 7일에 게시됨

저희 Dalgarno 국립공원은 전 세계에서 자연을 사랑하시는 분들께서 찾아 주시는 인기 휴가지입니다. 저희는 공원 전체에 걸쳐 300마일이 넘는 등산로를 보유하고 있습니다. www.hikingdestination.net과 같은 관광 전문 웹사이트들이 현재 저희 공원 내의 등산로를 담은 안내도를 판매하고 있습니다. 하지만 방문객들께서는 이 안내도들을 비용을 들이지 않고 이용하실 수 있다는 점에 유의하시기 바랍니다. **안내도를 다운로드하시려면, 상단의 "하이킹" 탭을 클릭하신 후, 명칭 또는 번호로 등산로를 선택하셔서 댁에 있는 컴퓨터로 출력하기만 하시면 됩니다.**

hiking trail 등산로   **throughout** ~ 전역에 걸쳐   **currently** 현재   **without cost** 비용을 들이지 않고

Q. 웹페이지는 무엇을 포함하고 있는가?
(A) 최고의 등산로에 대한 추천
(B) 무료 안내도를 받기 위한 설명

[문제 키워드] What / Web page / include
[해설] 지문 마지막에 안내도를 다운로드하기 위한 방법을 차례로 설명하는 내용이(~ these maps are available without cost. To download one, simply click the "Hiking" tab above ~) 있으므로 (B)가 정답이다.

[어휘] **acquire** ~을 얻다, 획득하다

실전 문제

01.(C) 02.(D) 03.(B) 04.(A) 05.(D) 06.(B)
07.(B) 08.(B) 09.(A) 10.(D)

01-02는 다음 웹페이지를 참조하시오.

One Earth: 더 나은 비즈니스 세미나

| 홈 | **소개** | 과거의 세미나 성공 사례 | 다가오는 일정 | 자주 하는 질문들 |

저희 One Earth는 모든 사람들이 경제 수준이나 국적 또는 사회적 배경에 상관 없이 서로 함께 하는 법을 배울 수 있다고 믿습니다.

저희가 무대 위로 모시는 [01]각 연설자들은 개인적인 경험에서 우러나오는 얘기를 전해 드립니다. 오직 전 세계 곳곳의 다른 곳에서 다양한 일을 해 본 후에야 진정으로 모든 장애물을 극복하고 한때 자신과 다르다고 여겼던 사람들과 함께 하는 법을 배울 수 있습니다.

저희 'One Earth: 더 나은 비즈니스 세미나'에 참석하심으로써, [02]여러분과 여러분의 직원들은 다른 국가의 기업들과 더욱 효과적으로 협업하는 방법을 배우실 수 있습니다. 그것이 바로 저희와 저희의 자원 봉사 연설자들이 여러분에서 저희 강연을 통해 얻어 가시기를 바라는 부분입니다.

have faith that ~임을 믿다   **regardless of** ~에 상관 없이   **economic** 경제의   **national** 국가의   **take the stage** 무대에 오르다   **overcome** ~을 극복하다   **obstacle** 장애물   **once** 한때   **cooperate** 협업하다, 협조하다   **effectively** 효과적으로   **take away from** ~로부터 얻어 가다, 가져가다

01. 추론 문제

One Earth의 연설자들에 관해 암시된 것은 무엇인가?
(A) 각자의 분야에서 전문가들이다.
(B) 각자 여러 언어를 구사한다.
(C) 다양한 근무 경험을 지니고 있다.
(D) 주기적으로 자원 봉사 활동을 한다.

[해설] 연설자가 언급된 두 번째 단락에 개인적인 경험(personal experiences)을 얘기해 준다는 말이 있고, 바로 뒤이어 그 내용이 전 세계 곳곳의 다른 곳에서 다양한 일을 해 본 것(having worked a variety of jobs in different places)과 관련되어 있음을 알리고 있으므로 다양한 근무 경험을 언급한 (C)가 정답이다.

paraphrasing   having worked a variety of jobs 다양한 일을 해봄 → diverse work experience 다양한 근무 경험

[어휘] **expert** 전문가   **respective** 각각의   **field** 분야   **diverse** 다양한   **regularly** 주기적으로

02. 목적 문제

'One Earth: 더 나은 비즈니스 세미나'의 한 가지 목적은 무엇인가?
(A) 취업 비자 제공하기
(B) 자원 봉사 활동 장려하기
(C) 국제 무역 용이하게 하기
(D) 국제적인 팀워크 개선하기

[해설] 마지막 단락에 해당 세미나를 통해 다른 국가의 기업들과 더욱 효과적으로 협업하는 방법을 배울 수 있다는(~ learn how to cooperate more effectively with businesses in other countries) 말이 쓰여 있는데, 이는 국제적인 팀워크 향상과 관련된 일이므로 (D)가 정답이다.

paraphrasing   cooperate more effectively with businesses in other countries 다른 국가의 기업들과 더욱 효과적으로 협업하기 → Improving international teamwork 국제적인 팀워크 개선하기

[어휘] **encourage** ~을 장려하다, 권하다   **facilitate** ~을 용이하게 하다   **improve** ~을 개선하다, 향상시키다

paraphrasing 정답   1. (b)   2. (a)   3. (c)

03-05는 다음 웹페이지 정보를 참조하시오.

http://www.seymourcity.gov

| 홈 | 공원 관리부 | **상공회의소** | 지역 의원 만나보기 | 연락처 |

[03]세이모어 시티 상공회의소(SCCC)는 거의 모든 분야를 포함하는 50곳이 넘는 지역 기업들을 대표합니다. 민간 부문에서 활동하고 계

내용이고, 빈칸 뒤는 마감일을 연장하겠다는 내용이다. 즉, 빈칸 앞은 원인, 빈칸 뒤는 결과에 해당하므로 '그러므로, 따라서'라는 의미로 인과 관계를 나타내는 접속부사인 (A) Therefore가 정답이다.

[어휘] additionally 추가로 however 그러나 for example 예를 들면

08. 동사의 형태

[해설] 주어 all reports 뒤에 들어갈 적절한 동사의 형태를 고르는 문제이다. 명사 report는 동사 collect의 주체가 될 수 없으므로 수동태인 (A) were collected가 정답이다.

PART 7 웹페이지

풀이 방법 해석

홈	자주 하는 질문들	나의 계정

축하 드립니다, Vanessa Graham 님! Sahara 비즈니스 프리미엄으로 업그레이드되셨습니다! 이제 당신은 당신의 레스토랑을 위해 sahara.com에서 구입하는 모든 대량 구매에 대해 특별 적립과 할인을 받을 수 있습니다.

당신의 계정 업그레이드로 누릴 수 있는 몇몇 혜택입니다.
* 추가 재고 검색 필터 옵션
* 명성 있는 요리사들의 요리법
* 모든 주문에 대한 무료 일반 배송
* 연중 무휴의 온라인 채팅 또는 전화상의 고객 지원

연습 문제

01.(A) 02.(A) 03.(A) 04.(B)

01.

[내 계정]
다시 방문하신 것을 환영합니다, Beverly Nolin 님! 귀하께서는 성공적으로 로그인하셨습니다. 마지막 로그인 시간은 9월 4일 오후 3시 52분이었습니다. 저희는 최근 웹사이트를 업그레이드했습니다. 귀하의 온라인 계정에 대한 다음과 같은 변동 사항에 유의해 주시기 바랍니다.

새로운 기능:
- 귀하의 **휴대전화 포인트를 신속하고 편리하게 충전**하실 수 있습니다.
- **실시간으로 데이터 사용량을 확인**하실 수 있습니다.
- 한 번의 비용 지불로 월 청구 요금을 납부하시거나 자동 이체를 설정하실 수 있습니다.
- 귀하의 구매 제품에 적용될 수 있는 품질 보증 관련 정보와 안전상의 리콜 여부를 확인하실 수 있습니다.

account 계정 feature 기능, 특징 top up ~을 가득 채우다, 보충하다 credit 포인트 in real time 실시간으로 bill 고지서, 청구서 set up ~을 설정하다 direct debit 자동 이체 warranty 품질 보증(서) recall (결함 제품의) 리콜, 회수

Q. Nolan 씨는 누구일 것 같은가?
(A) 휴대전화기 구매 고객

(B) 휴대전화기 기술자

[문제 키워드] Who / Ms. Nolan

[해설] 키워드 Ms. Nolan이 지문의 전체적인 소재이므로 지문 전반에서 단서를 파악해 각 선택지와 비교해야 한다. 초반부를 통해 Nolan 씨가 이 웹페이지에 접속한 사용자임을 알 수 있고, 지문 중반부에 제시된 휴대 전화 포인트 충전(Top up your cell phone credit ~), 데이터 사용량 확인 (Check your data usage ~) 등의 서비스를 이용할 수 있다는 말을 통해 휴대 전화기를 구매한 고객임을 알 수 있으므로 (A)가 정답이다.

02.

홈	부서	뉴스	연락처

저희 Jarvis 사에서는 부동산을 임대하는 것이 스트레스를 받는 경험일 수 있다는 사실을 알고 있습니다. 여러분께서는 세입자와 문제를 겪거나 시시각각 변화하는 규정을 준수하는 방법을 잘 알지 못하실 수 있습니다. 저희에게 부동산을 관리하도록 맡기시면, 시간을 절약하실 수 있을 뿐만 아니라 번거로운 일도 해결하실 수 있습니다. 저희는 세입자에 대한 신원 확인을 실시하고, 수리 작업에 필요한 조치를 취해 드리며, 임대료도 받아 드릴 것입니다. 추가로, **언제든지 필요하실 때 상담해 드릴 수 있는 변호사들을 직원으로 두고 있습니다.** 오늘 저희에게 연락 주셔서 저희가 어떻게 서비스를 제공해 드릴 수 있는지 알아보시기 바랍니다.

department 부서 property 건물, 부동산 tenant 세입자, 입주자 comply with ~을 준수하다 ever-changing 시시각각 변화하는 regulation 규정, 규제 hassle 번거로운 일 make arrangements for ~에 대한 조치를 하다, ~에 필요한 준비를 하다 rental payment 임대료 in addition 추가로 counsel ~에게 상담해 주다

Q. Jarvis 사를 이용하는 것의 혜택으로 언급된 것은 무엇인가?
(A) 법률 전문가들과의 상담
(B) 수리 작업에 대한 할인

[문제 키워드] What / mentioned / benefit / using Jarvis Ltd.

[해설] 키워드 Jarvis Ltd.가 지문의 전체적인 소재이므로 지문 전반에서 단서를 파악해 각 선택지와 비교해야 한다. 지문 후반부에 언제든지 상담해 줄 변호사들을 직원으로 두고 있다는(we have lawyers on staff who can counsel ~) 말이 있으므로 (A)가 정답이다.

[어휘] consultation 상담 legal 법률의 professional 전문가

03.

www.communitylink.com.au/award

저희 Community Link는 버스턴 시의 취약 계층 주민들께 가까이 다가가는 데 전념하고 있는 비영리 단체입니다. 저희는 지역 내에서 변화를 만들어 내기 위해 노력하고 계신 분들을 표창하기 위해 매년 Community Link 상을 수여합니다. 과거의 수상자들께서는 노숙자 보호소 개설과 성인 독서 수업, 공공 장소 정화 작업 외의 여러 일들을 포함해 수많은 프로젝트에 기여해 주셨습니다. **이 상의 후보로 지명하시고자 하는 분이 계실 경우, Eliza Sinclair 씨께 e.sinclair@communitylink.com.au로 이메일을 보내 주십시오.**

non-profit 비영리의 dedicated to -ing ~하는 데 전념하는, 헌신하는 reach out to ~에게 다가가다 vulnerable 취약한 present ~을 주다, 수여하다, 제공하다 recognize ~을 인정하다, 표창하다 locally 지역적으로 contribute to ~에 기여하다, 공헌하다 shelter 보호소, 쉼터 nominate A for B B에 대해 A를 후보로 지명하다

DAY 20 173

> **실전 문제**
> 01. (B)　02. (C)　03. (B)　04. (D)　05. (C)　06. (C)
> 07. (A)　08. (A)

01-04은 다음 회람을 참조하시오.

발신: Erica West
수신: 전 직원
제목: 사무실 위치 이전
날짜: 8월 23일

다음 주에, 우리는 Elm 가 527번지에 위치한 새 사무실로 이전할 예정입니다. ⁰¹**여러분 모두 이사 전문 업체 직원들을 위해 금요일 오후 시간을 활용하여 각자의 짐을 상자에 담아야 합니다.** ⁰²그분들께서 토요일에 새 사무실로 모든 물품을 옮겨 주실 것입니다. ⁰³월요일이 첫 날이므로, 오전 시간은 짐을 풀고 근무 자리를 준비하는 데 전념하게 될 것입니다. ⁰⁴월요일 점심 시간 이후에 정규 업무를 재개하겠습니다.

안녕히 계십시오.

Erica West
인사부 부장

relocation 위치 이전, 이사　pack A into B A를 B에 담아 꾸리다　mover 이사 업체 직원　be dedicated to -ing ~하는 데 전념하다　set up ~을 준비하다, 설치하다　workstation 근무 자리　regular 정규의, 일반의, 정기적인　operation 운영, 가동, 작동

01. 대명사 어휘

[해설] 앞 문장에 제시된 회사가 다른 곳으로 이전한다는 공지와 어울려야 하므로 of you와 결합해 수신인인 전체 직원을 가리킬 수 있는 대명사가 쓰여야 한다. 따라서 '모두, 전부'를 뜻하는 (B) All이 정답이다.

02. 알맞은 문장 고르기

(A) 우리는 적절한 가격대를 협의할 수 있었습니다.
(B) 고객들께서 우리의 위치에 대해 불만을 제기하셨습니다.
(C) 그분들께서 토요일에 새 사무실로 모든 물품을 옮겨 주실 것입니다.
(D) 이 지역에는 전문 이사 업체에 대한 선택권이 많지 않습니다.

[해설] 앞 문장에 이사 업체 직원(the movers)들을 위해 금요일 오후에 짐을 꾸리라고 요청하는 말이 있으므로 이 내용과 연계되는 것으로서, 이사 업체 직원들을 They로 지칭함과 동시에 그 이후에 발생될 일을 미래 시제 동사를 써서 알리는 (C)가 정답이다.

[어휘] negotiate ~을 협의하다, 협상하다　affordable 가격이 적절한, 저렴한　complain about ~에 대해 불만을 제기하다

03. 동명사 어휘

[해설] and로 연결된 setting up our workstations과 마찬가지로 월요일 아침에 해야 하는 일들 중의 하나를 나타낼 동명사가 필요한데, 새 사무실로 가서 근무 자리를 준비하기 위해 하는 일이어야 하므로 '짐 풀기'를 의미하는 (B) unpacking이 정답이다.

[어휘] fold ~을 접다　purchase ~을 구입하다　attach ~을 부착하다, 첨부하다

04. 동사의 시제

[해설] 월요일 오후에 있을 일을 나타내는 문장인데, 이는 앞선 문장에서 미래 시제 동사 will be dedicated로 표현된 월요일 오전에 해야 하는 일보다 나중에 일어날 일이므로 동일한 미래 시제인 (D) will resume이 정답이다.

05-08은 다음 이메일을 참조하시오.

발신: Toby Fischer
수신: Kelly Lloyd
제목: 실적 평가
날짜: 12월 18일

Kelly Lloyd 씨께

⁰⁵귀하의 소속 직원들에 대한 실적 평가 보고서 마감 기한이 12월 15일이었음을 다시 알려드리고자 이 이메일을 보냅니다. ⁰⁶**귀하의 부서를 제외하고 다른 모든 부서들로부터 그것들을 수령했습니다.** 세인트 루이스 무역 박람회에 회사 부스를 준비하느라 매우 바빴다는 것을 이해합니다. ⁰⁷따라서 마감 기한을 연장할 것이니 이번 주말까지 제출되어야 합니다.

⁰⁸모든 보고서는 인트라넷을 통해 취합되었으나 지금은 더 이상 웹페이지를 이용할 수 없습니다. 그러니, 직접 인사부에 제출해 주시기 바랍니다. 질문이 있으시거나 도움이 필요할 경우, Moorland 씨에게 연락하시기 바랍니다.

안녕히 계십시오.
Toby Fischer

performance 실적, 성과　evaluation 평가(서)　organize 준비하다, 정리하다　extend 연장하다　Intranet 인트라넷, 내부 전산망　in person 직접　personnel (조직의) 인원, (회사의) 인사과

05. 형용사 어휘

[해설] 빈칸 뒤에 제시된 날짜 15 December가 이메일 작성 날짜(December 18)보다 이전 시점인 점과 이후에 이어지는 내용에서 마감일을 연장해 주겠다고 한 점 등으로 보아 빈칸이 포함된 문장은 수신자에게 직원 실적 평가서 제출 마감일을 지키지 못했음을 상기시키는 내용임을 알 수 있다. 따라서 '~가 기한인'이라는 뜻으로 쓰이는 (C) due가 정답이다.

[어휘] posted 게시된　located 위치한　performed 수행된, 실시된

06. 알맞은 문장 고르기

(A) 평가 결과에 근거해 현금 보너스가 지급될 것입니다.
(B) 1월 2일 점심 시간 이전에 제 수신함에 들어 와 있어야 합니다.
(C) 귀하의 부서를 제외하고 다른 모든 부서들로부터 그것들을 수령했습니다.
(D) 일부 우리 직원들은 1월 2일부터 이곳에서 근무를 시작할 것입니다.

[해설] 앞 문장에서 수신자가 직원 실적 평가 보고서를 마감 기한까지 제출하지 못했음을 상기시켰으므로 이 내용과 관련된 것으로서, 앞서 언급한 보고서를 대명사 them으로 받아 다른 모든 부서로부터는 보고서를 수령한 상태임을 현재완료 시제를 써서 알리는 내용인 (C)가 정답이다.

[어휘] based on ~에 기초하여　grant 주다, 수여하다　place 놓다, 두다　except ~을 제외하고

07. 접속부사

[해설] 빈칸 앞은 무역 박람회 준비 업무 때문에 바빴던 상황을 이해한다는

모든 요소를 고려해야 한다.

[해설] 선택지가 다양한 명사들로 구성되어 있으므로 명사 어휘 문제이다. 빈칸 앞에 위치한 'take+목적어+into' 구조와 어울리는 명사가 필요하므로 이 구조와 함께 '~을 고려하다, 감안하다'라는 의미를 나타낼 때 사용하는 (C) account가 정답이다.

[어휘] factor 요소 value 가치 amount 양, 수량, 액수

24. 부정어 도치

그는 1만 달러가 넘게 잃은 후에는 주식 시장에 거의 투자하지 않았다.

[해설] 선택지가 다양한 부사들로 구성되어 있으므로 문법 문제이다. 빈칸 뒤에 조동사 did와 주어 he가 도치되어 있으므로 도치 구조를 이끄는 부사 (C) Scarcely가 정답이다.

[어휘] invest in ~에 투자하다 stock market 주식 시장 approximately 약, 대략 frequently 자주, 흔히

PART 6 알맞은 문장 고르기-선택지의 시제

풀이 방법 해석

발신: Joseph Swanson
수신: 지점장들
제목: Bloomer's Fashion
날짜: 2월 18일

지점장들께 알립니다.

여러분 모두가 우리 Bloomers' Fashion 지사의 세 곳을 보수하는 것에 대한 결정에 대해 알고 계시리라 생각합니다. 우리의 계획은 보수 공사가 완전히 끝날 때까지 그 세 곳을 임시적으로 닫는 것입니다. 선택된 그 지사들은 내부가 아주 오래되었습니다. 설문조사는 우리의 가장 큰 고객층이 10대라는 것을 보여줍니다. 이 변화는 우리 사업이 젊은 고객들의 관심을 계속 끄는 데 도움이 될 것입니다.

첨부된 것은 승인된 평면도와 보수 일정입니다. 그것에 대한 질문이 있으시면 Bolton 씨에게 언제라도 연락하세요.

Joseph Swanson
Bloomers' Fashion 대표이사

 연습 문제

01.(A) 02.(B) 03.(B) 04.(B)

01.

Julia Stark 씨가 이번 주말에 있을 음악 시상식에서 '올해의 앨범' 상을 수상할 예정입니다. -------.

be set to부정사 ~할 예정이다 win (상 등) ~을 받다, 타다

(A) 이는 그녀의 다섯 번째이자 3년 연속 수상이 될 것입니다.
(B) 그 콘서트 입장권은 기록적인 시간에 매진되었습니다.

[단서] is set to win

[해설] 앞 문장의 동사 표현(is set to win ~)은 미래의 일을 나타내므로 빈칸에도 미래 시제 동사 will be와 함께 해당 수상 사실과 관련된 미래의 일을 말하는 (A)가 정답이다.

[어휘] in a row 연속으로 sell out 매진되다, 품절되다 in record time 기록적인 시간에

02.

구리 공급의 급격한 감소로 인해, 대부분의 전선 제조사들은 지난 두 분기 동안 그 문제에 시달려 왔습니다. 40년이 넘는 역사를 지닌 우리 회사는 전에 이 문제를 여러 번 겪었으며, 그에 대비했습니다. -------.

drastic 급격한 copper 구리 supply 공급 electric wire 전선 manufacturer 제조사 suffer from ~에 시달리다, ~로 고통받다

(A) 우리는 이번 달에 할당량을 충족할 수 없을 것입니다.
(B) 우리는 전 세계적으로 판매 업체들을 다각화했습니다.

[단서] experienced, prepared

[해설] 앞 문장에 과거 시제 동사(experienced, prepared)와 함께 과거에 겪은 경험과 이에 대비해온 사실을 나타내고 있으므로 마찬가지로 과거 시제 동사(diversified)를 이용해 관련 대비책을 말하는 내용인 (B)가 정답이다.

[어휘] quota 할당량 diversify ~을 다각화하다 vendor 판매 업체

03.

불편을 드려 죄송하지만, 저희 카페는 현재 개조 공사로 인해 문을 닫았습니다. 저희는 불충분한 식사 공간과 관련해 많은 불만 사항을 접수했습니다. -------.

inconvenience 불편함 currently 현재 insufficient 불충분한 dining area 식사 공간

(A) 저희는 주말에 어떠한 예약도 받지 않습니다.
(B) 가장 바쁜 시간대에 긴 대기 줄이 있었습니다.

[단서] received

[해설] 빈칸 앞에 과거 시제 동사(received)와 함께 과거 시점에 불만 사항을 접수한 사실을 말하고 있으므로 마찬가지로 과거 시제 동사(was)를 이용해 그 불만 사항이 무엇이었는지를 알리는 내용에 해당되는 (B)가 정답이다.

04.

-------. 저희 요리사들이 최근 한 차례 실시된 고객 설문 조사 중에 받은 추천 사항들을 바탕으로 새로운 요리에 대한 조리법을 개발하고 있습니다. 여러분께서는 다음 달부터 이 요리들을 맛보실 수 있습니다.

develop ~을 개발하다 recipe 조리법 dish 요리 based on ~을 바탕으로 latest 최근의 round (특정한 일의) 한 차례, 한 회

(A) 비밀 BBQ 소스 맛이 이미 저희 레스토랑에서 병에 담겨 판매되었습니다.
(B) 저희 레스토랑의 메뉴에는 골라 먹을 수 있는 다양한 채식 요리가 특별히 포함될 것입니다.

[단서] next month

[해설] 빈칸 다음 문장들을 보면 현재 개발 중인 것이 미래 시점인 다음 달부터(next month) 이용 가능하다는 사실이 쓰여 있으므로 미래 시제 동사(will feature)와 함께 미래 시점에 생길 메뉴상의 특징을 말하는 (B)가 정답이다.

[어휘] feature ~을 특징으로 하다 vegetarian 채식의

13. 주격 관계대명사

Ray 씨는 연회장 B에서 개최될 예정인 은퇴 기념 만찬 행사를 기획하는 일을 맡고 있다.

[해설] 선택지가 다양한 의문사들로 구성되어 있으므로 문법 문제이다. 빈칸 뒤에 주어 없이 동사 is supposed로 시작되는 불완전한 절이 있으므로 주어 역할이 가능하면서 바로 앞에 위치한 선행사 retirement dinner를 수식할 수 있는 (A) which가 정답이다. (B) where와 (C) when은 완전한 절을 이끌고, (D) what은 선행사를 수식하지 않는다.

[어휘] in charge of ~을 맡고 있는, 책임지는   retirement 은퇴

14. 명사절의 역할: 목적어

누가 차량 충돌 사고에 대한 책임이 있는지에 관해 철저한 조사가 있을 것이다.

[해설] 선택지가 다양한 접속사와 의문사들로 구성되어 있으므로 문법 문제이다. 빈칸 이하는 전치사 as to의 목적어 역할을 할 명사절이 되어야 하므로 명사절 접속사가 필요하며, 동시에 이것은 is의 주어가 되어야 하므로 이 두 가지 역할이 가능한 (B) who가 정답이다. (A) that은 전치사의 목적어로 쓰이는 명사절을 이끌 수 없으며, (D) whether 뒤에는 완전한 절이 와야 한다.

[어휘] thorough 철저한   investigation 조사   as to ~에 관해

15. 과거분사

최근 선임된 내무부 장관이 내일 헌팅턴 시청에서 기자 회견을 열 예정이다.

[해설] 선택지가 다양한 품사의 단어들로 구성되어 있으므로 문법 문제이다. 빈칸 앞에 위치한 부사 recently의 수식을 받으면서 그 뒤에 위치한 Secretary of Internal Affairs를 수식할 분사가 빈칸에 쓰여야 한다. 직책은 다른 사람에 의해 선임되는 것이므로 수동의 의미를 나타낼 수 있는 과거분사 (D) appointed가 정답이다.

[어휘] Secretary of Internal Affairs 내무부 장관   press conference 기자 회견   appoint ~을 선임하다, 임명하다   appointment 임명, 약속, 예약

16. to부정사의 역할: 부사 역할

저조한 1분기 매출을 만회하기 위해, Bailey 자동차는 특별 판촉 행사를 만들어 내기로 결정했다.

[해설] 선택지가 다양한 전치사구로 구성되어 있으므로 문법 문제이다. 빈칸 뒤에 위치한 동사원형 make와 결합해야 하므로 동사원형과 함께 '~하기 위해'라는 의미를 나타낼 때 사용하는 (B) In order to가 정답이다.

[어휘] make up for ~을 만회하다, 보충하다   poor 저조한, 형편 없는   quarter 분기   sales 매출, 판매(량)   promotion 판촉, 홍보

17. 부정대명사

거의 모든 디자이너들이 그 패션 쇼를 위해 화려한 의상을 준비한 반면, 한 디자이너는 올 블랙 의류 라인을 선보였다.

[해설] 선택지가 다양한 품사의 단어들로 구성되어 있으므로 문법 문제이다. 접속사 while을 사이에 두고 앞뒤 내용이 대조가 되어야 의미가 자연스러워지므로 주절의 주어 Almost all of the designers와 대조되는 일부 디자이너를 가리킬 대명사가 빈칸에 쓰여야 알맞다. 따라서 designer를 대신할 수 있는 부정대명사 (A) one이 정답이다.

[어휘] wardrobe 의상   present ~을 선보이다, 발표하다

18. 명사의 위치: 형용사 뒤

Duncan 아카데미는 수업 일정을 편성할 수 있는 학사 관리 책임자를 필요로 한다.

[해설] 선택지가 다양한 품사의 단어들로 구성되어 있으므로 문법 문제이다. 부정관사 an과 형용사 academic 뒤에 위치한 빈칸은 이 둘의 수식을 받을 단수 명사 자리이므로 (C) administrator가 정답이다.

[어휘] in need of ~을 필요로 하는   coordinate ~을 편성하다, 조정하다   administrate ~을 관리하다, 운영하다(= administer)   administrational 관리의, 행정의

19. 동사 어휘

대부분의 레스토랑 소유주들은 매년 수익을 유지하기 위해 메뉴 가격을 인상하는 경향이 있다.

[해설] 선택지가 다양한 동사들로 구성되어 있으므로 동사 어휘 문제이다. 빈칸 뒤에 위치한 to부정사와 결합할 수 있는 동사가 필요하므로 to부정사와 함께 '~하는 경향이 있다'라는 의미를 나타내는 (A) tend가 정답이다.

[어휘] raise ~을 인상하다, 끌어올리다   maintain ~을 유지하다   profit 수익

20. 빈출 숙어

모든 직원들은 첨부된 슬라이드 파일을 검토해 봄으로써 새로운 영업 정책에 익숙해져야 한다.

[해설] 선택지가 다양한 동사들로 구성되어 있으므로 동사 어휘 문제이다. 빈칸 뒤에 위치한 'oneself+with+대상' 구문과 어울리는 동사가 필요하므로 이 구조로 쓰여 '~에 익숙해지다, ~을 숙지하다' 등을 의미할 때 사용하는 (B) familiarize가 정답이다.

[어휘] policy 정책   contribute ~을 기여하다, 기부하다   recognize ~을 인정하다, 표창하다   advertise ~을 광고하다

21. 빈출 숙어

모든 지출 비용 환급 요청서는 반드시 이번 주 금요일까지 원본 영수증과 함께 제출되어야 한다는 점을 명심하십시오.

[해설] 선택지가 다양한 동사들로 구성되어 있으므로 동사 어휘 문제이다. 빈칸 뒤에 위치한 'in mind' 및 that절과 어울리는 동사가 필요하므로 이들과 함께 쓰여 '~라는 점을 명심하다'라는 의미를 나타내는 (B) Keep이 정답이다.

[어휘] expense 지출 비용   reimbursement 환급

22. 가정법 미래 도치

저희 제품에 관심이 있으실 경우에 저희 영업 사원들이 안내 책자를 한 부 보내 드릴 것입니다.

[해설] 선택지가 다양한 품사의 단어들로 구성되어 있으므로 문법 문제이다. 빈칸 뒤로 주어 you와 be동사 원형이 이어져 있으므로 도치된 구조임을 알 수 있으며, 빈칸 이하가 '~에 관심이 있으면'과 같은 가정의 의미를 나타내야 자연스럽다. 따라서 가정법 접속사 if가 생략되고 조동사 should가 앞으로 이동한 가정법 미래 도치 구조가 되어야 알맞으므로 (B) should가 정답이다.

[어휘] representative 사원   brochure 안내 책자   be interested in ~에 관심이 있다

23. 빈출 숙어

새로운 사업을 시작할 때, 소유주는 건물 접근성과 간접비를 포함해 반드시

대신하다

02. so/neither 도치

Smith의 동료 직원들 중 한 사람이 덜 비싼 것으로 휴대전화 서비스 약정을 변경했으며, 그도 그렇게 했다.

[해설] 선택지가 쓰임이 다른 다양한 부사들로 구성되어 있다. 빈칸 뒤에 조동사 did와 주어 he가 도치되어 있으므로 도치 구조를 이끄는 부사 (B) so가 정답이다.

[어휘] coworker 동료 직원

03. 가정법 과거완료

모든 원료가 예정대로 배송되었다면 이번 달의 생산 할당량이 지난주에 충족되었을 것이다.

[해설] 선택지가 동사 ship(배송하다)의 다양한 형태로 구성되어 있으므로 문법 문제이다. 주절에 'would/could/might+have p.p.'가 올 경우, if절에는 가정법 과거완료를 나타내는 'had p.p.' 형태의 동사가 쓰이므로 (C) had been shipped가 정답이다.

[어휘] quota 할당량   raw material 원료

04. 빈출 숙어

개발팀은 기기를 더 크게 만들지 않고 배터리 수명을 연장할 수 있는 방법을 알아내기 위해 노력하고 있다.

[해설] 선택지가 다양한 동사 숙어들로 구성되어 있으므로 어휘 문제이다. 빈칸 뒤에 위치한 a way(방법)와 의미가 어울리는 숙어로서 특정 방법과 관련된 행위를 나타내기에 알맞은 것이 필요하므로 '~을 알아내다'라는 의미로 쓰이는 (C) figure out이 정답이다.

[어휘] development 개발   extend ~을 연장하다, 확장하다   device 기기, 장치   carry on ~을 계속하다   lag behind ~보다 뒤쳐지다   call off ~을 취소하다, 철회하다

05. 부정어 도치

Choi 씨는 노스사이드 내의 연립 주택으로 이사한 후로 좀처럼 주민 센터를 방문하지 않았다.

[해설] 선택지가 다양한 품사의 단어들로 구성되어 있으므로 문법 문제이다. 빈칸 뒤에 조동사 did와 주어 Mr. Donaldson이 도치되어 있으므로 도치 구조를 이끄는 부정의 의미를 가진 부사 (B) Rarely가 정답이다.

[어휘] rarely 좀처럼 ~하지 않는

06. 'only+부사구' 도치

오직 유효 운전 면허증을 지참하고 오실 경우에만 GRS Car Rental에서 차량을 대여하실 수 있습니다.

[해설] 선택지가 다양한 동사들로 구성되어 있으므로 문법 문제이다. 부사 only와 with 전치사구로 문장이 시작되고 있으므로 도치 구조가 되어야 하는데, 빈칸 뒤에 위치한 주어 you, 형용사 able과 어울리는 동사는 be동사이므로 (D) are가 정답이다.

[어휘] valid 유효한

07. 가정법 과거완료 도치

Kelly 씨가 왼쪽 전조등을 수리했었다면, 경찰로부터 벌금을 피할 수 있었을 것이다.

[해설] 선택지가 다양한 동사들로 구성되어 있으므로 문법 문제이다. 각 선택지가 조동사 또는 동사이므로 접속사 없이 두 개의 절이 하나의 문장으로 연결되려면 도치 구조가 되어야 한다. 주절의 동사 'would have p.p.'를 통해 가정법 과거완료 문장임을 알 수 있으므로 'If+주어+had p.p.' 구문에서 if가 생략되고 주어와 had가 도치된 구조를 만드는 (C) Had가 정답이다.

[어휘] fine 벌금

08. 빈출 숙어

재고를 파악하기 위해 Barney's 식료품점에 새로운 소프트웨어 시스템이 도입되었다.

[해설] 선택지가 다양한 명사들로 구성되어 있으므로 명사 어휘 문제이다. 빈칸 앞뒤에 위치한 동사 keep, 전치사 of와 어울리는 명사가 필요하므로 이 둘과 함께 keep track of로 쓰여 '~을 파악하다, 추적하다'라는 의미를 나타내는 (D) track이 정답이다.

[어휘] introduce ~을 도입하다, 소개하다   inventory 재고(품), 재고 목록   function 기능, 역할, 행사

09. so/neither 도치

Carlson 감독은 그 프로 야구팀에 합류하지 않기로 결정했으며, 일부 선수들도 그랬다.

[해설] 선택지가 부사와 대명사로 구성되어 있으므로 문법 문제이다. 빈칸 뒤에 조동사 did와 주어 some players가 도치되어 있으므로 도치 구조를 이끄는 부사 (B) neither가 정답이다.

[어휘] clearly 분명히

10. 최상급 비교의 형태

올 한 해는 10여 년 만에 디젤 차량 판매량의 가장 급격한 감소를 기록했다.

[해설] 선택지가 다양한 품사의 단어들로 구성되어 있으므로 문법 문제이다. 정관사 the와 명사 drop 사이에 위치한 빈칸은 형용사 자리인데, 비교 범위에 해당되는 기간 전치사구 in over a decade와 어울리려면 최상급 형용사가 쓰여야 한다. 따라서 (C) sharpest가 정답이다.

[어휘] drop in ~의 감소   vehicle 차량   sales 판매(량), 매출   sharp 급격한, 날카로운   sharpen ~을 날카롭게 하다   sharply 급격히, 날카롭게

11. 비교급 강조 부사

Wade Fashion의 가격은 다른 계절들보다 여름에 훨씬 더 높다.

[해설] 선택지가 부사와 형용사로 구성되어 있으므로 문법 문제이다. 빈칸 뒤에 위치한 than과 짝을 이뤄 비교를 나타내야 하므로 비교급 형용사의 형태인 (B) higher가 정답이다.

[어휘] significantly (비교급 수식) 훨씬   highly 매우, 대단히, 크게

12. 조건 부사절 접속사

Ritter 아울렛에서 판매하는 어떤 상품이든 계절 재고 정리 세일에서 구입하지만 않았다면 반품될 수 있다.

[해설] 선택지가 접속사와 부사로 구성되어 있으므로 문법 문제이다. 빈칸 앞뒤로 완전한 절이 각각 있으므로 빈칸은 이 절들을 연결할 접속사 자리이다. 빈칸 이하가 '계절 재고 정리 세일에서 구입되지만 않았다면'과 같은 부정 조건을 나타내야 자연스러우므로 '~하지 않는다면'이라는 의미의 접속사 (C) unless가 정답이다.

[어휘] merchandise 상품   clearance sale 재고 정리 세일   regardless (of) 상관 없이

10. 세부사항 문제

Bailey 씨는 어떻게 해당 호텔에 관해 알게 되었는가?
(A) 온라인 광고를 통해서
(B) 친구의 추천을 통해서
(C) 협회 소식지를 통해서
(D) 신문 기사를 통해서

[해설] 세 번째 지문 맨 마지막에, 우연히 온라인 배너 광고를 클릭하여 자신이 묵은 호텔을 찾았다고(Little did I know that when I clicked that online banner by chance that I'd find such a great little gem) 알리고 있으므로 온라인 광고가 제시된 (A)가 정답이다.

`paraphrasing` online banner 온라인 배너 → online advertisement 온라인 광고

[어휘] association 협회

`paraphrasing 정답` 1. (b)   2. (a)   3. (c)

DAY 20

PART 5 문법 | 가정법/도치

확인 문제 해석

① 만약 그가 택시를 탔다면, 회의에 제때 도착했었을 것이다.
② 만약 당신이 설명서를 철저히 검토했었다면, 그것을 빠르게 조립했었을 것이다.
③ 정보가 더 필요하시면, 저에게 이메일을 보내 주세요.
④ 지정된 주차장에만 직원들은 그들의 차를 주차한다.
⑤ 나는 지난 분기에 교육에 참석했고 Min 씨도 그랬다(교육에 참석했다).

 연습 문제

01.(B)   02.(C)   03.(A)   04.(D)   05.(A)   06.(B)

01.

1. 선택지 보고 문법/어휘 문제 파악하기 ☑ 문법 문제 ☐ 어휘 문제
2. 빈칸 분석하기 주절의 동사 would have hired
   → ☑ 가정법 과거완료 ☐ 가정법 미래 문장임을 알 수 있다.
3. 정답 선택하기 정답 (B)

그녀가 계약을 따냈다면 개인 보조를 채용할 수 있었을 것이다.

02.

1. 선택지 보고 문법/어휘 문제 파악하기 ☑ 문법 문제 ☐ 어휘 문제
2. 빈칸 분석하기 빈칸 뒤에 완전한 절이 2개 있지만 ☑ 접속사 ☐ 전치사가 없으므로 도치 구문이다.
   → 도치 구문을 이끌 수 있는 조동사가 정답이다.
3. 정답 선택하기 정답 (C)

더 많은 정보가 필요하시면 온라인을 방문하시거나 직통 전화로 전화하세요.

03.

1. 선택지 보고 문법/어휘 문제 파악하기 ☑ 문법 문제 ☐ 어휘 문제
2. 빈칸 분석하기 빈칸 뒤에 완전한 절이 2개 있지만 ☑ 접속사 ☐ 전치사가 없으므로 도치 구문이다.
   → 주절의 동사 could have attended
   → ☑ 가정법 과거완료 ☐ 가정법 미래 도치이다.
3. 정답 선택하기 정답 (A)

더 큰 장소에서 열렸다면 더 많은 사람들이 콘서트에 참석할 수 있었을 것이다.

04.

1. 선택지 보고 문법/어휘 문제 파악하기 ☑ 문법 문제 ☐ 어휘 문제
2. 빈칸 분석하기 빈칸 앞에 'do동사+주어'가 있으므로 scarcely가 문장 맨 앞으로 나가 도치된 구문임을 알 수 있다.
   → 동사 자리에는 ☑ 동사원형 ☐ 과거분사 형태가 들어가야 한다.
3. 정답 선택하기 정답 (D)

그녀는 그녀의 친구들에게 휴대전화로 그녀의 사진을 거의 보내지 않는다.

05.

1. 선택지 보고 문법/어휘 문제 파악하기 ☑ 문법 문제 ☐ 어휘 문제
2. 빈칸 분석하기 빈칸 뒤에 있는 것 ☐ 부사구+주어+동사 ☑ 전치사구+조동사+주어+동사원형
   → 도치 구문을 이끌 수 있는 것을 골라야 한다.
3. 정답 선택하기 정답 (A)

유효한 신분증이 있어야만 사람들은 공항에서 자동차를 렌트할 수 있다.

06.

1. 선택지 보고 문법/어휘 문제 파악하기 ☐ 문법 문제 ☑ 어휘 문제
2. 빈칸 분석하기 빈칸 뒤에 있는 명사구 (vacation requests)
   명사구의 의미 (휴가 신청)
   → '승인하기 전에 ------할 것이다'라는 문맥에 어울리는 동사가 정답이다.
3. 정답 선택하기 정답 (B)

부서장은 휴가 신청을 승인하기 전에 그것들을 검토해야 한다.

실전 문제					
01.(C)	02.(B)	03.(C)	04.(C)	05.(B)	06.(D)
07.(C)	08.(D)	09.(B)	10.(C)	11.(B)	12.(C)
13.(A)	14.(B)	15.(D)	16.(B)	17.(A)	18.(C)
19.(A)	20.(B)	21.(B)	22.(B)	23.(C)	24.(C)

01. 가정법 미래 도치

교대 근무를 하러 오실 수 없을 경우에, Denver 씨에게 연락하시면 그분이 당신 대신 일할 사람을 찾을 것입니다.

[해설] 선택지가 다양한 품사의 단어들로 구성되어 있으므로 문법 문제이다. 빈칸 뒤로 주어 you와 be동사 원형이 이어져 있으므로 도치된 구조임을 알 수 있으며, '~할 수 없으면'과 같은 가정의 의미가 되어야 자연스럽다. 따라서 가정법 접속사 If가 생략되고 조동사 should가 앞으로 이동한 가정법 미래 도치 구조가 되어야 알맞으므로 (C) Should가 정답이다.

[어휘] come in for ~하러 오다   shift 교대 근무(조)   cover for ~을

이 공사를 진행하게 될 08Vitella 사는 비용을 할인해 주었는데, 해당 부지가 지역 사회를 위해 사용될 것이기 때문이다. 08시 당국자들은 이 워터파크가 높은 수준으로 제때 완공될 경우에 이 업체에게 향후의 공사 계약들을 수주시킬 것이라고 밝혔다.

approve ~을 승인하다   wading pool 어린이용 물 놀이터   supporter 지지자, 후원자   tourism 관광업   account for ~을 차지하다   economy 경제   make a bid 입찰하다   have a good chance of ~할 가능성이 높다   thanks to ~로 인해, ~덕분에   site 부지, 장소   for community use 지역 사회를 위해 사용되는   officials 당국자, 관계자   grant ~을 승인하다   contract 계약(서)   on time 제때   to a high standard 높은 수준으로

수신: Gregory Duvall <g.duvall@vitellainc.com>
발신: Heather Phillips <h.phillips@vitellainc.com>
날짜: 12월 17일
제목: Grayburg Adventures

Gregory 씨께

Grayburg Adventures를 완공하는 데 귀하와 귀하의 팀이 보여 주신 노고에 감사 드리고자 합니다. 08제가 시 의회의 Jill Berry 씨와 막 이야기를 했는데, 전반적인 작업 완성도를 열렬히 칭찬하시면서 대단히 만족해 하고 계십니다. 정말 잘해 주셨습니다!

Heather

council 의회   pleased 만족한, 기쁜   eagerly 열렬히, 간절히   compliment ~을 칭찬하다

www.wayside-hotel.net/testimonials

| 홈 | 객실 예약 | 포토 갤러리 | **고객 추천 후기** | 연락처 |

Wayside 호텔 고객 추천 후기

6일 전에 Carmen Bailey 씨가 게시함

저는 제 친구들과 가족 전부에게 Wayside 호텔을 반드시 추천할 것입니다. 저는 최근에 그레이버그를 방문했는데, 09주의 주니어 수영 대회의 시간 기록원으로 참석하도록 요청받았기 때문입니다. 남서부 수영 협회의 일원으로서, 저는 행사 참석을 위해 자주 출장을 다니기 때문에, 지역 전체에 걸쳐 수많은 호텔에서 머무른 경험이 있습니다. Wayside 호텔은 제가 본 호텔들 중에서 분명 최고의 가치를 지니고 있습니다. 깨끗하고 넓은 객실과 친절한 직원들이 있습니다. 저는 심지어 그전까지 이 호텔에 관해 들어 보지도 못했습니다. 10제가 우연히 그 온라인 배너 광고를 클릭해 이와 같이 훌륭한 작은 보석을 발견할 줄은 꿈에도 생각하지 못했습니다.

testimonial 고객 추천 후기   be invited to부정사 ~하도록 요청받다   timer 시간 기록원   frequently 자주, 흔히   throughout ~ 전역에 걸쳐   region 지역   value 가치   spacious 넓은   Little did I know that ~할 줄은 꿈에도 생각하지 못했다   by chance 우연히   gem 보석

06. 목적 문제

기사의 목적은 무엇인가?
(A) 곧 있을 시 재정 지원 관련 투표에 대해 이야기하기 위해
(B) 그레이버그에 위치한 지역 업체들을 홍보하기 위해
(C) 경연대회의 수상자들에 관해 보도하기 위해
(D) 공사 프로젝트에 대한 계획을 알리기 위해

[해설] 첫 지문 시작 부분에 그레이버그 북부에 위치할 워터파크인 Grayburg Adventures 공사에 대한 계획이 승인되었다는(Plans have been approved for the construction of Grayburg Adventures, a water park ~) 사실과 함께 이 공사와 관련된 정보가 제공되고 있으므로 (D)가 정답이다.

[어휘] vote 투표   funding 재정 지원   promote ~을 홍보하다   local 지역의, 현지의   competition 경연대회

07. 동의어 문제

기사에서 두 번째 단락, 두 번째 줄의 표현 "accounts for"와 의미가 가장 가까운 것은 무엇인가?
(A) 계산하다
(B) 해당하다
(C) 정당화하다
(D) 보고하다

[해설] account for 뒤로 15퍼센트라는 비율(about fifteen percent)과 '경제'라는 범주가 나타나 있으므로 경제에서 차지하는 비율을 말하기 위해 account for가 쓰였음을 알 수 있다. 이는 다시 말하면 15퍼센트라는 비율에 해당한다는 말과 같으므로 '~에 해당하다'를 뜻하는 (B) represents가 정답이다.

08. 추론 문제 - 연계 문제

Vitella 사에 관해 암시된 것은 무엇인가?
(A) 시 의회의 한 사람이 소유하고 있다.
(B) 한 가지 사업에 대해 예산보다 비용이 적게 들었다.
(C) 향후에 그레이버그에서 있을 작업을 제안받을 것이다.
(D) 2월에 한 가지 일을 맡아 하기 시작했다.

[해설] Vitella Inc.가 제시된 첫 지문 마지막 단락에 워터파크가 높은 수준으로 제때 완공될 경우에 이 업체에게 향후 공사 계약을 수주시킬 것이라는(Vitella Inc., ~ City officials said they would grant future contracts to the business if the water park is completed ~) 말이 있고, 두 번째 지문에는 공사에 대단히 만족해 하고 있다는 말이 있으므로(Jill Berry of the city council, ~ eagerly complimenting the overall quality of the work) 앞으로 추가 작업 계약이 이뤄질 것으로 판단할 수 있다. 따라서 (C)가 정답이다.

[어휘] own ~을 소유하다   come in under budget 예산보다 비용이 덜 들다   venture (모험적) 사업   task 일, 업무

09. True 문제 - 연계 문제

Bailey 씨에 관해 무엇이 사실일 것 같은가?
(A) 그레이버그에서 자랐다.
(B) 전문 수영 코치이다.
(C) Phillips 씨와 회의를 했다.
(D) Grayburg Adventures에 가봤다.

[해설] Bailey 씨가 쓴 후기인 세 번째 지문에, 자신이 State Junior Swim Meet 행사의 시간 기록원으로 참석한 사실이 쓰여 있는데(I was invited to be a timer at the State Junior Swim Meet), 이 행사 이름이 제시된 첫 지문 두 번째 단락에 그 워터파크에서 State Junior Swim Meet를 주최한다는(to host the State Junior Swim Meet at the water park) 말이 나타나 있다. 여기서 말하는 the water park가 Grayburg Adventures이므로 Bailey 씨가 Grayburg Adventures에 가봤다는 사실을 알 수 있다. 따라서 (D)가 정답이다.

[어휘] grow up 자라다

[어휘] similar 유사한 direct ~을 감독하다 based on ~을 기반으로 하는, 바탕으로 하는 spare 여분의 wilderness 야생, 황야 tactics 전술

paraphrasing 정답 1. (c) 2. (a) 3. (b)

03-05는 다음 설문지를 참조하시오.

Murphy 렌탈

최근에 저희 Murphy 렌탈을 이용해 주셔서 감사 드립니다. 저희는 고객들께 합리적인 청소용품과 장비를 제공해 드리기 위해 애쓰고 있습니다. 아래의 양식을 통해 여러분께서 의견을 공유해 주신다면 감사하게 여길 것입니다. ⁰³답변을 제출해 주시는 모든 고객들께 다음 번 이용 시 10퍼센트의 할인을 받으실 수 있는 쿠폰을 우송해 드립니다.

고객 성함: Lori Elliot   날짜: 3월 17일
우편 주소: Fox가 152번지, 프레즈노, 캘리포니아 주 93724
사용 제품: Primeway 스팀 카펫 청소기
배송/⁰⁵수거 날짜: 3월 4일/3월 7일

다음 사항에 대해 1점(매우 불만족)에서 ⁰⁴5점(매우 만족)의 등급으로 평가해 주시기 바랍니다. 이용하지 않으신 서비스에 대해서는 해당 항목을 빈칸으로 남겨 두시면 됩니다.

웹사이트
- ⁰⁴필요로 했던 것을 신속히 찾을 수 있었다. __5__
- 웹사이트가 최신식으로 보인다고 생각했다. __2__
- 웹사이트에서 지불 관련 정보를 제공하기가 편했다. __4__

직원
- 상담 전화를 받는 고객 서비스 직원들이 친절하고 아는 것이 많았다. ____
- 기기를 가져다준 직원이 시간을 엄수했다. __3__
- 기기를 수거해 간 직원이 시간을 엄수했다. __5__

추가 의견: 기기 배송이 늦기는 했지만, ⁰⁵그 기기를 수거해 간 기사님으로부터 깊은 인상을 받았습니다. 그분께서는 집안을 통과해 기기를 옮기는 동안 새롭게 청소된 제 카펫에 어떠한 물이나 용액도 떨어지지 않도록 비닐로 꼼꼼하게 기기를 포장하셨습니다.

patronage 이용, 애용 strive to부정사 ~하기 위해 애쓰다 affordable 합리적인, 저렴한 supplies 용품, 물품 equipment 장비 share ~을 공유하다 drop-off 갖다주기, 내려놓기 pick-up 수거하기, 가져가기 rate ~을 평가하다, 등급을 매기다 statement 말, 글, 진술, 성명 disagree 동의하지 않다 state-of-the-art 최신의 appearance 모습, 외관 knowledgeable 아는 것이 많은 additional 추가의 be impressed with ~에 깊은 인상을 받다 thoroughly 철저히 wrap ~을 포장하다, 싸다 drip 떨어지다 solution 용액 carry ~을 옮기다, 나르다 through ~을 지나, 통과해

03. 세부사항 문제

Murphy 렌탈은 설문지를 작성한 고객들에게 어떻게 감사의 표시를 하는가?
(A) 계정으로 포인트를 발급해 줌으로써
(B) 경품 추첨 행사에 참가시킴으로써
(C) 할인 쿠폰을 발송해 줌으로써
(D) 무료 청소용품을 제공해 줌으로써

[해설] 첫 단락에 답변을 제출하는 모든 고객들에게 10퍼센트의 할인을 받을 수 있는 쿠폰을 우송해 준다고(All customers who submit their answers will be mailed a voucher for ten percent off their next purchase) 알리고 있으므로 (C)가 정답이다.

paraphrasing be mailed a voucher for ten percent off 10퍼센트 할인 쿠폰이 우송되다 → sending them a discount coupon 할인 쿠폰을 발송하다

[어휘] issue ~을 발급하다 credit (매장 등의) 포인트 account 계정, 계좌 enter ~을 참가시키다, 가입시키다 prize drawing 경품 추첨 행사

04. 세부사항 문제

Elliot 씨가 회사의 웹사이트에 관해 언급한 것은 무엇인가?
(A) 현대적으로 보인다고 생각했다.
(B) 다시 방문할 계획이다.
(C) 자신의 지불 금액을 수납하지 않았다.
(D) 탐색하기 편리했다.

[해설] 중간 부분의 웹사이트 평가 항목에서, '필요로 했던 것을 빠르게 찾을 수 있었다'는 항목에 대해 5점을 주었는데(I was able to find what I needed quickly. 5) 바로 윗부분에 5점은 '매우 만족함'을(5 (Strongly Agree)) 의미하는 것으로 나타나 있다. 이는 웹사이트 내에서의 탐색이 편리했다는 말과 같으므로 (D)가 정답이다.

[어휘] accept ~을 받아들이다 payment 지불(금) navigate 탐색하다, 찾아 다니다

05. 세부사항 문제

Elliot 씨가 3월 7일에 서비스를 제공한 직원에 관해 언급한 것은 무엇인가?
(A) 기기에 관한 질문에 답변해 주었다.
(B) 더럽히지 않기 위해 신중을 기했다.
(C) Elliot 씨가 일부 가구를 옮기는 것을 도와 주었다.
(D) 제시간에 도착하지 못했다.

[해설] 지문 상단에 3월 7일이 수거 날짜로(Pick-up Dates) 쓰여 있고, 이 수거 작업과 관련해 마지막 단락에 수거 담당 기사가 카펫에 물이나 용액이 떨어지지 않도록 비닐로 꼼꼼하게 기기를 포장했다는(He thoroughly wrapped it in plastic so that it would not drip any water or solution ~) 말이 쓰여 있다. 따라서 그 기사는 바닥을 엉망으로 만들지 않기 위해 신중하게 일을 한 것으로 볼 수 있으므로 (B)가 정답이다.

[어휘] make a mess 엉망으로 만들다, 어지럽히다 on time 제 시간에

paraphrasing 정답 1. (c) 2. (a) 3. (b)

06-10은 다음 기사와 이메일, 그리고 온라인 후기를 참조하시오.

그레이버그 지역 뉴스

2월 5일 — ^{06, 09}그레이버그 북부에 위치할 워터파크인 Grayburg Adventures 공사에 대한 계획이 승인되었다. 이 복합 건물에는 세 가지 워터 슬라이드와 어린이용 물 놀이터, 그리고 올림픽 경기장 규모의 수영장이 포함된다. 이 공사는 3월 말에 시작되어 연말쯤 완료될 것으로 예상된다.

이 워터파크를 지지하는 사람들은 그 시설이 지역 내에 더 많은 관광객들을 유치할 것이라고 생각한다. 관광 사업이 지역 경제의 약 15퍼센트를 ⁰⁷차지하고 있기 때문에, 더 많은 관광객을 끌어들이는 일이 긍정적인 효과를 가져올 것이며, 이는 특히 호텔들과 레스토랑들, 그리고 상점들에 해당된다. 이 도시에서는 ⁰⁹내년 초에 이 워터파크에서 주의 주니어 수영 대회를 개최하기 위해 입찰을 한 상태이며, 제공 가능한 현대적인 시설들 덕분에 선정될 가능성이 높다.

[해설] 키워드 Mr. Thorpe가 제시되는 부분에서 단서를 찾아야 한다. 이 이름이 쓰여 있는 마지막 부분은 수신함으로 쿠폰과 특가 서비스를 받기 위해(If you would like to be sent occasional coupons and special deals to your inbox ~) 이름과 이메일 정보를 입력하는 항목이므로 (A)가 정답이다.

[어휘] be dissatisfied with ~에 만족하지 못하다

03.

후기 작성자 - Crystal Rhodes

저는 현재 3주째 Gilroy-90을 사용하고 있는데, 대체로 사용 결과에 만족하고 있습니다. 이 제품은 제 옷을 매우 깨끗하게 만들어 주며, **작동 중에 큰 소음을 발생시키지 않습니다.** 또한 나중에 작동을 시작하도록 기계를 설정할 수 있는데, 이는 바쁜 제 일정에 있어 편리한 부분입니다. 선택할 수 있는 여러 가지 작동 사이클이 있지만, 아쉽게도, 어느 것에도 절수 기능은 없습니다. 이것이 바뀔 수만 있다면 그렇게 하고 싶은 유일한 점입니다.

run 작동되다, 돌아가다   cycle (기계 등이 한 차례 도는) 사이클
feature 기능, 특징

Q. Rhodes 씨가 해당 세탁기와 관련해 언급하는 것은 무엇인가?
(A) 물을 많이 사용하지 않는다.
(B) 조용하게 작동된다.

[문제 키워드] What / indicate / washing machine

[해설] about 뒤의 키워드 washing machine이 지문의 전체적인 소재이므로 지문 전반에서 단서를 파악해 각 선택지와 비교해야 한다. 지문 초반부에 그 제품이 작동 중에 큰 소음을 내지 않는다고(it doesn't make much noise when it's running) 했으므로 (B)가 정답이다.

04.

Wellbright 전자 의견 제공 양식

저희 Wellbright 전자를 선택해 주셔서 감사 드립니다. 잠시 시간 내어서 의견을 공유해 주시기 바랍니다.

고객 성명: Connie Sandford   주소: Cheshire 로 972번지

의견: 저는 최근 건물 전체에 전기 배선을 다시 해야 했습니다. 여름 휴가 기간에 맞춰 반드시 모든 것이 완료되기를 원했습니다. **저희 집에 작업을 해주신 팀원들께서는 제 모든 질문에 답변해 주셨으며, 프로젝트 완료 시에 모든 먼지와 부스러기를 진공 청소기로 확실하게 청소해 주셨습니다.** 저는 이 업체를 친구들과 가족에게 분명히 추천해 줄 것입니다.

entire 전체의   property 건물, 부동산   rewire 전기 배선을 다시 하다   in time for ~의 때에 맞춰   crew (함께 작업하는) 팀, 조   vacuum up 진공 청소기로 청소하다   dust 먼지   debris 부스러기, 잔해

Q. Sandford 씨는 작업 인원에 관해 무엇을 언급하는가?
(A) 프로젝트를 위해 제때 도착했다.
(B) 나중에 직접 말끔히 청소했다.

[문제 키워드] What / Ms. Sandford / mention / work crew

[해설] 키워드 work crew가 제시되는 부분에서 단서를 찾아야 한다. 지문 중반부에 작업팀 일원들이 작업 후에 먼지와 부스러기를 진공 청소기로 확실히 청소해 주었다(The crew members ~ they made sure to vacuum up any dust and debris at the completion of the project)고 했으므로 (B)가 정답이다.

[어휘] clean up after ~ 뒤를 깨끗이 청소하다

실전 문제

| 01.(B) | 02.(A) | 03.(C) | 04.(D) | 05.(B) | 06.(D) |
| 07.(B) | 08.(C) | 09.(D) | 10.(A) | | |

01-02는 다음 서평을 참조하시오.

<Into the Mountains>

Katie Kramer는 <Into the Mountains>와 함께 다시 한번 대성공을 거뒀습니다. 이 작품은 평원에 자리한 거주지를 떠나 자신의 부족민들을 이끌고 **01계속되는 폭풍우를 피할 곳을 찾아 근처의 산속으로 어쩔 수 없이 올라가 들어가는** 한 부족장을 따라 전개됩니다.

비록 Kramer가 자신의 **02<Water Ways>** 시리즈 속 등장 인물로부터 탈피하고 있기는 하지만, 이 책의 주요 등장 인물들과 유사하게 연관 짓기가 쉽습니다. <Water Ways>와 마찬가지로, 등장 인물들은 위험하고 죽어가는 것처럼 보이는 세상 속에서 생존하기 위한 방법들을 생각해 내려 애쓰는 상황에 직면합니다.

land ~을 획득하다, 차지하다   huge success 대성공   chief 추장   tribe 부족   be forced to부정사 어쩔 수 없이 ~하다   homeland 모국, 거주 구역   plain 평원   seek ~을 찾다, 구하다   shelter from ~을 피할 수 있는 곳   take leave of ~에서 탈피하다, 벗어나다   similarly 마찬가지로, 유사하게   relate to ~와 연관 짓다   be faced with ~에 직면하다, ~와 마주하다   come up with ~을 생각해 내다

01. 주제 문제

<Into the Mountains>는 무슨 종류의 책인가?
(A) 역사 교과서
(B) 모험 소설
(C) 개인 회고록
(D) 여행 가이드

[해설] 작품 내용이 대략적으로 설명된 첫 단락에, 폭풍우를 피할 곳을 찾아 근처의 산속으로 어쩔 수 없이 들어가는(lead his people ~ up into the nearby mountains to seek shelter from a series of storms) 부족민들을 묘사하고 있는데, 이는 일종의 모험 상황에 해당되므로 (B)가 정답이다.

[어휘] fiction 소설   memoir 회고록

02. 추론 문제

Katie Kramer에 관해 암시된 것은 무엇인가?
(A) 일련의 유사한 책들을 출간했다.
(B) <Water Ways>를 바탕으로 한 영화를 감독했다.
(C) 여유 시간에 등산을 하러 간다.
(D) 야생에서 생존하는 전술에 관한 강습을 받았다.

[해설] 두 번째 단락에 기존에 출간된 <Water Ways> 시리즈 속 주요 등장 인물들과 유사하게 연관 짓기가 쉽다는 말이(~ Water Ways series, the main characters in this book are similarly easy to relate to) 쓰여 있는 것으로 볼 때, 앞서 유사한 책들을 썼음을 알 수 있으므로 이를 언급한 (A)가 정답이다.

paraphrasing   similarly easy to relate to 유사하게 연관 짓기가 쉬운 → similar books 유사한 책들

사를 목적어로 취해 '~ 동안 내내'라는 의미를 나타낼 때 사용하는 (A) throughout이 정답이다. 나머지 전치사들은 기간 명사가 아닌 시점 명사와 함께 사용한다.

06. 알맞은 문장 고르기

(A) 저희 성수기가 바로 코앞으로 다가왔습니다.
(B) 저희 웹사이트에서 신나는 놀이 기구를 보실 수 있는 동영상을 확인해 보십시오.
(C) 저희는 5월 1일부터 9월 말일까지 일주일 내내 문을 엽니다.
(D) 동봉해 드린 것은 우선 출입증이므로 귀하께서는 대기 시간을 줄이실 수 있습니다.

[해설] 빈칸 뒤에 이어지는 문장을 보면, '다시 말해, 즉' 등의 의미로 다른 말로 설명할 때 사용하는 접속부사가 쓰여 있으므로 That is 뒤에 제시된 대기 줄을 건너뛸 수 있다는 말과 동일한 의미에 해당되는 문장을 고르면 된다. 따라서 동봉된 출입증으로 대기 시간을 줄일 수 있다고 한 (D)가 정답이다.

[어휘] peak season 성수기 right around the corner 바로 코앞에 닥친 Enclosed is A 동봉해 드린 것은 A입니다 so that (결과) 그러므로, 그 결과 (목적) ~할 수 있도록 reduce ~을 줄이다, 감소시키다

07. 명사 어휘

[해설] times와 복합 명사를 구성하며, 줄을 서지 않고도 들어 갈 수 있는 VIP 회원이 다른 VIP 회원들로 인해 대기하게 되는 경우를 나타내야 하므로 '피크 시간대, 가장 바쁜 시간대'라는 의미를 나타낼 때 사용하는 (B) peak가 정답이다.

08. 동명사 어휘

[해설] 고객인 상대방을 가리키는 you를 목적어로 취해 업체 측에서 고대하는 일을 나타내야 하는데, 공원에서(at the park) 하는 일을 나타내야 하므로 '~을 맞이하다, 받아들이다' 등을 뜻하는 (A) having이 정답이다. (D) visiting이 쓰이면 고객인 상대방을 방문한다는 의미가 되므로 어색하다.

PART 7 후기/설문조사

풀이 방법 해석

작성자: Bianca Wade

저는 최근에 I-81을 따라서 했던 장거리 자동차 여행 중에 Conway 휴게소에 들러 그곳에 있는 동안 Kessler Deli에서 음식을 먹어보았어요. 직원들은 샌드위치를 만드느라 매우 바빴는데도 활기차고 에너지가 넘쳤어요. 저의 첫 방문이어서 어떤 줄로 가야 하는지 혼란스러웠는데 그들이 어디로 가야 하는지 알려주며 저를 도와주었어요. 메뉴에 있는 모든 것들이 맛있어 보였는데, 저는 특별한 소스가 들어 있는 클럽 샌드위치와 구운 감자칩이 곁들여 나오고 음료가 제공되는 Clubber Combo를 주문했어요.

모든 게 맛있었지만, 먹는 동안 소스가 손 전체에 묻었어요. 저는 그들이 준 일반적인 마른 냅킨을 사용했는데 그 후에도 손이 끈적거려서 바로 씻어야 했어요.

전반적으로, 이곳은 식사하기에 훌륭한 곳이고 다음에 이 지역을 지날 때 꼭 다시 올 거예요.

 연습 문제

01.(B) **02.**(A) **03.**(B) **04.**(B)

01.

Vernon 호텔 – 콩코드, 뉴햄프셔 주
"가격 대비 훌륭한 가치!"

저는 최근에 처음으로 Vernon 호텔에 머물렀는데, 싱글룸의 가격이 매우 합리적이라고 생각했습니다. 저는 비행기를 타고 콩코드로 갔기 때문에, 이 호텔의 공항 셔틀 버스 서비스를 이용해야 했습니다. 저는 이 버스가 공항에서 15분마다 한 번씩 출발한다는 사실을 믿을 수 없었으며, 이는 정말로 편리했습니다. 또한 깨끗하고 편안했습니다. 유일한 제 불만은 이 호텔 구내 레스토랑의 메뉴가 매우 제한적이라는 점입니다. 하지만 이는 작은 문제에 불과한 것이었습니다.

value 가치 reasonable 합리적인 depart 출발하다, 떠나다
convenient 편리한 comfortable 편안한 complaint 불만
on-site 구내의, 건물 내의 minor (중요도 등이) 작은, 사소한

Q. 무엇이 해당 호텔과 관련해 후기 작성자에게 깊은 인상을 남겼는가?
(A) 식사 선택권
(B) 교통편 서비스

[문제 키워드] What / impressed / reviewer / hotel

[해설] 키워드인 impressed가 직접적으로 언급되어 있지 않으므로 패러프레이징된 부분인 I couldn't believe를 찾는다. 지문 중반부에 공항 셔틀 버스 서비스의 좋은 점을(~ departs every fifteen minutes from the airport, which was really convenient. It was also clean and comfortable) 언급하고 있으므로 (B)가 정답이다.

[어휘] impress ~에게 깊은 인상을 남기다

02.

Abner 호텔 고객 설문 조사
저희는 여러분의 의견을 소중히 여기고 있습니다! 최근 저희 시설에서 머무신 경험이 어떠셨는지 말씀해 주십시오.

다음 항목들에 대해 1점(나쁨)에서 10점(훌륭함)의 단위로 어떻게 평가하시겠습니까? 이용하지 않은 편의 시설에 대해서는 N/A(해당 사항 없음)로 표기해 주십시오.

예약 과정: __10__   직원: __10__
객실 크기: __9__   식당: __9__
객실 청결도: __10__   구내 체육관: __N/A__

때때로 전송되는 쿠폰과 특가 서비스를 수신함으로 받아 보기를 원하실 경우, 성함과 연락처를 아래에 추가해 주시기 바랍니다.
성명: Noah Thorpe   E-mail: n.thorpe@winifredexpress.com

value ~을 소중히 여기다 facility 시설(물) rate ~을 평가하다, 등급을 매기다 on a scale of ~의 단위로 applicable 적용될 수 있는
amenities 편의 시설 process 과정 cleanliness 청결(도)
on-site 구내의, 건물 내의 occasional 때때로 발생되는 deal 거래 조건, 거래 제품 inbox 수신함

Q. Thorpe 씨에 관해 암시된 것은 무엇인가?
(A) 이메일로 제공 서비스를 받아 보기를 원한다.
(B) 해당 호텔의 체육관에 만족하지 못했다.

[문제 키워드] What / suggested / Mr. Thorpe

04.

> -------. 추가로, 귀하께서는 잠재적으로 수익성 있는 투자에 관한 발표를 하도록 요청받으실 수 있습니다.
>
> in addition 추가로 potentially 잠재적으로 profitable 수익성 있는 investment 투자

(A) 이 유명 기관은 일부 세계에서 가장 부유한 고객들을 보유하고 있습니다.
(B) 그 직책의 주요 직무는 주식 시장의 동향을 분석하는 일이 될 것입니다.

[단서] In addition, provide presentations
[해설] 빈칸 뒤에 추가 정보를 말할 때 사용하는 접속부사 In addition과 함께 수익성 있는 투자에 관한 발표를 할 수도 있다는 말이 쓰여 있으므로 빈칸에도 이와 유사한 일이 제시되어야 한다. 따라서 수익성 있는 투자와 관련된 일로서 주식 시장의 동향 분석이 언급된 (B)가 정답이다.

[어휘] renowned 유명한 institution 기관, 협회 responsibility 직무, 책무 analyze ~을 분석하다 stock market 주식 시장

실전 문제
01.(D) 02.(C) 03.(A) 04.(D) 05.(A) 06.(D)
07.(B) 08.(A)

01-04는 다음 이메일을 참조하시오.

> 수신: Emily Porter
> 발신: custserv@northstarair.net
> 날짜: 11월 7일
> 제목: NSA 마일리지 보상
>
> Porter 씨께
> North Star 항공사 마일리지 보상 프로그램에 가입하신 것을 축하 드립니다! 01방금 예약하신 항공편은 두 배의 마일리지 점수가 쌓입니다. 따라서 귀하께서는 현재 일등석으로 업그레이드하실 수 있는 자격에 충분한 마일리지를 보유하고 계십니다! 02이 항공편에서 업그레이드하기를 원하실 경우, 미리 저희 서비스팀에 알려 주시기만 하면 됩니다. 이 제공 서비스는 해당 항공편의 모든 일등석 좌석이 예약될 때까지 유효합니다.
> 03또한 향후에 저희 항공편을 업그레이드하실 수 있도록 귀하의 포인트를 남겨 두는 것으로 결정하셔도 됩니다. 04저희는 귀하가 선택하실 수 있는 많은 항공사들이 있다는 것을 잘 알고 있기에, North Star 항공사를 선택해 주신 것에 대해 감사 드립니다.
> 안녕히 계십시오.
> NSA 고객 서비스팀

reward 보상 join ~에 가입하다, 함께 하다 accordingly 따라서, 이에 따라 qualify for ~에 대한 자격을 얻다 in advance 미리, 사전에 offer 제공(되는 것) good 유효한

01. 알맞은 문장 고르기

(A) 웹사이트에서 공항 시설물의 목록과 안내도를 찾아보실 수 있습니다.
(B) 귀하의 항공편이 취소되었다는 사실을 알려 드리게 되어 유감스럽게 생각합니다.
(C) 출발 및 도착 안내판에서 새로운 정보를 확인해 보시기 바랍니다.
(D) 방금 예약하신 항공편은 두 배의 마일리지 점수가 쌓입니다.

[해설] 빈칸 뒤에 결과를 나타내는 접속부사 Accordingly와 함께 일등석으로 업그레이드 가능한 수준의 마일리지를 보유하게 되었다는 결과를 언급하고 있으므로 그 원인에 해당되는 것으로서 두 배의 마일리지를 얻었다는 사실을 나타내는 (D)가 정답이다.

[어휘] facility 시설(물) regret to부정사 ~해서 유감이다 inform A that A에게 ~라고 알리다 check A for B B가 있는지 A를 확인하다 departure 출발 arrival 도착 A earn B A로 인해 B를 얻다, A가 B의 결과를 가져오다

02. 동사의 형태

[해설] to부정사와 결합해 상대방이 원하는 일을 조건으로 나타내는 If절이 되어야 알맞으므로 '~하기를 원하다, ~하고자 하다' 등의 의미를 나타낼 때 사용하는 (C) would like가 정답이다.

03. 인칭대명사

[해설] 전치사 with의 목적어로 쓰일 대명사는 상대방이 갖고 있는 포인트를 그대로 뒀다가(save your points) 사용하는 업체를 가리켜야 하는데, 이는 이메일을 보낸 곳에 해당되므로 '우리'를 의미하는 (A) us가 정답이다.

04. 형용사 어휘

[해설] 사람 주어에 대한 보어로 쓰일 수 있으면서 that절과 결합해 사용하는 형용사가 필요하므로 이와 같은 역할이 가능한 (D) aware가 정답이다. (A) necessary나 (B) obvious는 It ~ that 구조로 된 가주어/진주어 문장에서 보어로 쓰인다.

[어휘] necessary 필요한, 필수의 obvious 명백한 responsible 책임지고 있는, 맡고 있는

05-08은 다음 편지를 참조하시오.

> Burns 씨께
> 저희가 귀하의 신청서를 처리해 드렸으며, 귀하께서는 이제 Seven Flags 놀이공원의 VIP 회원이 되셨습니다! 05현재 귀하께서는 연중 언제든지 저희 놀이공원에 출입하실 수 있습니다. 06동봉해 드린 것은 우선 출입증이므로 귀하께서는 대기 시간을 줄이실 수 있습니다. 다시 말해, 각 놀이 기구마다 그저 이 출입증을 입장 관리 직원에게 제시하는 것만으로도 대기하는 줄을 건너뛰어 들어가실 수 있습니다. 07피크 시간대에는 인기 있는 놀이 기구를 타려면 우선 출입증을 지닌 VIP 회원들께서도 줄 서 기다리실 수 있다는 점에 유의하시기 바랍니다.
> 귀하께서는 저희 우편물 발송 대상자 명단에 올라 있는 분이시므로, 저희 Seven Flags에서 발생되는 어떠한 변동 사항에 관한 최신 소식도 받아보실 수 있습니다. 08곧 저희 놀이공원에서 귀하를 맞이할 수 있기를 고대합니다!
> 안녕히 계십시오.
> Seven Flags 놀이공원

process ~을 처리하다 application 신청(서), 지원(서) access ~에 출입하다, ~을 이용하다 at any time 언제든지 that is 다시 말해, 즉 skip ahead 앞으로 건너뛰다 ride 놀이 기구 by (방법) ~함으로써 fast pass 우선 출입증 mailing list 우편물 발송 대상자 명단

05. 전치사 어휘

[해설] 빈칸 뒤에 위치한 명사구 the year는 기간을 나타내므로 기간 명

[어휘] apply for ~을 신청하다 shift 교대 근무(조)

23. 빈출 숙어

Oliver's Kitchen의 고객들은 고품질의 메뉴 선택권과 함께 신속한 배달 서비스를 기대할 수 있다.

[해설] 선택지가 다양한 전치사들로 구성되어 있으므로 전치사 어휘 문제이다. 빈칸 앞에 위치한 동사 count와 결합 가능한 전치사가 필요한데, 이 문장에서는 두 가지 좋은 서비스에 대해 '~을 기대하다'라는 의미를 구성할 수 있는 (B) on이 정답이다. (A) for는 count for로 쓰여 '~에 대해 의지하다, 중요하다' 등을 의미하므로 이 문장에 맞지 않는다.

[어휘] high quality 고품질의, 고급의

24. 빈출 숙어

자원 봉사 활동에 참여하는 학생들은 Mason 대학교에 입학 허가를 받을 가능성이 크다.

[해설] 선택지가 다양한 동사들로 구성되어 있으므로 동사 어휘 문제이다. 빈칸 뒤에 위치한 part in과 결합 가능한 동사로서 '~에 참여하다'라는 의미를 구성할 때 사용하는 (D) take가 정답이다.

[어휘] get accepted to ~에 입학 허가를 받다

PART 6 알맞은 문장 고르기-빈칸 뒤에 접속부사

풀이 방법 해석

수신: Jeffrey Longino
발신: customerservice@ezebookz.com
날짜: 5월 12일
제목: 성공적인 등록

Longino 씨께

모든 종류의 책과 잡지의 디지털 버전 이용에 있어 선도적인 공급자인 E-Z E-books의 회원이 되어주셔서 감사합니다. 귀하의 독서 선호도가 분석되어 저희의 데이터 베이스에 입력되었습니다. 이러한 방식으로, 저희는 다른 어떠한 경쟁사들보다 귀하에게 더 적합한 책 추천을 해드릴 수 있습니다.

귀하는 현재 Silver Star 회원입니다. 그러므로 1주일에 최대 3권까지 이용할 수 있습니다. e북은 저희의 웹사이트나 모바일 앱에서 다운로드 받으실 수 있습니다.

다시 한번 E-Z E-books에 가입해주셔서 감사합니다.

E-Z E-books 서비스 팀

연습 문제

01.(A)   02.(B)   03.(A)   04.(B)

01.

우리는 매 분기에 고객 설문 조사를 실시합니다. 3분기에 대한 설문 조사 결과가 나왔습니다. -------. 따라서, 인사부에서 다음 달에 걸쳐 일련의 교육을 실시할 것입니다.

conduct ~을 실시하다, 수행하다   quarter 분기   therefore 따라서, 그러므로   personnel department 인사부   a series of 일련의 training 교육

(A) 많은 고객들은 우리 영업 사원들이 제품을 잘 알지 못한다고 불만을 제기했습니다.
(B) 잠깐 시간 내셔서 우리의 최신 고객 설문 조사 결과를 훑어 보시기 바랍니다.

[단서] survey results, therefore, conduct training

[해설] 빈칸 뒤에 결과를 나타낸 접속부사 Therefore와 함께 직원 교육을 하겠다는 말이 쓰여 있으므로 빈칸에는 그 원인에 해당되는 문장이 필요하다. 따라서 직원 교육이 필요한 이유로서 많은 고객들이 사원들과 관련해 제기한 불만 사항이 언급된 (A)가 정답이다.

[어휘] be unfamiliar with ~을 잘 알지 못하다, ~에 익숙하지 않다   look over ~을 훑어 보다   latest 최신의

02.

-------. 게다가, 매달 말일에 가장 높은 수치를 기록한 직원은 특별상을 받게 될 것입니다.

moreover 게다가, 더욱이   associate 직원   prize 상, 상품

(A) 반드시 친절한 미소로 우리 매장에 있는 모든 고객들을 맞이해 주시기 바랍니다.
(B) 여러분이 도움을 드린 고객께서 신용카드를 만들면 해당 직원은 5달러의 인센티브를 받게 됩니다.

[단서] moreover, a special prize

[해설] 빈칸 뒤에 추가 사항을 제시할 때 사용하는 접속부사 Moreover와 함께 직원에게 제공되는 혜택이 제시되어 있다. 따라서 그와 유사한 것으로서 직원에게 주어지는 또 다른 혜택에 해당되는 내용을 담은 (B)가 정답이다.

[어휘] greet ~을 맞이하다   incentive 인센티브, 장려금   assist ~을 돕다

03.

지난 분기에 대한 지출 보고서가 이용 가능합니다. -------. 결과적으로, 회사에서는 일등석 항공편, 비즈니스 클래스 항공편 또는 5성급 호텔에 대한 비용을 더 이상 환불해 주지 않을 것입니다.

expense 지출 (비용), 경비   consequently 결과적으로   no longer 더 이상 ~ 않다   refund ~을 환불해 주다

(A) 예산 관리팀에 따르면, 우리의 출장 경비가 너무 높습니다.
(B) 이사회는 여러분 중 일부가 업무로 출장 가야 한다는 점을 이해합니다.

[단서] consequently, will no longer refund

[해설] 빈칸 뒤에 결과를 나타내는 접속부사 Consequently와 함께 회사에서 앞으로 환불해 주지 않는 대상이 제시되어 있으므로 빈칸에는 그 원인에 해당되는 문장이 쓰여야 한다. 따라서 출장 경비가 너무 높다는 사실이 언급된 (A)가 정답이다.

[어휘] according to ~에 따르면   budget 예산   board of directors 이사회   travel 출장 가다, 여행하다

[해설] 선택지가 형용사와 부사로 구성되어 있으므로 문법 문제이다. 빈칸 앞에 위치한 more와 함께 비교를 나타낼 형용사 또는 부사가 필요한데, 동사 locate를 수식해 상품을 찾는 방식을 나타낼 부사가 쓰여야 알맞으므로 (C) quickly가 정답이다.

[어휘] rearrange ~을 다시 정리하다, 재배치하다 warehouse 창고 locate ~의 위치를 찾다 merchandise 상품

13. 최상급 비교의 형태

<Nashville Monthly Update>는 테네시 지역에서 컨트리 음악과 관련해 가장 널리 구독되는 잡지이다.

[해설] 선택지가 다양한 품사의 단어들로 구성되어 있으므로 문법 문제이다. 빈칸 뒤에 온 명사 magazine을 수식하는 과거분사 subscribed를 수식할 수 있으면서 정관사 the와 결합 가능한 것은 최상급 부사이므로 (A) most widely가 정답이다.

[어휘] subscribe ~을 구독하다 widely 널리, 폭넓게 widen ~을 넓히다, 확대하다

14. 원급: as ~ as 사이에 명사

가능한 한 많은 자원 봉사 프로그램에 참여하는 것은 어렵지만 일반적으로 매우 보람 있는 일이다.

[해설] 선택지가 형용사와 부사로 구성되어 있으므로 문법 문제이다. 빈칸 뒤에 위치한 as possible과 짝을 이뤄 원급 비교를 나타내는 as가 포함된 것 중에서, 복수 명사 volunteer programs를 수식할 수 있는 many가 결합된 (B) as many가 정답이다.

[어휘] participate in ~에 참여하다 rewarding 보람 있는

15. 시간 부사절 접속사

커피 매장들이 플라스틱 컵에 대해 1달러의 비용을 청구하기 시작한 이후로, 발생되는 쓰레기 양이 상당히 감소했다.

[해설] 선택지가 접속사와 전치사로 구성되어 있으므로 문법 문제이다. 빈칸이 속한 절에는 과거 시제 동사(started)가, 주절에는 현재완료 시제 동사(has decreased)가 쓰여 있으므로 과거의 어느 시점 이후의 영향을 나타내는 문장임을 알 수 있다. 따라서 '~ 이후로'라는 의미로 과거의 시작점을 나타내는 부사절 접속사 (A) Since가 정답이다.

[어휘] generate ~을 발생시키다 decrease 감소하다 significantly 상당히, 많이 whereas ~인 반면 as long as ~하는 한, ~하기만 하면

16. 조건 부사절 접속사

새 금전 등록기를 이용한 일일 매장 운영은 점원들이 교육을 완료하기만 하면 순조롭게 진행될 것이다.

[해설] 선택지가 접속사와 전치사로 구성되어 있으므로 문법 문제이다. 빈칸 뒤에 주어와 동사가 포함된 절이 있으므로 이 절을 이끌 접속사가 필요한데, '점원들이 교육을 완료하기만 하면'과 같이 조건을 나타내는 의미가 되어야 자연스럽다. 따라서 '~하는 한, ~하기만 하면'을 뜻하는 조건 부사절 접속사 (C) as long as가 정답이다.

[어휘] operation 운영, 영업, 가동 go smoothly 순조롭게 진행되다 clerk 점원 if so 그렇다면 prior to ~에 앞서

17. 비교급: more ~ than 사이에 형용사/부사

Rachel Cain 인사부장은 다른 어떤 부서장들보다 더욱 면밀히 모든 지원서를 검토한다.

[해설] 선택지가 형용사와 부사로 구성되어 있으므로 문법 문제이다. more와 than 사이에 위치해 비교급을 구성할 형용사 또는 부사가 필요한데, 동사 reviews를 수식해 검토하는 방식을 나타낼 부사가 쓰여야 알맞으므로 (A) closely가 정답이다.

[어휘] application 지원(서) department head 부서장 closely 면밀히

18. 수량 형용사

Duncan 마케팅은 여러 업체에 많은 다른 약정 서비스를 제공한다.

[해설] 선택지가 다양한 품사의 단어들로 구성되어 있으므로 문법 문제이다. 동사 offers와 목적어 different service plans 사이에 위치한 빈칸은 이 목적어를 수식할 형용사 자리인데, 복수 명사구이므로 복수 명사 앞에 사용하는 (A) many가 정답이다. (D) plenty를 쓰려면 plenty of 형태가 되어야 한다.

[어휘] service plan 약정 서비스 plenty 많음, 풍부함

19. 동사 어휘

시상식에서 수상 소감을 말하던 중에, Warwick 씨는 자신의 성공이 가족의 지지에 기인한다고 말했다.

[해설] 선택지가 다양한 동사들로 구성되어 있으므로 동사 어휘 문제이다. 빈칸 뒤에 '결과+to+원인'을 나타내는 명사구가 있으므로 이와 같은 구조와 함께 '~가 …에 기인하다'라는 의미를 나타낼 때 사용하는 동사 (B) attributed가 정답이다.

[어휘] acceptance speech 수상 소감 support 지지, 후원

20. 빈출 숙어

사진 촬영을 기다리는 동안, 모든 신입 사원들은 보안 출입증을 받기 위한 서류를 작성하도록 요청받는다.

[해설] 선택지가 다양한 숙어들로 구성되어 있으므로 어휘 문제이다. paperwork를 목적어로 취해 서류를 대상으로 할 수 있는 행위를 나타낼 숙어가 필요하므로 '~을 작성하다'를 뜻하는 (D) fill out이 정답이다.

[어휘] paperwork 서류 (작업) security badge 보안 출입증 turn down ~을 거절하다 take over ~을 인계받다 give up ~을 포기하다

21. 비교급: more ~ than 사이에 형용사/부사

Russo Appliances는 경쟁사들보다 더욱 경쟁력을 갖추기 위해 무료 배송 서비스를 제공하고 있다.

[해설] 선택지가 다양한 품사의 단어들로 구성되어 있으므로 문법 문제이다. 빈칸 앞에 위치한 more와 함께 비교급을 나타낼 수 있는 것은 형용사 또는 부사인데, become의 보어 역할을 해야 하므로 형용사 (B) competitive가 정답이다.

[어휘] competitor 경쟁사 compete 경쟁하다 competitive 경쟁력 있는, 경쟁적인 competition 경쟁, 경연 대회 competitively 경쟁적으로

22. 빈출 숙어

Glimmerglass 제조사는 생산 지연을 만회하기 위해 자사의 공장 직원들에게 추가 교대 근무를 신청하도록 요청했다.

[해설] 선택지가 다양한 동사들로 구성되어 있으므로 동사 어휘 문제이다. 빈칸 뒤에 위치한 up for와 결합 가능한 동사로서 '~을 만회하다, 보충하다'라는 의미를 구성할 때 사용하는 (C) make가 정답이다. (A) save는 save up for로 쓰일 수 있지만, '~을 위해 저축하다'라는 의미를 나타내므로 이 문장에 맞지 않는다.

safely가 정답이다.

[어휘] task 업무, 일 site 현장, 부지 carry out ~을 수행하다 injury 부상

02. 비교급: more ~ than 사이에 형용사/부사

Nielsen 식료품점의 어떠한 고객 불만 사항이든지 예전보다 더욱 지체 없이 해결되어야 한다.

[해설] 선택지가 다양한 품사의 단어들로 구성되어 있으므로 문법 문제이다. more와 than 사이에 위치해 비교급을 구성할 형용사 또는 부사가 필요한데, 바로 앞에 위치한 동사 be resolved를 수식해야 하므로 부사인 (B) promptly가 정답이다.

[어휘] resolve ~을 해결하다 prompt 즉각적인; ~ 정각에; ~하도록 촉발하다 promptly 즉시, 지체 없이

03. 비교급 비교의 형태

Collins 씨는 다른 지원자들이 가진 것보다 더 많은 자격증을 지니고 있다.

[해설] 선택지가 접속사와 전치사로 구성되어 있으므로 문법 문제이다. 빈칸 앞에 위치한 more와 짝을 이뤄 비교의 의미를 나타낼 때 사용하는 (A) than이 정답이다.

[어휘] certification 자격증, 증명서 applicant 지원자

04. 빈출 숙어

구입하신 Tony 디지털 오락 시스템을 설치하실 때 제공된 설명을 신중히 따르시기 바랍니다.

[해설] 선택지가 다양한 숙어들로 구성되어 있으므로 어휘 문제이다. 빈칸에 쓰일 숙어는 특정 시스템과 관련해 제공된 설명을 따라야 하는 목적에 해당되는 의미를 나타내야 알맞으므로 '~을 설치하다'라는 뜻으로 쓰이는 (D) set up이 정답이다.

[어휘] directions 설명(서), 지시 make sense 이치에 맞다 cope with ~에 대처하다 name after ~을 따서 이름 짓다

05. 단수 주어+단수 동사 / 복수 주어+복수 동사

Morris 씨와 Kemp 씨는 패션 위크 행사를 취재하기 위해 파리로 출장을 갔다.

[해설] 선택지가 동사 travel의 다양한 형태로 구성되어 있으므로 문법 문제이다. 빈칸 앞뒤로 주어와 전치사구만 있으므로 빈칸이 문장의 동사 자리인데, 주어 Ms. Morris and Mr. Kemp는 복수이므로 수 일치에 상관 없이 사용할 수 있는 과거 시제 동사 (C) traveled가 정답이다.

[어휘] cover ~을 취재하다, (주제 등) ~을 다루다 travel 출장 가다

06. 최상급: the most 뒤에 형용사/부사

평론가들은 그 3부작에서 두 번째 속편이 가장 인상적이었다는 데 동의한다.

[해설] 선택지가 다양한 품사의 단어들로 구성되어 있으므로 문법 문제이다. 빈칸 앞에 위치한 the most와 함께 최상급을 구성할 수 있는 것은 형용사 또는 부사인데, be동사 was 뒤에서 보어 역할을 해야 하므로 형용사 (D) impressive가 정답이다.

[어휘] sequel 속편 trilogy 3부작 impress ~에게 깊은 인상을 남기다 impression 인상, 감명 impressively 인상적으로 impressive 인상적인

07. 비교급 강조 부사

자동화된 장비 덕분에, 조립 라인이 훨씬 더 빨리 상품을 생산할 수 있다.

[해설] 선택지가 다양한 품사의 단어들로 구성되어 있으므로 문법 문제이다. 빈칸 바로 뒤에 위치한 비교급 부사 faster를 수식해 강조하는 역할을 해야 하므로 '훨씬, 상당히'라는 의미로 비교급을 수식할 수 있는 (C) a lot이 정답이다.

[어휘] equipment 장비 assembly 조립 be capable of -ing ~할 수 있다 goods 상품 seldom 거의 ~않는

08. 최상급: the most 뒤에 형용사/부사

Ayden Cooke 씨가 발명한 에너지 발생 송수관 터빈이 지금까지 중에서 그의 가장 혁신적인 아이디어로 여겨진다.

[해설] 선택지가 다양한 품사의 단어들로 구성되어 있으므로 문법 문제이다. 빈칸 앞에 위치한 one's(his) most와 함께 최상급을 구성해 바로 뒤에 위치한 명사 idea를 수식할 수 있는 것은 형용사이므로 (C) innovative가 정답이다.

[어휘] generating 발생시키는, 일으키는 invent ~을 발명하다 innovation 혁신(적인 것) innovate ~을 혁신하다 innovative 혁신적인 innovatively 혁신적으로

09. 최상급 관용 표현

보안 검색대를 거칠 수 있도록 최소한 15분 일찍 도착하셔야 합니다.

[해설] 선택지가 부사구와 상관접속사로 구성되어 있으므로 문법 문제이다. 빈칸 뒤에 수사 표현이 포함된 명사구 15 minutes가 있으므로 수사 표현 앞에 사용하는 (C) at least가 정답이다.

[어휘] go through ~을 거치다, 통과하다 security checkpoint 보안 검색대

10. 원급: as ~ as 사이에 형용사/부사

이리 지역에서 Bird Auto만큼 단골 고객들에게 즉각 대응하는 자동차 수리소는 없다.

[해설] 선택지가 다양한 품사의 단어들로 구성되어 있으므로 문법 문제이다. 'as ~ as'의 구조로 원급 비교를 나타낼 때 두 as 사이에 원급 형용사나 부사가 쓰여야 하는데, be동사 are 뒤에서 보어 역할을 해야 하므로 형용사 (B) responsive가 정답이다.

[어휘] loyal customer 단골 고객 response 대응, 응답 responsive 즉각 대응하는 respond 대응하다, 응답하다 responsively 즉각 대응하여

11. 비교급: more ~ than 사이에 형용사/부사

Saunders 엔지니어링은 시중에 나와 있는 다른 것들보다 더 효율적인 엔진을 만들었다.

[해설] 선택지가 다양한 품사의 단어들로 구성되어 있으므로 문법 문제이다. more와 than 사이에 위치해 비교급을 구성할 형용사 또는 부사가 필요한데, be동사 is 뒤에서 보어 역할을 해야 하므로 형용사 (A) efficient가 정답이다.

[어휘] on the market 시중에 나온 efficient 효율적인 efficiency 효율(성) efficiently 효율적으로

12. 비교급 비교의 형태

Zavala Home Online은 주문받은 상품을 더욱 신속히 찾을 수 있도록 본사 창고를 다시 정리했다.

10. 세부사항 문제

Knutson 씨는 무슨 변화에 찬성할 것 같은가?
(A) 더 조용한 방 이용하기
(B) 더 많은 휴식 시간 추가하기
(C) 건물을 현대화하기
(D) 온라인으로 강의 제공하기

[해설] 두 번째 지문 끝부분에 Knutson 씨는 오전과 오후에 짧은 휴식 시간이 있다면 사람들이 정보를 더 잘 받아들일 것 같다고(~ people would absorb the information better if there were short rest times in mid-morning and mid-afternoon) 알리면서 휴식 시간의 중요성을 강조하고 있다. 따라서 더 많은 휴식 시간을 추가하는 일에 찬성할 것으로 생각할 수 있으므로 (B)가 정답이다.

`paraphrasing` rest times 휴식 시간 → breaks 휴식 시간

[어휘] in favor of ~을 찬성하는   add ~을 추가하다   modernize ~을 현대화하다

`paraphrasing 정답` 1. (a)   2. (d)   3. (e)   4. (b)   5. (c)

DAY 19

PART 5   문법 | 비교 구문

확인 문제 해석
❶ 이 컬러 프린터는 흑백 프린터만큼 빠르게 출력할 수 있다.
❷ 이 아파트는 내 아파트보다 더 넓어 보인다.
❸ 우리의 새 아이스크림 맛은 기존 것들보다 훨씬 더 인기가 있다.
❹ 이 태양광 패널들은 저희 제품 가운데 가장 효율이 뛰어납니다.
❺ 당신은 늦어도 수요일까지 보고서를 제출해야 합니다.

연습 문제
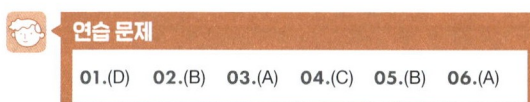
01.(D) 02.(B) 03.(A) 04.(C) 05.(B) 06.(A)

01.
1. 선택지 보고 문법/어휘 문제 파악하기 ☑문법 문제 ☐어휘 문제
2. 빈칸 분석하기 빈칸 앞과 뒤에 as가 있다.
   → ☑원급 구문 ☐최상급 구문
   → 빈칸 앞 as 앞에 ☑완전한 절 ☐불완전한 절이 있다.
   → 빈칸에는 ☐형용사 ☑부사가 들어가야 한다.
3. 정답 선택하기 정답 (D)

그 직책을 위한 추천서를 가능한 한 지체없이 제출해 주세요.

02.
1. 선택지 보고 문법/어휘 문제 파악하기 ☑문법 문제 ☐어휘 문제
2. 빈칸 분석하기 빈칸 앞에 more, 빈칸 뒤에 than이 있다.
   → ☑비교급 구문 ☐최상급 구문
   → 빈칸 앞 more 앞에 ☐완전한 절 ☑불완전한 절이 있다.
   → 빈칸에는 ☑형용사 ☐부사가 들어가야 한다.
3. 정답 선택하기 정답 (B)

Keystone 조리도구의 기구들은 다른 브랜드들의 것보다 더 비싸다.

03.
1. 선택지 보고 문법/어휘 문제 파악하기 ☑문법 문제 ☐어휘 문제
2. 빈칸 분석하기 빈칸 앞에 more, 빈칸 뒤에 ☑전치사 ☐부사가 있다.
   → 빈칸에는 ☑명사 ☐형용사가 들어가야 한다.
3. 정답 선택하기 정답 (A)

대부분의 항공사 승객들은 그들에게 주어지는 것보다 더 많이 가방을 놓을 공간을 원한다.

04.
1. 선택지 보고 문법/어휘 문제 파악하기 ☑문법 문제 ☐어휘 문제
2. 빈칸 분석하기 빈칸 앞에 the most가 있다.
   → ☐비교급 구문 ☑최상급 구문
   → 빈칸 앞 be동사 is의 보어 역할을 하는 것이 들어가야 한다.
   → 빈칸에는 ☑형용사 ☐부사가 들어가야 한다.
3. 정답 선택하기 정답 (C)

Sparkle Spark는 시판되는 가장 효과적인 세정제 중 하나이다.

05.
1. 선택지 보고 문법/어휘 문제 파악하기 ☑문법 문제 ☐어휘 문제
2. 빈칸 분석하기 빈칸 뒤에 있는 것 → ☑비교급 구문 ☐최상급 구문
   → 빈칸 뒤 구문을 강조할 수 있는 부사가 정답이다.
3. 정답 선택하기 정답 (B)

수력 전기 에너지는 기존에 예상했던 것보다 훨씬 더 수익성이 있는 것으로 판명되었다.

06.
1. 선택지 보고 문법/어휘 문제 파악하기 ☐문법 문제 ☑어휘 문제
2. 빈칸 분석하기 빈칸 뒤에 있는 명사구 (your extra work)
   명사구의 의미 (추가 근무)
   → 이것을 '월말 보너스로 ------할 것이다'라는 문맥에 어울리는 동사가 정답이다.
3. 정답 선택하기 정답 (A)

그 레스토랑은 월말 보너스로 추가 근무에 대해 보상할 것이다.

실전 문제

01.(D)	02.(B)	03.(A)	04.(D)	05.(C)	06.(D)
07.(C)	08.(C)	09.(C)	10.(B)	11.(A)	12.(C)
13.(A)	14.(B)	15.(A)	16.(C)	17.(A)	18.(A)
19.(B)	20.(D)	21.(B)	22.(C)	23.(B)	24.(D)

01. 원급: as ~ as 사이에 형용사/부사

작업 현장의 모든 업무는 어떠한 사고나 부상도 피할 수 있도록 가능한 한 안전하게 수행되어야 한다.

[해설] 선택지가 형용사와 부사로 구성되어 있으므로 문법 문제이다. 'as ~ as possible'은 원급 비교를 나타내므로 원급 부사 또는 형용사가 빈칸에 쓰여야 하는데, 동사 be carried out을 수식해야 하므로 원급 부사인 (D)

바랍니다). RBEA 회원들께서는 참가비에 대해 20퍼센트의 회원 전용 할인을 받으실 수 있습니다. www.bertraminst.com에서 온라인으로 등록하시기 바랍니다.

올해의 교육 내용은 다음과 같습니다.
"생산성 이용: 시간을 최대로 활용하는 법" - 발표자: Celina Enriquez
"최신 기술에 능통한 사람들을 위한 회계 연습" - 발표자: Larry Bluhm
[09]"팀 관리에 있어 해야 할 것과 하지 말아야 할 것" - 발표자: Jasmine Mata

[08]외부 지역으로부터 이동해 워크숍에 참석하는 분이실 경우, Carriage 호텔에서 특별 할인을 받으실 수 있도록 조치해 두었습니다. 이 시설과 할인받는 방법에 관해 더 많은 정보를 얻으시려면 555-0978로 Nicole Montford 씨에게 연락하시기 바랍니다.

improve ~을 향상시키다 proceedings 행사 so that (목적) ~할 수 있도록 view ~을 보다 as a way to부정사 ~하는 방법의 하나로 cover (주제 등) ~을 다루다 last 지속되다 sack lunch 도시락 nearby 근처의 exclusive 독점의, 전용의 fee 요금 harness ~을 이용하다 productivity 생산성 make the most of ~을 최대한 활용하다 accounting 회계 tech savvy 최신 기술에 능통한 do's and don'ts 해야 할 것과 하지 말아야 할 것 supervise ~을 관리하다 arrange ~을 조치하다, 마련하다

Bertram 협회의 강의와 워크숍에 관한 의견을 제공해 주셔서 감사 드립니다. 저희는 여러분의 의견을 소중히 여기고 있으며, 향후 활동을 개선하는 데 이를 활용할 것입니다.

성명: Beth Knutson   강의/워크숍: 집중 워크숍

1. Bertram 협회를 친구에게 얼마나 추천하고 싶으신가요?
   아주 많이
2. 전반적인 강의/워크숍에 대해 얼마나 만족스러우셨나요?
   대체로 만족함
3. 건물과 시설에 대해 얼마나 만족스러우셨나요?
   매우 만족함
4. 강의/워크숍에서 가장 마음에 드셨던 부분은 무엇이었나요?
   [09]Mata 씨께서 가르치셨던 시간이 대단히 도움이 되었는데, 제가 현재 맡고 있는 역할에 딱 맞는 것이기 때문입니다. 저는 그분이 제시한 실제 예시들이 정말로 마음에 들었으며, 이것이 내용을 더욱 쉽게 연관 지을 수 있게 만들어 주었습니다.
5. 저희가 다음 번에 이 강의/워크숍을 어떻게 개선할 수 있을까요?
   비록 집중 워크숍이기는 했지만, 점심 시간이 유일하게 교육이 없는 시간이었다는 점이 놀라웠습니다. [10]제 생각엔 오전 중에 그리고 오후 중에 짧은 휴식 시간이 있다면 사람들이 정보를 더 잘 받아들일 것 같습니다.

likely 가능성 있는, ~할 것 같은 extremely 대단히, 매우 fit perfectly with ~에 완벽하게 어울리다 current 현재의 role 역할 content 내용(물) relatable 연관 지을 수 있는 intensive 집중적인 absorb ~을 받아들이다 mid-morning 오전 중반 시간

06. 세부사항 문제

작년과 비교해 볼 때 워크숍과 관련해 무엇이 변경되었는가?
(A) 향후 활용을 위해 녹화될 것이다.
(B) 행사 당일에 더 일찍 시작될 것이다.
(C) 여러 명의 발표자들을 특징으로 할 것이다.
(D) 다른 장소에서 개최될 것이다.

[해설] 첫 지문 첫 단락에 처음으로 행사들을 촬영할 예정이라는(For the first time, we are filming the proceedings ~) 말과 함께 나중에 다시 볼 수 있게 하려 한다고 알리고 있으므로 (A)가 정답이다.

paraphrasing are filming 촬영하다 → be recorded 녹화되다

[어휘] compared to ~와 비교해, ~에 비해 feature ~을 특징으로 하다

07. True 문제

워크숍 참가자들에 관해 언급된 것은 무엇인가?
(A) 반드시 지역 비즈니스 엘리트 협회 회원이어야 한다.
(B) 워크숍이 끝난 후에 수료증을 받을 것이다.
(C) 각자의 식사를 준비해야 한다.
(D) 현장 입구에서 등록비를 지불할 수 있다.

[해설] 첫 지문 첫 단락에 1시간의 점심 식사 시간이 있다는 말과 함께 도시락을 챙겨 오거나 근처의 카페들 중 한 곳을 방문하라고 알리고 있으므로(~ with a one-hour lunch break (please bring a sack lunch or visit one of the nearby cafés)) 각자 식사를 알아서 해결해야 한다는 의미로 쓰인 (C)가 정답이다.

paraphrasing bring a sack lunch or visit one of the nearby cafés 도시락을 챙겨 오거나 근처의 카페를 방문하다 → make their own arrangements for a meal 각자 식사에 대한 준비를 하다

[어휘] certificate of completion 수료증 make one's own arrangements for 각자 ~에 대한 준비를 하다, 조치하다

08. 세부사항 문제

광고에 따르면, 사람들은 왜 Montford 씨에게 연락해야 하는가?
(A) 개인 시간에 대한 일정을 잡기 위해
(B) 워크숍에 등록하기 위해
(C) 웹사이트의 문제점을 알리기 위해
(D) 숙소에 관해 문의하기 위해

[해설] Montford 씨의 이름이 언급된 첫 지문 마지막 단락에, Carriage Hotel의 시설과 그곳에서 할인받는 방법에 관해 Nicole Montford 씨에게 연락하도록(~ we have arranged a special discount at Carriage Hotel. Contact Nicole Montford at 555-0978 for more information about that facility and how to receive the discount) 권하고 있으므로 숙소에 관한 문의를 뜻하는 (D)가 정답이다.

[어휘] inquire about ~에 관해 문의하다 accommodations 숙소, 숙박 시설

09. True 문제 - 연계 문제

Knutson 씨에 관해 암시된 것은 무엇인가?
(A) 기술을 이용해 일하는 것을 즐긴다.
(B) 생산적인 상태를 유지하는 데 문제가 있다.
(C) 외부 지역으로부터 방문한다.
(D) 다른 직원들을 관리한다.

[해설] Knutson 씨가 기입한 설문지 양식인 두 번째 지문 4번 항목에 Mata 씨가 가르쳤던 시간이 자신의 역할과 관련해 대단히 도움이 되었다는(The session taught by Ms. Mata was extremely helpful because it fits perfectly with my current role) 말이 있는데, 첫 지문에서 Mata 씨가 발표하는 시간의 주제가 "팀 관리에 있어 해야 할 것과 하지 말아야 할 것"이라고("The Do's and Don'ts of Supervising Your Team" - Presenter: Jasmine Mata) 쓰여 있다. 따라서 Knutson 씨는 관리자의 역할을 맡고 있음을 알 수 있으므로 (D)가 정답이다.

[어휘] productive 생산적인 oversee ~을 감독하다, 관리하다

01. 추론 문제

Goodwin 대학교에 관해 암시된 것은 무엇인가?
(A) Goodwin 지역 전역에 걸쳐 다수의 캠퍼스가 있다.
(B) 자체 농업 프로그램으로 알려져 있다.
(C) 최근에 일부 부지를 매입했다.
(D) 지역 주민들에게 장학금을 제공한다.

[해설] Goodwin University의 이름이 제시되는 두 번째 항목에, '새로 매입한 서쪽 구획(Newly Acquired Western Plot)'이라는 말이 쓰여 있는데, 이는 부지를 새로 매입한 것을 의미하므로 (C)가 정답이다.

paraphrasing Newly Acquired Western Plot 새로 매입한 서쪽 구획 → recently purchased some land 최근에 일부 부지를 매입했다

[어휘] throughout ~ 전역에 걸쳐 agricultural 농업의 offer ~을 제공하다 scholarship 장학금

02. True 문제

작업 현장에 관해 암시된 것은 무엇인가?
(A) 걸어서 접근해야 한다.
(B) 행사를 주최하기 위해 이용될 것이다.
(C) 기숙사 옆에 위치해 있다.
(D) 아름다운 화단을 특징으로 한다.

[해설] Vehicle Access 항목에 No라고 되어 있으므로 차량이 접근할 수 없음을 알 수 있다. 따라서 (A)가 정답이다.

[어휘] by foot 걸어서 host ~을 주최하다 dormitory 기숙사 feature ~을 특징으로 하다 flower bed 화단

paraphrasing 정답   1. (d)   2. (b)   3. (e)   4. (a)   5. (c)

03-05는 다음 거래 내역서를 참조하시오.

Margot Supplies 고객용 거래 내역서

고객 성명: Justine Goetz   전화번호: 733-555-7901
배송 주소: Stark 가 392번지, 롬바드, 일리노이 주 60148
주소 형태: [X] 상업용 [ ] 주거용
지불 방법: 신용카드 XXXX-XXXX-XXXX-6798 05주문 날짜: 7월 29일

제품 번호	브랜드 / 설명	단가	수량	총액
G0944	Stylz / 03머리에 볼륨을 주는 샴푸	12.99달러	15	194.85달러
04L7406	Fay / 03딥 컨디셔닝 트리트먼트	19.99달러	8	159.92달러
S3185	Dario / 03엑스트라 강력 헤어 젤	5.99달러	20	119.80달러
Z8520	Nolette / 03종일 지속되는 곱슬거림 방지 세럼	24.99달러	12	299.88달러
04쿠폰 적용됨: 할인 코드 FAYSUMMER, 모든 Fay 제품에 대해 15% 할인. 05모든 주문품은 전액 무료로 익일 배송해 드립니다!		소계		774.45달러
		할인		-23.99달러
		세금		46.47달러
저희 Margot Supplies의 고객이 되어 주셔서 감사 드립니다!		총액		796.93달러

invoice 거래 내역서, 송장 commercial 상업의 residential 주거의 anti-frizz 곱슬거림을 방지하는 apply ~을 적용하다 order 주문(품) ship ~을 배송하다, 선적하다 overnight delivery 익일 배송 absolutely free 전액 무료로

03. 직업 문제

Goetz 씨는 어디에서 근무할 것 같은가?
(A) 철물점에서
(B) 미용실에서
(C) 커피숍에서
(D) 배송회사에서

[해설] 도표 중간 부분에 제시된 구매 제품 설명 항목을 보면, 샴푸와 컨디셔닝 트리트먼트, 헤어 젤, 곱슬거림 방지 세럼이 쓰여 있다. 이 제품들은 모두 머리에 사용하는 것들이므로 (B)가 정답이다.

[어휘] hardware store 철물점

04. 세부사항 문제

Goetz 씨는 어느 제품에 대해 할인을 받았는가?
(A) G0944
(B) L7406
(C) S3185
(D) Z8520

[해설] 도표 왼쪽 하단에 할인 관련 정보가 제시되어 있는데, 할인 코드 FAYSUMMER와 함께 모든 Fay 제품에 대해 15퍼센트가 할인된다고 (Coupon Applied: Discount code FAYSUMMER, 15% off all Fay products) 쓰여 있다. 표의 제품 브랜드 항목에서 Fay 제품에 해당되는 품목 번호를 확인하면 L7406이므로 (B)가 정답이다.

05. 추론 문제

거래 내역서에 의해 암시된 것은 무엇인가?
(A) 상품이 7월 30일에 도착할 것으로 예상된다.
(B) Goetz 씨는 Margot Supplies의 단골 고객이다.
(C) 주문 사항에 대해 배송비가 청구될 것이다.
(D) Goetz 씨가 구매를 위해 매장 포인트를 일부 사용했다.

[해설] 왼쪽 하단에 모든 주문품은 익일 배송된다고(All orders are shipped by overnight delivery absolutely free) 쓰여 있고, 오른쪽 상단에 주문 날짜가 7월 29일로(Order Date: July 29) 표기되어 있으므로 다음 날인 7월 30일에 배송된다는 것을 알 수 있다. 따라서 (A)가 정답이다.

[어휘] regular customer 단골 고객 be charged for ~에 대해 청구되다, 부과되다 store credit 매장 포인트 purchase 구매(품)

paraphrasing 정답   1. (d)   2. (c)   3. (b)   4. (e)   5. (a)

06-10은 다음 광고와 양식을 참조하시오.

Bertram 협회의 도움으로 여러분의 경력을 한 단계 끌어올려 보십시오! 저희 Bertram 협회는 지역 비즈니스 엘리트 협회(RBEA)와의 제휴를 통해 비즈니스 전문가들께서 능력을 향상시키는 데 도움을 드리기 위해 제3회 연례 집중 워크숍을 제공합니다. 06처음으로, 행사들을 촬영할 예정이므로 참가자들께서는 행사 중에 다뤄진 주제들을 되새겨 보는 방법의 하나로 나중에 이 동영상을 시청하실 수 있습니다. 교육 시간은 오전 9시부터 오후 5시까지 진행되며, 071시간의 점심 식사 시간이 있습니다(도시락을 챙겨 오시거나 근처의 카페들 중 한 곳을 방문하시기

DAY 18 157

voucher 쿠폰, 상품권   issue ~을 발급하다; 발급   A entitle B to C A로 인해 B가 C할 수 있다, A가 B에게 C에 대한 자격을 주다   holder 소지자, 보유자   complimentary 무료의   on-site 구내의, 건물 내의   be combined with ~과 결합되다   value 가치   at the time of ~할 시에   booking 예약   present ~을 제시하다   authorize ~을 승인하다

Q. 쿠폰에 언급되지 않은 것은 무엇인가?
(A) 언제 만료되는지
(B) 어느 곳에서 유효한지

[문제 키워드] What / NOT indicated / voucher

[해설] 키워드 voucher가 지문의 전체적인 소재이므로 지문 전반에서 단서를 파악해 각 선택지와 비교해야 한다. 지문 전체적으로 만기일과 관련된 정보는 제시되어 있지 않으므로 (A)가 정답이다. 중반부에 사용 가능한 장소들이(It can be used ~ Castillo Hotel Seattle, Castillo Hotel Portland, or Castillo Hotel Sacramento) 제시되어 있으므로 (B)는 맞는 내용이다.

[어휘] expire 만료되다   valid 유효한

03.

Lander 댄스 스튜디오가
정성을 다해 여러분을 초대합니다.

Garden of Wonders
7월 12일 토요일 오후 7시

Nova Plaza에서 전문 댄서들과 아마추어 댄서들의 춤 공연을 관람하시면서 5가지 코스로 된 연회를 즐기시기 바랍니다. 행사 입장권 판매에서 오는 모든 수익금은 춤 수업 수강생들을 위한 시의 유일한 비영리 스튜디오인 Lander 댄스 스튜디오로 직접 전달됩니다.

현장에서 대리 주차 서비스를 이용하실 수 있으며, 이번 행사의 복장 규정은 정장입니다. 여러분을 뵐 수 있기를 고대합니다!

amateur 아마추어의   proceeds 수익금   non-profit 비영리의   formal 정식의, 격식을 갖춘

Q. Garden of Wonders는 무슨 종류의 행사인가?
(A) 댄스 경연 대회
(B) 기금 마련 만찬

[문제 키워드] What / event / Garden of Wonders

[해설] 키워드 Garden of Wonders가 지문의 전체적인 소재이므로 지문 전반에서 단서를 파악해 각 선택지와 비교해야 한다. 초반부에 '연회(banquet)'라는 말이 있고, 그 수익금이 한 댄스 스튜디오에 전달된다는 말이 뒤이어 제시되어 있으므로(All proceeds ~ go directly to Lander Dance Studio ~) 기금 마련을 위한 행사임을 알 수 있다. 따라서 (B)가 정답이다.

04.

지역 사진촬영술 컨퍼런스
10월 8일-**10일** · Finnegan 컨벤션 센터
10월 10일 금요일 일정

판매 업체 부스   오전 9:00-정오
중앙 홀에서 카메라 부대용품과 장비가 판매됩니다.

인맥을 쌓기 위한 점심 식사   정오-오후 1:30
출장 요리로 제공되는 점심 식사를 즐기시면서 분야의 다른 전문가들과 교류해 보십시오.

"자연과 함께 하는 삶"   오후 1:30-오후 3:00
자연 사진 작가 Craig Mahmood 씨께서 사진 촬영 중에 자연의 아름다움을 담는 것에 관해 강연을 하실 예정입니다.

"디자인의 7대 요소"   오후 3:30-오후 5:00
〈Images Magazine〉의 Vera Bradley 편집자께서 뛰어난 구도의 핵심 요소들에 관해 이번 강연을 진행하실 예정입니다.

accessories 부대용품   equipment 장비   on sale 판매 중인   luncheon 점심 식사, 오찬   catered 출장 요리로 제공되는   professional 전문가   field 분야   capture (사진 등에) ~을 담아 내다, 포착하다   element 요소   present ~을 제공하다, 제시하다   composition 구도, 구성

Q. 지역 사진촬영술 컨퍼런스의 마지막 날에 관해 암시된 것은 무엇인가?
(A) 폐회식이 포함될 것이다.
(B) 오전에 아무런 강연도 없다.

[문제 키워드] What / suggested / final day

[해설] 키워드 final day가 지문의 전체적인 소재이므로 지문 전반에서 단서를 파악해 각 선택지와 비교해야 한다. 오전 일정이 제시된 첫 번째 칸에 제품 판매와 관련된 행사만(Camera accessories and equipment will be on sale in the main hall) 제시되어 있으므로 강연이 없다는 사실을 언급한 (B)가 정답이다.

실전 문제

| 01.(C) | 02.(A) | 03.(B) | 04.(B) | 05.(A) | 06.(A) |
| 07.(C) | 08.(D) | 09.(D) | 10.(B) | | |

01-02는 다음 양식을 참조하시오.

Jocelyn's 정원 관리 & 조경 서비스
서비스 주문 양식

서비스 요청 날짜: 8월 25일
장소: Goodwin 대학교 (⁰¹새로 매입한 서쪽 구획)
고객 성함: Brenna Cruz
휴대전화 번호: 555-4323
계약 번호: GH32354354
작업 예상 시간: 6시간
업무: 무성하게 풀이 자란 구역에 대한 정리 작업, 잡초 제거, 구역 가장자리 주변에 나무 심기
요청 식물: 소나무 38그루(중간 크기)
⁰²차량 접근: 불가능
수도 공급원: 있음
기타 세부 사항 / 특정 요청 사항: 8월 10일에 학생들이 입주하기 시작합니다. 모든 작업이 이 날짜 전에 완료되어야 합니다.

order form 주문 양식, 주문서   acquire 획득하다, 취득하다   plot 작은 구획의 땅   estimated 예상되는   task 일, 업무   overgrown (풀 등이) 무성하게 자란, 제멋대로 자란   remove ~을 제거하다   weeds 잡초   edge 가장자리   pine tree 소나무   access 접근, 이용; ~에 접근하다, ~을 이용하다   source 공급원

05. 알맞은 문장 고르기

(A) 설명 책자의 도표에 쓰여 있는 기호들을 참고하시기 바랍니다.
(B) 예를 들자면, 유류 물질이나 액체 화학 물질이 바닥에 쏟아지는 일 같은 것입니다.
(C) 우리에게는 외부 업체와 맺은 계약이 있습니다.
(D) 모든 생산직 직원들은 현장 교육에 참석해야 합니다.

[해설] 앞 문장에서 일을 하는 동안 위험한 상황에 접할 수 있다는 말이 쓰여 있으므로 예시를 나타낼 때 사용하는 접속부사 For example과 함께 위험한 상황에 해당되는 일을 언급한 (B)가 정답이다.

[어휘] refer to ~을 참고하다   symbol 기호, 부호   liquid 액체   spill ~을 쏟다, 흘리다(spilt는 과거분사)   contract 계약(서)   outside 외부의   on-the-job training 현장 교육

06. 명사 어휘

[해설] 동사 take와 함께 사용되는 명사로서 위험 상황에 대해 안전 장치를 하고 표지판을 세우는 일을 하나로 아우를 수 있는 것이 필요하므로 '조치'를 의미하는 (A) measures가 정답이다.

[어휘] account 계정, 계좌   opportunity 기회

07. 명사 자리

[해설] 동명사 ignoring과 명사 regulations 사이에 위치한 빈칸은 명사를 수식하는 형용사 또는 복합 명사를 구성하는 또 다른 명사가 쓰일 수 있는 자리이다. 이 문장에서는 regulations와 함께 '안전 규정'이라는 뜻이 되어야 자연스러우므로 이 의미에 해당되는 복합 명사를 구성하는 (A) safety가 정답이다. 형용사 (C) safe가 쓰이면 '안전한 규정'이라는 어색한 의미가 된다.

08. 동사의 형태

[해설] be동사(have been)와 결합할 수 없는 부사 (A) clearly, 주어와 동격이 되지 않는 명사 (C) clearance를 제외하면 과거분사 (B)와 현재분사 (D)만 남는다. 동사 clear는 목적어가 필요한 타동사인데 빈칸 뒤에 목적어가 없으므로 수동태로 쓰여야 하므로 과거분사 (B) cleared가 정답이다.

[어휘] clearly 분명히, 명확히   clearance 정리 (세일)

PART 7 양식-일정표/초대장/영수증 등

풀이 방법 해석

Riverside 사 송장
수신: Golden Horizon 여행사
운영팀장 Cecil Fulton 귀하
배송지: Celtic 로 419번지, 글렌빌

품목/서비스	단가	수량	총액
A4 용지	15.00달러	4	60.00달러
A3 용지	20.00달러	2	80.00달러
토너 (X모델 시리즈)	17.00달러	2	34.00달러
토너 (AZ 모델 시리즈)	35.00달러	1	35.00달러
*USB 스틱	40.00달러	1	40.00달러
합계			249.00달러

*모든 컴퓨터 모델에 연결할 수 있음

Riverside 사를 선택해 주셔서 감사합니다! 어떠한 문제, 질문이 있으시거나 저희에게 피드백을 제공하고 싶으시면 Alissa Gill에게 a.gill@riverside.com으로 연락하세요.

 연습 문제

01.(A)   02.(A)   03.(B)   04.(B)

01.

현금 지급액 수령증
날짜: 11월 2일
직원 성명: Isabelle Dunbar
부서: 영업부

지급 비용 내역	금액
공항을 오가는 택시 요금과 영업부장들을 위해 마련된 워크숍에 참가하기 위한 몬트리올 출장 중의 모든 식사에 대해 사용할 현금을 수령함. 11월 5일에 토론토에서 몬트리올로 출발하며, 11월 8일 복귀 예정임.	300.00달러

비용 지급인: Nicholas Mitchell
비용 수령인: Isabelle Dunbar
서명: Isabelle Dunbar

receipt 수령, 받음, 영수증   payment 지급(액)   sales 영업, 판매(량)   fare (교통편) 요금   take part in ~에 참가하다   designed for ~을 위해 마련된, 고안된   issue ~을 지급하다, 발급하다

Q. Dunbar 씨는 몬트리올에서 무엇을 할 계획인가?
(A) 교육 시간에 참석하기
(B) 사업 계약서에 서명하기

[문제 키워드] What / Ms. Dunbar / do / Montreal

[해설] 키워드 Montreal이 제시되는 부분에서 단서를 찾아야 한다. 지문 중반부에 몬트리올은 Dunbar 씨가 워크숍 참가를 위해 가는 곳으로(~ a business trip to Montreal, where I will take part in a workshop ~) 제시되어 있으므로 교육 시간 참석을 의미하는 (A)가 정답이다.

02.

Castillo 호텔: 고객용 쿠폰
발급 대상자: Bethany Namara

이 쿠폰 소지자는 직접 선택한 1시간의 무료 마사지 한 가지를 받으실 자격이 있습니다. 이 쿠폰은 구내에서 스파 서비스를 제공하는 어느 Castillo 호텔 지점에서든지 사용하실 수 있습니다(Castillo 호텔 시애틀 지점, Castillo 호텔 포틀랜드 지점 또는 Castillo 호텔 새크라멘토 지점).

이 쿠폰은 다른 제공 서비스와 결합되어 쓰일 수 없으며, 현금 가치를 지니지 않습니다. 예약 시에 안내 담당 직원에게 쿠폰을 제시할 것임을 알리시기 바랍니다.

발급일: 1월 10일   승인 책임자: Carl Turner

04.

여러분 모두 요즘 정부 연구 보조금에 대한 경쟁이 매우 치열하다는 사실을 알고 계실 것입니다. 그 중 하나를 받기 위해, 모든 필수 서류들이 때에 맞춰 잘 준비되어야 합니다. -------. 작업 진행표에 따라 여러분의 부서가 무엇을 준비해야 하는지를 보실 수 있으실 것입니다.

competition 경쟁   grant 보조금   intense 치열한   win (상 등) ~을 받다, 타다   required 필수의   well prepared 잘 준비된   in a timely manner 때에 맞춰   department 부서   according to ~에 따라   timeline (시간 순서로 된) 진행표

(A) 5만 달러의 보조금이 작년에 Camden 조사 단체에 주어졌습니다.
(B) 그러므로, 제가 여러분께 준비 사항 점검표를 나눠 드리겠습니다.

[단서] should be well prepared, what ~ needs to prepare

[해설] 빈칸 앞에는 필수 서류를 잘 준비해야 한다는 말이 있으므로 결과를 나타내는 접속부사 Therefore와 함께 그와 같은 주의 사항에 따른 결과로서 준비 과정에 필요한 사항을 담은 점검표를 나눠 주겠다고 하는 (B)가 정답이다.

[어휘] award A to B A를 B에게 주다, 수여하다   therefore 그러므로, 따라서   distribute ~을 나눠 주다, 배부하다

실전 문제

01.(A)   02.(D)   03.(D)   04.(A)   05.(B)   06.(A)
07.(A)   08.(B)

01-04는 다음 설명을 참조하시오.

반품 및 교환 절차

⁰¹이 파트에서는, 고객 서비스 문제에 대한 간단한 해결책을 찾아보실 수 있습니다. 우리는 모든 반품 및 교환 요청을 처리하는 것이 쉽지 않다는 것을 알고 있습니다. 일부 고객들은 단순히 마음을 바꿀 수도 있고, 다른 이들은 우리 제품에 매우 화를 내기도 합니다. 우리 Fashion de Florence에서는, 고객들을 가장 소중하게 여깁니다. ⁰²따라서, 우리에게는 고객이 항상 옳다는 모토가 있습니다. 고객들이 제품을 반품하거나 교환하기 위해 가져올 때, 질문을 하지 마십시오. ⁰³그저 금전 등록기를 사용해 해당 거래를 처리하십시오. ⁰⁴이 정책 덕분에, 우리 매장은 지역에서 가장 고객 친화적인 소매점이라는 명성을 유지할 수 있습니다.

procedure 절차   handle ~을 처리하다   be upset with ~에 화를 내다   bring in ~을 가져오다   register 금전 등록기   transaction 거래   thanks to ~로 인해, ~ 덕분에   reputation 명성, 평판   customer-friendly 고객 친화적인   retail store 소매점   region 지역

01. 명사 어휘

[해설] 빈칸 앞에 간단한 해결책(simple solution)이라는 말이 있으므로 이 표현과 문맥상 어울려 쓰일 수 있는 어휘가 들어가야 한다. 따라서 '문제, 사안'이라는 의미로 쓰이는 (A) issues가 정답이다.

02. 알맞은 문장 고르기

(A) 근처에 책임자가 없을 경우, 금전 등록기 옆에 있는 전화기를 이용하십시오.
(B) 터치 스크린을 이용해 가격표에 적혀 있는 숫자를 입력하십시오.
(C) 할인된 가격이 특정 상품에는 적용되지 않을 수 있습니다.
(D) 따라서, 우리에게는 고객이 항상 옳다는 모토가 있습니다.

[해설] 앞 문장에 고객을 가장 소중하게 여긴다는 말이 있으므로 결과를 나타내는 접속부사 Hence와 함께 그에 따라 발생된 결과로서 생겨난 모토가 언급된 (D)가 정답이다.

[어휘] supervisor 책임자, 상사   nearby 근처에   price tag 가격표   apply A to B A를 B에 적용하다   certain 특정한, 일정한   merchandise 상품   hence 따라서, 이러한 이유로   motto 모토, 좌우명

03. 동사 어휘

[해설] 빈칸 앞에 금전 등록기를 사용하라는 말이 있는데, 거래(transaction)와 관련해 금전 등록기를 사용하는 목적에 해당되는 동사가 빈칸에 쓰여야 알맞으므로 '~을 처리하다'를 뜻하는 (D) process가 정답이다.

[어휘] replace ~을 교체하다, 대체하다

04. 동사의 형태

[해설] 앞 문장을 보면, 명령문 구조로 하지 말아야 하는 일(~ do not question them)과 해야 하는 일(Simply use ~)이 제시되어 있는데, 이는 현재 또는 앞으로 직원들에게 항상 요청하는 일에 해당된다. 따라서 그에 따른 결과로서 현재 또는 앞으로 뛰어난 명성을 유지하는 일이 가능하다는 의미가 되어야 하므로 가능성을 나타내는 조동사 can이 포함된 (A) can maintain이 정답이다.

[어휘] should have p.p. (과거의 일에 대한 후회) ~했어야 했다

05-08은 다음 회람을 참조하시오.

발신: 공장 관리 책임자
수신: 생산직 직원들
날짜: 3월 19일
제목: 안전

동료 직원 여러분께

근무 현장에 있는 동안에는 항상 안전에 유념하시기 바랍니다. 우리는 다양한 유독성 화학 물질을 원료로 사용하고 있기 때문에, 일일 업무를 하는 동안 위험한 상황을 접할 수도 있습니다. ⁰⁵예를 들자면, 유류 물질이나 액체 화학 물질이 바닥에 쏟아지는 일 같은 것입니다. 이와 같은 어떠한 잠재적 위험 상황이 발생될 경우, 즉시 상사에게 알리시기 바랍니다. ⁰⁶그들이 해당 위험 상황에 대해 안전 장치를 하고 적절한 표지판을 세우는 조치를 취할 것입니다. ⁰⁷안전 규정 무시를 의미하는 경우라면 절대로 편법을 사용하지 마시기 바랍니다. 해당 특정 상황이 발생되면 무엇을 따라야 하는지가 나와 있는 점검표를 참고하시기 바랍니다. ⁰⁸어떠한 위험 상황이든 처리되지 않았을 경우에 직원들은 절대로 업무를 재개하지 말아야 합니다. 감사합니다.

colleague 동료 직원   while ~하는 동안   job site 근무 현장   toxic 유독성의   chemical 화학 물질   raw material 원료, 원자재   face ~을 접하다, 마주하다   hazardous 위험한   task 업무, 일   potential 잠재적인   hazard 위험 (요소)   immediately 즉시   secure ~에 안전 장치를 하다   put up ~을 세우다, 내걸다   appropriate 적절한   take shortcuts 편법을 쓰다, 요령을 피우다   ignore ~을 무시하다   regulation 규정, 규제   consult ~을 참고하다   particular 특정한   resume ~을 재개하다

exceptionally 예외적으로 relatively 상대적으로, 비교적

22. 부사 어휘

모든 제품은 일과를 마감하는 시점에 창고에서 배송되기 전에 철저히 테스트되고 있다.

[해설] 선택지가 다양한 부사들로 구성되어 있으므로 부사 어휘 문제이다. 빈칸에 쓰일 부사는 동사 are tested를 뒤에서 수식해 제품이 배송되기 전에 테스트되는 방식을 나타내야 하므로 '철저히'라는 의미로 쓰이는 (B) thoroughly가 정답이다.

[어휘] ship out ~을 배송하다, 발송하다 warehouse 창고 casually 간편하게, 격식 없이 impartially 편견 없이, 차별 없이 approximately 약, 대략

23. 시간 부사절 접속사

교육 시간은 모든 직원들이 휴가에서 복귀할 때까지 연기되었다.

[해설] 선택지가 접속사와 전치사로 구성되어 있으므로 문법 문제이다. 빈칸 앞뒤로 위치한 두 절을 연결할 접속사가 필요하므로 유일한 접속사인 (C) until이 정답이다.

[어휘] postpone ~을 연기하다 upon ~하자마자

24. 부사 어휘

아이들은 박물관 투어 가이드가 전달하는 발표 내용을 유심히 들었다.

[해설] 선택지가 다양한 부사들로 구성되어 있으므로 부사 어휘 문제이다. 빈칸에 쓰일 부사는 동사 listened를 뒤에서 수식해 아이들이 가이드의 발표 내용을 듣는 방식을 나타내야 하므로 '유심히'를 뜻하는 (A) attentively가 정답이다.

[어휘] enormously 엄청나게, 대단히 individually 개별적으로 definitely 분명히

PART 6 알맞은 문장 고르기 - 선택지에 접속부사

풀이 방법 해석

여기 Bryant 회계에서 당신이 일하는 동안 절차상의 또는 정책상의 규정을 검토하기 위해서는 이 안내서를 참고하세요. 우리 사업체는 수천 명의 고객들이 있고, 우리가 모든 거래의 정확한 기록을 보유하는 것은 중요합니다. 우리의 사이버 보안 팀 덕분에 우리는 우리 고객들의 계정의 안전함과 프라이버시를 보장할 수 있습니다. 그들은 우리의 네트워크가 해킹당하지 않도록 막는 일을 아주 잘해주고 있습니다. 그럼에도 불구하고, 몇몇 보안 절차는 모든 직원들이 지켜주셔야 합니다. 예를 들어, 여러분은 매달 변경되어야 하는 안전한 비밀번호를 사용해야 합니다.

 연습 문제

01.(B) 02.(A) 03.(B) 04.(B)

01.

귀사의 매장 정책에는 전액 환불을 받기 위해서는 제품이 일주일 내로 반품되어야 한다고 명확히 명시되어 있습니다. -------. 주문한 제품이 도착했을 때 저는 출장 때문에 외부 지역에 가 있었습니다. 제가 이 제품에 결함이 있었다는 것을 알게 되었을 즈음에, 저는 이미 그 시기를 놓쳤습니다. 저는 귀사에서 저를 도와 주실 수 있으신지 알고 싶습니다.

policy 정책, 방침 state that (문서 등에) ~라고 명시되어 있다 within ~ 이내에 full refund 전액 환불 out of town 다른 지역에 가 있는 on business 출장으로 defective 결함이 있는 window 시기, 시간대 find out ~을 확인하다, 알아내다 whether A or not A인지 아닌지

(A) 또한, 웹사이트에 귀사의 정책이 변경되었다고 언급되어 있습니다.
(B) 하지만 저는 이번 경우에 대해 예외를 적용해 주실 수 있기를 바랍니다.

[단서] policy clearly states, I was out of town

[해설] 빈칸 앞에는 반품과 관련해 꼭 지켜야 하는 기간이, 빈칸 이후로는 환불 조건을 지킬 수 없었던 상황에 대한 설명이 쓰여 있어 대조적인 흐름이 되어야 한다. 따라서 대조를 나타내는 접속부사 However와 함께 정책 사항에 반하는 일로서 자신의 경우를 예외로 해달라고 부탁하는 (B)가 정답이다.

[어휘] make an exception 예외로 하다 case 경우, 사례

02.

공사팀이 다음 달에 저희 식료품 매장의 여러 구역을 개조할 것입니다. 이들은 대부분의 작업이 저희 정규 영업 시간을 피해 실시될 것이라고 말해 주었습니다. -------. 저희는 미리 불편함과 발생 가능성 있는 소음에 대해 사과 드립니다.

crew (함께 작업하는) 팀, 조 grocery store 식료품 매장 perform ~을 실시하다, 수행하다 inconvenience 불편함

(A) 그럼에도 불구하고, 일부 작업은 저희 매장이 영업하는 동안 완료되어야 합니다.
(B) 그곳은 지역 내에서 가장 높은 평가를 받는 공사 업체입니다.

[단서] performed outside of ~ business hours, inconvenience

[해설] 빈칸 앞에 영업 시간이 아닐 때 공사가 진행된다는 말이 있으므로 '그럼에도 불구하고'라는 의미를 지니는 접속부사 Nevertheless와 함께 그 공사와 관련해 영업 시간 중에 진행해야 하는 일부 작업이 있음을 언급하는 (A)가 정답이다.

[어휘] nevertheless 그럼에도 불구하고 while ~하는 동안 highly rated 높은 평가를 받는, 높은 등급을 받은 region 지역

03.

이번 프로모션 기간 동안 상용 고객 클럽 회원들은 포인트를 두 배로 받게 됩니다. -------. 그러니 이번 여름 휴가를 위해 저희 웹사이트를 서둘러 로그인하셔서 귀하의 항공편을 예약하세요.

promotion 판촉, 홍보 hurry 서두르다 book 예약하다 flight 항공편

(A) 따라서, 이것은 오늘부터 2주 동안 지속될 것입니다.
(B) 게다가, 귀하는 무료 좌석 업그레이드 추첨에 자동으로 응모됩니다.

[단서] receive double points , book your flight

[해설] 빈칸 앞에서 클럽 회원의 이점을 말하고 있으므로 추가 정보를 나타내는 in addition과 함께 또 다른 좋은 점을 알리는 내용을 담은 (B)가 정답이다.

[어휘] last 지속되다 in addition 추가로, 게다가 automatically 자동으로

라서 '~하지 않는다면'이라는 뜻으로 부정 조건을 나타내는 부사절 접속사 (C) Unless가 정답이다.

[어휘] unexpected 예기치 못한

11. 주격 관계대명사

Lainey 사는 고객 서비스 분야에서 경력이 있는 사람들을 모집하고 있다.

[해설] 선택지가 다양한 의문사로 구성되어 있으므로 문법 문제이다. 빈칸 뒤에 주어 없이 동사 have로 시작되는 불완전한 절이 있으므로 동사 have의 주어 역할을 함과 동시에 앞에 위치한 사람 선행사 people을 수식할 때 사용하는 주격 관계대명사 (A) who가 정답이다.

12. 이유 부사절 접속사

Cummings 보험사는 여러 추가 직원들을 고용할 계획이기 때문에 더 큰 사무실로 이전할 예정이다.

[해설] 선택지가 접속사와 전치사로 구성되어 있으므로 문법 문제이다. 빈칸 앞뒤로 위치한 두 절을 연결할 접속사가 필요한데, '추가 직원들을 고용할 계획이기 때문에 더 큰 사무실로 이전한다'와 같이 이유를 나타내야 적절하다. 따라서 '~이기 때문에'라는 뜻으로 이유를 나타내는 부사절 접속사 (D) since가 정답이다.

[어휘] additional 추가의   while ~인 반면, ~하는 동안

13. 부사 어휘

주민들은 세인트루이스 지역에서 또 다른 폭풍우로 인해 발생 가능한 홍수에 대해 크게 우려하고 있다.

[해설] 선택지가 다양한 부사들로 구성되어 있으므로 부사 어휘 문제이다. 빈칸에 쓰일 부사는 형용사 concerned를 앞에서 수식해 우려하는 정도를 나타내야 하므로 '크게, 깊이'를 의미하는 (C) deeply가 정답이다.

[어휘] be concerned about ~에 대해 우려하다   flooding 홍수   rigidly 엄격히, 완고하게   firmly 확고히, 굳게

14. 주격 관계대명사

Pottsdale 주민 센터는 자원 봉사 활동에 대해 지역 주민을 표창하는 시상식 행사를 조직한다.

[해설] 선택지가 다양한 품사의 단어로 구성되어 있으므로 문법 문제이다. 빈칸 뒤에 주어 없이 동사 recognizes로 시작되는 불완전한 절이 있으므로 불완전한 절을 이끌며 앞에 위치한 선행사 awards ceremony를 수식할 수 있는 관계대명사 (B) which가 정답이다.

[어휘] organize ~을 조직하다   recognize ~을 표창하다, 인정하다   local 지역 주민   volunteering work 자원 봉사 활동

15. 양보 부사절 접속사

골드 회원들에게는 무료 투자 관련 조언과 상담 서비스가 제공되지만, 다른 은행 고객들은 그와 같은 서비스에 대해 비용을 지불해야 합니다.

[해설] 선택지가 다양한 품사의 단어로 구성되어 있으므로 문법 문제이다. 콤마 앞뒤로 위치한 두 절을 연결할 접속사가 필요한데, '골드 회원들에게는 무료 서비스가 제공되지만, 다른 은행의 고객들은 돈을 내야 한다'와 같은 양보의 의미가 되어야 적절하다. 따라서 '~이지만, ~인 반면'이라는 뜻으로 양보를 나타내는 부사절 접속사 (D) whereas가 정답이다.

[어휘] investment 투자(액)   counseling 상담

16. 시간 부사절과 주절의 시제 관계

Serrano 씨는 연구실에서 퇴근하기 전에 반드시 일일 업무 보고서를 제출해야 한다.

[해설] 선택지가 동사 leave의 다양한 형태로 구성되어 있으므로 문법 문제이다. 주절에 일반적으로 해야 하는 일을 나타내는 동사 must submit가 쓰여 있으므로 before절에도 일반적인 일을 나타내는 현재 시제가 필요하므로 (B) leaves가 정답이다.

[어휘] submit ~을 제출하다   laboratory 연구실, 실험실   leave ~에서 퇴근하다, 나가다

17. 조동사 + 동사원형

Pierson 전자의 주가 폭등은 그들의 모바일 기기의 성공에 기인하는 것으로 볼 수 있다.

[해설] 선택지가 동사 atribute(~에 기인하다)의 다양한 형태로 구성되어 있으므로 문법 문제이다. 빈칸 앞에 조동사(can)가 있으므로 동사원형이 와야 한다. 따라서 (A) be attributed가 정답이다.

[어휘] spike in ~의 폭등, 급등   stock value 주가

18. 이유/양보 전치사

지역 주민들이 제기하는 불만에도 불구하고, Stark 건설사는 일정대로 유지하기 위해 계속 야간에 작업했다.

[해설] 선택지가 다양한 전치사들로 구성되어 있으므로 전치사 어휘 문제이다. '주민들의 불만에도 불구하고, 계속 야간에 작업한다'와 같은 의미가 되어야 알맞으므로 '~에도 불구하고'를 뜻하는 전치사 (A) In spite of가 정답이다.

[어휘] resident 주민   thanks to ~ 때문에, ~ 덕분에   apart from ~ 외에는

19. 부사 어휘

이륙에 앞서 반드시 안전 벨트가 단단히 착용되도록 하시기 바랍니다.

[해설] 선택지가 다양한 부사들로 구성되어 있으므로 부사 어휘 문제이다. 빈칸에 쓰일 부사는 동사 is와 fastened 사이에서 이들을 수식해 안전 벨트를 착용하는 방식을 나타내야 하므로 '단단히, 튼튼하게'라는 뜻으로 쓰이는 (D) securely가 정답이다.

[어휘] fasten ~을 고정시키다, 매다   takeoff 이륙   broadly 폭넓게, 대체로   exactly 정확하게   merely 그저, 단지

20. 접속사 vs. 전치사 vs. 부사 구분

심사위원단이 최종 결정에 이르자마자 수상자들이 발표될 것이다.

[해설] 선택지가 다양한 품사의 단어들로 구성되어 있으므로 문법 문제이다. 빈칸 앞뒤에 각각 완전한 절이 위치해 있으므로 빈칸은 이 절들을 연결할 접속사 자리이다. 따라서 유일한 접속사인 (C) as soon as가 정답이다. (A) upon은 전치사, (B) nearly와 (D) moreover는 부사이다.

[어휘] winner 수상자   panel judge 심사위원단   reach ~에 도달하다, 이르다   nearly 거의   moreover 더욱이

21. 부사 어휘

Rossville 중고차 사의 소유주는 고객들이 돈으로 바꾸기를 원하는 모든 차량들을 직접 점검한다.

[해설] 선택지가 다양한 부사들로 구성되어 있으므로 부사 어휘 문제이다. 빈칸에 쓰일 부사는 동사 inspects를 앞에서 수식해 모든 차량을 점검하는 방식을 나타내야 하므로 '직접'을 의미하는 (C) personally가 정답이다.

[어휘] inspect ~을 점검하다   vehicle 차량   trade in A for B A를 B로 바꾸다, 교환하다   credit 입금(액)   aggressively 공격적으로

실전 문제

01.(A)	02.(A)	03.(B)	04.(A)	05.(B)	06.(B)
07.(C)	08.(D)	09.(B)	10.(C)	11.(A)	12.(D)
13.(C)	14.(B)	15.(D)	16.(B)	17.(A)	18.(A)
19.(D)	20.(A)	21.(C)	22.(B)	23.(C)	24.(A)

01. 접속사 vs. 전치사 vs. 부사 구분

명단에 포함된 모든 사람이 도착한 후에, Glover 씨는 환영 연설을 하기 위해 무대 뒤편에서 나왔다.

[해설] 선택지가 다양한 품사의 단어들로 구성되어 있으므로 문법 문제이다. 빈칸 뒤에 콤마 앞과 뒤에 모두 완전한 절이 위치해 있으므로 빈칸은 이 절들을 연결할 접속사 자리이다. 따라서 유일한 접속사인 (A) After가 정답이다. (B) about은 전치사, (C) Last와 (D) Only는 부사이다.

[어휘] come out from ~에서 밖으로 나오다

02. 부사 어휘

함께 프로젝트를 작업했기 때문에, 두 팀의 구성원들의 보너스가 균등하게 지급되었다.

[해설] 선택지가 다양한 부사들로 구성되어 있으므로 부사 어휘 문제이다. 빈칸에 쓰일 부사는 동사 were distributed를 뒤에서 수식해 보너스를 지급하는 방식을 나타내야 하는데, 함께 작업한 사람들에게 배분되는 방식과 관련되어야 하므로 '균등하게'를 뜻하는 (A) equally가 정답이다.

[어휘] distribute ~을 나눠 주다, 배부하다   commonly 흔히   eagerly 열망하여, 간절히   particularly 특히, 특별히

03. 조건 부사절 접속사

귀하의 예약에 관한 질문이 있으실 경우, 저희 서비스팀으로 이메일을 보내주십시오.

[해설] 선택지가 다양한 품사의 단어들로 구성되어 있으므로 문법 문제이다. 빈칸 뒤에 콤마를 사이에 두고 주어와 동사가 포함된 절과 명령문 절이 위치해 있으므로 빈칸은 이 절들을 연결할 접속사 자리이다. 그런데 빈칸이 속한 절은 조건을 나타내는 부사절이어야 하므로 조건 부사절 접속사인 (B) If가 정답이다. (C) Then은 부사이다.

[어휘] reservation 예약

04. 양보 부사절 접속사

비록 우회해야 하기는 했지만, Wallace 씨는 주택 공개 행사장에 일찍 도착했다.

[해설] 선택지가 다양한 접속사들로 구성되어 있으므로 어휘 문제이다. 빈칸 뒤에 위치한 두 절이 '우회해야 했지만 일찍 도착했다'와 같이 양보의 의미를 나타내야 알맞으므로 '(비록) ~이기는 하지만'을 뜻하는 양보 부사절 접속사 (A) Although가 정답이다.

[어휘] take a detour 우회하다   make it to ~에 도착하다, 가다   unless ~하지 않는다면   since ~하기 때문에, ~한 이후로   so that (목적) ~할 수 있도록

05. 이유 부사절 접속사

오전에 수업을 들으러 가기 때문에, Dunlap 씨는 늦은 시간대에만 교대 근무한다.

[해설] 선택지가 다양한 품사로 된 단어로 구성되어 있으므로 문법 문제이다. 빈칸 뒤에 콤마를 사이에 두고 각각 완전한 절이 위치해 있으므로 빈칸은 이 절들을 연결할 접속사 자리이다. 그런데 빈칸이 속한 절은 이유를 나타내는 부사절이 되어야 알맞으므로 이유 부사절 접속사인 (B) Because가 정답이다. (A) Due to는 전치사, (D) Consequently는 부사이다.

[어휘] shift 교대 근무(조)   consequently 결과적으로

06. 목적 부사절 접속사

Lawrence 고등학교는 학생들이 유인물에 집중할 수 있도록 스마트폰 사용을 금지하고 있다.

[해설] 선택지가 접속사와 전치사로 구성되어 있으므로 문법 문제이다. 빈칸 앞뒤에 각각 완전한 절이 위치해 있으므로 빈칸은 이 절들을 연결할 접속사 자리이다. 그런데 빈칸 이하 부분이 스마트폰 사용을 금지하는 목적에 해당되므로 목적 부사절 접속사인 (B) so that이 정답이다. (A) such as와 (C) ahead of는 전치사이다.

[어휘] ban ~을 금지하다   concentrate on ~에 집중하다   ahead of ~보다 앞서   while ~하는 동안, ~이기는 하지만

07. 복합관계부사

jennyscloset.com에서 50달러 이상에 해당되는 주문을 하실 때마다 무료 배송 서비스를 받으세요.

[해설] 선택지가 다양한 접속사들로 구성되어 있으므로 어휘 문제이다. 빈칸 이하의 절은 무료 배송 서비스를 받을 수 있는 조건을 나타낸다. 따라서 '~할 때마다, ~할 때는 언제든지'라는 의미로 조건을 의미할 수 있는 복합관계부사 (C) whenever가 정답이다.

[어휘] place an order 주문하다   in that ~라는 점에서   though 비록 ~이기는 하지만

08. 양보 부사절 접속사

탑승에 앞서 보안 검색대에서 확인을 받았다 하더라도 모든 탑승객들의 수하물이 반드시 세관 구역에서 점검되어야 한다.

[해설] 선택지가 접속사와 전치사로 구성되어 있으므로 문법 문제이다. 빈칸 앞뒤로 완전한 절이 있으므로 이 절들을 연결할 접속사가 필요하다. '설사 보안 검색대에서 확인되었다 하더라도, 세관 구역에서 점검되어야 한다'는 맥락의 양보의 의미가 되어야 알맞으므로 '~라 하더라도'를 뜻하는 양보 부사절 접속사 (D) even if가 정답이다.

[어휘] inspect ~을 점검하다   customs 세관   prior to ~에 앞서

09. 시간 부사절 접속사

경연 대회 결선 진출자들은 일단 심사위원단에 의해 선정되면 통보를 받을 것이다.

[해설] 선택지가 접속사와 전치사로 구성되어 있으므로 문법 문제이다. 빈칸 앞뒤로 완전한 절이 있으므로 이 절들을 연결할 접속사가 필요하며, '선정되면 통보받을 것이다'와 같은 의미가 되어야 자연스럽다. '일단 ~하면, ~하는 대로'라는 뜻으로 쓰이는 시간 부사절 접속사 (B) once가 정답이다.

[어휘] finalist 결선 진출자   notify ~에게 통보하다   panel 위원단   against ~에 반대해, ~에 기대어

10. 조건 부사절 접속사

예기치 못한 지연 문제가 있지 않다면, 주문품들은 보통 영업일로부터 이틀 후에 배송될 것입니다.

[해설] 선택지가 다양한 품사의 단어들로 구성되어 있으므로 문법 문제이다. 콤마 앞뒤로 위치한 두 절을 연결할 접속사가 필요한데, '지연 문제가 있지 않다면 보통 ~ 배송된다'와 같은 부정 조건과 결과가 이어져야 적절하다. 따

(A) 신속 배달 서비스에 대해 확인할 것이다.
(B) 추가 재료를 주문할 것이다.
(C) 참석자 수에 관해 문의하고 싶어 한다.
(D) 배송 날짜가 재조정되어야 한다는 것에 동의한다.

[해설] 제시된 문장은 '내가 요청하겠다'라는 의미로 해석할 수 있다. 이는 바로 앞 문장에서 언급한 마지막 순간에 배송을 해 주는 일과(They should be able to make a last-minute delivery) 관련된 확인 요청을 의미하는데, 이는 뒤늦게 주문을 해도 신속히 배송을 해줄 수 있는지 확인할 것이라는 의미이므로 (A)가 정답이다.

[어휘] check on ~을 확인하다 inquire about ~에 관해 문의하다 attendance 참석, 참석자 수

09. 세부사항 문제

Jones 씨에 의해 무슨 정보가 제공되는가?
(A) 왜 한 장소가 선택되었는지
(B) 제품을 어디로 배송해야 하는지
(C) 행사가 언제 시작될 것인지
(D) 행사에 얼마나 많은 사람들이 참석하는지

[해설] Jones 씨의 이름이 언급된 1시 25분 메시지에 Jones 씨가 막 전화를 해서 연회에 80명의 사람들이 온다고 말한 사실을(~ Mr. Jones just called. He said that there will be 80 people at their banquet ~) 알리고 있으므로 (D)가 정답이다.

[어휘] venue 장소

10. 세부사항 문제

Faulkner 씨는 곧이어 무엇을 할 것 같은가?
(A) 주문량 늘리기
(B) 식사 시간 갖기
(C) 메뉴 변경하기
(D) 고객 맞이하기

[해설] 1시 20분에는 Faulkner 씨가 공급업체에 50인분을 만든다고 얘기한 사실이 쓰여 있는데(I already told our supplier that we'll make 50 servings), Delacruz 씨가 1시 25분 메시지에서 80명의 사람들이 오는 것으로 확인받은 사실을(He said that there will be 80 people at their banquet tonight) 알리고 있다. 따라서 Faulkner 씨는 추가 주문을 해야 하는 상황이므로 (A)가 정답이다.

paraphrasing 정답 1. (d) 2. (e) 3. (c) 4. (a) 5. (b)

DAY 18

PART 5 문법 | 부사절 접속사

확인 문제 해석

❶ 그는 자격증을 취득했기 때문에 그 직책에 지원할 수 있었다.
❷ Aaron 씨는 차가 도로에서 고장이 났기 때문에 회의를 놓쳤다.
❸ 인터넷 연결이 매우 불안정해서 그 회사는 인터넷 서비스 공급업체를 변경했다.
❹ 달리 명시되지 않으면 모든 문의 이메일은 Wilson 씨에게 전달되어야 한다.

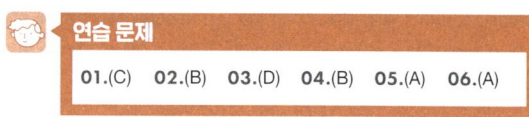

연습 문제

01.(C) 02.(B) 03.(D) 04.(B) 05.(A) 06.(A)

01.

1. 선택지 보고 문법/어휘 문제 파악하기 ☑문법 문제 ☐어휘 문제
2. 빈칸 분석하기 빈칸 뒤에 있는 것 ☑완전한 절 2개 ☐불완전한 절 1개와 완전한 절 1개
   → 빈칸에는 ☑접속사 ☐전치사가 들어가야 한다.
3. 정답 선택하기 정답 (C)

Nixon 씨가 회의에 참석할 수 없다면 Tyler 씨가 그녀를 대신할 것입니다.

02.

1. 선택지 보고 문법/어휘 문제 파악하기 ☐문법 문제 ☑어휘 문제
2. 빈칸 분석하기 빈칸 뒤에 있는 동사 (wrapped)
   → '보호를 위해 ------ 포장되어 있다'는 문맥에 어울리는 부사가 들어가야 한다.
3. 정답 선택하기 정답 (B)

저희의 초콜릿이 묻혀진 쿠키는 보호를 위해 개별 포장 되어 있습니다.

03.

1. 선택지 보고 문법/어휘 문제 파악하기 ☐문법 문제 ☑어휘 문제
2. 빈칸 분석하기 빈칸 앞 내용과 뒤 내용의 의미 관계가 ☑대조되는 내용 ☐목적을 나타내는 내용이 되는 것이 자연스럽다.
3. 정답 선택하기 정답 (D)

Peck 씨는 경기가 불황임에도 불구하고 그의 사업체를 열기로 결정했다.

04.

1. 선택지 보고 문법/어휘 문제 파악하기 ☐문법 문제 ☑어휘 문제
2. 빈칸 분석하기 빈칸 뒤에 있는 2개의 문장의 의미 관계가 ☐대조되는 내용 ☑이유를 나타내는 내용이 되는 것이 자연스럽다.
3. 정답 선택하기 정답 (B)

Hanson 씨가 퇴직하기 때문에, 인사부는 대체할 사람을 찾고 있다.

05.

1. 선택지 보고 문법/어휘 문제 파악하기 ☐문법 문제 ☑어휘 문제
2. 빈칸 분석하기 빈칸 앞뒤 문장의 의미 관계가 ☑목적을 나타내는 내용 ☐대조되는 내용이 되는 것이 자연스럽다.
3. 정답 선택하기 정답 (A)

White 씨는 그 직책에 자격을 갖출 수 있도록 그녀의 자격증을 갱신했다.

06.

1. 선택지 보고 문법/어휘 문제 파악하기 ☑문법 문제 ☐어휘 문제
2. 빈칸 분석하기 빈칸 뒤에 있는 것 ☑완전한 절 2개 ☐불완전한 절 1개와 완전한 절 1개
   → 빈칸에는 ☑접속사 ☐전치사가 들어가야 한다.
3. 정답 선택하기 정답 (A)

농촌 지역이 홍수를 겪을 때마다 농산물의 평균 가격이 상당히 상승한다.

flooring 바닥재 electricity 전기 move into ~로 이사하다
lease contract 임대 계약(서) at the last minute 마지막 순간에
insulate ~에 단열 처리를 하다 crew (함께 일하는) 팀, 조 coat (페인트 등의) 칠 at least 최소한, 적어도 so that (목적) ~할 수 있도록 take care of ~을 처리하다 set 준비된

04. 추론 문제

Denzel 법률에 관해 암시된 것은 무엇인가?
(A) 아주 좋은 평판을 얻고 있다.
(B) 새로운 사무실로 이전할 것이다.
(C) 최근에 개조 공사를 거쳤다.
(D) 직원을 더 모집할 계획이다.

[해설] 첫 메시지에 Denzel Legal 사를 위한 사무실 준비 작업이(office preparations for Denzel Legal) 언급되고 있고, 2시 37분 메시지에는 그 회사가 일정대로 그 사무실로 이전하는 일(their company can move into the office)이 언급되어 있으므로 Denzel Legal 사가 새 사무실로 이전한다는 것을 알 수 있다. 따라서 (B)가 정답이다.

[어휘] reputation 명성, 평판 undergo ~을 거치다, 겪다 recruit ~을 모집하다

05. 세부사항 문제

Hayes 씨는 무엇을 여전히 해야 하는가?
(A) 일부 바닥재 설치하기
(B) 고객 계약서 업데이트하기
(C) 전기 회로 연결하기
(D) 벽에 2차 페인트칠하기

[해설] 2시 40분 메시지에 Hayes 씨가 1차로 칠한 것이 완전히 마른 뒤에 내일 작업을 할 계획이라고(we plan on doing that tomorrow so that the first coat can finish drying) 알리고 있는데, 이때 doing이 의미하는 것은 두 번째 페인트 작업을 의미하므로 (D)가 정답이다.

[어휘] electric circuit 전기 회로

06. 의도 파악 문제

오후 2시 43분에, Stone 씨가 "Sounds like we're all set, then"이라고 썼을 때 의미한 것은 무엇이겠는가?
(A) 사무실이 편리한 곳에 위치해 있다.
(B) 사무실이 제때 준비될 것이다.
(C) 배송 물품이 이미 도착했다.
(D) 고객이 업데이트를 요청했다.

[해설] 제시된 문장은 '준비가 모두 된 것 같다'라는 의미로 해석 가능하다. 이는 앞서 2시 41분에 Stone 씨가 모든 것이 처리되는 건지(everything will be taken care of?) 묻자 Hayes 씨가 그렇다고 말한 뒤에 이어지는 반응이다. 따라서 첫 메시지에 언급된 Denzel Legal 사를 위한 사무실 준비 작업이(office preparations for Denzel Legal) 완료된 것을 의미하는 말이므로 (B)가 정답이다.

[어휘] conveniently located 편리한 곳에 위치한 on time 제때 shipment 배송(품)

paraphrasing 정답 1. (e) 2. (d) 3. (b) 4. (c) 5. (a)

07-10은 다음 온라인 채팅을 참조하시오.

Alex Bowen (오후 1:17)
모두 오늘 저녁에 있을 [07]Wilber 기술 서비스의 연회에 대한 준비가 되셨나요?

Bailey Delacruz (오후 1:18)
제가 어제 Sanders 씨와 얘기해 봤지만, 최종 인원수와 관련해서 제게 아직 다시 전화를 주지 않으셨어요.

Alex Bowen (오후 1:19)
[07]우리는 지금 당장이라도 음식 준비를 시작해야 해요. 그쪽 행사에 우리가 음식을 충분히 제공하지 못하면 어쩌죠?

Rosa Faulkner (오후 1:20)
[10]제가 이미 우리 공급업체에 50인분을 만들 거라고 얘기해 놨어요.

Alex Bowen (오후 1:21)
하지만 그쪽에서는 50명과 80명 사이라고 말했어요. 우리가 재료를 충분히 주문하지 못하면 어떻게 하죠?

Rosa Faulkner (오후 1:22)
[08]마지막 순간에 배송을 해줄 수 있을 겁니다. 제가 요청할게요.

Alex Bowen (오후 1:23)
Bailey 씨, Sanders 씨께 전화하셔서 최종 답변을 확인해 주시면 좋겠어요.

Rosa Faulkner (오후 1:24)
아직 저쪽에서 트럭이 출발하지 않았기 때문에 우리가 변경할 시간이 있어요.

Bailey Delacruz (오후 1:25)
실은, [09, 10]Jones 씨가 막 전화하셨어요. 오늘 저녁에 있을 연회에 80명의 사람들이 올 거라고 하셨어요.

Alex Bowen (오후 1:26)
음, 큰일 날 뻔했네요. 잠시 후에 준비 구역에서 뵙겠습니다.

banquet 연회 head count 인원 수 any minute now 지금 당장이라도 supplier 공급업체 serving 1인분 order ~을 주문하다 ingredient (음식) 재료, 성분 last-minute 마지막 순간의 that was close 큰일 날 뻔했다, 아슬아슬했다 prep area 준비 구역 in a bit 잠시 후에, 곧

07. 직업 문제

메시지 작성자들은 무슨 분야에서 근무할 것 같은가?
(A) 기술 지원
(B) 연예
(C) 출장 요리 제공
(D) 관광

[해설] 첫 메시지에 언급된 Wilber Tech Services 사의 연회(Wilber Tech Services banquet) 준비와 관련해, 1시 19분 메시지에 음식 준비를 시작하는 일과 함께 음식을 충분히 제공하지 못할 경우에 대한 우려를 나타내는(We have to start preparing the food ~. What if we don't provide enough ~) 말이 있으므로 음식 제공 업체임을 알 수 있다. 따라서 (C)가 정답이다.

[어휘] field 분야, 업계 catering 출장 요리 제공(업)

08. 의도 파악 문제

오후 1시 22분에 Faulkner 씨가 "I'll ask"라고 썼을 때 의미하는 바는 무엇이겠는가?

실전 문제

01. (A) 02. (D) 03. (C) 04. (B) 05. (D) 06. (B)
07. (C) 08. (A) 09. (D) 10. (A)

01-03는 다음 온라인 채팅을 참조하시오.

Juliette Buckley [오후 2:19]
지난 회의 시간에, Wilson 건설을 위한 캠페인을 시작하기 위한 모든 준비가 거의 다 되었어요. 현재 상황은 어떤가요?

Rory Palmer [오후 2:20]
실은, ⁰¹그쪽에서 광고에 다른 로고를 사용하고 싶다고 얘기했어요. 우리는 초기 디자인 단계로 되돌아가야 했어요.

Juliette Buckley [오후 2:21]
그렇게 해도 기존의 마감 시한을 맞출 수 있으세요?

Jeff Cummings [오후 2:22]
⁰²저희 팀에서 사람을 보내 도와 드릴 수 있어요. 그렇게 하는 게 필요하실 겁니다. 여러분 중에 그쪽 업체와 전에 일해 본 적이 있는 분 있으세요?

Ingrid Hamill [오후 2:23]
⁰³제가 해본 적이 있는데, 그때는 별 문제 없었어요.

Rory Palmer [오후 2:24]
Jeff 씨가 도와 줄 사람을 보내 주신다면, 분명 저희 팀에서 해낼 수 있을 거예요.

Juliette Buckley [오후 2:25]
알겠습니다, 좋아요. 다시 한번 감사합니다, Jeff 씨.

launch ~을 시작하다, 출시하다 stand (특정 상황, 관계, 입장 등에) 있다 commercial 광고 (방송) initial 처음의 phase 단계 pull A off A를 해 내다, 성사시키다

01. 주제 문제
메시지 작성자들은 무슨 종류의 문제에 관해 이야기하고 있는가?
(A) 고객이 변경을 요청했다.
(B) 공간이 충분하지 않을 것이다.
(C) 일이 너무 복잡하다.
(D) 파일이 삭제되었다.

[해설] 2시 20분 메시지에 Palmer 씨가 고객사로부터 다른 로고를 사용하고 싶다고 전달받은 부분을(they said that they want to use a different logo in the commercials) 언급한 뒤로 그 일의 진행 방법을 논의하고 있다. 따라서 이와 같은 고객의 요청을 언급한 (A)가 정답이다.

[어휘] sufficient 충분한 task 일, 업무 complicated 복잡한

02. 세부사항 문제
Cummings 씨는 자신이 무엇을 할 것이라고 말하는가?
(A) 개인적으로 일을 도와 주기
(B) 마감 시한 연장을 승인해 주기
(C) 고객과 협의하기
(D) 한 직원에게 일을 다시 배정하기

[해설] Cummings 씨가 2시 22분에 쓴 메시지를 보면, 자신의 팀에서 사람을 보내 도와 줄 수 있다고(I can send someone from my team to help) 알리는 말이 있는데, 이는 그 사람에게 새롭게 업무를 배정하는 것과 같으므로 (D)가 정답이다.

paraphrasing send someone 사람을 보내다 → Reassign an employee 한 직원에게 일을 다시 배정하기

[어휘] assist with ~을 돕다 grant ~을 승인하다 extension (기한 등의) 연장 negotiate with ~와 협의하다 reassign ~에게 다시 배정하다, 다시 할당하다

03. 의도 파악 문제
오후 2시 22분에 Cummings 씨가 "Haven't any of you worked with them before"라고 썼을 때 의미한 것은 무엇이겠는가?
(A) 프로젝트의 책임을 맡고 싶어 한다.
(B) 미숙한 동료 직원들에 대해 우려하고 있다.
(C) 고객에 관해 더 많은 정보가 필요하다.
(D) 일련의 계약 협상에서 배제되었다.

[해설] 제시된 문장은 앞서 언급된 고객사와 전에 일해 본 사람이 있는지를 묻는 질문이다. 바로 뒤이어 Hamill 씨가 자신이 해본 적이 있고 그때는 별 문제 없었다고(I have, but I didn't have any problems when I did) 대답하는 상황이다. 따라서 앞서 언급된 로고 변경 문제와 관련해 이 회사가 전에도 그런 적이 있었는지를 확인하기 위한 질문이라는 것을 알 수 있으며, 이는 결국 그 회사와 관련된 추가 정보를 얻고자 하는 것이므로 (C)가 정답이다.

[어휘] take charge of ~의 책임을 맡다 inexperienced 미숙한, 경험이 부족한 coworker 동료 직원 be left out of ~에 배제되다, 제외되다 contract 계약(서) negotiation 협상, 협의

paraphrasing 정답 1. (b) 2. (e) 3. (a) 4. (c) 5. (d)

04-06은 다음 온라인 채팅을 참조하시오.

Rebecca Stone (오후 2:35)
⁰⁴, ⁰⁶Denzel 법률을 위한 사무실 준비는 어떻게 되어 가고 있나요?

Carson Guerrero (오후 2:36)
제가 새로운 바닥재를 설치하는 일을 완료했어요. 전기 작업이 제 예상보다 조금 더 시간이 걸리긴 했지만요.

Rebecca Stone (오후 2:37)
저는 ⁰⁴그 회사가 일정대로 그 사무실로 이전할 수 있을지 분명히 해 두고 싶습니다. 마지막 순간에 그쪽 임대 계약을 변경해야 하는 일은 하고 싶지 않아요.

Carson Guerrero (오후 2:38)
그럴 필요는 없을 것 같습니다.

Nathan Hayes (오후 2:39)
벽마다 단열 작업이 되어 있고, 제 팀이 이미 그 벽에 1차 페인트칠 작업을 완료했습니다.

Carson Guerrero (오후 2:39)
⁰⁵보통 최소 두 번은 칠을 입히지 않나요?

Nathan Hayes (오후 2:40)
네, ⁰⁵1차로 칠한 것이 완전히 마를 수 있도록 내일 그 작업을 할 계획입니다.

Rebecca Stone (오후 2:41)
알겠습니다, ⁰⁶그럼 모든 것이 처리되는 건가요?

Nathan Hayes (오후 2:42)
⁰⁶네, 전혀 걱정하실 필요 없습니다.

Rebecca Stone (오후 2:43)
아주 좋습니다. 그렇다면 모든 준비가 되어 있는 것 같네요.

Warren Delarosa [오전 10:55]
제 작업팀이 약 15분 후에 그쪽으로 갈 수 있습니다.

truckload 트럭 한 대 분량 **unload** (짐 등) ~을 내리다 **boxed-up** 상자에 담아 꾸린 **belongings** 개인 물품, 소지품 **property** 건물, 부동산 **crew** (함께 작업하는) 팀, 조 **head that way** 그쪽으로 향하다, 그 방향으로 가다

Q. 오전 10시 54분에, Abbott 씨가 "Is that all"이라고 썼을 때 의미한 것은 무엇이겠는가?
(A) 일부 물품이 분실되는 것을 걱정하고 있다.
(B) 일이 완료되었는지 확인하고 싶어 한다.

[문제 키워드] At 10:54 A.M. / what / Ms. Abbott / mean / "Is that all"

[해설] 10시 54분 메시지에서 Abbott 씨는 '그게 전부인지' 물으면서 거의 완료되었으면 Kaminski 씨 댁에 도움이 좀 필요할 것 같다고(If you're almost finished, we could use some help ~) 알리고 있다. 따라서 주어진 표현은 현재 진행 중인 작업의 완료 여부를 확인하는 질문임을 알 수 있으므로 (B)가 정답이다.

02.

Luiz Pereira [오후 2:25]
6월 30일에 있을 행사에 대한 준비 작업은 어떻게 되어 가고 있나요?

Irene Tillis [오후 2:26]
Alliance 공원을 음식 축제 장소로 최종 확정했습니다. 시에서 보내온 서류를 오늘 아침에 막 받았습니다.

Kreran Byrne [오후 2:27]
정말 잘됐네요! 그럼 제가 전단지 디자인 작업을 시작할 수 있겠어요. 저는 요리 시연회와 아주 다양한 부스들을 강조하고 싶습니다.

Luiz Pereira [오후 2:28]
아주 잘해 주셨습니다, Irene 씨. 그리고 Kieran 씨, 금요일에 열리는 회의에 가져오실 수 있도록 초안을 준비해 보세요.

paperwork 서류 (작업) **flyer** 전단지 **emphasize** ~을 강조하다 **demonstration** 시연(회) **the wide variety of** 다양한 **booth** 부스, 칸막이 공간 **draft** 초안

Q. 메시지 작성자들은 무엇을 논의하고 있는가?
(A) 야외 축제
(B) 요리 경연 대회

[문제 키워드] What / writers / discussing

[해설] 2시 26분 메시지에서 Tillis 씨가 Alliance Park를 축제 장소로 확정했다고(~ finalized Alliance Park as the location for the food festival) 알린 후에 행사 준비에 필요한 작업에 관해 이야기하고 있으므로 (A)가 정답이다.

[어휘] competition 경연 대회

03.

Mattie Worden [오전 9:44]
이월 주문되었던 목재 캐비닛의 작업 진행 상황은 어떤가요? **우리 단골 고객들 중의 한 분이신 Kirk 씨께서 여전히 기다리고 계십니다.**

Stefan Baier [오전 9:49]
오늘 아침부터 다시 재고가 들어와 있는 상태입니다. 그분에게 전화하셔서 제품이 준비되어 있다고 말씀 드리고 싶어 하셨잖아요?

Mattie Worden [오전 9:50]
정확한 배송 상세 정보를 알려 드릴 수 있게 된 후에나 할 겁니다.

Demi Elliot [오전 9:51]
그분께서 바로 이곳 시내의 Elsie 로 3828번지에 계시기 때문에, 제 팀이 오늘 4시에서 5시 사이에 배송해 드릴 수 있습니다.

Mattie Worden [오전 9:52]
감사합니다. **제가 그분께 알려 드릴게요.**

status 진행 상황, 상태 **be on backorder** 이월 주문되다 **regular client** 단골 고객 **be in stock** 재고가 있다 **as of**+시점 ~부터

Q. Worden 씨는 곧이어 무엇을 할 것 같은가?
(A) 배송 주소 업데이트하기
(B) 고객에게 연락하기

[해설] 9시 52분 메시지에서 Worden 씨가 그 사람에게 알려 주겠다고 말하고 있는데(I'll let him know), 여기서 him은 처음에 단골 고객으로 언급된 Kirk 씨를(Mr. Kirk, one of our regular clients) 가리키므로 (B)가 정답이다.

04.

Sharon Wynn [오후 3:11]
Ocello 산업을 대상으로 하는 **영업용 홍보 발표가 겨우 이틀밖에 남지 않았어요. 슬라이드가 완료되었나요?**

Thomas Ventura [오후 3:12]
네, 모든 그래픽과 최신 수치도 추가했습니다. 심지어 제가 Bajpai 씨와 여러 차례 연습도 해봤기 때문에, 타이밍을 완벽히 익혀 두었습니다.

Sharon Wynn [오후 3:14]
그렇다니 기쁩니다.

Mina Bajpai [오후 3:15]
저는 오늘 유인물을 완료할 겁니다. 인상적으로 보일 수 있게 컬러 인쇄를 하고 두꺼운 용지를 사용하도록 인쇄소에 전달할 예정입니다.

Sharon Wynn [오후 3:16]
전부 준비가 된 것 같네요.

sales pitch 영업용 홍보 발표, 제품 구매 권유 **add** ~을 추가하다 **latest** 최신의 **figure** 수치, 숫자 **have A down** A를 완벽히 익히다, 숙지하다 **instruct A to**부정사 A에게 ~하도록 전하다, 지시하다, 설명하다 **thick** 두꺼운 **impressive** 인상적인

Q. 오후 3시 16분에, Wynn 씨가 "Seems like it's all set"이라고 썼을 때 의미한 것은 무엇이겠는가?
(A) 자신의 팀이 발표 준비가 된 것으로 생각한다.
(B) 자신이 이미 일부 장비를 설치해 두었다.

[문제 키워드] At 3:16 P.M. / what / Ms. Wynn / mean / "Seems like it's all set"

[해설] 첫 메시지에서 Wynn 씨가 영업용 홍보 발표에 쓸 슬라이드 완료 여부를(The sales pitch ~ Are the slides finished?) 묻자 Ventura 씨가 그렇다고(Yes) 답변하고 있고, 그 뒤로 Bajpai 씨가 유인물 작업 일정과 방법을 설명하고 있다. 따라서 마지막에 Wynn 씨가 '전부 준비된 것 같다'고 말하는 것은 해당 발표 행사 준비가 완료된 것으로 생각한다는 뜻이므로 (A)가 정답이다.

04. 접속부사

[해설] 빈칸 다음에 맛있는 음식이 아주 없어지는 것은 아니라는 말이 쓰여 있는 데, 이는 앞선 단락에서 말하는 인기 아이스크림 매장이 영원히 문을 닫는 것과 대조되는 내용에 해당된다. 따라서 '그럼에도 불구하고'라는 의미로 대조적인 내용을 말할 때 사용하는 (D) Nevertheless가 정답이다.

[어휘] hence 따라서, 이런 이유로 meantime 그 동안, 그 사이에 accordingly 그에 따라, 그 결과 nevertheless 그럼에도 불구하고

05-08은 다음 정보를 참조하시오.

Marissa Barnes

05Marissa Barnes 씨는 자신이 투자의 전문가임을 거듭해서 입증해 왔습니다. 10년 넘게, 그녀는 자신의 투자 선택에 대해 지속적으로 최소 15퍼센트의 수익을 올렸습니다. 06많은 유명인들과 사업가들은 그녀에게 그들의 자산을 맡겨 왔습니다. 이들은 다른 어떤 투자를 통해 얻는 것보다 그녀와 함께 얻는 더 높은 수익에 만족감을 드러냈습니다. 그녀는 2005년에 경영학 학위를 받으며 Wilson 대학교를 졸업했습니다. Goldberg 은행에서 짧은 인턴 생활을 마친 후, Knox 금융에 채용되어 시장 분석가로 근무했습니다. 07하지만, 그녀는 진정으로 빛을 발하기 시작했던 고객 서비스 부서로 곧바로 전근되었습니다. 08Barnes 씨는 역사상 가장 유명한 투자가들 중의 한 명으로 알려지게 되었습니다.

prove A as B A가 B임을 입증하다 expert 전문가 investing 투자 earn (돈) ~을 벌다, (수익) ~을 올리다 investment 투자(금) earnings 수익, 소득 degree 학위 business administration 경영학 recruit ~을 채용하다, 모집하다 analyst 분석가 transfer ~을 전근시키다 shine 빛을 발하다 investor 투자자

05. 인칭대명사

[해설] 빈칸 앞에 쓰인 동사 prove는 목적어를 필요로 하는 타동사인데, 빈칸에 쓰일 인칭대명사는 주어인 Marissa Barnes 자신을 가리켜야 문맥에 적합하므로 재귀대명사인 (C) herself가 정답이다. 재귀대명사는 행위 주체와 대상자가 동일할 경우에 사용한다.

06. 알맞은 문장 고르기

(A) 많은 유명인들과 사업가들은 그녀에게 그들의 자산을 맡겨 왔습니다.
(B) Barnes 씨와 약속 일정을 잡으시려면 Knox 금융에 연락하십시오.
(C) 지금이 신생 기업에 대한 투자를 시작하기에 완벽한 시기입니다.
(D) 재무 관련 상담 서비스는 온라인으로 이용 가능합니다.

[해설] 빈칸 다음 문장에 제시된 대명사 They가 가리키는 사람이 포함된 문장이 필요하므로 이 대명사로 받을 수 있는 대상인 '많은 유명인과 사업가들'과 Barnes 씨를 가리키는 her가 함께 언급된 (A)가 정답이다.

[어휘] celebrity 유명인 entrust A to B A를 B에게 맡기다 invest in ~에 투자하다 startup company 신생 기업 financial 재무의, 재정의, 금융의

07. 접속부사

[해설] 빈칸 앞에는 시장 분석가로 일을 시작했다는 말이, 빈칸 뒤에는 금방 다른 부서로 전근되었다는 말이 쓰여 있어 갑작스런 상황의 변화가 발생되었음을 알리는 흐름임을 알 수 있다. 따라서 '하지만' 등의 의미로 상황 반전이나 대조의 의미를 나타낼 때 사용하는 (B) However가 정답이다.

[어휘] specifically 구체적으로 말하면

08. 동사의 형태

[해설] 앞 문장에 과거 시제 동사 began과 함께 과거의 특정 시점에 빛을 발하기 시작했다는 말로 명성을 얻은 시작점이 언급되어 있으므로 그 이후로 가장 유명한 투자자라는 입지를 유지해 왔음을 나타낼 동사가 쓰여야 한다. 따라서 과거에 시작된 일이 현재까지 지속되는 상태를 나타낼 때 사용하는 현재완료 시제 (B) has become이 정답이다.

PART 7 온라인 채팅

풀이 방법 해석

Virgil Dyer [오전 10:24]
새 전시는 잘 준비되고 있나요? 갤러리와의 계약은 마무리되었나요?

Melody Kim [오전 10:25]
네, 마무리되었어요. 2월에 저희에게 30개의 조각상을 보낼 거예요.

Virgil Dyer [오전 10:26]
좋네요! 그렇다면, 안내책자를 준비할 때가 되었군요.

Melody Kim [오전 10:27]
Robert가 이미 그 작업을 시작했어요.

Virgil Dyer [오전 10:28]
이 전시가 많은 외국인 관광객들을 끌어모을 테니, 여러 언어로 제공하고 싶네요.

Robert Fennell [오전 10:29]
제가 거의 다 했어요. 주로 사진입니다. 견본을 인쇄할 수 있어요.

Melody Kim [오전 10:30]
인쇄하기 전에 몇 가지를 수정해야 할 거예요.

Robert Fennell [오전 10:31]
알겠어요. 어떤 것들이요?

Melody Kim [오전 10:32]
스페인어로도 설명을 포함시킬 수 있도록 사진 크기를 좀 줄이고 싶어요.

Robert Fennell [오전 10:33]
그렇게 할 수 있을 것 같네요.

연습 문제

01.(B) **02.**(A) **03.**(B) **04.**(A)

01.

Jeanne Abbott [오전 10:50]
Bedford 씨의 이사에 대한 작업은 어떻게 되어 가고 있나요?

Warren Delarosa [오전 10:53]
첫 번째 트럭 분량으로 가구를 옮겼습니다. 지금 상자에 담아 꾸렸던 그분의 물품들을 새 건물에 막 내리고 있습니다.

Jeanne Abbott [오전 10:54]
그게 전부인가요? 거의 완료되셨으면, Kaminski 씨 댁에 도움이 좀 필요할 것 같아요. 큰 물품들이 많이 있거든요. Dwyer 가 560번지입니다.

01.

우리 사무실은 몇몇 예정된 전자 장비 유지 보수 작업으로 인해 이번 주 수요일에 문을 닫을 것입니다. 하지만 직원들께서는 당일에 여전히 9시부터 5시까지 원격으로 근무하셔야 합니다.

due to ~로 인해   electronic 전자 장비의   maintenance 유지 관리   work from a remote location 원격으로 근무하다

[단서] office will be closed, still expected to work

[해설] 사무실이 수요일에는 문을 닫지만 당일에 여전히 다른 곳에서 근무해야 한다는 의미가 되어야 알맞으므로 빈칸 앞뒤가 대조적인 흐름임을 알 수 있다. 따라서 '하지만'이라는 의미로 역접 관계를 나타낼 때 사용하는 (B) However가 정답이다.

[어휘] moreover 더욱이, 게다가

02.

귀하께서는 파일을 업로드하시거나 다운로드하시기 위해 회사 네트워크에 접속하실 수 있는 권한을 부여받으셨습니다. 아쉽게도, 보안 목적으로 인해 건물 외부에 있는 사람은 누구도 접속할 수 없습니다.

authorize A to부정사 A가 ~하도록 승인하다   access ~에 접속하다, ~을 이용하다   inaccessible 접속할 수 없는, 이용할 수 없는

[단서] You are authorized, it is inaccessible to anyone outside

[해설] 빈칸 앞에는 네트워크 접속이 승인된 사실이, 빈칸 뒤에는 네트워크에 접속할 수 없는 조건이 언급되어 있어 대조적인 내용을 말하는 흐름임을 알 수 있다. 따라서 '안타깝게도, 아쉽게도'라는 의미로 역접 관계를 나타낼 때 사용하는 (A) Unfortunately가 정답이다.

[어휘] similarly 마찬가지로, 유사하게

03.

귀하의 지난번 주문에 문제가 있었다는 내용을 듣게 되어 사과 드립니다. 매장 정책에 따라, 저는 동일한 가격의 매장 포인트로 제공해 드릴 수 있습니다. 그렇지 않을 경우, 이 제품을 여전히 원하시면 귀하의 주소로 새 것을 보내 드릴 수 있습니다.

as per ~에 따라   policy 정책   store credit 매장 포인트   equal 동일한, 동등한   value 가격, (금전적) 가치

[단서] offer a store credit, send a new one

[해설] 빈칸 앞에는 매장 포인트를 제공하겠다는 말이, 빈칸 뒤에는 새 것을 집으로 보내 주겠다는 말이 쓰여 있는 것으로 보아 문제 해결과 관련해 선택 가능한 두 가지 대조적인 방법을 제시하는 맥락임을 알 수 있다. 따라서 '그렇지 않으면'이라는 의미로 서로 다른 선택 사항을 언급할 때 사용하는 (A) Otherwise가 정답이다.

[어휘] otherwise 그렇지 않으면

04.

악천후로 인해, 제 작업팀은 오늘 공사 현장에서 어떤 일도 완료할 수 없었습니다. 그럼에도 불구하고 저희는 일정보다 앞서 있었기 때문에 여전히 마감시한을 맞출 수 있을 것입니다.

inclement weather 악천후, 궂은 날씨   construction site 공사 현장

[단서] not able to get any work done, still be able to meet the deadline

[해설] 빈칸 앞에는 어떤 일도 완료할 수 없었다는 말이, 빈칸 뒤에는 여전히 마감시한을 맞출 수 있다는 말이 쓰여 있어 대조적인 사실을 언급하는 흐름임을 알 수 있다. 따라서 '그럼에도 불구하고'라는 의미로 역접 관계를 나타낼 때 사용하는 (B) Nevertheless가 정답이다.

[어휘] likewise 마찬가지로

> **실전 문제**
> 01.(B) 02.(C) 03.(C) 04.(D) 05.(C) 06.(A)
> 07.(B) 08.(B)

01-04는 다음 기사를 참조하시오.

뉴 브런즈윅 (6월 7일) ─ 아이스크림과 스낵 제품으로 지역의 사랑을 받아 온 업체가 곧 영원히 문을 닫을 예정이다. 01Cold Cones의 소유주인 Jim Brady 씨가 은퇴할 계획을 발표했다. 올여름이 지나면, 한때 인기있었던 이 아이스크림 매장은 개조되어 커피숍으로 바뀔 것이다. 02Brady 씨는 자신의 딸이 이 가족 사업을 이어받기를 희망했다. 그녀는 대신 광고 업계에서 경력을 추구하기로 결정했다. 03현재 그녀는 눈길을 끄는 슬로건인 'Finesse가 바로 최고급입니다'를 만들어 낸 것으로 자신의 공로를 인정받은 Finesse Fashion에서 근무 중이다.

04그럼에도 불구하고, 뉴 브런즈윅에 맛있는 특별 음식이 완전히 사라지는 것은 아니다. 해당 아이스크림 매장을 대체하는 커피숍은 다양한 맛의 아이스크림 제품을 포함해 디저트로 가득한 메뉴를 특징으로 할 것이다.

local favorite 지역 사람들이 가장 좋아하는 것   for good 영원히   owner 소유주   once-popular 한때 인기 있었던   be renovated into 개조되어 ~로 바뀌다   pursue ~을 추구하다   instead 대신   currently 현재   catchy 눈길을 끄는   completely 완전히, 전적으로   out of ~이 없는   treat 특별 음식, 한턱, 대접

01. 동사의 형태

[해설] 동사 has announced의 목적어로 쓰인 명사 plan은 to부정사와 결합해 '~하려는 계획'이라는 의미로 사용하므로 (B) to retire가 정답이다.

02. 알맞은 문장 고르기

(A) 영업 마지막 날에 대한 예약을 받는 중이다.
(B) Brady 씨가 남은 시즌 동안 특가 상품을 내놓을 예정이다.
(C) Brady 씨는 자신의 딸이 이 가족 사업을 이어받기를 희망했다.
(D) 고객들은 곧 이 레스토랑의 웹사이트를 통해 배달 주문을 할 수 있을 것이다.

[해설] 빈칸 다음 문장에 제시된 대명사 She로 받을 수 있는 사람이 포함된 문장이 필요하므로 이 대명사가 지칭하는 대상으로서 Brady 씨의 딸이 언급된 문장인 (C)가 정답이다.

[어휘] the rest of ~의 나머지   take over ~을 이어받다, 물려받다   place a delivery order 배달 주문을 하다   via ~을 통해

03. 동사 어휘

[해설] 빈칸 앞뒤에 각각 위치한 be동사, 전치사 with와 결합 가능한 과거분사가 필요하므로 이 둘과 함께 '~에 대한 공을 인정받다'라는 의미를 나타낼 때 사용하는 (C) credited가 정답이다.

[어휘] propose ~을 제안하다   be credited with ~로 인정받다, 명성을 얻다   increase ~을 증가시키다

speech를 수식할 수 있는 (C) convincing이 정답이다. (D) convinced는 사람에 대해서만 사용한다.

[어휘] strategy 전략   convincingly 설득력 있게   convince ~을 설득하다

17. 동명사의 역할: 타동사의 목적어 역할

모든 재정 자문들이 중복되는 일을 없앨 수 있도록 회사 내 부서들을 개편하도록 권하고 있다.

[해설] 선택지가 동사 reorganize의 다양한 형태와 명사로 구성되어 있으므로 문법 문제이다. 빈칸 앞에 위치한 동사 recommend의 목적어 역할을 함과 동시에 그 뒤에 위치한 명사구를 목적어로 취할 수 있는 것은 동명사이므로 (D) reorganizing이 정답이다. 명사 (C) reorganization이 쓰이려면 뒤에 전치사가 동반되어야 한다.

[어휘] financial advisor 재정 자문   overlapping 중복되는   reorganize ~을 개편하다

18. 사람 명사/사물 명사/추상 명사의 구분

Clooney 씨의 계산에 따르면, 공사를 제때 완료하기 위해 여섯 명의 추가 직원들이 필요할 것이다.

[해설] 선택지가 다양한 품사의 단어들로 구성되어 있으므로 문법 문제이다. 소유격 Mr. Clooney's 뒤는 명사 자리이며, Based on의 목적어로서 추가 직원들이 필요하다는 판단의 근거가 되어야 하므로 '계산'을 의미하는 (C) calculations가 정답이다.

[어휘] based on ~을 바탕으로   additional 추가의   on time 제때   calculator 계산기   calculation 계산   calculate ~을 계산하다

19. 부사 어휘

목스빌의 기차역이 8월쯤에 전면적으로 운영될 것이다.

[해설] 선택지가 다양한 부사들로 구성되어 있으므로 부사 어휘 문제이다. 빈칸에 쓰일 부사는 바로 뒤에 위치한 형용사 operational을 수식해 기차역의 운영 방식과 관련된 의미를 나타내야 하므로 '전적으로, 완전히'를 뜻하는 (B) completely가 정답이다.

[어휘] operational 운영되는, 가동되는   voluntarily 자발적으로   generously 아낌없이, 후하게   relatively 상대적으로, 비교적

20. 부사 어휘

우리는 커피를 좀 더 마시기 위해 회의를 잠시 중단할 것이다.

[해설] 선택지가 다양한 부사들로 구성되어 있으므로 부사 어휘 문제이다. 빈칸에 쓰일 부사는 앞에 위치한 동사 pause를 수식해 회의를 중단하는 방식을 나타내야 하므로 '잠깐, 간단히' 등을 의미하는 (A) briefly가 정답이다.

[어휘] cordially 진심으로, 다정하게   randomly 무작위로   nearly 거의

21. 수량 표현+of+관계대명사

자원 봉사자들로 구성된 대규모의 사람들이 행사장에 나타났는데, 이들 중 대부분은 정부 직원들이었다.

[해설] 선택지가 접속사와 전치사구로 구성되어 있으므로 문법 문제이다. 빈칸 뒤에 동사 were로 시작되는 불완전한 절이 있으므로 주어 역할을 함과 동시에 이 절을 이끌 수 있는 것으로 수량 표현과 관계대명사가 결합된 구조인 (C) most of whom이 정답이다.

[어휘] volunteer 자원 봉사자   show up 나타나다, 모습을 보이다

22. 부사 어휘

지점장의 책무는 직무 설명서에 상당히 명확하게 규정되어 있다.

[해설] 선택지가 다양한 부사들로 구성되어 있으므로 부사 어휘 문제이다. 빈칸에 쓰일 부사는 앞에 위치한 be동사 are과 과거분사 defined 사이에서 직무 설명서에 규정된 방식을 나타내야 하므로 '명확히'를 뜻하는 (C) clearly가 정답이다.

[어휘] responsibility 책무, 책임   branch 지점, 지사   quite 상당히, 꽤   define ~을 규정하다   company's handbook 직무 설명서   promptly 즉각적으로   unusually 평소와 달리, 유난히   widely 널리, 폭넓게, 대단히

23. 명사절 접속사 구분: what vs. that

무엇이 잠재 고객들과 논의되어야 하는지가 부장 회의에서 결정될 것이다.

[해설] 선택지가 절을 이끌 수 있는 단어들로 구성되어 있으므로 문법 문제이다. 빈칸 뒤에 두 개의 동사가 있으므로 will be determined 앞까지가 문장의 주어 역할을 하는 명사절이어야 한다. 그런데 빈칸 뒤에 주어 없이 동사 needs로 이어지는 불완전한 절이 있으므로 불완전한 절을 이끄는 명사절 접속사 (B) What이 정답이다. (A) That이 명사절 접속사로 쓰일 때는 완전한 절을 이끈다.

[어휘] potential 잠재적인   determine ~을 결정하다

24. 부사 어휘

처음에 인턴으로 일을 시작한 사람들만이 홍보 담당 직원 자리에 지원할 수 있는 자격이 있다.

[해설] 선택지가 다양한 부사들로 구성되어 있으므로 부사 어휘 문제이다. 빈칸에 쓰일 부사는 바로 뒤에 위치한 과거 시제 동사 started를 수식해 과거에 시작한 일을 강조하는 의미를 나타내야 알맞으므로 '처음에'를 뜻하는 (C) initially가 정답이다.

[어휘] be eligible to부정사 ~할 수 있는 자격이 있다   apply for ~에 지원하다   PR 홍보(= Public Relations)   representative 직원   compulsorily 강제적으로   accidentally 우연히, 실수로   strategically 전략적으로

PART 6   접속부사 – 역접

풀이 방법 해석

Henry Martin의 법률 사무소

수상 경력이 있는 기관인 Henry Martin의 법률 사무소는 법정 소송 사건들에서 승소한 것으로 명성이 나 있다. 수석 변호사인 Martin 씨는 2001년부터 500명이 넘는 개인 고객들을 법정에서 대변했다. 그의 카리스마와 전문 지식은 동료 변호사들과 법정 공무원들 모두에 의해 인정받고 존경받는다. 그는 역사상 가장 훌륭한 법정 변호사들 중 한 명으로 명성을 쌓았다. 그 결과, 그를 법정에서 맞닥뜨려야 했던 많은 변호사들은 자신들의 고객에게 합의에 동의할 것을 권했다. 그럼에도 불구하고, 그는 직접 고객들을 대변하는 것에서 물러나 그의 회사에 있는 다른 변호사들에게 자문가로서의 역할만 하겠다고 결정했다.

연습 문제

01.(B)   02.(A)   03.(A)   04.(B)

where는 완전한 절을 이끌며 장소 선행사를 수식한다.

[어휘] generate ~을 발생시키다, 만들어 내다   efficiently 효율적으로

06. 선행사에 따른 관계대명사 구별

Min's Kitchen의 식사 키트를 구입한 고객들의 25%가 정기 배송 서비스에 가입했다.

[해설] 선택지가 접속사와 대명사로 구성되어 있으므로 문법 문제이다. 빈칸과 동사 signed up 사이에 동사 purchased으로 시작되는 불완전한 절이 있는데, 이 절은 빈칸 앞에 위치한 사람 선행사 customers를 설명하는 내용에 해당된다. 따라서 사람 선행사를 수식하는 관계대명사 (B) who가 정답이다. (D) what을 쓰려면 선행사가 없어야 한다.

[어휘] customer 고객   purchase 구매하다   sign up 가입하다   delivery 배송

07. 관계대명사와 관계부사 구별

과학자들은 낮 시간에 낮잠을 자는 직원들이 직장에서 더욱 생산적이라고 주장한다.

[해설] 선택지가 다양한 관계사들로 구성되어 있으므로 문법 문제이다. 빈칸 뒤에 불완전한 절이 있으므로 관계부사 (A)와 (D)는 제외시킨다. (B)와 (C) 중에서 선행사 employees가 사람이므로 사람 선행사를 수식하는 관계대명사 (C) who가 정답이다.

[어휘] claim that ~라고 주장하다   take a nap 낮잠을 자다   productive 생산적인

08. 소유격 관계대명사

이 버스 일일 승차권은 문화 지구 내 위치한 호텔에 투숙하는 관광객들에게 매우 유용합니다.

[해설] 선택지가 다양한 품사의 단어들로 구성되어 있으므로 문법 문제이다. 빈칸 뒤에 위치한 hotels는 그 앞에 위치한 tourists이 투숙하는 곳으로 판단할 수 있으므로 소유격 관계대명사인 (C) whose가 정답이다.

[어휘] bus pass 버스 정기 승차권   tourist 여행객   district 구역

09. 부사 어휘

소유하고 계신 Hodges 잔디 깎기 기계의 칼날은 계속 기계가 제대로 작동할 수 있도록 주기적으로 세척하고 갈아 주셔야 합니다.

[해설] 선택지가 다양한 부사들로 구성되어 있으므로 부사 어휘 문제이다. 빈칸에 쓰일 부사는 앞에 위치한 분사 working을 수식해 기계가 작동되는 방식을 나타내야 하는데, 칼날을 주기적으로 관리하는 목적과 관련되어야 하므로 '제대로 작동되다'라는 의미를 구성하는 (D) properly가 정답이다.

[어휘] blade 칼날   lawnmower 잔디 깎기 기계   sharpen ~을 날카롭게 하다   regularly 주기적으로   formally 공식적으로   typically 일반적으로, 전형적으로

10. 수량 표현+of+관계대명사

여러 종류의 영화 상이 <High Tide>에게 돌아갔으며, 그 중 하나는 '올해의 영화' 상이었다.

[해설] 선택지가 다양한 품사의 단어들로 구성되어 있으므로 문법 문제이다. 수량 표현 one of의 수식을 받음과 동시에 was로 이어지는 불완전한 절을 이끌 수 있는 접속사가 필요하므로 이 역할이 가능한 관계대명사 (A) which가 정답이다.

11. 관계부사

컨벤션 센터 주변에 있는 대부분의 호텔들은 투숙객들이 출력이나 팩스 전송을 할 수 있는 비즈니스 라운지를 가지고 있다.

[해설] 선택지가 접속사와 대명사로 구성되어 있으므로 문법 문제이다. 빈칸 이하의 절은 빈칸 앞에 위치한 a business lounge를 수식하므로 장소 선행사를 수식하는 관계부사 (B) where가 정답이다.

[어휘] print out 출력하다

12. 전치사+관계대명사

폭풍우가 몰아치는 날씨가 예보되었기 때문에 직원 가족들이 초대되는 야유회 행사가 연기되었다.

[해설] 선택지가 접속사와 대명사로 구성되어 있으므로 문법 문제이다. 빈칸과 동사 has been postponed 사이에 완전한 구조로 된 절이 있으며, 이 절은 사물 선행사 picnic을 설명하는 내용이다. 따라서 사물 선행사 picnic을 수식하는 관계대명사가 전치사와 결합된 구조인 (B) to which가 정답이다. (D) that이 선행사를 수식하는 관계대명사로 쓰이려면 뒤에 불완전한 절이 와야 한다.

[어휘] postpone ~을 연기하다   stormy 폭풍우가 몰아치는   predict ~을 예보하다, 예측하다

13. 명사절 접속사의 종류: 의문부사

그 배송 기사는 어디에 배송 물품을 놓아야 하는지 물었다.

[해설] 선택지가 다양한 의문사로 구성되어 있으므로 문법 문제이다. 빈칸 이하의 절이 타동사 asked의 목적어 역할을 할 명사절이 되어야 하는데, 빈칸 뒤에 완전한 절이 왔으므로 완전한 명사절을 이끄는 의문부사 (B) where가 정답이다.

14. 부사 어휘

Newark 실험실의 연구원들은 더 나은 독감 백신을 개발하기 위해 모든 임상 실험 결과를 신중히 검토하고 있다.

[해설] 선택지가 다양한 부사들로 구성되어 있으므로 부사 어휘 문제이다. 빈칸에 쓰일 부사는 앞에 위치한 동사 are reviewing을 수식해 실험 결과를 검토하는 방식을 나타내야 하므로 '신중히, 조심스럽게'를 의미하는 (B) carefully가 정답이다.

[어휘] clinical test 임상 실험   flu 독감   undoubtedly 의심의 여지 없이   relatively 상대적으로, 비교적   accordingly 그에 맞춰, 그런 이유로

15. 명사절 접속사의 종류: 의문부사

언제 새 휴대전화기가 출시되어야 하는지에 대해 격렬한 논쟁이 벌어졌다.

[해설] 선택지가 접속사와 대명사로 구성되어 있으므로 문법 문제이다. 빈칸 이하의 절은 전치사 about의 목적어 역할을 할 명사절이 되어야 하는데, 빈칸 뒤에 완전한 절이 있으므로 완전한 절을 이끄는 명사절 접속사 (C) when이 정답이다. (B) that은 전치사의 목적어 역할을 하는 명사절을 이끌 수 없으며, (D) whose는 절 앞에 사용하지 않는다.

[어휘] harsh 격렬한, 가혹한   debate 논쟁, 토론   release ~을 출시하다

16. 현재분사

Holloway 씨는 온라인 마케팅 전략의 필요성에 관해 설득력 있는 연설을 했다.

[해설] 선택지가 동사 convince의 다양한 형태와 부사로 구성되어 있으므로 문법 문제이다. 부정관사 a와 명사 speech 사이에 위치한 빈칸은 명사를 수식할 분사가 쓰일 자리인데, '설득력 있는'이라는 의미로 사물 명사

→ 빈칸부터 September 10까지가 주어진 new film을 뒤에서 수식하므로 ☐ 명사절 접속사 ☑ 형용사절 접속사가 들어가야 한다.

3. 정답 선택하기 정답 (B)

9월 10일에 개봉될 Studio 83의 새 영화는 Betty Abbott가 감독했다.

02.

1. 선택지 보고 문법/어휘 문제 파악하기 ☐ 문법 문제 ☑ 어휘 문제
2. 빈칸 분석하기 빈칸 뒤에 있는 동사 (scheduled)
   빈칸 뒤에 있는 접속사 (but)
   → 문맥상 ☐ 원인과 결과 ☑ 반대되는 내용이 되어야 함을 파악한다.
3. 정답 선택하기 정답 (A)

당신의 연설은 원래 오전 10시로 예정되어 있었지만 이후 시간으로 지연되었습니다.

03.

1. 선택지 보고 문법/어휘 문제 파악하기 ☑ 문법 문제 ☐ 어휘 문제
2. 빈칸 분석하기 문장의 주어 (Amanda Burke)
   문장의 본동사 (will appear)
   → 빈칸에는 ☐ 대명사 ☑ 접속사가 들어가야 한다.
   → 정답이 될 수 있는 후보 2개 (A, C)
   → 빈칸부터 will be exhibited까지가 주어진 Amanda Burke를 수식하는 데, 빈칸 바로 뒤에 ☑ 명사 ☐ 형용사가 있다.
3. 정답 선택하기 정답 (C)

자신의 그림이 전시될 Amanda Burke는 지역 뉴스에 출연할 것이다.

04.

1. 선택지 보고 문법/어휘 문제 파악하기 ☑ 문법 문제 ☐ 어휘 문제
2. 빈칸 분석하기 문장의 주어 (the new apartment)
   문장의 본동사 (feels)
   → 빈칸 바로 뒤에 ☑ 동사 ☐ 부사가 있고 선행사가 ☐ 사람 ☑ 사물임을 파악한다.
3. 정답 선택하기 정답 (A)

의자와 테이블이 구비된 새 아파트는 비좁게 느껴진다.

05.

1. 선택지 보고 문법/어휘 문제 파악하기 ☑ 문법 문제 ☐ 어휘 문제
2. 빈칸 분석하기 빈칸 뒤에 있는 것 ☑ 완전한 절 ☐ 불완전한 절
   → 빈칸에는 ☐ 관계대명사 ☑ 관계부사가 들어가야 한다.
   → 정답이 될 수 있는 후보 2개 (B, C)
   → 선행사가 ☑ 장소 ☐ 이유를 나타낸다.
3. 정답 선택하기 정답 (B)

컬러 복사본을 인쇄할 수 있는 비즈니스 센터를 이용하세요.

06.

1. 선택지 보고 문법/어휘 문제 파악하기 ☑ 문법 문제 ☐ 어휘 문제
2. 빈칸 분석하기 빈칸 앞 콤마(,) 앞에 있는 것 ☑ 완전한 절 ☐ 불완전한 절
   빈칸 뒤에 있는 것 ☑ 동사 ☐ 부사
   → 빈칸에는 ☐ 대명사 ☑ 접속사가 들어가야 한다.
   → most of 앞의 선행사가 ☑ 사람 ☐ 사물이다.
3. 정답 선택하기 정답 (C)

우리는 대략 30명의 지원자들을 면접을 봤는데, 그들 모두 열정적으로 보였다.

실전 문제

01.(A)	02.(B)	03.(C)	04.(B)	05.(C)	06.(B)
07.(C)	08.(C)	09.(D)	10.(A)	11.(B)	12.(B)
13.(B)	14.(B)	15.(C)	16.(C)	17.(D)	18.(C)
19.(B)	20.(A)	21.(C)	22.(C)	23.(B)	24.(C)

01. 형용사절 구별

교육을 담당하고 있는 Bryant 씨는 다음 달에 워크숍을 개최할 계획을 세우고 있다.

[해설] 선택지가 다양한 품사의 단어들로 구성되어 있으므로 문법 문제이다. 빈칸이 포함된 절은 문장의 주어와 동사 사이에 콤마와 함께 삽입된 형용사절이므로 형용사절 접속사인 관계대명사 (A) who가 정답이다.

[어휘] in charge of ~을 담당하는

02. 선행사에 따른 관계대명사 구별

Fowler 씨는 극심한 차량 혼잡이 발생되는 구역들을 피하는 우회 도로를 이용하기로 결정했다.

[해설] 선택지가 다양한 품사의 단어들로 구성되어 있으므로 문법 문제이다. 빈칸 뒤에 불완전한 절이 있는데, 이 절은 빈칸 앞에 위치한 사물 선행사 bypass를 설명하는 내용에 해당된다. 따라서 사물 선행사를 수식하는 관계대명사 (B) that이 정답이다.

[어휘] bypass 우회 도로

03. 소유격 관계대명사

Cuddy 씨는 내일 발표를 하는 그녀의 매니저에게 설문 조사 결과를 보냈다.

[해설] 선택지가 다양한 관계대명사로 구성되어 있으므로 문법 문제이다. 빈칸 뒤에 위치한 presentation은 그 앞에 위치한 manager의 업무로 판단할 수 있으므로 소유 관계에 해당된다. 따라서 소유격 관계대명사인 (C) whose가 정답이다.

[어휘] survey result 설문 결과   presentaion 발표

04. 주격 관계대명사

자신의 오래된 책을 기증한 Galloway는 도서판매 기간 동안 도서관에서 자원봉사하기로 했습니다.

[해설] 선택지가 다양한 품사의 단어들로 구성되어 있으므로 문법 문제이다. 빈칸은 문장의 주어와 동사 사이에 콤마와 함께 삽입된 형용사절의 동사 donated의 주어 자리이므로 주격 관계대명사 (B) who가 정답이다. (C) that은 삽입절을 이끌지 못한다.

[어휘] donate 기부하다   volunteer 자원봉사를 하다

05. 선행사에 따른 관계대명사 구별

에너지를 더욱 효율적으로 발생시키는 새로운 터빈이 개발되는 중이다.

[해설] 선택지가 접속사와 대명사로 구성되어 있으므로 문법 문제이다. 빈칸과 동사 is 사이에 동사 generates로 시작되는 불완전한 절이 있는데, 이 절은 빈칸 앞에 위치한 사물 선행사 turbine을 설명하는 내용에 해당된다. 따라서 사물 선행사를 수식하는 관계대명사 (C) that이 정답이다. (B)

[어휘] approve ~을 승인하다 additional 추가의 payment 지불(금) colleague 동료 직원

paraphrasing 정답   1. (b)   2. (c)   3. (a)

08-10은 다음 문자 메시지 대화를 참조하시오.

William Emery [오전 11:03]
Susan, 오늘 데이터베이스와 관련해 혹시 무슨 문제라도 겪고 계신가요?

Susan Vaca [오전 11:04]
아뇨, 저한테는 정상적으로 작동되고 있는 것 같은데요. 왜 물으시는 거죠?

William Emery [오전 11:05]
제가 ⁰⁸요약 보고서 때문에 신발 시장에 관한 분석 조사를 마무리 지으려는 중입니다. 그런데, 로그인하려고 하면, 계속 오류 메시지가 나타나고 있어요. 정확한 로그인 정보와 비밀번호를 사용하고 있는데도 말이에요. ⁰⁹저는 그저 지난 3년 동안의 우리 지역에 대한 통계 자료 내역이 들어 있는 파일들의 사본만 다운로드하면 됩니다.

Susan Vaca [오전 11:06]
제가 처리해 드릴 수 있어요.

William Emery [오전 11:07]
⁰⁹정말 고맙습니다! 제게 큰 도움이 될 거예요.

Susan Vaca [오전 11:10]
제가 이메일로 보내 드리면 될까요?

William Emery [오전 11:11]
실은, 그 파일 크기가 그렇게 하기에는 너무 많이 클 거라고 생각해요. ¹⁰제가 그냥 외장 하드 드라이브를 갖고 당신 사무실에 곧 들를게요.

behave (기계 등이) 작동되다, 돌아가다   normally 정상적으로   analysis 분석 (자료)   summary 요약   sign in 로그인하다   demographics 통계 자료   breakdown 내역(서), 명세(서)   region 지역   handle ~을 처리하다   far 아주, 대단히   stop by ~에 들르다   external hard drive 외장 하드 드라이브   shortly 곧

08. 세부사항 문제

Emery 씨는 무슨 종류의 프로젝트를 맡아 일하고 있는가?
(A) 신발 디자인
(B) 데이터베이스 업그레이드
(C) 직원 평가
(D) 연구 조사 문서

[해설] 11시 5분 메시지에서 Emery 씨는 요약 보고서 때문에 신발 시장에 관한 분석 조사(analysis of the footwear market for my summary report)를 마무리 지으려는 중이라고 알리고 있으므로 연구 조사 문서 작업을 뜻하는 (D)가 정답이다.

[어휘] work on ~을 맡아 작업하다, ~에 대한 일을 하다   evaluation 평가(서)

09. 의도 파악 문제

오전 11시 6분에, Vaca 씨가 "I can handle that"이라고 썼을 때 무엇을 하기로 동의하는가?
(A) Emery 씨의 비밀번호를 재설정해 줄 것이다.
(B) 계약서 사본을 출력해 줄 것이다.
(C) 몇몇 파일을 다운로드해 줄 것이다.
(D) IT 부서에 연락할 것이다.

[해설] 앞선 메시지에서 Emery 씨가 특정 통계 자료가 들어 있는 파일들의 사본만 다운로드하면 된다고(I just need to download a copy of files ~) 알리자 Vaca 씨가 "I can handle that"이라고 답변했고, 바로 뒤이어 Emery 씨가 고맙다는 말과 큰 도움이 될 것이라는 말을 전하는 상황이다. 따라서 파일 다운로드를 도와 주겠다는 의미로 쓰인 말임을 알 수 있으므로 이에 해당되는 (C)가 정답이다.

[어휘] reset ~을 다시 설정하다, 다시 맞추다   contract 계약(서)

10. 세부사항 문제

Emery 씨는 곧 무엇을 할 계획인가?
(A) 자신의 컴퓨터 점검받기
(B) 발표하기
(C) Vaca 씨가 보낸 이메일 읽기
(D) 직접 Vaca 씨를 방문하기

[해설] 맨 마지막 메시지에서 Emery 씨가 외장 하드 드라이브를 갖고 Vaca 씨의 사무실에 곧 들르겠다고(I'll just stop by your office with an external hard drive shortly) 알리고 있으므로 직접 방문한다고 한 (D)가 정답이다.

paraphrasing   stop by your office 당신의 사무실에 들르다 → Visit Ms. Vaca in person 직접 Vaca 씨를 방문하다

[어휘] in person 직접 (가서)

paraphrasing 정답   1. (a)   2. (c)   3. (b)

DAY 17

PART 5   문법 | 형용사절 접속사

확인 문제 해석

❶ 그녀는 컴퓨터 소프트웨어를 다운받았는데, 그것의 일련번호를 이메일로 받았다.
❷ Terry는 2년 전에 인턴으로 일했던 지원자들 중 한 명이다.
❸ 그는 새 레스토랑을 열 상업용 부동산을 찾고 있다.
❹ 나는 5개의 제안서를 검토했는데, 그것 중 2개가 우리의 요구에 충족한다.
❺ Smith 씨가 주최한 자선 파티는 꽤 성공적이었다.

연습 문제

01.(B)   02.(A)   03.(C)   04.(A)   05.(B)   06.(C)

01.

1. 선택지 보고 문법/어휘 문제 파악하기   ☑ 문법 문제   ☐ 어휘 문제
2. 빈칸 분석하기   문장의 본동사 (is directed)
   빈칸 뒤에 있는 것 ☑ 동사 ☐ 부사
   → 빈칸에는 ☐ 전치사 ☑ 접속사가 들어가야 한다.

(B) 병원 예약 시간에 다녀오기
(C) 자신의 차량 수리받기
(D) 고객과 만나기

[해설] 첫 문장에 Meyers 씨와 업무상 점심 식사를 했다는 말이 있으므로 고객과 만나는 시간을 가진 것으로 판단할 수 있다. 따라서 (D)가 정답이다.

paraphrasing business lunch with ~와 함께 한 업무상 점심 식사 → Met with a client 고객과 만났다

[어휘] colleague 동료   fix ~을 고치다, 바로 잡다

04. 세부사항 문제

Rhodes 씨는 Pearson 씨에게 무엇을 하도록 요청하는가?
(A) 회의 일정 재조정하기
(B) 책임자와 이야기하기
(C) 몇몇 구직 지원자들을 환영하기
(D) 대회의실 예약하기

[해설] 두 번째 문장과 세 번째 문장에 단체 면접 시간(the group interview)에 늦을 수도 있으니 로비에서 모든 사람들을 맞이해 달라고(Could you greet everyone in the lobby ~) 요청하고 있으므로 (C)가 정답이다.

paraphrasing greet ~을 맞이하다 → Welcome ~을 환영하다

[어휘] director 책임자, 관리자, 임원, 이사   job candidate 구직 지원자   reserve ~을 예약하다

paraphrasing 정답   1. (c)   2. (b)   3. (a)

05-07은 다음 문자 메시지 대화를 참조하시오.

Ashley McHale [오전 9:43]
안녕하세요, Darrell 씨. 부탁 하나 들어줄 수 있어요?

Darrell Lawson [오전 9:46]
무슨 일이시죠?

Ashley McHale [오전 9:47]
제가 오늘 오후 1시에 05잠재 고객들로 구성된 그룹을 이끌고 체육관을 견학시켜 드릴 예정인데, 06제가 킥복싱 수업을 하기로 되어 있다는 사실을 지금 막 알았어요.

Darrell Lawson [오전 9:53]
제가 몇몇 추가 교대 근무를 맡을 생각이에요. 무슨 레벨이죠?

Ashley McHale [오전 9:54]
06중급 수업이고, 오후 1시 30분부터 2시 30분까지 진행됩니다.

Darrell Lawson [오전 9:55]
제가 할게요.

Ashley McHale [오전 9:56]
06고마워요! 정말로 감사 드립니다.

Darrell Lawson [오전 9:57]
07출석 예정인 회원들의 이름을 미리 확인하는 것이 가능할까요?

Ashley McHale [오전 9:58]
물론이죠. 이메일로 받아 보시겠어요, 아니면 출력본으로 뽑아 드릴까요?

Darrell Lawson [오전 9:59]
무엇이든 더 편리하신 것으로 해 주세요.

prospective 잠재적인, 유망한   look to부정사 ~하고 싶어 하다   pick up ~을 얻다, 획득하다   shift 교대 근무(조)   add A to B A를 B에 추가하다   intermediate 중급의   run 진행되다, 운영되다   I'm on it. 제가 하겠습니다. 제가 맡겠습니다.   find out ~을 확인하다, 알아보다   in advance 미리, 사전에   in attendance 출석하는, 참석하는

05. 세부사항 문제

오늘 누가 McHale 씨와 견학을 할 것인가?
(A) 잠재 회원들
(B) 기업 투자자들
(C) 구직 지원자들
(D) 피트니스 강사들

[해설] 견학 일정이 언급되는 9시 47분 메시지에 McHale 씨가 잠재 고객들로 구성된 그룹을 이끌고 체육관을 견학시켜 줄 예정이라고(I'm showing a group of prospective customers around the gym today) 알리고 있는데, 여기서 잠재 고객은 체육관 회원이 될 가능성이 있는 사람들을 가리키므로 (A)가 정답이다.

paraphrasing prospective customers 잠재 고객들 → Potential members 잠재 회원들

[어휘] potential 잠재적인   corporate 기업의   investor 투자자   applicant 지원자   instructor 강사

06. 의도 파악 문제

오전 9시 55분에, Lawson 씨가 "I'm on it"이라고 썼을 때 의미하는 것은 무엇이겠는가?
(A) 교대 근무 시간 일정표를 검토할 것이다.
(B) McHale 씨를 위해 일부 정보를 찾을 것이다.
(C) 운동 수업을 가르칠 시간이 난다.
(D) 레벨이 맞다는 것을 확인해 줄 수 있다.

[해설] 앞서 9시 47분에 McHale 씨가 자신이 킥복싱 수업을 하기로 되어 있다(I'm supposed to teach a kickboxing class)는 말과 함께 그것이 중급 수업이고 1시 30분부터 2시 30분까지(Intermediate, and it runs from 1:30 P.M. to 2:30 P.M.) 진행된다고 알린 뒤에 Lawson 씨가 "I'm on it"이라고 말하자 McHale 씨가 감사의 말을 전하는 상황이다. 따라서 Lawson 씨가 그 수업을 대신해 줄 수 있다는 의미로 쓰인 말이라는 것을 알 수 있으므로 (C)가 정답이다.

07. 세부사항 문제

Lawson 씨는 McHale 씨에게 무엇을 하도록 요청하는가?
(A) 추가 비용 지불 승인하기
(B) 계획에 관해 동료 직원과 이야기하기
(C) 몇몇 홍보용 자료 준비하기
(D) 참가자들에 관한 정보 제공하기

[해설] 9시 57분 메시지에서 Lawson 씨가 출석 예정인 회원들의 이름을 미리 확인하는 것이 가능할지(Would it be possible to find out in advance the names of the members who will be in attendance?) 묻는 것으로 그 회원들의 이름을 알려 달라고 요청하고 있으므로, '참가자 관련 정보의 제공'을 의미하는 (D)가 정답이다.

paraphrasing the names of the members who will be in attendance 출석 예정인 회원들의 이름 → information about participants 참가자들에 관한 정보

는 처음에 언급된 현수막 주문과(Have you placed the order for our banners yet?) 관련해 변경해야 하는 수량을 나타낸다. 따라서 주문 수량을 변경할 수 있다는 점에 대한 안도를 나타내는 말임을 알 수 있으므로 (B)가 정답이다.

[어휘] opportunity to부정사 ~할 수 있는 기회

04.

> Giorgio Pirozzi [오전 11:43]
> 저는 Goldcliff 콘퍼런스 홀에 와 있습니다. 안타깝게도, 이곳의 연회실은 우리가 시상식 만찬 행사를 개최하기를 원하는 날에 예약되어 있어요.
>
> Wooseok Lee [오전 11:47]
> 이용 가능한 다른 방들이 있나요?
>
> Giorgio Pirozzi [오전 11:48]
> 네, 약 200명의 사람들을 수용할 수 있는 작은 방이 있어요. 하지만 말씀드린 다른 연회실처럼 최근에 리모델링되어 있지는 않습니다. 오셔서 한번 보시겠어요?
>
> Wooseok Lee [오전 11:49]
> 제가 지금 우리의 신규 고객이신 Lara Kennedy 씨의 사무실에서 일을 마무리하는 중입니다. 곧 그쪽으로 가겠습니다.

ballroom 연회실   wrap A up A를 마무리하다   shortly 곧, 머지 않아

Q. Lee 씨는 어디에서 Pirozzi 씨를 만날 계획인가?
(A) 콘퍼런스 행사장에서
(B) 신규 고객의 사무실에서

[문제 키워드] Where / Mr. Lee / meet / Mr. Pirozzi

[해설] 키워드인 meet이 직접적으로 언급되어 있지 않으므로 패러프레이징된 부분인 be there를 찾는다. 11시 49분 메시지에서 Lee 씨는 Pirozzi 씨에게 곧 그곳으로 가겠다고(I'll be there shortly) 알리고 있는데, 첫 메시지에서 Pirozzi 씨는 현재 Goldcliff Conference Hall에 있다고(I'm here at the Goldcliff Conference Hall) 말했으므로 (A)가 정답이다.

실전 문제

| 01.(A) | 02.(B) | 03.(D) | 04.(C) | 05.(A) | 06.(C) |
| 07.(D) | 08.(D) | 09.(C) | 10.(D) | | |

01-02는 다음 문자 메시지 대화를 참조하시오.

> Gary Johnson [오후 4:07]
> ⁰¹제 컴퓨터가 네트워크에 다시 접속되지 않고 있어요. 오셔서 한번 확인해 주시겠어요?
>
> Rachel Morrow [오후 4:08]
> 죄송하지만, 제가 이미 교육 때문에 밖에 나왔어요. 오늘은 복귀하지 않을 겁니다. 하지만 Vanessa Reynolds 씨가 아직 사무실에 있는 것 같아요.
>
> Gary Johnson [오후 4:09]
> 알겠습니다. 그분께 연락해 보도록 할게요.
>
> Rachel Morrow [오후 4:10]
> 그건 그렇고, ⁰²근무하시는 층에 계시는 모든 분들이 곧 새 컴퓨터를 지급받는다고 들었어요.
>
> Gary Johnson [오후 4:11]
> 그럴 때도 됐죠! 좋은 소식 알려 주셔서 감사합니다.

leave for ~하러 떠나다, 출발하다   get in touch with ~와 연락하다   by the way (화제 전환 시) 그건 그렇고   It's about time. 그럴 때가 됐다.

01. 추론 문제

Morrow 씨에 관해 무엇이 사실일 것 같은가?
(A) IT 부서에 근무하고 있다.
(B) 보통 오후 4시에 퇴근한다.
(C) 최근에 새로운 장비를 설치했다.
(D) 사무용품을 구입하는 책임을 맡고 있다.

[해설] 첫 메시지에서 Johnson 씨가 자신의 컴퓨터가 네트워크에 접속되지 않는다는(My computer can't connect to the network) 문제점과 함께 이를 해결할 수 있도록 Morrow 씨에게 도움을 요청하고 있으므로 Morrow 씨는 컴퓨터 관련 업무를 하는 IT 부서의 직원임을 알 수 있다. 따라서 (A)가 정답이다.

[어휘] install ~을 설치하다   equipment 장비   in charge of ~을 책임지고 있는   supplies 용품, 물품

02. 의도 파악 문제

오후 4시 11분에 Johnson 씨가 "It's about time"이라고 썼을 때 의미한 것은 무엇이겠는가?
(A) 자신의 네트워크 연결 상태를 복구했다.
(B) 장비 업그레이드를 계속 원해 왔다.
(C) Reynolds 씨가 만날 시간이 없다고 말했다.
(D) Morrow 씨가 요청에 응하는 데 너무 오래 걸리고 있다.

[해설] 바로 앞선 메시지에서 Morrow 씨가 상대방인 Johnson 씨가 근무하는 층에 있는 모든 사람들이 새 컴퓨터를 지급받는다는 사실을(everyone on your floor will get new computers soon) 언급한 뒤로 'It's about time'이라고 반응하고 있다. 그리고 바로 뒤이어 좋은 소식에 고맙다고 인사하는 것으로 보아, 컴퓨터 장비가 곧 교체되어야 하는 상황이었음을 알 수 있으므로 이와 같은 장비 교체를 바라 왔다는 의미로 쓰인 (B)가 정답이다.

[어휘] restore ~을 복구하다, 복원하다   respond to ~에 응하다   request 요청(서)

paraphrasing 정답 1. (a)   2. (c)   3. (b)

03-04는 다음 문자 메시지를 참조하시오.

> 수신: Haley Pearson
> 발신: Clark Rhodes
> 전송 시간: 화요일 오후 1:32
>
> ⁰³Meyers 씨와 업무상의 점심 식사를 마치고 돌아가는 길인데 교통이 혼잡합니다. 지금 제가 차 안에 있기는 하지만, 영업직 ⁰⁴단체 면접 시간에 조금 늦을 수도 있습니다. 로비에서 모든 분들을 맞이해 대회의실 C로 안내해 주시겠습니까? 감사합니다!

congested 혼잡한   sales position 영업직   direct A to B A를 B로 안내하다

03. 세부사항 문제

Rhodes 씨는 점심 시간에 무엇을 했을 것 같은가?
(A) 그의 동료에게 이메일 보내기

DAY 16   139

PART 7 문자 메시지

풀이 방법 해석

Howard Ball [오전 9:39]
Kelly, Fulbright 여행사를 위한 팸플릿 진행 상황이 어때요?

Kelly Banks [오전 9:40]
그들이 세 번 접히는 것을 흑백으로 2천 부 필요로 했었죠, 맞죠? 내일 아침에 완료될 거예요.

Howard Ball [오전 9:41]
그들이 지금 막 전화해서 흑백이 아니라 컬러로 원한다고 했어요.

Kelly Banks [오전 9:42]
정말요? 그럼 이것에 대해 Aaron을 불러들여야 겠네요.

Howard Ball [오전 9:43]
Aaron, 당신의 인쇄기들이 내일까지 세 번 접히는 팸플릿을 컬러로 2천 부 완료할 수 있을까요?

Aaron Foster [오전 9:44]
지금 바로 시작해야겠지만, 할 수 있어요.

Howard Ball [오전 9:45]
아주 좋아요. 그들에게 알릴게요.

 연습 문제

01.(B) 02.(A) 03.(B) 04.(A)

01.

Earl Ledezma [오전 10:15]
여전히 과학 컨벤션 행사를 위해 발표자가 한 분 더 필요합니다. 아이디어가 있으신 분 계신가요?

Georgia Behrens [오전 10:16]
제가 Springfield 대학에 계신 **Jeremiah Otis 박사님**의 아주 흥미로운 강연을 온라인으로 봤습니다. 행사 일정에 그분이 추가되면 정말 좋을 텐데요. **하지만 그날 박사님이 시간이 있으실지는 잘 모르겠습니다.**

Earl Ledezma [오전 10:17]
제가 확인해 볼게요.

Georgia Behrens [오전 10:18]
감사합니다. 이번 주 후반에 만나서 이에 대해 더 논의해 봅시다.

presenter 발표자   **addition** 보탬(이 되는 것), 추가(되는 것)

Q. 오전 10시 17분에, Ledezma 씨가 "I'll check on it"라고 썼을 때 의미한 것은 무엇이겠는가?
(A) Springfield 대학에서 열리는 행사를 위해 자리를 예약해 볼 것이다.
(B) Otis 박사가 시간이 나는지를 알아볼 것이다.

[문제 키워드] At 10:17 A.M. / what / Mr. Ledezma / mean / "I'll check on it"

[해설] 10시 16분 메시지에서 Behrens 씨가 Jeremiah Otis 박사를 언급하면서 그분이 당일에 시간이 있을지 모르겠다고(I'm not sure whether he is free on that day) 하자, Ledezma 씨가 '내가 확인해 보겠다'고 답변하는 상황이다. 따라서 Otis 박사가 시간이 나는지를 확인해 보겠다는 뜻임을 알 수 있으므로 (B)가 정답이다.

[어휘] reserve ~을 예약하다   find out ~을 알아보다

02.

[오후 1:02] Kasumi Yamaoka
혹시 점심 식사를 마치고 오셨나요?

[오후 1:03] Adam Emerson
네, 막 왔어요. 왜 그러시죠?

[오후 1:04] Kasumi Yamaoka
제가 오늘 오후에 있을 회의를 위해 데이터베이스에서 일부 연구 자료를 다운로드한 다음에 출력해야 하는데, **제 비밀번호에 뭔가 문제가 생겼어요. 입력할 때 계속 오류 메시지가 떠요.**

[오후 1:05] Adam Emerson
그동안 제 사무실로 오셔서 제 계정을 이용하셔도 됩니다.

[오후 1:06] Kasumi Yamaoka
감사합니다! 곧 뵙겠습니다.

account 계정   **in the meantime** 그 사이에, 그러는 동안

Q. Yamaoka 씨는 무슨 문제점을 언급하는가?
(A) 비밀번호가 작동되지 않는다.
(B) 프린터에 잉크가 다 떨어졌다.

[문제 키워드] What problem / Ms. Yamaoka / mention

[해설] 키워드인 problem이 직접적으로 언급되어 있지 않으므로 패러프레이징된 부분인 something is wrong을 찾는다. 1시 4분 메시지에서 Yamaoka 씨가 비밀번호에 뭔가 문제가 있다는 말과 함께 계속 오류 메시지가 뜬다고(~ something is wrong with my password. I keep getting an error message ~) 알리고 있으므로 (A)가 정답이다.

[어휘] out of A A가 다 떨어진, 다 쓴

03.

David Chung [오후 3:09]
혹시 우리 현수막들을 주문하셨나요?

Corrine Burcham [오후 3:10]
아직이요. 막 인쇄소에 왔어요. 시내 구역에 교통이 너무 혼잡해서요.

David Chung [오후 3:11]
아, 정말 운이 좋네요! Kaster 씨께서 모든 출입구에 현수막을 걸고 싶어 하신다는 사실을 막 알게 되어서, **1개가 아니라 3개가 필요해요.**

Corrine Burcham [오후 3:12]
그렇게 처리할 수 있습니다. 전부 같아야 하는 게 맞죠?

David Chung [오후 3:13]
네, 맞아요, 감사합니다!

place an order for ~을 주문하다   **banner** 현수막   **congested** 혼잡한   **hang** ~을 걸다   **take care of** ~을 처리하다

Q. 오후 3시 11분에 Chung 씨가 "Oh, how lucky"라고 썼을 때 의미한 것은 무엇이겠는가?
(A) 교통혼잡을 피할 수 있는 더 좋은 방법을 찾았다.
(B) 변동 사항을 요청할 수 있는 기회를 놓치지 않았다.

[문제 키워드] At 3:11 P.M. / what / Mr. Chung / mean / "Oh, how lucky"

[해설] 해당 표현이 제시된 문장에 1개가 아니라 3개가 필요하다는(~ we need three of them instead of one) 말이 함께 제시되어 있는데, 이

해 사과 드립니다. ⁰⁴기술자가 해당 작업을 완료한 후에는, 고객 만족도 설문지를 작성하실 수 있도록 저희 웹사이트를 방문해 주시기 바랍니다. 미리 감사의 말씀 드립니다.

안녕히 계십시오.

Houston 가전제품

inform A that A에게 ~라고 알리다   drain hose 배수용 호수   prone to ~하기 쉬운   leak (물, 가스 등) 새다, 누설되다   damage 피해, 손상, 손해   set up ~을 정하다, 준비하다   fill out ~을 작성하다

01. 형용사 어휘

[해설] part를 수식해 기계 부품의 특성을 나타낼 형용사가 필요한데, 바로 다음 문장에 호스에 누수 현상이 발생될 가능성이 있다는 말과 어울려야 하므로 '결함이 있는'을 뜻하는 (C) faulty가 정답이다.

[어휘] discounted 할인된   changeable 변하기 쉬운, 바꿀 수 있는

02. 접속부사

[해설] 빈칸 앞에는 '누수 발생 가능성'이라는 문제점이, 빈칸 뒤에는 피해가 생기기 전에 반드시 교체하도록 촉구하는 내용이 쓰여 있으므로 각각 원인과 결과에 해당함을 알 수 있다. 따라서 '그러므로, 따라서' 등의 의미로 결과를 나타낼 때 사용하는 (B) Therefore가 정답이다.

[어휘] apart from ~ 외에는, ~을 제외하고, ~뿐만 아니라   regardless (of) (~에) 상관 없이   still 그런데도

03. 알맞은 문장 고르기

(A) 새로운 호스 설치 작업에 대해서는 청구 요금이 발생되지 않을 것입니다.
(B) 가까운 소매 대리점으로 귀하의 기기를 반품하시기 바랍니다.
(C) 저희는 귀하를 7월 첫째 주로 일정을 잡았습니다.
(D) 저희 제품의 특징이 회사 웹사이트에 게시되어 있습니다.

[해설] 빈칸 앞에는 문제점과 함께 기술자를 보내는 조치 방법이, 빈칸 뒤에는 불편함에 대해 사과하는 내용이 제시되어 있으므로 해당 호스 부품 교체 작업과 관련된 것으로서 청구 요금이 발생되지 않는다는 정보를 제시하는 (A)가 정답이다.

[어휘] charge 청구 요금, 부과 요금   installation 설치   return ~을 반품하다, 반납하다   appliance (가전) 기기   retail location 소매 대리점   feature 특징, 기능

04. 동사의 형태

[해설] 빈칸 앞에 쓰인 주어 the technician이 작업을 완료하는 시점은 앞서 언급된 We will send a technician ~ 부분과 같이 미래의 일인데, 여기서 After절은 현재 시제 동사로 미래를 대신하는 시간/조건 부사절의 하나에 해당되므로 현재 시제인 (D) completes가 정답이다.

05-08은 다음 편지를 참조하시오.

12월 23일
Barry Harper
Pollock 로 4160번지
오마하, 네브래스카 주 68102

Harper 씨께,

<Airplane Planet> 잡지를 구독해 주셔서 감사 드립니다. ⁰⁵저희는 항공기와 항공 산업에 관한 가장 최신의 정보를 제공해 드리는 데 전념하고 있습니다. ⁰⁶저희 잡지의 모든 내용물은 오직 전현직 비행사와 항공기 설계자에 의해서만 작성됩니다. 이분들의 경험이 항공 분야의 새로운 발전상을 분석하고 이해하는 데 도움이 됩니다. ⁰⁷이러한 이유로, 이분들의 기사와 설명은 모두 신뢰할 수 있는 것입니다. ⁰⁸저희 잡지에 글을 기고하시는 데 관심이 있으실 경우, 귀하의 자격 인증서와 어떠한 관련 증빙 서류든지 꼭 포함시켜 주시기 바랍니다.

안녕히 계십시오.

<Airplane Planet> 구독 신청 관리팀

subscribe to ~을 구독하다, ~의 서비스에 가입하다   up-to-date 최신의   aviation 항공 산업, 항공술   analyze ~을 분석하다   development 발전(상), 개발   field 분야   commentary 설명, 해설   reliable 신뢰할 수 있는   credentials 자격 인증서   relevant 관련된   references 증빙 서류

05. 동사의 형태

[해설] 동사 commit은 목적어를 필요로 하는 타동사인데, 빈칸 뒤에 전치사 to만 있으므로 수동태로 쓰여야 한다. 따라서 (B) are committed가 정답이다. 참고로, 'be committed to -ing'는 하나의 표현으로 기억해 두는 것이 좋다.

06. 알맞은 문장 고르기

(A) 올해 말까지 귀하의 구독 신청을 갱신하실 수 있습니다.
(B) 이 편지에 동봉된 멤버십 관련 약관을 읽어 보시기 바랍니다.
(C) 저희 잡지의 모든 내용물은 오직 전현직 비행사와 항공기 설계자에 의해서만 작성됩니다.
(D) 귀하의 구독 신청에는 저희 잡지의 디지털 버전에 대한 이용 권한도 포함되어 있습니다.

[해설] 빈칸 뒤에 이어지는 문장에 특정 대상을 지칭하는 Their와 함께 그들의 경험이 크게 도움이 된다고 알리고 있으므로 그 대상에 해당되는 사람들을 언급해 그들이 하는 일을 설명하는 (C)가 정답이다.

[어휘] renew ~을 갱신하다   terms and conditions (계약 등의) 약관   contents 내용물   current 현재의   former 전직의, 과거의   access to ~에 대한 이용, 접근, 접속   as well ~도, 또한

07. 접속부사

[해설] 빈칸 앞에는 특정 인물들의 경험이 큰 도움이 된다는 말이, 빈칸 뒤에는 그 사람들이 쓴 기사가 신뢰할 수 있다는 말이 쓰여 있으므로 각각 원인과 결과에 해당되는 흐름임을 알 수 있다. 따라서 '이러한 이유로'라는 의미로 결과를 나타낼 때 사용하는 (B) For this reason이 정답이다.

[어휘] despite that 그러함에도 불구하고   in part 부분적으로는, 일부   conversely 반대로, 역으로

08. 동사의 형태

[해설] 전치사 in의 목적어 역할을 함과 동시에 그 뒤에 이어진 전치사 to와 결합해 사용할 수 있는 단어가 필요하므로 동명사 (A) contributing이 정답이다. 명사인 (B) contribution은 셀 수 있는 명사에 해당되므로 부정관사 a가 함께 쓰여야 한다.

[어휘] contribute 기고하다   contribution 기고, 기부, 기여

PART 6 접속부사 – 인과

풀이 방법 해석

McBee 씨께,

저희는 귀하가 요청하신 대로 12월 9일 귀하의 카드로 결제된 28.73달러 금액의 거래 두 건을 검토하였고, 실수로 두 번 청구된 것으로 결론지었습니다.

그러므로 저희는 두 번째 것을 취소하였습니다. 또한, 귀하의 지불 잔액에서 28.73달러를 제외시켰습니다. 그게 다가 아닙니다. 사과하기 위해 저희는 3월까지 귀하의 지불 잔액에 대해 이자를 동결하기로 결정하였습니다. 귀하가 이 조치에 만족하시길 바랍니다. 저희 신용 회사는 귀하를 고객으로 모실 수 있어서 기쁘고 함께 계속 거래하기를 기대합니다.

Southfield Credit 고객 서비스 드림

연습 문제

01.(B) 02.(A) 03.(A) 04.(A)

01.

등록 인원 부족으로 인해, 귀하께서 신청하신 ES201 강의는 이번 학기에 수업을 하지 않을 것입니다. 결과적으로, 정규 학생 신분을 유지하기 위해, 귀하께서는 반드시 다른 3학점짜리 강의를 선택하셔야 합니다.

due to ~로 인해 lack of ~의 부족 registration 등록 sign up for ~을 신청하다, ~에 등록하다 semester 학기 maintain ~을 유지하다 full time student 정규 학생 status 신분, 상태 credit 학점

[단서] will not be taught, select another ~ course

[해설] 빈칸 뒤에 다른 3학점짜리 강의를 선택해야 한다는 말이 있는데, 이는 ES201 강의가 열리지 않는 것에 따른 결과에 해당된다. 따라서 '결과적으로'라는 의미로 결과를 나타낼 때 사용하는 (B) Consequently가 정답이다.

[어휘] in contrast 대조적으로

02.

경매 행사에서 판매될 일부 미술품은 한 점에 1백만 달러가 넘는 가치를 지니고 있습니다. 이러한 이유로, 해당 행사에 가장 신뢰할 수 있는 사설 경비 업체가 고용되었습니다.

artwork 미술품 auction 경매 be valued at ~의 가치를 지니고 있다 piece 한 점, 작품 reliable 신뢰할 수 있는 private security 사설 경비 업체 hire ~을 고용하다

[단서] is valued at over a million dollars, the most reliable ~ hired

[해설] 빈칸 뒤에 가장 신뢰할 수 있는 경비 업체가 고용되었다는 말이 있는데, 이는 일부 미술품이 매우 비싸다는 사실에 따른 조치에 해당된다. 따라서 원인과 결과가 이어지고 있음을 알 수 있으므로 '이러한 이유로'라는 의미로 인과 관계를 나타낼 때 사용하는 (A) For this reason이 정답이다.

[어휘] additionally 추가적으로

03.

그 국제 영화제가 과거 그 어느 때보다 올해 세계적으로 더 많은 주목을 받았습니다. 따라서, 저희는 미리 저희 도시에 있는 호텔 객실을 예약하시도록 적극 권해 드립니다.

draw attention 주목을 끌다, 관심을 끌다 highly recommend (that) ~하도록 적극 권하다 book ~을 예약하다 in advance 미리, 사전에

[단서] more global attention ~ ever before, book ~ in advance

[해설] 세계적으로 더 많은 주목을 받음에 따라 미리 객실을 예약을 하도록 권하는 내용이 되어야 알맞다. 따라서 빈칸 앞뒤는 원인과 결과에 해당하므로 '따라서, 그러므로'라는 의미로 결과 앞에 사용하는 (A) Therefore가 정답이다.

04.

로튼의 시장인 Tommy Savage는 시의 비즈니스 관련 규제를 상당히 줄일 예정이라고 발표했습니다. 결과적으로, 여러 전국적인 체인점들이 향후 수개월 내로 로튼 지역에 지점을 개설하는 데 관심을 표명했습니다.

mayor 시장 significantly 상당히, 많이 reduce ~을 줄이다, 감소시키다 regulation 규제, 규정 national 전국적인 express ~을 표현하다, 나타내다 interest in ~에 대한 관심

[단서] reducing ~ regulations, opening branches

[해설] 비즈니스 관련 규제를 상당히 줄인다고 발표한 것에 따라 업체들이 해당 지역에 지점을 개설하는 데 관심을 나타냈다는 의미가 되어야 알맞으므로 두 문장이 각각 원인과 결과를 나타냄을 알 수 있다. 따라서 '결과적으로'라는 의미로 결과 앞에 사용하는 (A) As a result가 정답이다.

[어휘] on the contrary 그와는 반대로

실전 문제

01.(C) 02.(B) 03.(A) 04.(D) 05.(B) 06.(C)
07.(B) 08.(A)

01-04는 다음 편지를 참조하시오.

Houston 가전제품
Davisson 가 3665번지
코너스빌, 인디애나 주 47331

6월 30일

Brianne Wallace
Deer Haven 로 1875번지
그린빌, 사우스캐롤라이나 주 29601

Wallace 씨께,

01Swisher 7 식기 세척기 모델에 결함이 있는 부품이 있다는 사실을 알려드리게 되어 유감스럽게 생각합니다. 저희는 짧은 시간 사용에도 불구하고 배수용 호스에 누수가 발생되기 쉽다는 점을 발견했습니다. **02**따라서, 귀하의 자택에 물로 인한 피해를 야기하기 전에 반드시 교체되어야 합니다. 예약 일정을 잡으실 수 있도록 555-1320으로 저희 서비스 센터에 연락 주시기만 하면 됩니다. 편하신 시간에 귀하의 자택으로 기술자를 보내 드릴 것입니다. **03**새로운 호스 설치 작업에 대해서는 청구 요금이 발생되지 않을 것입니다. 이와 같은 불편함에 대

14. 명사절 접속사 구분: what vs. that

경제 전문가들은 무엇이 아시아 주식 시장의 하락에 영향을 미쳤는지를 알아내기 위해 노력하고 있다.

[해설] 선택지가 다양한 품사의 단어들로 구성되어 있으므로 문법 문제이다. 빈칸 뒤에 주어 없이 동사 influenced로 시작되는 불완전한 절이 있으므로 이 동사의 주어 역할을 함과 동시에 불완전한 절을 이끄는 접속사 (B) what이 정답이다. (D) that도 불완전한 절을 이끌 수 있지만, 선행사를 수식해야 하므로 빈칸 앞에 선행사가 쓰여 있지 않은 이 문장에는 맞지 않는다.

[어휘] economist 경제 전문가 figure out ~을 알아내다 influence ~에 영향을 미치다 drop 하락, 감소 stock 주식

15. 명사절 접속사의 종류: 복합관계형용사

Horton & Associates는 1,500명이 넘는 사람들을 수용할 수 있는 어느 행사장에서든 자사의 연례 시상식을 개최할 것이다.

[해설] 선택지가 다양한 품사의 단어들로 구성되어 있으므로 문법 문제이다. 빈칸 뒤에 위치한 venue를 수식함과 동시에 절을 이끌 수 있는 복합관계형용사 (D) whichever가 정답이다.

[어휘] annual 연례의 venue 행사장 accommodate ~을 수용하다

16. 상관접속사

적절한 연구 논문에는 그 안에 인용된 모든 자료에 대한 참고 문헌뿐만 아니라 공동 저자의 이름도 포함되어 있어야 한다.

[해설] 선택지가 다양한 품사의 단어들로 구성되어 있으므로 문법 문제이다. 빈칸 앞뒤에 위치한 명사구들은 모두 동사 include의 목적어가 되어야 하므로 대등한 관계의 두 요소를 연결할 '~뿐만 아니라 …도'라는 의미로 쓰이는 상관접속사 (C) as well as가 정답이다.

[어휘] proper 적절한 coauthor 공동 저자 reference 참고 문헌 source 자료, 출처 cite ~을 인용하다 unless ~하지 않는다면 despite ~에도 불구하고 in advance 미리, 사전에

17. 수동태와 능동태의 구분

육류 가격의 급격한 증가는 Burger Baron이 대부분의 메뉴에 대해 더 높은 가격을 청구하게 했다.

[해설] 선택지가 동사 cause의 다양한 형태로 구성되어 있으므로 문법 문제이다. 빈칸 앞에 명사구와 to부정사, 전치사구만 있으므로 빈칸이 문장의 동사 자리이며, 빈칸 뒤에 위치한 Burger Baron을 목적어로 취하려면 능동태가 되어야 하므로 (C) caused가 정답이다.

[어휘] sharp 급격한 rise in ~의 증가 charge ~을 청구하다, 부과하다

18. 부사 종류: 강조 부사

회사 지출 비용에 대해 항목별로 구분한 도표가 정확히 어디에서 비용 삭감이 이뤄져야 하는지를 보여 주었다.

[해설] 선택지가 다양한 품사의 단어들로 구성되어 있으므로 문법 문제이다. 동사 showed와 목적어 역할을 하는 where 명사절 사이에 위치한 빈칸은 강조 역할을 할 부사 자리이므로 (B) exactly가 정답이다.

[어휘] itemized 항목별로 구분한 table 도표 make cuts 삭감하다 exact 정확한; ~을 강요하다 exactly 정확히 exactness 정확(함)

19. 부사 어휘

Lansdale Footwear는 주말에도 근무할 의향이 있는 유능한 영업 사원들을 적극적으로 찾고 있다.

[해설] 선택지가 다양한 부사들로 구성되어 있으므로 부사 어휘 문제이다. 빈칸에 쓰일 동사는 is와 seeking 사이에 들어가 직원을 구하는 방식을 나타내야 하므로 '적극적으로'를 뜻하는 (D) actively가 정답이다.

[어휘] seek ~을 찾다, 구하다 competent 유능한 representative 직원 be willing to부정사 ~할 의향이 있다 nearly 거의 randomly 무작위로

20. 명사절 접속사의 종류: 의문부사

Godfrey 씨는 왜 Lang 씨가 공급업체를 바꾸기로 결정했는지를 궁금해하고 있다.

[해설] 선택지가 다양한 의문사들로 구성되어 있으므로 문법 문제이다. 빈칸 뒤에 위치한 절을 이끌어 타동사 wondering의 목적어 역할을 할 명사절 접속사가 필요하다. 빈칸 뒤에 완전한 절이 있으므로 완전한 절을 이끄는 명사절 접속사 (A) why가 정답이다. (B) whom과 (C) which는 불완전한 절을 이끌어야 하며, (D) whenever는 부사절 접속사이다.

[어휘] switch ~을 바꾸다 supplier 공급업체

21. 부사 어휘

Acosta 법률 사무소에서 근무하는 무급 인턴 직원들은 일반적으로 타이핑이나 문서 복사와 같은 사무 업무를 처리한다.

[해설] 선택지가 다양한 부사들로 구성되어 있으므로 부사 어휘 문제이다. 빈칸에 쓰일 부사는 동사 handle을 앞에서 수식하는 역할을 하는데, handle이 현재 시제이므로 현재 시제 동사와 어울려 일반적인 일을 나타낼 때 사용하는 (A) generally가 정답이다.

[어휘] non-paid 무급의 handle ~을 처리하다 task 업무, 일 precisely 정확히 suddenly 갑자기 reasonably 합리적으로

22. 명사절의 역할: 보어

매달 첫 번째 월요일은 공과금 고지서가 고객들에게 발송되는 때이다.

[해설] 선택지가 다양한 의문사들로 구성되어 있으므로 문법 문제이다. be동사 is 뒤로 빈칸과 함께 하나의 절이 이어지는 구조이므로 이 절은 is 뒤에서 보어 역할을 하는 명사절이 되어야 한다. 그런데 특정 날짜에 해당되는 주어와 동격이 되어야 하므로 '때'를 나타내는 명사절 접속사 (C) when이 정답이다.

[어휘] utility bill 공과금 고지서

23. 부사 어휘

<Burning Bridges>를 관람한 사람들 중에서 대략 절반이 그 영화가 지루했다고 말한다.

[해설] 선택지가 다양한 부사들로 구성되어 있으므로 부사 어휘 문제이다. 빈칸에 쓰일 부사는 '절반'이라는 규모를 나타내는 half를 수식해야 하므로 '대략'이라는 의미로 근사치를 말할 때 사용하는 (C) Roughly가 정답이다.

[어휘] smoothly 순조롭게, 부드럽게

24. 부사 어휘

공청회에 참석한 일부 패널 위원들은 해안가 지역을 개발하는 계획에 대해 격렬하게 논쟁을 벌였다.

[해설] 선택지가 다양한 부사들로 구성되어 있으므로 부사 어휘 문제이다. 빈칸에 쓰일 부사는 동사 argued를 뒤에서 수식해 논쟁을 하는 방식을 나타내야 하므로 '격렬하게'를 뜻하는 (B) forcefully가 정답이다.

[어휘] panel (토론회 등의) 패널 public hearing 공청회 argue 논쟁하다 waterfront 해안가 permanently 영구적으로

03. 부사 어휘

전동 공구의 사용으로 인해, Dunlap 산업의 생산 속도가 훨씬 더 빨라졌다.

[해설] 선택지가 다양한 부사들로 구성되어 있으므로 부사 어휘 문제이다. 빈칸에 쓰일 부사는 비교급 부사 faster를 앞에서 수식해야 하므로 '훨씬, 상당히'라는 의미로 비교급을 강조할 때 사용하는 (D) considerably가 정답이다.

[어휘] thanks to ~로 인해 ~ 덕분에   power tool 전동 공구   production 생산   exclusively 오로지, 독점적으로   potentially 잠재적으로   professionally 전문적으로

04. 명사절 접속사의 종류: 복합관계대명사

적재 구역에서 근무하는 임시 직원들은 회사 유니폼 대신에 원하는 것은 무엇이든 입는 것이 허용된다.

[해설] 선택지가 다양한 품사의 단어들로 구성되어 있으므로 문법 문제이다. 빈칸 뒤에 위치한 절을 이끌어 타동사 wear의 목적어 역할을 할 명사절 접속사가 필요하므로 선택지 중 유일하게 접속사 역할이 가능한 (B) whatever가 정답이다.

[어휘] temporary 임시의, 일시적인   loading zone 적재 구역

05. 명사절 접속사의 종류: 의문대명사

그 책의 표지에서 수정되어야 하는 것은 철자가 틀린 저자 이름이다.

[해설] 선택지가 다양한 의문사와 복합관계대명사로 구성되어 있으므로 문법 문제이다. 선택지의 의문사들 중에서 동사 should be revised의 주어로 쓰일 수 있으면서 문장 전체의 주어 역할을 할 명사절을 이끌 수 있는 의문대명사 (D) What이 정답이다. (C) Which는 선택 대상에 대해 사용한다.

[어휘] revise ~을 수정하다   cover 표지   misspelled 철자가 틀린   whoever ~하는 누구든

06. to부정사와 사용되는 명사절 접속사

Nikita's 인테리어 디자인은 매우 인기가 많은데, 그곳은 고객의 만족도를 유지하는 법을 알고 있기 때문이다.

[해설] 선택지가 여러 품사로 구성되어 있으므로 문법 문제이다. 빈칸 뒤에 위치한 to부정사와 결합 가능한 것은 의문사인데, to 이하 부분이 완전한 구조이므로 의문부사 (B) how가 정답이다. (A) what 뒤에는 주어나 목적어 등이 빠진 불완전한 구조가 이어져야 한다.

[어휘] satisfied 만족하는

07. 명사절 접속사의 종류: 의문형용사

논의는 어느 제품이 먼저 광고될 예정인지에 관해서일 것이다.

[해설] 선택지가 다양한 품사의 단어들로 구성되어 있으므로 문법 문제이다. 빈칸 앞에 본동사 will be가 있고 빈칸 뒤에 명사, 그 뒤에 불완전한 절이 있으므로 명사절 접속사가 들어가야 한다. 따라서 명사 product를 수식하면서 명사절을 이끄는 접속사 역할을 하는 (C) Which가 정답이다.

[어휘] advertise ~을 광고하다

08. 명사절의 역할: 목적어

Fowler 씨는 직원들의 출장비 환급 요청이 승인되어야 하는지를 결정하는 일을 책임지고 있다.

[해설] 선택지가 다양한 품사의 단어들로 구성되어 있으므로 문법 문제이다. decide는 타동사이므로 동명사로 쓰일 때도 목적어가 필요하다. 따라서 빈칸 이하의 절이 목적어 역할을 하는 명사절이 되어야 하므로 명사절 접속사 (D) whether가 정답이다. (B) after는 부사절 접속사이다.

[어휘] in charge of ~을 책임지는   travel expense 출장비   reimbursement 환급   approve ~을 승인하다

09. 명사절 접속사의 종류: 복합관계대명사

매장을 가장 먼저 여는 사람은 누구든지 보안 경보 장치를 끄고 금전 등록기를 켜야 한다.

[해설] 선택지가 다양한 품사의 단어들로 구성되어 있으므로 문법 문제이다. 빈칸 뒤에 동사가 두 개 있으므로 두 번째 동사 should shut off 앞까지가 주어 역할을 하는 명사절이 되어야 한다. 따라서 opens의 주어 역할을 하면서 명사절을 이끌 수 있는 접속사로 쓰이는 (A) Whoever가 정답이다.

[어휘] shut off ~을 끄다, 차단하다   turn on ~을 켜다, 틀다   cash register 금전 등록기

10. 명사절 접속사의 종류: 의문대명사

이용 가능한 여러 기업 금융 선택권들 사이에서, 어느 것이 가장 좋은 서비스를 제공해 주는지를 결정하는 것은 쉽지 않다.

[해설] 선택지가 다양한 의문사들로 구성되어 있으므로 문법 문제이다. 선택지의 의문사들 중에서 주어가 없는 불완전한 절을 이끌 수 있는 것은 의문대명사 (B) which이다. 나머지는 모두 의문부사이므로 뒤에 완전한 절이 와야 한다.

[어휘] among ~ 사이에서   determine ~을 결정하다   serve ~에게 서비스를 제공하다

11. 부사 어휘

Merrimack Flooring은 고객들에게 최고의 추천 사항을 제공하기 위해 지역 공급업체들과 긴밀히 협력하고 있다.

[해설] 선택지가 다양한 부사들로 구성되어 있으므로 부사 어휘 문제이다. 빈칸에 쓰일 부사는 자동사 works를 뒤에서 수식해 지역 업체들과 협력하는 방식을 나타내야 하므로 '긴밀히'라는 뜻으로 쓰이는 (C) closely가 정답이다.

[어휘] supplier 공급업체   abruptly 갑자기, 불쑥   heavily (양, 정도 등) 많이, 심하게

12. 명사절 접속사의 종류: whether

종업원이 추가 시간 근무를 했는지를 바탕으로, 월말 보너스 액수가 다를 수 있다.

[해설] 선택지가 다양한 품사의 단어들로 구성되어 있으므로 문법 문제이다. 빈칸과 콤마 사이에 위치한 절은 전치사 on의 목적어 역할을 할 명사절이 되어야 하므로 명사절 접속사 (D) whether가 정답이다. (B) following과 (C) despite는 전치사이다.

[어휘] based on ~을 바탕으로   amount 액수   vary 다르다, 차이가 나다   despite ~에도 불구하고

13. 명사절 접속사의 종류: 복합관계형용사

회사 노트북들에 대해 예정된 정기 점검으로 인해, 어느 것이든 빌려 가신 것을 내일까지 돌려 주시기 바랍니다.

[해설] 선택지가 다양한 접속사로 구성되어 있으므로 문법 문제이다. 빈칸 뒤에 위치한 ones를 수식함과 동시에 절을 이끌 수 있는 복합관계형용사 (A) whichever가 정답이다.

[어휘] due to ~로 인해   regular 정기적인   inspection 점검   bring back ~을 돌려 주다   check out ~을 빌려 가다, 대출하다

DAY 16

PART 5 문법 | 명사절 접속사

확인 문제 해석

❶ 회의에서 저희가 논의한 것을 당신께 보내 드릴 것입니다.
❷ 대표이사는 다음 분기에 매출이 향상될 것으로 예상했다.
❸ 이 소책자는 각 직원들이 비상 시 취해야 할 조치를 명시하고 있다.
❹ Miller 씨는 그의 부서가 개편될지 안 될지에 대해 걱정한다.
❺ 그녀는 언제 <Bahamas Post>를 구독하기 시작했는지 잊어버렸다.
❻ 이 할인권은 누구든 우리 서비스에 관심이 있는 사람에게 줄 것이다.

 연습 문제

01.(B) 02.(C) 03.(B) 04.(B) 05.(D) 06.(D)

01.
1. 선택지 보고 문법/어휘 문제 파악하기 ☑문법 문제 □어휘 문제
2. 빈칸 분석하기 문장의 본동사 (is)
   → 본동사 앞에 동사 need를 가진 절이 있다.
   → 빈칸에는 □전치사 ☑접속사가 들어가야 한다.
3. 정답 선택하기 정답 (B)

당신이 가져와야 할 것은 녹음 또는 메모를 할 기기입니다.

02.
1. 선택지 보고 문법/어휘 문제 파악하기 ☑문법 문제 □어휘 문제
2. 빈칸 분석하기 문장의 본동사 (explained)
   빈칸 뒤에 있는 것 ☑완전한 절 □불완전한 절
   → 빈칸에는 □전치사 ☑접속사가 들어가야 한다.
   → 빈칸부터 문장 끝까지가 동사의 목적어 역할을 하므로 ☑명사절 접속사 □부사절 접속사가 들어가야 한다.
3. 정답 선택하기 정답 (C)

Solomon 씨는 마케팅 팀이 더 효율적으로 운영되기 위해 자원이 더 필요하다고 설명했다.

03.
1. 선택지 보고 문법/어휘 문제 파악하기 ☑문법 문제 □어휘 문제
2. 빈칸 분석하기 문장의 본동사 (is)
   빈칸 뒤에 있는 것 ☑완전한 절 □불완전한 절
   → 빈칸에는 □전치사 ☑접속사가 들어가야 한다.
   → 빈칸부터 문장 끝까지가 be동사의 보어 역할을 하므로 ☑명사절 접속사 □부사절 접속사가 들어가야 한다.
3. 정답 선택하기 정답 (B)

Smith 씨의 강점은 그녀가 해외에서 일한 폭넓은 경험이 있다는 것이다.

04.
1. 선택지 보고 문법/어휘 문제 파악하기 ☑문법 문제 □어휘 문제
2. 빈칸 분석하기 빈칸 앞에 있는 것 ☑전치사 □부사
   빈칸 뒤에 있는 것 ☑완전한 절 □불완전한 절
   → 빈칸에는 □전치사 ☑접속사가 들어가야 한다.
   → 빈칸부터 문장 끝까지가 전치사의 목적어 역할을 하므로 ☑명사절 접속사 □부사절 접속사가 들어가야 한다.
3. 정답 선택하기 정답 (B)

Duffy 교수는 주식 시장에 투자하는 것이 수익성이 있는지에 대한 생각을 공유할 것이다.

05.
1. 선택지 보고 문법/어휘 문제 파악하기 □문법 문제 ☑어휘 문제
2. 빈칸 분석하기 빈칸 뒤에 있는 과거분사 (priced)
   → 의미 (가격이 책정된)
   → 이 과거분사와 짝꿍 표현으로 쓰이는 부사가 정답이다.
3. 정답 선택하기 정답 (D)

Caesar's 자동차 대리점은 적정한 가격이 책정된 차량을 보유하고 있는 것으로 잘 알려져 있다.

06.
1. 선택지 보고 문법/어휘 문제 파악하기 ☑문법 문제 □어휘 문제
2. 빈칸 분석하기 문장의 본동사 (indicate)
   빈칸 뒤에 있는 것 ☑완전한 절 □불완전한 절
   → 빈칸에는 □의문대명사 □복합관계대명사 ☑의문부사가 들어가야 한다.
3. 정답 선택하기 정답 (D)

당신이 어디에서 일하고 싶은지 명시하세요.

실전 문제

01.(A)	02.(A)	03.(D)	04.(B)	05.(D)	06.(B)
07.(C)	08.(D)	09.(A)	10.(B)	11.(C)	12.(D)
13.(A)	14.(B)	15.(D)	16.(C)	17.(C)	18.(B)
19.(D)	20.(A)	21.(A)	22.(C)	23.(C)	24.(B)

01. 명사절의 역할: 주어

Pro Laptop X 시리즈가 단종될 것인지 아닌지는 올해의 매출에 달려 있다.

[해설] 선택지가 접속사와 부사로 구성되어 있으므로 문법 문제이다. 빈칸 뒤에 동사가 두 개 있으므로 두 번째 동사 depends 앞까지가 주어 역할을 하는 명사절이 되어야 한다. 따라서 명사절 접속사 (A) Whether가 정답이다. (B) Although와 (C) However는 부사절 접속사이다.

[어휘] discontinue ~을 단종하다 depend on ~에 달려 있다, ~에 따라 다르다 sales 매출, 판매(량) although 비록 ~이기는 하지만 however 아무리 ~하더라도, 하지만 nearly 거의

02. 명사절의 역할: 목적어

내일 있을 회의에서, 우리 부장님께서 누가 이 새로운 프로젝트를 이끌 것인지를 발표할 것이다.

[해설] 선택지가 접속사와 대명사로 구성되어 있으므로 문법 문제이다. 동사 will announce 뒤로 빈칸과 또 다른 동사 will lead가 이어지는 구조이므로 빈칸 이하 부분이 will announce의 목적어 역할을 하는 명사절이 되어야 한다. 그런데 will lead의 주어가 빠진 불완전한 절이므로 불완전한 절을 이끄는 명사절 접속사 (A) who가 정답이다.

그의 별난 유머 감각은 The Lund가 유치하고자 하는 젊은 비즈니스 전문가들에게 꼭 들어맞는 것일 수도 있다. DJ Raghu Nayar 씨도 오늘 앞서 우리 지역에서 모습이 포착된 바 있다.

The Lund는 온라인으로 예약을 받고 있으며, 객실 점유율은 이미 매우 높은 상태이다. 사람들은 (¹⁰**전문적으로 가꿔진 정원**과 고급 레스토랑을 포함해), 이 새로운 시설이 제공해 주는 것을 보고 싶어할 뿐만 아니라 1박에 불과 125달러인 개장 기념 요금도 이용하기를 원하는 것으로 보인다.

keep A under wraps A를 비밀에 부치다   settle ~을 결정하다
heavily guarded secret 극비 사항   undisclosed 비공개의   build interest 관심을 높이다   intrigue 흥미   speculate that ~라고 짐작하다   be restricted to ~로 제한되다   invitee 초대된 사람   venue 행사장   in addition 추가로   gig 공연   quirky 별난   right fit for ~에 꼭 맞는 것   seek to부정사 ~하려 시도하다   occupancy rate 점유율   expertly 전문적으로   manicured 잘 다듬어진
take advantage of ~을 이용하다   introductory rate (초기에 손님을 많이 끌어모으기 위한) 개장 기념 요금

5월 15일 목요일 오전 9:05
수신: Yun Mao
발신: Stefan Berg

¹¹이미 이슬비가 내리기 시작했으며, 오늘 늦게는 더 강한 비가 예상되고 있습니다. 우리는 차선책으로 정해둔 장소로 축하 연회를 옮길 수밖에 없습니다. ¹²주 공연자는 지금 음향 장비를 설치하고 있습니다. 제가 일부 내용을 들어 봤는데, 정말 웃기고 재미있습니다. 우리 초청객들께서 이 특별 깜짝 공연을 아주 마음에 들어 하실 것 같습니다.

drizzle 이슬비가 내리다   heavy (정도, 양 등이) 강한, 많은   have no choice but to부정사 ~할 수밖에 없다, 어쩔 수 없이 ~해야 하다   backup 차선책의, 예비의   site 장소, 현장   set up ~을 설치하다   equipment 장비   material (공연 등의) 내용   hilarious 정말 웃기는, 아주 재미 있는

08. 세부사항 문제

5월 13일에 무슨 종류의 행사가 예정되어 있는가?
(A) 교육 세미나
(B) 시상식
(C) 지역사회 모금 행사
(D) 개장식

[해설] May 13이라는 날짜를 찾을 수 있는 첫 지문의 시작 부분에 '개장식(Ribbon-Cutting Ceremony)'이라는 말이 있고, 바로 아래 부분에 개장하게 되어 기쁘다는(We are pleased to open our doors) 말이 함께 쓰여 있으므로 (D)가 정답이다.

paraphrasing   Ribbon-Cutting Ceremony 개장식
→ grand opening 개장식

[어휘] fundraiser 모금 행사, 기금 마련 행사

09. 동의어 문제

기사에서 첫 번째 단락, 두 번째 줄의 단어 "settled"와 의미가 가장 가까운 것은 무엇인가?
(A) 달성된
(B) 최종 확정된
(C) 피로가 풀린

(D) 보상받은

[해설] is settled의 주어로 공연자를 뜻하는 the entertainer가 쓰여 있는데, 바로 뒤에 그 사람과 관련된 정보가 극비 사항으로 유지되고 있다는 말이 쓰여 있다. 따라서 공연자가 결정된 상태지만 극비로 유지되고 있는 맥락이므로 '결정된'과 유사하게 '최종 확정된'이라는 의미로 쓰이는 (B)가 정답이다.

10. True 문제

The Lund에 관해 언급된 것은 무엇인가?
(A) 유명 건축가에 의해 설계되었다.
(B) 사업체의 체인점 중 하나이다.
(C) 잘 관리된 옥외 공간이 있다.
(D) 도심 구역에 위치해 있다.

[해설] 두 번째 지문 세 번째 단락에 전문적으로 가꿔진 정원(its expertly manicured gardens)이 있다는 말이 있으므로 잘 관리된 옥외 공간이 있다고 한 (C)가 정답이다.

paraphrasing   expertly manicured gardens 전문적으로 가꿔진 정원 → well-kept outdoor space 잘 관리된 옥외 공간

[어휘] architect 건축가   well-kept 잘 관리된

11. 세부사항 문제 – 연계 문제

처음에 어디에서 음료가 제공될 것인가?
(A) 중앙 로비에서
(B) Crystal Ballroom에서
(C) Rose Lounge에서
(D) Mountainview Terrace에서

[해설] 첫 지문에서 3시에 첫 번째로 음료가 제공됨(Cocktail reception)을 알 수 있고, 이에 해당되는 부가 설명이 언급된 하단 부분에 악천후 시에 Rose Lounge로 옮긴다고(In case of poor weather, the reception will be moved to the Rose Lounge) 나타나 있다. 이와 관련해, 마지막 지문에 비가 내리고 있어서 차선책으로 정해둔 장소로 옮겨야 한다고(~ heavier rains are expected ~ We have no choice but to move the reception to our backup site) 쓰여 있으므로 Rose Lounge에서 칵테일이 제공되는 연회가 진행될 것을 알 수 있다. 따라서 (C)가 정답이다.

12. 추론 문제 – 연계 문제

행사에서 누가 특별 공연자일 것 같은가?
(A) Natalie Palmero 씨
(B) Adelaide Sagese 씨
(C) Jerry Dunston 씨
(D) Raghu Nayar 씨

[해설] 마지막 지문에 주 공연자가 장비를 설치하는 중이고 일부 내용을 들어 보니 아주 웃기고 재미있다는(The main performer ~ I've heard some of the material, and it's hilarious) 말이 쓰여 있다. 이와 같은 특징을 보일 수 있는 사람이 두 번째 지문 두 번째 단락에 언급된 코미디언 Jerry Dunston 씨인 것으로(comedian Jerry Dunston ~ His quirky humor) 유추할 수 있으므로 (C)가 정답이다.

paraphrasing 정답   1. (b)   2. (a)   3. (c)

정을 이뤘다. 올해, 시인들은 '자연'이라는 주제로 각자 창작품을 만들도록 안내 받은 반면, 과거에 열린 행사들은 주제에 대해 어떠한 제약도 없었다. Nolan Becker 씨와 Altea Santana 씨가 각각 참가작 <The Blackbird Cries>와 <Sweet River>로 2위와 3위 상을 수상했다.

올해로 5년째 개최되는 행사였기 때문에, 주최측에서는 지난 5년간의 수상작들과 '가작'으로 지정받은 작품들을 ⁰⁷<Springfield Voices>라고 불리는 시집에 포함시키기로 결정했다. 이는 앞으로 계속될 것으로 예상되는 시리즈의 1권이다. 이 시집은 지역 내에서 발행될 것이며, ⁰⁷다음 달에 도서관에서 판매될 것이다. 모든 수익금은 사우스필드의 지역 프로젝트에 자금을 제공하는 데 사용된다.

지역 내의 향후 활동에 관한 추가 정보를 원하면, www.gosouthfield.com/events를 방문하기 바란다.

top ~을 뛰어넘다, 능가하다 entry 참가자, 참가작 fist place 대상, 1등상 on display 전시 중인, 진열 중인 culminate 절정을 이루다 give a reading 낭독하다 distribute ~을 나눠 주다, 배부하다 be directed to부정사 ~하도록 안내받다 whereas ~인 반면 put restrictions on ~을 제약하다 submission 제출(한 것) respectively 각각 Honorable Mention 가작(당선 작품에 버금가는 작품) designation 지정 collection of poetry 시집 volume (잡지의) 권 ongoing 계속되는 locally 지역에서, 지역적으로 proceeds 수익금 go toward (비용 등) ~에 사용되다

05. 주제 문제

기사에서 무슨 종류의 행사가 이야기되고 있는가?
(A) 글짓기 경연대회
(B) 연례 모금 행사
(C) 미술 축제
(D) 기념일 파티

[해설] 첫 단락 초반부에 5th Annual Southfield Poetry Contest에서 있었던 일을 소개하면서 아마추어 시인들이(poets) 각자 시(poem)를 써서 제출하고 이에 대해 상을 준 행사로 설명되고 있으므로 (A)가 정답이다.

paraphrasing Poetry Contest 시 경연대회 → writing competition 글짓기 경연대회

[어휘] competition 경연대회 fundraiser 모금 행사

06. 세부사항 문제

기사에 따르면, Suarez 씨는 금요일 저녁에 무엇을 했을 것 같은가?
(A) 상금 받기
(B) 작품을 큰 소리로 읽기
(C) 다른 사람들의 작품 평가하기
(D) 인터뷰에 참가하기

[해설] Suarez 씨의 이름이 언급된 첫 단락 시작 부분에 금요일에 열린 행사에서 대상을 받았다고(Theresa Suarez, took home first place) 쓰여 있고, 같은 단락 중반부에 5위 안에 들어간 5명의 수상자들이 각자의 시를 그 자리에서 낭독한(the top five winners gave a live reading of their poems) 사실이 함께 쓰여 있다. 따라서 Suarez 씨가 큰 소리로 작품을 읽었음을 알 수 있으므로 (B)가 정답이다.

paraphrasing gave a live reading of their poems 시를 그 자리에서 낭독했다 → Read a composition aloud 작품을 큰 소리로 읽기

[어휘] accept ~을 받아들이다 cash prize 상금 composition (글, 음악 등의) 작품 aloud 큰 소리로 assess ~을 평가하다

07. True 문제

<Springfield Voices>에 관해 언급된 것은 무엇인가?
(A) 5년 전에 처음 출간되었다.
(B) Becker 씨가 홀로 만든 것이다.
(C) 베스트셀러가 되었다.
(D) 6월부터 판매될 것이다.

[해설] <Springfield Voices>가 언급된 두 번째 단락에 다음 달부터 판매되는 것으로(available for sale at the library next month) 쓰여 있는데, 지문 첫 머리에 쓰여 있는 기사 작성 날짜가 5월 3일로(May 3) 되어 있으므로 6월부터 판매된다는 것을 알 수 있다. 따라서 (D)가 정답이다.

paraphrasing available for sale 판매가 가능한 → be sold 판매되다

[어휘] solely 오로지, 단독으로

paraphrasing 정답 1. (c) 2. (b) 3. (a)

08-12은 다음 초청장과 기사, 그리고 문자 메시지를 참조하시오.

The Lund의 소유주와 전 직원들이 진심어린 마음으로
여러분을 초대합니다.

The Lund 호화 쇼
⁰⁸개장식
5월 13일 목요일 오후 3시

⁰⁸저희가 개장과 함께 출장 여행객들에게 고급 숙소를
제공해 드릴 수 있게 되어 기쁘게 생각합니다.

¹¹오후 3시: Mountainview 테라스에서 진행되는 칵테일 축하 연회*
이 행사는 초청객에 한해 입장 가능하므로 이 카드를 제시해 주십시오.

오후 4시: Crystal Ballroom에서 진행되는 개장식 및 식후 행사.
다과가 제공됩니다.

The Lund는 Sherman 가 5700번지에 위치해 있습니다.
무료 주차 가능합니다.

¹¹* 악천후 시에, 축하 연회는 Rose 라운지로 옮겨 진행됩니다.

cordially 진심으로 extravaganza 화려한 행사, 호화 쇼 Ribbon-Cutting Ceremony 개장식, 개관식 accommodations 숙소, 숙박시설 present ~을 제시하다 by invitation only 초청객에 한해 출입 가능 refreshments 다과 serve (음식 등) ~을 제공하다 in case of ~의 경우에

공연자의 이름을 비밀에 부친 The Lund

5월 11일 — The Lund 호화 쇼가 불과 며칠 후면 시작되며, 주요 공연 시간의 출연자가 ⁰⁹결정된 가운데, 그것이 누구인지에 관한 정보는 극비 사항으로 유지되어 왔다. "저희는 그분의 이름을 비공개로 유지하는 것이 저희 행사에 대한 관심과 흥미를 높이는 방법일 것이라고 생각했습니다"라고 The Lund의 지배인 Stefan Berg 씨가 말했다. "하지만 저희는 저희가 제공해 드리는 것에 대해 모든 분들께서 즐거워하실 것으로 확신합니다."

The Lund의 소유주인 Natalie Palmero 씨가 가수 Adelaide Sagese 씨와 가족간의 친밀한 유대 관계를 형성하고 있기 때문에, 많은 이들은 그녀가 바로 그 미스터리 손님일 것이라 짐작하고 있다. 참석자 명단은 오직 초청객들에 한해 제한되어 있기 때문에, 행사장에 대형 스타가 출연하더라도 놀라운 일이 아니다. 추가로, ¹²코미디언 Jerry Dunston 씨가 여러 공연을 위해 우리 도시에 와 있지만, 그의 웹사이트에는 목요일 저녁 일정에 대해 아무것도 기재해 두지 않았다.

실전 문제

01.(D) 02.(B) 03.(C) 04.(C) 05.(A) 06.(B)
07.(D) 08.(D) 09.(B) 10.(C) 11.(C) 12.(C)

01-04는 다음 기사를 참조하시오.

브룩스빌 (9월 18일) — 작곡가 Mary Cornwall 씨와 극작가 Bob Ballard 씨가 브룩스빌 단숨에 사로잡을 새로운 공연을 만들기 위해 합심했다. **01** 뮤지컬 <Alongside Me>는 12월 중순으로 예상되는 이 공연의 상연 종료 시점까지 이미 입장권이 매진되어 대단한 히트를 쳤다. —[1]—.

모든 훌륭한 공연에는 훌륭한 무대가 필요하며, 이 작품의 준비 과정에서 편법은 사용되지 않았다. —[2]—. 인테리어 디자이너 Lily O'Hare 씨가 고용되어 배경을 구성하는 여러 세트들을 디자인했다. **02** 전체 무대는 장면마다 자연스러운 전환이 이루어지게 하기 위해 회전하도록 디자인되었다.

04 주인공은 Suzanne Coeur 씨가 맡아 데뷔 공연을 펼치고 있다. —[3]—. **04** 그녀의 연기와 음악은 너무 인상적이어서 다른 어떤 경험 많은 배우들에도 필적할 만하다. 여러 영화 제작자들이 각자의 스튜디오로 그녀를 합류시키기 위해 경쟁하고 있다.

"저는 최선을 다해 왔으며, 모든 분들이 이 공연을 얼마나 사랑해 주시고 계신지를 보니 정말 겸손해질 따름입니다"라고 한 인터뷰에서 Coeur 씨가 밝혔다. "**03** 저는 12월 23일에 있을 자선 행사에서 저희가 무대에서 사용한 물품들을 경매로 판매하는 것을 정말로 고대하고 있습니다."

이 공연의 두 번째 시즌은 분명 곧 다시 찾아올 것이다. —[4]—. 발표되자마자, 입장권이 빠르게 매진될 것임을 예상해야 할 것이다.

composer 작곡가 playwright 극작가 take A by storm A를 단숨에 사로잡다 projected 예상되는 take shortcuts 편법을 쓰다, 요령을 피우다 make up ~을 구성하다 entire 전체의 rotate 회전하다, 돌다 seamless (진행 등이) 자연스러운, 순조로운 lead role 주인공 range 범위 impressive 인상적인 rival ~에 필적하다, ~에 비할 만하다 compete 경쟁하다 be humbled by ~에 겸손함을 느끼다 auction ~을 경매로 팔다 charity 자선 행사

01. 목적 문제

기사는 왜 쓰여졌는가?
(A) 극장을 홍보하기 위해
(B) 입장권에 대한 불만을 제기하기 위해
(C) 젊은 극작가의 프로필을 알리기 위해
(D) 연극 공연물에 관해 얘기하기 위해

[해설] 첫 단락에 뮤지컬 <Alongside Me>를 언급하면서 공연 기간이 아직 한참 남은 시점에 이미 입장권이 매진될 정도로 대단한 히트를 쳤다고 (The musical Alongside Me has been such a hit ~) 알린 후에 이 공연과 관련된 상세 정보를 전달하는 것으로 지문이 전개되고 있으므로 (D)가 정답이다.

paraphrasing musical 뮤지컬 → theatrical performance 연극 공연물

[어휘] profile ~의 프로필을 말하다 theatrical 연극의

02. True 문제

<Alongside Me>에 관해 사실인 것은 무엇인가?
(A) 1인 공연이다.
(B) 회전하는 세트를 특징으로 한다.
(C) 여러 상을 받았다.
(D) 경험 많은 여배우가 주연을 맡는다.

[해설] 두 번째 단락 끝부분에 자연스러운 장면 전환을 위해 무대가 회전하도록 디자인되어 있다는(The entire stage was designed to rotate ~) 말이 있으므로 이를 언급한 (B)가 정답이다.

[어휘] feature ~을 특징으로 하다 win (상 등) ~을 받다, 타다

03. 세부사항 문제

기사에 따르면, 12월 23일에 무슨 일이 있을 예정인가?
(A) <Alongside Me>의 두 번째 시즌이 시작될 것이다.
(B) 일부 출연진이 사인을 해줄 것이다.
(C) 무대 소품이 경매로 판매될 것이다.
(D) 연출자가 연설을 할 것이다.

[해설] December 23이 언급된 네 번째 단락에, 12월 23일에 있을 자선 행사에서 무대에서 사용한 물품들을 경매로 판매할 수 있기를 바란다는(~ auctioning the things we used on stage for charity on December 23) 말이 쓰여 있는데, 이는 무대 소품을 경매에 내놓겠다는 뜻이므로 (C)가 정답이다.

paraphrasing the things we used on stage 무대에서 사용한 물품 → Stage props 무대 소품

[어휘] take place (일, 행사 등이) 일어나다, 발생되다 sign autographs 사인을 해주다 props 소품 auction off ~을 경매로 처분하다 director 연출자, 감독

04. 문장 삽입 문제

[1], [2], [3] 그리고 [4]로 표시된 위치들 중에서, 다음 문장이 들어가기에 가장 적절한 곳은 어디인가?

"이는 공연을 관람한 사람들이라면 누구에게든 충격으로 다가온다."

(A) [1]
(B) [2]
(C) [3]
(D) [4]

[해설] 제시된 문장은 특정한 일을 지칭하는 This와 함께 그것이 공연을 본 사람들에게 충격적일 것이라는 의미를 나타낸다. 따라서 관람객들에게 충격적일 만한 사실이 언급된 문장을 찾아야 하며, 세 번째 단락에서 Suzanne Coeur 씨가 주인공을 맡아 데뷔 공연을 펼친다는 의미로 쓰인 문장 뒤에 위치한 [3]에 들어가, 막 데뷔한 배우답지 않게 뛰어난 연기를 선보여 충격적이라고 말하는 흐름이 되어야 알맞으므로 (C)가 정답이다.

paraphrasing 정답 1. (c) 2. (b) 3. (a)

05-07는 다음 기사를 참조하시오.

사우스필드 지역의 창의성 축하 행사

07 5월 3일 — 100명이 넘는 다른 참가자들의 작품을 누르고 **05, 06** Theresa Suarez 씨의 시 <Summer Winds>가 금요일에 열린 제5회 연례 사우스필드 시 경연대회에서 대상을 차지했다. 사우스필드 지역의 아마추어 시인들이 4월 한 달 동안에 걸쳐 사우스필드 공립 도서관에 각자의 작품을 제출했다. 출품작들은 2주 동안 해당 도서관에 전시되었으며, 이 행사는 **06** 5위 안에 들어간 5명의 수상자들이 각자의 시를 그 자리에서 낭독하고 트로피가 수여된 시상식과 함께 절

01.

Leverton 현대 미술관은 조각가 Teresa Ashton 씨의 작품 전시회인 <Shadows of Time>의 종료 날짜를 연기할 계획임을 발표했다. —[1]—. 이 행사는 애초에 2월 28일까지만 운영될 예정이었으나, 현재 추가로 3주 더 일반 대중에게 공개될 것이다. **이 전시회는 행사 첫날 겨우 21명의 사람들만 참석함으로써 더딘 출발을 보였다.** —[2]—. 하지만 독특한 조각 과정에 관한 입소문이 나면서 지역 주민들이 Ashton 씨의 조각품들에 대해 곧 관심을 갖게 되었다.

sculptor 조각가 run 운영되다, 진행되다 the public 일반 대중 additional 추가적인 exhibit 전시품 get off to ~으로 시작하다 resident 주민 gain interest in ~에 관심을 갖다 word spread 입소문이 났다 sculpting 조각 process 과정

Q. [1]과 [2]로 표시된 위치들 중에서, 다음 문장이 들어가기에 가장 적절한 곳은 어디인가?

"비평가들 또한 작품에 대해 비판적인 평론을 썼다."

(A) [1]
(B) [2]

[문제 키워드] critics, also, unfavorable

[해설] 제시된 문장은 추가 정보를 말할 때 사용하는 also(또한)와 함께 '비평가들도 비판적으로 평가했다'는 의미를 나타낸다. 따라서 전시회 시작 당시의 부정적인 상황을 언급한 문장 뒤에 위치한 [2]에 들어가 그와 같은 상황에 대한 추가 정보를 덧붙이는 흐름이 되어야 알맞으므로 (B)가 정답이다.

[어휘] critic 비평가 unfavorable 비판적인

02.

다시 정상 궤도에 올라선 콘서트 홀 개조 공사

Platinum 콘서트 홀의 주 공연장을 개조하는 계획이 다시 한번 진행되고 있다. —[1]—. **현재, 지역 기업가 Andre Desmond 씨의 아낌없는 기부로 인해 이 프로젝트는 앞으로 나아갈 수 있게 되었다.** "우리는 이 프로젝트를 전면적으로 취소해야 할지 우려하고 있었습니다"라고 이 홀의 책임자 Vivian Ross 씨가 말했다. "Desmond 씨의 도움을 통해, 우리가 간절히 필요로 하는 개선 작업을 할 수 있습니다." —[2]—. 이 개조 공사에는 해진 좌석 교체와 오래된 목조물 복구, 그리고 추가 조명을 더하는 일이 포함될 것이다.

back on track 다시 정상 궤도에 오른 underway 진행되는 generous 아낌없는, 너그러운 entrepreneur 기업가 make an improvement 개선하다, 향상시키다 desperately 간절히, 필사적으로 worn 해진, 닳은 restore ~을 복구하다, 회복시키다 woodwork 목조물 add ~을 추가하다 additional 추가적인 temporarily 일시적으로

Q. [1]과 [2]로 표시된 위치들 중에서, 다음 문장이 들어가기에 가장 적절한 곳은 어디인가?

"이 작업은 자금 부족으로 인해 일시적으로 중단된 바 있다."

(A) [1]
(B) [2]

[문제 키워드] had been temporarily halted

[해설] 제시된 문장은 특정 작업을 지칭하는 The work와 함께 '자금 부족으로 인해 일시적으로 중단되었다'는 의미를 나타낸다. 따라서 현재 다시 작업이 시작될 수 있게 된 원인이 제시된 문장 앞에 위치한 [1]에 들어가 과거와 현재의 상황이 대비되는 흐름이 되어야 알맞으므로 (A)가 정답이다.

[어휘] halt ~을 중단시키다 lack of ~의 부족 funding 자금 (조달)

03.

6월 10일 — 어젯밤에 열린 시상식에서, **Chester Burgess 씨가 하트포드 예술 협회(HAA)로부터 평생 공로상을 수상했다. 이 상은 하트포드에 거주하면서 예술계에 공헌하고 있는 예술가, 공연자 또는 극장 관련 근무자에게 매년 주어진다.** Burgess 씨는 의상 디자인 작업으로 알려진 분으로서, 30년 넘게 Sheridan 극장과 기타 단체들을 위해 물품을 준비해 주었다. Burgess 씨의 작품 샘플은 HAA의 웹사이트인 www.haa1.org에서 찾아볼 수 있다.

theater-related 극장과 관련된 contribute to ~에 공헌하다, 기여하다 be known for ~로 알려져 있다

Q. Burgess 씨에 관해 암시된 것은 무엇인가?
(A) 한 극장의 소유주이다.
(B) 하트포트 주민이다.

[문제 키워드] What / suggested / Mr. Burgess

[해설] about 뒤의 키워드 Mr. Burgess가 지문의 전체적인 소재이므로 지문 전반에서 단서를 파악해 각 선택지와 비교해야 한다. 지문 초반부에 Burgess 씨가 받은 상은 하트포드 지역에 거주하는 공연 관련 업계 종사자들에게 주는 상이라는(Chester Burgess accepted the Lifetime Achievement Award ~ The award is given every year ~ who is living in Hartford) 말이 있으므로 (B)가 정답이다.

[어휘] resident 주민

04.

웨스트뷰 항구 분기 평가

4월 4일

해당 항구 운영 위원장이 웨스트뷰 항구에 대한 분기별 평가 내용을 공개했는데, 엄청나게 성장했음을 보여준다. 이 항구를 이용하는 화물 선박의 숫자가 작년의 같은 기간에 비해 12퍼센트 증가했다. **이 선박들은 석탄과 철제 물품에서부터 가구와 고급 제품에 이르기까지 모든 것을 수송한다.** 이와 같은 성장 덕분에, 웨스트뷰 항구는 내년 말까지 지역 내에서 가장 큰 고용 주체가 될 궤도에 올라섰다.

quarterly 분기의 commissioner 운영 위원장 release ~을 공개하다, 출시하다 indicate ~을 나타내다, 가리키다 significant 상당한, 많은 growth 증가, 성장 cargo 화물 compared to ~에 비해 coal 석탄 iron 철제(품) owing to ~ 덕분에 be on track to부정사 ~할 궤도에 오르다 employment 고용

Q. 기사에서 웨스트뷰 항구에 관해 언급된 것은 무엇인가?
(A) 다양한 상품을 운송하는 데 이용되고 있다.
(B) 일부 열차 선로 근처에 위치해 있다.

[문제 키워드] What / mentioned / Westview Port

[해설] about 뒤의 키워드 Westview Port가 지문의 전체적인 소재이므로 지문 전반에서 단서를 파악해 각 선택지와 비교해야 한다. 지문 중반부에 해당 항구를 이용하는 선박들이 석탄과 철제 물품, 가구, 고급 제품 등 많은 것을 운송한다고(These ships carry everything from coal and iron to furniture and luxury items) 알리고 있으므로 (A)가 정답이다.

[어휘] transport ~을 운송하다 goods 상품

facility 시설(물) Jacuzzi 자쿠지(욕조의 한 형태) added 추가된
fee 요금 note that ~라는 점에 주목하다, 유의하다 in advance
미리, 사전에

01. 형용사 어휘

[해설] 빈칸 뒤에 위치한 복수 명사 changes를 수식할 수 있어야 하므로 이와 같은 역할이 가능한 (B) a few가 정답이다. (A) each와 (D) another는 단수 명사를, (C) much는 셀 수 없는 명사를 수식한다.

02. 알맞은 문장 고르기

(A) 추가 타월은 프런트 데스크에서 받아 이용하실 수 있습니다.
(B) 인명 구조원 직책에 공석이 하나 있습니다.
(C) 카탈로그는 온라인에서 보실 수 있습니다.
(D) 공사 담당 팀은 오직 낮 시간에만 작업할 수 있습니다.

[해설] 빈칸 앞 부분에 제시된 수영장 시설 이용과 관련된 정보와 연계되는 것으로서 추가 타월을 이용하는 방법을 알리는 내용에 해당되는 (A)가 정답이다.

03. 접속부사

[해설] 빈칸 앞 단락에는 수영장 시설 이용과 관련된 정보가, 빈칸 뒤에는 또 다른 시설물인 비즈니스 센터 이용과 관련된 정보가 제시되어 있다. 따라서 시설물 이용과 관련된 추가 정보를 전달하고 있으므로 '또한'이라는 의미로 추가 사항을 말할 때 사용하는 (D) Also가 정답이다.

[어휘] after all 결국 without ~ 없이, ~하지 않고 unless ~하지 않는다면, ~가 아니라면

04. 형용사 어휘

[해설] 빈칸 뒤에 위치한 fee를 수식해 요금의 수준과 관련된 의미를 나타내기에 적절한 형용사가 필요하므로 '아주 적은, 명목상의'라는 뜻으로 쓰이는 (D) nominal이 정답이다.

[어휘] occasional 때때로 발생되는, 가끔 있는 precise 정확한 initial 최초의, 처음의

05-08은 다음 기사를 참조하시오.

Red Jet 항공사 덕분에 항공 여행이 이제 막 조금 더 편안해졌다. 05Red Jet 사는 자사의 각 비행기에서 세 열의 좌석을 없앴다. 이는 모든 탑승객들에게 다리 공간이 2인치 더 생기게 해주는 것이다. 06이것이 얼마 안 돼 보이긴 하겠지만, 작은 공간이라도 큰 효과를 발휘한다. 이는 탑승객들이 자신의 앞쪽에 있는 좌석을 실수로 발로 차는 경우를 줄이는 데 도움이 될 것이다. 07추가로, 탑승객들이 편히 쉬고 잠을 자는 데 도움이 될 수 있도록 모든 좌석이 부드러운 극세사 쿠션으로 재단장되었다. 08Red Jet 항공사가 좌석 공간을 넓혔기 때문에, 더 많은 사람들이 일반석에서도 편안하게 비행을 즐길 수 있을 것이다.

thanks to ~로 인해, ~ 덕분에 allow ~을 가능하게 하다 leg room 다리 공간 go a long way 큰 효과를 내다, 크게 도움이 되다 reduce ~을 줄이다, 감소시키다 instance when ~하는 경우, 사례 be refitted with ~로 재단장되다, 재정비되다 microfiber 극세사 fall asleep 잠들다 expand ~을 넓히다, 확장하다 in comfort 편안하게

05. 알맞은 문장 고르기

(A) 다가오는 연휴 시즌에 대해 항공 요금이 인하되었다.
(B) Red Jet 사는 자사의 각 비행기에서 세 열의 좌석을 없앴다.
(C) 승무원이 안전벨트 사용법을 시범 보일 것이다.
(D) 탑승객들의 안전은 우리의 최우선 사항이다.

[해설] 빈칸 뒤에 제시된 다리 공간이 2인치 늘어났다는 말과 연계되는 것으로서 그와 같은 공간을 확보할 수 있게 한 조치로 항공기 내의 일부 좌석을 없앴다는 사실을 언급한 (B)가 정답이다.

[어휘] fare (교통편의) 요금 remove ~을 제거하다, 없애다
demonstrate ~을 시범 보이다, 시연하다 top priority 최우선 사항

06. 동사의 형태

[해설] 조동사 may와 부정어 not 뒤에는 동사원형이 쓰여야 하므로 동사원형인 (A) seem이 정답이다.

07. 접속부사

[해설] 빈칸 앞에는 추가로 공간이 생긴 것에 따른 장점이, 빈칸 뒤에는 새롭게 단장된 좌석의 특징이 언급되어 있다. 따라서 추가적인 서비스 혜택을 알리는 흐름임을 알 수 있으므로 '추가로, 게다가'라는 의미로 추가 사항을 말할 때 사용하는 (D) In addition이 정답이다.

[어휘] nevertheless 그럼에도 불구하고

08. 명사 어휘

[해설] 동사 has expanded의 목적어로서 확장 또는 확대가 가능한 대상을 나타낼 명사가 필요한데, 빈칸 앞에서 좌석 공간을 늘린 것에 대해 다루었으므로 '좌석 (공간), 자리' 등을 의미하는 (D) seating이 정답이다.

PART 7 기사 (2) 문화/예술/지역사회 관련 기사

풀이 방법 해석

연예 뉴스

리보니아(9월 7일) — 10년 전 해체한 인기 록그룹 Thunder Head가 재결합할 예정이며, 전국 투어로 무대에 돌아올 것이라고 발표했다.

Thunder Head는 15년 전에 결성되어 즉시 유명해졌다. 그들의 콘서트는 매진되었고 그들이 발매한 2장의 앨범은 300만장의 판매고를 올렸다. 하지만, 그룹의 매니저인 Tim Dawkins에 따르면, 갑작스런 명성은 그 뮤지션들이 감당하기에 너무 컸다.

"미디어의 갑작스런 모든 관심이 그 당시에 그들에게는 너무 큰 것이었어요." Dawkins 씨는 말했다. "이제 그들이 서로 문제를 해결하고 개인 학업을 추구할 시간을 가졌으니 그들은 다시 돌아올 준비가 되었습니다. 그들이 3월부터 8월까지 투어를 하게 될 것을 알리게 되어 기쁩니다."

공연 티켓은 그룹의 팬페이지에서 구입할 수 있다.

 연습 문제

01.(B)   02.(A)   03.(B)   04.(A)

PART 6 접속부사 - 첨가

풀이 방법 해석

저희 Donut Delight는 항상 맛있는 도넛을 만드는 것으로 유명했습니다. 그것들은 전국의 대형 슈퍼마켓과 대부분의 편의점 둘 다에서 살 수 있습니다. 하지만 이번 4월에 저희는 몇몇의 건강한 식품들을 소개할 것입니다. 우리 문화의 식습관에 대한 많은 우려가 있었습니다. 고객들을 진심으로 아끼는 회사로서, Donut Delight는 이제 통밀 머핀과 같은 건강한 음식을 제공할 것입니다. 게다가, 저희는 원래의 레시피를 변경하여 도넛의 지방과 설탕 함유량을 10퍼센트 줄였습니다. 이제 여러분은 저희 제품을 먹으면서 기분이 더 좋아지실 것입니다. 저희의 최신 맛을 경험하기 위해 지역 슈퍼마켓에 오늘 방문하세요!

 연습 문제

01.(B) 02.(B) 03.(B) 04.(A)

01.

Hopewell 보험사의 가족이 되신 것을 환영합니다! 프리미엄 회원으로서, 귀하께서 필요로 하시는 어떠한 의료 처방에 대해서도 완전히 보장될 것입니다. 게다가, 병원비의 90퍼센트가 보장될 것이며, 여기에는 입원비도 포함됩니다.

prescription 처방전, 처방약 **completely** 완전히, 전적으로 **cover** (비용 등) ~을 부담하다, (보험으로) 보장하다

[단서] medical prescriptions, hospital fees

[해설] 빈칸 앞에는 의료 처방과 관련된 비용 부담 정도가, 빈칸 뒤에는 병원비 보장 정도가 언급되어 있다. 따라서 보장 서비스와 관련된 추가 정보를 제시하는 흐름이므로 '더욱이, 게다가' 등의 의미로 추가 정보를 덧붙일 때 사용하는 (B) Moreover가 정답이다.

[어휘] on the other hand 다른 한편으로는, 반면에

02.

Milford 직업 박람회가 7월 3일 토요일 오전 10시부터 오후 4시까지 Milford 지역 문화 센터에서 개최될 것입니다. 구직자들은 현장 면접에 대비해 여러 장의 이력서를 지참하셔야 합니다. 게다가, 미래의 고용주들의 마음을 끄는 데 도움이 될 수 있도록 어떠한 형태의 증빙 서류든지 제시하실 것을 권합니다.

hold ~을 개최하다, 열다 **job seeker** 구직자 **copy** 한 장, 사본 **résumé** 이력서 **in preparation for** ~에 대비해 **on-site** 현장의 **be encouraged to**부정사 ~하도록 권장되다 **present** ~을 제시하다, 보여주다 **references** 증빙 서류 **appeal to** ~의 마음을 끌다 **employer** 고용주

[단서] bring ~ résumés, present any types of references

[해설] 빈칸 앞에는 이력서를 지참하도록 당부하는 말이, 빈칸 뒤에는 어떠한 증빙 서류든 제시하도록 권하는 말이 쓰여 있다. 따라서 추가적인 권고 사항을 언급하고 있으므로 '게다가, 더욱이'라는 의미로 추가 사항을 말할 때 사용하는 (B) Furthermore가 정답이다.

03.

이사 전문 업체가 우리의 새 사무실로 가져갈 수 있게 각자의 물품을 상자에 담아 포장할 것을 전 직원께 요청드립니다. 추가로, 각자의 업무 공간 주변을 청소하는 것을 도와 주시기 바랍니다.

ask A to부정사 A에게 ~하도록 요청하다 **box up** ~을 상자에 넣어 포장하다, 꾸리다 **so that** (목적) ~할 수 있도록 **assist with** ~하는 것을 돕다

[단서] box up their belongings, assist with cleaning

[해설] 빈칸 앞에는 물품을 상자에 담아 두도록 요청하는 말이, 빈칸 뒤에는 청소를 돕도록 당부하는 말이 쓰여 있다. 따라서 직원들에게 바라는 일을 추가로 알리는 흐름임을 알 수 있으므로 '추가로'라는 의미로 쓰이는 (B) In addition이 정답이다.

04.

Gold Class 회원께서는 공항에서 할인을 받고 전국에 있는 호텔들을 선택하실 수 있습니다. 또한, 국내 항공권을 구입하실 때 두 배로 보상 마일리지를 받습니다.

receive ~을 받다 **reward** 보상 **domestic** 국내의

[단서] receive discounts, get double reward miles

[해설] 빈칸 앞 문장에서 공항 및 호텔 관련 혜택이, 빈칸 뒤에는 보상 마일리지 관련 혜택이 제시되어 있다. 따라서 추가적인 혜택을 알리는 흐름임을 알 수 있으므로 '또한'을 의미하는 (A) Also가 정답이다.

[어휘] rather 다소, 오히려, 좀, 약간

실전 문제

01.(B) 02.(A) 03.(D) 04.(D) 05.(B) 06.(A)
07.(D) 08.(D)

01-04는 다음 이메일을 참조하시오.

수신: Marcus Hill <mhill@eronmail.com>
발신: Bull Mountain Hotel
날짜: 2월 7일
제목: 귀하의 숙박
첨부: 시설

고객님께

다음 주에 저희 호텔에서 귀하를 모실 수 있기를 고대합니다. **01**저희 호텔에 최근에 몇몇 변동 사항이 생겨 귀하께 알려 드리고자 합니다. 실내 수영장 개조 공사 작업이 완료된 상태이며, 현재 자쿠지와 아동용 수영장이 있습니다. 실내 수영장은 오전 6시부터 오후 10시까지 운영됩니다. **02**추가 타월은 프런트 데스크에서 받아 이용하실 수 있습니다. **03**또한, 무엇이 되었든 비즈니스 관련 목적으로 머무르시는 경우에는 새롭게 추가된 비즈니스 센터를 이용할 수 있습니다. **04**복사기와 프린터, 팩스 기기를 아주 저렴한 요금에 이용하실 수 있습니다.

저희 Bull Mountain 호텔을 선택해 주셔서 미리 감사 드립니다. 다음 주에 뵙겠습니다.

안녕히 계십시오.

Bull Mountain 호텔 서비스팀

14. to부정사의 역할: 부사 역할

이전의 세미나 참석자들께서 남긴 추천 후기를 더 보기를 원하시거나 다음 워크숍에 등록하기를 원하시는 분은 저희 교육 센터의 웹페이지를 방문하시기 바랍니다.

[해설] 선택지가 동사 register의 다양한 형태로 구성되어 있으므로 문법 문제이다. 이미 문장의 동사 visit이 있으므로 register는 준동사로 쓰여야 하는데, 웹사이트를 방문하는 목적을 의미해야 알맞으므로 목적을 나타낼 때 사용하는 to부정사 (B) to register가 정답이다.

[어휘] testimonial 추천 후기 former 이전의 attendee 참석자

15. 시간 부사절과 주절의 시제 관계

모든 지원자들의 이력서를 검토한 후에, Estes 씨는 면접을 볼 사람들을 결정할 것이다.

[해설] 선택지가 동사 decide의 다양한 형태로 구성되어 있으므로 문법 문제이다. After절에 현재 시제 동사(reviews)가 쓰일 때, 주절에는 미래 시제 동사가 사용되므로 (B) will decide가 정답이다.

[어휘] applicant 지원자

16. 위치/방향 전치사

해링턴 시장은 Sunset 고속도로를 따라 나무를 심을 것을 제안했다.

[해설] 선택지가 다양한 전치사들로 구성되어 있으므로 전치사 어휘 문제이다. Sunset Highway는 도로를 의미하므로 길이나 거리 등을 나타내는 명사와 함께 '~을 따라'라는 의미로 쓰이는 전치사 (A) along이 정답이다.

[어휘] mayor 시장 through ~을 통해 forward 앞으로; ~을 전송하다

17. 부사의 역할과 위치: 동사 뒤 수식

사람들은 Louisville 테마 파크의 놀이기구에서 부상을 당하는 것을 염려하지만, 이는 단 한 번 발생된 일이었다.

[해설] 선택지가 부사와 전치사로 구성되어 있으므로 문법 문제이다. 자동사 happened를 뒤에서 수식할 부사가 빈칸에 필요하므로 이 역할이 가능한 부사 (A) once가 정답이다. (D) ever는 일반 동사 앞에 쓰인다.

[어휘] get injured 부상당하다 ride 놀이기구

18. 인칭대명사 구분: 주격

주문하실 준비가 되시면 종업원을 부르시는 대신 테이블에 놓인 태블릿을 이용하십시오.

[해설] 선택지가 다양한 인칭대명사로 구성되어 있으므로 문법 문제이다. 접속사 if와 동사 are 사이에 위치한 빈칸은 if절의 주어 자리이므로 주격 대명사 (D) you가 정답이다.

[어휘] instead of ~ 대신 order 주문하다

19. 부사 어휘

직원들은 분기마다 발급되는 수표의 형태로 초과 근무에 대한 보상을 받을 것이다.

[해설] 선택지가 다양한 부사들로 구성되어 있으므로 부사 어휘 문제이다. 빈칸에 쓰일 부사는 현재 시제 동사 is issued를 뒤에서 수식해야 하므로 이 역할이 가능한 것으로서 반복 주기를 나타내는 (A) quarterly가 정답이다. (C) typically도 현재 시제 동사와 어울려 일반적인 일을 나타낼 때 사용하지만 동사 뒤에 위치하지 않는다.

[어휘] overtime 초과 근무 compensation 보상 in the form of ~의 형태로 check 수표 issue ~을 발급하다, 지급하다 quarterly 분기마다 conveniently 편리하게 typically 일반적으로 largely 대체로, 크게

20. 상관접속사

경영 기술 워크숍 행사에는 강연뿐만 아니라 직접 해 보는 실습도 포함되어 있다.

[해설] 선택지가 다양한 품사의 단어들로 구성되어 있으므로 문법 문제이다. 빈칸 앞에 위치한 not only와 짝을 이뤄 not only A but also B(A뿐만 아니라 B도) 구문으로 쓰이는 (D) but also가 정답이다.

[어휘] hands-on 직접 해 보는 exercise 실습, 실행 as if 마치 ~한 것처럼 aside from ~ 외에는 on top of ~뿐만 아니라

21. 부사 어휘

Willingboro 산업은 주기적으로 포커스 그룹 시간을 가지므로, 그곳의 제품들은 대량 생산되기 전에 고객들에 의해 검토된다.

[해설] 선택지가 다양한 부사들로 구성되어 있으므로 부사 어휘 문제이다. 빈칸에 쓰일 부사는 현재 시제 동사 holds를 앞에서 수식해야 하므로 이 역할이 가능한 것으로서 현재 시제 동사와 함께 반복 주기를 나타낼 때 사용하는 (D) regularly가 정답이다.

[어휘] focus group 포커스 그룹(시장 조사 등을 위해 모인 사람들의 그룹) mass produce ~을 대량 생산하다 mutually 서로, 상호간에 readily 손쉽게, 선뜻 abruptly 갑자기, 불쑥 regularly 주기적으로

22. 부사 어휘

자격을 얻지 못하는 것을 피하기 위해 지원 가이드라인을 정확하게 따르는 것이 중요하다.

[해설] 선택지가 다양한 부사들로 구성되어 있으므로 부사 어휘 문제이다. 빈칸에 쓰일 부사는 follow를 수식해 가이드라인을 따르는 방식을 나타내야 하는데, 자격을 얻지 못하는 일을 피할 수 있는 방식이어야 하므로 '정확하게'를 의미하는 (B) precisely가 정답이다.

[어휘] disqualified 자격을 잃은 potentially 잠재적으로 efficiently 효율적으로

23. 등위접속사 so

Henderson 씨가 지금부터 우리 사무실에서 근무할 예정이므로 이곳에서 환영 받는 기분을 느낄 수 있도록 도와주십시오.

[해설] 선택지가 부사와 접속사로 구성되어 있으므로 문법 문제이다. 빈칸 앞뒤로 각각 주어와 동사가 포함된 절이 있으므로 이 절들을 연결할 접속사가 빈칸에 필요하다. '근무를 시작하는 것'과 '환영해 주는 것'은 원인과 결과로 볼 수 있으므로 '~이므로' 등의 의미로 원인과 결과를 이어주는 접속사 (A) so가 정답이다. (B) then과 (D) ever는 부사이다.

[어휘] then 그렇다면, 그 후에, 그때 once 일단 ~하는 대로, (과거에) 한 때

24. 부사 어휘

회사의 새 마케팅 전략은 과거에 있었던 것과는 현저하게 다르다.

[해설] 선택지가 다양한 부사들로 구성되어 있으므로 부사 어휘 문제이다. 빈칸에 쓰일 부사는 바로 뒤에 위치한 형용사 different를 수식해 차이가 나는 정도를 나타내야 하므로 '현저하게, 두드러지게'라는 의미로 강조할 때 사용하는 (D) markedly가 정답이다.

[어휘] strategy 전략 separately 따로, 분리되어 mutually 서로, 상호간에 securely 안전하게

04. 부사 어휘

Hopewell 자동차 제조업체의 주가가 계속 꾸준히 상승할 것으로 예상된다.

[해설] 선택지가 다양한 부사들로 구성되어 있으므로 부사 어휘 문제이다. 빈칸에 쓰일 부사는 바로 앞에 위치한 rising을 수식해 상승하는 방식을 나타내야 하므로 증감을 나타내는 동사와 어울려 '꾸준히'라는 의미로 사용되는 (A) steadily가 정답이다.

[어휘] stock value 주가 rise 증가하다, 오르다 exclusively 오로지, 독점적으로 partly 부분적으로 formally 공식적으로, 정식으로

05. 등위접속사

많은 동료 직원들은 Nick Gruber 씨의 리더십이 강력하고 열정적이라고 생각한다.

[해설] 선택지가 다양한 품사의 단어들로 구성되어 있으므로 문법 문제이다. 빈칸에 쓰일 단어는 뒤에 and로 연결된 passionate와 마찬가지로 to be의 보어 역할을 하는 형용사여야 하므로 (A) strong이 정답이다. (D) strongest는 최상급 형태이므로 the와 함께 사용한다.

[어휘] colleague 동료 직원 passionate 열정적인 strongly 강력히 strength 힘, 장점

06. 상관접속사

Maison de Marseille의 메뉴에 올라 있는 모든 식사는 수프와 샐러드 둘 다 함께 제공된다.

[해설] 선택지가 다양한 품사의 단어들로 구성되어 있으므로 문법 문제이다. 빈칸 뒤에 두 명사가 'A and B'로 연결되어 있으므로 이와 같은 구조와 함께 'A와 B 둘 다'라는 의미의 상관접속사로 쓰이는 (C) both가 정답이다.

[어휘] unless ~하지 않는다면

07. 등위접속사 and/or

재무 또는 관련 분야의 학위를 소지하고 있는 사람은 누구든지 그 일자리에 지원하도록 권장된다.

[해설] 선택지가 전치사와 접속사로 구성되어 있으므로 문법 문제이다. 빈칸 앞뒤에 각각 위치한 명사 finance와 명사구 a related field는 모두 전치사 in의 목적어가 되어야 알맞으므로 '또는'이라는 의미로 대등한 관계의 단어나 구를 연결하는 접속사 (B) or가 정답이다.

[어휘] degree 학위 related 관련된 field 분야 be encouraged to 부정사 ~하도록 권장되다 apply for ~에 지원하다

08. 상관접속사

다가오는 마라톤 경주 중에, 버스와 전차 모두 시내 지역에서 운행되지 않을 것이다.

[해설] 선택지가 부사와 접속사로 구성되어 있으므로 문법 문제이다. 빈칸 앞에 위치한 neither와 짝을 이뤄 'A도 B도 아닌'이라는 의미의 상관접속사로 쓰이는 (A) nor가 정답이다.

[어휘] operate 운행되다, 운영되다

09. 부사 어휘

자격을 갖춘 후보자들은 마감 시한을 놓치지 않기 위해 지체 없이 지원서를 제출하도록 권장됩니다.

[해설] 선택지가 다양한 부사들로 구성되어 있으므로 부사 어휘 문제이다. 빈칸에 쓰일 부사는 submit을 수식해 지원서 제출 방식을 나타내야 하는데, 마감시한을 놓치지 않는 방식에 해당되어야 하므로 '즉시, 지체 없이'를 뜻하는 (C) promptly가 정답이다.

[어휘] qualified 자격을 갖춘, 적격인 candidate 후보자 so as (not) to부정사 ~하도록[하지 않도록] fully 완전히, 전적으로 separately 따로, 분리되어 primarily 주로

10. 과거분사

Bartlett Legal의 공석에 제출된 모든 지원서들이 Jen Bartlett 씨에 의해 개인적으로 검토될 것이다.

[해설] 선택지가 동사 submit의 다양한 형태와 명사로 구성되어 있으므로 문법 문제이다. 뒤에 이미 문장의 동사 will be reviewed가 있으므로 동사 submit은 빈칸에 준동사로 쓰여 주어 applications(지원서)를 수식하는 역할을 해야 한다. 지원서는 사람에 의해 제출되는 대상이므로 수동의 의미를 나타낼 수 있는 과거분사 (C) submitted가 정답이다.

[어휘] application 지원(서) submit ~을 제출하다 submission 제출(된 것)

11. 분사구문

Steward Tech 사는 자사의 직원들을 더욱 효율적으로 근무하게 하는 것을 선호함에 따라 불필요한 보안 조치를 없앴다.

[해설] 선택지가 동사 prefer의 다양한 형태와 명사로 구성되어 있으므로 문법 문제이다. 이미 문장의 동사 removed가 있으므로 prefer는 준동사로 쓰여야 한다. 효율적으로 근무하게 하는 것을 선호한다는 사실이 불필요한 조치를 없앤 이유이므로 이유 부사절 'as it prefers ~'에서 접속사와 주어가 생략되고 분사구문으로 바뀐 구조를 만드는 분사 (D) preferring이 정답이다.

[어휘] remove ~을 없애다, 제거하다 unnecessary 불필요한 measures 조치 let ~하게 하다 efficiently 효율적으로 preference 선호(하는 것)

12. 동명사 숙어 표현

상급 목공 과정을 이수하자마자 수료증이 발급될 것입니다.

[해설] 선택지가 다양한 품사의 단어들로 구성되어 있으므로 문법 문제이다. 전치사 Upon의 목적어 역할을 하면서 명사구(your advanced carpentry courses)를 목적어로 취할 수 있는 것은 동명사이므로 (C) completing이 정답이다. 명사 (D) completion이 쓰이려면 뒤에 전치사가 함께 쓰여야 한다.

[어휘] upon -ing ~하자마자 advanced 상급의, 진보한 carpentry 목공 certificate 수료증, 인증서 issue ~을 발급하다 complete ~을 이수하다, 완료하다; 완료된 completion 완료, 완수

13. 'to -ing'와 'to부정사'의 구분

대부분의 주민들은 커닝엄 외곽 지역에 추가 발전소를 건설하는 것에 반대했다.

[해설] 선택지가 다양한 품사의 단어들로 구성되어 있으므로 문법 문제이다. 빈칸 앞에 위치한 'object to'에서 to는 전치사이므로 그 뒤에 명사나 동명사가 이어져야 하는데, 빈칸 뒤에 위치한 명사구(an additional power plant)를 목적어로 취해야 하므로 동명사인 (D) constructing이 정답이다. 명사 (B) construction이 쓰이려면 뒤에 전치사가 동반되어야 한다.

[어휘] resident 주민 object to -ing ~하는 것에 반대하다 additional 추가의 power plant 발전소 on the outskirts of ~의 외곽에

DAY 15

PART 5 문법 | 등위접속사와 상관접속사

확인 문제 해석

① 본 트레이닝은 인턴과 신입 사원을 대상으로 합니다.
② 이 물품은 일시 품절 상태이지만 오후에 다시 채워질 것입니다.
③ 당신은 현 회원이므로 이 무료 물품을 받을 수 있습니다.
④ 회사가 출장 예산을 삭감했으므로 우리는 소형차를 빌려야 한다.
⑤ 그는 사무실 컴퓨터에서도 휴대 기기에서도 이메일 계정에 접속하지 않았다.

 연습 문제

01.(B) 02.(B) 03.(C) 04.(A) 05.(C) 06.(A)

01.
1. 선택지 보고 문법/어휘 문제 파악하기 ☑문법 문제 ☐어휘 문제
2. 빈칸 분석하기 빈칸 앞에 있는 것 ☑완전한 절 ☐불완전한 절
   빈칸 뒤에 있는 것 ☐부사 ☑동사
   → 빈칸에는 ☐전치사 ☐부사 ☑접속사가 들어가야 한다.
3. 정답 선택하기 정답 (B)

내 주문품은 늦게 발송되었지만 예정된 날짜에 도착했다.

02.
1. 선택지 보고 문법/어휘 문제 파악하기 ☑문법 문제 ☐어휘 문제
2. 빈칸 분석하기 빈칸 앞에 있는 것 ☑완전한 절 ☐불완전한 절
   빈칸 뒤에 있는 것 ☑완전한 절 ☐불완전한 절
   → 빈칸에는 ☐전치사 ☑접속사가 들어가야 한다.
   → 빈칸 앞뒤 내용의 관계 ☑원인과 결과 ☐상반되는 내용
3. 정답 선택하기 정답 (B)

Singleton 씨가 휴가를 가서, Jensen 씨가 그를 대신할 것이다.

03.
1. 선택지 보고 문법/어휘 문제 파악하기 ☑문법 문제 ☐어휘 문제
2. 빈칸 분석하기 빈칸 뒤에 있는 접속사 (or)
   → 위의 것과 짝을 이루어 상관접속사를 완성하는 것이 정답
3. 정답 선택하기 정답 (C)

당신은 우리에게 이메일을 보내거나 24시간 상담전화에 전화해서 연락할 수 있습니다.

04.
1. 선택지 보고 문법/어휘 문제 파악하기 ☑문법 문제 ☐어휘 문제
2. 빈칸 분석하기 빈칸 앞에 있는 상관접속사의 일부 표현 (neither)
   → 위의 것과 짝을 이루어 상관접속사를 완성하는 것이 정답이다.
3. 정답 선택하기 정답 (A)

공사로 인해, Main 가와 Houston 가의 진입로로 둘 다 진입할 수 없습니다.

05.
1. 선택지 보고 문법/어휘 문제 파악하기 ☐문법 문제 ☑어휘 문제
2. 빈칸 분석하기 빈칸 뒤에 있는 동사 (located)
   → 의미 (위치해 있다)
   → 이 동사와 함께 쓰이는 부사가 정답이다.
3. 정답 선택하기 정답 (C)

새 사무실 건물은 지하철역 가까이에 편리하게 위치해 있다.

06.
1. 선택지 보고 문법/어휘 문제 파악하기 ☑문법 문제 ☐어휘 문제
2. 빈칸 분석하기 and 앞에 있는 단어의 품사 ☐명사 ☑형용사
   → 빈칸에는 ☐부사 ☑형용사가 들어가야 한다.
3. 정답 선택하기 정답 (A)

Travel Trunk의 여행 가방은 튼튼하고 들기에 가벼운 것으로 알려져 있다.

실전 문제

01.(B)	02.(B)	03.(D)	04.(A)	05.(A)	06.(C)
07.(B)	08.(A)	09.(C)	10.(C)	11.(D)	12.(C)
13.(D)	14.(D)	15.(B)	16.(A)	17.(A)	18.(D)
19.(A)	20.(D)	21.(D)	22.(B)	23.(D)	24.(D)

01. 등위접속사 so

Carr 씨는 인상적인 학력을 지니고 있으므로 연구부에 훌륭한 자산이 될 것이다.

[해설] 선택지가 전치사와 접속사로 구성되어 있으므로 문법 문제이다. 빈칸 앞뒤로 각각 주어와 동사가 포함된 절이 있으므로 이 절들을 연결할 접속사가 빈칸에 필요하다. '인상적인 학력 소지'와 '부서의 훌륭한 자산이 되는 것'은 원인과 결과로 볼 수 있으므로 '~이므로' 등의 의미로 원인과 결과를 이어주는 접속사 (B) so가 정답이다. 참고로, (D) regarding은 전치사이다.

[어휘] impressive 인상적인   asset 자산   regarding ~와 관련해

02. 상관접속사

불편함에 대해 보상해 드리기 위해, 귀하의 다음 번 주문에 대해 무료 배송 또는 15퍼센트의 할인 중 하나를 제공해 드리겠습니다.

[해설] 선택지가 다양한 품사의 단어들로 구성되어 있으므로 문법 문제이다. 빈칸 뒤에 두 명사구가 'A or B'의 구조로 연결되어 있으므로 이와 같은 구조와 함께 'A와 B 둘 중 하나'라는 의미의 상관접속사로 쓰이는 (B) either가 정답이다.

[어휘] make up for ~에 대해 보상하다, 만회하다   inconvenience 불편함   offer 제공하다   toward (방향) ~쪽으로, (목적) ~을 위해

03. 등위접속사 and/or

이상적인 후보자는 최소 3년간의 경력과 훌륭한 의사소통 능력을 지니고 있어야 할 것이다.

[해설] 선택지가 부사와 접속사로 구성되어 있으므로 문법 문제이다. 빈칸 앞뒤에 각각 위치한 두 명사구 three years of experience와 excellent communication skills는 모두 동사 have의 목적어가 되어야 하므로 대등한 관계의 단어나 구를 연결하는 접속사 (D) and가 정답이다.

[어휘] ideal 이상적인   at least 최소한   as well ~도, 또한

하고 오후에는 좀 더 편안한 분위기가 되며, 저녁에는 에너지가 넘친다고 (The mood at lunchtime is serious, ~ it takes on a more relaxed quality. Then in the evening, we energize the space ~) 설명하고 있다. 이는 시간대 별로 분위기가 달라진다는 의미이므로 (A)가 정답이다.

[어휘] depending on ~에 따라 다른, ~에 달려 있는   promote ~을 촉진시키다   party 사람, 단체   improve ~을 향상시키다, 개선하다

paraphrasing 정답 1. (b)   2. (c)   3. (a)

10-13은 다음 기사를 참조하시오.

기술 박람회에 참가하는 ZoomCore

메드포드 (11월 10일) — 컴퓨터 제조업체 ZoomCore 사가 다음 달에 2주 동안 열리는 Medford 기술 박람회에 사상 처음으로 참가할 예정이라고 발표했다. —[1]—.

박람회에서 신제품을 선보이는 일은 ZoomCore와 같은 신생 전자제품 업체들에게 있어 일반적으로 위험한 기회로 여겨진다. 대부분은 모든 지원을 잃거나 [13]투자자들로부터 [10]상당한 관심과 자금을 확보하는 것 중의 하나로 나뉜다. —[2]—.

ZoomCore 사가 출시하는 컴퓨터들은 온라인 게임을 즐기는 사람들 사이에서 대단한 인기를 누려 왔다. "느긋하게 쉬려 할 때 느리게 작동되는 컴퓨터만큼 더 좌절감을 주는 것은 거의 없습니다"라고 Gordon Willis 대표이사는 말했다. —[3]—. "[11]저희는 지금까지 중에서 최고의 게임용 컴퓨터들을 도입하기 위해 몇몇 맞춤 개조 작업을 했으며, 사람들에게 새롭고 흥미로운 게임 경험을 제공해 드리고 있습니다."

—[4]—. Willis 씨는 자사에서 설치하려고 계획 중인 화면 디스플레이가 사람들이 마치 프로 게이머들 중의 한 명이 된 것처럼 느끼게 만들어 줄 것이라고 말했다. 그는 "한 번도 겪어 보지 못한 종류의 경험이 될 것입니다"라고 공식 성명에서 밝혔다. "행사에 참석할 수 없는 분들을 위해, [12]저희 회사의 웹사이트를 통해 박람회 현장에서 저희가 하고 있는 일들을 확인해 보실 수 있습니다."

manufacturer 제조사   risky 위험한   electronics 전자 제품   either A or B A 또는 B 둘 중의 하나   lose ~을 잃다, 분실하다   gain ~을 얻다   considerable 상당한, 많은   funding 자금 (제공)   investor 투자자   release ~을 출시하다, 내놓다   frustrating 좌절감을 주는   custom 맞춤 제작의   modification 개조, 변경   bring in ~을 도입하다   press release 공식 성명, 보도 자료

---

10. 동의어 문제

두 번째 단락, 두 번째 줄의 단어 "considerable"과 의미가 가장 가까운 것은 무엇인가?
(A) 끈질긴
(B) 상당한
(C) 사려 깊은
(D) 의식하는

[해설] 해당 문장에서 considerable은 투자자들로부터 얻는 관심과 자금의 정도를 나타내기 위해 사용된 형용사이다. 따라서 그 관심과 자금의 정도가 크다는 의미를 나타낸다는 것을 알 수 있으므로 이와 유사한 단어로 '상당한'을 뜻하는 (B)가 정답이다.

11. 세부사항 문제

기사에 따르면, ZoomCore 사는 박람회에서 무엇을 공개할 계획인가?
(A) 새롭게 개발된 몇몇 게임

(B) 혁신적인 컴퓨터 디자인
(C) 최신 그래픽과 사운드 카드
(D) 맞춤 변경 작업이 된 컴퓨터

[해설] 박람회에서 공개되는 제품의 특성이 언급된 세 번째 단락에, 최고의 게임용 컴퓨터들을 도입하기 위해 맞춤 개조 작업을 한 사실이(We made some custom modifications to bring in our best gaming computers yet ~) 언급되어 있으므로 (D)가 정답이다.

paraphrasing   custom modifications 맞춤 개조 작업 → customized changes 맞춤 변경 작업

[어휘] unveil 공개하다, 발표하다   revolutionary 혁신적인   top-of-the-line 최신의, 최고급의   customized 맞춤 제작된, 주문 제작된

12. 세부사항 문제

ZoomCore 사는 박람회에서 무엇을 할 계획인가?
(A) 프로 게이머 대변인을 고용할 것이다.
(B) 몇몇 제품을 할인된 가격에 제공할 것이다.
(C) 온라인으로 방송할 것이다.
(D) 개인 맞춤 설정을 선택하는 방법을 시연할 것이다.

[해설] 지문 맨 마지막에, 행사에 참석할 수 없는 사람들을 위해 웹사이트를 통해 박람회 현장에서 전하는 모습을 볼 수 있다고(you can see what we are doing at the expo through our company website) 알리고 있는데, 이는 온라인 방송을 하겠다는 말이므로 (C)가 정답이다.

[어휘] spokesperson 대변인   broadcast ~을 방송하다   demonstrate ~을 시연하다   personalized 개인 맞춤의

13. 문장 삽입 문제

[1], [2], [3] 그리고 [4]로 표시된 위치들 중에서, 다음 문장이 들어가기에 가장 적절한 곳은 어디인가?

"높아지고 있는 ZoomCore의 인기를 감안해, 분석가들은 이 업체가 많은 지원을 이끌어 낼 것으로 예상하고 있다."

(A) [1]
(B) [2]
(C) [3]
(D) [4]

[해설] 제시된 문장은 ZoomCore가 많은 지원을 받게 될 것이라는 의미다. 이는 자금 지원과 관련된 내용이므로 투자자들로부터의 관심과 자금 확보가 언급된 문장 뒤에 위치한 [2]에 들어가 ZoomCore가 그 대상이 될 것이라고 말하는 흐름이 되어야 적절하므로 (B)가 정답이다.

[어휘] rising 높아지는, 상승하는   analyst 분석가   backing 지원

paraphrasing 정답 1. (a)   2. (c)   3. (b)

05. True 문제

REP에 관해 암시된 것은 무엇인가?
(A) 그에 대한 참여는 자발적이다.
(B) 그것을 고안한 사람이 교육을 제공한다.
(C) Wilhelm 씨의 반대에 부딪히고 있다.
(D) 폭넓은 경험을 필요로 한다.

[해설] 두 번째 단락 시작 부분에, 직원들이 REP 선택 여부를 결정한다고 (Employees who opt into REP ~) 한 것으로 보아 이는 직원들이 이 프로그램에 자발적으로 참여함을 알 수 있으므로 (A)가 정답이다.

paraphrasing opt into ~하기로 선택하다 → voluntary 자발적인

[어휘] voluntary 자발적인 be opposed by ~의 반대에 부딪히다 extensive 폭넓은, 광범위한

06. 문장 삽입 문제

[1], [2], [3] 그리고 [4]로 표시된 위치들 중에서, 다음 문장이 들어가기에 가장 적절한 곳은 어디인가?

"이는 그들을 지나치게 피곤한 상태로 만들 수 있으며, 비효율성의 원인이 된다."

(A) [1]
(B) [2]
(C) [3]
(D) [4]

[해설] 제시된 문장은 특정 대상을 지칭하는 단수 대명사 It과 복수 대명사 them이 함께 쓰여 있으며, them을 지나치게 피곤하게 만들어 비효율성의 원인이 된다는 의미를 나타내고 있다. 따라서 일반적인 직장인의 통근 시간이 1시간이 넘는다는 의미의 문장 뒤에 위치한 [4]에 들어가 그에 따른 부정적인 영향을 말하는 흐름이 되어야 자연스러우므로 (D)가 정답이다.

[어휘] leave A 형용사 A를 ~한 상태로 만들다 overly 지나치게 contribute to ~에 대한 원인이 되다 inefficiency 비효율(성)

paraphrasing 정답 1. (b) 2. (c) 3. (a)

07-09은 다음 기사를 참조하시오.

뉴올리언스 한복판에서 즐기는 식사: Hillview Café
Lorraine Ferguson 작성

3월 12일 ― 개업한 지 25년 만에, Hillview Café가 새로운 국면에 접어들었습니다. **07이 레스토랑은 지난달에 Tyrone Manning 씨에게 매각되었으며, 그는 이 식당의 탁월함을 유지하기 위해 부단히 노력하고 있습니다.** 저는 이번 주 초에 Manning 씨와 함께 자리했습니다.

LF: **08최근 <Dining Daily>에 실린 평가에서, Casey Rigsby 씨는 본인의 식사 경험을 '모든 감각을 충족하는 기쁨'이라고 불렀습니다.** 어떻게 이와 같은 극찬을 듣게 되신 건가요?

TM: 저희 수석 요리사이신 Scott Cobos 씨께서 아주 다양한 입맛을 지닌 분들의 마음에 드는 요리들로 구성된 폭넓은 메뉴를 만들어 주셨습니다. Hillview Café에서 10년 동안 근무하신 끝에, Cobos 씨께서는 식사 손님들이 가장 좋아하는 일부 요리들을 완성하셨습니다. 그분은 또한 새로운 것들도 기꺼이 시도해 보시고 있습니다.

LF: 이름에 '카페'라는 단어가 들어가 있지만, 이 레스토랑은 흔히 '고급 식당'으로 분류되고 있습니다. 어떤 분위기를 만드시려고 노력 중이신지 설명해 주실 수 있으신가요?

TM: 놀라운 음식과 함께, 저희는 최고 수준의 서비스를 제공해 드리기 위해 애씁니다. 동시에, 저희는 스스로 너무 진지하게 생각하지 않습니다. **09점심 시간대의 분위기는 업무상 만남을 가지는 분들이 많아서 진지합니다. 오후 시간대에는, 좀 더 편안한 상태로 바뀌기 시작합니다. 그런 다음 저녁이 되면, 저희는 라이브 음악과 화려한 조명으로 공간에 활기를 불어 넣습니다.**

in business 영업 중인, 운영 중인 phase 국면, 단계 dining establishment 식당 (건물) achieve ~을 달성하다, 이루다 high praise 극찬 extensive 폭넓은, 광범위한 dish 요리, 음식 appeal to ~의 마음을 끌다 be willing to부정사 기꺼이 ~하다, ~할 의향이 있다 be classified as ~로 분류되다 atmosphere 분위기 along with ~와 함께 strive to부정사 ~하기 위해 애쓰다 top-notch 최고 수준의, 일류의 take on (특정 모습이나 성질 등) ~을 띠다, 나타내다 relaxed 편안한, 느긋한

07. 목적 문제

기사의 목적은 무엇인가?
(A) 한 레스토랑의 기념일 파티를 홍보하기 위해
(B) 메뉴의 새로운 품목들을 소개하기 위해
(C) 한 업체의 소유권 변화를 집중 조명하기 위해
(D) 전문 요리사가 지닌 요리 팁을 제공하기 위해

[해설] 첫 단락에 Hillview Café가 지난달에 Tyrone Manning 씨에게 매각되었다는 말과 함께(The restaurant was sold to Tyrone Manning last month ~) 그 식당의 훌륭함을 지속하기 위해 노력하고 있다고 알리면서 그 사람과의 인터뷰 내용을 소개하고 있다. 따라서 업체 소유권의 변화와 관련된 인터뷰임을 알 수 있으므로 (C)가 정답이다.

paraphrasing The restaurant was sold to Tyrone Manning 레스토랑이 Tyrone Manning 씨에게 매각되었다 → business's change in ownership 업체의 소유권 변화

[어휘] introduce ~을 소개하다 highlight ~을 집중 조명하다, 강조하다 ownership 소유권

08. 추론 문제

Rigsby 씨는 누구일 것 같은가?
(A) 잡지사 영업 사원
(B) 레스토랑 지배인
(C) 전문 요리사
(D) 음식 평론가

[해설] Rigsby 씨의 이름이 언급된 두 번째 단락에 그 사람이 <Dining Daily>에 실린 평가에서 자신의 식사 경험에 관한 내용을(In a recent review in Dining Daily, Casey Rigsby called her dining experience ~) 썼다는 말이 있으므로 음식 평론을 하는 사람임을 알 수 있다. 따라서 (D)가 정답이다.

[어휘] salesperson 영업 사원 critic 평론가, 비평가

09. True 문제

Hillview Café의 분위기에 관해 언급된 것은 무엇인가?
(A) 하루 중의 시간대에 따라 변화된다.
(B) 식사 손님들 사이의 대화가 활발하게 한다.
(C) 몇몇 고객들로부터 안 좋은 평가를 받았다.
(D) 새로운 장식물로 인해 개선되었다.

[해설] Hillview Café의 분위기를 설명한 마지막 단락에, 점심 때는 진지

mass-producer 대량 생산업체 assembly line (공장 등의) 조립라인 facility 시설(물) found ~을 설립하다 carpentry 목공 apprentice 견습생 woodworking 목공 작업 crank out (대량으로) ~을 쏟아내다 make a profit 이윤을 얻다 household 가정 achieve ~을 달성하다 employ ~을 고용하다 intend to부정사 ~할 계획이다, 작정이다

01. 주제 문제

기사의 주제는 무엇인가?
(A) Lisette 사가 새로운 라인의 맞춤 제작 제품들을 제공하고 있다.
(B) Lisette 사가 공급업체들 중의 하나를 인수했다.
(C) Lisette 사가 업계의 선도적인 고용주이다.
(D) Lisette 사가 세계적으로 성장해 왔다.

[해설] 첫 단락에 Lisette 사가 Belford 벌목의 사업 인수를 발표한 사실과 함께 Belford 벌목이 목재를 공급한 회사였다는 내용이(Lisette Inc. recently announced its business takeover of Belford Logging ~ supplied by Belford Logging) 있으므로 '공급업체의 인수'를 의미하는 (B)가 정답이다.

paraphrasing business takeover 사업 인수 → has acquired 인수했다

[어휘] acquire ~을 인수하다, 획득하다 supplier 공급업체 leading 선도적인, 앞서 가는 employer 고용주 field 업계, 분야

02. 세부사항 문제

Lisette 사는 무엇을 생산하는가?
(A) 빠르게 조립된 가구
(B) 목재 요리 도구
(C) 목공 작업용 공구
(D) 정원 장식용품

[해설] 두 번째 단락에 해당 회사가 조립 라인을 통해 가구를 만드는 주요 대량 생산업체(a major mass-producer of assembly line furniture)라는 말과 함께 매일 수십 개씩 완료할 수 있다고(finish dozens every day) 알리고 있으므로 '빠르게 조립된 가구'를 뜻하는 (A)가 정답이다.

[어휘] assemble ~을 조립하다 wooden 목재의 utensil 도구 tool 공구, 도구

03. True 문제

Medina 씨에 관해 언급된 것은 무엇인가?
(A) 원래 오클라호마 시티 출신이다.
(B) 10월에 대표이사직에서 물러날 것이다.
(C) 자신의 회사를 지속적으로 확장하고 싶어 한다.
(D) 여전히 취미로 전통적인 목공 작업을 한다.

[해설] 네 번째 단락에 나타난 Medina 씨의 인터뷰 내용에 전국의 모든 가정에 Lisette 사 브랜드를 보유하게 하는 일을 달성할 때까지 성장을 멈추지 않을 것이라는(I don't plan to stop growing until I achieve that) 말이 있는데, 이는 '사업의 지속적인 성장'을 의미하는 것이므로 (C)가 정답이다.

paraphrasing don't plan to stop growing 성장을 멈추지 않을 계획이다 → continue expanding her company 회사를 지속적으로 확장하다

[어휘] step down as ~의 자리에서 물러나다 expand ~을 확장하다, 확대하다 practice ~을 실행하다, 연습하다

paraphrasing 정답 1. (a) 2. (b) 3. (c)

04-06은 다음 기사를 참조하시오.

'사무실'의 의미 변화

5월 19일 — Richland 디자인 사에서는, '사무실'이라는 단어가 물리적인 장소 이상의 개념이 되어 가고 있다. —[1]—. 이 회사는 '원격 근무 프로그램,' 즉 REP를 도입했는데, 이는 직원들에게 더 흔하게 알려져 있는 것이다. 이 프로그램은 직원들에게 재택 근무를 하는 데 필요한 수단을 제공한다. Richland 디자인 사의 대표인 Timothy Wilhelm 씨는 [04]잠재적인 구직 지원자들이 더욱 가고 싶어 하는 회사를 만들기 위한 노력의 일환으로 이와 같은 변화를 채택했다. —[2]—. [04]"최고의 재능을 지닌 분들을 데려오기 위해서는, 최고의 업무 환경을 제공해야 합니다"라고 Wilhelm 씨가 말했다. "저희 쪽과 같이 대단히 경쟁이 치열한 업계에서는 제대로 된 팀원들을 보유하는 것이 성공하기 위한 유일한 방법입니다. —[3]—."

[05]REP를 시작하기로 결정하는 직원들은 일주일에 최대 4일까지 원격으로 근무하는 것을 선택할 수 있다. 주변 환경의 변화로 인해 창의성을 높일 수 있을 뿐만 아니라, 이와 같은 관행은 또한 시간이 오래 걸리고 스트레스를 유발하는 통근에 대한 필요성도 없애 준다. 최근의 설문 조사에 따르면, [06]일반적인 직장인이 주중에 매일 1시간이 넘는 시간을 통근하는 데 소비하는 것으로 나타난다. —[4]—. REP 지지자들은 이 문제에 대처할 수 있기를 바라고 있다.

physical 물리적인 launch ~을 시작하다, ~에 착수하다 adopt ~을 채택하다 in an effort to부정사 ~하기 위한 노력의 일환으로 desirable 호감이 가는, 사람들이 원하는 potential 잠재적인 job candidate 구직 지원자 working conditions 업무 환경 highly 대단히, 매우 competitive 경쟁적인 industry 업계 opt into ~을 하기로 결정하다, 선택하다 remotely 원격으로, 먼 거리에서 in addition to ~뿐만 아니라 scenery (주변) 배경 boost ~을 높이다, 증대시키다 eliminate ~을 없애다, 제거하다 commute 통근 according to ~에 따르면 average 일반적인, 평균의 supporter 지지자, 후원자 combat ~을 방지하다

04. 세부사항 문제

기사에 따르면, Richland 디자인 사는 왜 정책을 변경했는가?
(A) 직원들의 생산성 수준을 높이기 위해
(B) 일부 고객들의 불만 사항에 대응하기 위해
(C) 더욱 뛰어난 자질을 지닌 직원들을 끌어들이기 위해
(D) 경쟁사의 조치를 따라 하기 위해

[해설] 정책 변경의 목적이 제시된 첫 단락 중반부에, 잠재적인 구직 지원자들에게 더욱 호감이 가는 회사를 만들어 최고의 재능을 지닌 사람들을 데려오기(~ adopted the change in an effort to make the company more desirable to potential job candidates ~ "In order to bring in the best talent ~) 위함이라고 했다. 따라서 '더욱 뛰어난 직원을 끌어들이기 위해서'라는 의미로 쓰인 (C)가 정답이다.

paraphrasing bring in the best talent 최고의 재능을 지닌 사람들을 데려오기 → attract more highly qualified workers 더욱 뛰어난 자질을 지닌 직원을 끌어들이기

[어휘] productivity 생산성 respond to ~에 대응하다 highly qualified 뛰어난 자격을 지닌 competitor 경쟁사 action 조치, 움직임

DAY 14 121

하는지를 말하는 흐름이 되어야 알맞으므로 (B)가 정답이다.

02.

(12월 7일) — 유명한 부동산 개발업자 Andrew Logan은 지금의 자리에 오르기 위해 열심히 일했다. 그가 처음 애리조나에서 부동산 개발 분야에 입문했을 때, 그는 한 가지 큰 문제가 있다는 것을 알아차렸다. "저는 집을 짓는 데 필요한 기술을 가진 사람들이 필요했지만, 그들을 찾기가 너무 어려웠습니다"라고 Logan 씨는 인터뷰에서 말했다. "이미 훈련을 받은 사람들은 종종 다른 곳으로 가버렸습니다." 그것이 그가 직원들을 우선시하기 시작한 이유이다. "일단 저는 좋은 사람을 찾으면, 그들이 나를 위해 일하는 것이 행복하다는 것을 확실하게 했습니다."

real estate 부동산 developer 개발업자 field 분야 major 큰, 주요한 trained 훈련된, 숙련된

Q. Logan 씨는 사업에 어떤 문제가 있었는가?
(A) 숙련된 직원이 충분하지 않았다.
(B) 적당한 가격의 부동산이 없었다.

[문제 키워드] problem / Mr. Logan / have / his business

[해설] 키워드인 problem을 지문에서 찾는다. 지문 중반부에 그가 알아차린 큰 문제점이 숙련된 사람들을 찾기 힘들었다는(I needed people who already had the skills necessary to build houses, but they were so hard to find) 내용이 언급되어 있으므로 (A)가 정답이다.

03.

5월 10일 — Munford 시의회는 시내에 대규모 예술 프로젝트에 투자하기로 합의했다. 도시의 상가 구역의 건물 벽에 벽화를 그리기 위해 Munford 현대 미술 아카데미와 협력할 것이다. 젊은 예술가들이 약간의 노출을 받는 동시에 방문객들의 관심을 끌 수 있는 좋은 방법이 될 것이다. 시의원 Joe Rogers는 이 프로젝트가 1년 안에 제값을 할 것이라고 말한다. "우리는 벽화 앞에서 사진을 찍기 위해 여기로 오는 **수많은 관광객들 유치할 것입니다**"라고 의회가 이 문제에 대한 투표를 하기 전에 그는 말했다. "Sebring이 비슷한 일을 한 후, 매년 20%의 더 많은 관광객을 끌어들이기 시작했습니다."

council 의회 downtown 시내 collaboration 협력, 협조 mural 벽화 district 구역 exposure 노출 pay for itself 비용만큼 돈이 절약되다, 제값을 하다 similar 비슷한, 유사한

Q. 프로젝트의 어떤 장점이 언급되는가?
(A) Munford의 관광업을 촉진할 것이다.
(B) Munford 미술관으로 관심을 끌 것이다.

[문제 키워드] benefit / project

[해설] 키워드 project가 지문의 전체적인 소재이므로 지문 전반에서 단서를 파악해 각 선택지와 비교해야 한다. 지문 후반부에 수많은 관광객을 유치할 것이라는(We'll have tons of tourists coming here) 이점이 쓰여 있으므로 관광업을 촉진할 것이라고 하는 (A)가 정답이다.

[어휘] benefit 이점 tourism 관광업 draw attention 관심을 끌다

04.

침묵의 소리

톨레도 — Lammar Café로 들어서면, 미국의 50년대 스타일의 장식물이 여러분을 맞이할 것이다. 햄버거와 밀크셰이크 같은 클래식한 메뉴 품목들과 과거의 유니폼을 입은 종업원들로 인해, 여러분은 시간을 거슬러 올라간 것 같은 생각이 들 것이다. —[1]—. 이 레스토랑은 진짜로 당시와 같은 분위기를 유지하기 위해 한층 더 노력하고 있는데, **휴대전화 사용이 허용되지 않는다. 이 방침은 엄격히 준수되고 있으며, 휴대전화를 사용하다 발각되는 사람은 누구든지 밖에서 전화를 받도록 요청받는다.** —[2]—. 하지만, 대부분의 손님들은 전화기를 계속 확인하는 일을 하지 않으면서 레스토랑에 자리한 순간의 경험을 즐긴다.

décor 장식(물) vintage 고풍스러운, 구식의 wait staff 종업원 go the extra mile 한층 더 노력하다 authentic 진짜와 똑같은, 진품의 policy 정책, 방침 strictly 엄격히 follow ~을 준수하다, 따르다 patron 손님, 고객 present 자리에 있는, 참석한 constantly 지속적으로

Q. [1]과 [2]로 표시된 위치들 중에서, 다음 문장이 들어가기에 가장 적절한 곳은 어디인가?

"일부 고객들은 이 규칙에 적응하는 데 어려움이 있음을 인정한다."

(A) [1]
(B) [2]

[해설] 제시된 문장은 특정 규칙을 지칭하는 the rule과 함께 '일부 고객이 그 규칙에 적응하는 데 어려움이 있음을 인정한다'는 의미를 나타낸다. 따라서 휴대전화 사용이 허용되지 않는다는 말과 함께 발각될 경우의 조치가 언급된 문장 뒤에 위치한 [2]에 들어가 그 규칙에 따른 어려움을 말하는 흐름이 되어야 알맞으므로 (B)가 정답이다.

[어휘] admit ~을 인정하다 adjust to ~에 적응하다

실전 문제

| 01.(B) | 02.(A) | 03.(C) | 04.(C) | 05.(A) | 06.(D) |
| 07.(C) | 08.(D) | 09.(A) | 10.(B) | 11.(D) | 12.(C) |
| 13.(B) |

01-03는 다음 기사를 참조하시오.

오클라호마 시티 (3월 19일) — **01 Lisette 사가 최근 Belford 벌목 사의 사업 인수를 발표했다. 이는 그 회사가 사용하는 대부분의 목재가 Belford 벌목에 의해 공급되었다**는 점을 감안하면 전반적인 회사 운영비를 줄이는 데 도움이 될 것이다.

Lisette 사는 맞춤 제작 가구 디자인 회사로 처음 출발했지만, 불과 몇 년 만에, **02 조립 라인을 통해 가구를 만드는 주요 대량 생산업체**로 탈바꿈했다. 수제 의자 또는 탁자는 만드는 데 몇 주가 걸릴 수도 있지만, 이곳 오클라호마 시티에 위치한 이 회사의 시설은 **02 매일 수십 개씩 완료할 수 있다.**

Lisette 사는 고등학교 졸업 후에 견습생으로 목공을 배운 Lisette Medina 씨에 의해 설립된 회사이다. "제가 처음에는 전통적인 목공 작업의 중요성을 배우기는 했지만, 사업은 취미로 하는 것이 아니라 이윤을 얻기 위해 제품을 빠르게 쏟아내야 한다고 생각합니다"라고 그녀는 인터뷰에서 밝혔다.

Belford 벌목 사의 인수에 관해 질문했을 때, Medina 씨는 회사에 대한 희망 사항을 공유해 주었다. "**03 제 목표는 전국의 모든 가정마다 Lisette 사 브랜드를 보유하게 하는 것입니다. 저는 그것을 달성할 때까지 성장을 멈추지 않을 계획입니다**"라고 Medina 씨는 말했다.

Lisette 사는 현재 12,000명의 직원을 고용하고 있으며, 올해 10월에 문을 열 또 다른 생산 시설을 위해 추가 직원을 고용할 계획이다.

takeover 인수, 매입 operation expenses 운영비 supply ~을 공급하다 custom 맞춤 제작의 turn into ~로 탈바꿈하다, 변모하다

120 기적의 토익 RC

중앙 로비의 안내 데스크로 가셔서 Dominick Arias를 찾으십시오. 이 분은 귀하와 함께 근무하게 될 저희 사원급 연구원들 중의 한 분입니다. ⁰⁷이분께서 귀하의 첫 출근일에 필요한 모든 사항을 알고 계십니다. 이분께서 귀하의 사원증에 필요한 사진을 촬영할 수 있도록 보안팀으로 안내해 드릴 것입니다. ⁰⁸그것이 발급되기까지는 이틀 정도 걸릴 것입니다. 귀하께서는 그곳에서 임시 사원증을 받게 되실 것입니다. 오리엔테이션과 환영회가 그 후에 열립니다.

질문이 있으실 경우, 언제든지 제게 알려 주시기 바랍니다.

안녕히 계십시오.

Melissa Frey
인사부장, Hanover 연구실

application 지원(서) position 직책, 일자리 choose ~을 선발하다, 선택하다 among ~ 중에서 candidate 지원자 management 경영(진) well qualified 뛰어난 자격을 갖춘 a wide range of 아주 다양한 task 업무, 일 reception desk 안내 데스크 ask for ~을 찾아 오다 escort A to B A를 B로 안내하다 badge 신분증 temporary 임시의, 일시적인 remaining 남은, 나머지의 reception 환영회 follow 뒤따르다

05. 동사의 형태

[해설] 다음 문장에 과거 시제 동사 were chosen을 써서 상대방이 이미 과거 시점에 선택된 사람임을 나타내고 있으므로 지원서(your application)를 받은 것도 과거에 완료된 일이어야 알맞다. 따라서 완료된 일의 상태가 현재까지 지속되는 것을 나타낼 때 사용하는 현재완료 시제 (A) have accepted가 정답이다. 과거진행 시제인 (D) were accepting이 쓰이면 상대방의 지원서를 과거에 계속 받고 있었다는 의미가 되어 어색하다.

06. 동사 어휘

[해설] 빈칸이 속한 문장은 상대방을 선발한 이유와 관련되어야 하며, 목적어로 쓰인 a wide range of tasks와 의미가 어울려야 하므로 '~을 수행하다, ~하다'라는 의미를 나타내는 (B) perform이 정답이다.

[어휘] train ~을 교육하다 request ~을 요청하다 cancel ~을 취소하다

07. 동사의 형태

[해설] 빈칸 앞에 이미 문장의 동사 knows가 있으므로 또 다른 동사 need가 빈칸에 쓰이려면 준동사의 형태가 되어 빈칸 이하 부분이 everything을 수식하는 역할을 해야 알맞다. everything은 사람에 의해 필요해지는 대상에 해당되므로 수동의 의미를 나타낼 수 있는 과거분사 (C) needed가 정답이다.

08. 알맞은 문장 고르기

(A) 사원증을 재발급하려면 5달러를 지불하셔야 합니다.
(B) 처음에는 저희 시설 내에서 찾아다니시는 데 어려움을 겪으실 수 있습니다.
(C) 언제든지 회사 홈페이지에서 하나 다운로드하시기 바랍니다.
(D) 그것이 발급되기까지는 이틀 정도 걸릴 것입니다.

[해설] 앞 문장에 사원증(your badge)을 만드는 데 필요한 일이 언급되어 있으므로 your badge를 It으로 지칭해 그것이 발급되는 데 걸리는 시간을 알려 주는 (D)가 정답이다. 처음 출근하는 사람에게 전달하는 정보이므로 사원증 재발급 비용이 언급된 (A)는 적절하지 않다.

[어휘] reissue ~을 재발급하다 have difficulty -ing ~하는 데 어려움을 겪다 navigate (길, 방향 등) ~을 찾아다니다 facility 시설 at first 처음에는 issue ~을 발급하다

PART 7 기사 (1) 비즈니스 기사

풀이 방법 해석

Helena Saunders의 또 다른 모바일 히트

개발자 Helena Saunders는 수백만 명에 의해 다운로드되고 사용되는 또 다른 모바일 앱을 출시했다. Saunders 씨는 패션 비즈니스를 공부했고 패션디자인 회사에서 그녀의 경력을 시작하려고 했었지만, 그녀가 독학한 취미인 모바일 앱을 개발하는 것이 상당히 더 유망한 것으로 드러나자 그러한 바람을 접기로 결심했다.

그녀의 앱의 탁월함은 그것의 단순함에 있는 것 같다. 대부분의 사람들은 전적으로 주의를 쏟지 않아도 되는 앱을 사용하고 싶어 한다.

그녀의 첫 번째 앱은 옷을 왼쪽 또는 오른쪽으로 넘기는 것만 포함했었다. 그것은 선호도를 기억하여 그에 기반한 비슷한 스타일을 추천해주었다. 소매 업체들은 빠르게 그 앱에 자금을 댔다. 이번에는, 친구들을 찾는 앱을 개발했는데, 이것은 그들의 위치와 옷 선호도에 기반한 것으로 첫 번째 달에만 300만 명이 넘는 사용자들에 의해 다운로드 되었고 갈수록 증가하고 있다.

 연습 문제

01.(B) 02.(A) 03.(A) 04.(B)

01.

디저트를 먹을 배를 남겨두세요

Timber Grill의 소유주이자 요리사인 Lloyd Merrit 씨는 단순히 스테이크 이상의 것을 제공하고 싶어 했다. ―[1]―. 그는 '그릴 위의 음식'이라는 이 레스토랑의 테마 안에 포함되는 달콤한 디저트 요리를 만들기 위해 노력했다. 수개월간의 실험 끝에, 그는 마침내 자신의 대표 요리로 Grilled Peaches를 결정하게 되었다. **Merrit 씨는 주스 혼합물에 복숭아를 밤새 담가 둔 후에 계피와 기타 향료를 혼합한 것과 섞는다.** ―[2]―. 매일 밤마다 식사 공간이 가득 차는 것을 보면, Merrit 씨의 노력이 결실을 맺은 것이 분명하다.

stay within ~의 범위 내에 머물러 있다 theme 주제, 테마 experimentation 실험 settle on ~을 결정하다 signature (제품 등이) 대표적인, 고유의 soak A in B A를 B에 담그다, 흠뻑 적시다 blend 혼합(물) sprinkle A with B A를 B와 섞다 spice 향료 pay off 결실을 맺다, 성과를 내다

Q. [1]과 [2]로 표시된 위치들 중에서, 다음 문장이 들어가기에 가장 적절한 곳은 어디인가?

"완성된 제품은 고객들이 또 먹고 싶어서 계속 다시 찾아 오게 만드는 맛있는 특별 요리다."

(A) [1]
(B) [2]

[문제 키워드] finished product

[해설] 제시된 문장은 완성된 제품이 지니는 특징을 말하고 있으므로 제조 방식이 설명된 문장 뒤에 위치한 [2]에 들어가 완성된 제품이 어떤 역할을

03.

Bowen 씨께

귀하의 주문 사항을 검토한 바, 저희는 귀하께 비용이 과다 청구되었음을 인정합니다. 19.93달러의 차액이 귀하의 계좌로 환불되었습니다. 이것이 귀하의 신용카드에 반영되었음을 확인하실 수 있습니다.

upon -ing ~하자마자, ~한 즉시 overcharged 과다 청구된 refund ~을 환불하다 account 계좌 see that ~임을 확인하다, 알다

[단서] was refunded

[해설] 앞 문장에 과거 시제 동사 was refunded와 함께 이미 차액이 환불되었음을 알리고 있으므로 반영된 시점도 과거여야 한다. 따라서 현재까지 지속되는 과거의 일을 나타내는 현재완료 시제인 (B) has been reflected가 정답이다.

[어휘] reflect ~을 반영하다

04.

Michaels 씨께

회사에서 귀하의 자카르타 지사로의 전근 지원서를 거절했다는 사실을 알려드리게 되어 유감스럽습니다. 안타깝게도, 현재 그곳에는 공석이 남아 있지 않지만, 자리가 생길 경우에 다시 한번 지원해 주시기를 권해 드립니다.

regret to부정사 ~해서 유감이다 inform A that A에게 ~라고 알리다 application 지원(서), 신청(서) transfer to ~로 전근하다 branch 지사, 지점 opening 공석 encourage A to부정사 A에게 ~하도록 권하다, 장려하다 apply 지원하다, 신청하다

[단서] regret to inform

[해설] 통보 사실이 언급되는 that절에 빈칸이 속해 있는데, 특정 사실을 통보하는 경우에 이미 과거 시점에 결정된 내용을 알리는 것이므로 현재까지 지속되는 과거의 일을 나타내는 현재완료 시제 (B) has declined가 정답이다.

[어휘] decline ~을 거절하다

실전 문제

01. (C) 02. (B) 03. (B) 04. (A) 05. (A) 06. (B)
07. (C) 08. (D)

01-04는 다음 기사를 참조하시오.

Dino Diner

01 유명 영화 시리즈 <Dinosaur District>를 테마로 한 새 레스토랑이 이곳 코빙턴에 개업했다. 소유주 Travis Short 씨는 영화의 테마를 활용하는 것이 마케팅에 도움이 된다고 주장한다. "물론, 저는 해당 스튜디오에 저작권료를 지불해야 합니다. 하지만 이는 대부분의 레스토랑이 광고 방송과 브랜드 작업에 소비해야 하는 것보다 적은 액수입니다"라고 그가 한 인터뷰에서 밝혔다.

02 지난 주말에 있었던 이 레스토랑의 성대한 개업식 이후로, 상당히 많은 관심을 받아 오고 있다. **03** 가족들은 자리를 안내받기까지 최대 2시간까지 줄을 서서 기다렸다. "저희 아이들이 <Dinosaur District> 영화를 너무 좋아해서, 기다릴 만한 가치가 있어요"라고 이 레스토랑에 관해 부모 한 사람이 말했다.

04 Dino Diner는 곧 코빙턴의 명소로 알려질 것으로 보인다.

themed after ~을 테마로 한 owner 소유주 claim that ~라고 주장하다 royalty 저작권료 spend A on B (돈, 시간 등) A를 B에 소비하다 commercial 광고 방송 branding 브랜드 작업 a considerable deal of 상당히 많은 attention 관심, 주목, 주의 worth+명사 ~할 만한 가치가 있는 parent 부모 중 한 명 regarding ~와 관련해 it seems like ~한 것 같다 known as ~로서 알려지다 landmark 명소, 인기 장소

01. 동사의 형태

[해설] 우선, 빈칸 앞에는 주어와 themed가 이끄는 수식어가, 빈칸 뒤에는 부사와 in 전치사구만 있으므로 빈칸이 문장의 동사 자리이다. 두 번째 단락에서, 과거 시점에 개업식이 있었다는(grand opening last weekend) 것으로 보아 이미 개업한 상태임을 알 수 있으므로, 과거에 발생한 일이 현재까지 이어지는 상태를 나타낼 때 사용하는 현재완료 시제 (C) has opened가 정답이다.

02. 동사 어휘

[해설] 빈칸 뒤에 위치한 a considerable deal of attention을 목적어로 취해 '많은 관심을 받아 오고 있다'라는 의미가 되어야 가장 자연스러우므로 '~을 받다'를 뜻하는 (B) received가 정답이다.

[어휘] award ~을 수여하다, 주다 complete ~을 완료하다, 완수하다

03. 알맞은 문장 고르기

(A) 점심과 저녁 식사 시간 근무조로 일할 배송 기사들을 구하는 중이다.
(B) 가족들은 자리를 안내받기까지 최대 2시간까지 줄을 서서 기다렸다.
(C) 이 레스토랑의 메뉴가 그곳 웹사이트에 게시되어 있다.
(D) 포장 음식 전용 창구가 곧 설치될 것이다.

[해설] 빈칸 앞에 언급된, 사람들의 많은 관심(a considerable deal of attention)과 다음 문장에 나타난 기다릴 만한 가치가 있다는 점(worth the wait)과 연계되는 문장이 필요하므로 자리를 안내받기까지 긴 시간이 소요됨을 언급한 (B)가 정답이다.

[어휘] wanted 구인 중인 shift 교대 근무(조) takeout window 포장 음식 전용 창구 install ~을 설치하다

04. 부사 어휘

[해설] 미래 시제 동사 will become과 의미가 어울리는 시점 부사가 쓰여야 하므로 '곧, 머지 않아'라는 의미로 쓰이는 (A) soon이 정답이다. 나머지 부사들은 모두 과거 시점을 나타낸다.

[어휘] recently 최근에 once (과거의) 한때, 한번

05-08은 다음 이메일을 참조하시오.

수신: William McBride
발신: Melissa Frey
날짜: 11월 9일
제목: Hanover 연구실에 오신 것을 환영합니다!

McBride 씨께

05 저희 Hanover 연구실은 A팀의 사원급 연구원 직책에 대한 귀하의 지원서를 받았습니다. 귀하께서는 많은 지원자들 가운데서 선발되셨습니다. **06** 저희 인사부와 경영진은 귀하께서 매우 뛰어난 자격을 갖추고 있으며, 아주 다양한 업무들을 수행할 준비가 되어 있으시다고 생각합니다. 귀하의 첫 출근일은 11월 14일 월요일이 될 것입니다.

빈칸 뒤에 위치한 명사구 an attached tow cable(부착된 견인용 케이블)은 Washington 트럭 모델의 특징 중 하나로 생각할 수 있으므로 '~을 특징으로 하다'를 뜻하는 동사 (A) features가 정답이다.

[어휘] latest 최신의   attached 부착된   tow cable 견인용 케이블   conduct ~을 수행하다   address ~을 처리하다   force ~에게 강요하다

20. 동사 어휘

Kenosha's Citizen Recognition Day 행사 중에, Julia Wings 씨가 자선 행사 참여에 대해 상을 받았다.

[해설] 선택지가 다양한 동사들로 구성되어 있으므로 동사 어휘 문제이다. 명사 award를 목적어로 취해 '상'에 대해 할 수 있는 행위를 나타낼 동사가 필요하므로 '~을 받아들이다, 수락하다'를 뜻하는 동사 (C) accepted가 정답이다.

[어휘] charity 자선 (활동)   revise ~을 수정하다   contribute ~에 기여하다, 공헌하다, 기부하다   assume ~라고 생각하다, (책임 등) ~을 맡다

21. 동사 어휘

Pham 씨는 다가오는 Boston 리더십 세미나를 위해 10개의 좌석을 예약했다.

[해설] 선택지가 다양한 동사들로 구성되어 있으므로 동사 어휘 문제이다. 특정 세미나 행사를 위해 10개의 좌석(10 seats)과 관련해 할 수 있는 일을 나타낼 동사가 필요하므로 '~을 예약하다'를 뜻하는 (D) reserved가 정답이다.

[어휘] upcoming 다가오는, 곧 있을   raise ~을 증가시키다, 끌어 올리다   indicate ~을 나타내다, 가리키다

22. 동사 어휘

Cindy Bauer 씨의 미용실은 고객을 위한 서비스를 개선하기 위해 할 수 있는 모든 것을 다하고 있다.

[해설] 선택지가 다양한 동사들로 구성되어 있으므로 동사 어휘 문제이다. 빈칸에 쓰여 to부정사를 구성할 동사는 서비스와 관련해 모든 것을 다하는 목적을 나타내야 하므로 '~을 개선하다'를 뜻하는 (B) enhance가 정답이다.

[어휘] distribute ~을 배부하다, 나눠 주다   enhance ~을 개선하다   claim ~을 주장하다, 요구하다   combine ~을 결합하다, 조합하다

23. 동사 어휘

Nishida 씨는 주말쯤에 자신의 분기별 판매 할당량을 초과할 기세를 보이고 있다.

[해설] 선택지가 다양한 동사들로 구성되어 있으므로 동사 어휘 문제이다. 특정 시점까지 판매 할당량과 관련해 할 수 있는 일을 나타내기에 적절한 동사가 필요하므로 '~을 초과하다'를 뜻하는 (C) exceed가 정답이다.

[어휘] be on pace to부정사 ~할 기세를 보이다   quarterly 분기의   sales 판매(량), 매출   quota 할당량   determine ~을 결정하다, 밝혀내다   succeed 성공하다   exceed ~을 초과하다   reveal ~을 드러내다, 폭로하다

24. 동사 어휘

Cox 부동산은 지난주에 이메일을 통해 주택 공개 행사에 대한 초대장을 발송했다.

[해설] 선택지가 다양한 동사들로 구성되어 있으므로 동사 어휘 문제이다. 명사 invitations를 목적어로 취해 '초대장'과 관련된 행위를 나타내기에 적절한 동사가 필요하므로 '~을 발송하다, 보내다'를 뜻하는 (A) extended가 정답이다.

[어휘] invitation 초대(장)   via ~을 통해   recover ~을 회복하다, 되찾다   notify ~에게 통보하다

PART 6 시간 표현이 없는 현재완료 시제

풀이 방법 해석

Medina가 이름을 떨치다

가수 Alex Medina가 지역 학교를 위한 기금 모금 프로젝트를 진행함으로써 지역 사회에 기여했다. "한 유명인이 이 기금 모금 행사에 앞장서 준 덕분에 학교가 필요한 기금을 모았을 뿐만 아니라 학생들에게 소중한 경험을 제공함으로써 전체 프로젝트가 큰 성공을 거뒀습니다"라고 Troy 고등학교의 교장인 Tina Sharpton이 말했다.

프로젝트 동안 모인 기금은 Troy 학군 전체에 걸쳐 컴퓨터실을 업데이트하는 데 사용될 것이다. 정부 공무원들에게 여러 번 요청했음에도 불구하고 기금은 8년 넘게 승인되지 않았다. 학생들은 이번 업그레이드에 대해 흥분과 열광을 드러냈다. 그들은 이전에 있던 구식의 기기 대신 현재의 기술을 사용하게 되기를 간절히 원하고 있다.

  연습 문제

01.(A)   02.(B)   03.(B)   04.(B)

01.

Beach Burgers가 로스앤젤레스에 또 한 곳의 지점을 열었으며, 이는 현재 이곳이 남부 캘리포니아 지역에서 가장 인기 있는 패스트푸드 체인임을 의미하는 것입니다. 이 업체는 샌디에이고 시내 중심가에서 소규모 가족 중심으로 운영되는 푸드 트럭으로 시작했습니다.

branch 지점   family-run 가족 중심으로 운영되는

[단서] it is now the most popular, started as

[해설] 빈칸 뒤에 현재(now) 가장 인기 있는 체인임을 의미한다는 말로 보아, 이는 이미 과거 시점에 지점을 하나 더 연 사실을 알 수 있으므로 과거에 발생된 일이 현재까지 영향을 미칠 때 사용하는 현재완료 시제인 (A) has opened가 정답이다.

02.

부동산 개발 업체들이 Centerville 극장의 철거를 요구하고 있다. 많은 지역 주민들이 이 생각에 반대하고 있는데, 이 장소가 아주 작은 이 마을에서 라이브 공연을 제공하는 유일한 곳으로 남아 있기 때문이다.

real estate 부동산   developer 개발 업체, 개발자   call for ~을 요구하다   against ~에 반대하여   venue 장소, 행사장

[단서] demolishment, are against the idea

[해설] because 앞에 위치한 주절은 많은 주민들이 현재(are) 반대하고 있다는 내용인데, 이는 과거에서 현재까지 해당 극장이 유일한 공연 장소로 존재해 온 사실을 바탕으로 하는 것이다. 따라서 과거에서 현재까지의 지속 상태와 관련한 현재완료 시제 (B) has remained가 정답이다.

[어휘] remain ~로 남아 있다, 유지되다

DAY 14   117

같은 자선 단체에 기부될 것이다.

[해설] 선택지가 동사 collect의 다양한 형태로 구성되어 있으므로 문법 문제이다. 빈칸 뒤에 문장의 동사 will be donated가 있으므로 또 다른 동사 collect는 준동사로 쓰여야 한다. 따라서 분사들 중의 하나를 골라야 하는데, 빈칸이 수식하는 toys and clothing은 사람에 의해 수집되는 대상에 해당되므로 수동의 의미를 나타낼 수 있는 과거분사 (D) collected가 정답이다.

[어휘] resident 주민 donate A to B A를 B에 기부하다 charity 자선 단체 collect ~을 모으다, 수집하다

09. 분사구문

새 사무용 의자 세트를 조립할 때는 설명서를 참조해 주세요.

[해설] 선택지가 동사 assemble의 다양한 형태로 구성되어 있으므로 문법 문제이다. 접속사 when 뒤에서 주어 없이 동사가 바로 쓰이려면 분사구문의 형태가 되어야 하는데, 빈칸 뒤에 위치한 명사구를 목적어로 취해야 하므로 현재분사인 (C) assembling이 정답이다.

[어휘] assemble 모으다, 조립하다 consult 참조하다 manual 설명서

10. 현재분사로만 출제되는 분사구문

Camacho 백화점은 8월 5일 토요일부터 무료 메이크업 강좌를 제공할 것이다.

[해설] 선택지가 동사 begin의 다양한 형태와 명사로 구성되어 있으므로 문법 문제이다. 빈칸 앞에 이미 문장의 동사 will offer가 있으므로 또 다른 동사 begin은 준동사로 쓰여야 한다. 따라서 현재분사의 형태인 (A) beginning이 정답이다. 명사 (C) beginner는 makeup classes와 복합명사를 구성하지 않으므로 오답이다.

[어휘] offer ~을 제공하다 free 무료의

11. 과거분사

사무 공간 부족으로 인해 Hammington 법률사무소는 새 업무 빌딩으로 이전할 것이다.

[해설] 선택지가 동사 remodel의 다양한 형태로 구성되어 있으므로 문법 문제이다. 빈칸 앞에 부사, 뒤에 명사가 있으므로 office building을 수식할 분사가 빈칸에 필요한데, 건물은 리모델링되는 것이므로 분사 (A)와 (B) 중 수동의 의미를 나타내는 (B) remodeled가 정답이다.

[어휘] lack 결핍, 부족 space 공간 relocate 이전하다 remodel 개조하다, 리모델링하다

12. 명사를 뒤에서 수식하는 분사

Hancock 농장에서 사용되는 화학 살충제가 식수에서 발견되었다.

[해설] 선택지가 다양한 품사의 단어들로 구성되어 있으므로 문법 문제이다. 빈칸과 전치사구 by Hancock Farms는 주어 Chemical pesticides를 뒤에서 수식하는 수식어구를 구성해야 하므로 빈칸에는 분사들 중의 하나가 들어가야 한다. 빈칸 뒤에 목적어 없이 by 전치사구(~에 의해)가 바로 이어지고 있으므로 목적어를 취하지 않는 과거분사 (B) used가 정답이다.

[어휘] chemical pesticide 화학 살충제 usefully 유용하게

13. 과거분사

새로운 본사 사무실에 대해 제안된 평면도가 반드시 내일 제출되어야 한다.

[해설] 선택지가 동사 propose의 다양한 형태와 명사로 구성되어 있으므로 문법 문제이다. 정관사 The와 명사 floor plan 사이에 위치한 빈칸은 명사를 수식할 수 있는 분사가 필요한 자리이다. floor plan은 사람에 의해 제안되는 것이므로 수동의 의미를 나타낼 수 있는 과거분사 (C) proposed가 정답이다.

[어휘] floor plan 평면도 headquarters 본사 submit ~을 제출하다 proposal 제안(서) propose ~을 제안하다

14. 감정 동사의 분사 구분

저희 호텔에서 도움이 필요하실 때는 언제든지 저희 직원들이 기꺼이 도와 드릴 것입니다.

[해설] 선택지가 동사 delight의 다양한 형태로 구성되어 있으므로 문법 문제이다. 빈칸 앞뒤에 각각 위치한 be동사, to부정사와 결합될 수 있는 것이 필요하므로 이 둘과 함께 '기꺼이 ~하다, ~해서 기쁘다'라는 의미를 나타낼 때 사용하는 (C) delighted가 정답이다. 참고로, delighted는 사람에 대해서만 사용한다.

[어휘] assist ~을 돕다 delight ~을 기쁘게 하다; 기쁨

15. 동명사의 역할: 주어 역할

대부분의 사업가들은 은행에서 사업 대출을 승인받는 것이 가장 스트레스를 받는 일이라고 알렸다.

[해설] 선택지가 동사 obtain의 다양한 형태로 구성되어 있으므로 문법 문제이다. 빈칸 뒤에 위치한 명사구(approval ~ bank)를 목적어로 취해 that절의 동사 is의 주어 역할을 할 수 있는 것은 동명사이므로 (D) obtaining이 정답이다.

[어휘] approval 승인 loan 대출 task 일, 업무 obtain ~을 얻다, 획득하다

16. to부정사의 역할: 명사 역할

다음 작품에 출연하는 배우들이 다음 주에 예행 연습을 시작할 계획이다.

[해설] 선택지가 동사 begin의 다양한 형태로 구성되어 있으므로 문법 문제이다. 빈칸 앞에 위치한 plan은 to부정사와 결합해 '~할 계획이다'라는 의미를 나타내므로 (B) to begin이 정답이다.

[어휘] production (영화, 연극 등의) 작품 rehearse 예행 연습하다

17. 단순 시제: 미래

Northern 마케팅 사는 내년 초쯤에는 두 배나 많은 고객들을 보유하게 될 것이다.

[해설] 선택지가 동사 have의 다양한 형태로 구성되어 있으므로 문법 문제이다. 미래 시점 표현 by the beginning of next year와 시제가 어울려야 하므로 미래 시제 동사인 (B) will have가 정답이다.

[어휘] twice as many 두 배나 많은

18. '타동사+목적어+전치사' 숙어

Grisham 컨설팅 사는 자사의 사무실을 개조하는 데 많은 액수의 자금을 쏟아부었다.

[해설] 선택지가 다양한 전치사들로 구성되어 있으므로 전치사 어휘 문제이다. 문장의 동사로 쓰인 put은 'put A into B'의 구조로 쓰여 '(돈, 시간 등) A를 B에 쏟다'라는 의미를 나타내므로 (B) into가 정답이다.

[어휘] a large amount of 많은 액수의, 많은 양의 funding 자금

19. 동사 어휘

최신 Washington 트럭 모델은 차량에 부착된 견인용 케이블을 특징으로 한다.

[해설] 선택지가 다양한 동사들로 구성되어 있으므로 동사 어휘 문제이다.

05.

1. 선택지 보고 문법/어휘 문제 파악하기 ☑문법 문제 ☐어휘 문제
2. 빈칸 분석하기 빈칸 앞에 있는 것 ☑완전한 절 ☐불완전한 절
   → 빈칸에는 ☐문장의 필수 성분 ☑수식어 역할을 하는 것이 들어가야 한다.
   → 정답의 후보 2개 (B, C)
   → parking lot과의 의미 관계 ☐능동 ☑수동
3. 정답 선택하기 정답 (B)

저희 호텔 고객들만을 위해 지정된 주차장에 차량을 주차해 주세요.

06.

1. 선택지 보고 문법/어휘 문제 파악하기 ☑문법 문제 ☐어휘 문제
2. 빈칸 분석하기 빈칸 앞에 있는 것 ☑접속사 ☐전치사
   → 빈칸이 포함된 절에 동사가 없으므로 ☐명사 ☑분사가 들어가야 한다.
   → 정답의 후보 2개 (B, D)
   → 주절의 주어 you와의 의미 관계 ☑능동 ☐수동
3. 정답 선택하기 정답 (D)

허가증을 신청하실 때, 귀하의 현재 우편 주소를 포함시켜야 합니다.

실전 문제

01.(C)	02.(C)	03.(A)	04.(D)	05.(B)	06.(C)
07.(C)	08.(D)	09.(C)	10.(A)	11.(B)	12.(B)
13.(C)	14.(C)	15.(D)	16.(B)	17.(B)	18.(B)
19.(A)	20.(C)	21.(D)	22.(B)	23.(C)	24.(A)

01. 분사의 역할: 명사 수식

제안된 일부 행사 장소들은 동시에 10개가 넘는 행사들을 개최하기에는 적합하지 않다.

[해설] 선택지가 동사 suggest의 다양한 형태와 명사로 구성되어 있으므로 문법 문제이다. 정관사 the와 명사 venues 사이에 위치한 빈칸은 형용사 자리이므로 형용사와 같은 역할을 하는 과거분사 (C) suggested가 정답이다. 명사 (D) suggestion은 venues와 복합 명사를 구성하지 않으므로 오답이다.

[어휘] venue 행사장 be suitable for ~에 적합하다 suggest ~을 제안하다 suggestion 제안, 의견

02. 과거분사

모든 필수 자재들을 작업 현장으로 들여왔으므로, Manning Tower 공사가 드디어 시작될 수 있다.

[해설] 선택지가 동사 require의 다양한 형태와 명사로 구성되어 있으므로 문법 문제이다. 정관사 the와 명사 materials 사이에 위치한 빈칸은 형용사 자리이며, 분사로 대체할 수 있다. 또한 materials는 사람에 의해 필요해지는 대상에 해당되므로 수동의 의미를 나타내는 과거분사 (C) required가 정답이다.

[어휘] material 자재, 재료 job site 작업 현장 required 필수의, 필요한 requirement 필수 요건

03. 현재분사로만 출제되는 분사구문

빠르게 다가오는 마감 시한으로 인해, 기의 모든 팀원들이 다음 주에 소과 근무를 해야 한다.

[해설] 선택지가 동사 approach의 다양한 형태로 구성되어 있으므로 문법 문제이다. 부사 rapidly와 명사 deadline 사이에 위치한 빈칸은 부사의 수식을 받으면서 명사를 수식할 분사가 쓰일 자리인데, approach의 분사가 명사를 수식할 때는 현재분사로만 사용되므로 (A) approaching이 정답이다.

[어휘] due to ~로 인해 deadline 마감 시한 approach 다가오다, 다가가다

04. 과거분사

Wenger 씨는 인턴 사원을 뽑는 데 어려움이 있었는데, 모든 지원자들이 자격을 갖추고 있었기 때문이다.

[해설] 선택지가 동사 qualify의 다양한 형태와 명사로 구성되어 있으므로 문법 문제이다. be동사 were 뒤에 위치한 빈칸은 as절의 주어(all of the applicants)에 대한 보어이므로 분사 또는 명사 중에서 골라야 한다. 지원자들은 자격이 주어지는 입장이므로 수동의 의미를 나타낼 수 있는 과거분사 (D) qualified가 정답이다.

[어휘] applicant 지원자 qualify 자격을 갖추다, ~에게 자격을 갖춰 주다 qualification 자격 요건 qualified 자격을 갖춘, 적격인

05. 현재분사

그 연구는 플라스틱 제품이 해양 생태계에 미치는 지속적인 영향에 초점을 맞출 것이다.

[해설] 선택지가 동사 last의 다양한 형태로 구성되어 있으므로 문법 문제이다. 정관사 the와 명사 effect 사이에 위치한 빈칸은 명사 수식이 가능한 분사가 쓰일 수 있는 자리인데, 자동사 last는 현재분사의 형태로만 명사를 수식할 수 있으므로 (B) lasting이 정답이다.

[어휘] effect 영향 ecosystem 생태계 last 지속되다 lasting 지속되는

06. 과거분사

예정된 공연 시간보다 최소 30분 전에 극장에 도착하시기 바랍니다.

[해설] 선택지가 동사 schedule의 다양한 형태로 구성되어 있으므로 문법 문제이다. 소유격 대명사 your와 명사구 show time 사이에 위치한 빈칸은 명사를 수식할 수 있는 분사가 쓰여야 하는 자리이다. 공연 시간은 사람에 의해 예정되는 대상이므로 수동의 의미를 나타내는 과거분사 (C) scheduled가 정답이다.

[어휘] at least 최소한 prior to ~ 전에, ~에 앞서

07. 감정 동사의 분사 구분

Timmy Buck 씨의 고객들은 그의 맞춤 제작 가구에 대해 거의 항상 만족한다.

[해설] 선택지가 동사 satisfy의 다양한 형태로 구성되어 있으므로 문법 문제이다. 빈칸 앞뒤에 각각 위치한 be동사 are, 전치사 with와 결합 가능한 것이 필요하므로 이 둘과 함께 '~에 만족하다'라는 의미를 나타낼 때 사용하는 (C) satisfied가 정답이다. 참고로, satisfied는 사람에 대해서만 사용한다.

[어휘] custom-made 맞춤 제작된 satisfy ~을 만족시키다 satisfactory 만족스러운

08. 명사를 뒤에서 수식하는 분사

지역 주민들을 통해 모은 모든 장난감과 의류는 Open Arms Society와

주문하려면 제품 비용의 절반(18달러)을 지불해야 하는데 나머지 절반은 회사에서 낸다고(There is also an optional sweater available ~ should pay for half the cost of the item ($18), and the company will cover the cost of the other half) 쓰여 있으므로 (A)가 정답이다.

paraphrasing the company will cover the cost of the other half 회사에서 나머지 절반의 비용을 충당할 것이다 → be partially paid for by the company 회사에 의해 일부 비용이 지불된다

[어휘] partially 일부, 부분적으로 row 열, 줄

08. 추론 문제 – 연계 문제

Ramos 씨에 관해 암시된 것은 무엇인가?
(A) 2월 1일에 유니폼을 받을 것이다.
(B) 최대 수량의 세트를 주문했다.
(C) Acre 여행사에서 관리자로 근무하고 있다.
(D) 두 가지 다른 사이즈의 옷을 필요로 한다.

[해설] Ramos 씨의 이름은 유니폼 신청서인 두 번째 지문의 신청자 이름 항목에서 찾아볼 수 있다. 그 아래의 색상 표기 항목에 보라색으로(Color Needed: [✔] Purple) 표기되어 있는데, 첫 지문 두 번째 단락에 보라색은 관리자들이 입는 유니폼 색상이라고(managers will wear purple uniforms) 쓰여 있으므로 Ramos 씨는 관리자 직책을 맡고 있음을 알 수 있다. 따라서 (C)가 정답이다.

[어휘] the maximum number of 최대 수량의

09. 동의어 문제

양식에서 첫 번째 단락, 두 번째 줄의 단어 "elect"와 의미가 가장 가까운 것은 무엇인가?
(A) 반품하다
(B) 결정하다
(C) 투표하다
(D) 거절하다

[해설] 해당 문장에서 elect가 포함된 If절은 사전에 확인해 보지 않고 사이즈를 주문하는 경우를 말하고 있는데, 이는 신청자 개인의 결정에 따르는 일에 해당된다. 따라서 If절의 동사로 쓰인 elect가 '결정하다, 선택하다' 등의 의미로 쓰였다는 것을 알 수 있으므로 이와 같은 뜻을 가진 (B)가 정답이다.

10. True 문제

주문 양식에서 암시된 것은 무엇인가?
(A) 인사팀이 유니폼을 위해 직원들의 치수를 측정할 것이다.
(B) 라지 사이즈의 유니폼이 다 떨어질 수 있다.
(C) Ramos 씨는 직접 몇몇 사이즈를 확인했다.
(D) Ramos 씨는 로고 부착 위치에 대해 선호하는 부분이 없다.

[해설] 두 번째 지문 맨 아래 부분에 로고 위치에 대해 어떤도 상관 없다고(Logo Position: ~ [✔] Any Available) 표기되어 있으므로 선호하는 위치가 없다고 한 (D)가 정답이다.

[어휘] measure ~의 치수를 측정하다 run out 다 떨어지다, 다 쓰다 in person 직접 preference 선호(하는 것) placement 배치, 설치

paraphrasing 정답 1. (a) 2. (e) 3. (d) 4. (c) 5. (b)

DAY 14

PART 5 문법 | 분사

확인 문제 해석

1. 누수 때문에 카펫이 손상된 것 같다.
2. 모든 IT 기업들은 고객들이 서비스에 만족하도록 유지해야 한다.
3. 이메일에 첨부된 파일을 참조하세요.
4. 외국어를 배우는 데 관심이 있는 모든 이들이 저희에게 연락을 합니다.
5. 저희 공장을 견학하실 때 사진을 찍어서는 안 됩니다.
6. 양식에 명시되어 있는 것처럼 저희가 모든 권리를 갖습니다.

연습 문제

01.(B) 02.(C) 03.(B) 04.(A) 05.(B) 06.(D)

01.

1. 선택지 보고 문법/어휘 문제 파악하기 ✔ 문법 문제 ☐ 어휘 문제
2. 빈칸 분석하기 빈칸 앞에 있는 것 ☐ 형용사 ✔ 관사
   빈칸 뒤에 있는 것 ✔ 명사 ☐ 동사
   → 빈칸에는 ✔ 형용사 역할을 하는 것 ☐ 동사 역할을 하는 것이 들어가야 한다.
3. 정답 선택하기 정답 (B)

패키지에 있는 설명서를 참고하세요.

02.

1. 선택지 보고 문법/어휘 문제 파악하기 ✔ 문법 문제 ☐ 어휘 문제
2. 빈칸 분석하기 빈칸 앞에 있는 것 ✔ 2형식 동사 ☐ 5형식 동사
   → 빈칸에는 ✔ 보어 ☐ 목적어가 들어가야 한다.
3. 정답 선택하기 정답 (C)

워크숍 덕분에 모든 직원들이 승강기를 작동시키는 데 숙련되었다.

03.

1. 선택지 보고 문법/어휘 문제 파악하기 ☐ 문법 문제 ✔ 어휘 문제
2. 빈칸 분석하기 빈칸 뒤에 있는 목적어 (issues)
   → 이 목적어와 짝꿍 표현으로 쓰이는 동사가 정답이다.
3. 정답 선택하기 정답 (B)

자문단은 해양 보존에 대한 사안을 처리할 것이다.

04.

1. 선택지 보고 문법/어휘 문제 파악하기 ✔ 문법 문제 ☐ 어휘 문제
2. 빈칸 분석하기 빈칸 앞에 있는 것 ☐ 전치사 ✔ 관사
   빈칸 뒤에 있는 것 ✔ 명사 ☐ 동사
   → 빈칸에는 ☐ 명사 ✔ 형용사 들어가야 한다.
   → 정답 후보 2개 (A, B)
   → sales와의 의미 관계 ✔ 감정의 원인 ☐ 감정을 느끼는 주체
3. 정답 선택하기 정답 (A)

Xenon-8의 실망스러운 매출은 제품 라인을 변경하게 했다.

appliances in the employee lounge ~ be sure to leave the item like you found it. Spills should be cleaned up right away, and old food should be thrown out), 이는 직원 휴게실 이용과 관련된 요청 사항에 해당되므로 (D)가 정답이다.

[어휘] installation 설치   nomination 후보 추천, 후보 지명   instructions 지침, 지시, 설명   reserve ~을 예약하다   regarding ~에 관한   break room 휴게실

04. 세부사항 문제

회사는 지난달에 무엇을 했는가?
(A) 직원들로부터 의견을 취합했다.
(B) 몇몇 신규 장비를 구입했다.
(C) 더 작은 건물로 이전했다.
(D) 직원 근무 시간을 변경했다.

[해설] last month라는 시점이 언급된 두 번째 단락 시작 부분에 지난 달에 직원 설문 조사를 한 사실이(based on your comments in last month's staff survey) 나타나 있으므로 직원들의 '의견 취합'을 의미하는 (A)가 정답이다.

paraphrasing   staff survey 직원 설문 조사 → Gathered feedback from employees 직원들로부터 의견 취합하기

[어휘] gather ~을 모으다   equipment 장비   relocate to ~로 이전하다

05. 추론 문제

일부 팀들은 이번 달에 무엇을 할 것 같은가?
(A) 직원 성과 검토하기
(B) 개조 공사를 위한 요청서 제출하기
(C) 일부 회의를 외부 장소에서 개최하기
(D) 업계 콘퍼런스에 참석하기

[해설] this month라는 시점이 언급된 마지막 단락에 이번 달에 두 곳의 회의실이 이용 불가능한 상태가 되면서 회의실 대신 휴게실을 사용하는 빈도가 늘었다고 알리면서 빈 방이 없으면 근처의 카페로 가라고(If you cannot find an open room in our office, please go to a nearby café) 요청하고 있다. 이는 휴게실에서 회의를 하는 대신에 외부의 장소를 이용하라는 말이므로 (C)가 정답이다.

paraphrasing   go to a nearby café 근처의 카페로 가다 → off-site 외부의 장소에서

[어휘] performance 성과, 실적   off-site 외부 장소에서   industry 업계, 분야

paraphrasing 정답   1. (a)   2. (d)   3. (b)   4. (c)   5. (e)

06-10은 다음 회람과 양식을 참조하시오.

수신: Acre 여행사 전 직원
발신: Connie Kirk, 총무부장
날짜: 1월 6일
제목: 직원 유니폼

우리 회사의 복장 규정 정책에 대한 변경 사항을 알려 드리고자 합니다. 다음 달부터, 전 직원들께서는 각자의 비즈니스 정장 대신 유니폼을 착용하셔야 합니다. 모두 아시다시피, ⁰⁶우리는 최근에 회사명과 로고를 변경했습니다. 유니폼을 추가하는 것이 고객들께서 이와 같은 변화에 더욱 쉽게 적응하시도록 하는 데 도움이 되는 **방법**으로 회사 자문 위원회에 의해 추천되었습니다.

새로운 로고는 보라색과 하늘색으로 되어 있으므로 ⁰⁸관리자들께서는 보라색 유니폼을 착용하시는 반면, 나머지 직원들께서는 하늘색 유니폼을 착용하시게 될 것입니다. 각 유니폼 세트는 바지 한 벌과 단추 잠금 방식의 반팔 셔츠로 구성되어 있습니다. 직원들께서는 무료로 최대 네 세트까지 유니폼을 받으실 자격이 있으십니다. 또한 회색으로 된 스웨터도 옵션으로 이용 가능합니다. ⁰⁷한 벌 이상의 스웨터를 주문하고자 하시는 분들께서는 제품 비용의 절반(18달러)을 지불하셔야 하며, 회사에서 나머지 절반의 비용을 충당해 드릴 것입니다.

이번 주말까지 유니폼 신청 양식을 작성 완료해 주시기 바랍니다. 유니폼은 1월 27일에 도착할 것이며, 직원들께서는 2월 1일부터 착용하기 시작하셔야 합니다. 여러분의 협조에 감사 드립니다.

dress code 복장 규정   policy 정책   attire 복장, 의복   add ~을 추가하다   consultant 자문, 고문   get used to ~에 적응하다   transition 변천, 이행   whereas ~인 반면에   trousers 바지   short-sleeved 반팔의   button-up 단추 잠금 방식의   be eligible to부정사 ~할 자격이 있다   half 절반   cover (비용 등) ~을 충당하다

유니폼 신청 양식

각 유니폼의 샘플이 사이즈 별로 인사부에 비치되어 있다는 점을 알아 두시기 바랍니다. 사전에 확인해 보시지 않고 사이즈를 주문하기로 ⁰⁹결정하셔서 너무 작거나 클 경우, 교체 비용은 개인 책임입니다.

⁰⁸직원 이름: Lyle Ramos   사이즈: 라지
세트 요청 수량: 3   스웨터 요청 수량: 0
⁰⁸필요한 색상: [✔] 보라색   [ ] 하늘색
¹⁰로고 위치: [ ] 앞면 오른쪽   [ ] 앞면 왼쪽   [ ] 뒷면 중앙
¹⁰[✔] 어디든 상관 없음

elect to부정사 ~하기로 결정하다, 선택하다   in advance 사전에, 미리   replacement 교체, 대체

06. 세부사항 문제

Kirk 씨는 유니폼의 무슨 이점을 언급하는가?
(A) 고객들이 새 브랜드에 적응하는 데 도움을 줄 것이다.
(B) 팀워크에 대한 감각을 향상시켜 줄 것이다.
(C) 직원들을 더욱 편안하게 만들어 줄 것이다.
(D) 전문성의 수준을 증대시켜 줄 것이다.

[해설] 첫 지문 첫 단락에 유니폼 착용이 필요한 목적으로 고객들이 변경된 회사명과 로고에 더욱 쉽게 적응하게 만들 것이라고(we have recently changed our business's name and logo. Adding uniforms ~ a way to help our clients get used to the transition more easily) 알리고 있으므로 (A)가 정답이다.

paraphrasing   changed our business's name and logo 회사의 이름과 로고를 변경했다 → rebranding 새 브랜드

[어휘] adjust to ~에 적응하다   rebranding 새 브랜드 (작업)   improve ~을 향상시키다

07. True 문제

스웨터에 관해 언급된 것은 무엇인가?
(A) 회사에 의해 일부 비용이 지불될 것이다.
(B) 모든 직원들이 착용해야 한다.
(C) 네 가지 사이즈로 이용 가능하다.
(D) 일렬로 된 단추가 있다.

[해설] 스웨터가 언급된 첫 지문 두 번째 단락에, 한 벌 이상의 스웨터를

(A) 회사의 이름이 변경될 것이다.
(B) 신임 대표이사가 소개될 것이다.

[문제 키워드] what / happen / August

[해설] 키워드 August가 제시되는 부분에서 단서를 찾아야 한다. 지문 초반부에 8월 1일부터 Norfolk-GP라는 이름으로 운영되기 시작한다고(~ will begin operating under the name Norfolk-GP from August 1) 알리고 있는데, 이는 회사 이름의 변경을 의미하므로 (A)가 정답이다.

실전 문제

| 01.(C) | 02.(B) | 03.(D) | 04.(A) | 05.(C) | 06.(A) |
| 07.(A) | 08.(C) | 09.(B) | 10.(D) | | |

01-02는 다음 회람을 참조하시오.

수신: Evanston 사 전 직원
제목: 업무 시간 정책
날짜: 8월 18일

우리 경영진은 사무실에 근무하는 **01대다수의 직원들에게 취학 연령의 아이들이 있어** 때때로 9시에서 5시까지 근무하는 일정을 준수하기 어렵다는 점에 주목하게 되었습니다. 이분들을 수용하기 위해, 우리는 새로운 정책을 시행하기로 결정했습니다.

여러분이 사무실에서 보내는 시간은 사무실 입구에 설치된 시간 기록계에 의해 공식적으로 측정되고 있습니다. 우리 대표이사님께서 좀 더 유연한 근무 시간을 허용하시는 데 동의해 주셨습니다. 여러분이 오전 10시에서 오후 2시 사이의 시간대에 사무실에서 근무하는 한, 각자의 일정에 따라 주당 40시간의 근무 시간 중 나머지를 자유롭게 채우실 수 있습니다. 이를 통해 여러분은 개인적인 휴무를 사용할 필요 없이 **02아이들의 방과 후 행사에 참석할 수 있을 것입니다.** 이 정책과 관련해 문의사항이 있으신 분은 인사부로 전달해 주시기 바랍니다.

policy 정책   school-age 취학 연령의   follow ~을 따르다, 준수하다   accommodate ~을 수용하다   initiate ~을 시행하다   measure ~을 측정하다   time clock 시간 기록계   flexible 유연한, 탄력적인   so long as ~하는 한   fill ~을 채우다, 메우다   remainder 나머지, 남은 것   according to ~에 따라   time off 휴무, 휴가   direct A to B (질문 등) A를 B로 전달하다, 보내다

01. True 문제

Evanston 사 직원들에 관해 언급된 것은 무엇인가?
(A) 주간 근무 시간 기록지를 작성해야 한다.
(B) 일부가 건의서를 제출했다.
(C) 대부분에게 학교를 다니는 아이가 있다.
(D) 일부는 오직 원격으로만 근무한다.

[해설] 첫 단락 시작 부분에 대다수의 직원들에게 취학 연령의 아이들이 있다는(the majority of the employees in our office have school-age children) 내용이 있으므로 (C)가 정답이다.

paraphrasing have school-age children 취학 연령의 아이들이 있다 → have kids in school 학교를 다니는 아이가 있다

[어휘] fill out ~을 작성하다   time sheet 근무 시간 기록지   suggestion card 건의서   remotely 원격으로

02. 세부사항 문제

회람에 따르면, 새로운 정책으로 인해 직원들이 무엇을 할 수 있는가?

(A) 더 많은 사교 생활 이끌어 가기
(B) 학교 행사에 참석하기
(C) 야간 강좌 수강하기
(D) 재택 근무 하기

[해설] 새로운 정책에 따른 영향이 언급된 두 번째 단락에 아이들의 방과 후 행사에 참석할 수 있을 것이라는(This will allow you to go to your kids' afterschool events) 말이 있으므로 이에 해당되는 (B)가 정답이다.

paraphrasing go to your kids' afterschool events 아이들의 방과 후 행사에 참석하다 → Attend school events 학교 행사에 참석하기

[어휘] lead ~을 이끌다   work from home 재택 근무를 하다

paraphrasing 정답   1. (c)   2. (a)   3. (d)   4. (e)   5. (b)

03-05는 다음 이메일을 참조하시오.

날짜: 11월 30일
수신: 전 직원
발신: Leslie Carone
제목: 직원 휴게실

공용 공간은 특별히 주의해 다뤄져야 한다는 점을 명심하시도록 직원 여러분께 요청 드립니다. **03직원 휴게실에서 전자레인지나 냉장고와 같은 기기들을 사용하신 후에는 반드시 처음 보셨던 상태대로 유지해 주시기 바랍니다.** 흘린 것은 즉시 닦아 내셔야 하며, 오래된 음식은 버려 주시기 바랍니다.

경영진은 **04지난달에 있었던 직원 설문 조사에서 나온 여러분의 의견을 바탕으로** 이 문제에 대한 조치를 취하려고 합니다. 많은 분들께서 청결 문제로 인해 직원 휴게실이 시간을 보내고 휴식을 취하기에 적합한 공간이 아니라는 불만을 제기해 주셨습니다. 우리는 이 부분과 함께 우리의 주목을 끈 기타 문제들을 처리하기 위해 노력하고 있습니다.

우리는 또한 해당 휴게실이 팀 회의용으로 사용되지 말아야 한다는 점을 각 팀장님들께 상기시켜 드리고자 합니다. 일부 직원들께서 다른 회의실들이 예약되어 있을 때 그곳에서 회의를 하셨는데, 특히 개조 공사를 거치는 동안 **05이번 달에 두 곳의 회의실이 이용 불가능한 상태가 되면서 더 그러했습니다. 우리 사무실에서 빈 방을 찾을 수 없으실 경우, 근처의 카페로 가시기 바랍니다.** 이와 같은 경우에 팀에 할당된 자금을 음료 구입에 사용하시면 됩니다. 예산 제한과 관련해 질문이 있으실 경우에는 재무팀에 이야기하시기 바랍니다.

shared area 공용 공간   treat ~을 다루다   appliances (가전) 기기   microwave 전자레인지   refrigerator 냉장고   spill 흘림, 엎지름   throw out ~을 버리다   take action 조치를 취하다   matter 문제   based on ~을 바탕으로   suitable 적합한, 어울리는   cleanliness 청결(도)   work toward ~을 위해 노력하다   address ~을 처리하다, 다루다   undergo ~을 거치다, 겪다   renovation 개조, 보수   beverage 음료   budget 예산

03. 주제 문제

주로 무엇이 이야기되고 있는가?
(A) 새 기기의 설치
(B) 팀장 후보자 추천
(C) 회의실 예약을 위한 지침
(D) 휴게실에 관한 요청 사항

[해설] 첫 단락에 직원 휴게실에서 기기를 사용할 때 주의해야 할 점과 음식물 처리에 관련된 주의 사항들을 설명하고 있는데(After using the

주차증을 받으시려면 인사부에 여러분의 차량을 등록해야 합니다. 운전 면허증, 주 등록증 사본 그리고 차량이 보험에 가입되었다는 증명서를 가지고 오세요. 주차증은 발행되는 데 꼬박 하루가 걸리므로 주차비를 지불해야 하기 전에 반드시 차량을 등록하세요.

건물 관리팀의 설명에 따르면 이 같은 변화는 주차장이 무료였던 탓에 직원이 아닌 사람들이 모든 주차 공간을 차지하는 데 따른 불만 때문입니다. 이로써 건물 직원들이 주차 공간을 찾기가 더 쉬워질 것입니다.

연습 문제
01.(B)　02.(B)　03.(A)　04.(A)

01.

수신: 모든 직원
발신: Miles Lopez
제목: 지역 봉사자
날짜: 4월 16일

이번 주말에 McMahon 공원의 쓰레기를 치우기 위한 특별한 자원봉사 행사가 있을 예정입니다. 공원은 회사 건물 바로 맞은편에 위치하고 있으며, 공원이 더 나아 보이게 도움으로써, 우리는 또한 사무실을 방문하는 고객들을 위해 이미지를 개선합니다. 아침이나 오후 근무 시간에 자원봉사를 하신 분들은 다음 주 월요일 오전에 반차를 받을 것입니다.

coming 다가오는　half-day off 반차

Q. 직원들은 무엇을 하도록 요청되는가?
(A) 월요일에 재택 근무를 하기
(B) 공원 청소 행사에 참여하기

[문제 키워드] What / staff / asked to do

[해설] 주말에 자원봉사 행사가 있을 것임을(This coming weekend there will be a special volunteer event to remove trash from McMahon Park) 소개하며, 후반부에 참여하는 직원은 반차를 받을 것이라는 내용이 있으므로 (B)가 정답이다.

02.

수신: Lauria 기업 전 직원
발신: Bryce Zwick
날짜: 1월 10일
제목: 읽어 보십시오

수년간 헌신적으로 재직해 오시면서, 인도네시아에서의 첫 번째 해외 제휴 관계에 대한 성공적인 협상을 마치신 끝에, **Marshall Doughty 사업 개발부장님께서 이달 말에 자리에서 물러나실 계획입니다.** 모든 직원들은 1월 31일 목요일 오후 4시에 대회의실에서 Doughty 부장님을 위해 열리는 송별회에 참석해 주시기 바랍니다. **Doughty 부장님의 후임자께서 그 다음 주에 근무를 시작하실 것입니다. 그분의 성함은 Michelle Howard 씨이며**, 이분께서 우리와 한 배에 타게 된 것을 기쁘게 생각합니다.

negotiation 협상, 협의　overseas 해외의　dedicated 헌신적인, 전념하는　step down from ~에서 물러나다　farewell reception 송별회　replacement 후임(자), 대체(자)　on board 승선한, 탑승한

Q. 회람은 무엇을 공지하는가?

(A) 다가오는 기업 합병
(B) 인사 변동 사항

[문제 키워드] What / memo / announcing

[해설] 지문 초반부에는 Marshall Doughty 씨가 자리에서 물러난다는(~ Marshall Doughty plans to step down ··) 사실을, 후반부에는 그 사람의 후임자와 관련된(Mr. Doughty's replacement will begin work ~) 정보를 알리고 있는데, 이는 모두 인사 변동 내용에 해당하므로 (B)가 정답이다.

[어휘] personnel 인사(부), 직원들

03.

수신: Shine 극장 전 직원
발신: Fiona Wells
제목: 좌석 관련 정책
날짜: 4월 16일

티켓 구입 시에 고객들께 곧 있을 우리의 좌석 관련 정책 변동 사항을 설명해 드리는 것이 중요합니다. 현재는 관객들이 늦게 도착할 경우에 안내원이 즉시 좌석으로 모셔 가고 있습니다. 5월 1일부터, 늦게 오시는 분들이 공연장으로 들어가려면 공연 휴식 기간까지 대기해야 할 것입니다. **우리는 이것이 공연자들과 다른 관객들 모두가 방해를 덜 받게 하는 데 도움이 되기를 바랍니다.**

policy 정책　currently 현재　latecomer 늦게 오는 사람
cut down on ~을 줄이다　distraction 방해(가 되는 것)

Q. Wells 씨는 왜 정책을 변경할 계획인가?
(A) 공연에 지장을 주는 일을 피하기 위해
(B) 입장권 판매 수를 증가시키기 위해

[문제 키워드] Why / Ms. Wells / change / policy

[해설] 키워드 policy가 지문의 전체적인 소재이므로 지문 전반에서 단서를 파악하여 각 선택지와 비교해야 한다. 지문 마지막에 정책 변경을 통해 공연자들과 다른 관객들이 방해를 덜 받기를 바란다고(~ cut down on distractions for both the performers and the other audience members) 알리고 있으므로 (A)가 정답이다.

[어휘] disrupt ~에 지장을 주다, 방해가 되다

04.

수신: Norfolk 금융 전 직원
발신: Ashia Havaldar
날짜: 7월 2일
제목: 최종 마무리된 협상

GP International 사와의 협상이 성공적이었음을 알려 드리게 되어 기쁩니다. 우리는 향후 몇 주 동안에 걸쳐 두 회사 사이의 합병을 최종 마무리해 **8월 1일부터 Norfolk-GP라는 이름으로 운영되기 시작할 것입니다.** Norfolk의 Avery Madera 현 대표이사님께서 계속해서 모든 수준에서 회사 운영을 총괄하실 텐데, GP 사의 대표이사님께서 은퇴하실 계획이시기 때문입니다. 다가오는 몇 달 동안 일부 조직 개편이 있을 수 있지만, 우리의 계획에는 어떠한 해고 조치도 포함되어 있지 않습니다.

merger 합병　operate 운영되다　under the name (of) ~라는 이름으로　oversee ~을 총괄하다　operation 운영, 경영, 가동　restructuring 조직 개편, 구조 조정　layoff 해고

Q. 회람에 따르면, 8월에 무슨 일이 있을 것인가?

Loretta Watts

under one's agreement ~의 동의 하에 24/7 일주일 내내 하루 24시간 work out 운동하다 be proud of ~을 자랑스럽게 여기다 challenge 어려움, 힘듦 obstacle 지장이 되는 것, 방해(물) certified 공인된, 인증된 be willing to부정사 기꺼이 ~하다 lose weight 체중을 줄이다 get in shape 좋은 몸 상태를 유지하다, 좋은 몸매를 유지하다

01. 동사의 형태

[해설] 빈칸 앞에 위치한 주어 This e-mail은 사람에 의해 보내지는 대상이므로 send의 주체가 될 수 없다. 따라서 동사 send가 수동태로 쓰여야 알맞으므로 유일하게 수동태에 해당되는 (D) has been sent가 정답이다.

02. 알맞은 문장 고르기

(A) 더 상세한 정보는 저희 웹사이트에 게시되어 있습니다.
(B) 이것이 저희가 이 지역에서 가장 많은 회원들을 보유하고 있는 이유입니다.
(C) Barn 체육관에 대한 귀하의 관심에 감사 드립니다.
(D) 사물함 열쇠 교체에 대해 5달러의 서비스 수수료가 있을 것입니다.

[해설] 앞 문장에 매일 24시간으로 운영되고 있어서 언제든지 운동할 수 있다는 장점이 언급되어 있으므로 이를 This로 지칭해 그와 같은 장점에 따른 결과로서 가장 많은 회원을 보유하고 있다는 사실을 말하는 (B)가 정답이다.

[어휘] fee 수수료, 요금 replacement 교체(품)

03. 동사 어휘

[해설] 빈칸이 속한 절(you 이하 부분)은 바로 앞에 제시된 선행사 every challenge and obstacle을 수식하는 역할을 하는데, 어려움과 장애물을 운동을 할 때 맞닥뜨리게 되는 것에 해당하므로 '~을 접하다, 마주하다' 등의 의미로 쓰이는 (B) face가 정답이다.

04. 동명사 어휘

[해설] 동사 Thank와 함께 쓰이는 전치사 for 뒤에는 감사하는 이유가 제시되어야 하는데, 빈칸 뒤에 위치한 a member of Barn Gym과 의미가 어울려야 하므로 '회원이 된 것에 대해 감사하다'라는 의미가 되어야 자연스럽다. 따라서 명사 보어와 함께 '~가 되다'라는 의미로 쓰이는 become의 동명사인 (B) becoming이 정답이다.

[어휘] arrange 마련하다, 정리하다 cooperate 협조하다

05-08은 다음 편지를 참조하시오.

Simmons 씨께

지난 화요일, 10월 29일에 귀하의 오후 동안 인터넷에 접속할 수 없었다는 불만을 제기하셨습니다. ⁰⁵Riverfront Palace 아파트에 거주하는 이용자들로부터 많은 신고가 있었습니다. ⁰⁶저희는 하드웨어 유지보수 작업이 잠시 동안만 진행될 것으로 예상했습니다. 안타깝게도, 저녁 6시 30분까지 작동이 완전히 복구되지 않았습니다. 조사 끝에, 저희는 건설 작업자들이 당신의 아파트의 노후된 가스 파이프를 점검하고 교체하는 동안 본선이 끊어진 탓에 정전이 발생했음을 알게 되었습니다. ⁰⁷한 작업자가 파이프를 교체하면서 저희의 인터넷 선을 실수로 끊은 것입니다.

⁰⁸혼란에 대해 사과 드립니다. 저희는 하루 서비스의 금액을 차감하는 것으로 보상해 드릴 것입니다. 1.25달러이고 다음 달 청구서에 반영될 것입니다. 이 사안에 대한 더 많은 정보를 원하시면, 저희 고객 센터에 전화하시거나 웹사이트에 방문해 주세요.

Fernando Gomez
고객 서비스 부서 책임자

make a complaint 불만을 제기하다 subscriber 이용자, 가입자 investigation 조사 outage 정전 accidentally 우연히, 실수로 compensate 보상하다 deduction 공제(액)

05. 동사의 형태

[해설] 선행사 subscribers를 수식하는 관계절의 동사 자리이다. subscribers가 복수 명사이고 문맥상 현재 거주하고 있는 사람들이 되어야 하므로 현재 시제 복수 동사인 (A) reside가 정답이다.

[어휘] reside 거주하다

06. 알맞은 문장 고르기

(A) 수리 작업은 원래 다음 주 월요일로 예정되어 있었습니다.
(B) 저희는 하드웨어 유지보수 작업이 잠시 동안만 진행될 것으로 예상했습니다.
(C) 건물의 대부분의 주민들은 우리의 기본 인터넷 서비스를 이용합니다.
(D) 귀하의 계약이 다음 달에 만료될 것임을 상기시켜 드립니다.

[해설] 뒤에 역접의 의미를 갖는 부사 unfortunately가 있고 그 뒤에 6시 30분까지 복구되지 않았다는 내용이 있으므로, 앞에는 이와 상반되는 내용이 들어가야 한다. 따라서 원래는 간단한 작업일 것으로 예상했는데 6시 30분까지 끝나지 않았다는 문맥이 되는 것이 자연스러우므로 (B)가 정답이다.

[어휘] maintenance 유지보수 briefly 잠시, 간단히 expire 만료되다

07. 분사구문

[해설] 접속사 while 앞에 주어와 동사를 완전히 갖춘 완전한 절이 있으므로 while ~ pipe까지는 수식어 역할을 한다. 따라서 접속사 뒤에 쓰여 수식어구를 만들 수 있는 분사 (B) replacing이 정답이다.

08. 명사 어휘

[해설] 앞 단락의 내용이 아파트 주민들이 인터넷 서비스가 한동안 끊겨 불만을 제기한 내용이므로 '중단, 혼란'의 의미를 갖는 (D) disruption이 정답이다.

[어휘] malfunction 오작동 cancellation 취소

PART 7 회람

풀이 방법 해석

수신: Windrose Tower 지점 직원들
발신: Serena Carrillo
제목: 주차
날짜: 1월 16일

직원 여러분들은 주목해 주세요.

이번 주말, Windrose Tower는 건물 주차장 입구에 감시를 하는 부스와 요금소를 설치할 예정입니다. 주차증을 소지하지 않은 사람들은 시간당 5달러의 요금을 지불해야 합니다. 인사부에서 주차증을 받기까지 1주일의 유예기간이 있을 것입니다.

PART 6 Thank you for/apologize for+명사

풀이 방법 해석

수신: Linda Groves
발신: Jessica Curry
날짜: 5월 12일
제목: 당신의 첫날입니다!

Groves 씨께

당신은 인턴으로 합격하셨습니다! 이곳 Sugar Land의 프로그램에 합류해 주셔서 감사합니다. 앞으로 몇 달 동안 당신이 저희의 팀과 함께하게 되어서 기쁩니다. 6월 1일에 오실 때는, 이 수락 이메일의 사본과 사진이 있는 신분증을 가지고 오세요. 보안 팀이 보안 신분증을 만드는 것을 도와줄 것입니다. 그러고 나서, 인사부 사무실로 가시게 될텐데 그곳에서 Anita Park를 찾으시면 됩니다. 그녀가 시설을 안내해드리고 첫 서류 작성을 도와드릴 거예요. 질문이나 우려되는 것이 있으면 저나 Park 씨에게 연락주세요.

Jessica Curry
인사부 부장, Sugar Land 사

연습 문제

01.(B) 02.(A) 03.(A) 04.(A)

01.

지난번 Delta 미용실 방문과 관련해 제공해 주신 의견에 감사 드립니다. 저희는 항상 고객들의 말씀에 끝까지 귀 기울이려고 합니다.

provide ~을 제공하다   hear out ~을 끝까지 듣다

[단서] eager to hear out

[해설] Thank 뒤에 이어지는 전치사 for의 목적어는 감사의 이유를 나타내는데, 항상 고객의 의견을 듣고 싶다고 했으므로 '의견'을 의미하는 (B) feedback이 정답이다.

[어휘] purchase 구입(품)

02.

Johnson 씨께

저희는 귀하의 불만 사항을 검토했으며, 귀하께서는 주문하신 Baby Blue 대신에 Sky Blue를 받으신 것으로 결론을 내렸습니다. 저희는 이 실수에 대해 사과 드립니다. 이 문제를 어떻게 해결하고 싶으신지 저희에게 알려 주시기 바랍니다.

complaint 불만   conclude that ~라고 결론 내리다   instead of ~ 대신에   resolve ~을 해결하다

[단서] were sent the Sky Blue instead of the Baby Blue

[해설] apologize 뒤에 이어지는 전치사 for의 목적어는 사과의 이유를 나타내는 데, 앞서 고객이 잘못된 주문품을 받았다고 했으므로 이를 대신할 명사로 '실수'를 뜻하는 (A) error가 정답이다.

[어휘] delay 지연, 지체

03.

Harper 씨께

Highland 장학금 프로그램에 대한 귀하의 기부에 감사 드립니다. 모든 기부금은 학생들이 교재 비용과 수업료를 지불하는 데 도움이 됩니다.

contribution 기부(금), 기여, 공헌   pay for ~에 대한 비용을 지불하다   tuition 등록금, 수강료

[단서] contribution

[해설] Thank 뒤에 이어지는 전치사 for의 목적어는 감사의 이유를 나타내며, 기부금이 학생들에게 도움이 된다는 말과 연결되어야 하므로 '기부(금)'을 뜻하는 (A) donation이 정답이다.

[어휘] volunteering 자원 봉사

04.

주민 여러분께

우리 아파트 단지의 쓰레기 처리 구역이 주차장 뒤편으로 옮겨졌습니다. 저희는 이로 인해 초래될 수 있는 어떠한 혼란에 대해서도 사과 드립니다.

resident 주민   disposal 처리, 처분   complex (복합) 단지

[단서] disposal area ~ moved

[해설] apologize 뒤에 이어지는 전치사 for의 목적어는 사과의 이유를 나타내는데, 쓰레기 처리 구역이 옮겨진 것에 따라 발생 가능한 문제를 의미해야 하므로 '혼란'을 뜻하는 (A) confusion이 정답이다.

[어휘] promotion 홍보, 승진

실전 문제

01.(D) 02.(B) 03.(B) 04.(A) 05.(A) 06.(B)
07.(B) 08.(D)

01-04는 다음 이메일을 참조하시오.

수신: j.archer@jfob.net
발신: l.watts@gymbarn.net
날짜: 4월 7일
제목: 환영합니다

Archer 씨께

Barn 체육관에 오신 것을 환영합니다. **01**이 이메일은 귀하의 동의 하에 보내드리는 것입니다. 저희는 일주일 내내 하루 24시간 운영되므로 언제든지 오셔서 운동하실 수 있습니다. **02**이것이 저희가 이 지역에서 가장 많은 회원들을 보유하고 있는 이유입니다. 저희는 Barn 체육관이 그렇게 하는 유일한 곳이기 때문에 매우 자랑스럽게 여기고 있습니다. 말씀 드릴 것이 한 가지 더 있습니다. **03**저희는 귀하께서 운동을 시작하시는 시점 또는 운동 중에 접하게 되시는 모든 어려움과 지장이 되는 것들을 전적으로 이해합니다. 데스크로 오시거나 주변에 있는 저희 직원들 중 한 명에게 질문하기만 하시면 됩니다. 저희 모든 직원들은 공인된 트레이너들이며, 귀하께서 체중을 줄이시고 일생 중 가장 뛰어난 몸 상태를 유지하는 데 기꺼이 도움이 되어 드릴 것입니다. **04**저희 Barn 체육관의 회원이 되신 것에 대해 다시 한번 감사 드립니다.

안녕히 계십시오.

15. 동명사의 역할: 전치사의 목적어 역할

Atlantic Airways는 상하기 쉬운 상품을 해외로 운송하는 일을 전문으로 해 왔다.

[해설] 선택지가 동사 transport의 다양한 형태와 명사로 구성되어 있으므로 문법 문제이다. 전치사 in의 목적어 역할을 함과 동시에 명사구 perishable goods를 목적어로 취할 수 있는 것은 동명사이므로 (A) transporting이 정답이다.

[어휘] perishable 상하기 쉬운 goods 상품 transport ~을 운송하다 transportation 운송, 교통(편)

16. to부정사의 역할: 부사 역할

정부는 지역 경제를 개선할 수 있도록 소기업들을 위한 일련의 면세 혜택을 제안했다.

[해설] 선택지가 동사 improve의 다양한 형태와 명사로 구성되어 있으므로 문법 문제이다. 앞에 이미 문장의 동사 proposed가 있으므로 빈칸은 동사 자리가 아니며, 면세 혜택을 제안한 목적을 나타내야 알맞으므로 to부정사인 (A) to improve가 정답이다. 이때의 to부정사는 '~하기 위해서'라는 의미의 부사적 용법으로 쓰였다. 명사 (C) improvement는 앞뒤에 위치한 명사들과 어순이 맞지 않는다.

[어휘] propose ~을 제안하다 tax exemption 면세 local economy 지역 경제 improve ~을 개선하다

17. 시간 부사

Bauer 씨는 현재 인턴 사원으로 근무하고 있으며 다음 달에 정규직 사원으로 고용될 것이다.

[해설] 선택지가 다양한 부사들로 구성되어 있으므로 부사 어휘 문제이다. 빈칸에 쓰일 부사는 현재 시제 동사 works를 수식해야 하므로 현재 시제와 어울리는 (A) currently가 정답이다.

[어휘] currently 현재 formerly 이전에, 과거에 shortly 곧, 머지않아

18. 수량 형용사

수요의 감소로 인해, Blanchard Auto는 과거의 여러 해에 비해 더 적은 수의 자동차를 제조할 것이다.

[해설] 선택지가 다양한 형용사들로 구성되어 있으므로 형용사 어휘 문제이다. 빈칸 뒤에 위치한 than과 짝을 이뤄 비교를 나타내야 하므로 비교급 형용사의 형태인 (A) fewer가 정답이다.

[어휘] decrease in ~의 감소 demand 수요 manufacture ~을 제조하다 previous 이전의, 과거의

19. 동사 어휘

고용 계약서는 직책의 일일 업무들과 금전적 보상에 관한 내용을 다룬다.

[해설] 선택지가 다양한 동사들로 구성되어 있으므로 동사 어휘 문제이다. 빈칸 뒤에 위치한 명사구는 고용 계약서(employment contract)에 들어 있는 내용에 해당되므로 '(주제 등) ~을 다루다'라는 의미로 쓰이는 (D) covers가 정답이다.

[어휘] responsibility 업무, 직무 compensation 보상 transfer ~을 전근시키다 prohibit ~을 금지하다

20. 동사 어휘

교대 근무 책임자들이 Sutton 제조사의 조립 라인에 설치된 새로운 장비의 사용법을 시연한다.

[해설] 선택지가 다양한 동사들로 구성되어 있으므로 동사 어휘 문제이다. 새로운 장비의 사용법과 관련해 책임자들이 할 수 있는 일을 나타낼 동사로 적절한 것이 필요하므로 '~을 시연하다'를 뜻하는 (B) demonstrate가 정답이다. (A) specialize는 자동사이므로 바로 목적어를 취할 수 없다.

[어휘] supervisor 책임자, 상사 equipment 장비 assembly 조립 recover ~을 회복하다, 되찾다 stimulate ~을 자극하다

21. 동사 어휘

모든 식품 용기들은 운송 중에 내용물이 상하는 것을 방지하도록 적절히 밀폐되어야 한다.

[해설] 선택지가 다양한 동사들로 구성되어 있으므로 동사 어휘 문제이다. 빈칸 뒤에 위치한 '목적어+from -ing' 구조와 어울리는 동사로서 '~가 …하는 것을 방지하다, 막다'라는 의미를 나타낼 때 사용하는 (A) prevent가 정답이다.

[어휘] container 용기, 그릇 seal ~을 밀폐시키다 properly 적절히, 제대로 contents 내용(물) spoil 상하다 while in transit 운송 중에 grant ~을 승인하다

22. 동사 어휘

신입 사원들을 수용하기 위해, Rios 마케팅은 스크랜튼 시내 지역 근처에 더 큰 사무실을 찾고 있다.

[해설] 선택지가 다양한 동사들로 구성되어 있으므로 동사 어휘 문제이다. 신입 사원들을 수용하기 위해 더 큰 사무실을 대상으로 할 수 있는 일을 나타낼 동사가 필요하므로 '~을 찾다, 구하다'를 뜻하는 (C) seeking이 정답이다.

[어휘] accommodate ~을 수용하다 conclude ~을 끝맺다, 결론 내다 aim ~을 목표로 하다

23. 동사 어휘

대부분의 승객들은 Sonic Airlines 항공기 내의 줄어든 다리 공간에 대해 불만을 표출했다.

[해설] 선택지가 다양한 동사들로 구성되어 있으므로 동사 어휘 문제이다. 감정 명사 frustration(불만, 좌절감)을 목적어로 취할 수 있는 동사가 필요하므로 '~을 표현하다'를 뜻하는 (D) expressed가 정답이다.

[어휘] frustration 불만, 좌절감 decreased 줄어든 leg room 다리 공간 ensure ~을 보장하다, ~하는 것을 확실히 하다 resolve ~을 해결하다

24. 동사 어휘

빅토리아에 있는 대부분의 기념품 매장들이 연중으로 운영되기는 하지만, 일부는 겨울 동안 문을 닫는다.

[해설] 선택지가 다양한 동사들로 구성되어 있으므로 동사 어휘 문제이다. 빈칸 뒤에 목적어 없이 전치사구가 이어져 있으므로 유일한 자동사인 (B) operate가 정답이다. 나머지 동사들은 모두 타동사이므로 뒤에 목적어가 있어야 한다.

[어휘] throughout the year 연중으로 shut down 문을 닫다 engrave ~을 새기다 operate 운영되다 initiate ~을 개시하다 compile (자료 등을 모아) ~을 정리하다

로 문법 문제이다. 빈칸 앞에 위치한 동사 consider는 동명사를 목적어로 취하므로 (B) delegating이 정답이다.

[어휘] management 경영(진)　recruit ~을 채용하다, 모집하다　task 업무, 일　agency 대행사　delegate ~을 위임하다　delegation 대표단

04. 동명사의 역할: 전치사의 목적어 역할

Callahan's는 엄청난 보상 포인트를 제공함으로써 지역에서 가장 인기 있는 주택 개조 전문 매장이 되었다.

[해설] 선택지가 동사 offer의 다양한 형태로 구성되어 있으므로 문법 문제이다. 전치사 by의 목적어 역할을 함과 동시에 명사구 huge reward points를 목적어로 취할 수 있는 것은 동명사이므로 (B) offering이 정답이다.

[어휘] home improvement 주택 개조　region 지역　reward 보상

05. 동명사의 역할: 타동사의 목적어 역할

엔진을 점검한 후에, 그 정비공은 차량을 새 것으로 교체하도록 제안했다.

[해설] 선택지가 동사 replace의 다양한 형태와 명사로 구성되어 있으므로 문법 문제이다. 빈칸 앞에 위치한 동사 suggest의 목적어 역할을 함과 동시에 명사구 the car를 목적어로 취할 수 있는 것은 동명사이므로 (C) replacing이 정답이다.

[어휘] inspect ~을 점검하다　mechanic 정비공　replace A with B A를 B로 교체하다

06. 동명사의 역할: 주어 역할

Holder's 은행의 사무실을 개조하는 계약을 따낸 것이 우리 회사에서 Harman 씨가 처음으로 이룬 성과였다.

[해설] 선택지가 동사 secure의 다양한 형태와 명사로 구성되어 있으므로 문법 문제이다. 빈칸 뒤에 위치한 명사구(the contract ~ office)를 목적어로 취해 전체 문장의 동사 was의 주어 역할을 할 수 있는 것은 동명사이므로 (D) Securing이 정답이다.

[어휘] contract 계약(서)　accomplishment 성과, 업적　secure (계약 등) ~을 따내다, 확보하다

07. 동명사의 역할: 주어 역할

깨끗하고 건강에 도움이 되는 업무 환경을 유지하는 것이 인사부의 주요 직무들 중 하나이다.

[해설] 선택지가 동사 maintain의 다양한 형태로 구성되어 있으므로 문법 문제이다. 빈칸 뒤에 위치한 명사구(a clean ~ environment)를 목적어로 취해 동사 is의 주어 역할을 할 수 있는 것은 동명사이므로 (C) Maintaining이 정답이다.

[어휘] work environment 업무 환경　responsibility 책임, 의무　maintain ~을 유지하다

08. 동명사의 역할: 전치사의 목적어 역할

새 지게차 모델인 Titan 2000은 한 번에 최대 4톤까지 짐을 처리할 수 있는 것으로 드러났다.

[해설] 선택지가 동사 handle의 다양한 형태로 구성되어 있으므로 문법 문제이다. 전치사 of의 목적어 역할을 함과 동시에 명사구 up to 4 tons of load를 목적어로 취할 수 있는 것은 동명사이므로 (C) handling이 정답이다.

[어휘] prove oneself+형용사 ~한 것으로 드러나다, 입증되다　capable of -ing ~할 수 있는, ~할 능력이 있는　at once 한 번에　handle ~을 처리하다, 다루다　handler (동물) 조련사

09. 동명사의 역할: 타동사의 목적어 역할

Bolton 씨와 그녀의 팀원들은 차량 대여 계약서의 조항들을 수정하는 일을 완료했다.

[해설] 선택지가 동사 revise의 다양한 형태와 명사로 구성되어 있으므로 문법 문제이다. 빈칸 앞에 위치한 동사 finish의 목적어 역할을 함과 동시에 명사구 the terms and conditions를 목적어로 취할 수 있는 것은 동명사이므로 (C) revising이 정답이다.

[어휘] terms and conditions (계약서 등의) 조항, 약관　contract 계약(서)　revise ~을 수정하다　revision 수정

10. 동명사의 역할: 전치사의 목적어 역할

보관 창고 직원들은 매장의 모든 재고 상품을 관리하는 일을 책임지고 있다.

[해설] 선택지가 동사 manage의 다양한 형태로 구성되어 있으므로 문법 문제이다. 전치사 for의 목적어 역할을 함과 동시에 명사구 all inventory items를 목적어로 취할 수 있는 것은 동명사이므로 (B) managing이 정답이다.

[어휘] stockroom 보관 창고　inventory 재고(품), 재고 목록

11. 동명사의 역할: 타동사의 목적어 역할

사용자 설명서는 사용 직후에 핸드 믹서기를 세척하도록 권하고 있다.

[해설] 선택지가 동사 clean의 다양한 형태와 명사로 구성되어 있으므로 문법 문제이다. 빈칸 앞에 위치한 동사 recommend의 목적어 역할을 함과 동시에 명사구 the hand mixer를 목적어로 취할 수 있는 것은 동명사이므로 (D) cleaning이 정답이다.

[어휘] user's manual 사용자 설명서

12. 동명사의 역할: 주어 역할

모퉁이마다 현금 자동 입출금기를 설치한 것은 British Star 은행의 고객들이 매우 편리함을 느끼게 했다.

[해설] 선택지가 동사 install의 다양한 형태와 명사로 구성되어 있으므로 문법 문제이다. 빈칸 뒤에 위치한 명사구(automated ~ corner)를 목적어로 취해 동사 has made의 주어 역할을 할 수 있는 것은 능동태 동명사이므로 (D) Installing이 정답이다.

[어휘] automated teller machine 현금 자동 입출금기　convenient 편리한　install ~을 설치하다　installation 설치

13. 동명사 숙어 표현

모든 영업 사원들은 주말 동안에 걸쳐 매장의 진열 방식을 변경하느라 바빴다.

[해설] 선택지가 동사 change의 다양한 형태로 구성되어 있으므로 문법 문제이다. 빈칸 앞에 위치한 be busy는 'be busy -ing'의 구조로 쓰여 '~하느라 바쁘다'라는 의미를 나타내므로 (A) changing이 정답이다.

[어휘] representative 직원　display 진열, 전시　layout 배치, 구획

14. 'to -ing'와 'to부정사'의 구분

저희는 가까운 미래에 당신과 함께 사업을 할 수 있기를 고대하고 있습니다.

[해설] 선택지가 동사 do의 다양한 형태로 구성되어 있으므로 문법 문제이다. 빈칸 앞에 위치한 look forward to는 동명사와 결합하므로 (C) doing이 정답이다.

을 의미하므로 (A)가 정답이다.

paraphrasing carpool 카풀 → share rides 함께 타고 다니기

[어휘] ride (차량 등의) 타고 가기

paraphrasing 정답 1. (b) 2. (c) 3. (d) 4. (e) 5. (a)

DAY 13

PART 5 문법 | 동명사

확인 문제 해석

❶ 설문 조사 양식을 작성하는 데 불과 몇 분밖에 걸리지 않습니다.
❷ 재정 자문은 증권 시장에 추가 자금을 투자할 것을 권고했다.
❸ 그 오래된 극장을 보존하는 것에 관한 열띤 논쟁이 있었다.
❹ Wong 씨는 온라인 보안 시스템 개발을 전문으로 한다.
❺ 그녀는 일일 보고서 제출을 담당한다.
❻ Bell 씨는 자유 시간 대부분을 소설을 쓰는 데 보냈다.
❼ 나는 아침 5시에 일어나는 데 익숙하다.
❽ Harrison 쇼핑몰의 개장은 다음 주로 예정될 것이다.

 연습 문제

01.(A) 02.(C) 03.(B) 04.(D) 05.(D) 06.(C)

01.

1. 선택지 보고 문법/어휘 문제 파악하기 ☑문법 문제 ☐어휘 문제
2. 빈칸 분석하기 빈칸 앞에 있는 것 ☑타동사 ☐자동사
   → 빈칸은 ☑목적어 ☐보어 자리이다.
   → 정답 후보 2개 (A , B)
   → 빈칸 바로 뒤에 ☑명사 ☐전치사가 있다.
3. 정답 선택하기 정답 (A)

Bay Shore 식당에서 식사를 할 때 사람들은 일반적으로 테이블을 예약할 것을 권장한다.

02.

1. 선택지 보고 문법/어휘 문제 파악하기 ☑문법 문제 ☐어휘 문제
2. 빈칸 분석하기 빈칸 앞에 있는 것 ☐명사 ☑전치사
   → 빈칸에는 ☐동사 ☑동명사가 들어가야 한다.
3. 정답 선택하기 정답 (C)

나이 제한을 없앰으로써, Bristol 놀이공원은 방문율이 15퍼센트 증가했다.

03.

1. 선택지 보고 문법/어휘 문제 파악하기 ☑문법 문제 ☐어휘 문제
2. 빈칸 분석하기 빈칸 앞에 있는 것 ☑타동사 ☐자동사
   → 빈칸은 ☐주어 ☑목적어 자리이다.
3. 정답 선택하기 정답 (B)

이 공장 견학 동안 전선이나 호스를 밟지 말아 주세요.

04.

1. 선택지 보고 문법/어휘 문제 파악하기 ☑문법 문제 ☐어휘 문제
2. 빈칸 분석하기 빈칸 앞에 있는 동사 (keep)
   → ☑동명사 ☐to부정사와 함께 쓰인다.
3. 정답 선택하기 정답 (D)

Billy 가를 타기 위해서는 이 우회 안내판을 따라가기만 하면 됩니다.

05.

1. 선택지 보고 문법/어휘 문제 파악하기 ☐문법 문제 ☑어휘 문제
2. 빈칸 분석하기 빈칸 뒤에 있는 전치사 (in)
   → 이 전치사와 함께 쓰이는 동사가 정답이다.
3. 정답 선택하기 정답 (D)

Chester 은행의 Concord 씨는 담보 대출과 기업 대출을 전문으로 한다.

06.

1. 선택지 보고 문법/어휘 문제 파악하기 ☑문법 문제 ☐어휘 문제
2. 빈칸 분석하기 빈칸 앞에 있는 것 ☐부정사 to ☑전치사 to
   → 빈칸에는 ☐동사원형 ☑동명사가 들어가야 한다.
3. 정답 선택하기 정답 (C)

포틀랜드의 주민들은 새로 개조된 도서관을 방문하기를 고대하고 있다.

실전 문제

01.(C)	02.(B)	03.(B)	04.(B)	05.(C)	06.(D)
07.(C)	08.(B)	09.(C)	10.(B)	11.(D)	12.(D)
13.(A)	14.(C)	15.(A)	16.(A)	17.(A)	18.(A)
19.(D)	20.(B)	21.(A)	22.(C)	23.(D)	24.(B)

01. 동명사의 역할: 전치사의 목적어 역할

석유 파동에 직면한 후, Farrell Auto는 현재 전기 자동차를 개발했다.

[해설] 선택지가 동사 face의 다양한 형태로 구성되어 있으므로 문법 문제이다. 전치사(또는 접속사) After 뒤에서 주어 없이 동사가 쓰이려면 동명사(또는 분사)의 형태가 되어야 하는데, 빈칸 뒤에 목적어가 있으므로 목적어를 취할 수 있는 동명사(현재분사) (C) facing이 정답이다.

[어휘] oil crisis 석유 파동   develop ~을 개발하다   face ~에 직면하다   electric 전기의

02. to부정사의 태

코미디언 Johnny Orwell 씨가 한때 인기 있었던 TV 프로그램 <My Friends>의 다음 시즌 대본을 쓰도록 고용되었다.

[해설] 선택지가 동사 write의 다양한 형태로 구성되어 있으므로 문법 문제이다. 빈칸 앞에 이미 문장의 동사 was hired가 있으므로 write는 준동사로 쓰여야 하는데, 빈칸 뒤에 위치한 명사구를 목적어로 취해야 하므로 능동태 to부정사 형태인 (B) to write가 정답이다.

[어휘] hire ~을 고용하다   once-popular 한때 인기 있었던

03. 동명사의 역할: 타동사의 목적어 역할

경영진은 채용 업무를 외부의 대행사에 위임하는 것을 고려하고 있다.

[해설] 선택지가 동사 delegate의 다양한 형태와 명사로 구성되어 있으므

(B) 상업 미술관에서
(C) 공립 도서관에서
(D) 예술 연구소에서

[해설] 첫 단락 끝부분에 at the site of the show, the Penfield Public Library라는 말로 행사장이 공립 도서관임을 알 수 있으므로 (C)가 정답이다.

[어휘] institute 연구소, 기관, 협회

06. 세부사항 문제

방문객들은 행사장에서 무엇을 할 기회를 가질 것인가?
(A) 미술가의 강연 듣기
(B) 가장 좋아하는 그림에 투표하기
(C) 경품 추첨 행사에 등록하기
(D) 일부 미술 작품에 대해 입찰하기

[해설] 두 번째 단락 중간 부분에, 행사 중에 사전에 선정된 작품들에 대한 경매 행사가 열린다는(there will be an auction for several pre-selected pieces) 말이 있는데 이는 가격 입찰을 통해 미술 작품을 구매하는 행사를 의미하므로 (D)가 정답이다.

paraphrasing auction for several pre-selected pieces 사전에 선정된 여러 작품들에 대한 경매 행사 → Bid on some artwork 일부 미술 작품에 대해 입찰하기

[어휘] vote on ~에 대해 투표하다   drawing 추첨 행사   bid on ~에 입찰하다

07. 추론 문제

Austin 씨는 누구일 것 같은가?
(A) 행사 기획자
(B) 미술 평론가
(C) 미술관 소유주
(D) 지역 기자

[해설] Austin 씨의 이름이 제시된 마지막 단락에, 자원 봉사자가 필요하다는 말과 함께 시간을 낼 수 있는 사람은 Noreen Austin 씨에게 연락하도록(If you are able to share your time, please contact Noreen Austin) 요청하고 있으므로 Austin 씨는 행사 진행과 관련 있는 사람임을 알 수 있다. 따라서 '행사 기획자'를 뜻하는 (A)가 정답이다.

[어휘] critic 평론가, 비평가

paraphrasing 정답 1. (d)   2. (a)   3. (e)   4. (b)   5. (c)

08-10은 다음 공지를 참조하시오.

Cessna 대로에 관한 공지

교통국(DOT)에서는 Cessna 대로의 변화에 관한 계획을 최종 확정했습니다. ⁰⁸3월 20일부터, 각 방향으로 추가 차로를 개설하기 위해 주요 간선 도로의 전 구간에서 도로 공사가 시작될 것입니다. 그 결과로, 앞으로 6개월 동안 부분적인 도로 폐쇄가 수시로 있을 것입니다. 이 공사는 Plymouth 다리에서 용도가 전환된 여분의 자금을 활용해 실시될 예정입니다. 이 다리는 최근 안전 평가 과정을 거쳤으나 수리 작업이 필요하지 않은 관계로, 예상 수리 작업을 위해 할당되었던 재원이 Cessna 대로의 예산에 추가되었습니다. ⁰⁹이 다리는 이번 달에 다시 페인트 작업이 될 예정이었지만, 해당 작업은 1월 초로 연기되었습니다.

해당 공사가 진행되는 동안 Valena 지역 내에서 교통 혼잡이 문제가 될 것으로 예상됩니다. ¹⁰주민들과 방문객들께서는 모두 도로의 차량 수를 감소시키기 위해 가능한 한 카풀을 하시도록 권해 드립니다.

roadwork 도로 공사   entire 전체의   thoroughfare 주요 간선 도로   additional 추가의   lane 차로   closure 폐쇄   on and off 수시로, 때때로   carry out ~을 실시하다, 수행하다   surplus 여분의   fund 자금   redirected from ~에서 용도가 전환된   undergo ~을 거치다, 겪다   assessment 평가   allocate ~을 할당하다, 배정하다   budget 예산   postpone ~을 연기하다   traffic congestion 교통 혼잡   issue 문제, 사안   neighborhood 지역, 인근   while ~하는 동안   resident 주민   carpool (함께 차를 타는) 카풀   cut down on ~을 감소시키다, 단축하다

08. 목적 문제

공지의 한 가지 목적은 무엇인가?
(A) 수리 작업 일정의 변동 사항을 알리는 것
(B) 공사 프로젝트에 관한 상세 정보를 제공하는 것
(C) 도로에 관한 의견을 요청하는 것
(D) 운전자들에게 안전 문제에 관해 주의를 주는 것

[해설] 지문 시작 부분에 3월 20일부터 각 방향으로 추가 차로를 개설하기 위해 주요 간선 도로의 전 구간에서 도로 공사가 시작된다는(Beginning March 20, roadwork will begin on the entire length of the thoroughfare to build an additional lane) 말과 함께 해당 공사와 관련된 정보를 제시하고 있으므로 (B)가 정답이다.

[어휘] roadway 도로   warn A about B A에게 B에 관해 주의를 주다

09. True 문제

Plymouth 다리에 관해 언급된 것은 무엇인가?
(A) Cessna 대로로 가는 우회 경로이다.
(B) 안전 점검을 통과하지 못했다.
(C) 내년이나 되어야 다시 페인트칠이 될 것이다.
(D) 작년에 개통되었다.

[해설] Plymouth 다리 관련 정보가 제시된 첫 단락 끝부분에, 그 다리에 다시 페인트를 칠하는 작업이 1월 초로 연기되었다고(The bridge was supposed to be repainted this month, but that work has been postponed to early January) 쓰여 있는데, 이는 내년이나 되어야 그 작업이 시작된다는 말이므로 (C)가 정답이다.

paraphrasing has been postponed to early January 1월 초로 연기되었다 → not be repainted until next year 내년이나 되어야 다시 페인트칠이 된다

[어휘] alternative route 우회 경로   inspection 점검

10. 세부사항 문제

지역 주민들은 무엇을 하도록 권장되는가?
(A) 가능한 한 차량을 함께 타고 다니기
(B) 온라인으로 폐쇄 구간 확인하기
(C) 대중교통 이용하기
(D) 교통국에 문제점 알리기

[해설] 지역 주민들에 대한 권장 사항이 제시된 마지막 단락에, 주민들과 방문객들 모두 차량 수를 감소시킬 수 있도록 가능한 한 카풀을 하라고(Residents and visitors alike are encouraged to carpool whenever they can) 권하고 있는데, 카풀은 함께 차를 타고 다니는 것

stations 컴퓨터 사용 공간을 더 제공하다

[어휘] resident 주민 assistance 도움 relocate to ~로 이전하다

02. 세부사항 문제

공지에 따르면, 공지를 읽는 사람들은 왜 Templeton 씨에게 연락해야 하는가?

(A) 인쇄본으로 된 정기 간행물을 요청하기 위해
(B) 출판물을 구독하기 위해
(C) 정식 항의서를 제출하기 위해
(D) 개조 공사에 입찰하기 위해

[해설] 지문 하단 부분을 통해 Templeton 씨가 공지 작성자임을 알 수 있고, 두 번째 단락에서 잡지의 원본 인쇄물을 찾아야 할 경우에 자신에게 연락해 달라고(If you need to find an original print copy of a magazine, please contact me ~) 알리고 있으므로 (A)가 정답이다.

paraphrasing original print copy of a magazine 잡지의 원본 인쇄물 → periodicals in print 인쇄본으로 된 정기 간행물

[어휘] periodical 정기 간행물 subscribe to ~을 구독하다 publication 출판물 submit ~을 제출하다 formal 정식의, 공식적인 complaint 항의(서) place a bid for ~에 입찰하다

paraphrasing 정답 1. (e) 2. (c) 3. (b) 4. (d) 5. (a)

03-04는 다음 공지를 참조하시오.

탬파 주민 여러분께 알립니다.

시 의회에서는 시내 버스의 엔진을 하이브리드 엔진으로 전환하기 위해 투표를 진행했습니다. [03]이 변화를 통해 유해 배기 가스를 최대 70%까지 감소시키게 될 것입니다. 또한, 모든 버스 정류장에는 일부 전력을 자체적으로 공급하고 야간에 전기 소비량을 줄일 수 있도록 태양열 전지판이 설치될 것입니다.

이 제안은 시의 공원 관리부 소속 고위 관계자인 [04]**Emma Stanton** 씨께서 제시해 주셨습니다. 그분의 사무실에는 우리가 [04]**환경에 끼치는 영향을 줄이는 데 도움이 되는 방법과 관련해 일반 시민들로부터 아이디어를 모으는 데 사용되는 상담 서비스 전화가 놓여 있습니다. 주민 여러분께서 그 전화번호인 555-7234로 전화하셔서 생각을 공유해 주시기를 강력히 요청 드립니다.**

resident 주민 council 의회 vote 투표하다 convert A to B A를 B로 전환하다 harmful 유해한 emission 배기 가스, 배출물 be fitted with ~가 설치되다, 갖춰지다 solar panel 태양열 전지판 partially 일부, 부분적으로 proposal 제안(서) put forward ~을 제안하다, 제시하다 gather ~을 모으다 impact on ~에 대한 영향 be urged to부정사 ~하도록 강력히 요청 받다, 촉구되다

03. True 문제

탬파의 시내 버스에 관해 언급된 것은 무엇인가?
(A) 승객들을 위해 더 많은 좌석이 생길 것이다.
(B) 야간에는 덜 자주 운행될 것이다.
(C) 오직 재생 가능 에너지만 사용할 것이다.
(D) 곧 공해를 덜 유발시키게 될 것이다.

[해설] 지문 시작 부분에 시내 버스의 엔진을 바꿈으로써 유해 배기 가스를 최대 70%까지 감소시킬 수 있다고(~ reduce harmful emissions by up to 70%) 알리고 있는데, 이는 공해를 줄이는 방법에 해당되므로 이와 같은 의미로 쓰인 (D)가 정답이다.

paraphrasing reduce harmful emissions 유해 배기 가스를 줄이다 → cause less pollution 공해를 덜 유발시키다

[어휘] run 운행되다, 가동되다 frequently 자주 renewable energy 재생 가능 에너지

04. 세부사항 문제

공지를 읽는 사람들은 왜 Stanton 씨에게 연락할 수도 있는가?

(A) 친환경적인 변화를 추천하기 위해
(B) 공립 공원에 관한 우려를 나타내기 위해
(C) 캠페인 보조자로서 자원하기 위해
(D) 공공 문제에 대해 투표하기 위해

[해설] Stanton 씨의 이름이 제시된 두 번째 단락에, 환경에 도움이 될 수 있는 아이디어를 시민들로부터 얻는 데 사용되는 상담 전화가 있다는 말과 함께 그 전화번호로 연락해 생각을 공유해 달라고 요청하고 있다(Her office has a hotline ~ help reduce our impact on the environment. Residents are urged to call it ~). 이는 환경에 도움이 되는 일을 추천하는 것을 의미하므로 (A)가 정답이다.

[어휘] environmentally friendly 친환경적인 express ~을 나타내다, 표현하다 concern 우려, 걱정 assistant 보조, 조수 cast a vote 투표하다 issue 문제, 사안

paraphrasing 정답 1. (c) 2. (b) 3. (a) 4. (e) 5. (d)

05-07은 다음 공지를 참조하시오.

제2회 연례 펜필드 지역사회 아트 쇼

제2회 연례 펜필드 지역사회 아트 쇼 행사가 10월 11일 토요일로 예정되어 있습니다. 전문 미술가로 활동하고 계시는 분이든 또는 이제 막 시작하시는 분이든 상관 없이, 저희는 여러분의 작품을 꼭 확인해 보기를 원합니다! 등록 양식은 www.penfieldart.com에서 온라인으로 이용하실 수 있습니다. 작품은 Ellsworth 예술 연구소 또는 [05]**행사장인 펜필드 공립 도서관**으로 10월 8일까지 제출하셔야 합니다.

시내에 위치한 상업 미술관인 Broyles 미술관 소속 직원들께서 조명 시설과 작품 배치에 관한 전문 지식을 공유해 주시는 방법으로 미술품 전시에 도움을 주시겠다고 너그러운 마음으로 자원해 주셨습니다. [06]**행사 기간 중에, 사전에 선정된 여러 작품들에 대한 경매 행사가 열립니다.** 추가로, 심사위원들께서 작품을 평가하시고 여러 부문에 걸쳐 시상해 주실 것입니다.

이번 행사를 성공적으로 개최하기 위해, 저희는 작품 설치/철거, 방문객 맞이, 그리고 매점 근무에 도움을 주실 [07]**자원 봉사자가 필요합니다.** 시간을 내 주실 수 있는 분께서는, 555-7931로 Noreen Austin 씨께 연락 주시기 바랍니다.

registration form 등록 양식 drop off ~을 갖다주다, 내려놓다 site 장소, 현장, 부지 on or before+날짜 (기한) ~까지 commercial 상업의 generously 너그럽게, 후하게 expertise 전문 지식 arrange ~을 배치하다, 정렬하다 piece 작품 pre-selected 사전에 선정된 in addition 추가로 judge 심사위원 assess ~을 평가하다 give away 나눠 주다 take-down 철거, 해체 concession stand 구내 매점

05. 세부사항 문제

미술 전시 행사가 어디에서 열릴 것인가?
(A) 지역 문화 센터에서

렇게 작은 공간을 임대하기로 결정했습니다. 이와 같은 비용 절감은 저렴한 가격의 형태로 고객들에게 그 혜택이 돌아갑니다. 여러분의 양해에 감사 드립니다.

premises (건물 등의) 구내, 공간   have A on hand ~을 보유하다, 준비해 두다   operating costs 운영비   savings 비용 절약

Q. Dream 레스토랑은 비용을 줄이기 위해 무엇을 하는가?
(A) 짧은 영업 시간 제공하기
(B) 작은 장소에서 업체 운영하기

[문제 키워드] What / Restaurant / do / reduce costs

[해설] 키워드인 reduce costs가 직접적으로 언급되어 있지 않으므로 패러프레이징된 부분인 keep operating costs down을 찾는다. 지문 후반부에 운영비를 낮게 유지하기 위해 작은 공간의 임대를 결정했다고(We have chosen to rent such a small space ~ to keep operating costs down) 알리고 있으므로 (B)가 정답이다.

[어휘] run ~을 운영하다

03.

교통국에서는 5월 10일 금요일부터 5월 15일 수요일까지 **Kenner 가에 도로 재포장 공사를 실시할** 예정입니다. 도로와 보도 모두 이용 불가능하게 될 것이므로 Prospect Business Complex(PBC)의 정문은 이 기간에 잠가 둘 것입니다. 18번 가 쪽에 위치한 측면 출입구는 여전히 이용할 수 있으며, 해당 건물의 주차 상황에 대해서는 아무런 영향도 없을 것입니다. 질문이나 우려 사항이 있으신 분은 PBC 건물 관리 책임자인 Judith Timms 씨에게 555-3697번으로 연락하시기 바랍니다.

resurface (도로, 바닥 등) ~을 재포장하다   sidewalk 보도   inaccessible 이용 불가능한, 접근할 수 없는   effect on ~에 대한 영향   concern 우려, 걱정

Q. PBC에 관해 암시된 것은 무엇인가?
(A) 교통국 사무실 공간을 제공하고 있다.
(B) Kenner 가 쪽에서 정문에 접근할 수 있다.

[문제 키워드] What / suggested / PBC

[해설] about 뒤의 키워드 PBC가 제시되는 부분에서 단서를 찾아야 한다. 초반부에 언급된 Kenner 가의 도로 재포장 공사(resurfacing Kenner Street)와 관련해, 중반부에 도로를 이용할 수 없어 Prospect Business Complex (PBC)의 정문을 그 기간에 잠가 둘 것이라고(The main entrance to Prospect Business Complex (PBC) will be locked ~) 되어 있는데, 이는 Kenner 가에 정문이 있음을 암시하므로 (B)가 정답이다.

[어휘] house ~에 공간을 제공하다   access ~에 접근하다, ~을 이용하다

04.

Harrisburg 공립 도서관 방문객들께 알립니다.

Harrisburg 공립 도서관은 8월 1일부터 8월 7일까지 제2회 연례 여름 문학 축제를 주최하게 되어 기쁘게 생각합니다. 이 축제 기간 내내, 저희는 **Wanda Girard 씨와 Dawn Matz 씨, 그리고 Francis Kline 씨와 같은 재능 있는 작가들**이 진행하는 강연들을 특별히 마련할 것입니다. 참가자들께서는 또한 Wanda Girard 씨의 최신 도서인 <Sunflower Days>를 구입할 기회를 얻게 될 것인데, 이 책은 <National Express Magazine>의 문학 평론가 Danielle Jordison 씨에 의해 '반드시 읽어야 할 마음을 울리는 책'이라고 불렸습니다.

literary 문학의   feature ~을 특징으로 하다   talented 재능 있는   author 작가, 저자   move (마음 등) ~을 뭉클하게 하다, ~에 감동을 주다

Q. Kline 씨는 누구인가?
(A) 작가
(B) 문학 평론가

[문제 키워드] Who / Mr. Kline

[해설] 키워드인 Mr. Kline이 제시되는 부분에서 단서를 찾아야 한다. 해당 이름이 제시되는 중반부에 Kline씨는 재능 있는 작가들 중의 한 명으로(~ featuring lectures from talented authors such as Wanda Girard, Dawn Matz, and Francis Kline) 언급되고 있으므로 (A)가 정답이다.

[어휘] critic 평론가

실전 문제

| 01.(B) | 02.(A) | 03.(D) | 04.(A) | 05.(C) | 06.(D) |
| 07.(A) | 08.(B) | 09.(C) | 10.(A) |

01-02는 다음 공지를 참조하시오.

오클랜드 도서관 회원 여러분!

저희는 요즘 인쇄 매체를 이용하는 대신 온라인상에서 대부분의 조사가 실시되고 있음을 알고 있습니다. 따라서, 저희는 일부 잡지 인쇄물의 구독 서비스를 취소하고 **01컴퓨터실 공간의 규모를 넓히기로 결정했습니다.**

이전에 잡지 인쇄물들을 보관하는 데 사용되었던 장소가 **01현재 10대의 추가 컴퓨터들을 놓을 공간을 확보하기 위해** 개조되고 있습니다. **02잡지의 원본 인쇄물을 찾으셔야 하는 분들께서는 제게 연락하셔서** 해당 잡지의 이름과 발간 날짜를 말씀해 주십시오. 필요할 경우에 공급받을 수 있도록 제가 해당 잡지사에 연락하겠습니다.

감사합니다.

02Larry Templeton
선임 사서, 오클랜드 도서관
555-8712

conduct ~을 실시하다, 수행하다   subscription 구독 (서비스)   formerly 이전에, 과거에   store ~을 보관하다   make room for ~에 필요한 공간을 확보하다   additional 추가의   date of issue 발간 날짜

01. 세부사항 문제

오클랜드 도서관에 대해 무엇이 언급되었는가?
(A) 지역 주민들을 위한 강좌를 열기 시작할 것이다.
(B) 컴퓨터 사용 공간을 더 제공할 것이다.
(C) 온라인 조사 지원 서비스를 제공할 것이다.
(D) 더 넓은 건물로 이전할 것이다.

[해설] 첫 단락에 컴퓨터실 공간의 규모를 넓히기로(increase the size of our computer lab area) 결정한 사실과 함께, 두 번째 단락에 10대의 추가 컴퓨터들을 놓을 공간을 확보하기 위해 개조하고 있다는(is being renovated to make room for an additional 10 computers) 말이 있으므로 이와 같은 공간의 용도가 언급된 (B)가 정답이다.

paraphrasing   make room for an additional 10 computers 10대의 추가 컴퓨터들을 놓을 공간을 확보하다 → provide more computer

(D) 한정된 기간에 한해, 단체 관람객들을 위한 할인도 있습니다.

[해설] 빈칸 앞 문장에 언급된 유명 배우들(famous movie actors)로 출연진이 구성되어 있다는 사실과 연계되는 것으로서 그 배우들을 They로 지칭해 그들의 실제 모습을 본 소감을 나타내는 (B)가 정답이다.

[어휘] refund 환불 exchange 교환 policy 정책 complicated 복잡한

05-08은 다음 쿠폰을 참조하시오.

할인 쿠폰

MB Parker's의 모든 직원들이 귀하의 생일을 축하 드립니다! ⁰⁵귀하의 성원에 대한 감사의 표시로 이 쿠폰을 발급해 드립니다. ⁰⁶귀하께서는 저희 매장에서 50달러 상당의 어느 구매품에 대해서든 이 쿠폰을 사용할 자격이 있으십니다! 계산 담당 직원에게 제시하기만 하시면 됩니다. ⁰⁷이것은 심지어 온라인 구매 제품에 대해서도 적용됩니다. 이 카드의 뒷면에 코드가 쓰여 있으므로 계산할 때 입력하시면 됩니다. ⁰⁸이 특별 제공 쿠폰은 재고 정리 상품에는 적용되지 않습니다. 12월 31일까지 유효합니다.

voucher 쿠폰, 상품권 as a token of ~의 표시로 loyalty 성원, 충성(도) be eligible to부정사 ~할 자격이 있다 present A to B A를 B에게 제시하다 cashier 계산 담당 직원 check out 계산하다 offer 제공(품) clearance merchandise 재고 정리 상품 valid 유효한

05. 명사 어휘

[해설] as a token of의 목적어에 해당되는 빈칸은 쿠폰을 발급하는 이유와 관련되어야 하며, 빈칸 뒤에 쓰인 전치사 of와 어울림과 동시에 고객의 성원이나 충성도 등을 뜻하는 your loyalty와도 의미가 연결되어야 하므로 '~에 대한 감사의 뜻으로'라는 표현을 만들 때 사용하는 (B) appreciation이 정답이다.

[어휘] donation 기부(금) satisfaction 만족(도) attachment 첨부(된 것)

06. 동사의 형태

[해설] 빈칸 앞에 위치한 be eligible은 to부정사와 함께 '~할 자격이 있다'라는 의미로 사용하므로 (C) to use가 정답이다.

07. 알맞은 문장 고르기

(A) MB Parker's의 회원 프로그램에 가입해 주셔서 감사 드립니다.
(B) 저희 매장에서 귀하의 특별한 날을 즐기시기를 바랍니다.
(C) 저희 웹사이트 www.mbparkers.com에서 매장 지점들을 확인하십시오.
(D) 이것은 심지어 온라인 구매 제품에 대해서도 적용됩니다.

[해설] 앞 문장에서 쿠폰을 it으로 지칭해 그것을 실제 매장에서 사용하는 방법을 알려 주고 있으므로 이 내용과 연계되는 것으로서 쿠폰을 This로 지칭해 추가 사용처를 알려 주고 있는 (D)가 정답이다.

[어휘] join ~에 가입하다, 합류하다 location 지점, 위치 apply A to B A를 B에 적용하다 purchase 구매(품)

08. 동사의 형태

[해설] 지문 중간에서, 현재 시제 동사를 써서 현재 자격이 있음을 나타낸 You are eligible ~ 구문과 마찬가지로, 재고 정리 상품이 제외된다는 점도 이 쿠폰이 지니는 특징으로서 일반적인 사실에 해당하므로 현재 시제 동

사가 쓰여야 자연스럽다. 단수 주어 This special offer와 수 일치가 되어야 하므로 (B) exempts가 정답이다.

[어휘] exempt 면제하다

PART 7 공지 (2) 공공장소에서의 공지

풀이 방법 해석

Buffalo 기차역을 이용하시는 승객들께

최근에 폭풍우가 동쪽으로 가는 기차들의 선로 일부분에 심각하게 피해를 입혔습니다. 수리를 하기 위해 Buffalo와 Albany 사이를 운행하는 기차편의 횟수가 9월 7일부터 21일까지 상당히 줄어들 것입니다.

취소된 기차의 티켓을 이미 구입하셨다면, 저희 고객 서비스 부서의 Louis Sinclair를 찾으셔서 가장 빨리 이용 가능한 기차로 바꾸시기 바랍니다. 이로 인한 불편함에 미리 사과드립니다.

 연습 문제

01.(A) 02.(B) 03.(B) 04.(A)

01.

Camden 은행 고객들께 알립니다.

Austin 가 942번지에 위치한 Camden 은행 지점이 직원 교육으로 인해 7월 8일과 9일에 문을 닫습니다. 예금 인출과 고지서 비용 납부 등과 같은 많은 서비스들은 여전히 해당 건물 외부의 정문 근처에 위치한 ATM을 통해 이용할 수 있을 것입니다. 고객들께서는 또한 온라인으로 거래하실 것이 권장됩니다. 그 대신에, Lewbow 가 1356번지에 위치한 저희 지점이 이 기간에 계속 문을 열 것입니다. 이로 인해 야기될 수 있는 불편함에 대해 사과드립니다.

branch 지점, 지사 staff training exercise 직원 교육 make a withdrawal 예금을 인출하다 pay bill 고지서 비용을 납부하다 carry out ~을 수행하다 transaction 거래 alternatively 그 대신에, 그렇지 않으면

Q. 공지의 목적은 무엇인가?
(A) 일시적인 폐쇄를 알리기 위해
(B) 신규 서비스를 홍보하기 위해

[문제 키워드] purpose

[해설] 지문 시작 부분에 특정 은행 지점이 문을 닫는 시점을 알리면서(The Camden Bank branch at 942 Austin Street will be closed July 8-9 ~) 그에 따른 조치를 제시하고 있으므로 (A)가 정답이다.

[어휘] temporary 일시적인 promote ~을 홍보하다

02.

Dream 레스토랑 고객들께 알립니다.

저희 주문 카운터 근처에 있는 테이블은 식사용이 아닌 오직 고객 대기용으로만 사용된다는 점에 유의하시기 바랍니다. 모든 음식은 반드시 포장용으로만 주문되니 식당에서 가져가셔야 합니다. 저희는 영업장 내에서 식사를 하신 이후에 깨끗이 정리하는 일을 할 직원을 보유하고 있지 않습니다. **저희는 운영비를 낮게 유지하기 위해 레스토랑용으로 이**

01.

박스 오피스를 뒤흔드는 속편
Barry Sherman 작성

몬트리올 (6월 2일) — 오래 기다려 온 2010년 히트 영화 <Cop Chase>의 속편이 어제 극장에서 개봉되었으며, 입장권 판매 기록을 경신했습니다. 이 영화는 기존 영화의 출연진에 속했던 배우들이 카메오로 출연하고 있지만, 주로 젊은 새 주인공에 초점을 맞추고 있습니다.

prequel (시간적으로 앞선 내용을 다룬) 속편 release ~을 개봉하다, 출시하다 sales 판매(량), 매출, 영업 cast 출연진 mainly 주로 focus on ~에 초점을 맞추다 protagonist 주인공

[단서] cameos from the original film's cast
[해설] 빈칸 바로 뒤에서 말하는 기존 출연진의 카메오 출연은 변하지 않는 특징에 해당되므로 일반적인 사실 등을 나타낼 때 사용하는 현재 시제인 (A) features가 정답이다.

02.

Little Rock 민박에 머물러 주셔서 감사 드립니다. 아침으로 선호하시는 식사를 표기해 주시기 바랍니다. 모든 아침 식사 옵션에는 직접 선택하신 베트남 스타일의 커피와 과일 바구니가 포함됩니다. 이 카드를 직원에게 되돌려 주시기 바랍니다.

indicate ~을 표기하다, 나타내다 preference 선호(하는 것) come with ~을 포함하다, ~가 딸려 있다 return A to B A를 B에게 되돌려 주다

[단서] Every breakfast option
[해설] 모든 아침 식사 옵션에 포함되는 음식은 특정 시점에만 적용되는 것이 아닌 일반적인 특징에 해당되므로 일반적인 사실을 말할 때 사용하는 현재 시제로 쓰인 (B) comes가 정답이다.

03.

20년 전 지역 B&B 숙박업체로 설립된 Paradise 리조트는 전국적인 리조트 체인이 되었습니다. 당사는 호텔, 숙박 시설, 프라이빗 콘도 등 다양한 숙박 시설을 갖추고 있습니다. Paradise 리조트에서 여러분들은 실망하지 않을 것입니다.

establish 설립하다 bed and breakfast 아침 식사를 제공하는 숙박 accommodation 숙박시설 lodge 산장, 숙소

[단서] has become
[해설] 리조트 체인이 되었다는 현재 완료 시제를 사용했으므로 현재 숙박 시설을 갖추고 있고 제공한다는 것을 나타낼 수 있는 현재 시제인 (A) feature가 정답이다.

04.

Willis 씨께

이 편지는 귀하의 <Today's Style> 구독 서비스가 4월 17일에 만료될 것이라는 점을 상기시켜 드리기 위한 것입니다. 저희는 만료일 2주 전에 이를 알려드리는 메시지를 보내 드리고 있습니다. 귀하께서는 이 편지에 답장하시거나 저희 서비스 센터로 전화하시는 방법으로, 또는 저희 웹사이트를 방문하셔서 회원 자격을 갱신하실 수 있습니다.

reminder (메시지 등의) 상기시키는 것 subscription 구독 서비스 expire 만료되다 expiration 만료, 만기 renew ~을 갱신하다 by (방법) ~함으로써 either A, B, or C A나 B 또는 C 중의 하나 respond to ~에 답장하다

[단서] This letter is a reminder
[해설] 서비스 만료일 2주 전에 메시지를 보내는 일은 해당 업체에서 일반적으로 하는 일에 해당되므로 일반적인 사실을 나타낼 때 사용하는 현재 시제로 쓰인 (A) send가 정답이다.

실전 문제

01.(B) 02.(A) 03.(C) 04.(B) 05.(B) 06.(C)
07.(D) 08.(B)

01-04는 다음 후기를 참조하시오.

[01] <Rolling Thunder>는 모든 연령대의 사람들에게 즐거움을 주는 뮤지컬입니다. 저는 가족과 함께 관람했습니다. 저희 모두는 다른 대부분의 뮤지컬들보다 훨씬 더 재미있다고 생각했습니다. [02] 저희는 처음부터 끝까지 계속 웃었습니다! 대본과 악보가 한 유명 코미디언에 의해 쓰여졌다는 사실이 전혀 놀랍지 않습니다. [03] 또한, <Rolling Thunder>는 쉽게 알아 볼 수 있는 유명 영화 배우들로 구성된 출연진을 특징으로 합니다. [04] 그들은 화면에서 보이는 모습 바로 그대로였습니다. 전반적으로, 저는 이 공연에 대해 별점 5점의 점수와 함께 최고라는 찬사를 보냅니다.

It comes as no surprise that ~라는 점이 놀랍지 않다, ~한 것이 당연하다 script 대본 score 악보 cast 출연진 recognize ~을 알아보다 overall 전반적으로 rating (평가) 점수, 등급 two thumbs up 최고, 강력 추천작, 끝내주는 것

01. 형용사 자리

[해설] 부정 관사 an과 명사 musical 사이에 위치한 빈칸은 명사를 수식할 형용사 자리인데 musical이 즐거움을 주는 주체에 해당되므로 '즐겁게 만드는, 즐겁게 해주는'이라는 의미로 쓰이는 (B) entertaining이 정답이다. (D) entertained는 '즐거움을 느낀'을 의미하므로 사람에 대해 사용한다.

[어휘] entertain ~을 즐겁게 해주다

02. 명사 어휘

[해설] 빈칸은 전치사 to의 목적어 자리로서 빈칸 앞에 위치한 from start와 짝을 이루는 종료 시점을 나타내야 알맞으므로 '끝, 마지막 부분'을 뜻하는 (A) finish가 정답이다.

[어휘] search 검색, 수색, 찾기 decline 감소, 하락

03. 동사의 형태

[해설] 빈칸 뒤 who절에서 현재 시제 동사 are를 써서 일반적으로 쉽게 알아볼 수 있다는 사실을 나타낸 것과 같이, 빈칸이 포함된 구절 역시 유명 배우들로 출연진이 구성되어 있다는 일반적인 사실을 나타내야 알맞으므로 동일한 현재 시제인 (C) features가 정답이다.

04. 알맞은 문장 고르기

(A) 저는 티켓 환불과 교환 정책이 매우 복잡하다고 생각했습니다.
(B) 그들은 화면에서 보이는 모습 바로 그대로였습니다
(C) 저희가 앉아 있던 곳에서 무대가 잘 보이지 않았습니다.

자리이며, 3인칭 단수 주어 Ms. Peterson과 수 일치에 상관 없이 사용할 수 있는 과거 시제 (B) predicted가 정답이다.

[어휘] hospitality industry 접객 업계   boom 호황을 누리다, 붐을 일으키다   predictable 예측 가능한   prediction 예측, 예상

17. 주어와 동사의 수 일치

해외에서 근무할 수 있는 기회를 제공하기 때문에 이 직책에 대한 해외 지원자들의 숫자가 두 배가 되었다.

[해설] 선택지가 다양한 품사의 단어들로 구성되어 있으므로 문법 문제이다. 접속사 since 앞에 빈칸이 있고, 그 앞에 명사와 전치사구들만 쓰여 있으므로 빈칸은 주절의 동사 자리이다. 또한 단수 주어 The number와 수 일치가 되어야 하므로 (C) has doubled가 정답이다.

[어휘] applicant 지원자   abroad 해외에서   double 두 배로 되다[만들다]   doubly 두 배로, 두 가지로

18. 사람 명사 vs. 사물 명사

두 기술자들 중의 누구도 낡은 트럭 모델을 처리하는 것을 꺼려하지 않았다.

[해설] 선택지가 다양한 품사의 단어들로 구성되어 있으므로 문법 문제이다. 정관사 the 뒤에 위치한 빈칸은 the의 수식을 받으면서 전치사 of의 목적어 역할을 할 명사 자리인데, 형용사 보어 reluctant(꺼리는)는 사람에 대해 사용하므로 사람 명사인 (B) technicians가 정답이다.

[어휘] be reluctant to부정사 ~하는 것을 꺼리다   handle ~을 처리하다, 다루다   technical 기술적인   technician 기술자

19. 동사 어휘

컴퓨터 공학 학위를 소지하는 것이 Louisville 디자인에서의 승진 기회를 향상시켜 준다.

[해설] 선택지가 다양한 동사 어휘들로 구성되어 있으므로 동사 어휘 문제이다. 컴퓨터 공학 학위를 갖고 있는 것과 승진 기회 사이의 의미 관계를 나타낼 동사가 필요하므로 '~을 개선하다, 향상시키다'를 뜻하는 (B) improves가 정답이다.

[어휘] degree 학위   promotion 승진   recruit ~을 모집하다   unveil ~을 공개하다

20. 동사 어휘

이사회는 새로운 광고 캠페인이 자사의 매장으로 더 많은 고객들을 끌어들일 것이라고 생각한다.

[해설] 선택지가 다양한 동사 어휘들로 구성되어 있으므로 동사 어휘 문제이다. 새로운 광고 캠페인과 더 많은 고객들 사이의 의미 관계를 나타낼 동사가 필요하므로 '~을 끌어들이다'라는 의미로 쓰이는 (C) attract가 정답이다.

[어휘] board members 이사회, 이사진   ad 광고   resolve ~을 해결하다   evolve 발전하다, ~을 발전시키다

21. 동사 어휘

업그레이드된 이 화상 회의 시스템을 통해, Bishop 산업의 직원들은 해외에서 근무하고 있는 사람들과 의사소통할 수 있다.

[해설] 선택지가 다양한 동사 어휘들로 구성되어 있으므로 동사 어휘 문제이다. 빈칸 뒤에 위치한 전치사 with와 어울리는 자동사가 필요하므로 with와 함께 '~와 의사소통하다'라는 의미를 구성하는 (B) communicate가 정답이다.

[어휘] teleconferencing 화상 회의   overseas 해외에서   initiate ~을 시작하다   encounter ~와 맞닥뜨리다, 마주하다   emphasize ~을 강조

하다

22. 동사 어휘

귀하의 해외 배송을 더 신속히 처리하기를 원하실 경우, Customs Bypass 옵션을 선택하셔야 합니다.

[해설] 선택지가 다양한 동사 어휘들로 구성되어 있으므로 동사 어휘 문제이다. 해외 배송과 관련해 특정 옵션을 선택하는 이유와 관련된 동사가 빈칸에 쓰여야 알맞으므로 '~을 더 신속히 처리하다'라는 의미로 쓰이는 (C) expedite가 정답이다.

[어휘] shipment 배송(품)   implement ~을 시행하다   enforce ~을 집행하다   relocate ~을 이전하다, 옮기다

23. 동사 어휘

Hahn's 금융은 새 회계사들을 수용하기 위해 다음 달에 더 넓은 사무 공간으로 이전할 예정이다.

[해설] 선택지가 다양한 동사 어휘들로 구성되어 있으므로 동사 어휘 문제이다. 더 넓은 사무실로 이전하는 일과 새로운 직원들 사이의 의미 관계를 나타낼 동사가 필요하므로 '~을 수용하다'라는 의미로 쓰이는 (B) accommodate가 정답이다.

[어휘] relocate to ~로 이전하다   accountant 회계사   ensure ~을 보장하다, ~임을 확실히 하다   respond 대응하다, 응답하다   issue ~을 발급하다, 지급하다

24. 동사 어휘

Alexander Hunt 씨가 제18회 연례 몬터레이 골프 선수권 대회의 우승자로 드러났다.

[해설] 선택지가 다양한 동사 어휘들로 구성되어 있으므로 동사 어휘 문제이다. 빈칸 뒤에 위치한 'as+자격/신분' 전치사구와 어울리는 자동사가 필요하므로 '~로 드러나다, 떠오르다'라는 의미를 나타낼 때 사용하는 (A) emerged가 정답이다.

[어휘] rely (on) (~에) 의지하다, (~를) 신뢰하다   delegate ~을 위임하다, 맡기다

PART 6 일반적인 사실을 나타내는 현재 시제

풀이 방법 해석

VIP Sky Club에 합류하신 것을 축하드립니다! 귀하의 회원 가입에 따라 오는 많은 혜택들이 있습니다.

귀하는 이제 각각 초고속 인터넷 사용, 편안한 라운지 의자, 그리고 샤워실을 특징으로 하는 저희의 공항 라운지들을 사용하실 수 있습니다.

저희의 공항 라운지들은 무료 간식과 음료 바도 제공하는데, 수프와 샌드위치를 제공하는 작은 식당도 함께 있습니다. 하지만 그곳에서 드시는 것에 대해서는 돈을 지불하셔야 합니다.

저희는 귀하가 여행하시는 동안 편안한 쉴 곳을 제공해드릴 수 있어 기쁩니다.

 연습 문제

01. (A)   02. (B)   03. (A)   04. (A)

[어휘] contract 계약(서) be set to부정사 ~할 예정이다 consider-ing ~하는 것을 고려하다 switch ~을 바꾸다 expire 만료되다

05. to부정사의 역할: 명사 역할

Goodlettsville 도서관은 컴퓨터와 다른 장비를 업그레이드하기 위한 충분한 기금을 마련하기 원한다.

[해설] 선택지가 동사 raise의 다양한 형태로 구성되어 있으므로 문법 문제이다. 빈칸 앞에 위치한 동사 wish는 to부정사를 목적어로 취하는 동사이므로 (A) to raise가 정답이다.

[어휘] fund 기금, 자금 equipment 기구, 장비

06. to부정사의 역할: 부사 역할

귀하의 잡지 구독 서비스를 갱신하시려면, 직원에게 전화해 말씀하시기만 하면 됩니다.

[해설] 빈칸 뒤에 동사원형인 renew가 있으므로 동사원형과 결합해 to부정사를 구성하는 (A) To가 정답이다. 이때의 to부정사는 '~하기 위해서'라는 의미로 부사의 역할을 한다.

[어휘] renew ~을 갱신하다 subscription 구독, 가입 서비스 representative 직원

07. to부정사의 역할: 명사 역할

고객 서비스 책임자들이 고객 전화에 대한 대응 시간을 줄이기 위해 애쓰고 있다.

[해설] 선택지가 동사 reduce의 다양한 형태와 명사로 구성되어 있으므로 문법 문제이다. 빈칸 앞에 위치한 동사 strive는 to부정사를 목적어로 갖는 동사이므로 (B) to reduce가 정답이다.

[어휘] strive to부정사 ~하기 위해 애쓰다 response 대응, 반응 reduce ~을 줄이다, 감소시키다 reduction 감소, 할인

08. to부정사의 역할: to be 용법

그 경기의 개회식이 월요일 오전 9시 정각에 시작될 예정이다.

[해설] 선택지가 동사 commence의 다양한 형태와 명사로 구성되어 있으므로 문법 문제이다. 빈칸 앞에 위치한 be동사는 'be to부정사'의 구조로 예정된 일을 나타내므로 to부정사를 구성하는 동사원형 (C) commence가 정답이다.

[어휘] promptly 정확히 제시간에, 지체 없이 commence 시작되다 commencement 시작, 개시

09. 5형식 동사+목적어+to부정사

이 지역의 풍차들이 도시 내 모든 가정에 필요한 전기를 충분히 생산할 것으로 예상된다.

[해설] 선택지가 동사 generate의 다양한 형태와 명사로 구성되어 있으므로 문법 문제이다. 빈칸 앞에 위치한 수동태 동사 be expected는 to부정사와 결합되므로 (D) to generate가 정답이다.

[어휘] windmill 풍차 sufficient 충분히 generation 세대 generate ~을 생산하다, 만들어 내다

10. 5형식 동사+목적어+to부정사

Billy's 패션 사의 고객들은 그 상점의 웹사이트를 방문해 의견을 제공하도록 요청받는다.

[해설] 선택지가 동사 visit의 다양한 형태와 명사로 구성되어 있으므로 문법 문제이다. 빈칸 앞에 위치한 수동태 동사 be asked는 to부정사와 함께 쓰이므로 (C) to visit이 정답이다.

[어휘] feedback 의견

11. to부정사의 역할: 형용사 역할

지역의 유명인을 광고에 내보내는 것은 새로운 시장에서 브랜드의 입지를 확고히 할 수 있는 효과적인 방법이다.

[해설] 선택지가 동사 establish의 다양한 형태와 명사로 구성되어 있으므로 문법 문제이다. 빈칸 앞에 위치한 명사 way는 to부정사와 함께 쓰이므로 (A) to establish가 정답이다.

[어휘] endorse (유명인이 광고에서) ~을 홍보하다, ~을 승인하다 celebrity 유명인 effective 효과적인 presence 존재(감) establish ~을 확립하다 establishment 확립, 수립, 시설

12. to부정사의 역할: 형용사 역할

근로 생산성을 향상시키기 위해 Creep Paper는 유연 근무제를 도입했다.

[해설] 선택지가 동사 improve의 다양한 형태와 명사로 구성되어 있으므로 문법 문제이다. 빈칸 앞에 위치한 'In an effort'는 to와 결합해 '~하려는 노력으로'라는 뜻으로 쓰이므로 (B) to improve가 정답이다.

[어휘] productivity 생산성 flexible 유연한 working hours 근무시간

13. to부정사의 역할: 명사 역할

대부분의 지역 음식점들은 지역에서 재배된 농산물과 고기 그리고 과일을 사용하는 경향이 있다.

[해설] 선택지가 다양한 품사의 단어들로 구성되어 있으므로 문법 문제이다. 빈칸 앞에 위치한 동사 tend는 to부정사를 목적어로 취하므로 (B) to use가 정답이다.

[어휘] tend to부정사 ~하는 경향이 있다 locally 지역에서, 지역적으로 grown 재배된 produce 농산물

14. to부정사의 역할: 부사 역할

겨울 연휴 기간 중에 배송을 더 신속히 처리하기 위해, Antonio's Tea Factory는 시간제 창고 근무자들을 고용하고 있다.

[해설] 선택지가 전치사와 접속사로 구성되어 있으므로 문법 문제이다. 빈칸 뒤에 동사원형인 expedite가 위치해 있으므로 동사원형과 함께 쓰일 수 있는 (D) In order to(~하기 위해)가 정답이다.

[어휘] in order to부정사 ~하기 위해 expedite ~을 더 신속히 처리하다 shipping 배송 warehouse 창고

15. 단순 시제: 과거

지난 분기에, Decker 가구 사는 작년 동안 판매한 것보다 더 많은 의자를 판매했다.

[해설] 선택지가 동사 do의 다양한 형태로 구성되어 있으므로 문법 문제이다. 빈칸은 비교를 나타내는 접속사 than이 이끄는 절의 동사 자리인데, 과거의 기간을 나타내는 during the previous year와 어울려야 하므로 과거 시제 동사인 (C) did가 정답이다.

[어휘] quarter 분기

16. 주어와 동사의 수 일치

Peterson 씨는 다음 분기에 콜로라도 지역의 접객 업계가 호황을 누릴 것이라고 예측했다.

[해설] 선택지가 다양한 품사의 단어들로 구성되어 있으므로 문법 문제이다. 주어와 빈칸 뒤로 that절이 바로 이어져 있으므로 빈칸은 문장 전체의 동사

DAY 12

PART 5 문법 | to부정사

확인 문제 해석

1. 대부분의 부모들은 그들의 자녀가 과외 활동에 참여하도록 권장한다.
2. 요크셔 시는 시내에 새 주차장을 지을 계획이 있다.
3. 워크숍 자리를 확보하기 위해서는 미리 예약해 주세요.
4. Lee 씨는 인터뷰를 실시하도록 요청받았다.
5. 모든 구독자들은 무료 아이템을 받을 수 있다.
6. 이 모바일 앱은 당신이 사용 가능한 자산을 찾도록 도와줍니다.

연습 문제

01.(C) 02.(B) 03.(C) 04.(B) 05.(D) 06.(A)

01.

1. 선택지 보고 문법/어휘 문제 파악하기 ☐ 문법 문제 ☑ 어휘 문제
2. 빈칸 분석하기 빈칸 앞 문장의 주어 (the store manager)
   주어가 '고객 불만에 즉시 --------해야 한다'는 문맥을 완성하는 동사가 정답이다.
3. 정답 선택하기 정답 (C)

상점 매니저는 어떠한 고객의 불만에라도 즉시 응대해야 한다.

02.

1. 선택지 보고 문법/어휘 문제 파악하기 ☑ 문법 문제 ☐ 어휘 문제
2. 빈칸 분석하기 빈칸 앞에 있는 동사 (asked)
   빈칸 앞의 동사가 취하는 목적격 보어의 형태 ☑ to부정사 ☐ 동명사
3. 정답 선택하기 정답 (B)

Fuller 씨의 상사들은 그에게 건물의 인테리어 평면도를 설계할 것을 요청했다.

03.

1. 선택지 보고 문법/어휘 문제 파악하기 ☑ 문법 문제 ☐ 어휘 문제
2. 빈칸 분석하기 빈칸 앞에 있는 명사 (effort)
   빈칸 앞의 명사를 수식할 수 있는 ☐ 형태 동명사 ☑ to부정사
3. 정답 선택하기 정답 (C)

매출을 증가시키기 위해, Galvan 철물점은 광고 캠페인을 진행하기 시작했다.

04.

1. 선택지 보고 문법/어휘 문제 파악하기 ☑ 문법 문제 ☐ 어휘 문제
2. 빈칸 분석하기 빈칸 앞에 있는 것 ☑ 완전한 문장 ☐ 불완전한 문장
   → 빈칸에는 ☐ 동사 역할 ☑ 부사 역할을 하는 것이 와야 한다.
3. 정답 선택하기 정답 (B)

Fowler 슈퍼마켓은 더 많은 고객들을 끌어모으기 위해 회원 할인을 제공하기 시작했다.

05.

1. 선택지 보고 문법/어휘 문제 파악하기 ☑ 문법 문제 ☐ 어휘 문제
2. 빈칸 분석하기 빈칸 앞에 있는 동사 (help)
   빈칸 앞의 동사가 취하는 목적격 보어의 형태 ☑ 동사원형 ☐ 동명사
3. 정답 선택하기 정답 (D)

보상 프로그램은 당신이 단골 고객층을 확보하는 데 도움이 될 것입니다.

06.

1. 선택지 보고 문법/어휘 문제 파악하기 ☑ 문법 문제 ☐ 어휘 문제
2. 빈칸 분석하기 빈칸 앞에 있는 형용사 (eager)
   빈칸 앞의 형용사를 수식할 수 있는 형태 ☐ 동사원형 ☑ to부정사
3. 정답 선택하기 정답 (A)

Guerra 산업은 대중에게 최신 태블릿 기기를 소개하고 싶어 한다.

실전 문제

01.(B)	02.(D)	03.(D)	04.(C)	05.(A)	06.(A)
07.(B)	08.(C)	09.(D)	10.(C)	11.(A)	12.(B)
13.(B)	14.(C)	15.(C)	16.(B)	17.(C)	18.(B)
19.(B)	20.(C)	21.(B)	22.(C)	23.(B)	24.(A)

01. to부정사의 역할: 명사 역할

이 모바일 애플리케이션을 통해 언제든지 원하실 때 주문품을 추적하실 수 있습니다.

[해설] 선택지가 동사 track의 다양한 형태로 구성되어 있으므로 문법 문제이다. 빈칸 앞에 위치한 동사 allow는 'allow+목적어+to부정사'의 구조로 쓰이므로 to부정사인 (B) to track이 정답이다.

[어휘] order 주문(품) track ~을 추적하다

02. to부정사를 취하는 형용사

Gong 법률 사무소는 운영비를 줄일 수 있었다.

[해설] 선택지가 동사 reduce의 다양한 형태와 명사로 구성되어 있으므로 문법 문제이다. 빈칸 앞에 위치한 be able은 to부정사와 결합하여 '~할 수 있다'라는 뜻으로 쓰이므로 (D) to reduce가 정답이다.

[어휘] reduce 줄이다, 감소하다 operational 운영의 expense 비용

03. to부정사의 역할: 명사 역할

그 교수는 모든 학생들에게 마감 시한 전에 과제물을 제출하도록 권한다.

[해설] 선택지가 동사 submit의 다양한 형태와 명사로 구성되어 있으므로 문법 문제이다. 빈칸 앞에 위치한 동사 encourage는 'encourage+목적어+to부정사'의 구조로 사용되므로 to부정사인 (D) to submit이 정답이다.

[어휘] encourage A to부정사 A에게 ~하도록 권하다, 장려하다 prior to ~ 전에, ~에 앞서 submit ~을 제출하다

04. to부정사를 취하는 형용사

Sullivan 케이블 사와의 현 계약이 다음 달에 만료될 예정이기 때문에, 회사에서는 공급업체를 바꾸는 것을 고려하고 있다.

[해설] 선택지가 동사 expire의 다양한 형태로 구성되어 있으므로 문법 문제이다. 빈칸 앞에 위치한 is set은 to부정사와 결합해 '~할 예정이다'라는 뜻으로 쓰이므로 (C) to expire가 정답이다.

paraphrasing　dialog between our company and newspapers, magazines, and blogs 회사와 신문사, 잡지사, 그리고 블로그들 사이의 소통 → communication with media outlets 언론 매체들과의 의사소통

[어휘] recruit ~을 모집하다　industry 업계　media outlet 언론 매체

07. 세부사항 문제

Barron 씨는 다음 달에 무엇을 할 것인가?
(A) 해외로 전근하기
(B) 은퇴 생활에 들어가기
(C) 신문사와 인터뷰하기
(D) 자신의 후임자 찾기

[해설] Barron 씨의 이름이 언급된 마지막 단락에 다음 달에 캐나다의 밴쿠버 지사를 떠나 아일랜드의 더블린 지사에서 홍보부를 이끌 것이라는(Suzanne Barron, who will leave our Vancouver branch in Canada next month to head up the PR department in our Dublin branch in Ireland) 말이 있는데, 이는 다른 국가로의 전근을 의미하는 것이므로 (A)가 정답이다.

[어휘] transfer 전근하다　overseas 해외로　retirement 은퇴, 퇴직　replacement 후임(자), 대체(자)

paraphrasing 정답　1. (c)　2. (d)　3. (e)　4. (a)　5. (b)

08-10은 다음 공고를 참조하시오.

직원들께 알립니다:

우리 Bachman 회계는 현재 회사의 사업 확장을 용이하게 하기 위해 여러 직책에 신입 사원을 모집하고 있습니다. 지난 몇 달 동안에 걸쳐, **08우리의 고객층이 상당히 넓어졌는데, 이는 과거에 지역 내에서 가장 규모가 큰 회계 업체였던 Kembery 사가 문을 닫은 이후로** 개인 고객과 기업 고객들 모두 어쩔 수 없이 회계와 관련하여 새로 도움을 줄 곳을 찾아야 했기 때문입니다.

더 많은 직원들에 대한 필요성을 해결하기 위해, 우리는 09(A)구인 웹사이트에 채용 공고를 업로드하고 09(D)지역 신문에 광고를 해왔습니다. 또한 몇몇 우리 인사부 직원들은 입소문을 내기 위해 09(B)밀러 시 채용 박람회 행사장에서 부스도 운영했습니다. 하지만, 이와 같은 많은 노력에도 불구하고, 우리는 여전히 여러분의 도움이 필요합니다. 여러분께서 누구든 우리 팀에 적합할 만한 분을 알고 계시면, 그분들께 우리의 공석에 관해 알려 드리기 바랍니다. 어느 분이든 직원이 개인적으로 추천한 분께 특별히 관심을 기울일 것이므로, **10여러분께서 아시는 분이 지원한 경우, 그분의 성함과 전화번호, 그리고 이메일 주소를 3월 31일까지 r_conner@bachmanacc.com으로 Rosario Conner 씨께 보내 주시기 바랍니다.**

recruit ~을 모집하다　facilitate ~을 용이하게 하다　expansion (사업) 확장　customer base 고객층　be forced to부정사 어쩔 수 없이 ~하다　accounting 회계　assistance 도움　go out of business 문을 닫다, 폐업하다　address ~을 해결하다, 처리하다　job descriptions 채용 공고　operate ~을 운영하다　booth 부스, 칸막이 공간　get the word out 소문을 내다　good fit 적합한 사람

08. 세부사항 문제

공고 내용에 따르면, 무엇이 Bachman 회계의 성장에 도움이 되었는가?
(A) 수개월 동안의 엄청난 광고
(B) 직원 교육에 대한 투자
(C) 주요 경쟁사의 폐업
(D) 신규 서비스의 출시

[해설] 회사의 성장과 그 이유가 언급된 첫 단락에, 과거에 지역 내에서 가장 규모가 큰 회계 업체였던 Kembery 사가 문을 닫은 이후로 고객층이 넓어졌다고 제시되어 있으므로(customer base has grown significantly, ~ after Kembery Inc. — previously the largest accounting firm in the area — went out of business) '주요 경쟁사의 폐업'을 뜻하는 (C)가 정답이다.

paraphrasing　went out of business 문을 닫았다 → closure 폐업

[어휘] investment in ~에 대한 투자　closure 폐업　competitor 경쟁사, 경쟁자　launch 출시, 공개

09. Not True 문제

Bachman 회계가 활용한 채용 방법으로 언급되지 않은 것은 무엇인가?
(A) 온라인에 구인 공고 게시하기
(B) 채용 박람회 참석하기
(C) 채용 대행업체 이용하기
(D) 신문 광고 내기

[해설] Bachman Accounting 사가 직원 모집을 위해 노력한 일이 언급된 두 번째 단락에, we have uploaded job descriptions on career Web sites를 통해 '온라인 구인 공고 게시'를 뜻하는 (A)를, 그 뒤에 이어지는 advertised in the local newspaper에서 '신문 광고'를 뜻하는 (D)를, 그리고 바로 이어서 제시된 operated a booth at the Miller City Career Fair에서 '채용 박람회 참석'을 언급한 (B)를 확인할 수 있다. 하지만 채용 대행업체를 이용했다는 내용은 없으므로 (C)가 정답이다.

[어휘] method 방법　fair 박람회　recruitment firm 채용 대행업체　place an advertisement 광고를 내다

10. 세부사항 문제

직원들은 3월 31일까지 무엇을 하도록 요청받는가?
(A) 공석에 대한 직무 내용 검토하기
(B) 구직 지원자들에 대한 연락처 제출하기
(C) 단체 교육 시간에 등록하기
(D) 제휴 관계를 맺을 업체 추천하기

[해설] March 31이 제시된 지문 마지막 부분에, 아는 사람이 지원한 경우에 그 사람의 이름과 전화번호, 그리고 이메일 주소를 3월 31일까지 Rosario Conner 씨에 보내도록(~ please send the person's name, phone number, and e-mail address to Rosario Conner at r_conner@bachmanacc.com by March 31) 요청하고 있는데, 이는 연락처를 제출하라는 말이므로 (B)가 정답이다.

paraphrasing　person's name, phone number, and e-mail address 이름과 전화번호 그리고 이메일 주소 → contact information 연락처

[어휘] job duty 직무　job candidate 구직 지원자　sign up for ~에 등록하다, ~을 신청하다

paraphrasing 정답　1. (c)　2. (e)　3. (a)　4. (d)　5. (b)

paraphrasing 정답 1. (e)   2. (d)   3. (b)   4. (a)   5. (c)

03-04는 다음 공지를 참조하시오.

헌신적인 봉사를 기리며

우리 브렌트우드 지역 센터의 운영진은 Shirley Galloway 씨께 대단히 깊은 감사의 말씀을 드리고자 합니다. Galloway 씨는 25년 전에 브렌트우드 지역으로 이주하셨으며, 그 이후로 틈날 때마다 여러 가치 있는 프로젝트에 헌신해 오셨습니다. 예를 들어, 자원 봉사자로서 브렌트우드 도서관에서 ⁰³원어민이 아닌 분들을 대상으로 하는 일련의 영어 강좌들을 만드셨으며, 이는 지난 15년 동안 계속 운영되어 오고 있습니다. 브렌트우드 독서 클럽과 뒷마당 정원 협회 같은 여러 지역사회 단체의 일원으로서, Galloway 씨는 우리 도시의 많은 주민들과 서로 알고 지내 오셨습니다. ⁰⁴10년 전에 우리 팀에 합류하기에 앞서, Galloway 씨는 많은 사회 문제들을 해결하기 위한 조치를 취하는 데 있어 가장 좋은 방법들을 알아 보기 위해 우리 지역 전체를 찾아 다니셨습니다.

우리는 4월 20일 금요일 오후 3시에 브렌트우드 지역 센터에서 Galloway 씨를 위한 환송회를 개최할 예정입니다. 주민 여러분께 이 행사에 참석하실 것을 권해 드립니다.

dedicated 헌신적인, 전념하는 **service** 봉사, 근무, 재직 **dedicate A to B** (시간, 노력 등) A를 B에 쏟다, 바치다 **worthwhile** 가치 있는 **found** ~을 만들다, 세우다, 설립하다 **volunteer** 자원 봉사자 **run** 운영되다, 지속되다 **resident** 주민 **region** 지역 **method** 방법 **take action** 조치를 취하다 **resolve** ~을 해결하다 **farewell reception** 환송회

03. 세부사항 문제

공지에 따르면, Galloway 씨는 어떻게 지역 사회에 도움을 주어 왔는가?
(A) 원예 동호회를 만듦으로써
(B) 어학 교육 프로그램을 시작함으로써
(C) 도서관에 재정적인 기여를 함으로써
(D) 공직에 출마함으로써

[해설] Galloway 씨가 기여한 분야의 예시가 언급된 중반부에, 원어민이 아닌 사람들을 대상으로 하는 일련의 영어 강좌들을 만들었다는(she founded a series of English classes for non-native speakers) 말이 있으므로 어학 교육 프로그램의 시작을 언급한 (B)가 정답이다.

paraphrasing a series of English classes 일련의 영어 강좌 → language education program 어학 교육 프로그램

[어휘] make a financial contribution to ~에 재정적으로 기여하다 run for political office 공직에 출마하다

04. 세부사항 문제

Galloway 씨는 브렌트우드 지역 센터에서 얼마나 오랫동안 근무했는가?
(A) 25년
(B) 15년
(C) 10년
(D) 5년

[해설] Galloway 씨의 근무 시작 시점은 지문 중반부에 언급된 Before joining our team 10 years ago에서 확인할 수 있다. 이는 10년 전에 합류했다는 의미이므로 (C)가 정답이다.

paraphrasing 정답 1. (e)   2. (c)   3. (a)   4. (d)   5. (b)

05-07은 다음 공지를 참조하시오.

우리 Tetreault 컨설팅 사의 성공은 직원 여러분의 헌신과 전문성에 크게 의존하고 있습니다. 우리는 여러분께서 경력상의 능력을 갈고 닦으며 발전을 이루는 데 도움이 될 수 있도록 점점 더 높은 수준의 책임을 제공하는 정책에 전념하고 있습니다. 이와 같은 관점에서, ⁰⁵우리는 9월 1일부로 홍보 부이사이신 Ron Marchant 씨께서 신임 홍보 이사가 되신다는 사실을 알려 드리게 되어 기쁘게 생각합니다.

지난 몇 년 동안에 걸쳐, Marchant 씨께서는 우리 회사에 대한 사람들의 인식을 관리하기 위해 부단히 노력해 오셨습니다. Marchant 씨의 능력은 해당 분야에 속한 다른 분들에 의해 인정받아 왔는데, 권위 있는 Mela-Amaya 상에 네 차례나 후보자로 지명되신 끝에, 마침내 지난 가을에 그 상을 받아 댁으로 가져가셨기 때문입니다. ⁰⁶직접 개발하신 News Network 프로그램을 통해, Marchant 씨는 우리 회사와 신문사, 잡지사 그리고 블로그들 사이에의 소통을 크게 개선시키셨습니다.

Marchant 씨는 ⁰⁷다음 달에 캐나다의 밴쿠버 지사를 떠나 아일랜드의 더블린 지사에서 홍보부를 이끌게 될 Suzanne Barron 씨의 후임으로 근무하실 것입니다. 우리는 새로운 역할을 맡게 Marchant 씨와 Barron 씨 두 분 모두에게 행운을 빌어 드립니다.

heavily 크게, 많이, 대단히 **dependent on** ~에 의존하는 **dedication** 헌신, 공헌 **professionalism** 전문성, 직업 의식 **be committed to** ~에 전념하다 **policy** 정책 **hone** ~을 갈고 닦다, 연마하다 **progress** 진보하다, 발달하다 **in light of** ~에 비추어, ~을 감안해 **as of** (날짜) ~부로, ~부터 **manage** ~을 관리하다 **perception** (사람들의) 인식 **be recognized by** ~에 의해 인정받다 **field** 분야 **be nominated for** ~에 대한 후보로 지명되다 **prestigious** 권위 있는 **replace** ~을 후임이 되다, 대체하다 **head up** ~을 이끌다, 책임지다

05. 주제 문제

공지는 주로 무엇에 관한 것인가?
(A) 정책의 변화
(B) 직원의 승진
(C) 회사의 새로운 위치
(D) 회사의 업적

[해설] 첫 단락 마지막 부분에 9월 1일부로 홍보 부이사인 Ron Marchant 씨가 신임 홍보 이사가 된다는 사실을 알리고 있는데, 이는 부이사에서 이사로 승진된다는 말이므로 (B)가 정답이다.

[어휘] promotion 승진, 진급 achievement 업적, 성취

06. True 문제

Marchant 씨에 관해 언급된 것은 무엇인가?
(A) 권위 있는 대학교를 졸업했다.
(B) 회사를 위해 여러 신규 고객들을 모집했다.
(C) 여러 차례 업계 내의 상을 받았다.
(D) 언론 매체들과의 의사소통을 개선시켰다.

[해설] 두 번째 단락 마지막 부분에 직접 개발한 프로그램을 통해, 회사와 신문사, 잡지사 그리고 블로그들 사이의 소통을 크게 개선시켰다는 말이 있으므로(he greatly improved the dialog between our company and newspapers, magazines, and blogs) 언론 매체들과의 의사소통을 개선시켰다고 한 (D)가 정답이다.

03.

우리 골프 리조트에서 여름철은 가장 바쁜 시기이므로 우리는 이 기간에 **직원들이 쓸 수 있는 휴가 일수를 제한하기 시작할 것입니다.** 우리는 각 교대 근무 시간에 반드시 충분한 수의 직원들이 근무하게 함으로써 우리의 서비스 수준을 유지하는 데 도움이 되기 바랍니다. 6월 1일부터, 여러분은 오직 3일간만 연속으로 휴가를 쓰는 것이 허용될 것입니다. 더 많은 정보를 원하시는 분은, 인사부 직원에게 이야기하시기 바랍니다.

restrict ~을 제한하다 shift 교대 근무(조) in a row 연속으로

Q. 공지의 목적은 무엇인가?
(A) 교대 근무를 대신할 지원자를 요청하는 것
(B) 휴가 정책에 관한 새로운 소식을 전하는 것

[문제 키워드] purpose / notice

[해설] 지문 시작 부분에 직원들의 휴가 일수를 제한하기 시작할 것이라고 (we will begin restricting the number of vacation days) 알린 후에 관련 세부 사항을 전달하고 있으므로 (B)가 정답이다.

[어휘] cover (일 등) ~을 대신해 주다 policy 정책

04.

직원 여러분께 알립니다! 이 기회를 빌어 저를 소개하고자 합니다. 제 이름은 Tabitha Conley이며, 신임 건물 관리 책임자입니다. 제 다음 달 목표는 우리 건물이 정부에서 발표한 최신 **화재 안전 관리 요건**을 준수할 수 있도록 조정하는 것입니다. 이 일에는 자동 스프링클러와 같은 새 장비를 설치하는 작업이 수반될 것입니다. 이번 주 후반에, **우리가 준수해야 하는 규정과 관련된 상세 정보를 이메일로 보내 드리겠습니다.** 질문이 있으신 분은 제게 알려 주시기 바랍니다.

aim 목표, 목적 adapt ~을 조정하다, 적응시키다 comply with ~을 준수하다(= follow) requirement 요건, 필요 조건 issue ~을 발표하다 involve ~을 수반하다, 포함하다

Q. Conley 씨는 무엇을 할 것이라고 말하는가?
(A) 규제에 관한 정보 배포하기
(B) 직원들에게 새 장비 사용법 가르치기

[문제 키워드] What / Ms. Conley / do

[해설] 키워드 Ms. Conley가 지문의 전체적인 소재이므로 지문 전반에서 단서를 파악해 각 선택지와 비교해야 한다. 지문 중반부에 화재 안전 관리 요건(fire safety requirements)을 언급한 후, 후반부에서는 준수해야 하는 규정 관련 정보를 이메일로 보내겠다고(I will e-mail the details about the rules ~) 했으므로 (A)가 정답이다.

[어휘] distribute ~을 배포하다, 배부하다 regulation 규제, 규정

실전 문제

| 01.(B) | 02.(A) | 03.(B) | 04.(C) | 05.(B) | 06.(D) |
| 07.(A) | 08.(C) | 09.(C) | 10.(B) | | |

01-02는 다음 공지를 참조하시오.

공지: Lowe, Cortese & Associates에서의 변화

우리 회사에서 요구하는 일련의 특별한 자격 요건을 지닌 구직 지원자를 찾기 위한 철저한 조사 과정 끝에, **01우리 Lowe, Cortese & Associates 팀에 가장 최근에 합류하게 된 일원인 Marie Katz 씨를 소개해 드리게 되어 기쁘게 생각합니다. Katz 씨께서는 재산법에 중점을 둔 고위 직책의 역할**을 맡게 되실 것입니다. Katz 씨의 과거 근무 경력에는 Dwight, Webster, 그리고 Gilbert 사에서 부동산 관련 소송 처리를 맡으신 일이 포함되어 있습니다. 전문 지식 및 인상적인 의사소통 능력과 함께, Katz 씨께서는 업무상 연락 관계에 있는 분들과 단골 고객들로 구성된 자신의 폭넓은 인맥을 우리에게 연결해 주실 것입니다. 우리는 Katz 씨의 도움으로 회사의 재산법 담당 부서 확장이라는 목표에 도달할 수 있으리라 생각합니다. 모든 직원들은 다음 주에 Katz 씨의 경력 사항과 고객들을 대하는 접근법에 관해 더 많이 알게 될 기회가 있을 것인데, 그 이유는 **02주간 회의가 시작될 때 Katz 씨께서 간단한 발표를 하실 것**이기 때문입니다.

exhaustive 철저한 job candidate 구직 지원자 qualifications 자격 요건 firm 회사, 업체 take on ~을 맡다 role 역할 senior 고위의, 상급의 associate 직원 property law 재산법 handle ~을 처리하다 real estate 부동산 case 소송 사건 expertise 전문 지식 impressive 인상적인 professional contacts 업무상 연락 관계에 있는 사람들 loyal customer 단골 고객 expand ~을 확대하다, 확장하다 approach 접근법 deal with ~을 대하다, 다루다 brief 간단한, 짧은

01. 목적 문제

공지의 목적은 무엇인가?
(A) 고객들에게 수수료 변경을 알리기 위해
(B) 회사에 입사한 한 변호사를 환영하기 위해
(C) 법률회사의 공석을 알리기 위해
(D) 새로운 법률 규제를 소개하기 위해

[해설] 지문 시작 부분에 가장 최근에 입사한 직원을(the newest member) 소개한다는 말과 함께 그 사람이 재산법에 중점을 두고 일할 것이라고(focusing on property law) 쓰여 있다. 따라서 새로 입사한 변호사를 환영할 목적이라는 (B)가 정답이다.

[어휘] legal fee (변호사의) 수임료 promote ~을 알리다, 홍보하다 job opening 공석 introduce ~을 소개하다 regulation 규제, 규정

02. True 문제

Katz 씨에 관해 사실인 것은 무엇인가?
(A) 동료 직원들에게 발표를 할 것이다.
(B) 의사소통 워크숍을 진행할 것이다.
(C) 모든 신규 고객들을 맡을 것이다.
(D) 주간 회의에 빠질 것이다.

[해설] 지문 맨 마지막 문장에, Katz 씨를 she로 지칭해 주간 회의가 시작될 때 간단하게 발표를 할 것이라고(she will give a brief presentation at the beginning of the weekly meeting) 쓰여 있으므로 (A)가 정답이다.

paraphrasing give a brief presentation 간단한 발표를 하다 → give a talk 발표하다

[어휘] coworker 동료 직원 lead ~을 진행하다, 이끌다 be absent from ~에서 빠지다, 부재 중이다

mayor 시장 neighboring 인접한, 인근의 competition 경쟁, 경기, 시합 promote ~을 홍보하다, 판촉하다 be designed to부정사 ~하기 위해 고안되다 grant 보조금 benefit from ~로부터 혜택을 보다, 이득을 얻다 attempt to부정사 ~하려는 시도

05. 동사의 형태

[해설] 뒤에 이어지는 문장을 보면, 빈칸 바로 다음에 언급된 a friendly competition의 개최 시기가 나와 있는데, 미래 시점(Starting next month)에 시작되는 일임을 알 수 있으므로 참가 시점을 나타내는 동사도 미래 시제인 (B) will partake가 정답이다.

[어휘] partake 참가하다

06. 알맞은 문장 고르기

(A) 많은 레스토랑과 상점들이 이 경쟁에 참가하고 싶어 한다.
(B) 포츠빌에는 보통 연중 이맘때쯤에 이글턴보다 방문객들이 더 많다.
(C) 각 도시에서 그것들을 나눠 줄 10곳의 유명 명소들을 선정했다.
(D) 둘 중 어느 도시든 방문하는 누구에게나 대중교통 할인 서비스가 이용 가능하다.

[해설] 빈칸 앞 문장에서 언급한 스탬프를 받는 일(who collect all of the stamps)과 연계되는 문장이 필요하므로 해당 스탬프를 them으로 지칭하여 받을 수 있는 장소 정보가 제시된 (C)가 정답이다.

[어휘] around this time of year 연중 이맘때쯤 pick ~을 선정하다, 고르다 give A out A를 나눠 주다

07. 동사 어휘

[해설] as와 함께 사용될 수 있는 자동사로서 city passports의 용도와 관련된 의미를 나타낼 수 있어야 하므로 as와 함께 '~의 역할을 하다'라는 뜻을 나타낼 때 사용하는 (D) serve가 정답이다.

[어휘] observe ~을 관찰하다, 보다, 준수하다 receive ~을 받다

08. 복합관계부사

[해설] town을 수식함과 동시에 동사 wins의 주어 역할이 가능한 복합 관계 형용사가 필요한데, 지문 첫 부분에 언급된 것과 같이 두 곳의 도시(two neighboring towns) 중 하나가 그 대상이므로 '~하는 어느 쪽이든지'라는 의미를 나타낼 때 사용하는 (C) Whichever가 정답이다.

PART 7 공지 (1) 사내 공지

풀이 방법 해석

공지: 세계화 학과 전공

Columbine 대학의 총장으로서, William Collins 교수님을 모시게 되어 영광입니다. 그는 세계화 학과의 학과장이 될 것입니다. 10년 전에, 그는 국제 무역 관계에 대한 논문을 완성했고 그 이후로 그의 분야에서 존경받는 인물 중 한 명이 되었습니다. 그를 저희의 일부로 받아들임으로써 우리 학교의 명성이 높아질 것이고 경영, 마케팅, 무역 및 국제 관계에 관심이 있는 학생들을 훨씬 더 많이 끌어들일 것입니다.

세계화 학과는 가을 학기부터 우리 학생들이 전공이나 부전공 과목으로 들을 수 있게 됩니다. Collins 교수님은 다음 주 화요일 오후 2시-3시까지 Kennedy 강당에서 전공에 대해 발표를 할 것입니다.

 연습 문제

01.(A) **02.**(B) **03.**(B) **04.**(A)

01.

A 주차장이 다음 주 월요일부터 2주간 개조 공사를 위해 폐쇄될 것임을 다시 한번 알려드립니다. B 주차장이 개방될 것이지만 고객과 회사 차량들만을 위해 확보될 것입니다. 이 기간 동안, 모든 직원들은 버스나 지하철로 통근하실 것이 권장됩니다. **우리는 Central 역에서 불과 두 블록 떨어져 있어요.** 차량을 가져오셔야 한다면 직접 비용을 부담하셔서 도로 주차를 이용하셔야 합니다.

이것이 야기할 불편함에 대해 사과 드리며 양해해 주셔서 감사합니다.

실장
애틀란타 케이블 & 인터넷

be reserved for ~를 위해 확보해 두다 commute 통근하다 at one's expense 사비로

Q. 애틀란타 케이블 & 인터넷에 대해 암시된 것은 무엇인가?
(A) 대중교통에 가까이 위치해 있다.
(B) 주차 비용을 상환해 줄 것이다.

[문제 키워드] What / suggested / Atlanta Cable & Internet

[해설] 키워드 Atlanta Cable & Internet의 실장이 직원들에게 공지한 내용이다. 주차장 공사로 인해 대중교통을 이용할 것을 권장하면서 우리는 Central 역에서 불과 두 블록 떨어져 있다(We are just two blocks away from Central Station)고 했다. 따라서 (A)가 정답이다.

02.

저는 우리가 훨씬 더 빠르고 안전한 근무 환경을 갖게 될 것이라는 것을 안내하게 되어 기쁩니다. 3월 1일부터, 비밀번호를 입력해서 들어오는 모든 문들이 여러분의 생체 측정 데이터, 즉 지문에 의해 출입할 수 있는 문들로 교체될 것입니다. 이것은 피자 배달원들이나 택배 배달원들과 같이 승인되지 않은 사람들에게 비밀번호가 노출되기 때문입니다. **그러므로, 이번 주 말까지 보안실로 오셔서 보안 데이터 시스템에 여러분의 지문을 등록하고 동의서에 서명해 주시기 바랍니다.** 이것은 오직 보안 목적을 위해서만 사용될 것이라는 점을 약속 드립니다.

secure 안전한 PIN 비밀번호(personal identification number) biometric 생체 측정의 fingerprint 지문 unauthorized 승인되지 않은 courier 배달원 agreement form 동의서

Q. 직원들은 이번 주 말까지 무엇을 해야 하는가?
(A) 비밀번호 재발급하기
(B) 그들의 생체 측정 정보 등록하기

[문제 키워드] What / employees / do / by the end of this week

[해설] 키워드 by the end of this week가 언급된 지문 후반부에서 이번 주 말까지 지문을 등록하라고(enter your fingerprint into our security data system, and sign an agreement form by the end of this week) 했으므로 (B)가 정답이다.

03.

Kelly 건설사가 계약을 따냈으며, Carson 극장을 개조할 것입니다. 공사는 5월 7일에 시작되어 늦어도 6월 12일까지 완료될 예정입니다. 이 개조 공사로 인해 그 극장이 더 많은 관람객을 수용할 수 있게 될 것입니다.

win a contract 계약을 따내다   complete ~을 완료하다   no later than 늦어도 ~까지   accommodate ~을 수용하다   audience 관객, 청중

[단서] Work is scheduled to begin on 7 May
[해설] 다음 문장에서 공사 시작 예정일을 명시했으므로 극장 개조 작업은 미래에 발생할 일임을 알 수 있다. 따라서 미래 시제인 (A) will renovate가 정답이다.

04.

우리 회사는 일련의 변화들을 통해 자사의 이미지를 업그레이드하고 있습니다. 우리는 지역 자선 단체에 기부하기 시작했으며, 다음 주부터 우리의 새 로고를 특징으로 하는 유니폼이 지급될 것입니다.

through ~을 통해   a series of 일련의   donate to ~에 기부하다   charity 자선 단체, 자선 활동   as of ~부터   feature ~을 특징으로 하다   distribute ~을 나눠 주다

[단서] We have begun donating, as of next week, will be distributed
[해설] 다음 문장에 이미 기부를 시작한 일과 다음 주에 유니폼을 지급하는 일이 언급되어 있으므로 현재도 계속 이미지 업그레이드가 진행되는 과정임을 알 수 있다. 따라서 현재 진행 시제인 (A) is upgrading이 정답이다.

실전 문제

01. (D)   02. (C)   03. (D)   04. (A)   05. (B)   06. (C)
07. (D)   08. (C)

01-04는 다음 보도 자료를 참조하시오.

저희 Snowbird 베이커리는 모두 매일 아침 갓 구운 최상의 빵과 케이크 그리고 쿠키를 제공하는 것으로 잘 알려져 있습니다. 01저희는 3년 연속 "솔트레이크 시티 최고의 제과점"으로 지명되었습니다. 02그럼에도 불구하고, 저희 Snowbird 베이커리의 소유주이신 Emily Donahue 씨께서는 운영 방식에 변화를 주기로 결정하셨습니다. 이 달 1일부터, 저희는 흥미로운 신규 서비스를 제공하고 있습니다. 03결혼식이나 기타 기념 행사들과 같은 특별 행사를 위해 주문 제작 케이크를 만드시려면 미리 저희에게 연락 주시기 바랍니다. 원하시는 맛과 디자인을 선택하시면 저희가 제작해 드립니다. 04게다가, 저희는 심지어 무료로 행사장까지 배송도 해 드릴 것입니다. 이는 오직 솔트레이크 시티 시 경계 내에 거주하는 고객들만 이용 가능합니다.

be well known for ~로 잘 알려져 있다   offer ~을 제공하다   finest 최상의, 최고의   be named A A로 지명되다, 임명되다   nevertheless 그럼에도 불구하고   make a change to ~을 변화시키다, 변경하다   operation 운영, 가동, 작동   in advance 미리, 사전에   custom 주문 제작의, 맞춤 제작의   city limits 시 경계

01. 형용사 어휘

[해설] three와 years 사이에 위치하여 지속 기간을 나타낼 수 있는 형용사로서, '연이은, 연속된'이라는 의미로 지속성을 강조하는 역할을 하는 (D) consecutive가 정답이다.

[어휘] occasional 때때로 생기는, 가끔 하는   precise 정확한   initial 최초의

02. 동사의 형태

[해설] 주어로 쓰인 사람 명사와 to부정사 사이에 위치한 빈칸은 문장의 동사 자리이므로 동사가 아닌 (B)를 제외한 나머지 선택지 중에서 알맞은 시제로 된 것을 찾아야 한다. 빈칸 뒤에 이어지는 문장에 현재진행 시제(are offering)를 써서 현재 새로운 조치가 지속되고 있다고 말하는 것으로 볼 때, 이미 과거 시점에 변동 사항이 결정된 일임을 알 수 있으므로 과거 시제인 (C) decided가 정답이다.

03. 명사 어휘

[해설] 빈칸 뒤에 예시로 제시된 결혼식이나 기념 행사를 하나로 아우를 수 있는 범주에 해당되는 명사가 필요하므로 special과 함께 '특별 행사'라는 의미를 나타낼 수 있는 (D) occasions가 정답이다.

[어휘] deal 거래 (조건), 계약   appreciation 감사, 감상, 감탄   promotion 승진, 홍보, 판촉

04. 알맞은 문장 고르기

(A) 게다가, 저희는 심지어 무료로 행사장까지 배송도 해 드릴 것입니다.
(B) 저희 매장은 개조 공사 프로젝트로 인해 일시적으로 문을 닫을 예정입니다.
(C) 저희 모든 고객들께 지속적으로 충실히 성원을 보내 주신 것에 대해 감사 드립니다.
(D) 각각의 저희 제품이 지닌 영양 가치는 저희 웹사이트에 게시되어 있습니다.

[해설] 빈칸 다음 문장에, 앞서 언급된 특정 대상을 지칭하는 This와 함께 이용 가능 대상자 범위를 알리는 내용이 왔다. 따라서 This에 해당되는 것으로서 주문 제작 제품에 대한 배송 서비스의 특징을 설명한 (A)가 정답이다.

[어휘] in addition 게다가, 추가로   even 심지어 (~도)   free of charge 무료로   temporarily 일시적으로   continuous 지속적인   loyal 충실한   support 성원, 지지   nutritional values 영양 가치

05-08은 다음 기사를 참조하시오.

투어 게임 (12월 9일) — 05서로 인접한 두 도시 포츠빌과 이글턴의 시장들이 친선을 도모하는 경쟁에 참가한다. 다음 달부터 시작하여, 가장 많은 관광객들을 유치하는 도시가 승리를 거두게 된다. 이 콘테스트는 도시 여행증에 모든 스탬프를 받는 사람들의 숫자에 의해 승부가 결정될 것이다. 06각 도시에서 그것들을 나눠 줄 10곳의 유명 명소들을 선정했다. 07이 친선 경쟁을 홍보하기 위해, 선정된 명소들 근처에 위치한 상점과 레스토랑에서 사용할 수 있는 할인 우대증의 역할을 할 수 있도록 도시 여행증이 고안되었다. 승리를 거두는 도시는 해당 도시의 도서관 개조 공사에 필요한 보조금을 받게 될 것이다. 08어느 도시가 승리를 거두든지, 두 도시 모두 분명 관광 산업을 증대시키기 위한 시도를 통해 혜택을 볼 것이다.

품 코너에서 근무할 수 있다.

[해설] 선택지가 다양한 동사들로 구성되어 있으므로 동사 어휘 문제이다. 빈칸이속한 once절은 다른 제품 코너에서 근무하기 위한 조건을 나타내야 하므로 온라인 교육(online training)과 관련해 해야 하는 일을 나타낼 동사로 '~을 이수하다'를 뜻하는 (A) completed가 정답이다.

[어휘] sales associate 영업 직원 department (백화점 등의) 코너, 매장 once 일단 ~하고 나면, ~하자마자 defer ~을 미루다 encounter ~와 맞닥뜨리다, 마주치다 earn ~을 벌다, 얻다

21. 동사 어휘

농산물 가격은 곡물 수확량 규모와 무엇이 현재 제철인지에 따라 다를 것이다.

[해설] 선택지가 다양한 동사들로 구성되어 있으므로 동사 어휘 문제이다. depending on 이하 부분은 조건을 나타내므로 '~에 따라 다를 것이다'와 같이 차이를 나타내는 동사가 빈칸에 필요하다. 따라서 '다르다, 차이가 나다'를 뜻하는 (B) differ가 정답이다.

[어휘] produce 농산물 depending on ~에 따라, ~에 달려 있는 crop yield 곡물 수확량 currently 현재 in season 제철인 rely 의지하다, 신뢰하다

22. 동사 어휘

Hurst 씨는 자신의 직원들이 워크숍 참석을 통해 얻은 경험을 공유할 수 있기를 기대한다.

[해설] 선택지가 다양한 동사들로 구성되어 있으므로 동사 어휘 문제이다. they 이하 부분은 바로 앞에 위치한 명사 experience를 수식하는 역할을 해야 한다. 따라서 experience는 특정 행사의 참석을 통해 얻은 경험을 의미해야 하므로 '~을 얻다'를 뜻하는 (A) gained가 정답이다.

[어휘] share ~을 공유하다 remove ~을 제거하다

23. 동사 어휘

태평양 연안의 기상 자문은 쓰나미가 하와이를 강타할 것으로 예상될 때 비상 탈출 경보를 발령한다.

[해설] 선택지가 다양한 동사들로 구성되어 있으므로 동사 어휘 문제이다. 목적어에 해당되는 evacuation alert와 의미가 어울리는 동사가 필요하므로 '비상 탈출 경보를 발령하다'라는 의미가 되게 하는 (C) issues가 정답이다.

[어휘] evacuation alert 비상 탈출 경보 enforce ~을 집행하다 launch ~을 시작하다, 출시하다 issue ~을 발령하다, 발급하다

24. 동사 어휘

이번 달에, Farrell 컨설팅 사는 처음 찾는 고객과 소기업들을 응대하는 데 필요한 일련의 공식 가이드라인을 시행했다.

[해설] 선택지가 다양한 동사들로 구성되어 있으므로 동사 어휘 문제이다. 목적어에 해당되는 an official set of guidelines와 의미가 어울리는 동사가 필요하므로 '일련의 가이드라인을 시행하다'라는 의미가 되게 하는 (D) implemented가 정답이다. (C) differed는 자동사이므로 목적어를 취할 수 없다.

[어휘] deal with ~을 대하다, ~을 다루다 encounter ~와 맞닥뜨리다, ~와 마주하다 oversee ~을 총괄하다, 감독하다 differ 다르다, 차이가 나다 implement ~을 시행하다

PART 6 뒤의 내용이 단서인 동사 시제

풀이 방법 해석

하트퍼드(3월 17일) — Designs by Diaz가 기자 회견에서 해외 시장으로 진출할 것이라고 발표했다. 그들의 첫 번째 해외 지사는 올해 말에 열 것이다. 회사는 최근에 승진한 직원들을 마드리드의 새 지사를 운영하게 할 계획이다. 지금까지, 가정용품을 공급하는 이 회사는 전국적으로 27개의 지사가 있다. 각 지점은 훌륭한 고객 만족 등급을 받았다. CEO인 Marcus Diaz는 이 추세가 계속되기를 희망한다. 그는 마드리드 지사가 국내 지사들만큼 성공적이라면, 내년쯤 바르셀로나에 또 다른 지사를 열고 싶다고 말했다.

연습 문제

01.(A)   02.(B)   03.(A)   04.(A)

01.

포틀랜드 지역 토박이 미술가인 Meredith Black 씨가 포틀랜드 지역 문화 센터에서 10점의 조각품을 선보일 것이라고 발표했습니다. 이 행사는 내년 여름에 7월 19일부터 한 달간 개최될 예정입니다.

native to ~ 토박이인, ~ 태생의 sculpture 조각품 take place (행사, 일등이) 개최되다, 발생되다

[단서] The event is scheduled to take place next summer

[해설] 다음 문장에서 미래의 특정 기간에 열리는 행사라고 했으므로 조각품을 전시하는 시점도 미래임을 알 수 있다. 따라서 미래 시제인 (A) will present가 정답이다.

[어휘] present ~을 선보이다, 소개하다, 제공하다

02.

Greene 씨께

저희 레스토랑에서의 식사 경험과 관련해 제공해 주신 의견에 감사 드립니다.

이미 아시다시피, 저희는 저희 레스토랑 직원들이 각자의 휴대전화를 꺼두어야 한다는 내용의 새 정책을 시행했습니다. 이를 도입한 이후로, 이미 고객 평가가 별 1개만큼 향상되었습니다!

dining experience 식사 경험 policy 정책 introduce ~을 도입하다, 소개하다 improve 향상되다, 개선되다

[단서] Since introducing it

[해설] 다음 문장에 과거의 시작 시점을 나타내는 Since와 함께 새로운 정책이 도입된 이후의 긍정적인 결과를 제시했으므로 이미 정책을 시행한 상태임을 알 수 있다. 따라서 과거 시제인 (B) implemented가 정답이다.

[어휘] implement ~을 시행하다

[해설] 선택지가 동사 offer의 다양한 형태로 구성되어 있으므로 문법 문제이다. 빈칸 앞뒤로 주어와 목적어, 그리고 전치사구만 있으므로 빈칸이 문장의 동사 자리이며, upcoming은 미래 시제 동사와 쓰이므로 (A) will offer가 정답이다.

[어휘] catering 출장 뷔페 upcoming 곧 있을, 다가오는 banquet 연회

10. 완료 시제: 현재완료

지난 3개월 동안 Balatas 컨트리클럽은 클럽하우스와 스파 시설을 개보수했다.

[해설] 선택지가 동사 renovate의 다양한 형태와 파생어 명사로 구성되어 있으므로 문법 문제이다. 빈칸 앞뒤로 주어와 목적어만 있으므로 빈칸이 문장의 동사 자리이다. 과거에서 현재까지의 기간을 나타내는 Over 전치사구와 어울리려면 현재완료 시제가 쓰여야 하므로 (B) has renovated가 정답이다.

[어휘] past 지난 renovate 개조하다, 보수하다

11. 완료 시제: 현재완료

지난 10월 이후로, Tony's 자동차 용품 사의 부동액 매출이 증가해 왔다.

[해설] 선택지가 동사 increase의 다양한 형태와 파생어 부사로 구성되어 있으므로 문법 문제이다. 빈칸 앞뒤로 전치사구와 명사구만 있으므로 빈칸이 문장의 동사 자리인데, 과거의 시작점을 나타내는 Since 전치사구와 어울리려면 현재완료 시제가 필요하므로 (D) have increased가 정답이다.

[어휘] sales 매출, 판매(량) antifreeze 부동액 increase 증가하다 increasingly 점점 더

12. 시간 부사절과 주절의 시제 관계

Stanford 사가 공석을 공지했을 때, 지원자들이 이력서를 제출하기 시작했다.

[해설] 선택지가 동사 begin의 다양한 형태로 구성되어 있으므로 문법 문제이다. 빈칸 앞뒤로 주어와 명사구만 있으므로 빈칸이 주절의 동사 자리인데, When절에 쓰인 과거 시제 동사(announced)와 시제가 일치되어야 하므로 동일 과거 시제 동사인 (B) began이 정답이다.

[어휘] job opening (직장의) 빈자리 applicant 지원자 submit ~을 제출하다 résumé 이력서

13. 미래를 대신하는 현재진행 시제

그 주차장은 바닥 재포장 공사가 실시되는 동안 일시적으로 폐쇄될 것이다.

[해설] 선택지가 동사구 carry out의 다양한 형태로 구성되어 있으므로 문법 문제이다. 빈칸 앞에 접속사 while과 명사구만 있으므로 빈칸이 while절의 동사 자리이며, while절은 주절의 동사(will be closed)와 동일 시제를 사용해야 하므로 미래를 대신하는 현재진행 시제 (B) is being carried out이 정답이다.

[어휘] temporarily 일시적으로 resurfacing (바닥 등의) 재포장 carry out ~을 실시하다, 수행하다

14. 조건 부사절과 주절의 시제 관계

고객이 서비스 약정을 변경하기를 원할 경우, 지점장은 반드시 어떠한 계약 변경 사항이든 승인해야 한다.

[해설] 선택지가 동사 want의 다양한 형태로 구성되어 있으므로 문법 문제이다. If절(조건 부사절)에 속한 빈칸 앞뒤로 주어와 to부정사구만 있으므로 빈칸이 If절의 동사 자리이며, 주절에 조동사 must가 쓰일 경우에 If절의 동사는 현재 시제여야 하므로 (A) wants가 정답이다.

[어휘] branch 지점, 지사 approve ~을 승인하다 contract 계약(서)

15. 수동태의 형태

표면이 부드럽게 마감되기 위해서는, 새 페인트를 칠하기 전에 기존의 어떠한 페인트 층이든 반드시 제거되어야 한다.

[해설] 선택지가 동사 remove의 다양한 형태로 구성되어 있으므로 문법 문제이다. 빈칸 앞뒤로 명사구와 전치사구만 있으므로 빈칸이 문장의 동사 자리이며, 주어 paint layers는 사람에 의해 제거되는 대상이므로 수동의 의미를 나타낼 수 있도록 remove가 수동태로 쓰여야 한다. 따라서 유일한 수동태인 (B) must be removed가 정답이다.

[어휘] smoothly 부드럽게 surface 표면 original 기존의, 원래의 layer (쌓인) 층, 막 apply ~을 바르다 remove ~을 제거하다

16. '자동사+전치사' 숙어

이번 주에 어떠한 자선 활동이든 참가하는 학생들은 지역 기업들이 기부한 무료 제품을 받을 자격이 있다.

[해설] 선택지가 다양한 전치사들로 구성되어 있으므로 전치사 어휘 문제이다. 빈칸 앞에 분사로 쓰인 동사 participate는 전치사 in과 짝을 이루는 자동사이므로 (A) in이 정답이다.

[어휘] charity 자선 (활동) be eligible for ~에 대한 자격이 있다 contribute ~을 기부하다

17. '타동사+목적어+전치사' 숙어

Golden Airlines는 자사의 국제 항공편 탑승객들에게 고급 식사를 제공한다.

[해설] 선택지가 다양한 전치사들로 구성되어 있으므로 전치사 어휘 문제이다. 빈칸 앞에 쓰인 동사 serve는 'serve+음식+to+사람'의 구조로 쓰이므로 (A) to가 정답이다.

[어휘] gourmet 고급의 passenger 탑승객

18. 부사의 역할과 위치: 동사 사이에서 수식

새 공급업체와 함께한 지 불과 한 달 만에, 이미 두 번의 미비한 배송 문제가 있었다.

[해설] 선택지가 부사와 형용사로 구성되어 있으므로 문법 문제이다. 현재완료 구문에서 have와 been 사이에 빈칸이 있으므로 빈칸은 동사를 수식할 부사 자리이며, 현재완료 시제에서 동사를 수식하는 부사로 자주 쓰이는 (C) already가 정답이다.

[어휘] supplier 공급업체 incomplete 미비한, 불완전한 shipment 배송(품) reasonably 합리적으로 moreover 더욱이, 게다가

19. 동사 어휘

새 지역 구획 법안으로 인해 Parker's Pizza가 주거 지역에 지점을 열 수 있었다.

[해설] 선택지가 다양한 동사들로 구성되어 있으므로 동사 어휘 문제이다. 빈칸 뒤에 위치한 '목적어+to부정사' 구조와 어울리는 동사로서 '~가 …할 수 있게 하다'라는 의미를 나타내는 (D) enabled가 정답이다.

[어휘] zoning law 지역 구획 법안 branch 지점 residential 주거의 emphasize ~을 강조하다 implement ~을 시행하다

20. 동사 어휘

Wilson 백화점에서는 영업 직원들이 온라인 교육을 이수하고 나면 다른 제

DAY 11 91

05.

1. 선택지 보고 문법/어휘 문제 파악하기 ☑문법 문제 ☐어휘 문제
2. 빈칸 분석하기 빈칸 앞에 있는 것 ☑시간 부사절의 주어 ☐시간 부사절의 동사
   → 빈칸은 ☐목적어 ☑동사 자리이다.
   주절의 동사의 시제 ☐현재 시제 ☑미래 시제
   → 빈칸에는 ☑현재 시제 동사 ☐미래 시제 동사가 들어가야 한다.
3. 정답 선택하기 정답 (B)

그녀의 전근 신청이 승인되면, Alicia Wise는 우리 부서에 합류할 것이다.

06.

1. 선택지 보고 문법/어휘 문제 파악하기 ☐문법 문제 ☑어휘 문제
2. 빈칸 분석하기 빈칸 뒤 목적어 (its variety of flower baskets)
   목적어 뒤에 나오는 전치사 (to)
   → 위의 전치사와 함께 쓰이는 동사가 답이다.
3. 정답 선택하기 정답 (A)

Manorville Flower는 그들의 다양한 꽃바구니를 시 경계 내에 있는 주소지로 배송한다.

실전 문제

01.(B)	02.(C)	03.(A)	04.(C)	05.(A)	06.(D)
07.(D)	08.(C)	09.(A)	10.(B)	11.(D)	12.(B)
13.(B)	14.(A)	15.(B)	16.(A)	17.(A)	18.(C)
19.(D)	20.(A)	21.(B)	22.(A)	23.(C)	24.(D)

01. 단순 시제: 미래

향후 몇 주 동안 모든 직원들은 온라인 교육 과정을 이수할 것이다.

[해설] 선택지가 동사 complete의 다양한 형태로 구성되어 있으므로 문법 문제이다. 빈칸 앞뒤로 주어와 목적어만 있으므로 빈칸은 문장의 동사 자리이며, 미래 시간 전치사구 During the next few weeks와 어울리는 미래 시제 동사가 필요하므로 (B) will complete가 정답이다.

[어휘] complete ~을 완수하다, 완료하다

02. 단순 시제: 과거

Cervantes 씨는 지난주에 한 시장 분석가와 함께 새로운 사업에 대한 자신의 아이디어를 논의했다.

[해설] 선택지가 동사 discuss의 다양한 형태와 파생어 명사로 구성되어 있으므로 문법 문제이다. 빈칸 앞뒤로 주어와 목적어, 전치사구만 있으므로 빈칸은 문장의 동사 자리이며, 과거 시점 표현 last week과 어울리는 과거 시제 동사가 필요하므로 (C) discussed가 정답이다.

[어휘] analyst 분석가   discussion 논의   discuss ~을 논의하다

03. 단순 시제: 미래

레이크빌의 새 아파트 단지에서 근무할 추가 시설 관리 직원이 돌아오는 이번 가을에 고용될 것이다.

[해설] 선택지가 동사 hire의 다양한 형태로 구성되어 있으므로 문법 문제이다. 빈칸 앞뒤로 주어와 전치사구들만 있으므로 빈칸은 문장의 동사 자리이며, 미래 시점 표현 this coming autumn과 어울리는 미래 시제 동사가 필요하므로 (A) will be hired가 정답이다.

[어휘] maintenance 시설 관리   hire ~을 고용하다

04. 완료 시제: 현재완료

2006년에 영업을 시작한 이후로 줄곧, Mercado 사는 11월에 직원 성과를 평가해 왔다.

[해설] 선택지가 동사 evaluate의 다양한 형태로 구성되어 있으므로 문법 문제이다. 빈칸 앞뒤로 주어와 목적어, 전치사구만 있으므로 빈칸은 문장의 동사 자리이며, '~한 이후로 줄곧'이라는 의미의 'Ever since+과거 시제 동사' 구문의 종속절과 어울리는 현재완료 시제 동사가 주절에 필요하므로 (C) has evaluated가 정답이다.

[어휘] ever since ~ 이후로 줄곧   performance 성과, 실적, 수행 능력   evaluate ~을 평가하다

05. 완료 시제: 현재완료

Logan 씨는 지난 3개월 동안 Inno Tech 사에서 유급 인턴으로 근무해 오고 있다.

[해설] 선택지가 동사 work의 다양한 형태로 구성되어 있으므로 문법 문제이다. 빈칸 앞뒤로 주어와 전치사구들만 있으므로 빈칸은 문장의 동사 자리이며, 과거에서 현재까지의 기간을 나타내는 for the last three months와 어울리는 현재 완료 시제 동사가 필요하므로 (A) has been working이 정답이다.

[어휘] paid 유급의

06. 시간 부사절과 주절의 시제 관계

Jensen 씨는 내일 철저한 조사를 끝내고 나서 공장 관리자에게 보고할 예정이다.

[해설] 선택지가 동사 finish의 다양한 형태로 구성되어 있으므로 문법 문제이다. 주절에 미래 시제 동사(will report)가 쓰일 경우에 after 절(시간 부사절)에는 현재 시제 동사가 쓰여야 하므로 (C) finishes가 정답이다.

[어휘] report 보고하다   thorough 철저한   inspection 조사

07. 조건 부사절과 주절의 시제 관계

날씨가 좋을 경우, Duchess Heights Mall의 개장식이 예정대로 옥외에서 개최될 것이다.

[해설] 선택지가 동사 hold의 다양한 형태로 구성되어 있으므로 문법 문제이다. If절(조건 부사절)에 현재 시제 동사(is)가 쓰일 경우에 주절에는 미래 시제 동사가 쓰여야 하므로 (D) will be held가 정답이다. 미래완료 시제인 (B) will have been held는 특정 미래 시점 표현과 함께 그 시점에 완료되는 일을 나타낼 때 사용한다.

[어휘] favorable 좋은, 호의적인

08. 단순 시제: 과거

Lutz 씨는 지난 월요일에 특별 경영진 회의를 소집했으며, 고객 불만이 최근 증가한 것에 대해 사과했다.

[해설] 선택지가 동사 apologize의 다양한 형태와 파생어 명사로 구성되어 있으므로 문법 문제이다. 주절에서 회의를 소집한 시점을 나타내는 과거 시제 동사 called와 동일 시점에 사과했다는 의미가 되어야 알맞으므로 과거 시제인 (C) apologized가 정답이다.

[어휘] call ~을 소집하다   rise in ~의 증가   complaint 불만

09. 단순 시제: 미래

Clara Grill은 곧 있을 Canada Investment의 연회에서 케이터링 서비스를 제공할 예정이다.

like the location, initial salary, position responsibilities, and shifts that we're hiring for) 알 수 있다. 그런데 두 번째 지문인 광고의 내용을 보면, 광고 앞부분에 위치(main headquarters building in Semmes, AL.), 근무 교대(Monday through Friday, 9-5), 각 직책별 직무가 언급되어 있지만 초봉이 언급되지 않았으므로 (B)가 정답이다.

[어휘] request 요청하다   include 포함하다   wage 급여

08. 세부사항 문제

지원자들은 어떻게 Core Tech에 입사 지원을 할 수 있는가?
(A) 인사 담당자에게 연락해서
(B) 본사에 신청서를 발송해서
(C) 온라인 지원서를 작성해서
(D) 면접 행사에 참석해서

[해설] 지원 방법이 언급된 두 번째 지문 마지막 단락에, 지원하려면 Core Tech 웹사이트를 방문하여 초기 지원서를 작성하라고(To apply for any of these positions, visit Core Tech's Web site and fill out an initial application) 알리고 있으므로 (C)가 정답이다.

[어휘] candidate 지원자   apply for 지원하다   mail 우편으로 보내다   application 지원

09. 추론 문제 – 연계 문제

Byrd 씨에 대해 무엇이 암시되는가?
(A) 곧 승진할 것이다.
(B) 매우 창의적이다.
(C) 세부적인 것에 신경을 쓴다.
(D) 신원 조회를 통과했다.

[해설] Byrd 씨의 이름은 마지막 지문의 도표에서 제품 디자인(Product Design) 신입 사원 명단에서 확인할 수 있는데, 이 업무 담당 직원은 뛰어난 창의력이 요구된다고(A strong sense of creativity is a must for this position) 했으므로 정답은 (B)이다.

[어휘] imply 암시하다   promotion 승진   attentive 주의 깊은, 신경을 쓰는

10. True 문제

7월 9일 행사에서 품질 관리팀 구성원에 대해 나타난 것은?
(A) 화상 회의를 통해 만날 것이다.
(B) 경쟁에 참가할 것이다.
(C) 신원 조회를 위해 서류를 제출할 것이다.
(D) 신기술에 대한 그들의 생각을 토론할 것이다.

[해설] 7월 9일의 일정표인 두 번째 지문에서, 품질 관리팀은 경쟁적인 적용 연습에 참여한다고(Participate in competitive exercises) 했으므로 이를 competition으로 표현한 (B)가 정답이다.

paraphrasing   competitive exercises 경쟁적인 활동 → competition 경쟁

[어휘] take part in 참여하다, 참가하다   competition 대회, 경쟁   submit 제출하다   document 서류

paraphrasing 정답   1. (a)   2. (b)   3. (c)

DAY 11

PART 5   문법 | 시제

확인 문제 해석

① 그들은 보통 회의를 화요일에 연다.
② 판촉 행사는 다음 주에 열릴 것이다.
③ 그녀는 지난달에 지사를 방문했다.
④ Claire는 2015년부터 부서장으로 일하고 있다.
⑤ Morris 씨는 그녀가 주문을 취소하려고 전화하기 전에 주문품을 발송했다.
⑥ Lee 씨는 곧 있을 취업 박람회에서 상을 수여할 것이다.

 연습 문제

01.(A)   02.(C)   03.(B)   04.(D)   05.(B)   06.(A)

01.
1. 선택지 보고 문법/어휘 문제 파악하기   ☑ 문법 문제   ☐ 어휘 문제
2. 빈칸 분석하기   빈칸 앞에 있는 것 ☑ 주어+부사   ☐ 동사+부사
   → 빈칸은 ☑ 동사   ☐ 목적어 자리이다.
   → normally와 어울려 쓰일 수 있는 ☐ 미래 시제 동사   ☑ 현재 시제 동사가 들어가야 한다.
3. 정답 선택하기   정답 (A)

보조 교수는 주로 학생들이 제출한 글쓰기 과제를 확인한다.

02.
1. 선택지 보고 문법/어휘 문제 파악하기   ☑ 문법 문제   ☐ 어휘 문제
2. 빈칸 분석하기   빈칸 뒤에 있는 것 ☑ 과거 시제 표현   ☐ 미래 시제 표현
   → 빈칸은 ☑ 과거 시제 동사   ☐ 미래 시제 동사 자리이다.
3. 정답 선택하기   정답 (C)

Pelham 전자는 3년 전에 발명가인 William Tanner에 의해 설립되었다.

03.
1. 선택지 보고 문법/어휘 문제 파악하기   ☑ 문법 문제   ☐ 어휘 문제
2. 빈칸 분석하기   빈칸 뒤에 있는 것 ☐ 과거 시제 표현   ☑ 미래 시제 표현
   → 빈칸은 ☐ 과거 시제 동사   ☑ 미래 시제 동사 자리이다.
3. 정답 선택하기   정답 (B)

개인 뱅킹 강좌가 다음 주에 Landry 주민 센터에서 열릴 것이다.

04.
1. 선택지 보고 문법/어휘 문제 파악하기   ☑ 문법 문제   ☐ 어휘 문제
2. 빈칸 분석하기   빈칸 뒤에 있는 시간 표현 (over the last five years)
   → 빈칸은 ☑ 현재완료 시제 동사   ☐ 미래 시제 동사 자리이다.
3. 정답 선택하기   정답 (D)

Greene 씨는 그의 제과점을 지난 5년 동안 운영해 왔다.

[해설] 두 번째 단락 시작 부분에 영업 시간이 월요일부터 금요일까지라고 (our opening hours, Monday to Friday) 쓰여 있으므로 주말에는 문을 닫는다는 것을 알 수 있으므로 (B)가 정답이다.

paraphrasing opening hours, Monday to Friday 영업 시간이 월요일부터 금요일까지 → closed on the weekend 주말에는 문을 닫음

[어휘] field 분야 loan 대출 exclusively 오로지, 독점적으로

05. 세부사항 문제

해당 직책의 무슨 혜택이 언급되어 있는가?
(A) 유급 휴가
(B) 분기별 직원 회식
(C) 구내 식당 내 무료 식사
(D) 성과급

[해설] 근무 환경과 관련된 정보가 제시된 두 번째 단락 끝부분에, 분기별 목표를 달성하는 데 따른 보너스를 지급받는다고(employees earn generous bonus payments for meeting their quarterly targets) 했는데, 이는 성과급 제도가 있다는 뜻이므로 (D)가 정답이다.

paraphrasing bonus payments for meeting their quarterly targets 분기별 목표를 충족하는 데 대한 보너스 → Performance bonuses 성과급

[어휘] benefit 혜택, 이점 performance 성과, 실적

paraphrasing 정답 1. (c) 2. (d) 3. (a) 4. (b) 5. (e)

06-10은 다음 이메일, 광고, 그리고 일정표를 참조하시오.

수신: Josephine Greer <j.greer@coretech.com>
발신: Calvin Bauer <c.bauer@coretech.com>
날짜: 5월 21일
제목: 채용

안녕하세요 Josephine,

우리 회사 구인 광고를 내는 데 당신의 도움이 필요해요. 아시다시피 [06]지금이 학기말이고 잠재력을 갖춘 많은 젊은이들 졸업할 거예요. 따라서 빨리 움직여야 합니다. 급히 알려 드려 죄송합니다. 하지만 저희 부서가 CT Tablet의 출시로 매우 바빴던 점 양해 바랍니다. [07]공고를 올릴 때 위치, 초봉, 직책별 임무, 근무 시간대 등의 정보를 포함하는 것을 잊지 말아 주세요. 미리 감사드립니다.

진심으로,

Calvin Bauer
R&D 매니저, Core Tech

recruitment 채용 semester 학기 potential 잠재력 department 부서 launch 출시 initial salary 초봉 in advance 미리

Core Tech의 핵심 멤버가 되세요!

인기 있는 전자제품 제조업체인 Core Tech는 몇몇 신입급 직책을 채울 열성적인 인재를 찾고 있습니다. [07]현재 저희는 월~금요일, 오전 9시~오후 5시까지 근무하는 기본 근무 시간대 근로자만 채용합니다. 다음의 모든 일자리들은 앨라배마주 Semmes에 있는 본사 건물에 위치합니다.

[07]채용 중인 자리:
- 인사 담당자: 정기 직원 교육 계획 수립 지원, 다른 직원들에 관련된 기밀 문서 처리 및 급여 또는 업무 환경 관련 문제가 있는 직원 지원합니다. 신원 조회를 통과해야 합니다.
- [09]제품 디자인: 당사의 혁신적인 제품 디자이너들과 함께 전자제품을 개발하고 업그레이드합니다. 뛰어난 창의력이 요구되는 자리입니다.
- 품질 관리: 모든 Core Tech 제품은 대중에게 공개되기 전 철저한 테스트를 수행합니다. 디테일에 대한 매우 세심한 주의가 요구되는 자리입니다.

[08]이 자리에 지원하려면 Core Tech 웹사이트를 방문하셔서 초기 지원서를 작성해 주세요. 초기 검토 기간이 끝난 후 합격자분들은 화상 회의를 통한 일차 면접을 진행하게 됩니다.

core 핵심적인 manufacturer 제조자, 생산 회사 enthusiastic 열성적인 headquarters 본사, 본부 handle 다루다 confidential 기밀의 regarding ~에 관한 background check 신원 조회 thorough 철저한 unveil 공개하다 via ~을 통해, 경유하여

Core Tech 신입 사원 오리엔테이션: 7월 9일

Core Tech 본사 사무실: 8554 Tunbridge Road, Semmes, AL 36575

부서	신규 입사자	메모
인사 담당자	Natalie Phelps Eric Bradley	신원 조회 실시 예정
[09]제품 디자인	Liam Glenn **Ashley Byrd**	혁신 기술에 대한 아이디어 공유
품질 관리	Simone Lowery Audrey Blackwell	[10]경쟁적인 활동에 참가

innovative 혁신적인 participate in ~에 참가하다 competitive 경쟁적인 exercise 활동

06. 세부사항 문제

Bauer 씨는 왜 Greer 씨에게 일을 빨리 하라고 요청하는가?
(A) 곧 회사의 바쁜 시즌이 시작될 것이다.
(B) 제품 출시를 위해서는 더 많은 인력이 필요하다.
(C) 많은 학생들이 곧 대학을 졸업할 것이다.
(D) 일부 직원이 경쟁사에 입사했다.

[해설] Bauer 씨가 쓴 이메일 전반부에, 지금이 학기말이고 잠재력을 갖춘 많은 젊은이들 졸업할 것이므로 빨리 움직여야 한다고(it's the end of the semester, and a lot of young people with a lot of potential will be graduating) 했으므로 (C)가 정답이다.

[어휘] task 일, 업무 launch 출시 graduate 졸업하다 soon 곧 competitor 경쟁자, 경쟁사

07. Not True 문제 – 연계 문제

Bauer 씨가 요청한 어떤 정보가 광고에 포함되지 않았는가?
(A) 사용 가능한 교대조
(B) 초봉
(C) 직무
(D) 작업 장소

[해설] 이메일의 마지막 부분에서 Bauer 씨가 광고에 포함하도록 요청한 정보는 위치, 초봉, 직책별 임무, 근무 교대임을(include information

01-02는 다음 광고를 참조하시오.

Emberton 국립 공원에서 현재 여름 기간에 근무하실 등산 가이드를 찾고 있습니다. **01)과거에는 단 6개월만 일반 대중에게 개방되었던 공원이 현재는 지속적으로 이용 가능합니다.**

해외 방문객들을 수용하기 위해, **02(B)반드시 영어와 다음 언어들 중의 한 가지에 능통하셔야 합니다**: 스페인어, 프랑스어 또는 표준 중국어. 저희가 상세 안내도와 교육은 제공해 드리겠지만, **02(C)반드시 매일 최대 20마일에 달하는 등산 활동을 감당하실 수 있을 정도로 충분히 건강하신 분이어야 합니다.**

이 자리에 지원하시려면, www.emberton.gov를 방문하시기 바랍니다. **02(A)채용된 지원자들께서는 반드시 어느 시간대든 유동적으로 근무할 수 있어야 하는데,** 교대 근무 조가 주중과 주말에 모두 배정되기 때문입니다.

currently 현재 seek ~을 찾다, 구하다 the public 일반 대중 continuously 지속적으로 accessible 이용 가능한, 접근 가능한 accommodate ~을 수용하다 overseas 해외의 be fluent in ~에 능통하다, ~에 유창하다 fit 건강한, 준비된 handle ~을 처리하다, 다루다 apply for ~에 지원하다 applicant 지원자 shift 교대 근무(조) assign ~을 배정하다, 할당하다

01. 세부사항 문제

Emberton 국립 공원에 최근 변경된 것은 무엇인가?
(A) 웹사이트에서 안내도를 제공한다.
(B) 현재 연중으로 개방된다.
(C) 여름에 입장료가 무료이다.
(D) 새로운 등산로를 만들었다.

[해설] 과거와 현재 사이의 차이점이 언급된 첫 단락에, 단 6개월만 일반 대중에게 개방되었던 공원이 현재 지속적으로 이용 가능하다는(Previously open to the public just six months of the year, the park is now continuously accessible) 말로 변화된 부분을 알리고 있으므로 이를 언급한 (B)가 정답이다.

paraphrasing continuously accessible 지속적으로 이용 가능한 → open year-round 연중으로 개방된

[어휘] year-round 연중으로, 일 년 내내 admission 입장(료) hiking trails 등산로

02. Not True 문제

해당 일자리에 대한 자격 요건으로 언급되지 않은 것은 무엇인가?
(A) 유동적인 일정으로 근무할 수 있는 능력
(B) 두 가지 언어에 대한 유창함
(C) 높은 수준의 신체적 건강함
(D) 공원의 등산로 시스템에 관한 지식

[해설] 두 번째 단락의 you must be fluent in English and one of the following languages 부분에서 '두 가지 언어에 대한 유창함'을 언급한 (B)를, 그 뒤에 이어지는 you must be fit enough to handle hikes of up to 20 miles per day에서 '신체적 건강함'을 말한 (C)를, 그리고 마지막 단락의 Successful applicants must be free to work anytime을 통해 '유동적인 근무 일정'을 말한 (A)를 확인할 수 있다. 하지만 등산로 시스템에 관한 지식은 두 번째 단락에 언급된 바와 같이 채용된 이후에 교육을 통해 얻을 수 있는 지식이므로 (D)가 정답이다.

[어휘] flexible 유동적인, 탄력적인 fluency in ~의 유창함 physical 신체의 fitness 건강(함)

paraphrasing 정답 1. (d) 2. (e) 3. (c) 4. (a) 5. (b)

03-05는 다음 구인 공고를 참조하시오.

대출 담당 직원 모집

Sutter 은행 그랜드 래피즈 지역의 지점에 근무할 **03(D)매우 체계적인** 정규직 대출 담당 직원을 찾습니다. 이 직책에는 잠재 대출자들을 평가해 적격 여부를 결정하고 해당 고객들이 필요로 하는 것을 충족할 대출 상품을 추천해 드리는 업무가 포함됩니다. 저희 Sutter 은행은 빠르게 진행되는 업무 환경이므로, **03(A)반드시 여러 업무를 동시에 처리할 수 있으면서 높은 수준의 정확성을 유지할 수 있는 분이어야 합니다. 03(B)은행 또는 신용 조합에서 최소 2년간 근무한 경력이 필수입니다.**

대출 담당 직원은 **04)저희 영업 시간인 월요일부터 금요일, 오전 9시부터 오후 6시까지 매주 40시간 근무합니다.** 저희 직원들은 친절하고 따뜻하며, 직원들은 편리한 구내 식당과 무료 지하 주차장을 이용하실 수 있습니다. 저희 Sutter 은행은 어디에도 뒤지지 않는 급여와 의료 보험, 그리고 초과 근무 수당을 제공하고 있습니다. 추가로, **05)직원들은 분기 목표를 달성하는 데 따른 넉넉한 보너스도 지급받습니다.**

이 직책에 지원하시려면, 이메일 제목에 "직책 번호 0927"을 명기해 이력서와 자기소개서를 hr@sutterbank.com으로 보내 주시기 바랍니다.

loan officer 대출 담당 직원 look for ~을 찾다, 구하다 involve ~을 수반하다, 포함하다 assess ~을 평가하다 potential 잠재적인 borrower 대출자, 빌리는 사람 determine ~을 결정하다 eligibility 자격이 있음, 적격임 accuracy 정확성 credit union 신용 조합 take advantage of ~을 이용하다 on-site 구내의, 부지내의 competitive 어디에도 뒤지지 않는, 경쟁력 있는 wage 급여 paid overtime 초과 근무 수당 generous 넉넉한, 후한 earn bonus payments 보너스를 지급받다 quarterly 분기의 subject line 제목을 쓰는 칸

03. Not True 문제

해당 직책에 대해 우대되는 자격 요건으로 언급되지 않은 것은 무엇인가?
(A) 동시에 여러 업무를 수행할 수 있는 능력
(B) 금융 기관에서의 과거 근무 경력
(C) 금융 또는 회계 전공 대학 학위
(D) 뛰어난 체계적 업무 처리 능력

[해설] 첫 단락의 who is very well organized 부분에서 '체계적인 업무 능력'을 언급한 (D)를, 같은 단락 후반부의 you must be able to multitask에서 '다중 업무 능력'을 말한 (A)를, 그리고 바로 뒤이어 제시되는 At least 2 years' experience working at a bank or credit union 부분에서 '과거의 금융 기관 근무 경력'을 말한 (B)의 내용을 확인할 수 있다. 하지만 금융이나 회계 분야의 학위와 관련된 요건은 제시되어 있지 않으므로 (C)가 정답이다.

[어휘] simultaneously 동시에 financial institution 금융 기관 degree 학위 accounting 회계 organizational skills 체계적인 처리 능력

04. 추론 문제

Sutter 은행에 관해 암시되는 것은 무엇인가?
(A) 업계에서 가장 높은 급여를 지급한다.
(B) 주말에는 문을 닫는다.
(C) 최근에 신규 지점을 열었다.
(D) 오직 사업체들을 대상으로만 대출을 제공한다.

DAY 10

01.

보조 요리사 구함

저희 Oakland Steakhouse는 시내 지점에서 근무할 보조 요리사를 구하고 있습니다. 직무에는 재료 준비와 음식 플레이팅, 용품 정리, 그리고 주방 청결 유지가 포함됩니다. 이상적인 후보자는 근면한 근무 태도와 빠르게 진행되는 환경에서 근무할 수 있는 능력의 소유자여야 합니다. 저희는 적합한 분을 교육할 의향이 있지만, 선정된 지원자는 반드시 캘리포니아 주에서 발급하는 유효한 보건 및 식품 취급 자격증 소지자여야 합니다. 지원서를 다운로드하시려면 www.oaklandsteakhouse.com을 방문하시기 바랍니다.

assistant 보조, 조수   seek ~을 찾다, 구하다   duty 직무
ingredient (음식) 재료   plate (음식) ~을 접시에 담아 장식하다
supplies 용품, 물품   ideal 이상적인   fast-paced 빠르게 진행되는
be willing to부정사 ~할 의향이 있다   train ~을 교육하다
applicant 지원자   valid 유효한   food-handling 식품 취급
certificate 자격증, 면허증   issue ~을 발급하다

Q. 해당 직책의 한 가지 자격 요건은 무엇인가?
(A) 주에서 발급하는 보건 관련 자격증
(B) 해당 분야에서의 과거 근무 경력

[문제 키워드] What / one requirement

[해설] 지문 후반부에 캘리포니아 주에서 발급하는 유효한 보건 및 식품 취급 자격증 소지자여야 한다고(~ valid health and food-handling certificate issued by the state of California) 알리고 있으므로 (A)가 정답이다.

[어휘] certification 자격 증명서

02.

Mays 출판에서 그래픽 디자이너를 찾습니다.

Mays 출판은 <Garden Art Monthly>나 <Dog World>와 같은 인기 있는 서적들을 포함해 아주 다양한 취미 관련 잡지들을 출간하고 있습니다. 저희는 현재 그래픽 디자인팀을 확장시키고 있습니다. 해당 직책은 정규직이지만, **직원들은 주당 5일 중에서 2일은 재택 근무 하는 것이 허용됩니다.** 이상적인 후보자는 최소 3년의 그래픽 디자인 경력을 보유하고 있거나, 관련 분야에서 학사학위를 소지하고 있어야 합니다. 지원하시려면, hr@mayspublishing.com으로 이력서와 샘플 포트폴리오를 보내 주시기 바랍니다.

seek ~을 찾다, 구하다   currently 현재   expand ~을 확대하다, 확장하다   be permitted to부정사 ~하도록 허용되다   ideal 이상적인
candidate 후보자, 지원자   at least 최소한

Q. Mays 출판의 그래픽 디자이너에 관해 언급된 것은 무엇인가?
(A) 반드시 학사 학위를 소지하고 있어야 한다.
(B) 시간제로 원격 근무를 할 수 있다.

[문제 키워드] What / indicated / Mays Publishing's graphic designers

[해설] 지문 중반부에 5일 중 2일은 재택 근무 할 수 있다는(~ permitted to work from home two of the five days) 내용이 있으므로 이와 같은 원격 근무 혜택을 언급한 (B)가 정답이다.

[어휘] bachelor's degree 학사 학위   related 관련된   remotely 원격으로

03.

SUP Shipping – 물류 센터 직원 채용 진행 중

아이오와 주 Elgin의 Clemont Street 200에 위치한 SUP Shipping 물류 센터 내 여러 직책에서 일할 의욕적이고 활기 넘치는 지원자들을 모집합니다. 1교대는 새벽 4시부터 8시까지입니다. **물류 센터 직원들은 행선지에 따라 운전기사들의 경로를 용이하게 만들어 주기 위해 컨베이어 벨트로부터 박스를 옮겨서 배송 트럭에 정리하는 일을 하게 됩니다.** 일반적으로 들게 될 상자 무게는 최대 50파운드까지로 예상됩니다. 경쟁력 있는 급여 및 제한된 범위의 의료 보험이 제공됩니다. 직접 내방하거나 www.sup.com/openings에서 온라인으로 지원하세요.

energetic 활기찬, 의욕적인   position 직책   shift 교대 근무
facilitate 용이하게 하다   health care 건강 보험   in person 직접

Q. 물류 센터 직원의 임무는 무엇인가?
(A) 목적지에 따라 패키지 정리하기
(B) 고객들에게 패키지를 배달하기

[문제 키워드] What / duty / distribution associate

[해설] 중반부에 물류 센터 직원이 하게 될 일이 언급되어 있는데, 행선지에 따라 박스를 정리하는 일을 하게 될 것이라고(Distribution associates pull boxes from the conveyor belts and arrange them in delivery trucks based on where they are going in order to facilitate the drivers' routes) 했으므로 정답은 (A)이다.

[어휘] sort 분류하다   package 패키지, 소포   destination 목적지

04.

창고 유통 업무 책임자 구함

저희 Leeson 화장품과 함께 흥미롭고 성공적인 직장 생활을 즐겨 보시기 바랍니다. 저희는 전국에서 가장 규모가 큰 화장품 공급업체들 중의 하나이며, 현재 애틀랜타 지점의 창고 유통 업무 책임자를 필요로 하고 있습니다. 업무에는 재고 수준을 신중히 점검함으로써 반드시 상품이 정시에 배송되도록 하는 일이 포함됩니다. **지원자들은 반드시 최소 2년간의 관리자 직급 근무 경력을 지니고 있어야 합니다.** 지원서는 6월 1일까지 접수되며, 증빙 서류는 면접 단계 이후에 확인될 것입니다.

warehouse 창고   distribution 유통, 배급   supplier 공급업체
cosmetics 화장품   duty 직무   ensure 반드시 ~하도록 하다, ~을 보장하다   goods 상품   stock 재고(품)   management role 관리자 직급   application 지원(서)   accept ~을 받아들이다
references 증빙 서류

Q. 구인 광고에서 제공되지 않는 정보는 무엇인가?
(A) 면접 날짜
(B) 요구되는 경력

[문제 키워드] What / NOT provided / job advertisement

[해설] 지문 전체적으로 면접 날짜는 언급되어 있지 않으므로 (A)가 정답이다. 지문 후반부에 관리자 직급 경력이 있어야 한다고(Applicants must have at least two years' experience ~) 했으므로 (B)는 맞는 내용이다.

실전 문제

| 01.(B) | 02.(D) | 03.(C) | 04.(B) | 05.(D) | 06.(C) |
| 07.(B) | 08.(C) | 09.(B) | 10.(B) | | |

비싼

03. 접속부사

[해설] 빈칸 앞에는 물건을 상자에 담아 두라고 요청하는 말이, 빈칸 뒤에는 주변 공간을 깨끗이 치우라고 요청하는 말이 쓰여 있으므로 추가 요청 사항을 덧붙이는 흐름임을 알 수 있다. 따라서 '추가로, 게다가'라는 의미로 추가 정보를 언급할 때 사용하는 (B) In addition이 정답이다.

[어휘] regardless (of) (~에) 상관 없이   as such 그러한 이유로, 그와 같이   somehow 어떻게든, 왠지

04. 알맞은 문장 고르기

(A) 포장용 라벨은 인사부 사무실에서 받아 사용하실 수 있을 것입니다.
(B) 다음 주에 Downy 여행사 직원들을 만날 기회가 있을 것입니다.
(C) 그 이사 전문 업체는 뛰어난 서비스로 인해 여러 상을 수상한 바 있습니다.
(D) 각자 짐을 풀 수 있도록 월요일에 조금 일찍 도착하시도록 요청 드립니다.

[해설] 빈칸 다음 문장에 특정한 일을 지칭하는 That과 함께 그 일이 지연 없이 업무를 시작하게 해줄 것이라고 알리고 있으므로 이에 해당되는 것으로서 월요일에 일찍 도착해 짐을 풀도록 요청하는 내용의 (D)가 정답이다.

[어휘] receive ~을 받다   award 상   unpack (짐 등) ~을 풀다

05-08은 다음 설명을 참조하시오.

DVR 설치 방법
다시는 가장 좋아하는 프로그램을 놓치는 일이 절대 없도록 Rockwell DVR을 설치하시기 바랍니다. 05심지어 되감기 또는 빨리 넘기기를 통해 가장 좋아하시는 부분으로 넘어가실 수도 있습니다.
06구체적으로 시간과 채널을 선택하시는 것으로 시작해 보십시오.
07Rockwell DVR은 최대 500시간까지 프로그램 또는 영화를 저장할 수 있습니다. 녹화해 두신 것을 시청하시려면, '내 녹화 자료' 목록에서 선택하십시오. 08프로그램들이 실제 방송 날짜와 시간을 기준으로 시간 순으로 목록에 나타날 것입니다.
프로그램이 이미 녹화되었는지 여부를 해당 DVR이 인식하지 못할 수 있습니다. 녹화 프로그램 목록에 재실행 항목이 여러 번 나타날 수 있다는 점 명심하시기 바랍니다.

instructions 설명, 안내, 지시   set up ~을 설치하다   rewinding 되감기   fast-forwarding 빨리 넘기기   select ~을 선택하다, 고르다   view ~을 시청하다, 보다   in chronological order 시간 순으로, 연대 순으로   broadcast 방송   detect ~을 감지하다, 발견하다   keep in mind that ~라는 점을 명심하다   rerun 반복 재생, 재방송, 재실행   appear 나타나다

05. 동사 어휘

[해설] 전치사 to와 어울리는 자동사로서 by 전치사구에서 말하는 되감기와 빨리 넘기기를 통해 할 수 있는 일을 나타낼 동사가 필요하므로 '건너 뛰다'라는 의미를 나타내는 (B) skip이 정답이다.

[어휘] reset 다시 맞추다, 재설정하다   inquire 문의하다

06. 부사 자리

[해설] 전치사 by와 목적어 역할을 하는 동명사 사이에 위치한 빈칸은 동명사를 수식할 부사 자리이므로 부사인 (C) specifically가 정답이다.

[어휘] specify ~을 명시하다   specification (제품) 사양, 설명서   specific 구체적인, 명확한

07. 알맞은 문장 고르기

(A) Rockwell DVR은 최대 500시간 동안 프로그램 또는 영화를 저장할 수 있습니다.
(B) 비밀번호로 특정 프로그램을 잠금 설정하시려면 '시청 제한' 옵션을 이용하십시오.
(C) 무엇이든 녹화하시기 전에 설명서를 꼭 신중하게 읽어 보시기 바랍니다.
(D) 개인 설정에 대한 드롭다운 화면이 나타날 것입니다.

[해설] 빈칸 뒤에 녹화해 둔 것을 시청하는 방법을 설명하고 있으므로 프로그램 녹화와 관련된 특징을 언급하는 문장으로서 최대 녹화 시간을 알려주는 (A)가 정답이다.

[어휘] store ~을 저장하다, 보관하다   Parental Controls (부모의) 시청 제한   dropdown (세부 항목이 아래로 펼쳐지는 방식의) 드롭다운   personal settings 개인 설정   appear 나타나다

08. 동사의 형태

[해설] 빈칸이 속한 문장은 앞서 동사 choose와 함께 명령문으로 녹화 프로그램 목록에서 선택하라고 한 것에 따라 그 이후에 진행되는 일을 나타내야 자연스럽다. 명령문에 제시된 행위 이후에 발생되는 일을 나타낼 때는 미래 시제 동사를 사용하므로 (B) will be listed가 정답이다. (D) will have been listed는 미래 완료 시제인데, 미래완료 시제는 미래의 완료 시점을 나타내는 표현이 동반되어야 하므로 오답이다.

PART 7 광고 (2) 구인 광고

풀이 방법 해석

Carbone Trucking은 더 많은 운전사들이 필요합니다

원래 렉싱턴에 기반을 둔 Carbone Trucking은 지난 10년 동안 동해안에 있는 기업들에게 트럭을 제공한 믿을 만한 트럭 회사입니다. 이제, 그 성공과 명성을 바탕으로 캐나다와 멕시코뿐만 아니라 전국에 걸쳐 배달을 시작할 계획입니다.

그렇게 하기 위해, 더 많은 운전사들이 필요합니다. 자격 요건은 아래와 같습니다.

- 유효한 1종 운전 면허증 소지자
- 2년간 무사고 운전 경력
- 운전과 관련한 범죄 기록 없어야 함
- 여권 신청 자격이 되어야 함
- 신체적으로 정신적으로 건강해야 함

직접 또는 온라인으로 지원하세요. 운전사 직책에 고려되기 위해서는 당신이 주로 가는 병원에서 발급한 건강 증명서를 제시해야 한다는 것을 알아두세요.

연습 문제

01. (A)   02. (B)   03. (A)   04. (A)

연습 문제

01. (B) **02.** (B) **03.** (A) **04.** (B)

01.

잠시 시간 내어 Barbeque Town의 웹사이트로 가셔서 저희 온라인 설문지를 작성해 주시기 바랍니다. 제출하시자마자 15퍼센트 할인 쿠폰을 발급받게 되실 것입니다.

proceed to ~로 가다   fill out ~을 작성하다   upon -ing ~하자마자, ~한 즉시

[단서] Please take a moment to ~, Upon submitting it

[해설] 앞 문장에 명령문 구조로 요청 사항을 전달하고 있는데, 이는 미래 시점의 일에 해당되므로 그에 따라 쿠폰을 발급받는 일도 미래의 일이어야 한다. 따라서 (B) will be issued가 정답이다.

[어휘] issue ~을 발급하다

02.

친애하는 Patel 씨께

7월 7일로 예정되어 있는 경력 개발 세미나에 등록해 주셔서 감사합니다. 양식에 따르면 귀하는 여행가방을 선물로 선택하셨습니다.

sign up 가입하다   upcoming 예정된, 다가오는   according to ~에 따라

[단서] According to your form

[해설] 세미나에 등록하며 작성한 양식에서 선물을 선택했음을 알 수 있다. 따라서 과거 시제인 (B) chose가 정답이다.

03.

이 편지는 저희 Lexington 사의 수석 회계 담당자 직책에 대한 귀하의 지원서를 받았음을 확인해 드리기 위한 것입니다. 일반적으로 저희가 지원서를 처리하는 데 2주의 시간이 소요됩니다. 그 기간이 지난 후에 직원이 귀하께 연락드릴 것입니다.

application 지원(서)   accountant 회계사   process ~을 처리하다   representative 직원

[단서] takes two weeks for us to process

[해설] 앞 문장에서 지원서 처리에 2주가 걸린다고 한 것으로 보아 앞으로 2주 후에 결과와 관련해 직원이 연락할 것이라는 뜻이므로 미래 시제 동사 (A) will contact가 정답이다.

04.

수신: Samuel Dent <samueldent@aoo.com>
발신: 고객 서비스부 <cs@passionapparel.com>
날짜: 5월 11일
제목: 반품 요청

Dent 씨께

5월 9일에, 저희는 귀하께서 반품으로 저희에게 돌려 보내 주신 스웨터를 받았습니다. 배송 요금을 환불해 드리지 않는 것이 저희 매장의 정책임을 상기시켜 드리고자 합니다. 따라서 저희는 영업일로 5일 후에 귀하께서 해당 제품에 대해 지불하신 전액인 17.99달러의 금액을 귀하의 계좌로 입금해 드릴 것입니다.

policy 정책   shipping fee 배송 요금   thus 따라서, 그에 따라   credit ~에 입금하다   account 계좌, 계정   amount 금액, 액수   pay for ~에 대한 비용을 지불하다

[단서] May 11, May 9

[해설] 상단의 이메일 발송 날짜가 May 11이고, 빈칸 앞에 적힌 날짜가 May 9인 것으로 보아 과거 시점에 발생된 일을 말하는 문장임을 알 수 있으므로 과거 시제인 (B) received가 정답이다.

실전 문제

01. (B) **02.** (A) **03.** (B) **04.** (D) **05.** (B) **06.** (C)
07. (A) **08.** (B)

01-04는 다음 이메일을 참조하시오.

발신: 인사부
수신: 전 직원
날짜: 3월 9일
제목: 사무실 이전

대표이사님께서 지난주에 기자 회견을 통해 공식적으로 Downy 여행사의 인수를 발표하셨습니다. 01대표님께서는 우리가 현재 사용 중인 사무실이 새로운 직원들을 모두 수용하기에는 너무 협소하다는 점을 인정하셨습니다. 023월 14일 월요일부로 우리는 Broadway 가 481번지에 위치한 더 넓은 사무실로 이전할 예정입니다.

이사 전문 업체가 모든 사무용 장비와 가구를 새로운 사무실로 가져다줄 것입니다. 이 업체에서 3월 12일 토요일에 모든 것을 옮길 예정이므로 금요일 저녁에 퇴근하시기 전에 각자의 물품을 상자에 담아 두시기 바랍니다. 03추가로, 각자의 업무 공간 주변을 깨끗이 치우시도록 요청 드립니다. 이사 업체 직원들이 청소 서비스도 제공해야 할 경우에는 요금을 청구할 것입니다.

한 가지 더 말씀 드릴 것은 상자들이 각자의 새 책상 위에 놓여질 것이라는 점입니다. 04각자 짐을 풀 수 있도록 월요일에 조금 일찍 도착하시도록 요청 드립니다. 그렇게 하시면 어떤 지연도 없이 일일 업무를 시작할 수 있게 될 것입니다.

Yulia Franco

acquisition 인수   current 현재의   accommodate 수용하다   belongings 소지품

01. 동사의 형태

[해설] 주어 He와 that절 사이에 빈칸이 있으므로 빈칸은 문장의 동사 자리임을 알 수 있다. 따라서 (C)를 제외한 나머지 동사들 중에서 시제가 알맞은 것을 찾아야 하는데, 앞 문장에 제시된 announced와 마찬가지로 해당 과거 시점에 인정한 일을 나타내야 알맞으므로 동일한 과거 시제인 (B) admitted가 정답이다.

02. 형용사 어휘

[해설] 명사 office를 수식해 새로 이전할 사무실의 특징을 나타낼 형용사가 필요한데, 앞서 언급된 현재 사용 중인 사무실이 너무 좁다는(too small) 점에 따른 조치와 관련되어야 하므로 '넓은'을 뜻하는 (A) spacious가 정답이다.

[어휘] luminous 야광의   traditional 전통적인, 일반적인   expensive

17. 전치사 regarding

전기 작업을 위한 예정된 정전과 관련된 통지서가 지역 주민들에게 발송될 것이다.

[해설] 선택지가 다양한 전치사들로 구성되어 있으므로 전치사 어휘 문제이다. 빈칸 뒤에 위치한 명사구(a ~ work)는 통지서(notification)에 포함된 내용에 해당되므로 주제 등을 나타낼 때 '~와 관련된'이라는 의미로 쓰이는 (C) regarding이 정답이다.

[어휘] notification 통지(서)   blackout 정전   resident 주민   regarding ~와 관련된   according to ~에 따르면

18. 재귀대명사: 재귀 용법

Moss 씨는 자신이 극도의 압박감 속에서도 효과적으로 일할 수 있는 사람임을 입증해 왔다.

[해설] 선택지가 다양한 인칭대명사들로 구성되어 있으므로 문법 문제이다. 동사 has proven 뒤에 위치한 빈칸은 이 동사의 목적어 자리인데, 목적어로 쓰일 대명사가 가리키는 사람이 주어 Ms. Moss와 일치하므로 행위 주체와 대상이 동일할 때 사용하는 재귀대명사 (B) herself가 정답이다.

[어휘] be capable of -ing ~할 수 있다   effectively 효과적으로   pressure 압박(감)

19. 수동태와 능동태의 구분

IT 부서는 금요일에 새로운 소프트웨어가 모든 업무 공간에 설치될 것이라고 공지했다.

[해설] 선택지가 동사 install의 다양한 형태로 구성되어 있으므로 문법 문제이다. that절에 속한 빈칸 앞뒤로 주어와 전치사구만 있으므로 빈칸이 that절의 동사 자리인데, 빈칸 뒤에 목적어 없이 전치사구만 있으므로 수동태 동사가 필요하다. 따라서 유일한 수동태 동사인 (C) will be installed가 정답이다.

[어휘] workstation 업무 공간, 근무 자리   install ~을 설치하다

20. 형용사 어휘

가구를 조립하는 방법에 관한 상세 설명을 보시려면, 사용자 설명서를 참고하시기 바랍니다.

[해설] 선택지가 다양한 형용사들로 구성되어 있으므로 형용사 어휘 문제이다. 빈칸 뒤에 위치한 명사 instructions를 수식해 가구 조립에 관한 설명의 특성을 나타낼 형용사가 필요하므로 '상세한'을 의미하는 (C) detailed가 정답이다.

[어휘] instructions 설명, 안내, 지시   assemble ~을 조립하다   refer to ~을 참고하다   owner's manual 사용자 설명서   lasting 지속적인   challenging 어려운, 힘든   concentrated 집중된, 농축된

21. 수동태와 능동태의 구분

Ivory Academy는 모든 현 수강생들에 대한 상세 학업 기록을 보유하고 있다.

[해설] 선택지가 동사 keep의 다양한 형태로 구성되어 있으므로 문법 문제이다. 빈칸 앞뒤로 주어와 목적어 역할을 하는 명사와 전치사구만 위치해 있으므로 빈칸이 문장의 동사 자리이다. 3인칭 단수 주어(Ivory Academy)와 수 일치가 되면서 목적어(detailed academic records)를 취할 수 있는 능동태 동사의 형태인 (B) keeps가 정답이다.

[어휘] current 현재의   attendee 수강생, 참석자

22. 형용사 어휘

Adkins 자동차 대여 업체는 여름이 지속되는 동안 상당한 수요 증가를 예측하고 있다.

[해설] 선택지가 다양한 형용사들로 구성되어 있으므로 형용사 어휘 문제이다. 빈칸 뒤에 위치한 명사 increase를 수식할 형용사가 필요하므로 증가 정도를 나타낼 수 있는 것으로서 '상당한, 많은'을 의미하는 (D) considerable이 정답이다.

[어휘] predict ~을 예측하다   increase in ~의 증가   demand 수요   duration 지속 기간   flexible 유연한, 탄력적인   comprehensive 종합적인   preliminary 예비의

23. 수동태와 능동태의 구분

Hailey Brown 씨의 시집은 Lucy Steele 씨가 작업한 삽화를 포함할 것이다.

[해설] 선택지가 동사 include의 다양한 형태와 형용사로 구성되어 있으므로 문법 문제이다. 빈칸 앞뒤로 주어와 목적어, 그리고 전치사구만 위치해 있으므로 빈칸이 문장의 동사 자리인데, 목적어(illustrations)를 취해야 하므로 능동태 동사의 형태인 (A) will include가 정답이다.

[어휘] poetry collection 시집   illustration 삽화

24. 형용사 어휘

<Beltran Times Newspaper>에서 근무하는 기자들은 자신들이 취재하는 내용에 대해 까다롭지 않다.

[해설] 선택지가 다양한 형용사들로 구성되어 있으므로 형용사 어휘 문제이다. be동사 are 뒤에 위치해 보어로서 주어 Reporters의 특성을 나타낼 형용사가 필요한데, 전치사 about과 어울리는 것으로서 취재 기사에 대한 선별과 관련된 의미를 나타내는 (C) selective가 정답이다.

[어휘] selective about ~에 대해 까다로운, 선별적인   cover ~을 취재하다   noteworthy 주목할 만한   overwhelming 압도적인   prominent 두드러진, 중요한, 유명한

PART 6   앞의 내용이 단서인 동사 시제

풀이 방법 해석

발신: 빌딩 관리실
수신: 모든 주민들
제목: 주차장 유지 보수
날짜: 7월 16일

지난 몇 달 동안, 저희는 우리 건물 주차장의 열악한 주차장 상태에 관한 여러 불평을 세입자들로부터 받았습니다. Dozer 건설사가 보수 공사 프로젝트를 하기로 선정되었는데 그들의 예상 완료 시점이 다른 업체들보다 상당히 빨랐기 때문입니다.

작업은 7월 24일에서 26일까지 진행될 것이고, 이 동안 우리 건물의 주차장은 출입이 금지될 것입니다. 그러므로 차량이 있는 주민들은 도로에 주차할 곳이나 다른 주차장을 찾으셔야 할 것입니다. 관리실은 그 기간 동안의 대체 주차 비용을 상환할 것입니다. 이 날짜 동안의 주차 영수증을 소지해 주세요.

Vanessa Lohan
Oakland Tower 건물 관리자

[어휘] as of ~부터, ~부로 be informed of ~에 관해 통보받다 sales 매출, 판매(량) incentive 인센티브, 보상책 informative 유익한

07. 수동태와 능동태의 구분

Roswell 은행은 신분 도용과 계좌 해킹으로부터 고객들을 보호하기 위한 새 보안 조치를 시행해 왔다.

[해설] 선택지가 동사 implement의 다양한 형태로 구성되어 있으므로 문법 문제이다. 빈칸 앞뒤로 주어와 목적어, 그리고 to부정사만 있으므로 빈칸이 문장의 동사 자리이다. 3인칭 단수 주어(Roswell Bank)와 수 일치가 되면서 목적어(new security measures)를 취할 수 있는 능동태 동사의 형태인 (B) has implemented가 정답이다.

[어휘] measures 조치 identity theft 신분 도용 account 계좌 implement ~을 시행하다

08. 수동태와 능동태의 구분

지역 내 여러 화물 운송 업체들을 인수한 이후, Silk Road Trucking 사는 자사의 서비스 구역을 확대할 예정이다.

[해설] 선택지가 동사 expand의 다양한 형태로 구성되어 있으므로 문법 문제이다. 빈칸 앞뒤에 주어와 목적어 역할을 하는 명사만 있으므로 빈칸이 문장의 동사 자리이며, 목적어(its service area)를 취하려면 능동태 동사가 필요하므로 (C) will be expanding이 정답이다.

[어휘] following ~ 후에 acquisition 인수, 매입 regional 지역의 trucking business 화물 운송 업체 expand ~을 확대하다, 확장하다

09. 수동태와 능동태의 구분

아시아의 여러 국가에 도입된 BlasTalk 소셜 네트워크 앱은 거의 1백만 명에 달하는 사용자들을 끌어 들였다.

[해설] 선택지가 동사 introduce의 다양한 형태로 구성되어 있으므로 문법 문제이다. 빈칸은 선행사 social networking app을 수식하는 that절의 동사 자리이며, 빈칸 뒤에 목적어 없이 전치사구만 있으므로 수동태 동사가 필요하다. 따라서 유일한 수동태 동사인 (C) was introduced가 정답이다.

[어휘] attract ~을 끌어 들이다 nearly 거의 introduce ~을 도입하다, 소개하다

10. 형용사 어휘

벼룩 시장에서 가판대 텐트의 윗부분을 덮는 데 필요한 내구성이 뛰어난 소재가 선택되어야 한다.

[해설] 선택지가 다양한 형용사들로 구성되어 있으므로 형용사 어휘 문제이다. '소재, 재료' 등을 의미하는 사물 명사 material을 수식해 그 특성을 나타낼 형용사가 필요한데, 가판대 텐트에 사용되는 소재여야 하므로 '내구성이 좋은'을 뜻하는 (B) durable이 정답이다. (C) eager와 (D) decisive는 사람 명사에 대해 사용한다.

[어휘] cover ~을 덮다 stall 가판대 flea market 벼룩 시장 cautious 신중한, 조심스러운 eager 열렬한, 간절히 바라는 decisive 결단력 있는, 결정적인

11. 수동태와 능동태의 구분

Hartford 사는 'Hartford 사: 직무 안내서'에서 직원들의 직무를 설명하고 있다.

[해설] 선택지가 동사 describe의 다양한 형태로 구성되어 있으므로 문법 문제이다. 빈칸 앞뒤로 주어와 목적어, 그리고 전치사구만 위치하고 있으므로 빈칸이 문장의 동사 자리인데, 목적어(employee responsibilities)를 취해야 하므로 능동태 동사인 (B) describes가 정답이다.

[어휘] responsibility 직무, 책무

12. 형용사 어휘

제품과 관련된 모든 공식적인 언급은 적절한 플랫폼에서 이뤄져야 한다.

[해설] 선택지가 다양한 형용사들로 구성되어 있으므로 형용사 어휘 문제이다. 빈칸 뒤에 위치한 platforms를 수식해 제품과 관련된 공식적인 언급이 이뤄지는 플랫폼의 특성을 나타내야 하므로 '적절한'을 의미하는 (B) appropriate이 정답이다.

[어휘] formal 공식적인 statement 언급, 진술, 성명(서) platform 플랫폼(사용 기반이 되는 시스템) lucrative 수익성이 좋은 impermissible 용인할 수 없는 exceptional 우수한, 특출한

13. 수동태와 능동태의 구분

Maxwell 제조사의 이사회는 생산비를 줄이기 위해 해외로 자사의 공장을 이전하는 것을 고려하고 있다.

[해설] 선택지가 동사 consider의 다양한 형태와 명사로 구성되어 있으므로 문법 문제이다. be동사 are과 함께 쓰일 수 있으면서 동명사 moving을 목적어로 취해야 하므로 능동태 현재 진행 시제를 구성하는 현재분사 (B) considering이 정답이다.

[어휘] board members 이사회 consider -ing ~하는 것을 고려하다 abroad 해외로 reduce ~을 줄이다 production costs 생산비 consideration 고려

14. 동사의 형태

영업부장은 회사가 수익에 대해 신기록을 세웠다고 공지했다.

[해설] 선택지가 동사 announce의 다양한 형태로 구성되어 있으므로 문법 문제이다. 빈칸 앞으로 주어와 that절만 위치해 있으므로 빈칸이 문장의 동사 자리이다. 3인칭 단수 주어(sales manager)와 수 일치에 상관 없이 쓰일 수 있으면서 목적어(that절)를 취할 수 있는 능동태 동사의 형태인 (C) announced가 정답이다.

[어휘] set a new record 신기록을 세우다 profit 수익

15. 동사의 형태

캐나다로 사업을 확장하기 전에, Tofu Table은 오직 채식 요리들만 제공했다.

[해설] 선택지가 동사 offer의 다양한 형태로 구성되어 있으므로 문법 문제이다. 주절에 속한 빈칸 앞뒤로 주어와 목적어만 쓰여 있으므로 빈칸이 문장의 동사 자리이다. 3인칭 단수 주어(Tofu Table)와 수 일치에 상관 없이 쓰일 수 있으면서 목적어(vegetarian dishes)를 취할 수 있는 능동태 동사의 형태인 (C) offered가 정답이다.

[어휘] expand into ~로 사업을 확장하다 offer ~을 제공하다

16. 1형식 동사

서비스 요금은 데이터 사용량 및 앱 내에서의 구매를 바탕으로 달마다 다를 수 있습니다.

[해설] 선택지가 다양한 동사들로 구성되어 있으므로 동사 어휘 문제이다. 빈칸 뒤에 목적어 없이 전치사구만 위치해 있으므로 자동사가 필요하며, 'from A to B' 구조의 전치사구와 어울려야 하므로 (A) vary가 정답이다.

[어휘] charge 청구 요금 based on ~을 바탕으로 purchase 구매(품) vary 다르다, 다양하다 form 형성되다, ~을 형성하다 supply ~을 공급하다 present ~을 제시하다, 발표하다

03.

1. 선택지 보고 문법/어휘 문제 파악하기 ☑문법 문제 □어휘 문제
2. 빈칸 분석하기 빈칸 앞에 있는 것 ☑주어 □동사
   - → 빈칸은 ☑동사 □목적어 자리이다.
   - → 빈칸 뒤에 목적어가 □있으므로 ☑없으므로 □능동태 동사
     ☑수동태 동사 자리이다.
3. 정답 선택하기 정답 (A)

당신의 은행 로그인 아이디와 비밀번호는 항상 안전하게 유지되어야 합니다.

04.

1. 선택지 보고 문법/어휘 문제 파악하기 □문법 문제 ☑어휘 문제
2. 빈칸 분석하기 빈칸 뒤의 명사 (schedule)
   - → 의미 (일정)
   - → 이 명사의 의미를 꾸며주면서 함께 쓰일 수 있는 형용사가 정답이다.
3. 정답 선택하기 정답 (C)

저는 다가오는 가을 축제의 임시 일정을 첨부했습니다.

05.

1. 선택지 보고 문법/어휘 문제 파악하기 ☑문법 문제 □어휘 문제
2. 빈칸 분석하기 빈칸 앞에 있는 것 ☑주어 □동사
   - → 빈칸은 ☑동사 □목적어 자리이다.
   - → 빈칸 뒤에 목적어와 보어가 나란히 나오지 않았으므로 □능동태 동사 ☑수동태 동사 자리이다.
3. 정답 선택하기 정답 (D)

Kelly Marx는 Houston Auto에서 올해의 영업사원으로 선정되었다.

06.

1. 선택지 보고 문법/어휘 문제 파악하기 ☑문법 문제 □어휘 문제
2. 빈칸 분석하기 빈칸 앞에 있는 것 ☑주어 □동사
   - → 빈칸은 ☑동사 □목적어 자리이다.
   - → 빈칸 뒤에 목적어가 □있으므로 ☑없으므로 □능동태 동사
     ☑수동태 동사 자리이다.
3. 정답 선택하기 정답 (B)

설문 조사 결과에 따르면 많은 고객들이 당사의 보증 수리 연장 프로그램에 관심이 있다.

실전 문제

01.(B)	02.(C)	03.(D)	04.(A)	05.(C)	06.(A)
07.(B)	08.(C)	09.(C)	10.(B)	11.(B)	12.(B)
13.(B)	14.(C)	15.(C)	16.(A)	17.(C)	18.(B)
19.(C)	20.(C)	21.(B)	22.(D)	23.(A)	24.(C)

01. 수동태와 능동태의 구분

Joyce 씨는 소개와 환영 연설로 교육 시간을 시작할 것이다.

[해설] 선택지가 동사 start의 다양한 형태로 구성되어 있으므로 문법 문제이다. 빈칸 앞뒤로 주어와 목적어에 해당되는 명사와 전치사구만 위치해 있으므로 빈칸이 문장의 동사 자리이며, the training session를 목적어로 취할 능동태 동사가 필요하므로 (B) will start가 정답이다.

[어휘] training session 교육 시간 introduction 소개 welcoming speech 환영 연설

02. 수동태의 형태

계약서의 모든 조항은 구체적으로 합의되어야 하며, 그래야 향후에 논쟁을 피할 수 있다.

[해설] 선택지가 동사 settle의 다양한 형태와 명사로 구성되어 있으므로 문법 문제이다. 빈칸 앞에 위치한 be동사와 결합 가능하면서 부사 specifically의 수식을 받을 수 있는 것은 분사인데, 빈칸 뒤에 목적어가 없으므로 수동태를 구성하는 과거분사 (C) settled가 정답이다.

[어휘] terms 조항, 조건 contract 계약(서) specifically 구체적으로 dispute 논쟁, 분쟁 settle ~을 합의하다, 해결하다 settlement 합의, 해결

03. 형용사 어휘

고객 설문 조사를 통해 얻은 새로운 결과물이 새 마케팅 캠페인에 적용 가능하다.

[해설] 선택지가 다양한 형용사들로 구성되어 있으므로 형용사 어휘 문제이다. be동사 are 뒤에 위치해 보어로서 주어 new findings의 특성을 나타낼 형용사가 필요한데, 바로 뒤에 위치한 'to+대상' 전치사구와 어울려야 하므로 '~에 적용 가능한'을 뜻하는 (D) applicable이 정답이다.

[어휘] findings 결과물 survey 설문 조사(지) tentative 잠정적인 extensive 폭넓은 urgent 긴급한 applicable 적용 가능한

04. 수동태와 능동태의 구분

지난해 통과된 법에 따라 모든 건설 현장은 엄격한 환경 지침에 의해 규제를 받고 있다.

[해설] 선택지가 동사 regulate의 다양한 형태로 구성되어 있으므로 문법 문제이다. 주절에 속한 빈칸 앞뒤로 주어와 전치사구만 있으므로 빈칸에는 주절의 동사가 필요하다. 빈칸 뒤에 목적어가 없으므로 유일한 수동태 동사인 (A) have been regulated가 정답이다.

[어휘] pass 통과하다 construction 건설 strict 엄격한 guideline 지침 regulate ~을 규제하다

05. 3형식 동사의 수동태

비록 기상학자들이 거대 눈보라를 예보하고 있기는 하지만, Schenectady 공립 학교의 수업은 취소되지 않았다.

[해설] 선택지가 동사 predict의 다양한 형태와 명사로 구성되어 있으므로 문법 문제이다. Even though절에 속한 빈칸 앞뒤로 주어와 목적어 역할을 하는 명사들만 있으므로 빈칸이 Even though절의 동사 자리이다. 빈칸 뒤에 목적어 a massive snowstorm이 있으므로 능동태 동사 (C) predict가 정답이다.

[어휘] meteorologist 기상학자 massive 거대한, 막대한 predictable 예측 할 수 있는 predict ~을 예보하다, 예측하다 prediction 예보, 예측

06. 4형식 동사의 수동태

어제부터, 모든 직원들이 새로운 영업 인센티브 프로그램에 관해 통보받아 알고 있다.

[해설] 선택지가 동사 inform의 다양한 형태와 형용사로 구성되어 있으므로 문법 문제이다. 빈칸 앞뒤에 주어와 전치사구만 있으므로 빈칸에 문장의 동사가 필요하다. 목적어 없이 of 전치사구가 바로 이어지려면 inform이 수동태로 쓰여야 하므로 유일한 수동태 동사의 형태인 (A) have been informed가 정답이다.

한 기술이 탑재되어 [10]매번 넣으시는 세탁물의 무게를 감지할 수 있습니다. —[3]—. [09(A)]또한 타이머 기능이 있어 세탁물을 넣으신 후 최대 12시간까지 미리 작동 설정을 하실 수 있습니다.

Najera-9 세탁기에는 모든 부품과 인력 작업에 대해 10년 기간의 품질 보증 서비스가 포함되어 있습니다. —[4]—. www.siebertapp.com을 통해, 또는 저희 지점들 중 한 곳에 들르셔서 오늘 주문하시기 바랍니다.

home appliances 가전 기기 latest 최신의 quality 품질 maintain ~을 유지하다 cubic feet 입방피트 stabilizing technology 안정화 기술 ensure that ~임을 보장하다, ~임을 확실히 해두다 hardly 거의 ~ 않다 disturb ~을 방해하다 unlike ~와 달리 conventional 종래의, 일반적인, 전통적인 detect ~을 감지하다 weight 무게 load 적재량; ~을 넣다, 싣다 up to 최대 ~까지 in advance 미리, 사전에

08. 세부사항 문제

Siebert 가전제품은 얼마나 오랫동안 영업을 해왔는가?
(A) 2년
(B) 5년
(C) 10년
(D) 20년

[해설] 첫 단락의 마지막 부분에, 20년 전에 문을 열었다는(since opening two decades ago) 말이 있으므로 20년 동안 영업을 해온 업체임을 알 수 있다. 따라서 (D)가 정답이다.

paraphrasing two decades 20년 → Twenty years 20년

[어휘] in business 영업 중인, 운영 중인

09. Not True 문제

Najera-9 세탁기의 특징으로 언급되지 않은 것은 무엇인가?
(A) 프로그램할 수 있는 타이머
(B) 큰 용량
(C) 에너지 효율성
(D) 조용한 작동

[해설] 기능상의 특징들이 언급된 두 번째 단락에, 시작 부분의 5.5 cubic feet of space, much more than most other brands를 통해 '큰 용량'을 언급한 (B)를, 그 뒤에 이어지는 it hardly makes a sound while in use에서 '조용한 작동 상태'를 뜻하는 (D)를, 그리고 마지막 문장인 It also has a timer that allows you to load the machine and then set it to start up to twelve hours in advance에서 '프로그래밍 가능한 타이머'를 언급한 (A)를 확인할 수 있다. 하지만 에너지 효율과 관련된 정보는 제시된 바가 없으므로 (C)가 정답이다.

paraphrasing hardly makes a sound while in use 사용 중에 소리가 거의 나지 않는다 → quiet operation 조용한 작동

[어휘] feature 특징, 기능 programmable 프로그램할 수 있는 capacity 용량, 수용량 efficiency 효율(성) operation 작동, 가동

10. 문장 삽입 문제

[1], [2], [3] 그리고 [4]로 표시된 위치들 중에서, 다음 문장이 들어가기에 가장 적절한 곳은 어디인가?

"이 센서 시스템 덕분에, 최대 40퍼센트까지 더 적은 물이 소비됩니다."

(A) [1]
(B) [2]
(C) [3]
(D) [4]

[해설] 제시된 문장은 특정 센서 시스템을 가리키는 this sensor system과 함께 그 시스템으로 인해 물을 더 적게 소비한다는 장점을 알리고 있다. 따라서 무게를 감지하는 기술이 들어 있다고 언급한 문장 다음에 위치한 [3]에 들어가 그 기술의 장점을 소개하는 흐름이 되어야 적절하므로 (C)가 정답이다.

[어휘] thanks to ~ 덕분에, ~로 인해

paraphrasing 정답 1. (b)　2. (e)　3. (d)　4. (c)　5. (a)

DAY 10

PART 5 문법 | 능동태와 수동태

확인 문제 해석

❶ 신청서는 7월 31일까지 제출되어야 한다.
❷ 이 종일 입장권이 있다면 원하는 모든 세미나에 참여하실 수 있습니다.
❸ 그 소프트웨어는 내일 아침 업그레이드될 것이다.
❹ Garfield 씨는 그들에게 파이를 보냈다.
❺ Bae 씨는 주간 회의에 참석할 것을 요청받았다.
❻ Donovan 씨는 촉박한 마감 시한에 대해 우려하고 있다.
❼ 이 사무실에는 실내 온도 조절기가 갖춰져 있다.

연습 문제

01.(B)　02.(C)　03.(A)　04.(C)　05.(D)　06.(B)

01.

1. 선택지 보고 문법/어휘 문제 파악하기 ☑ 문법 문제 ☐ 어휘 문제
2. 빈칸 분석하기 빈칸 앞에 있는 것 ☑ 주어 ☐ 동사
  → 빈칸은 ☑ 동사 ☐ 목적어 자리이다.
  → 빈칸 뒤에 목적어가 ☐ 있으므로 ☑ 없으므로 ☐ 능동태 동사 ☑ 수동태 동사 자리이다.
3. 정답 선택하기 정답 (B)

신선한 해산물을 실은 수송품이 매일 아침 Captain's Cabin으로 배달된다.

02.

1. 선택지 보고 문법/어휘 문제 파악하기 ☑ 문법 문제 ☐ 어휘 문제
2. 빈칸 분석하기 빈칸 앞에 있는 것 ☑ 주어 ☐ 동사
  → 빈칸은 ☑ 동사 ☐ 목적어 자리이다.
  → 빈칸 뒤에 목적어가 ☐ 있으므로 ☑ 없으므로 ☐ 능동태 동사 ☑ 수동태 동사 자리이다.
3. 정답 선택하기 정답 (C)

모든 상자들은 배가 Cheasapeake 만에 도착하자마자 점검되었다.

04. True 문제

Flowlex 매트에 관해 사실인 것은 무엇인가?
(A) 별도의 휴대용 용기가 딸려 온다.
(B) 다양한 사이즈로 구매 가능하다.
(C) 다수의 색상으로 디자인되어 있다.
(D) 요가 자세에 관한 동영상과 함께 판매된다.

[해설] 두 번째 단락 다섯 번째 항목에, 부대용품으로 편리하게 휴대할 수 있도록 끈이 달린 그물망 형태의 가방이 제공된다고(Mesh bag with strap for easy transport) 쓰여 있으므로 별도의 휴대용 용기가 딸려 있다고 한 (A)가 정답이다.

paraphrasing Mesh bag with strap for easy transport 편리한 휴대를 위한 끈이 달린 그물망 형태의 가방 → separate carrying container 별도의 휴대용 용기

[어휘] come with ~가 딸려 있다, 포함되어 있다 separate 별도의, 분리된 carrying 휴대용의

paraphrasing 정답 1. (a) 2. (e) 3. (d) 4. (c) 5. (b)

05-07은 다음 웹사이트 광고를 참조하시오.

Cuevas Solutions

주택은 주요 투자 항목이지만, 많은 사람들은 바깥 공간은 소홀히 여긴 채 주택 실내에만 중점을 둡니다. 05저희 Cuevas Solutions는 여러분의 뜰을 매력적이고 편리하게 이용하실 수 있는 공간으로 탈바꿈시키는 데 도움을 드릴 수 있습니다.

저희 모든 잠재 고객들께 처음 1회의 상담 서비스를 무료로 제공해 드리고 있습니다. 상담 중에, 저희 정원 디자인 전문가들 중 한 명이 다음과 같은 일을 할 것입니다.

- 06(C)선호하시는 사양에 관해 이야기 나누고, 상세 정보를 메모합니다
- 주택 내 일조 상태에 맞게 잘 자랄 수 있는 식물을 제안합니다
- 06(B)귀하의 뜰과 이용 가능한 공간의 면적을 측정합니다
- 06(D)예상되는 작업 비용에 대한 견적서를 제공합니다

저희에게 555-0671로 전화 주셔서 예약 일정을 잡으시기 바랍니다. 저희는 현재 체스터필드에 본사를 두고 있지만, 07오크몬에 있는 지사가 운영을 시작하는 대로 그곳에서도 곧 직원들을 보내 드릴 예정입니다.

investment 투자 neglect ~을 소홀히 하다 transform A into B A를 B로 탈바꿈시키다, 변모시키다 yard 마당, 뜰 inviting 매력적인 accessible 쉽게 이용 가능한 initial 처음의, 최초의 prospective 잠재적인, 유망한 favored 선호하는 lighting conditions 일조 상태 measure ~을 측정하다 dimensions 면적, 규격 quote 견적(서) set up ~의 일정을 정하다 be based in ~에 본거지를 두다 in operation 운영 중인, 영업 중인

05. 주제 문제

광고는 무엇을 홍보하고 있는가?
(A) 부동산 서비스
(B) 실내 디자인 업체
(C) 조경 서비스
(D) 판매용 원예 도구

[해설] 업체의 특성이 제시된 첫 단락에, 늘 매력적이고 편리하게 이용할 수 있는 공간으로 탈바꿈시키는 데 도움을 줄 수 있다는(~ can help you transform your yard into an inviting and accessible space) 말이 있는데 이는 조경 서비스를 제공한다는 뜻이므로 (C)가 정답이다.

paraphrasing transform your yard 뜰을 탈바꿈시키다 → Landscaping services 조경 서비스

[어휘] real estate 부동산 firm 업체, 회사 landscaping 조경 (작업) gardening 원예 tool 도구, 공구 for sale 판매용의

06. Not True 문제

맨 처음 상담에 포함되어 있지 않은 것은 무엇인가?
(A) 과거 작업의 사진 보여 주기
(B) 치수 측정하기
(C) 고객 선호 사항 기록하기
(D) 가격 견적서 제공하기

[해설] 맨 처음 상담 시 제공되는 서비스가 언급된 두 번째 단락에, 첫 항목인 Speak with you about your favored options, taking notes on the details에서 '선호 사항에 대한 기록'을 의미하는 (C)를, 세 번째 항목의 Measure the dimensions of your yard에서 '치수 측정 작업'을 뜻하는 (B)를, 그리고 마지막 항목의 Give you a quote 부분에서 '견적서 제공'을 의미하는 (D)를 확인할 수 있다. 하지만 과거에 했던 작업의 사진을 볼 수 있다는 말은 없으므로 (A)가 정답이다.

[어휘] take measurements 치수를 측정하다 preference 선호(하는 것) pricing 가격 (책정) estimate 견적(서)

07. 추론 문제

Cuevas Solutions에 관해 암시된 것은 무엇인가?
(A) 소유주가 모든 문의 사항을 처리한다.
(B) 환불 보장 서비스를 제공한다.
(C) 신규 지점을 열 계획이다.
(D) 동종 업계에서 최고 수준의 회사이다.

[해설] 마지막 단락에 오크몬에 있는 지사가 운영을 시작하는 대로 그곳에서도 곧 직원들을 보낼 것이라고(we will soon be sending crews from a branch in Oakmont once it is in operation) 알리고 있는데, 이는 신규 지사가 문을 연다는 뜻이므로 (C)가 정답이다.

[어휘] handle ~을 처리하다, 다루다 money-back guarantee 환불 보장 top-rated 최고 수준의, 최고 등급의 of its kind 동종 분야에서

paraphrasing 정답 1. (e) 2. (c) 3. (a) 4. (d) 5. (b)

08-10은 다음 광고를 참조하시오.

Siebert 가전제품의 새 세탁기를 놓치지 마십시오!

지난 5년 동안, 저희 Siebert 가전제품은 가전 기기 분야에서 최고의 판매량을 보여 온 브랜드였으며, 저희 회사의 최신 제품인 Najera-9 세탁기를 소개해 드리게 되어 기쁘게 생각합니다. —[1]—. 이 제품은 여러분께서 저희 상품에게 기대해 오셨던 것과 동일한 최고 수준의 품질을 지니고 있으며, 이는 08저희가 20년 전에 문을 연 이후로 계속 유지해 온 것입니다.

Najera-9 세탁기는 09(B)5.5입방피트의 공간을 제공하는데, 이는 대부분의 다른 브랜드보다 훨씬 더 넓습니다. —[2]—. 이 제품의 안정화 기술이 09(D)사용 중에 거의 소음이 나지 않도록 보장해 드리며, 이는 여러분께서 다른 사람들을 방해하지 않고도 밤늦게 세탁을 하실 수 있음을 의미합니다. 종래의 세탁기들과는 달리, Najera-9 세탁기에는 특별

DAY 09 79

Q. Bluebell Cleaners에 관해 사실인 것은 무엇인가?
(A) 판매용 청소 제품을 제공한다.
(B) 어떤 규모의 프로젝트든 처리할 수 있다.

[문제 키워드] What / true / Bluebell Cleaners

[해설] about 뒤의 키워드 Bluebell Cleaners가 지문의 전체적인 소재이므로 지문 전반에서 단서를 파악해 각 선택지와 비교해야 한다. 지문 초반부에 작업 규모에 구애받지 않는다는(No job is too big or too small) 말이 있으므로 (B)가 정답이다.

[어휘] handle ~을 처리하다

실전 문제

| 01.(A) | 02.(B) | 03.(C) | 04.(A) | 05.(C) | 06.(A) |
| 07.(C) | 08.(D) | 09.(C) | 10.(C) | | |

01-02는 다음 광고를 참조하시오.

선물을 고르기 어려우신가요? SmartShop 카드가 완벽한 해결책입니다! 저희 기프트 카드는 전국 각지에 위치한 수백 곳의 인기 소매 판매점에서 사용 가능하며, 10달러에서 500달러에 이르는 값어치를 지닌 카드를 구입하실 수 있습니다. 여러분께서는 또한, 대부분의 다른 기프트 카드들과는 달리, ⁰¹카드의 잔액에 만료일이 없다는 사실을 아주 마음에 들어 하실 것입니다. SmartShop 카드를 이용하시면, 여러분의 친구와 가족이 마음에 들어 하는 매장에서 직접 즐겁게 쇼핑하실 수 있습니다. ⁰²저희 웹사이트 www.smartshopcard.net을 방문하셔서 오늘 여러분의 카드를 구입해 보십시오. 그곳에서, 다양한 특별 행사에 어울리는 디자인 중에서 하나를 선택하실 수도 있습니다.

retail store 소매 판매점   across ~ 전역에서   purchase ~을 구입하다   value 값어치, 가치   range from A to B A에서 B의 범위에 이르다   the fact that ~라는 사실   unlike ~와 달리   expiration date 만료일   balance 잔액, 잔고   in person 직접 (가서)   order ~을 주문하다   among ~ 중에서, 사이에서   suitable for ~에 어울리는, 적합한   a wide range of 다양한   occasion 행사, 때, 경우

01. 세부사항 문제

SmartShop 카드에 대해 무엇이 언급되어 있는가?
(A) 잔액이 만료되지 않는다.
(B) 분실했을 경우에 쉽게 교체할 수 있다.
(C) 온라인에서 사용될 수 있다.
(D) 여러 국가에서 유효하다.

[해설] 지문 중반부에 카드의 잔액에 만료일이 없다고(there is no expiration date for the balance on the card) 언급되어 있으므로 이에 해당되는 (A)가 정답이다.

paraphrasing   no expiration date 만료일이 없음 → does not expire 만료되지 않는다

[어휘] credit 입금액, 잔액   expire 만료되다, 만기가 되다   replace ~을 교체하다, 대체하다   valid 유효한   several 여럿의, 몇몇의

02. 세부사항 문제

광고에 따르면, 고객들은 웹사이트에서 무엇을 할 수 있는가?
(A) 선물 추천 받기
(B) 카드 디자인 선택하기
(C) 선물 포장 요청하기
(D) 매장 목록 둘러 보기

[해설] Web site가 언급되는 후반부에, 사이트에서 다양한 특별 행사에 어울리는 디자인 중에서 하나를 선택할 수도 있다고(There you can also choose among designs suitable for a wide range of special occasions) 알리는 내용이 있으므로 이를 언급한 (B)가 정답이다.

paraphrasing   choose among designs 디자인 중에서 선택하다 → Select a card design 카드 디자인 선택하기

[어휘] wrapping 포장   browse ~을 둘러보다, 훑어보다

paraphrasing 정답   1. (e)   2. (c)   3. (d)   4. (a)   5. (b)

03-04는 다음 광고를 참조하시오.

Lavender 사에서 **Flowlex 요가 매트**를 소개해 드립니다.
여러분의 요가 실력을 한 단계 끌어 올려 보세요!
74.99달러

- 규격: 길이 75인치×폭 27인치, 요가 연습에 필요한 더 넓은 공간을 제공해 드립니다
- 두께: 0.25인치
- 재질: ⁰³자연 분해성 나노 고무 재질이 표면에 습기가 흡수되지 않도록 해 드립니다
- 자세 관련 표시: 매번 완벽한 자세를 잡을 수 있도록 도와 드리는 길잡이
- ⁰⁴부대용품: 편리한 휴대를 위해 끈이 달린 그물망 형태의 가방
- 환경 보호 의무: 오직 냄새 없는 무독성 재질만 사용, 완전히 재활용 가능한 포장재

dimensions 규격   thickness 두께   material 재질, 재료, 자재   biodegradable 자연 분해성의   nano-elastic 나노 고무의   draw A away from B A를 B에서 멀리 떨어뜨리다   outer layer 표면, 표층   pose 자세   guidance 길잡이, 안내   alignment 조정, 정렬, 가지런함   mesh 그물망   strap 멜빵, 끈   transport 옮김, 이송   environmental responsibility 환경 보호 의무   exclusive 유일한, 독점적인, 전용의   non-toxic 무독성의   odor-free 냄새 없는   fully 완전히, 전적으로

03. 세부사항 문제

Flowlex 매트의 나노 고무 기능이 하는 역할은 무엇인가?
(A) 매트가 동그랗게 말리는 것을 방지해 준다.
(B) 매트의 온도를 조절해 준다.
(C) 매트의 표면을 건조한 상태로 유지해 준다.
(D) 기분 좋은 향이 나온다.

[해설] 나노 고무가 언급된 두 번째 단락 세 번째 항목에, 자연 분해성 나노 고무 재질이 표면에 습기가 흡수되지 않도록 해 준다는(Biodegradable nano-elastic material draws moisture away from the outer layer) 특징이 설명되어 있으므로 표면의 건조함 유지를 언급한 (C)가 정답이다.

paraphrasing   draws moisture away from the outer layer 표면에 습기가 흡수되지 않도록 하다 → keeps the mat's surface dry 매트의 표면을 건조한 상태로 유지하다

[어휘] feature 기능, 특징   prevent A from -ing A가 ~하는 것을 방지하다   curl up 동그랗게 말리다   regulate ~을 조절하다   temperature 온도   surface 표면   release ~을 내보내다, 방출하다   pleasant 기분 좋게 하는   scent 향

연락처 정보: 555-7623의 Jessica로 연락주세요. 요청 시 톱의 사진을 올려 드립니다.

연습 문제

01. (A)   02. (A)   03. (A)   04. (B)

01.

O'Connell Paints 직원 감사 행사

직원들께 모든 제품에 대해 추가 할인을 제공합니다!
하루만 제공됩니다 (수요일, 11월 5일)

다음 특별 할인 혜택을 누리세요:
페인트 롤러 60% 할인
옥외 페인트 55% 할인
페인트 브러시 50% 할인
스텐실 도장 45% 할인

저희 매장은 행사일에는 직원 분들을 대상으로만 영업합니다. 다음 날에는 다시 정상 운영될 예정입니다.

Q. O'Connell Paints는 언제 다시 일반인에게 오픈될 것인가?
(A) 11월 6일
(B) 11월 5일

[문제 키워드] When / reopen to the public

[해설] 키워드인 reopen to the public이 제시되는 부분에서 단서를 찾아야 한다. 지문 마지막 부분에 행사일에는 직원들을 대상으로만 영업하고, 다음 날에 정상 운영으로 돌아간다고(We will return to normal operations on the following day.) 언급한다. 지문 앞부분에서 행사일이 11월 5일임을 확인할 수 있으므로 행사 다음 날인 (A) 11월 6일이 정답이다.

[어휘] appreciation 감사   extra 추가의, 여분의   outdoor 야외의
operation 영업, 운영

02.

Bromley 요리 학교

지난 20년 동안, 저희 Bromley 요리 학교는 장차 요리사가 되기를 원하시는 분들을 위해 최고 수준의 요리 수업을 제공해 왔습니다. 저희가 제공해 드리는 것을 놓치지 마시기 바랍니다.
· 경험 많은 강사들이 가르치는 소규모 수업
· 전 세계의 많은 음식을 요리해 볼 수 있는 기회
· 직장인 수강생들을 수용하기 위한 유연한 수업 일정

여러 레스토랑과 출장 요리 전문 업체들과의 폭넓은 교류 관계 덕분에, 저희가 보유한 취업 알선 지원 프로그램은 전국 최고 중의 하나입니다. 오늘 555-4416번으로 저희에게 전화 주십시오.

culinary 요리의   institute (교육) 기관   prospective 장차 ~가 되려는   instructor 강사   opportunity to부정사 ~할 수 있는 기회
flexible 유연한, 탄력적인   accommodate ~을 수용하다   vast 폭넓은, 광범위한   catering 출장 요리(업)   job placement 취업 알선
assistance 지원, 도움

Q. Bromley 요리 학교에 관해 언급된 것은 무엇인가?
(A) 식당들과 전문적인 관계를 유지하고 있다.
(B) 소속 강사들이 여러 다른 국가 출신이다.

[문제 키워드] What / indicated / Bromley Culinary Institute

[해설] about 뒤의 키워드 Bromley Culinary Institute가 지문의 전체적인 소재이므로 지문 전반에서 단서를 파악해 각 선택지와 비교해야 한다. 마지막 단락에 여러 레스토랑 및 출장 요리 업체들과 폭넓게 교류한다는(~ our vast network of restaurants and catering companies ~) 말이 있으므로 (A)가 정답이다.

[어휘] dining establishment 식당

03.

Bee Healthy Wraps
6개 들이 한 팩: 24.99달러

특징
· 마치 비닐 포장 랩처럼 용기에 들어 있는 음식물을 밀봉할 수 있습니다.
· 100% 밀랍으로 만들어져 있어, 무독성 제품입니다.
· 방수 기능이 있으며, **최대 10회까지 사용할 수 있습니다.**
· 냉장실 또는 냉동실에 넣어도 밀착성을 잃지 않습니다.
· 완전히 자연 분해성이며, 심지어 음식물 쓰레기와 함께 처리해도 됩니다.

각각의 Bee Healthy Wraps 팩에는 여섯 가지 서로 다른 화려한 패턴으로 된 6개의 30cm×30cm 랩이 들어 있습니다. 여러분의 주방에서 비닐 쓰레기를 내보내시기 바랍니다! 오늘 www.beehealthywraps.com에서 주문하십시오.

feature 특징   **beeswax** 밀랍   **nontoxic** 무독성의
water resistant 방수의   **grip** 꽉 붙잡음, 움켜쥠   **refrigerator** 냉장고   **freezer** 냉동고   **fully** 완전히, 전적으로
biodegradable 자연 분해성의   **be disposed of** 처리되다, 처분되다

Q. 제품의 무슨 이점이 언급되고 있는가?
(A) 재사용될 수 있다.
(B) 경량 제품이다.

[문제 키워드] What benefit / mentioned

[해설] 키워드 benefit이 지문 전체에 언급되므로 지문 전반에서 단서를 파악해 각 선택지와 비교해야 한다. 특징의 세 번째 항목에 최대 10회까지 사용될 수 있다는(able to be used up to ten times) 말이 있는데, 이는 재사용 가능성을 나타내는 것이므로 (A)가 정답이다.

[어휘] benefit 이점, 혜택   lightweight 경량의

04.

Bluebell Cleaners가 여러분의 집을 빛나게 해 드리겠습니다!
555-0336 ◆ www.bluebellcleaners.com

저희는 여러분의 집이 최고의 모습을 찾도록 도와 드릴 준비가 되어 있는 경험 많은 전문 청소팀을 보유하고 있습니다. **작업 규모에 구애받지 않습니다!** 저희가 자체 장비와 청소용 제품을 공급할 것입니다. 여러분께서는 친절한 저희 직원들에게 정확히 무엇이 필요한지만 말씀해 주시면 됩니다. 저희는 월요일부터 토요일까지, 심지어 촉박하게 연락 주셔도 이용 가능합니다. 오늘 전화하셔서 견적을 받아 보시거나 예약을 하시기 바랍니다.

crew (함께 작업하는) 팀, 조   supply ~을 공급하다   one's own 자체의, 고유의   equipment 장비   exactly 정확히   on short notice 급한 연락에도   estimate 견적(서)

01. 동사 어휘

[해설] space를 목적어로 취해 공간 활용과 관련된 일을 나타낼 동사가 필요한 데, 뒤에 제시된 by 전치사구에서 말하는 거실을 어수선하게 만드는 다른 리모컨들을 없애는 데 따른 결과에 해당되어야 하므로 '공간을 확보하다, 절약하다' 등의 의미를 나타낼 수 있는 (B) save가 정답이다.

[어휘] reform ~을 개선하다, 개혁하다 contribute ~을 기부하다, 기고하다, 기여하다 divide ~을 나누다

02. 부사 자리

[해설] 동사 press 앞에 위치한 빈칸은 press를 수식해 특정 버튼을 누르는 방식을 나타낼 부사가 쓰여야 하는 자리이므로 부사인 (C) gently가 정답이다.

[어휘] gentle 상냥한, 점잖은, 온화한, 부드러운 gentleness 상냥함, 점잖음, 온화함

03. 접속사 자리

[해설] 콤마를 기준으로 앞뒤에 완전한 절이 위치해 있으므로 빈칸은 이 절들을 연결할 접속사 자리이다. 따라서 유일한 접속사인 (C) When이 정답이다. (A) For와 (B) During은 전치사, (D) Even은 부사이다.

[어휘] even 심지어, (비교급 수식) 훨씬

04. 알맞은 문장 고르기

(A) 해당 기기의 설명서를 참고하셔야 할 수도 있습니다.
(B) 저희 제품과 연결되지 않는 어떠한 기기든지 알려 주십시오.
(C) 이 다목적 리모컨은 여러분의 삶을 더욱 간편하게 만들어 드릴 것입니다.
(D) 리모컨에 오직 인증된 배터리만을 사용하시기 바랍니다.

[해설] 앞 문장에서 언급한 '기기마다 버튼들의 기능이 다를 수 있다'는 내용과 연계되어야 하므로 그와 같은 경우에 대한 조치로 기기의 설명서를 참고하라고 언급한 (A)가 정답이다.

[어휘] consult (책, 자료 등) ~을 참고하다 approved 인증된, 인가된

05-08은 다음 이메일을 참조하시오.

발신: Gold House Investments
수신: Justin Lewis
날짜: 9월 18일
제목: 사무실 공사

안녕하세요, 저는 Gold House 투자의 David입니다. 05저희 사무실 개조를 위해 귀사를 선정했다는 사실을 알려 드리게 되어 기쁩니다. 제 동료 직원들과 저는 귀사의 작업에 관한 후기를 읽어 봤으며, 저희 모두는 귀사에서 저희 사무실 리모델링 작업을 하게 되기를 고대하고 있습니다.

06저희가 직접 뵙고 논의하고자 하는 몇몇 사안들이 있습니다. 예를 들어, 가능한 한 빨리 작업이 완료되기를 원하고 있기 때문에, 추가 비용이 들 수도 있겠지요. 07동시에, 저희에게는 지켜야 하는 엄격한 예산이 있습니다. 08이와 같은 세부 사항을 파악할 수 있도록 직접 만나 뵙는 것이 가장 좋을 것이라고 생각합니다.

감사합니다.
Henrietta White
부서장, Gold House 투자

associate 동료 직원 strict 엄격한 budget 예산 adhere to ~을 고수하다, 지키다 face-to-face 서로 대면하여 work out ~을 알아내다

05. 동사 어휘

[해설] our office를 목적어로 취해 사무실을 대상으로 할 수 있는 일을 나타낼 동사가 필요한데, 뒤에 이어지는 문장에 언급된 작업 결과물(your company's work), 사무실에 대한 리모델링 작업 요청(having you work on our office remodeling) 등의 내용과 어울려야 하므로 '~을 개조하다, 보수하다'를 의미하는 (A) renovate가 정답이다.

[어휘] replace ~을 교체하다, 대체하다

06. 알맞은 문장 고르기

(A) 저희는 고객 대기 공간을 확장하고자 합니다.
(B) 저희가 직접 뵙고 논의하고자 하는 몇몇 사안들이 있습니다.
(C) 회의 일정을 잡으시려면 저 또는 제 비서 중 한 명에게 연락 주십시오.
(D) 귀사의 웹사이트에 있는 이전 작업물의 사진들이 매우 인상적입니다.

[해설] 앞 단락에서는 특정 작업을 요청하고 싶다는 의사를 나타내고 있고, 빈칸 뒤에는 관련 비용 문제를 직접 만나서 알아보고 싶다는 말이 제시되어 있다. 따라서 함께 논의할 일이 있음을 알리는 의미로 쓰인 문장이 빈칸에 필요하므로 (B)가 정답이다.

[어휘] expand ~을 확장하다, 확대하다 issue 사안, 문제 in person 직접 (만나) either A or B A 또는 B 둘 중의 하나 impressive 인상적인

07. 접속부사

[해설] 빈칸 앞에는 신속한 작업에 따른 추가 비용 발생 가능성이, 빈칸 뒤에는 지켜야 하는 엄격한 예산이 있다는 사실이 제시되어 있다. 따라서 상대방이 알아두어야 하는 정보를 차례로 알리는 흐름이므로 '동시에'라는 의미로 고려해야 하는 대조적인 사실을 함께 언급할 때 사용하는 (B) At the same time이 정답이다.

[어휘] therefore 그러므로, 따라서 as much as ~만큼, ~ 정도 in return 답례로, 대신에

08. 동사의 형태

[해설] 빈칸 앞에 위치한 it would be best는 to부정사와 결합해 '~하는 것이 가장 좋을 것이다'라는 의미를 나타내므로 (B) to meet이 정답이다.

PART 7 광고 (1) 제품 및 서비스 광고

풀이 방법 해석

품목: RZ-7 원형 톱
수상 경력이 있는 LumberJack 브랜드로부터!
희망 가격: $100
위치: Wayzata, MN

제품 설명:
- 작년에 신품 구입. 원래 가격은 195달러였습니다.
- 6, 8, 10인치 톱날에 맞게 조정 가능합니다.
- 전원 코드는 선택 사항이며 배터리는 하루 내내 지속됩니다.

[어휘] ongoing 지속되는   drought 가뭄   have an effect on ~에 영향을 미치다   competent 유능한, 능숙한   suitable 적합한   confidential 기밀의

PART 6 뒤의 내용이 단서인 동사 어휘

풀이 방법 해석

설명: Morning Mate 커피 메이커 설정하기

Morning Mate 커피 메이커는 당신이 아침에 침대에서 나오자마자 신선하게 내린 커피 한잔이 당신을 기다리고 있게 합니다. 당신이 해야 할 일은 커피 가루를 넣고 타이머를 설정하는 것뿐입니다.

버튼을 눌러 커피가 준비되길 원하는 시간을 입력하기만 하면 됩니다.

디지털 인터페이스에 일련의 선택 목록이 보여집니다. 당신은 한 주의 그날 그날 다른 시간을 설정할 수 있습니다. 목록을 탐색하시려면 화살표 버튼을 사용하시기만 하면 됩니다.

당신의 맞춤 설정을 입력한 후, '저장' 버튼을 꼭 누르세요.

연습 문제

01.(A)   02.(B)   03.(B)   04.(A)

01.

계좌 소유 고객들께

저희 Wilson 은행에 당좌 예금 계좌를 개설해 주셔서 감사 드립니다! 첫 사용에 앞서 여러분의 은행 카드를 잊지 말고 활성화시키시기 바랍니다. 신규 카드에 부착된 스티커에 적힌 번호로 전화를 걸어서 그렇게 하실 수 있습니다.

account 계좌, 계정   holder 소유자, 보유자   checking account 당좌 예금 계좌

[단서] You can do so by calling the number

[해설] 다음 문장에 나온 특정 번호로 전화를 걸어서 할 수 있다는 내용으로 보아 이 방법으로 카드와 관련해 취할 수 있는 조치를 나타낼 동사를 골라야 한다. '~을 활성화하다'를 뜻하는 (A) activate가 정답이다.

[어휘] state (사람이) ~을 말하다, (문서 등에) ~라고 쓰여 있다

02.

Bensonville 법원에 신임 원로 판사가 선임되었습니다. Adams 판사는 법정 다툼 내용에 온정적으로 끝까지 귀 기울인 전력으로 인해 해당 직책에 선임되었습니다.

judge 판사   position 직책, 자리   thanks to ~로 인해, ~ 덕분에   compassionately 온정적으로, 자애롭게   legal battle 법정 다툼

[단서] Judge Adams was selected for the position

[해설] 다음 문장에 Adams 판사가 특정 직책에 선임된 이유가 언급되어 있으므로 그와 같은 일을 나타낼 동사로서 '선임되다'라는 수동의 의미를 구성할 수 있는 (B) appointed가 정답이다.

[어휘] retire 은퇴하다, 퇴직하다

03.

우리 마케팅팀은 우리 제품을 재활용하는 새로운 정책을 홍보할 것입니다. 최근에 시장 분석 전문가들은 대부분의 소비자들이 친환경적인 실천을 시행하는 회사들을 높이 평가하고 있다고 알렸습니다.

promote ~을 홍보하다   policy 정책, 방침   analyst 분석가   consumer 소비자   highly evaluate ~을 높이 평가하다   implement ~을 시행하다   environmentally friendly 친환경적인   practice 실천, 관행, 관례

[단서] environmentally friendly practices

[해설] 빈칸에 쓰일 동사는 새로운 정책과 관련되어야 하는데, 다음 문장에 언급된 '친환경적인 운영'이라는 말과 연계되어야 하므로 '~을 재활용하다'를 뜻하는 (B) recycle이 정답이다.

04.

처음으로 자동차 보험 상품을 구입하기를 원하실 경우에 번호표를 뽑으시기 바랍니다. 신규 보험 신청자는 운전 면허증과 차량 등록증을 제시해 주셔야 한다는 점에 유의하시기 바랍니다.

take a number (대기용) 번호표를 뽑다   insurance policy 보험 증서   present ~을 제시하다   car registration 차량 등록증

[단서] policy buyers

[해설] 다음 문장에 운전 면허증과 차량 등록증을 제시해야 한다고 했는데, 이는 자동차 보험 상품을 구입할 때 필요한 일로 판단할 수 있으므로 '~을 구입하다'를 뜻하는 (A) purchase가 정답이다.

[어휘] access ~을 이용하다, ~에 접근하다

실전 문제

01.(B)   02.(C)   03.(C)   04.(A)   05.(A)   06.(B)
07.(B)   08.(B)

01-04는 다음 설명을 참조하시오.

다목적 LM 리모컨 프로그래밍하기: 설명서

TV와 DVD 플레이어, 서라운드 음향 시스템을 비롯해 그 외의 여러 기기들을 제어할 수 있도록 다목적 LM 리모컨을 프로그램해 보시기 바랍니다. 01이를 통해 거실을 어수선하게 만드는 다른 리모컨들을 없앰으로써 커피 테이블에 공간을 확보하실 수 있습니다.

02먼저, 수신부를 향하게 하면서 "기기 프로그램하기"를 가볍게 누르십시오.

03리모컨의 불빛이 3회 깜빡이면, 해당 기기에 연결된 것입니다. 기기에 따라, 버튼마다 다른 기능이 있을 수 있습니다. 04해당 기기의 설명서를 참고하셔야 할 수도 있습니다.

리모컨 상단의 화면에서 연결된 기기의 목록을 확인해 보실 수 있습니다.

all-purpose 다목적의, 만능의   instructions 설명(서), 안내(서), 지시   get rid of ~을 없애다, 제거하다   clutter up ~을 어수선하게 만들다   device 기기, 장치   while ~하면서, ~하는 동안   receptor (전파 등의) 수신부   flash 깜빡이다   depending on (차이 등의 기준을 말할 때) ~에 따라   function 기능   view ~을 보다   at the top of ~의 상단에

DAY 09   75

14. 3형식 동사

모든 공석에 고려되기 위해서는 지원자들이 최소 학사 학위를 소지하고 있어야 한다.

[해설] 선택지가 다양한 동사들로 구성되어 있으므로 동사 어휘 문제이다. 빈칸 뒤에 위치한 '목적어+to부정사' 구조와 어울리는 동사로서 '~에게 …하도록 요구하다'라는 의미를 나타낼 때 사용하는 (B) require가 정답이다.

[어휘] open position 공석　candidate 지원자, 후보자　minimum 최소의, 최저의　bachelor's degree 학사 학위　expose ~을 노출시키다　obtain ~을 얻다, 획득하다

15. 1형식 동사

James Holt 씨와 Rebecca Smith 씨는 영국 왕실을 중점적으로 다루는 또 다른 책에 대해 협업했다.

[해설] 선택지가 다양한 동사들로 구성되어 있으므로 동사 어휘 문제이다. 빈칸 뒤에 위치한 전치사 on과 어울리는 자동사가 필요하므로 on과 함께 '~에 대해 협업하다, 공동 작업하다'라는 의미를 나타내는 (C) collaborated가 정답이다.

[어휘] focus on ~을 중점적으로 다루다　royal family 왕실, 왕족　initiate ~을 시작하다　explain ~을 설명하다　gather 모이다, ~을 모으다

16. 시간 부사

본사에서 전근된 뒤로, Clay 씨는 현재 보스턴 지사의 영업부를 총괄하고 있다.

[해설] 선택지가 다양한 부사들로 구성되어 있으므로 부사 어휘 문제이다. 현재 진행 동사 is supervising과 어울리는 부사가 빈칸에 필요하므로 현재 시점을 나타내는 부사 (A) now가 정답이다.

[어휘] transfer 전근하다　headquarter office 본사　supervise ~을 총괄하다, 감독하다　sales department 영업부　branch 지사, 지점

17. '자동사+전치사' 관용어구

많은 회사들이 재능 있는 소프트웨어 개발자들을 찾고 있다.

[해설] 선택지가 다양한 전치사들로 구성되어 있으므로 전치사 어휘 문제이다. 빈칸 앞에 위치한 자동사 look과 어울리는 전치사가 필요한데, '재능 있는 개발자를 찾고 있다'라는 의미가 되어야 적절하므로 '~을 찾다'라는 의미가 되게 하는 (B) for가 정답이다.

[어휘] look for ~을 찾다　talented 재능 있는　developer 개발자　throughout ~ 전체에 걸쳐, ~ 동안 내내

18. 형용사의 역할: 목적격 보어

Bannon 씨는 이번 토요일에 근무할 시간이 나지 않는다는 점을 분명히 했다.

[해설] 선택지가 다양한 품사로 된 단어들로 구성되어 있으므로 문법 문제이다. 빈칸 앞에 위치한 동사 make는 'make+목적어+목적격 보어'의 구조로 쓰이므로 목적격 보어 역할이 가능한 형용사 (A) clear가 정답이다.

[어휘] clear 분명한; ~을 치우다　clearly 분명하게

19. 형용사 어휘

Richmond 부동산은 우수한 고객 서비스에 대해 지역 비즈니스 상을 수상했다.

[해설] 선택지가 다양한 형용사들로 구성되어 있으므로 형용사 어휘 문제이다. 전치사 for의 목적어인 customer service를 수식해 상을 받은 이유에 해당하는 서비스의 특징을 나타낼 형용사가 필요하므로 '우수한, 특출한' 등을 뜻하는 (D) exceptional이 정답이다.

[어휘] local 지역의, 현지의　feasible 실현 가능한　complex 복잡한　drastic (변화 등이) 급격한

20. 단수 주어+단수 동사 / 복수 주어+복수 동사

고객들은 새로운 셀프 계산대에 대해 긍정적으로 반응했다.

[해설] 선택지가 동사 respond의 여러 형태와 명사로 구성되어 있으므로 문법 문제이다. 빈칸 앞뒤로 주어와 부사, to 전치사구만 있으므로 빈칸이 문장의 동사 자리이며, 복수 주어 Customers와의 수 일치에 상관 없이 사용할 수 있는 과거 시제 동사 (A) responded가 정답이다.

[어휘] respond to ~에 반응하다, 대답하다　self-checkout counter 셀프 계산대　response 반응, 대답

21. 형용사 어휘

고소 공포증으로 인해, Freeman 씨는 동료 직원들과 등산 여행을 함께 하기 꺼려 했다.

[해설] 선택지가 다양한 형용사들로 구성되어 있으므로 형용사 어휘 문제이다. 빈칸 앞뒤에 각각 위치한 be동사 was, to부정사와 어울리는 형용사가 필요하므로 이 둘과 함께 '~하기를 꺼리다'라는 의미를 만들 때 사용하는 (D) reluctant가 정답이다.

[어휘] due to ~로 인해　fear of heights 고소 공포증　colleague 동료 직원　remarkable 놀랄 만한　confidential 기밀의　accessible 접근 가능한, 이용 가능한

22. 단수 주어+단수 동사 / 복수 주어+복수 동사

그 부서는 내일 밖으로 점심 식사 하러 가는 것으로 Ingram 씨의 승진을 축하할 것이다.

[해설] 선택지가 동사 celebrate의 다양한 형태로 구성되어 있으므로 문법 문제이다. 빈칸 앞에 위치한 3인칭 단수 주어 The department와의 수 일치에 상관 없이 사용할 수 있는 미래 시제 동사 (A) will be celebrating이 정답이다.

[어휘] department 부서　promotion 승진

23. 형용사 어휘

축구 경기장 5개와 맞먹는 공간인 Frazier 대저택의 정원 전체가 공원으로 변화되었다.

[해설] 선택지가 다양한 형용사들로 구성되어 있으므로 형용사 어휘 문제이다. 빈칸 뒤에 위치한 area of 5 football fields는 Frazier Mansion의 규모를 쉽게 설명하기 위해 사용된 명사구이다. 따라서 '맞먹는, 상당하는'이라는 의미를 지니는 (A) equivalent가 정답이다.

[어휘] entire 전체의　convert A into B A를 B로 변화시키다, 전환하다　exemplary 모범이 되는　apparent 명백한

24. 형용사 어휘

지속되고 있는 가뭄이 농부들과 식품 가격에 모두 상당한 영향을 미치고 있다.

[해설] 선택지가 다양한 형용사들로 구성되어 있으므로 형용사 어휘 문제이다. 빈칸 뒤에 위치한 명사 effect를 수식해 영향을 미치는 정도를 나타낼 형용사가 필요하므로 '상당한, 많은'을 의미하는 (B) substantial이 정답이다.

[해설] 선택지가 동사 hire의 다양한 형태로 구성되어 있으므로 문법 문제이다. 빈칸 앞뒤로 주어와 목적어, 그리고 for 전치사구만 있으므로 빈칸이 문장의 동사 자리이며, 3인칭 단수 주어 Donna's Fabric과 수 일치가 되는 형태인 (A) is hiring이 정답이다.

[어휘] meet ~을 충족시키다 rush order 긴급 주문 temporary 임시의 warehouse 창고 packaging 포장

04. 수 일치의 예외

대부분의 의사들은 당뇨병 환자들에게 매일 식사와 운동을 기록하도록 권고하고 있다.

[해설] 선택지가 동사 record의 다양한 형태로 구성되어 있으므로 문법 문제이다. that절에 속한 빈칸 앞뒤로 주어와 목적어, 부사만 있으므로 빈칸이 that절의 동사 자리이다. 그런데 recommend와 같이 주장/요구/의무 등을 나타내는 동사의 목적어로 쓰이는 that절의 동사는 동사원형만 가능하므로 (A) record가 정답이다.

[어휘] patient 환자 diabetes 당뇨병 record 기록하다

05. 주격 관계대명사 뒤 동사의 수 일치

연락처 정보를 업데이트하는 모든 사용자에게 무료 배송 코드가 제공됩니다.

[해설] 선택지가 동사 update의 다양한 형태로 구성되어 있으므로 문법 문제이다. 주격 관계대명사 who 뒤에 위치한 빈칸은 who절의 동사 자리이며, 이때 선행사와 수가 일치되어야 하므로 단수 대명사 anyone에 맞는 동사 형태인 (B) updates가 정답이다.

[어휘] contact 연락처 free shipping 무료 배송

06. 단수 주어+단수 동사 / 복수 주어+복수 동사

루이지애나에 위치한 Anderson 농장은 홍수로 인해 힘든 시기를 겪었다.

[해설] 선택지가 동사 experience의 다양한 형태와 형용사로 구성되어 있으므로 문법 문제이다. 빈칸 앞뒤로 각각 주어와 목적어, 그리고 전치사구들만 위치해 있으므로 빈칸이 문장의 동사 자리이며, 3인칭 단수 주어 Anderson Farm과의 수일치에 상관 없이 사용할 수 있는 과거 시제 동사 (B) experienced가 정답이다.

[어휘] hardship 힘듦, 어려움, 고난 due to ~로 인해 flooding 홍수 experience ~을 겪다, 경험하다 experiential 경험상의

07. 주어와 동사 사이에 수식어구가 있는 유형

귀하의 제품에 대한 배송 날짜는 주문이 이뤄지는 시간에 따라 다릅니다.

[해설] 선택지가 동사 depend의 다양한 형태와 형용사로 구성되어 있으므로 문법 문제이다. 빈칸 앞뒤로 주어와 전치사구만(the order 이하는 time을 수식) 있으므로 빈칸이 문장의 동사 자리이며, 3인칭 단수 주어 delivery date와 수 일치가 되는 형태인 (B) depends가 정답이다.

[어휘] shipment 배송(품) depend on ~에 따라 다르다, ~에 달려 있다 place an order 주문하다 dependent 의존적인, 의지하는

08. 형용사 어휘

Estrada 제조사는 여러 주요 자동차 회사에 신뢰할 만한 자동차 부품을 공급한다.

[해설] 선택지가 다양한 형용사들로 구성되어 있으므로 형용사 어휘 문제이다. 빈칸 뒤에 위치한 명사구 auto parts를 수식해 여러 주요 회사에 공급하는 부품의 특성을 나타낼 형용사가 필요하므로 '신뢰할 만한'을 의미하는 (B) reliable이 정답이다.

[어휘] supply ~을 공급하다 part 부품 vulnerable 취약한 previous 이전의, 과거의 immediate 즉각적인

09. 단수 주어+단수 동사 / 복수 주어+복수 동사

뉴스 기자로 근무했을 당시, Graves 씨는 도시에 있는 여러 주요 기업가들을 인터뷰했다.

[해설] 선택지가 동사 interview의 다양한 형태와 명사로 구성되어 있으므로 문법 문제이다. 주절에 속한 빈칸 앞뒤로 주어와 목적어, 전치사구만 있으므로 빈칸이 주절의 동사 자리이며, 3인칭 단수 주어 Ms. Graves와의 수 일치에 상관 없이 사용할 수 있는 과거 시제 (C) interviewed가 정답이다.

[어휘] leading 주요한, 선도적인 business owner 기업가

10. 단수 주어+단수 동사 / 복수 주어+복수 동사

Edwards 씨는 주간 회의 시간에 새로운 프로젝트와 관련된 모든 질문에 답변할 것이다.

[해설] 선택지가 동사 answer의 다양한 형태로 구성되어 있으므로 문법 문제이다. 빈칸 앞뒤로 주어와 목적어, 그리고 전치사구들만 위치해 있으므로 빈칸에 문장의 동사가 필요하며, 3인칭 단수 주어 Ms. Edwards와의 수 일치에 상관 없이 사용할 수 있는 미래 시제 동사 (C) will answer가 정답이다.

[어휘] regarding ~와 관련된

11. 주어와 동사 사이에 수식어구가 있는 유형

컨벤션에 참가한 거의 모든 회원들로부터 피드백 양식을 걷었다.

[해설] 선택지가 동사 collect의 다양한 형태와 명사로 구성되어 있으므로 문법 문제이다. 빈칸 앞뒤로 각각 명사구와 전치사구만 위치해 있으므로 빈칸이 문장의 동사 자리이며, 복수 주어 Feedback forms와 수 일치가 되는 형태인 (A) were collected가 정답이다.

[어휘] form 양식, 형식 nearly 거의 attend 참석하다

12. 단수 주어+단수 동사 / 복수 주어+복수 동사

쓰레기 수거 요금을 철회하는 것이 사람들로 하여금 쓰레기를 적절히 재활용하도록 장려할 수 있다.

[해설] 선택지가 동사 encourage의 다양한 형태로 구성되어 있으므로 문법 문제이다. 빈칸 앞뒤로 동명사구와 목적어, 그리고 to부정사구만 있으므로 빈칸이 문장의 동사 자리이며, 단수 취급 하는 동명사구 주어와의 수 일치에 상관 없이 사용할 수 있는 (D) can encourage가 정답이다.

[어휘] waive ~을 철회하다, 포기하다 encourage A to부정사 A에게 ~하도록 장려하다, 권하다 properly 적절히, 제대로

13. 주어와 동사 사이에 수식어구가 있는 유형

활발하게 작업이 이뤄지는 현장에 들어가는 사람들은 장화나 안전모와 같은 안전 장비를 착용해야만 한다.

[해설] 선택지가 동사 force의 다양한 형태와 형용사로 구성되어 있으므로 문법 문제이다. 빈칸 앞에는 주어와 entering이 이끄는 수식어구가, 빈칸 뒤에는 to부정사구만 있으므로 빈칸이 문장의 동사 자리이며, 복수 주어 People과 수 일치가 되는 형태인 (C) are forced가 정답이다.

[어휘] active 활발한, 적극적인 job site 작업 현장 be forced to부정사 어쩔 수 없이 ~해야 하다, ~하도록 강요받다 safety gear 안전 장비 forceful 단호한, 강력한

[어휘] donate ~을 기부하다 supplies 물품, 용품 sign up for ~에 등록하다, ~을 신청하다 volunteer to부정사 자원해서 ~하다 instructor 강사

paraphrasing 정답   1. (c)   2. (d)   3. (a)   4. (e)   5. (b)

DAY 09

PART 5 문법 | 주어와 동사의 수 일치

확인 문제 해석

① Mario Pizzas는 3개월마다 메뉴를 업데이트한다.
② 많은 지원자들이 로비에서 기다리는 중이다.
③ 내가 온라인으로 예약한 회의실을 다른 누군가가 사용 중이다.
④ 그는 지난주에 열린 테니스 경기에서 우승했다.
⑤ 일부 정보는 더 이상 쓸모 없는 것이었다.
⑥ 세입자는 욕조가 무상으로 수리되어야 한다고 주장했다.

연습 문제

01.(B)   02.(C)   03.(B)   04.(B)   05.(C)   06.(D)

01.
1. 선택지 보고 문법/어휘 문제 파악하기 ☑문법 문제 □어휘 문제
2. 빈칸 분석하기 빈칸 앞에 있는 문장의 주어 ☑단수 주어 □복수 주어
   → 빈칸은 ☑단수 동사 □복수 동사 자리이다.
3. 정답 선택하기 정답 (B)

Rockaway 산업은 전 세계의 국가들에게 태양 전지판을 제공한다.

02.
1. 선택지 보고 문법/어휘 문제 파악하기 ☑문법 문제 □어휘 문제
2. 빈칸 분석하기 빈칸 앞에 있는 문장의 주어 (officials)
   → □단수 주어 ☑복수 주어
   → 빈칸은 □단수 동사 ☑복수 동사 자리이다.
3. 정답 선택하기 정답 (C)

정부 공무원들은 매 분기마다 우리의 주요 시설을 점검한다.

03.
1. 선택지 보고 문법/어휘 문제 파악하기 □문법 문제 ☑어휘 문제
2. 빈칸 분석하기 빈칸 앞 전치사 due to의 의미 (~ 때문에)
   → 빈칸 뒤에는 회의에 참석하지 못한 □결과 ☑이유가 이어져야 한다.
3. 정답 선택하기 정답 (B)

나는 상사와의 선약 때문에 회의에 참석할 수 없었다.

04.
1. 선택지 보고 문법/어휘 문제 파악하기 ☑문법 문제 □어휘 문제
2. 빈칸 분석하기 빈칸 앞 which가 수식하는 선행사 (policy)
   → 선행사가 ☑단수 □복수이다.
   → 빈칸은 ☑단수 동사 □복수 동사 자리이다.
3. 정답 선택하기 정답 (B)

이것은 지난달에 시행된 보안 정책에 대한 업데이트입니다.

05.
1. 선택지 보고 문법/어휘 문제 파악하기 ☑문법 문제 □어휘 문제
2. 빈칸 분석하기 빈칸 앞에 있는 문장의 주어 (one)
   → 주어가 ☑단수 □복수이다.
   → 빈칸은 ☑단수 동사 □복수 동사 자리이다.
3. 정답 선택하기 정답 (C)

선임 회계사 중 한 명이 Seymour Financial에서 교육을 진행한다.

06.
1. 선택지 보고 문법/어휘 문제 파악하기 ☑문법 문제 □어휘 문제
2. 빈칸 분석하기 빈칸 앞 who가 수식하는 선행사 (anyone)
   → 선행사가 ☑단수 □복수이다.
   → 빈칸은 ☑단수 동사 □복수 동사 자리이다.
3. 정답 선택하기 정답 (D)

전근을 신청하고 싶은 사람은 누구든지 인사부 직원에게 연락해야 한다.

실전 문제

01.(C)	02.(C)	03.(A)	04.(A)	05.(B)	06.(B)
07.(B)	08.(B)	09.(C)	10.(C)	11.(A)	12.(D)
13.(C)	14.(B)	15.(C)	16.(A)	17.(C)	18.(A)
19.(D)	20.(A)	21.(D)	22.(A)	23.(A)	24.(B)

01. 단수 주어+단수 동사 / 복수 주어+복수 동사

Jordan 씨는 이미 로마 지사로 전근 갔기 때문에, 신임 교육 책임자가 본사에 필요하다.

[해설] 선택지가 동사 relocate의 다양한 형태로 구성되어 있으므로 문법 문제이다. Since절에 속한 빈칸 앞뒤로 주어와 to 전치사구만 있으므로 빈칸이 Since절의 동사 자리이며, 3인칭 단수 주어 Mr. Jordan과 수 일치가 되는 형태인 (C) has relocated가 정답이다.

[어휘] relocate to ~로 옮기다, 전근 가다   headquarters 본사

02. 형용사 어휘

Everwood Landscaping이 선정된 것은 모든 서비스 요건을 합리적인 가격에 충족하겠다고 약속했기 때문이다.

[해설] 선택지가 다양한 형용사들로 구성되어 있으므로 형용사 어휘 문제이다. 빈칸 뒤에 위치한 명사 price를 수식해 가격 수준을 나타낼 형용사가 필요하므로 '합리적인'을 뜻하는 (C) reasonable이 정답이다.

[어휘] promise to ~하기로 약속하다   fulfill ~을 이행하다, 충족하다   requirement 필요 조건   at a reasonable price 합리적인 가격에   informative 유익한   unforeseen 예측하지 못한   former 이전의, 전직의

03. 단수 주어+단수 동사 / 복수 주어+복수 동사

긴급 주문을 맞추기 위해 Donna's Fabric은 포장 라인에 임시 창고 근로자들을 고용하고 있다.

Jackie Hannan
Brookview 로 3976번지
채프먼, 캔자스 67431

Hannan 씨께

Chapman 공립 도서관에 연락해 주셔서 감사드립니다. 저희는 이용객들의 의견을 [09]소중히 여기고 있기 때문에 시간 내어 연락 주신 것에 대해 감사드립니다. 저희가 다음 달부터 여러 가지 새로운 강좌를 연다는 사실을 알게 되시면 기쁘실 것이라고 생각합니다. 따라서 귀하께서 관심이 가는 것을 찾으시길 바랍니다.

Storyworld	5~7세의 어린 독자들을 위한 기초 독서 수업	매주 월요일 오후 4:30
[10]Book Explorers	공상 과학 소설에 관심 있는 십대들을 위한 독서 동아리	매달 첫째 수요일, 오후 7:00
[07]Lab Leaders	컴퓨터실에서 모여 인터넷 서핑 방법, 태블릿 PC 사용법, 그리고 스마트폰 앱 다운로드 방법을 배워 보세요.	매주 목요일 오후 2:30
Career Success	대중 연설, 발표, 협상에 대한 능력을 향상시킴으로써 업무 능력을 한 단계 끌어올려 보세요.	매주 화요일 오후 7:30

도서관 대출 데스크에 방문하시면 상기 강좌들 중 어느 것이든지 등록하실 수 있습니다. [11]저희는 또한 오전에 열리는 어린이 활동을 위해 마커 펜, 색종이, 풀을 비롯한 기타 물품들을 기부해 주시기를 이용객들께 요청드리고 있습니다. 관심이 있으시면, s.cobb@chapmanlibrary.org로 Spencer Cobb 씨에게 이메일 보내 주시기 바랍니다.

곧 저희 도서관에서 뵐 수 있기를 바랍니다!

Marie Devon
수석 사서, Chapman 공립 도서관

---

value ~을 소중하게 여기다 get in touch 연락하다 of interest to ~의 관심을 끄는 interested in ~에 관심이 있는 browse ~을 둘러보다 strengthen ~을 향상시키다, 강화하다 public speaking 대중 연설 negotiate 협상하다 register for ~에 등록하다 contribute ~을 기부하다 glue 풀

07. 추론 문제 - 연계 문제

Hannan 씨는 어느 강좌에 관심이 있을 것 같은가?
(A) Storyworld
(B) Book Explorers
(C) Lab Leaders
(D) Career Success

[해설] Hannan 씨가 쓴 이메일인 첫 지문 첫 단락에 노인들을 위한 수업 개설에 관해 문의하면서 자신과 나이가 비슷한 많은 사람들이 기술에 관해 배우고 싶어한다고(~ many people at my age, including myself, would like to learn more about technology) 언급했는데, 두 번째 지문의 도표에서 이와 관련된 수업은 인터넷 서핑과 태블릿 PC 사용법 등이 포함된 Lab Leaders이므로 (C)가 정답이다.

08. 세부사항 문제

Hannan 씨는 도서관에 대해 무엇을 마음에 들어 하는가?
(A) 다양한 현대 서적들
(B) 아주 다양한 강좌들
(C) 아는 것이 많은 직원들
(D) 편리한 이용 시간

[해설] 첫 지문 두 번째 단락에, Hannan 씨는 항상 도서관 직원들의 많은 경험과 박식함에 깊은 인상을 받는다고(I'm always impressed with how experienced and well-informed your employees are) 했으므로 이에 해당되는 (C)가 정답이다.

paraphrasing well-informed 박식한 → knowledgeable 아는 것이 많은

[어휘] the wide range of 아주 다양한 knowledgeable 아는 것이 많은 convenient 편리한

09. 동의어 문제

편지에서, 첫 번째 단락, 첫 번째 줄의 단어 "value"와 의미가 가장 가까운 것은 무엇인가?
(A) ~에 대해 마음을 쓰다
(B) 추정하다
(C) ~에 동의하다
(D) ~의 비용이 들다

[해설] value의 목적어로 '이용객들의 의견'을 의미하는 the opinions of our patrons가 쓰여 있는데, 도서관의 입장에서 이용객들의 의견은 중요하게 생각해야 하는 대상에 해당된다. 따라서 이와 유사한 의미로 '~에 대해 마음을 쓰다' 등을 뜻하는 (A)가 정답이다.

10. True 문제

Book Explorers에 대해 언급된 것은 무엇인가?
(A) 글쓰기 연습을 포함한다.
(B) 도서관에서 가장 인기 있는 강좌이다.
(C) 모든 연령대의 사람들을 위해 고안된 것이다.
(D) 한 달에 한 번 모인다.

[해설] Book Explorers가 제시된 두 번째 단락의 도표를 보면 매달 첫 번째 수요일에(1st Wednesday of the month) 강좌가 있는 것을 알 수 있는데, 이는 한 달에 한 번 강좌가 열린다는 뜻이므로 (D)가 정답이다.

paraphrasing 1st Wednesday of the month 매달 첫 번째 수요일 → once a month 한 달에 한 번

11. 세부사항 문제

도서관 이용객들은 왜 Cobb 씨에게 연락해야 하는가?
(A) 일부 물품을 기부하기 위해
(B) 강좌에 등록하기 위해
(C) 자원해서 강사가 되기 위해
(D) 강좌에 대해 건의하기 위해

[해설] Cobb 씨의 이름이 언급된 두 번째 지문 후반부에, 마커 펜, 색종이, 풀을 비롯한 기타 물품들을 기부해 줄 것을 이용객들에게 요청하고 있다는(We are also asking patrons to contribute ~) 말과 함께 기부를 원할 경우에 Spencer Cobb 씨에게 이메일을 보내라고(If you are interested in doing so, please e-mail Spencer Cobb at ~) 알리고 있으므로 '물품 기부'를 의미하는 (A)가 정답이다.

paraphrasing contribute 기부하다 → donate 기부하다

04-06은 다음 편지를 참조하시오.

Daisy Tyler
Southlands 로 177번지
토론토, 온타리오
M5V 2L6

Tyler 씨께

Gallivan 로에 위치한 임대 건물에 문제가 있다는 사실을 알려 드리게 되어 유감스럽게 생각합니다. **04귀하께서 8월 1일에 그곳으로 귀하의 여행사 사무실을 이전하실 계획이었다는 점**을 알고 있습니다. 안타깝게도, 현재의 세입자를 내보내는 데 문제를 겪고 있기 때문에, 새로운 이사 날짜는 8월 8일이 될 것입니다.

귀하의 현재 임대 계약이 7월 31일에 만료되기 때문에, 이는 귀하께 심각한 문제를 초래함을 알고 있습니다. 다행히도, 제가 제안해 드릴 수 있는 두 가지 해결책이 있습니다. 첫째로, **05Paloma 가에 있는 Fordham 빌딩에 이용 가능한 공간이 있습니다. 월 임대료는 동일하며, 지하철역뿐만 아니라 두 곳의 버스 정류장이 걸어서 가기에 매우 가까운 곳에 있다는 추가 장점이 있습니다.** 아니면, 귀하께서 그럼에도 불구하고 제때에 현재의 장소를 떠날 수 있도록 **06저희 회사에서 귀사의 모든 사무용 가구와 기타 물품들을 임시로 보관할 장소를 임대하는 데 드는 비용을 부담하겠습니다.** 이 선택 사항들을 좀 더 논의해 볼 수 있도록 제게 연락 주시기 바랍니다.

안녕히 계십시오.

Alex Wright
Ace 부동산

regret to부정사 ~해서 유감이다   issue 문제, 사안   rental property 임대 건물   evict ~을 내보내다, 쫓아내다   current 현재의   tenant 세입자   lease 임대 계약(서)   expire 만료되다   benefit 장점, 혜택   alternatively (대안을 말할 때) 또는, 그렇지 않으면   cover (비용) ~을 충당해 주다   temporary 임시의   storage unit 보관소, 창고   site 장소, 위치   on time 제때

04. 세부사항 문제

Tyler 씨는 8월에 무엇을 할 계획인가?
(A) 또 다른 직원을 고용하기
(B) 임대 계약 갱신하기
(C) 휴가 떠나기
(D) 자신의 회사 이전하기

[해설] August라는 시점이 언급된 첫 단락에, 수신인인 Tyler 씨가 8월 1일에 특정 건물로 여행사 사무실을 이전할 계획이라는(planning on moving your travel agency's offices there on August 1) 말이 있으므로 (D)가 정답이다.

paraphrasing moving 이사하기 → Relocate 이전하다

[어휘] renew ~을 갱신하다   rental agreement 임대 계약(서)   relocate ~을 이전하다

05. True 문제

Fordham 빌딩에 관해 언급된 것은 무엇인가?
(A) 현대적인 디자인으로 되어 있다.
(B) Gallivan 로에 위치해 있다.
(C) 대중교통과 가깝다.
(D) 일시적으로 이용이 불가하다.

[해설] Fordham Building이 언급된 두 번째 단락에, Fordham Building이 지하철역뿐만 아니라 두 곳의 버스 정류장이 걸어서 가기에 매우 가까운 곳에 있다는(being a very short walk from a subway station and two bus stops) 사실을 알리고 있으므로 대중교통과 가깝다고 한 (C)가 정답이다.

paraphrasing a subway station and two bus stops 지하철역과 두 곳의 버스 정류장 → public transportation 대중교통

[어휘] be located on ~에 위치해 있다   public transportation 대중교통   temporarily 일시적으로   unavailable 이용이 불가능한

06. 세부사항 문제

Wright 씨는 무엇에 대한 비용을 지불하겠다고 제안하는가?
(A) 일부 물품을 보관하는 것
(B) 방을 재단장하는 것
(C) 구인 광고 하는 것
(D) 손상된 가구 교체하는 것

[해설] 비용 지불과 관련된 내용이 제시된 두 번째 단락 후반부에, 상대방 회사의 모든 사무용 가구와 기타 물품들을 임시로 보관할 장소를 임대하는 데 드는 비용을 부담하겠다고(my company can cover the cost of renting a temporary storage unit) 제안하고 있으므로 물품 보관을 의미하는 (A)가 정답이다.

[어휘] store ~을 보관하다   redecorate ~을 재단장하다, 다시 꾸미다   advertise ~을 광고하다   job opening 공석, 빈 자리   replace ~을 교체하다   damaged 손상된

paraphrasing 정답   1. (b)   2. (c)   3. (a)

07-11은 다음 이메일과 편지를 참조하시오.

수신: Chapman 공립 도서관 <contact@chapmanlibrary.org>
발신: Jackie Hannan <jhannon@ctwmailbox.com>
날짜: 2월 4일
제목: 도서관 강좌

관계자께

저는 도서관의 단골 이용 이용객이며, 도서관 측에서 제공하는 대부분의 수업들이 어린이와 청년층에 맞춰져 있다는 사실을 알게 되었습니다. 도서관 활동에 젊은 사람들이 관심을 가지게 하는 것이 중요하다고 생각하기는 하지만, 나이가 든 이용객들에 대해서도 잊지 마셔야 합니다. **07특히 노인들을 위해 고안된 몇몇 수업들을 개설하는 것이 가능할까요? 제 자신을 포함해 제 나이대의 많은 사람들은 기술에 관해 더 많이 배우고 싶어 하는 것으로 알고 있습니다.**

그 외에는, 도서관의 서비스에 대해 다른 불만 사항은 없습니다. 저는 보통 최소한 일주일에 한 번은 도서관을 방문하고 있으며, **08항상 그곳의 직원들이 얼마나 경험이 많고 박식한지에 대해 깊은 인상을 받습니다.** 그분들은 복잡한 조사를 하는 저를 여러 차례 도와 주셨습니다.

귀하의 고려에 대해 감사 드립니다.

Jackie Hannan
Brookview 로 3976번지, 채프먼, 캔자스 67431

regular patron 단골 손님   the majority of 대부분의   be geared toward ~에게 맞춰져 있다   elderly 나이가 많은   designed for ~을 위해 고안된   senior citizen 노인   be impressed with ~에 깊은 인상을 받다   well-informed 박식한   on multiple occasions 여러 차례, 여러 경우에   consideration 고려

Decaro 씨께

저는 귀사의 마케팅 보조 직책에 지원한 Suzanne Kessler 씨를 대신해 편지를 씁니다. 저희 GPL 사에서 3년의 시간을 보내는 동안, Kessler 씨는 다수의 광고 캠페인 작업을 한 바 있습니다. 저는 항상 그녀의 독특한 관점과 혁신적인 아이디어에 깊은 인상을 받았습니다. Kessler 씨는 귀하의 팀에 아주 훌륭한 보탬이 될 것입니다. 세부적인 질문이 있으시다면 귀사의 채용 과정에 기꺼이 추가적으로 협조해 드리겠습니다.

Jack Collins
마케팅 부장, GPL 사

apply for ~에 지원하다   assistant 보조, 조수   numerous 다수의, 수많은   be impressed with ~에 깊은 인상을 받다   perspective 관점, 시각   addition 보탬, 추가(되는 것)   cooperate 협조하다   recruitment 채용   process 과정

Q. Collins 씨는 Kessler 씨에 관해 무엇을 언급하는가?
(A) 창의적인 아이디어를 갖고 있다.
(B) 협조적인 태도를 갖고 있다.

[문제 키워드] What / Mr. Collins / mention / Ms. Kessler

[해설] about 뒤의 키워드 Ms. Kessler가 지문의 전체적인 소재이므로 지문 전반에서 단서를 파악해 각 선택지와 비교해야 한다. 중반부에 Ms. Kessler를 her로 지칭해 독특한 관점과 혁신적인 아이디어가 있다고(her unique perspective and innovate ideas) 알리고 있는데, 이는 창의성을 말하는 것이므로 (A)가 정답이다.

[어휘] attitude 태도

실전 문제
01. (A) 02. (D) 03. (B) 04. (D) 05. (C) 06. (A)
07. (C) 08. (C) 09. (A) 10. (D) 11. (A)

01-03은 다음 편지를 참조하시오.

Penny Dumont
Strand 로 875번지
휴스턴, 텍사스 77032

Dumont 씨께,

곧 있을 귀하의 프로젝트에 대해 저희 Gemini 사를 고려해 주셔서 감사합니다. ―[1]―. 제가 직접 해당 건물을 방문해 봤기 때문에, 상세한 비용 책정 명세서를 제공해 드릴 수 있습니다(동봉 자료 참고). 01옥상 전체를 슬레이트 타일로 교체하는 데 드는 총 비용은 18,500달러입니다. 여기에는 인건비와 모든 자재비가 포함되어 있습니다. ―[2]―. 03해당 기간 이내로 작업 일정을 잡지 않으실 경우, 귀하의 건물을 다시 평가해야 할 수 있습니다. ―[3]―.

경험 많은 직원들과 높은 수준을 자랑하는 저희 Gemini 사를 선택해 주시기를 바랍니다. ―[4]―. 02저희 작업에 대해 과거의 고객들에게서 어떻게 생각하셨는지를 알아보고 싶으실 경우, 저희 웹사이트에서 '추천 후기' 페이지를 방문하시기 바랍니다. 작업 예약을 하시려면, 555-3776으로 전화 주십시오.

곧 연락 주시기를 바랍니다.

Nick Sussex
전문 기사, Gemini 사

now that ~이므로   property 건물, 부동산, 자산   in person 직접 (가서)   pricing 비용 (책정), 가격 (책정)   breakdown 명세서   rooftop (건물의) 옥상   enclosed 동봉된   entire 전체의   labor 노동, 근로   material 자재, 재료, 물품   assess ~을 평가하다   standard 기준, 표준   testimonial 추천 후기, 추천의 글

01. 세부사항 문제

Gemini 사는 무슨 종류의 업체일 것 같은가?
(A) 지붕 공사 전문 업체
(B) 택배 서비스 회사
(C) 장비 수리소
(D) 부동산 중개소

[해설] Gemini Co.의 주요 업무와 관련된 특성이 제시되는 첫 단락에 옥상 전체를 슬레이트 타일로 교체하는 일(replacing your entire rooftop ~)이 언급되어 있으므로 지붕 공사 업체를 의미하는 (A)가 정답이다.

paraphrasing replacing your entire rooftop 옥상 전체를 교체하는 일 → roofing 지붕 공사

[어휘] roofing 지붕 공사   courier 택배 서비스   equipment 장비

02. 세부사항 문제

Dumont 씨는 왜 웹사이트를 방문해야 하는가?
(A) 프로젝트 시작 날짜를 확인해 주기 위해
(B) 사내 소식지를 신청하기 위해
(C) 작업 사진 갤러리를 둘러보기 위해
(D) 다른 고객들의 의견을 읽어 보기 위해

[해설] 웹사이트가 언급된 두 번째 단락에, 과거의 고객들이 생각한 바를 웹사이트의 '추천 후기' 페이지에서 확인할 수 있다고(Should you wish to find out what our past clients thought ~ please visit the "Testimonials" page on our Web site) 알리고 있으므로 '다른 고객들의 의견을 읽어 보기 위해서'라고 한 (D)가 정답이다.

paraphrasing what our past clients thought 과거의 고객들이 생각한 것 → opinions of other customers 다른 고객들의 의견

[어휘] sign up for ~을 신청하다   browse ~을 둘러 보다

03. 문장 삽입 문제

[1], [2], [3] 그리고 [4]로 표시된 위치들 중에서, 다음 문장이 들어가기에 가장 적절한 곳은 어디인가?

"견적 비용은 6개월 동안 유효합니다."

(A) [1]
(B) [2]
(C) [3]
(D) [4]

[해설] 제시된 문장은 견적 비용이 6개월 동안 유효하다는 의미를 나타낸다. 따라서 이 기간을 that time period로 지칭해 그 기간이 지난 이후의 상황을 설명하는 문장 앞에 위치한 [2]에 들어가 견적 비용과 기간, 그리고 그 이후의 조치를 알리는 흐름이 되는 것이 적절하므로 (B)가 정답이다.

[어휘] quoted price 견적 비용   valid 유효한

paraphrasing 정답 1. (a) 2. (b) 3. (c)

샌프란시스코, 캘리포니아 94118

Edwards 씨께

귀하의 자동차에 대한 작업이 완료되었고 이제 가져가시도록 준비가 되었습니다.

팬벨트가 닳았고 완전히 교체되어야 했습니다. 전화상으로 이야기한 대로, 브레이크 패드도 상태가 좋지 않아서 그것들도 교체했습니다. 타이어는 무료로 위치를 바꾸어 드렸고, 오일을 갈고 부동액을 다시 채웠습니다. 작업에 대한 전체 송장은 인쇄되어 접수 데스크에 있습니다. 저희는 평일 오전 8시에서 저녁 7시까지 영업합니다.

Blackwell Shop을 선택해주셔서 감사합니다. 차량을 가져가신 후에, 저희 웹사이트에 가셔서 저희 서비스에 대한 의견을 남겨주세요. 또한, 서비스와 판촉 행사에 대한 업데이트를 확인하시려면 소셜미디어에서 저희를 팔로우해 주세요.

Annie Moore
고객 서비스 대표

 연습 문제

01. (A) 02. (A) 03. (B) 04. (A)

01.

Vaughn 씨께

저희 소프트웨어 시스템의 결함으로 인해, 10월 3일에 이뤄진 일부 은행 이체 거래가 고객들의 계좌에 이중으로 등록되었습니다. 그 결과, 귀하께 BTN 사로부터 각각 231.22달러씩 두 번 지급되었습니다. 두 번째 지급액은 귀하의 계좌로 입금되지 말아야 하는 것이므로, 이 오류를 바로 잡기 위해 저희는 231.22달러를 공제했습니다. **이 금액 이체와 관련해 문의 사항이 있으실 경우, 언제든지 제게 555-4630번으로 전화 주시기 바랍니다.** 이로 인해 초래된 불편함에 대해 사과의 말씀 드립니다.

Dean Abbott
계좌 관리 담당, Warren 은행

glitch 결함, 문제 **transfer** 이체, 송금 **duplicate** 이중의, 중복된 **entry** 입력, 등록 **account** 계좌, 계정 **issue** ~을 지급하다 **payment** 지불(액) **deposit** ~을 입금하다 **deduct** ~을 공제하다

Q. Vaughn 씨는 왜 Abbott 씨에게 연락해야 하는가?
(A) 문의를 하기 위해
(B) 거래를 확인해 주기 위해

[문제 키워드] Why / Ms. Vaughn / contact / Mr. Abbott

[해설] 키워드인 contact가 지문에 직접적으로 언급되어 있지 않으므로 패러프레이징된 부분인 call 주변에서 단서를 찾는다. 지문 후반부에 문의 사항이 있을 경우에 편지 발신인인 자신에게 전화하라고(If you have any questions about this transfer, please feel free to call me ~) 알리고 있으므로 (A)가 정답이다.

02.

Sandra Manning
Mulvey 로 1820번지
위니펙, 매니토바 주 R3M 2A6

Manning 씨께

저희 Riverview 가구에서 맞춤 제작한 오크 나무 캐비닛을 구입해 주셔서 감사드립니다. **저희는 귀하의 제품에 대한 생산 단계를 완료했으며, 현재 배송될 준비가 되어 있습니다.** 이 제품은 저희 창고에서 4월 4일에 출발할 예정이며, 4월 7일 오후 1시에서 5시 사이에 배달될 것입니다. 저희는 귀하의 대금을 전액 수납했습니다. 곧 다시 서비스를 제공해 드릴 수 있기를 바랍니다.

안녕히 계십시오.

Ken Tetreault
고객 서비스 직원, Riverview 가구

custom 맞춤 제작의 **stage** 단계 **ship** ~을 배송하다 **warehouse** 창고 **payment** 지불(액) **in full** 모두, 전부

Q. 편지의 목적은 무엇인가?
(A) 주문 현황을 확인해 주는 것
(B) 배송 지연에 대해 사과하는 것

[문제 키워드] purpose

[해설] 지문 초반부에 제품 생산을 마치고 배송될 준비가 되어 있다고(We have completed the production stage of your item, and it is now ready to be shipped) 밝히는 부분이 목적에 해당되는데, 이는 주문품과 관련된 상황을 알려 주는 것이므로 (A)가 정답이다.

[어휘] status (진행상의) 현황, 상황

03.

Burris 씨께

국립 과학 협회를 대신해, 귀하의 회원 자격이 곧 다가오는 11월 30일에 만료된다는 사실을 알려 드리고자 합니다. —[1]—. 아시다시피, 회원 혜택에는 과학 행사와 워크숍 참석, 과학 관련 도서의 할인, 그리고 저희 웹사이트상의 콘텐츠에 대한 독점 이용 권한이 포함되어 있습니다. —[2]—. **귀하의 회원 혜택을 계속해서 누리시기를 원하시면 작성 완료하셔서 다시 우편으로 보내 주시기 바랍니다.** 귀하가 저희 특별 그룹의 일원으로 계속 남아 있으시기를 바랍니다!

Kieran Foster

on behalf of ~을 대신해, 대표해 **expire** 만료되다 **benefit** 혜택, 이득 **exclusive** 독점적인 **access to** ~에 대한 이용, 접근

Q. [1]과 [2]로 표시된 곳 중 아래 문장이 들어가기에 가장 적절한 곳은 어디인가?

"동봉해 드린 회원 자격 갱신 양식을 확인해 보시기 바랍니다."

(A) [1]
(B) [2]

[해설] 제시된 문장은 '회원 자격 갱신 양식을 동봉했다'는 의미다. 따라서 이 양식을 it으로 지칭하여 함께 양식을 가지고 해야 할 일을 알리는 문장 앞에 위치한 [2]에 들어가 필요한 조치 사항을 전달하는 흐름이 되어야 적절하므로 (B)가 정답이다.

[어휘] renewal 갱신

04.

인사부장 Latonia Decaro
Roanoke 사
Hill 가 611번지
댈러스, 텍사스 주 75204

account 계정, 계좌 frequent customer 단골 고객 reward A with B 보상으로 A에게 B를 주다, B로 A에게 보답하다 credit 입금(액) check out 비용을 지불하고 나가다

01. 한정사 어휘

[해설] 빈칸 뒤에 위치한 credit은 바로 앞 문장에 언급된 a credit of $10를 가리키므로 앞서 제시된 것을 대신할 때 사용하는 지시형용사 (B) This가 정답이다.

02. 동사 어휘

[해설] 빈칸은 명심해야 하는 일을 나타내는 that절에 속해 있는데, 부정어 not이 쓰여 있어 앞 문장에서 말하는 어떤 물품에 대해서도 사용 가능하다는 점과 달리 배송비는 적용 대상이 아니라는 의미가 되어야 알맞다. 따라서 전치사 to와 어울려 '~에 적용되다'라는 뜻으로 쓰이는 (B) apply가 정답이다.

[어휘] accrue 누적되다, ~을 축적하다 direct ~을 감독하다, 지시하다, (길 등을) 안내하다, (문의 사항 등을) 보내다

03. 접속사 자리

[해설] 빈칸 앞뒤로 각각 주어와 동사가 포함된 두 개의 절이 있으므로(명령문인 앞 절은 주어 you가 생략됨) 빈칸은 접속사 자리이다. 따라서 접속사인 (C) whereas와 (D) before 중에서 의미가 적절한 것을 골라야 하는데, 비용을 지불하고 나가기 전에 혜택 적용 버튼을 눌러야 하므로 '~하기 전에'를 뜻하는 (D) before가 정답이다.

[어휘] around ~ 주변에, ~을 둘러 within ~ 이내에 whereas ~인 반면

04. 알맞은 문장 고르기

(A) 최근에 저희 매장을 방문해 주신 것에 대해 다시 한번 감사 드립니다.
(B) 잠시 시간 내시어 온라인 설문지를 작성해 주시기 바랍니다.
(C) 특가 제공 서비스는 오직 한정된 기간에만 이용 가능하다는 점에 유의하시기 바랍니다.
(D) 저희 회사에는 하루 24시간, 일주일 내내 온라인으로 연락 가능한 서비스 직원들이 있습니다.

[해설] 앞 문장에 질문이 있을 경우에 서비스 담당 부서로 연락하라고 권하는 말이 있으므로 해당 서비스 운영 방식을 알리는 (D)가 정답이다.

[어휘] fill out ~을 작성하다 questionnaire 설문지 representative 직원

05-08은 다음 이메일을 참조하시오.

수신: Howard Foley <h.foley@fmail.net>
발신: Customer Service Team <service@wildwheelsmag.net>
날짜: 2월 2일
제목: 취소

구독자께

05이 이메일은 귀하께서 <Wild Wheels Magazine> 구독 서비스를 취소하셨기 때문에 보내 드리는 것입니다. 실수로 '구독 취소'를 누르신 경우에는, 저희에게 연락 주시기 바랍니다. 06저희가 즉시 귀하의 구독 서비스를 복구시켜 드릴 수 있습니다. 07귀하의 서비스 취소 번호는 HF9241입니다. 저희 서비스 담당 직원과 얘기하실 때 사용하시기 바랍니다.

귀하의 1년 구독 서비스는 여전히 2개월의 기간이 남아 있다는 점을 명심하시기 바랍니다. 08이 기간이 만료될 때까지 저희 잡지를 계속 받

아 보실 수 있습니다.

안녕히 계십시오.

<Wild Wheels Magazine>

cancellation 취소 subscriber 구독자, 서비스 가입자 cancel ~을 취소하다 subscription 구독 서비스 unsubscribe 구독을 취소하다, 서비스를 취소하다 accidentally 실수로 in correspondence with ~와 연락을 주고 받는, 편지를 주고 받는 representative 직원 expire 만료되다

05. 접속사 자리

[해설] 빈칸 앞뒤로 각각 주어와 동사가 포함된 두 개의 절이 있으므로 빈칸은 이 절들을 연결할 접속사 자리이다. 따라서 접속사인 (B) if와 (C) because 중에서 의미가 어울리는 것을 찾아야 하는데, 빈칸 뒤에서 말하는 구독 서비스를 취소한 일이 이메일을 보내는 이유에 해당되므로 '~ 때문에'를 뜻하는 (C) because가 정답이다.

[어휘] due to ~로 인해 then 그럼, 그렇다면, 그때, 그런 다음

06. 동사 어휘

[해설] 빈칸이 포함된 문장은 앞 문장에서 말한 실수로 '구독 취소'를 눌러서 업체에 연락했을 경우에 따르는 조치 사항을 나타내야 자연스럽다. 따라서 구독 서비스를 다시 이용할 수 있게 해 준다는 의미에 해당되는 동사가 필요하므로 '~을 회복시키다, 되살리다' 등을 뜻하는 (B) restore가 정답이다.

[어휘] transfer ~을 전근시키다, 옮기다 collect ~을 수거하다, 수집하다, 모으다

07. 알맞은 문장 고르기

(A) 이 이메일에 답변하지 마시기 바랍니다.
(B) 그 시간 이후에 자동으로 그것이 갱신될 것입니다.
(C) 질문이나 우려 사항이 있으시면, 고객 서비스부로 연락하십시오.
(D) 귀하의 서비스 취소 번호는 HF9241입니다.

[해설] 빈칸 뒤에 특정 대상을 지칭하는 that과 함께 담당 직원과 얘기할 때 그것을 사용하라는 문장이 나온다. 따라서 that에 해당될 만한 것으로서 서비스 취소 번호를 알려주는 (D)가 정답이다.

[어휘] respond to ~에 답변하다, 응답하다 renew ~을 갱신하다 concern 우려, 걱정

08. 동사의 형태

[해설] 빈칸 뒤에 위치한 명사구 our magazine과 결합해 동사 continue의 목적어 역할을 할 수 있는 것이 빈칸에 필요하므로 동명사인 (D) receiving이 정답이다. 형용사 (A) receivable과 명사 (B) receipts는 바로 뒤에 our가 올 수 없다.

[어휘] receivable 받을 수 있는, (돈 등을) 받아야 할 receipt 영수증, 받음, 수령

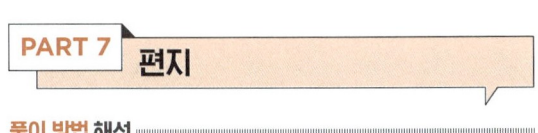

풀이 방법 해석

Blackwell Shop
2003 Geary 로

PART 6 앞의 내용이 단서인 동사 어휘

풀이 방법 해석

수신: Richard Saldana <rsaldana@rmail.net>
발신: Member Services <mserv@joblink.net>
날짜: 9월 15일
제목: 등급 업그레이드

회원님께

이 이메일은 귀하가 Job Link의 회원 등급을 골드 패키지로 업그레이드하신 것을 확인하기 위함입니다. 당신의 사업체는 이제 다양한 기능을 사용할 수 있습니다. 일자리를 게시하고, 프로필에 접근하고 경력이나 전문성 등을 지정하여 검색할 수 있습니다. 편하신 때에 저희 웹사이트인 www.joblink.net/login에 접속하셔서 그렇게 하시면 됩니다.

저희 Job Link는 귀하의 회사의 프라이버시를 존중한다는 것을 유념해 주세요. 귀하가 게시해달라고 요청한 회사의 세부 정보만 보이도록 합니다.

Job Link 회원 서비스

연습 문제

01.(A) 02.(A) 03.(B) 04.(B)

01.

오늘 경험이 어떠셨나요? Lily's Garden은 여러분께서 저희 레스토랑에 관해 해주시는 말씀을 들어 보기를 원하므로, 잠시 시간 내셔서 설문지를 작성해 주시기 바랍니다. 이렇게 해주시면, 다음 번에 이곳에서 식사하실 때 10퍼센트 할인을 받으실 수 있는 쿠폰을 지급받으시게 됩니다.

experience 경험 **take a moment to**부정사 잠시 시간 내서 ~하다 **fill out** ~을 작성하다

[단서] restaurant

[해설] 앞 문장에서 레스토랑 이용 경험에 관한 설문지를 작성하도록 요청하고 있으므로 다음 번에 할인을 받기 위한 행위와 관련된 동사로서 '식사하다'를 뜻하는 (A) dine이 정답이다.

[어휘] negotiate 협상하다

02.

National Arbor Group(NAG)은 전국에 걸쳐 산림을 복구하는 데 전념하고 있습니다. 현재까지, 5,000평방마일이 넘는 범위에 나무들을 심어 왔습니다.

be dedicated to -ing ~하는 데 전념하다 **restore** ~을 복구하다, 회복시키다 **to date** 현재까지 **square miles** 평방마일

[단서] restoring forests

[해설] 앞 문장에서 산림을 복구하는 데 전념하는 단체임을 알리고 있으므로 이와 관련해 나무로 할 수 있는 행위를 나타낼 동사로 '~을 심다'를 뜻하는 (A) planted가 정답이다.

[어휘] log ~을 벌목하다

03.

Rochester Roofing은 불과 몇 명밖에 되지 않는 직원들로 5년 전에 설립되었지만, 빠르게 뛰어난 명성을 얻었습니다. 수요에 발맞추기 위해, 설립자 Kelly Moss 씨는 20명의 추가 직원을 고용했습니다.

found ~을 설립하다 **gain** ~을 얻다, 획득하다 **outstanding** 뛰어난 **reputation** 명성, 평판 **keep up with** (속도, 진척 등) ~와 발맞추다, ~을 따라 잡다 **demand** 수요, 요구

[단서] To keep up with demand

[해설] 앞서 언급된 빠르게 뛰어난 명성을 얻었다는 말은 회사의 발전을 의미하므로 수요를 따라잡기 위해 추가 직원과 관련해 한 일을 나타낼 동사로 '~을 고용하다'를 뜻하는 (B) hired가 정답이다.

04.

개조 공사가 주방 공간을 확장시켜 주고 드라이브스루 창구를 추가해 줄 것입니다. 이는 우리가 서비스를 제공할 수 있는 고객들의 숫자를 극대화해 줄 것입니다.

renovation 개조, 보수 **expand** ~을 확장하다, 확대하다 **add** ~을 추가하다

[단서] expand, add

[해설] 앞서 언급된 주방 공간의 확장과 드라이브스루 창구 추가가 고객 숫자에 미치는 영향과 관련된 동사가 필요하므로 '~을 극대화하다, 최대화하다'를 뜻하는 (B)가 정답이다.

[어휘] reduce ~을 감소시키다

실전 문제

01.(B) 02.(B) 03.(D) 04.(D) 05.(C) 06.(B)
07.(D) 08.(D)

01-04는 다음 이메일을 참조하시오.

수신: t.jensen@rmail.net
발신: custserv@borneo.net
날짜: 10월 7일
제목: Borneo 계정

고객님께,

단골 고객이 되어 주신 것에 대해, 저희 Borneo.net이 보답해 드리기 위해 귀하께 10달러의 금액을 지급해 드렸습니다. [01]이 지급액은 저희 웹사이트의 어떤 물품에 대해서도 사용하실 수 있습니다. [02]이 금액이 배송비에는 적용되지 않는다는 점을 명심하시기 바랍니다. 다음 번에 www.borneo.net에 로그인하실 때, '내 계정' 페이지를 확인해 보십시오. [03]이 지급액을 사용하기 위해서는, 비용을 지불하고 나가시기 전에 '마이 크레딧' 버튼을 누르기만 하시면 됩니다.

어떤 질문이든지 있으실 경우에는 언제든지 저희 서비스 담당 부서로 편하게 연락 주시기 바랍니다. [04]저희 회사에는 하루 24시간, 일주일 내내 온라인으로 연락 가능한 서비스 직원들이 있습니다.

안녕히 계십시오.

Borneo 온라인 아울렛 서비스팀

[해설] 선택지가 다양한 동사들로 구성되어 있으므로 동사 어휘 문제이다. 빈칸 뒤에 to부정사가 있으므로 to부정사를 목적어로 취하는 동사 (B) plans가 정답이다. (D) suggests는 동명사를 목적어로 취한다.

[어휘] personnel department 인사부   a series of 일련의   supply ~을 공급하다   remain ~한 상태로 유지되다

15. 5형식 동사

최근의 설문 조사에 따르면 대부분의 온라인 고객들은 신속한 계산 기능이 사용하기 매우 편리하다고 생각하는 것으로 나타난다.

[해설] 선택지가 다양한 동사들로 구성되어 있으므로 동사 어휘 문제이다. 빈칸 뒤에 위치한 '목적어(the quick check-out)+목적격 보어(convenient)' 구조와 어울리는 동사가 필요하므로 이 구조로 쓰여 '~을 …하다고 생각하다'라는 의미를 나타내는 동사 (D) find가 정답이다.

[어휘] check-out 계산(대)   convenient 편리한   place ~을 놓다, 두다   join ~에 함께 하다, 합류하다

16. 장소 전치사

주요 생산 시설 견학이 Massey 씨의 출장 일정표에 올라 있다.

[해설] 선택지가 다양한 전치사들로 구성되어 있으므로 전치사 어휘 문제이다. itinerary는 '일정(표)'를 의미하며, 일정표 등의 문서에 적힌 것을 나타낼 때는 전치사 on을 사용하므로 (A) on이 정답이다.

[어휘] facility 시설(물)   itinerary 일정(표)   business trip 출장

17. 부사의 역할과 위치: 형용사 수식

Randall 씨는 남달리 유능한 직원들을 모집하는 것을 알려져 있다.

[해설] 선택지가 다양한 품사의 단어들로 구성되어 있으므로 문법 문제이다. be동사 are와 보어로 쓰인 형용사 competent 사이에 위치한 빈칸은 형용사를 수식할 부사 자리이므로 부사 어미 -ly로 끝나는 (A) exceptionally가 정답이다.

[어휘] be known for ~로 알려져 있다   recruit ~을 모집하다   competent 유능한   exceptionally 남달리, 유난히, 이례적으로   exception 예외   except ~을 제외하다

18. 명사의 역할: 목적어 역할

개발자들이 기능을 감소시키지 않고 AirLite 태블릿의 배터리 수명을 증가시키기 위해 노력하고 있다.

[해설] 선택지가 다양한 품사의 단어들로 구성되어 있으므로 문법 문제이다. 빈칸은 전치사 without의 목적어로 쓰인 동명사 reducing의 목적어 자리이므로 명사 (D) functionality가 정답이다.

[어휘] developer 개발자   function 기능하다   functionally 기능적으로   functional 기능하는   functionality 기능성

19. 형용사 어휘

Collins 씨는 주가와 시장을 예측하는 혁신적인 컴퓨터 소프트웨어 프로그램들을 개발했다.

[해설] 선택지가 다양한 형용사들로 구성되어 있으므로 형용사 어휘 문제이다. 빈칸 뒤에 위치한 명사구 computer software programs를 수식해 그 특성을 나타내기에 적절한 형용사가 필요하므로 '혁신적인'을 의미하는 (D) innovative가 정답이다.

[어휘] develop ~을 개발하다   predict ~을 예측하다   stock value 주가   severe 극심한, 혹독한

20. 동사의 형태

경영진은 추가 직원을 고용함으로써 개별 업무량을 줄여 주겠다고 약속했다.

[해설] 선택지가 동사 promise의 다양한 형태로 구성되어 있으므로 문법 문제이다. 빈칸 앞에 위치한 has와 결합 가능한 것이 필요하므로 현재완료 시제를 구성할 때 사용하는 과거분사 형태인 (B) promised가 정답이다.

[어휘] promise to부정사 ~하겠다고 약속하다   reduce ~을 줄이다   individual 개별의, 개인의   workload 업무량

21. 형용사 어휘

대학교 의류 제품에 대해 20퍼센트 할인을 받기 위해서는, 학생들은 반드시 유효한 학생증을 보여 줘야 한다.

[해설] 선택지가 다양한 형용사들로 구성되어 있으므로 형용사 어휘 문제이다. 빈칸 뒤에 위치한 명사구 student ID(학생증)를 수식하기에 적절한 형용사가 필요한데, 증명서로서의 역할과 관련된 특성을 나타내야 하므로 '유효한'이라는 뜻으로 쓰이는 (D) valid가 정답이다.

[어휘] in order to부정사 ~하기 위해   steady 한결같은, 꾸준한   common 흔한   valid 유효한

22. 3형식 동사

기자 회견 중에, Whitman 씨는 자신의 회사가 HB 산업을 인수할 것이라고 공식적으로 발표했다.

[해설] 선택지가 다양한 동사들로 구성되어 있으므로 동사 어휘 문제이다. 빈칸 뒤에 that절이 바로 이어져 있으므로 that절을 목적어로 취하는 동사 (C) announced가 정답이다. (A) told의 경우, 'tell+사람 목적어+that절'의 구조로 쓰인다.

[어휘] press conference 기자 회견   officially 공식적으로   acquire ~을 인수하다, 매입하다   remain ~한 상태로 유지되다   outline ~을 간략히 설명하다

23. 형용사 어휘

잘 상하는 모든 식품을 가능한 한 오래 신선하게 유지하기 위해, Mullins Shipping 사는 압축 포장 기계를 사용한다.

[해설] 선택지가 다양한 형용사들로 구성되어 있으므로 형용사 어휘 문제이다. 빈칸에 들어가 명사 items를 수식할 형용사는 가능한 한 오래 신선하게 유지될 필요가 있는 제품의 특성과 관련되어야 하므로 '잘 상하는'을 뜻하는 (C) perishable이 정답이다.

[어휘] shrink-wrapping 수축 포장   mandatory 의무적인   noteworthy 주목할 만한   thorough 철저한

24. 동사의 형태

주민들은 Newton 도서관의 원래 건물이 철거되는 대신 박물관으로 복구되어야 한다고 주장했다.

[해설] 선택지가 동사 restore의 다양한 형태로 구성되어 있으므로 문법 문제이다. 빈칸이 속한 that절에 빈칸 앞뒤로 각각 명사구와 as 전치사구만 위치해 있으므로 빈칸이 that절의 동사 자리이다. 따라서 동사인 (D) should be restored가 정답이다.

[어휘] resident 주민   argue that ~라고 주장하다   demolish ~을 철거하다   restore ~을 복구하다, 복원하다

04. 동사의 형태

Deacon 제조사의 부서장들은 개조 공사 계획에 새로운 휴게실 공간과 카페를 포함시키기로 결정했다.

[해설] 선택지가 다양한 품사의 단어들로 구성되어 있으므로 문법 문제이다. 빈칸 앞뒤로 명사와 전치사구, 그리고 to부정사구만 위치해 있으므로 빈칸이 문장의 동사 자리이다. 따라서 동사의 형태인 (B) have decided가 정답이다.

[어휘] supervisor 부서장, 책임자, 상사 decide to부정사 ~하기로 결정하다 renovation 개조, 보수 decision 결정

05. 동사의 형태

Lawson County Fair의 입장권 매출이 행사 기획자들이 예상했던 것을 초과했다.

[해설] 선택지가 다양한 품사의 단어들로 구성되어 있으므로 문법 문제이다. 빈칸 앞뒤로 명사와 전치사구, 그리고 what이 이끄는 명사절이 있으므로 빈칸이 문장의 동사 자리이다. 따라서 과거 시제 동사의 형태인 (C) exceeded가 정답이다.

[어휘] sales 매출, 판매(량) planner 기획자 predict ~을 예상하다 exceed ~을 초과하다 excessive 과도한

06. 형용사 어휘

Franco Home의 은식기류는 가격이 적당하지만, 신중히 다루지 않으면 녹에 취약하다.

[해설] 선택지가 다양한 형용사들로 구성되어 있으므로 형용사 어휘 문제이다. 빈칸 뒤에 위치한 'to+부정적인 요소'와 어울리는 형용사가 필요하므로 이와 같은 전치사구와 함께 '~에 취약한, 피해를 입기 쉬운' 등의 의미를 나타낼 때 사용하는 (B) vulnerable이 정답이다.

[어휘] silverware 은식기류 affordable 가격이 알맞은 rust 녹 handle ~을 다루다 remarkable 놀랄 만한 exemplary 모범적인, 본보기가 되는 subsequent 그 다음의

07. 명령문

비바람으로 인한 피해를 방지하기 위해, 주택 외벽에 날씨의 영향을 받지 않는 페인트를 사용하십시오.

[해설] 선택지가 다양한 품사의 단어들로 구성되어 있으므로 문법 문제이다. 목적을 나타내는 In order to부정사 구문 이후로 빈칸과 명사구만 있으므로 주어 없이 동사만으로 문장을 구성할 수 있는 형태인 명령문을 이끄는 동사원형 (C) use가 정답이다.

[어휘] in order to부정사 ~하기 위해 prevent ~을 방지하다 damage 피해, 손상 elements 비바람, 폭풍우 weather resistant 날씨의 영향을 받지 않는

08. 동사의 형태

Lucian 사에서는 휴가를 떠나기 전에 부서장의 승인이 필수이다.

[해설] 선택지가 동사 require의 다양한 형태로 구성되어 있으므로 문법 문제이다. 빈칸 앞에 위치한 be동사 is와 결합 가능한 형태가 필요한데, 빈칸 뒤에 목적어가 없으므로 타동사 require가 수동태로 쓰여야 한다. 따라서 과거분사 (C) required가 정답이다.

[어휘] supervisor 부서장, 책임자, 상사 approval 승인 take leave 휴가를 떠나다 require ~을 필요로 하다 required 필수의, 필요한

09. 조동사+동사원형

직사광선이 그림을 손상시킬 수 있기 때문에, 그 미술품들은 박물관 지하에 전시되어 있다.

[해설] 선택지가 동사 damage의 다양한 형태로 구성되어 있으므로 문법 문제이다. 조동사 can 뒤에는 동사원형이 쓰여야 하므로 (C) damage가 정답이다.

[어휘] artwork 미술품 display ~을 진열하다, 전시하다 basement 지하(실) damage ~을 손상시키다, ~에 피해를 입히다

10. 2형식 동사

모든 고객 파일을 디지털화하는 작업이 엄청난 일인 것으로 드러나고 있다.

[해설] 선택지가 다양한 동사들로 구성되어 있으므로 동사 어휘 문제이다. 빈칸 뒤에 위치한 'to be 명사 보어' 구조와 어울려야 하므로 '~하는 것으로 드러나다, 판명되다'라는 의미를 나타낼 때 사용하는 2형식 동사 (B) proving이 정답이다.

[어휘] digitize ~을 디지털화하다 prove to be A A한 것으로 드러나다 enormous 엄청난, 막대한 task 일, 업무 seek ~을 찾다, 구하다 place ~을 놓다, 두다

11. 3형식 동사

Perfect Fit은 지하에 실내 수영장과 400미터 트랙을 갖고 있다.

[해설] 선택지가 다양한 동사들로 구성되어 있으므로 동사 어휘 문제이다. 빈칸 뒤에 위치한 명사구 an indoor swimming pool과 400 meter track은 Perfect Fit이라는 체육 시설에 속하는 하나의 공간에 해당하므로 '~을 특징으로 하다, 포함하다'등을 의미하는 타동사 (D) features가 정답이다. (A) arrives와 (B) completes는 자동사로만 쓰이며, (C) refers는 자동사와 타동사로 모두 쓰이지만 의미가 맞지 않는다.

[어휘] indoor 실내의 track 경주로, 트랙 basement 지하실

12. 3형식 동사

당신의 동료들이 이곳에서의 당신의 직책에 해당되는 다른 상세 정보를 제공해 줄 것입니다.

[해설] 선택지가 다양한 동사들로 구성되어 있으므로 동사 어휘 문제이다. 빈칸 뒤에 위치한 '사람+with+사물' 구조와 어울리는 동사가 필요하므로 이 구조로 쓰여 '~에게 …을 제공하다'를 의미하는 (C) provide가 정답이다.

[어휘] specific to ~에 특정하게 해당되는 position 직책, 일자리 describe ~을 설명하다

13. 형용사 어휘

무대 감독은 500달러의 비용이 공연에 필요한 소품을 구입하는 데 충분할 것이라고 추산했다.

[해설] 선택지가 다양한 형용사들로 구성되어 있으므로 형용사 어휘 문제이다. be동사 뒤에 위치한 빈칸에 쓰일 형용사는 that절의 주어 $500가 지니는 비용 가치와 관련된 의미를 나타내야 하므로 '충분한'을 뜻하는 (A) sufficient가 정답이다.

[어휘] estimate that ~라고 추정하다 acquire ~을 얻다, 획득하다 props 소품 flexible 유연한, 탄력적인 capable 능력 있는, 할 수 있는 calculating 계산적인

14. 3형식 동사

인사부는 다음 달에 일련의 워크숍을 개최할 계획이다.

DAY 08

PART 5 문법 | 동사의 형태 변화와 종류

확인 문제 해석

❶ Moore 씨는 그녀의 직원들에게 이메일을 보냈다.
❷ 그 주문품은 내일 도착할 것이다.
❸ 더 자세한 정보를 얻으시려면 그저 저희 웹사이트를 방문하시기만 하면 됩니다.
❹ Long 씨는 건축 법규를 준수했다.
❺ Emerson 화학은 선두 기업이 되었다.
❻ Wilkinson 씨는 프로젝트 마감 시한이 연장되어야 한다는 데 동의했다.
❼ Miller 씨는 그녀의 컴퓨터를 안전하게 두었다.

연습 문제

01.(C) 02.(A) 03.(C) 04.(C) 05.(B) 06.(B)

01.
1. 선택지 보고 문법/어휘 문제 파악하기 ☑문법 문제 ☐어휘 문제
2. 빈칸 분석하기 문장에 없는 요소 ☐주어 ☑동사
   → 빈칸은 ☐주어 형태 ☑동사 형태를 완성할 자리이다.
3. 정답 선택하기 정답 (C)

엘크턴의 시민들은 그들의 공공 도서관을 지키기 위해 10만 달러를 기부했다.

02.
1. 선택지 보고 문법/어휘 문제 파악하기 ☑문법 문제 ☐어휘 문제
2. 빈칸 분석하기 빈칸 앞에 있는 것 ☐전치사 ☑조동사 ☐부사
   → 빈칸은 ☑동사원형 ☐명사 자리이다.
3. 정답 선택하기 정답 (A)

이 정수 장치 중 하나는 작은 마을에 식수를 충분히 공급할 수 있습니다.

03.
1. 선택지 보고 문법/어휘 문제 파악하기 ☐문법 문제 ☑어휘 문제
2. 빈칸 분석하기 빈칸 앞의 be동사, 빈칸 뒤의 전치사 for와 함께 짝꿍으로 쓰이는 형용사가 정답이다.
3. 정답 선택하기 정답 (C)

이 호텔 방은 4명 이상이 여행하는 가족에게 적합하다.

04.
1. 선택지 보고 문법/어휘 문제 파악하기 ☐문법 문제 ☑어휘 문제
2. 빈칸 분석하기 빈칸 뒤에 있는 전치사 (in)
3. 정답 선택하기 함께 쓰이는 동사가 정답 (C)

매년 수천 명의 사람들이 연례 메이슨 시 마라톤에 참가한다.

05.
1. 선택지 보고 문법/어휘 문제 파악하기 ☐문법 문제 ☑어휘 문제
2. 빈칸 분석하기 빈칸 뒤에 있는 것 ☐주격 보어 ☑명사절
   → 빈칸은 ☐2형식 동사 ☑3형식 동사 자리이다.
3. 정답 선택하기 정답 (B)

Benjamin Jones는 그가 내년에 화이트스톤의 시장으로 출마할 것이라고 발표했다.

06.
1. 선택지 보고 문법/어휘 문제 파악하기 ☐문법 문제 ☑어휘 문제
2. 빈칸 분석하기 빈칸 뒤에 있는 것 ☑명사구+명사구 ☐명사구+형용사 보어
   → 빈칸은 ☑4형식 동사 ☐5형식 동사 자리이다.
3. 정답 선택하기 정답 (B)

Gourmet Market은 매장 회원들에게 추가 할인을 제공한다.

실전 문제

01.(D)	02.(B)	03.(B)	04.(B)	05.(C)	06.(B)
07.(C)	08.(C)	09.(C)	10.(B)	11.(D)	12.(C)
13.(A)	14.(B)	15.(D)	16.(A)	17.(A)	18.(D)
19.(D)	20.(B)	21.(D)	22.(C)	23.(C)	24.(D)

01. 동사의 형태

전문 재정 자문가인 Rose Weiss 씨는 하루 단위로 세계 통화 시장을 평가한다.

[해설] 선택지가 다양한 품사의 단어들로 구성되어 있으므로 문법 문제이다. 빈칸 앞뒤로 각각 주어와 목적어에 해당되는 명사구들만 위치해 있으므로 빈칸은 문장의 동사 자리이다. 따라서 동사인 (D) evaluates가 정답이다.

[어휘] financial advisor 재정 자문 currency market 통화 시장
on a daily basis 하루 단위로, 매일 evaluation 평가(서) evaluator 평가자 evaluate ~을 평가하다

02. 동사의 형태

응급 의료 상황 전문가들은 어떤 종류의 상황에 대해서도 침착한 상태를 유지하도록 지시받는다.

[해설] 선택지가 다양한 품사의 단어들로 구성되어 있으므로 문법 문제이다. 빈칸 앞뒤에 각각 위치한 be동사 are와 to부정사와 결합할 수 있는 단어가 필요하므로 이 둘과 함께 '~하도록 지시받다'라는 의미를 나타낼 때 사용하는 (B) instructed가 정답이다.

[어휘] professional 전문가 remain ~한 상태를 유지하다 calm 침착한 instruct ~에게 지시하다 instructor 강사

03. 형용사 어휘

DeRosa 은행은 전적으로 안전하고 24시간 감시되는 금고실에 접근할 수 있는 권한을 VIP 고객들에게 제공하고 있다.

[해설] 선택지가 다양한 형용사들로 구성되어 있으므로 형용사 어휘 문제이다. 빈칸에 쓰일 형용사는 선행사 vault space(금고실)의 특성을 나타내기에 알맞은 것이어야 하므로 '안전한'을 의미하는 (B) secure가 정답이다.

[어휘] access to ~에 대한 접근, 이용 vault space 금고실
completely 전적으로, 완전히 around the clock 24시간
accustomed 익숙한 secure 안전한 additional 추가적인 relevant 관련된

on short notice 급한 연락에도 (불구하고), 급한 공지에도

06. 추론 문제

Kramer 씨에 관해 암시된 것은 무엇인가?
(A) 수상 후보로 지명되었다.
(B) 작년 행사에서 발표자였다.
(C) 자신의 세무 대리 전문 회사를 시작했다.
(D) Maldano 씨의 이전 직장 동료이다.

[해설] Kramer 씨가 언급된 초반부에, 그 사람이 작년에 했던 세무 소프트웨어 선택에 관한 유익한 연설이 많은 참가자들에게 유용했다는(His informative talk last year on selecting tax software was helpful to a lot of participants ~) 말이 있으므로 작년 행사에서 연설을 한 사람임을 알 수 있다. 따라서 (B)가 정답이다.

[어휘] be nominated for ~에 대한 후보로 지명되다   tax preparation 세무 대리(업)   former 이전의, 과거의   colleague 동료

07. 세부사항 문제

Soto 씨는 내일 무엇을 보낼 계획인가?
(A) 최종 확정된 일정표
(B) 발표 슬라이드에 필요한 이미지
(C) 시스템 요구 사항이 담긴 목록
(D) 콘퍼런스 참가자들로부터 받은 질문

[해설] 발신인인 Soto 씨가 내일 보내겠다고 말하는 것은 마지막 문장에 제시되는데, 질의응답 시간을 준비하는 데 도움이 될 수 있도록 내일 그것들을 보내겠다고(I'll send those to you tomorrow ~) 알리는 부분이 있다. 여기서 그것들(those)은 바로 앞서 언급된 사람들이 제출한 질문들을(we asked people to submit questions ~) 가리키므로 (D)가 정답이다.

[어휘] requirement 요구 사항, 필요 조건

paraphrasing 정답   1. (a)   2. (c)   3. (b)

08-10은 다음 이메일을 참조하시오.

수신: <selmavernon@antonioco.com>
발신: <randolphi@nbexpo.net>
날짜: 5월 20일
제목: 전국 비즈니스 엑스포

Vernon 씨께

[08]전국 비즈니스 엑스포(NBE)를 대표해, Hopkins Plaza에서 개최되는 올해의 행사에 등록해 주셔서 감사드립니다. 이틀 간의 VIP 패키지에 대한 귀하의 등록은 확인되었으며, 귀하께서는 엑스포가 시작되는 6월 7일보다 약 일주일 앞서 우편으로 환영 책자 묶음을 받으시게 됩니다.

모든 참가자들께서는 행사 현장에 계시는 동안 반드시 NBE에서 발급한 신분증을 착용하셔야 합니다. [09]귀하는 등록 페이지에서 사진을 업로드하지 않으신 것으로 보입니다. 귀하의 신분증을 제작해 환영 책자 묶음과 함께 제때 발송해 드릴 수 있도록 사진 한 장을 제게 이메일로 보내 주시겠습니까? 이렇게 하지 않으실 경우, 입구에서 문제를 겪으실 수도 있습니다. [10]시내에 있는 Hopkins Plaza가 시내에 위치해 있는 탓에 그곳의 주차장이 매우 협소하다는 점에 유의하시기 바랍니다. 외부 지역에서 방문하시는 경우, 호텔에서 버스나 택시를 이용하실 것을 권해 드립니다.

안녕히 계십시오.

Ivan Randolph

on behalf of ~을 대표해   register for ~에 등록하다   registration 등록   packet 책자 묶음, 자료 묶음   approximately 약, 대략   issue ~을 발급하다   premises (건물) 구내, 부지, 현장   in time 제때   from out of town 외부 지역으로부터

08. 추론 문제

Randolph 씨는 누구일 것 같은가?
(A) 호텔 소유주
(B) 경영학 교수
(C) 행사 기획자
(D) 인쇄소 직원

[해설] 지문 하단 부분을 통해 Randolph 씨가 발신인임을 알 수 있으며, 첫 문장에서 전국 비즈니스 엑스포(NBE)를 대표해 올해의 행사에 등록한 것에 대해 감사하게 생각한다는(On behalf of the National Business Expo (NBE), I would like to thank you for registering for this year's event ~) 말로 자신의 신분을 암시하고 있다. 따라서 이와 같은 인사를 할 수 있는 입장에 있는 사람으로 적절한 (C)가 정답이다.

09. 세부사항 문제

Randolph 씨는 Vernon 씨에게 무엇을 하도록 요청하는가?
(A) 사진 제출하기
(B) VIP 패키지로 업그레이드하기
(C) 지정 좌석 선택하기
(D) 등록 양식에 서명하기

[해설] Randolph 씨의 요청 사항이 언급된 두 번째 단락에서 Vernon 씨가 등록 페이지에서 사진을 업로드하지 않았기 때문에 사진 한 장을 이메일로 보내 달라고(~ you did not upload a photograph of yourself on the registration page. Could you please e-mail one to me ~) 요청하는 내용이 있으므로 (A)가 정답이다.

paraphrasing   e-mail one 이메일로 보내다 → Submit 제출하다

[어휘] designated 지정된

10. True 문제

Hopkins Plaza에 관해 언급된 것은 무엇인가?
(A) 작년 엑스포 행사의 개최 장소였다.
(B) 차량을 위한 공간이 제한되어 있다.
(C) 셔틀버스 서비스를 운영하고 있다.
(D) 6월 7일에 완전히 예약되어 있다.

[해설] 두 번째 단락에 Hopkins Plaza의 주차장이 매우 협소하다는(~ Hopkins Plaza's downtown location, its parking lot is very small) 특징이 제시되어 있으므로 이에 해당되는 (B)가 정답이다.

paraphrasing   very small 매우 협소한 → limited space 제한된 공간

[어휘] vehicle 차량   operate ~을 운영하다   completely 완전히, 전적으로   booked 예약된

paraphrasing 정답   1. (c)   2. (b)   3. (a)

[어휘] expire 만료되다 recently 최근에 renew 갱신하다 payment 납부, 지불

paraphrasing 정답   1. (b)   2. (a)   3. (c)

03-04는 다음 이메일을 참조하시오.

수신: Charlene Yee <yeechar@geosales.com>
발신: Lexington Supermarket <info@lexingtonsuper.com>
날짜: 12월 13일
제목: 기회를 놓치지 마세요!

Yee 씨께

03Lexington 슈퍼마켓 보상 카드(LSRC)의 최근 수령인들 중 한 분으로서, 귀하께서는 이용 가능하신 옵션들을 알고 계셔야 합니다. 대부분의 쇼핑객들께서는 저희 Lexington 슈퍼마켓에서 지불하는 1달러에 대해 1포인트를 적립할 수 있다는 사실을 알고 계십니다. 저희는 또한 지정된 달에 귀하께 두 배의 포인트를 제공해 드리는 브랜드들을 담은 목록인 월간 <Lexington Spotlight>도 발송해 드리고 있습니다.

하지만, 귀하께서 오직 Lexington 슈퍼마켓에서만 LSRC 회원 혜택을 이용하고 계실 경우, 가능한 가장 빠른 방법으로 포인트를 쌓지 못하시게 됩니다. 대신, 04저희 제휴 업체에서 제공하는 포인트 적립 기회를 활용하셔야 하는데, 여기에는 Western 철도와 McGrath 의류, Evergreen 영화관을 비롯한 다수의 업체들이 포함되어 있습니다. 귀하의 포인트를 훨씬 더 많이 늘리실 수 있도록 이 업체들을 방문하실 때 LSRC를 꼭 제시하시기 바랍니다.

저희 매장에서 쇼핑해 주셔서 감사드립니다!

LSRC 팀

recipient 수령인, 받는 사람   earn 받다, 얻다; 얻게 하다   designated 지정된   benefit 혜택   take advantage of ~을 이용하다   present ~을 제시하다   boost ~을 늘리다, 증대하다

03. 세부사항 문제

Yee 씨는 왜 이메일을 받는가?
(A) 일정량의 식료품을 구입했다.
(B) 고객 설문지에 답변했다.
(C) 일부 슈퍼마켓 쿠폰을 다운로드했다.
(D) 최근에 단골 고객용 프로그램에 가입했다.

[해설] 첫 문장에 Lexington 슈퍼마켓 보상 카드(LSRC)의 최근 수령인들 중 한 사람으로서(As one of the newest recipients of Lexington Supermarket Rewards Card (LSRC) ~) 이용 가능한 옵션들을 알고 있어야 한다고 알리고 있는데, 이는 단골 고객들이 이용하는 카드일 것이므로 (D)가 정답이다.

[어휘] respond to ~에 답변하다, 응답하다   questionnaire 설문지   sign up for ~에 가입하다, ~을 신청하다   loyalty program 단골 고객용 프로그램

04. 세부사항 문제

Yee 씨는 무엇을 하도록 권장받는가?
(A) 우편물 발송 대상자 명단에 이름 추가하기
(B) 가장 좋아하는 브랜드에 대한 후기 제공하기
(C) 다른 업체에서 회원 카드 사용하기
(D) 혜택 관련 정책의 변경 사항 확인하기

[해설] 권장되는 일이 언급되는 두 번째 단락에, 제휴 업체에서 제공하는 포인트 적립 기회를 활용하라고(you should take advantage of the point-earning opportunities offered by our partners ~) 권장하는 말과 함께 해당 업체들을 소개하고 있으므로 다른 업체에서의 카드 사용을 의미하는 (C)가 정답이다.

[어휘] add A to B A를 B에 추가하다   mailing list 우편물 발송 대상자 명단

paraphrasing 정답   1. (b)   2. (c)   3. (a)

05-07은 다음 이메일을 참조하시오.

수신: Felicia Maldano <fmaldano@m1-solutions.net>
발신: Mickey Soto <mickey@tpcevent.org>
날짜: 11월 10일
제목: 세무 전문가 콘퍼런스

Maldano 씨께

저는 다가오는 세무 전문가 콘퍼런스에서 회계사들을 위한 고객 서비스 팁을 주제로 한 귀하의 강연을 들을 수 있기를 진심으로 고대하고 있습니다. 05Timothy Kramer 씨가 아파서 최종 순간에 취소하셔야 했기 때문에 그분의 오전 시간을 대신해 주시는 것에 대해 다시 한번 감사드립니다. 06세무 소프트웨어 선택에 관해 그분께서 작년에 해주신 유익한 연설이 많은 참가자들에게 유용했기 때문에, 올해 그분의 전문 지식을 듣지 못하게 되어 아쉬울 것입니다. 하지만, 귀하께서 선정하신 주제에 관해 이미 많은 긍정적인 의견을 들었기 때문에, 좋은 평가를 받게 될 것이라고 생각합니다. 귀하의 발표에 수반되는 어떠한 사진이나 그래픽 자료가 있으실 경우, 내일 일과가 끝날 때까지 제게 보내 주셔야 저희 시스템과의 호환성 여부를 다시 한번 확인할 수 있습니다. 또한, 저희 웹사이트에서, 사람들에게 콘퍼런스 주제에 관련된 질문을 제출하도록 요청했습니다. 07마지막 순서로 진행되는 질의응답 시간을 준비하시는 데 도움이 될 수 있도록 내일 귀하께 그 질문들을 보내 드리겠습니다.

안녕히 계십시오.

Mickey Soto

accountant 회계사   cover ~을 대신하다, 대신 맡다   at the last minute 최종 순간에   illness 아픔, 병   informative 유용한, 정보를 주는   it is a shame to부정사 ~해서 아쉽다, 안타깝다   expertise 전문 지식   well received 좋은 평가를 받는   accompany ~에 동반되다   compatibility 호환(성)

05. 세부사항 문제

Soto 씨는 왜 Maldano 씨에게 감사하는가?
(A) Kramer 씨를 위해 메모를 준비했다.
(B) Soto 씨의 연설에 대한 주제를 제안했다.
(C) 콘퍼런스 예산에 기부금을 냈다.
(D) 급한 연락에도 일을 수락했다.

[해설] 지문 초반부에 Timothy Kramer 씨가 아파서 최종 순간에 취소를 하는 바람에 그 사람이 맡았던 오전 시간을 대신하는 것에 대해 감사하다고(~ for covering Timothy Kramer's morning session, as he had to cancel at the last minute ~) 인사하는 부분을 통해 급히 대체할 사람으로 이메일의 수신인인 Maldano 씨를 찾았다는 것을 알 수 있으므로 (D)가 정답이다.

[어휘] donate 기부하다, 기부금을 내다   budget 예산   task 일, 업무

03.

수신: Priya Chetti <pchetti@alvareztransportation.com>
발신: Miguel Guerrero <miguel.g@alvareztransportation.com>
날짜: 11월 13일
제목: 회신: 잊으신 물품

Chetti 씨께

저희 셔틀 버스에 귀하의 가방 중 하나를 놓고 내리셨다는 말을 듣게 되어 유감입니다. 종착점이 지난 후에 버스에 남겨지는 모든 물품은 공항의 4번 터미널에 위치한 제 사무실로 보내집니다. 귀하의 문의 사항을 더 깊이 조사해 보기 위해, 브랜드 같은 기타 상세 정보와 함께 그 가방의 크기와 색상을 알아야 합니다. 가급적 빨리 제게 이메일을 보내 주시기 바랍니다.

안녕히 계십시오.

Miguel Guerrero

leave A on B A를 B에 놓고 가다, 남겨 놓다 remain 남아 있다
investigate ~을 조사하다 inquiry 문의 along with ~와 함께
at your earliest convenience 가급적 빨리

Q. Chetti 씨는 무엇을 하도록 요청받는가?
(A) Guerrero 씨의 사무실 방문하기
(B) 추가 정보 제공하기

[문제 키워드] What / Ms. Chetti / asked to do

[해설] 키워드인 Ms. Chetti에게 요청하는 일을 묻고 있으므로 요청 관련 단서가 제시되는 부분을 찾아야 한다. 지문 중반부에 자신이 알아야 하는 세부 사항들을 언급하면서 이메일을 보내 달라고 요청하고 있으므로(I would need to know the size and color ~ Please e-mail me ~) 추가 정보 제공을 의미하는 (B)가 정답이다.

[어휘] additional 추가적인

04.

수신: 전 직원 <staff@phelpsltd.com>
발신: Brady Patton <bpatton@phelpsltd.com>
날짜: 1월 8일
제목: 점심 시간 강연

우리 직원들의 직업 능력 개발을 지원하기 위한 노력의 일환으로, 우리 Phelps 사는 매달 직원들을 위해 월간 강연 행사 개최를 시작할 것입니다. 첫 번째 강연은 1월 28일 정오부터 오후 1시까지 대회의실에서 열립니다. 주제는 '과학 기술 시간 절약 방법'입니다. 이 행사에 참여하기를 원하실 경우, 출장 요리 업체를 통한 점심 식사가 제공될 것이므로 인사부에서 신청하시기 바랍니다. 이 시간이 유익하기를 바랍니다.

Brady Patton

professional development 직업 능력 개발 timesaver 시간 절약 방법 informative 유익한

Q. 1월 28일 행사에 관해 언급되지 않은 것은 무엇인가?
(A) 참가자들이 반드시 미리 등록해야 한다.
(B) 모든 직원들에게 필수이다.

[문제 키워드] NOT mentioned / January 28 event

[해설] about 뒤의 키워드 the January 28 event가 지문의 전체적인 소재이므로 지문 전반에서 단서를 파악해 각 선택지와 비교해야 한다. 지문 전체적으로 모든 직원에게 필수적이라는 말은 없으므로 (B)가 정답이다. 중반부에 인사부에 신청하라는(~ please sign up in the HR office ~) 말이 있으므로 (A)는 맞는 내용이다.

[어휘] register 등록하다 in advance 미리, 사전에 required 필수인

실전 문제

| 01.(A) | 02.(B) | 03.(D) | 04.(C) | 05.(D) | 06.(B) |
| 07.(D) | 08.(C) | 09.(A) | 10.(B) | | |

01-02는 다음 이메일을 참조하시오.

수신: Sean Briggs
발신: Filmore Furniture
날짜: 9월 1일
제목: 뉴스레터

친애하는 Briggs 씨께,

저희 Filmore Furniture는 리클라이너 의자의 재고를 확대했습니다. 구매 내역에 따르면, [01] 귀하는 아마 Hopeland ReMax에 관심이 있으실 것입니다. 이 안락의자에는 내장 컵 홀더, 휴대용 전자기기를 충전할 수 있는 USB 포트, 그리고 세 가지 다른 속도의 마사지 기능이 있습니다. 저희 전시장에 오셔서 체험해 보시기 바랍니다!

참고로 말씀드리면, [02] 귀하께서는 실버에서 골드 회원으로 업그레이드되셨으므로 무료 배송 서비스를 받으실 수 있음을 알려 드립니다. 여기에는 배송, 설치, 그리고 오래된 가구의 수거까지 모두 포함되어 있습니다.

진심으로,

Dayana Hamilton
세일즈 매니저, Filmore Furniture

furniture 가구 expand 확장하다, 확대하다 inventory 재고 charge 충전하다 electronic 전자의 showroom 전시장 qualify for 자격이 되다 installation 설치

01. 목적 문제

Hamilton 씨는 왜 이메일을 보냈는가?
(A) 인기 있는 제품을 소개하기 위해
(B) 구매에 대한 피드백을 요청하기 위해
(C) 회사의 정책을 설명하기 위해
(D) 배송 현황을 보고하기 위해

[해설] 첫 문단에서 리클라이너 의자의 재고를 확대했다며 특정 모델인 Hopeland ReMax를 소개하고(you may be interested in the Hopeland ReMax) 있으므로 정답은 (A)이다.

[어휘] introduce 소개하다 request 요청하다 policy 정책 status 상태, 현황

02. True 문제

Briggs 씨의 멤버십에 대해 언급된 것은 무엇인가?
(A) 곧 만료될 것이다.
(B) 최근에 업그레이드되었다.
(C) 자동으로 갱신될 것이다.
(D) 월회비 납부를 요구한다.

[해설] 멤버십 관련 내용이 제시된 후반부에 실버에서 골드 회원으로 업그레이드되었다고(now that you have been upgraded from a Silver to a Gold member) 했으므로 정답은 (B)이다.

07. 알맞은 문장 고르기

(A) 행사에서 Paulie's Pasta Palace의 출장 요리가 제공될 것입니다.
(B) 일 년 내내 보여 주신 노고와 노력에 대해 여러분 모두에게 감사 드립니다.
(C) 표를 제출하시는 대로 주차에 대한 요금이 환급될 것입니다.
(D) 우리는 당일 행사를 위해 지붕이 설치된 구역과 두 개의 바비큐 화덕을 예약해 두었습니다.

[해설] 빈칸 앞에는 버스 출발 시간이, 빈칸 뒤에는 요리하는 음식의 종류가 제시되어 있다. 따라서 뒤에 이어지는 문장과 연계되는 것으로서 음식 조리와 관련해 예약한 시설물을 언급하는 (D)가 정답이다.

[어휘] cater ~에 출장 요리를 제공하다 effort 노력 reimburse ~을 환급해 주다 reserve ~을 예약하다 covered 지붕이 있는, 지붕으로 덮인 pit 구덩이

08. 형용사 어휘

[해설] 빈칸 뒤에 제시된 activity와 관련된 정보가 제시된 다음 문장에, 도착하는 대로(once we arrive) 팀을 구성해 하는 활동이라고 언급하는 것으로 보아 가장 먼저 진행되는 활동임을 알 수 있으므로 (D) first가 정답이다.

[어휘] recurring 재발하는, 되풀이되는 timely 때에 맞춘, 시기 적절한

PART 7 이메일 (2) 정보 전달 이메일

풀이 방법 해석

수신: allstaff@cedarburg.net
발신: c.martell@cedarburg.net
날짜: 8월 3일 화요일
제목: 사무실 통풍구

동료 여러분께,

아시다시피, 우리 건물의 중앙 통풍구에 문제가 있습니다. 그것에 대한 작업이 내일 아침에 시작될 예정이나, 기술자들이 몇 시에 끝날지는 확실하지 않다고 합니다. 그러므로 경영진은 내일 여러분들이 모두 집에서 일하는 것이 최상의 방안이라는 결정을 내렸습니다.

떨어져서 일하므로, 메신저 프로그램에 접속한 상태를 유지하고 휴대폰을 휴대하시기 바랍니다. 그렇게 함으로써 우리는 사무실에 같이 있는 것처럼 효율적으로 서로 연락할 수 있습니다.

이로 인한 불편에 대해 사과드립니다.

Cindy Martell

연습 문제

01.(B)　02.(A)　03.(B)　04.(B)

01.

발신: Fabian Vela <f_vela@brunsonconsulting.net>
수신: 전 직원 <allstaff@brunsonconsulting.net>
날짜: 6월 19일
제목: 주차장 바닥 재포장

직원 여러분께

7월 1일부터 7월 5일까지, 우리 사무실의 주차장이 바닥 재포장 공사 작업이 진행되는 동안 주차장 출입이 제한될 것입니다. 우리는 Faribault 빌딩의 관리 책임자와 협의했으며, 우리 직원들이 그곳의 주차장을 사용하게 하는 데 동의해 주셨습니다. 그렇게 하기를 원하실 경우, 반드시 인사부에서 출입증을 받아 가셔야 합니다. 그렇지 않으면, 그곳의 보안팀이 주차장에 진입하지 못하게 할 것입니다.

Fabian Vela

resurfacing (도로, 바닥 등의) 재포장 off limits 출입이 제한된 while ~하는 동안 undergo ~을 거치다, 겪다 negotiate with ~와 협의하다, 협상하다 pick up ~을 가져가다 otherwise 그렇지 않으면 cooperation 협조

Q. Faribault 빌딩에 관해 암시된 것은 무엇인가?
(A) 그곳의 주차장이 수리될 것이다.
(B) 주차장이 출입증을 필요로 한다.

[문제 키워드] What / suggested / Faribault Building

[해설] about 뒤의 키워드 Faribault Building이 제시된 부분에서 단서를 찾을 수 있다. 해당 명칭이 제시되는 중반부에 그 건물 주차장을 이용하려면 출입증을 받아야 한다고(~ the Faribault Building, and he has agreed to allow our employees to use their lot. If you wish to do so, you must pick up a pass ~) 알리고 있으므로 (B)가 정답이다.

02.

수신: Roseway Jewelry Clerks <clerklist@rosewayjewelry.com>
발신: Sierra Green <sgreen@rosewayjewelry.com>
날짜: 12월 18일
제목: 매장 점원들을 위한 정보

다음 달 1일부터, 우리 Roseway Jewelry는 제품이 원래의 포장 용기에 들어 있다 하더라도 유효한 영수증이 없으면 더 이상 반품을 받지 않을 것입니다. 우리는 이 변동 사항을 웹사이트에 공지했으며, 매장 전역에 공지를 게시했습니다. 하지만 고객들이 여전히 이 변동 사항에 관해 질문을 할 수 있으므로, 반품이 허용되는 것인지 아닌지를 확신할 수 없을 경우에는 책임자에게 전달하시기 바랍니다.

Sierra Green, 점장

clerk 점원 accept ~을 받아들이다 valid 유효한 receipt 영수증 even if (설령) ~한다 하더라도 packaging 포장재 throughout ~ 전역에 direct A to B A를 B에게 전달하다, 보내다 whether or not ~인지 아닌지

Q. 이메일의 목적은 무엇인가?
(A) 새로운 정책을 설명하기 위해
(B) 보석 제품 세일을 알리기 위해

[문제 키워드] purpose

[해설] 지문 초반부에 다음 달부터 유효한 영수증이 없으면 반품을 받지 않는다고(From the 1st of next month, Roseway Jewelry will no longer accept returns without a valid receipt ~) 알리면서 관련 정보를 제시하고 있는데, 이는 정책상의 변화를 뜻하는 말이므로 (A)가 정답이다.

[어휘] policy 정책

[단서] your driver's license will be suspended

[해설] 다음 문장에 특정 시점까지 납부하지 않으면 운전 면허가 정지된다는 말이 있는데, 이는 최후의 통보에 해당되는 조치로 볼 수 있으므로 '최종적인'을 뜻하는 형용사 (A) final이 정답이다.

[어휘] current 현재의

실전 문제

01.(B) 02.(C) 03.(D) 04.(D) 05.(B) 06.(A)
07.(D) 08.(D)

01-04는 다음 정보를 참조하시오.

> Douglas Cain
>
> 많은 분들께서 Douglas Cain 씨의 성공적인 농구 선수 경력으로 인해 Cain 씨의 이름을 알고 있습니다. 01농구 선수로서 공식적으로 은퇴한 이후로, Cain 씨는 전국으로 방송되는 스포츠 TV 채널에서 스포츠 해설가로서 일해 왔습니다. 여기 여러분들이 흥미롭다고 느끼실 만한 이야기가 하나 더 있습니다. 여러분들은 아마 Christopher Douglass 라는 이름이 익숙하실 수 있는 데, 이는 Cain 씨의 필명입니다. 02Cain 씨는 과거에 이룬 성공이 자신의 책 매출에 영향을 미칠까 염려했기 때문에 실명을 사용하지 않기로 결정했습니다. 03이것은 그가 오로지 그의 글을 바탕으로만 평가받게 합니다. 04자신의 필명으로 인해, Cain 씨는 스타 선수와 찬사를 받는 작가 둘 모두에 대한 명성을 별도로 누릴 수 있습니다.

retire 은퇴하다 commentator 해설가 nationwide 전국적인 pen name 필명 influence ~에 영향을 미치다 sales 매출, 판매(량) thanks to ~로 인해, ~ 덕분에 fame 명성 athlete 운동 선수 acclaimed 찬사를 받는

01. 동사의 형태

[해설] 과거 시제 동사 retired와 함께 과거의 시작점을 나타내는 Since절이 쓰이면, 주절에는 그 이후의 지속 상태를 나타내는 현재완료 시제가 짝을 이뤄 사용되므로 (B) has served가 정답이다.

02. 형용사 어휘

[해설] 빈칸 뒤에 쓰인 success는 자신이 쓴 책의 매출에 영향을 미치는 원인으로서 지문 시작 부분에 언급된 '성공적인 선수 생활(his successful basketball career)'을 가리킨다. 그런데 이미 공식적으로 과거 시점에 은퇴했다는(officially retired) 언급으로 보아, 과거 시점의 성공을 가리키므로 '과거의, 이전의' 등을 뜻하는 (C) former가 정답이다.

[어휘] following 다음의, 아래의 unexpected 예기치 못한 temporary 일시적인, 임시의

03. 알맞은 문장 고르기

(A) 그의 인기 도서 시리즈는 프로 선수로서의 경력을 바탕으로 하고 있습니다.
(B) 팀의 여러 동료 선수들이 그가 쓴 글의 초안에 대해 의견을 제공해 주었습니다.
(C) 그의 책이 베스트셀러 목록에 올랐다는 사실에 의해 입증됩니다.
(D) 이것은 그가 오로지 그의 글을 바탕으로만 평가받게 합니다.

[해설] 앞 문장에 Cain 씨가 자신의 책에 실명을 사용하지 않았다는 말이 있으므로 이 내용과 연계되는 것으로서 오로지 그가 쓴 글에 의해서만 평가 받는다고 한 (D)가 정답이다.

[어휘] be based on ~을 바탕으로 하다, 기반으로 하다 several 여럿의, 몇몇의 early draft 초안 prove ~을 입증하다 evaluate 평가하다

04. 부사 자리

[해설] 주어 Mr. Cain과 동사 enjoy, 그리고 동사의 목적어와 이 목적어를 수식하는 of 전치사구까지 갖춘 완전한 문장이므로 빈칸에는 부가적인 요소에 해당되는 부사가 쓰여야 알맞다. 따라서 (D) separately가 정답이다.

[어휘] separation 분리, 구분 separate ~을 분리하다, 갈라 놓다; 분리된, 떨어진

05-08은 다음 이메일을 참조하시오.

> 수신: 전 직원
> 발신: Danielle Frost
> 날짜: 8월 8일
> 제목: 회사 야유회
> 첨부: 지도
>
> 동료 직원들께 알립니다.
>
> 올해 우리 회사의 연례 야유회 행사가 8월 21일 금요일로 예정되어 있습니다. 05몸이 아파서 빠지시거나 휴가 중인 분이 아니시라면 참석해 주시기 바랍니다. 06우리는 10시 30분에 함께 사무실에서 출발할 것이며, Gardena 공원까지 전세 버스로 이동합니다. 07우리는 당일 행사를 위해 지붕이 설치된 구역과 두 개의 바비큐 화덕을 예약해 두었습니다. 우리는 통째로 된 옥수수와 치즈버거, 그리고 핫도그를 요리할 계획입니다. 식사와 관련된 제약이나 음식 알레르기가 있으신 분은 미리 제게 알려 주십시오. 08행사 계획상의 첫 번째 활동은 얼티밋 프리스비입니다. 도착하는 대로 부서장님들에 의해 팀이 결정될 것입니다. 저는 분명 우리 모두가 올해도 다시 한번 아주 즐거운 시간을 보낼 것이라고 생각합니다. 그곳에서 뵙겠습니다.
>
> 안녕히 계십시오.
>
> Danielle Frost
> 부장, 인사부

associate 동료 직원 chartered bus 전세 버스 corn on the cob 통째로 된 옥수수 dietary 식사의 restriction 제약, 제한 inform ~에게 알리다 in advance 미리, 사전에 agenda 활동 계획 ultimate frisbee 얼티밋 프리스비(팀을 나눠 플라스틱 원반을 주고받으며 하는 경기) department head 부서장 once (일단) ~하는 대로, ~하자마자

05. 접속사 어휘

[해설] 빈칸 바로 뒤에는 참석할 수 없는 조건이 제시되어 있는데, 콤마 뒤에 위치한 주절에는 참석해야 한다는 말이 쓰여 있다. 따라서 빈칸이 속한 절은 부정 조건을 나타내는 의미가 되어야 알맞으므로 '~하지 않는다면, ~가 아니라면' 등의 의미로 부정 조건을 제시할 때 사용하는 접속사 (B) Unless가 정답이다.

[어휘] whereas ~인 반면 so much as ~조차도, ~까지도

06. 동사의 형태

[해설] 야유회 장소로 떠나는 시점을 파악해야 한다. 상단에 제시된 이 이메일의 작성 날짜인 8 August이고 첫 문장에 제시된 행사 날짜는 21 August이다. 즉, 야유회는 미래에 있을 행사이므로 미래 시제인 (A) will depart가 정답이다.

다. 명사 performances를 수식해 웹사이트에서 목록을 통해 확인하는 공연의 특성을 나타낼 형용사가 필요하므로 '다가오는, 곧 있을'을 의미하는 (C) upcoming이 정답이다.

[어휘] view ~을 보다 performance 공연 potential 잠재적인 standard 기준의, 표준의 capable 능력 있는, 할 수 있는

23. 두 단어 이상으로 이루어진 전치사

주 의회는 반복되는 여름 폭우와 극심한 겨울 가뭄에 따른 결과로 저수지를 만들기로 결정했다.

[해설] 선택지가 다양한 전치사구들로 구성되어 있으므로 전치사 어휘 문제이다. 빈칸 뒤에 위치한 '여름 폭우와 극심한 겨울 가뭄'은 저수지를 만들게 된 원인으로 볼 수 있다. 따라서 원인 앞에 사용해 '~에 따른 결과로'라는 의미로 쓰이는 (B) as a result of가 정답이다.

[어휘] council 의회 reservoir 저수지 repeated 반복되는 severe 극심한, 심각한 drought 가뭄 in order for ~을 위해 apart from ~ 외에는 such as ~와 같은

24. 형용사 어휘

우리 회사가 고객층을 확대하기를 원한다면, 우리가 광고 캠페인을 시작하는 것이 필수적이다.

[해설] 선택지가 다양한 형용사들로 구성되어 있으므로 형용사 어휘 문제이다. 'It is ~ that절'로 된 가주어/진주어 구문에서 is 뒤에 위치해 보어로 쓰일 형용사 필요하므로 이 역할이 가능한 (A) essential이 정답이다. '광고 캠페인을 시작하는 것이 필수적이다'라는 의미가 되므로 문맥상으로도 자연스럽다.

[어휘] expand ~을 확대하다 customer base 고객 층 launch ~을 시작하다, ~에 착수하다 ad 광고 essential 필수적인 bound 가능성 있는, 해야 하는, ~를 향하는 steady 꾸준한 routine 일상적인

PART 6 순서를 나타내는 형용사 어휘

풀이 방법 해석

수신: 행사 참가자들
발신: Janet Wheeler <j.wheeler@bosem.org>
날짜: 12월 18일
제목: 경영주 세미나
첨부 파일: 피드백 양식

참가자분들께

필모어에서의 지난주 경영주 세미나에 와주셔서 감사합니다. 귀하에게 도움이 되고 유익했길 바랍니다. 귀하의 지원과 참석 덕분에, 올해의 마지막 세미나는 대성공이었습니다. 저희는 내년 라인업을 변경하는 것을 현재 고려하고 있고 귀하의 의견을 듣고 싶습니다. 잠시 시간을 내시어 첨부된 피드백 양식을 작성하셔서 저희에게 보내주세요. 귀하와 귀하의 사업체에게 더 나은 서비스를 제공하기 위해 저희가 무엇을 할 수 있을지 알고 싶습니다.

경영주 세미나의 다음 차례는 휴스턴에서 열릴 것입니다. 저희 기관이 일정을 짤 것이고 여러분들 모두에게 알려드릴 것입니다.

Janet wheeler
선임 기획자, 경영주 세미나

 연습 문제

01.(A) 02.(A) 03.(B) 04.(A)

01.

워크숍 참가자들께

지난주에 열린 Leaders in Retail Workshop 행사에 참석해 주셔서 감사 드립니다. 다음 번 저희 워크숍 시리즈를 개선할 수 있도록, 이번 행사에 참석하셨던 모든 분들로부터 의견을 취합하고자 합니다.

participant 참가자 attend ~에 참석하다 in order to부정사 ~할 수 있도록 improve ~을 개선하다 gather ~을 모으다

[단서] improve, gather feedback

[해설] 개선의 대상이 되는 워크숍은 앞으로 열릴 워크숍이어야 하므로 순서상 다음 것을 나타낼 때 사용하는 (A) next가 정답이다.

02.

Stanza Band가 5월 18일 토요일에 Turner 음반 가게에서 특별 어쿠스틱 공연을 펼칠 예정입니다. 이 밴드의 매니저는 곧 열릴 공연 당일에 공개될 예정인 앨범에 실린 신곡들과 함께 그들의 첫 앨범에 담겨 있는 곡들을 연주할 것이라고 발표했습니다.

along with ~와 함께 release ~을 공개하다, 출시하다

[단서] will be doing, will perform

[해설] 빈칸 뒤에 쓰인 show는 앞선 문장들에 언급된 미래 시점(will be doing, will perform, is scheduled)에 있을 공연이므로 앞으로의 일과 관련해 '곧 있을'을 의미하는 형용사 (A) upcoming이 정답이다.

[어휘] upcoming 곧 있을, 다가오는

03.

귀하의 제품 구입에 감사 드립니다. 귀하의 이전 주문을 통해 받으셨던 15퍼센트 할인 쿠폰이 성공적으로 적용되었습니다. 귀하께서는 8월 7일 화요일까지 이번 배송 제품을 받으실 것으로 예상하실 수 있습니다.

purchase 구입(품) obtain ~을 얻다, 획득하다 order 주문(품) successfully 성공적으로 apply ~을 적용하다 receive ~을 받다 shipment 배송(품)

[단서] obtained

[해설] 빈칸이 속한 that절의 동사 obtained가 과거 시제이므로 과거의 주문을 통해 받은 쿠폰임을 알 수 있다. 따라서 과거 시제 동사와 어울리는 형용사로 '이전의, 과거의'를 뜻하는 (B) previous가 정답이다.

04.

Connors 씨께

이 메시지는 1월 9일에 귀하께 발급된 주차 위반 딱지에 대한 벌금을 납부할 것을 알려 드리는 최종 통지서입니다. 4월 3일까지 San Jose 법원으로 45달러를 납부하지 않으실 경우 귀하의 운전 면허는 정지될 것입니다.

notification 통지(서) parking ticket 주차 위반 딱지 issue ~을 발급하다 payment 지불(액) suspend ~을 정지시키다, 중단하다

[해설] 선택지가 다양한 전치사들로 구성되어 있으므로 전치사 어휘 문제이다. 빈칸 뒤에 위치한 시점 표현 October 20까지 폐쇄되는 상태가 지속되므로 '~까지'라는 의미로 지속 상태를 나타낼 때 사용하는 (A) until이 정답이다.

[어휘] since ~하기 때문에　repair 수리　block ~을 가로막다　until (지속) ~까지　through ~을 통해　behind (위치) ~ 뒤에, (진행 등) ~보다 뒤처져

13. 전치사 with

어린 아이들을 동반하는 여행객들이 먼저 비행기에 탑승하도록 허용될 것입니다.

[해설] 선택지가 다양한 전치사들로 구성되어 있으므로 전치사 어휘 문제이다. 빈칸 앞뒤에 각각 위치한 Travelers와 small children의 의미로 보아 '아이와 함께 하는 여행객'이라는 뜻이 되어야 적절하므로 '~와 함께'를 나타내는 전치사 (A) with가 정답이다.

[어휘] be allowed to부정사 ~하도록 허용되다　board ~에 탑승하다 beside ~ 옆에

14. 위치/방향 전치사

모든 학과에 걸쳐 국제 학생들은 인턴 근무에 지원하도록 권장됩니다.

[해설] 선택지가 다양한 전치사들로 구성되어 있으므로 전치사 어휘 문제이다. 빈칸 뒤에 위치한 all departments(모든 학과)는 국제 학생들이 소속된 범위에 해당하므로 '~ 전체에 걸쳐'라는 의미로 범위를 나타낼 때 사용하는 (C) across가 정답이다.

[어휘] department 학과　be encouraged to부정사 ~하도록 권장되다 apply for ~에 지원하다　below (위치) ~보다 아래에, (수준 등) ~에 못 미치는　across ~ 전체에 걸쳐　since ~ 이후로

15. 부사의 역할과 위치: 동사 앞 수식

마이애미 지사로 전근한 이후에도, Stein 씨는 여전히 보스턴에 있는 이전 동료들과 연락하고 있다.

[해설] 선택지가 형용사와 부사로 구성되어 있으므로 문법 문제이다. 주어와 동사 사이에 빈칸이 있으므로 동사를 수식할 부사 자리인데, 전근한 이후에도(transferred) 계속하여 연락을 유지하고(keeps) 있는 상태를 나타내고 있으므로 '여전히'라는 뜻으로 지속의 의미를 지닌 부사 (B) still이 정답이다.

[어휘] even after ~한 이후에도　transfer to ~로 전근하다　keep in touch with ~와 연락하다　coworker 동료 직원　previous 이전의, 과거의　fully 완전히, 모두, 전적으로

16. 시간 부사

Hammond 은행에서 가장 경험이 많은 직원인 Trisha Bowden 씨는 전에 호주에서 3년간 살았다.

[해설] 선택지가 다양한 부사들로 구성되어 있으므로 부사 어휘 문제이다. 빈칸 뒤에 위치한 과거 시제 동사 lived와 어울리는 부사가 필요하므로 '이전에, 과거에'라는 의미로 과거 시제 동사와 함께 사용하는 (C) previously가 정답이다.

[어휘] experienced 경험이 많은　additionally 추가로

17. 재귀대명사: 강조 용법

물류 관리 책임자인 Wendy Clay 씨는 자사에서 보유하고 있는 새 전기 자동차들을 직접 점검하기를 원한다.

[해설] 선택지가 다양한 인칭대명사로 구성되어 있으므로 문법 문제이다. 빈칸을 제외하고도 주어와 동사(wants), 그리고 to부정사의 목적어(the fleet's new electric vehicles)까지 갖춘 완전한 문장이다. 따라서 부사처럼 부가적인 요소로 쓰이는 재귀대명사 (D) herself가 정답이다.

[어휘] chief 책임자, 팀장　logistics 물류 (관리)　inspect ~을 점검하다 fleet (회사 등이 보유한 전체 차량 등의) 무리　vehicle 차량

18. 인칭대명사 구분: 주격

Deegan 씨는 한 인턴 직원의 도움이 없었다면 제시간에 설계도를 완성하지 못했을 것이라고 말했다.

[해설] 선택지가 다양한 인칭대명사로 구성되어 있으므로 문법 문제이다. 접속사 that과 that절의 동사 wouldn't have completed 사이에 위치한 빈칸은 이 that절의 주어 자리이므로 주격 대명사 (C) he가 정답이다.

[어휘] would have p.p. ~했었을 것이다　complete ~을 완료하다 blueprint 설계도　on time 제시간에　without ~가 없었다면, 아니었다면　assistance 도움

19. 형용사 어휘

Howe's Shipping의 기사들은 모든 지역 도로의 폐쇄 상황을 알고 있어야 한다.

[해설] 선택지가 다양한 형용사들로 구성되어 있으므로 형용사 어휘 문제이다. 빈칸 앞뒤에 각각 위치한 be동사, 전치사 of와 어울려야 하므로 be aware of의 형태로 '~을 알고 있다'라는 의미를 구성할 때 사용하는 (D) aware가 정답이다.

[어휘] be supposed to부정사 ~할 의무가 있다, ~하기로 되어 있다 closure 폐쇄　opposite 반대의, 맞은편의　delicate 섬세한, 약한, 깨지기 쉬운

20. 전치사 as

회계 책임자로서, Shields 씨는 고객들에게 재정적 조언을 제공해 줄 것으로 기대된다.

[해설] 선택지가 다양한 전치사들로 구성되어 있으므로 전치사 어휘 문제이다. 빈칸 뒤에 위치한 an account manager은 직책에 해당하므로 '~로서'라는 의미로 자격이나 신분을 나타낼 때 사용하는 (B) As가 정답이다.

[어휘] account manager 회계 책임자　be expected to부정사 ~할 것으로 기대되다, 예상되다　financial 재정의, 재무의

21. 형용사 어휘

어떠한 사고나 부상이든 피하려면, 안전 장비를 착용하는 것이 작업 현장에 있는 모든 사람들에게 의무이다.

[해설] 선택지가 다양한 형용사들로 구성되어 있으므로 형용사 어휘 문제이다. be동사 is 뒤에 위치한 빈칸에 쓰일 형용사는 주어 wearing safety gear(안전 장비 착용)의 특성을 나타내는 보어 역할을 해야 하므로 '의무적인'을 뜻하는 (B) mandatory가 정답이다.

[어휘] avoid ~을 피하다　injury 부상　safety gear 안전 장비 job site 작업 현장　notable 주목할 만한　mandatory 의무적인 disruptive 지장을 주는　ambiguous 애매모호한

22. 형용사 어휘

다가오는 공연에 대한 전체 목록을 보시려면, 저희 극장의 웹페이지를 방문하십시오.

[해설] 선택지가 다양한 형용사들로 구성되어 있으므로 형용사 어휘 문제이

02. 분사 형태 전치사

여름 시즌용 신제품들을 포함해 대부분의 저희 재고품들이 절반 가격으로 할인될 것입니다.

[해설] 선택지가 include의 다양한 형태로 구성되어 있으므로 문법 문제이다. 빈칸 뒤에 위치한 명사구는 재고의 일부에 해당되므로 '~을 포함해'라는 의미로 일부 사용하는 전치사 (D) including이 정답이다.

[어휘] inventory 재고(품), 재고 목록 be half off 절반이 할인되다 include ~을 포함하다 including ~을 포함해

03. 전치사 for

Peyton 씨는 지역사회 자원봉사 프로그램에 대한 헌신에 대해 상을 받았다.

[해설] 선택지가 다양한 전치사들로 구성되어 있으므로 전치사 어휘 문제이다. 빈칸 뒤에 위치한 his dedication은 상을 받은 이유에 해당되므로 이유를 나타낼 때 사용하는 전치사 (A) for가 정답이다.

[어휘] dedication to ~에 대한 헌신, 전념

04. 형용사 어휘

직원들로부터 DIY 작업 팁을 얻는 데 익숙한 Cruz Hardware 고객들은 그 대신 회사 웹사이트를 참고해야 할 것이다.

[해설] 선택지가 다양한 형용사들로 구성되어 있으므로 형용사 어휘 문제이다. 빈칸 앞뒤에 각각 위치한 be동사 are, to -ing와 어울려 be accustomed to -ing의 형태로 '~하는 데 익숙하다'라는 의미를 나타낼 때 사용하는 (A) accustomed가 정답이다.

[어휘] be accustomed to -ing ~하는 데 익숙하다 DIY (제작, 수리 등을) 소비자가 직접 하는 것 refer to ~을 참고하다 instead 대신에 specific 특정한, 구체적인 sustainable (환경적으로) 지속 가능한 general 일반적인

05. 전치사 except

제조사에서 곧바로 배송되는 상품을 제외하고, 주문품들이 영업일로 이틀 후에 도착할 것이다.

[해설] 선택지가 전치사와 접속사로 구성되어 있으므로 문법 문제이다. 빈칸 뒤에 위치한 명사 merchandise(shipped 이하는 분사구)를 목적어로 취할 전치사가 필요하며, 빈칸 이후의 내용은 제외 대상에 해당되는 조건으로 볼 수 있으므로 '~을 제외하고'를 뜻하는 전치사 (D) except가 정답이다. (B) however는 부사 또는 접속사로 쓰이며, (C) whereas는 접속사이다.

[어휘] merchandise 상품 ship ~을 배송하다 directly from ~에서 곧바로 manufacturer 제조사 however 아무리 ~하더라도, 하지만 whereas ~인 반면

06. 장소 전치사

서명된 계약서의 이 원본을 디지털 잠금 장치가 되어 있는 캐비닛 안에 보관하십시오.

[해설] 선택지가 다양한 전치사들로 구성되어 있으므로 전치사 어휘 문제이다. 빈칸 뒤에 위치한 the cabinet은 계약서를 보관하는 장소에 해당되므로 공간의 내부를 나타낼 때 사용하는 (A) in이 정답이다.

[어휘] original 원본의 signed 서명이 된 contract 계약(서)

07. 두 단어 이상으로 이루어진 전치사

계약서에 따르면, 비용 지불은 매달 1일에 이뤄져야 합니다.

[해설] 선택지가 다양한 전치사구들로 구성되어 있으므로 전치사 어휘 문제이다. '계약서'를 뜻하는 contract는 비용 지불과 관련된 정보를 확인할 수 있는 자료에 해당된다. 따라서 '~에 따르면'이라는 의미로 근거 또는 출처를 나타낼 때 사용하는 (A) According to가 정답이다.

[어휘] contract 계약(서) be to부정사 ~해야 하다, ~할 예정이다 make a payment 비용을 지불하다 aside from ~ 외에는 prior to ~에 앞서, ~ 전에 thanks to ~로 인해, ~ 덕분에

08. 형용사 어휘

San Andrade 태양열 발전소는 재사용 가능한 에너지로부터 전기를 얻는 지역내 주요 전기 공급원이다.

[해설] 선택지가 다양한 형용사들로 구성되어 있으므로 형용사 어휘 문제이다. '전기 공급원'을 의미하는 electricity source를 수식해 그것이 지역 내에서 지니는 중요성과 관련된 의미를 나타낼 형용사가 쓰여야 적절하므로 '주요한'을 뜻하는 (A) primary가 정답이다.

[어휘] solar plant 태양열 발전소 region 지역 source 공급원, 원천 reusable 재사용 가능한 previous 이전의, 과거의 diverse 다양한 ample 충분한, 풍부한

09. 두 단어 이상으로 이루어진 전치사

누구든 구내 식당을 이용하는 사람은 회사 내에서 어느 직책을 맡고 있든 상관없이 깨끗이 청소해야 한다.

[해설] 선택지가 형용사와 부사로 구성되어 있으므로 문법 문제이다. 빈칸 뒤에 'of which절'의 구조가 이어져 있는데, 이와 같은 구조와 결합 가능한 것으로서 '~하는 것에 상관없이'라는 의미를 나타낼 때 사용하는 (C) regardless가 정답이다.

[어휘] cafeteria 구내 식당 clean up ~을 깨끗이 청소하다 regardless of ~에 상관없이 hold ~을 맡다, 보유하다 partial 부분적인

10. 두 단어 이상으로 이루어진 전치사

빠르게 새 시즌 준비를 하기 위해, 새 배송 물품 도착에 앞서 선반 공간이 치워져야 한다.

[해설] 선택지가 전치사와 부사로 구성되어 있으므로 문법 문제이다. 선반 공간을 치우는 일은 새로운 배송 물품이 도착하기 전에 이뤄져야 하는 일이므로 '~에 앞서'를 뜻하는 전치사 (A) ahead of가 정답이다.

[어휘] in order to부정사 ~하기 위해 prepare for ~을 준비하다, ~에 대비하다 clear ~을 치우다 shipment 배송(품) arrival 도착 alongside ~ 옆에 (나란히), ~와 함께 within ~ 이내에

11. 동명사와 자주 쓰이는 전치사

당선되자마자, Townsend 시장은 시의 환경 미화 캠페인을 위한 제안을 내놓았다.

[해설] 선택지가 다양한 전치사들로 구성되어 있으므로 전치사 어휘 문제이다. 당선된 일과 제안을 내놓은 일 사이의 순서를 나타낼 전치사가 빈칸에 쓰여야 알맞으므로 '~하자마자'를 뜻하는 전치사 (A) Upon이 정답이다.

[어휘] upon -ing ~하자마자 elect ~을 선출하다 release ~을 공개하다, 내놓다 proposal 제안 beautification (환경) 미화

12. 기간 전치사

Stewart 로에 일부 도로 수리 작업이 있기 때문에, 10월 20일까지 폐쇄될 것이다.

10. 세부사항 문제

Barrera 씨는 회사가 무엇을 해줄 것으로 기대하는가?
(A) 실수에 대해 사과하기
(B) 수수료 면제하기
(C) 환불하기
(D) 빠른 배송을 이용하기

[해설] 지문 후반부에 자신이 충실한 고객이기 때문에 다른 Brickson 전동 드릴을 속달 배송 서비스로 한 번 더 보내 주길 기대한다고(I expect that you will send me another Brickson power drill via express delivery service) 했으므로 (D)가 정답이다.

paraphrasing express delivery service 빠른 배송 서비스 → express shipping 빠른 배송

[어휘] apologize 사과하다 waive 면제하다 issue 발행하다, 발부하다 refund 환불 shipping 배송

paraphrasing 정답 1. (c) 2. (b) 3. (a)

DAY 07

PART 5 | 문법 | 전치사 (2)

확인 문제 해석

① 그녀는 발표 후에 잠재 고객들의 질문에 답변했다.
② 당신은 수수료와 함께 신청서를 제출해야 합니다.
③ 공사장에 들어가기 전에 보호용 헬멧을 착용해 주세요.
④ 당신은 무료 아이템을 이용할 자격을 얻게 될 것입니다.
⑤ 그는 그의 상사로부터 허가를 얻었다.
⑥ 일부 주민들은 그 건설 계획에 반대한다.
⑦ 이 유리는 열에 취약하다.
⑧ 모든 직원들은 항상 그들의 보안 배지를 보이도록 요청받는다.

연습 문제

01.(B) 02.(C) 03.(C) 04.(D) 05.(D) 06.(D)

01.

1. 선택지 보고 문법/어휘 문제 파악하기 ☐ 문법 문제 ☑ 어휘 문제
2. 빈칸 분석하기 빈칸 앞 내용 ☑ 불만이 있다 ☐ 고객이 많다
   빈칸 뒤 내용 ☐ 음식이 맛있다 ☑ 대기 시간이 길다 ☐ 주차 공간이 없다
3. 정답 선택하기 앞뒤 내용을 연결해 줄 수 있는 어휘 (B)

Benny's Bento Box의 긴 대기 시간과 관련한 여러 불만이 있었다.

02.

1. 선택지 보고 문법/어휘 문제 파악하기 ☐ 문법 문제 ☑ 어휘 문제
2. 빈칸 분석하기 빈칸 앞 내용 ☑ 콩류와 견과류의 쓰임 ☐ 콩류와 견과류의 종류

빈칸 뒤 내용 ☐ 장소 ☑ 식재료 ☐ 회사명
3. 정답 선택하기 앞뒤 내용을 연결해 줄 수 있는 어휘 (C)

콩과 견과는 고기 대신 단백질의 급원으로 사용될 수 있다.

03.

1. 선택지 보고 문법/어휘 문제 파악하기 ☐ 문법 문제 ☑ 어휘 문제
2. 빈칸 분석하기 빈칸 뒤에 있는 것 ☐ to부정사 ☑ 동명사
   빈칸 앞뒤 문맥을 이어주는 의미 ☑ ~함으로써 ☐ ~하기 전에
3. 정답 선택하기 (C)

이 업그레이드된 소프트웨어를 설치함으로써 더 많은 주문을 더 빨리 처리하실 수 있을 것입니다.

04.

1. 선택지 보고 문법/어휘 문제 파악하기 ☐ 문법 문제 ☑ 어휘 문제
2. 빈칸 분석하기 빈칸 뒤의 명사구 (Mr. Hudson's direction)
   이 명사구의 의미 (Hudson 씨의 관리)
3. 정답 선택하기 명사구와 함께 쓰여 관용어구를 만드는 전치사 (D)

지난 3년 동안, Tao Car Tuning은 Hudson 씨의 관리 하에 수익을 증가시켰다.

05.

1. 선택지 보고 문법/어휘 문제 파악하기 ☐ 문법 문제 ☑ 어휘 문제
2. 빈칸 분석하기 빈칸 앞에 있는 동사 attract의 의미 (끌어들이다)
   빈칸 뒤에 있는 명사 clients의 의미 (고객)
   → 문맥상 위의 동사, 명사와 함께 쓰일 수 있는 형용사를 답으로 고른다.
3. 정답 선택하기 정답 (D)

이 세미나는 당신의 사업체에 잠재적 고객을 끌어들일 기본적인 전략을 다룹니다.

06.

1. 선택지 보고 문법/어휘 문제 파악하기 ☐ 문법 문제 ☑ 어휘 문제
2. 빈칸 분석하기 빈칸 앞 명사 (proximity)
3. 정답 선택하기 위의 명사와 함께 쓰이는 전치사 (D)

수원지 근처에 있기 때문에, 공장들은 폐기물을 버릴 때 주의한다.

실전 문제

01.(B) 02.(D) 03.(A) 04.(A) 05.(D) 06.(A)
07.(A) 08.(A) 09.(C) 10.(A) 11.(A) 12.(A)
13.(A) 14.(C) 15.(B) 16.(C) 17.(D) 18.(C)
19.(D) 20.(B) 21.(B) 22.(C) 23.(B) 24.(A)

01. 전치사 between

시상식에서 신임 최고 재무 이사님의 자리가 Pennington 씨와 Pratt 씨 사이에 마련되었다.

[해설] 선택지가 전치사와 접속사로 구성되어 있으므로 문법 문제이다. 빈칸 뒤에 'A and B'의 구조로 쓰인 두 명사구를 목적어로 취해야 하므로 이와 같은 표현 구조와 함께 사용하는 전치사 (B) between이 정답이다.

[어휘] CFO 최고 재무 이사 arrange ~을 마련하다 throughout ~ 전체에 걸쳐, ~ 동안 내내

dedicated to ~에 전념하는 issue 문제, 사안 affect ~에 영향을 미치다 city council 시 의회 proposal to부정사 ~하자는 제안 demolish ~을 철거하다, 허물다 portion 일부, 부분 expand ~을 확장하다 current 현재의 take A into consideration A를 고려하다 resident 주민 serve as ~의 역할을 하다 habitat 서식지 rare 희귀한 multi-story 여러 층으로 된 take up ~을 차지하다 additional 추가적인 fellow 동료의, 같은 처지의 voice 목소리를 내다 support 지지 alternative 대안 upcoming 곧 있을, 다가오는 the rest of ~의 나머지 take A under advisement A를 심사 숙고하다

05. 목적 문제

Cheng 씨는 왜 이메일을 보냈는가?
(A) Ruiz 씨에게 동호회에 가입하도록 요청하기 위해
(B) 지역 사회 행사에 자원하기 위해
(C) 한 프로젝트에 대한 우려를 표명하기 위해
(D) 공원을 청소하는 날을 계획하기 위해

[해설] 지문 시작 부분에, 발신인인 Cheng 씨는 지역 문화 센터와 그곳의 주차장을 확장하기 위해 Hutchinson 공원의 일부를 철거하자는 의회의 제안이 모든 요소를 고려하지 않은 것 같아 걱정스럽다고(the city council's proposal to demolish a portion of Hutchinson Park ~ I am worried that the current plans ~) 알리고 있는데, 이 부분이 이메일의 목적에 해당된다. 즉 프로젝트에 대한 우려 표명을 하기 위한 이메일이므로 (C)가 정답이다.

[어휘] invite A to부정사 A에게 ~하도록 요청하다 join ~에 가입하다, 합류하다 volunteer 자원하다 express ~을 표현하다 concern 우려, 걱정 cleanup 정화, 청소

06. True 문제

Hutchinson 공원에 대해 암시된 것은 무엇인가?
(A) Cheng 씨의 집에서 가까운 곳에 있다.
(B) 지역에서 가장 큰 공원이다.
(C) 다양한 야생 동물의 서식지이다.
(D) 여러 층으로 된 주차장이 있다.

[해설] Hutchinson 공원에 관해 설명하는 중반부에, 많은 희귀 조류 종뿐만 아니라 다른 작은 동물들에게 있어 필수적인 서식지의 역할을 하고 있다고(it serves as an essential habitat for a number of rare bird species, as well as other small animals) 알리는 내용이 있는데, 이는 여러 동물의 서식지임을 뜻하는 것이므로 (C)가 정답이다.

paraphrasing habitat 서식지 → home 서식지

[어휘] home to ~의 서식지 a variety of 다양한 wildlife 야생동물

07. 세부사항 문제

Cheng 씨는 다음 주에 무엇을 할 계획인가?
(A) 공청회 참석하기
(B) Ruiz 씨의 사무실 방문하기
(C) 선거에서 투표하기
(D) 온라인으로 몇몇 의견 게시하기

[해설] 'next week'라는 시점이 언급된 후반부에, 다음 주에 곧 열리는 시 의회 회의에서 대안에 대해 지지의 목소리를 낼 것이라고(~ will voice our support for this alternative at the upcoming city council meeting next week) 언급하고 있으므로 공청회 참석을 의미하는 (A)가 정답이다.

[어휘] public meeting 공청회 vote 투표하다 election 선거

paraphrasing 정답   1. (a)   2. (c)   3. (b)

08-10은 다음 이메일을 참조하시오.

수신: Maine Hardware <cust.serv@mainehardware.com>
발신: Henry Barrera <h.barrera@rmail.com>
날짜: 6월 9일
제목: 주문번호 HR2285544

관련자 분께,

저는 지난주 귀사의 온라인 스토어에서 Brickson 전동 드릴과 몇몇 다른 도구들을 주문했어요. 소포가 오늘 도착했는데 드릴에 문제가 있다는 것을 알고는 매우 실망했어요. ⁰⁸지침에 따랐고 심지어 배터리 교체까지 해봤지만 전원이 켜지지 않았어요. ⁰⁹데크를 설치하기 위해 고용되었기 때문에 이번 주말에 그 전동 공구가 꼭 필요해요. 만약 제가 이 프로젝트를 연기해야 한다면 제 고객은 행복해하지 않을 거예요. 그 드릴을 가급적 빨리 교체하는 것이 중요합니다. 제가 충실한 고객이기 때문에 ¹⁰다른 Brickson 전동 드릴을 빠른 배송 서비스로 한 번 더 보내 주셨으면 합니다. 오늘 오후에 우체국에 가서 원래 드릴을 다시 보내 드리겠습니다.

진심으로,

Henry Barrera

hardware 철물, 장비 tool 도구 instruction 설명서, 지침 turn on 켜지다 postpone 연기하다 loyal 충실한, 충성심이 있는 express 급행의, 신속한

08. 세부사항 문제

Barrera 씨의 주문에 있는 아이템에 무슨 문제가 있는가?
(A) 잘못된 브랜드이다.
(B) 결함이 있다.
(C) 부품이 빠져 있다.
(D) 제시간에 도착하지 않았다.

[해설] 초반부에 드릴에 문제가 있다는 것을 알고는 매우 실망했다며 지침에 따랐고 심지어 배터리 교체까지 해봤지만 전원이 켜지지 않았다고(I followed the instructions and even tried changing the battery, but it will not turn on) 했으므로 (B)가 정답이다.

[어휘] order 주문 defective 결함이 있는 on time 제시간에

09. 세부사항 문제

Barrera 씨가 왜 급히 제품을 교체해 달라고 요청하는가?
(A) 일을 완료하기 위해 그것이 필요하다.
(B) 새 주소로 이사를 갈 계획이다.
(C) 선물로 그것을 주길 원한다.
(D) 홈 프로젝트를 시작하기로 되어 있다.

[해설] 지문 중반부에 데크를 설치하기 위해 고용되었기 때문에 이번 주말에 그 전동 공구가 꼭 필요하다고(I need that power tool this weekend because I've been hired to build a deck) 했으므로 (A)가 정답이다.

[어휘] request 요청하다 replace 교체하다 urgently 급하게 complete 완료하다, 완성하다 be supposed to ~하기로 되어 있다, ~할 예정이다

leather 가죽 armchair 안락의자 out of stock 재고가 없는 indicate ~을 표기하다, 나타내다 shipment 배송(품) manufacturer 제조사 chestnut 밤나무, 밤색 make an adjustment 조정하다, 수정하다 inconvenience 불편

01. 목적 문제

이메일의 목적은 무엇인가?
(A) 의견을 제공해 준 것에 대해 고객에게 감사를 전하기 위해
(B) 대금을 수령했음을 확인해 주기 위해
(C) 고객에게 배송 지연에 대해 알리기 위해
(D) 배송비 변경을 설명해 주기 위해

[해설] 지문 시작 부분에 재고가 없는 관계로 제조사로부터 2주나 지나야 새로운 배송 물품을 받을 예정이라서 예상보다 훨씬 더 늦게 상대방에게 전달될 것이라고(~ I'm afraid this item will arrive at your home much later than expected) 언급되어 있는데, 이는 배송 지연을 알리는 것이므로 (C)가 정답이다.

[어휘] receipt 수령, 받음 payment 지불 비용 inform A of B A에게 B를 알리다 fee 요금

02. 세부사항 문제

Hart 씨는 무엇을 하도록 제안하는가?
(A) 다른 색상 선택하기
(B) 서둘러 주문하기
(C) 다른 지점에 확인해 보기
(D) 온라인 카탈로그 보기

[해설] 제안 사항이 언급된 중반부에, 체스넛 브라운 색상 대신에 초콜릿 브라운 색상을 선택하는 것은 어떤지(how about choosing chocolate brown instead of chestnut brown?) 제안하고 있으므로 (A)가 정답이다.

paraphrasing choosing 선택하기 → selecting 선택하기

[어휘] rush 서두르는

paraphrasing 정답 1. (a) 2. (b) 3. (c)

03-04는 다음 이메일을 참조하시오.

수신: Judy Yu
발신: William Ponce
날짜: 6월 18일
제목: 귀하의 최근 출장

친애하는 Judy,

지난주 출장에서 쓴 경비를 보고하는 메일을 받았어요. 하지만 문제가 있는 것 같습니다. **03**첨부 파일을 열고자 했을 때 파일이 손상되었다는 오류 메시지가 나타났습니다. 지금은 우리 회사가 전자 영수증을 받는 것으로 알고 있지만, 이 경우에는 **04**각 업무 관련 비용에 대한 구매 증명을 보내 주셔야 합니다. IT 팀은 이미 이 문제에 대해 통보받았지만, 그동안 당신이 그 서류를 보내줄 때까지 환불을 처리할 수 없습니다.

미리 양해해 주셔서 감사합니다!

William Ponce

expense 비용 business trip 출장 attachment 첨부 파일 corrupt (파일을) 손상시키다 receipt 영수증 proof of purchase 구매 증명 in the meantime 그동안 process 처리하다

reimbursement 비용 환급

03. 세부사항 문제

Ponce 씨는 어떤 문제점을 언급하는가?
(A) 일부 고객들이 계약을 거절했다.
(B) 일부 파일은 볼 수 없었다.
(C) 출장이 연기되었다.
(D) 회사 방침이 바뀌었다.

[해설] 전반부에서 첨부 파일을 열려고 했을 때 파일이 손상되었다는 오류 메시지가 나타났다는(When I tried to open the attachments, I got an error message saying that the files had been corrupted) 문제점을 알리고 있으므로 이를 언급한 (B)가 정답이다.

[어휘] client 고객 reject 거절하다 contract 계약 view 보다 postpone 연기하다

04. 세부사항 문제

Yu 씨는 Ponce 씨에게 무엇을 보내야 하는가?
(A) 비상 연락 정보
(B) 수정된 사업 계약서
(C) 고객 미팅 결과
(D) 영수증 사본

[해설] 후반부에 업무 관련 비용에 대한 구매 증명을 보내 달라고(send me a proof of purchase for each of your business related expenses) 요청하고 있는데 이는 영수증 사본을 보내 달라는 말이므로 (D)가 정답이다.

paraphrasing proof of purchase 구매 증명 → receipt 영수증

[어휘] emergency contact 비상 연락처 revised 개정된

paraphrasing 정답 1. (b) 2. (c) 3. (a)

05-07은 다음 이메일을 참조하시오.

수신: Abigail Ruiz <ruiza@caxtonltd.com>
발신: Hua Cheng <chenghua@orlandns.org>
날짜: 6월 30일
제목: 지역 문화 센터

Ruiz 씨께

제 이름은 Hua Cheng이며, 저는 올랜드에 영향을 미치는 환경 문제에 전념하고 있는 지역 단체인 Orland Nature Society의 대표입니다. **05**저는 지역 문화 센터와 그곳의 주차장을 확장하기 위해 **Hutchinson 공원의 일부를 철거하자는 시 의회의 제안서를 최근에 읽었습니다.** 저는 현재의 그 계획이 모든 요소를 고려하지 않았다는 점이 걱정스럽습니다. 비록 Hutchinson 공원이 주민들 사이에서 그렇게 인기 있는 곳은 아니지만, **06**많은 희귀 조류 종뿐만 아니라 다른 작은 동물들에게 있어 필수적인 서식지의 역할을 하고 있습니다. 이곳은 반드시 보호되어야 합니다. 저는 지역 문화 센터를 위해 여러 층으로 된 주차장을 짓는 것이 해결책이 될 수 있다고 생각하는데, 어떠한 추가적인 공간도 차지하지 않을 것이기 때문입니다. **07**제 단체의 몇몇 동료 회원들과 저는 다음 주에 곧 열리는 시 의회 회의에서 이와 같은 대안에 대해 지지의 목소리를 낼 것입니다. 귀하를 비롯해 의회의 다른 분들께서 저희 의견을 심사숙고해 주시기를 바랍니다.

Hua Cheng

답이다.

02.

수신: Serrano Apparel <customerservice@serranoapparel.com>
발신: Roy Newman <roy_newman@victoriasales.com>
날짜: 3월 28일
제목: 결함이 있는 제품

고객 서비스부에 보냅니다,

저는 지난주에 귀사의 웹사이트를 통해 대님 재킷 하나를 구입했는데(주문 번호 29805), 소매 중의 하나에 접합 부분이 뜯겨 있습니다. 제가 이 제품을 어떻게 교환받을 수 있는지 알려 주시기 바랍니다. 저는 가능한 한 빨리 이 문제가 처리되었으면 하는데, 제가 다음 주에 샌디에이고로 여행을 갈 때 이 재킷을 가져가고 싶기 때문입니다. 제게 555-5490으로 전화로 연락하실 수 있습니다.

Roy Newman

defective 결함이 있는 **seam** 접합 부분, 이음매 **sleeve** 소매 **torn** 뜯긴, 찢긴 **replacement** 교체(품), 대체(품)

Q. Newman 씨는 왜 문제점이 빨리 해결되기를 원하는가?
(A) 세일 행사를 이용하고 싶어 한다.
(B) 곧 다른 지역으로 갈 계획이다.

[문제 키워드] Why / Mr. Newman / problem / settled / quickly

[해설] 키워드인 quickly가 직접적으로 언급되어 있지 않으므로 패러프레이징된 부분인 as soon as possible을 찾는다. 지문 중반부에 빨리 처리되기를 원하는 이유로 샌디에이고 여행을 간다는 사실이(I'd like this matter to be taken care of as soon as possible, as I'm going on a trip to San Diego ~) 언급되어 있으므로 (B)가 정답이다.

03.

수신: Patrick Webster <webster.p@montgomeryautos.com>
발신: Roma Senhar <senhar.r@montgomeryautos.com>
날짜: 9월 3일
제목: 의무 교육

Webster 씨께

9월 22일에 직원들을 대상으로 열리는 **의무 교육 시간**에 관한 귀하의 메모를 받았습니다. 안타깝게도, 저희 팀은 일정이 겹칩니다. 저희는 그 주 내내 전국 자동차 박람회에 가 있을 것입니다. 그 교육을 녹화해 주시겠습니까? 그렇게 해주시면, 저희 팀이 돌아와서 동영상으로 그것을 시청할 수 있습니다. 저는 이것이 교육을 연기하는 일을 피할 수 있는 가장 좋은 해결책이라고 생각합니다. 어떻게 생각하시는지 제게 알려 주시기 바랍니다.

Roma Senhar

mandatory 의무적인 **scheduling conflict** 일정의 겹침 **entire** 전체의 **postpone** ~을 연기하다

Q. Senhar 씨는 Webster 씨에게 무엇을 하도록 요청하는가?
(A) 교육 시간 날짜 변경하기
(B) 교육을 동영상으로 만들기

[문제 키워드] What / Ms. Senhar / ask / Mr. Webster / do

[해설] 요청 사항이 언급되는 중반부에 그 교육을 녹화해 달라고 요청하고 (Could you record the session? That way, my team can watch it on video ~) 있으므로 (B)가 정답이다.

04.

수신: Niagara Power Company <billing@npc.com>
발신: Penelope Snowe <p.snowe@nmail.com>
날짜: 7월 3일
제목: 연체료

관계자께,

저는 지난달 몇 주 동안 출장 중이었습니다. 제가 돌아왔을 때, 귀사에서 온 월 전기 요금이 이미 납부 기한이 지났다는 것을 알게 되었습니다. 이번에는 5달러의 연체료를 내겠지만, 다시는 이런 문제가 생기길 원치 않습니다. **매달 당좌 계좌에서 전기 요금이 바로 인출되게 하려면 무엇을 해야 하는지 알려 주세요.**

진심으로,

Penelope Snowe

out of town 도시를 떠난 **electric bill** 전기 요금 **past due** 납부 기한이 지난 **late fee** 연체료 **checking account** 당좌 계좌

Q. Snowe 씨에 대해 사실인 것은?
(A) 그녀는 자동 결제를 설정하기를 원한다.
(B) 그녀는 최근에 새로운 직업을 위해 인터뷰했다.

[문제 키워드] What / true / Ms. Snowe

[해설] 지문 후반부에 매달 당좌 계좌에서 전기 요금이 바로 인출되게 하려면 무엇을 해야 하는지 알려 달라고(Please let me know what I need to do to have the amount of my electric bill directly taken from my checking account each month) 했으므로 (A)가 정답이다.

실전 문제

| 01.(C) | 02.(A) | 03.(B) | 04.(D) | 05.(C) | 06.(C) |
| 07.(A) | 08.(B) | 09.(A) | 10.(D) | | |

01-02는 다음 이메일을 참조하시오.

수신: Joseph Bader <baderjoseph@cedartech1.com>
발신: Riddell Inc. <orders@riddellinc.com>
날짜: 10월 11일
제목: Riddell 사에서 보내 드리는 메시지

Bader 씨께

귀하께서 최근에 저희 Riddell 사에서 주문하신 가죽 안락의자는 재고가 없는 상태입니다. 이 사실이 저희 온라인 카탈로그에 표기되었어야 했지만 그렇지 못했습니다. [01]**2주는 지나야 저희가 제조사로부터 새로운 배송 물품을 받을 예정이기 때문에**, 이 제품은 예상보다 훨씬 더 늦게 귀하의 자택에 도착할 것 같습니다. 기다리는 것을 원치 않으실 경우, [02]**체스넛 브라운 색상 대신에 초콜릿 브라운 색상으로 선택하시는 건 어떠신가요?** 그렇게 차이가 나는 색상은 아니며, 이르면 내일 아침까지도 배송될 수 있습니다. 귀하의 계정 페이지를 방문하셔서 수정하실 수 있습니다.

귀하의 양해에 감사드리며, 불편에 대해 사과드립니다.

Charles Hart
고객 서비스 직원, Riddell 사

[어휘] frequent 자주 가다

04. 동사 어휘

[해설] 빈칸에 쓰일 동사는 바로 뒤에서 입장료가 무료라고 언급한 것의 원인과 관련되어야 적절하므로 '~에 자금을 제공하다'라는 의미로 쓰이는 (A) funds가 정답이다. fund가 동사로도 쓰인다는 것을 기억해 두면 좋다.

[어휘] rent ~을 대여하다, 임대하다 transfer ~을 옮기다, 전근시키다

05-08은 다음 후기를 참조하시오.

> ⁰⁵<Over That Hill>은 성인들도 즐겁게 읽을 수 있는 흥미로운 아동 도서이다. 이 책의 주인공은 달팽이다. 하지만 이 달팽이는 사람들이 예상하는 것보다 훨씬 더 속도가 빠르다. ⁰⁶동물보다 더 빨리 달릴 수 있는데 현실에서는 절대로 할 수 없는 일이다! ⁰⁷<Over That Hill>에는 누구나 쉽게 관련지을 수 있는 몇몇 현실적인 상황들이 나온다. 나는 주인공이 어떻게 느꼈을지를 쉽게 이해할 수 있었다. ⁰⁸훌륭한 줄거리뿐만 아니라 삽화도 너무나 아름답다. 이 책을 읽고 나서, 나는 어린 아이들이 있는 내 친구들 모두에게 주기 위해 한 권씩 구입했다.

snail 달팽이 though (문장 끝이나 중간에서) 하지만 realistic 현실적인 illustration 삽화 absolutely 완전히, 전적으로

05. 형용사 자리

[해설] 빈칸 앞에 위치한 be동사와 결합 가능한 것으로서 that절이 수식하는 선행사, 즉 <Over That Hill>이라는 책의 특성을 나타낼 형용사가 쓰여야 알맞으므로 '즐거운'을 뜻하는 (D) enjoyable이 정답이다.

06. 알맞은 문장 고르기

(A) 일부 아이들은 그 결말에 실망할 것이다.
(B) 안타깝게도, 이 책은 온라인으로만 구입할 수 있다.
(C) 저자는 이 이야기가 원래 성인들을 대상으로 했던 것이라고 말했다.
(D) 현실에서는 절대로 할 수 없을 정도로 동물보다 더 빨리 달릴 수 있다!

[해설] 앞 문장에 책의 주인공인 달팽이가 속도가 빠르다는 말이 쓰여 있으므로 이 내용과 연계되는 것으로서 해당 달팽이를 She로 지칭해 책 속의 내용과 현실 사이의 차이를 언급한 (D)가 정답이다.

[어휘] author 저자, 작가 state that ~라고 말하다, 언급하다 be meant for ~을 대상으로 하다, ~을 위한 것이다 outrun ~보다 더 빨리 달리다

07. 동사 어휘

[해설] 빈칸 뒤에 전치사가 있으므로 목적어를 필요로 하지 않는 자동사가 필요한데, to와 어울려 쓰이는 자동사여야 하므로 to와 함께 '~에 관련되다'라는 의미를 나타낼 때 사용하는 자동사 (C) relate가 정답이다.

[어휘] greet ~을 맞이하다, 환영하다 overcome ~을 극복하다

08. 전치사 어휘

[해설] 빈칸 뒤에 '훌륭한 줄거리'를 뜻하는 명사구가 있고 그 뒤로 삽화가 굉장히 아름답다는 말이 이어져 있으므로 추가적인 장점을 언급하는 흐름임을 알 수 있다. 따라서 '~뿐만 아니라, ~ 외에도'라는 의미로 추가 정보를 제시할 때 사용하는 (D) Aside from이 정답이다.

[어휘] far from 결코 ~가 아닌, ~에서 멀리 떨어진 close to ~와 가까운 ahead of ~보다 앞선, ~ 앞에

PART 7 이메일 (1) 문제 제기 이메일

풀이 방법 해석

수신: cust.serv@primoauto.com
발신: d.wade@bmail.com
날짜: 8월 9일
제목: 주문 #8784484

친애하는 서비스 직원 분께,

지난주에 당신 가게에서 제 차에 쓸 새 공기 필터를 찾고 있었는데, 직원이 제게 필요한 사이즈가 없다고 했고 하나 주문하는 걸 도와줬습니다. 그는 그것이 보통 당신의 상점에 없기 때문에 제품에 대해 제가 배송비를 지불해야 할 것이라 말했습니다.

주문품을 받고, 저는 송장을 보았습니다. 배송비 3달러, 필터 7달러로 총 10달러를 청구받았습니다. 하지만 이번 주 귀사의 매장 판매 전단에 7달러에 주문한 것과 똑같은 제품이 나와 있습니다. 제가 그곳에 있었을 때 당신의 직원이 실수를 한 것 같습니다. 제가 당신의 매장에서 그것을 픽업할 수 없었기 때문에, 저에게 배송비를 환불해야 한다고 생각합니다. 당신이 이것을 할 수 있는지 알려주십시오.

진심으로,

Devin Wade

 연습 문제

01. (A)   02. (B)   03. (B)   04. (A)

01.

수신: Paper Express <info@paper-express.net>
발신: Crystal Cho <ccho@wendtinsurance.com>
날짜: 11월 16일
제목: 주문 번호 49580

Paper Express 사에 보냅니다,

저는 최근 Wendt 보험사에서 사용할 용지를 대량으로 주문했습니다. 여기에는 A3와 A4 사이즈 두 가지 모두로 된 일반 백색 복사 용지와 줄이 그어진 메모장들, 그리고 고급 이력서 용지가 포함되어 있습니다. **이 주문품은 이틀 전에 도착할 예정이었지만, 저희는 여전히 받지 못한 상태입니다.** 이 문제를 자세히 살펴봐 주셨으면 하는데, 며칠 내로 제품을 받지 못하면 다른 곳에서 용지를 구입해야 할 것이기 때문입니다.

Crystal Cho

place a large order 대량으로 주문하다 pads of ~의 여러 묶음 résumé 이력서 matter 일, 문제, 사안 elsewhere 다른 곳에서

Q. 이메일의 목적은 무엇인가?
(A) 배송 지연을 알리는 것
(B) 주문 사항에 물품을 추가하는 것

[문제 키워드] purpose

[해설] 중반부에 이틀 전에 도착할 예정이었던 주문품을 여전히 받지 못한 상태라고(The order was supposed to arrive two days ago, but we still don't have it) 알리는 것이 이메일의 목적에 해당되므로 (A)가 정

press conference 기자 회견   quarterly 분기의   board 이사회
branch 지사, 지점

(A) 그녀는 회사를 해외로 확장하려는 의도를 발표했다.
(B) 그 회사는 고품질 제품으로 알려져 있다.

[단서] Michelle Baker, held a press conference

[해설] 앞서 기자 회견을 한 사람으로 언급된 Michelle Baker를 대신하는 She와 함께 그 사람이 기자 회견에서 발표한 내용을 전달하는 (A)가 정답이다.

[어휘] intention 의도   be known for ~로 알려져 있다

02.

Lucas 제조사의 직원들이 파업에 돌입했습니다. --------. 노조 대표인 Janet Bay 씨가 내일 오후에 회사의 이사진과 만날 예정입니다.

go on strike 파업에 돌입하다   union 노동 조합   be set to부정사 ~할 예정이다

(A) 작년에 20퍼센트의 수익 증가가 기록되었습니다.
(B) 그들은 급여 인상과 의료 보험 혜택을 요구하고 있습니다.

[단서] Employees, have gone on strike

[해설] 앞 문장에 언급된 Employees를 대신하는 They와 함께 파업에 돌입한 직원들의 요구 사항을 제시한 (B)가 정답이다.

[어휘] rise in ~의 증가   profit 수익   demand ~을 요구하다   health benefits 의료 보험

03.

<News 5>는 중요한 국내 사건들에 대해 균형 잡힌 보도를 하는 것으로 뛰어난 명성을 얻었습니다. --------. 이 행사는 이번 주 토요일 오후 8시에 개최될 것입니다.

earn a reputation for ~에 대해 명성을 얻다   outstanding 뛰어난

(A) 새로운 보도팀이 해외 사건을 취재하는 데 필요합니다.
(B) 그것은 연례 TV 시상식에서 Excellence in Journalism Award 부문에 선정되었습니다.

[단서] News 5 has earned ~ reputation

[해설] 앞 문장에 <News 5>라는 방송 프로그램의 특징이 언급되어 있으므로 이 프로그램을 지칭하는 It과 함께 그 특징에 따라 발생된 긍정적인 결과를 언급하는 (B)가 정답이다.

[어휘] reporting 보도   cover ~을 취재하다, 보도하다   annual 연례의, 해마다의

04.

Sally's Seafood Shack 팀의 일원으로서, 여러분은 깨끗한 유니폼을 입고 출근하셔야 합니다. --------. 그것들을 매니저 사무실로 제출하기만 하시면 됩니다.

be expected to부정사 ~하도록 요구받다, ~할 것으로 기대되다
submit 제출하다

(A) 영수증이 있으실 경우에 우리가 여러분의 세탁 비용을 환급해 드릴 것입니다.
(B) 다음 달 내내 진행되는 특별 판촉 행사가 있을 것입니다.

[단서] As a member of ~ team, you are expected to

[해설] 앞 문장에 한 업체의 소속 직원들을 대상으로 하는 공지 사항이 언급되어 있으므로 공지 주체와 대상자를 하나로 아우르는 We와 함께 유니폼 착용 관련 정책 사항을 알리는 (A)가 정답이다.

[어휘] reimburse ~을 환급하다   expense 지출 (비용)   receipt 영수증   promotion 판촉, 홍보, 승진   run 진행되다, 운영되다

실전 문제

| 01.(B) | 02.(C) | 03.(B) | 04.(A) | 05.(D) | 06.(D) |
| 07.(C) | 08.(D) |

01-04는 다음 기사를 참조하시오.

빛의 축제

뉴 로셀 시에서는 빛의 축제와 함께 새해를 기념할 예정이다. **01**이 연례 행사는 거의 20년 전에 처음 시작된 이후로 줄곧, 지역 전역으로부터 관광객들을 유치해 왔다. 올해는, 센트럴 파크가 여러 줄로 늘어선 화려한 조명들로 꾸며질 것이다. **02**이 조명들은 해질 무렵에 점등되어 자정까지 계속 불을 밝힐 것이다. 이 새로운 특징적 요소와 함께, 일몰 후에 더 많은 사람들이 방문할 것으로 예상된다. 연인과 가족, 그리고 친구들이 모두 아름다운 풍경을 감상하고 사진을 찍기 위해 함께 모여든다. **03**전문 사진작가들 또한 이 구역에 자주 돌아다니면서 공원을 찾는 사람들을 위해 사진을 찍어 주겠다고 종종 제안한다. **04**시에서 이 축제에 재정을 지원하고 있어 입장료가 모든 사람에게 무료이므로 1월에 조명들이 철거되기 전까지 뉴 로셀 시의 센트럴 파크에 방문해 보기 바란다.

annual 연례의   region 지역   adorn A with B A를 B로 꾸미다, 장식하다   string 줄, 끈   feature 특징(적인 것)   admire ~을 감상하다   scenery 풍경, 경치   offer to부정사 ~하겠다고 제안하다   admission 입장(료)   take down ~을 철거하다, 허물다

01. 접속사 자리

[해설] 빈칸 앞뒤로 각각 완전한 절이 위치해 있으므로 빈칸은 접속사 자리이다. 따라서 유일하게 접속사에 해당하는 (B) since가 정답이다.

02. 알맞은 문장 고르기

(A) 축제에 관한 정보는 관광국에서 배부할 것이다.
(B) 작년의 축제를 촬영한 사진들이 시 웹사이트에 게시되어 있다.
(C) 이 조명들은 해질 무렵에 점등되어 자정까지 계속 불을 밝힐 것이다.
(D) 주차권은 시청에서 받을 수 있다.

[해설] 앞 문장에 공원이 화려한 조명들(colorful lights)로 꾸며진다는 말이 있으므로 colorful lights를 They로 지칭해 그 조명들이 불을 밝히는 시간대를 언급한 (C)가 정답이다.

[어휘] distribute ~을 퍼뜨리다, 배포하다, 유통시키다   turn on ~을 켜다   remain ~한 상태로 계속 남아 있다, 유지되다   lit 불이 켜진   parking pass 주차권   obtain ~을 얻다, 획득하다

03. 동사의 형태

[해설] 전문 사진작가들이 공원에서 하는 일을 나타낸 문장인데, 앞 문장에서 현재 시제 동사 come을 써서 일반적으로 발생되는 일임을 나타낸 것과 마찬가지로 여기서도 역시 현재 시제로 써야 하므로 (B) frequent가 정답이다.

DAY 06 49

account 계정, 계좌   accounting 회계

17. 기간 전치사

Valdez 사의 주가가 지난 세 번의 분기 동안 지속적으로 증가했다.

[해설] 선택지가 다양한 전치사들로 구성되어 있으므로 전치사 어휘 문제이다. 빈칸 뒤에 위치한 the past three quarters는 기간을 나타내는 명사구이므로 '~ 동안'이라는 의미로 기간을 나타낼 때 사용하는 (A) for가 정답이다.

[어휘] stock value 주가   rise 증가하다   steadily 지속적으로, 꾸준히   quarter 분기

18. 명사의 위치: 형용사 뒤

지난 1년 동안 영화 재생 서비스 가입자 수가 현저하게 증가되어 왔다.

[해설] 선택지가 increase의 다양한 형태로 구성되어 있으므로 문법 문제이다. 형용사 noticeable과 전치사 in 사이에 위치한 빈칸은 명사 자리이며, 단수를 나타내는 부정관사 a와 어울려야 하므로 단수형 명사인 (D) increase가 정답이다.

[어휘] noticeable 현저한, 주목할 만한   increase in ~의 증가   streaming service 재생 서비스   subscription (서비스) 가입

19. 형용사 어휘

유급 교육 및 수강료 환불 프로그램으로 인해, Vargas Tech는 입사해 근무하기에 전망이 밝은 회사이다.

[해설] 선택지가 다양한 형용사들로 구성되어 있으므로 형용사 어휘 문제이다. 유급 교육 및 수강료 환불 프로그램은 직원들에게 이득이 되는 조건들이므로 이와 관련된 의미로서 '전망이 밝은, 유망한'이라는 뜻으로 긍정적인 특성을 나타낼 수 있는 (B) promising이 정답이다.

[어휘] thanks to ~로 인해, ~ 덕분에   paid 유급의   tuition 수강료   reimbursement 환급   work for ~에서 근무하다   presiding 통솔하는

20. 전치사의 위치: 명사(구) 앞

Hooper 산업은 경험 부족에도 불구하고 Antwan Ray 씨를 소프트웨어 엔지니어로 고용했다.

[해설] 선택지가 전치사와 접속사로 구성되어 있으므로 문법 문제이다. 빈칸 뒤에 위치한 명사구 his lack of experience를 이끌 수 있는 것은 전치사이며, '경험 부족에도 불구하고 고용했다'라는 의미가 되어야 적절하므로 '~에도 불구하고'를 뜻하는 전치사 (D) despite가 정답이다.

[어휘] hire ~을 고용하다   lack of ~의 부족   although 비록 ~이지만   as if 마치 ~한 것처럼   since ~이기 때문에, ~한 이후로

21. 형용사 어휘

학사 학위 이상의 학위를 소지하고 계실 경우, 해당 직책에 지원하실 수 있는 자격이 있으십니다.

[해설] 선택지가 다양한 형용사들로 구성되어 있으므로 형용사 어휘 문제이다. 사람 주어 you에 대한 보어로 쓰일 수 있는 형용사로서 빈칸 앞뒤에 각각 위치한 be동사 are, to부정사와 결합 가능한 (B) eligible이 정답이다. (D) common은 가주어 It이 쓰인 문장에 어울린다.

[어휘] bachelor's degree 학사 학위   be eligible to부정사 ~할 수 있는 자격이 있다   apply for ~에 지원하다   position 직책   steady 같은, 꾸준한   exclusive 독점적인, 전용의   common 흔한

22. 형용사 어휘

Brandt 씨는 기자 회견 중에 오직 세미나 주제와 관련된 질문에 대해서만 답변할 것이다.

[해설] 선택지가 다양한 형용사들로 구성되어 있으므로 형용사 어휘 문제이다. that절이 수식하는 선행사 questions의 보어가 될 형용사로 빈칸 뒤에 위치한 전치사 to와 어울려 '~와 관련된'이라는 의미를 나타낼 수 있는 (B) relevant가 정답이다.

[어휘] press conference 기자 회견   routine 일상적인   collective 공동의, 집단적인   defective 결함이 있는

23. 시간 전치사

고객들은 주문을 하기에 앞서 온라인에서 가격을 비교해 보는 경향이 있다.

[해설] 선택지가 다양한 전치사들로 구성되어 있으므로 전치사 어휘 문제이다. 주문을 하기 전에 가격을 먼저 비교해 본다는 문맥이 되는 것이 자연스러우므로 '~ 전에, ~에 앞서'를 뜻하는 전치사 (C) prior to가 정답이다.

[어휘] tend to부정사 ~하는 경향이 있다   compare ~을 비교하다   place an order 주문하다   aside from ~ 외에는, ~을 제외하고   in spite of ~에도 불구하고   across from ~의 맞은편에

24. 형용사 어휘

Channel 7 News는 정확한 일기 예보를 하는 것으로 알려져 있다.

[해설] 선택지가 다양한 형용사들로 구성되어 있으므로 형용사 어휘 문제이다. 빈칸에 쓰일 형용사는 weather forecasts를 수식해 일기 예보의 특성을 나타내야 하므로 '정확한'이라는 의미로 쓰이는 (B) accurate이 정답이다.

[어휘] comparable 필적할 만한, 비교할 만한   accurate 정확한   temporary 일시적인   equal 동등한

PART 6   알맞은 문장 고르기-선택지에 대명사

풀이 방법 해석

집에서 요리를 많이 하는 사람으로서, Mix o' Matic은 훌륭한 주방 도구입니다. 일반적인 믹서기보다 사용하기 더 편리합니다. 속도 조절 다이얼이 하나만 있거든요! 그럼에도 불구하고 심지어 아이들이 다루기에도 안전하게 만드는 특별한 특징들이 있습니다. 예를 들어, 날에 손가락이 너무 가까이 가면 날을 멈추게 하는 센서가 있습니다. 무엇보다도, 세척하기가 훨씬 더 쉽습니다. 그게 아마도 Mix o' Matic에 대해 제가 가장 좋아하는 점인 것 같습니다.

 연습 문제

01.(A)   **02.**(B)   **03.**(B)   **04.**(A)

01.

West Side 산업의 대표이사 Michelle Baker 씨가 분기 이사회 회의 후에 어제 기자 회견을 열었다. -------. 이는 몬트리올과 토론토에 지사를 개설함으로써 시작될 것이다.

06. 장소 전치사

주소지에 사람이 아무도 없을 경우에는 문 옆에 배송 상자나 소포를 두십시오.

[해설] 선택지가 다양한 전치사들로 구성되어 있으므로 전치사 어휘 문제이다. 빈칸 앞뒤에 각각 위치한 명사 boxes or packages와 the door 사이의 위치 관계를 나타낼 전치사가 필요하므로 '~ 옆에'를 뜻하는 (A) beside가 정답이다.

[어휘] leave ~을 남기다, 놓다 present 있는 since ~ 이후로 toward (방향) ~ 쪽으로, (목적) ~을 위해

07. 시점 전치사 vs. 기간 전치사

저희 배송 트럭들 중 한 대가 고장 났기 때문에 주문품 배송은 오후나 되어야 이뤄질 것입니다.

[해설] 선택지가 다양한 전치사들로 구성되어 있으므로 전치사 어휘 문제이다. 시점 표현 the afternoon을 목적어로 취해야 하므로 시점 명사와 함께 사용하는 전치사 (B) until이 정답이다. (C) for는 숫자 표현이 포함된 기간 명사와 함께 사용한다.

[어휘] order 주문(품) not A until B B나 되어야 A하다 make a delivery 배송하다 break down 고장 나다 among ~ 사이에서

08. 시점 전치사

직원들은 내일 저녁 6시 30분까지 시상식 만찬에 오도록 초대받았다.

[해설] 선택지가 다양한 전치사들로 구성되어 있으므로 전치사 어휘 문제이다. 빈칸 뒤에 위치한 6:30 tomorrow evening은 만찬에 도착하는 일을 완료하는 기한에 해당되므로 '~까지'라는 의미로 기한을 나타낼 때 사용하는 (A) by가 정답이다.

[어휘] award dinner 시상식 만찬

09. 인칭대명사 구분: 소유격

저희 Daytona 호텔에서는 고객께 가능한 한 최고의 서비스를 제공해 드리기 위해 애쓰고 있습니다.

[해설] 선택지가 다양한 인칭대명사로 구성되어 있으므로 문법 문제이다. 전치사 to와 명사 guests 사이에 위치한 빈칸은 명사를 수식해야 하므로 이 역할이 가능한 소유격 대명사 (C) our가 정답이다.

[어휘] strive to부정사 ~하기 위해 애쓰다

10. 기간 전치사

다음 학년도에 걸쳐, 역사학 교수들이 새로운 교육 과정을 만들어 낼 것으로 예상된다.

[해설] 선택지가 다양한 품사의 단어들로 구성되어 있으므로 문법 문제이다. 빈칸 뒤에 위치한 기간 명사구 the next academic year를 목적어로 취할 전치사가 필요하므로 '~ 동안에 걸쳐'라는 의미로 기간 명사와 함께 사용하는 전치사 (A) Over가 정답이다.

[어휘] be expected to부정사 ~할 것으로 예상되다 create ~을 만들어 내다 curriculum 교육 과정

11. 형용사 어휘

Hughes 씨는 아이들을 가르쳐 본 경험이 많지 않을지 모르지만, 그의 학력은 그 범위가 넓다.

[해설] 선택지가 다양한 형용사들로 구성되어 있으므로 형용사 어휘 문제이다. be동사 is 뒤에 위치한 빈칸은 but절의 주어 his background in education의 특성을 나타내는 보어에 해당되므로 '폭넓은, 광범위한'이라는 의미로 학력 범위를 나타낼 수 있는 (C) extensive가 정답이다.

[어휘] background in education 학력 preferred 선호되는 harsh 가혹한, 혹독한 challenging 어려운, 힘든

12. 기간 전치사

통화 가치가 하루 중 내내 변동될 수 있지만, Sydney 은행은 24시간 내에 가장 좋은 환율을 제공한다.

[해설] 선택지가 다양한 전치사들로 구성되어 있으므로 전치사 어휘 문제이다. 빈칸 뒤에 위치한 the day는 기간의 의미가 내포된 명사이므로 '~ 동안 내내'라는 의미로 기간 명사와 함께 사용하는 전치사 (A) throughout이 정답이다.

[어휘] although 비록 ~이지만 currency value 통화 가치 vary 변동되다, 다르다 exchange rate 환율 concerning ~와 관련해 as for ~에 관해서라면 below (위치) ~ 아래에, (수준 등이) ~에 못 미치는

13. 전치사 over

작년에 75,000톤이 넘는 소고기를 고객들에게 공급했던 Dakota Livestock이 어제 한 캐나다 회사에 인수되었다.

[해설] 선택지가 전치사들로 구성되어 있으므로 전치사 어휘 문제이다. 동사 supplied의 목적어로 쓰인 75,000 tons와 같은 수사 표현 앞에 위치해 '~을 넘어서, ~ 이상'이라는 의미로 쓰이는 전치사 (B) over가 정답이다.

[어휘] supply ~을 공급하다 acquire ~을 인수하다, 매입하다 over ~가 넘는 through ~을 통해

14. 부사 어휘

공급업체와 관련된 문제로 인해, Jay's 이탈리안 레스토랑은 최근 해산물 요리를 제공하지 않고 있다.

[해설] 선택지가 다양한 부사들로 구성되어 있으므로 부사 어휘 문제이다. 현재완료 시제로 쓰인 동사 has offered와 의미가 어울리는 부사로 '최근에'를 뜻하는 (B) recently가 정답이다.

[어휘] due to ~로 인해 supplier 공급업체 offer ~을 제공하다 greatly 대단히 shortly 곧, 머지 않아 willingly 기꺼이, 흔쾌히

15. 부사의 역할과 위치: 형용사 수식

포커스 그룹은 대부분의 사람들이 구식 보드 게임을 하는 데 극히 낮은 관심을 보인다는 사실을 나타냈다.

[해설] 선택지가 다양한 품사의 단어들로 구성되어 있으므로 문법 문제이다. 부정관사 an과 명사를 수식하는 형용사 low 앞에 위치한 빈칸은 형용사를 수식할 부사 자리이므로 (B) extremely가 정답이다.

[어휘] focus group 포커스 그룹(시장 조사 등을 위해 구성된 그룹) indicate that ~임을 나타내다 interest in ~에 대한 관심 old-fashioned 구식의 extreme 극도의, 극심한; 극단, 극도 extremely 극히, 극도로 extremity 극한, 극도

16. 형용사의 역할: 주격 보어

Stein 투자사는 현재 고객들의 손실에 대한 책임이 있다.

[해설] 선택지가 다양한 품사의 단어들로 구성되어 있으므로 문법 문제이다. 빈칸 앞에 위치한 동사 become은 형용사 보어 또는 명사 보어와 함께 사용하는데, 이 문장에서는 주어의 상태와 관련된 의미가 되어야 적절하므로 형용사인 (D) accountable이 정답이다.

[어휘] accountable for ~에 대한 책임이 있는 loss 손실, 손해

01.
1. 선택지 보고 문법/어휘 문제 파악하기 ☐ 문법 문제 ☑ 어휘 문제
2. 빈칸 분석하기 빈칸 앞에 있는 동사 exchange의 의미 (교환하다)
   빈칸 뒤에 있는 명사 merchandise의 의미 (상품)
   → 문맥상 위의 동사, 명사와 함께 쓰일 수 있는 형용사를 답으로 고른다.
3. 정답 선택하기 정답 (D)

당신은 구입한 지 7 영업일 이내에 결함이 있는 상품을 반품하거나 교환할 수 있습니다.

02.
1. 선택지 보고 문법/어휘 문제 파악하기 ☑ 문법 문제 ☐ 어휘 문제
2. 빈칸 분석하기 빈칸 뒤에 있는 것 ☑ 동명사 ☐ 동사원형
   → 빈칸은 ☐ 부사 ☑ 전치사 자리이다.
3. 정답 선택하기 정답 (B)

모든 연구원들은 실험실에 들어가기 전에 보안 검사를 받아야 한다.

03.
1. 선택지 보고 문법/어휘 문제 파악하기 ☐ 문법 문제 ☑ 어휘 문제
2. 빈칸 분석하기 빈칸 뒤 명사가 의미하는 것 ☑ 구체적인 장소 ☐ 기간
3. 정답 선택하기 정답 (D)

방문객들은 McCarthy 타워에서 파노라마식의 도시 전경을 즐길 수 있습니다.

04.
1. 선택지 보고 문법/어휘 문제 파악하기 ☑ 문법 문제 ☐ 어휘 문제
2. 빈칸 분석하기 빈칸 뒤에 있는 것 ☐ 동사구 ☑ 명사구
   → 빈칸은 ☐ 부사 ☑ 전치사 자리이다.
3. 정답 선택하기 정답 (C)

비가 오는 날씨에도 불구하고 그 축구 경기는 예정대로 열렸다.

05.
1. 선택지 보고 문법/어휘 문제 파악하기 ☐ 문법 문제 ☑ 어휘 문제
2. 빈칸 분석하기 빈칸 앞뒤 문맥을 연결할 수 있는 의미 ☐ ~ 옆에
   ☐ ~ 너머 ☑ ~ 동안
   → 정답의 후보 2개 (B, D)
   → 빈칸 뒤 명사가 ☑ 확정된 기간을 나타내는 명사 ☐ 구체적인 숫자 표현으로 나타낸 기간이다.
3. 정답 선택하기 정답 (B)

성수기 동안에는 모든 서빙 직원들이 초과 근무를 하도록 요구된다.

06.
1. 선택지 보고 문법/어휘 문제 파악하기 ☑ 문법 문제 ☐ 어휘 문제
2. 빈칸 분석하기 빈칸 뒤에 있는 접속사 (and)
3. 정답 선택하기 정답 (A)

치즈 제품은 우유와 고기 섹션 사이에 있습니다.

실전 문제

01.(A)	02.(B)	03.(B)	04.(A)	05.(C)	06.(A)
07.(B)	08.(A)	09.(C)	10.(A)	11.(C)	12.(A)
13.(B)	14.(B)	15.(B)	16.(D)	17.(A)	18.(D)
19.(B)	20.(D)	21.(B)	22.(B)	23.(C)	24.(B)

01. 전치사의 위치: 명사(구) 앞

Main 가의 도로 공사 작업으로 인해, 운전자들은 Forrest 로를 따라 우회할 것이 권장된다.

[해설] 선택지가 전치사와 접속사로 구성되어 있으므로 문법 문제이다. 빈칸 뒤에 위치한 명사구 road work on Main Street를 이끌 수 있는 것은 전치사이므로 유일한 전치사인 (A) Due to가 정답이다.

[어휘] take a detour 우회하다 along (길 등) ~을 따라 due to ~로 인해 as long as ~하는 한 whereas ~인 반면 even though 비록 ~이지만

02. 형용사 어휘

Dawson Academy의 일부 학생들은 시험을 완료하는 데 충분한 시간이 주어지지 않는다는 불만을 제기하고 있다.

[해설] 선택지가 다양한 형용사들로 구성되어 있으므로 형용사 어휘 문제이다. time을 수식해 시험 시간과 관련된 특성을 나타낼 형용사가 필요한데, 불만의 원인이 되려면 학생들에게 시간이 많이 주어지지 않는다는 맥락이 되어야 한다. 따라서 '충분한'을 뜻하는 (B) adequate이 정답이다.

[어휘] concentrated 집중된, 농축된 continual 끊임 없는 bound 가능성이 큰, 해야 하는, ~로 향하는

03. 전치사의 위치: 동명사 앞

Todd 씨는 주간 경영진 회의를 시작하기 전에 유인물을 나눠 주었다.

[해설] 선택지가 다양한 품사로 된 단어들로 구성되어 있으므로 문법 문제이다. starting으로 시작되는 동명사구를 이끌 수 있는 것은 전치사인데, 일의 전후 관계를 나타내야 하므로 '~ 전에'를 뜻하는 전치사 (B) before가 정답이다. (A) so that은 접속사, (D) therefore는 부사이다.

[어휘] pass around ~을 나눠 주다 handout 유인물 so that (목적) ~할 수 있도록 along (길 등) ~을 따라 therefore 따라서, 그러므로

04. 장소 전치사 at / on / in

Burke 씨는 Bronson 주민 센터에서 교육 워크숍을 진행할 것이다.

[해설] 선택지가 다양한 전치사들로 구성되어 있으므로 전치사 어휘 문제이다. Bronson Community Center는 행사가 개최되는 특정 장소에 해당되므로 구체적인 장소 명사 앞에 사용하는 전치사 (A) at이 정답이다.

05. 시간 전치사

<Innovations Monthly> 구독자들은 온라인으로 등록한 후에 그 잡지의 디지털 버전을 이용할 수 있다.

[해설] 선택지가 다양한 전치사들로 구성되어 있으므로 전치사 어휘 문제이다. 온라인으로 등록한 후에 디지털 버전을 이용할 수 있는 것이므로 '~ 후에'를 뜻하는 전치사 (C) after가 정답이다.

[어휘] subscriber 구독자, 서비스 가입자 access ~을 이용하다, ~에 접근하다 register 등록하다 onto (이동) ~ 위로

하지만, ¹⁵질이 좋지 않은 용지를 사용하면 항상 너무 저렴해 보이기 때문에 그런 용지로 프로그램을 주문하지 마시기 바랍니다. 선택할 수 있는 것들을 직접 확인해 보시고 적합한 것을 고르셔야 할 것입니다.

도와주셔서 감사합니다!

Cody

devise ~을 고안하다 exception 예외 match ~와 맞다, 어울리다 achievement 업적, 성과 recognize ~을 인정하다, 표창하다 give A emphasis A를 강조하다 account 계정, 계좌 budget 예산 flimsy 질이 좋지 않은, 조잡한 in person 직접 (가서) suitable 적합한

11. 세부사항 문제 - 연계 문제

5월 10일에 누가 꽃을 받을 것인가?
(A) Neilson 씨
(B) Silva 씨
(C) Fugere 씨
(D) Anagal 씨

[해설] 첫 지문 첫 단락에서 각 부문 수상자들을 위해 꽃다발을 구입해야 한다고(we should buy a bouquet of flowers for each category winner) 했고, 5월 10일 행사 일정이 제시된 두 번째 지문에 나타난 수상자들 중의 한 명이 Kaumari Anagal 씨(Kaumari Anagal – Top Annual Sales)이므로 (D)가 정답이다.

12. 동의어 문제

첫 번째 이메일에서, 두 번째 단락 두 번째 줄의 단어 "clear"와 의미가 가장 가까운 것은 무엇인가?
(A) 밝은
(B) 명백한
(C) 비어 있는
(D) 공개된

[해설] 해당 문장에서 clear는 특정 활동이 지니는 의의를 설명하는 표현에 사용한 것으로서 사람들에게 전달되는 메시지의 특성을 나타낸다. 따라서 '분명한, 명확한' 등의 의미로 사용되었으므로 '명백한'이라는 의미로 쓰이는 (B)가 정답이다.

13. True 문제

5월 10일 행사에 관해 사실인 것은 무엇인가?
(A) 식사가 포함된다.
(B) 오직 신입 직원들만을 위한 것이다.
(C) 참석자들은 손님을 데리고 올 수 있다.
(D) 오후 8시에 종료된다.

[해설] 5월 10일 행사 일정이 제시된 두 번째 지문에, 오후 6:30에 뷔페 저녁 식사(Buffet dinner) 순서가 있으므로 식사가 포함된다고 한 (A)가 정답이다.

paraphrasing Buffet dinner 뷔페 저녁 식사 → meal 식사

[어휘] attendee 참석자

14. 추론 문제 - 연계 문제

Sahaku 씨에 관해 언급된 것은 무엇인가?
(A) 작년에 회사 내에서 가장 높은 수준의 판매 실적을 올렸다.
(B) 행사에서 자신의 파트가 강조되기를 원하지 않는다.
(C) Vergara Enterprises에서 근무한 지 반 년이 채 되지 않았다.
(D) Neilson 씨 다음으로 간단히 연설을 할 계획이다.

[해설] Sahaku 씨는 두 번째 지문에서 '환영의 상'을 받는 사람으로 제시되어 있는데(Muneto Sahaku – Welcome Award), 세 번째 지문 첫 단락에 환영의 상은 지난 6개월 내에 합류한 사람을 위한 것이라고(Since this award is for someone who has joined our team in the last six months) 쓰여 있으므로 Sahaku 씨는 근무를 시작한 지 6개월이 채 되지 않았음을 알 수 있다. 따라서 (C)가 정답이다.

[어휘] ceremony 식, 의식 emphasize ~을 강조하다 give a speech 연설하다 brief 간단한, 잠시의

15. 세부사항 문제

Tolbert 씨는 무엇을 하도록 요청받는가?
(A) 디자인에 몇몇 그래픽 추가하기
(B) 더 저렴한 프린터 찾아보기
(C) 프로그램을 위해 견고한 용지 선택하기
(D) 모든 이들의 이름의 철자 확인하기

[해설] Tolbert 씨가 수신인으로 되어 있는 마지막 지문 마지막 단락에, 질이 좋지 않은 용지에 프로그램이 인쇄되도록 주문하지 말라는(please do not order the programs on flimsy paper) 말과 함께 직접 확인하고 선택하라는(You'll have to check their options in person and choose ~) 내용이 있으므로 (C)가 정답이다.

[어휘] add A to B A를 B에 추가하다 sturdy 튼튼한, 견고한 spelling 철자

paraphrasing 정답 1. (b) 2. (a) 3. (c)

DAY 06

PART 5 문법 | 전치사 (1)

확인 문제 해석

① 저희 배송이 엔진 고장으로 인해 늦어지고 있습니다.
② 온라인 양식을 작성하심으로써 저희 경연 대회에 참여하실 수 있습니다.
③ 고객들은 우리가 웹사이트에서 제공하는 것에 관한 세부 사항을 더 알고 싶어 한다.
④ 대부분의 여행객들은 겨울에 우리 도시를 방문한다.
⑤ 고객 회의는 1월 31일까지 연기될 것이다.
⑥ 주가가 지난 5년 동안 증가해 왔다.
⑦ 저희 웹사이트에 당신의 피드백을 남겨 주세요.
⑧ 새 광고 덕분에 판매가 증가하고 있다.
⑨ 새 커피 기계에 관한 세부사항은 설명서에 쓰여 있다.

연습 문제

01.(D) 02.(B) 03.(D) 04.(C) 05.(B) 06.(A)

을 받으라고(sign up for a membership and get 20% off your first purchase) 쓰여 있으므로 해당 할인은 한 번만 제공되는 것임을 알 수 있다. 따라서 (D)가 정답이다.

07. 세부사항 문제

기사에 따르면, Highlander는 최근에 무엇을 했는가?
(A) 제품 회수를 했다.
(B) 소유권을 변경했다.
(C) 업계의 상을 수상했다.
(D) 새로운 지점을 열었다.

[해설] 두 번째 지문 첫 번째 단락에 연례 엑스포에서 3년 연속으로 최고 품질 브랜드로 선정되었다고(it has been named Highest Quality Brand) 했으므로 (C)가 정답이다.

[어휘] recall 제품 회수   ownership 소유권   branch 지점

08. 동의어 문제

기사에서, 2문단 세번째 줄의 단어 "steer"와 의미상 가장 가까운 것은
(A) 끌어들이다
(B) 이끌다
(C) 구매하다
(D) 시도하다

[해설] 해당 문장에서 steer는 뒤에 나오는 in the right direction과 결합하여 '~를 어디로 몰다'라는 의미를 나타내므로 보기 가운데 '이끌다'의 의미를 가진 (B)가 정답이다.

09. True 문제

Krauss 씨에 대해 나타난 것은?
(A) 그는 혼자 캠핑 가는 것을 더 좋아한다.
(B) 그는 Black Hills 지역에서 자랐다.
(C) 그는 폭풍우 때 캠핑을 갔다.
(D) 그는 텐트를 치기 위해 야영장 직원의 도움이 필요했다.

[해설] Krauss 씨가 쓴 후기인 세 번째 지문의 중반부에서 캠핑장 직원이 악천후를 경고했다는(warned us of bad weather) 것과 밤새도록 바람이 울부짖고 비가 내리는 소리를 들었다는(heard the wind howl and rain come down all night) 내용을 바탕으로 Krauss 씨가 폭풍우 때 캠핑을 갔다는 것을 알 수 있으므로 (C)가 정답이다.

10. 추론 문제 – 연계 문제

Krauss 씨는 자신의 Highlander 캠핑 텐트에 대해 무엇을 암시하는가?
(A) 그가 회원으로 구입한 첫 번째 물건이었다.
(B) 선택적 지지대 없이도 충분히 견고하다.
(C) 성인 2명에게 충분히 크지 않았다.
(D) 물을 막는 데 효과가 없다.

[해설] 마지막 지문 첫 문장에 20% 할인된 가격에 텐트를 구입했다고(we purchased a Highlander Camping Tent with a 20% discount) 했는데, 첫 번째 지문의 웹페이지에 20% 첫 구매 할인 혜택을 받으라고(get 20% off your first purchase) 했으니 이를 고려했을 때 후기에 언급된 할인은 첫 구매로 인한 것임을 알 수 있다. 따라서 (A)가 정답이다.

[어휘] sturdy 튼튼한   effective 효과적인

paraphrasing 정답   1. (a)   2. (c)   3. (b)

11-15는 다음 두 이메일과 행사 정보를 참조하시오.

수신: Cody Gwinn
발신: Judith Franklin
날짜: 4월 14일
제목: 5월 10일 행사

Cody 씨께

5월 10일 행사에 필요한 용품을 구입하는 일을 도와 주시겠다고 승낙해 주셔서 감사합니다. 이미 얘기를 나눴던 물품들 외에도, **[11]각 부문 수상자들을 위해 우리가 꽃다발을 구입해야 한다고 생각하는데**, 이에 따라 총 4개가 필요합니다.

추가로, 다양한 부서에 소속된 대표 직원들이 무대 위에서 여러 활동을 할 것입니다. 제 생각에는 이것이 우리 회사에서 팀워크를 대단히 소중하게 여긴다는 사실을 전달할 **[12]분명한** 메시지가 될 것 같습니다. Kimberly 씨가 현재 프로그램 초안을 맡아 작업하고 있으니, 이에 대한 어떤 아이디어든지 있으실 경우, 그녀가 그것을 제게 보내기 전에 그녀에게 말씀하십시오.

감사합니다!

Judith

assist with ~을 돕다   supplies 용품, 물품   representative 직원, 대표자   perform ~을 하다, 수행하다   on-stage 무대에서 하는   highly valued 대단히 소중하게 여겨지는   currently 현재   draft 초안

Vergara Enterprises
연례 사내 연회

5월 10일 금요일 Eagle Plaza (1층 대연회장)
오후 6:00   도착 및 칵테일 제공
[13]오후 6:30   뷔페 저녁 식사
오후 7:30   환영 연설, Phil Neilson 영업부장
오후 7:45   연설, Juan Silva 인사부장
오후 8:00   연례 직원상 시상, Naomi Fugere IT 부장
            Ronnie Tavares – 최우수 창의적 아이디어상
            [11]Kaumari Anagal – 최우수 연간 판매 실적상
            [14]Muneto Sahaku – 환영의 상
            Edith Bannon – 평생 공로상

annual 연례의, 연간의   banquet 연회   ballroom 대연회장
distribution of honors 시상(식)   lifetime achievement 평생 공로

수신: Kimberly Tolbert
발신: Cody Gwinn
날짜: 4월 15일
제목: 프로그램 초안

안녕하세요, Kimberly 씨

보내 주신 프로그램 초안을 받았습니다. 고안해 주신 일정이 잘 진행될 것으로 생각되는데, 한 가지만 예외입니다. **[14]제 의견으로는, 환영의 상이 첫 번째로 주어져야 할 것 같습니다. 이 상은 지난 6개월 내에 우리 팀에 합류한 분을 위한 것이기 때문에,** 다른 상들에 의해 인정받는 업적 수준에 그다지 걸맞지 않습니다. 프로그램 순서에서 너무 뒤쪽에 배치함으로써 이 상이 너무 많이 강조되는 것을 원치 않습니다.

그 외에는, 프로그램이 아주 좋아 보이기 때문에 인쇄 준비가 된 것 같습니다. 평소와 마찬가지로 Yancy 프린팅을 이용하시기 바랍니다. 우리 회사는 그 업체 계정이 있습니다. 우리가 예산을 꼭 유념해야 하기는

03. 세부사항 문제

Prestige Solar에서 제공하는 서비스는 무엇인가?
(A) 건축 허가를 돕는 일
(B) 월간 생산량 보고서를 제공하는 일
(C) 태양열 전지판을 청소하는 일
(D) 자금 조달에 필요한 은행 승인을 받는 일

[해설] Prestige Solar의 서비스가 언급된 두 번째 지문 세 번째 단락에, 전지판 표면에 축적되는 먼지와 오염 물질에 대한 정기적인 제거 작업을 해준다는(we can take care of the regular removal of dust and grime buildup ~) 정보가 있으므로 (C)가 정답이다.

paraphrasing removal of dust and grime buildup 먼지와 오염 물질의 제거 → Cleaning 청소

[어휘] assist with ~에 대해 돕다　building permit 건축 허가　seek ~을 구하다, 추구하다　approval 승인

04. 추론 문제 - 연계 문제

랭포드 공장에 관해 암시된 것은 무엇인가?
(A) 회사에서 가장 규모가 큰 시설이다.
(B) 지난 5년 이내에 건축되었다.
(C) 그곳의 제품이 안전 관련 리콜을 필요로 했다.
(D) 그곳의 개조 작업이 지연되었다.

[해설] 세 번째 지문의 시작 부분에 작업 장소가 랭포드로 되어 있고(Proposed Installation Address: 4549 Carriage Lane, Langford) 작업 시작 요청일이 9월 5일로 되어 있는데(Requested Start Date of Work: September 5), 첫 지문 첫 단락에 9월에 Colchester에서 가장 규모가 큰 공장에서 작업이 시작된다는(The work will begin at Colchester's largest plant in September) 말이 있다. 즉, 랭포드 공장이 가장 규모가 큰 시설임을 알 수 있으므로 (A)가 정답이다.

[어휘] facility 시설(물)　construct ~을 건축하다, 짓다　goods 제품, 상품　recall (결함 제품에 대한) 리콜, 회수

05. 세부사항 문제 - 연계 문제

7월 12일에 무슨 일이 있을 것 같은가?
(A) Prestige Solar가 선금을 지급받을 것이다.
(B) Prestige Solar가 설치 작업을 시작할 것이다.
(C) Colchester에 기술자가 방문할 것이다.
(D) Colchester가 견적서를 받을 것이다.

[해설] 7월 12일이라는 날짜와 관련해, 마지막 지문에 평가일이 7월 11일(Assessment Date: July 11)로 되어 있고, 두 번째 지문 마지막 단락에 평가 다음 날에 대략적인 비용을 보여 주는 보고서를 받을 수 있다는(~ visit your property on the assessment date, and the following day you will receive a report outlining the approximate costs) 정보가 있으므로 7월 12일에 대략적인 비용을 확인할 수 있는 견적서를 받는다는 것을 알 수 있다. 따라서, (D)가 정답이다.

paraphrasing a report outlining the approximate costs 대략적인 비용을 개괄적으로 설명하는 보고서 → an estimate 견적서

[어휘] deposit 선금, 예치금　estimate 견적(서)

paraphrasing 정답　1. (b)　2. (a)　3. (c)

06-10은 다음 웹페이지와 기사, 그리고 후기를 참조하시오.

www.highlander.com/featuredproducts

| 홈 | 주요 제품 | 회원 | 자주 묻는 질문 |

Highlander 캠핑 텐트(성인 2명)

특징:
* 설치가 쉬움
* 8개의 고정펙이 함께 제공됨
* 거센 바람과 비에 견딜 수 있도록 지지대(옵션)가 있음
* 이중 메쉬 라이닝으로 건조하게 유지해 주며 벌레를 막음

가격: 200달러

저희 매장으로 오셔서 **06, 10 회원 가입을 하시고 20% 첫 구매 할인 혜택을 받으세요!**

featured product 주요 제품　set up 설치하다　stake 텐트 고정펙　support bar 지지대　withstand 견디다　sign up for ~을 신청하다　membership 회원 자격

Highlander가 다시 해내다

5월 5일 – Highlander는 하이킹, 캠핑, 낚시와 같은 활동을 위한 야외 장비에서 가장 유명한 브랜드 중 하나로 알려져 있다. 3년 연속으로, 아웃도어 마니아들을 위한 연례 엑스포(AEOE)에서 **07 최고 품질 브랜드로 선정되었다.** 올해, 그것의 가장 인기 있는 품목은 성인 두 명을 위해 디자인된 텐트였다.

Scott McCulloch CEO는 "이런 영예를 다시 한 번 받게 돼 너무 기쁩니다"고 말했다. "항상 그렇듯이, 우리는 고객들이 요구하는 것을 경청합니다. 그것은 우리의 개발팀을 올바른 방향으로 **08 이끄는** 데 도움이 됩니다."

be known for ~로 알려지다　outdoor gear 야외용 장비　designed 설계된　honor 명예

---

www.productbuzz.com/outdoors

제품: Highlander 캠핑 텐트
후기 작성자: Jorge Krauss

제 가장 친한 친구와 저는 Black Hills로 캠핑 여행을 떠났습니다. 준비하기 위해, **10 20% 할인된 Highlander 캠핑 텐트를 구매했는데**, 그렇게 해서 기쁩니다. Highlander 브랜드는 품질로 유명하며 우리를 실망시키지 않았습니다. 우리가 캠핑장에 도착했을 때, **09 그곳의 직원들은 우리에게 악천후를 경고했어요.** 텐트를 설치한 후에는 옵션인 서포트 바도 사용했습니다. **09 밤새도록 바람이 울부짖고 비가 내리는 소리를 들었음에도 불구하고**, 우리는 텐트 안에서 건조한 상태를 유지했습니다. 저는 이 제품을 진지한 캠핑족에게 추천합니다.

prepare for ~을 준비하다　campground 캠핑장　optional 옵션인　howl 울부짖다　serious 진지한

06. 세부사항 문제

새로운 회원들에게 제공되는 것은?
(A) 제품 보증 연장
(B) 무료 특급 배송
(C) 캠핑 용품
(D) 일회성 할인

[해설] 첫 번째 지문 마지막 단락에 회원 가입을 하고 20% 첫 구매 할인

[해설] 키워드 Stacey가 언급된 세 번째 지문에서 먼저 단서를 찾아야 한다. 이 지문 중반부에 Nicholson 씨가 필요로 한 정보를 Stacey 씨가 제공한 사실이(~ Stacey was able to provide you with the information ~) 쓰여 있는데, 이는 두 번째 지문에 언급된 지도를 출력해준 일을(She printed out a map for me ~) 가리킨다. 여기서 'She'는 앞 문장에 언급된 안내 담당 직원을(The receptionist even ~) 가리키므로 (A)가 정답이다.

실전 문제

01.(D)	02.(B)	03.(C)	04.(A)	05.(D)	06.(D)
07.(C)	08.(B)	09.(C)	10.(A)	11.(D)	12.(B)
13.(A)	14.(C)	15.(C)			

01-05는 다음 기사와 정보, 그리고 양식을 참조하시오.

친환경적으로 변화하는 Colchester

3월 23일 — 자동차 부품 제조사인 Colchester 사는 자사의 공장들을 더욱 환경 친화적으로 만들기 위한 개조 계획을 발표했다. 회사의 임원들은 지속 가능한 에너지원으로 옮겨 가기를 원하고 있는데, 가스로 동력을 얻는 기계의 인기가 곧 ⁰¹지나갈 것이라고 생각하기 때문이다. 이 프로젝트에는 태양열 전지판의 설치, 빗물 집수 시스템의 추가, 그리고 벽면 단열재의 개선 작업이 포함될 것이다. ⁰²벌링턴과 랭포드, 그리고 밸리뷰의 공장에 근무하는 모든 직원들은 그 공장들에 대한 작업이 실시되는 동안 일시적으로 다른 곳에서 근무하게 될 것이다. ⁰⁴해당 작업은 9월에 Colchester에서 가장 규모가 큰 공장에서부터 시작될 것이며, 나머지 두 곳은 내년 초에 개선 작업을 거칠 예정이다.

"저희는 환경에 유익한 관행에 앞장 서게 되어 기쁘게 생각합니다"라고 ⁰²밸리뷰 공장 감독자인 John Lomas 씨가 말했다. 회사 관계자들은 다른 현장들에 근무조를 추가로 배치하는 방법으로 동일한 수준으로 생산량을 유지할 수 있기를 바라고 있다.

go green 친환경적으로 바꾸다 manufacturer 제조사 executive 임원 sustainable (환경적으로) 지속 가능한 solar panel 태양열 전지판 improve ~을 개선하다 insulation 단열(재) temporarily 일시적으로 relocate ~을 이전하다 carry out ~을 실시하다 undergo ~을 거치다, 겪다 modification 개선, 개조, 변경 lead the way in ~에 앞장서다 practice 관행, 관례 beneficial 유익한 foreman (공사 현장 등의) 감독, 주임 officials 관계자들, 당국자들 additional 추가적인 shift 교대 근무(조) site 장소, 현장

Prestige Solar: 회사 개요

여러분의 건물에 태양열 전지판을 추가하는 것을 고려하고 계신다면, 저희 Prestige Solar가 그 과정의 매 순간에 도움을 드릴 수 있습니다.

상담: 경험 많은 저희 기술자들이 전력 생산을 최대화할 수 있도록 가장 좋은 전지판 배치 방법에 관해 조언해 드릴 것입니다.

지속적인 도움: 품질 보증 기간 중의 수리 작업은 추가 비용 없이 제공됩니다. 게다가, 효율을 최대화하기 위해 ⁰³전지판 표면에 축적되는 먼지와 오염 물질에 대한 정기적인 제거 작업을 해드릴 수 있습니다.

자금 조달: 선불로 태양열 전지판 비용을 지불하실 준비가 되지 않으셨나요? 최장 5년에 걸쳐 태양열 전지판 비용을 나눠 할부로 지불하실 수 있습니다.

무료 최초 상담 서비스 일정을 정하실 수 있도록 저희에게 연락 주십시오. ⁰⁵저희 직원들 중의 한 명이 평가 당일에 귀하의 건물을 방문할 것이며, 다음 날에 대략적인 비용을 개괄적으로 설명하는 보고서를 받아 보실 수 있습니다.

property 건물, 자산, 부동산 consultation 상담 placement 배치 output 생산(량), 출력 ongoing 지속되는 warranty 품질 보증(서) at no extra cost 추가 비용 없이 take care of ~을 처리하다 removal 제거 dust 먼지 grime 오염 물질, 때 buildup 축적 surface 표면 efficiency 효율 financing 재무, 자금 조달 up front 선불로 bill 고지서 installment 할부(금) spread out (균등하게) ~을 나누다 set up ~을 정하다, 설정하다 initial 최초의 assessment 평가 outline ~을 개괄적으로 설명하다 approximate 대략적인

Prestige Solar
신규 고객 예약 양식

회사명: Colchester 회사 담당자: Nathaniel Lewis
이메일 주소: n.lewis@colchestermfg.com 전화 번호: 555-1039
설치 제안 장소: Carriage 로 4549번지, ⁰⁴랭포드

⁰⁵평가일: 7월 11일
⁰⁴작업 시작 요청일: 9월 5일

상기 예약 일정을 변경하시거나 취소하셔야 할 경우, 가능한 한 빨리 저희에게 연락 주시기 바랍니다. Prestige Solar에 대한 귀사의 관심에 감사드립니다!

booking 예약 representative 대표자, 대리인 proposed 제안된 installation 설치 interest in ~에 대한 관심

01. 동의어 문제

기사에서 첫 번째 단락, 네 번째 줄의 단어 "pass"와 의미가 가장 가까운 것은 무엇인가?
(A) ~을 채택하다
(B) 뛰어나다
(C) ~을 앞지르다
(D) 끝나다

[해설] 해당 문장에서 pass는 가스로 동력을 얻는 기계의 인기와 관련된 의미를 나타내는데, 이는 지속 가능한 에너지원으로 옮겨 가기를 원하는 회사의 입장과 대조되는 부분이다. 따라서 그 인기가 줄어들거나 사라진다는 의미로 pass가 쓰였음을 알 수 있으므로 '끝나다'를 뜻하는 (D)가 정답이다.

02. 추론 문제

Lomas 씨에 관해 암시된 것은 무엇인가?
(A) 경영팀에 가장 최근에 들어온 사람이다.
(B) 잠시 동안 다른 곳에서 근무할 것이다.
(C) 환경 연구에 대한 학위를 보유하고 있다.
(D) 생산량 향상에 대한 전략을 제공했다.

[해설] John Lomas는 첫 지문 두 번째 단락에 밸리뷰 공장 감독자라고 쓰여 있는데(John Lomas, foreman of the Valleyview plant), 앞 단락에 벌링턴과 랭포드, 그리고 밸리뷰 지역의 공장에 근무하는 모든 직원들이 일시적으로 근무지를 옮긴다는(All employees at plants in Burlington, Langford, and Valleyview will be temporarily relocated ~) 말이 있으므로 다른 곳에서 근무할 것이라고 한 (B)가 정답이다.

paraphrasing be temporarily relocated 일시적으로 전근되다 → work at another site for a short time 잠시 다른 곳에서 근무하다

[어휘] degree 학위 strategy 전략 production 생산(량)

(C) 저희가 귀하의 배터리를 폐기하고 무료로 새것을 드릴 것입니다.
(D) 저희 프로그램의 새 회원으로 귀하를 맞이하게 되어 매우 기쁩니다.

[해설] 앞 문장에 배터리를 언제든지 매장으로 갖고 오라고 권하고 있으므로 그 배터리를 yours로 지칭해 그것을 폐기하고 새것을 주겠다는 내용의 조치 사항을 언급한 (C)가 정답이다.

[어휘] dispose of ~을 처리하다, 처분하다   for free 무료로

PART 7 삼중 지문 연계 문제

풀이 방법 해석

Jacksonville이 가로등을 교체할 것이다

5월 6일- 다음 주 동안, Zamora Lighting이 Jacksonville 시내 지역의 가로등을 교체할 것이다.

근로자들이 외부의 지연이나 방해 없이 가로등을 설치할 수 있도록 우회로가 지정될 것이다. 도로의 각 구역에는 아침과 저녁의 교통량이 많은 시간대를 피하기 위해 평일 오전 10시에서 오후 4시 사이에 작업이 이루어질 것이다. 일정과 새로운 소식에 대한 내용은 시 웹사이트에서 볼 수 있고 지역 신문에 실릴 것이다.

가로등 설치 일정
5월 14일 월요일: 휴일, 작업 없음
5월 15일 화요일: Divison 가
5월 16일 수요일: Ridgewood 가
5월 17일 목요일: Mayfield 로
5월 18일 금요일: Edgewater 가
작업이 완료되면 양방향 도로가 재개통될 것입니다.

Garrett 씨께,

이 작업이 5월 16일 수요일에 귀하의 사업체에 끼칠 불편함에 대해 사과드립니다. 해당 도로를 도보로 통행하는 것은 여전히 허용될 것이므로 귀사의 고객들은 계속하여 귀사를 이용할 수 있을 것임을 양해 부탁드립니다. 그날은 Mayfield 로에 거리 주차를 하실 것을 권장드립니다.

양해해주셔서 감사합니다.

Randall Boone

Q. Garrett 씨에 대해 사실인 것은 무엇인가?
(A) 대중교통으로 통근한다.
(B) Ridgewood 가에 사업체를 소유하고 있다.
(C) 주로 Mayfield 가에 주차한다.
(D) 현재 휴가 중이다.

 연습 문제

01. (B)   02. (A)

01-02

Amethyst 스파 마사지 치료

저희는 1시간짜리의 마사지 서비스에 대해 다음과 같은 선택권을 제공해 드리게 되어 기쁘게 생각합니다.
태국식 마사지: 60달러

스웨덴식 마사지: 70달러
01 핫 스톤 마사지: 80달러
스포츠 마사지: 90달러

예약을 원하시면, 555-6112번으로 전화 주십시오. 저희는 매일 오전 7시부터 오후 9시까지 영업합니다.

offer ~을 제공하다   following 다음의, 아래의
book an appointment 예약하다

www.spa-reviews101.com

저는 최근에 처음으로 Amethyst 스파를 방문했는데, 훌륭한 경험이었습니다. 제가 받은 1시간짜리 마사지는 몸을 아주 편하게 해주었으며, 01 제가 지불한 80달러의 가치가 충분히 있었습니다. Amethyst 스파의 모든 직원들은 매우 친절하고 전문적이었습니다. 심지어 02 안내 담당 직원은 자신의 업무 범위를 벗어나는 일에도 저를 도와주었습니다. 제가 집에 전화기를 놓고 나왔기 때문에 한 특정 레스토랑으로 가는 길 안내를 부탁했었습니다. 02 그 직원은 제가 길을 잃지 않도록 지도를 출력해 주었습니다! 저는 분명 단골 고객이 될 계획입니다.

01 Stephanie Nicholson, Willow Lake

relaxing 편안하게 하는, 느긋한   well worth 충분히 ~의 가치가 있는
entire 전체의   receptionist 안내 담당자   go above and beyond (권한, 직무 등을) 넘어서다   regular customer 단골 손님

수신: Stephanie Nicholson <nicholsons@inbox22.com>
발신: Jasmine Rafferty <jasmine@amethystspa.com>
날짜: 7월 9일
제목: 감사합니다!

Nicholson 씨께

저희 스파에 대한 귀하의 최근 이용 후기에 감사 드립니다. 저희는 알맞은 가격에 우리 도시에서 최고의 스파 치료 서비스를 제공해 드리기 위해 애쓰고 있습니다. 02 Stacey 씨가 귀하께서 필요로 하셨던 정보를 제공해 드릴 수 있었다니 기쁩니다. 다음 달에, 저희는 고객들께서 받으시는 각 스파 치료에 대해 포인트를 쌓으실 수 있는 고객 보상 프로그램을 시작할 계획입니다. 저희는 귀하를 곧 다시 볼 수 있기를 바랍니다.

안녕히 계십시오.

Jasmine Rafferty
소유주, Amethyst 스파

strive to부정사 ~하기 위해 애쓰다   affordable (가격이) 알맞은
launch ~을 시작하다, 출시하다   earn ~을 얻다, 받다

01. Nicholson 씨는 방문 중에 무슨 서비스를 받았는가?
(A) 스웨덴식 마사지
(B) 핫 스톤 마사지

[문제 키워드] What service / Ms. Nicholson / receive

[해설] 키워드 Ms. Nicholson이 언급된 두 번째 지문에서 먼저 서비스와 관련된 단서를 찾아야 한다. 이 지문 초반부에 80달러의 비용을 지불했다는 (the $80 that I paid for it) 언급이 있는데, 첫 지문에서 이 비용에 해당되는 서비스가 'Hot Stone Massage: $80'이므로 (B)가 정답이다.

02. Stacey는 누구인가?
(A) 안내 담당 직원
(B) 마사지 치료사

[문제 키워드] Who / Stacey

01-04는 다음 설명을 참조하시오.

> Frankfurt 가죽 신발: 관리와 유지
>
> Frankfurt Cobbler Company는 고객들께 구매 가능한 최고의 품질을 지닌 수제 가죽 신발을 제공해 드리기 위해 최선을 다하고 있습니다. **01**그럼에도 불구하고, 심지어 최고의 품질을 지닌 제품도 적절히 관리되지 않을 경우에 그 가치를 잃게 됩니다. **02**신발을 습한 장소에 보관하는 것을 피하셔야 하지만, 반드시 장기간 직사 광선에 노출된 상태로 놓아 두지 마시기 바랍니다. 또한, 더러워질 경우에는 천으로 닦아 주시기 바랍니다. **03**이와 같은 사항들이 신발의 수명을 크게 연장하는 데 도움이 될 것입니다. 새 밑창 교환 등과 같은 일반 수선 작업은 2년 기간의 일반 품질 보증 서비스 하에 보장됩니다. **04**이 기간이 지난 후에는, 유지 관리 서비스에 대해 요금이 청구될 것입니다. 이와 같은 경우에, 저희 공인 서비스 센터 중의 한 곳으로 방문하시기 바랍니다.

> leather 가죽 maintenance 유지 관리 lose one's value 가치를 잃다 care for ~을 관리하다, 돌보다, 보살피다 properly 적절히, 제대로 humid 습한 exposed to ~에 노출된 for extended periods 장기간 extend ~을 연장하다 standard 일반의, 표준의 sole 밑창 cover (손해 등) ~을 보장하다 warranty 품질 보증(서) certified 공인된, 인증된

01. 접속부사

[해설] 빈칸 앞뒤의 내용을 보면, 최고의 품질을 지닌 제품임에도 불구하고 제대로 관리를 하지 않으면 가치를 잃는다는 흐름이 되어야 적절하므로 '그럼에도 불구하고'라는 의미로 대조적인 관계를 나타낼 때 사용하는 접속부사 (D) Nevertheless가 정답이다.

[어휘] likewise 마찬가지로 therefore 그러므로, 따라서 otherwise 그렇지 않으면, 그 외에는

02. 동사의 형태

[해설] 빈칸 앞에 동사 avoid가 이미 있으므로 또 다른 동사인 store는 준동사의 형태로 쓰여야 하는데, avoid는 동명사를 목적어로 취하므로 (A) storing이 정답이다.

[어휘] store ~을 보관하다, 저장하다

03. 지시대명사

[해설] 빈칸 뒤에 신발의 수명을 늘리는 데 도움이 된다는 말이 쓰여 있는데, 이는 앞서 제시된 몇 가지 주의 사항들을 통해 달성할 수 있는 일이다. 따라서 빈칸에는 이 몇몇 주의사항들을 대신 지칭할 수 있는 지시대명사가 필요하므로 '이것들'을 뜻하는 (C) These가 정답이다.

04. 알맞은 문장 고르기

(A) 이 기간이 지난 후에는, 유지 관리 서비스에 대해 요금이 청구될 것입니다.
(B) 아직도 그렇게 하지 않으신 경우에는, 저희 홈페이지에 후기를 남겨 주시기 바랍니다.
(C) 더 정확한 세부 사항을 보시려면 계약서를 참고하시기 바랍니다.
(D) Frankfurt Cobbler Company를 선택해 주셔서 감사합니다.

[해설] 빈칸 앞에 제시된 품질 보증 서비스와 연계되는 내용이 쓰여야 자연스러우므로 이 서비스 기간을 that period로 지칭해 해당 기간 이후에 발생되는 일을 알리는 (A)가 정답이다.

[어휘] charge A for B A에게 B에 대한 요금을 청구하다, 부과하다 leave ~을 남기다 refer to ~을 참고하다 precise 정확한

05-08은 다음 이메일을 참조하시오.

> 날짜: 11월 7일
> 수신: Emma Douglass <edouglass@lmail.net>
> 발신: Henrietta White <hwite@fullertonmobile.net>
> 제목: 휴대전화
>
> Douglass 씨께
>
> 지난주에 귀하의 FT4 휴대전화 개통을 도와 드릴 수 있어서 기뻤습니다. 안타깝게도, 귀하께서 갖고 계신 특정 모델과 관련해 알려 드릴 좋지 않은 소식이 있습니다. **05**해당 제조사에서 그 모델이 과도하게 충전될 경우에 일부 배터리가 부풀어 오르는 경우를 발견했습니다. **06**이는 전기 회로를 과열시키거나 더 심할 경우에 화재로 이어질 수 있습니다.
>
> **07**귀하께서 결함이 있는 배터리를 갖고 계신지 그렇지 않은지를 알아보시려면, 전화기 뒤쪽의 덮개를 열어 "제품 ID 번호"를 찾아보시기 바랍니다. 그 번호가 "PD2"로 끝나는 경우, 언제든지 저희 매장으로 배터리를 갖고 오시기를 권해 드립니다. **08**저희가 귀하의 배터리를 폐기하고 무료로 새것을 드릴 것입니다.
>
> 감사합니다.
>
> Henrietta White
> 책임자, Fullerton 모바일

> assist A with B B에 대해 A를 돕다 activation 활성화 manufacturer 제조사 swollen 부풀어 오른 overcharge 과도하게 충전되다 lead to ~로 이어지다, ~의 결과를 낳다 overheat ~을 과열시키다 circuitry 전기회로 determine ~을 알아내다, 밝히다 faulty 결함이 있는 cover 덮개 look for ~을 찾다

05. 동사 어휘

[해설] 빈칸 뒤에 목적어(some batteries)와 과거분사(swollen)가 나오는데, 둘 사이의 의미 관계로 볼 때 '목적어+목적 보어'의 구조임을 알 수 있으므로 이와 같은 구조와 함께 사용하는 5형식 동사 find의 과거 시제 (A) found가 정답이다.

[어휘] exchange ~을 교환하다 repair ~을 수리하다

06. 지시대명사

[해설] 조동사 could 앞에 위치한 빈칸은 주어 자리이므로 주어 역할이 가능한 대명사 (A) Some과 (C) This 중에서 하나를 골라야 하는데, 앞선 문장에서 말하는 문제점에 따른 결과를 나타내는 문장이 되어야 하므로 앞 문장에 제시되는 특정 내용을 하나의 단어로 지칭할 때 사용하는 (C) This가 정답이다. 참고로, (D) Hence는 부사이다.

[어휘] hence 따라서, 이런 이유로

07. 접속사 어휘

[해설] 빈칸 앞에 to부정사로 쓰인 동사 determine은 목적어를 필요로 하는 타동사이며, 빈칸 뒤에 이어지는 절이 목적어 역할을 하는 명사절이 되어야 알맞으므로 명사절을 이끄는 접속사 (B) whether가 정답이다.

[어휘] so that (목적) ~할 수 있도록, (결과) 그러므로, 그 결과 although 비록 ~이기는 하지만

08. 알맞은 문장 고르기

(A) 귀하께서는 매달 쿠폰 북을 발송 받을 것입니다.
(B) 첨부된 건의 양식을 작성하셔서 저희에게 다시 보내 주시기 바랍니다.

만 지속될 것이다.

[해설] 선택지가 다양한 부사들로 구성되어 있으므로 부사 어휘 문제이다. 자동사 last와 부사적으로 쓰인 기간 표현 one week 사이에 빈칸이 위치해 있으므로 이 기간 표현을 강조하는 역할을 하는 부사 (A) only가 정답이다.

[어휘] last 지속되다   clearly 명확히   mostly 대부분   scarcely 좀처럼 ~ 않다

24. 명사 어휘

오랜 협의 끝에, Stanford 씨는 건물주와 현 임대 계약서의 내용을 조정하기로 합의했다.

[해설] 선택지가 다양한 명사들로 구성되어 있으므로 명사 어휘 문제이다. 빈칸 앞뒤에 각각 위치한 동사 make, 전치사 to와 어울리는 명사가 필요하므로 이 둘과 함께 쓰여 '~을 조정하다'라는 의미를 나타내는 (B) adjustments가 정답이다.

[어휘] negotiation 협의   current 현재의   contract 계약(서)   benefit 혜택, 이득   objective 목적, 목표

PART 6 앞 문장의 내용을 요약하는 지시대명사

풀이 방법 해석

다른 TradeNet 고객들에게 물건을 배송하는 것:

저희 TradeNet에서는 사람들에게 물건을 사고, 팔고, 거래하는 플랫폼을 제공합니다. 그러므로, 보내시는 분은 받으시는 분에게 물건을 보내기 전에 적절히 포장할 책임이 있습니다. 보내는 사람으로서, 훼손을 피하기 위해 보내는 물건을 잘 포장하는 것이 여러분에게 이득이 될 것입니다.

저희는 강한 피드백 교환 시스템을 바탕으로 운영된다는 것을 유념해 주세요. 이것은 거래에 수반된 모든 사람들의 진실성에 의존합니다. TradeNet 회원들에게는 모든 거래에 대한 솔직한 후기를 남길 것이 요구됩니다. 악명이 높은 누군가로부터 구매할 의향이 있는 사람들은 별로 없을 겁니다. 이러한 방식으로, 저희는 높은 수준의 고객 만족도를 유지할 수 있습니다.

 연습 문제

01.(B)   02.(A)   03.(B)   04.(B)

01.

지금 이 순간부터, 우리 은행의 고객들께서는 개인 모바일 기기를 통해 각자의 모든 계좌에 접속하실 수 있습니다. 고객들께서는 현재의 잔액을 확인하시고 다른 계좌로 금액을 이체하실 수 있으며, 월간 내역서를 확인하실 수 있습니다. 이는 고객 만족도를 상당히 증가시켜 줄 것으로 예상됩니다.

access ~에 접속[접근]하다, ~을 이용하다   account 계좌   device 기기, 장치   balance 잔액   transfer ~을 이체하다, 옮기다   statement 내역서   considerably 상당히, 많이

[단서] access all of their accounts ~ devices

[해설] 빈칸이 속한 문장에서 말하는 '고객 만족도 증가'는 앞 문장에 언급된 서비스 변동 사항들에 따른 결과로 볼 수 있으므로 앞 문장 전체를 대신할 수 있는 (B) This가 정답이다.

02.

Santa Monica 콘도미니엄

폐전자제품 처리 규정

우리는 재활용 쓰레기통 바로 옆에 전자제품을 재활용할 수 있는 공간을 마련할 것입니다. 모든 소형 휴대용 전자제품은 무료로 폐기할 수 있습니다. 하지만 냉장고, 세탁기, 식기세척기, 대형 오븐 등 더 큰 것들에 대해서는 폐기 수수료가 부과됩니다. 이것은 다음 달부터 시행될 예정입니다.

arrange 마련하다   recycle 재활용하다   portable 휴대용의   dispose of ~을 버리다, 처리하다   incur 발생시키다   fee 수수료, 요금   implement 시행하다

[단서] Electronic Waste Disposal Policy

[해설] 빈칸이 속한 문장에서 말하는 '다음 달부터 시행되는'은 앞서 언급된 쓰레기 처리 규정이므로 이를 가리킬 때 사용하는 (A) This가 정답이다.

03.

Crabtree 사무용 책상을 구입해 주셔서 감사 드립니다! 모든 저희 제품들처럼, 조립 과정을 필요로 하므로 설명서를 참조하십시오. 이것이 시장에서 저희 제품 가격을 아주 경쟁력 있게 만들어 준다는 점을 명심하시기 바랍니다.

purchase ~을 구입하다   assembly 조립   refer to ~을 참조하다   instructions 설명, 지시, 안내   competitive 경쟁력 있는

[단서] it requires assembly

[해설] 빈칸이 속한 문장에서 말하는 '경쟁력 있게 만드는' 일은 앞서 언급된 제품을 조립해야 한다는 특징에 따른 것이므로 앞서 나온 내용 전체를 가리킬 때 사용하는 (B) this가 정답이다.

04.

저는 주문품이 7월 7일에 도착할 수 있는지 여쭤 보고자 합니다. 제 회사가 시카고에서 열리는 무역 박람회에 참석할 계획인데, 그곳에서 저희가 새로운 안내 책자를 배부해야 합니다. 그렇지 않을 경우, 그것이 저희 일정에 일부 변동을 초래하게 될 것입니다.

trade fair 무역 박람회   distribute ~을 배부하다, 나눠 주다   brochure 안내 책자, 소책자

[단서] whether the order may arrive on July 7

[해설] 빈칸은 일정 변동을 초래하는 원인에 해당되는데, 이 변동은 앞서 언급된 주문품 도착 시점에 따른 것이므로 앞서 언급된 내용을 가리킬 때 사용하는 (B) that이 정답이다.

실전 문제

01.(D)   02.(A)   03.(C)   04.(A)   05.(A)   06.(C)
07.(B)   08.(C)

DAY 05

13. 재귀대명사 숙어

Mullen 씨의 부서에 인턴 직원 한 명이 배정되었으므로, 그녀 혼자 이 프로젝트를 할 필요가 없을 것이다.

[해설] 선택지가 다양한 인칭대명사로 구성되어 있으므로 문법 문제이다. by의 목적어 자리인 빈칸에 쓰일 대명사는 주어 she를 가리키므로 주어와 전치사의 목적어가 동일할 때 사용하는 재귀대명사 (C) herself가 정답이다. 'by oneself'를 하나의 숙어로 기억해 두는 것이 좋다.

[어휘] assign ~을 배정하다 division (회사 등의) 부, 과 by oneself 혼자, 스스로

14. 형용사의 역할: 주격 보어

Tatum 씨의 연구에 따르면 대부분의 철새들이 이동하는 경로는 추적 기술의 도움을 받아 예측 가능한 것으로 나타난다.

[해설] 선택지가 다양한 품사의 단어들로 구성되어 있으므로 문법 문제이다. be동사 are 뒤에 위치한 빈칸은 that절의 주어(most migratory birds' travel routes)에 대한 보어 자리이므로 형용사 어미 -able로 끝나는 (C) predictable이 형용사 보어로 쓰여 '철새 이동 경로가 예측 가능하다'라는 의미가 되게 하는 것이 알맞다.

[어휘] migratory bird 철새 tracking 추적 predict ~을 예측하다 predictable 예측 가능한 prediction 예측

15. 형용사의 역할: 주격 보어

아직 자신의 학위 과정을 완료하지 못했기 때문에, Sanchez 씨는 그 직책에 지원하는 것을 꺼려하고 있다.

[해설] 선택지가 다양한 품사의 단어로 구성되어 있으므로 문법 문제이다. be동사 is 뒤에 위치한 빈칸은 주어 Mr. Sanchez에 대한 보어 자리이며, to부정사와 함께 'be reluctant to부정사'의 구조로 '~하기를 꺼려하다'라는 의미를 나타낼 때 사용하는 형용사 (B) reluctant가 정답이다.

[어휘] complete ~을 완료하다 degree 학위 apply for ~에 지원하다 reluctantly 꺼려하여, 마지못해 reluctance 꺼림, 마지못해 함 reluctancy 꺼림, 내키지 않음

16. 인칭대명사 구분: 소유격

온라인 쇼핑의 인기로 인해, Vincent Accessory는 자사의 온라인 매장을 시작할 것이다.

[해설] 선택지가 다양한 품사로 된 단어로 구성되어 있으므로 문법 문제이다. 동사 launch와 목적어로 쓰인 명사구 online store 사이에 위치한 빈칸은 명사구를 수식할 단어가 필요한 자리이므로 이 역할이 가능한 소유격 대명사 (C) its가 정답이다.

[어휘] due to ~로 인해 launch ~을 시작하다, ~에 착수하다 beyond (위치) ~ 너머에, (시간) ~을 지나, (능력 등) ~을 넘어서는

17. 빈도 부사

팀 프로젝트를 배정할 때, Hines 씨는 흔히 각자의 장점을 바탕으로 직원들을 여러 그룹으로 나눈다.

[해설] 선택지가 다양한 부사들로 구성되어 있으므로 부사 어휘 문제이다. 빈칸에 쓰일 부사는 동사 divides를 수식해야 하는데, divides가 현재 시제이므로 현재 시제 동사와 함께 사용하는 빈도 부사 (C) frequently가 정답이다.

[어휘] assign ~을 배정하다 divide A into B A를 B로 나누다 based on ~을 바탕으로 individual 각각의, 개인의 strength 장점 noticeably 두드러지게 apparently 보아 하니, 명백히 frequently 흔히, 자주 substantially 상당히, 많이

18. 사람 명사/사물 명사/추상 명사의 구분

이 할당 업무에 추가적인 도움이 필요하실 것이므로 보조 직원이 당신에게 지명될 것입니다.

[해설] 선택지가 다양한 품사의 단어들로 구성되어 있으므로 문법 문제이다. 부정 관사 an과 동사 will be appointed 사이에 위치한 빈칸은 주어 역할을 할 명사 자리인데, will be appointed의 주어로서 지명되는 대상이 되는 것은 사람이므로 사람 명사인 (A) assistant가 정답이다.

[어휘] appoint ~을 지명하다, 임명하다 assignment 할당 업무 assistant 보조, 조수 assistance 도움 assist ~을 돕다

19. 명사 어휘

대표이사는 성공적인 신제품 출시를 위해 관련된 모든 부서 전체에 걸쳐 전적인 협조를 요청한다.

[해설] 선택지가 다양한 명사들로 구성되어 있으므로 명사 어휘 문제이다. 동사 requires의 목적어로서 모든 부서에 걸쳐 요구할 수 있는 것을 나타낼 명사가 필요하므로 '협조'를 의미하는 (B) cooperation이 정답이다.

[어휘] full 전적인, 모든 related 관련된 launch 출시, 공개 demonstration 시연(회) cooperation 협조 assurance 장담, 보장 overview 개요

20. 명사 어휘

프린터를 켜기 전에 사용자 설명서를 참고하시기 바랍니다.

[해설] 선택지가 다양한 명사들로 구성되어 있으므로 명사 어휘 문제이다. user's와 결합해 동사 consult의 목적어로서 기기 사용 전에 참고할 수 있는 것을 나타낼 명사가 필요하므로 user's와 함께 '사용자 설명서'라는 표현을 만드는 (C) manual이 정답이다.

[어휘] consult ~을 참고하다 turn on ~을 켜다, 틀다 assent 찬성, 승인 route 경로 manual 설명서 crisis 위기

21. 시간 부사

Highland 은행은 한 세기보다 조금 더 이전에 Edinburgh에서 설립되었다.

[해설] 선택지가 부사와 전치사로 구성되어 있으므로 문법 문제이다. 기간 표현 over a century와 어울려 과거 시점을 나타낼 때 사용하는 부사 (A) ago가 정답이다. (B) prior to는 전치사이고, (C) beginning은 시점 표현과 함께 전치사적으로 쓰인다.

[어휘] found ~을 설립하다 prior to ~ 전에, ~에 앞서 apart 따로, 떨어져

22. 명사 어휘

Martins 교수는 Kansas 대학교 인근에 있는 연립 주택을 찾고 있다.

[해설] 선택지가 다양한 명사들로 구성되어 있으므로 명사 어휘 문제이다. 빈칸 앞뒤에 각각 위치한 전치사 in, of와 결합해 두 건물들 사이의 거리 관계를 나타내는 표현을 완성해야 하므로 '~의 인근에 있는'이라는 뜻을 나타낼 때 사용하는 (C) vicinity가 정답이다.

[어휘] look for ~을 찾다 in the vicinity of ~의 인근에 있는 direction 방향, 지시, 감독 hazard 위험 landmark 명소

23. 강조 부사

Salem Bedding의 창립 기념일 세일 행사는 오늘부터 오직 일주일 동안

01. 숫자 표현과 사용되는 부사

Gibson 제조사는 지난 분기 동안에만 약 15퍼센트의 성장을 기록했다.

[해설] 선택지가 다양한 품사의 단어들로 구성되어 있으므로 문법 문제이다. 빈칸에는 수사 표현 15%를 앞에서 수식할 부사가 와야 하므로 '약, 대략'이라는 의미로 숫자 표현을 수식하는 (B) approximately가 정답이다.

[어휘] growth 성장   quarter 분기   approximation 근사치, 비슷한 것   approximate 근사치의; ~와 비슷하다

02. 숫자 표현과 사용되는 부사

대략 60만명의 승객들이 매주 Penn Station을 통해 여행을 한다.

[해설] 선택지가 다양한 부사들로 구성되어 있으므로 부사 어휘 문제이다. 수사 표현 600,000을 앞에서 수식할 부사가 빈칸에 쓰여야 알맞으므로 이 역할이 가능한 (C) Roughly가 정답이다.

[어휘] persistently 끈질기게   initially 처음에   casually 무심코

03. 시간 부사

출장에서 돌아오시는 대로 영수증을 회계부로 꼭 제출해 주시기 바랍니다.

[해설] 선택지가 다양한 부사들로 구성되어 있으므로 부사 어휘 문제이다. 빈칸 앞뒤에 위치한 as와 어울려 주어와 동사(you return)가 포함된 절을 이끌 접속사를 구성할 수 있는 (C) soon이 정답이다.

[어휘] accounting department 회계부   far 멀리, 떨어져   brightly 밝게, 환하게

04. 명사 어휘

Holland 씨는 자신의 아파트에서 걸어서 갈 수 있는 거리에 있는 시간제 일자리를 얻고 싶어 한다.

[해설] 선택지가 다양한 명사들로 구성되어 있으므로 명사 어휘 문제이다. 빈칸 앞에 위치한 walking과 결합 가능한 명사로 '걸어서 갈 수 있는 거리'라는 의미를 나타낼 때 사용하는 (B) distance가 정답이다.

[어휘] within walking distance of ~에서 걸어서 갈 수 있는 거리에   stance 입장, 태도   proximity 인접(성)   range 종류, 범위

05. 의미가 달라지는 '-ly' 부사

Lincoln Lane Pizza는 최근에 점점 더 많은 수의 포장 주문을 받아 왔다.

[해설] 선택지가 형용사와 부사로 구성되어 있으므로 문법 문제이다. 현재완료 시제 동사 has received와 어울리는 부사로 '최근에'를 의미하는 (B) lately가 정답이다. (A) late은 '늦게'를, (C) later는 '나중에'를 의미한다. (D) latest는 '최신의'를 의미하는 형용사이다.

06. 접속부사

전문 음식 평론가들이 낮은 평가를 하기는 했지만, Ronny's Diner는 그럼에도 불구하고 Kingston 주민들 사이에서 가장 좋아하는 식당으로 유지되고 있다.

[해설] 선택지가 부사와 전치사로 구성되어 있으므로 문법 문제이다. '비록 ~이지만'을 나타내는 접속사 Although가 이끄는 절과 의미상 어울리는 부사로서 '그럼에도 불구하고'를 뜻하는 (D) nevertheless가 정답이다.

[어휘] critic 평론가   remain ~로 유지되다, 남아 있다   eatery 식당   moreover 더욱이   along (길 등) ~을 따라

07. 빈출 부사 enough

많은 양의 고기와 높게 쌓아 올린 감자튀김이 포함된 Steak Platter는 배가 고픈 성인 2명이 먹기에 충분히 많다.

[해설] 선택지가 형용사와 부사로 구성되어 있으므로 문법 문제이다. 빈칸에는 형용사 big 뒤에서 수식할 부사가 쓰여야 알맞으므로 형용사를 뒤에서 수식해 '충분히 ~한'이라는 의미를 나타낼 때 사용하는 (C) enough가 정답이다.

[어휘] portion 일부, 몫, 1인분   pile ~을 쌓다   firmly 굳게, 확고히

08. 명사 어휘

이 모바일 앱은 더욱 편리하게 저희 치과 진료소에 예약 일정을 잡거나 일정을 재조정하는 데 도움을 줍니다.

[해설] 선택지가 다양한 명사들로 구성되어 있으므로 명사 어휘 문제이다. 빈칸 앞에 위치한 두 동사 arrange, reschedule의 목적어로 어울리는 명사는 일정과 관련된 것이어야 하므로 '예약, 약속' 등을 의미하는 (D) appointments가 정답이다.

09. 부정 부사

Manaford Auto 사의 트럭들은 매우 견고해서 좀처럼 유지 관리를 필요로 하지 않는다.

[해설] 선택지가 다양한 부사들로 구성되어 있으므로 부사 어휘 문제이다. that절의 주어 they와 동사 require 사이에 위치할 수 있으면서 현재 시제와 어울리는 빈도 부사 (C) seldom이 정답이다.

[어휘] so A that B 너무 A해서 B하다   sturdy 견고한   maintenance 유지 관리   shortly 곧, 머지 않아   seldom 좀처럼 ~ 않다

10. 명사의 위치: 소유격 뒤

어떠한 연체료도 발생하는 일이 없도록 납부 기한 이전에 금액을 지불하시기 바랍니다.

[해설] 선택지가 다양한 품사의 단어들로 구성되어 있으므로 문법 문제이다. 빈칸은 소유격 대명사 your의 수식을 받으면서 동사 submit의 목적어 역할을 할 명사 자리이므로 명사 어미 -ment로 끝나는 (D) payment가 정답이다.

[어휘] due date 납부 기한, 제출 기한   incur (비용 등) ~을 발생시키다   late charge 연체료   payable 지불할 수 있는   payment 지불(액)

11. 빈도 부사

분기마다 한 번씩, Lawrence 건설사는 소속 직원들에게 초과 근무 보너스를 지급한다.

[해설] 선택지가 부사와 전치사로 구성되어 있으므로 문법 문제이다. 빈칸 뒤에 위치한 'per+명사'와 어울려 '~마다 한 번씩'이라는 반복 주기를 나타내는 부사 (A) Once가 정답이다.

[어휘] quarter 분기   once 한 번   since ~ 이후로   along (길 등) ~을 따라

12. 빈도 부사

Gentry 보안 업체는 경비를 보도록 고용된 구역들을 일상적으로 순찰한다.

[해설] 선택지가 다양한 부사들로 구성되어 있으므로 부사 어휘 문제이다. 빈칸에 쓰일 부사는 현재 시제 동사 patrols를 앞에서 수식해야 하므로 현재 시제 동사와 어울려 빈도를 나타낼 때 사용하는 (D) routinely가 정답이다.

[어휘] patrol ~을 순찰하다   hire ~을 고용하다   additionally 추가적으로   routinely 일상적으로

informed that all seaside rooms were already booked) 정보를 통해 알 수 있는 내용인 (B)가 정답이다.

[어휘] be dissatisfied with ~에 대해 불만스러워하다 make a complaint about ~에 대해 불만을 제기하다 cleanliness 청결 상태

14. 동의어 문제

쿠폰에서 첫 번째 단락, 첫 번째 줄의 단어 "appreciate"와 의미가 가장 가까운 것은 무엇인가?
(A) ~을 강화하다
(B) ~을 칭찬하다
(C) ~을 알다
(D) ~을 감탄하다

[해설] appreciate의 목적어로 쓰인 that절은 업체 측에서 고객을 대할 때 항상 알고 있어야 하는 사항에 해당된다. 따라서 appreciate이 '알다, 인식하다' 등의 의미임을 알 수 있으며, 이와 같은 뜻으로 쓰이는 또 다른 동사인 (C)가 정답이다.

15. 추론 문제 – 연계 문제

Agano 씨는 어느 도시에서 일하고 있을 것 같은가?
(A) 로스앤젤레스
(B) 샌프란시스코
(C) 프레즈노
(D) 롱 비치

[해설] 발신인이 Agano 씨로 되어 있는 첫 지문 두 번째 단락의 끝부분에, 자신이 무료 쿠폰을 첨부했다고(I have attached a voucher ~) 언급하고 있는데, 이 쿠폰에 해당되는 두 번째 지문의 하단에 '발행 지점, Montrose 호텔 고객 관리부, 프레즈노(Issued by Montrose Hotel Guest Relations, Fresno ~)'라고 쓰여 있으므로 (C)가 정답이다.

paraphrasing 정답 1. (b) 2. (e) 3. (d) 4. (c) 5. (a)

DAY 05

PART 5 문법 | 부사 (2)

확인 문제 해석

① Houston Software는 정기적으로 제품을 업데이트한다.
② 제품 디자인 부서는 월요일 아침에는 고객과의 회의를 거의 하지 않는다.
③ 저희는 최종 면접을 위해 당신에게 곧 연락드릴 것입니다.
④ 저희 회원증이 있으시면 40%까지 절약하실 수 있습니다.
⑤ 우리는 최근에 우리의 웹사이트를 다시 디자인했다.
⑥ 그 디자인은 매우 매력적이어서 젊은 고객들의 관심을 끌 것이다.
⑦ 마감일이 연장되었다. 그럼에도 불구하고, 그는 제때 보고서를 제출하지 않았다.

 연습 문제

01.(C) 02.(A) 03.(A) 04.(D) 05.(A) 06.(C)

01.
1. 선택지 보고 문법/어휘 문제 파악하기 ☑문법 문제 ☐어휘 문제
2. 빈칸 분석하기 빈칸 뒤에 있는 것 ☐명사 ☑형용사 ☐부사
   → 빈칸은 ☐명사 ☑부사 자리이다.
3. 정답 선택하기 정답 (C)

매우 효율적인 자동화된 조립 라인은 생산을 적어도 30퍼센트 증가시킬 것이다.

02.
1. 선택지 보고 문법/어휘 문제 파악하기 ☐문법 문제 ☑어휘 문제
2. 빈칸 분석하기 빈칸 뒤에 있는 것 ☑현재 시제 ☐과거 시제 ☐미래 시제
   빈칸 뒤 동사의 의미 (열다, 개최하다)
   → 동사의 시제와 의미에 어울리는 부사가 정답이다.
3. 정답 선택하기 정답 (A)

Garner 씨는 판매 수치를 개선하기 위한 전략을 논의하기 위해 자주 회의를 연다.

03.
1. 선택지 보고 문법/어휘 문제 파악하기 ☐문법 문제 ☑어휘 문제
2. 빈칸 분석하기 빈칸 앞의 in, 빈칸 뒤의 of와 짝꿍으로 쓰이는 명사가 정답이다.
3. 정답 선택하기 정답 (A)

3월 20일에 Vincent Books는 국경일을 기념하여 문을 닫을 것이다.

04.
1. 선택지 보고 문법/어휘 문제 파악하기 ☐문법 문제 ☑어휘 문제
2. 빈칸 분석하기 빈칸 앞에 있는 것 ☑미래 시제 동사 ☐현재 시제 동사
3. 정답 선택하기 정답 (D)

합병은 이사회가 최종 협의에 도달하면 곧 승인될 것이다.

05.
1. 선택지 보고 문법/어휘 문제 파악하기 ☑문법 문제 ☐어휘 문제
2. 빈칸 분석하기 빈칸 뒤에 있는 것 ☐명사구 ☑전치사구
   → 빈칸은 ☐형용사 ☑부사 자리이다.
3. 정답 선택하기 정답 (A)

인턴십을 시작했을 때조차도 Singh 씨는 기대를 뛰어 넘어 업무를 수행했다.

06.
1. 선택지 보고 문법/어휘 문제 파악하기 ☐문법 문제 ☑어휘 문제
2. 빈칸 분석하기 빈칸 뒤에 있는 것 ☑숫자 표현 ☐미래 시제 동사
3. 정답 선택하기 정답 (C)

Meyers 주방장은 과일 파이를 만들 때 설탕 약 1티스푼만큼 넣을 것을 권한다.

실전 문제

01.(B)	02.(C)	03.(C)	04.(B)	05.(B)	06.(D)
07.(C)	08.(D)	09.(C)	10.(D)	11.(A)	12.(D)
13.(C)	14.(C)	15.(C)	16.(C)	17.(C)	18.(A)
19.(B)	20.(C)	21.(A)	22.(C)	23.(A)	24.(B)

Sprague City's Summer Concert Series) 되어 있으므로 (D)가 정답이다.

[어휘] bad weather 악천후   raise funds 기금을 모으다

10. 세부사항 문제

웹사이트 방문자들은 왜 주어진 링크를 클릭해야 하는가?
(A) 일정표를 보기 위해
(B) 그들의 의견을 공유하기 위해
(C) 좌석을 예약하기 위해
(D) 지도를 다운로드하기 위해

[해설] 링크 정보가 언급된 두 번째 지문 두 번째 단락에, 관람 지역이 표시된 지역 안내도를 언급하며 "here(여기에서)"라는 클릭 유도 표기를 제시한 후, 직접 다운로드하려면 링크를 따라가라고(Follow the link to download a copy for yourself) 알리고 있으므로 (D)가 정답이다.

[어휘] share ~을 공유하다   feedback 의견   reserve ~을 예약하다

paraphrasing 정답   1. (c)   2. (d)   3. (a)   4. (b)   5. (e)

11-15는 다음 이메일과 쿠폰을 참조하시오.

수신: Patricia Lowry <p.lowry@scribnersolutions.com>
발신: Tatsuhi Agano <tatsuhiagano@montrosehotel.com>
날짜: 11월 6일
제목: 귀하의 Montrose 호텔 숙박
첨부: montrose.쿠폰

Lowry 씨께,

저희 Montrose 호텔의 롱 비치 지점에서 겪으신 부정적인 경험에 대해 사과의 말씀을 드리고자 합니다. [12, 13]귀하께서는 메시지를 통해 11월 2일부터 11월 4일까지 해변 전망으로 된 객실을 하나 예약하셨지만 체크인하셨을 때 해변 전망의 객실들이 모두 이미 예약되었다는 통보를 받았다고 알려 주셨습니다. [11]불과 2주 전에 이곳에서 근무를 시작한 저희 직원들 중 한 명이 귀하께서 객실 예약 전화를 하셨을 때 정확하게 예약 양식을 작성하지 않았던 것 같습니다. 결과적으로, 귀하께서는 정원 전망으로 된 객실을 받으셨습니다.

저는 당시 근무 중이던 책임자 [12]Tyrone Soto 씨가 귀하께서 체크인하신 직후에 해당 사안에 관해 알게 되자마자 귀하의 객실로 무료 와인 한 병을 보내 드렸다는 말을 들었습니다. 추가로, 제가 캘리포니아에 있는 저희 지점들(로스앤젤레스, 샌프란시스코, 프레즈노, 또는 롱 비치) 중 한 곳에서 [15]무료 1박을 하실 수 있는 쿠폰을 첨부해 드렸습니다. 증정용으로 귀하께 제공해 드립니다.

[15]Tatsuhi Agano 드림
고객 관리 책임자, Montrose 호텔

negative 부정적인   indicate that ~임을 나타내다, 보여 주다
be placed in ~에 배치되다, 놓이다   complimentary 무료의
issue 사안, 문제   shortly after ~한 직후에   in addition 추가로
with one's compliments ~가 증정하는, 서비스로 제공하는

Montrose 호텔: 1박 쿠폰   번호: 05485
발행 대상자: Patricia Lowry   날짜: 11월 6일
저희 Montrose 호텔은 신뢰할 수 있는 서비스가 저희 고객들께 필수적이라는 점을 [14]인식하고 있으며, 귀하의 기대치에 미치지 못한 점에 대해 사과의 말씀을 드립니다. 이 쿠폰을 소지하시면 캘리포니아 지역을 기반으로 하는 서의 호텔의 어느 시점에서나시 니엑스 툼에서 1박을 하

실 수 있습니다(뒷면에서 주소를 확인 가능). 만료일은 없습니다.
[15]발행 지점, Montrose 호텔 고객 관리부, 프레즈노, 캘리포니아 93740. 문의 사항이나 우려 사항이 있으신 분은 저희 직통 전화 1-800-555-8338로 전화 주시기 바랍니다.

issue ~을 발행하다, 발급하다   reliable 신뢰할 수 있는
expectation 기대(치)   entitle A to B A에게 B에 대한 자격을 주다
holder 소유자, 보유자   based (지역명과 함께) ~을 기반으로 하는
reverse 뒷면의, 반대의   expiration date 만료일, 만기일   hotline 직통 전화

11. 세부사항 문제

Agano 씨에 따르면, 무엇이 문제를 야기했는가?
(A) 경험이 부족한 직원
(B) 맞지 않는 지불금
(C) 일부 결함이 있는 소프트웨어
(D) 일부 일시적인 폐쇄 사례들

[해설] Agano 씨가 쓴 이메일인 첫 지문 첫 단락에, 불과 2주 전에 근무를 시작한 직원이 객실 예약과 관련해 정확하게 예약 양식을 작성하지 않았던 것 같다는(one of our employees ~ did not complete the reservation form correctly ~) 말로 문제의 원인을 설명하고 있으므로 경험이 부족한 직원을 뜻하는 (A)가 정답이다.

paraphrasing   started working here two weeks ago 2주 전에 근무를 시작함 → inexperienced 경험이 부족한

[어휘] inexperienced 경험이 부족한   incorrect 부정확한   payment 지불(비용)   faulty 결함이 있는   temporary 일시적인   closure 폐쇄(사례)

12. 세부사항 문제

11월 2일에 Montrose 호텔에서 무슨 일이 있었는가?
(A) Lowry 씨가 Agano 씨와 만났다.
(B) Agano 씨가 객실 쿠폰을 발행했다.
(C) Soto 씨가 전화로 예약을 받았다.
(D) Lowry 씨가 무료 음료를 받았다.

[해설] 11월 2일이라는 날짜는 첫 지문 첫 단락에 Lowry 씨의 투숙 기간이 시작되는 날짜로(from November 2 to November 4) 제시되어 있고, 다음 단락에 Lowry 씨가 체크인한 직후에 객실로 무료 와인 한 병을 보냈다는(~ sent a complimentary bottle of wine to your room ~ shortly after you checked in) 말이 쓰여 있다. 따라서 Lowry 씨가 11월 2일에 체크인한 직후에 무료 음료를 받았음을 알 수 있으므로 (D)가 정답이다.

paraphrasing   a complimentary bottle of wine 무료 와인 → free beverage 무료 음료

[어휘] take a booking 예약을 받다   beverage 음료

13. True 문제

Lowry 씨에 관해 암시된 것은 무엇인가?
(A) 자신의 객실 크기에 불만족스러워했다.
(B) 예약한 유형의 객실을 제공받지 못했다.
(C) 호텔의 청결 상태에 대해 불만을 제기했다.
(D) 호텔의 정원이 방문용으로 개방되어 있을 것이라고 생각했다.

[해설] 첫 지문 첫 단락에, 해변 전망으로 된 객실을 하나 예약했지만 체크인했을 때 해변 전망의 객실이 모두 이미 예약되었다는 통보를 받았다는(~ you had reserved a room with a seaside view ~ you were

06-10은 다음 웹사이트와 공지를 참조하시오.

```
www.spraguecity.gov
┌─────┬──────┬─────┬─────────┬─────────┐
│  홈  │비즈니스│ 호텔 │ 인근 지역 │ 외식 공간 │
└─────┴──────┴─────┴─────────┴─────────┘
```

⁰⁶스프라그 시의 여러 지역들

⁰⁷세군도 하이츠는 시내 쇼핑 구역의 심장부로서, 세상에 존재하는 모든 제품을 찾아볼 수 있는 전문 매장들과 부티크가 있습니다. 노상 주차가 월요일부터 금요일까지 무료이며, 여러 곳의 버스 정류장들이 있어 대중교통을 이용해 이 지역에 쉽게 이를 수 있습니다.

허먼 힐즈는 현대적인 시설물 사이로 여기저기 흩어져 있는 역사적인 건물들로 인해 신구의 조화를 이루고 있는 곳입니다. ⁰⁹Gerhart 경기장은 스포츠 경기 대회와 스프라그 시의 여름 콘서트 시리즈를 포함해 연중 다양한 행사들이 열리는 본거지입니다.

⁰⁸⁽ᴮ⁾클라우드는 고층 아파트 건물들이 주를 이루고 있지만, 이 고급 주거 건물들 사이로 ⁰⁸⁽ᴰ⁾전국적으로 유명한 Pontiac 비스트로를 포함해 이곳 저곳에 위치한 레스토랑들을 찾을 수 있습니다. ⁰⁸⁽ᴬ⁾Trisler 호수 주변으로 길이 나 있어 산책하기에 아주 좋은 곳입니다.

에머슨 파크는 다수의 녹지 공간과 정원, 그리고 대형 골프장 때문에 적절하게 이름이 붙여진 곳입니다. 이 지역은 야외 공간을 즐기기에 완벽한 곳입니다.

neighborhood 지역, 구역 dining out 외식 everything under the sun 세상에 존재하는 모든 것 free of charge 무료의 reach ~에 도달하다, 이르다 bring together old and new 신구 조화를 이루다 dotted among ~ 사이로 여기저기 흩어져 있는 year-round 연중, 일년 내내 competition 경기 대회 be dominated by ~가 주를 이루다 high-rise 고층의 dwelling 주거 건물, 주택 nationally 전국적으로 renowned 유명한 stroll 산책 be aptly named 적절히 이름이 지어지다 numerous 수많은, 다수의 green space 녹지 공간

불꽃놀이 행사를 위한 기금 마련 행사, 성공을 거두다

스프라그 시의 지역 단체들이 자금 부족으로 인해 취소 위협을 받고 있었던 시의 연례 불꽃놀이 행사를 위한 자금을 마련하기 위해 힘을 모았습니다. 다행히도, Sprague Unity and Community Caretakers의 도움과 지역 주민들의 아낌 없는 지원을 통해, 이 행사는 계속될 것입니다.

모든 분들께서 얼마든지 이 흥미로운 행사의 일부가 되실 수 있으며, 이 행사는 ⁰⁹여름 콘서트 시리즈 개막 공연의 마지막 순서로 예정되어 있습니다. 입장료는 무료이지만, 좌석이 빠르게 가득 메워질 것으로 예상됩니다. 또한 이 지역 주변으로 아주 좋은 관람 지점이 있으며, ¹⁰여기의 지역 안내도에도 지점들이 표기되어 있습니다. 직접 사본을 다운로드하시려면 링크를 따라가시기 바랍니다. 불꽃놀이 행사의 대략적인 시작 시간은 오후 9시입니다.

fundraiser 기금 마련 행사, 모금 행사 fireworks show 불꽃놀이 행사 band together 힘을 모으다 raise funding 자금을 마련하다, 모금하다 under threat of ~의 위협을 받는 lack of ~의 부족 generous 아낌 없는, 너그러운, 후한 local 지역 주민 go on 계속되다 admission 입장(료) fill up 가득 차다 viewing point 관람 지점 marked on ~에 표기된 approximate 대략적인

06. 추론 문제

웹사이트 내용은 누구를 대상으로 작성되었을 것 같은가?
(A) 연례 대회 참가자들
(B) 스프라그 시를 방문하는 관광객들
(C) 공무원 직의 지원자들
(D) 스프라그 시의 사업가들

[해설] 웹사이트의 한 페이지에 해당되는 첫 지문 첫머리에, '스프라그 시의 지역들(Neighborhoods in Sprague City)'이라는 제목과 함께 네 곳의 지역들이 지닌 특징을 설명하고 있는데, 이는 관광 관련 정보에 해당되므로 (B)가 정답이다.

[어휘] candidate 지원자, 후보자 government position 공무원 일자리

07. 세부사항 문제

웹사이트에 따르면, 세군도 하이츠에서 이용 가능한 것이 무엇인가?
(A) 지하철역
(B) 고급 레스토랑들
(C) 매일 무료 주차
(D) 아주 다양한 상점들

[해설] 세군도 하이츠가 언급된 첫 지문 첫 단락을 살펴보면, 시내 상점가의 심장부로서, 부티크들과 전문 매장들이 있다고(offers boutiques and specialty shops) 쓰여 있으므로 다양한 상점들을 의미하는 (D)가 정답이다.

paraphrasing boutiques and specialty shops 부티크와 전문 매장 → A wide variety of stores 아주 다양한 상점들

[어휘] available 이용 가능한 fine-dining 고급 식사를 할 수 있는 a wide variety of 아주 다양한

08. Not True 문제

클라우드에 관해 사실이 아닌 것은 무엇인가?
(A) 수역 근처에 있다.
(B) 주로 주거 지역이다.
(C) 음악인들에게 인기 있는 곳이다.
(D) 한 유명 레스토랑의 본거지이다.

[해설] 클라우드를 설명한 첫 지문 세 번째 단락에, 고층 아파트가 주를 이루는 곳이라는 정보를(dominated by high-rise apartment buildings) 통해 (B)를, 호수 주변에 길이 있다는(The path around Trisler Lake) 정보를 통해 (A)를, 그리고 전국적으로 유명한 Pontiac 비스트로를(the nationally renowned Pontiac Bistro) 비롯해 여러 레스토랑이 있다는 부분을 통해 (D)를 확인할 수 있다. 하지만 음악인들에게 인기가 있다는 점과 관련된 정보는 찾아볼 수 없으므로 (C)가 정답이다.

[어휘] body of water (호수, 바다 등의) 수역 primarily 주로 residential 주거의 site 장소, 위치

09. True 문제 - 연계 문제

불꽃놀이 행사에 관해 언급된 것은 무엇인가?
(A) 악천후로 인해 취소될 수 있다.
(B) 스프라그 시에서 처음으로 열릴 예정이다.
(C) 지역 사회 프로젝트를 위한 기금을 모을 것이다.
(D) Gerhart 경기장에서 개최될 것이다.

[해설] 우선, 불꽃놀이 행사 관련 정보가 제시된 두 번째 지문 두 번째 단락에, 여름 콘서트 시리즈 개막 공연의 마지막 순서라고(the finale of the opening performance of the Summer Concert Series) 쓰여 있는데, 첫 지문 두 번째 단락에 Gerhart Stadium에서 여름 콘서트 시리즈가 열린다고(Gerhart Stadium ~ including sports competitions and

01-05는 다음 회람과 일정표를 참조하시오.

수신: SoloCon Inc. 전 직원
발신: Annie Knox
제목: 곧 있을 변경
발송: 9월 12일
첨부 파일: work schedule

⁰¹경영진은 Lexington Tower에서 일하는 직원들을 대상으로 한 대부분의 설문 조사를 검토했으며 일부 공간을 개조하기로 합의했습니다. 여러분의 구역에서 작업이 진행되는 날에는 사무실에서 근무할 수 없을 것이기 때문에, ⁰⁴여러분의 구역이 개보수되기 전날에 노트북이 지급될 것입니다. 여러분의 구역이 준비되고 난 다음 날에 오시면 그것을 반품하시면 됩니다. 회사 노트북을 사용할 때는 표준 사무실 규정을 따르세요. 신뢰할 수 없는 출처인 링크를 클릭하거나 자료를 다운로드하지 마시기 바랍니다.

각 팀에 더 많은 자유가 주어질 것입니다. 각 팀은 사무실로 돌아온 후 ⁰²가구를 어디에 놓을지 투표할 것입니다. 모든 고객 기록을 디지털화했기 때문에 파일 캐비닛이 더 이상 필요하지 않은 팀의 경우, ⁰³파일 캐비닛이 당사 소유가 아니므로 단순히 폐기할 수 없음을 주의하십시오. 여러분이 그것들을 없애고 싶다면, 제가 건물 관리자에게 알리겠습니다.

management 경영진   survey 설문 조사   staff 직원   renovate 개보수하다   issue 지급하다   section 구역   regulation 규정   digitize 디지털화하다

SloCon Inc. 일정

날짜	팀(들)	담당자
⁰⁴9월 23일	인사	Richard Moss
9월 24일	영업	Jessica Meyers
9월 25일	회계, 연구 개발	Bob Hager, Michelle White

contact (연락을 받는) 담당자   personnel 인사   accounting 회계

01. 목적 문제

Knox 씨는 왜 직원들에게 회람을 보냈는가?
(A) 새로운 팀원을 소개하기 위해
(B) 보수 공사를 발표하기 위해
(C) 회사 방침을 명확히 하기 위해
(D) 피드백을 요청하기 위해

[해설] 발신인이 Knox 씨로 되어 있는 첫 지문의 첫 단락에, 직원들을 대상으로 한 대부분의 설문 조사를 검토한 후 일부 공간을 개조하기로 했다고(~ agreed to renovate some spaces) 알린 후에, 개보수 공사를 위해 직원들이 해야 할 일을 설명하는 것으로 내용이 전개되고 있으므로 (B)가 정답이다.

[어휘] company policy 회사 정책   request 요청하다

02. 세부사항 문제

회람에 따르면, 팀원들은 무엇에 투표할 것인가?
(A) 어디로 이전할지
(B) 어떤 가구를 교체할 것인지
(C) 언제 프로젝트를 시작할 것인지
(D) 어떻게 사무용 가구를 배열할 것인지

[해설] 팀이 언급된 첫 지문 두 번째 단락에 각 팀이 가구를 어디에 놓을지 투표할 것이라고(Each team will vote on where to place its furniture) 나와 있으므로 (D)가 정답이다.

paraphrasing   place 놓다 → arrange 배열하다

[어휘] relocate 이전하다   replace 교체하다   arrange 배열하다

03. 추론 문제

SoloCon Inc.의 파일 캐비닛에 대해 무엇이 암시되는가?
(A) 그것들은 Lexington Tower의 재산이다.
(B) 그것들은 올해 초에 구입되었다.
(C) SoloCon Inc.에 대한 민감한 정보를 포함하고 있다.
(D) 충분히 크지 않다.

[해설] 파일 캐비닛이 언급된 첫 지문 두 번째 단락에 해당 캐비닛은 당사의 소유가 아니라고 단순히 폐기할 수 없다고(we cannot simply throw them out as they do not belong to us) 알리고 있으므로 (A)가 정답이다.

04. 세부사항 문제 - 연계 문제

인사팀의 구성원들에게 언제 노트북이 지급될 것인가?
(A) 9월 22일에
(B) 9월 23일에
(C) 9월 24일에
(D) 9월 25일에

[해설] 노트북 전달 시점이 언급된 첫 지문 첫 단락에 해당 구역이 개보수되기 전날에 노트북이 지급될 것이라고 했는데(a laptop will be issued to you on the day before your section is renovated), 두 번째 지문의 도표에서 인사팀의 경우 개보수에 해당되는 날짜가 9월 23일이므로 이 날짜보다 하루 전인 (A)가 정답이다.

05. True 문제

회계팀에 대해 나타난 것은 무엇인가?
(A) SoloCon Inc.의 모든 거래를 처리한다.
(B) 매주 팀 회의를 개최한다.
(C) 다른 팀보다 인원 수가 적다.
(D) 다른 팀과 사무실 공간을 공유한다.

[해설] 회계팀 관련 정보는 두 번째 지문의 도표에 표기된 Sep. 25 Accounting/R&D에서 찾을 수 있는데, 25일에 개보수가 이루어지는 부서로서 R&D팀이 같은 날 개보수 공사가 있는 것으로 보아 회계팀이 R&D팀과 사무실 공간을 공유하는 것을 알 수 있으므로 (D)가 정답이다.

[어휘] handle 처리하다   transaction 거래   share 공유하다

paraphrasing 정답   1. (b)   2. (d)   3. (a)   4. (e)   5. (c)

08. 알맞은 문장 고르기

(A) 이와 같은 일이 발생할 경우에, 전선이 녹거나 심지어 불이 붙을 수도 있습니다.
(B) 손상되었거나 결함이 있는 제품은 소매점으로 반품되어야 합니다.
(C) 센서가 금속을 감지하면, 자동으로 발열 요소를 차단합니다.
(D) 토스터를 활용해 만드는 훌륭한 조리법과 관련된 아이디어를 얻으실 수 있습니다.

[해설] 앞 문장에서 전선을 토스터 옆에 기대어 놓거나 위에 걸쳐 놓는 것이 문제점의 하나라고 언급한 것과 연계되는 문장이 필요하므로 이러한 행위를 such an event로 지칭해 그에 따른 부정적인 결과를 언급하는 (A)가 정답이다.

[어휘] in case of ~의 경우에   catch fire 불이 붙다   damaged 손상된   faulty 결함이 있는   retailer 소매점   detect ~을 감지하다, 발견하다   shut off ~을 차단하다, 정지시키다   heat element 발열 요소

PART 7 이중 지문 연계 문제

풀이 방법 해석

수신: Tyler Hawkins
발신: Britney Krueger
날짜: 10월 27일
주제: 모니터

Tyler 씨께

당신의 요청에 따라, 우리 사무실을 위한 새 모니터의 몇몇 사양을 살펴보았습니다. TechMate에서 우리에게 적당한 몇몇 사양을 찾을 수 있었고, 저는 Clearview 20X, Crystal 9.7, ViewMaster 6, 그리고 Classic 45로 범위를 좁혔습니다.

저 4개의 모델 중, Clearview 20X는 유일하게 에너지 평가에서 별 다섯 개를 받았는데, 우리 회사의 전기료를 줄이는 데 도움을 줄 것입니다. MagiScreen 500도 에너지 평가에서 별 다섯 개를 받았지만 비용이 우리의 예산을 초과할 것이기 때문에 언급하지 않았습니다. Crystal 9.7은 매력적인 화면 디자인을 갖고 있지만, 에너지 평가에서 가장 낮습니다.

직접 상품 후기를 자유롭게 살펴보시기 바랍니다. 준비되시면 어떤 모델을 몇 개 주문할지 제게 알려주세요.

Britney Krueger

수신: Britney Krueger
발신: Tyler Hawkins
날짜: 10월 28일
제목: 회신: 모니터

Britney 씨께

정보 감사합니다. 아주 도움이 되었어요. 우리가 구입할 수 있는 에너지 평가 별 다섯 개의 것으로 합시다. 우리의 운영비를 줄일 수 있는 것을 찾아서 잘한 것 같아요. 단지 걱정되는 것은, 우리가 모두 한 번에 사야 할지 잘 모르겠네요. 우리가 정확히 몇 개가 필요할지 알기까지 우선 당신의 사무실 것만 한 개 사도록 하죠. 다음 주쯤 인사부에서 정확히 몇 명의 신입사원이 우리 회사에 들어올지 알려줄 거예요.

Tyler Hawkins

Q. Hawkins 씨는 Krueger 씨에게 어떤 모니터 모델을 주문하라고 하는가?
(A) Clearview 20X
(B) Crystal 9.7
(C) ViewMaster 6
(D) Classic 45

 연습 문제

01.(A)

01.

<생물학 강연 시리즈>
Kramer 협회에서 일반인들을 위해 1월 한 달 내내 진행되는 무료 강연

1월 7일: 줄기 세포와 그 치료 역할
1월 14일: 소화 작용 이해
1월 21일: 산림 보존의 중요성
1월 28일: 유전학의 역사

모든 강연은 100A 강의실에서 진행됩니다. 좌석은 선착순으로 이용 가능합니다.

biology 생물학   stem cells 줄기 세포   role 역할   digestion 소화   conservation 보존, 보호   genetics 유전학   on a first-come, first-served basis 선착순으로

유명 생물학자 Paul Camacho 박사가 새로운 다큐멘터리 <Into the Lab>의 첫 공개 상영회를 발표했으며, 이는 2월 25일에 Logan Theater에서 상영될 것이다. 이 다큐멘터리 영화는 기획 단계에서부터 결과 분석에 이르기까지 실험 과정 전반에 걸쳐 단계별로 Camacho 박사와 연구팀의 모습을 담고 있다. **이 실험은 줄기 세포와, 그것이 어떻게 의학 요법에 도움이 되고 영향을 미칠 수 있는지에 관한 새로운 정보를 제공해 주었으며, 이는 Camacho 박사가 최근 Kramer 협회에서 열린 강연 중에 다룬 주제이다.**

debut 처음 선보이는   step-by-step 단계별로   analyze ~을 분석하다   cover (주제 등) ~을 다루다

Q. Camacho 박사는 언제 Kramer 협회에서 강연을 했을 것 같은가?
(A) 1월 7일
(B) 1월 21일

[문제 키워드] When / Dr. Camacho / give a lecture

[해설] 키워드 Dr. Camacho가 언급된 두 번째 지문에서 먼저 강연과 관련된 단서를 찾아야 한다. 이 지문 마지막 문장에 Camacho 박사가 Kramer Institute에서 열린 강연에서 줄기 세포를 주제로 다뤘다고(~ stem cells ~ a topic that Dr. Camacho recently covered during the lecture at the Kramer Institute) 쓰여 있는데, 첫 지문에 줄기 세포가 강연 주제인 날짜가 1월 7일이므로(January 7: Stem Cells ~) (A)가 정답이다.

실전 문제

01.(B)	02.(D)	03.(A)	04.(A)	05.(D)	06.(B)
07.(D)	08.(C)	09.(D)	10.(A)	11.(A)	12.(D)
13.(B)	14.(C)	15.(C)			

[단서] sales, These

[해설] 빈칸 앞에 위치한 These와 함께 앞 문장에 언급된 판매량(sales)을 가리키는 명사가 필요하므로 '수치, 숫자'를 뜻하는 (A) numbers가 정답이다.

실전 문제

01.(C) 02.(A) 03.(B) 04.(B) 05.(B) 06.(A)
07.(A) 08.(A)

01-04는 다음 편지를 참조하시오.

로즈우드 케이블 서비스
College 가 1111번지
로즈우드, 오하이오 43070

로즈우드 케이블 고객께

⁰¹이 편지는 5월 1일부터 특정 서비스에 대한 요금이 인하된다는 사실을 알려드리기 위한 것입니다. 저희 VIP 패키지는 한 달에 50달러에서 43달러로, 스페셜 패키지는 한 달에 40달러에서 35달러로 변경됩니다. ⁰²이 할인 서비스는 저희가 시장에서 더욱 경쟁력 있는 업체가 되기 위해 제공되는 것입니다. 귀하의 서비스를 상위 패키지들 중의 하나로 업그레이드하기를 원하실 경우에 오늘 전화 주시기 바랍니다. ⁰³5달러의 추가 비용만 내시면 가장 많은 TV 채널을 이용하시게 될 것입니다. ⁰⁴또한, 귀하의 인터넷 속도가 500 Mbps로 빨라질 것이므로, 현재보다 두 배나 더 빠르게 다운로드를 하실 수 있습니다.

as of ~부터, ~부로 reduce ~을 인하하다, 할인하다 competitive 경쟁력 있는 upper 상위의, 상급의 twice+형용사 두 배 ~한 current 현재의

01. 동사의 형태

[해설] 빈칸 뒤에 위치한 '사람 목적어+that절'과 결합 가능하면서 편지의 목적을 나타내는 의미를 구성할 수 있어야 하므로 to부정사인 (C) to inform이 정답이다.

[어휘] inform (A that) (A에게 ~라고) 알리다 informative 유용한 정보를 주는, 유익한

02. 명사 어휘

[해설] 지시형용사 These의 수식을 받아야 하므로 앞선 문장에서 These로 가리킬 만한 명사를 찾아야 한다. 앞 문장에서 패키지별로 요금이 내려감을 알리고 있는데, 이는 요금 할인을 뜻하므로 (A) discounts가 정답이다.

[어휘] submission 제출(되는 것) budget 예산 extension 연장, 확장, 확대, 내선 전화 (번호)

03. 알맞은 문장 고르기

(A) 더 많은 사람들을 저희에게 소개해 주실수록, 더 많은 할인을 받으실 수 있는 자격이 주어집니다.
(B) 5달러의 추가 비용만 내시면 가장 많은 TV 채널을 이용하시게 될 것입니다.
(C) 이용 가능한 채널과 인터넷 선택권을 담은 전체 목록을 보시려면 저희 웹사이트를 방문하시기 바랍니다.
(D) 로즈우드 케이블은 10년 넘게 이 지역에서 자랑스럽게 서비스를 제공해 오고 있습니다.

[해설] 빈칸 다음에 추가 정보를 말할 때 사용하는 Also와 함께 이용 속도가 빨라진다는 장점을 언급했으므로 빈칸에도 앞 문장에서 말하는 패키지 업그레이드에 따른 혜택의 하나가 언급되어야 알맞다. 따라서 5달러의 추가 비용으로 가장 많은 채널을 이용할 수 있다는 의미인 (B)가 정답이다.

[어휘] refer A to B (서비스 등을 이용하도록) A를 B에게 소개하다 eligible for ~에 대한 자격이 있는 additional 추가의

04. 접속사 어휘

[해설] 빈칸 앞뒤로 각각 완전한 절이 있으므로 빈칸은 접속사 자리이다. 인터넷 속도 개선과 두 배 더 빠른 다운로드는 각각 원인과 결과에 해당되므로 결과를 나타내는 접속사인 (B) so가 정답이다. 참고로, (A) then은 부사이다.

[어휘] then 그럼, 그렇다면, 그러고 나서, 그때

05-08은 다음 설명을 참조하시오.

기기 사용과 예방 조치: Delicious Dawn 토스터

⁰⁵Delicious Dawn 토스터는 안전하고 사용하기 편리한 주방 기기로 고안된 제품입니다. ⁰⁶하지만, 이 토스터 모델이 위험한 상태가 될 수 있는 특정 사용 방식들이 있는데, 이로 인해 기기에 손상을 초래하거나 심지어 주방에 화재를 일으킬 수도 있습니다. 버터나 치즈, 또는 잼 등과 같은 음식물이 녹아 기기의 전열선 안으로 흘러 들어갈 수 있습니다. ⁰⁷이 음식 재료들은 토스터 기기 오작동의 일반적인 원인입니다. 또 다른 흔한 문제점은 전선을 기기 옆에 기대어 놓거나 위에 걸쳐지도록 놓아 두는 것으로부터 비롯됩니다. ⁰⁸이와 같은 일이 발생할 경우에, 전선이 녹거나 심지어 불이 붙을 수도 있습니다. 제품의 품질 보증서에는 위에 기재된 어떠한 상황들도 언급하고 있지 않다는 점에 유의하시기 바랍니다.

precaution 예방 조치 appliance (가전) 기기 melt 녹다, ~을 녹이다 drip down into ~ 안으로 흘러 들어가다 common 일반적인, 흔한 malfunction 오작동 rest (사물) 놓여 있다, 그대로 있다 warranty 품질 보증(서)

05. 동사의 형태

[해설] 제품의 특징을 나타내는 문장이 되어야 하므로 빈칸 앞뒤에 각각 위치한 be동사, to부정사와 함께 '~하도록 고안되다, 설계되다' 등의 의미를 나타낼 때 사용하는 (B) designed가 정답이다.

[어휘] design ~을 고안하다, 디자인하다

06. 형용사 어휘

[해설] 제품의 상태를 나타낼 형용사가 필요한데, 기기를 손상시키거나 화재를 일으키는 원인과 관련된 상태여야 하므로 '위험한'을 뜻하는 (A) hazardous가 정답이다.

[어휘] seasoned (사람) 경험 많은, (음식) 양념을 한 effective 효과적인 settled 안정적인, (생활 등이) 자리 잡힌

07. 명사 어휘

[해설] 지시형용사 These의 수식을 받아야 하므로 앞선 문장에서 These로 가리킬 수 있을 만한 명사를 찾으면 butter, cheese, or jam이 해당되는데, 이것들은 음식물이므로 '음식 재료'라는 의미로 쓰이는 (A) ingredients가 정답이다.

[어휘] device 기기, 장치 chemical 화학 물질, 화학 제품 tool 도구, 기구, 수단

아주 다양한 매트리스 제품을 보유하고 있다.

[해설] 선택지가 다양한 품사의 단어들로 구성되어 있으므로 문법 문제이다. 명사 mattresses를 수식하는 형용사 priced를 앞에서 수식할 부사가 필요하므로 부사 어미 -ly로 끝나는 (B) reasonably가 정답이다.

[어휘] reasonably priced 합리적인 가격의 reasonable 합리적인, 타당한 reasoning 추론 reason 이유, 사유

24. 명사 어휘

환경 문제와 연관되어 있는 모든 관련 당사자들이 최종 회의에서 결국 합의에 이르렀다.

[해설] 선택지가 다양한 명사들로 구성되어 있으므로 명사 어휘 문제이다. 동사 표현 come to와 어울리는 명사로서 최종 회의에서 나타난 결과와 관련된 의미의 어휘가 알맞으므로 '합의, 동의'를 뜻하는 (A) agreement가 정답이다.

[어휘] related 관련된 party 당사자 involved in ~에 연관된 come to an agreement 합의에 이르다 advance 진보, 발전 achievement 성취 admission 등록, 입장

PART 6 지시형용사 뒤 명사 어휘

풀이 방법 해석

워싱턴 스트리밍 서비스
79 Waterway 로
타코마, 워싱턴 80314

스트리밍 서비스 고객님들께,

좋은 소식입니다! 2월 1일부로, 귀하께서 워싱턴 스트리밍 서비스로 시청할 수 있는 방송과 영화의 목록이 확대될 것입니다. 동일한 월 이용료로, 이제 귀하는 작년에 최신으로 방영되었던 많은 텔레비전 방송을 보실 수 있습니다.

이러한 추가는 Wolf 방송사와의 협력 덕분입니다.

방송망의 여러 인기 있는 TV 시리즈가 저희의 홈페이지에 완전히 올라와 있습니다. 온라인 엔터테인먼트 제공자로 WSS를 선택해주셔서 감사합니다.

고객 서비스 팀
워싱턴 스트리밍 서비스

 연습 문제

01.(A) 02.(B) 03.(B) 04.(A)

01.

장학금 기회

4월 12일 — 전국 각지의 학생들이 Extracurricular Leader 장학금 중 하나를 받기 위해 서둘러 신청서를 제출하고 있다. 교재 비용을 부담하는 것에서부터 등록금 전액을 납부하는 것에 이르기까지 비용 가치가 다양한 여러 다른 장학금들이 있다. 이 기금은 다양한 분야에 속해 있는 기업가들에 의해 제공된다.

scholarship 장학금 rush to부정사 서둘러 ~하다 put in ~을 제출하다 application 신청(서) vary in ~가 다양하다 value 가치 cover (비용 등) ~을 충당하다 fully pay for ~에 대한 비용을 전액 지불하다 tuition 등록금, 수강료 field 분야

[단서] scholarships, These

[해설] 빈칸 앞에 위치한 These는 앞서 언급된 a number of different ones, 즉 여러 가지 장학금(scholarships)을 가리키므로 이를 대신할 명사로 '기금, 자금'을 뜻하는 (A) funds가 정답이다.

02.

Barnes 씨께

저는 잉글랜드에 있는 사탕 매장 체인인 London's Sweet Tooth의 소유주입니다. Rotterdam Chocolates 사가 뛰어난 명성을 지니고 있으므로 저는 이곳 잉글랜드에 있는 제 매장에서 판매할 수 있도록 귀사의 제품을 대량으로 구매하고자 합니다. 이 제휴 관계는 양측 회사 모두에게 대단히 유익할 수 있으므로 곧 귀하로부터 답변을 들을 수 있기를 고대합니다.

owner 소유주 outstanding 뛰어난 reputation 명성, 평판 in bulk 대량으로 for sale 판매용으로 highly 대단히, 매우 beneficial 유익한

[단서] I would like to purchase your product ~ in England, This

[해설] 빈칸 앞에 위치한 This는 앞서 언급된 제품을 대량으로 들여와 판매하는 일을 가리키는데, 이는 사업상의 거래이므로 이를 대신할 명사로 '제휴 관계'를 뜻하는 (B) partnership이 정답이다.

[어휘] resource 자원, 재원

03.

지역 주민들 여러 분께서 태양열 전지판으로 도시 전역의 옥상들을 뒤덮자는 아이디어를 공유해 주셨습니다. 이 제안은 전력 문제에 있어 우리 도시가 외부 공급원에 의존할 필요성을 감소시켜 줄 수 있습니다.

resident 주민 cover ~을 덮다 rooftop 옥상 solar panel 태양열 전지판 rely on ~에 의존하다

[단서] shared an idea, This

[해설] 빈칸 앞에 위치한 This는 앞 문장에 언급된 지역 주민들이 특정 아이디어를 공유한 일을 가리키는데, 이는 제안 사항에 해당되므로 '제안(서)'를 의미하는 (B) proposal이 정답이다.

[어휘] entry 출입, 참가, 출품(작)

04.

수신: 영업팀
발신: Melissa Franken, 대표이사
제목: 분기 보고서

저는 가장 최근의 분기 보고서에 대해 우려하는 바입니다. 우리 판매량이 지난 몇 개월에 걸쳐 거의 15퍼센트 하락한 것으로 보입니다. 이 수치는 용납될 수 없는 것이며, 우리는 올 연말에 목표를 충족할 수 있도록 일부 대대적인 변화를 기해야 합니다.

sales 판매(량), 영업, 매출 quarterly 분기의 drop 하락하다 nearly 거의 unacceptable 받아들일 수 없는

전 장비가 필수다.

[해설] 선택지가 다양한 품사의 단어들로 구성되어 있으므로 문법 문제이다. be동사 are 뒤에서 보어로 쓰인 형용사 dangerous를 수식할 부사가 필요하므로 부사 (C) highly가 정답이다. (A) high도 부사로 쓰이지만 형용사를 앞에서 수식하지 않는다.

[어휘] flammable 가연성의   liquid 액체   handle ~을 다루다, 처리하다   height 높이, 키, 고도   highly 매우, 대단히, 크게   heighten 고조되다, ~을 고조시키다

13. 명사 어휘

어떠한 독성 물질이든 책임자의 감독하에 적절하게 처리되어야 한다.

[해설] 선택지가 다양한 명사들로 구성되어 있으므로 명사 어휘 문제이다. the supervisor's의 수식을 받아야 하므로 사람의 행동이나 감정과 관련있으면서, 무언가의 범위를 나타내는 전치사 under의 목적어가 되어야 하므로 '감독, 지휘' 등을 뜻하는 (B) direction이 정답이다.

[어휘] toxic 독성의   material 물질, 물체, 재료   dispose of ~을 처리하다, 처분하다   properly 적절히, 제대로   supervisor 책임자, 부서장, 상사   failure 실패, 하지 못함

14. 형용사의 역할: 명사 수식

그 워크숍은 리더십 능력을 키우는 데 필요한 여러 주목할 만한 시간들을 특징으로 할 것이다.

[해설] 선택지가 다양한 품사의 단어들로 구성되어 있으므로 문법 문제이다. 형용사 several과 명사 sessions 사이에 위치한 빈칸은 명사를 수식할 또 다른 형용사가 쓰일 수 있는 자리이므로 형용사 어미 -able로 끝나는 (B) notable이 정답이다.

[어휘] feature ~을 특징으로 하다   notably 특히, 현저히   note ~을 주목하다, ~에 유의하다   noted 유명한

15. 형용사의 역할: 주격 보어

일련의 토론 끝에, 노동 조합은 근무 환경과 관련된 경영진의 조건에 동의했다.

[해설] 선택지가 다양한 품사의 단어들로 구성되어 있으므로 문법 문제이다. be동사 was 뒤에 위치한 빈칸은 주어 labor union을 설명하는 보어 자리인데, labor union의 의견과 관련된 형용사 보어가 쓰여야 알맞으므로 형용사 어미 -able로 끝나는 (D) agreeable이 정답이다.

[어휘] debate 토론, 논쟁   labor union 노동 조합   management 경영(진)   terms 조건, 조항   agreeable 동의하는, 기분 좋은

16. 부사의 역할과 위치: 동사 앞 수식

Tucson Petrol의 최고 경영자는 본사를 Fresno로 이전하는 것에 대해 공식적으로 발표했다.

[해설] 선택지가 다양한 품사의 단어들로 구성되어 있으므로 문법 문제이다. 동사 announced 앞에 위치한 빈칸은 동사를 수식할 부사 자리이므로 부사 어미 -ally로 끝나는 (B) formally가 정답이다.

[어휘] announce 발표하다   relocation 이전, 이주   headquarters 본사

17. 인칭대명사 구분: 주격

Cobb 씨가 개조 공사에 필요한 예산을 받는 대로, 몇몇 장식을 선택할 수 있도록 추천해 줄 것이다.

[해설] 선택지가 다양한 품사의 단어들로 구성되어 있으므로 문법 문제이다. 주절의 동사 will recommend 앞에 위치한 빈칸은 주절의 주어 자리이므로 주격 대명사 (B) she가 정답이다.

[어휘] once (일단) ~하는 대로, ~하자마자   budget 예산   renovation 개조, 보수   décor 장식(품)

18. 명사의 위치: 소유격 뒤

Janson 씨의 결단력이 거래 계약을 선택할 때 특히 도움이 된다.

[해설] 선택지가 다양한 품사의 단어들로 구성되어 있으므로 문법 문제이다. 소유격 Ms. Janson's 다음은 이 소유격의 수식을 받을 명사 자리이므로 명사 어미 -ness로 끝나는 (D) decisiveness가 정답이다.

[어휘] contract 계약(서)   decisive 결단력 있는, 결정적인   decidedly 단호히, 분명히   decisiveness 결단력, 단호함

19. 명사 어휘

부서장들은 가이드라인에 따라 직원 성과를 평가해야 한다.

[해설] 선택지가 다양한 명사들로 구성되어 있으므로 명사 어휘 문제이다. 빈칸 앞에 위치한 employee와 어울려 복합 명사를 구성할 수 있는 것으로서 '직원 성과'라는 의미를 나타내는 (A) performance가 정답이다.

[어휘] evaluate ~을 평가하다   according to ~에 따라   performance 성과, 실적, 수행 능력   resource 자원, 재원   inspection 점검, 조사   agreement 계약(서), 합의(서)

20. 부사의 역할과 위치: 동사 사이에서 수식

Jo 제약에서 근무한 지 불과 2년 만에, Lawson 박사는 성공적으로 새로운 백신을 개발했다.

[해설] 선택지가 다양한 품사의 단어들로 구성되어 있으므로 문법 문제이다. 현재완료 시제 구문으로, has와 과거분사 developed 사이에 위치한 빈칸은 동사 사이에서 수식하는 부사 자리이므로 부사 어미 -ly로 끝나는 (B) successfully가 정답이다.

[어휘] develop ~을 개발하다   successful 성공적인   successfully 성공적으로   succeed 성공하다   success 성공

21. 명사 어휘

그 책임자는 모든 조립 라인들이 계획대로 가동되고 있다고 보고했다.

[해설] 선택지가 다양한 명사들로 구성되어 있으므로 명사 어휘 문제이다. be동사 are 뒤에 위치한 in과 어울려 보어 역할을 할 전치사구를 구성할 명사가 필요하므로 in과 함께 '가동 중인'이라는 의미로 기계 작동 상태를 나타낼 때 사용하는 (C) operation이 정답이다.

[어휘] assembly 조립   shift 교대 근무(조)   benefit 혜택, 이득

22. 명사 어휘

Ace 비즈니스 호텔은 청결한 객실과 합리적인 요금으로 항상 Twain 씨의 기대치를 충족시킨다.

[해설] 선택지가 다양한 명사들로 구성되어 있으므로 명사 어휘 문제이다. Ms. Twain's의 수식을 받아야 하므로 사람의 감정이나 행동과 관련된 명사가 필요한 데, 동사 meets의 목적어로서 충족 가능한 것이어야 하므로 '기대(치)'를 의미하는 (D) expectations가 정답이다.

[어휘] affordable 합리적인, 타당한   rate 요금   alternative 대안, 대체(물)   destination 목적지   objective 목표, 목적

23. 부사의 역할과 위치: 형용사 수식

Beltran 가구는 자사의 웹사이트에서 구매 가능한 것으로 합리적인 가격의

[해설] 선택지가 다양한 품사의 단어들로 구성되어 있으므로 문법 문제이다. 주어와 동사 place 사이에 위치한 빈칸은 동사를 수식할 부사 자리이므로 부사 어미 -ally로 끝나는 (C) strategically가 정답이다.

[어휘] place ~을 배치하다, 놓다 habitat 서식지 capture (사진 등으로) ~을 포착하다, 담아 내다 strategy 전략 strategically 전략적으로 strategic 전략적인

02. 부사의 역할과 위치: 동사 사이에서 수식

Kessler의 자동차들은 배기 가스와 연료 소비 모두를 감소시킬 수 있도록 특별히 디자인되어 있다.

[해설] 선택지가 다양한 품사의 단어들로 구성되어 있으므로 문법 문제이다. 수동태 구문을 이루는 be동사 are과 과거분사 designed 사이에 위치한 빈칸은 동사 사이에서 수식하는 부사 자리이므로 부사 어미 -ally로 끝나는 (B) specially가 정답이다.

[어휘] automobile 자동차 reduce ~을 감소시키다 emission 배기 가스, 배출물 consumption 소비 specialize (in) 전문으로 하다 specialty 전공, 전문 분야, 특산품

03. 형용사의 역할: 주격 보어

Callahan 케이블이 제공하는 서비스 약정은 경쟁사들이 제공하는 것에 필적할 만하다.

[해설] 선택지가 다양한 품사의 단어들로 구성되어 있으므로 문법 문제이다. be동사 are 뒤에 위치한 빈칸은 주어 Service plans를 설명하는 보어 자리이므로 전치사 to와 어울려 '~에 필적할 만하다'이라는 의미를 만드는 형용사 (D) comparable이 정답이다.

[어휘] competitor 경쟁사, 경쟁자 compare ~을 비교하다 comparison 비교

04. 명사 어휘

Donaldson 씨는 아시아에 위치한 지사로 전근할 의향이 전혀 없었다.

[해설] 선택지가 다양한 명사들로 구성되어 있으므로 명사 어휘 문제이다. 동사 had의 목적어로서 사람(Ms. Donaldson)의 감정이나 행동과 관련된 적절한 명사가 빈칸에 필요하므로 '의향, 의도' 등을 의미하는 (B) intention이 정답이다.

[어휘] transfer to ~로 전근하다 branch office 지사 improvement 개선, 향상 malfunction (기계 등의) 오작동

05. 부사의 역할과 위치: 동사 사이에서 수식

우리는 다큐멘터리 촬영 경험이 있는 계약직 사진 작가들을 적극적으로 모집하고 있다.

[해설] 선택지가 다양한 품사의 단어들로 구성되어 있으므로 문법 문제이다. 현재진행형 구문으로, be동사 are와 현재분사 recruiting 사이에 위치한 빈칸은 동사 사이에서 수식하는 부사 자리이므로 부사 어미 -ly로 끝나는 (C) actively가 정답이다.

[어휘] recruit ~을 모집하다 contract 계약 actively 적극적으로 activate ~을 활성화하다

06. 부사의 역할과 위치: 동사 앞 수식

Soother 패치는 하부 요통으로 종종 고통받는 사람들에게 도움이 된다.

[해설] 선택지가 다양한 품사의 단어로 구성되어 있으므로 문법 문제이다. 주격 관계대명사 who와 동사 suffer 사이에 위치하여 동사를 수식하는 부사 (C) sometimes가 정답이다.

[어휘] suffer from ~로 고통 받다 lower back pain 하부 요통

07. 부사의 역할과 위치: '타동사+목적어' 뒤

최신 의류 제품 라인 덕분에, Bush 패션은 자사의 고객층을 상당히 확대해 왔다.

[해설] 선택지가 다양한 품사의 단어들로 구성되어 있으므로 문법 문제이다. 동사 has expanded의 목적어 its customer base 다음이자 문장 맨 마지막에 위치한 빈칸은 동사 has expanded를 수식할 부사 자리이므로 부사 어미 -ly로 끝나는 (C) considerably가 정답이다.

[어휘] expand ~을 확대하다 customer base 고객층 consider ~을 고려하다 considering ~을 고려하면 considerably 상당히 consideration 고려

08. 부사의 역할과 위치: 전치사구 수식

Malone 씨는 가급적이면 내일까지 특송 서비스를 통해 자신의 주문품을 받을 것으로 기대했다.

[해설] 선택지가 다양한 품사의 단어들로 구성되어 있으므로 문법 문제이다. 배송 시점을 나타내는 by 전치사구를 앞에서 수식할 수 있는 것은 부사이므로 부사 어미 -ly로 끝나는 (B) preferably가 정답이다.

[어휘] express 특송의, 급행의 prefer ~을 선호하다 preferably 가급적이면 preference 선호(하는 것) preferable 선호하는

09. 부사의 역할과 위치: 분사 수식

대형 주차장 옆에 편리하게 위치한 Mooney's Steakhouse는 점심 식사 모임 장소로 인기 있는 곳이다.

[해설] 선택지가 다양한 품사의 단어들로 구성되어 있으므로 문법 문제이다. 빈칸에는 위치를 나타내는 과거분사 situated가 이끄는 분사구문을 수식할 부사가 와야 하므로 부사 어미 -ly로 끝나는 (C) Conveniently가 정답이다.

[어휘] convenient 편리한 convenience 편의 (시설), 편리 conveniently 편리하게

10. 부사의 역할과 위치: 전치사구 수식

시험지를 제출하기 전에 각 답안을 신중하게 검토해 보시기 바랍니다.

[해설] 선택지가 다양한 품사의 단어들로 구성되어 있으므로 문법 문제이다. 빈칸에는 검토 시점을 나타내는 prior to 전치사구를 앞에서 수식할 부사가 와야 알맞으므로 부사 어미 -ly로 끝나는 (D) carefully가 정답이다.

[어휘] prior to ~ 전에, ~에 앞서 turn in ~을 제출하다 careful 조심하는, 신중한 carefully 조심스럽게, 신중히

11. 부사의 역할과 위치: 형용사 수식

<Fortune Magazine>은 George Nichols를 수학에 가장 특출한 재능을 지닌 십대들 중의 한 명으로 순위에 올렸다.

[해설] 선택지가 다양한 품사의 단어들로 구성되어 있으므로 문법 문제이다. 빈칸에는 the most와 함께 최상급을 구성하는 형용사 gifted를 앞에서 수식할 부사가 와야 알맞으므로 부사 어미 -ly로 끝나는 (D) exceptionally가 정답이다.

[어휘] excepted 제외되어, 예외인 exception 제외, 예외 exceptional 특출한, 이례적인 exceptionally 특출하게, 이례적으로

12. 부사의 역할과 위치: 형용사 수식

제트 연료와 같은 가연성 액체들은 매우 위험하기 때문에, 다룰 때 특별 안

(C) 단체 할인을 받아 구할 수 있다.
(D) 매진될 것으로 예상된다.

[해설] 입장권 관련 정보가 담긴 마지막 단락에, 입구에서 입장권 판매가 이뤄지지 않는다는(there will be no ticket sales at the door) 말이 있는데, 이는 미리 구입해야 한다는 뜻이므로 (A)가 정답이다.

[어휘] in advance 미리, 사전에 acquire ~을 얻다, 획득하다 sell out 매진되다

13. 문장 삽입 문제

[1], [2], [3] 그리고 [4]로 표시된 위치들 중에서, 다음 문장이 들어가기에 가장 적절한 곳은 어디인가?

"올해는, 그 숫자가 천 명을 초과할 것으로 예상된다."

(A) [1]
(B) [2]
(C) [3]
(D) [4]

[해설] 제시된 문장은 특정 수치를 언급하는 that number를 써서 '그 수치가 1,000(one thousand)을 넘을 것'이라는 의미를 나타낸다. 따라서 작년에 920명의 참가자들이 행사에 참여했음을 알리는 문장 다음에 위치한 [4]에 들어가 올해의 예상 수치를 말하는 흐름이 되어야 적절하므로 (D)가 정답이다.

[어휘] surpass ~을 초과하다

paraphrasing 정답   1. (b)   2. (a)   3. (c)

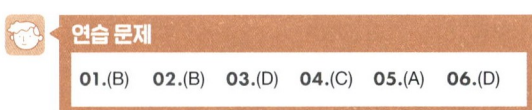

DAY 04

PART 5 문법 | 부사 (1)

확인 문제 해석

① 저희 직원들이 귀하의 전화에 즉시 답할 것입니다.
② 그 회사는 설립 이래로 꾸준히 성장해 왔다.
③ Jade 씨는 새 인턴들과 긴밀히 일해야 한다.
④ 그것을 별도로 포장해 주세요.
⑤ 그는 유난히 긍정적인 설문 조사 결과를 받았다.
⑥ Peterson 씨는 친절하게도 자진해서 그의 시간을 냈다.
⑦ 그 회사는 지속적으로 고객 서비스를 개선하기 위해 정기 설문 조사를 수행해 왔다.
⑧ 계산대 옆에 전략적으로 위치한 그 진열대에는 할인 중인 물품들이 있다.

연습 문제

01.(B) 02.(B) 03.(D) 04.(C) 05.(A) 06.(D)

01.

1. 선택지 보고 문법/어휘 문제 파악하기 ☑문법 문제 ☐어휘 문제
2. 빈칸 분석하기 빈칸 뒤에 있는 것 ☐동사 ☑형용사
   → 빈칸은 ☐명사 ☑부사 자리이다.
3. 정답 선택하기 정답 (B)

매우 인기 있는 행사인 Fireworks Over Fresno가 이번 주 토요일 밤에 열립니다!

02.

1. 선택지 보고 문법/어휘 문제 파악하기 ☑문법 문제 ☐어휘 문제
2. 빈칸 분석하기 빈칸 뒤에 있는 것 ☑주격 보어인 형용사 ☐동사
   → 빈칸은 ☐명사 ☑부사 자리이다.
3. 정답 선택하기 정답 (B)

원본 영수증이 있으면 어떠한 구매라도 전액 환불 가능합니다.

03.

1. 선택지 보고 문법/어휘 문제 파악하기 ☐문법 문제 ☑어휘 문제
2. 빈칸 분석하기 빈칸 앞에 있는 for 뒤에 있는 reasons와 짝꿍 표현으로 쓰이는 명사가 정답이다.
3. 정답 선택하기 정답 (D)

보안상의 이유로 당신은 이 방문자 출입증을 항상 제시해야 합니다.

04.

1. 선택지 보고 문법/어휘 문제 파악하기 ☑문법 문제 ☐어휘 문제
2. 빈칸 분석하기 빈칸 앞에 있는 것 ☑자동사 ☐타동사
   → 빈칸은 ☐명사 ☑부사 자리이다.
3. 정답 선택하기 정답 (C)

테스트 그룹들은 Richie's의 새 아이스크림 맛에 호의적인 반응을 보였다.

05.

1. 선택지 보고 문법/어휘 문제 파악하기 ☑문법 문제 ☐어휘 문제
2. 빈칸 분석하기 빈칸 앞에 있는 것 ☑자동사 ☐타동사
   → 빈칸은 ☐명사 ☑부사 자리이다.
3. 정답 선택하기 정답 (A)

성공은 Nashua Tech에서 성실하게 일한 직원들 덕분이라고 본다.

06.

1. 선택지 보고 문법/어휘 문제 파악하기 ☑문법 문제 ☐어휘 문제
2. 빈칸 분석하기 빈칸 앞에 있는 것 ☐능동태 동사 ☑수동태 동사
   → 빈칸은 ☐명사 ☑부사 자리이다.
3. 정답 선택하기 정답 (D)

몇몇 품목들은 Emerson 시에 있는 우리 창고에서 곧장 배송된다.

실전 문제

01.(C)	02.(B)	03.(D)	04.(B)	05.(C)	06.(C)
07.(C)	08.(B)	09.(C)	10.(D)	11.(D)	12.(C)
13.(B)	14.(B)	15.(D)	16.(B)	17.(D)	18.(D)
19.(A)	20.(B)	21.(C)	22.(D)	23.(B)	24.(A)

01. 부사의 역할과 위치: 동사 앞 수식

Global Geography의 사진 기자들은 야생 동물의 자연스러운 이미지를 포착하기 위해 서식지에 전략적으로 카메라를 배치한다.

에 어제 잠재 투자자들이 방문했고 건물을 둘러보는 바람에(~ we had some prospective investors visit the office yesterday, and Mr. Toscano showed them around the building) 완료되지 못했다고 했다. 따라서 방문객들의 견학을 언급한 (C)가 정답이다.

paraphrasing showed them around the building 건물을 둘러보게 했다 → were taking a tour 견학했다

[어휘] task 일, 업무 budget 예산 approve ~을 승인하다 shipment 배송(품) take a tour 견학하다 disagree 동의하지 않다

08. 의도 파악 문제

오전 9시 8분에, Bauer 씨가 "I've got it covered"라고 썼을 때 의미한 것은 무엇이겠는가?
(A) 몇몇 설문지들을 취합할 것이다.
(B) 몇몇 장비를 빌릴 것이다.
(C) 몇몇 무거운 물건들을 옮길 것이다.
(D) 최종 보고서를 이메일로 보낼 것이다.

[해설] 9시 8분 메시지의 앞부 내용을 보면, Goyal 씨가 손수레를 빌려야 하는데 건물 관리인을 찾을 수 없다고(~ the building manager has one I can borrow, but I haven't been able to track him down) 말하자 Bauer 씨가 "I've got it covered"라고 응답했고, 바로 뒤이어 Goyal 씨가 감사의 인사를 한다(Thanks, Anke! That would be really helpful). 따라서 Bauer 씨가 물건을 빌리는 일에 도움을 주기 위해 한 말임을 알 수 있으므로 (B)가 정답이다.

[어휘] borrow ~을 빌리다 equipment 장비

09. 세부사항 문제

10시에 무슨 일이 있을 것인가?
(A) 몇몇 직원들이 회의에 참석할 것이다.
(B) 몇몇 작업자들이 건물에 도착할 것이다.
(C) Goyal 씨가 수리 업체에 연락할 것이다.
(D) Mazzi 씨가 주차 자리를 맡아 둘 것이다.

[해설] 10시라는 시점은 9시 4분 메시지에 언급된 Eureka Repairs의 작업팀 도착 시간인 오전 11시(A crew from Eureka Repairs is coming today at 11 A.M.)와, 9시 10분 메시지에 그들이 도착하기 1시간 전에 주차 자리 확보를 위해 표지판을 세워 놓겠다고(I'll put up a sign an hour before they get here to hold a spot) 말하는 부분을 통해 파악할 수 있다. 따라서 9시 10분 메시지 작성자인 Mazzi 씨가 10시에 주차 자리를 맡아 둘 것이므로 (D)가 정답이다.

paraphrasing hold 확보하다 → reserve 따로 잡아 두다

[어휘] reserve 따로 잡아 두다

paraphrasing 정답 1. (b) 2. (a) 3. (c)

10-13은 다음 기사를 참조하시오.

연례 행사를 위해 모이는 기자들
Mandy Nadeau 작성

밴쿠버 (4월 29일) — 이번 주말, Stroude 광장은 캐나다인 특파원 콘퍼런스(CCC)에 참석하는 기자들로 가득 찰 것이다. —[1]—. 참가자들은 Antoine Lawrence 씨와 같이 수상 경력이 있는 기자들이 진행하는 강연과 글쓰기 능력에 관한 워크숍, 그리고 인맥을 쌓을 수 있는 기회들로 구성된 이틀간의 행사를 즐길 수 있다. 10신문 기자 협회(NWG)의 **Donald Zimmerman 대표가 소속 동호회 회원들에게 전문성 개발**

기회를 제공하기 위한 방법으로 10년 전에 이 행사를 처음 설립했다. —[2]—. 그 이후로, 11성장을 거듭해 전통적인 인쇄물 언론 분야든 또는 온라인 기반의 뉴스 사이트든 상관없이 캐나다 전역의 기자들을 포함하기에 이르렀다.

행사 기획자인 Louise Baxter 씨는 이 행사에 대한 관심에 기뻐하고 있다. —[3]—. "90퍼센트가 넘는 참가자들이 다음 해에 다시 행사장을 찾고 있는데, 이는 CCC가 얼마나 유익한지를 입증하는 것입니다"라고 Baxter 씨는 밝혔다. 13신규 참가자들의 숫자 또한 지속적으로 증가하고 있다. 작년에, 920명의 참가자들이 처음으로 행사에 참석했다. —[4]—.

하루 입장권은 75달러에, 양일 입장권은 130달러에 구입 가능하다. 참가자들은 지난해와 달리 12입구에서 입장권 판매가 이뤄지지 않는다는 점에 유의해야 한다. 추가 정보와 모든 활동이 담긴 일정표를 보기 위해서는, www.cancorcon.ca를 방문하기 바란다.

gather 모이다 be filled with ~로 가득 차다 establish ~을 설립하다, 확립하다 throughout ~ 전역의 online-based 온라인 기반의 be pleased with ~에 대해 기뻐하다 interest in ~에 대한 관심 attendee 참석자 demonstrate ~을 증명하다 figure 숫자, 수치 newcomer 새로 온 사람 rise 증가하다 steadily 지속적으로, 꾸준히 complete 완전한, 모두 갖춰진

10. 세부사항 문제

누가 Canadian Correspondents Conference를 설립했는가?
(A) Nadeau 씨
(B) Lawrence 씨
(C) Zimmerman 씨
(D) Baxter 씨

[해설] Canadian Correspondents Conference 관련 배경 정보가 제시된 첫 단락에, Newspaper Writers Guild(NWG)의 Donald Zimmerman 대표가 10년 전에 처음 설립했다고(Donald Zimmerman, ~ first established the event ten years ago) 언급했으므로 (C)가 정답이다.

paraphrasing established 설립했다 → founded 설립했다

[어휘] found ~을 설립하다

11. True 문제

콘퍼런스에 참석하는 기자들에 관해 언급된 것은 무엇인가?
(A) 일부가 상을 받을 것이다.
(B) 전 세계에서 찾아온다.
(C) 대부분이 워크숍에 관심이 있다.
(D) 다양한 형식으로 글을 쓴다.

[해설] 첫 단락 마지막에, 전통적인 인쇄물 언론 분야이든 또는 온라인 기반의 뉴스 사이트든 상관없이 캐나다 전역의 기자들을 포함하는 행사라는(~ journalists throughout Canada, whether in traditional print journalism or in online-based news sites) 내용이 나오는데, 이는 기사 제공 방식의 다양함과 관련된 말이므로 이에 해당되는 (D)가 정답이다.

[어휘] be presented with ~을 받다 format 형식

12. 추론 문제

콘퍼런스 입장권에 관해 암시된 것은 무엇인가?
(A) 반드시 미리 구입되어야 한다.
(B) 오직 NWG 회원에게만 판매된다.

eligibility 자격 증명 서류

[어휘] proof 증명(서)   eligibility 자격이 있음, 적격임   applicant 지원자   evaluation 평가(서)

04. 직업 문제

Herrera는 무슨 종류의 업체일 것 같은가?
(A) 소프트웨어 판매 회사
(B) 그래픽 디자인 회사
(C) 미술 학원
(D) 컴퓨터 프로그래밍 서비스 회사

[해설] 회사의 특징이 설명된 첫 단락에, 인쇄물과 온라인 마케팅에 필요한 콘텐츠 제공, 로고 제작, 스마트폰 애플리케이션용 삽화 작업이 언급되어 있는데(~ contents for print and online marketing, ~ logo creation or artwork for smartphone applications), 이는 그래픽 디자인 작업에 해당되므로 (B)가 정답이다.

paraphrasing logo creation or artwork 로고 제작, 삽화 → graphic design 그래픽 디자인

[어휘] institute 학원, 기관, 협회

05. 문장 삽입 문제

[1], [2], [3] 그리고 [4]로 표시된 위치들 중에서, 다음 문장이 들어가기에 가장 적절한 곳은 어디인가?

"이 증빙 서류마다 현재 또는 과거의 직무에 관한 설명이 포함되어 있어야 합니다."

(A) [1]
(B) [2]
(C) [3]
(D) [4]

[해설] 제시 문장은 특정 증빙 서류를 지칭하는 these references라는 표현을 써서 '현재 하는 일과 과거에 했던 일을 설명하는 내용이 포함되어 있어야 한다'는 의미를 나타낸다. 이는 두 번째 단락 시작 부분에서 언급하는 근무 경력 증명 자료로서 의뢰인에게서 받는 추천서의 조건에 해당한다. 따라서 [3]에 들어가 그 추천서에 대해 부연 설명하는 흐름이 되어야 적절하므로 (C)가 정답이다.

[어휘] references 증빙 서류   description 설명, 묘사   current 현재의   job duty 직무

paraphrasing 정답   1. (b)   2. (c)   3. (a)

06-09는 다음 온라인 채팅을 참조하시오.

Daksha Goyal [오전 9:03]
오늘 직원 휴게실의 출입이 제한된다는 사실을 잊지 마세요. 지난달에 모든 분들이 작성한 직원 설문지를 바탕으로, ⁰⁶우리는 대부분의 사람들이 직원 휴게실이 너무 어둡다고 생각했다는 사실을 알아냈기 때문에, 페인트를 다시 칠할 예정입니다.

Anke Bauer [오전 9:04]
직원 소식지에서 그와 관련된 내용을 읽은 것이 기억나요. ⁰⁹Eureka Repairs의 작업팀이 오늘 오전 11시에 오는 게 맞죠?

Daksha Goyal [오전 9:05]
그렇습니다. 하지만 휴게실이 아직 준비가 되어 있지 않아요. 지금 제가 밖으로 가구를 옮기고 있습니다.

Camelia Mazzi [오전 9:05]
⁰⁷그 일은 어제 오후에 완료되었어야 하는 것 아닌가요?

Daksha Goyal [오전 9:06]
네, ⁰⁷하지만 어제 몇몇 잠재 투자자들께서 사무실을 방문하셨고, Toscano 씨께서 그분들께 우리 건물을 둘러보시게 해 드렸어요. 우리는 복도에 많은 가구가 놓여 있는 것을 원치 않았는데, 좋지 않은 인상을 남길 거라고 생각했기 때문입니다.

Camelia Mazzi [오전 9:07]
이해가 되네요. 도움이 필요하신가요?

Daksha Goyal [오전 9:07]
저, 제가 손수레 없이는 들지 못할 것 같은 몇몇 물품들이 있어요. ⁰⁸제가 빌릴 수 있는 것이 건물 관리인에게 하나 있는 것 같은데, 어디에 계신지 계속 찾을 수 없었어요.

Anke Bauer [오전 9:08]
제가 처리해 드릴게요.

Daksha Goyal [오전 9:09]
⁰⁸고마워요, Anke 씨! 그렇게 해 주시면 정말로 도움이 될 거예요. 구하시는 대로 3층으로 갖고 올라와 주세요.

Camelia Mazzi [오전 9:10]
그리고 Eureka Repairs의 트럭이 주차할 수 있는 공간이 있는지도 분명히 해 두는 게 좋을 거예요. ⁰⁹입구 옆에 자리를 확보할 수 있도록 그분들이 이곳으로 오기 1시간 전에 제가 표지판을 세워 둘게요.

off limits 출입이 제한된   fill out ~을 작성하다   determine that ~임을 알아내다, 밝혀내다   crew (함께 작업하는) 팀, 반, 작업자들   prospective 잠재적인, 유망한   investor 투자자   make a bad impression 좋지 않은 인상을 남기다   make sense 이해가 되다, 앞뒤가 맞다   lift ~을 들어 올리다   track A down ~을 찾아내다, 추적하다   cover ~을 대신하다, 맡다   put up ~을 세워 놓다, 내걸다   hold a spot 자리를 확보하다

06. 추론 문제

Goyal 씨가 직원 휴게실에 관해 암시하는 것은 무엇인가?
(A) 새로운 조명 시스템이 필요하다.
(B) 회의실로 사용될 수 있다.
(C) 몇몇 새 가구가 들어올 것이다.
(D) 벽 색상이 변경될 것이다.

[해설] Goyal 씨가 쓴 첫 메시지에서, 대부분의 사람들이 직원 휴게실이 너무 어둡다고 생각한다는 이유로 페인트를 다시 칠한다고(~ the employee lounge was too dark, so it's going to be repainted) 알리는 말이 있는데, 이는 색상 변경을 의미하는 것이므로 (D)가 정답이다.

paraphrasing be repainted 다시 페인트칠이 되다 → color will be changed 색상이 변경되다

[어휘] lighting 조명

07. 세부사항 문제

왜 어제 한 가지 일이 지연되었는가?
(A) 예산이 승인되지 않았었기 때문에
(B) 배송 물품이 도착하지 않았기 때문에
(C) 몇몇 방문객들이 견학을 하고 있었기 때문에
(D) 직원들이 예산에 대해 동의하지 않았기 때문에

[해설] '이제'라는 시점은 9시 5분에 Mazzi 씨가 쓴 메시지에서 찾을 수 있는데, 어제 완료되었어야 하는 일이 아니었는지 묻자, 바로 다음 메시지

실전 문제

01.(C)	02.(B)	03.(B)	04.(B)	05.(C)	06.(D)
07.(C)	08.(B)	09.(D)	10.(C)	11.(D)	12.(A)
13.(D)					

01-02는 다음 문자 메시지 대화를 참조하시오.

Irene Jones [오전 10:03]
01 Dawson 법률 사무소의 사무실 이전은 어떻게 되어 가고 있나요?

Kevin Bradley [오전 10:07]
01, 02 사무용 가구를 모두 싣고 현재 새로 입주할 장소로 이동하는 중입니다.

Irene Jones [오전 10:08]
벌써요? 실은 Covina 사가 Gordon 가로 이전하는 데 제가 도움이 좀 필요해서요.

Kevin Bradley [오전 10:09]
가능한 한 빨리 제가 그리로 가겠지만, 먼저 마무리 지어야 할 추가 문서 작업이 좀 있을 거예요.

Irene Jones [오전 10:10]
무슨 일이라도 있으셨나요?

Kevin Bradley [오전 10:11]
그쪽에서 마지막 순간에 추가 포장재와 테이프를 요청하는 바람에 거래 내역서 내용을 조정해야 해요.

Irene Jones [오전 10:12]
알겠어요. 그 일을 마무리 지으시면 제게 알려 주세요.

load up ~을 다 싣다   on one's way to ~로 이동 중인   paperwork 문서 작업   packing materials 포장재   at the last minute 마지막 순간에   adjust ~을 조정하다   invoice 거래 내역서

01. 직업 문제

Bradley 씨는 무슨 종류의 업체에서 근무하는가?
(A) 법률 회사
(B) 가구 매장
(C) 이사 전문 회사
(D) 부동산 중개업소

[해설] 첫 메시지에서 Jones 씨가 Dawson 법률 사무소의 사무실 이전 작업(the office move for Dawson Legal)에 대한 진행 상황을 묻자, 바로 뒤이어 Bradley 씨가 사무용 가구를 모두 싣고 그 업체가 새로 입주할 장소로 이동하는 중이라고(The office furniture is all loaded up, and we're on our way to their new location) 알리고 있다. 따라서 이삿짐을 나르는 상황임을 알 수 있으므로 (C)가 정답이다.

[어휘] firm 회사   real estate 부동산   agency 회사, 대행사

02. 의도 파악 문제

오전 10시 8분에 Jones 씨가 "Already"라고 썼을 때 의미하는 것은 무엇이겠는가?
(A) 거래 내역서와 관련해 고객과 얘기했다.
(B) 작업이 더 오래 걸릴 것으로 예상했다.
(C) 약속 시간을 놓쳤다.
(D) 일정을 잘 모른다.

[해설] 10시 7분 메시지에서 Bradley 씨가 사무용 가구를 모두 싣고 업체가 새로 입주할 장소로 이동하는 중이라고(The office furniture is all loaded up, and we're on our way to their new location) 알리자 '벌써요?'라고 반응하는 상황이다. 이는 그렇게 빨리 작업이 진행될 줄 몰랐다는 뜻으로 더 오래 걸릴 것으로 생각했음을 의미하는 말이다. 따라서 (B)가 정답이다.

[어휘] task 일, 업무   be unsure of ~에 확신이 없다

paraphrasing 정답   1. (b)   2. (a)   3. (c)

03-05는 다음 편지를 참조하시오.

Melissa Alger
Richmond 가 143번지
맨체스터
M1 2PZ

Alger 씨께,

저희 Herrera의 공석에 대한 귀하의 지원서를 접수했습니다. 귀하께서 제출하신 이미지들은 인상적이고 예술적이며, 저희는 귀하의 능력이 저희 팀에 큰 보탬이 될 수 있다고 생각합니다. —[1]—. 04 저희는 주로 인쇄물과 온라인 마케팅에 필요한 콘텐츠를 제공하고 있지만, 일부 프로젝트에는 로고 제작이나 스마트폰 애플리케이션용 삽화 작업이 포함됩니다. —[2]—.

03, 05 이 직책에 고용되시기 위해서는, 반드시 최소 2년간의 해당 업계 근무 경력을 증명하셔야 합니다. 귀하께서는 프리랜서이시기 때문에, 귀하의 고객 세 분으로부터 받은 추천서 제출을 통해 이 부분이 확인될 수 있습니다. 그 목적은 다양한 소프트웨어 프로그램에 대한 것뿐만 아니라, 제때 그리고 요구 조건에 맞게 프로젝트를 진행하는 것과도 관련된 귀하의 경험을 확인하기 위한 것입니다. —[3]—. 저희가 필요로 하는 모든 것을 받는 대로, 진행 가능한 면접 시간과 관련해 귀하에게 다시 연락 드리겠습니다.

귀하로부터 다시 연락받을 수 있기를 고대합니다. —[4]—.

안녕히 계십시오.

Annie Joplin
Herrera

application 지원(서)   open position 공석, 빈 자리   impressive 인상적인   artistic 예술의, 예술적인   addition 보탬, 추가(되는 것)   demonstrate ~을 증명하다   at least 최소한, 적어도   field 업계, 분야   submission 제출   letter of recommendation 추천서   aim 목적   deliver ~을 진행하다, 행하다   on time 제때   regarding ~와 관련해

03. 목적 문제

편지는 왜 보내졌는가?
(A) 채용 면접 일정을 정하기 위해
(B) 자격 증명 서류를 요청하기 위해
(C) 한 지원자에게 일자리를 제안하기 위해
(D) 직원 평가서를 제공하기 위해

[해설] 첫 단락의 배경 설명에 이어, 두 번째 단락에 최소 2년간의 업계 근무 경력을 증명해야 한다는 말과 함께 의뢰인으로부터 받은 추천서 제출을 통해 이를 확인할 수 있다는(~ can be confirmed through the submission of letters of recommendation) 말로 보아 증명 서류를 요청하기 위한 편지임을 알 수 있으므로 (B)가 정답이다.

paraphrasing   letters of recommendation 추천서 → proof of

PART 7 의도 파악 문제/문장 삽입 문제

01. 의도 파악 문제
풀이 방법 해석

Miles Bowen [오후 5시 18분] Chad, 사무실에 있어요?
Chad Sellers [오후 5시 19분] 네. 뭐 잊은 거 있어요?
Miles Bowen [오후 5시 20분] Fairburn에 있는 고객들에게 택배로 보내기로 한 서류가 있습니다. 당신이 그것을 처리해 줄 수 있다고 생각하나요?
Chad Sellers [오후 5시 22분] 그건 문제가 되지 않을 거예요. 어떤 문서입니까?
Miles Bowen [오후 5시 23분] 오늘 날짜가 적힌 Fairburn 표시가 된 파일입니다. 제 책상 옆에 있는 파일 캐비닛에 있어요.
Chad Sellers [오후 5시 25분] 키패드 자물쇠가 달려 있어요.
Miles Bowen [오후 5시 26분] 아, 암호를 모르세요? 5772입니다.
Chad Sellers [오후 5시 28분] 네, 찾았어요. 이미 택배 기사에게 찾으러 오라고 했나요?
Miles Bowen [오후 5시 29분] 방금 했어요. 도와주셔서 감사합니다.

Q. 오후 5시 25분에, Sellers 씨가 "키패드 자물쇠가 달려 있어요"라고 쓸 때, 무슨 의미인 것 같은가?
(A) 그는 엉뚱한 곳에 있다.
(B) 그는 약간의 정보가 필요하다.
(C) 그는 보안 부서를 방문해야 한다.
(D) 그는 파일에 접근할 권한이 없다.

02. 문장 삽입 문제
풀이 방법 해석

즉시 보도용

연락처: Diyah Shah, 555-6852

Palmdale(6월 3일) — Pacific Trucking은 영업 지역을 확대할 계획을 발표하게 되어 기쁘게 생각합니다. — [1] —. 원래는 당사는 태평양 시간대 및 산악 표준 시간대에 해당하는 주들에 대해서만 상품을 운송했지만, 곧 미국 본토 전역을 커버할 예정입니다.

신규 수요를 충족시키기 위해, Pacific Trucking은 빠르면 다음 주부터 채용을 시작할 것입니다. — [2] —. 확장의 초기 단계에는, 100명의 정규직 운전자를 채용할 것입니다.

Pacific Trucking은 성공적이고 매우 존경받는 고용주입니다. — [3] —. 모든 직원들은 저렴한 요금으로 건강 및 치과 진료 보험을 이용할 수 있습니다. 만약 이미 트럭을 소유하고 있고 Pacific Trucking 운전기사가 되고 싶다면, 여러분은 회사의 환경 기준에 맞게 트럭을 개조해야 합니다. — [4] —. 만기일이 가깝다면, 합격되기 전에 갱신하도록 요청을 받을 수 있습니다. 자세한 내용은 www.pacifictrucking.com/careers를 참조하시기 바랍니다.

Q. [1], [2], [3] 그리고 [4]로 표시된 곳 중 다음 문장이 들어가기에 가장 알맞은 곳은?

"유효한 사업용 운전면허 소지자만이 운전직에 지원해야 합니다."

(A) [1]
(B) [2]
(C) [3]
(D) [4]

 연습 문제
01.(B) 02.(A)

01.

Makenna Lyons [오후 3시 18분]
Danny, 문제가 생겼어요. 방금 우리 해산물 공급 업체에서 연락이 왔어요. 그들은 오늘 사고로 인해 신선한 생선을 저희 식당에 가지고 올 수 없다고 했어요.

Danny Goodman [오후 3시 20분]
정말요? 하지만 오늘은 금요일인데요. 오늘 저녁 특선 요리는 생선 튀김이라구요.

Makenna Lyons [오후 3시 21분]
알아요, 그리고 그들을 실망시키고 싶지 않아요. 오늘 대체 특선을 생각해 주시겠어요?

Danny Goodman [오후 3시 23분]
냉장고를 확인해 볼게요.

Makenna Lyons [오후 3시 34분]
훌륭해요. 당신을 믿어요!

---

supplier 공급업체 disappoint 실망시키다 replacement 대체
freezer 냉동고 count on ~을 의지하다

Q. 오후 3시 23분에, Goodman씨가 "냉장고를 확인해 볼게요"라고 쓸 때, 무슨 의미인가?
(A) 그는 장치를 검사할 것이다.
(B) 그는 새로운 요리를 만들 것이다.

[문제 키워드] At 3:23 P:M / Mr. Goodman / "I'll check out freezer"

[해설] 3시 21분 메시지에서 오늘 대체 요리 특선을 생각해 주겠냐는 (Could you come up with a replacement special for today?) 요청에 대해 "냉장고를 확인해 보겠다"라고 답하는 상황이다. 따라서 특선 요리에 대해 알아볼 의사가 있음을 알 수 있으므로 (B)가 정답이다.

[어휘] examine 검사하다 device 장치 dish 요리

02.

자선 단체인 Backyard Ball은 최근 점점 더 많은 관심을 받고 있다. 그것은 처음에 아이들이 하루에 적어도 한 시간 동안 밖에 나가 놀도록 장려하기 위한 노력으로 설립되었다. 이 단체의 인기가 급상승한 것은 전 농구 스타 Eric Banks 덕분일 것이다. — [1] —. 고향인 Detroit에서 열린 몇몇 경기에 그가 캐주얼 코치로 처음 모습을 드러낸 이후 Backyard Ball의 멤버십은 500% 이상 성장했다. — [2] —.

---

initially 처음에 appearance 출현, 외모

Q. [1]과 [2]로 표시된 위치 중에서, 다음 문장이 들어가기에 가장 적절한 곳은 어디인가?

"Banks 씨는 작년에 은퇴 후 그 프로그램에 합류했다."
(A) [1]
(B) [2]

[해설] 제시된 문장은 Banks 씨와 지문 전체에서 소개되고 있는 Backyard Ball 프로그램과의 관계를 나타낸다. 이 내용은 문맥상 Banks 씨라는 사람에 대한 소개가 끝난 뒤에 나와야 적절하며 동시에 그의 프로그램 참여가 결과인 멤버십 증가보다 앞서 위치해야 의미가 자연스럽게 연결된다. 따라서 (A)가 정답이다.

⁰¹Gavin 가전제품을 대표해, 귀하의 자택에 최근 Gavin 46S 에어컨을 설치하신 것에 대해 축하의 말씀 드립니다. 하지만 저희 제조 공장들 중 한 곳에서 출시하는 일부 기기에서 발견된 제품 결함으로 인해, 특정 모델에 부품 교체가 필요합니다.

⁰²모든 Gavin 46S 모델 제품에 이와 같은 결함이 있는 것은 아닙니다. 귀하의 제품이 부품 교체를 필요로 하는 것인지 확인하실 수 있도록, 플라스틱 덮개 아래 쪽에 쓰여 있는 일련번호를 살펴보십시오. ⁰³그 번호가 "ITV"로 시작될 경우, 귀하의 모델은 부품 교체를 필요로 하는 것입니다. 저희에게 전화 주셔서 수리 기사가 언제 새 부품을 갖고 귀하의 자택을 방문하면 되는지 알려 주시기 바랍니다. ⁰⁴저희 Gavin 가전제품은 전액 무료로 부품을 교체해 드릴 것입니다.

이와 같은 불편함에 대해 사과의 말씀 드립니다. 귀하의 양해와 협조에 미리 감사 드립니다.

Ruben Huntz
고객 서비스 지원팀, Gavin 가전제품

defect 결함 on behalf of ~을 대표해, 대신해 unit 기구, 장치 detect ~을 발견하다, 감지하다 manufacturing plant 제조 공장 replacement 교체(품) beneath ~ 아래에 hood 덮개, 뚜껑 absolutely free of charge 전액 무료로

01. 명사 어휘

[해설] 축하의 말을 전하는 이유로서 recent의 수식을 받아 에어컨 제품 구매와 관련해 자택 내에서 발생 가능한 일을 나타낼 명사가 필요하므로 '설치'를 의미하는 (A) installation이 정답이다.

[어휘] content 내용(물) reception 접수처, (축하) 연회

02. 알맞은 문장 고르기

(A) 저희 웹사이트에서 만족도 설문지를 작성해 주시기 바랍니다.
(B) Gavin 가전제품은 자사의 모든 제품에 대해 품질 보증 서비스를 제공합니다.
(C) 모든 Gavin 46S 모델 제품에 이와 같은 결함이 있는 것은 아닙니다.
(D) 더 오래된 특정 모델들은 이러한 기능이 없을 수 있습니다.

[해설] 바로 다음 문장에서 교체 부품이 필요한 제품인지 확인하는 방법을 알려 주는 것으로 보아 부품 교체가 일부 제품에만 필요함을 알 수 있으므로 모든 제품에 결함이 있는 것은 아니라는 의미인 (C)가 정답이다.

[어휘] fill out ~을 작성하다 questionnaire 설문지 warranty 품질 보증(서) contain ~을 포함하다, ~가 들어 있다 feature 기능, 특징

03. 인칭대명사

[해설] 앞 문장에서 확인하라고 한 일련 번호(the serial number)를 보고 부품 교체 필요 여부를 판단하는 방법을 설명하는 문장이므로 단수 사물 명사인 the serial number를 대신할 수 있는 (C) it이 정답이다.

04. 형용사 어휘

[해설] 빈칸 뒤에 위치한 of charge와 함께 쓰일 수 있는 것으로서 부품 교체 작업에 대한 비용 처리와 관련된 의미가 되어야 하므로 '무료로'라는 뜻을 나타낼 때 사용하는 (C) free가 정답이다.

[어휘] ahead 앞으로, 앞에, 미리 prior 사전의, 우선하는, 이전의

05-08은 다음 편지를 참조하시오.

Eagle WiFi 서비스 가입자께

⁰⁵11월 1일부터로, 귀하의 WiFi 인터넷 서비스에 일부 변동 사항이 시행될 것입니다. ⁰⁶귀하께서는 안전한 비밀번호를 사용하셔야 하며, 특정 웹사이트에 접속하기 위해서는 나이를 증명하셔야 합니다. 이와 같은 조치는 모든 서비스 가입자들의 안전을 위해 시행되는 것입니다. 또한, 귀하의 네트워크 보안을 감시하고 향상시키기 위해 여러 IT 전문가들이 고용되었습니다. ⁰⁷저희는 귀하와 같은 모든 서비스 가입자들께서 더욱 안전하고 보호된 서비스를 즐기실 수 있기를 바랍니다. ⁰⁸새로운 보안 조치와 관련된 더 상세한 정보는 저희 웹사이트에서 찾아보실 수 있습니다.

subscriber 서비스 가입자, 구독자 implement ~을 시행하다, 실시하다 prove ~을 증명하다, 입증하다 access ~에 접속하다, ~을 이용하다 measures 조치, 방안 put A into place A를 실시하다, 시행하다 improve ~을 향상시키다

05. 형용사 자리

[해설] 변동 사항이 시행된다는 사실을 알리는 문장이므로 빈칸 뒤에 위치한 November 1이 시작 시점임을 알 수 있다. 따라서 날짜와 함께 '~부터 발효되는'이라는 의미를 나타낼 때 사용하는 (D) Effective가 정답이다.

[어휘] effect 효과, 영향; ~을 초래하다 effective (규정 등이) 발효되는, 시행되는, 효과적인

06. 동사 어휘

[해설] 변동 사항과 관련해 상대방에게 요청하는 일을 나타내는 문장이 되어야 알맞으므로 be동사, to부정사와 함께 '~해야 하다'라는 의미를 만들 때 사용하는 (A) required가 정답이다. (C) devoted는 to 뒤에 동명사가 쓰여야 하며, (D) decided는 수동태가 아닌 decide to부정사의 구조로 쓰인다.

[어휘] devote (노력, 시간 등) ~을 쏟다, 바치다

07. 인칭대명사

[해설] 전치사 like의 목적어 자리인 빈칸에는 바로 앞에 제시된 all subscribers와 동일한 입장에 있는 사람을 나타내야 하는데, subscribers는 이 편지를 읽는 사람, 즉 상대방을 지칭하므로 (C) you가 정답이다.

08. 알맞은 문장 고르기

(A) 저희 콜 센터 직원들을 통해 매일 24시간 서비스를 받으실 수 있습니다.
(B) 새로운 보안 조치와 관련된 더 상세한 정보는 저희 웹사이트에서 찾아보실 수 있습니다.
(C) 귀하의 컴퓨터를 안전하게 유지하기 위해 사용하실 수 있는 몇몇 소프트웨어 프로그램이 있습니다.
(D) 서비스 수수료는 귀하의 계좌에서 자동으로 공제될 것이라는 점에 유의하시기 바랍니다.

[해설] 변동 사항과 관련된 정보를 모두 전달한 후에 마지막 문장으로 제시되기에 적절한 것을 골라야 하므로 해당 변동 사항을 '새로운 조치(the new security measures)'로 지칭해 관련 추가 정보를 찾아볼 수 있는 방법을 알리는 (B)가 정답이다.

[어휘] representative 직원 around the clock 24시간 fee 수수료, 요금 deduct A from B A를 B에서 공제하다 account 계좌, 계정

으로 확대하는 것이다.

[해설] 선택지가 다양한 명사로 이루어져 있으므로 명사 어휘 문제이다. 문장의 동사가 'be to do' 구조이므로 이와 어울리는 어휘를 찾아야 하는데, '목표들 중의 하나는 ~하는 것이다'라는 의미가 되는 것이 가장 적합하므로 (B) objectives가 정답이다.

[어휘] primary 주요한 expand A into B A를 B로 확대하다, 확장하다 presence 존재(감), 있음 payment 지불(액) objective 목표 clearance 정리, 치움 restoration 복원, 복구

24. '형용사+명사' 짝꿍 표현

건물 관리팀은 지난 한 달간 쓰레기를 10퍼센트 줄이는 데 들인 공동의 노력에 대해 모든 입주자들에게 감사하고 있다.

[해설] 선택지가 다양한 품사의 단어들로 구성되어 있으므로 문법 문제이다. 소유격 대명사 your와 명사 effort 사이에 위치한 빈칸은 명사를 수식하는 형용사 자리이므로 형용사 어미 -ive로 끝나는 (D) collective가 정답이다.

[어휘] resident 입주자, 주민 effort 노력 reduce ~을 줄이다, 감소시키다 collect ~을 수집하다, 모으다 collector 수집가 collective 공동의, 집단적인

PART 6 앞 문장의 명사를 받는 인칭대명사

풀이 방법 해석

날짜: 6월 15일
수신: Rebecca Wagner <r.wagner@hmail.com>
발신: 고객 서비스 <custserv@everbrite.com>
제목: 감사합니다!

Wagner 씨께

이 이메일은 저희의 EverBrite 태블릿 기기에 대한 후기를 보내주신 것에 감사드리기 위함입니다. 저희 회사는 저희가 무엇을 잘못하고 있고 상품과 서비스를 어떻게 개선시킬 수 있는지 알게 해주는 귀하와 같은 고객들에 의지합니다.

감사의 의미로 첨부된 쿠폰을 받아 주세요. 모든 온라인에서 또는 매장을 직접 방문하여 EverBrite 상품을 구입할 때 사용하실 수 있습니다. 귀하의 이전 구매가 선물이었다고 하셨습니다. 이제, 나가셔서 저희의 플래그십 매장에서 진행 중인 특별 주말 할인 이벤트에서 새 EverBrite 태블릿을 구입하실 수 있습니다.

다시 한번 감사합니다.

서비스 부서, EverBrite 전자기기

 연습 문제

01.(B) 02.(A) 03.(B) 04.(B)

01.

Bishop 씨께

MoreHome.com을 통해 주문하신 식기 세트에 관한 의견을 제공해 주셔서 감사 드립니다. 저희는 일부 그릇이 도착하자마자 금이 가 있었다는 얘기를 듣게 되어 유감으로 생각합니다. 저희가 무료로 그것들을 교체해 드리겠습니다.

cracked 금이 간, 갈라진 replace ~을 교체하다 free of charge 무료로

[단서] some of the bowls

[해설] 동사 replace의 목적어로서 교체 대상이 되어야 하는 것은 앞 문장에 언급된 some of the bowls이므로 복수 사물 명사를 대신할 수 있는 (B) them이 정답이다.

02.

이 편지는 Cricket 가 41번지에 위치한 아파트에 대한 제 임대 계약과 관련된 것입니다. 저는 3개월 일찍 이사 가려고 합니다. 제 회사가 저를 디트로이트로 전근시킬 예정입니다.

in regards to ~와 관련된 move out 이사 나가다 transfer A to B A를 B로 전근시키다

[단서] rental contract I have, I will be moving out

[해설] 빈칸 뒤에 위치한 company는 앞 문장에 언급된 바와 같이 이 글의 작성자인 I가 다니는 회사여야 하므로 동일한 1인칭 대명사인 (A) My가 정답이다.

03.

친애하는 Harris 씨,

이 메일은 지난 금요일까지였던 여름 휴가 요청에 대해 알려 드리기 위한 것입니다. 귀하를 제외한 모든 직원이 제시간에 제출했습니다.

remind 상기시키다 request 요청 due ~로 예정된

[단서] remind you

[해설] 앞 문장에서 '귀하에게 알려 드리기 위한' 것이라고 편지의 목적이 나왔으므로 글의 흐름상 2인칭 대명사인 (B) you가 정답이다.

04.

Vanessa Bosch 씨와 Christopher Wilde 씨가 모두 올 연말에 은퇴하기로 발표하셨습니다. 이분들께서는 모두 합쳐 80년의 마케팅 경력을 지니고 있으십니다.

retirement 은퇴, 퇴직 combined 합쳐진, 결합된

[단서] Both Vanessa Bosch and Christopher Wilde

[해설] 앞 문장에 언급된 Vanessa Bosch 씨와 Christopher Wilde 씨의 경력 기간을 합산한 내용이 되어야 알맞으므로 3인칭 복수 대명사인 (B) They가 정답이다.

실전 문제

01.(A) 02.(C) 03.(C) 04.(C) 05.(D) 06.(A)
07.(C) 08.(B)

01-04는 다음 이메일을 참조하시오.

날짜: 5월 29일
수신: Thomas Ackerman <tackerman@cmail.net>
발신: Ruben Huntz <rhuntz@gavinappliance.net>
제목: 제품 결함

Ackerman 씨께

이므로 형용사 어미 -al로 끝나는 (C) chronological이 정답이다.

[어휘] arrange ~을 정리하다 in chronological order 날짜순으로, 연대순으로 chronicle 연대기, 기록 chronology 연대표, 연대순 chronologically 연대순으로

13. 형용사의 역할: 명사 수식

Alley Pizza는 어느 지역으로든 신뢰할 만한 배달 서비스를 제공하는 것으로 알려져 있다.

[해설] 선택지가 다양한 품사의 단어들로 구성되어 있으므로 문법 문제이다. 소유격 대명사 its와 명사 delivery 사이에 위치한 빈칸은 명사를 수식할 형용사 자리이므로 형용사 어미 -able로 끝나는 (D) reliable이 정답이다.

[어휘] rely (on) 신뢰하다, 의지하다 reliable 신뢰할 만한

14. 형용사 구분: 일반 형용사 vs. 분사 형용사

Bale 씨는 인상적인 성과로 이달의 사원으로 선정되었다.

[해설] 선택지가 다양한 품사의 단어들로 구성되어 있으므로 문법 문제이다. 소유격 his와 performance 사이에 위치한 빈칸은 명사를 수식할 형용사 자리인데, 명사 performance를 수식해야 하므로 '인상적인'을 뜻하는 (D) impressive가 정답이다. (B) impressed(깊은 인상을 받은)는 사람에 대해서만 사용한다.

[어휘] name 지명하다 impress ~에게 깊은 인상을 남기다, 감명을 주다 performance 성과

15. 형용사 구분: 일반 형용사 vs. 분사 형용사

철저한 테스트를 거친 후에, 그 시제품은 대량 생산을 위한 승인을 받을 것이다.

[해설] 선택지가 다양한 품사의 단어들로 구성되어 있으므로 문법 문제이다. 동명사 undergoing과 명사 목적어 tests 사이에 위치한 빈칸은 명사를 수식할 형용사 자리인데, 사물 명사 tests를 수식해야 하므로 '철저한'을 뜻하는 (C) exhaustive가 정답이다. (B) exhausted(지친)는 사람에 대해서만 사용한다.

[어휘] undergo ~을 거치다, 겪다 prototype 시제품 mass production 대량 생산 exhaust ~을 지치게 만들다 exhaustion 탈진, 소진

16. 명사 어휘

Daniel's Builders는 공사 현장에 들어갈 때 모든 공사 작업자들이 안전 조치를 따르도록 요구한다.

[해설] 선택지가 다양한 명사로 이루어져 있으므로 명사 어휘 문제이다. 빈칸 앞의 safety만으로는 동사 follow의 목적어로서 준수 대상을 나타내기에 의미가 부족하므로 '안전 조치'라는 복합 명사를 구성하는 또 다른 명사 (A) measures가 정답이다.

[어휘] demand that ~하도록 요구하다 construction site 공사 현장 measures 조치 advance 진보, 발전 perspective 관점, 시각 property 건물, 부동산

17. 대명사 those

Hoffmann 씨는 유사한 학력을 지닌 대부분의 사람들보다 더 많은 현장 경험을 가지고 있다.

[해설] 선택지가 다양한 인칭대명사로 구성되어 있으므로 문법 문제이다. 전치사 of의 목적어 역할을 함과 동시에 with 전치사구의 수식을 받아야 하므로 이와 같은 역할이 가능한 대명사로 '~하는 사람들'이라는 의미로 쓰이는 (B) those가 정답이다.

[어휘] field experience 현장 경험 educational 교육의, 교육적인

18. 재귀대명사: 재귀 용법

Fisherman's 요리 경연대회 행사 기간 중에, 해산물 요리 샘플을 마음껏 드실 수 있습니다.

[해설] 선택지가 다양한 인칭대명사로 구성되어 있으므로 문법 문제이다. 빈칸은 동사 help의 목적어 자리인데, 이 목적어가 가리키는 대상이 주어 you와 같으므로 행위 주체와 대상이 동일할 때 사용하는 재귀대명사 (D) yourself가 정답이다.

[어휘] help oneself to ~을 마음껏 먹다

19. 명사 어휘

오직 몇몇 후보자들만이 우리 인사부에서 요구하는 모든 자격 요건을 갖추고 있다.

[해설] 선택지가 다양한 명사로 이루어져 있으므로 명사 어휘 문제이다. 동사 possess의 목적어로 어울리는 명사로서 후보자들이 지니고 있는 것을 나타내야 하므로 '자격 요건'을 의미하는 (A) qualifications가 정답이다.

[어휘] candidate 후보자 possess ~을 소유하다 alternative 대안, 대체(하는 것) engagement 약속(된 일), 참여

20. 형용사의 역할: 명사 수식

운영팀은 고객들이 제기한 건설적인 비판을 검토하는 시간을 가졌다.

[해설] 선택지가 다양한 품사의 단어들로 구성되어 있으므로 문법 문제이다. 정관사 the와 명사 criticism 사이에 위치한 빈칸은 명사를 수식할 형용사 자리이므로 형용사 어미 -ive로 끝나는 (B) constructive가 정답이다.

[어휘] criticism 비판 construct ~을 건설하다, 짓다 constructive 건설적인 construction 건설, 공사

21. 명사 어휘

이사회는 다음 분기부터 매출을 증대하기 위한 혁신적인 접근법을 활용하기로 결정했다.

[해설] 선택지가 다양한 명사로 이루어져 있으므로 명사 어휘 문제이다. 동사 utilize의 목적어로서 매출 증대를 위해 활용할 수 있는 것을 나타낼 명사가 필요하다. 따라서 형용사 innovative와 함께 '혁신적인 접근법'이라는 의미를 만드는 (B) approach가 정답이다.

[어휘] utilize ~을 활용하다 boost ~을 증대하다 sales 매출, 영업, 판매 industry 업계, 산업 approach 접근법 stretch (도로 등의) 긴 구간, (지속되는) 기간 phase 단계, 국면

22. 형용사의 역할: 명사 수식

Wilkerson 씨는 대중 연설에 관한 소중한 의견과 개인적인 팁을 제공해 주었다.

[해설] 선택지가 다양한 품사의 단어들로 구성되어 있으므로 문법 문제이다. 형용사 some과 명사 comments 사이에 위치한 빈칸은 명사를 수식할 또 다른 형용사가 필요한 자리이므로 형용사 어미 -able로 끝나는 (C) valuable이 정답이다.

[어휘] value 가치; ~을 소중히 여기다 valuable 소중한 valuably 값비싸게

23. 명사 어휘

이 프로젝트의 주요 목표들 중 하나는 성공적으로 우리의 입지를 유럽 시장

01. 형용사의 역할: 명사 수식

Lorenzo 마케팅은 올해의 의류 제품 라인에 대한 혁신적인 광고를 만든 공을 인정받고 있다.

[해설] 선택지가 다양한 품사의 단어들로 구성되어 있으므로 문법 문제이다. 정관사 the와 명사 advertisement 사이에 위치한 빈칸은 명사를 수식할 형용사 자리이므로 형용사 어미 -ive로 끝나는 (C) innovative가 정답이다.

[어휘] be credited with ~에 대한 공을 인정받다 innovate 혁신하다 innovative 혁신적인

02. 형용사의 형태: 형용사 어미

서랍 속에 놓여져 있기는 했지만, 그 손전등은 여전히 작동 가능한 상태이다.

[해설] 선택지가 다양한 품사의 단어들로 구성되어 있으므로 문법 문제이다. be동사 is 뒤에 위치할 수 있으면서 부사 still의 수식을 받을 수 있는 것은 형용사이므로 형용사 어미 -al로 끝나는 (C) functional이 정답이다.

[어휘] be left in ~에 놓여 있다, 남겨져 있다 drawer 서랍 function 기능; 기능하다 functional 기능을 하는, 기능적인

03. 형용사의 형태: '-ly' 형용사

좌석이 매진될 가능성이 있기 때문에, Hayden 극장은 훨씬 미리 공연 입장권을 예매하도록 권한다.

[해설] be동사 are 뒤에서 보어 역할을 할 단어가 필요한데, 주어인 좌석(seats)과 관련된 상태를 나타낼 형용사가 쓰여야 알맞으므로 형용사 어미 -ly로 끝나는 (D) likely가 정답이다.

[어휘] well in advance 훨씬 미리 likelihood 가능성

04. 형용사의 역할: 주격 보어

안전한지 확인하기 위해 경비원들이 한 시간마다 그 시설물을 순찰한다.

[해설] 선택지가 다양한 품사의 단어들로 구성되어 있으므로 문법 문제이다. be동사 is 뒤에서 it에 대한 보어 역할을 할 단어가 필요한데, it이 지칭하는 the facility의 보안 상태를 나타낼 형용사가 쓰여야 알맞으므로 (A) secure가 정답이다.

[어휘] patrol ~을 순찰하다 facility 시설(물) secure 안전한; ~을 확보하다 security 보안

05. 파생어 형용사

Trujillo 직원들에게 지급되는 연휴 보너스는 한 해의 수익에 달려 있다.

[해설] 선택지가 다양한 품사의 단어들로 구성되어 있으므로 문법 문제이다. be동사 is 뒤에서 보어 역할을 할 단어가 필요한데, 전치사 on과 어울려야 하므로 'be dependent on'의 구조로 '~에 달려 있다, ~에 따라 다르다'라는 의미로 쓰이는 (C) dependent가 정답이다.

[어휘] profit 수익 depend 의존하다, 믿다 dependable 믿을 수 있는

06. 형용사의 역할: 명사 수식

그 새로운 독립 연구는 고단백 식단의 유익한 효과에 초점을 맞추고 있다.

[해설] 선택지가 다양한 품사의 단어들로 구성되어 있으므로 문법 문제이다. 정관사 the와 명사 effects 사이에 위치한 빈칸은 명사를 수식할 형용사 자리이므로 형용사 어미 -al로 끝나는 (B) beneficial이 정답이다.

[어휘] independent 독립적인 focus 초점을 맞추다 protein 단백질 diet 식단

07. 명사 어휘

Baker 씨는 자신만의 속도로 일을 할 수 있기 때문에 프리랜서가 되고 싶어 했다.

[해설] 선택지가 다양한 명사로 이루어져 있으므로 명사 어휘 문제이다. 전치사 at의 목적어로 쓰일 수 있는 명사로 프리랜서가 되고 싶은 이유에 해당하는 업무처리 방식과 관련된 의미를 나타내야 하므로 '자신만의 속도로'라는 의미를 만드는 (C) pace가 정답이다.

[어휘] at one's own pace 자신만의 속도로 load 적재량, 업무량 entry 출품작, 참가작

08. 형용사의 역할: 주격 보어

Wilkerson Café는 인근 레스토랑들과의 경쟁력을 유지하기 위해 특별 점심 메뉴를 제공하고 있다.

[해설] 선택지가 다양한 품사의 단어들로 구성되어 있으므로 문법 문제이다. 빈칸 앞에 위치한 동사 stay는 형용사 보어와 결합해 2형식 동사로 쓰이므로 형용사 어미 -ive로 끝나는 (D) competitive가 정답이다.

[어휘] compete 경쟁하다, 겨루다 competitively 경쟁적으로 competitor 경쟁사, 경쟁자 competitive 경쟁력 있는, 경쟁하는

09. 형용사의 역할: 명사 수식

승객들을 아주 다양한 목적지로 데려다 주는 Horizon Airlines는 그 서비스 면에서 최고의 업체로 뽑혔다.

[해설] 선택지가 다양한 품사의 단어들로 구성되어 있으므로 문법 문제이다. 부정관사 a와 명사 range 사이에 위치한 빈칸은 명사를 수식하는 형용사 자리이므로 (A) wide가 정답이다.

[어휘] be voted A A로 뽑히다 widen 넓어지다, ~을 넓히다 widely 널리, 폭넓게, 대단히

10. 명사 어휘

저희 멤버십에 등록하실 경우, 저희 전문가들과 무료 상담을 받을 자격을 얻으시게 됩니다.

[해설] 선택지가 다양한 명사로 이루어져 있으므로 명사 어휘 문제이다. 회원 등록을 함으로써 전문가들로부터 무료로 받을 수 있는 혜택을 나타낼 명사가 빈칸에 쓰여야 알맞으므로 형용사 free와 함께 '무료 상담'이라는 의미를 구성할 수 있는 (D) consultation이 정답이다.

[어휘] be eligible to부정사 ~할 자격을 얻다 expert 전문가 comparison 비교 continuity 지속성, 연속성 consultation 상담

11. 'be+형용사+전치사' 표현

설문 조사에 따르면 고객들은 장애인들을 위한 새 주차 공간에 대해 감사하게 생각하는 것으로 나타나 있다.

[해설] 선택지가 다양한 품사의 단어들로 구성되어 있으므로 문법 문제이다. be동사 are 뒤에서 customers에 대한 보어 역할을 할 단어가 필요한데, 전치사 of와 어울려야 하므로 'be appreciative of'의 구조로 '~에 감사하다'라는 의미로 쓰이는 (D) appreciative가 정답이다.

[어휘] handicapped 장애가 있는 appreciate ~에 대해 감사하다

12. 형용사의 역할: 명사 수식

모든 잡지와 신문들이 발간 날짜순으로 정리되어 있다.

[해설] 선택지가 다양한 품사의 단어들로 구성되어 있으므로 문법 문제이다. 전치사 in과 명사 order 사이에 위치한 빈칸은 명사를 수식할 형용사 자리

10. 세부사항 문제

웹페이지에 따르면, 고객들은 어떻게 음식 재료에 관한 구체적인 정보를 얻을 수 있는가?
(A) 안내 데스크에 전화함으로써
(B) 요리사와 이야기함으로써
(C) 온라인 메뉴를 읽어 봄으로써
(D) 스마트폰 앱을 다운로드함으로써

[해설] 음식 재료 관련 정보를 얻는 방법이 제시된 마지막 단락에, 요리사를 찾아 문의함으로써 음식에 들어가는 것에 관해 더 알아볼 수 있다고(~ find out more about what is in each dish by asking for the chef ~) 알리고 있다. 즉, 요리사와 이야기해야 한다는 말이므로 (B)가 정답이다.

paraphrasing asking for (이야기하기 위해) ~을 찾다 → speaking to ~와 이야기하다

[어휘] specific 구체적인, 특정한   ingredient 음식 재료, 성분

paraphrasing 정답   1. (b)   2. (a)   3. (c)

DAY 03

PART 5   문법 | 형용사

확인 문제 해석

1. 그녀는 Kim 씨의 직속상관이다.
2. 그 사교 행사는 유대 관계를 강하게 만들어 주었다.
3. 월 임대료는 감당할 만하다(가격이 적당하다).
4. 이 제품은 환경친화적인 재료로 만들어진다.
5. 그녀는 파손된 물건을 반품하고 싶어 했다.
6. 그 회사는 상당한 성장을 경험했다.
7. Texas Inn의 숙박 요금은 비싸지 않다.
8. 냉동차 안의 상하기 쉬운 제품을 안전하게 수송해 주세요.
9. 그 관리자는 설문 조사 수행을 책임지고 있다.
10. 많은 참가자들이 지역 축제에 참석할 것으로 기대된다.
11. 그 회사는 광고에 돈을 적게 쓰기로 결정했다.

연습 문제

01.(B)   02.(B)   03.(C)   04.(D)   05.(A)   06.(B)

01.

1. 선택지 보고 문법/어휘 문제 파악하기   ☑ 문법 문제   ☐ 어휘 문제
2. 빈칸 분석하기   빈칸 뒤에 있는 것   ☐ 동사   ☐ 부사   ☑ 명사
   → 빈칸에는 ☑ 형용사 ☐ 동사가 들어가야 한다.
3. 정답 선택하기   정답 (B)

여러분은 어떤 아이템도 경쟁력 있는 가격에 구입하실 수 있습니다.

02.

1. 선택지 보고 문법/어휘 문제 파악하기   ☑ 문법 문제   ☐ 어휘 문제
2. 빈칸 분석하기   빈칸 앞에 있는 것   ☑ 명사의 소유격   ☐ 명사의 복수형
   빈칸 뒤에 있는 것   ☐ 동사   ☐ 부사   ☑ 명사
   → 빈칸에는 ☑ 형용사 ☐ 동사가 들어가야 한다.
3. 정답 선택하기   정답 (B)

Trent Home Goods는 이 나라의 선도적인 주방 기기 제조업체가 되었다.

03.

1. 선택지 보고 문법/어휘 문제 파악하기   ☐ 문법 문제   ☑ 어휘 문제
2. 빈칸 분석하기   빈칸 앞에 있는 동사 (obtain)
   동사의 의미 (얻다, 획득하다)
   → 이 동사와 어울려 쓸 수 있는 명사가 정답이다.
3. 정답 선택하기   정답 (C)

회사 차량을 사용하기 위해서는 모든 직원들은 그들의 상사에게 승인을 받아야 한다.

04.

1. 선택지 보고 문법/어휘 문제 파악하기   ☑ 문법 문제   ☐ 어휘 문제
2. 빈칸 분석하기   빈칸 앞에 있는 것   ☑ 2형식 동사   ☐ 4형식 동사
   → 빈칸은 ☐ 목적어 ☑ 주격 보어 자리이다.
   → 따라서 ☑ 형용사 ☐ 동사가 와야 한다.
3. 정답 선택하기   정답 (D)

대량 생산 방식 덕분에 이제 많은 가정용품들이 일반 대중들이 구입할 수 있게 되었다.

05.

1. 선택지 보고 문법/어휘 문제 파악하기   ☑ 문법 문제   ☐ 어휘 문제
2. 빈칸 분석하기   빈칸 앞에 있는 것   ☐ 2형식 동사   ☑ 5형식 동사
   → 빈칸은 ☐ 목적어 ☑ 목적격 보어 자리이다.
   → 따라서 ☑ 형용사 ☐ 부사가 와야 한다.
3. 정답 선택하기   정답 (A)

프로선수들은 팀워크를 유지하기 위해 매일매일 연습해야 한다.

06.

1. 선택지 보고 문법/어휘 문제 파악하기   ☑ 문법 문제   ☐ 어휘 문제
2. 빈칸 분석하기   빈칸 앞에 있는 것   ☑ 2형식 동사   ☐ 4형식 동사
   → 빈칸은 ☐ 목적어 ☑ 주격 보어 자리이다.
   → 따라서 ☑ 형용사 ☐ 동사가 와야 한다.
   → 정답이 될 수 있는 후보 (B, C)
3. 정답 선택하기   정답 (B)

현금 보너스의 액수는 그들의 연간 총 매출에 달려 있다.

실전 문제

01.(C)	02.(C)	03.(D)	04.(A)	05.(C)	06.(B)
07.(C)	08.(D)	09.(A)	10.(D)	11.(D)	12.(C)
13.(D)	14.(D)	15.(C)	16.(A)	17.(B)	18.(D)
19.(A)	20.(B)	21.(B)	22.(C)	23.(B)	24.(D)

particularly 특히　waste 폐기물　founder 설립자　effect on ~에 대한 영향　lead the way in ~하는 데 있어 앞장서다　contribute to ~에 기여하다, 공헌하다　experiment 실험　focused on ~에 초점이 맞춰진　development 개발, 발전　material 자재, 재료, 물품　result in ~의 결과를 낳다　insulation 절연(재), 단열(재)　make use of ~을 활용하다　sustainable 지속 가능한　keynote address 기조 연설

05. 추론 문제

O'Donnell 씨에 관해 암시된 것은 무엇인가?
(A) 한 행사의 심사 위원이 되기 위해 신청했다.
(B) 수년간 PSD의 일원이었다.
(C) 환경 친화적인 건물을 설계했다.
(D) Cooper 씨에게 제안 사항을 제출했다.

[해설] 지문 초반부에, Making a Difference Award의 수상자로 Leah O'Donnell 씨가 선정된 사실(Leah O'Donnell as this year's recipient), 환경 지속 가능성에 기여하는 건축가에게 주는 상이라는 점(~ given annually to an architect who is dedicated to sustainability), Jenkins Bank Tower 프로젝트를 통해 상을 받았다는 점(the Jenkins Bank Tower, which won her the award) 등을 통해 그녀가 환경 친화적인 건물을 디자인했음을 알 수 있으므로 (C)가 정답이다.

[어휘] sign up 신청하다　judge 심사위원

06. 세부사항 문제

5년 전에 무슨 일이 있었는가?
(A) PSD가 일부 연구에 투자하기 시작했다.
(B) PSD가 Cooper 씨에 의해 설립되었다.
(C) O'Donnell 씨는 업계에서 주는 상을 처음 받았다.
(D) O'Donnell 씨가 Jenkins Bank에 고용되었다.

[해설] '5년 전'이라는 시점은 지문 중반부에 언급된다. 지난 5년 동안 PSD가 새로운 건설 자재 개발에 초점을 맞춘 연구와 실험에 재정적으로 기여해왔다는(~ contributing financially to key studies and experiments focused on the development ~) 말이 있는데, 이는 연구에 돈을 투자한 것이므로 (A)가 정답이다.

paraphrasing contributing financially 재정적으로 기여함 → investing 투자함

[어휘] invest in ~에 투자하다　found ~을 설립하다

07. 세부사항 문제

O'Donnell 씨는 5월에 무엇을 할 계획인가?
(A) 업계 행사에서 연설하기
(B) 새로운 자재 개발 시작하기
(C) 한 프로젝트에 필요한 자금 마련하기
(D) 온라인 강의하기

[해설] '5월'이라는 시점이 언급된 마지막 부분에, 5월에 개최되는 업계 컨퍼런스에서 그녀가 기조 연설을 한다고(her upcoming keynote address at May's industry conference) 알리고 있으므로 (A)가 정답이다.

paraphrasing keynote address 기조 연설 → speak 연설하다

[어휘] raise funds 자금을 마련하다, 모금하다

paraphrasing 정답 1. (a)　2. (c)　3. (h)

08-10은 다음 웹페이지를 참조하시오.

http://www.longoriahotel.com
Longoria 호텔에서 현재 이용 가능한 룸 서비스
Longoria 호텔에 투숙하시는 고객들께서는 이제 객실에서 편안하게 [09]저희 호텔 내 레스토랑인 Indigo의 맛있는 요리를 즐기실 수 있습니다. 이 서비스는 해당 레스토랑의 정규 영업시간 동안 이용 가능합니다. [08]불과 14.95달러의 비용만으로, 두 가지 곁들임 요리가 포함된 특별 주 요리를 드실 수 있으며, 이는 매일 다르게 제공됩니다. 또한 주 요리와 애피타이저, 그리고 디저트를 개별적으로 주문하실 수도 있습니다.

식사 비용은 객실로 청구되므로 현금을 미리 준비하실 필요가 없습니다. 바쁜 기간에는 주문하신 음식을 받기까지 시간이 더 걸린다는 점을 감안해 주시기 바랍니다. 식사를 마치신 후에는, [09]객실 문 밖의 복도에 쟁반과 접시를 놓아 두기만 하시면, Indigo 직원이 그 물품들을 회수해 갈 것입니다.

주문을 하시려면, 객실 전화로 03번을 누르시면 됩니다. [10]음식 알레르기가 있으시거나 기타 식사 관련 제약이 있으실 경우, 레스토랑에 연락하실 때 요리사를 찾아 문의하시면 각 음식에 들어가는 것에 관해 더 알아보실 수 있습니다.

on-site 구내의, 부지 내의　featured 특별한, 특징적인　entrée 주 요리　individually 개별적으로　in advance 미리, 사전에　retrieve ~을 회수하다, 되찾아 가다　place an order 주문하다　dietary 식사의　restriction 제한, 제약

08. True 문제

Longoria 호텔의 룸 서비스 식사에 관해 언급된 것은 무엇인가?
(A) 긍정적인 평가를 받았다.
(B) 24시간 이용 가능하다.
(C) 오늘의 특별 요리가 포함되어 있다.
(D) 현금으로 구입해야 한다.

[해설] 첫 단락에 매일 다르게 제공되는 특별 주 요리를 먹을 수 있다는 말이 있는데(~ get our featured entrée with two side dishes, which is different every day), 이는 '오늘의 특별 요리'를 의미하는 것이므로 (C)가 정답이다.

[어휘] favorable 긍정적인, 호의적인　rating 평가 점수, 등급　around the clock 24시간

09. 세부사항 문제

누가 호텔 고객들이 사용한 그릇을 수거할 것인가?
(A) 호텔 지배인
(B) 안내 데스크 접수 담당자
(C) 시설 관리부 직원
(D) 레스토랑 직원

[해설] 그릇 수거 방식이 언급된 두 번째 단락에, Indigo 직원이 쟁반과 접시를 회수해 간다고 되어 있는데(an Indigo employee will retrieve the items), 첫 단락에 Indigo는 호텔에 있는 레스토랑이라고(our on-site restaurant, Indigo) 쓰여 있으므로 레스토랑 직원인 (D)가 정답이다.

paraphrasing employee 직원 → staff member 직원

[어휘] receptionist 안내 직원　housekeeping 시설 관리(부)

01. 세부사항 문제

Sparrow Messaging은 사용자들이 무엇을 할 수 있게 해주는가?
(A) 인터넷에 신속히 연결하기
(B) 불필요한 소프트웨어 프로그램 삭제하기
(C) 바이러스 방지 소프트웨어에 드는 비용 절약하기
(D) 온라인 회의 동영상 촬영 및 저장하기

[해설] 첫 단락에 사용자가 누릴 수 있는 장점으로, 바로가기 (아이콘)을 채워 넣을 필요가 없다는 말과 함께(clutter ~ with shortcuts to multiple different programs) 불필요한 프로그램을 삭제하는 것이 도움이 된다고 (You will find that deleting all the unnecessary programs ~) 했으므로 (B)가 정답이다.

paraphrasing unnecessary programs 불필요한 프로그램 → unneeded software programs 불필요한 소프트웨어 프로그램

[어휘] unneeded 불필요한

02. True 문제

Sparrow Messaging에 관해 사실인 것은 무엇인가?
(A) 정기적으로 업데이트된다.
(B) 긍정적인 평가를 받았다.
(C) 고객 만족 보장 서비스를 포함한다.
(D) 장기 계약에 대해 할인을 제공한다.

[해설] 정식 버전에 관한 설명이 제시되는 맨 마지막 부분에, 무료 소프트웨어 업데이트를 매달 받는다는(You will get free monthly software updates ~) 사실이 언급되어 있으므로 이에 해당되는 (A)가 정답이다.

paraphrasing get monthly software updates 매달 소프트웨어 업데이트를 받다 → updated regularly 정기적으로 업데이트된다

[어휘] regularly 정기적으로 satisfaction 만족 guarantee 보장 long-term 장기간의 contract 계약(서)

paraphrasing 정답   1. (c)   2. (a)   3. (b)

03-04는 다음 양식을 참조하시오.

Cleveland 호텔: 이벤트 홀 예약 양식

저희 Cleveland 호텔에서 여러분의 행사를 개최하기로 결정해 주셔서 감사합니다! 저희가 귀하와 일행을 최선을 다해 모실 수 있도록 이 양식을 작성해 주시기 바랍니다. 03**요청 사항을 바탕으로 대략적인 견적서를 이메일로 보내 드리겠습니다.**

연락 담당자: _____
이메일: _____
휴대 전화: _____
행사 날짜: _____
선호하시는 홀: [ ] Diamond Ballroom   [ ] Crystal Hall
[ ] 04**Flower Garden (외부 공간)**
좌석 배치: [ ] 둥근 탁자 [ ] 강연 [ ] 결혼식 [ ] 기타: _____
대략적인 손님 숫자: _____
시청각 장비 대여 여부: [ ] 예   [ ] 아니오
고객용 객실 이용 여부: [ ] 예, 대략적으로 _____   [ ] 아니오

reservation 예약 fill out ~을 작성하다 accommodate ~을 수용하다 approximate 대략적인 estimate 견적서 based on ~에 따라, ~을 바탕으로 preference 선호(하는 것) audio/visual equipment 시청각 장비 approximately 약, 대략

03. 세부사항 문제

Cleveland 호텔 직원이 무엇을 할 것인가?
(A) 가격 견적서 발송하기
(B) 전체 행사 녹화하기
(C) 시청각 장비 수리하기
(D) 곧 있을 행사를 위한 식사 준비하기

[해설] 첫 단락에 요청 사항을 바탕으로 대략적인 견적서를 이메일로 보내 준다고 쓰여 있는데(We will e-mail an approximate estimate ~), 이는 서비스 비용과 관련된 견적서를 의미하므로 (A)가 정답이다.

paraphrasing approximate estimate 대략적인 견적서 → price quote 가격 견적서

[어휘] price quote 가격 견적서 videotape ~을 녹화하다 entire 전체의

04. 추론 문제

Cleveland 호텔에 관해 암시된 것은 무엇인가?
(A) 최근에 개장했다.
(B) 야외 행사를 주최한다.
(C) 몇몇 출장 요리 선택권을 제공한다.
(D) 대규모 단체 고객들에게 할인을 제공한다.

[해설] 지문 중반부의 항목들 중에서, 행사 장소의 하나인 Flower Garden이 외부 공간이라고(outside) 쓰여 있으므로 야외 행사도 주최한다는 사실을 알 수 있다. 따라서 이를 언급한 (B)가 정답이다.

paraphrasing outside 외부의 → outdoor 야외의

[어휘] catering 출장 요리 제공(업)

paraphrasing 정답   1. (c)   2. (b)   3. (a)

05-07은 다음 기사를 참조하시오.

PSD, 권위 있는 상을 시상하다
Carolyn Hewitt 작성

2월 15일 — The Partnership for Sustainable Design(PSD)이 05**Making a Difference Award의 올해 수상자로 Leah O'Donnell** 씨를 선정했다. 이 상은 환경의 지속 가능성에 기여하고 있는 건축가에게 해마다 주어진다. O'Donnell 씨는 이 단체가 이상적으로 여기는 인물의 훌륭한 본보기였으며, 특히 05**그녀에게 수상의 영광을 안겨준 최근의 프로젝트 Jenkins Bank Tower**를 통해 그러한 모습이 드러났다. "저희 PSD는 새로운 건물들이 새로운 폐기물을 만들어 낼 필요가 없다고 생각합니다"라고 PSD의 설립자이자 대표인 Andre Cooper 씨가 말했다. PSD는 건설 업계가 환경에 미치는 영향을 최소화하기 위해 20년 동안 노력해 왔다. 06**지난 5년 동안, PSD는 새로운 건설 자재 개발에 초점을 맞춘 주요 연구와 실험에 재정적으로 기여하는** 일에 앞장서 왔다. 그와 같은 한 가지 프로젝트에서는 재활용 플라스틱 병으로 만들어진 독특한 유형의 절연재 개발이라는 결과를 낳았다. O'Donnell 씨는 Jenkins Bank Tower 건물 전체에 걸쳐 이 자재를 활용했으며, 심지어 환경적으로 지속 가능한 건축 자재에 관해 웹에 기반을 둔 강의를 하기도 했다. 이 주제는 뉴욕에서 07**5월에 개최되는 업계 콘퍼런스에서 있을 그녀의 기조 연설**에서도 반복해서 언급될 것으로 예상된다.

present ~을 주다, 제시하다 prestigious 권위 있는 recipient 수상자 sustainability 환경 지속 가능성 ideal 이상적인 인물

그 기간 동안은, 거리에 주차하시거나 길 건너편에 있는 주차장을 이용하실 것을 요청드립니다. 작업 기간 동안 발생하는 주차 비용은 관리실에 모든 영수증을 제출하시면 다음 달 임대료에서 차감될 것입니다.

이곳 The Lofts의 시설을 개선시키는 것이 기대가 됩니다.

Sharon Lowery

Q. Lowery 씨는 누구겠는가?
(A) 공사 근로자
(B) 건물 관리인
(C) 경비원
(D) 배달 운전 기사

참여자 자체를 포함한다. **사전 등록이 권장되지만, 행사 당일 달릴 준비가 되어 나타나는 사람도 참가가 허용된다.** 더 많은 정보를 위해서, www.run4acure.com의 이벤트 웹 사이트를 참조하면 된다.

host 개최하다   charity event 자선행사   raise money 기금을 모으다   participate in ~에 참가하다   donation 기부   advance registration 사전 등록

Q. 행사에 대한 사실이 아닌 것은?
(A) 참가자는 자신의 후원자를 찾아야 한다.
(B) 참가자는 사전에 등록하여야 한다.

[문제 키워드] What / NOT true / event

[해설] about 뒤의 키워드 the event가 지문의 전체적인 소재이므로 지문 전반에서 단서를 찾아 각 선택지와 비교해야 한다. 지문 중반 이후 사전 등록이 권장되지만 행사 당일 달릴 준비가 되어 나타나는 사람도 참가가 허용된다는(Advance registration is encouraged, but those who show up ready to run on the day of the event will also be allowed to participate in the run) 말이 있으므로 (B)가 정답이다. 앞부분에 참가자들이 후원자를 찾도록 요청받는다는(are asked to find sponsors to agree to make a donation) 말이 있으므로 (A)는 지문 내용과 일치한다.

 연습 문제

01.(B)   02.(B)

01.

Luciano Romani (오전 9:05)	안녕하세요, 저는 Tidwell Communications에 근무하는 기술자 Luciano Romani입니다. 오늘 초고속 인터넷 선을 설치하기 위해 귀하의 자택을 방문할 예정입니다. 오후 4시와 6시 사이에 누가 계신가요?
Theresa Harrison (오전 9:08)	네. 제가 준비해야 하는 특별한 것이라도 있나요?
Luciano Romani (오전 9:09)	가구와 기타 물품들을 벽에서 치워주시기만 하시면 됩니다. 그리고, 다른 기사 한 명이 저와 함께 갈 것입니다. 이 기사는 신입 사원들을 대상으로 하는 저희 현장 경험 프로그램에 참여 중입니다.
Theresa Harrison (오전 9:10)	그건 괜찮습니다.

install ~을 설치하다   be cleared away from ~로부터 치워지다   on-the-job 현장의   new hire 신입 사원

Q. Romani 씨의 동료 직원에 관해 언급된 것은 무엇인가?
(A) 일정 관리상의 착오를 일으켰다.
(B) 교육 과정을 밟는 중이다.

[문제 키워드] What / mentioned / Mr. Romani's coworker

[해설] about 뒤의 키워드가 Mr. Romani's coworker이므로 Romani의 메시지에서 단서를 찾을 수 있다. 9시 9분 메시지에 신입 사원이 받아야 하는 현장 경험 프로그램 때문에 기사 한 명이 같이 간다고(~ another technician will be with me. He's part of our on-the-job experience program for new hires) 언급하고 있는데, 이는 그 기사가 교육을 받는 중이라는 뜻이므로 (B)가 정답이다.

[어휘] undergo ~을 거치다, 겪다   process 과정

02.

치료를 위해 뛰다

5월 8일 — Stockbridge College는 암 연구를 위한 기금을 마련하기 위해 이번 달 말에 특별한 자선 행사를 개최할 것이다. 이 행사에 참여하기를 원하는 사람들은 그들이 달리는 매 마일마다 기부하는 것에 동의할 후원자를 찾도록 요청받는다. 스폰서는 기업 또는 개인이 될 수 있으며,

실전 문제

01.(B)   02.(A)   03.(A)   04.(B)   05.(C)   06.(A)
07.(A)   08.(C)   09.(D)   10.(B)

01-02는 다음 온라인 광고를 참조하시오.

Sparrow Messaging

Sparrow Messaging(SM)은 안전한 메신저 소프트웨어 프로그램으로서 다른 메신저 서비스들에 비해 여러 장점들을 제공합니다. SM은 다양한 기능을 수행하기 때문에, 사용자들께서는 업무용 컴퓨터의 바탕화면에 여러 가지 다른 프로그램들의 ⁰¹바로가기 (아이콘)을 채워 넣으실 필요가 없습니다. 여러분의 업무용 컴퓨터에서 불필요한 모든 프로그램들을 삭제하는 것이 더욱 효율적으로 컴퓨터를 가동하는 데 도움이 된다는 사실을 알게 되실 것입니다.

SM의 기능들: 그저 인터넷에 연결만 하면
– 안전하게 메시지를 주고받을 수 있습니다
– 어떠한 크기나 유형의 파일도 전송하실 수 있습니다
– 다자 간 통화 연결이 가능합니다
– 화상 회의에 참여하실 수 있습니다

지금 SM을 사용해 보십시오!

체험판(무료): 여기를 클릭하세요
SM 설치 프로그램을 다운로드해 SM 체험판을 이용해 보십시오. 하지만 이 버전에서는 일부 기능을 이용할 수 없다는 점에 유의하시기 바랍니다.

정식 오피스 버전(매달 7.99달러): 여기를 클릭하세요
SM의 모든 기능을 이용하실 수 있습니다. ⁰²향상된 보안 기능이 포함된 무료 소프트웨어 업데이트를 매달 받게 될 것입니다.

secure 안전한   benefit 장점, 혜택   perform ~을 수행하다   function 기능(= feature)   clutter A with B A를 B로 채워 넣다   shortcut 지름길, 바로가기 (아이콘)   run 가동되다, 운영되다   efficiently 효율적으로   transfer ~을 전송하다   multi-party 다수의   video conference 화상 회의   trial version 체험판   be aware that ~라는 점에 유의하다, 주목하다

02. 알맞은 문장 고르기

(A) 특정 약품과 치료제는 이용하지 못할 수도 있습니다.
(B) 의료 전문가들의 명단은 회사 웹사이트에서 찾아보실 수 있습니다.
(C) 모든 직원들은 서명하기 전에 보험 증서를 철저히 검토해봐야 합니다.
(D) 일단 승인되고 나면, 의료 지출 비용이 매달 1일에 환급될 것입니다.

[해설] 앞 문장에 보험 신청서를 승인받는 방법이 제시되어 있으므로 이 문장과 연계되는 내용을 골라야 한다. 승인 이후에 발생되는 일로서 의료 비용 환급 조치를 언급한 (D)가 정답이다.

[어휘] certain 특정한 medication 약(품) treatment 치료(제) professional 전문가 insurance policy 보험 증서 thoroughly 철저히 once 일단 ~하면 expense 지출 비용 reimburse ~을 환급해 주다

03. 동사의 형태

[해설] 문장 전체의 동사 believe 바로 뒤에 위치한 빈칸에 또 다른 동사 keep이 쓰이려면 준동사가 되어야 하므로 동명사의 형태인 (B) keeping이 정답이다. 참고로, 빈칸에서 healthy까지는 believe의 목적어 역할을 하는 that절(that은 생략) 내의 주어에 해당된다.

04. 동사 어휘

[해설] 직원들에게 건강을 잘 유지하도록 요청하는 문장이 되어야 적절하므로 '~하도록 각별한 주의가 요구되다, ~하도록 촉구되다' 등을 의미하는 be urged to부정사 구문을 만드는 (C) urged가 정답이다.

[어휘] appeal (to) (~의) 관심을 끌다 rotate 교대로 하다, 교대 근무를 하다 house ~에 공간을 제공하다, (건물 등이) ~을 보유하다

05-08은 다음 공지를 참조하시오.

> [05]우리 St. Louis Manufacturing은 본사 공장의 효율성에 크게 중점을 두고 있습니다. 전체 생산 공정은 폐기물과 시간을 감소시킬 수 있도록 설계되어 있습니다. 하지만 개선의 여지가 더 남아 있을 수 있으므로, 직원들은 추천 사항들이 생각날 경우에 얘기해 주셔야 합니다. [06]생산 라인 책임자와 얘기를 나누거나 사무실 옆에 위치한 건의함을 활용해 그렇게 할 수 있습니다. [07]유용한 아이디어를 제공하는 직원들은 매 분기 마지막 날에 보너스를 받게 될 것입니다. 그 액수는 그 아이디어가 이곳 공장의 업무 환경이나 생산성을 얼마나 효과적으로 향상시킬 수 있는지를 바탕으로 할 것입니다. [08]또한, 해당 직원의 사진도 휴게실의 Wall of Brilliance에 게시될 것입니다.

put a strong emphasis on ~에 크게 중점을 두다 efficiency 효율성 entire 전체의 process 공정, 과정 be designed to부정사 ~하도록 설계되다, 고안되다 wasted materials 폐기물 room for improvement 개선의 여지 line manager (생산, 조립 등의) 라인 책임자 suggestion box 건의함 be based on ~을 바탕으로 하다, 기반으로 하다 effectiveness 효과(성) improve ~을 향상시키다 conditions (작업 등의) 환경

05. 명사 어휘

[해설] 전치사 at의 목적어로서 이 공지가 전달되는 곳을 가리키는 명사가 빈칸에 필요한데, 지문 후반부에 해당 장소를 지칭하는 here at the plant와 연계되어야 하므로 '공장'을 뜻하는 또 다른 명사인 (D) factory가 정답이다.

06. 동사의 형태

[해설] 빈칸 뒤에 or로 연결된 동사 use와 마찬가지로 명령문 형태로 요청하는 의미가 되어야 알맞으므로 동사 원형인 (D) Speak가 정답이다.

07. 알맞은 문장 고르기

(A) 그렇게 하는 직원들은 공장 직원 안내서에 기재됩니다.
(B) 경영진은 직원 휴게실을 개조할 계획입니다.
(C) 최첨단 기술이 우리 조립 라인마다 활용되고 있습니다.
(D) 유용한 아이디어를 제공하는 직원들은 매 분기 마지막 날에 보너스를 받게 될 것입니다.

[해설] 빈칸 뒤에 부연 설명으로 제시된 문장의 주어 Its amount(액수)가 가리킬 수 있는 대상이 포함된 문장이 필요하므로 아이디어 채택에 따른 보상으로 보너스 지급을 언급한 (D)가 정답이다. (A)도 일종의 보상 혜택으로 볼 수는 있지만 Its amount에 해당되는 것이 없으므로 오답이다.

[어휘] handbook 안내서 break room 휴게실 cutting edge 최첨단의 assembly 조립

08. 접속부사

[해설] 사진이 게시되는 것은 앞선 문장에 언급된 보너스 지급 외의 추가 혜택에 해당되므로 '또한' 등의 의미로 추가 정보를 언급할 때 사용하는 접속부사 (B) Also가 정답이다.

[어휘] hence 따라서, 그런 이유로 otherwise 그렇지 않으면, 그 외에는 similarly 유사하게

PART 7 True·Not True 문제/추론 문제

01. True·Not True 문제
풀이 방법 해석

> Wright Hardware는 이제 Mason 브랜드 전동 공구를 취급합니다! Mason 브랜드 제품을 구매할 때 어느 Wright Hardware 지점에서든 본 쿠폰을 제시하면 10% 할인 혜택을 받을 수 있습니다!
>
> *다른 브랜드에는 적용되지 않습니다.
> *오퍼는 3월 1일에 만료됩니다.

Q. 쿠폰에 대한 설명으로 사실인 것은?
(A) 3월까지 유효하다.
(B) 온라인 구매 시 사용할 수 있다.
(C) 특정 브랜드에서만 사용할 수 있다.
(D) 고객당 1개 품목에 한하여 적용된다.

02. 추론 문제
풀이 방법 해석

> 수신: m.jones@nmail.net
> 발신: s.lowery@thelofts.org
> 제목: 유지보수
>
> 주민 여러분들께
>
> The Lofts의 주차장이 이달 말에 재포장되고 다시 페인트칠 될 것입니다. 작업은 8월 15일 금요일에 시작해서 8월 17일 일요일에 끝날 것입니다.

PART 6 뒤의 내용이 단서인 명사 어휘

풀이 방법 해석

이곳 Dole Tech에서는, 만족이 최우선 순위입니다. 그게 저희 회사가 고객들을 만족시켜 드리는 제품을 개발하기 위해 노력하는 이유입니다. 설문조사가 수시로 시행되고, 포커스 집단 조사가 매달 개최됩니다. 각각의 결과는 저희의 주간 사보에 실립니다. 이 절차가 직원 여러분들 각자가 새 제품, 디자인, 그리고 특징에 대한 혁신적이고 인기 있는 아이디어를 떠올리도록 돕기를 바랍니다. 여러분들 모두가 우리가 그 목표를 성취할 수 있도록 돕는 그 어떤 것이라도 제출하도록 권장하는 바입니다.

연습 문제

01.(A) 02.(B) 03.(B) 04.(A)

01.

Jefferson 씨께,
곧 떠나실 귀하의 여행과 관련된 일부 세부 사항들을 제공해 드리고자 합니다. 귀하께서는 시애틀까지 Golden Air를 이용하실 것이며, 귀하의 항공편은 월요일 오전 8시에 출발합니다. 셔틀 버스를 이용해 공항에서 호텔까지 이동하시게 됩니다.

details 세부사항 **regarding** ~에 관하여 **upcoming** 곧 있을, 다가오는 **leave** 출발하다, 떠나다

[단서] take Golden Air to Seattle, flight will leave

[해설] 다음 문장에 항공편 목적지와 출발 시간 정보가 제시된 것으로 보아 여행 일정을 알려주는 내용임을 알 수 있으므로 '여행, 출장' 등을 뜻하는 (A) travel이 정답이다.

02.

Moyer 씨께,
저희는 지난 주문의 지연 문제에 대한 귀하의 불만 사항을 접수했습니다. 저희 창고들 중의 하나를 심각하게 강타한 예기치 못한 폭풍으로 인해, 저희는 귀하의 주문품을 제때 발송할 수 없었습니다. 귀하의 주문 사항을 가능한 한 빨리 완료하기 위해 저희가 할 수 있는 최선을 다하고 있습니다.

complaint 불평, 불만 **order** 주문(품) **unexpected** 예기치 못한 **severely** 심하게, 혹독하게 **warehouse** 창고 **ship out** ~을 발송하다 **on time** 제때

[단서] we were not able to ship out your order on time

[해설] 다음 문장에 제때 주문품을 발송하지 못한 일이 언급된 것으로 보아 지연 문제에 대한 불만이 제기되었음을 알 수 있으므로 '지연, 지체'를 의미하는 (B) delay가 정답이다.

[어휘] defect 결함

03.

Hattiesburg Daily (11월 19일) — 해티스버그의 Marilyn Ellis 시장은 시의 대중교통망의 확대를 유청했다. Ellis 시장은 더 많은 버스와 노선들이 특히 교통 혼잡 시간대에 도로 위의 차량 운전자 수를 감소시키는 데 도움이 될 것이라고 생각하고 있다.

call for ~을 요청하다 **decrease** ~을 감소시키다 **the number of** ~의 수 **particularly** 특히 **rush hour** 교통 혼잡 시간대

[단서] more buses and routes

[해설] 다음 문장에 더 많은 버스와 노선들을 통해 교통 문제를 해결하려 한다는 말이 있는데, 이는 교통 시스템의 확대를 의미하는 것이므로 '확대, 확장'을 뜻하는 (B) expansion이 정답이다.

[어휘] obligation 의무

04.

카터스빌 — 지역 주민들이 Cartersville Pizzeria에서 곧 있을 배달 정책 변경에 기뻐하고 있습니다. 유명한 이 피자 전문점은 어떤 배달 기사도 정식으로 고용한 적이 없었지만, Home Service 사와 거래 계약을 이뤄냈으며, 이 업체가 주문품을 여러분의 집 앞까지 곧장 가져다 드릴 것입니다.

resident 주민 **policy** 정책, 방침 **work out** ~을 이뤄내다, 해결하다 **deal** 거래, 계약 **directly to** ~로 곧장

[단서] drivers, bring orders directly to your front door

[해설] 다음 문장에 한 업체를 고용해 배달 서비스를 제공하려는 계획이 언급된 것으로 보아 배달 정책의 변경을 말하는 내용임을 알 수 있으므로 '배달'을 뜻하는 (A) delivery가 정답이다.

실전 문제

01.(B) 02.(D) 03.(B) 04.(C) 05.(D) 06.(D)
07.(D) 08.(B)

01-04는 다음 공지를 참조하시오.

[01]Rosa 산업은 직원들을 가장 중시하는 것으로 잘 알려진 곳입니다. 우리 경영진은 직원들의 배우자와 자녀들을 위한 비용을 전액 부담하는 새로운 의료 보험 패키지를 포함시키기로 결정을 내렸습니다. 모든 보험 신청서는 승인을 받을 수 있도록 인사부로 송부되어야 합니다. [02]일단 승인되고 나면, 의료 지출 비용이 매달 1일에 환급될 것입니다. [03]우리는 소속 직원들과 그들이 사랑하는 사람들의 건강을 유지하는 것이 시간이 지남에 따라 더욱 더 회사의 생산성을 증대시킬 것이라 믿습니다. [04]모든 직원들은 스스로와 가족들, 그리고 회사를 위해 각자의 건강을 유지하도록 각별한 주의가 요구됩니다.

management 경영진 **medical insurance** 의료 보험 **fully cover** ~에 대한 비용을 전액 부담하다 **spouse** 배우자 **claim** 신청(서) **be forwarded to** ~로 전송되다, 보내지다 **personnel department** 인사부 **productivity** 생산성 **maintain** ~을 유지하다 **for the sake of** ~을 위해서

01. 명사 어휘

[해설] 다음 단락에 제시되는 내용(our workers and their loved ones ~)을 통해 지문에서 언급하는 의료 보험 서비스가 회사 내 직원들을 위한 것임을 알 수 있으므로 putting과 first 사이에 위치해 가장 중시하는 대상을 나타낼 명사로 적합한 (B) employees가 정답이다.

[어휘] donor 기부자 faculty (대학의) 교수진

맞으므로 소유대명사 (D) theirs가 정답이다.

[어휘] ensure that ~인지 확실히 하다, 반드시 ~하도록 하다 takeout order 포장 주문(품)

15. 재귀대명사: 강조 용법

그가 영업 경험이 가장 많기 때문에, Rolle 씨는 직접 그 VIP 고객을 응대하기로 결정했다.

[해설] 선택지가 다양한 인칭대명사로 구성되어 있으므로 문법 문제이다. 전치사 with의 목적어 the VIP client 다음이자 문장 맨 마지막에 위치한 빈칸은 부사처럼 부가적인 요소가 필요한 자리이다. 따라서 부사적으로 쓰여 강조 용법으로 사용되는 재귀대명사 (D) himself가 정답이다.

[어휘] sales 영업, 판매(량) deal with ~을 대하다, 처리하다

16. 복합 명사

Carson City에서 곧 있을 자원 봉사 활동들이 그 도시의 웹사이트에 게시되어 있다.

[해설] 선택지가 다양한 품사의 단어로 구성되어 있으므로 문법 문제이다. 명사 volunteer 단독으로는 형용사 upcoming의 수식을 받기에 의미상 부족하므로 '자원 봉사 활동'이라는 복합 명사를 구성하는 또 다른 명사 (C) activities가 정답이다.

[어휘] upcoming 곧 있을, 다가오는 active 활동적인, 적극적인 activate ~을 활성화하다 activation 활성화

17. 사람 명사 vs. 사물 명사

연구 보조금 신청자들은 그 연구 센터의 웹사이트에서 각자의 상황을 확인할 수 있다.

[해설] 선택지가 다양한 품사의 단어들로 구성되어 있으므로 문법 문제이다. 바로 뒤에 위치한 for 전치사구의 수식을 받음과 동시에 동사 can check의 주어 역할을 할 명사가 필요한데, can check의 주체는 사람이어야 하므로 사람 명사인 (D) Applicants가 정답이다.

[어휘] grant 보조금 status (진행상의) 상황 application 신청(서), 지원(서), 적용, 응용 apply 신청하다, 지원하다, ~을 적용하다 applicant 신청자, 지원자

18. 재귀대명사: 재귀 용법

새로 고용된 직원들은 그들이 여러 컴퓨터 소프트웨어 프로그램에 익숙해질 수 있도록 기회를 얻는다.

[해설] 선택지가 다양한 인칭대명사로 구성되어 있으므로 문법 문제이다. 빈칸은 to familiarize의 목적어 자리인데, 이 목적어로 쓰일 대명사가 주어 newly hired workers를 가리켜야 어울린다. 따라서 행위 주체와 대상이 동일할 때 사용하는 재귀대명사 (C) themselves가 정답이다.

[어휘] familiarize oneself with ~에 익숙해지다, ~을 익히다

19. 명사 어휘

부품 비용과 관련된 모든 부분은 계약서의 조항에 따라 제조사에 의해 충당될 것이다.

[해설] 선택지가 다양한 명사로 이루어져 있으므로 명사 어휘 문제이다. 전치사 under의 목적어로서 계약서상의 내용과 관련된 명사가 빈칸에 들어가야 알맞으므로 '조항, 조건' 등을 의미하는 (B) terms가 정답이다.

[어휘] related 관련된 cover (비용 등) ~을 충당하다 manufacturer 제조사 under the terms of ~의 조항에 따라 stretch (도로 등의) 긴 구간, (지속되는) 기간

20. 인칭대명사 구분: 목적격 vs. 소유대명사

내 친구 중 한 명이 도쿄 국제공항에서 우리를 차로 데리러 올 것이다.

[해설] 선택지가 다양한 인칭대명사로 구성되어 있으므로 문법 문제이다. 전치사 of 뒤에 위치한 빈칸은 of의 목적어 자리인데, a friend of와 결합해 '내 친구 중의 한 명'이라는 의미를 나타낼 때는 소유대명사를 사용하므로 (D) mine이 정답이다.

[어휘] pick up ~을 차로 데리러 가다

21. 명사 어휘

Harris는 다가오는 무역 박람회에 대비해 회사 안내 책자를 업데이트할 것이다.

[해설] 선택지가 다양한 명사로 이루어져 있으므로 명사 어휘 문제이다. 빈칸 앞뒤에 각각 위치한 전치사 in, for와 어울리는 명사가 필요하므로 '~에 대비해'라는 의미를 나타낼 때 사용하는 (C) preparation이 정답이다.

[어휘] brochure 안내 책자 trade fair 무역 박람회 deliberation 심사숙고 reduction 감소, 할인 reputation 명성, 평판

22. 재귀대명사: 재귀 용법

고용 계약서는 동료들끼리 서로 각자의 연봉을 이야기할 수 없다는 점을 명시하고 있다.

[해설] 선택지가 다양한 인칭대명사로 구성되어 있으므로 문법 문제이다. 전치사 among의 목적어 자리인 빈칸에 쓰일 대명사는 that절의 주어 coworkers를 가리켜야 알맞으므로 주어와 전치사의 목적어가 동일할 때 사용하는 재귀대명사 (A) themselves가 정답이다.

[어휘] employment contract 고용 계약서 specify that ~임을 명시하다 coworker 동료 직원 among themselves 자기들끼리

23. 명사 어휘

인사부장은 지난달에 열정적으로 신입 사원들을 위한 오리엔테이션을 진행했다.

[해설] 선택지가 다양한 명사로 이루어져 있으므로 명사 어휘 문제이다. 빈칸 앞에 위치한 전치사 with와 어울려 오리엔테이션을 진행한 방법을 나타낼 수 있는 명사가 필요하므로 '열정적으로'라는 의미를 구성할 때 사용하는 (A) enthusiasm이 정답이다.

[어휘] HR manager 인사부장 lead ~을 진행하다, 이끌다 expense 지출 (비용) objection 이의, 반대 assurance 장담, 확언

24. 명사 어휘

공장 책임자들은 새로운 안전 규정의 준수 여부를 확실히 해두기 위해 조립 라인을 둘러봐야 한다.

[해설] 선택지가 다양한 명사로 이루어져 있으므로 명사 어휘 문제이다. 빈칸 뒤에 위치한 전치사 with와 어울리는 명사로서 안전 규정과 관련해 조립 라인을 둘러 보는 이유를 나타낼 수 있는 명사가 필요하므로 '준수, 따름' 등을 의미하는 (A) compliance가 정답이다.

[어휘] assembly 조립 ensure ~을 확실히 해두다 compliance with ~에 대한 준수, 따름 regulation 규정, 규제

[어휘] commute 통근하다 the majority of ~의 대부분, 대다수 in favor of ~을 찬성하는, ~에 호의적인 add ~을 추가하다

04. 인칭대명사 구분: 소유격

Walker 씨가 비즈니스 목적으로 파리에 갈 때마다, 자신의 통역사를 동반할 것이다.

[해설] 선택지가 다양한 인칭대명사로 구성되어 있으므로 문법 문제이다. 전치사 by와 목적어로 쓰인 명사 interpreter 사이에 위치한 빈칸은 명사 interpreter를 수식해야 하므로 이 역할이 가능한 소유격 대명사 (A) her가 정답이다.

[어휘] be accompanied by ~을 동반하다 interpreter 통역사

05. 명사 어휘

숙박 기간 중에 무제한으로 실내 수영장과 피트니스 센터를 이용하실 수 있습니다.

[해설] 선택지가 다양한 명사로 이루어져 있으므로 명사 어휘 문제이다. 빈칸 앞에 위치한 동사 have, 뒤에 위치한 'to+장소 명사구'와 어울려 '~을 이용할 수 있다'라는 의미를 구성할 때 사용하는 (A) access가 정답이다.

[어휘] rate 요금, 속도, 비율 policy 정책 charge 청구(액)

06. 재귀대명사: 강조 용법

Miller 씨는 무료 제품이나 유급 휴가 또는 현금 보너스 중에서 직접 휴가 보상을 선택하도록 허용되었다.

[해설] 선택지가 다양한 인칭대명사로 구성되어 있으므로 문법 문제이다. 주어 Mr. Miller와 동사 was allowed 사이에 위치한 빈칸은 부사처럼 부가적인 요소에 해당되는 단어가 필요한 자리이다. 따라서 부사적으로 쓰여 강조를 나타낼 때 사용하는 재귀대명사 (D) himself가 정답이다.

[어휘] reward 보상 paid day off 유급 휴무(일)

07. 재귀대명사: 재귀 용법

그 자체로도 가격이 합리적인 UPhone 스마트폰은 장기 서비스 약정을 할 경우 큰 폭으로 할인된다.

[해설] 선택지가 다양한 인칭대명사로 구성되어 있으므로 문법 문제이다. by의 목적어 자리인 빈칸에 쓰일 대명사는 주어 UPhone smartphones를 가리키므로 주어와 전치사의 목적어가 동일할 때 사용하는 재귀대명사 (B) themselves가 정답이다.

[어휘] affordable 합리적인 가격의 greatly 크게, 대단히, 매우 service plan 서비스 약정

08. 사람 명사 vs. 사물 명사

Dustin Flooring에서 함께 일하는 동료 직원들은 Sean Reynolds 씨가 부서장으로 승진할만한 자격이 있었다는 데 동의한다.

[해설] 선택지가 다양한 품사의 단어들로 구성되어 있으므로 문법 문제이다. 정관사 the와 전치사 to 사이에 위치한 빈칸은 the의 수식을 받을 명사 자리인데, deserved(~을 받을 자격이 있다)의 목적어가 될 수 있는 것은 사물 명사이므로 (B) promotion이 정답이다.

[어휘] fellow 동료; 동료의, 같은 처지의 supervisor 부서장, 상사 promotion 승진 promoter (행사 등의) 기획자 promote ~을 승진시키다

09. 명사 어휘

Scott 씨는 사무실 임대 계약서를 마지막 순간에 수정하고 싶어했다.

[해설] 선택지가 다양한 명사로 이루어져 있으므로 명사 어휘 문제이다. 동사 make의 목적어로 쓰일 수 있으면서 빈칸 뒤에 위치한 전치사 to와 어울려 '~을 수정하다'라는 의미를 구성할 때 사용하는 (D) modification이 정답이다.

[어휘] make a modification to ~을 수정하다 last-minute 마지막 순간의 agreement 계약(서), 합의(서) obligation 의무 admission 입장(료), 입학 (허가)

10. 인칭대명사 구분: 주격

McBride 씨가 프로젝트 팀장으로 임명되었는데, 그가 처음에 아이디어를 제안했기 때문이다.

[해설] 선택지가 다양한 인칭대명사로 구성되어 있으므로 문법 문제이다. 접속사 since와 동사 proposed 사이에 위치한 빈칸은 since절의 주어 자리이므로 주격 대명사 (B) he가 정답이다.

[어휘] be named A A로 임명되다 initially 처음에, 최초로 propose ~을 제안하다

11. 부정대명사

연구 보고서가 무슨 주제에 관해 쓰여지든 상관없이, 모든 것은 동료 집단에 의해 검토되어야 한다.

[해설] 선택지가 대명사와 형용사로 구성되어 있으므로 문법 문제이다. 동사 should be reviewed 앞에 위치한 빈칸은 주어 자리이며, 앞서 언급된 research papers 전체를 가리켜야 알맞으므로 '모든 것'을 뜻하는 대명사 (B) all이 정답이다. (A) other와 (D) every는 형용사이고, (C) both는 대명사이기는 하지만 두 가지를 가리킬 때 사용한다.

[어휘] regardless of ~에 상관없이 peer 동료, 또래

12. 인칭대명사 구분: 목적격 vs. 소유대명사

Body Ball은 짧고 간단한 운동을 통해 근육을 키우고 지방을 태워 몸을 탄력 있게 만들도록 도와드릴 수 있습니다.

[해설] 선택지가 다양한 인칭대명사로 구성되어 있으므로 문법 문제이다. 동사 help는 'help+목적어+원형 부정사'의 구조로 사용하므로 목적격 대명사 (A) you가 정답이다. '당신의 것'을 뜻하는 소유대명사 (B) yours는 의미가 맞지 않으며, 주어와 동사의 목적어가 서로 다르므로 재귀대명사도 빈칸에 쓰일 수 없다.

[어휘] tone ~을 탄력 있게 만들다 workout 운동

13. 인칭대명사 구분: 소유격

두 교사들이 그들의 자원 봉사 활동에 대해 지역 리더십 시상식에서 표창받았다.

[해설] 선택지가 다양한 인칭대명사로 구성되어 있으므로 문법 문제이다. 전치사 for와 for의 목적어로 쓰인 명사구 volunteer work 사이에 위치한 빈칸은 명사구를 수식해야 하므로 이 역할이 가능한 소유격 대명사 (B) their가 정답이다.

[어휘] recognize ~을 표창하다, 인정하다 volunteer 자원 봉사

14. 인칭대명사 구분: 목적격 vs. 소유대명사

카페 고객들은 나가기 전에 포장 주문품이 자신의 것인지 확실히 하기 위해 영수증에 적힌 주문 번호를 확인해야 한다.

[해설] 선택지가 다양한 인칭대명사로 구성되어 있으므로 문법 문제이다. be동사 is 뒤에 위치한 빈칸은 that절의 주어 takeout order를 설명하는 보어 자리이다. 따라서 '포장 주문품 = 그들의 것'이라는 의미가 되어야 알

DAY 02

PART 5 문법 | 대명사

확인 문제 해석

1. 그들은 행사에 참여하도록 요청받는다.
2. Park 씨는 그녀의 소포를 속달 우편으로 보낼 것이다.
3. 저는 당신의 것을 제외하고 팀원 대부분의 휴가 신청서를 받았습니다.
4. 그들은 매장을 청결하고 깔끔하게 유지하는 데 헌신했다.
5. Olson 씨는 혼자서 문제를 해결했다.
6. 우리 신차는 다른 자동차 제조사들의 것보다 더 연료 효율이 높다.
7. 1년 회원권을 가진 분들께는 주간 뉴스레터를 보내 드립니다.
8. 몇몇은 새로운 사무실 건물로 이동하기로 되어 있다.
9. 후보자들 중 아무도 자격이 없다.
10. 악천후로 인해 많은 오전 항공편이 결항되었다.

연습 문제

01. (A) 02. (C) 03. (D) 04. (D) 05. (D) 06. (A)

01.
1. 선택지 보고 문법/어휘 문제 파악하기 ☑ 문법 문제 ☐ 어휘 문제
2. 빈칸 분석하기 빈칸 뒤에 있는 것 ☐ 명사 ☑ 동사 ☐ 부사
   → 빈칸에는 ☑ 주어 ☐ 목적어 역할을 할 수 있는 것이 들어가야 한다.
3. 정답 선택하기 정답 (A)

그는 가능한 최상의 서비스를 제공하는 데 전념한다.

02.
1. 선택지 보고 문법/어휘 문제 파악하기 ☑ 문법 문제 ☐ 어휘 문제
2. 빈칸 분석하기 빈칸 뒤에 있는 것 ☑ 명사 ☐ 동사 ☐ 전치사
   → 빈칸에는 ☐ 목적격 대명사 ☑ 소유격 대명사가 들어가야 한다.
3. 정답 선택하기 정답 (C)

오늘 우리의 점심 식사 메뉴는 채소가 곁들여진 구운 연어입니다.

03.
1. 선택지 보고 문법/어휘 문제 파악하기 ☑ 문법 문제 ☐ 어휘 문제
2. 빈칸 분석하기 빈칸 뒤에 있는 것 ☐ 명사 ☑ 동사 ☐ 부사
   → 빈칸에는 ☑ 주어 ☐ 목적어 역할을 할 수 있는 것이 들어가야 한다.
3. 정답 선택하기 정답 (D)

예전의 태블릿이 더 가볍긴 하지만, 내 것은 배터리 수명이 더 길다.

04.
1. 선택지 보고 문법/어휘 문제 파악하기 ☑ 문법 문제 ☐ 어휘 문제
2. 빈칸 분석하기 빈칸 앞에 있는 것 ☑ 완전한 문장 ☐ 불완전한 문장
   → 빈칸에는 ☐ 소유격 대명사 ☑ 재귀대명사가 들어가야 한다.
3. 정답 선택하기 정답 (D)

Sanders 씨는 가능한 판매업체들에 직접 연락하길 원했다.

05.
1. 선택지 보고 문법/어휘 문제 파악하기 ☑ 문법 문제 ☐ 어휘 문제
2. 빈칸 분석하기 빈칸 뒤에 있는 것 ☐ 명사 ☑ 관계대명사 ☐ 인칭대명사
   → 빈칸에는 ☑ 선행사 역할을 하는 것 ☐ 지시사 역할을 하는 것이 들어가야 한다.
3. 정답 선택하기 정답 (D)

이 좌석 구역은 온라인으로 미리 티켓을 구입한 사람들을 위해 마련된 것입니다.

06.
1. 선택지 보고 문법/어휘 문제 파악하기 ☐ 문법 문제 ☑ 어휘 문제
2. 빈칸 분석하기 빈칸 앞 until further와 짝꿍 표현으로 어울려 쓰이는 명사가 정답이다.
3. 정답 선택하기 정답 (A)

뒤쪽 주차장은 추후 공지가 있을 때까지 이용할 수 없을 것입니다.

실전 문제

01. (D)	02. (A)	03. (C)	04. (A)	05. (A)	06. (D)
07. (B)	08. (B)	09. (D)	10. (B)	11. (B)	12. (A)
13. (B)	14. (D)	15. (D)	16. (C)	17. (D)	18. (C)
19. (B)	20. (D)	21. (C)	22. (A)	23. (D)	24. (A)

01. 부정대명사

Stein 산업은 현재 컴퓨터 프로그래밍에 뛰어난 경력을 지닌 사람은 누구든지 채용할 생각이다.

[해설] 선택지가 다양한 대명사로 구성되어 있으므로 문법 문제이다. 빈칸은 to부정사 to recruit의 목적어 자리인데, 바로 뒤에 위치한 with 전치사구의 수식을 받을 수 있어야 하므로 이 두 가지 역할이 모두 가능한 (D) anyone이 정답이다.

[어휘] currently 현재 look to부정사 ~할 생각이다 strong background 뛰어난 경력

02. 인칭대명사 구분: 소유격

독창적인 가족 요리 비법을 특징으로 하는 유명 요리사 Peter Ware 씨가 자신이 쓴 판매용 요리책의 출시를 발표했다.

[해설] 선택지가 다양한 인칭대명사로 구성되어 있으므로 문법 문제이다. 전치사 of와 of의 목적어로 쓰인 명사 cookbook 사이에 위치한 빈칸은 명사 cookbook을 수식할 단어가 필요한 자리이므로 소유격 대명사의 강조 형태인 (A) his own이 정답이다.

[어휘] feature ~을 특징으로 하다 recipe 요리법 celebrity 유명 인사 release 출시, 공개 for sale 판매용 one's own 자신만의, 고유의

03. 인칭대명사 구분: 목적격 vs. 소유대명사

시내에서 일하는 많은 사람들이 버스로 통근하고 있으며, 그들 중 대부분은 버스전용 차로를 추가하는 것에 대해 찬성하고 있다.

[해설] 선택지가 다양한 인칭대명사로 구성되어 있으므로 문법 문제이다. 전치사 of 뒤에 위치한 빈칸은 of의 목적어 자리이므로 목적격 대명사 (C) them이 정답이다. 소유대명사 (D) theirs도 목적어 역할은 가능하지만 '그들의 것'을 나타내므로 문장의 의미에 맞지 않는다.

05. 주제 문제

Sunset Valley는 무엇일 것 같은가?
(A) 컨벤션 센터
(B) 건강 관리 스파 시설
(C) 피트니스 시설
(D) 채용 대행업체

[해설] 해당 업체의 서비스 종류가 제시된 세 번째 단락에 증기 목욕, 마사지, 뷰티 트리트먼트(steam baths, massages, beauty treatments)가 언급되어 있으므로 이와 같은 서비스를 이용할 수 있는 곳에 해당되는 (B)가 정답이다.

[어휘] job recruitment 인력 채용, 직업 알선   agency 대행업체, 대행사

06. True 문제

광고에서 Sunset Valley에 관해 무엇을 알 수 있는가?
(A) 최근에 상을 받았다.
(B) 텔레비전 프로그램에 특별히 소개될 것이다.
(C) 전직 건축가에게 최근에 매각되었다.
(D) 경쟁사들보다 인기가 더 많다.

[해설] 첫 단락 마지막에 지역 내 다른 시설보다 더 많은 방문객이 찾는다고(we have more visitors than any other facility in the area) 알리고 있는데, 이는 인기가 더 많다는 뜻이므로 (D)가 정답이다.

paraphrasing more visitors 더 많은 방문객 → more popular 인기가 더 많은

[어휘] win an award 상을 받다   feature ~을 특별히 포함하다, 특집으로 싣다   former 전직의, 이전의   competitor 경쟁사, 경쟁자

07. 세부사항 문제

전일 패키지 이용 고객은 무엇에 대해 추가 비용을 낼 수 있는가?
(A) 야간 숙박 시설
(B) 집으로 가져갈 수 있는 피부 관리 제품
(C) 건강 평가 서비스
(D) 공항에서 출발하는 교통편

[해설] 추가 비용 관련 정보가 제시된 마지막 단락에 아주 적은 비용으로 받을 수 있는 추가 종합 건강 검진 서비스가(an additional overall health assessment offered for a nominal fee) 있다고 알리고 있으므로 (C)가 정답이다.

paraphrasing assessment 평가 → evaluation 평가

[어휘] accommodation 숙박 시설   evaluation 평가(서)

paraphrasing 정답 1. (a)   2. (c)   3. (b)

08-10은 다음 소책자를 참조하시오.

Paradise Hotel & Resort에 오신 것을 환영합니다! ⁰⁸귀가가 여기서의 투숙을 즐기시는 동안, 수상 경력이 있는 저희 편의 시설 중 일부를 이용하세요. 이 모든 시설은 주말에도 운영됩니다.

Supreme Spa (13세 이상)
저희 호텔에서 편안한 스포츠 마사지, 피부 관리, 진흙 목욕을 받으시기 바랍니다. ⁰⁹적은 비용을 내시면, 객실로 아로마 테라피를 가져다 드립니다. 저희의 폭넓은 선택지에서 양초와 오일의 향을 고를 수 있습니다. (매일)

Mini-Pool (4-10세)
¹⁰아이들을 위한 아쿠아봉와 장난감이 충분하지만, 손님들이 직접 가져오셔도 좋습니다. 이 구역은 안전 요원이 근무 중일 때만 개장합니다. (금-화요일)

Ball Play Room (3-12세)
¹⁰오랫동안 가장 인기있는 시설인 저희 볼풀에서 아이들로 하여금 다른 아이들과 함께 점프하고 놀 수 있게 하세요. 각 어린이 그룹에는 적어도 한 명의 성인 보호자가 필요합니다. (매일)

Dance Floor (전 연령)
댄스 플로어는 싱글, 커플, 가족, 친구들을 환영합니다. 현지 공연자들의 라이브 음악에 밤새 춤을 춰보세요. (금-수요일)

amenities 편의 시설   relaxing 편안한   nominal 아주 얼마 안 되는   scent 향   on duty 근무 중인   ball pit 볼풀   performer 공연자

08. 목적 문제

이 안내 책자의 목적은 무엇인가?
(A) 투숙객에게 시설에 대해 알리는 것
(B) 특별 행사에 대해 발표하는 것
(C) 몇몇 자원봉사자를 뽑는 것
(D) 관광객들에게 길을 알려주는 것

[해설] 첫 단락에서 투숙을 즐기는 동안 편의 시설 중 일부를 이용하라는(be sure to make use of some of our award-winning amenities) 말과 함께 네 가지 시설에 관한 정보를 알리는 것으로 지문이 구성되어 있으므로 (A)가 정답이다.

[어휘] inform 알리다   announce 발표하다   recruit 모집하다   give direction to ~로 가는 길을 알려주다

09. True 문제

Supreme Spa에 대해 사실인 것은 무엇인가?
(A) 인증된 직원들을 고용한다.
(B) 예약을 요구한다.
(C) 추가 비용이 발생할 수 있다.
(D) 호텔 바깥에 위치하고 있다.

[해설] Supreme Spa가 소개된 두 번째 단락에 적은 비용을 내면 객실로 아로마 테라피를 가져다 준다는(For a nominal fee, they also bring aroma therapy to your room) 말이 있으므로 (C)가 정답이다.

[어휘] certified 인증받은   incur 발생시키다

10. 세부사항 문제

책자에 따르면 Mini-Pool과 Ball Play Room의 공통점은 무엇인가?
(A) 둘 다 어린이를 위한 것이다.
(B) 둘 다 매주 매일 문을 연다.
(C) 둘 다 각각의 아이들을 감독할 어른이 필요하다.
(D) 둘 다 방문객들로 하여금 자신의 장비를 가져오도록 권장한다.

[해설] Mini-Pool은 어린이들을 위한 아쿠아봉과 장난감이 충분하다는(have plenty of pool noodle and toys for the kids) 정보와 Ball Play Room은 아이들로 하여금 다른 아이들과 놀 수 있게 하라는(let loose to jump and play with others) 정보를 통해 어린이들을 위한 시설임을 알 수 있으므로 (A)가 정답이다.

paraphrasing 정답 1. (b)   2. (c)   3. (a)

[해설] 지문 전반부에 제품을 사용한 적이 없으며, 원래 중고품 항목에 있었으나(This was originally listed under items) 수정되었음을 알리는 내용(that has been corrected)이 있으므로 제품의 상태에 대한 명확한 설명을 뜻하는 (A)가 정답이다.

[어휘] clarify 명확히 하다 promote 홍보하다 kitchen appliance 주방 기기

02. 세부사항 문제

공지에 따르면, 사람들은 왜 Dickson 씨에게 전화해야 하는가?
(A) 쿠폰을 적용하기 위해
(B) 조리법을 얻기 위해
(C) 신속한 배송을 위해
(D) 가격을 협상하기 위해

[해설] Dickson 씨의 이름이 제시된 문장에 긴급하게 받아야 하는(need to receive it urgently) 사람들은 연락하고 했고, 다음 문장에 특급 배송 가능성에 대해(the possibility of express shipping) 언급하고 있으므로 (C)가 정답이다.

paraphrasing contact 연락하다 → call 전화하다

[어휘] apply 신청하다 recipe 조리법 expedite 신속히 하다 negotiate 협상하다

paraphrasing 정답 1. (c) 2. (b) 3. (a)

03-04는 다음 공지를 참조하시오.

Bridgehampton 슈퍼마켓 고객 여러분께

환경에 대한 우려로 인해, 03 저희 슈퍼마켓은 더 이상 비닐 봉지는 제공하지 않을 것이며 종이 봉지만을 제공할 것입니다. 저희는 또한 종이 봉지에 대해 요금을 부과할 것입니다. 재활용 가능한 친환경적인 봉지는 각 계산대에서 구매하여 이용하실 수 있습니다. 또한, 저희 Bridgehampton 슈퍼마켓은 다른 업체들과 연합해 쓰레기를 줄이기로 약속했습니다. 따라서, 04 저희는 상하기 쉬운 모든 상품을 유통 기한 이틀 전에 식품 자선 단체에 기부할 예정입니다.

Bridgehampton Supermarket 경영진

environmental 환경적인 concern 우려, 걱정 charge ~을 부과하다, 청구하다 fee 요금, 수수료 environmentally friendly 환경 친화적인 reusable 재활용 가능한 register 계산대 pledge to부정사 ~하겠다는 약속, 맹세 therefore 따라서, 그러므로 donate ~을 기부하다 perishable 잘 상하는 goods 상품 charity 자선 단체 expiration date 유통 기한, 만료일

03. 목적 문제

공지의 주요 목적은 무엇인가?
(A) 정책 변화를 알리는 것
(B) 재활용 프로그램을 홍보하는 것
(C) 오염에 관한 인식을 높이는 것
(D) 청소 프로젝트에 필요한 자원 봉사자를 모집하는 것

[해설] 지문 시작 부분에 비닐 봉지가 아닌 종이 봉지만을 제공할 것이라고(our supermarket will no longer be providing plastic bags, only paper ones) 알린 후에, 그와 관련된 이용 방법 및 앞으로의 계획을 언급하고 있다. 이는 내부 정책의 변화에 해당하므로 (A)가 정답이다.

[어휘] policy 정책 promote ~을 홍보하다 raise awareness about ~에 대한 인식을 드높이다 pollution 오염, 공해

04. 세부사항 문제

Bridgehampton 슈퍼마켓은 어떻게 쓰레기를 줄일 계획인가?
(A) 가격을 인하함으로써
(B) 자선 기부를 함으로써
(C) 낭비 행위에 대해 벌금을 부과함으로써
(D) 소량으로 식품을 구비해 놓음으로써

[해설] 쓰레기를 줄이기 위한 방법이 언급되는 마지막 부분에, 상하기 쉬운 상품을 유통 기한이 되기 전에 자선 단체에 기부하겠다고(we will be donating all perishable goods to food charities ~) 알리고 있으므로 이 방법에 해당하는 (B)가 정답이다.

paraphrasing donating all perishable goods to food charities 상하기 쉬운 모든 상품을 자선 단체에 기부하다 → making charitable donations 자선 기부하기

[어휘] reduce ~을 인하하다, 줄이다 charitable 자선의 make a donation 기부하다 wasteful 낭비하는 stock (제품 등) ~을 구비하다, 갖춰 놓다 amount 양, 수량

paraphrasing 정답 1. (b) 2. (c) 3. (a)

05-07은 다음 광고를 참조하시오.

밤낮으로 일만 하고 계신가요? Sunset Valley에서 스스로에게 휴식을 선물해 보세요!

현대적인 시설: 세계적으로 인정받는 건축가에 의해 설계되어 새롭게 지어진 저희 시설에서 휴식에 집중해 보십시오. 저희는 20에이커 넓이의 삼림 지대에 위치하고 있어 자연과 교감하며 정신 없이 바쁜 도시의 일상에서 벗어날 수 있게 해 드리며, 05지역 내 다른 어떤 시설보다 더 많은 방문객들께서 찾아오고 계십니다.

Naturemade 제품: 저희는 자연에서 유기농으로 재배된 재료로 개발된 피부 관리 제품 라인인 Naturemade만을 사용합니다. 모든 고객들께서는 각자 소장하실 수 있는 샘플 크기의 Naturemade 제품을 몇 가지 받으시게 됩니다.

일체 비용이 포함된 패키지: 경험 많은 저희 직원들이 여러분께서 원하는 것을 모두 맞춰 드리고 스트레스를 해소하실 수 있도록 도움을 드리겠습니다. 저희 전일 패키지를 이용하시면, 06증기 목욕, 마사지, 뷰티 트리트먼트 등과 같은 6가지의 1시간짜리 트리트먼트 서비스를 제공해 드립니다. 이 트리트먼트 서비스들을 서로 혼합하여 여러분께 가장 적합한 조합을 만드실 수 있으며, 모두 하나로 묶어 저렴한 가격에 이용하실 수 있습니다. 07아주 적은 비용으로 제공되는 추가 종합 건강 검진 서비스도 있습니다. 외부 지역에서 찾아오시는 분일 경우, 믿고 이용하실 수 있는 저희 공항 셔틀버스로 공항에서부터 무료로 모셔 오기도 합니다. 555-3389로 오늘 저희에게 전화 주십시오.

around the clock 밤낮으로, 하루 24시간 rest 휴식 facility 시설(물) immerse oneself in ~에 몰두하다 hectic 정신 없이 바쁜 exclusively 오로지, 독점적으로 ingredient 재료, 성분 trial-size 샘플 크기의 inclusive 비용이 모두 포함된 pamper ~가 원하는 것을 모두 맞춰 주다 relieve ~을 덜어 주다, 완화시키다 match (비슷한 것끼리) ~을 맞추다, 연결시키다 suit ~에게 적합하다 additional 추가적인 assessment 평가 nominal fee 아주 적은 요금, 최소한의 요금 from out of town 외부 지역에서 pick A up (차로) A를 태우러 가다, 데려오다 reliable 믿을 수 있는

Q. 이메일의 목적은 무엇인가?
(A) 출장 정책 변경을 발표하는 것
(B) 향후 여행 세부 정보 제공하는 것
(C) 휴가를 요청하는 것
(D) 복리후생을 설명하는 것

02. 세부사항 문제

풀이 방법 해석

> Trujillo Education 리더십 세미나
>
> Trujillo Education(TE)은 직업 훈련을 전문으로 하는 국제적으로 유명한 교육 기업입니다. 저희 모든 프로그램에는 다음이 포함됩니다:
> – 업계 전문가들의 담화
> – 모든 사람이 참여할 수 있는 능동적인 워크샵 세션
> – 참가자들이 다운로드할 수 있는 보충 자료
>
> 새로운 특전을 활용하도록 인사 담당자와 교육 담당자분들을 초대합니다. 내년 1월부로, TE를 초청해 직원 대상 특별 세션을 실시하는 어떤 기업이든 20% 할인 혜택을 받으실 것입니다. 프로그램에 대해 더 알아 보시려면 웹 사이트 www.te.edu를 방문하십시오.

Q. 1월에 무슨 일이 일어날 것인가?
(A) 워크샵 일정이 변경될 것이다.
(B) 새로운 연사가 Trujillo Education에 합류할 것이다.
(C) 수료증이 발급될 것이다.
(D) 기업 할인이 제공될 것이다.

 연습 문제

01.(A)   02.(B)

01.

> RISOR (5월 5일) — Agder Amateur Baseball League(AABL) 가 올해 챔피언십 시리즈 개최 장소로 Risor Stadium을 선정했다. 그 경기장은 편안하고 넓은 좌석과 더불어 버스와 지하철 두 노선 모두 편리한 위치로 인해 선정되었다. 언제나 그랬듯이, 이 시리즈는 최고의 기록을 가진 두 AABL 팀 사이에서 펼쳐질 것이다. 물론, Risor Raiders는 올 시즌 가장 큰 경기에서 홈그라운드 이점을 누릴 수 있는 팀 중 하나가 되기를 바라고 있다. 팀 기록과 다가오는 경기의 티켓에 대한 업데이트는 AABL 웹사이트에서 찾을 수 있다.

location 장소   **hold** 개최하다   **spacious** (공간이) 넉넉한   **seating** 좌석   **convenient** 편리한   **homefield** 홈 구장   **advantage** 이점

Q. 기사는 주로 무엇에 관한 것인가?
(A) 스포츠 경기
(B) 음악 콘서트

[문제 키워드] article / mainly about

[해설] 초반부에 Risor Stadium이 올해 챔피언십 시리즈를 개최할 장소로 선정된 사실을 알린 후 그 경기와 관련된 정보를 제공하고 있으므로 (A)가 정답이다.

02.

> 저희 RG Homecare는 고객들의 안전과 편의를 최우선으로 여기고 있습니다. 저희는 고장 난 보일러가 스트레스일 수 있다는 사실을 알고 있습니다. 이것이 바로 저희가 모든 회원들께 24시간 고객 상담 전화 서비스를 제공하는 이유이며, 수리 기사가 방문하는 횟수에는 제한이 없습니다. 저희는 항상 추가 비용 없이 필수 수리 작업을 해 드릴 것입니다.
>
> 스탠다드 회원제와 함께, 저희는 **프리미엄 회원제**도 제공하고 있으며, 프리미엄 회원 고객들께서는 다음과 같은 혜택을 누리실 수 있습니다.
> · 추가 비용 없이 배수 장치나 파이프에 생기는 막힘 현상 처리
> · **일 년에 한 번 보일러와 난방 시스템에 대한 정기 유지 관리 서비스 제공**
> · 수리 작업 일정에 대한 우선권

convenience 편의   **make a repair** 수리하다   **necessary** 필요한   **for no additional charge** 추가 비용 없이   **entitle A to B** A가 B할 수 있다, A에게 B에 대한 자격을 주다   **blockage** 막힘   **drain** 배수구   **routine** 정기적인   **maintenance** 유지 관리   **priority** 우선(권)

Q. 프리미엄 회원들이 독점적으로 이용할 수 있는 것은 무엇인가?
(A) 무제한 수리 서비스
(B) 연례 점검

[문제 키워드] available exclusively / Premium Members

[해설] 문제 키워드인 Premium Members가 언급된 부분을 지문에서 먼저 찾는다. Premium Members에 대한 혜택이 제시된 두 번째 단락의 두 번째 항목에 일 년에 한 번씩 제공되는 서비스가 제시되어 있으므로(A routine maintenance check ~ once a year) 이를 '연간 점검'으로 바꿔 표현한 (B)가 정답이다.

[어휘] **exclusively** 독점적으로   **inspection** 점검

실전 문제

01.(A)   02.(C)   03.(A)   04.(B)   05.(B)   06.(D)
07.(C)   08.(A)   09.(C)   10.(A)

01-02는 다음 온라인 공지를 참조하시오.

> http://www.2ndhandxchange.com/appliance#627464
> 제품: Chez Chef 브랜드 슬로우 쿠커(3.5L)
> 가격: 20달러
>
> 저는 이 제품을 작년에 집들이 선물로 받았고 사용해 본 적이 없습니다. 원래 소매가는 45달러입니다. **01이 내용은 원래 중고품 항목에 나열되었지만, 웹 사이트 서비스 부서에 상황을 설명한 후 수정되었습니다.** 이 제품은 Chez Chef의 슬로우 쿠커 조리법 책자도 함께 제공됩니다.
>
> *2nd Hand Xchange에서 물건을 구매하는 것에 관심이 있지만 **02긴급히 받으셔야 할 분들은 555-6752로 Lori Dickson에게 연락하시기 바랍니다.** 그녀는 판매자에게 특급 배송 가능 여부에 대해 연락할 것입니다. 추가 요금이 부과될 수 있습니다.*

housewarming gift 집들이 선물   **retail price** 소매가   **list** 나열하다   **used item** 중고품   **booklet** 소책자   **urgently** 긴급하게   **express shipping** 특급 배송

01. 목적 문제

공지가 게시된 한 가지 이유는 무엇인가?
(A) 제품의 상태를 명확히 하기
(B) 제품 사용법을 설명하기
(C) Chez Chef 브랜드를 홍보하기
(D) 주방 기기를 소개하기

장소에 해당되므로 be동사 is와 수동태를 구성해 수동의 의미를 나타내는 과거분사 (D) reserved가 정답이다. 명사인 (B) reservation이 be동사 뒤에 보어로 쓰일 경우, 주어와 동격이 되어야 하지만 the entire place와 동격이 될 수 없으므로 오답이다.

[어휘] reservation 예약

03. 명사 어휘

[해설] 음식 먹기 콘테스트에서 참가자들에게 쿠폰의 형태로 주어지는 것을 나타낼 명사가 빈칸에 필요하므로 '경품, 상품' 등을 뜻하는 (A) Prizes가 정답이다.

[어휘] sales 매출, 판매(량), 영업   receipt 영수증, 받음, 수령

04. 알맞은 문장 고르기

(A) 대부분의 고객들은 주문품을 포장해 가는 것을 선호합니다.
(B) 모든 음식이 반드시 지정된 제한 시간 내에 소비되어야 합니다.
(C) 이는 식욕이 왕성한 사람들이 친구들과 함께 다시 찾아오도록 해 주는 것입니다.
(D) 다른 사람들이 앉을 수 있도록 빨리 먹고 가는 사람들에게 할인이 제공됩니다.

[해설] 바로 앞 문장에 '쿠폰을 제공하는 일'이 언급되어 있으므로 이를 This로 지칭해 그에 따른 긍정적인 효과를 나타내는 (C)가 정답이다. 앞 문장에 콘테스트를 마친 다음에(then) 진행되는 일이 언급되어 있으므로 콘테스트 진행 방식에 해당되는 (B)를 다시 언급하는 것은 흐름상 자연스럽지 못하다.

[어휘] take one's orders to go 주문품을 포장해 가다   consume ~을 소비하다, 먹다   specified 지정된, 명시된   encourage A to부정사 A가 ~하도록 만들다, 장려하다   appetite 식욕

05-08은 다음 기사를 참조하시오.

> Veggie Village: 웨스트 힐의 새로운 스타
> Veggie Village가 작년에 Jaycee Andrade 씨의 소유 하에 카페를 하나 개점했으며, Andrade 씨는 지역에서 공수해 오는 유기농 제품을 제공하기 위한 목적으로 해당 공간을 임대하기 시작했다. **05 모든 천연 재료의 공급처가 이 카페의 메뉴에 기재되어 있다. 06 그녀는 제휴 관계를 맺은 공급업체를 홍보하는 데 도움을 주기 위해 이렇게 하고 있다.**
> **07 상류층 고객들을 끌어들이기 위해, Andrade 씨는 다양한 허브 티와 채식용 샐러드를 제공하고 있다.** 또한, 반려 동물에게 매우 친화적인 환경을 제공하고 있어 고객들이 카페 내부로 강아지와 고양이를 데리고 들어올 수 있다. **08 이곳에서는 심지어 반려 동물을 위한 물그릇도 제공하고 있으며, 판매용 간식까지 있다.**
> 비록 가격이 조금 고가일 수는 있지만, Veggie Village는 친구나 반려 동물과 함께 건강에 좋은 브런치를 즐기기에 아주 좋은 편안한 분위기를 갖춘 곳이다.

under the ownership of ~의 소유 하에   with the intention of ~하려는 목적으로   locally sourced 지역에서 공급받는   partially 일부, 부분적으로   supplier 공급업체   high society 상류 사회   serve (음식 등) ~을 제공하다, 내오다   vegetarian 채식주의자   pet-friendly 반려 동물에게 친화적인   environment 환경   on the high end 고가인   comfortable 편안한   atmosphere 분위기

05. 명사 어휘

[해설] natural과 의미가 어울리는 명사로서 앞서 언급된, 지역에서 공급받는 유기농 제품과 관련해 메뉴에 기재될 수 있는 것을 나타내야 하므로 '음식 재료'를 의미하는 (A) ingredients가 정답이다.

06. 형용사 자리

[해설] 소유격 대명사와 명사 사이에 위치한 빈칸은 명사를 수식하는 형용사 또는 복합 명사를 구성하는 또 다른 명사가 쓰일 수 있는 자리인데, '제휴를 맺은 공급업체'라는 의미가 되어야 적절하므로 형용사 역할을 하는 과거분사 (C) partnered가 정답이다. 명사인 (B) partnership은 suppliers와 복합 명사를 구성하지 않는다.

[어휘] partner ~와 제휴 관계를 맺다   partnership 제휴 관계

07. 동사의 형태

[해설] 명사구 members of high society를 목적어로 취해 Andrade 씨가 다양한 허브 티와 채식용 샐러드를 제공하는 목적을 나타내야 적절하므로 to부정사인 (D) To attract가 정답이다.

[어휘] attraction 명소, 인기 장소   attract 끌어들이다, 끌어 모으다

08. 알맞은 문장 고르기

(A) 이곳에서는 심지어 반려 동물을 위한 물그릇도 제공하고 있으며, 판매용 간식까지 있다.
(B) 하지만 메뉴에서 고를 수 있는 모든 것이 채식용 음식인 것은 아닙니다.
(C) 계절에 따라 메뉴 품목 이용 가능 여부가 달라질 수 있다.
(D) 고객들은 실내 또는 뒤쪽의 테라스 중 어디에 앉을지 결정할 수 있다.

[해설] 앞 문장에 언급된 '반려 동물에게 친화적인 환경'에 대한 부연 설명이 이어지는 것이 적절하므로 반려 동물을 위한 서비스를 구체적으로 설명하는 (A)가 정답이다.

[어휘] have A for sale 판매용으로 A가 있다   availability 이용 가능 여부   depending on ~에 따라, ~에 달려 있는   either A or B A 또는 B 둘 중의 하나   patio 테라스

PART 7 주제·목적 문제/세부사항 문제

01. 주제/목적 문제

풀이 방법 해석

> 발신: Deborah Watson <d.watson@littech.com>
> 수신: 영업팀 <sales@littech.com>
> 제목: 앞으로의 출장
>
> 영업팀 구성원들에게 알려 드립니다.
>
> 10월 1일자로 우리 회사의 출장 관련 공식 방침에 몇 가지 수정 사항이 있을 예정이니 참고하시기 바랍니다. 영수증은 계속 제출되어야 하지만, 인쇄된 영수증 대신 전자 영수증을 받을 것입니다. 또한, 몇몇 분들은 20달러의 일일 경비가 하루 경비로 더 이상 충분하지 않다고 언급했습니다. 검토 후, 경영진은 25달러로 올리는 것에 합의했습니다. 이 문제에 대해 궁금한 점이나 고민이 있으시면 언제든지 편하게 연락하세요.
>
> 진심으로,
>
> Deborah Watson
> LIT Tech 인사부장

PART 6 앞의 내용이 단서인 명사 어휘

풀이 방법 해석

디케이터의 딥디쉬(두꺼운 피자나 파이)
Pirelli's Pizza & Pie는 많은 관광객들은 끌어모으고 거의 모든 지역 지도에 표시되어 있다. 이곳 디케이터 시내의 Main 가에 있는 이곳은 2005년 이후로 명소로 자리잡고 있다. 설립자인 Luigi Pirelli는 시카고의 유명한 딥디쉬 피자에 기반한 창의적인 메뉴를 가지고 레스토랑을 열고 싶어 했고, 큰 성공을 한 것으로 증명되었다.

메뉴에 있는 품목들을 제대로 요리하기 위해서는, 큰 벽돌 오븐이 필요하다. Pirelli's Pizza & Pie의 주방은 사실 그것들을 여러 개 가지고 있는데, 하루 종일 뜨겁게 유지된다. 그것들은 레스토랑 오픈 1시간 전인 매일 오전 10시에 불이 붙여진다.

Pirelli 씨는 이전하거나 다른 지점을 열고자 하는 바람은 없다고 했다. 그러므로, 당신이 다음 번에 디케이터에 있을 때는 이 지역 명소를 꼭 방문하길 바란다!

연습 문제
01.(A) 02.(B) 03.(A) 04.(A)

01.

Loganville 극장이 2개월간의 개조 공사 끝에 다시 개장합니다! 이제 지역 주민들이 다시 한 번 공연을 즐기실 수 있는 곳이 생깁니다.

renovation 개조, 보수   local 지역 주민

[단서] The Loganville Theater

[해설] 앞 문장에 언급된 극장 재개장에 따라 공연을 다시 즐길 수 있다는 흐름이 되어야 알맞으므로 '공연, 연주(회)' 등을 뜻하는 (A) performances가 정답이다.

02.

Blackburn Marketing 사의 Martin Blackburn 대표이사가 기자 회견에서 자신의 회사가 Arizona Ads 사를 인수할 것이라고 발표했다. "이 인수는 그곳의 직원들이 지닌 경험을 통해 우리가 전국적인 수준에서 경쟁하는 데 도움이 될 것입니다."라고 그는 기자들에게 말했다.

press conference 기자 회견 take over ~을 인수하다, 인계받다
compete 경쟁하다   on a national level 전국적인 수준에서

[단서] his company will take over Arizona Ads

[해설] 앞 문장에 Arizona Ads 사를 인수한다는 내용이 있으므로 이를 한 단어로 나타낼 명사로 '인수, 매입, 획득' 등을 의미하는 (B) acquisition이 정답이다.

[어휘] establishment 설립, 확립, 기관, 시설

03.

친애하는 Han 씨께,

귀하의 주문이 일정대로 금일 도착하지 못했다는 소식에 유감스럽습니다. 해당 배송 지연은 기사 수의 부족으로 인해 발생한 것입니다.

deliver 배달하다   as scheduled 일정대로   insufficient 부족한

[단서] not delivered

[해설] 앞 문장에 언급된 주문이 도착하지 못했다는 소식을 나타낼 명사가 필요하므로 '지연, 연기' 등을 뜻하는 (A) delay가 정답이다.

04.

Hancock Kids의 매니저는 그 밴드가 자선 공연을 위해 로디 지역을 방문할 예정이라고 발표했다. 모든 수익금은 현재 암 치료 센터가 지어지고 있는 Lodi 아동 병원에 전달될 것이다.

benefit (모금을 위한) 자선 (행사), 혜택, 이득   cancer 암
construct ~을 짓다, 건설하다

[단서] benefit performance

[해설] 앞 문장에 자선 공연을 위해 방문한다는 말이 있으므로 그에 따라 발생되는 수익금이 병원에 쓰인다는 흐름이 되어야 알맞다. 따라서 '수익금'을 의미하는 (A) proceeds가 정답이다.

[어휘] sales 영업, 매출, 판매(량)

실전 문제
01.(D) 02.(D) 03.(A) 04.(C) 05.(A) 06.(C)
07.(D) 08.(A)

01-04는 다음 기사를 참조하시오.

브리스톨의 Monster Meats

브리스톨에 가 본 적이 있으신 분이라면, Oak 로에 위치해 있으며 Danielle Greene 씨가 운영하는 유명 레스토랑인 Monster Meats를 아마 들어 보았을 것입니다. ⁰¹테이블이 빠르게 가득 차기 때문에 미리 전화해 보는 것을 적극 권장합니다. ⁰²때때로 저녁에는, 장소 전체가 개인 파티나 특별 행사를 위해 예약되기도 합니다.

메뉴를 홍보하기 위해, Greene 씨는 무엇이든 자신이 메뉴에 추가하기로 결정하는 새로운 음식을 바탕으로 음식 먹기 콘테스트를 개최합니다. ⁰³그런 다음에 쿠폰의 형태로 참가자들에게 경품이 제공됩니다. ⁰⁴이는 식욕이 왕성한 사람들이 친구들과 함께 다시 찾아오도록 해 주는 것입니다.

브리스톨을 방문할 계획이신 분은 꼭 Monster Meats에 자리를 예약해 보십시오. 먼저 전화를 해 보셔야 한다는 점만 잊지 않으시면 됩니다!

managed by ~가 운영하는   fill up 가득 차다   entire 전체의
promote ~을 홍보하다   based on ~을 바탕으로, 기반으로
add A to B A를 B에 추가하다   in the form of ~의 형태로
participant 참가자

01. 부사

[해설] 빈칸에 쓰일 부사(구)는 전화를 걸 때 권장되는 방식을 나타내야 하는데, 테이블이 빨리 가득 차서 자리를 구하지 못하는 상황을 피할 수 있는 방식이어야 하므로 '미리, 사전에'를 의미하는 (D) in advance가 정답이다.

[어휘] as well 마찬가지로, ~도   in addition 추가로   instead 대신

02. 동사의 형태

[해설] 빈칸 앞에 주어로 쓰인 the entire place는 사람에 의해 예약되는

해 있는데, sale과 복합 명사를 이뤄 '정리 세일'이라는 구체적인 의미가 되어야 알맞으므로 명사 (B) clearance가 정답이다.

[어휘] hold ~을 개최하다   make room for ~에 필요한 공간을 확보하다   merchandise 상품   clear ~을 치우다, 정리하다; 분명한, 명확한   clearance 정리, 치우기

15. 명사의 위치: 관사 뒤

Washington 가구점의 수익성에 관해 발간된 보고서가 많은 투자자들의 관심을 끄는 데 도움이 되었다.

[해설] 선택지가 다양한 품사의 단어로 구성되어 있으므로 문법 문제이다. 정관사 the와 전치사 of 사이에 위치한 빈칸은 the의 수식을 받을 명사 자리이므로 명사형 어미 -ty로 끝나는 (D) profitability가 정답이다.

[어휘] publish ~을 발간하다   attention 관심, 주목   investor 투자자   profitably 유익하게   profit 수익; 이익이 되다   profitable 수익성이 있는   profitability 수익성

16. 관사 없는 명사 자리

해외 시장에 진입하기 위한 시도는 문화적 차이와 같은 요소들을 고려해야 한다.

[해설] 선택지가 다양한 품사의 단어로 구성되어 있으므로 문법 문제이다. 빈칸은 형용사 foreign(해외의)의 수식을 받으면서 to부정사 to enter의 목적어 역할을 할 명사 자리인데, 부정 관사가 없으므로 가산 명사 market이 복수형으로 쓰여야 한다. 따라서 (D) markets가 정답이다.

[어휘] attempt to부정사 ~하기 위한 시도   consider ~을 고려하다   factor 요소   such as ~와 같은   cultural differences 문화적 차이

17. 명사의 위치: 형용사 뒤

몇몇 주요 IT 기업들을 유치한 이래로 Petersburgh시는 엄청난 인구 증가를 경험했다.

[해설] 선택지가 다양한 품사로 된 단어로 구성되어 있으므로 문법 문제이다. 형용사 tremendous(엄청난) 뒤에 위치한 빈칸은 형용사의 수식을 받을 명사 자리이므로 명사형 어미 -th로 끝나는 (C) growth가 정답이다.

[어휘] population 인구   attract 유치하다, 끌어들이다

18. 명사의 위치: 형용사 뒤

그 회사들은 소유주들이 상호 합의에 이를 수 있다면 올해 중에 합병될 것이다.

[해설] 선택지가 다양한 품사의 단어로 구성되어 있으므로 문법 문제이다. 형용사 mutual(상호간의) 뒤에 위치한 빈칸은 형용사의 수식을 받을 명사 자리이므로 명사형 어미 -ment로 끝나는 (D) agreement가 정답이다.

[어휘] merge 합병되다   owner 소유주   agree 합의하다, 동의하다   agreeable 기분 좋은, 선뜻 동의하는

19. 명사 어휘

지역 축제를 사람들에게 알리기 위한 노력의 일환으로, 도시에 있는 대부분의 업체들이 자사의 매장과 사무실마다 포스터를 부착하는 데 동의했다.

[해설] 선택지가 다양한 명사로 이루어져 있으므로 명사 어휘 문제이다. 빈칸 앞뒤에 각각 위치한 전치사 In, to부정사와 어울려 '~하기 위한 노력의 일환으로'라는 의미를 나타낼 때 사용하는 (B) effort가 정답이다.

[어휘] publicize ~을 사람들에게 알리다   local 지역의   business 업체, 회사   agree to부정사 ~하는 데 동의하다   put A in B A를 B에 놓다, 두다   entry 출품작   advance 진보, 발전   earnings 수입, 소득

20. 명사의 위치: 관사 뒤

필수 경력의 부족으로 Hillman 씨는 2차 면접 기회를 얻지 못했다.

[해설] 선택지가 다양한 품사의 단어로 구성되어 있으므로 문법 문제이다. 부정관사 a와 전치사 of 사이에 위치한 빈칸은 명사 자리이므로 (C) lack이 정답이다. 동명사 (D) lacking은 부정관사의 수식을 받지 못한다.

[어휘] required experience 필수 경력   round 회차

21. 명사 어휘

회사 차량을 이용하기 위해서는, 소속 부서장으로부터 서면 허가를 받으셔야 합니다.

[해설] 선택지가 다양한 명사로 이루어져 있으므로 명사 어휘 문제이다. 동사 obtain의 목적어로서 회사 차량을 이용하기 위해 부서장으로부터 받아야 하는 것을 나타낼 명사가 필요하므로 '허가'라는 의미로 쓰이는 (A) permission이 정답이다.

[어휘] in order to부정사 ~하기 위해   obtain ~을 얻다, 획득하다   written 서면으로 된   supervisor 부서장, 책임자, 상사   concentration (정신) 집중   application 신청(서), 지원(서), 적용, 응용   notice 공고, 통지

22. 명사의 위치: 형용사 뒤

VitaBlast는 일반적으로 아침 식사를 거르는 사람들을 위한 인기 있는 건강 보조 식품이다.

[해설] 선택지가 다양한 품사의 단어로 구성되어 있으므로 문법 문제이다. 형용사 popular(인기 있는), dietary(식사의, 음식물의)와 전치사 for 사이에 위치한 빈칸은 이 두 형용사의 수식을 받을 명사 자리이므로 명사형 어미 -ment로 끝나는 (C) supplement가 정답이다.

[어휘] normally 일반적으로   skip ~을 건너뛰다   supplementary 보충의   supplement 보충(물); ~을 보충하다

23. 명사 어휘

Prince 씨가 부재 중인 동안 비서가 휴가 신청서를 처리할 것이다.

[해설] 선택지가 다양한 명사로 이루어져 있으므로 명사 어휘 문제이다. 비서가 대신 일을 처리하는 원인과 관련된 명사가 필요하므로 'Prince 씨의 부재'라는 의미를 나타내는 (D) absence가 정답이다.

[어휘] assistant 비서, 보조, 조수   take care of ~을 처리하다   in one's absence ~가 부재 중인 동안   property 건물, 부동산   ability 능력   load 짐(의 양), 적재량, 업무량

24. 명사 어휘

저희 새 자동 추적 시스템이 귀사의 생산성을 증대시킬 것입니다.

[해설] 선택지가 다양한 명사로 이루어져 있으므로 명사 어휘 문제이다. 동사 increase의 목적어로서 증가시킬 수 있는 대상을 나타낼 명사가 필요하므로 '생산성'이라는 의미로 쓰이는 (A) productivity가 정답이다.

[어휘] automated tracking system 자동 추적 시스템   achievement 업적, 달성   patience 인내(심)   addition 추가(되는 것)

문법 문제이다. 빈칸 앞에 위치한 형용사 lower(더 낮은)의 수식을 받으면서 동사 gives의 목적어 역할을 할 명사가 빈칸에 들어가야 하는데, 부정관사가 없으므로 가산명사 rate의 복수 형태인 (B) rates가 정답이다.

[어휘] contract 계약(서)   rate ~을 평가하다, 등급을 매기다; 요금, 속도, 비율   rater 평가자

04. 명사의 위치: 형용사 뒤

Longwood Hotel & Spa를 찾는 고객들은 제공되는 아주 다양한 서비스에 흔히 기뻐한다.

[해설] 선택지가 다양한 품사의 단어로 구성되어 있으므로 문법 문제이다. 형용사 wide와 전치사 of 사이에 빈칸이 있으므로 명사 자리이며 wide, of와 어울려 '아주 다양한'이라는 의미를 구성할 때 사용하는 (C) variety가 정답이다.

[어휘] be delighted by ~에 기뻐하다   the wide variety of 아주 다양한   variation 변형, 차이   various 다양한   vary 다양하다, 서로 다르다

05. 명사의 위치: 관사 뒤

수익의 증가 덕분에, 이사회는 회사의 전 직원을 대상으로 하는 보너스에 대해 동의했다.

[해설] 선택지가 동사 또는 명사로 쓰이는 rise의 다양한 형태로 이루어져 있으므로 문법 문제이다. 부정 관사 a와 전치사 in 사이에 위치한 빈칸은 명사 자리이므로 명사인 (A) rise가 정답이다. 동명사 (C) rising은 부정 관사 a의 수식을 받지 못한다.

[어휘] thanks to ~로 인해, ~ 덕분에   profit 수익   board of directors 이사회   company-wide 회사 전체의   rise 증가; 증가하다

06. 명사 어휘

그 인기로 인해, 미리 티켓을 구입하실 것을 강력히 권해 드립니다.

[해설] 선택지가 다양한 명사로 이루어져 있으므로 명사 어휘 문제이다. 빈칸 앞에 위치한 전치사 in과 어울려 '미리, 사전에'라는 의미로 티켓 구입 시기를 나타낼 전치사구를 구성할 수 있는 (C) advance가 정답이다.

[어휘] due to ~로 인해   popularity 인기   strongly 강력히   purchase ~을 구입하다   view 관점, 견해, 경치   environment 환경   perspective 시각, 관점

07. 명사의 위치: 형용사 뒤

Lenny's 농장은 10년 넘게 그 지역에서 가장 큰 유기농 농산물 공급업체였다.

[해설] 선택지가 다양한 품사의 단어로 구성되어 있으므로 문법 문제이다. 최상급 형용사 the largest와 전치사 of 사이에 위치한 빈칸은 the largest의 수식을 받을 명사 자리이므로 명사형 어미 -er로 끝나는 (C) supplier가 정답이다.

[어휘] organic 유기 농법의   produce 농산물   region 지역   decade 10년   supply ~을 공급하다   supplier 공급업체   supplies 용품, 물품

08. 명사의 위치: 관사 뒤

모든 세입자들은 마감일 전까지 비용을 납부하도록 요구된다.

[해설] 선택지가 다양한 품사로 된 단어로 구성되어 있으므로 문법 문제이다. 부정관사 a와 전치사 before 그리고 on 사이에 위치한 빈칸은 명사 자리이므로 명사형 어미 -ment로 끝나는 (B) payment가 정답이다.

[어휘] tenant 세입자   be asked to ~요청하다   due date 마감일

09. 명사의 역할: 주어 역할

귀하의 부서는 우리 매장에서 결함이 있는 상품과 관련된 모든 문제들을 처리하고 있습니다.

[해설] 선택지가 다양한 품사의 단어로 구성되어 있으므로 문법 문제이다. 소유격 대명사 Your와 동사 handles 사이에 위치한 빈칸은 주어 역할을 할 명사 자리이므로 명사형 어미 -ment로 끝나는 (C) department가 정답이다. 동명사 (D) departing은 의미상 적합하지 않다.

[어휘] handle ~을 처리하다   related to ~와 관련된   defective 결함이 있는   merchandise 상품   depart 출발하다   department 부서

10. 명사의 역할: 목적어 역할

지난해 동안 Tacoma Industrial의 빠른 성장은 많은 관심을 끌어 왔다.

[해설] 선택지가 다양한 품사의 단어로 구성되어 있으므로 문법 문제이다. 빈칸은 타동사 attracted(~을 끌어들이다)의 목적어로 쓰일 명사 자리인데, '관심을 끌다'라는 의미가 되어야 적절하다. interest가 '관심'을 의미할 때는 단수로 쓰이므로 (D) interest가 정답이다.

[어휘] rapid 빠른   growth 성장   interest 관심, 이자, 이익; ~의 관심을 끌다   interested 관심이 있는

11. 명사의 위치: 형용사 뒤

여러분의 구역에 적용될 수 있는 어떠한 제한 사항에 대해서든 저희 서비스 범위 안내도를 꼭 확인해 보시기 바랍니다.

[해설] 선택지가 다양한 품사의 단어로 구성되어 있으므로 문법 문제이다. 형용사 any와 that절 사이에 위치한 빈칸이므로 이 둘의 수식을 받을 명사 자리이다. 따라서 명사형 어미 -tion으로 끝나는 (A) restrictions가 정답이다.

[어휘] coverage (도달) 범위   apply to ~에 적용되다   restriction 제한   restrict ~을 제한하다   restrictive 제한하는

12. 명사 어휘

이 침실 두 개짜리 아파트는 지하철역과의 접근성으로 인해 훨씬 더 비싸다.

[해설] 선택지가 다양한 명사로 이루어져 있으므로 명사 어휘 문제이다. 빈칸 뒤에 위치한 'to+장소 명사구'와 어울릴 수 있는 명사로 '~와의 접근성'이라는 의미를 나타낼 때 사용하는 (B) proximity가 정답이다.

[어휘] a lot (비교급 수식) 훨씬   due to ~로 인해   attempt 시도   reminder (상기시키는) 공지, 메모

13. 명사의 역할: 목적어 역할

많은 직원들이 각자의 직업 생활을 개선하는 방법에 관한 조언을 얻기 위해 Douglass 씨에게 상담을 한다.

[해설] 선택지가 다양한 품사의 단어로 구성되어 있으므로 문법 문제이다. 두 전치사 for, about 사이에 위치한 빈칸은 for의 목적어 역할을 할 명사 자리이므로 명사형 어미 -ice로 끝나는 (D) advice가 정답이다.

[어휘] consult ~에게 상담하다   improve ~을 개선하다   professional 직업의, 전문적인   advisory 자문의, 고문의

14. 복합 명사

Famous 패션은 새로운 상품을 놓는 데 필요한 공간을 확보하기 위해 대대적인 정리 세일 행사를 개최하고 있다.

[해설] 선택지가 다양한 품사의 단어로 구성되어 있으므로 문법 문제이다. 형용사 massive(대규모의, 대량의)와 명사 sale(세일) 사이에 빈칸이 위치

DAY 01

PART 5 | 문법 | 명사

확인 문제 해석

❶ 모든 회원들이 합의에 도달했다.
❷ 그의 승진이 곧 발표될 것이다.
❸ 그녀는 임시 직원이었다.
❹ 선임 정비사 직의 지원자들은 자격증을 소지하고 있어야 한다.
❺ Gagne 씨는 정보를 필요로 한다.
❻ Vincent 실험실은 현재 인턴을 고용하고 있다.
❼ 연사들은 리셉션에 초대된다.
❽ 이 직위는 컴퓨터 공학에 대한 폭넓은 전문 지식을 요구한다.
❾ 많은 참석자들이 오후 시간에 참석할 것이다.
❿ 평면도는 그 건축가에 의해 체크될 것이다.
⓫ 당신은 이 신청서를 작성해야 한다.

연습 문제

01.(D) 02.(B) 03.(B) 04.(B) 05.(C) 06.(A)

01.
1. 선택지 보고 문법/어휘 문제 파악하기 ☑문법 문제 ☐어휘 문제
2. 빈칸 분석하기 빈칸 앞에 있는 것 ☐관사 ☐명사 ☑소유격
   → 빈칸은 ☑명사 ☐동사 자리이다.
3. 정답 선택하기 정답 (D)

이사진들의 기대는 유럽 시장으로의 확장에 기반한 것이다.

02.
1. 선택지 보고 문법/어휘 문제 파악하기 ☐문법 문제 ☑어휘 문제
2. 빈칸 분석하기 빈칸 앞 동사 (complete)
   → 동사의 의미 (작성하다, 완성하다)
   → 이 동사와 어울려 쓰일 수 있는 명사가 답이다.
3. 정답 선택하기 정답 (B)

Kent Market에서 더 절약을 하고 싶으시면, 저희 회원 가입을 위해 신청서를 작성해 주세요.

03.
1. 선택지 보고 문법/어휘 문제 파악하기 ☑문법 문제 ☐어휘 문제
2. 빈칸 분석하기 빈칸 앞에 있는 것 ☐관사 ☑타동사 ☐자동사
   → 빈칸은 ☑명사 ☐동사 자리이다.
3. 정답 선택하기 정답 (B)

업무 시간을 바꾸기 전에 직속 상사에게 반드시 허가를 받아야 한다.

04.
1. 선택지 보고 문법/어휘 문제 파악하기 ☑문법 문제 ☐어휘 문제
2. 빈칸 분석하기 빈칸 앞에 있는 것 ☐소유격 ☑형용사 ☐부사
   → 빈칸은 ☑명사 ☐동사 자리이다.
   → 정답이 될 수 있는 후보 2개 (B , D)

3. 정답 선택하기 정답 (B)

Hancock 가문은 100년 전에 자선 단체를 설립했다.

05.
1. 선택지 보고 문법/어휘 문제 파악하기 ☑문법 문제 ☐어휘 문제
2. 빈칸 분석하기 빈칸 앞에 있는 것 소유격 ☑형용사 ☐부사
   → 빈칸은 ☑복수 명사 ☐단수 명사 ☐동사 자리이다.
3. 정답 선택하기 정답 (C)

모든 참석자들은 강의 후에 이름표, 펜, 그리고 메모지를 받을 것이다.

06.
1. 선택지 보고 문법/어휘 문제 파악하기 ☑문법 문제 ☐어휘 문제
2. 빈칸 분석하기 빈칸 앞에 있는 것 형용사 ☑타동사 ☐자동사
   → 빈칸은 ☑명사 ☐동사 자리이다.
   → 정답이 될 수 있는 후보 3개 (A, B, C)
   → 빈칸 앞에 an이 없으므로 ☑불가산 명사 ☐가산 명사가 들어가야 한다.
3. 정답 선택하기 정답 (A)

이 워크숍은 현재 구직 중인 모든 사람들을 돕기 위해 특별히 의도되었습니다.

실전 문제

01.(D) 02.(C) 03.(B) 04.(C) 05.(A) 06.(C)
07.(C) 08.(B) 09.(C) 10.(D) 11.(A) 12.(B)
13.(D) 14.(B) 15.(D) 16.(D) 17.(C) 18.(D)
19.(B) 20.(C) 21.(A) 22.(C) 23.(D) 24.(A)

01. 명사의 위치: 형용사 뒤

귀하의 서비스 약정 상세 정보에 대한 모든 설명을 보시려면 Horizon Mobile과의 계약서를 참조하시기 바랍니다.

[해설] 선택지가 다양한 품사로 된 단어로 구성되어 있으므로 문법 문제이다. 빈칸 앞에 형용사 full(완전한)이 있고, 빈칸 뒤에 전치사 of가 있으므로 빈칸에는 명사가 들어가야 한다. 따라서 명사형 어미 -tion으로 끝나는 (D) description이 정답이다.

[어휘] refer to ~을 참조하다 contract 계약(서) descriptive 설명하는 description 설명

02. 명사의 역할: 주어 역할

Daytona 지점 사무실로 출퇴근하는 관리자들은 수당을 받을 권리가 있다.

[해설] 선택지가 다양한 품사로 된 단어로 구성되어 있으므로 문법 문제이다. 빈칸 뒤에 위치한 분사 commuting의 수식을 받아 주어로 쓰일 명사가 빈칸에 필요한데, 동사 are와 수 일치가 되는 복수 명사가 들어가야 하므로 (C) Supervisors가 정답이다.

[어휘] commute 출퇴근하다 branch 지점 be entitled to ~할 권리가 있다 allowance 수당, 용돈

03. 관사 없는 명사 자리

Donner Cable 사는 2년 이상의 계약을 보유한 고객들에게 더 낮은 요금을 제공한다.

[해설] 선택지가 동사 rate(평가하다)의 다양한 형태로 이루어져 있으므로

토익 기본서

20일 만에 끝내는 기적의 토익 RC

해설집